Concerning Alexander the Great

A Reconstruction of Cleitarchus

By

Andrew Michael Chugg

2015 & 2021

First Edition, February 2015
Second Edition, April 2021

© 2015 by Andrew Michael Chugg. All rights reserved.
ISBN 978-1-9163997-0-9

Dedicated to the Third Diogenes

Thirteenth Member of the Pantheon
By Order of the Senate of Rome

Concerning Alexander the Great

Contents

Introduction	1
PART ONE	7
Book 1: Spring 336BC - 27th September 336BC - 15th October 335BC	8

The Birth & Ancestry of Alexander; Philip Dispatches an Expeditionary Force to Asia Minor; The Assassination of Philip at the Equinoctial Festival; The Accession of Alexander & the Funeral of Philip; The Recalcitrance of Thebes & the Assembly at Corinth; The Meeting with Diogenes; The Situation in the Persian Empire; The Balkan Campaign & the Battle with the Triballians; Rebellion in Greece & the Investment and Fall of Thebes; The Fate of Thebes Decided by the League at Corinth; The Visit to the Oracle at Delphi.

Book 2: 16th October 335BC - 5th October 334BC — 29

Preparations for the Asian Expedition; Crossing the Hellespont; The Visit to Troy; The Battle of the Granicus; The Surrender of Magnesia; The Siege of Miletus; The Dismissal of the Fleet; The Siege of Halicarnassus; The Capture of the Fortress of the Marmares.

Book 3: 6th October 334BC - 24th September 333BC — 45

Alexander Encouraged by Omens; The Arrest of Alexander Lyncestes; The Retreat of the Sea; The Gordian Knot; The Death of Memnon; Darius at Babylon; Alexander's Advance into Cilicia; Alexander Falls Sick at Tarsus; The Warning Concerning Philip the Doctor and Alexander's Recovery.

Book 4: 25th September 333BC - 13th October 332BC — 63

The Battle of Issus; An Interview with the Queens; The Treasures at Damascus; The First Letter from Darius; A New King for Sidon; The Siege of Tyre.

Book 5: 14th October 332BC – 1st October 331BC — 102

Second Peace Offer from Darius; The Siege of Gaza; Occupation of Egypt; Expedition to Siwa; Foundation of Alexandria; The March back to Byblos; The Preparations of Darius; Alexander's Advance into Mesopotamia; Crossing the Tigris; Death of Stateira; Third Peace Offer from Darius; The Battle of Arbela.

PART TWO — 151

Book 6: October 2nd 331BC – July 330BC — 152

The Escape of Darius and the Capture of Treasure at Arbela; Mennis and the Cave of Naphtha; The Occupation of Babylon; the Seizure of Susa; The Capture of the Susian Gates; Meeting with the Mutilated Greeks; The Burning of Persepolis; The Pursuit of Darius and his Murder by Bessus.

Book 7: July 330BC – June 329BC   195

The Advance to Hecatompylus; Description of Hyrcania and the Caspian Sea; Surrender of Artabazus & the Greek Mercenaries; Theft of Bucephalus; Surrender of Nabarzanes; Visit of the Amazon Queen; Adoption of Persian Dress; Revolt of Satibarzanes; The Philotas Affair; Assassination of Parmenion; The Euergetae; First Crossing of the Paropamisus Range.

Book 8: July 329BC – Autumn 328BC   242

Alexander's Advance to the River Oxus; Bessus Betrayed to Alexander; The Fate of the Branchidae; Alexander Wounded near Maracanda; The Revolt of Spitamenes; Alexander's Advance to the River Tanais; Annihilation of a Macedonian Column by Spitamenes and Alexander's Counterattacks; Capture of the Rock of Ariamazes.

Book 9: Autumn 328BC – May 327BC   271

The Hunt in Basista; The Killing of Cleitus; The Treaty with Sisimithres; The Decapitation of Spitamenes; The Proskynesis Experiment; The Conspiracy of the Pages; The Army Caught in a Blizzard; The Marriage to Roxane.

Book 10: June 327BC – June 326BC   297

The Invasion of India; Feting by Nysa; The Siege of Mazaga; The Capture of Aornus and The Battle Against Porus on the Hydaspes.

Book 11: July 326BC – Late Spring 325BC   326

Eastwards Through India; The Mutiny on The Hyphasis and the Return to the Kingdom of Porus; The River Voyage Downstream; The Siege of the Town of the Oxydracae; Alexander's wound and his Recovery.

Book 12: Late Spring 325BC – June 324BC   354

Southern India and its Ocean; The March through the Kedrosian Desert; The Dionysiac Comus and The Return to Persia.

Book 13: July 324BC – July 323BC & Beyond   375

The Flight of Harpalus; The Exiles Decree; The Mutiny at Opis; The Death of Hephaistion; The Cossaeans; Death in Babylon; Aftermath & Entombment.

Key Historical Issues   409

- Alexander's Ancestry   409
- The Date of Alexander's Birth   411
- The Date of Accession of Alexander the Great   413
- Alexander's Half-Brothers   418
- Alexander and Diogenes   419
- The Delphic Oracle and Alexander   420
- Justification of the Invasion of Asia   420

Alexander's Emulation of Achilles	421
Alexander's Forces at the Granicus	422
The Date of the Battle of the Granicus	423
Alexander's Route between the Granicus and Sardis	423
The Passage of Mount Climax	424
The Arrest of Alexander Lyncestes	424
Geographical Eccentricities: Turkey as a Peninsula	425
Why Did Alexander Head North from Pisidia?	425
Was Philip the Doctor Suborned by Darius?	426
The Three Peace Offers from Darius	427
Dating Issues Including the Fall of Tyre and Arbela	427
The Appointment of the King of Sidon	429
Did Alexander Visit Upper Egypt?	430
The Location of the Battle of Arbela or Gaugamela	432
The Sack and Burning of Persepolis	436
Did Darius Agree to Surrender in July 330BC?	437
Alexander's Route: Battle of Issus to Death of Darius	439
Alexander's Emulation of Cyrus and the Persianising	441
Geographical Errors between the Caspian and India	445
The Visit of the Queen of the Amazons	447
Prophthasia	449
The Culpability of Philotas and Parmenion	451
The Condemnation of the Branchidae	456
The Killing of Cleitus	458
The Culpability and Fates of Callisthenes and the Pages	461
The Marriage to Roxane	465
Alexander's Route Through Afghanistan	467
Alexander's Route Through India	472
Fragments from Cleitarchus' Thirteenth Book	473
Babylon as the Metropolis	475
Re-Ordering Curtius on the Mutiny at Opis	476
The Palace Hypaspists and the Somatophylakes	477

The Large Lacuna in the Tenth Book of Curtius	481
Hephaistion's Pyre	482
Hephaistion the Demigod	489
The Cause of the Death of Alexander	490
How Did the Leading Men Split after Alexander's Death?	493
Arrhidaeus the Fool	495
The First Division of the Satrapies	496
Last Plans	502
Antipater & Cassander as Regicides	505
The Itinerant Corpse	506
Is Arrian Reliable?	511
The Nature and Genesis of Cleitarchus' Account	**529**
Introduction	529
Connecting the Timespan and the Number of Books	531
Locating Jacoby's Fragments and the Book Boundaries	534
Vestiges of Cleitarchus' Book Structure in Diodorus	538
Book Boundaries and Fragment Locations in Cleitarchus	542
Sources of Cleitarchus	551
The Date of the Indica of Megasthenes	565
Dating Cleitarchus from the Vulgate & Fragments	567
Conclusive Clues in a Papyrus on Cleitarchus' Career	572
Unattributed Fragments: the Einquellenprinzip	577
Cleitarchan Style & Themes	580
Cleitarchus in Diodorus 17 and Curtius	584
Is Curtius Mainly Translating Cleitarchus?	586
Cleitarchus in Trogus	591
Cleitarchus in the Metz Epitome	592
Cleitarchus in Plutarch	596
Other Anonymous Fragments	597
Poetical Devices in Cleitarchus	597
The Character and Value of Cleitarchus	598
Feasibility of Reconstruction	599

The Methodology of the Reconstruction	600
Conclusions	601
Organisation and Sources	609
Bibliography	643
Modern References	643
Selected Ancient Sources	649
Acknowledgements	652
Index	653

Introduction

In spite of the objections of Tarn, I regard it as certain that whatever source Diodorus used, it was the same as that employed by Curtius. Schwartz assembled a formidable list of parallels between the two writers, without exhausting the subject. It is adequate to prove the point. To reconstruct this source would be a useful task.

C. Bradford Welles[1]

Cleitarchus, then, is elusive. Is he also irretrievable? My feeling is that it is possible to reconstruct something of his work, but the exercise of doing so is particularly arduous.

A. B. Bosworth[2]

Insofar as we have detailed and complete accounts of the lives of any of the great historical figures from antiquity it is generally because their contemporaries were inspired to write about them and those writings have in some way come down to us, albeit sometimes by devious routes. Alexander the Great is an interesting case in point. We know that numerous of his fellow Greeks were moved to compose extensive and elaborate accounts of his reign and his campaigns and many of those authors actually participated in the events that they recounted. However, none of those primary accounts survives today except in fragments quoted by secondary writers. Instead we rely on a couple of traditions of historiography, for which the earliest manuscripts had their origins in the era of the Roman Empire, three or more centuries after Alexander's death. Nevertheless, these Roman writers themselves necessarily relied on the primary accounts for their information, although they were not always as careful as we might wish in their treatment of the original material.

The first of these surviving traditions of Alexander historiography is sometimes termed the Official Tradition. It comprises just three extant works: the *Anabasis Alexandrou* and the *Indica* of Arrian and the anonymous *Itinerarium Alexandri*. In fact the latter may well be a derivative from Arrian's works and is also rather small-scale in comparison. Thus it is not much of an exaggeration to equate the Official Tradition with Arrian himself. He was an interesting and not altogether insignificant historical character in his own right. For example, he served as governor of Cappadocia under the Emperor Hadrian and also held office as the Archon of Athens. However, his reputation is founded mainly on his literary works and on his two works on Alexander most particularly. He has been greatly respected by modern historians, because he tells us that he based his works on the accounts of Aristobulus, Nearchus and Ptolemy, three of Alexander's senior officers. Hence he has been regarded as conveying the viewpoint of the upper echelons within Alexander's regime. But what Arrian's readers need to know, yet

---

[1] C. Bradford Welles, *Loeb edition of Diodorus Siculus*, Vol. 8 (Harvard, 1963), Introduction, 12.

[2] A.B. Bosworth, *From Arrian to Alexander* (Oxford, 1988), Introduction, 13.

are not usually told, is that he largely edits out the more salacious details and anecdotes concerning Alexander's private life, because he does not believe that this is suitable material for a published history and because he doubts the veracity of sources that peddle such material. Furthermore, he is rather superficial on Alexander's motives and aspirations, so that it can be hard for his readers to gain any real impression as to why the king took the decisions, which drove each successive episode of his career. In summary, Arrian provides a rather dull catalogue of events that is lacking in human insight. Furthermore, his accuracy relative to alternative versions on certain matters is open to question.

The antidote to Arrian is provided by the so-called Vulgate Tradition. The surviving ancient works, which derive from this tradition are particularly Curtius's *Deeds of Alexander*, the seventeenth book of the *Library of History (Bibliotheke)* by Diodorus Siculus, the eleventh and twelfth books of Justin's *Epitome of the Philippic History of Pompeius Trogus* and the so-called *Metz Epitome*. In addition, Plutarch's *Life of Alexander* and also his essay *On the Fortune or Virtue of Alexander* from his *Moralia* have substantial Vulgate elements, but appear also to incorporate some elements from the Official Tradition. The Vulgate sources are replete with scurrilous and salacious stories, which nevertheless mainly embody a large element of truth. They seethe with gossip and comments on Alexander's purposes and motives and are gaudy with colourful descriptions of the places and geography and of the fauna and flora that Alexander's expedition encountered.

There is also a third tradition that merits a mention. That is the amalgamation of semi-legendary accounts of episodes in Alexander's career most commonly called the *Alexander Romance*. It appears to have been edited together from earlier tales in Egypt in about the third century AD. Its oldest surviving manuscript was penned in Greek, which seems to have been its original language, but it was translated into many other antique languages around fifteen centuries ago as it rapidly grew in popularity: these include Latin, Syriac, Armenian, Arabic, Persian and Ethiopic versions, all of which survive today. A few of the manuscripts implausibly claim authorship by Callisthenes, Alexander's court historian. This is the basis for an alternative name for this tradition of *Pseudo-Callisthenes*. However, this tradition is of very limited historical value, since it is heavily contaminated by myth and fictional embellishments. In the *Romance* Alexander's conquests proceed in erratic geographical leaps and bounds that bear scant resemblance to his actual itinerary.

Instead, it is the Vulgate Tradition that is the focus for the present reconstruction for the simple reason that the great majority of its material seems to have derived from a single lost account of Alexander's reign, penned by a scholar of the Cynical school called Cleitarchus, who compiled it in Alexandria in Egypt between about 280-250BC. The fact that the majority of the surviving accounts derive from Cleitarchus makes it feasible for a good approximation to the original to be reconstructed by a process of triangulating backwards in time to define an original

Introduction

text that could reasonably have spawned the various parallel accounts of each episode in the surviving Vulgate sources.

Virtually every sentence and phrase of my reconstruction of Cleitarchus is derived directly from text in the antique source manuscripts of the Vulgate. That is to say that *all* its material can be found in authoritative antique manuscripts. There are no inventions and indeed it could be added that I have often eschewed emendations of the source manuscripts by modern editors, who sometimes seem lacking in empathy with the perspective of Alexander's early historians in the particular context of their times and have not always been sufficiently diligent in cross-checking the sense of their modifications relative to the full range of surviving material on Alexander. The sense of my words in reconstructing Cleitarchus is therefore very much true to the gist of the Vulgate accounts and there is no fiction to be found here, unless that fiction had already become established within the texts two thousand years ago, when the Vulgate became frozen into its surviving manuscript tradition.

However, my reconstructed text is not merely a simple translation of passages from the surviving secondary sources. Instead it has been necessary to meld together overlapping and intersecting accounts and continually to assess which source should have pre-eminence in the case of (usually slight) disparities. Furthermore, I have thought it fitting to attempt to echo the evidently flowery literary style of Cleitarchus to some extent, especially in the case of speeches and descriptive passages. To this end I have sometimes employed poetical devices including rhythmic or metrical passages, incidental rhyming or simple assonance and alliteration. However, it would also be true to say that some of this embroidery is already reflected in the surviving Latin and Greek texts of Curtius, Diodorus and even Justin and Plutarch. In this sense my own text is not merely a reconstruction, but also an evocation of the original. It is especially fitting that the reconstruction should retain Cleitarchus' colourful sensationalism and prurience in contrast to the dull propriety and declared self-censorship of Arrian's *Anabasis Alexandrou*.

Different passages may be attributed to Cleitarchus with widely varying degrees of confidence. Therefore, I have indicated the approximate confidence level using a textual hierarchy running from a lowest through three intermediate steps to a highest, the latter being defined as attributed fragments of Cleitarchus from surviving ancient texts. This is implemented as follows: *italic*; plain text; ***italicized bold***; **simple bold**; <u>**underlined simple bold**</u>. Subject to a few minor exceptions, it is possible to read the reconstruction at a variety of confidence levels by ignoring all text below the desired level of fidelity.

This reconstruction is particularly founded on the premise that Curtius and Diodorus (Book 17 & Book 18.1-4) are largely abridgements of the History of Alexander by Cleitarchus, whereas Justin (Books 11 to 13.4) and Plutarch's *Life of Alexander* are considered to contain substantial Cleitarchan elements. The precise degree to which each surviving source reflects the Cleitarchan archetype is argued in detail in the section of this book that analyses The Nature and Genesis of Cleitarchus' Account, but the broad interrelationship between various of the lost and extant ancient sources is outlined in Figure A. Although I cannot be absolutely sure that Curtius did not employ another major source, the process of performing the reconstruction has had the incidental consequence of accumulating many minor points of evidence such as to formulate a cumulatively strong case that Curtius is in fact substantially (though not entirely) a Latin translation of a moderately abridged version of Cleitarchus' Greek text. In particular, it has transpired that this hypothesis resolves virtually all difficulties without generating significant inconsistencies.

Nevertheless, reconstructed text solely based on material from only one of Curtius or Diodorus 18.1-4 or Justin 11-13.4 or the *Metz Epitome* or Plutarch's works on Alexander is indicated at a relatively lower level of confidence. Higher confidence is assigned to material exclusively derived from Diodorus 17. Still higher confidence is vested in cases where there are detailed matches between these sources and the highest confidence rests with the attributed fragments of Cleitarchus, although they are sadly sparse.

If the premise of a common source for the surviving texts were correct, then it would be expected that a relatively smooth and coherent version of the prototype could be reconstructed by merging them. However, if any of the extant sources had employed a significant secondary source, then it would be anticipated that the attempt to define a prototype that explained all the material in each of them should encounter numerous intractable contradictions. It is a conclusion of this project that it has been possible to reconstruct Alexander's entire reign including the events leading up to his accession without encountering significant contradictions when integrating all the appertaining material in Curtius, Diodorus and the *Metz Epitome* (with the obvious exception of a few passages in Curtius where that author is clearly offering his own comments and one instance, where he attacks Cleitarchus by name with reference to Ptolemy's version in a matter that concerned Ptolemy.) This is an important result, because it tends to reinforce the premise that Curtius, Diodorus and the *Metz Epitome* at least are essentially abridgements of Cleitarchus. Such an inference is not at all obvious in reading those sources individually, due to great variations in the degree of epitomisation and different abridgers having chosen to focus on different aspects of the story.

In the case of Justin, we know from his manuscripts that he epitomised Trogus, although the latter probably used Cleitarchus or else used Timagenes, who in turn used Cleitarchus. More difficulties tend to arise in reconciling his words with the tradition from the other Vulgate texts, as might reasonably be expected for such indirect transmission. A straightforward example is that Justin is more negative about Alexander's treatment of Philotas and Parmenion than either Curtius or Diodorus. Another example would be Justin's assertion (11.10.14) that Tyre fell through treachery, which does not appear to follow the Cleitarchan line. Yet in fact these incongruities are easily explained as either incidental consequences of

Introduction

successive stages of epitomisation via Trogus or else as among the many misunderstandings and over-simplifications, which are plainly attributable to Justin's rather careless epitomisation of Trogus. The process of reconstruction has also indicated significant amounts of Cleitarchan material in Plutarch, by virtue of some striking parallels between my text (reconstructed from Curtius and Diodorus) and some of Plutarch's anecdotes. But it is equally obvious that Plutarch used many early sources (as too did Cleitarchus himself), so I have in general used Plutarch's material sparingly and attributed it a low confidence as deriving from Cleitarchus.

Neither do I intend that this should be the final and immutable version of the reconstruction, but rather hope that it may evolve and be revised in the light of new evidence or arguments as they emerge in the future.

The reconstructed text of Cleitarchus comprising thirteen books, one for each year of Alexander's reign, immediately follows on from this introduction. Subsequently, four additional sections provide material that supports and justifies technical aspects of the reconstruction. Firstly, a section on Key Historical Issues looks at how Cleitarchus viewed the most controversial events and outcomes of the reign and particularly compares and contrasts Cleitarchus' interpretations with the viewpoint of Arrian and his Official Tradition. Then a section on the Nature and Genesis of Cleitarchus' Account defines and analyses what we can know and infer about Cleitarchus and the structure and contents of his single surviving work. Next a chronologically organised Table defines the episode by episode Organisation and Contents of the reconstruction including the ancient source references and some modern references, which have discussed the Cleitarchan version of each respective episode. Finally, I have incorporated a bibliography defining the key ancient and modern references, of which I have made use in planning and performing the reconstruction. A few acknowledgements and an index to the entire tome are to be found at its very end.

Finally, I would also commend the account of Cleitarchus to those readers who have little interest in the technical niceties of source research for Alexander studies. Cleitarchus' account rested on its literary merits for centuries in winning its place as the most popular version of Alexander's campaigns among the Hellenistic Greeks and the Romans. I believe that it retains good measures of readability, atmosphere, coherence and accuracy even in the present metamorphosed and imperfect form, sufficient anyway that it may be read in isolation as an authentic breath of the distant past by readers who are relatively unfamiliar with the particulars of the history of the most glamorous king who ever reigned.

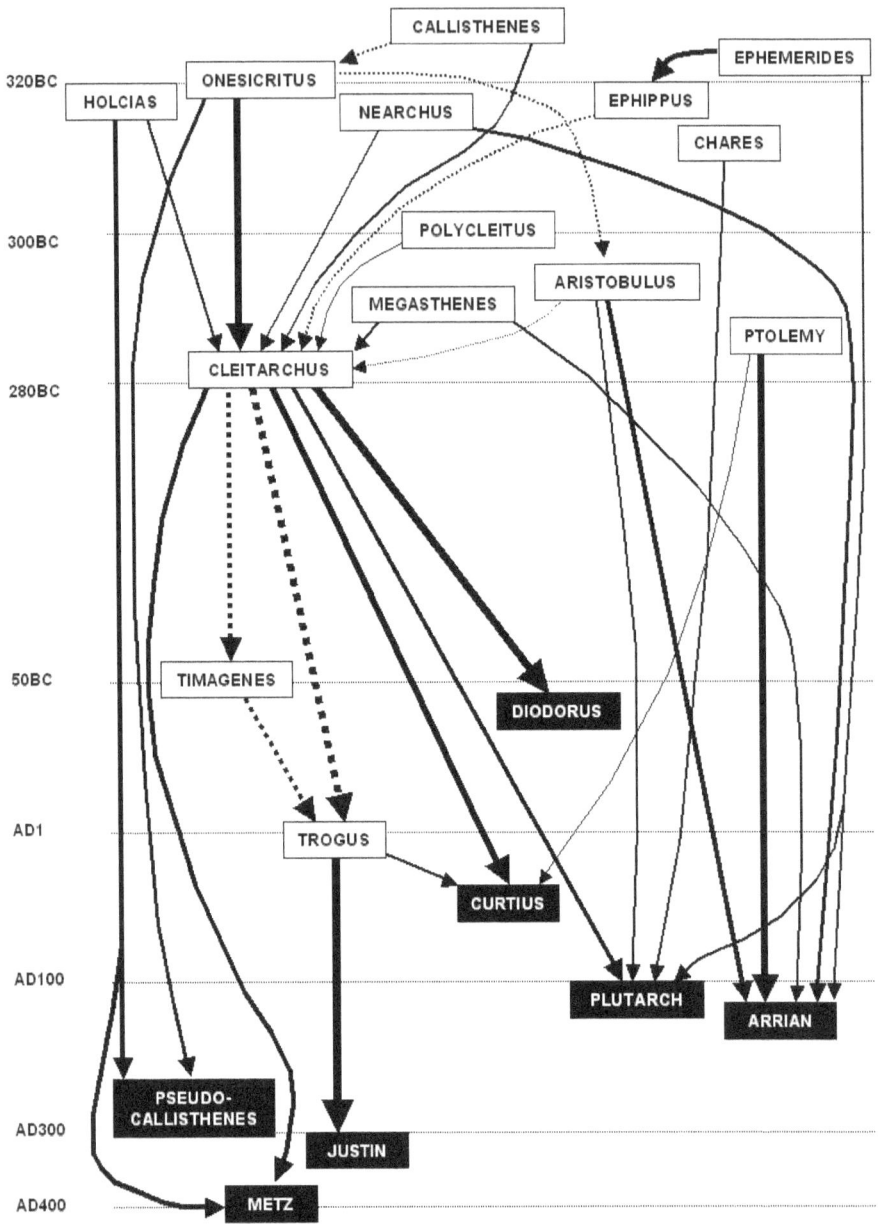

Figure A. Relationships between ancient authors on Alexander's campaigns especially pertaining to Cleitarchus (white in black box = extant; and vice versa).

PART ONE

Riding on a cotton cloud, his victims to espy,
Zeus flings all his thunderbolts out of a clear blue sky,
For I have seen electric storms cross sunny summer days
And shivered as I fell beneath that god's almighty gaze.

KEY
<u>**Underlined bold text for attributed Fragments of Cleitarchus**</u>
Bold text where there is overwhelming evidence
Bold italic text where there exists direct-firm evidence
Normal text where direct-weak evidence applies
Italic text where the evidence is conjectural

Book 1: Spring 336BC - 27th September 336BC - 15th October 335BC

The Birth & Ancestry of Alexander; Philip Dispatches an Expeditionary Force to Asia Minor; The Assassination of Philip at the Equinoctial Festival; The Accession of Alexander & the Funeral of Philip; The Recalcitrance of Thebes & the Assembly at Corinth; The Meeting with Diogenes; The Situation in the Persian Empire; The Balkan Campaign & the Battle with the Triballians; Rebellion in Greece & the Investment and Fall of Thebes; The Fate of Thebes Decided by the League at Corinth; The Visit to the Oracle at Delphi.

1.1 *In a short space of time Alexander accomplished colossal deeds and in the size of his successes he exceeds by virtue of his perspicacity and bravery the cases of all other kings within recorded history. It took just twelve years for his conquest of much of Europe and almost all of Asia to unfold and he won a resounding renown to rival that of the heroes and godlings of old. But it would be pointless actually to mention any victory of his monarchy initially, since his successes shall successively attest adequately to the glare of his glory as we proceed to relate his entire story.* Instead let us begin with his genealogy. **Alexander is considered to be a descendant of Heracles** *via* ***Caranus*** **on the basis of his paternity and** *through* ***Neoptolemus*** *the son of Achilles* **he could claim Aeacid ancestry in his mother's family tree.**[3] *All this is accepted universally.* **Hence from both his parents his physiological and psychological inheritance befitted him for accomplishments of outstanding excellence.** *Furthermore, Alexander's mother Olympias on the night he was conceived dreamt that she was coupled with a colossal serpent. Nor by this vision was she in the least deceived, for she bore in her womb a person of supernatural achievement.*

1.2 *Shortly we shall continue by recording all the incidents concerning the king that were of consequence, with due care for the correct chronology of events. But firstly it may be stated that as the one hundred and sixth Olympiad was being celebrated* **Alexander was born on the sixth day after the New Moon in the month of Hecatombaeon,**[4] **which is called Loios in Macedon, and it was upon this same date that the Temple**

---

[3] Paternal ancestry from Heracles and maternal ancestry from Aeacus are mentioned at the outset of their accounts of Alexander by Plutarch, *Alexander* 1.5 and Diodorus 17.1.5; the only likely common source for these details in these authors would be Cleitarchus.

[4] This can be shown to correspond to the twentieth of July 356BC in the Julian calendar with reference to calculations of ancient lunar eclipses. These occur at full moon, whereas Greek months began with the new moon. Hecatombaeon began with the first new moon after the summer solstice, which took place on approximately 27th June in the Julian calendar in Alexander's era.

Book 1: Spring 336BC - 27th September 336BC - 15th October 335BC

of Artemis in Ephesus was destroyed by arson. It was in respect of this that Hegesias the Magnesian made a remark sufficiently windy as to have blown out that great conflagration: namely that it was no wonder that Artemis's shrine suffered such a catastrophe, since the goddess was preoccupied with midwifery at Alexander's delivery! But all the augurs that were then in Ephesus became agitated, taking the temple's ruin as a sign that further ruin was fated and smiting their own faces, they wailed that woes and worse for Asia had that day been generated.

Figure 1.1. The birth of Alexander (Merian 1640)

1.3 *Some other omens occurred at Alexander's birth to presage his future prominence. On the day he was born two eagles perched all day long upon the roof-crest of his father Philip's residence, foretelling that he would bring both Europe and Asia jointly under his governance.* **Philip had just captured Potidaea, when three pieces of news reached him in quick succession: firstly, that the Illyrians had been overcome in a pitched battle by Parmenion; secondly, that his horse racing in the Olympic Games had won a victory and, finally, word of Alexander's nativity. Naturally, these things filled him with pride and the seers caused his spirits to be further magnified by declaring that a son whose birth had been seen to coincide with three victories would always be victorious worldwide.**

1.4 *As a boy Alexander was provided with a comprehensive elementary education and as an adolescent, he famously improved on this for five years under Aristotle's tuition. At the beginning of the spring immediately preceding the one hundred and eleventh Olympiad, Philip sent forward* three of his commanders into the Troad, which lay within the compass of Persian sovereignty. These were Parmenion, Amyntas and Attalus, with whose sister Philip had recently been joined in matrimony,[5] having divorced Olympias the mother of Alexander on suspicion of adultery.

1.5 *Meanwhile, whilst awaiting the gathering of his Greek allies, on the 27th day of Boedromion Philip celebrated the marriage of his daughter Cleopatra to that Alexander whom he had installed as king of Epirus. It was an autumnal equinoctial ritual in that year of the one hundred and eleventh Olympic festival, a day of especial splendour for the sake of each sovereign's royal grandeur: the one the giver of the bride and the other who was to wed her. Nor was there any lack of entertainment and Philip, unattended by his bodyguards, went to view a theatrical event marching midway between his son and son-in-law, the two Alexanders. But Pausanias, a youth from the Macedonian nobility, unsuspected by any bystanders, stationed himself in a narrow alley and slew Philip as he was passing, so that a day designated for rejoicing was sullied by mourning for a killing.*

1.6 *Attalus had raped this Pausanias at puberty and to this indignity was added still further injury. For Attalus invited him to a party and gave him neat wine to get him boozy, whereupon not just Attalus himself but indeed the entire company used him as a whore quite freely, making him among those of his own age the object of merciless mockery. Taking this very badly, Pausanias brought complaints before Philip very frequently. But being turned away on various pretexts, not without some ribaldry, and witnessing the honouring of his enemy with the command of an army, he refocussed his fury upon Philip personally and the vengeance that he could not procure as a complainant he exacted as a judge with unbalanced judgement.*

1.7 *Philip was forty-seven at the time of his assassination, his reign having reached a twenty-five-year duration.[6] He was the father of a son by a dancing girl from Larissa additionally. This was that Arrhidaeus who succeeded Alexander eventually. And Philip had a number of other sons by various wives, as monarchs do typically, some of these being slain by the sword, whereas the rest died naturally.[7]*

1.8 *Philip's forces comprised various clans, who differed in their reaction to his assassination. Some, believing themselves the victims of illegitimate oppression, revived hopes of emancipation. Others, being weary of farflung military operations, were pleased to forego the prospective expedition. And not a few grieved that a torch lit for the celebration of the daughter's wedding was diverted for the purpose of performing her father's funeral pyre ignition. The sudden transformation of the situation had also left Philip's Friends in a state of virtual consternation as they took firstly their aggravation of Asia and secondly the incompleteness of European*

---

[5] She was Cleopatra and the sister of Attalus in Diodorus 17.2.3 and Justin 9.5.9, but she is called Eurydice (possibly an honorific title for the king's spouse) in Arrian, *Anabasis* 3.6.5 and Athenaeus 13.557D writes that Cleopatra was the niece of Attalus and the sister of Hippostratus.

[6] Philip died on the autumnal equinox (as I earlier argued in an Appendix to *Alexander the Great in Afghanistan*) in 336BC having been born in 382BC and having (effectively) ascended the throne in 360BC, so these figures for his lifespan and length of reign from Justin 9.8.1 are relatively accurate given that Greek chronologists sometimes included parts of years in their tallies.

[7] We know, for example, that Ptolemy was said by several ancient sources to have been the son of Philip by Arsinoe and that Philip had seven or eight official wives.

Book 1: Spring 336BC - 27th September 336BC - 15th October 335BC

subjugation into consideration. Then, thirdly, there were the Illyrians, the Thracians, the Dardanians and the other foreign peoples of doubtful loyalties and dubious dispositions. It would not be possible to stop all of these nations, if they should simultaneously launch rebellions.

Figure 1.2. The assassination of Philip by Pausanias (André Castaigne 1898)

1.9 Alexander's accession remedied the dangerous situation arising from his father's assassination. *He established his authority much more firmly than any had thought likely. He was just twenty years of age and therefore not universally respected at that stage. But for his years he exhibited a very promising degree of self-control and moderation, so that it seemed that he stayed his hand more often than he took action. First of all, he rapidly* *requisitioned the support of the Macedonians by making judicious proclamations. He exempted his countrymen from every obligation except that they serve as soldiers in defence of the nation and this won him the support of the entire population, such that they* conceded that their king was changed only in his person and that there was no deterioration in the wise policies of the administration.

1.10 *Thereafter Alexander addressed the envoys that had been attending the wedding in a friendly manner, urging that the allegiance with which the Greeks had favoured his father should be extended to his successor. But he also set his soldiers to incessant training in the use of their weaponry, holding military exercises in order to instill discipline in the army.*

1.11 The king's first care was for his father's funeral, at which he had the conspirators killed on the cairn first of all. The only man spared was a brother of these, a nobleman named Alexander Lyncestes, for he had been the first to salute him as king and he wished to preserve this prophet of his crowning. He also contrived the killing of a rival for the kingship, his half-brother Caranus, dammed by a different wife of Philip.[8]

1.12 *There remained a possibility that Attalus would be a challenger for the monarchy as he was the brother of Cleopatra, Philip's last lady, so Alexander determined to forestall any such rivalry.* And this seemed especially wise, because **Cleopatra had borne a child to Philip a few days before his demise. Philip had sent Attalus on into Asia with the vanguard battalions in joint-command with Parmenion and his mild manner and benevolence**

---

[8] It is clear that this Caranus (named after the putative progenitor of the Argead dynasty) was not an infant son of Philip and Cleopatra: she had just one child by Philip, a girl named Europa (Athenaeus 13.557e; Justin 9.7.12; Diodorus 17.2.3; Pausanias 8.7.7; cf. Plutarch, *Alexander* 10.4) and there was not time for another; furthermore, an infant was not likely to have been a serious rival to Alexander in these circumstances, where the Macedonians were looking for dynamic and proactive leadership. However, it is highly probable that Philip had other sons in addition to Alexander and Arrhidaeus, as indeed is stated by Justin 9.8.3. It is suggested that Ptolemy was Philip's illegitimate son by several sources (Pausanias 1.6.2; Curtius 9.8.22; *Armenian Alexander Romance* 269) and there is no significant evidence to contradict them. Although Caranus is not mentioned by Satyrus in his list of Philip's wives and their children (Athenaeus 13.557b-e), neither is Ptolemy. It is anyway the case that absence of evidence is not evidence of absence and there is no reason to believe that Satyrus's list was comprehensive. I would therefore suspect that Caranus was a grown-up son of Philip by some woman with whom his relationship was of dubious legitimacy. Justin 11.2.3 uses the word *noverca* (step-mother) to describe this woman's relationship to Alexander, but he does so as a way of identifying Caranus as both a son of Philip and Alexander's half brother. It is for example possible that Justin's source stated that Caranus was a son of Philip and a half-brother to Alexander and that Justin (or Trogus) inferred that his mother was Alexander's *noverca*. It is additionally possible that Philip had recognised Caranus as a legitimate son, even if his mother had not been formally married to Philip (this may have been the position in the case of Arrhidaeus). It is also possible that Caranus was the son of another wife as listed by Satyrus (e.g. Meda). In short, there is no substantive basis to challenge the evidence of Justin 11.2.3 that Alexander had a half-brother called Caranus killed at the time of his accession, because Caranus had made himself a rival for the throne.

in bestowing benefactions had won him his troops' approbation. It seemed probable that he might seek to seize the sovereignty in alliance with such of the Greeks as opposed Alexander's authority. Therefore, the king selected a certain Hecataeus from among his supporters and sent him off to Asia with a band of trusted soldiers with instructions to bring Attalus back alive if feasible, but otherwise to slay him as soon as possible. So, he went over into Asia, attached himself to Attalus and Parmenion and awaited an opportunity to accomplish his mission.

1.13 Alexander was gravely concerned that a great many of the Greek nations were keen to kindle rebellions. In Athens, where Macedon was continually the target of Demosthenes' agitation, the news of Philip's assassination was the cause of celebration, for the Athenians would not readily concede primacy among the Greeks to the Macedonian monarchy. They contacted Attalus secretly and agreed to collaborate with him actively and they lobbied many another city to launch a bid for its liberty.

1.14 There was a vote taken by the Aetolians to reinstate those Acarnanians that had been exiled on Philip's instructions. A certain Aristarchus convinced the Ambraciot citizenry to expel the garrison that Philip had lodged in their city and to convert their country into a democracy. The Thebans voted similarly to force the garrison in their Cadmeia to flee and not to allow Alexander to establish his supremacy. The Spartans solely had never recognised Philip's hegemony and nor would they now acknowledge Alexander's authority.[9] Elsewhere in the Peloponnese, the Argives, Eleians, Arcadians and neighbouring cities engaged upon recovering their ancient liberties. And many tribes threatened disorder from beyond the northern Macedonian border as the widespread spirit of insurrection propelled their peoples in that direction.

1.15 *Yet* despite the danger and adversity that confronted his realm in every quarter, Alexander, *who had but recently attained his majority, both swiftly and decisively* put everything in order. Some he won over by persuasion and diplomacy, others he petrified into passivity, but the rest had to to be reduced through compulsion and harried into humility. Firstly, he treated with the Thessalians, recalling their common ancestries due to his descent from Heracles and Achilles respectively through his father's and his mother's genealogies. Boosting their confidence in him through compliments and lucrative promises, *he reminded them of how they had benefited from his father's services. Then through a formal vote of the Thessalian League Alexander convinced them to recognise him as their supreme commander and to tender him their taxes and revenues in place of his father.* Thereafter he gained the backing of the border tribes similarly, thereby freeing himself to march down to Thermopylae, where

---

[9] Diodorus 17.3.4 appears mistakenly to interchange the Spartans and the Arcadians.

he convened an Amphictyonic assembly and had it pass a resolution recognising his leadership of the Greek polity. He next admitted envoys from the Ambraciots to an audience and convinced them by taking them into his confidence that they had merely been fractionally early in celebrating the liberty that he had been about to confer upon them voluntarily.

1.16 *In order to cow the recalcitrants he led forward the Macedonian army mobilised for militancy.* With forced marches he reached Boeotia and encamped hard by the Cadmeia, casting the Theban nation into a state of consternation. Instantly that they heard that Alexander had entered Boeotian territory, the Athenians abandoned the disdain in which they had held him initially, so forcefully did the young king's impetus and rapidity wreck the resolve of every adversary. Accordingly, the Athenians voted to take into their city such of their property as was scattered across their territory and to attend to the repair of their battlements, but additionally they sent emissaries to Alexander to crave his indulgence for their not having more speedily recognised his over-arching authority.

1.17 *The emissaries even included Demosthenes, though he did not remain with the rest, but turned back to Athens at Cithaeron, either nervous on account of his anti-Macedonian policies or simply wishing to give the Persian king no reason to place his loyalties in question.* For he was widely believed to have received vast fees from that direction in payment for his activities to thwart Macedonian domination. It was this indiscretion that is said to have been referenced by Aischines in a speech in which he denounced Demosthenes for corruption: "Whereas it is true that currently the king's gold has left him temporarily in a state of satiation, even this will not give him permanent satisfaction, for no amount of money has ever been enough to glut the greed of such a person."[10] Alexander spoke pleasantly to the delegation, relieving the Athenian populace of their considerable trepidation.

1.18 *Thereafter,* following his father's precedent, **the king convened an assembly at Corinth comprising representatives from the city-states.** And when he had gathered the customary delegates, he addressed the meeting with expressions of moderation and persuaded it to appoint him supreme commander of the forces of the Greek nation. *He also had them commit themselves to participate in an expedition to be launched against Persia seeking retribution for the crimes that the Persians had perpetrated against the Greek population.* Thereafter many statesmen and philosophers came before him to congratulate him on these achievements and he supposed that Diogenes of Sinope, who was living in the city, would likewise come to pay his compliments. But since that philosopher conspicuously ignored Alexander and sat in the suburb of Craneion relishing his leisure, the cynic was subjected

---

[10] This speech suvives independently: Aischines 3.173.

Book 1: Spring 336BC - 27th September 336BC - 15th October 335BC

to a visit by the king, who came upon him whilst he was sunbathing. Diogenes sat up on seeing such a crowd approaching and fixed his gaze upon the king. Then, when that sovereign gave him greeting and asked whether he might grant him anything, he replied: "You can move a little out of my sun, which you are shading." It is said that Alexander was so full of admiration for the haughtiness and affectation of a man who thought him unworthy of attention that he turned to his attendants who were ridiculing the philosopher's priorities and confided: "Were I not Alexander I would like to be Diogenes".[11] **All his objectives having been achieved happily, Alexander returned to Macedonia with his army.**

1.19 Having followed the unfolding of Greek events, it is timely to turn our attention to various Asian incidents, where, in the aftermath of Philip's assassination, Attalus had actually plotted rebellion. He had allied himself with the Athenians against Alexander in order that they could act in unison. But he wavered subsequently and, salvaging the letter delivered from Demosthenes, he dispatched it to Alexander, seeking through protestations of loyalty to cleanse himself of all taint of treachery. Nevertheless, Hecataeus complied with the king's commands literally and arranged for Attalus to perish through perfidy. From that point on the Macedonian army in Asia was free from any incitement to rebellion with Attalus eliminated and Alexander enjoying the absolute loyalty of Parmenion.

1.20 *As Alexander's story is shortly to concern the empire of the Persians, it is necessary to comprehend both the Greek and the Persian situations. While Philip yet held the Macedonian monarchy, Ochus ruled the Persians and persecuted his people cruelly and harshly. Since he was detested for his pernicious personality, the chiliarch Bagoas, a eunuch physically, but a rampant rogue in actuality, assassinated him using poison administered by a particular physician and set upon the throne Arses, his youngest son. The brothers of the new king he likewise liquidated, though they had barely reached their majority, in order that the youth should be isolated and remain subservient to his authority. But the young ruler intimated that he viewed Bagoas's crimes with indignation and was willing to see the*

---

[11] The story of the meeting of Alexander and Diogenes is told by Valerius Maximus 4.3 ext. 4a and Plutarch, *Alexander* 14.1-3 and is also mentioned in his *Moralia* 331E-332C & 605D and there is a variant version of the same event in Diogenes Laertius, *Diogenes* 6, whilst Arrian, *Anabasis* 7.1.5-7.3.6 draws a parallel between Diogenes of Sinope and the *gymnosophists* whom Alexander encountered in India. The ultimate source for the meeting is almost certainly Onesicritus, who was both Alexander's chief pilot and a pupil of Diogenes. It is almost certain that Cleitarchus used Onesicritus as a major source and Cleitarchus was himself associated with the Cynics and took a keen interest in the *gymnosophists* and Calanus in particular. For all these reasons, it is likely that he included an account of this meeting in his history of Alexander's reign and Plutarch's version is the best model for his original. The version in Valerius Maximus may suggest it was in Trogus and that he took it from Cleitarchus (or from Timagenes, who took it from Cleitarchus). I have argued in Appendix A of the 2nd edition of my book on *Alexander's Lovers* (2012) that Alexander (at least in part) meant that he would like to be known by the Homeric epithet of Diogenes meaning roughly "sprung from Zeus".

eunuch castigated for his every indiscretion. Hence Bagoas forestalled Arses in this aim by slaying him and his offspring while he was in but the third year of his reign. This completed the extirpation of the dynasty, so that none was left to claim the throne from the immediate royal family. Consequently, Bagoas selected Darius, a member of the aristocracy, and installed him in the position of supreme authority. He was the son of Arsanes and the grandson of that Ostanes who was a brother of the former king, Artaxerxes.[12] As for Bagoas, he suffered an ironic fate such as it will be instructive to relate. With his usual ruthlessness, he attempted to poison Darius. But the plot being disclosed, the king proposed that the eunuch should drink to his health and, handing over his cup, compelled him to drink his medicine himself.

Figure 1.3. Alexander meets Diogenes at Corinth (relief in the Villa Albani, Rome)

---

[12] Artaxerxes II (405-359BC).

Book 1: Spring 336BC - 27th September 336BC - 15th October 335BC

1.21 *The selection of Darius for the throne was based on his exhibited bravery, for he was outstanding amongst the Persians in this quality. Once when king Artaxerxes was warring with the Cadusians, one famed for his fearlessness and might called for a volunteer among the Persians to meet him in a hand-to-hand fight. None but Darius,* then named Codommanus, *dared to duel with this opponent and he slew the man in the event. Consequently, the king honoured him with many excellent presents, while the Persians put him at the pinnacle of valiance. It was on account of this eminence that he was deemed worthy to be installed in the monarchy. And it was at about the time of Philip's murder that all this took place in parallel to Alexander becoming king of the Macedonian race. Such was the man that fate fielded to contend with Alexander's virtuosity and they fought one another in many momentous matches for the supremacy. These our detailed narrative shall describe successively and thus we shall proceed to chronicle this history.*

1.22 *Darius ascended the throne ahead of Philip's assassination and he planned to push the incipient war back into the Macedonian nation, but with Philip's extinction the king was relieved of all anxiety, being contemptuous of Alexander's immaturity. Rapidly, however, when Alexander's vigour and velocity had secured him in the rule of all Greek territory and made manifest the young man's extraordinary ability, Darius became more wary and began seriously to ready his soldiery. He refurbished numerous war galleys and mobilised many mighty armies, simultaneously commissioning his ablest commanders, including Memnon of Rhodes, in both courage and cunning the most talented of officers. The king consigned five thousand mercenaries to his command and sent him to seize Cyzicus with this band. Accordingly, Memnon marched his men across Mount Ida to reach Cyzican land.*[13]

1.23 *Some tell the tale that this sierra took its name from that daughter of Melisseus called Ida. It is the tallest massif in the Hellespontine area with a notable cave at its core, where Alexander judged the goddesses of yore.*[14] *This is the mountain that the Idaean Dactyls are supposed to have dwelt upon, having learnt from the Mother of the Gods*[15] *the skill of making iron. A weird phenomenon is recorded pertaining to this height, which elsewhere has never come to light. At about the season of the rising of the Dog Star,*[16] *standing upon the topmost scar the stillness of the air gives the*

---

[13] Mt Ida is the massif to the southeast of the Troad, whereas Cyzicus is on the southern shore of the Propontis (Sea of Marmara), so this implies that Memnon marched northwards from a location on the Ionian shore of Asia Minor.

[14] This is Alexander the youngest son of King Priam of Troy, who is also known as Paris.

[15] Probably Rhea is meant.

[16] Probably the Heliacal rising of Sirius, circa 20th July.

sense that the summit is elevated above the winds' turbulence and, though it still be dark below, up there you can see the sun's rising glow. Its rays do not emanate from an orb in this situation, but its light is cast up from many a direction so as to give a perfect impression of numerous blazes beyond the horizon. Progressively, these merge into a single conflagration having a breadth of three plethra of rotation.[17] Eventually, as daylight draws near, the normal solar sphere begins to appear, casting its usual illumination.

1.24 *Having crossed this mountain* **Memnon advanced upon Cyzicus with himself and his officers wearing Macedonian headgear, so that those in the city thought that it was Calas, their friend and ally,** *Attalus's successor,*[18] **who had decided to appear. Therefore, they naturally flung their gates open wide, but recognised their error just before Memnon got inside. Thus, thwarted Memnon departed and set to ravaging and plundering their countryside,** *but, whilst he was consequently preoccupied, the city of Grynion was stormed by Parmenion,*[19] *who sold its whole population into slavery. But when he invested Pitanê, Memnon manifested himself promptly and intimidated the Macedonian army into withdrawing from the city. Subsequently, Calas, commanding a combined contingent of mercenaries and Macedonians, was confronted in the Troad by a much mightier army of the Persians, so he retired into the Rhoeteion promontory on account of his numerical inferiority.*

1.25 *Considering that the diaffection in Greece had been suppressed, Alexander carried his campaigning into Thracian regions of unrest. Many of the tribes inhabiting this territory had been seized by a spirit of militancy, but were inspired to tender their submission in the face of his aggression.* Having met Syrmus at the Danube and trounced the Triballians, **he veered westwards against the Paeonians, the Illyrians and the neighbouring nations. Numerous of the natives had fomented insurrections. These he vanquished and established his own control over their dominions. He had not yet completed these operations, when messengers informed him that many of the Greeks had launched rebellions. Sundry cities had actually acted to end their alliance with the Macedonians, the most prominent being Thebes** and Athens. In many cases they had besieged their Macedonian garrisons, having defected from Alexander and gone over to the Persians.

---

[17] If the three lateral plethra be assumed to lie at a radius of a stade (= six plethra), they subtend around thirty modern degrees. This would be sensible, whereas the alternative interpretation that the solar glare was 300 feet wide is nonsensical.

[18] Calas was the son of a certain Harpalus from the family of the lords of Elimiotis in Macedonia. He is not necessarily the son of Alexander's treasurer, but might instead be a close relative. He appears from the circumstances to have replaced Attalus.

[19] Memnon's raid on Cyzicus and the stratagem of the hats is recorded by Polyaenus 5.44.5 in a way that is consistent with the thinner outline in Diodorus 17.7.8.

Book 1: Spring 336BC - 27th September 336BC - 15th October 335BC

1.26 *The orator Demosthenes had instigated these insurrections, so Alexander was told, for he had succumbed to bribery by the Persians, having accepted a considerable quantity of gold. Demosthenes had broadcast assertions that the entire army of the Macedonians had been wiped out by the Triballians. He brought before the Athenian assembly a witness who was anxious to explain that he had personally suffered an injury in a battle in which the king had been slain. Nearly all the city-states were credulous of this intelligence and underwent a change in their allegiance.* **Alexander was moved to make a rapid return to Macedonia on receiving this information, being keen to suppress the unrest with no hint of hesitation.**

1.27 The Thebans were primarily eager to expel the Macedonian garrison from their citadel called the Cadmeia, which they promptly invested, whereupon Alexander and his army suddenly manifested themselves before the walls of the city and encamped in its immediate vicinity. Prior to their arrival the Thebans had had sufficient opportunity to encircle the Cadmeia with a deep ditch and palisade, so as to stop the troops trapped within receiving reinforcements or other forms of aid. They had also issued an appeal to the Arcadians, Argives and Eleians for assistance and they sent the Athenians a request for reinforcements. Then, when Demosthenes donated a shipment of arms for their defence, they outfitted all citizens lacking panoplies with these presents. But in response to the requests for reinforcements, the Peloponnesians sent soldiers as far as the isthmus, where they awaited the outcome of events on account of the imminence of the king's presence. Whereas the Athenians, under Demosthenes' influence, voted in support of the Thebans but failed to send forth their contingents, whilst awaiting the war's developments. In the Cadmeia, Philotas, the commander of the garrison, watched the Thebans making immense siege preparations, so he made a stockpile of every projectile that could be used as a weapon and did what was feasible to reinforce his fortifications.

1.28 So it was that when the king appeared suddenly out of Thrace with his whole army, aid for Thebes from her allies was proving desultory, whereas the forces of her foes possessed an apparent and patent superiority. Nevertheless, her leaders convened in council to consider a resolution on their city's defence and they were unanimously determined to fight for their autonomy and independence. The motion was duly passed by the assembly and all were ready zealously to run every risk in pursuit of victory.

1.29 Initially, Alexander gave the Thebans time to ponder and held his forces back, believing that a single city would never dare to resist such an army's attack. For at that juncture the king commanded more than thirty thousand infantry and no fewer than three thousand cavalry, all battle-hardened veterans of Philip's reign, who had hardly had a single setback in any campaign. This was that very army, of which the prowess and loyalty enabled him to conquer the Persian Empire subsequently. Had the

Thebans adjusted their position in the light of their situation and had they asked the Macedonians for peace and a partnership treaty, the king would have agreed to their proposals gladly and would have conceded their every entreaty, for he was keen to assuage any Greek acrimony, so that he could be free to pursue the Persian war with impunity.

1.30 But ultimately, he recognised that he was despised by the Theban citizenry, so he determined that he should completely destroy their city and by this exhibition of ferocity to blunt the enthusiasm of any other that might dare to confront him in enmity. He readied his forces for a fight then announced through a herald that any Theban still might decide to come over to him and delight in the communal peace, as was every Greek's right. With matching verve, the Thebans thundered from a tall tower in reply that anyone wishing to defy the tyrant of Greece might join with the Great King and Thebes in freeing the Greeks as their ally. This designation stung Alexander, who fell into a fierce anger, saying that he would see that the severest penalty would be visited upon the Theban community. Seething in his soul, he assembled siege engines for his attack and whatever else was needed to bring about a sack.

1.31 As the news spread throughout Greece that the Thebans were confronted by catastrophe, people were pained by the anticipated calamity, but none dared to deliver them any assistance, considering that the city had by a rushed and rash resistance realised a conspicuous threat to its existence. Nevertheless, the Thebans themselves ran the risk resolutely and willingly, though they were disturbed by certain signs sent by the gods and by various words of prophecy.

1.32 Firstly there was a fine web of gossamer found in the temple of Demeter, grown to the size of a cloak when spread and iridescent all around like a rainbow overhead. Concerning this the oracle at Delphi sent this response to their query: "To all mortals the gods have sent this omen; to the Boeotians firstly and then to the neighbouring men." Whereas the ancestral oracle of Thebes had proffered this answer: "The woven web is well for one, but ill for another." This sign had transpired three months prior to Alexander's appearance before the city's wall, but at the very time of the king's arrival the statues in the agora suddenly became wet with beads of moisture giving the appearance of sweat. Furthermore, people reported to the city's commissioners that the marsh at Onchestus was emitting a sound most like a moan, while at Dirke the waters were disturbed by a ripple of a blood-red tone. Lastly, it was reported by rovers returning from Delphi that that they had seen bloodstains on the roof of the sanctuary that the Thebans had funded using Phocian money.[20]

---

[20] The Phocians had been expelled from the Amphictyonic League in 346BC and forced to pay reparations.

Book 1: Spring 336BC - 27th September 336BC - 15th October 335BC

1.33 *Experts in the interpretation of auguries confided that the web predicted the departure of the city's deities and its iridescence indicated a storm of calamities. The sweating of the statues portended a colossal catastrophe and the appearance of blood in many a locality meant that a wholesale slaughter would take place throughout the city. They concluded that the gods were unambiguously forecasting dire adversity, so they urged that the outcome of the conflict should not be chanced in hand-to-hand hostilities, but that the city should seek a safer solution through discussions with its adversaries.*

1.34 *Yet still the enthusiasm of the Thebans for a contest was not curbed. On the contrary in their keenness, they were completely unperturbed as they reminisced concerning their triumph at Leuctra and their other victories, where they had won against the odds through their fighting abilities to the amazement of the rest of the Greek communities. Thus, they gave vent to their patriotic spirit bravely rather than wisely and flung themselves precipitously towards the annihilation of their country.*

1.35 *In the space of just three days the king had made ready everything required for his assault upon the city. He split his forces into three brigades and ordered the first to attack the palisades that had been raised before the city and the second to confront the serried Theban infantry. The third he held in reserve to reinforce any harried section of his army and to relieve them in the line progressively. On their side the Thebans corralled their cavalry within their stockades and deployed their freedmen, immigrants and refugees to defend the palisades, whilst their citizens made ready to engage before the city with the king's brigades, which outnumbered them very heavily. Meanwhile, their wives and offspring surged into the sanctuaries and beseeched their deities to deliver Thebes from her enemies.*

1.36 *As the Macedonians advanced and each regiment approached their Theban opposition, the trumpets blared to signal a confrontation and the soldiers of both sides yelled the battle cry in unison and propelled their javelins in their adversaries' direction. All their missiles having soon been cast, everyone engaged with their swords at last in a hand-to-hand struggle and thus began a titanic battle. An inexorable force was exerted by the Macedonian ranks on account of their numbers and the power of their phalanx, but the Thebans outshone them in sheer athleticism due to relentless training in their gymnasium. In addition, they fought in a condition of exaltation, each completely uncaring concerning the peril of his situation. Those injured in either army were very many and quite a few fell in the face of blows from the enemy. The air shook with the shouts of men locked in deadly disputations: moans and groans and yells and exhortations. Among the Macedonians their fellows roused them to live up to their lustrous reputations, whilst among the Thebans they urged* remembrance of children and elderly relations in danger of slavery and their country with all their property exposed to Macedonian fury. The battles of Leuctra and Mantinea should be watchwords for their victory, being famous throughout Greece for deeds of bravery. Thus, for a long while the outcome hung in the balance, on account of the extraordinary valour of the combatants.

1.37 *Finally, Alexander perceived that the Thebans were still standing staunchly in defence of their liberty, but that his Macedonians were showing signs of flagging in their exertion, so he ordered his reserve battalions to go into action. As they charged suddenly against the fatigued Theban ranks, they slew a fair few through the impact of their phalanx. Yet still the Thebans would not concede victory, but on the contrary, being filled with the will to win, they scorned all jeopardy. Their morale was such that they shouted openly that the Macedonians had made manifest their inferiority. Normally, when an adversary attacks in rotation, it is sensible for soldiers to be fearful of the force of the fresh formation. But the Thebans were an exception on that occasion in facing each new threat with increased determination as their enemy threw fresh troops into action to replace those on the verge of exhaustion.*

1.38 *Therefore the resolution of the Thebans proved indefatigable in the face of frontal assault by Alexander's hosts, but the king noticed a postern gate, the guards of which had abandoned their posts. He hastened Perdiccas with a substantial detachment of troops at his side to seize the unprotected portal and to force their way inside. The officer and his task force speedily penetrated into the city via this entry, while the Thebans, having withstood the first onslaught of the enemy, were confronting the second resolutely, still buoyed up by expectations of victory. But when they understood that their city had been invaded in some parts, they immediately began to withdraw within its ramparts. Yet in the course of this activity, their cavalry careered into their infantry and trampled and killed very many, whilst the horsemen themselves rode riotously on into the city and moved into a maze made up of many a narrow alley, where they foundered in fosses and fell upon their own weaponry. Simultaneously, the Macedonian garrison in the Cadmeia surged out of the citadel, fell upon the Thebans and, catching them in confusion, slew quite a few of them as well.*

1.39 *Inevitably, while the city was being sacked, it was the scene of sundry retributions within the circuit of its fortifications. The Macedonians were incensed by the Theban proclamation's arrogance, so they attacked the inhabitants with more than usual violence. They flung themselves upon these unfortunates yelling and cursing and slew everyone they encountered without relenting. Equally, the Thebans clung to a forlorn hope of victory, valuing their lives but cheaply whenever they encountered*

Book 1: Spring 336BC - 27th September 336BC - 15th October 335BC

an enemy and drawing his blows personally by tangling with him desperately. In the taking of that city, no Theban thought to beg the Macedonians for mercy nor was any seen to crouch down and cling to the knees of their conquerors cravenly. But neither did the agony brought upon them by their bravery elicit pity from any adversary. Nor did the day's duration even allow sufficiently for the extent of the cruelty that might have been inflicted by their implacability. In summary, the entire city was sacked indiscriminately. Universally, children were dragged into captivity, shrieking the names of their mothers quite piteously.

1.40 *Invariably, households were seized with their entire complement, thus accomplishing the city's enslavement. Of the men remaining, some, though injured and dying, grappled with the enemy, but were themselves slaughtered as they sought to slay their adversary. Others, equipped with nothing more than a broken spear, confronted their assailants as they drew near, for though their lives were forfeit in these final fights, they held their freedom and their rights even more dear. As the mayhem spread and every part of the place became clogged with the dead, no witness could have failed to pity the plight of the people of that benighted city. For even other Greeks –* Phocians, *Thespians, Orchomenians, Plataeans plus sundry others at odds with the Thebans - who had joined in campaigning with the king, surged into the city alongside him and gave vent to their own loathing, compounding its citizens' suffering.*[21]

1.41 *So the city was the scene of many a sickening sin. Greeks were callously killed by natives of their own nation and families were mercilessly murdered by their kin. Even a shared slang failed to secure any cessation. Ultimately, when night fell finally, their residences had been ransacked thoroughly and women, children and the elderly were torn from temples where they had sought sanctuary and subjected to ravishment and unrestrained inhumanity.*

1.42 *Among the numerous and grievous calamities that befell the city, some Thracian cavalry broke into the house of Timocleia, a lady of firm fidelity and modesty and while the rest were plundering her patrimony, she was raped by their leader most shamefully and grilled as to whether there were any gold or silver hidden about the property.*[22] *She admitted to it as though making*

---

[21] Though near neighbours of the Thebans, we know that these cities had suffered greatly during the preceding era of Theban domination: the Phocians in particular had had a penal decree enacted against them by the Amphictyonic Council in 356BC through the agency of the Thebans, so they were not reticent in exacting revenge when this opportunity presented itself.

[22] The story of Timocleia is not told by either of the main Cleitarchan sources for the destruction of Thebes (i.e. Diodorus and Justin), but only by Plutarch, *Alexander* 12 and Polyaenus, *Stratagems* 8.40; however, Plutarch tells it at a point where he appears to be using Cleitarchus for the 6000 Theban dead and 30,000 captives and it is the kind of digression that both Justin and Diodorus would have avoided for the sake of brevity in their epitomes. Plutarch also tells the story in more detail in his *Moralia* 259D-260D and he attributes it to Aristobulus in *Moralia* 1093C; this does not exclude it having been told by Cleitarchus also (either inspired by Aristobulus or following other

a confession and led him by himself into the garden showing him to a dry well and telling him that when the city fell she had solely and personally cast into it her most precious property. Then as the Thracian was peering down into the pit, she got behind him and pushed him into it and flung many rocks over its rim, so that she was soon certain of having killed him. Afterwards, when the Thracians led her with her hands bound before Alexander, she showed by her carriage and her gait that she was a personage of great dignity and hauteur, so calmly and fearlessly did she follow those that led her. Then when the king demanded to know her identity, she replied that Theagenes had been her brother, who had marshalled the men that had fought Philip for Greek liberty and who had fallen at Chaeronea, where he was a commander. Consequently, being greatly impressed by her response and by her actions equally, Alexander directed that she and her children should be set free.

1.43 Over six thousand Thebans were slain in their city with more than thirty thousand being taken into captivity[23] *and an incredible amount of property was seized as booty.* **The king** *buried the Macedonian dead, who numbered in excess of five hundred, then he summoned the representatives of the Greek people to decide the fate of Thebes in the League Council. When the debate began, those that were hostile to the* **Thebans,** including the Phocians, Plataeans, Thespians and Orchomenians, allies of Alexander who now shared in his victory, **proposed that the city should suffer the most severe penalty.** For they were retaliating regarding the ravaging of their own cities firstly and in respect of the ruthlessness of the Thebans secondly. Thirdly, **they castigated them for their** current and also **past support of Persia in undermining Greek liberty.** *For in the reign of Xerxes they had actually fought their fellow Greeks in alliance with the Persian invaders and they alone among Greeks were feted by the Persian kings as collaborators, so that they set thrones before their sovereigns to seat the Theban ambassadors.* This had made Thebes a pariah among every Greek nation, which was evident from the Greeks having sworn an oath to efface the place upon the Persians' capitulation. Additionally, *they told tales of previous Theban iniquities, with which they had filled all their theatrical tragedies, in order to foment ill feeling against them, not merely for their current treacheries but also for immemorial infamies.*

1.44 Then Cleadas, one of the Theban captives, was permitted to address the ambassadors. Thebes had not rebelled against the king, he said, whom they had heard had been killed, but instead against the king's successors. Whatever fault were found with them was due to their credulity rather than attributable to treachery and for this they had already paid a surpassing penalty through the annihilation of the young men in their army. The only people left were a harmless crowd of women and the arthritic elderly, who had been subjected to rape and

---

accounts) and this is supported by some disparities between Plutarch's versions, e.g. Timocleia pushes the Thracian into the well in the *Life of Alexander*, but waits for him to climb down in the *Moralia*; therefore I have included the story of Timocleia here tentatively.

[23] Plutarch, *Alexander* 11.6 & Diodorus 17.14.1.

Book 1: Spring 336BC - 27th September 336BC - 15th October 335BC

violence respectively, more awful than anything they had ever endured previously. It was no longer on behalf of their compatriots that they made their plea, since too few remained to matter greatly, but for the guiltless soil of their dear country and for a city that had not merely bred men, but also the occasional deity. For Cleadas now directed his appeal towards Alexander's idolatry for Heracles, a son of their city and the progenitor of the Argead dynasty[24] and to his father Philip's youthful sojourn in their community. He implored Alexander to spare a city that venerated as divinities the forefathers of his family born in its vicinity, a city that had additionally overseen the training of that most illustrious king.

1.45 But bitter enmities prevailed over entreaties and **the sentiments of the council were inflamed against Thebes, so that they ultimately voted to raze the city, to sell the captives into slavery, to outlaw the Thebans in all Greek territory and to forbid every Greek from offering them sanctuary. In accordance with the council's decree, Alexander demolished the entire city** and distributed its lands among those that shared in his victory, *thus providing a shocking warning of the degree of calamity that rebellion could bring. After freeing the priests, various Macedonian agents, those who had opposed rebellion and Pindar's house and descendants,* **the king auctioned off all its imprisoned inhabitants,** their prices being buoyed up by hatred for aggressors, rather than the mercantile motives of any bidder. Nevertheless, <u>their total value amounted to less than four hundred and forty talents of silver. For they were parsimonious and niggardly in their culinary tendencies, making meals out mincemeat in leaves, boiled vegetables, various tiny fish such as anchovies, sausages, beef ribs and a porridge of peas. Attaginus, the son of Phrynon entertained Mardonius and fifty other Persians with these, although Herodotus in his ninth book says that Attaginus was in receipt of generous monies.[25] At Plataea, the Greeks need not have provided them with potent opposition, for they could not have won against any kind of competition, having already been neutralised by such nauseating nutrition.</u>[26]

1.46 The Athenians were mortified by the fall of Thebes and threw open their gates to the refugees in contravention of the League's decrees. This so provoked the king that, when Athens sent emissaries to entreat him to refrain from further hostilities, **Alexander demanded that ten Athenian statesmen that were his key enemies be delivered up to him** before he would agree to the city's pleas. ***Demosthenes and Lycurgus were the foremost of these***, who had emboldened their countrymen in their mutinies. ***So, the city convened an***

---

[24] Justin 11.4.5 suggests that the Aeacidae (Alexander's mother's family) traced their descent from Heracles, but it was Alexander's father's family, the Argead kings of Macedon, which actually vaunted this particular semi-legendary genealogy, so I have inferred a transcriptional error.

[25] Herodotus, *Histories* 9.15-16.

[26] Jacoby Fragment 7 of Cleitarchus from the 1st book of his History Concerning Alexander preserved in Athenaeus 148D-F.

assembly and the emissaries were listened to attentively, but after they had heard out their story, the populace was immersed in misery and perplexity. Though keen to preserve the honour of their country, they were traumatised by the Theban tragedy and being forewarned by the cataclysm suffered by their neighbour, they were haunted by their own impending danger.

Figure 1.4. Timocleia brought before Alexander with hands bound (Domenichino)

1.47 *After many had spoken in the assembly, Phocion the Good, who was opposed to Demosthenes' party, declared that the men demanded should be mindful of the example set by Leos' and Hyacinthus' daughters and go gladly to their deaths to preserve their country from awful slaughters and he castigated the cowardice and pusillanimity of those that refused to lay down their lives for their city.[27] The citizens nevertheless rejected his recommended recourse and riotously drove him from the podium and when Demosthenes delivered a diligently contrived discourse, they were overcome by sympathy for their leaders and desired to save them. Ultimately, it is attested that Demades was persuaded by a bribe of five*

---

[27] The Delphic oracle required Leos to have his three daughters sacrificed in order to save Athens from famine, e.g. Pausanias, *Description of Greece* 1.5.2. Hyacinthus of Lacedaemon moved to Athens and caused his four daughters to be sacrificed at the tomb of the Cyclops Geraestus in order to deliver the city from famine and plague: see Pseudo-Apollodorus, *Bibliotheca* 3.15.8; Hyginus, *Fabulae* 238.

talents from Demosthenes' adherents to advise that the assembly should seek to save those threatened with a death sentence, so he read out a decree that was full of subtle refinements. It provided for an appeal to be made on behalf of the men chosen coupled with a resolution to bring the full force of the law into action against anyone convicted of its infraction. The citizens approved Demades' motion, endorsed the decree and dispatched a delegation. Those envoys sent to Alexander included Demades and they were also instructed to present the city's pleas on behalf of the Theban refugees, specifically that Athens be permitted to give sanctuary to Theban escapees.

1.48 *On this mission Demades* intimated to Alexander that Athens would go to war before she would surrender any Athenian commander and he *achieved all the aims with which he had been sent through eloquent argument. He persuaded the king to agree that the men need not be placed in his custody and that the orators among them would retain their liberty and additionally that the Thebans could remain in his city.* But the generals were banished from Athenian territory and defected to Darius immediately, providing the Persians with no mean augmentation of their military potency.

1.49 At this point the king made a pilgrimage to Delphi to visit the Oracle of Apollo, wishing to consult the god concerning the Asian campaigns that were to follow.[28] But it happened that he visited on one of the days when prophecy is prohibited on account of its inauspiciousness, so he first of all addressed a summons to the prophetess. Then, when she refused to perform her prognostication, pleading its illegality in mitigation, he went up personally and sought to drag her to the shrine forcefully. Whereupon, as though conquered by his tenacity, she declared: "You are invincible, my boy!" On hearing which, he replied: "I need no further prophecy, having received an oracle that fills me with joy."

1.50 These were the concerns of Alexander *in the first year of his reign.*

---

[28] Alexander's consultation of the Delphic Oracle is mentioned retrospectively by Diodorus 17.93.4, agreeing with Plutarch, *Alexander* 14.4, which shows that this story was probably in Cleitarchus, but that Diodorus omitted it in epitomising the main account of the event. This was the basis on which he was known as the invincible Alexander long before he was called Alexander the Great (Hypereides, the contemporaneous Athenian orator and later Livy 9.18 also called Alexander invincible.) The historicity of the visit is supported by an inscription from Delphi recording a gift to the shrine at this time of 150 gold coins minted in the name of Philip II [SIG³ 251H, col. II, lines 9-10 (p.436-7)].

Figure 1.5. The Pythia (Delphic prophetess) and Alexander (André Castaigne 1898)

Book 2: 16ᵗʰ October 335BC - 5ᵗʰ October 334BC

Preparations for the Asian Expedition; Crossing the Hellespont; The Visit to Troy; The Battle of the Granicus; The Surrender of Magnesia; The Siege of Miletus; The Dismissal of the Fleet; The Siege of Halicarnassus; The Capture of the Fortress of the Marmares.

2.1 *This book recounts the events concerning Alexander in the second year of his reign.*

2.2 *The king convened a meeting of his generals and his foremost Friends after having returned with his army to Macedonia. At this council he tabled for discussion his plan for the invasion of Asia in terms of the timing of the onslaught and how the war should be fought. Antipater and Parmenion advised him first to father an heir and only then to engage upon so ambitious an affair. But Alexander contradicted them, being eager to get the enterprise underway and consequently antagonistic towards any delay. He observed: "It would be scandalous for me, as the successor to the command of our invincible national army and as the person appointed by the Greeks to lead the offensive in the fighting, to settle down at home consumating my marriage pending the production of offspring." He went on to lecture them on the advantages of the operation and roused their enthusiasm for the forthcoming contest through this oration. At Dium in Macedonia he made the gods lavish offerings and held a theatrical festival dedicated to Zeus and the Muses that had been founded by Archelaus, one of their former kings. He continued the celebrations for nine days, dedicating each day to one of the Muses. He also erected a pavilion to hold a hundred couches and invited to a banquet his Friends and his commanders as well as the* Greek *city-states' ambassadors. By conducting the festivities with great splendour and personally hosting the entertainment of a great number as well as distributing sacrificial beasts and all else required to celebrate such feasts to each and every soldier, he put his army in a hearty humour.*

2.3 Before setting off for the war in Asia Alexander *purged each of the relatives of his stepmother that Philip had raised into the higher echelons and promoted to commander. Nor did he spare such of his own family as seemed suited for the crown, so that, whilst he was fighting far away, there should not remain in Macedon a means of bringing him down. He also* inducted the more talented of the tributary rulers *from Thrace* to serve *honourably* as his auxiliaries, whilst leaving the more laggardly *and men of meaner birth* to look after their territories, *thereby lessening the risk of mutinies.*[29]

---

[29] Reported by Justin 11.5.3 and elaborated by Frontinus, *Stratagems* 2.11.3.

Figure 2.1. The departure of Alexander for Asia (Petrty, 1909)

2.4 Thus it was that, eight hundred and twenty years after the Heraclid invasion[30] and while Euainetos was still the Athenian Archon, Alexander, having mustered his forces in Macedon, **advanced his army** to the **Hellespontine shore, where he embarked his troops upon ships for ferrying from Europe to Asia.**[31] *From there the sight of Asia inspired him with extraordinary ardour and he set up altars to the twelve gods to make offerings for a successful war.*

2.5 *But the king would not embark until he had subjected the finances of his companions to review and allotted to one a farmstead, to the next a village and to another some hamlet's or harbour's revenue. When finally, he had disbursed or dispersed nearly all the crown property, Perdiccas made the enquiry: "But, Sire, what is left for your own treasury?" And when the king responded: "My hopes and expectations," Perdiccas replied: "In these then we shall share, who participate in the expedition as your companions." Subsequently, he refused his allotted property and some of the rest of Alexander's Friends declined their share similarly.* However, Alexander bestowed possessions readily on such companions as coveted and welcomed his charity, so that his distributions exhausted practically all his Macedonian patrimony, *but he declared that Asia would compensate him sufficiently.*

2.6 *The king sacrificed beasts before any of his vessels left the shore, imploring that the gods grant him victory in a war, in which he was chosen to seek vengeance for so many Persian assaults upon Greece of yore. And he had traced characters in dye upon the hand of the officiating priest,*

---

[30] Allegedly the return from exile of the descendants of Heracles, Alexander's paternal ancestors, this traditional event is commonly identified with the Dorian invasion of Greece. The point of this mention of Alexander's ancestors would appear to be an attempt to legitimise Alexander's conquests: the implication is that he was merely reclaiming lands that had once been occupied by his forebears. Cleitarchus was writing as a Greek citizen of Alexandria in the mid-3rd century BC. In Hellenistic geography Egypt, defined as the black land of the Nile valley, was the last nation of Asia before Libya, which began at the edge of the desert on its western bank (there was no Suez Canal to provide an alternative physical boundary to the Nile). Thus, the legitimisation potentially extended even to the Greek rule of Ptolemaic Egypt.

[31] Jacoby Fragment 7 of Cleitarchus from the *Stromata* of Clement of Alexandria 1.139.4.

the same hand as he used to lift the innards of the beast. These letters indicated that the king would be granted victory and the warm liver revealed their imprint when displayed to the army, thus boosting morale, as success seemed to have been promised by the deity.[32] Alexander asserted: "The empire of the Persians has ripened long enough and is ready for reaping, so it is time it were taken over by others for safer keeping." Neither was the army's thinking at odds with their sovereign's expectations. Oblivious of their wives and children and the homesickness of farflung military operations, it was as if the Persian gold and the wealth of the entire Orient were already their personal compensations, so it was not warfare and its perils that they pondered but rather the plunder from those nations.

2.7 Alexander *himself sailed across to the Troad with sixty ships of war, and he* **hurled his spear into the enemy ground as his vessel drew near the shore and was first to spring fully armed down onto the land** *as if dancing on a floor.* **This signified that he received Asia from the gods as a spear-gain.** *And he sacrificed further victims with the prayer that those lands should not be reluctant to accept his reign.* **At Troy the king visited the tombs of Achilles, Ajax and the other heroes who had died in the Trojan War, making offerings to each of them as to an ancestor,**[33] *and as a token of honour he did more.* He poured oil to anoint Achilles' gravestone and ran a race by it against his companions, in the nude as is the custom, then wreathing it with garlands, whilst Patroclus' grave was likewise honoured by Hephaistion,[34] the king hailed the hero as happy in life to have had a faithful comrade and to have been granted a great proclaimer of his fame after he became a shade.[35] As Alexander was touring and inspecting the sights of the city, he was asked whether the lyre of Paris were what he wished to see? But he responded: "That instrument I would view indifferently, but it would make me most happy to see the lyre of Achilles, with which he hymned the heroic deeds of men of gallantry."[36]

2.8 The king then took a true tally of his army. The count of infantry was found to be twelve thousand that were Macedonian, seven thousand allies and five thousand mercenaries, all under the command of Parmenion. And Alexander had been joined by Odrysians, Triballians and Illyrians amounting to seven thousand. Additionally, the archers and the Agrianians, as they were known, comprised another thousand. Thus, the infantry totalled thirty-two thousand. In counting the cavalry there were eighteen hundred that were Macedonian in the charge of Philotas the son of Parmenion plus another eighteen hundred of which most were Thessalians led by Calas the son of Harpalus with six hundred from the

---

[32] The story of the dyed liver is recounted by Frontinus, *Stratagems* 1.11.14 in what is believed to be a fragment of Trogus, who in turn used Cleitarchan sources.

[33] Alexander's mother's family were Aeacidae, who claimed descent from Aeacus, the grandfather of both Achilles and Ajax.

[34] Aelian, *Varia Historia* 12.7 and Plutarch, *Alexander* 15.4 and Cicero, *Pro Archias Poeta* 24.

[35] Patroclus being the loyal friend and Homer being the post-mortem publicist.

[36] The anecdote of the lyre is common to Plutarch, *Alexander* 15.5 and Aelian, *Varia Historia* 9.38.

rest of the Greek nations under the command of Erigyius.[37] **Nine hundred Thracian scouts and Paeonians completed the total of forty-five hundred horse. In crossing from Europe to Asia, these men comprised Alexander's invasion force.** They were supported by one hundred and eighty-two vessels at sea. *Left in Europe under Antipater there were twelve thousand foot and fifteen hundred cavalry.*

Figure 2.2. Alexander anoints the tomb of Achilles before racing (André Castaigne 1898)

2.9 *With such puny punching power it is unclear whether it is more remarkable that he conquered the whole world or that he dared to make the assault at all. When he was raising his forces for such a perilous quarrel, he did not choose vigorous youths in the first flower of manhood, but veterans rather, many of them actually retired from battle, who had served with his uncles and with his father.*[38] *It might have been supposed that he had not selected soldiers, but veteran*

---

[37] Diodorus 17.17.4 implies that the six hundred other Greeks were separate from eighteen hundred Thessalians, but he then agrees with Justin 11.6.2 that the cavalry totalled four thousand five hundred, despite having seemingly listed five thousand one hundred. The solution is obvious: very probably in Diodorus's source's text the six hundred other Greeks were a component of the second block of eighteen hundred cavalry, of which the remaining twelve hundred were Thessalians. Since Justin and Diodorus agree exactly on the totals of both cavalry and infantry (disagreeing in detail with Plutarch, *Alexander* 15.1 [30,000-43,000 foot & 4000-5000 horse], Arrian, *Anabasis* 1.11.3 [not much more than 30,000 foot & 5000 horse] and numbers from Aristobulus [30,000 foot & 4000 horse], Ptolemy [30,000 foot & 5000 horse] and Anaximenes [43,000 foot & 5500 horse] cited by Plutarch, *Moralia* 327D-E), it is almost certain that their figures are from Cleitarchus, who is the only likely common source of Diodorus and Justin.

[38] The Macedonian throne had been occupied successively by Philip's brothers, Alexander (369-367BC) and Perdiccas (367-359BC), prior to Philip's accession in 359BC. A soldier who had

Book 2: 16th October 335BC - 5th October 334BC

combat instructors. Furthermore, it is said that sixty was the minimum age of the officers, so, if you had scrutinised the camp headquarters, you would have said it seemed like an assembly of some bygone government's senators. Therefore, in battle nobody thought to flee, but rather they only contemplated victory, for they could not place any hope in their speed of flight and so they had to rely upon their weapon wielding might.

2.10 In setting out from the Troad *against the enemy, Alexander barred his troops from pillaging Asian territory, instructing that they should spare their own estate and not wreck what they had come to appropriate.* **As they passed the sacred enclosure of Athena, an augur, named Aristander,[39] noticed a statue of Ariobarzanes, former satrap of Phrygia, cast down upon the ground before the shrine[40] and he spotted other favourable signs around the same time. He came before the king announcing that he was destined to win a victory in a colossal clash of cavalry, especially if the battle should be within Phrygia's boundary. He added that Alexander would personally slay in the onslaught a famous marshal among the enemy. This was his prophecy concerning the king's destiny from that which the gods had allowed him to see and Athena, particularly, would aid Alexander in achieving glory.**

2.11 Alexander *hailed the seer's augury and* **made ostentatious offerings to Athena,** *dedicating his own armour to the deity.* **Then he took the finest of the panoplies that had been left in the sanctuary and he donned it and fought in it during the initial hostilities. The first battle was indeed to be decided by his own bravery, when he was to clinch a famous victory. But this was to occur some days subsequently.**

2.12 The Persian satraps and generalissimos had not taken the field in time to oppose the crossing of the Macedonians. *Rather they chose to allow Alexander to advance within their dominions, for Darius deemed it more glorious to eject incursions than to forestall invasions.* **But they mustered their men and convened a council to consider how they might contend with Alexander. Memnon the Rhodian, celebrated for his strategic expertise, counselled that they should avoid face-to-face hostilities, but that they should ravage the countryside, so as to prevent the progress of their adversaries, because they could not be supplied. Simultaneously, they should send their navy and a land army across to Macedonia, so as to transfer the focus of the fighting into European territory. Subsequent events were to provide ample demonstrations that these were the wisest of recommendations, but**

---

campaigned with Alexander would therefore have been serving for at least 33 years in 334BC and would have been at least approaching fifty years of age.

[39] The manuscripts read "Alexander", but the name of the augur whose predictions are widely celebrated by both the Vulgate and the Official traditions of Alexander historiography is an obvious correction, rather than believe that Aristander had a rival not mentioned elsewhere and sharing the name of the king.

[40] Ariobarzanes was Satrap of Phrygia from 388-361BC, but was then arrested and punished as a rebel, which probably explains why his statue had been cast down.

Memnon nevertheless failed to convince any Persian commander, since his plan was incompatible with their sense of honour. Thus, they took the decision to seek a confrontation and, gathering forces from all directions, they grew to heavily outnumber the Macedonians. Then they went forward into Hellespontine Phrygia, where they encamped in the plains of Adrasteia *beside the Granicus River, using its course as a defensive barrier.*[41]

2.13 *When Alexander learnt of the assemblage of the foreign force, he advanced rapidly to encamp facing them across the Granicus River's course. As they held the high ground there was no move from the Persian army, who intended to take the opportunity provided by the transit of the river to fall upon their enemy, for they thought easily to win the fray, whilst the Macedonian phalanx were in disarray. But at the rising of the sun* on the sixth day of Thargelion[42] ***Alexander decisively charged*** his cavalry *across the river and deployed his troops in battle order before the Persians could provide contention. But in response they sent forward their own massed cavalry across the Macedonian front in its entirety, for they preferred to engage horse with horse rather than risk their infantry.*

2.14 *The Persian left wing was formed from the contingents of cavalry commanded separately by Memnon of Rhodes and the satrap Arsames. The horsemen from Paphlagonia were next in line under the command of Arsites. Then came the Hyrcanian cavalry headed up by the satrap of Ionia, Spithridates. The right wing was formed from a thousand Medes plus two thousand horsemen under Rheomithres as well as Bactrians equal in number to these. The centre comprised echelons of other nationalities gathered in great numbers and selected for their valorous qualities. The Persians totalled more than ten thousand cavalry supported by no fewer than one hundred thousand infantry, but the latter stood behind the front and did not go into action, since the cavalry really should have been sufficient to confront each and every Macedonian.*

---

[41] Adrasteia was a nymph associated with Hellespontine Phrygia. She was a minor deity who defended the righteous. Strabo 13.1.11 confirms that the Granicus River flowed through the Plains of Adrasteia, where Justin 11.6.10 also placed the battle. Its site is believed to lie around the junction of the Kocabas Çay and the Biga Çay near the modern Dimetoka (e.g. Hammond, *JHS* 100, 1980, 76ff).

[42] I infer a mention of the Attic Lunar date by Cleitarchus by analogy with his subsequent reference to the date of Gaugamela/Arbela; it was Thargelion according to Plutarch, *Camillus* 19.4; Plutarch, *Alexander* 16.2 confirms that the Macedonian month was Daisios, equivalent to the Attic Thargelion; Aelian, *Varia Historia* 2.25 implies 6th Thargelion (~20th May 334BC in the Julian calendar) – he does not name the battle, saying only that Alexander defeated the Persians, but the Granicus is the only such engagement that occurred in Thargelion.

Book 2: 16th October 335BC - 5th October 334BC

Figure 2.3. Alexander about to attack across the Granicus (Petrty, 1909)

2.15 *As the horsemen of both sides clashed tumultuously, the Thessalian cavalry stationed on the left wing under Parmenion valiantly met the charge of their opposition, whilst the king, accompanied by his elite cavalrymen on the right wing, personally led a lunge against the Persians and, upon closing, began to inflict casualties beyond counting.*

2.16 *However, the foreigners fought fiercely in venturing to test their tenacity against Macedonian gallantry as Fortune focussed the finest fighters into the same vicinity in order to settle the assignment of victory. Spithridates, the satrap of Ionia, son-in-law of King Darius and a Persian ancestrally, being a man of exceptional gallantry flung himself upon the Macedonian lines with a considerable contingent of cavalry. Escorted by a formation of forty Royal Relatives, noteworthy for their bravery, he weighed in heavily upon the enemy. Fighting fiercely, he slew a few of his adversaries, then set upon the rest inflicting many injuries. Considering that the impetus of this onslaught seemed to pose some danger, Alexander steered his steed towards the satrap and rode straight at the foreigner.*

2.17 *To the Persian it appeared that this opportunity for single combat was heaven-sent. He hoped that Asia might be relieved of a dire threat by his own heroic achievement: that the infamous bravura of Alexander would be thwarted by his personal intervention and that he would preserve from degradation the glorious Persian reputation. Firstly, he flung his javelin* with so much verve and cast it with such might that it lodged in Alexander's cuirass having pierced through his shield and the shoulder-plate on his right. The king plucked out the dangling missile and spurred his steed, so as to drive his lance through the centre of the satrap's chest by employing the impetus from his speed.[43] At this the surrounding ranks of both armies gasped at the thrill of such an outstanding display of skill. But the spike of the lance snapped off on striking Spithridates' breastplate and, whilst its headless shaft was recoiling, the Persian drew his sword and came at the king. But Alexander regained his grip upon his lance sufficiently quickly as to thrust at the face of his adversary and to strike it fiercely. The Persian was toppled from his mount, but even as he fell, Rhosaces, his brother galloped into the quarrel *with a yell*. He swung his sword at the king's head with such fury that it cracked his helm and inflicted a grazing scalp injury. But, as the foreigner endeavoured to deliver another blow to the same split, Cleitus the Black charged in, slicing down upon the Persian's arm and thereby severing it.

Figure 2.4. Spithridates attacks Alexander (engraved by Audran after Charles Le Brun)

2.18 *The Royal Relatives now crowded around the two dismounted men in tight formation. Initially they cast their javelins upon Alexander, then, moving in, did all that they might to massacre the monarch of the Macedonian nation. But though he had to fight numerous, fierce engagements, nevertheless he was not overwhelmed by the numbers of his*

---

[43] The text of Diodorus 17.20.4 uses the correct technical term, *xyston*, which was the Macedonian cavalry sarissa, a three-metre-long lance that Alexander is depicted wielding in the Alexander Mosaic from Pompeii (see Figure 4.3 in this reconstruction – Battle of Issus). Stirrups had not been invented in Alexander's era, because, if Alexander had maintained a tight grip at impact to force the spearhead home, the reactionary force would have thrown him backwards, tumbling him from his mount. This is why Alexander is not gripping his *xyston* under-arm, but is merely guiding it home, in the Alexander Mosaic.

Book 2: 16th October 335BC - 5th October 334BC

assailants. *Despite taking two blows to his cuirass, another to his helm and three upon that same shield that he had taken from Athena's shrine, yet he did not surrender, but, buoyed up by spiritual exultation, he overcame every danger. In the course of this scrum, several of the other noble Persian commanders were overcome. The most illustrious amongst those that fell were* Atizyes *and* Pharnaces, *the brother of Darius's wife, and* Mithrobuzanes, *who commanded the Cappadocians, as well.*

2.19 *Now that numerous of their commanders had been liquidated and the Macedonians had outfought every Persian regiment, firstly those confronting Alexander were routed, then the rest followed their precedent. Consequently, the king was considered generally to have earnt the laurels through his bravery and was thought of as the foremost forger of their victory. And besides him, the Thessalian Cavalry gained great celebrity for their gallantry, supported by the superb horsemanship of their companies and their incomparable combative capabilities. Subsequent to the rout of the Persian cavalry, there was an engagement between each side's infantry, but this contest continued but briefly. The Persians were disheartened by the flight of their cavalry and this undermining of their morale induced them speedily to flee,* defeated more by Alexander's strategy than by the valour of his army.

2.20 The Persian casualties were very heavy: **the tally of the Persian dead exceeded ten thousand amongst their infantry and included no fewer than two thousand of their cavalry and more than twenty thousand were taken into captivity.** But in Alexander's army just nine infantrymen fell and only one hundred and twenty of his cavalry. These latter the king buried munificently, so as to console his surviving cavalry, and he commemorated them with equestrian statuary and granted their relatives tax immunity.

2.21 *Forming up his forces again, Alexander led them down into Lydia and took control of the city of the Sardians including its citadels. Furthermore, its satrap* Mithrenes *voluntarily surrendered its cache of treasure and valuables.*[44]

---

[44] Alexander's route from the Granicus to Sardis has been a matter of dispute. Donald Engels in *Alexander the Great and the Logistics of the Macedonian Army* p.33 argued that he doubled back to Troy and then continued southwards hugging the coastline. This was mainly because he thought Alexander had founded Alexandria Troas fifteen miles south of Troy at this time. But this seems to be wrong. Pliny *NH* 5.124 says that its name was changed from Antigonia to Alexandria, perhaps by Lysimachos in 301BC after the defeat of Antigonus at Ipsus. It is anyway quite possible that Alexander visited the spot whilst initially at Troy, since it was within range of cavalry patrols from his camp on the Scamander River. Furthermore, it is most unlikely that Alexander would have retreated from the site of his victory. Rather we should expect him to have pursued the main bulk of the retreating Persian forces. Diodorus states that these made for Miletus, perhaps by cutting up the river valleys behind their position on the Granicus and coming back down to the Aegean coastline near Adramyttium. Alternatively, and I think less credibly in view of the ruggedness of the terrain, they might have made a beeline for Sardis with Alexander on their heels, before continuing

2.22 *In the wake of his victory a substantial portion of Asia Minor defected to Alexander including the city of Magnesia on the River Maeander, where they had erected a monument to Themistocles in their agora. For* **Themistocles** *became their governor after he* **had his audience with Xerxes.** *But, when the Persian king required aggression against Greece of* **Themistocles**, *he* **slew a bull at the altar and caught its blood in a large beaker. Then, when the whole bowl had been downed, he soonafter fell dead upon the ground.**[45]

2.23 *Memnon had taken refuge within the city of Miletus accompanied by the survivors of the fray among the Persians, so Alexander encamped nearby and deployed his troops in shifts every day to make continual assaults upon its fortifications. Those besieged readily repelled the attacks from their walls initially, for many soldiers had congregated in the city and they possessed vast stocks of ammunition and other weaponry appropriate to the emergency. But the king confirmed his faithfulness to his intentions by deploying siege engines, so as to shake the fortifications and he prosecuted the siege most aggressively, both by land and by sea. Then the Macedonians managed to make an entry through the collapsing masonry, so that the defenders were finally forced to flee in the face of Macedonian superiority. Immediately, the Milesian citizenry bowed down before the king in entreaty and placed themselves and their city beneath his authority. Some of the Persians perished at the hands of their enemy, whilst others broke out of the city and sought sanctuary. The remainder were taken into captivity. Alexander treated the Milesians kindly, but sold all the rest into slavery.*

2.24 *Alexander could find no further use for his navy, the funding of which was proving quite costly. Hence, he dismissed his fleet with the exception of a flotilla assigned to siege engine transportation. The Athenian allies were among these, comprising a contingent of twenty galleys.*

---

on to Miletus. Some Persian forces may have retreated due east to Dascylion, since Alexander sent Parmenion off that way (Arrian, *Anabasis* 1.17.2).

[45] Jacoby Fragment 33 of Cleitarchus from Plutarch, *Themistocles* 27.1-2 and Jacoby Fragment 34 of Cleitarchus from Cicero, *Brut.* 42-43. Cleitarchus evidently discussed the exile of Themistocles, when he entered the service of the Persian king (actually Artaxerxes I) and became the Persian governor of Magnesia. Clearly this is very likely to have been located within his text at the point that Alexander passed Magnesia. The truth of Cleitarchus' version of Themistocles' suicide has been doubted, since Thucydides 1.138 gave a less sensationalist, contemporaneous version, in which he had died of some disease, though it was rumoured that he had taken poison. It is likely that Cleitarchus compared and contrasted Themistocles' career with that of Alexander, but there is unfortunately no manuscript basis on which to attempt to reconstruct this.

Figure 2.5. The capture of Miletus (André Castaigne 1898)

2.25 *There are those that sanction the sense of Alexander's strategy in demobilising his navy. For Darius had yet to be dealt with, so a big battle seemed inevitable and the king reckoned that the Macedonian line would be less likely to give, if he denied his men the option of sailing away from trouble. He had practised the same tactic, they say, by putting the Granicus River at his rear, for nobody could consider running away, when the fate of any that were chased into its course was clear. They note that there is similarly the example of Agathocles, king of the Syracusan territory, who adopted Alexander's strategy some years subsequently and unexpectedly gained a comprehensive victory.[46] He sailed over to Libya*

---

[46] This mention of Agathocles is from Diodorus 17.23.2-3, but Diodorus 20.7 recounts in more detail the story of Agathocles' having literally burnt his boats during his invasion of Libya in 310BC. It is likely that Diodorus summarised a comparison between the naval divestments of Alexander

with a scanty army and burnt his boats so that his troops had no hope of being able successfully to flee, thus compelling them to fight most nobly and consequently to win a victory against the tens of thousands constituting the Carthaginian army.

2.26 The majority of the Persians and their mercenaries, following the fall of Miletus, congregated under the ablest of their commanders at Halicarnassus. This was the Carians' largest municipality, which incorporated the seat of their ruling dynasty and there were plenty of citadels within this city. At around this time, Memnon dispatched to Darius his wife[47] and offspring, because he considered that consigning them into the care of the king would be beneficial to their safe-keeping and, simultaneously, Darius would be the more willing to entrust Memnon with supreme command whilst holding a surety against double-dealing. And so it proved to be, since Darius immediately sent dispatches to the people living beside the sea to obey Memnon diligently. Accordingly, having thus established his supremacy, he made all the requisite arrangements to withstand a siege in the Halicarnassians' city.

2.27 King Alexander sent his siege engines and supplies to Halicarnassus by sea, whilst he himself marched into Caria with his entire army, winning over the cities that lay along his route through acts of philanthropy. He favoured the Greek municipalities with the greatest beneficence, granting them tax immunity and independence. He also offered them his assurance that Greek liberation was his main motivation for prosecuting his war against the Persian nation. He was met by a lady named Ada during this journey. She was by birth a member of the Carian royal family. When she submitted her suit to repossess her ancestral sovereignty, he ordained that she should succeed to the Carian monarchy. Thus, he gained the Carians' loyalty, through the patronage that he bestowed upon this lady. For immediately, embassies were sent by every city, conferring golden wreaths upon the king and undertaking to co-operate with him completely.

2.28 Upon reaching the environs of Halicarnassus Alexander established an encampment and proceeded to prosecute an energetic and comprehensive investment. Initially, he employed his troops in shifts to launch continual assaults upon the fortifications, using up all the hours of daylight in fighting operations. Subsequently, he moved up all manner of siege machinery and filled in the ditches that ran before the walls of the city with each gang of his labourforce sheltered beneath a shanty and he

---

and Agathocles from an account in Cleitarchus, because in Book 17 he calls Agathocles a king, whereas in Books 16, 18, 19 and 20 he calls him a tyrant or dynast. Such a disparity in terminology is suggestive of different sources. It would follow that Cleitarchus wrote after 310BC.

[47] This was Barsine, the daughter of Artabazus, who was destined to become Alexander's mistress and who eventually bore him a son named Heracles, who appears in Book 13.

shook the towers and the curtain walls down by bringing his battering rams to bear upon the town. Whenever he caused a section of the ramparts to crumble, he strove in a hand-to-hand struggle to force an entry across the rubble.

2.29 But at first the Macedonians were readily repulsed by Memnon, for he had mustered many men within his Carian bastion. He sallied forth from the city with men in the dead of night at a site where the siege engines had been busy and set them all alight. Fierce fighting followed before the fortifications, in which far more faculty was shown by the Macedonians, but numerical superiority and fire power favoured the Persians. For they had the aid of men manning the ramparts, whence they slew some foes and crippled others by using ballistas to shoot darts.

2.30 The trumpets on either side sounded the call to arms simultaneously and cheers resounded widely as the troops urged on courageous comrades of whichever nationality in performing feats of bravery. Some sought to extinguish fires that flared up amidst the machinery. Others engaged in deadly hand-to-hand combat with the enemy, inflicting baleful butchery. Others again erected replacement ramparts behind those that had failed and of far more substantial construction than those originally assailed. The commanders reporting to Memnon stood in the thick of the action promising precious prizes to those that fought with distinction, so that the greed was great for victory on both sides of the confrontation. Everywhere there were to be witnessed warriors being wounded by their adversaries or being carried unconscious away from the hostilities. Others stood guard over the recumbent bodies of their buddies, wrestling to rescue them from the predations of their enemies. Still others on the verge of succumbing to a torrent of terrors were rallied and revitalised as fighters by the exhortations of their commanders. Ultimately, some of the Macedonians were slain on the threshold of entering the city, including a commander called Neoptolemus, a man from a family ranking among the nobility.[48]

2.31 Two towers were battered down along with a pair of curtain walls of the town subsequently. At this point men from Perdiccas's battalion, having drunk excessively, launched an impetuous nighttime assault upon the citadel of the city. Detecting the disorderliness of these aggressors, Memnon's men sallied forth in superior numbers, massacring many Macedonians and routing the others. As news of this action spread, very many Macedonians sped to the aid of their comrades and a major fight unfolded. When Alexander and his noblemen arrived in the vicinity, the Persians were flung back and confined within the city, so then the king

---

[48] Arrian, *Anabasis* 1.20.10 suggests that Neoptolemus the son of Arrabaeus had deserted to the enemy, but Diodorus 17.25.5 may be preferable, since his brother Amyntas continued as a trusted senior officer in Alexander's army. Possibly Arrian had read that Neptolemus had been slain *amongst the enemy* or had *given himself up to the enemy* (before being summarily executed).

sent forward an emissary to call for a truce to fetch the Macedonians who had fallen before the fortifications. Ephialtes and Thrasybulus, Athenians fighting beside the Persians, aired their opinions that the corpses should be denied a funeral, but Memnon ruled that the bodies should be given up for burial.

2.32 *Later on at a council of the commanders Ephialtes recommended that they should not tarry until the city fell and they were taken into captivity. He urged instead that the mercenary officers should lead a sally fighting in the front ranks against the enemy. Memnon perceived that Ephialtes was keen to vaunt his gallantry and he vested high hopes in his powerful physique and bravery, so he permitted him to proceed to lead an attack upon their adversary. Accordingly, Ephialtes assembled two thousand troops picked by hand and gave each of a group of them a firebrand and assigned the rest to contend with any enemy band. Then, when dawn had barely broken, he abruptly had all the gates flung wide open and issued forth with his band of men, detailing the torchbearers to set the siege engines alight, causing a colossal conflagration promptly to ignite. He himself led the rest in a close-packed phalanx formed up to a depth of many ranks and he attacked the Macedonians as they came up to give aid in extinguishing the flames flaring up from the raid. When the king realised what was occurring, he ranged his finest fighters in the front ranks and posted elite troops in supporting banks. At their backs he deployed a third formation also comprising men with a stalwart fighting reputation. He himself took command at the head of all and made a sturdy stand against foes, who thought their push had made them irresistible. He also sent men off to extinguish the blazes and to salvage the siege engines in those places.*

2.33 *When both sides yelled out simultaneously and the trumpets blared to signal the advance, they fought with terrific tenacity on account of the valour of the combatants and the fervour of their rivalry. The Macedonians managed to prevent the spread of the conflagration, but Ephialtes' men had the better of them in the confrontation and he himself, being physically far superior to his adversaries, personally slew many that engaged him in hand-to-hand hostilities. The besieged sent showers of missiles from elevated stations within their recently erected makeshift fortifications and thereby slew many of the Macedonians. For a tower had been erected a hundred cubits tall, which was crammed with catapults shooting bolts down upon them all. Even as many Macedonians were expiring in the face of the hail of darts and the rest were retiring, Memnon charged into the fray with a much larger force and the king found himself wanting for any effective recourse.*

2.34 *Just at that juncture, when the soldiers from the city appeared to be prevailing in this struggle, there came an incredible reversal in the course*

Book 2: 16th October 335BC - 5th October 334BC

of the battle. The oldest Macedonians, who were excused from combat on grounds of their senescence, but who had fought under Philip and triumphed in many engagements, were prompted by the crisis to reproduce their prior prowess. Being by far their betters in battle-experience and perseverance and led by Atarrhias,[49] *they rudely rebuked the lack of resilience among the young men who were evading the violence. They stood shoulder to shoulder with their shields interlocked to confront every adversary, who thought himself already assured of victory. They managed to slay Ephialtes together with many of his auxiliaries and they compelled the remnants of the enemy to retire to take refuge within the city. The Macedonians got inside the curtain wall amidst their fleeing adversaries as darkness began to fall, but the king commanded that the bugler sound the recall, so they fell back to their encampment one and all.*

2.35 *However, Memnon convened a council of the satraps and his leading men and determined that the* lower *city should be forsaken. They ensconced their finest fighters with plenty of supplies in the citadel and evacuated the bulk of their forces to Kos together with the rest of their resources as well. When at dawn the next day Alexander discovered their departure, he levelled the lower city, so as to invest the citadel with a ditch and rampart of imposing stature.*

2.36 *The king detailed a section of his army and those that held its command to march inland with the mission of annexing the nations that lay at hand. All the territories as far as Greater Phrygia were subdued by these deputies, who fed their forces with spoils gleaned from the hostilities.*[50] *Alexander himself seized control of the coastline all the way to Cilicia, conquering many cities and dauntlessly besieging and capturing the strongholds in their territories.* The capture of one of these was quite extraordinary, entailing such ironies that we should not neglect its story.

2.37 *A stronghold that is virtually impregnable sits on a huge crag in the limits of the Lycian territories. It is occupied by a people, who are known as the Marmares. As Alexander was marching through, these men mauled the Macedonian rear guard, slaying not a few, and making off with many beasts of burden and numerous slaves too. This infuriated the king, who set to besieging their fortress, dedicating every effort to taking this fastness.*

---

[49] Curtius 8.1.36 has Cleitus state that Atarrhias had called back the younger men when they were retreating from the battle at Halicarnassus. Curtius probably took this information from Cleitarchus. It follows that Cleitarchus had probably also mentioned Atarrhias's role in the context of his description of the siege of Halicarnassus.

[50] Arrian, *Anabasis* 1.24.3, notes that Parmenion was sent into Phrygia via Sardis at this point. This was probably part of the same expedition into Phrygia mentioned by Diodorus 17.27.6.

2.38 *Initially, the elders among the Marmares counselled their younger men to cease resisting Alexander and to try to persuade him to forgive them. But they rejected reconciliation, eagerly preferring to die honourably and simultaneously with the end of liberty in their nation. In that case, the elders suggested* ironically, *they might each personally like to do away with their wives, their progeny and the elderly members of their family. Then those with enough strength and agility could save themselves simply by smashing their way through the enemy under cover of night and reaching safety amidst the mountains in the vicinity.[51] The younger men reckoned that this made sense actually. Consequently, orders were issued that each man should repair to his own home to prepare for the atrocity by supping on the choicest food and drink in company with his family.*

2.39 *Some six hundred of them,[52] however, flinched from the act of killing their kindred face to face, but burnt them in their houses in its place, whilst they fled their families' fates by flinging wide the city's gates and making for the mountains with their mates. Thus, the younger fellows effectuated their decision, each condemning his kindred to be inhumed within his habitation, whilst he himself stole through the midst of the encamped opposition and headed for the hills in full flight, cloaked in the darkness of that damnable night.*

2.40 These were the concerns of Alexander *in the second year of his reign.*

---

[51] The implication is that the elders put forward the suggestion that the men murder their families superciliously as a ridiculous alternative and were surprised when it was taken seriously. This was why the story interested Cleitarchus (as an adherent of the Cynical school of philosophy) and an appreciation of its irony might also explain its retention by Diodorus in his epitome.

[52] The source text for this subsection (Diodorus 17.28.4) may be slightly corrupt or lacunose.

Book 3: 6th October 334BC - 24th September 333BC

Alexander is Encouraged by Omens; The Arrest of Alexander Lyncestes; The Retreat of the Sea; The Gordian Knot; The Death of Memnon; Darius at Babylon; Alexander's Advance into Cilicia; Alexander Falls Sick at Tarsus; The Warning Concerning Philip the Doctor and Alexander's Recovery.

3.1 *This book recounts the events concerning Alexander in the third year of his reign.*

3.2 *In this year Darius sent funds to Memnon and appointed him as his general controlling every aspect of the war. Memnon assembled a multitude of mercenaries, manning three hundred ships, and prosecuted the conflict with great vigour. He captured Chios, then, on sailing across to Lesbos, he easily seized Antissa, Methymna, Pyrrha and Eressos. Additionally, the major city of Mytilene, which was amply furnished with supplies and defenders, he nevertheless took after arduously besieging it for many days with the loss of a substantial number of his soldiers. Word spread rapidly concerning the general's activities and most islands in the Cyclades sent him embassies. When the rumour reached Greece that Memnon and his fleet were about to set sail for Euboea, the cities of that island were flung into a state of fear. However, such Greeks as favoured the Persians, especially the Spartans, grew hopeful of a turnaround in their international relations. Memnon distributed bribes liberally and won many Greeks over to the Persian side. However, Fortune curtailed his opportunity to establish his superiority, for he fell sick and died, gripped by a deadly malady, and with his extinction Darius's cause also sank into oblivion.*

3.3 *Meanwhile Alexander was in a state of uncertainty regarding his future itinerary. Eagerness to confront Darius and risk a battle afflicted him frequently, but equally regularly he resolved to bolster himself strategically by securing all the territory along the shore of the sea together with its resources and honing his army, before marching up-country to vie for the sovereignty.*

3.4 *In the land of Lycia near the city of Xanthus at this juncture a spring began to gush up from its depths and overflow, bringing up a bronze tablet inscribed with antique characters, foretelling the fall of the Persian empire with the Greeks effecting its overthrow. Alexander was so inspired by this prophecy that he eagerly pursued the capture of the coast as far as Cilicia and Phoenicia as his strategic priority.*

3.5 *Alexander lingered for several days in Phaselis on the coast of Pamphylia, where he noticed that a statue of its citizen, the late Theodectas, had been erected in the agora. One evening after* supper he led a comus to the likeness, whilst merry with wine and he crowned it with a wreath of vine as a congenial tribute in his revelry to their affiliation through Aristotle and philosophy.[53]

3.6 *Whilst he was tarrying at Phaselis,* **it was communicated to Alexander on the basis of information from a prisoner that a plot was being hatched against him by the Lyncestian Alexander, the son-in-law of that Antipater who had been left as Macedonia's governor.**[54] **Furthermore,** at this time Alexander's mother wrote to the king offering him helpful advice and specifically warning that he should be wary of the Lyncestian Alexander. This was a man of outstanding bravery and absolute audacity, who attended the king as a member of his group of Friends in a trusted capacity. But there were credible circumstances to support the accusation, so he was arrested, fettered and placed in detention pending arraigning him at a *later* court session, **for the king feared that his** *immediate* **execution might trigger a Macedonian insurrection.**

3.7 *Alexander marched on past a mountain along the Pamphylian shoreline where the surging surf came rolling right up to its roots most of the time, hardly ever exposing the rocky passage beneath the craggy and precipitous incline. But on this occasion, there was a withdrawal of the sea, though with solemnity rather than alacrity, as if it somehow perceived the king's proximity and wished by this sign to perform obeisance to his majesty.*[55]

3.8 Having set the affairs of Lycia and Pamphylia in order and after dispatching Cleander with funds to hire mercenaries in the vicinity of the Peloponnese, Alexander moved his army to the city of Celaenae.[56] At that time the Marsyas flowed through the middle of this town, a river of which Greek fable sings the renown. Its source gushes forth from the crest of a crag, whence it cascades downunder impacting upon a rock below with a tremendous thunder. Thence it fans out to water the surrounding plains, pure and translucent, since it carries no silt or grains. Hence its hue, like unto a becalmed sea, has fostered poetic fantasy, for it is rumoured that nymphs reside upon the boulder, gripped by an infatuation with the river. And it is still called the Marsyas, whilst it flows within the walls of

---

[53] Theodectas had been a pupil of Aristotle and had authored around fifty tragedies.

[54] Arrian, *Anabasis* 1.25 locates the arrest of Alexander Lyncestes at Phaselis and names the prisoner-informer as Sisines, Darius's messenger to Lyncestes, who was intercepted by Parmenion. This might be the same Sisines, whom Alexander subsequently had eliminated just before the Battle of Issus according to Curtius 3.7.11 and Section 4.6 below, in which case he was perhaps a double agent.

[55] The famous episode of the passage of the coastline beneath Mount Climax, is here based on Plutarch, *Alexander* 17.3, which is probably alluding to the Cleitarchan version, and Jacoby Fragment 31 of Callisthenes, whom Cleitarchus himself probably followed. Arrian, *Anabasis* 1.26.1 notes that it was necessary for the north (i.e. offshore) wind to blow to keep the sea off this beach.

[56] At this point the surviving parts of Curtius open: much material is irretrievable from Book 3 of Cleitarchus prior to this point in consequence of the loss of the early books of Curtius.

the city, but they name it the Lycus, when it roils out beyond the ramparts with greater volume and velocity.[57]

Figure 3.1. The sea withdraws to make way for Alexander's army (André Castaigne 1898)

---

[57] *Lycus* means wolf.

3.9 When Alexander made his entry, the town itself had been deserted by its inhabitants, but on undertaking to assault the citadel into which they had fled for their safety, he sent his herald in advance to announce that they would be subject to the harshest penalty, should they not surrender promptly. They led this emissary up a tower made very lofty by both its construction and its situation and bade that he appraise the extent of its elevation and report to Alexander. For they saw that the king and their own population did not share the same estimation of their unassailable location. They themselves appreciated the impregnability of their position and they would remain loyal *to Darius* to the point of extinction. However, when they perceived that their citadel was tightly besieged and every day saw their supplies reduce, they negotiated a sixty-day truce on the basis that, unless Darius sent a relieving army before its expiry, they would surrender their city. And when no help from that sovereign was forthcoming, on the appointed day, they gave themselves up to the king.

3.10 Thereafter, envoys from the Athenians came before Alexander, requesting the return of their countrymen captured at the Granicus River. The king responded that he would not only order their compatriots' restitution, but also the return of the rest of the Greeks, as soon as his Persian war had reached its conclusion. For the time being, Darius was the object of his attention, whom he learnt had not yet crossed the Euphrates, so he was concentrating all his forces from every direction in order to enter upon the decisive engagement of so great a war with all his capabilities.

3.11 *The army was now being guided through Phrygia,* a country settled with hamlets rather than cities. *Between greater and lesser Phrygia is situated the city of Gordion* equidistant from the Pontic and Cilician seas. *This town* sits beside the River Sangarius and it *hosts the celebrated palace of Midas.* We are taught that between these two seas lies the narrowest Asian territory, since the seas squeeze the terrain into a neck that is rather scrawny.[58] And because surf virtually rings this land, though it clings to the continent, it gives the impression of an island. And, but for the intervention of this slender impediment, the seas would be mated at the place where they are currently separated.

3.12 A desire gripped Alexander to acquire Gordion, *not so much for the sake of its gold as* **because he had heard that the yoke of Gordius occupied a spot within its temple of Zeus and that ancient prophecies had foretold that all Asia would be controlled by the man who managed to unravel its knot.**

3.13 *The cause of this conundrum being presented was as follows: Gordius was ploughing in those parts with oxen he had rented, when he began to be circled by birds of every variety. So he set out to consult the augurs in a nearby city and at its gate he met a maiden of exquisite beauty*

---

[58] This geographical concept of an isthmus in eastern Turkey, though also reflected elsewhere in ancient texts, is not very accurate, although there is a slight narrowing of Anatolia between the Gulf of Issus and the Euxine (Pontic Sea); cf. Strabo 12.1.3 and Pliny, *NH* 6.2.7.

Book 3: 6th October 334BC - 24th September 333BC

and asked her by whom he might best be provided with an augury? She was adept in the art of prophecy through parental instruction, so on hearing the reason for his consultation, she confided that it portended his future kingship and she proposed matrimony, in order that she might share in this expectation. Such a delightful proposition seemed like the first benefit of his royalty. After their wedding dissension arose within the Phrygian nation and when they consulted the oracles about ending the fighting, the reply was that this would require the appointment of a king. Enquiring further as to the identity of this sovereign, they were bidden to regard as their ruler upon their return him whom they first met journeying to the temple of Zeus in a wagon. It was Gordius they saw coming, so they straightaway saluted him as their king. He installed in the temple of Zeus that wagon, in which he had been riding when they hailed him as their king, consecrating it to regal majesty. He was succeeded by his son Midas, whom Orpheus initiated into the sacred mysteries and who filled Phrygia with suchlike ceremonies, whereby he was better guarded all his life than by armies.

3.14 When Alexander had brought Gordion under his control, he entered the temple of Zeus and asked to be shown that wagon with the yoke *tied to its pole* **in which it was recorded by tradition that Gordius the father of Midas had ridden.** *On inspecting it, the king saw that it scarely differed in ostentation from those in menial, everyday utilisation. Its remarkable feature was the yoke, which was fastened with a multiplicity of ligatures all tightly entangled and concealing their junctures.* **Alexander was gripped by a great longing to fulfil the prophecy by loosing the binding and consequently to become Asia's king.** *He was surrounded by a crowd of Phrygians and Macedonians, the former poised in anticipatory suspense and the latter anxious on account of the rashness of their king's overconfidence. For* **the fastenings were affixed so firmly, that where a bond began or where it ended could be comprehended neither by eye nor by study.** *And the king's attempted untangling made his men nervous especially, lest a futile effort should be interpreted as a foreboding of what was yet to be. But* **having struggled for ages with the concealed knots quite vainly***: "What does it matter how it is undone?" said he, and* **by slashing with his sword he severed every cord,** *such that the knots were plain to see,* **thereby either circumventing or else fulfilling the oracular prophecy.**

3.15 Thereafter, since Alexander had resolved to confront Darius directly, wherever he might be, in order to leave his rear secured safely, he gave the governance of his fleet on the Hellespontine coastline to Amphoterus and he conferred the command of its troops upon Hegelochus with the task of trying to free Lesbos, Chios and Kos from the garrisons of his enemy. He gave these officers five hundred talents to fund their campaigning activities and he sent six hundred to Antipater and those guarding the Greek cities. He also summoned ships from his allies in accordance with their treaties to hold the Hellespont against his adversaries. For he was not yet aware of the death of Memnon, so it was him that he focussed all his attentions upon, knowing full well that everything would be easy, if nothing were perpetrated by Memnon personally.

Figure 3.2. Alexander cuts the knot at Gordion (Antonio Tempesta, 1608)

3.16 Now Alexander arrived at Ankyra, whence, after performing a headcount of his contingents, he entered Paphlagonia. *He next reached the land of the Heneti, adjoining the Paphlagonian territory.* This entire region offered the king its submission, handing over hostages, by which arrangement it maintained exemption from any tribute payment, for it had not even made such a contribution to the Persian government. Calas was appointed governor of that area and, after inducting troops that had just arrived from Macedonia, Alexander headed for Cappadocia.

3.17 *That Memnon would transfer the war's focus from Asia into Europe had been counted upon by Darius. Hence when the death of Memnon was related, the Persian king was correspondingly agitated. Thus, he set aside all other hopes of a resolution, being minded to settle the crisis in person.* For he deplored everything that his satraps had done, reckoning many of them to have been guilty of negligence and all of them to have been prone to accidents. Hence, he encamped in Babylonia and made a parade of all his regiments, so that they might engage in the war with the more valiance. And he built a stockade that could contain a host of ten thousand armed soldiers and commenced counting his contingents by adopting Xerxes' procedures.[59]

3.18 From dawn to dusk his regiments marched into the enclosure in the order that had been bidden. Being then sent forth they filled the fields of Mesopotamia

---

[59] Xerxes had likewise counted his forces at Doriscus on the coast of Thrace west of the River Hebrus, as is described by Herodotus 7.59.

Book 3: 6th October 334BC - 24th September 333BC

with a next to innumerable mass of foot and horsemen, giving the impression of exceeding their actual tally. There were one hundred thousand Persians including thirty thousand cavalry, whilst the Medes totalled ten thousand cavalry and fifty thousand infantry. There were two thousand Barcanian cavalrymen, each armed with a double-headed axe and a buckler and these were accompanied by ten thousand infantrymen equipped in the same manner. Forty thousand foot and seven thousand cavalry had been sent by the Armenians and six thousand of their ablest horsemen had been mustered by the Hyrcanians bolstered by a thousand cavalry from the Tapurians. The Derbices had mobilised foot soldiers numbering forty thousand, mostly armed with bronze or iron tipped spears, but some with their wooden tips fire-hardened. These too were accompanied by cavalry totalling two thousand. An army of eight thousand infantry and two hundred cavalry had come from the Caspian Sea. With them were men of another obscure nationality, who amounted to two thousand infantry and twice as many cavalry. These forces were reinforced by thirty thousand Greek mercenaries made up of outstanding young auxiliaries. However, Darius was in too much of a hurry to permit an opportunity to send for the Sogdians and the Bactrians together with the Indians and the other inhabitants from the vicinity of the Red Sea, regarding whose identity even he himself was hazy. But indeed, there was nothing in which he was less lacking than numerical superiority.

3.19 *Darius* was thoroughly pleased with the spectacle provided by his massed battalions and he ***convened his Council of Friends for a review of his options: either to appoint a captain-general to march down to the coast with charge of his army or for himself, the king, to take command and personally to engage with the Macedonian enemy. Some of his courtiers called for the king to command personally, claiming that the Persians would then fight more enthusiastically*** and so seeking by flattery to appeal to his vanity. ***However*, Charidemus the Athenian *was amongst this company, a man whose gallantry and leadership ability in warfare were respected widely. Charidemus harboured bitter hostility towards Alexander, because he had been exiled from Athens on his order.*[60]** *He* **counselled Darius** *that he should not rashly risk his throne on such adventurous activities, but should retain his onerous responsibilities and remain as ruler of Asia, whilst sending a general of proven capabilities to conduct the hostilities. A force*

---

[60] Charidemus was one of the ten Athenian generals and politicians of whom Alexander demanded the surrender following the fall of Thebes, but only Charidemus is actually recorded to have been exiled (1.46-48 above and Diodorus 17.15 & 17.25.6, Plutarch, *Demosthenes* 23.3, Arrian, *Anabasis* 1.10.4-6). At this point Diodorus 17.30.2 makes Charidemus a long-standing war comrade and advisor of King Philip, but this is most unlikely in his case – rather this description perfectly fits Amyntas the son of Antiochus, who had also defected to Darius circa 335BC and was also prominent in Cleitarchus's account. Diodorus at 17.48.2 speaks of Amyntas as though he had already mentioned him, although he had not. Diodorus has evidently somehow become confused between the two principal defectors at Darius's court. It appears (see Curtius 3.8.1-2) that a little later Amyntas and his men similarly advised Darius to go back to Mesopotamia and were also disparaged by Darius's retinue.

one hundred thousand men strong would constitute a sufficient throng, provided that a third were Greek mercenaries. And Charidemus insinuated that he himself would happily assume responsibility for the successful implementation of this strategy.

3.20 The king was persuaded by these arguments initially, but his Friends opposed them forcefully and they even aired the suspicion that Charidemus coveted the captaincy in order that he could betray the Persian Empire to its Macedonian enemy. And so, turning back to Charidemus, the king enquired as to whether Darius himself seemed inadequately equipped to crush his adversary? Then Charidemus, *being rather riled by the accusations, and oblivious of his own status and of royal vanity*, began vociferously to cast aspersions on Persian gallantry: *"Perhaps you do not wish me to respond truthfully, but, unless I now speak plainly, I shall some other time confess my views vainly. These forces, so finely outfitted, this rabble roused out of their habitations from across the entire Orient and from so many distinct nations might well be able to overawe the neighbouring people. They glint with gold embroidered purple and their arms and sumptuous accoutrements sparkle to such a degree that nobody could conceive of so much finery that had not beheld them in actuality. But the Macedonian army in the field, though admittedly coarse and shabby, never yields: its wedges of close-packed, tenacious soldiers, being sheltered by their lances and shields. This robust array of infantry they call the phalanx, where man-by-man and lance-by-lance they are packed in serried ranks. Attentive to the mere nod of their officer, they are trained to follow the standards and to keep their station. As one man they obey each order, for the troops are as adept as their commander in holding their ground, outflanking the opposition, scuttling to either wing and changing formation."*

3.21 *"Nor should you imagine that grasping after silver and gold has kept them in business. Up until now poverty has been their schoolmistress. When they are weary, the bare soil is their bed. They consider themselves well enough fed by whatever food they can cook in the course of campaigning. When they rise from their rest there is night still remaining. Do you sincerely suppose that the Thessalian, Acarnanian and Aetolian cavalry, bands unbeaten by their foes, will be repulsed by slings and spearpoints hardened in fire? Matching might is what you require. You should seek military aid from that country in which the enemy were made. Send that gold and silver of yours to hire proper warriors!"*

3.22 Darius *was easygoing and mild tempered by nature, but even people's characters are considerably corrupted by power.* Being unable to bear the truth, *he* took offence at Charidemus' expostulations and seized him by the belt as was the custom of the Persians, consigning him to his attendants' custody and ordering that they should inflict the death penalty,

Book 3: 6th October 334BC - 24th September 333BC

though he was his guest and a refugee. So then Charidemus was dragged off to his execution, *just when he was making a most salutary exhortation. Even in this situation, Charidemus did not forsake his candour*, crying: "I have at hand my death's avenger. That very man against whom I have advised you shall soon exact the penalty due for the scorning of my counsel and my unjust slaughter. *You shall repent your intractibility as you witness the overthrow of your sovereignty, and, truly, you that have been altered so dramatically by the exercise of royal authority shall be a lesson to posterity that when men surrender themselves to destiny, they forget their true identity.*" In the course of this declamation, his throat was slit by those assigned to perform his execution. Charidemus had enjoyed great expectations that came to naught on account of his outspoken interjections. Once the king's temper had cooled, he was racked by remorse and confessed that the Greek's arguments had had some force. Yet to undo his death was beyond even Darius's authority, *so he simply commanded that Charidemus be accorded a decent funeral ceremony.*

3.23 Thimodes the son of Mentor was a young man of great ebullience, who was ordered by the king to fetch from Pharnabazus all those foreign troops in whom Darius vested most reliance in order to engage their efforts in the war presently. And he assigned to Pharnabazus himself the command that had been held by Memnon previously. *And having looked for a more gifted general unsuccessfully, he himself determined to lead his army down to the sea.*

3.24 With Darius *fretting over his pressing cares, in his sleep as well he* was disturbed by threatening nightmares, *either aroused by pure anxiety or by the forebodings of a prophetic mentality.* Alexander's camp seemed in his vision to be glowing with a great blaze of fire and a little later Alexander was led before him in Darius's own one time attire *when he was a royal courier.* Then he was riding his steed through Babylon, whereupon Darius' view of both horse and rider was suddenly gone *when Alexander entered the temple of Belus as he rode on.* Furthermore, diverse interpretations from the seers compounded the king's concern. Some asserted that his dream was auspicious for the king, because he had seen the camp of his enemy burn and because Alexander had been bereft of his royal clothing and dressed as a Persian of little standing. However, others said otherwise, being minded to hypothesise that the manifestation of the Macedonian camp aglow foretold that Alexander would also shine so. That he was destined to seize the rule of Asia was beyond denying, since Darius had been dressed likewise when hailed as king. Also, as you usually find, anxiety had brought old omens to mind. It was recalled that at the outset of his reign Darius had ordered that the shape of the Persian sabre's scabbard should be altered to fit the form that the Greeks favoured. And the Chaldeans had promptly prognosticated that the empire of the Persians would pass to those that they had imitated. However, **Darius** himself was utterly at ease with the response of the seers that he advertised to his subsidiaries, and *therefore also* with his slumber's auguries, so he **advanced his camp to the river Euphrates.**

3.25 *At Babylon Darius congregated all his contingents and he reviewed his relatives and Friends and chose those that showed any competence. He assigned some to commands suited to their abilities and designated others to be his equerries. And everyone had arrived at Babylon, when the time had come to march on.* **The number of Darius's soldiers exceeded four hundred thousand infantry together with no fewer than one hundred thousand cavalry.** *Such was the host with which he set out for Cilicia from Babylon accompanied by his mother, his wife, two daughters and a son.*

3.26 It was a national custom of the Persians not to set off on a march before dawn. Thus, it was already daylight when the signal was given from the king's tent by blowing a horn. Above this pavilion, where it might be viewed by everyone, there shone a crystal-caged effigy of the sun. Their marching order was the following. Borne before them on silver altars was the fire said to be sacred and everlasting. Next came the Magi singing a traditional anthem. Three hundred and sixty-five young men clad in claret cloaks followed after them, exactly equal to the days of a year in their count, for the Persians too define the year as comprising days in that amount. Just after, white horses drew the carriage consecrated to Zeus. This was trailed by an equine leviathan, which they called the steed of the Sun. The horse-drovers were furnished with golden switches and garbed in white gear and ten carriages much embellished with gold and silver were immediately to their rear. These were followed by cavalrymen from twelve different nations that wielded disparate weaponry and fought in differing fashions.

3.27 Next after came those that the Persians call the Immortals, a ten thousand strong contingent. No others were more decorated with luxurious barbarian adornment. For they sported golden torques and gold embroidered apparel and they also wore long-sleeved tunics embellished with many an actual jewel. After a slight gap came those called the king's kinsmen, comprising a force of fifteen thousand men. This mob of almost feminine foppishness was conspicuous for its lavishness rather than for its combativeness. Next after them came the so-called Spear-Bearers regiment, who customarily had custody of the royal raiment. These preceded the king's chariot directly, which conveyed him raised up quite prominently. Both sides of his chariot were decorated with reliefs of the gods figured with gold and silver embossing. Scintillating gems adorned its yoke, from which sprouted two golden idols a cubit in height depicting Ninus and Belus, one on either side. And betwixt this pair *of gods* was sanctified a gold-wrought eagle with its wings spread wide.

Book 3: 6th October 334BC - 24th September 333BC

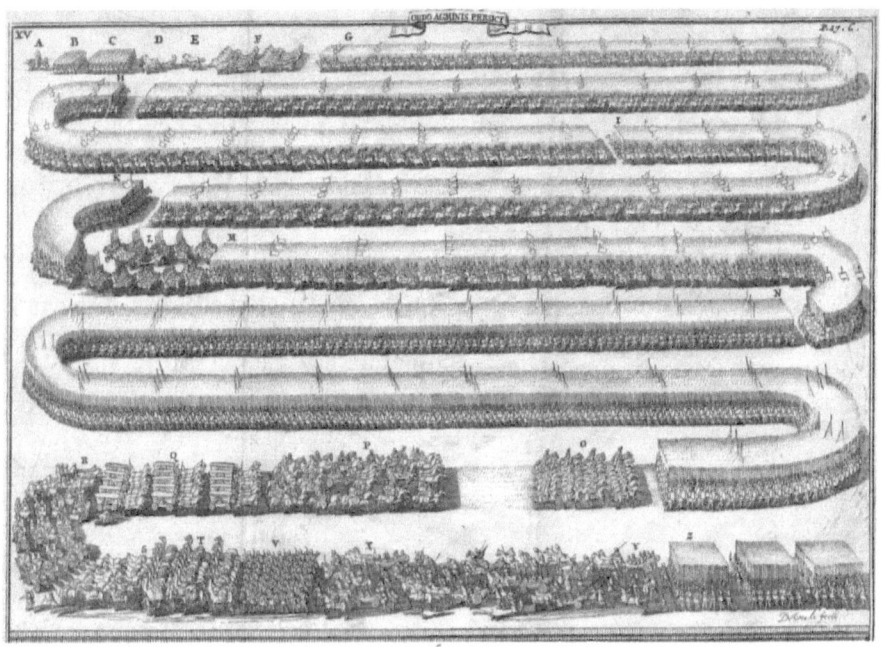

Figure 3.3. The marching order of the Persians (1685)

3.28 The king's apparel achieved pre-eminence by virtue of its extravagance: his tunic was woven with a central white band, the rest being dyed purple and the fabric of his mantle was cloth of gold embroidered with golden hawks whose beaks appeared to be clashing. He was girdled by a gilt belt in feminine fashion,[61] to which he had secured his scimitar in a gem-encrusted scabbard. The royal headdress, called a cidaris by the Persians, was bound with a band of imperial purple with white divisions. Trailing his chariot came ten thousand spearmen shouldering pikes with shafts embellished with silver and tipped with golden spikes. To the left and to the right of the chariot of the sovereign marched an escort of around two hundred of the king's most illustrious kin.[62] Thirty thousand infantry followed by four hundred of the king's own cavalry[63] brought up the rear of the main body.

3.29 Then after a gap of a stade in one carriage the wife of Darius was conveyed and there also rode in another Sisygambis, Darius's mother. A crowd of women were riding on horseback in attendance upon the royal ladies and they were followed by fifteen harmamaxes.[64] The king's children, their duennas and a herd

---

[61] This was the *zona* belt that was strapped just below the breasts.

[62] Probably honorary as well as actual relatives of the king, given their large numbers.

[63] The text has horses, but the idea of four hundred riderless steeds in such a column is preposterous so there has probably been some confusion between *eques* and *equus* in the Latin.

[64] A type of covered wagon or carriage: cf. Xenophon, *Anabasis* 1.2.16; Arrian, *Anabasis* 3.19.2.

of eunuchs occupied these, the latter being not at all looked down upon by the people of those countries. Next the three hundred and sixty-*five*[65] royal concubines were conveyed, even these being regally bedizened and arrayed. Six hundred mules and three hundred camels after these carried the king's *campaigning* monies, preceded by a detachment of archers. Just after were driven the wives of the king's friends and relations and legions of minions and camp followers. Last came a rearguard of bands of lightly armed soldiers together with their respective commanders.

3.30 Conversely, had people stopped to study the Macedonian army, they would have seen a different sort of pageantry. Its men and their mounts glowed with the gleam of bronze and steel rather than with the flash of gilding and motley. It was a force ready and willing to make a stand or else to manoeuvre upon command; impeded neither by its baggage nor by seething numbers and attentive not just to the signals of its leader, but also to his merest gestures. That army could camp in any location and requisition satisfactory supplies in any situation. Thus, Alexander did not want for warriors in his battlelines, whereas Darius, monarch over such a multitude, was reduced by the narrow confines of the territory to the same numerical deficiency that he had scorned in his enemy.

3.31 *Alexander himself had been monitoring the progress of Memnon in winning over Chios and the cities of Lesbos to his side and in taking Mytilene by storm before he had died. He had learnt that Memnon planned to sail to Macedonia with a fleet of three hundred warships and an infantry army to prosecute the hostilities, whilst there was a willingness to revolt in most of the Greek cities. This caused Alexander considerable worry, but when people arrived with news of Memnon's expiry, the king was relieved of this anxiety.*[66]

3.32 Alexander now awarded Abistamenes the satrapy of Cappadocia and set out for Cilicia with his whole army. He reached the place that is known as the Camp of Cyrus, since it was the site of that king's permanent base, when he led his forces into Lydia to confront Croesus. That spot lies a distance of fifty stades from the pass that affords access to Cilicia, the narrowest of defiles that the local people call "The Gates", because its natural rock formations resemble man-made fortifications. In consequence of Alexander's advance, the man who was was in

---

[65] Manuscripts of Curtius 3.3.24 seem to have omitted the final five and Curtius 6.6.8 (cccclx) is also usually amended, particularly on the basis of Diodorus 17.77.6.

[66] Alexander's northward progression in the early months of 333BC could be seen as a move to secure the hinterland of Asia Minor or to meet up with reinforcements from Macedonia or to find a smoother route into Cilicia. But I find none of these explanations wholly convincing. Instead, the historical context seems to be as related here in the Vulgate: Memnon was posing an acute threat to Alexander's rear, so the king hedged on whether to return to Macedonia or confront Darius directly by adopting this northwards route. It was the news of Memnon's death (in late spring) reaching Alexander (circa June) not long after he left Gordion that was decisive in moving him through the passes in the Taurus range and down into Cilicia.

Book 3: 6th October 334BC - 24th September 333BC

control of Cilicia, Arsames, having in mind what Memnon had urged at the outbreak of hostilities, put into effect a policy that had once been salutary: he laid waste to Cilicia with fire and sword in order to inflict deprivation upon the enemy. He destroyed whatever had any utility in order to leave derelict and wrecked such land as he could not personally protect.

3.33 However, it would have been far more efficacious to have occupied the pinched perforation that affords access to Cilicia with a strong garrison and to have held the heights that overlook that passage conveniently, whence he would have been able to block or crush the oncoming enemy with impunity. Instead, leaving a mere handful to hold the mountain tracks, he himself retreated, laying waste to the lands that he ought to have been preserving from such attacks. Consequently, those he left behind, considering themselves to have been abandoned to perdition, lacked the resolution to stand firm upon even a glimpse of the opposition, though even fewer than they would have been capable of holding their position. For an unbroken sierra of steep and rugged ranges encloses Cilicia. These mountains soar up out of the sea and curve around in a sort of arc returning to another section of the shore at their opposite extremity. Three passes, each very narrow and craggy, run through those heights where they reach furthest from the sea and one of these needs to be used to gain entry to that satrapy.

3.34 Similarly, where the land levels towards the sea, streams frequently interrupt its continuity and the renowned rivers Pyramus and Cydnus eddy their way across the country. But it is rather for its waters' clarity than for its breadth that the Cydnus is noteworthy. For it is received by siltless soil upon spilling from its springs quite gently and there are no torrents emptying into its placid course to produce any turbidity. Hence it stays unclouded and at the same time most chilly, since it is shaded by its banks quite prettily, and it still looks just the same as at its source, where it issues into the sea. Many were the monuments in that territory that are celebrated in poetry but had been worn away on account of their antiquity. They were shown the sites of the cities of Lyrnesus and Thebes, plus Typhon's cave and the grove of Corycus where saffron thrives as well as the locations of other things of which nothing but the fame survives.

3.35 ***Alexander*** *now received word that Darius was approaching with a vast army. Hence,* being worried that the narrow routes through the Taurus range might expose him to jeopardy, *he **entered** a*nother ***pass called "The Gates"*** in a great hurry, *covering a distance of five hundred stades in a single day's journey.* Having studied the place's topography, it is said that Alexander was never more struck by the excellence of his luck, for he conceded that he could have been routed by mere boulders had there been anyone to launch them down upon his oncoming soldiers. The way was barely wide enough for four men-at-arms to march abreast and its route was overhung by a mountain crest and was not just narrow, but was repeatedly ruptured by cascading torrents that spewed forth from the range's fundaments. Nevertheless, the king had commanded his lightly armed Thracians to go ahead up the mountain tracks and reconnoitre in order that no concealed enemies should spring out to launch attacks. A company of archers had also taken up a position on the ridge, keeping their bows strung since they had been warned that they were not engaging upon a march but a scrimmage. In this fashion the army got through to the town of Tarsus at the very moment when it was being set ablaze by the Persians, so that that a sumptuous citadel should not be acquired by the Macedonians. But Alexander had sent Parmenion ahead with a disencumbered detachment to extinguish the conflagration and, as soon as he saw that the foreign forces had fled upon his encroachment, he surged into a city saved by his intervention.

3.36 That river already remarked upon, **called the Cydnus, flows through the middle of Tarsus.** The town was at that time simmering in the swelter of summer,[67] during which the Cilician coastline is seared by the sun's glare rather more than elsewhere. The warmest period of the day was underway, when, **swathed in sweat and dust, Alexander reached that spot.** *Encouraged by the crystal-clear waters, he was tempted to take a bathe being then rather hot. Accordingly, he cast off his* arms and *clothing in full view of the army,* reckoning that it would be fitting to show that he was happy with care of his body that was available rapidly and readily. *Then* he flung himself into the river, *but he was scarcely fully immersed when* his limbs were locked in the shiver of a sudden rigor, *whereupon he became suffused with pallor and almost all of the living warmth was drained from his figure by the icy water. His attendants received the king into their arms, since* it looked like he was dying *and he was rendered quite speechless. Thus, they carried him off to his tent on the verge of unconsciousness.*

3.37 Profound anxiety pervaded the camp, already leaning towards lamentation. Tearfully, they bemoaned the fact that in the course of such swift and dashing action the most illustrious king of any period within recollection had been laid low neither in a fray nor even by a foe, but had been snatched away and snuffed out by mere immersion. Darius was fast approaching their position, a victor even before sighting his opposition. Consequently, they would have to withdraw into territory through which they had paraded in victory, where everything had been laid waste either by themselves or by the enemy. In retreating through an empty wilderness, even if nobody sought to make them his quarry, they could be overcome by hunger and scantiness. And who would direct them as they fled? Who would dare to lead men that Alexander had formerly led? Supposing they were to get as far as the Hellespont in making their withdrawal, who would ready a fleet to ferry them across its channel? Then, forgetting the trouble they themselves were in, they turned their pity once more towards their sovereign, lamenting that in the full bloom of his youth with so clever head, their ruler and

---

[67] It was approximately the early part of September, because Alexander had recovered from his ensuing illness by 24th September, when this book ends.

Book 3: 6th October 334BC - 24th September 333BC

their comrade-in-arms moreover had been sundered from them and was drifting amidst the dead.

3.38 In the meantime, Alexander had begun to breathe more easily. He regained his senses gradually and then he started to recognise the friends stood around him when he opened his eyes. Indeed, it seemed that his sickness had diminished in its severity for one reason only: that he had become conscious of the enormity of the catastrophe. However, a troubled mind harrowed him in tangible ways, for it was reported that Darius would reach Cilicia in four days. Consequently, he complained that he was being delivered up to Darius through incapacitation, that a great victory was being snatched from his possession and that he was being scuppered in his own pavilion through an ignominious and ignoble extinction. So, having admitted both his friends and his physicians, he observed: "As you can see, Fortune has ambushed me at the crux of our undertaking. I can virtually hear the din that the enemy's arms are making. And I, who instigated hostilities before, am now myself called out to wage war. For sure, when he wrote such haughty letters before, Darius brought my fate into consideration, but without good reason, if it be permitted that I be cured in accordance with my inclination. My timescales cannot be extended to allow for sluggish physicians and a leisurely remedy. It would be better for me to expire speedily than suffer too tardy a recovery. Therefore, if there is any doctor here that can provide me with succour or possesses some medical flair, know that I do not so much seek a remedy in order to dodge death but rather to embroil myself in deadly warfare."

3.39 Everybody was struck with great anxiety by the king's reckless impetuosity. Hence, they all began to beg Alexander individually not to be rushed into raising his risk of mortality, but to submit to his physicians' authority. The innocuousness of unproven cures was subject to suspicion, when the enemy were even trying to bribe his comrades to bring about his extinction. For Darius had issued a proclamation that a thousand talents would be given to the perpetrator of Alexander's assassination. Thus, they supposed that nobody would ever be so audacious as to try out a remedy that could be deemed suspicious on account of its novelty.

3.40 Among the notable physicians, who had accompanied the king from Macedonia there was a certain Philip, a native of Acarnania. *He was completely loyal to Alexander. During the king's boyhood he had been appointed as his doctor and he had been made a royal companion, so he had an exceptional affection for Alexander, not just as his sovereign, but also indeed as a foster-son.* He promised to supply a cure that was swiftly efficacious, though not exactly sudden, and to relieve so raging a fever with a medical potion. *His offer pleased nobody save him at whose risk it was tendered, for the king considered that anything was more easily endured than to remain morbidly immured. Arms and the clash of armies were a vision before his eyes and he believed that his own presence would catalyse the winning of the prize, if he could but stand forward of his standards, so* *he was just dejected that the draught was not to be drunk for three more days, for so the physician had directed.*

3.41 In the interim he received a note from Parmenion, his most loyal lieutenant, cautioning Alexander not to put Philip in charge of his treatment on the basis that he had been corrupted by Darius's announcements of the expectation of marriage to his sister and the thousand talents.[68] This letter filled Alexander's mind with great anxiety and he weighed up privately whichsoever hopes or fears favoured either policy: "Should I stick with the draught drinking, when, if I am given poison, it shall virtually seem that I have coming whatever then may happen? On the other hand, shall I discredit the loyalty of my physician? Or shall I therefore suffer my extinction in my own pavilion? But indeed, it is better to die by another's wicked action than to perish through my own apprehension." *After subjecting the ramifications to lengthy contemplation, telling nobody what had been communicated, he sealed the letter with his ring's impression and tucked it beneath the pillow upon which he lay prostrated.*

3.42 *The day designated by the doctor dawned after two days had been dissipated in similar meditation and* Philip *and the king's Friends* entered with the cup in which he had formulated the potion. *Studying him and grasping the note from Parmenion in his left hand,* Alexander *sat up in bed to take the draught and dauntlessly* drained the whole cup. *Then* he bade that Philip should read the letter and he fixed his eyes upon his face, reckoning that any pangs of conscience would give rise to some discernible trace. But the physician, having read the note through to its conclusion, did not express anxiety so much as indignation. *Casting both the epistle and his mantle before Alexander's couch, he vouched: "Sire, my existence has of course always depended upon Your Eminence, but now I truly judge that*

---

[68] It would seem unlikely that Parmenion was actually revealing fresh intelligence against Philip or that he meant that Philip had actually received a secret offer from Darius. It seems to have been public knowledge that Darius had offered a thousand talents to anyone who disposed of Alexander (see 3.39 above deriving from Curtius 3.5.16) and Arrian, *Anabasis* 1.25.3 notes that Alexander Lyncestes had been offered 1000 talents to betray Alexander. The offer of the hand of the sister of Darius may have been read over from a codicil to the reward for Lyncestes. Note that it is Darius's daughter's hand in Plutarch, *Alexander* 19.3, but Pseudo-Callisthenes 2.8.5 agrees that it was his sister and names her as Dadipharta. At this point Darius was too far away even to have heard of Alexander's illness let alone to have had time to order an attempt to bribe his physician. Plutarch, *Alexander* 19.1 says Darius thought Alexander lingered in Cilicia due to cowardice. Parmenion must instead have raised general concerns regarding trusting in a single physician who knew of Darius's public offer. Parmenion seems to have been on hand in the Cleitarchan text (he had led the advance party into Tarsus at Curtius 3.4.15, though Justin 11.8.5 strangely puts him in Cappadocia), so the question also arises as to why he chose to communicate his concerns by letter instead of in person. Probably, it was impossible to speak to Alexander privately during his illness, because he was constantly attended. Therefore, a note may have offered the most secure means for communicating what was intended as secret advice.

Book 3: 6th October 334BC - 24th September 333BC

my very breath is drawn via your sacred and revered countenance. The accusation of murderous treachery that has been slung at me shall certainly be washed away by your recovery. And you will grant life to me, when saved through my proficiency. I beseech you to put aside your trepidation and allow the medication to be drawn into your circulation. Put your mind at rest for a while, despite its disturbance by the futile concerns of your companions, who, though staunchly loyal, are troubling you through the extent of their suspicions."

3.43 These words not only made the king feel confident of his safety, but even cheerful and hopeful of a full recovery. Accordingly, he replied: "Philip, if the gods had allowed you to investigate my opinion of you in your preferred fashion, you would have chosen another way, but you certainly could not have wished for a better indication than this test today. Having received this letter, I nevertheless drank the potion that you had prepared for me. And now, believe me, I am no less concerned to prove your loyalty than to make a good recovery." And having made this declaration, he offered his right hand to the physician.

3.44 But such was the potency of the potion that what ensued seemed to support Parmenion's accusation. *For at first,* **Alexander's respiration grew shallow and laborious** *and, losing his voice, he became almost unconscious.* **But Philip left nothing untried: it was by him personally that poultices were applied and it was he that roused the king from his torpid decline, at one point using the odour from victuals and at another the whiff of wine. As soon as he sensed that Alexander had returned to his senses, he continually put him in mind sometimes of his mother and sister or at other times of his impending opportunity to become so glorious a victor.** Then the medication circulated through every artery and gradually its efficacy could be felt throughout his body. Firstly, he recovered *his mental acuity and then, more speedily than expected, also* his physical vitality, *for after* having spent three days in that state of infirmity, he made an appearance before the army, *since no Macedonian would be reassured without personally witnessing his king's recovery.* Nor were the troops keener to gawk at the king himself than at his physician. As if a god had come amongst them, they gratefully grasped Philip's right hand one by one. **The king rewarded his healer with magnificent presents and appointed him to his coterie of Friends, the courtiers of firmest allegiance.**

3.45 For indeed it is hard to convey how great and beyond the traditional veneration of his people for their kings was their devotion to this particular sovereign or, it might be said, their burning affection. In the first place, there was nothing he undertook that did not seem to enjoy divine assistance. Since Fortune was with him in every instance, even his rashness resulted in brilliance. His age too, though seemingly scarcely mature enough for deeds of such magnificence, yet having proven quite sufficient, glamorised all his achievements. Furthermore, there were things customarily considered of no consequence, but generally especially gratifying to the men of his regiments: taking his exercise in their company; dressing and behaving hardly differently from the ordinary citizenry and manifesting a military man's energy. By these characteristics, whether they were innate gifts or had been consciously engineered, he had made himself as much beloved as revered.

3.46 These were the concerns of Alexander *in the third year of his reign.*

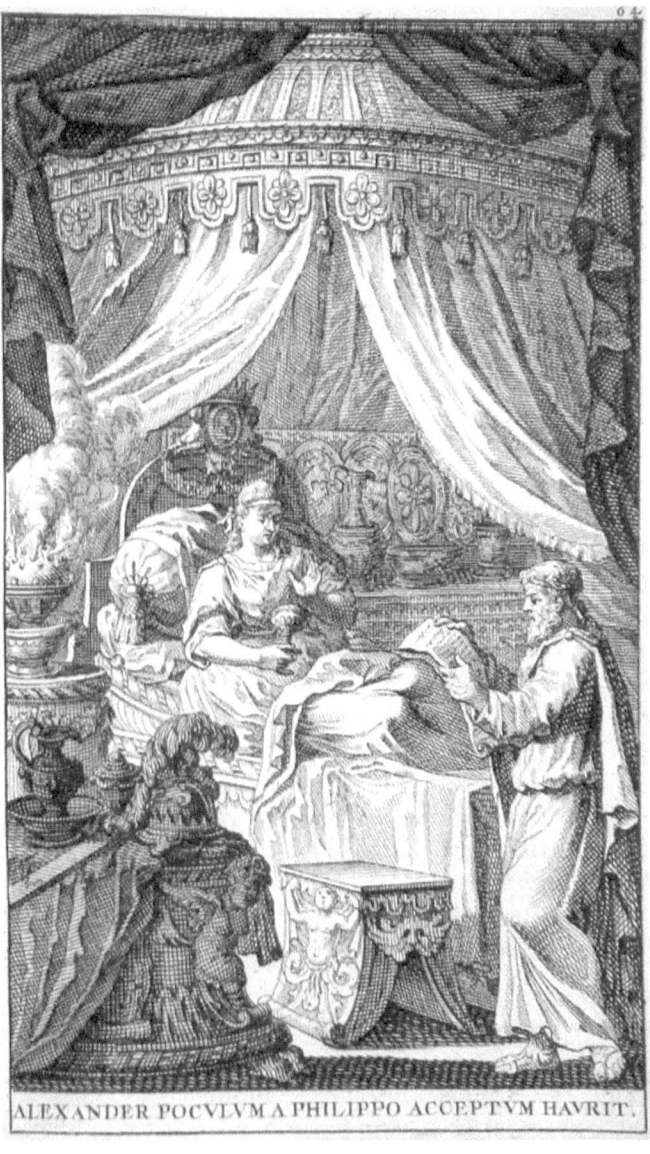

Figure 3.4. Alexander downs Philip's potion (1696)

Book 4: 25th September 333BC - 13th October 332BC

The Battle of Issus; An Interview with the Queens; The Treasures at Damascus; The First Letter from Darius; A New King for Sidon; The Siege of Tyre.

4.1 *This book recounts the events concerning Alexander in the fourth year of his reign.*

4.2 Darius, having received news of Alexander's sickness, hastened to reach the Euphrates with all the swiftness that so encumbered a host could achieve. He built a bridge across the river, but still just five days later had got his army over in order to occupy Cilicia the sooner. Meanwhile Alexander, *having* recovered from his illness, *arrived in Anchiale, which was built by Sardanapalus. Here he pitched his tent in the course of moving up country against the Persians. Not far away lay the tomb of Sardanapalus upon which stood a statue in stone with the fingers of its right hand converged as though they were being snapped. Upon it was inscribed in Syrian characters: "In a single day Sardanapalus the son of Anacyndaraxes constructed Tarsus and Anchiale. Other things not being worth this much, let you eat, drink and be merry." He meant it seems that other things are not worth a snap of the fingers.* **Sardanapalus died eventually from senility after having been deposed from his Syrian sovereignty.**[69]

4.3 Now Alexander reached the city of Soli. Having brought it under his authority, he exacted a bond of two hundred talents from its citizenry and stationed a garrison of his soldiers in its citadel. Then with games and a furlough he repaid the prayers that had been offered to make him well, making plain how sincere he was in his disdain for the foreigners, since the games were celebrated in Aesculapius's and Athena's honours.[70] The joyous news was brought, whilst Alexander was viewing competitions, that at Halicarnassus his men had outfought the forces of the Persians. Additionally, the Myndii and the Caunii and the greater part of their regions had been brought within his dominions.

4.4 Hence having staged a pageant through the games he moved camp, bridged the River Pyramus and reached the city of Mallus, whence, after another overnight encampment, he arrived at the stronghold of Castabalum. There the king met **Parmenion**, who **had been sent ahead to reconnoitre the route through the** *Syrian* **Gates, the pass that they must traverse** in order to reach a town called Issus. **Having** *driven off the Persians and* **taken possession of the narrowest part of the pass, he had left a skeleton garrison in place.** Then

---

[69] Jacoby Fragment 2 of Cleitarchus from Book 4 of his History Concerning Alexander preserved by Athenaeus 12.39 (530A): Syrian means Assyrian (a Cleitarchan idiosyncrasy); Cleitarchus may well have sourced this snippet of Persian history from the *Persica* written by his father Deinon.

[70] The god of healing and the goddess of wisdom: Alexander was vaunting his recovery from illness as being due to the intercession of these deities on his behalf.

Parmenion had seized Issus, which had also been abandoned by the barbarians. Having fanned out from there, he had expelled those who had held the high hills in the hinterland and had posted garrisons everywhere so as to secure their track. Thereafter, as was said beforehand, as both harbinger and perpetrator of these deeds he came straight back.

4.5 From there **Alexander moved his army to Issus,** *which he held by intimidating its populace.* There he took counsel as to whether they should carry on any further or else wait where they were for the scheduled arrival of fresh troops from Macedonia? Parmenion considered that there was no better locale for them to give battle, for in that place the frontline forces of each king would be equal, since the narrows could not accommodate a vast array of people. Alexander's side should avoid wide plains and open country, where they could be surrounded and crushed by an outflanking strategy. Parmenion feared that their own fatigue, rather than their enemies' bravery, would deny them the victory, for fresh Persians would confront them continually, were they able to deploy their ranks more extensively. The logic of such sensible advice was readily appreciated, so it was amidst these mountain passes that their adversary was awaited.

4.6 There was a Persian called Sisines in Alexander's army. The Satrap of Egypt had once sent him to Philip and, being courted with gifts and every courtesy, he had elected exile in preference to his patrimony. Thereafter he followed Alexander into Asia, being considered amongst the most loyal of his allies. And it happened that a Cretan soldier handed him a letter, sealed with a signet ring, the device of which he did not recognise. It had been sent by Darius's chiliarch, Nabarzanes, exhorting Sisines to effect something in keeping with his ancestry and his loyalties, for this, wrote Nabarzanes, would bring him into great honour with their king. As his intentions were innocent, Sisines often endeavoured to bring the letter before Alexander, but finding the king to be overburdened by his duties and his preparations for war, he repeatedly procrastinated in favour of a better opportunity, thereby arousing suspicion that he was plotting treachery. For in fact the letter, prior to its delivery, had come into Alexander's possession. And he had read it and re-sealed it using a ring with an unknown impression and had bidden that it be given to Sisines to assess the loyalty of the barbarian. But since over several days Sisines failed to approach the king, it seemed he had suppressed the letter in the cause of heinous scheming. Hence, he was slain in the column by the Cretans whilst marching, undoubtedly at Alexander's bidding.

4.7 The Greek troops whom Thimodes had received from Pharnabazus had already reached Darius, constituting his primary and practically his solitary hope. They earnestly urged him to retrace his route and to return to the wide-open plains of Mesopotamia. Else, if he deplored that plan, that he should at least divide his copious forces, so that his realm's entire fighting strength should not be struck down by a single stroke of fortune. This advice was not so unpalatable to the king as to his paladins, who declared that the Greeks, being of unreliable and purchasable loyalty, were intent upon treachery and that they sought to

Book 4: 25th September 333BC - 13th October 332BC

fragment his army for the sake of no other strategy than that they might go off by some back way in order to betray to Alexander everything to which they had been party. Nothing, they said, would be more prudent than to surround them with his entire army and wipe them out with flights of javelins and archery as a warning that there would be no escape from punishment for perfidy. But Darius, being ethical and merciful, said that he would certainly not sanction such a sin as to order the butchery of his own soldiers, who had followed him trustingly. For who would ever afterwards entrust their safety to him among the foreign communities, if his hands were stained with the blood of so many of his own mercenaries? Nobody should lose his life as the price for having offered idiotic advice, for none would join in consultations, if it were perilous to make recommendations. Most particularly, they themselves were convened to counsel him daily and expressed many an opinion, but the man was not deemed to be of better loyalty, who spoke with more discretion.

4.8 Accordingly, although Darius offered the Greeks his personal thanks for their thoughtfulness, he bade that they be informed, nevertheless, that if he were to retrace his course, he would without doubt be surrendering his realm to the enemy force. The conduct of warfare relies upon reputability and he who retreats may be deemed to flee. And actually, there was scarcely any sense in protracting the hostilities, since in a desolate region, ravaged in turn by his own host and by his enemies, there were insufficient supplies for such a vast array, especially when winter was just getting underway. Nor was it possible to divide his army, if he were to comply with the custom of his ancestors, who had always engaged all of their warriors in the decisive battles of their wars. And, by Heracles! this erstwhile fearsome sovereign, who had been buoyed up by a false sense of confidence due to the absence of his opponents, had renounced rashness in favour of reticence on becoming aware of the imminence of Darius's presence and had ensconced himself amidst the mountain corridors in the manner of a skulking beast, which lurks in its forest lair on hearing the racket from rovers. And now he was even feigning infirmity to deceive his soldiery. But Darius would no longer be allowing him to refuse a decisive battle. In that hollow in which those cowards were cowering, he would crush them one and all... But this bravado was more for show rather than being justifiable.

4.9 Nevertheless, Darius *decided to disencumber his forces, so he* **diverted his non-combatants and his baggage train including his monies and valuables to Damascus in Syria** *with a token military escort.* However, the wife *(who was also his sister)* and the mother of Darius accompanied the main column as was the custom of their country's court. His *two* maiden daughters and infant son also remained with their father and **he advanced rapidly** *into Cilicia* **to engage with Alexander,** *knowing that the latter was in possession of the passes in the mountains and reckoning that he would not dare to do battle in the plains. Disrespecting the sparseness of the Macedonians, but much impressed by the enormity of the army of the Persians, the local inhabitants forsook Alexander in favour of Darius. So, with unstinting* *willingness they furnished the Persians with food and supplies, foreseeing their victory in their minds' eyes.*

4.10 It chanced that Alexander reached the pass that affords access into Syria on the same night that Darius arrived at the place that is called the Amanic Gates.[71] The Persians did not doubt that the Macedonians were on the run, having abandoned Issus, which they had previously taken, for indeed some of their wounded and sick were seized, having been unable to keep up with the column. At the instigation of Darius' paladins, who were rabid in their barbaric savagery, all these captives had their hands hacked off and the stumps cauterised. They were then led around in order that they be familiarised with his army, and when they had seen all there was to see, he bade them report to their king concerning everything that they had been witnessing. Then Darius moved his camp *from Issus* to base himself upon the River Pinarus[72] in order to stay at the backs of those he supposed to have run away. But the men whose hands he had severed made their way to the Macedonian encampment, saying that Darius was dogging their steps and was following them as fast as he was able. This was barely believable, so Alexander sent scouts back along the littoral to reconnoitre whether Darius himself was advancing in his rear or whether some general was trying to give the impression that the arrival of the entire Persian force was near.

4.11 But, whilst the scouts were retracing their tracks, a huge host was glimpsed in the distance. Thereafter all over the flats, fires began to flare and a blaze appeared to be burning everywhere without intermittence, since the sprawling horde of men had dispersed especially spaciously on account of their beasts of burden. Therefore, rejoicing that the contest would take place there, in that most ideally narrow of courses, as he had begged in his every prayer, Alexander commanded his forces to lay out their camp just where they were. However, as commonly occurs when the occasion of a decisive battle nears, **the king's confidence gave way to fears.** *The numerical superiority of the enemy was cause for anxiety and* he was afraid of Fortune herself, whose favour had furthered his affairs so prosperously and, not unreasonably considering what she had done for him, he was concerned about her inconstancy. Just a single night now lay between him and the outcome of such a critical fight. Conversely, he reckoned that the rewards outweighed the jeopardy and, although it was uncertain whether he would win a victory, it was at any rate certain that, should he die, it would be heroically and

---

[71] Alexander was heading southwards with the Mediterranean coast on his right, but Darius had moved northwards past him further inland and came through the Amanican Gates to appear in Alexander's rear (it seems rather unexpectedly). Alexander was compelled to perform a volte-face and to retrace his steps northwards to meet Darius in the narrow coastal plain near the River Pinarus a little way south of Issus.

[72] The Latin of Curtius 3.8.16 (*motis ergo castris superat Pinarum amnem*) has usually been translated to the effect that Darius moved his camp and crossed the River Pinarus, but Callisthenes (Polybius 12.17-22) wrote that Darius encamped on the banks of the River Pinarus, so Curtius likely meant that Darius moved his camp to lie literally on top of the Pinarus.

Book 4: 25th September 333BC - 13th October 332BC

with great glory. *Certainly, to delay the confrontation would be to increase their insecurity, for it would foster despondency in the ranks of his military.*

4.12 Therefore he told his soldiers to refresh themselves and thereafter at the third watch to be armed and ready. Alexander himself ascended to the crest of a lofty ridge and, lit by the enveloping light of multiple torches, he sacrificed to the guardian gods of the vicinity in accordance with the custom of his country. The third blast of the trumpet was heard by the troops as had been ordered and they were now well prepared for both marching and for battle. They were told to advance at the double, such that by dawn they had reached the narrow strip of land where they had determined that they should make their stand. Those **scouts sent forward on a foray reported that Darius lay thirty stades away,** *his forces drawn up for battle and making for a menacing spectacle.* **Thereupon Alexander** halted his formations, donned his armour and **decreed his dispositions.**

4.13 Panicked peasants brought the news to Darius of the arrival of his foes. He could hardly believe that those fugitives that he had been pursuing were actually advancing upon him. Therefore, no little stress obsessed the minds of all, for they were fitted out for marching rather than for combat, so they had to race to snatch up their arms for the spat. But the very haste of those that scurried about and their invocation of their colleagues to take up their arms instilled still greater trepidation. Others went up onto the mountain ridge in order to get a good view of the formation of the enemy forces, whilst many more bridled their horses. No single chain of command controlled this disorderly army, amongst which diverse disruptions had stirred everyone into a frenzy. Previously, Darius had ordained that the mountain ridge should be occupied by a detachment in order to engage his enemy's rear as well as his front. Also, along the shoreline that afforded his right flank protection he planned to throw forward further troops so as to harry his foe from every direction. Additionally, twenty thousand soldiers he had sent forward with a battalion of archers were ordered to ford the Pinarus River, which coursed between the rival arrays of soldiery, and told to block the advance of the Macedonian military. If they could not hold their ground, they were to withdraw into the mountains and covertly to go right around the endmost of the enemy. But Fortune upset these worthy intentions, proving more influential than all calculations. For out of fear some did not dare to execute their mission, whereas others vainly pursued its execution, since when some parts show indecision, the whole is thrown into confusion.

4.14 Darius deployed his forces in the following fashion. Nabarzanes covered the right wing with his cavalry bolstered by about twenty thousand slingers and archers. On the same wing, Thimodes led the Greek mercenary infantry, comprising thirty thousand soldiers, unquestionably the backbone of Darius's army and a match for the Macedonian phalangite fighters. On the left wing twenty thousand barbarian infantry were commanded by the Thessalian Aristomedes and the king deployed his most pugnacious peoples in support of these. Darius himself meant to fight on that side of his army accompanied by three thousand elite cavalry, his usual bodyguards, and forty thousand infantry. Then the Hyrcanian and Median cavalry came after these and adjoining them, extending both to their right and their left, were the cavalry of other nationalities. Six thousand slingers and javelin-flingers preceded these formations, whilst they were stood at their specified stations. Darius had arrayed his forces to fill up every accessible spot in that corridor, and the wings reached to the ridges on one side and on the other plastered the shore. The wife and mother of the king and the rest of the retinue of women were received into the core of the corps.

4.15 *Alexander conceived this to be a heaven-sent opportunity to cripple the power of the Persians in a single victory,* **so he arrayed his infantry and cavalry appropriately.** He placed his phalanx to the fore, for no others amongst the Macedonians were mightier in war. Nicanor, the son of Parmenion, had custody of the right wing with Coenus, Perdiccas, Meleager, Ptolemaeus[73] and Amyntas standing by him, each leading his own battalion. Craterus and Parmenion himself were on the left wing, which stretched to the sea, but Craterus was bidden to obey Parmenion. **Cavalry were stationed on either wing: the right flank was covered by the Macedonians in combination on their left with the Thessalians** and the left wing was held by the Peloponnesians. Ahead of this battlefront Alexander deployed a company of slingers intermingled with archers. Thracians and Cretans also sallied forward, since they too were only lightly armoured. But against those sent forth by Darius to make the mountain ridge their base he flung the Agrianians, just lately arrived from Thrace. Furthermore, he instructed Parmenion to expand his lines insofar as was feasible towards the sea in order to form his fighting front further away from the mountains, which were occupied by the foreign forces of his enemy. But, having dared neither to make a stand against the oncoming Macedonians nor to get in behind them as they passed them by, these particular barbarians, being especially intimidated by the sight of the slingers, had opted to fly. This eventuality secured the flank of Alexander's formation, which he had feared might be assailed from a greater elevation. *At first* the Macedonian phalanx advanced in a depth of thirty-two ranks, for the narrow corridor did not permit a more extensive cordon. But then the mountain gorges gradually began to broaden and afford more space, so that, not only could the infantry assume their normal number of ranks, but *the cavalry*, who had *occupied the whole front*, could also wheel into place around the flanks.[74]

---

[73] Ptolemaeus the son of Seleucus: he died in the ensuing battle.

[74] The account of the Battle of Issus by Alexander's court historian, Callisthenes of Olynthus, survives via Polybius 12.17-22; he explained that Alexander drew up his phalanx initially 32-deep as he came northwards back through the pass, but that he was able to reduce this to 16-deep then 8-deep as the coastal plain widened such that he was able to broaden his front; it seems likely that Cleitarchus drew upon this account.

Book 4: 25th September 333BC - 13th October 332BC

4.16 At this point the two armies came in sight of one another, though still beyond the range of spears, whereupon *the* foremost *Persians raised up rough and ragged cheers, which spread through all their half a million warriors. These were reciprocated by the Macedonians with more force than the strength of their numbers by virtue of the reverberations from the peaks and desolate mountain pastures.* For crags and highlands situated roundabout always echo and amplify any audible shout. **Alexander** *forged ahead of his foremost standards and* held up his hand frequently to halt his array*, so that they should not through impetuosity be winded when they entered the fray* and to accustom their vision to toleration of the sight of their seething opposition. **And as he rode along his ranks, he addressed his soldiers in various terms as suited their respective characters. The Macedonians, winners of so many wars in Europe,** *who not so much at his but rather their own instigation* **had engaged upon the subjection of Asia** *and the uttermost Orient,* **he reminded of the traditional bravery of their nation. They** *were the deliverers of all the world's territories, who* **would someday surpass the boundaries reached by Dionysus and Heracles.** *They would not only impose their yoke upon the Persians, but also upon all nations. Bactria and India would be provinces of the Macedonians. What they regarded with wonder currently was the least of what there was to see, but everything would be revealed to them by victory. Profitless endeavours amidst the pinnacles of Illyria or the crags of Thrace were not their destiny, but rather the riches of the entire East prospectively. And there would scarcely be any work for their swords, for a shove of their shields would shift those panic-stricken wavering hordes. In addition to this, Alexander hailed his father Philip, who had defeated the Athenians, and he put his men in mind of the subjugation of the Boeotians and the tearing down of their most renowned town. He recalled their battlefront at the Granicus at one juncture and the many cities that they had either stormed or received in surrender at another, reflecting that* **everything behind their backs had been overthrown and trampled in their tracks.** He also told them that the impending battle would be both the termination of their toil and the culmination of their glory.

4.17 When he came upon Greek troops, Alexander asked them to recall that it was the peoples of these countries that had formerly made war upon Greece, firstly through the arrogance of the first Darius and then that of Xerxes, who had required of them both land and water, so that neither drink from their springs nor their regular provender were left to those that had to surrender. By these enemies their temples had been ransacked and incinerated, their cities had been stormed and the stipulations of both human and divine law had been violated. He *even* bade the Illyrians and Thracians, those used to living by banditry, to peer carefully at the ranks of their enemy that were gleaming with gold and purple finery, not outfitted with arms but rather with booty. *Let them march forward like men and strip the gilding from those passive women, exchanging the* *rough relief of their mountains and bared sods, stiff with perpetual frost, for the fecund tracts and purlieus of the Persian squads.*[75]

Figure 4.1. Alexander addresses his officers before Issus (André Castaigne, 1898)

4.18 *Nor was Darius inactive in the motivation of his army, for he assumed the duties of his commanders in circulating past everybody, rousing individuals personally, reminding them of the Persians' immemorial illustriousness and the perpetual empire that the immortal gods had given them to possess.*

---

[75] There is also a suspicion of innuendo in the Latin of Curtius 3.10.10, where rough relief (*aspera iuga*) could also mean doxies and bared sods (*nudasque calles*) is similar to naked servant-boys.

Book 4: 25th September 333BC - 13th October 332BC

4.19 Now the armies came within mutual range of arrows *and on both sides the buglers blew the signal for them to come to blows.* Thereupon the Persians launched their cavalry in a dashing charge against the left wing of their adversary, for Darius opted to decide the contest between the horse, thinking that the phalanx was the flower of the Macedonian force. And already he was seeking to surround Alexander's right wing as well, but when the Macedonian saw this he bade two squadrons of his cavalry to go and hold onto the spur of the fell. The rest he had ride rapidly into the thick of the action, except that he detached the Thessalian horse from this confrontation, ordering their commander to circle back secretly behind his lines to join Parmenion, there to do diligently whatever could be done. And thereafter *the king defended himself valiantly, surrounded on all sides by* the Persians. *But* being crowded together and virtually entangled *these* were unable firmly to fling their javelins, yet they loosed them upon Alexander simultaneously so clustered that they collided as they converged, such that but a few struck weakly and ineffectually upon their adversary, whilst most dropped to earth harmlessly.

4.20 Therefore they promptly drew their swords, being obliged to engage in hand-to-hand combat, and the blood really began to gush and spurt after that. For the two forces were so closely locked together that their arms were clashing against one another and they were poking the points of their swords into the faces of each other. Not even the timid and the cowardly could give up the fight, but standing face to face they fought like duellists might, standing their ground until perchance victory made room for their advance. Therefore, they paced forward eventually only when they had struck down an enemy. But though they had been exhausted, they were engaged by a fresh adversary. And neither could the wounded depart the field as is otherwise customary, since their own side pressed upon them from behind and ahead lay the enemy.

Figure 4.2. Alexander's charge at Issus on the Alexander Sarcophagus from Sidon.

4.21 Alexander peered around in all directions in his anxiety to spot Darius, *who, being raised up by his chariot, was both a prime target for his enemy's offensive and an idol to furnish his own side with an incentive.* Upon sighting the Persian king, Alexander charged him with his cavalry trailing, *for he served himself as a soldier just as much as a commander,* coveting the chief accolade of slaying the Persian ruler and winning the victory by his personal endeavour. *By now the battle had engaged the entirety of both sides' cavalry and many fell casualty as the fray raged indecisively, due to the evenly matched capabilities of the adversaries. The scales swung this*

71

way and that as the lines swayed to and fro locked in mortal combat. **Damage was done by every spear cast and thrust of the sword, since an easy target was presented by the constricted horde. Many were overcome by their injuries whilst confronting their enemies, but they kept on fighting until their expiry, so that their life left them sooner than their bravery. And the commander of each company fought resolutely at its head, inspiring corresponding courage in the ranks that he led. Injuries were inflicted in many varieties in the context of many kinds of heated hostilities as they held out for their respective victories.**

4.22 Oxathres, the brother of Darius, discerning that Alexander was pressing towards his sibling, *was concerned lest there should be no stopping him, since he conceived that he would share in the fate of his king.* **Hence,** he interposed himself and the cream of his cavalry before the royal chariot directly, *considering that this exhibition of his brotherly fidelity would cause him to be exalted by the people of his country, who already admired his combative ability. Standing out sharply from the rest due to his panoply and the vigour of his body and distinguished by a rare courage and loyalty,* he *certainly* shone in that fight, *skillfully felling some that pressed forward recklessly and putting others to flight.* **But surrounding their king the Macedonian horsemen** *roused one another through mutual exhortation and in company with their sovereign they* **smashed through the cavalry lines of the opposition,** *each determined to dispatch Darius ahead of the competition without any thought of self-preservation. Then the carnage truly reached ruinous proportions.* **All around the chariot of Darius his most illustrious lords lay in legions,** *where, before the gaze of their king, they had died most gloriously, all face down as they had fallen in the fighting having received some frontal injury.* **Many of the most prominent Persian commanders perished in this struggle: among these Antixyes, Rheomithres and Sabaces, the Governor of Egypt,** *leaders of vast armies,* **were especially notable.** *Around them a less familiar crowd of infantry and cavalry were piled in a huddle.* **Of the Macedonians** *too not so very many but yet some of the most valiant* **were laid low and Alexander himself suffered a slight slashing blow to his right thigh** *from a blade, when he was mobbed by the foe.*

4.23 By this time the horses harnessed to the chariot of Darius had been struck by spears *and had become frenzied by the accumulations of corpses from the battle.* Hence, being stampeded by their pain *and their fears,* they had begun to thrash the yoke, rocking the king riding in the vehicle and conveying him almost into the midst of the enemy. <u>Darius</u> *personally wrestled with the reins, demeaning his customary dignity, then leapt out, dreading being delivered still living into the power of his adversary. He* mounted upon a spare for the team of four that was held by his retinue *for such an emergency*.⁷⁶ As he made the switch under constant attack in the mêlée, he panicked *and threw away his insignia shamefully, so that they should not betray him as he* <u>turned to flee</u>.⁷⁷ *Beholding their king in this condition, those around him followed his decision and then each neighbouring company successively resorted to desertion, so that the entirety of the Persian cavalry was soon retreating rapidly. Thus, indeed the rest were scared into scattering and such as were afforded a route for escaping raced away casting aside the arms that they had assumed but lately to protect their persons: in such a degree does panic produce a revulsion for precautions.*

Figure 4.3. Alexander threatens Darius at Issus (Alexander Mosaic, Pompeii)

4.24 The cavalry sent out by Parmenion were pressing hard upon the escaping enemy and luckily all of them on that wing had been persuaded to flee. But towards Parmenion's right the Persians were harrying the Thessalian horsemen vehemently and one squadron had been trampled by their charge already, whereupon the Thessalians suddenly wheeled their steeds about, abandoning their flight and hurling themselves back into the fight, felling with abundant butchery barbarians who were straggling through overconfidence in their victory.

---

⁷⁶ It is obvious from the very close parallels in the rest of their texts here that Diodorus 17.34.6-7 is following the same source as Curtius 3.11.11-12, but unnecessary difficulties have been created by rendering *tethrippon heteron* as "another chariot". Although *tethrippos* is used to mean a four-horse chariot (Latin: *quadriga*), it literally means the team of four horses themselves (i.e. *tetra-hippos*), so *tethrippon heteron* (literally "another four-horse") can instead mean a spare horse for the four-horse team. This allows agreement with Curtius that Darius escaped on a spare horse rather than in a second chariot. Arrian 2.11.4 also has Darius transfer to a horse, but later in his flight. The Alexander Mosaic vividly depicts this scene, including especially the terror of the chariot team and the spare horse being brought before Darius.

⁷⁷ That Cleitarchus (inevitably) recorded the defeat of Darius at Issus is confirmed by Cicero, *Ad f.* 2.10.3, which is Jacoby Fragment 8 of Cleitarchus.

Both the Persian mounts and their riders were weighed down with leaf armour to the knee, so, though they maintained maximum speed, they manoeuvred only with difficulty. Thus, naturally, by weaving about on their steeds the Thessalians engaged them with impunity. When this gainful engagement was reported to Alexander, who had not yet ventured to press the pursuit of his adversary, being now the victor universally, he began to harry the heels of the fleeing enemy. Not more than a thousand cavalry followed the king as he rode down this huge horde of his opponents, but who whilst winning or in flight holds a headcount of his contingents? Hence so very few Macedonians drove the Persians like cattle and their escape was protracted by the same panic that pushed them into flight from the battle. *As their paths passed through narrow defiles and across rough country they jostled and trampled one another and many perished without a blow from the enemy. For men were crammed together in a press, some without their armour, others retaining full battle dress. Some still with their swords bared slew others who were thereby skewered. But most of the cavalry spewed out into the open country, vigorously urging on their steeds and reaching the refuge of the allied cities. At this point the Macedonian phalanx and the Persian infantry clashed but briefly, for the collapse of the cavalry had presaged a complete and universal victory. All the Persians resorted to retreat quite rapidly and, as so many myriads sought safety via narrow routes, corpses soon covered the country.* Yet the Greeks who had stood with Darius with Amyntas as their commander, previously one of Alexander's officers but at that time a defector, being separated from the rest got out without any semblance of a rout.

4.25 *With the onset of night* the remnants of the army of the Persians easily managed to disperse in diverse directions. Some took the direct route to Persia, whilst others detoured amidst the crags and secluded mountain gorges. A few retreated to the camp of Darius, but now **the victors gave up the pursuit and** also **reached the royal tents looking for loot and found them crammed with every kind of opulence. The troops made off with an enormous mass of silver, gold and gorgeous garments, rather the apparatus of decadence than equipment for defence. And** they plundered still more extensively, **not just from the royal treasures, but also comprehensively from the king's relatives, friends and commanders.** The roads were strewn with more beggarly belongings, which their greed had scorned relative to richer pickings.

Book 4: 25th September 333BC - 13th October 332BC

Figure 4.4. The flight of Darius at Issus (André Castaigne, 1898)

4.26 *Then they got to the ladies:* not only the womenfolk of the royal family, but also those of the king's relatives and friends that had accompanied the army, conveyed in gilded wagons in conformance with an ancestral custom of the Persians. And each of them had with her a surfeit of splendiferous furnishings and feminine finery, befitting her fabulous wealth and luxury. The fate of these female captives was completely lamentable. Formerly, they had been loth to be driven even in a sumptuous vehicle reflecting their refinement and no part of their persons had lacked raiment. Now each erupted from her tent clad only in a single garment, a sort of shirt that she rent, wailing and invoking the deities in prostrating herself at her conqueror's knees. Her hands shook as she shed her jewellery and her hair flew as she fled through the rugged territory. Subsequently, these escapees were wont to coalesce, when each sought the aid of those equally in distress. Some of their captors hauled these unfortunate females by their hair, whilst others tore off their finery leaving them quite bare and applied slaps of their hands or thwacks of their spearshafts to drive them here and there. *And their adornments were prised from them the more forcefully when they prized them the more dearly. Neither were their persons even spared the thrusts of Macedonian lusts, such that the camp resounded with every sort of scream and screech according to the fate of each.* Thus, the victors debauched the most precious and esteemed chattels of the Persians, treating them as Fortune's benefactions. *The scene was lacking in no form of outrage, since the cruelty and licentiousness of the victors was visited upon persons of every rank and age.* Although *the most moderate of the Macedonians viewed these vicissitudes of Fortune with forbearance and felt pity for those that had been so violently rent from their former existence,* nevertheless, *with the confiscation of the comforts conferred by their exalted station, these women were corralled by the men of a hostile and foreign nation and herded into a hopeless and humiliating subjugation.*

4.27 Then indeed one could discern Fortune's fickle face, since those that adorned Darius's pavilion, lending lush luxury and plush opulence to the place, kept its contents in a comfortable condition now for Alexander, just as for their former master. For these alone the troops left unravished, since it was established by precedent that they should receive the conqueror in the conquered king's tent. But *in particular* the captured mother, wife and children of Darius had captivated the attention and the compassion of everyone. *The mother, not merely due to her majesty but also her maturity, merited veneration and* the wife *on account of her beauty, unmarred by adversity, deserved adoration.* She had enfolded in her embrace a son, who had not yet reached six years of age, *born into the prospect of his father's huge yet lately relinquished heritage. However,* two teenage maidens, her granddaughters, were clasped to the old lady's breast, *being, not merely for their own sake but for hers also, overwhelmingly distressed. His family were unaware of Darius's fate, whether he had survived or had perished in a disaster so great, but they saw their own tent looted by armed combatants, who behaved improperly out of ignorance.* The queens were surrounded by a vast crowd of Asian noblewomen with mangled hair and rent garments, oblivious of their former magnificence. These, falling to the ground implored their assistance, invoking them by royal and rulership titles that no longer had any relevance. The queens were incapable of

Book 4: 25th September 333BC - 13th October 332BC

providing any succour, *but, unmindful of their personal disaster, were demanding to know which wing Darius had fought upon and what exactly was the struggle's outcome? They insisted: "We are not yet captives, if our lord the king still lives!" But* Darius, with many a change of mount, had by then extended his flight across stades beyond count.

4.28 Hence the Royal Pages *now secured the tent of Darius and prepared a bath and Alexander's dinner. Then they awaited his return from the pursuit and by lighting torches they created a great glimmer, so that he should discover Darius's entire paraphernalia made ready for him as a harbinger of his conquest of the whole of Asia.*

4.29 In the course of that battle there were *neutralised or* slain more than one hundred thousand Persian infantry and not less than ten thousand cavalry *of whom forty thousand were taken into captivity*.[78] But on Alexander's side some four thousand five hundred men suffered injury and just three hundred foot were lost together with one hundred and fifty cavalry, so slight was the cost of so vast a victory.

4.30 *On determining the decisiveness of his defeat Darius dedicated himself to his deliverance, mounting steed after steed to speed his disappearance, desperate to evade Alexander's custody by reaching the Upper Satrapies and a degree of safety.* Alexander *pursued him avidly with the Companion Cavalry and the best of the rest of his horsemen, only too keen to get his quarry into his possession, though he had a headstart of four or five stades. So he* chased Darius in his flight *for two hundred stades* until both hope and the light began to fade, whereupon he turned back fatigued from tracking the renegade and returned to the camp *at about midnight with nothing to show but Darius's chariot and his bow as trophies of the fight.*[79] *Having washed off his weariness by bathing,* he bade that his closest Friends be invited to join him for dining, for a mere graze received upon his thigh was not going to deny him his revelling. But **the diners were dismayed by a sudden doleful din issuing from the neighbouring pavilion** and the detachment that was on watch at the king's tent armed themselves, fearing lest it mark the instigation of a more considerable commotion. **The cause of this unexpected fuss was that the mother and the wife of Darius together with their noblewomen were bewailing the supposed death of their king with much moaning and groaning. For one of the eunuchs** amongst these captives, who had chanced to stand outside their tent, had recognised Darius's mantle, which, as already noted, he had cast off the better to thwart his betrayal. It had been in the hands of him who had brought it back upon its discovery. But reckoning that it had been wrenched from the king's corpse, the eunuch **delivered a false report of**

---

[78] The Persian losses and casualties are agreed by Curtius 3.11.27, Diodorus 17.36.5, Plutarch 20.5, Arrian 2.11.8 and Justin 11.9.10.

[79] See Plutarch, *Alexander* 20.5-6 for Darius's headstart and Alexander's trophies.

Darius's expiry, *claiming that Alexander had returned from the chase after having stripped his body.*

4.31 On becoming aware of the women's error Alexander is said to have shed a tear for the downfall of Darius and the devotion of his kindred. *And initially he bade Mithrenes, who had surrendered Sardis and was fluent in the Persian language, to go give them solace. But then, fearing lest a visit from a turncoat should cause the captives to recapitulate their consternation and disconsolation,* he sent Leonnatus, one of his leading lords, bidding him mention their mistake in making a living man the object of their mourning and lamentation. *Leonnatus entered their pavilion with a handful of guardsmen and bade it be announced that he had been sent by his sovereign. But, when they espied the soldiers' arms, those that were in the foyer, reckoning that their mistresses were done for, scurried inside shrieking that they had lived their last day, killers of captives having arrived before their door. Hence, since they neither dared to let them in nor could keep them at bay, they silently awaited the victor's verdict and made no foray.*

4.32 *Having waited a while for someone to invite him in, Leonnatus left his escort in the foyer when nobody dared to meet him and went on in anyway. This act in itself upset the women, since he seemed not so much to have been admitted as to have forced his way in. Therefore, the queenmother, Sisygambis, and the consort prostrated themselves at his feet and began to plead that, before they themselves were liquidated, they should be allowed to bury the body of Darius as the customs of his country dictated. Having performed the last rites for their king, they would cease to shirk their own killing.* Then Leonnatus revealed that Darius still lived and that they themselves would not only enjoy immunity but would retain all the trappings of their original queenly dignity. *In the morning Alexander himself would come round. Then the mother of Darius at last allowed herself to be raised up from the ground. And in the light of Leonnatus's welcome revelation, the women ceased their lamentation and lauded Alexander as deserving of veneration.*

4.33 *At dawn* **the next day,** after having carefully conducted the burial of all the bodies he could discover of the Macedonians, Alexander bade that the same respect also be accorded to the corpses of the most distinguished Persians and he mandated the mother of Darius to bury those she wished according to the customs of their country. She confined herself to ordering the inhumation of a few of her close kin and those in a fashion befitting their current situation, judging that the magnificence of the funeral celebrations with which the Persians perform the last rites would be distasteful when the victors were receiving cheap cremations. Thereupon, having dealt properly with the remains of the dead, **Alexander** sent a herald ahead to the captives announcing his own approach and, curtailing the encroachment of his swarming coterie, he **entered their tent with**

solely Hephaistion in his company. This man was by far the dearest to the king of all his associates having been brought up alongside him and having shared in all of his secrets. He also enjoyed the unique privilege of being allowed to admonish Alexander, but he exercised this freedom in such a manner that it appeared rather to have been authorised by his sovereign than appropriated by Hephaistion. And, *although he was the same age,* he outstripped his ruler in *handsomeness and* physical stature *and the dress of each was similar.* Hence the queens supposed him to be the king and accordingly commenced their customary reverencing of him. Whereupon some of the eunuchs that had been taken prisoner gesticulated to show which was Alexander, so that Sisygambis fell at his feet *excusing her ignorance due to never before having seen the king.* But, *taking her hand to raise her,* this was the response of the ruler: "Mother, you did not err, for he too is Alexander." *By using a title to address her that was most familiar, he meant to proffer the promise of preferential treatment in the future to those who had been distraught a little earlier.*

Figure 4.5. Alexander and Hephaistion visit the Persian Royal Family (Charles Le Brun)

4.34 *Indeed, had he continued up to the end of his days to behave so chivalrously, I consider that he would have been more triumphant than he actually appeared to be, when he was emulating Dionysus's pageantry in processing victoriously from the Hellespont to the outer Ocean successively through every country. Then he would have suppressed his arrogance and fury, faults he never overcame fully. Then he would have refrained from slaying his friends at his suppers and would have dreaded to execute without trial distinguished officers, his close companions in* *the conquest of so many nations. But Fortune had not yet overinflated his ego. For he that bore her breath so temperately and moderately at its onset proved imprudent when she really began to blow. But at that time at any rate, he behaved in such ways that he surpassed in both propriety and clemency all the kings of former days.* He treated the remarkably lovely royal virgins as just as inviolate as if they had sprung from the same parents as he. And **the wife** as well, whom no other lady at that time excelled in beauty, **he was so far from subjecting to lechery that he took special care to prevent anyone from debauching her body whilst he held her in his custody. He commanded that all her accoutrements be returned to each lady, including her servants and her jewellery** *and he added many another lackey so as virtually to double the entirety. He promised to each of the daughters a dowry that exceeded that due from Darius in its bounty and he undertook to raise the boy with the dignity due to a son of his own and allowed him to retain his royalty.*

Figure 4.6. The Persian Queens greet Alexander and Hephaistion (André Castaigne, 1898)

4.35 Sisygambis responded tearfully: "O Sire, you deserve that we should pray for you as we prayed for Darius, our own sovereign, formerly and I see this as befitting a king who has surpassed him, not merely in prosperity, but also in equity. Indeed, you call me 'mother' and 'queen', but personally I avow myself to be your humble servant. I both retain the exalted status of my former existence and am able to cope with the constraints of the present. But it is for you to decide to what extent your authority over us is to be characterised by clemency rather than by cruelty." *As many of the women were shedding a tear,* **Alexander bade them all be of good cheer and called upon the young boy to come**

Book 4: 25th September 333BC - 13th October 332BC

near. *Then the son of Darius wrapped his arms around the king's neck in an embrace, fearless of the unfamiliar face, when Alexander lifted the child up to his shoulder.* Being touched by the six-year-old's composure, the king kissed him and caught the glance of Hephaistion, observing: "How I wish that Darius had inherited something of the same disposition!" *And with that they quit the pavilion.*

4.36 Alexander consecrated three altars on a bank of the River Pinarus to Zeus, Heracles and Athena, then he headed for Syria. Parmenion was sent ahead *with the Thessalian cavalry* to Damascus, where lay the treasure of Darius. However, he learnt that he had been preceded by a satrap of the Persian king and was concerned lest the contempt of his opponents were invited by the scantiness of his following, so he sought to fetch reinforcements. But by chance the scouts that had been sent forward by Parmenion came across a man from the Mardian nation, who, on being led before the commander, handed him a letter sent by the governor of Damascus to Alexander. He added that he was in no doubt that the governor would surrender all the royal chattels as well as the treasure. After ordering that they should guard the Mardian, Parmenion opened the letter, in which it was written that Alexander should promptly send one of his commanders with a few men in order to possess himself of that which Darius had deposited at Damascus. Accordingly, in order to return the Mardian to the defector he despatched an escort of wardens, but the man entered Damascus before daybreak having slipped from the grasp of these custodians.

4.37 This behaviour disturbed Parmenion, who feared treachery. Hence, he did not venture, whilst lacking guidance, to pursue an unfamiliar itinerary. Nevertheless, trusting in the good fortune of his king, he ordered that some peasants should be seized to serve as guides for their journey. These being acquired quite quickly, he reached the city in three days, where the governor had already been fearing for their faith in his fidelity. Therefore, he feigned but feeble faith in the fortress's fortifications in ordering that his monarch's funds, which the Persians term 'gaza', together with his most precious possessions should be carried forth as if he meant to flee, whilst actually intending to present it as a prize for the enemy. Many thousands of men and women followed him as he left the city, a throng that stirred the pity of everybody, save him to whose trust they had been committed. For so as to profit more from his perfidy, he was prepared to cast before their adversary a prize preferable to any amount of money: namely the nobles and the wives and children of Darius's aristocracy, and the envoys from the Greek cities as well, whom Darius had left in the hands of the defector as though within his most secure citadel.

4.38 'Gangabae' is the Persian term for bearers who carry burdens upon their shoulders. When they could not bear the rigours of the journey, since a storm had brought a sudden fall of snow and the ground was rigid with frigidity, these bearers decked themselves in robes adorned with purple and gold embroidery that they had been carrying in addition to the money. And none ventured to forbid them, for Darius's difficulties gave free rein even to the humblest of men. Hence, they presented Parmenion with the appearance of a military column of significant importance. Therefore, with due diligence as if for a proper engagement he curtly exhorted his forces to set spur to their steeds and swiftly to charge upon the enemy. But those laden with baggage let it fall and took to their heels as terror seized them all. The armed guards escorting them were likewise stricken by consternation and they threw away their arms in resorting to available routes for evasion. The governor, by acting as though he too were terror-stricken, ensured that complete panic set in. All the royal riches were strewn across the entire plain: the monies meant for the pay of vast levies; the regalia of numerous noblemen and the adornments of so many illustrious ladies; golden vessels and golden bridles; pavilions appointed with regal magnificence as well as many a conveyance, abandoned by its occupants, but still filled with immense opulence and presenting even looters with a pitiful appearance, if such sentiments could hold greed in abeyance. For from an array of riches reaching beyond belief and built up by so many years of toil some items were now seen to be rent by briars whilst others were trodden into the soil, as the hands of the pillagers proved inadequate to the scale of their spoil.

4.39 And then they came upon those who had been first to flee. Numerous women were dragging their tiny offspring along *in the emergency*. Among them were the three virgin daughters of Ochus, who prior to Darius had held the sovereignty. A revolution had formerly reduced them from the royalty of their father's estate, but on this occasion Fortune exacerbated their fate even more cruelly. There were also in the same huddle the wife of the aforementioned Ochus and the daughter of Oxathres, brother to Darius, plus the wife of Artabazus, his foremost noble, and his son, who was named Ilioneos.[80] In addition, they captured the wife together with the son of Pharnabazus, who had been designated commander of the entire coastline by Darius, as well as the three daughters of Mentor and the widow and son of Memnon, that most illustrious leader. Scarcely any noble house evaded this vast disaster.

4.40 But Alexander, reckoning self-restraint to be kinglier conduct than the ravishing of his enemies' women, neither violated these ladies nor any others before marriage with the exception of Barsine, the widow of Memnon. Since she had received a Greek education and was of a personable disposition and because Artabazus, her father, was the son of a king's daughter,[81] Alexander decided at the instigation of Parmenion, *as is stated by Aristobulus in his history*, to associate with a lady of such great beauty and distinguished ancestry. *The king eventually came to love his prisoner and later had a son whom he named Heracles by her.*

---

[80] Probably named after Troy (Ilion), reflecting the Phrygian satrapy of Artabazus.

[81] His father was another Pharnabazus, who had married Apame, the daughter of Artaxerxes II, some time between 392-387BC.

Book 4: 25th September 333BC - 13th October 332BC

4.41 Also taken at this time were the Spartans and those Athenians, who had violated their oath of alliance with Alexander by following the Persians. By far the most distinguished among the Athenians both by their birth and by their renown were Aristogeiton, Dropides and Iphicrates. Likewise, men of distinction at home among their fellow Spartans were Pasippus and Onomastorides together with Onomas and Callicratides. The sum of struck coinage captured was two thousand six hundred talents[82] and the weight of wrought silver amounted to five hundred talents. Furthermore, thirty thousand men together with seven thousand beasts of burden bearing goods upon their backs were taken. But divine vengeance rapidly wreaked due punishment upon the betrayer of such a tremendous treasure. For one of his henchmen slew the traitor and bore his head before his king, I suppose even in adversity deeming Darius worthy of reverencing. And this was an opportune solace for having been betrayed, since he was both avenged upon a renegade and he perceived that not everybody felt that his royal authority had begun to fade.

4.42 Though but lately the monarch of such an enormous army, which he had led into battle whilst raised up in his chariot as if celebrating a victory rather than contesting a tussle, Darius was now in flight through vast and virtually desolate regions, places he had previously all but filled with his immense formations. Just a few men accompanied the king, for not all had escaped in the same direction and those with him found their steeds failing, since they could not match their monarch's regular mount rotation. He first reached Onchae, where four thousand Greeks still greeted him as sovereign; **then Darius raced on towards Babylon via the Euphrates**, since it seemed to him that he would control only that which he managed rapidly to seize. And **upon reaching Babylon, Darius rallied the survivors from the Battle of Issus. His defiance was still fierce, despite the wretched reverse, but he wrote to Alexander offering a fabulous fee for the return of his wife and family.**[83]

4.43 Meanwhile Alexander now gave the governorship of the part of Syria called 'Hollow'[84] to Parmenion, by whom the treasures had been recovered at

---

[82] A talent was 6000 drachmae (normally) of silver – a weight of about 25 kilogams.

[83] Diodorus 17.39 goes on to describe details from the second letter of Darius to Alexander, which Curtius 4.5.1-8 places after the siege of Tyre and which Diodorus then omits. Curtius 4.1.7-14 cites the ransom and a return of Alexander to Macedonia for the first letter. Since Justin 11.12.1-5 broadly confirms Curtius's version, it appears that Diodorus has become confused between the two separate letters. This is probably also what led him to suggest that Alexander presented a forged version of the first letter to his council – a story of which there is no hint elsewhere. This is further supported by Diodorus 17.39.3-4 giving an account of Darius's renewed preparations for war, which matches details given by Curtius 4.6.1-2 just before the siege of Gaza and Curtius 4.9.1-5 after Alexander's return from Egypt. I am inclined to acquit Cleitarchus of the confusion arising in Diodorus 17.39 on the combined evidence of Curtius and Justin, who were assuredly also following the Alexandrian on the matter of the letters.

[84] Coele Syria, comprising the broad valley between the ranges of Mount Lebanon (Libanus and Antilibanus).

Damascus, bidding him to look after both the booty itself and the captives with careful attention. The Syrians, not yet having been sufficiently intimidated by their calamities in the conflict, rejected the new regime, but they were quickly subjugated and obediently did as they were directed. Then too the island of Aradus capitulated. Straton, who was then ruling this island, also controlled the coastline and many areas stretching far inland. After accepting his fealty Alexander moved his camp to Marathus, a *nearby coastal* city.[85] There **the letter from Darius reached the king**, who was greatly offended by its arrogant wording. It annoyed him especially that **Darius** had described himself as His Majesty but had not seen fit to favour Alexander with the same dignity. Moreover, he **had specified** rather than petitioned *that, upon accepting enough money to purchase Macedon in its entirety, Alexander should return his mother, wife and children* immediately. Then, if he wished, Alexander might fairly seek to fight for the supremacy. If, finally, he could consider counsel that was more cautionary, he would be satisfied with his own country: he would withdraw from the bounds of another's sovereignty and would be his ally in all amity. Darius stood ready both to swear to such terms and to accept Alexander's pledge of reciprocity.

4.44 Alexander's riposte was written much in this fashion: "Salutations to Darius from His Majesty King Alexander. That *former* Darius, whose name you have assumed, visited complete disaster upon the Greeks holding the Hellespontine shore and upon the Greek colonies of Ionia furthermore. Thereafter he traversed the seas with vast armies, so as to wage war upon Macedonia and the Greek cities. Then afterwards we were again assaulted by Xerxes from the same race, who brought a monstrous horde of barbarians for us to face. Though vanquished in a naval engagement, he nevertheless left Mardonius on Greek soil, so that even whilst absent he might fire our fields and despoil each associated settlement. And regarding Philip, my father, as is well known by everybody, he was slain by people whom your people had bribed with the prospect of a phenomenal fee. Your warfare is without chivalry, for, though you do not want for weaponry, you seek to purchase the life of every adversary, as when you wished recently to hire an assassin to do away with me for a thousand talents, despite your authority over such an enormous army.[86] Thus I am the defender in this war, rather than the aggressor. And the gods back the better motivated individual. I have put the better part of Asia in my power and I have bested you yourself in battle. Insofar as you have not even fought fairly in our warfare, I am under no obligation to offer you any salvation. Nevertheless, if you come to me in supplication, I promise that your mother, wife and children shall be returned to you without ransom. For I know both how to conquer and how to conciliate those that I have overcome. Yet if you fear to place yourself at my mercy, I will pledge my word

---

[85] Marathus faced the island of Aradus.

[86] The allusion is to the bribe of 1000 talents offered to Alexander Lyncestes and apparently available to others such as Philip the Doctor for arranging Alexander's death, cf. Curtius 3.6.4.

Book 4: 25th September 333BC - 13th October 332BC

that you may come before me in perfect safety. Finally, whenever in future you write to me, remember not only to do so as to a king, but also as to your own sovereign." For this letter's delivery, he made Thersippus his emissary.

4.45 Alexander marched down into Phoenicia and received the surrender of its people,[87] starting with Byblos, a fortified citadel. Thence **he reached Sidon**, a city celebrated for the fame of its founders and for its antiquity. **There Straton held the monarchy with the backing of Darius's authority. But because he had tendered his fealty under pressure from the populace rather than voluntarily, he was deemed unsuitable to continue in the sovereignty and Hephaistion was delegated to determine exactly who among the Sidonians was most worthy of supremacy.**[88] Just then Hephaistion was the guest of two young men, who were eminent among their countrymen, so initially he thought of them. But when they were offered the chance to reign, they declined on account of the custom of their country that, unless they were of the royal strain, no one was admitted to that exalted dignity. Hephaistion admired the magnanimity with which they spurned that which others sought with swords and for which they burned, so he **responded:** "My congratulations to you on having been the first to fathom how much more magnificent it is to refuse rulership than to accept it. But **please therefore propose somebody of royal genealogy**, who will remember that he owes to you his sovereignty."

4.46 They perceived that many, fixated by so great an opportunity, were flattering the particular friends of Alexander in coveting the monarchy. However, **they noted that none was more satisfactory than a certain Abdalonymus, who definitely had a distant connection with the royal tree, but was *employed in* cultivating a market garden** near the edge of the city, **making a meagre living on account of his poverty**. As is often the case, **the cause of his penury was his *innate niceness and* honesty** and intent as he was on his day-to-day activities he had hardly heard of the clash of arms that had reverberated throughout all Asia's territories. ***When Hephaistion agreed to his enthronement,*** the aforementioned dignitaries abruptly entered the garden with the official royal raiment, whilst, as it happened, **Abdalonymus was watering** *and weeding* **the allotment.**[89] Thereupon, after they had saluted him as their sovereign, one of them announced: "You need to exchange the

---

[87] Curtius 4.1.15 & Diodorus 17.40.2.

[88] Diodorus 17.47 recounts this story after the siege of Tyre after noting that the rulership of Tyre was given to Abdalonymus after its fall. I infer that Diodorus was prompted to tell the story retrospectively by the award of the territory of Tyre and that Diodorus himself told the story correctly of Sidon, but that an editor subsequently incorrectly corrected the name of the city to Tyre, because the earlier omission of the matter made it seem that all Abdalonymus's territory should be at Tyre.

[89] Curtius has Abdalonymus drawing out weeds, but Diodorus, Justin and Plutarch in his *Moralia* all agree that he was drawing water, so perhaps Curtius misunderstood his source.

ragged garments you are wearing for the regalia that you see me holding. Cleanse your person of its perpetual caking of mud and dust. **Adopt the demeanour of a monarch** and bring your characteristic moderation to the office, for which it is fitting and just. And when you sit upon the throne, directing the lives and the deaths of the citizens of your country, be careful not to forget the poverty, in which – no, because of which, by Heracles – **you are receiving the sovereignty."** To **Abdalonymus** it all seemed like a reverie. Occasionally, he queried as to whether those that were sporting with him so outrageously had taken leave of their sanity? But the dirt was washed off him whilst he wavered in dubiety and he **was wrapped in the robe** *emblazoned with gold and purple* as the emissaries swore their fidelity. *Then he was conducted through the marketplace in the same people's company, whilst they proclaimed his sovereignty,* so that he arrived at the palace as a king in actuality.

4.47 Readily thereafter, as is its tendency, rumour raced through the entire city. **Many showed enthusiasm** *and marvelled at Fortune's variability*, but others exhibited some animosity. The wealthiest citizens complained to Alexander's friends concerning the new king's penury and servility. Alexander ordered that he should appear before him immediately, and after looking at him lengthily, he declared: "The nature of your origins is not belied by your outward appearance, but it is nice that you have borne privation with resilience." And Abdalonymus responded: "I hope that I shall be able to suffer sovereignty with the same equanimity. These hands of mine supplied what I sought. I owned nothing, but lacked for naught." From Abdalonymus's conversation *Alexander* gained an impression of a noble disposition. Consequently, he *bade that* not only *the regal appurtenances of Straton*, but also many items from the Persian treasure *be given into his possession.* In addition, a region bordering upon the city was placed under his dominion *and the king invested him as a royal companion. Thus, his career provides an object lesson in the forcefulness of Fortune's intercession.*

4.48 So now all Syria was under Macedonian control and **Alexander marched on through Phoenicia, where, with the sole exception of Tyre, the cities submitted voluntarily.** Alexander encamped on the mainland from which this city was separated by a narrow channel of the sea. Tyre outstrips all the other cities of Syria and Phoenicia in both size and renown and it seemed simpler to enter into an alliance with Alexander rather than submit to his rule in this town. Therefore, *her envoys presented the king with the gift of a golden crown* and out of hospitality they sent him as well a profusion of provisions from their citadel. **Alexander** bade that these presents be received as signalling amity and he **addressed the envoys** kindly, **saying that he would appreciate the opportunity to sacrifice to Heracles**, whom the Tyrians reverenced particularly.[90] He noted: "The Macedonian monarchy believes that this deity was

---

[90] This was Melkart, the tutelary god of Tyre, whom the Greeks identified with Heracles by virtue of syncretism.

Book 4: 25th September 333BC - 13th October 332BC

the ancestor of our dynasty and additionally an oracle has alerted me that I should perform such a sacrifice actually." **The envoys replied that there was a temple of Heracles outside their main city in their settlement at Old Tyre,** *where he could perform the rite propitiously and in a temple of greater antiquity.* Alexander *had a tendency to lose his temper, so he* did not conceal his anger, but retorted: "*In essence you are placing your faith in your locality. As inhabitants of an island, you scorn this land army. But I shall shortly show that you are joined to this landmass integrally and* I would have you know that I shall either be permitted to make an entry or I shall storm my way into your city."

4.49 On being sent back with this response, the envoys commenced cautioning their countrymen that a king whom Syria and Phoenicia had admitted ought also to be allowed entry by them. **But the Tyrians confronted the threat of a siege with alacrity.** *They wished to ingratiate themselves with Darius by maintaining an untarnished loyalty and they supposed that he would reward with great generosity those that accorded him such fidelity. They would divert Alexander into a tedious and arduous campaign, buying Darius time to prepare to fight back again.* **For the Tyrians had sufficient confidence in the defensibility of their island emplacement** *and its fighting complement* **as to decide that they would withstand an investment.**

4.50 For **four stades separate the mainland from the city** across a choppy strait, which is particularly exposed to the African breeze that repeatedly rolls breakers inshore off the high seas. And nothing presented a hindrance more than this wind to the operations by means of which the connection of the island to the shore was being planned by the Macedonians. It is hard to lay down a mole even in calm and tranquil marine conditions, but in practice from its onset through the thrashing delivered by its dashing sea the African wind demolishes any agglomerations. No mole can be made so firm that the swell does not erode its foundations, either by seeping through the structure's concretions or else cascading over the crest of the construction in rougher wind conditions. In addition to this difficulty, there was another of like severity. The walls and towers of the city were surrounded by particularly deep stretches of the sea. They could not fire artillery, except from ships well out to sea. And approaching to set up scaling ladders was denied to infantry, since the ramparts dropped sheerly beneath the briny. In fact, **Alexander** lacked a navy, but he **saw that even if he could have sailed against the city**, drifting and unsteady, **he could have been kept off by the artillery on the parapets** *and by the fleet of the enemy.*

4.51 Meanwhile a thing inspired confidence in the Tyrians that sounds trivial. In accordance with their country's customs commissaries had come from the Carthaginians to celebrate an annual holy festival. For Carthage had been founded by the Tyrians, so the concern of the colonists for their ancestral abode was perpetual. Consequently, they commenced encouraging the Tyrians to brave the siege with tenacity, since reinforcements from Carthage would soon reach their city. For *at that time*, the seas were infested with Punic fleets quite extensively, thus **the Tyrians held high hopes for support from their Carthaginian colony.** *Their resolve was bolstered by Dido's story, for she had founded Carthage then carried on with the conquest of a third of the world's territory. They thought it would smack of ignominy, if their ladies should be deemed to have shown more bravery in the colonisation of a new country than they themselves displayed in defence of their liberty.*[91] Accordingly, **they** opted for war and **deployed artillery upon their parapets and turrets.** They issued weaponry to men in possession of their fighting faculties **and assigned artisans, in whom the city abounded, to their arms factories.** The whole city resounded with the din of preparations for hostilities. *Grappling irons too, which are called 'harpagones', they readied to fling upon the operations of their enemies, together with 'crows' and other contrivances for the defence of cities. They contrived all kinds of contraptions, so that inventive weapons were mounted around the entire circuit of their fortifications, especially on the side facing the Macedonian operations.*

4.52 However, when iron was introduced into the furnaces as required for forging and bellows fanned the fires to blazing, it is said that beneath the flames rivulets of blood began to appear, which the Tyrians took as a sign that the Macedonians had much to fear. **Among the Macedonians** likewise, **when some soldiers happened to be breaking up loaves of bread, they reported that they shed drops of blood before their eyes.** *The king being perturbed, the most insightful of the seers, Aristander, pronounced that had the crust of the loaves bled, it would have augured Macedonian disaster, but since the blood seeped internally, it foretold, on the contrary, the destined fall of the besieged city.* Both because his naval fleets were *as yet* distant and on account of the impediment that appeared to be posed to the rest of his agenda by a protracted investment, Alexander sent heralds to urge peace upon the Tyrians. But in violation of international conventions, they were killed and cast into the deep by the city's denizens. *Being* consequently incensed by the undeserved deaths of his emissaries already and *determined that the Macedonian army should not tolerate the insolence of a solitary undistinguished community,* Alexander resolved to besiege the city *with dauntless daring and unremitting energy.*

4.53 However, they had to pave their way by laying down a mole to connect the mainland to the city. Hence the morale of the troops was immensely undermined when they appreciated the profundity of the intervening stretch of sea, which could hardly be filled even with the intercession of deities. What boulders big enough could be found? Where would they obtain tall enough trees? In order to muster the material for such a massive mound, it would be necessary to strip bare entire territories. Additionally, the strait was strewn with surf and the

---

[91] This mention of Dido's foundation of Carthage taken from Justin 11.10.13 may superficially seem Roman in character, but modern scholarship traces the story of Dido back to Timaeus of Tauromenium, who appears to have been one of Cleitarchus's sources.

Book 4: 25th September 333BC - 13th October 332BC

more constrictedly it swirled between the island and the promontory, the fiercer grew its ferocity. But Alexander, who was no novice at manipulating the minds of military guys, declared that as he slept a vision of Heracles holding out his right hand had seemed to materialize. With Heracles opening his path and acting as his guide, he had made to enter the city and dreamt himself inside. Besides this he also made mention of the Tyrian execution of his heralds in violation of international convention. And in addition, he noted that this was the sole city to have had the temerity to interrupt the progression of their victory. Then to each commander the task of reproaching his men was delegated and the project got underway, when everyone had been sufficiently motivated.

4.54 **At the outset Alexander demolished Old Tyre** *on the mainland*, **so that a great stock of rock was at hand and he engaged many myriads**[92] **of men upon the labour of shifting stones to make a mole two plethra**[93] **wide from one side to the other.** From Mount Libanus he transported timber for raft and tower construction. *From the neighbouring cities he enlisted the endeavours of the entire population, thus realising a rapid progression of the operation, since his workers were legion.* And the structure had not yet risen above the swells, but had already reached a reasonable height above the bed of the sea, when **the Tyrians sailed up** *in cockleshells* **to assail the Macedonians with mockery.** *They marvelled that these warriors of dauntless reputation were bearing packs upon their backs like a bunch of beasts of burden and* **they wondered whether Alexander would win his contest with Poseidon?** But their taunts simply served to accentuate the soldiers' enthusiasm. Already the mole was gradually emerging above the surface of the sea and simultaneously it grew broader and crept towards the city.

4.55 At this point, though its accretion had barely been perceptible previously, **the Tyrians** *were perturbed on perceiving the mole's enormity and* **began to sail around the structure,** *still surrounded by sea,* **in many craft of shallow draught and additionally to shower missiles upon those at work in its lee** *with archers and slingers backed by ballista and catapult artillery. Therefore,* **many Macedonians were injured or killed with impunity,** *since the skiffs could either be engaged or withdrawn quite readily. Missiles of every variety rained down upon throngs of the unarmoured, such that no assailant missed his quarry, their targets being both unprotected and unprepared. For it was not just from the front that missiles would appear, but additionally from the rear, since the builders were spread across a pier not so very wide and none could manage to dodge a spear cast from either side.*

4.56 *Alexander responded rapidly to recover from the risk of a harrowing rout. He manned all his vessels and personally led them out, heading with*

---

[92] A *myriad* is literally 10,000 in Greek and is the word used by Diodorus 17.40.5.

[93] A *plethron* is one hundred feet.

all haste for the Tyrian harbours to block the retreat of the Phoenician aggressors. They reacted nervously, rowing back to Tyre as fast as they might, lest he seize their city, whilst it was depleted of those able to fight. Both fleets beat their oars to a rapid tempo, focussing furious effort upon the row, and, although the Macedonians were encroaching at speed, the Tyrians reached the harbourmouth with a slight lead, so they pushed on in to elude destruction, only losing the tail of their formation, so that Alexander was thwarted in this action.

4.57 *The king pressed on with the mole construction, but the Macedonians were diverted from the building operations into the protection of their own persons. Furthermore, the further from the shore that the mole was projected, the more the deeps swallowed up whatever was injected. Hence the king bade that awnings of hide and canvas be erected, such that his workmen were more adequately protected and he deployed a dense screen of ships upon the sea, so that his men might labour in more safety.* Additionally, on the crest of the mound he erected two towers, from which projectiles could be cast upon approaching craft in vast showers. In response the Tyrians directed their vessels to a section of the coast beyond their opponent's view and butchered those who were fetching rubble by landing a fighting crew. On Mount Libanus too the Arabian peasantry fell upon the Macedonians when they found them disorderly. They slew about thirty and took rather fewer into captivity.

4.58 These matters caused Alexander to split his army and, so as not to seem laggardly by besieging a single city, he left Perdiccas and Craterus in charge of that activity and himself headed for Arabia with a task force equipped lightly for for the sake of mobility. Meanwhile the Tyrians used sand and stones to weigh down the stern of a vessel of exceptional size such that its prow was prominently forced to rise. They bedaubed it with bitumen and sulphur and got it underway by means of oars. Then with massive momentum it mounted the causeway, when its sails too had caught the wind's full force. And upon torching its prow, its rowers leapt into skiffs just behind, which had trailed the ship's course with this mission in mind. But the blaze engulfing the galleon instigated a spreading conflagration, which, before any possibility of prevention, enveloped the towers and other gear that had been placed at the head of the pier. Then those that had leapt into the little boats flung torches and tinder to feed the flames around every structure. At this juncture not only had fire engulfed the tower gantries but even the platforms at their extremities, whereupon those located in the towers were either incinerated or, casting off their panoplies, they plunged headlong into the seas. However, choosing rather to capture than slay the swimmers, the Tyrians wielded staves and stones to mangle their fists, until they had been incapacitated and could be taken aboard without posing any risks.

Book 4: 25th September 333BC - 13th October 332BC

Figure 4.7. A raid upon the mole at Tyre (Roberts, mid-19th century)

4.59 Nor was it fire in isolation that wrecked Alexander's operation, but **it happened that** on that same day **a vigorous north-westerly gale dashed the whole depth of the sea against the mole.** *The structure split open at its seams under the recurrent concussion, so that the waters surged through, rupturing the core of the construction. Consequently, the stacks of stone that held up the heaped earth were demolished rapidly, so that* **a large part of the causeway collapsed into the depths of the sea.** When Alexander returned from Arabia presently, there were scarcely any traces of the erstwhile massive mound still remaining to be found.

4.60 In these circumstances, as occurs commonly when things go badly, each of them said that the others were blameworthy; although each might more reasonably have rued the savagery of the sea. *Despairing of salvaging a structure stricken by Nature's ire, Alexander considered abandoning the siege of Tyre, but* driven by relentless ambition the king renewed his engineering operation. He arranged for the front of the mole rather than its flank to face into the wind on this occasion, affording the rest of the works some protection, since they were as it were shielded behind this salient of the construction. He also extended the width of the causeway in order that towers erected in a central reservation should be out of range of enemy ammunition.

4.61 Furthermore, **Alexander sent men up the mountain to fell huge trees and to haul them back to base with their branches still in place. These he flung into the deep seas around the mound and piled up stones to pin them down. Then he resumed planting more trees upon such rockeries, before heaping earth upon the bases formed by these. So, by successively interspersing rocks and whole trees, it was as though he had knitted**

together the entire mole with stone and wood, such that the violence of the waves could now be withstood.

4.62 Nor were the Tyrians tardy in trying any trick that could be contrived to stop the mole making headway. Distinguished service was done by those that dived beneath the sea beyond visual range of the enemy and slipped unseen to reach the causeway. They placed hooks around protruding boughs to drag upon a tree and, when one came free, it carried much material with it into the depths of the sea. Thus, relieved of their ballast, tree trunks and logs were extricated without complications, until the entire structure supported upon them copied the collapse of its foundations.

4.63 The king was dispirited, so whether he would withdraw from the siege or press on was as yet uncertain, whereupon a fleet arrived from Cyprus and on the same occasion Cleander came with Greek troops fresh to the Asian invasion. The ships, numbering one hundred and ninety vessels, were divided into two wings by Alexander: the left was left in the charge of Pnytagoras, sovereign of Cyprus, with Craterus as joint-commander, whilst on the right a quinquereme served as the flagship for Alexander. Despite themselves possessing a significant navy, **the Tyrians were not prepared to risk engaging in a battle at sea. They merely deployed a total of three vessels just beyond their harbour's battlements and the king himself rammed and sank these opponents,** *before returning to his encampments.*

4.64 The next day, sailing his fleet right up to the fortifications, Alexander shattered the walls at all locations mainly by means of battering ram concussions. The breaches were rapidly repaired with rocks by **the Tyrians**, who also **initiated the construction of inner fortifications** *five cubits inside the outer* **for their preservation should the outer fail in further aggressions.** *This inner wall was ten cubits from face to face and they used earth and rubble to fill the intervening space.* But everywhere they were goaded by the threat of disaster. For, *a very short time after,* the mole had been *rebuilt by Alexander and by relentless labour he had* advanced *it* to within a spear cast of the ramparts of his enemy. *Then he moved up his artillery to the end of the promontory and caused his catapults to pelt the masonry, whilst his ballistas beset the men upon the parapet. And additionally, fusilades from his archers and slingers injured many who hastened hurriedly to man the walls of their city. While this assault was underway from the causeway,* the king *sailed his whole fleet around the city making a survey, meant to display his intent shortly to* beset the Tyrians simultaneously by land and by sea.

4.65 The Macedonians lashed pairs of quadriremes[94] together *so that their prows were in contiguity, but their sterns were as far apart as could be.*

---

[94] Galleys with 2 banks of oars on each side with 2 rowers per oar (Diodorus 17.43.4 has triremes, but Curtius 4.3.14 has the more detailed account with the larger and more unusual type of galley specified more than once). Quinqueremes probably had 3 banks of oars with 2+2+1=5 rowers.

Book 4: 25th September 333BC - 13th October 332BC

This gap at the rear was bridged with sail-yards and stout poles tied together tautly. Upon these they laid decking to support *the military together with* their siege engines and artillery. *Thus, configured* they rowed these quadriremes up to the city, where their projectiles were discharged upon the enemy *in safety, since their towering prows protected the soldiery.* Hence Alexander toppled a plethron's breadth[95] of the fortifications and into this breach burst the Macedonians, but they were showered with missiles by the Tyrians, who managed to put them to flight and afterwards repaired the breach under the cover of night.

4.66 With their siege engines and artillery *again* readied for a fight, Alexander instructed his fleet to surround the walls of Tyre in the middle of the night. The ships were already moving in on the city everywhere and the Tyrians were paralysed with despair, when thick cloud speedily spread in obscuring the sky and whatever light had filtered forth from the heavens began to die. Then the sea gradually grew increasingly choppy, until the gathering gale whipped up swells that caused collisions between the vessels. At that point the lashings that linked the quadriremes began to be rent asunder and the decking disintegrated, dragging the troops down under into the deep with a tremendous thunder. It was indeed hopeless to try to handle the coupled ships in such turbulence. The troops obstructed the labours of the sailors; the rowers disrupted the routine of the soldiers and competence deferred to ignorance, as so often happens in such an instance. For the helmsmen, used usually to giving direction, did then as they were bidden for fear of extinction. Finally, by thrashing the oars more vigorously, it was as if the sailors wrenched their ships from the clutches of the sea and beached them upon the shore with many having suffered some injury.

4.67 It happened that those same days saw the arrival of thirty Carthaginian emissaries, not so much a help to the besieged as a solace for their miseries. For they announced that Carthage was encumbered by a conflict around their home city, fought rather for survival than for supremacy. At that time the Syracusans were ravaging the African regions and had pitched their camp not far from the city walls of the Carthaginians. Despite the dashing of their high hopes due to this situation, **the Tyrians** were not crestfallen, but **voted to transport their women, children and elderly men to Carthage** in the envoys' care, *being all the braver in facing whatever they might have to bear through keeping those most dear to them from having to share in the communal jeopardy confronted by their city. And they did succeed in sending some of their spouses and offspring to safety, whilst themselves readying their own eighty triremes to engage with their enemy.*

---

[95] A plethron is 100 feet.

Figure 4.8. Alexander directs an assault upon Tyre (Antonio Tempesta, 1608)

4.68 A Tyrian citizen swore at a public assembly that he had had a dream in which Apollo,[96] *a deity they worshipped especially attentively,* had threatened to desert their city. *Additionally, in his vision the mole the Macedonians had laid across the sea had been transformed into a tract of forestry. It was believed by many that the man had concocted his story to gain Alexander's approbation, so there was a move to stone him among the younger sections of the population, but the archons arranged his extrication and he sought refuge in the Temple of Heracles, where he won sanctuary from the people's wrath through his pleas. Yet* despite that this visionary was a person of scant authority, being inclined to believe the worst in their anxiety, the Tyrians fettered the statue of Apollo with a golden halter, *which they chained to Heracles's altar. For they had consecrated their city to the majesty of* this *deity, so* they considered *that he* would confine Apollo to their locality. The Carthaginians had appropriated this statue from the Syracusan territory[97] and had set it up in their ancestral country. Indeed, after capturing other cities they had adorned Tyre rather than Carthage with much of the booty.

---

[96] Probably Baal or the Sun God.

[97] Curtius 4.3.22 says that the statue came from Syracuse, but Diodorus 13.108.3-4 would imply that it was actually captured in the suburbs of Gela on the southern shore of Sicily, so it would be better to infer that Cleitarchus wrote that it was taken from the Syracusan sphere of influence.

Book 4: 25th September 333BC - 13th October 332BC

4.69 *Some of the Tyrians actually advocated the revival of a rite that had been discontinued for many years: the sacrifice of a freeborn boy to Cronos. It appears that without the opposition of the archons, in accordance with whose counsel everything was done, humanity would have been vanquished by superstition.* This form of <u>Cronos veneration, a sacrilege rather than a sacrament, has been bequeathed to the Carthaginians by their founders, the Phoenicians. Whenever they are pressing for success in some emergency, they vow the forfeiture of one of their offspring as a burnt offering to the deity, provided that the outcome favours their policy. A bronze statue of Cronos stands in their city with hands cupped over a brazier ready to receive the boy for roasting. As the flame of the rite begins toasting his body, his limbs contract and his mouth seems to grin like a person laughing merrily, until he is devoured completely by the fire and his cinders sift down into the pyre.</u>[98]

4.70 *At this juncture, the causeway reached the ramparts and connected the city to the mainland, so that the fighting along the walls became hand-to-hand. The Tyrians witnessed at close range the peril posed by the Macedonian army and readily conceived the calamity that would be consequent upon the capture of their city. Therefore, they fought so unrestrainedly as to despise all jeopardy. When the Macedonians moved up towers as tall as the walls, lowering gangways to attack the battlements, the Tyrians relied upon the cunning of their engineers and deployed many unprecedented counter-measures in their defence. Using barbs to teethe their armaments, they forged large tridents and cast them at close range to strike their assailants. These lodged in the shields of their tower-top opponents. Next, they hauled upon cords attached to the tridents. Each victim was faced with the option of either dropping his protection and exposing his person to perforation by a shower of projectiles or plummeting from his tall tower and perishing through pitifully clinging to his sole safeguard against these missiles. Other Tyrians ensnared their prey by casting fishing nets over them as they were fighting their way across a gangway. With the Macedonians enmeshed and vulnerable, the Tyrians could tug them and topple them, plunging them into a fatal fall.*

4.71 The Tyrians tethered stout poles in order to scupper such ships as came beneath their walls, for they shot these from ballistas, so that when the tethers tautened, they would abruptly dive into the vessels. They also slung from these same poles both scythes and sickles to lacerate either their adversaries or their vessels. Additionally, **the Tyrians** *contrived other ingenious expedients in order to neuter Macedonian manliness. With these they* **subjected the most daring of their opponents to inescapable and pitiable distress. They fabricated shields out of bronze** *and steel* **and filled them with sand and**

---

[98] Jacoby Fragment 9 of Cleitarchus from Schol. Plato Resp. 337A (Photius: Σαρδόνιος γέλως) clearly derived from here in accordance with Curtius 4.3.23.

mire. Then they brought them to the boil by roasting them constantly over a fierce fire. When the sand was searingly hot, they used an appliance to upturn the pot, spewing the stuff from their battlements over those that were attacking with most valiance. *And no scourge was more feared than this, for* the searing sand sifted beneath their breastplates and cuirasses and the intense heat scorched their skin, *for the grains could not be shaken out once they had made their way in.* They shrieked out prayers like those under torture, but none could relieve them from their awful dolour. *Being deprived of their senses by the excruciating agony, they cast aside their arms and tore off their armour in their insanity. Defenceless and completely vulnerable to injury,* these soldiers died readily *without an opportunity to menace the enemy.*

4.72 *The Phoenicians effused fire, flung javelins and cast stones simultaneously, weakening the will of their assailants by the intensity of their artillery. They lowered long poles, each fitted with a blade like a sickle, and cut the cords carrying the rams, rendering them unserviceable. With their fire-throwers they flung great gobs of glowing metal into throngs of their foes, and these could not fail to find targets where so many stood packed so close.* Besides *all* this they hurled iron claws and crows[99] from their catapults, snagging those stood behind a tower's parapets and tugging them over their rims to make their exits. *With many men manning their battlements, the Tyrians kept all their engines busy in their defence and inflicted numerous casualties among their opponents. Thus, they caused complete consternation and the butchery of their barrage was barely consistent with contention, but the Macedonians did not lose their resolution. As those to the fore fell and bled, those further back moved up in their stead and were undeterred by the fearful fate of some or other comrade.*

4.73 *Alexander mounted boulder-flinging catapults at strategic locations, inducing reverberations where they struck the fortifications. From his siege towers, ballistas kept blasting bolts at the parapets taking a terrible toll of their Tyrian targets. Therefore, the defenders fashioned marble wheels*[100] *with a lattice of windows so as safely to view the scenery, for they*

---

[99] Types of grappling iron.

[100] Diodorus makes two separate mentions of these wheels at 17.43.1 and 17.45.3 respectively. This is one of several reasons to suppose that Diodorus is not telling the events of Tyre in strict chronological order or in the order given by Cleitarchus. Additionally, Diodorus tells all the omens and portents of the siege together at 17.41.5-8, whereas Curtius relates them separately at various points during the siege. It is much more likely that Diodorus should have gathered them together for his epitome than that Curtius scattered them about. Finally, it turns out to be feasible to merge the accounts of Curtius and Diodorus sensibly on the basis of the order of events given by Curtius, but the opposite strategy would appear to lead to a messy outcome. It seems that Diodorus read the whole account of the siege by Cleitarchus, and then penned his summary from memory, whereas Curtius gives something closer to a sentence-by-sentence translation. Nevertheless, Diodorus's account of Tyre is unusually full, revealing that Curtius omitted significant sections of their common

ranged them before the battlements and rotated them by means of machinery.[101] *In this way they deflected or destroyed missiles from the Macedonian artillery. Additionally, the Tyrians stuffed seaweed into stitched up hides or skins sewn together, rigging these to break the blows of the boulders by the sponginess within the leather. In short, the Tyrians tirelessly practised every technique for their protection and displayed great talents in their tactics for self-preservation. They showed valiance in confronting their opponents, forsaking the shelter of their towers and battlements and making forays onto the gangways to meet Macedonian bravery with matching gallantry. Grappling hand to hand, they duelled with every adversary in making a stalwart stand in defence of their city.*

4.74 *Some Tyrian warriors wielded axes for the lopping of any enemy limb that was exposed for the chopping. A Macedonian commander, called Admetus, was outstandingly sturdy and conspicuously courageous. He stood firm defiantly in the face of furious Tyrian attacks, dying instantly and heroically when his skull was split by the stroke of one such axe.*

4.75 *Alexander realised that the assaults by the Macedonians had been checked by the resistance of the Tyrians. With the coming of nightfall, he withdrew his troops with a trumpet call.* At this point the king, out of utter frustration, gave raising the siege and invading Egypt some serious consideration. *For having overrun the rest of Asia with great rapidity, he found himself idling in the vicinity of a single city and therefore foregoing many a glorious opportunity.* But he was as much embarrassed by the prospect of withdrawal as by remaining and he saw that his reputation, through which he overthrew more than through campaigning, would be much diminished, if he left Tyre to testify that he could be vanquished. Consequently, although just one of his Friends, Amyntas the son of Andromenes, called for the siege to be continued, he commanded that the assault should be renewed.

4.76 Therefore, in order that nothing be left untried, he moved up more ships with his elite soldiers inside. Whereupon **it happened that out of the waves they witnessed arise the back of a sea-monster of remarkable size. It thrashed its immense bulk up onto the mole that the Macedonians had engineered, rifting the surf asunder as its whole body reared. There it loitered for a while harmlessly, where both sides could see it clearly, before it plunged back down into the sea from the crest of the causeway and,** *alternately surging up out of the swell and disappearing beneath the spray,*

---

source and sometimes severely epitomised matters that Diodorus relates in more depth. In conclusion, Diodorus paid particular attention to events at Tyre, considering them historically important, whereas Curtius cut material that he found repetitive or stylistically sub-standard or which perhaps contradicted other accounts of the siege.

[101] This interpretation seems the best sense to be found in the rather obscure descriptions of these devices in Diodorus 17.43.1 and 17.45.3.

it dived down into the depths finally *not far away from the ramparts of the city.* Both sides drew superstitious comfort from the portent that they believed this event to represent. The Macedonians deemed Poseidon to have pointed the way for their works' enlargement, whereas the Tyrians supposed that the same deity had dragged the beast onto the mole to avenge its assault upon the sea, indicating that the structure would collapse imminently. *Through the attention that they paid to their own interests each camp was swayed to believe that the god would come to its aid.* But in celebrating the sign, the Tyrians turned to feasting and overindulgence in wine. And at sunrise, still the worse for its powers, they embarked upon ships wreathed with garlands and flowers; such was their eagerness to foresee the celebration of their actual victory rather than merely its augury.

4.77 It happened that Alexander had issued an order for his fleet to assault the seaward sector, having left thirty of his lesser vessels near the shore. The Tyrians captured two of the latter and sorely terrorised the remainder, until Alexander heard the clamour and sailed his navy to the source of the uproar. The first Macedonian ship to arrive at the scene was a quinquereme that was fleeter than the rest of the fleet. Two Tyrian galleys that it came between charged it abeam and the first of these it turned to meet. But it was rammed by the beak of the other, which it held fast reciprocally. Then, being still free to manoeuvre, the first galley tried to charge decisively from the opposite side. But arriving with remarkable timing a trireme from Alexander's navy rammed the galley, which would else have struck the quinquereme imminently, with such force that the Tyrian helmsman was flung from its stern into the sea. Soon after many more Macedonian vessels were arriving and the king was also fast approaching. Whereupon by backing water the Tyrians managed with difficulty to tear their entangled ship free and all their vessels made for port simultaneously. The king pursued them aggressively and, though the harbour denied him entry, since he was fended off from its walls by the Tyrian artillery, he nevertheless either captured or sank nearly all the ships of the enemy.[102]

4.78 The troops were permitted two days of inactivity. Then **Alexander addressed the Macedonians exhorting them to match his own gallantry. He** commanded that his army advance its navy and its siege engines concertedly and he began a general assault by land and by sea in order to cow the enemy by its sheer ubiquity. This onslaught was pressed with furious ferocity. *And he outfitted his vessels with gear for siege warfare, since he noticed that the wall near the naval base*[103] *was weaker than*

---

[102] Arrian, *Anabasis* 2.21.9, states that thirteen Tyrian vessels participated in this raid: three quinqueremes, three quadriremes and seven triremes. Their initial targets were anchored Cypriot vessels.

[103] Apparently on the southern side of the city facing Egypt – see Arrian, *Anabasis* 2.22.7.

elsewhere, so he lashed triremes together to bear his best engines in order to launch an attack just there.

4.79 *Now Alexander performed a feat of daring that was barely believable even by those that witnessed this bit of the battle.* With great bravery and even greater jeopardy, *for his royal raiment and glinting arms made him a magnet for Tyrian weaponry,* the king mounted his loftiest wooden siege gantry and swung a gangway across to reach the wall of the city. And it was a wondrous sight to see, when he made a solitary sortie to gain a footing on the battlements, neither fearing Fortune's jealousy nor the threat from the Tyrian defence. With his valour vaunted before the magnificent military that had already vanquished the Persian army, he called upon the Macedonians to follow as he fought his way forward, felling those Tyrians that came near with a thrust of his spear or a slash of his sword. And he pushed others off the parapet with his shield's rim, putting paid to his adversaries' valiant vim.

Figure 4.9. The fall of Tyre (1696)

4.80 At the same time in another zone the hammering of many rams had loosened the joints of the stone, so that a long stretch of the fortifications had begun to fall and the Macedonians were making an entry through this broad breach in the wall. Simultaneously, the fleet forced its way into the harbour, whilst the forces accompanying Alexander surged across the gangway and occupied towers abandoned by the enemy in the mêlée.

Thus, the city was taken *and a portion of the inhabitants, crushed by so many setbacks at once, turned to their temples for deliverance. But* most Tyrians were persistent in their resistance, *barricading their alleyways with impediments and* yelling mutual encouragements. Some of them hurled themselves at their adversaries expecting to die, but not without retribution. Others bolted the doors of their homes and forestalled their enemies by a death of their own volition. A great many got up onto the rooftops and pelted the advancing opposition with stones and whatever was at hand for ammunition. Alexander ordered that the roofs should be set ablaze and that all should be slain save those that had fled into the sanctuaries. Although he had heralds proclaim these decrees, no Tyrian under arms deigned to seek asylum with his deities. Boys and maidens had packed the temples, but the menfolk all stood in their houses' vestibules, facing up to the fury of their foes in wretched rabbles.

4.81 Nevertheless, the Sidonians, who were among the Macedonian occupiers, were the salvation of many. Although they had accompanied the victors in gaining entry to the city, they recalled their Tyrian consanguinity - for they considered that Agenor had founded both communities – so they covertly provided their protection to Tyrian refugees, abstracting them to Sidon by hiding them in their ships which they used as ferries. Fifteen thousand were rescued from the sack through such furtive activities. But **all save a few of the men under arms were slain in the spoliations and the scale of the bloodshed may be inferred from the fact that** *over seven thousand* **warriors were cut down within the fortifications.**[104] Subsequently, the king's fury furnished the victors with a tragic spectacle: two thousand Tyrian fighters left alive by the killing frenzy were crucified along a large length of the littoral.[105] *Alexander sold the women and children into slavery, for, although most of the non-combatants had been removed to Carthage* and *Sidon* *successfully, more than thirteen thousand were found to remain and entered captivity.* The king did no harm to the Carthaginian emissaries, but issued them with a declaration of hostilities, though these were left in abeyance on account of current exigencies.

---

[104] Curtius 4.4.14 has *VI milia* (6000), whilst Diodorus 17.46.3 gives "more than 7000" (Arrian, *Anabasis* 2.24.4 states 8000).

[105] The large-scale executions at Tyre were evidently prompted by the execution of Alexander's emissaries and Macedonian prisoners of war (Arrian, *Anabasis Alexandrou* 2.24.3) by the Tyrians during the siege in contravention of the normal rules of warfare plus the fact that the Macedonians considered that the Tyrians' use of red-hot sand had been excessively cruel.

Book 4: 25th September 333BC - 13th October 332BC

Figure 4.10. A view of Tyre still connected to the mainland by Alexander's mole (1889)

4.82 *So* **Tyre** *had suffered the siege courageously rather than judiciously and* **met with complete calamity in the seventh month**[106] **after she began her contumacy.** *Alexander removed the gold fetters from Apollo's statue and bade that he be called 'Apollo Philalexandros' too.*[107] *He performed elaborate sacrifices to Heracles, rewarded those of his men who had served heroically in the hostilities and held a lavish funeral for his casualties. Lastly, he installed Abdalonymus as king of* **Tyre** *in a further extension of his territories.*

4.83 These were the concerns of Alexander *in the fourth year of his reign.*

---

[106] Diodorus 17.46.5; Curtius 4.4.19; Plutarch, *Alexander* 24.3; Arrian, *Anabasis* 2.24.6 states that Tyre fell in the Attic month of *Hecatombaeon*, which began on the first New Moon after the Summer Solstice; Plutarch, *Alexander* 25.2 tells the story that Tyre fell on the last day of the month, which was originally designated the 30th, but that Alexander redesignated it as 28th in support of a prophecy of Aristander. This suggests that this month was "hollow", meaning that it had only 29 days and the 29th day was therefore called the 30th, since it was the last (a standard Greek practice). In 332BC the Summer Solstice fell on about 26th June and the next New Moon occurred on about 20th July, so the last day of *Hecatombaeon* would be about 17th August (all these dates being given according to the Julian Calendar.)

[107] *Philalexandros* is "lover of Alexander".

Book 5: 14th October 332BC – 1st October 331BC

Second Peace Offer from Darius; The Siege of Gaza; Occupation of Egypt; Expedition to Siwa; Foundation of Alexandria; The March back to Byblos; The Preparations of Darius; Alexander's Advance into Mesopotamia; Crossing the Tigris; Death of Stateira; Third Peace Offer from Darius; The Battle of Arbela.

5.1 *This book recounts the events concerning Alexander in the fifth year of his reign, but it begins by outlining events that transpired elsewhere in the aftermath of the battle at Issus.*

5.2 The widespread war that was being waged by the mightiest monarchs of Europe and Asia in the hope of having hold of the whole world had also engaged the arms of Greece and Crete. **Agis, the king of Sparta, mustered and hired eight thousand Greek mercenaries who had escaped from** Cilicia and returned to their homes following **the battle at Issus** in order to foment a war against Antipater, the viceroy of Macedonia, *so as to try to transform affairs in favour of Darius. He had both funds and ferries from the Persian king, so* he set sail for Crete, *where he captured most of the municipalities* and made them support the Persian side. The Cretans vacillated in their loyalties according to the country of their invaders, whether of Spartan or Macedonian nationality.

5.3 That Amyntas, who had fled from Macedonia and deserted to Darius, *fought for the Persians in Cilicia. He* got away from the field of battle at Issus with a following of four thousand Greeks and reached Tripolis *in Phoenicia ahead of Alexander.* There he selected *sufficient* ships *from the Persian fleet* to transport his troops, *incinerating the remainder.* Sailing them over to Cyprus, he recruited more soldiers and ships and decided to set out for Egypt, since he perceived that a person might possess as if it were really his right whatever he had seized in the existing circumstances. He was currently in conflict with both kings and always ready to sway with the swing of things. So, having impressed upon his troops the opportunities afforded by such tall undertakings, he informed them that **Sabaces, the governor of Egypt, had fallen in the hostilities at Issus.** Hence the Persian garrison was both leaderless and powerless, whereas the Egyptians, persistently oppressed by their occupiers, would regard Amyntas' men as allies rather than as enemies. They were driven by necessity to pursue every possibility, for, Fortune having forsaken their first opportunity, any future seemed preferable to their situation currently. Therefore, his troops clamoured collectively for him to lead them wherever he saw fit. **Hence,** reckoning whilst their hopes were high to exploit such spirit, **he sailed into the Pelusian mouth** *of the Nile,* deceitfully declaring that Darius had designated him as the substitute for Sabaces.

Book 5: 14th October 332BC – 1st October 331BC

5.4 Having thereby taken possession of Pelusium, Amyntas sailed his soldiers upriver to Memphis. At the news of this, the Egyptians, an irresolute people better at initiating than effectuating anything, all scurried forth from their various villages and towns intending to annihilate the Persian garrisons. These, although alarmed, nevertheless failed to forsake their hope of holding on to Egypt. But **in approaching Memphis Amyntas outfought the Persians in the fighting, forcing them to fall back into the city.** Then, *having encamped,* **the victors began looting estates in the country,** *carrying off everything* as *booty* as *though they were amongst the enemy. Thereupon* the *Persian commander,* **Mazaces, though he saw that the unsuccessful tussle had unsettled his soldiers psychologically, nevertheless pointed out that Amyntas's men were dispersed widely and had become incautious through overconfidence in their victory. Thus,** *jointly with the Egyptians* **the Persians were impelled** *confidently* **to charge forth from the city** *to recover what they had held previously. That strategy proved just as successful in its culmination as it was wise in its conception.* **Amyntas's men were slain one and all along with their leader.** Such was the forfeit ceded to both sovereigns by this commander, who showed no more loyalty in serving the king to whom he had defected than in his desertion of Alexander.

5.5 Similar fates befell other Persian officers. A group of Darius's commanders, who had survived the Battle of Issus, accompanied by all the contingents that had followed them in their flight, and also reinforced by young men from Cappadocia and Paphlagonia, **sought to bolster Persian interests** by recapturing Lydia. Alexander's general, Antigonus, was in control of that area and, despite having given up much of his garrison to Alexander, he nevertheless belittled the barbarians in leading his battalions out to do battle with them. There as **elsewhere** the fortunes of their foes fared unfavourably, for the Persians were put to flight in each of three fights at successive sites. In parallel, a Macedonian fleet gathered from Greece captured or capsized the ships of Aristomenes, whom Darius had sent into the war in order to recover the Hellespontine shore. In the wake of this, Pharnabazus, admiral of the Persian fleet, exacted money from the Milesians and installed a garrison in the chief town of Chios, setting sail for Siphnos via Andros with a hundred vessels. From these too he extorted funds and garrisoned their islands. *But the fights between all these were slighter matters than the one contest upon which all the others hung and to which Fortune's fixed gaze clung.*

5.6 *One day around that time a letter from Darius was delivered, but now written as to a ruler. He proposed that Alexander should join himself in matrimony to his daughter, whose name was Stateira, and that her dowry should be the region ranging between the Hellespont and the Halys River in its entirety.*[108] Darius would be satisfied with the lands looking east from that

---

[108] The Halys is the modern Kizil Irmak; Arrian, *Anabasis* 2.25.1 mentions the Euphrates in its stead; cf. Justin 11.12.3-4 & Diodorus 17.39.1 (mentioning the Halys river boundary.)

riverside. If perchance Alexander should hesitate to accept this offer, *let him ponder that* Fortune never lingers long in the same vicinity and *that* men inasmuch as they experience success are always proportionately the more exposed to jealousy. He feared lest, like the birds that are levitated into the heavens by their innate lightness, Alexander were to be carried away by a callow and hollow vanity. Nothing was harder at his age than to cope with such prodigious prosperity. Darius retained a multiplicity of resources and could not always be caught in confined courses. Alexander had to get across the Euphrates and the Tigris and then both the Araxes and the Choaspes, the massive moats of Darius's dominions. He would have to pass through *empty* plains, where he could be shamed by the sparsity of his battalions. How long would it take him to penetrate Media, Hyrcania, Bactria and India adjoining the Ocean, not to mention the Sogdian and Arachosian nations and the rest of the races extending to the Tanais River[109] and the Caucasus Mountains? He would use up his youth merely in traversing such expanses, even if his passage were uncontended. Furthermore, he should curtail his calls for Darius to come before him, since his arrival would see Alexander's life ended.

5.7 Alexander responded to those that had brought the letter that Darius was dangling what did not belong to him and wished to apportion what he had entirely relinquished. Lydia, Ionia, Aeolia and the Hellespontine coastline were being offered him as a dowry, the very prizes of his own victory! **Terms are dictated by the victor and conceded by the loser.** If Darius alone did not know which role they respectively occupied, then let Ares, *the god of war,* firstly decide. Let him also be aware that Alexander, when setting out overseas, had not targeted the takeover of Lydia nor Cilicia, since they would be trivial trophies for such wholesale hostilities, but rather of Persepolis, seat of all the Persian dynasties, and thereafter of Bactra, Ecbatana and the easternmost territories. Alexander was capable of following wheresoever Darius might flee, so let him cease to threaten with rivers one whom he knew to have crossed the sea. *Instead let Darius come before him in person to make his plea.*

5.8 But although the kings had at least been in correspondence with one another, the Rhodians were *meanwhile* ceding their city and their harbours to Alexander, who had consigned Cilicia to Socrates and had bidden Philotas to govern the region around Tyre. The section of Syria that is called hollow was set in the hands of Andromachus by Parmenion, so that the latter could participate in what remained of the invasion. And having bidden Hephaistion to sail the fleet along the Phoenician shores, **the king got to Gaza** with all his corps.

---

[109] Alexander's expedition mistook the modern Syr Darya for the Tanais (actually the Don), but the more correct ancient name was the Jaxartes.

Book 5: 14th October 332BC – 1st October 331BC

5.9 *In roughly that same period the biennial* **Isthmian Games** *were held*[110] *and were attended by a crowd drawn from all over Greece.* **In council there the delegates of the League of Corinth voted on behalf of the Greeks,** people of a pragmatic disposition, **that fifteen envoys should carry a crown of gold to the king** *in recognition of his deeds promoting their welfare and liberty* **and that they should tender the congratulations of the Greeks on his Cilician victory.**[111] These selfsame Greeks but a little bit beforehand had been attentive to unreliable reports with the intention of following wheresoever Fortune might waft their wavering thoughts.

5.10 All the while, not only was Alexander himself besieging cities that rejected the yoke of his dominion, but his marshals too, being excellent leaders, had launched many an invasion: Calas into Paphlagonia; Antigonus into Lycaonia. Balacrus, having bested Hydarnes, the Satrap of Darius, re-took Miletus and Amphoterus and Hegelochus with a fleet of one hundred and sixty vessels brought the islands between the Greek mainland[112] and Asia under the authority of Alexander. Having taken Tenedos too, they stood ready to occupy Chios at the urging of its denizens. But Pharnabazus, as the deputy of Darius, detained those who desired to defect to the Macedonians and delivered their city back into the hands of Apollonides and Athenogoras, gentlemen of the pro-Persian faction, with a token detachment of soldiers. Alexander's commanders maintained their siege of the city, reckoning not so much on their own efforts, but on the disaffection of those invested. Nor were they mistaken in this view, since a wrangle arising between Apollonides and the officers of the garrison furnished an opportunity to force an entry to the city. And when a regiment of Macedonians surged in through a shattered gateway, the citizens who had already plotted to betray the city joined forces with Amphoterus and Hegelochus. The men of the Persian garrison were slain and Pharnabazus, as well as Apollonides and Athenogoras, was handed over in fetters along with twelve triremes with their commandos and rowers and, besides these, thirty crewless vessels, fifty pirate sloops and three thousand Greeks, whom the Persians had hired as mercenary troops. These last were distributed to strengthen the Macedonian contingents, the pirates were subjected to capital punishments and the captured oarsmen were incorporated amongst the Macedonian ships' complements.

5.11 It chanced that ***Aristonicus, the despot of Methymna,***[113] being ignorant of everything that had occurred ***at Chios, approached the*** barrier at the ***harbour*** mouth **with** a flotilla of ***pirate vessels*** in the first watch of the night. When the

---

[110] The Isthmian Games were held biennially at Corinth in the Spring preceding the Summer of the Olympics and two years thereafter; since Alexander reached Gaza in the Autumn of 332BC, an Olympic year, the games referred to here must have been celebrated in the Spring of that year.

[111] I.e. the Battle of Issus.

[112] *Achaia* in the manuscripts, this being an Homeric name for mainland Greece.

[113] On the island of Lesbos.

guards demanded to know his identity, he retorted that it was Aristonicus come to visit Pharnabazus. They replied that Pharnabazus was resting right now and that it was not feasible to visit him at the moment. However, they assured him that the port's hospitality was available to his ally and auxiliary and that he would have access to Pharnabazus during the following day. Aristonicus did not then hesitate to lead the way through the entrance trailed by ten pirate sloops, and, whilst they were docking their ships at the harbour quay, the watch put back the barrier and alerted those on nearby sentry duty. Since none of the pirates dared to put up a fight, **all were clapped in irons** *that very night* **and turned over to the Macedonians,** Hegelochus and Amphoterus, subsequently.

5.12 From there the Macedonians sailed to Mytilene. This port had recently been seized by Chares of Athens, who held it with a garrison of two thousand Persians. But since he was unable to endure a siege, he surrendered the place in exchange for being allowed to scurry away unscathed, making for Imbros. The Macedonians spared those who switched sides without a fuss.

5.13 Despairing of the peace that he had supposed he could procure through letters and a delegation, Darius assiduously devoted himself once more to the restoration of his manpower and his capacity to wage war. Therefore, he commanded the leaders of his forces to gather in Babylonia, and also bade Bessus, Satrap of Bactria, to muster as massive an army as he could bring and to deliver it up to him. These Bactrians are amongst those peoples the most predatory and of an uncouth character and deeply disdainful of Persian luxury. Situated not so far from the Scythians, a most rapacious race used to living predaciously, they forever wear their weaponry. But Bessus discomforted Darius, who doubted his loyalty, for he barely tolerated his subordination with any equanimity. And since he aspired to sovereignty, treason was to be feared as his only available opportunity.

5.14 Meanwhile Alexander was diligently seeking to determine which domain was Darius's destination, but it could not be revealed, due to the Persian practice of keeping the secrets of their kings most carefully concealed. Neither intimidation nor temptation can elicit the communication of any confidential information. The ancient tradition of the kings insisted upon silence on pain of extermination. A loose tongue is more severely chastised than any other transgression and their Magi maintain that no major matter may be managed by those that find it hard to keep their silence, which Nature has designed to be quite effortless for mankind. On this account being ignorant of all the arrangements being made by his enemy, **Alexander marched upon Gaza and besieged the city.**

5.15 The governor of Gaza was Betis,[114] who exhibited extraordinary loyalty to his king in defending vast fortifications with a skeleton garrison. Alexander, having surveyed the site, bade that mines be begun since the light, friable soil

---

[114] Batis in Arrian, *Anabasis* 2.25.4, who states that he was a eunuch (and is echoed on this point in the Itinerarium Alexandri XVIIII [Volkmann's text]).

Book 5: 14th October 332BC – 1st October 331BC

suited a subterranean operation. For deep drifts of sand are driven across the land by the nearby sea, such that neither rock nor stone is prone to hinder excavation. Therefore, he began tunnelling in an area that could not be seen by the garrison and to divert their attention from these operations he bade that siege towers be advanced towards the fortifications. Yet the same soil was unsuitable for trundling towers, since the sand subsided beneath the wheels, repressing their progress and fracturing the platforms in the turrets. Many men were wounded with impunity, since the same efforts when withdrawing the towers as when they were advanced enhanced their vulnerability.

5.16 So the signal was issued for withdrawal and the next day Alexander commanded his men to ring the perimeter of the wall. And at the rising of the sun prior to advancing his army he besought the backing of the gods by sacrificing according to the custom of his country. It chanced that a raven unexpectedly released a clod that it was carrying in its talons, which fell so as to disintegrate upon hitting the head of the king. The bird itself perched upon a nearby tower that had become smeared with bitumen and sulphur, to which its wings adhered. Being thus frustrated in its attempts to fly free, those at hand took it into captivity. A review of the incident by an augur seemed timely, as Alexander was prone to a superstitious mentality. Consequently, Aristander, whom he held in the utmost credulity, foretold that the overthrow of the city was actually portended by this augury, but that there was a risk that Alexander would incidentally receive some injury. Hence, he cautioned the king not to initiate an assault on that particular day. Though vexed that this single city stood in the way of him entering Egypt risk free, Alexander nevertheless signalled a withdrawal in deference to his visionary.

5.17 This boosted the boldness of the besieged, who burst out from a gate to set upon their retreating enemy, reckoning that the irresolution of their opponents would be their own opportunity. But they threw themselves into the fighting with more fervour than firmness, for, when they saw the Macedonian banners perform a volte-face, they promptly checked their progress. Thereupon the clamour of those engaged reached *the king*, whereupon, heedless of his predicted peril, but donning a corselet, which he rarely wore, upon being harangued by his friends, he *fetched up at the fore of the fighting*. Upon spotting him, a certain Arab, *one of Darius's warriors, dared a deed larger than his luck. He* stuck his sword behind his shield and*, as though he were a turncoat, prostrated himself at the king's knees.* Alexander bade the supplicant arise and be inducted amongst his own levies. *But, suddenly seizing his sword* with his right hand, *the barbarian struck at the king*'s neck. *Yet Alexander, dodging the blow* with a slight twist of his torso, *slashed with his sword to sever* the vainly lunging limb of *his foe.* Thereby discharging the danger predicted for that day, he supposed it to have gone away.

5.18 But, as is proverbial, fate is inescapable, for whilst all too enthusiastically engaged in frontline combat, the king was struck by a bolt that drove through his corselet. As it was embedded in his shoulder, his physician Philip drew it forth, whereupon a gush of blood began to flow to everyone's consternation, since the corselet made it hard to know the depth of the projectile's penetration. Not even showing a shift in his complexion, Alexander bade that the bleeding be staunched and that the injury be dressed. He stood his ground before the standards for a long while, either disguising his pain or keeping it suppressed, until the blood that had been held back by the bandage a bit before began to seep persistently and the wound, which had not hurt whilst still benumbed, swelled with the congealing of the gore. In consequence he commenced losing consciousness and began to buckle at the knees, whereupon he was seized by the men around him and carried back to camp by these. And Betis returned to the city, believing that the king had been killed and exulting in his victory.

5.19 Yet even ere his injury had healed Alexander ordered that a mound be raised up equal in elevation to the fortifications and bade that the walls be undermined by multiple tunnels. The populace erected further fortifications upon the original battlements, but even these could not match the tallness of the towers mounted atop the mound of the Macedonians. Hence missiles also rained down upon the interior of the town. The ultimate downfall of the city was the undermining of a wall by a tunnel, since the enemy made an entry through its rubble. The king himself led the troops of the spearhead and, whilst he was rushing in rather recklessly, he was struck by a stone in the leg just below the knee. Despite his first wound not yet having fully scarred, he nevertheless leant upon his spear and fought on in the vanguard, the more fervently fired by fury in that he had twice received an injury in the siege of that city.

5.20 Having made an outstanding fighting stand and being weakened by many wounds, Betis was abandoned by his band, but nonetheless fought on unflaggingly, though his armour was slick with his own blood and that of his enemies equally. But when missiles flew from all around, *he was overwhelmed and bound by Leonnatus and Philotas.*[115] *These* **men led Betis** *alive* **before the king** and, although he was usually an admirer of valour even in an enemy, Alexander was carried away by the arrogant exuberance of youth in declaring: "You shall not die as you have wished, but rather be aware that you shall suffer whatever can be contrived against a prisoner." But Betis stared back at the king, his expression not merely undaunted but actually obstinate in saying not a single word in response to Alexander's threat. Then the king observed: "See how obdurate is his silence. He has not bent his knee nor uttered any plea for mercy. But I shall triumph over his tranquility and I shall certainly punctuate it with sighs, if not otherwise." Then Alexander's anger turned to violence, for already at that time his recent achievements were imbuing him with foreign manners. Indeed, whilst Betis yet breathed, **thongs were thrust through his ankles. These were bound to the**

---

[115] There appears to be a short lacuna in the manuscript text of Curtius at this point, which may tentatively be reconstructed from its context and a somewhat parallel account from Hegesias FGrH 142 F5.

king's chariot and he was dragged around the circuit of the city by its team with the king glorying in imitating Achilles, from whom he traced his ancestry, whilst imposing punishment upon his hapless enemy.

Figure 5.1. The siege of Gaza by André Castaigne (1898)

5.21 *Thus Alexander took Gaza violently after a two-month siege of the city.* There perished around ten thousand of the Arabs and Persians. Nor was it a bloodless conquest for the Macedonians. Certainly, that siege is celebrated, but not so much for the fame of the city as for Alexander's exposure to a double jeopardy. **After settling the affairs of Gaza, the king himself hastened on into Egypt** *with his whole army,* **sending Amyntas to Macedonia with ten triremes to seek fit youths as fresh recruits,** since even successes entailed attrition of his troops and Alexander set less store on soldiers from the vanquished nations than on those from his own shore.

5.22 *Long since* **antagonistic to the power of the Persians, whom they considered to have ruled them haughtily** *and extortionately, perpetrating sacrilege against many a temple,* **the Egyptians were enthused by the prospect of Alexander's arrival.** For indeed they had even received Amyntas gladly, though he was a renegade arriving with dubious authority. Therefore, a vast host of them had mustered at Pelusium, which seemed Alexander's likely point of entry. In fact, on the seventh day after marching his army away from Gaza, the king reached that region of Egypt that is now known as Alexander's Camp. Thence he ordered his infantry contingents to make for Pelusium, while he himself with a disencumbered task force of selected troops sailed up the Nile. Neither did the Persians oppose his advance, being additionally panicked by the *native* revolt. And when he was already not far from Memphis, Mazaces, the viceroy of Darius, announced his abdication and crossed the river[116] to hand over eight hundred talents and all the royal accoutrements to Alexander. Thus, **all of Egypt's cities came into the king's power without hostilities, since the natives welcomed Alexander on account of Persian impieties.** From Memphis he sailed on up the same stream, penetrating into the interior of Egypt **and he settled its affairs without tampering with any Egyptian national custom. Thereafter Alexander elected to visit the oracle of Zeus-Ammon.**

5.23 Even for a small band travelling lightly the journey that they undertook was barely endurable. The land and the sky are utterly dry, for there the barren sands lie, which, being scorched by the sun's glow, set the surface simmering and sear the soles of the feet, giving rise to unbearable heat. The struggle is not only against the temperature and the aridity, but also with most obstructive sands that are piled high and give way beneath the tread so that feet forge forwards with difficulty. Actually, the Egyptians pressed these problems excessively, but a burning desire obsessed the king's mind that he should consult Zeus, whom he, dissatisfied with pre-eminence among mortals, either believed or wished it to be believed was the founder of his dynasty. Therefore, in the company of those he had elected to take with him he travelled downriver to the Mareotic marsh. **Halfway along the coast, the king was met by envoys from Cyrene bearing** *a crown and other* **gorgeous gifts,** *including three hundred warhorses and five of their finest four-horse chariots.* Their purpose was to petition for peace and to invite him to visit their cities. **He received these emissaries and their gifts cordially and concluded a pact with them of alliance and amity. Then he continued to pursue his planned journey.**

5.24 After taking on water, *on the first day and even the second the effort seemed endurable, since the wilderness where they were was not yet so*

---

[116] Memphis stood on the west bank of the Nile, whilst Alexander was evidently approaching along the eastern bank.

very desolate and sterile, though the land was already barren and infertile. But when fields of tall dunes arose, *they vainly peered around for solid ground just as if they were cast upon a vast sea.* After four days *not a trace of a tree nor any shrubbery met their gaze.* The water *as well, which camels had carried in skins,* ran out *and there was none to be found in the simmering sand and arid ground. Additionally, the sun imbued everything with scorching heat and their mouths were dry and parched, when* suddenly, *whether by the gift of the gods or mere fortuity,* the sky was filled with clouds *and the sun was veiled, a huge help to those harried by the heat, despite their water supply having failed. But actually, when* the storms *also* showered down chutes of rain from a cloudburst, *each man caught it in whichever way he could. Some, having been enfeebled by thirst, even began to gobble it with their gaping mouths. Consequently, their drought was ended unexpectedly, when they filled their skins from a pooling in a dip in the ground that they found providentially.*

5.25 Four more days were spent traipsing through desert wastes. *But when they were not very far from the seat of the oracle,* the sand dunes rendered their route untraceable. At that point they encountered a flock of cawing crows to their right and the guide told the king that they were following the way to the temple in their flight. *They flew forward fitfully ahead of the standards and when progress was slow, the crows would alight, then again take flight, as though they strove to show the way to the site.* The king took this for an omen and, thinking the god to be glad of his arrival, he hurried onwards towards the oracle. *And first of all, he came upon the so-called Bitter Lake, then going on another hundred stades he skirted what are known as Ammon's cities* and after *a journey of a day* he at last approached the enclosure of the god's sanctuary.

5.26 *Extraordinary as it is to relate, though* the precinct is situated amidst desert dunes and waterless wastes devoid of every amenity, *it is so completely enveloped by thick forestry that the sunlight is all but filtered out by its dense canopy.* The wood is fifty stades in length and breadth and many freshwater springs well up haphazardly, irrigating its many types of tree, especially such as fruit generously. Its climate too, being most like to the warmth of spring, is wondrously temperate, cycling through all seasons of the year in the same wholesome state, *though surrounded by a searing hot landscape. It is said that the sacred enclosure was established by Danaos the Egyptian.* Towards the east the near neighbours of its vicinity are Ethiopian. *Southwards the place faces those Arabians who are known as Trogodytes, whose region runs on right to the Red Sea.* Other Ethiopians, *who are called Simui,* occupy the land that lies to the west. There are Nasamones to the north, *a Syrtican nation living off loot from the shipping, since they infest the shores and seize storm-tossed vessels that run aground in and about shoals that they have staked out.*

5.27 The inhabitants of the groves, who are called Ammonii, inhabit huts *in scattered groups*. The centre of the oasis is set aside as their citadel, the walls of which encircle it in three loops. The innermost circuit encloses the ancient palace of their kings. The next accommodates their wives', children's and concubines' dwellings *and the watchstations of that bailey*. There too lies the oracle of the god *and his sacred spring, the waters of which sanctify offerings dedicated to the deity*. The outermost ring encompasses the barracks of the royal guards as well as the posts for standing sentry.

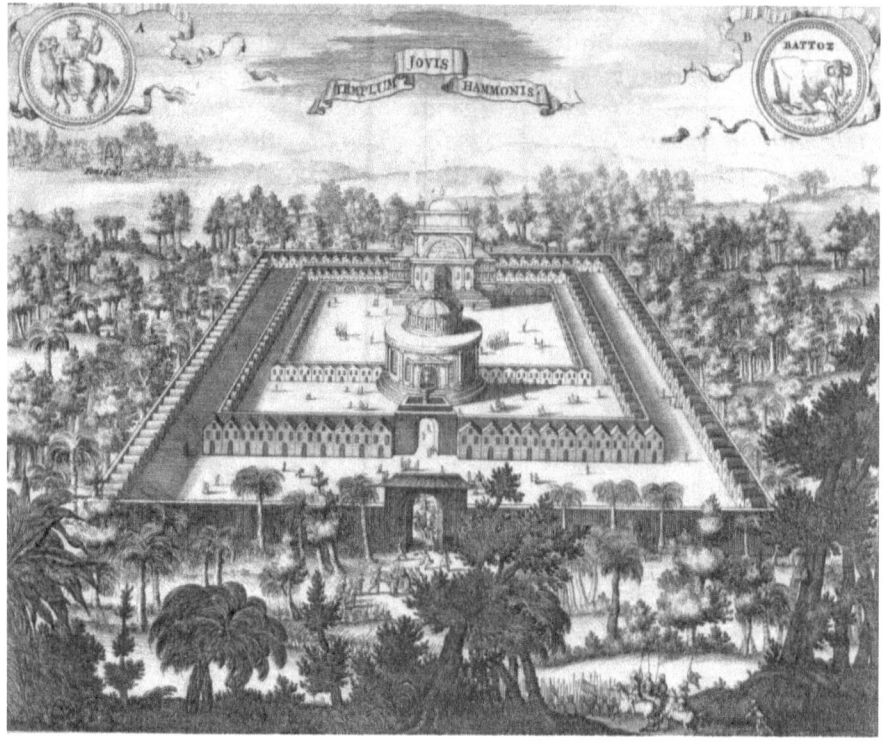

Figure 5.2. Imaginative reconstruction of the Temple of Ammon at Siwa (1685)

5.28 Outside the citadel but near at hand another shrine of Ammon lies in the shade of a grove of great trees, amidst which emerges a spring that is called the Source of the Sun *due to the way it varies. The temperature of its waters alters counterintuitively in a daily cycle of activity*. At dawn it streams forth lukewarm, but as the day passes it cools in proportion to the passage of time, until at noon, *when the heat is at its hottest*, it comes out coldest. Then again at a like rate it warms towards the twilight and seethes out in its hottest state at around midnight. Thereafter it resumes its cooling trend until its waters end up tepid once more by first light.

Book 5: 14th October 332BC – 1st October 331BC

5.29 That which is reverenced as the deity *does not have the same form with which carvers commonly characterise divinity. It* is embedded amidst an agglomeration of gems and emeralds *and most closely resembles a navel. It has a weird way of answering those that consult the oracle.* It is borne about on a golden boat by *eighty* priests *with multiple silver cups hung from either side of the vessel. With the god on their shoulders, they veer involuntarily under divine guidance.* A multitude of maidens and matrons follow and according to the custom of their country they descant discordant chants, *by which they believe Zeus is propitiated, such that his oracular response is validated.*

5.30 *On the particular occasion of the king's arrival,* when Alexander was admitted into the temple and had regarded the god for an interval, the eldest of the priests, who was their prophet, approached the king, saying, "Hail to the Son. And let you receive as from the god too this title." And Alexander himself replied, "I receive it gladly, Father. Henceforth I shall be called Diogenes,"[117] *for he had forgotten his mortality.* Then he enquired as to whether fate had destined him to rule the world in its entirety? The prophet went within the shrine and the bearers shouldered the deity, which teetered so as to speak symbolically. And the prophet, *practised in fluent flattery,* declared that the king's command of every land would most certainly come to be. Then Alexander spoke again: "O divinity, reveal this final thing to me: have I made all the murderers of my father pay the penalty or did any go free?" "Silence!" the prophet exclaimed, "No mortal may undermine the source of your paternity. Yet for the felling of Philip all the perpetrators have been punished properly." And he added, "The sublimity of your deeds shall be the proof of your descent from the deity and even as you have previously known nothing but victory, so you shall be invincible[118] *until you assume your own divinity and then* throughout eternity."

5.31 *After the sacrificial offerings,* rejoicing in the oracular pronouncements, Alexander honoured *both the priests and* the god with precious presents. *Then the king consented that his companions consult the oracle as well. They asked nothing more significant than whether the god ratified their reverence of their ruler with divine honours and the prophet pronounced that by this too Zeus would be gratified.*

---

[117] Diogenes was an epithet of several Homeric heroes, which may be translated as "Son of Zeus" or "sprung from Zeus".

[118] I.e. *Aniketos*, the title also endorsed by the Pythia at Delphi in the Cleitarchan tradition.

Figure 5.3. Alexander is greeted as the Son of Zeus by the eldest priest (1696)

Book 5: 14th October 332BC – 1st October 331BC

5.32 *On the basis of a sound and balanced estimation of its fidelity the responses of the oracle could be perceived as specious. But Fortune makes those in whom she has compelled confidence in her alone more gluttonous for glory than capable of coping with it. On that account Alexander not only allowed himself to be dubbed Diogenes, but even bade it and, although he meant to magnify the fame of his deeds with such a title, he actually marred it. And the Macedonians, though accustomed to the command of a king, nevertheless enjoyed a semblance of greater liberty than other monarchist men, so they contested his claim to immortality more stubbornly than was sensible either for their sovereign or for them. But let this be kept for its due occasion, for now I shall proceed with the rest of my narration.*

5.33 Alexander returned from Ammon by way of the Mareotic Lake, situated not far from the island of Pharos. He *had initially* intended to found a new city *upon the island itself. But, on surveying the topography of the vicinity, it was apparent that this location lacked the capacity to accommodate a substantial settlement, so he selected the site now occupied by Alexandria, which took its name from its founder.* **He left men from among his Friends behind whom he bade build his eponymous city between the marshes and the sea.** *Hence, he envisaged a circuit of eighty stades as its destiny and he bade that the governance of Egypt be accorded to this Macedonian colony. Here too Hegelochus anchored in order to bring the pirate, Aristonicus of Methymna, before the king. After Alexander had asked this man what he meant by harassing shipping, he answered with uncowed conceit: "The same as you mean by seizing the whole world; but because I do it with a single ship, I am labelled a bandit, whilst you are called a king, considering that you use a great fleet."*[119]

5.34 Then Alexander made for Memphis. He was afflicted by a desire that was not so much unjustified as inopportune to travel not just to Upper Egypt but to Ethiopia as well. Being eager to investigate the vestiges of antiquity, the renowned palace of Memnon and Tithonus was drawing him virtually beyond the limits of enlightenment. However, the impending war, of which by far the most challenging phase was yet to come, curtailed his time for sightseeing. Hence he gave the government of Egypt to Aeschylus of Rhodes and Peucestes of Macedon, allotting them four thousand troops to garrison the region and he called upon Polemon to defend the barriers across the Nile estuaries, assigning him thirty triremes to this end. Apollonius was placed in command of the Libyan lands adjoining Egypt and Cleomenes was to exact taxes, *tapping the wealth* from those Libyan tracts and from Egypt itself.

5.35 By bidding the inhabitants of the neighbouring cities to resettle in Alexandria, the king filled his new foundation with a populous populace. It is widely reported that when Alexander delineated the circuit of its future walls, as is the Macedonian tradition, *though* with barley meal *due to a lack of lime*, birds flocked to the location, making this meal their invitation to dine. And when many considered this a sombre sign, the seers dissented, saying that the city would

---

[119] That Hegelochus brought Aristonicus to Alexandria is suggested by Arrian, *Anabasis* 3.2.3-5.

acquire a large population through immigration and would supply sustenance to many a nation.

Figure 5.4. Alexander founds Alexandria by André Castaigne (1898)

5.36 Whilst Alexander was cruising downriver, Hector, a son of Parmenion, in the fairest flowering of his youth, was wishing to catch up with the king, to whom few were dearer. He therefore embarked upon a boat of slight capacity, which was crammed with far more than it could carry. And so, it immersed its entire complement as it eventually sank. Hector long contested with the current with his wet clothing and tightly fastened sandals impeding his swimming and he managed though semiconscious to reach the riverbank. But he was in a state of complete exhaustion and as he fought to resume his respiration, which panic and the peril had repressed, he gave up the ghost and died, since none came to his aid, the rest having got out on the opposite side. The king was gripped by great grief at his loss and on recovering his corpse gave him a magnificent funeral and send-off.

5.37 This mourning was magnified by news of the death of Andromachus, to whom he had given the government of Syria. He had been roasted alive by the Samaritans. In order to avenge his incineration, **Alexander advanced into Syria** with the greatest expedition and the perpetrators of the atrocity were given up to him upon his appearance in their nation. Thereafter he installed Memnon in Andromachus' position and those that had dealt death to his governor themselves incurred execution. Certain despots, including Aristonicus and Ersilaus of Methymna, he put in the hands of their own populations, who tortured them to death in revenge for their transgressions.

Book 5: 14th October 332BC – 1st October 331BC

5.38 Alexander next hearkened to the emissaries of the Athenians, the Rhodians and the Chians. The Athenians commended him on his victory and entreated that his Greek prisoners should be repatriated, whereas the Rhodians and the Chians lodged complaints against their garrisons. All of their petitions appeared correct and resolutions were put into effect. To recompense the citizens of Mytilene too, considering that they had stood by him outstandingly, he both defrayed the funds that they had laid out on the war and annexed to them a tremendous tract of adjoining territory. To the Cypriot sovereigns besides, who had not only defected from Darius, but had also sent Alexander a fleet whilst he invested Tyre, went honours commensurate with their helpfulness.

5.39 Since both Persian and Spartan soldiery was ravaging much of Crete's territory, Amphoterus, admiral of the fleet, was secondarily sent to set the island free, being bidden as his first priority to rid the sea of flotillas engaged in piracy. For it was plagued by many a plundering corsair, whilst both kings were engaged in warfare elsewhere. These things being set in train, the king dedicated a golden bowl and thirty goblets to Heracles of Tyre[120] and, intent upon confronting Darius again, he ordered a march to the River Euphrates to be proclaimed. *They went by way of Byblos, where* **Theias Byblios, who transcended all humanity in his handsomeness, was enamoured of his own daughter, called Myrra,**[121] *the result of their relationship being the birth of Adonis.*

5.40 Now Darius, on discovering the detour adopted by his foe from Egypt into Libya, pondered whether he should head for his realm's remoter reaches or linger in the vicinity of Mesopotamia. Undoubtedly, he would in person be able to incite the outlying peoples to participate in the war more successfully, as through his satraps he was rallying them only with difficulty. But when word spread abroad on good authority that Alexander with his entire army would pursue him unto whichever territory into which he might flee, being well aware of the vigour of his adversary, Darius decreed that all the contingents counted upon from distant nations should muster at Babylon. The Bactrians, Scythians and indeed the Indians having already gathered, in the same timeframe forces from the remaining peoples were successfully mustered.

5.41 Having swelled his ranks from every quarter, Darius directed an army *half again as large as he had led in Cilicia,* but with many men wanting for weaponry. These he furnished *with careful consideration,* making swords and lances *much longer than in the Cilician action, for he thought Alexander had derived advantage from their extension.* He manufactured mail for his cavalrymen and their mounts with overlapping leaves of steel. To those that before had had just a javelin, a sword and shield were given. Herds of

---

[120] The Greeks recognised the Tyrian god Melkart as a local version of Heracles.

[121] Jacoby Fragment 3 of Cleitarchus from Stobaeus *Florilegium*, IV 20, 73; it is an implication of the attribution of this fragment to the fifth book that Alexander marched up the coast past Byblos and that the unsubstantiated guess that the army marched inland from Tyre is mistaken.

horses were handed over to the foot to be broken in, so that his cavalry might be more numerous than previously. **He followed this** *up* **with** *what he believed would be a means of intimidating his foe in the form of* **two hundred scythed chariots, each drawn by four horses in a row,**[122] *such war vehicles being peculiar to those peoples.* Steel-tipped spears poked forward from their poles and triple scythes three spans long were affixed to either end of the yokes projecting beyond the beasts, cutting edges to the fore.[123] Upon the wheels many more blades were arrayed in opposing orientations. At the hubs another pair of scythes jutted straight out with their blades facing forwards. Still others were set in the rims, some slicing upwards and others slashing downwards. *Thus, whatever should get in the way of the charging horses stood to be cut to pieces.*

5.42 *Darius adorned his entire army with emblazoned armour and commissioned courageous commanders. When his forces had been outfitted in this fashion,* the king marched forth from Babylon with a throng *half* a million strong, at least a fifth of them on horseback.[124] He kept the celebrated Tigris on his right and used the Euphrates to screen the left flank of his track, *proceeding through fertile farmland fecund enough to furnish fodder for the beasts and food sufficient for so many men. They filled the fields of Mesopotamia.* Then, after traversing the Tigris, when he heard that his opponent was not far distant, he sent forward Satropates, a captain of his **cavalry**, with a thousand select horsemen. Six thousand again **were assigned to** his marshal, **Mazaeus, to block the fording of the river by his enemy.** His orders were additionally to devastate and incinerate the territory to which Alexander was about to make an entry. For Darius reckoned that his adversary could be incapacitated by *consequential* insufficiency, since he had nothing except what he seized by pillaging, whereas arrangements were in place to deliver supplies to Darius himself either overland or by river.

5.43 *It was* **Darius** *'s design that battle should be joined near Nineveh, since the plains thereabouts suited his intentions in affording him ample space to manoeuvre his army's vast formations. Hence, he* encamped by Arbela, an obscure village that was to achieve distinction through his own ruination. *Here he drilled his forces every day, so that they became responsive and*

---

[122] Curtius 4.9.4 is explicit that they were *quadrigae* (four horse chariots).

[123] A model of a 4th century BC Persian chariot was found amidst the Oxus treasure: it has four horses with two poles projecting from either side of the carriage and linked by a single yoke passing over the base of the neck of each beast.

[124] There is some disagreement in the sources on Darius's numbers. This may partly be explained by the assumption that the host that left Babylon (reported by Diodorus 17.39.4 & 17.53.3) was substantially larger than the 245,000 men (reported by Curtius 4.12.12), which Darius actually deployed in the field of battle. The fact that Justin 11.12.5 has exactly half the numbers in Diodorus may indicate that the latter has read "a million" for "half a million". The number mounted may originally have been given as a proportion of the total, which would have facilitated the corruption of Cleitarchus's figures in the surviving sources.

Book 5: 14th October 332BC – 1st October 331BC

proficient through practice and continual training. His key concern was that confusion could come about in battle due to the diversity of tongues among the contingents he was fielding. Caching most of his baggage and provisions at Arbela, he bridged the Lycus[125] and spent five days getting his army across just as in traversing the Euphrates *two years* previously.[126] Thence he advanced around eighty stades, encamping beside another tributary, known as the Boumelus[127] *locally*. This territory was advantageous for the deployment of his forces as it comprised featureless plains ideal for horses. Not even shrubs or stunted bushes obstructed the ground and it afforded a clear prospect into the far distance all around. And wherever anything protruded above the surrounding field, he bade that it be flattened and that every eminence be levelled.

5.44 Those *scouts* who gauged Darius' strength, insofar as it could be estimated remotely, could scarcely convince Alexander of their fidelity, given that so many thousands had *previously* been slain, when they reported that the force now fielded was larger again. However, as a despiser of every danger and especially the threat from being outnumbered, the king encamped beside the Euphrates on the eleventh day *after striking inland from the coast*. Having thrown bridges across the river, he commanded his cavalry to cross initially and his phalanx subsequently. Meanwhile Mazaeus arrived to oppose his crossing with six thousand horsemen, but did not dare to engage the Macedonian. After a few days had been afforded to his forces rather to raise their morale than to rest them, he began rapidly to advance against his enemy, fearing lest Darius should flee to remote regions of his realm, such that the pursuit would pass into a vast country entirely empty of occupation and devoid of rations. Therefore, on the four*teen*th day before *the battle at* Arbela he got to the Tigris river.

5.45 *Darius had deemed that Mazaeus might hold the ford and defend the rivercourse against the Macedonian offensive. But the general judged the torrent to be impassable due to its depth and the swiftness of its current, so his defence of it was inattentive. Instead, he engaged in the despoiling of the countryside and, when it was wasted far and wide, considered that the enemy could not be supplied. But Alexander advanced to the ford on the advice of a local guide. When he arrived the entire territory across the river was smoking from recent incineration, since Mazaeus was setting fire to whatever he came across* as though he were the enemy in the region. Initially, since the veil of the fumes had dimmed the daylight, Alexander halted for fear of ambush, but then when the scouts he sent forward declared all was clear, he advanced a few of his horse to attempt to ford the watercourse. While they were close to the banks the water reached no higher than their steeds' flanks, but at its mid-stream apex, they were in it up to their necks. Neither does any other river

---

[125] The Greater Zab? See the map in Figure B.

[126] On his way to Issus: Curtius 3.7.1.

[127] The Khazir?

in Eastern parts cascade with so ferocious a flow, for it not only conveys torrents from many tributaries but rocks also. It is in consequence of its careering current that it is called the Tigris, because in the Persian tongue they mean the "Arrow" by this.

5.46 Therefore, just as in battle array, **the infantry were flanked by the cavalry and** they lifted their weaponry above their heads, so that **they forayed into the channel** without difficulty. And first among the foot to emerge at the far bank was the king, where he waved his arms to show the shallows to his soldiers, whilst they were out of hearing. But **the water reached above their chests and they could barely keep a firm footing, since sometimes the slippery stones betrayed their steps and sometimes the swiftness of the current swept them into swimming. The task of those that bore burdens upon their shoulders was especially trying, since they could not right themselves and were swept into swirling vortices, impeded by their packs and shields.** And whilst they all strove to retrieve their plunder, they came into conflict with one another more than with the river and bunches of baggage that bobbed about butted many of them under. The king instructed them to concentrate upon keeping hold of their arms, since he would replace anything else *that mattered*. But they were not in a state to accept either his counsel or what he ordered: their dread drowned him out, and also their mutual recriminations as one after another tottered. Finally, they rose up out of the river where a slackening of the current had revealed shallows with nothing except a few packs lacking.

5.47 But Alexander devised a defence against the current's violence. He ordered all his troops firmly to link their hands together, so as to form a sort of barrage by bracing them one against another. The army could have been annihilated had there been an attempt to overwhelm it by any of its enemies, but the king's consistently favourable fortune warded off his adversaries. Similarly, he had crossed the Granicus whilst rank upon rank of infantry and cavalry stood riveted upon the far bank. So too he had concentrated his forces in the Cilician narrows in the face of such multitudinous foes. Even that recklessness that he displayed in abundance cannot be considered of consequence, since there was never the opportunity to conclude that he had acted rashly. Had Mazaeus fallen upon them whilst they were crossing the watercourse, doubtless he would have surprised them when in disarray, but he did not even start to charge them with his horse, until they had reached the riverbank and stood armed for the fray. The Persians had fielded no more than a thousand cavalry and Alexander, ascertaining their inadequacy, viewed them disdainfully and bade Ariston, the commander of his Paeonian cavalry, to charge them most sturdily. Those riders fought valiantly that day and Ariston especially. He thrust his lance straight through the throat of Satropates, the commander of these cavalry, then catching him as he fled through the midst of the enemy, he hurled him from his horse and hacked off his head with his sword, though he struggled violently. Returning with his trophy from the decapitation, he laid it at the king's feet amidst loud acclamation, *declaring: "In my country, O king, for such a gift as this one is given a gold cup."*

Book 5: 14th October 332BC – 1st October 331BC

"Yes," said Alexander, laughing, "An empty gift, but I shall drink your health in wine from one that is full up."[128]

5.48 ***As the crossing had been treacherous and an ordeal for his men Alexander encamped and rested his army that day*** and the next, ***then the day after that he ordered them to march on again.*** But *that night* at about the time of the first watch the Moon in eclipse began to hide her heavenly brilliance and then the stain of blood defiled her entire radiance,[129] and those who were already nervous in the run-up to such a decisive collision were consumed by colossal superstitious awe, which engendered a certain sense of trepidation *from what they saw*. They moaned that the gods were against their having been dragged to the ends of existence, where rivers refused to be forded, celestial bodies could not keep their characteristic incandescence and everywhere wilderness and wastelands were their environments. The blood of so many thousands *of men* was funding the wild aspirations of a single person, who hated his homeland, had disowned his father Philip and already in his own hubristic opinion was hailed in Heaven. Matters were moving towards mutiny, when the king, quite unmoved by everything, summoned his commanders and a crowd of his senior soldiers to his headquarters tent. And Alexander bade that the Egyptian seers, whom he considered most expert in astronomy and astrology, should announce their judgement. But despite being sufficiently well aware that cyclical celestial bodies exhibit predictable fluctuations and that the Moon wanes either when it is shaded by the Earth or else when the Sun comes close to it *in the sky*, these sages did not enlighten the troopers with the wisdom that they themselves had come by. Rather they declared that the Sun symbolised the Greek side whereas the Moon signified the Persian, so that whenever she went into shadow, it presaged calamity and overthrow for that nation. And they specified examples of Persian kings of yore, for whom an eclipse of the Moon had made manifest divine disfavour in war. Nothing moves a mob more effectively than superstition. Though otherwise anarchic, wild and fickle, they better obey the seers than their leaders, when they are seized by a false sense of religion. Therefore, this interpretation by the Egyptians, when communicated to the crowd, restored the optimism and loyalty of those who had been cowed.

5.49 Reckoning he ought *at once* to exploit their raised spirits, the king broke camp in the second watch of the night. The mountains called the Gordyaeans lay on his left and he had the Tigris on his right. After they had set out upon this march, scouts who had been sent ahead spying declared at dawn that Darius was arriving. Hence Alexander led his lines forward drawn up in fighting formation. But these were stragglers from the Persian concentration, just a thousand strong, who had

---

[128] An anecdote from Plutarch, *Alexander* 39.1.

[129] A Lunar Eclipse occurred on 20th September 331BC (Julian) with totality beginning at around 9pm local time eleven days before the battle (Plutarch, *Alexander* 31.4). This is consistent with the inference above (end of section 5.44) that Alexander reached the Tigris fourteen days before the battle.

given the impression of a colossal throng, since when the truth cannot be found fear compounds what is wrong. This being realised, the king led a few of his men in hot pursuit of the Persians as they fled back to their brothers, slaying some and seizing others. He sent horsemen on ahead of him to perform a reconnaissance and in order to extinguish the fires that the Persians had set in the settlements in the same instance. For the fugitives had hastily cast torches into the roof-thatch and upon piles of grain and, although the fire had caught hold in the upper reaches, the lower parts were not yet aflame. Hence, when the fires were quenched, the majority of the grain remained edible and supplies of other provisions also grew plentiful. This in itself fired the enthusiasm of the troops in their pursuit of their adversaries, for since they were burning the land and laying it to waste, in order to stop them ere they set everything ablaze, there was need for considerable haste. Therefore, what had been begun by necessity became sensible policy, for Mazaeus, who had been leisurely in setting the settlements alight previously, was now content to flee, relinquishing most things undamaged to his enemy. Alexander had determined that Darius lay no further than one hundred and fifty stades away, and so, being supplied with provisions to the point of satiety, he stayed for four days in the same locality.

5.50 Then dispatches from Darius were intercepted inciting the Greek allied troops either to slay or to betray their king and Alexander wondered whether he should recite them at an assembly, since he was satisfied that even these Greeks bore him sufficient goodwill and loyalty. But Parmenion deterred him, declaring that such offers would pollute the ears of the soldiers. A ruler is vulnerable to the treachery of even a single individual and greed makes nothing seem criminal. So, the king broke camp, complying with the counsel of his general.

5.51 Whilst he was en route, *a eunuch from among those detainees that attended upon* **the wife of Darius** *announced to Alexander that she was weakening and barely breathing. Exhausted by the continual toil of travelling and with her spirit ailing, she had collapsed into the arms of her mother-in-law and her maiden offspring* in the course of miscarrying.[130] *Thereafter she soon* passed away *and another eunuch arrived bearing that announcement. Hardly less than if news of the death of his own mother had been sent, the king exclaimed many a lament and with welling tears, such as Darius might have shed, he went off to the tent whither the mother of Darius sat beside the limp body of the dead. Here he relapsed into sorrow, when he saw her laid low upon the ground. Reminded too of earlier ills by this fresh wound, Sisygambis enfolded the marriageable maidens in her embrace, a solace and grace in their mutual mourning, though it ought to have been their mother that did the consoling. Her tiny grandson was*

---

[130] Though not in either Curtius or Diodorus, the miscarriage is adduced by both Plutarch, *Alexander* 30.1 and Justin 11.12.6, which makes it likelier than not that it was in Cleitarchus: perhaps due to disease simulating pregnancy as in the case of Queen Mary Tudor or else the outcome of an illicit liaison during her captivity with Alexander.

before her gaze, all the more pitiable because he was unaware of the malaise of calamity converging upon him most particularly.

Figure 5.5. The death of the wife of Darius (1696)

5.52 *It might have been thought that* **Alexander wept** *compulsively amidst his own family and that he did not offer but rather sought sympathy. Certainly, he abstained from nutrition* **and accorded her every funerary dignity** *in the fashion of the Persian nation,* deserving, by Heracles, even now of reaping him a reputation for real temperance and compassion. **He had seen her on just a single occasion** *when he went to visit the mother of Darius rather than his wife on the day of their capture and her exceptional* *loveliness had vindicated his virtue instead of leading him into lustful rapture.*

5.53 From among the eunuchs surrounding the queen and amid the commotion made by the mourners, Tyriotes slipped off on horseback *through a gate that was but lightly guarded, since it faced away from the enemy's soldiers. He was seized by the sentries on reaching Darius' encampment and being led into the royal tent by these, he moaned and rent his raiment. When Darius set eyes upon him, he was apprehensive in anticipation of various species of adversity and being unsure about which he should have most anxiety he said: "Your expression portrays some untold tragedy, but have a care not to spare the ears of an unfortunate fellow; I have learnt to live lucklessly and it is frequently a comfort in calamity for a man to know his destiny. Are you not in fact going to announce what I most sorely suspect yet dread to utter: that my family have been debauched, which is to me and I believe also to all of them viler than torture?" To this Tyriotes retorted: "Actually, that's far from the truth of the matter, for the greatest respect that can be paid to queens by their own people has been accorded to your kinsfolk by the conqueror. However, a little while ago your wife departed from this life."*

5.54 Then indeed not just groaning but also shrieking was heard through the whole encampment. Nor did Darius doubt that she had been slain because she could not endure her defilement and manic with misery he moaned: "What heinous iniquity have I committed, Alexander? Which of your kin did I kill that you vengefully repay my brutality? You abhor me without even any provocation, but supposing that you wage war against me justly, are you consequently obliged to make women the targets of your aggression?" Tyriotes swore by the gods of his homeland that she had not been subjected to anything appalling. Just as Darius had not stifled his tears, Alexander too had been greatly grieved by her death and had not held back from bawling. But this itself in the mind of her doting husband fired up further anxiety and suspicion, for he inferred that mourning the loss of a captive must indeed have been inspired by habitual sexual molestation. Hence, he dismissed all the onlookers and only retained Tyriotes. Now no longer crying, but rather sighing he said: "Do you not see, Tyriotes, that this is not the place for perjuries? The tools for torture are about to be brought in, but by the gods do not hold out for them, if you have any reverence for your sovereign. Being both youthful and her captor, did he not dare to do what I both wish to know but am ashamed to examine?"

5.55 *The eunuch volunteered his body for interrogation under torture, but invoked the attestations*[131] *of the gods that the queen had remained inviolate and had retained her honour.* Then, finally being brought to believe the eunuch's testimony, Darius veiled his head and wept a long while, until he wrenched the robe from his face and reached up his hands towards the heavens, declaring, tearful still: "O ancestral gods of my country, I had rather that you should maintain my throne's stability, *so that I might properly requite my adversary,* but if now there must come an end to my sovereignty *to appease divine jealousy,* I pray that none other should in future be the king of Asia save he that is so just an enemy and so merciful in victory."[132]

5.56 *And so, despite having turned all his attentions towards war when his peace overtures had twice been spurned, being swayed by the forbearance shown by his opponent,* Darius dispatched *ten* emissaries, *his key kinsmen,* bearing fresh terms for a peace settlement. Alexander convened his council *and bade that these envoys be brought in and the eldest among them was* their spokesman *and* said: "Darius has *felt no compulsion to appeal to you for peace on a third occasion, but rather this has been elicited by your fairness and moderation. We gain* no impression of his mother, wife and children being incarcerated, except insofar as they and Darius stay separated. You are scarcely less careful of the chastity of those that remain than a father would be, recognising them as queens and suffering them to retain the semblance of their former dignity. *Your countenance conveys the sort of sentiment I saw in the face of Darius, when he dispatched our embassy, yet he is mourning the death of a wife, you the loss of an enemy. You should already be stood in battle formation, had your attention to her funeral not entailed your detention.* What wonder that Darius should seek to make peace with a man of such a friendly disposition? What need is there of warfare between those who have risen above their dissension? Previously, *as well as a twenty thousand talent bounty,* he intended the River Halys at the Lydian border to be the boundary of your hegemony. Now he cedes everything between the Hellespont and the Euphrates as the dowry of his daughter, whom he offers you in matrimony. *Let you hold on to his son Ochus as hostage for his fidelity and inaction, but* let his mother and two virgin daughters be returned to us. *For their three persons* he prays that you accept *in compensation* thrice ten thousand talents of gold from us. *As the son-in-law of Darius, your role shall be hereditary in sharing control of the whole country.*"

---

[131] There is a pun in the Latin of Curtius such that the eunuch, lacking *testes*, invokes the *testes* of the gods on his behalf.

[132] This prayer of Darius appears in similar forms in: Curtius 4.10.34; Plutarch, *Alexander* 30.6; Plutarch, *Moralia* 338E-F; Arrian, *Anabasis* 4.20.3.

5.57 "Had I not noted your moderate disposition, I would withhold from hailing this as the moment when you should not solely accept but ought actually to seize a settlement. Consider how much lies in your wake. Understand how much you have still to take. An overextended empire is perilous, for what you cannot reach is hard to hold. Have you not observed that overladen ships cannot be controlled? I am not at all sure that Darius has not suffered so many losses on account of the room for diminutions provided by excessively vast dominions. Some things are more readily wrested away than retained. By Heracles! How much easier it is for our hands to grasp a thing than that the thing be completely contained. In itself the death of Darius' wife could be cautionary in that you already have less ability to behave compassionately."

5.58 Alexander bade that the emissaries should withdraw from his tent for him to discuss with his council what they had urged in settlement. The king encouraged each councillor to express his sentiment. For ages no one dared to speak his mind, since it was unclear which way the king inclined. But at last, Parmenion *mentioned that he had pressed previously for those prisoners detained at Damascus to be released to their ransomers, since a huge amount of money could be raised from those in fetters, whose handling was diverting many worthy warriors. And now too he earnestly advised that a solitary grandmother and a pair of girls should indeed be sold, being burdens both on the march and in battle order, in exchange for thirty thousand talents in gold. A rich realm could be reaped through negotiation, rather than hostilities, and nobody else had held the whole of the huge territories extending from the River Ister[133] to the Euphrates. Furthermore, Alexander ought to look back out of regard for Macedonia instead of staring forwards towards Bactria and India. He* concluded: "If I were Alexander, I would accept this offer."

5.59 The king *was displeased by this declamation, hence he* replied *at its conclusion:* "So too should I, if I were Parmenion. That is, I would prefer funds to fame. But as it is, my name is Alexander and, *being without any worry concerning penury,* I remember that I am a ruler rather than a trader. Indeed, I have nothing at all to retail, but in particular I do not put my majesty up for sale. If it should please us to repatriate our prisoners, then it would be more honorable to give them as gifts, than ransom them for a fee, *but thanks are worthless from an enemy.*"

5.60 Thereafter, having recalled the delegation, he gave them his answer in the following fashion: "Tell Darius from me that my acts of kindness and clemency were due to my natural inclinations rather than any attempt to appear friendly *or to instigate diplomacy*. I refrain habitually from warring with women and those I hold in captivity, *but it befits him to arm himself, who has aggrieved me.* Nevertheless, if he should ask for peace in good

---

[133] The Danube.

faith, unambiguously, I might perhaps consider granting his plea. But just as a world with two suns would not work properly, so the lands of men cannot be kept in peace and tranquillity, whilst two kings share the sovereignty.[134] Therefore, if Darius desires peace, he must cede me the supremacy, *though he may live on in luxury and rule every satrapy under my warranty.* Alternatively, he must *shortly* do battle with me to see who shall have the monarchy, *but he should have no higher hopes than previously.* And when, in actuality, he has recently sent letters to my soldiers inciting them to treachery and has just tried to bribe my friends to do away with me, I must pursue him to perdition as an assassin who resorts to chicanery, rather than as a legitimate adversary."

5.61 "In truth the terms for peace that you have delivered, were I to agree them, would cede Darius the victory. He offers me what is behind the Euphrates with generosity. Are you therefore oblivious of where you are even now addressing me? I am beyond the Euphrates, surely? Hence my encampment is beyond the broadest boundary of the territory he promises as a dowry. So that I may know that it is yours to surrender, expel me from this territory! And Darius would hand me his daughter with the same sort of generosity, though I know her to be betrothed to one who is his lackey. How highly indeed he honours me, if he prefers me to Mazaeus for propagating his dynasty! Go tell your king that both what he has lost already and what he yet retains are the stakes in our hostilities, since for both of our domains it is war that shall set the boundaries and which shall see that each of us obtains whatever the fortune of the forthcoming day decrees." **The envoys** *replied that, his heart being set upon war, he was acting with honesty in not beguiling them with hopes of a peace treaty. They begged to be allowed to return to their king immediately and advised Alexander that he too should make ready for butchery. Being then dismissed, they* reported that battle would be joined imminently.

5.62 Darius did not delay in moving Mazaeus forward with three thousand cavalry to guard the routes via which his enemy's advance was likely. Alexander, having performed the rites for the body of Darius' wife in due fashion, left all the more cumbersome components of his expedition within the existing ramparts with a skeleton garrison and advanced rapidly towards the opposition. He had split his infantry into two wings and had positioned cavalry around both flanks with the baggage trailing behind the army's ranks. Next, he sent Menidas ahead with veteran horsemen with the mission of determining Darius's location. But he, when he found Mazaeus ensconced nearby, did not dare to advance any further, and was able to announce only that he had heard the din of men and the whinnying of their mounts. Likewise, Mazaeus, upon discerning the scouts in the distance, scurried back to camp and announced the arrival of their opponents.

---

[134] The metaphor of the "two suns" is curiously missing from Curtius, but clearly derived from Cleitarchus, since it is found in both Diodorus 17.54.5 and Justin 11.12.15.

5.63 Therefore Darius, who had chosen open ground for the fray, ordered his troops to take up their weapons and arranged them in battle array. On his left wing there were Bactrian cavalry about a thousand strong with the same number of Dahae horsemen plus four thousand from Arachosia and Susianê to complete the *front of the* throng. These were backed up by a hundred scythed chariots and Bessus sat behind these four-horse vehicle positions with eight thousand more mounted Bactrians. Two thousand Massagetae brought up the rear of the formation. To these he had adjoined footsoldiers from many races, not intermingled, but each with their national forces. Next Ariobarzanes and Orontobates led the Persians supported by the Mardians and the Sogdians. These men commanded individual divisions, but Orsines, a descendant of the "Seven Persians", who also traced his ancestry to Cyrus, that most renowned ruler, was their overall commander. These were backed up by other tribes, which not even the record made by their allies adequately describes. Next after these nations came Phradates leading fifty four-horse chariots together with considerable Caspian formations. To the rear of the chariots were the Indians and the rest of the Red Sea residents, there to make up numbers rather than to act in offence. The rear of this section of the front was occupied by other scythed chariots, to which were attached the foreign recruits. Next to these came the so-called "Lesser" Armenians and next to them the Babylonians and both the Belitae and those that dwelt amidst the mountains of the Cossaeans. After these went the Gortuae, actually a Euboean band, sometime recruits of the Medes, but now degenerate and ignorant of the customs of their homeland. Beside them Darius placed the Phrygians and the Cataonians. Thereafter the Parthians finished off this formation. Such was his left wing for the confrontation.

5.64 The right wing was held by the nationals of Greater Armenia together with the Cadusian, the Cappadocian, the Syrian and the Median nations. Here too a force of fifty scythed chariots took up their stations. The fighting strength of the entire field army comprised forty-five thousand cavalry and two hundred thousand infantry. Arrayed in this fashion they advanced ten stades and were then told to stand under arms awaiting their enemy.

5.65 Alexander's army was gripped by panic, the cause of which was not clear, for they began to be agitated and frantic as an obscure dread breached the breast of every soldier. A shimmer in the sky like that from late-summer stubble burning seemed to reflect flames and they supposed that this was the glow from the camp-fires of the Persian hosts as though they had chanced upon their outposts. If Mazaeus, who was holding the highway, had fallen upon them whilst they were in this state of alarm, he could have inflicted huge harm. As it was, whilst he lurked at ease upon an eminence that he had seized, content to sit there inviolate, Alexander, recognising his army's disquiet, issued the signal for them to halt in their tracks, ordering that they should set aside their arms and relax. And he admonished them that there was no cause for consternation, since they were still far from the opposition. Eventually, they calmed down, retrieving both their arms

Book 5: 14th October 332BC – 1st October 331BC

and their doughty disposition. And nothing seemed more prudent in their present position than to fortify an encampment at that same location.

5.66 The next day, either due to loss of nerve or through having been ordered only to observe, Mazaeus accompanied by his elite cavalry relinquished the lofty eminence overlooking the Macedonian encampment and returned to Darius' presence. The Macedonians seized the same height he had yielded; since it was more secure than the level ground and the fighting formations their foe fielded could be monitored from that mound. But a mist that had emerged from the humid hills in their environment, even though it did not obscure an overview, prevented the discernment of each regiment and its deployment. They had flooded the plain with their vast array and the din from so many thousands of men even filled the ears of those stood far away. The king's resolution began to waver in weighing up whether Parmenion's plan or his own were better; however, they had reached a point whence the army could not be withdrawn without calamity except through victory. Consequently, concealing his concerns, the king commanded the advance of the mercenary Paeonian cavalry. He had himself, as has been related, deployed his phalanx into two wings and he had designated his cavalry to protect these wings. And now the brightening daylight had dispersed the haze, plainly revealing his adversary's battle arrays. And his Macedonians, whether out of enthusiasm or to relieve the prelude's tedium, emitted a mighty rallying cry in fighting fashion. The Persians reciprocated so that the woods and the vales resounded with fearsome bellows. And now the Macedonians could scarcely be dissuaded from charging upon their foes. Yet, reckoning it better to curtain his encampment upon that same elevation, Alexander bade that they throw up a fortification and when they rapidly completed this assignment, the king withdrew into his tent, whence he could survey the whole battlefront of his opponent.

5.67 Then indeed the entire form of the forthcoming contest was before his gaze. The arms and the banners of warriors and steeds made resplendent displays. Amongst the enemy everything was being made ready with meticulous care, as the fastidiousness of the commanders in riding up and down their lines made clear. And many inconsequential events, such as a murmur from the men, neighing from the nags and the glinting and glimmering of arms, disturbed a mind made anxious by the suspense. Therefore, either due to genuine irresolution or else in order to put his officers to the test, the king convened a council to consult as to which course of action would be for the best. **Parmenion,** the most expert of his marshals in the art of war, **advised that a sneak attack rather than a battle was called for. Their adversaries could be surprised in the dead of night.** Having incompatible customs and mutually unintelligible tongues and being startled out of their sleep by an unforeseen fright, how could they possibly unite in the confusion of a nocturnal fight? But in broad daylight, the Macedonians would from the first be faced by the fearsome figures of the Scythians and the Bactrians: their faces furry and their hair unkempt, not to mention their extraordinarily huge height. Troops are more than reasonably upset by such silly and absurd sorts of threat. In that situation such a multitude could engulf a smaller force, for the fight was being fought in a wideopen plain, rather than in a narrow and constricted Cilician course. Practically everyone concurred with Parmenion and Polyperchon swore that victory was unequivocally vested in that plan. It was the latter upon whom **Alexander** fixed his gaze and to whom he **delivered a counter-statement**, since he had recently reproached Parmenion more stingingly than he had meant and was reluctant to repeat that admonishment: "The skills in which you would school me are theft and skulduggery, for their only prayer lies in secrecy. I shall not suffer my reputation repeatedly to be undermined either by the absence of Darius or a confined pass or nocturnal chicanery. **I am resolved to attack in broad daylight, as I prefer to risk regretting the outcome** of this fight, **than be shamed by stealing my victory by night**.[135] Additionally, it has been reported to me that the barbarians are standing at arms and watching vigilantly, so that it would not actually be possible to come upon them unexpectedly. Therefore, it is for a pitched battle that I bid you to make ready." Then he sent them off to refresh themselves, having thus incited them against the enemy.

5.68 Darius, having inferred that his opponent would do as Parmenion had counselled, ordered that the steeds should stand bridled, that a large fraction of his army should stay armed and that the vigilance of the night watch should be redoubled. Consequently, his entire camp was effulgent with fire. In the company of his commanders and his relations he himself did the rounds of his regiments as they stood at their stations, invoking the Sun, Mithras and the sacred eternal flame to inspire them with courage in keeping with the record of their forbears and their immemorial fame. And certainly, said he, if the signs of divine support could be sensed by the human mind, then the gods stood behind them. They had, he added, recently struck a sudden terror into the minds of the Macedonians, who were still frantically casting aside their weapons and suitable suffering would soon be sought from these madmen by the deities of the domains of the Persians. Nor was their leader any saner than they, for in the way of a wild beast he had fixed his gaze upon his prey and was careering into the pitfall behind which this prize lay.

5.69 Amongst the Macedonians too there was similar apprehension, and they spent the night in fear, as if that were when the battle was in contention. Alexander, never in a greater state of agitation, bade that Aristander be called to preside over prayers and devotion. Robed in brilliant white, his head veiled, and holding out ahead of him the sacred fronds, the seer led the royal orisons to propitiate Zeus and Athena Nike *and after made offerings to Fear.*[136] Then, only when he had performed the sacrificial rite, **the king returned to his tent to rest for what was left of the night. But he could neither fall asleep nor relax: he**

---

[135] See Plutarch, *Alexander* 31.7 for Alexander refusing to steal a victory.

[136] See Plutarch, *Alexander* 31.4 for the sacrifice to *Phobos*.

Book 5: 14th October 332BC – 1st October 331BC

fretted *whether he should launch his attacks from the crest of the ridge against the Persian right wing or else rush head-on upon the enemy, whilst pondering whether swerving his front against their left wing would be preferable, irresolutely.* Eventually, at about the morning watch, his body being overburdened by his mind's anxiety, he slept exceptionally soundly. And already by daybreak Alexander's commanders had gathered to accept their orders, astonished by the unaccustomed silence enveloping the headquarters. *For on other occasions he had been in the habit of summoning them and sometimes chiding the tardy.* Now they were incredulous that he had actually failed to awake for the ultimate decisive tourney *and they began to believe that he was quailing in trepidation rather than sleeping restfully.* Yet none among his Bodyguards dared to enter his tent. *And now the moment was imminent, but without the orders of their commanders the troops could neither take up their arms nor form up by regiment.* After having waited a long while, Parmenion pronounced on his own authority that the soldiers should eat *and make ready.* But the king continued to slumber, though it had become necessary that the army should set forth urgently. Then, finally, Parmenion made entry to the king's tent, calling out his name repeatedly, but, when he could not rouse Alexander by voice alone, he shook him gently and confided: "It is fully light and our adversaries are advancing drawn up in fighting formation. Where's your lively disposition? Usually, indeed, you rouse the actual sentries."

5.70 Alexander retorted: "Do you suppose I could have slept before I had relieved my mind of all the anxieties that postponed my tranquillity?" *Then he ordered that the trumpet blast be blown that signalled the onset of hostilities.* And, when Parmenion relentlessly expressed his incredulity at Alexander's claim to have fallen asleep carefree, the king responded *grinning*: "It's not so surprising. When Darius was scorching the earth, devastating villages and spoiling provisions, it drove me round the bend, but now indeed what have I to fear, when he gives me a battle to contend? Now *that he has concentrated his contingents,* in a single day we shall make an end, curtailing the toil and risk that would otherwise extend. *By Heracles, he has fulfilled my heart's desire, but the reckoning behind this rationale shall subsequently transpire. Let you rejoin the regiments that you respectively lead. I shall join you imminently and explain how I wish you to proceed.*" Alexander was only in the habit of donning a cuirass on very rare occasions and then at the urging of his Friends rather than through apprehension at entering into hazardous situations, but that time at any rate he assumed this bodily protection then went forth to meet his legions. Never before had they seen their king possessed of such alacrity and from his dauntless expression they conceived a firm expectation of victory.

Figure 5.6. Alexander and Aristander sacrifice to Fear by André Castaigne (1898)

5.71 After having *a section of* the rampart levelled, **Alexander ordered** that his forces march forth and that *his line of battle be assembled.* The king stationed the royal cavalry squadron, called the Agema, under the command of Cleitus, dubbed the Black, on his right wing. Adjoining them were the rest of the Friends led by Philotas, Parmenion's son, who also had overall command of the other seven squadrons successively flanking him. *Last of these was the squadron of Meleager, which was followed by the phalanx.* Behind *the phalanx in reserve* stood the Silver Shield[137] infantry under the command of Nicanor *another* son of Parmenion. Next in line lay the regiment *from Elimiotis* led by Coenus and after him the Lyncestian and Orestian regiment was posted *under Perdiccas. Meleager commanded* the next regiment *and after him* Polyperchon led *the Stymphaean contingent. Then came the foreign troops, whose commander, Amyntas, was absent.* Philip the son of Balacrus, *who had only recently been received into alliance,* was running these regiments. *Such was the composition of the right wing. On the left,* Craterus held the next command. Here were the combined Peloponnesian and Achaean cavalry, then the horsemen from *Phthiotis and* Malis and mounted Locrians *and Phocians* adjoining them, *all led by Erigyius of Mytilene.* Their flank was covered *by the ranks* of the Thessalian cavalry, commanded by Philip. *They far excelled the rest in their combat capability and in their horsemanship. Next to them the king*

---

[137] The *argyraspides*: the name in given at this juncture by both Diodorus and Curtius, the latter using the correct Greek term; hence it must be taken from Cleitarchus. They are also called *hypaspists*; it seems that they only became *argyraspides* when Alexander distributed silver embossed shields in India (Curtius 8.5.4), so Cleitarchus might be using the term anachronistically here.

stationed the Achaean mercenaries. And the ranks of the infantry were covered by the cavalry. Such was the left-wing front. But in order that his shorter ranks could not be outflanked due to the numerical superiority of the enemy, the king *enclosed the back of his dispositions with robust battalions. He also* reinforced his flanks with reserves, not facing forwards, but rather towards the sides, *so that, if his foe should try to go around to attack behind his battle lines, they would stand ready to fight back. The Agrianians were here with Attalus as their commander and the Cretan bowmen were joined with them at this station. The hindmost ranks were rearward facing, so as to defend a ring around his entire formation. The Illyrians were in this location combined with mercenary squadrons and there too he set the lightly armed Thracians in position.* And by these dispositions he made his ranks so adaptable that those that stood at the rear to resist encirclement could nevertheless turn around and be faced to the front. Hence the front was not better defended than the flanks, nor were the flanks better protected than the hindmost ranks.[138]

5.72 *Having thus configured his army,* Alexander instructed his soldiery that *if the barbarians sent their scythed chariots against them with a great din, then* they should silently open their ranks to receive them as they impetuously rushed on in, for he had no doubt that they would gallop through without doing injury, so long as their path were blocked by nobody. *However, if the chariots were sent forth without any clamouring, then* they were to panic them by beating their shields with their spears *and hollering and to stab their javelins up through the hides of the frightened horses from both sides. Those commanding the wings were bidden to space their soldiers such that they should neither be outflanked due to standing too near to one another nor spread so much as to make their rearmost ranks disappear. The baggage along with every detainee, amongst whom the mother and offspring of Darius were kept in custody, he placed upon the high hill hard by the battlefield leaving a skeleton guard. As was customary, Parmenion was put in charge of the left wing, whilst* a station on the right wing was taken by the king.

5.73 They had still not closed to within a javelin's flight, when Bion, a turncoat, rushed across to reach **Alexander** as fast as he might, declaring that Darius had driven iron spikes into the dust, where he thought that his foe's cavalry would make their thrust and he had marked the place with care, so that his own side could avoid the snare. The king, having called for the informer to be escorted, convened his captains and told them what had been reported, warning them to avoid the designated vicinity and to highlight the danger to their cavalry.[139]

---

[138] Cf. Frontinus, *Strategemata* 2.3.19.

[139] These kinds of spikes are called caltrops: cf. Polyaenus 4.3.17.

5.74 However, the army was unable to hear the king when he issued exhortations, for their ears were filled with the furore from the two opposing formations. But cantering between his commanders and his companions in the sight of all he **voiced these expostulations:** "After traversing so many lands in the hope of the victory for which we shall be contending, just this single struggle is outstanding. **Recall the Granicus River, the crags of Cilicia** and Syria and Egypt conquered in the course of our journey. These should be your inspiration for high hopes of huge glory. **Having had repeatedly to be rallied from flight, it will only be if they cannot flee that the Persians will stand and fight.** It is now the third day that, white with terror, they have stood rooted to the spot weighed down by their arms and armour. There is no better indication of their desperation, than that they have subjected their towns and their farms to incineration, thereby conceding that whatever they do not destroy is ours to enjoy. And *you should not be much afraid of the boastful names of obscure nations, for it is irrelevant to the outcome of the war which of their number are Scythians and which Cadusians.* Insofar as they have so long stayed unfound, they are bound to be unrenowned, for the valorous are never without their reputations, whereas shirkers levered from their lairs contribute nothing but their appellations. Through their valiance the Macedonians have guaranteed that there is no place in the whole world unaware of the bravery of their breed. Take a good look at the rabble in the ranks of our enemies. Some have nothing but a javelin, whilst others fling stones from a sling. Few indeed have proper panoplies. Therefore, *though more stand on their side, more on our side shall be engaging.* Neither shall I expect you valiantly to charge into this contest, unless I myself am the exemplar of courage for all the rest. You shall find me fighting before of our foremost banner. Ornamenting my body, I bear many scars to attest to my valour. You know for yourselves that from the communal spoils I am almost alone in taking no share, but employ the prizes of victory for your care and accoutrement. But it is to the courageous that I have addressed this encouragement. Were there any here of a dissimilar disposition, I should have given them a different disquisition: that we have reached a point from which flight is not a possibility; that, after such expansive territory has been left in our tracks and we have put so many rivers and mountain ranges behind our backs, we must fight to make the journey to our own hearths in our home country." Thereby he inspired his commanders and the immediate bystanders amongst the military.

5.75 Darius was on his left wing ensconced amidst mass formations of his soldiery, choice cavalry and elite infantry, and he had expressed contempt for the thin ranks of his adversary, reckoning that the extension of Alexander's wings had made his battlefront empty. But, being raised up in his chariot, with outstretched arms he swept his gaze right and left around his surrounding arrays, saying: "We, that just recently were the lords of lands washed by the Ocean on the one hand and extending to the Hellespont at their western end, must fight now not for eminence but rather for our existence and for what matters more to you than existence: your very independence. This day shall see re-established or

Book 5: 14th October 332BC – 1st October 331BC

finished an empire larger than any other age has witnessed. At the Granicus the least part of our manpower engaged the enemy. Being vanquished in Cilicia, Syria could give us sanctuary and the Tigris and the Euphrates were deep defences of our territory. But we have arrived at a place, from which, if thrown back, there is no space left to flee. Everything in our rear has been consumed by these protracted hostilities. Our towns have lost their dwellers and our land lacks tillers. Our wives too and our children accompany our companies, ready prey for our adversaries, unless we interpose our bodies in defence of our dearest responsibilities."

5.76 "For my own part, I have fielded forces such as this almost immeasurable plain can scarcely contain. I have distributed arms and steeds and I have guaranteed that even so vast a multitude should not lack provisions and I have selected a location in which we can fully deploy our fighting divisions. Everything else lies within your power. You need merely dare to conquer, scorning their reputation, which is the most worthless weapon in confronting a brave warrior. What you have feared up until now as boldness was actually recklessness, which, having lost its initial impetus, like some bee that has shot its sting, becomes powerless. Furthermore, these plains have made manifest their sparseness, which the crags of Cilicia suppressed. Behold their thin lines, their widespread wings and their centre hollowed and frail, for he has averted his rearmost ranks from us, so that they are already turning tail. By Heracles, they can be trampled beneath the hooves of our horses, even if I send forth nothing but our scythed chariot forces. And we shall have won the war, if we win this fight, for they do not even have a chance at flight. The Euphrates over there and here the Tigris prohibit them from getting out of this."

5.77 "Furthermore, factors that formerly favoured them have now been turned about. Their army is laden with plunder, whereas ours is wieldy and lightly kitted out. Hence, hampered by loot lifted from us, we shall put them to the sword and the same stuff as provides our victory shall also provide its reward. But if the reputation of their nation disturbs any of you, know that it is the Macedonian panoplies that are there and not their actual bodies. For we in our turn have shed their blood in large amounts and losses are more serious amongst modest headcounts. And as for Alexander, however imposing he may appear to the cowardly and craven, he is but a single being and, if you hold with my opinion, a reckless and irrational person, who owes more to our quaking than to his own dash and daring. But it is impossible for anything to prove lasting without being based upon planning. Though fair winds may seem to blow, they eventually cease to pillow rashness. Furthermore, the twists of fate are fast and unpredictable and Fortune's favours are never reliable. Perchance the gods have ordained our fate thus: that the Persian Empire, which they have raised to a pinnacle of power as it thrived through three decades beyond two centuries, should be shaken rather than shattered by a shock of some gravity in order to remind us of our mortal frailties, which too easily slip from memory in the midst of prosperity. We were carrying out campaigning in Greece but recently. Now we are repulsing an assault upon us in our own country. We are tossed in our turn by Fortune's fickleness. Obviously, this Empire that is sought by both sides, one or other people will not possess. Nevertheless, even if no hope were left to us, we ought still to be spurred by dire necessity. For we have reached the worst extremity. My mother together with two daughters of mine and Ochus, conceived in the expectation of his inheritance of our dominions, and princes who are progeny of our royal houses and your erstwhile commanders, kept fettered like felons. Except for what is left to me in you, I am the greater part held hostage. Let us rescue my flesh and blood from bondage and bring back those dear to me, my mother and offspring. For your own children you would not shirk from dying. As for my wife, I lost her during her incarceration. But you may trust that all the rest are even now holding out their hands to you in supplication, imploring the gods of our nation, entreating your aid, your pity and your devotion, to set them free from their shackles, from slavery and from humiliating submission. Or do you suppose them patient with their enslavement to those of whom they disdain the government?"

5.78 "I see that the lines of the enemy are now advancing, but the closer I come to the contest the less content I can be with the words I have been pronouncing. By the gods of our country and by the eternal fire that is borne upon altars before us, and by the glow of the sun that ascends within the bounds of my empire and by the everlasting memory of Cyrus, who first wrenched the rulership from the Medes and the Lydians and apportioned it to the Persians, I beseech you to save from the utmost shame the people of Persia and our nation's name. Go forward in high spirits and full of confidence, in order that the glory got from your forefathers be left to your descendants. In your hands and by your right, you grip our liberty, our aspirations and our might. He who scorns death escapes mortality, but it always overtakes the most cowardly. A chariot conveys me, not only because of the customs of our country, but also to be seen the more conspicuously, and neither am I contrary to your copying me, whether I prove to set an example of cowardice or of bravery."

5.79 In the meantime **Alexander ordered his ranks to advance obliquely, both in order to circumvent the snares' vicinity and to intercept Darius, who had a wing to oversee. Darius too turned his own men in the same direction,** having bidden Bessus to urge the Massagetae cavalry on his left[140] to charge the flank of Alexander's wing formation. **Darius had the scythed chariots in front of his station, which upon his signal flung themselves collectively against the opposition. The charioteers galloped headlong** towards the enemy, *in order to fell more of the insufficiently forewarned warriors through their impetuosity. Accordingly, some were lacerated by the lances that lunged along far to the fore of the poles of the vehicles, whilst others were dissected by the scythes set on both sides of the curricles. Nor did the Macedonians give way steadily, but rather left their*

---

[140] Curtius 4.15.2 seems to say that the charge was against Alexander's left wing, but the Massagetae were stationed on Darius's extreme left wing near Bessus (Curtius 4.12.7).

lines disorderly as they scattered readily. And additionally, Mazaeus, master of most of the cavalry, *compounded the consternation by simultaneously* sending *his serried squadrons against the enemy.*[141] *And he ordered two thousand Cadusians and* a thousand *select Scythian horsemen to wheel around the flank of their adversary to capture the baggage* ensconced in its den. For he considered that the captives, who were also being guarded, would break out of their bonds upon perceiving the approach of their countrymen.

Figure 5.7. The charge of the scythed chariots by André Castaigne (1898)

5.80 But this did not escape the notice of Parmenion, who was on the left wing. Hence, he hastily dispatched Polydamas, both to point out their peril and to seek orders as to what they should be doing. Alexander, upon hearing Polydamas out, replied: "Go tell Parmenion that, if we are victorious in this contention, we shall not only recover what is ours, but shall also seize what belongs to the opposition. Therefore, let him not divert any men from his formation, but in order to be worthy of my father Philip and of me, let him scorn the loss of our luggage and fight the more valiantly." Meanwhile, **the barbarians having ransacked the baggage train and many of its guards having been slain, the captives were struck from their chains and, snatching whatever weapons were to hand, they joined their own side's cavalry band** to beset the Macedonians, who were thus encircled by a second strand. *There was uproar and havoc amongst the*

---

[141] From this point Curtius switches back and forth between the scythed chariot attack and the raid on the Macedonian base-camp, whereas Diodorus deals with the two actions successively. Since it is unlikely that Curtius would invent such alternations, whereas Diodorus had a strong motive to try to remove them in his ambition of producing a highly summarised account, I have concluded that the switchbacks are probably an authentic feature of Cleitarchus that Curtius reproduced.

tents at this rapid turn of events. The captive women attendant upon Sisygambis were joyous in announcing that Darius was victorious, their foes having been overthrown with great mayhem, even their baggage having ultimately been stripped from them. Most of them rushed to welcome the forces of their country, for they believed that the same outcome had been achieved universally and that the Persians were running around pillaging in the aftermath of victory. Yet Sisygambis, though the mother of Darius, remained emotionless and unmoving, when the captives exhorted her to raise her spirits from her grieving. *She uttered not one word and neither her pallor nor her expression altered, but* she sat unstirred, *I suppose* fearing to offend Fortune through premature jollity *or repudiate her gratitude for Alexander's generosity. And this she did in such a degree that those that beheld her were even unsure of her loyalty.*

5.81 In the meantime Menidas, a commander of cavalry for Alexander, arrived with a few squadrons to bring the baggage succour – it is unknown whether on his own initiative or by the king's order. But he could not cope with the Cadusians and Scythians charging, for on scarcely skirmishing he fled back to the king, not so much the baggage's saviour as a witness to its forfeiture. Alexander's setbacks had already upset his plans and he was worried, not without justification, that attention to the recovery of their possessions might divert his troops from the main action. Hence, he sent Aretes, the leader of the lancers that are called sarissaphoroi to contend with the Scythians. **Whilst this was happening, the chariots, which had thrown the ranks into confusion around the foremost standards, had** assailed the phalanx, *who linked shields and by drumming upon them with their spears raised a fearful din as commanded by the king. When their horses shied, most of the chariots veered about and careered back to collide with the ranks of their own side. Others were not deterred, but hurtled onward into the Macedonian lines and were received with stalwart resolve as* the troops channelled their ranks like valleys into which the chariots were trammelled. Wielding their spears *in concert,* they skewered *the flanks of* the horses *from both sides as they rushed recklessly on through these courses. Then they began to mob the chariots and to hurl forth their combatants. A huge number of crashed chariots and their crushed crews filled the field's expanse, for the charioteers could not control their terrified animals, which by incessantly thrashing their necks had not only cast off their yokes but had even overturned the vehicles. Those wounded dragged along the slain and could neither pull up in their panic nor progress due to the awful strain. Nevertheless,* a few of the chariots dodged their way through to the rear of the formation, condemning those they encountered to a wretched extinction, *for severed segments of men were strewn upon the soil. Such was the sharpness and velocity of the scythes, cunningly devised to despoil victims of their limbs, that arms were amputated with their shields and often slickly sliced necks sent heads tumbling into the fields with eyes wide open and a frozen*

Book 5: 14th October 332BC – 1st October 331BC

expression or else slashes to the ribs left a fatal incision. Since those freshly injured perceived no pain from their lacerations, though maimed and drained, they did not even set aside their weapons, until they had so copiously bled that they fell forward stone dead.

5.82 *As the main ranks began to close, they discharged their missiles using slings and bows and, after flinging their javelins, they came in contact and began to exchange blows. The cavalry were first into the fray and, the Macedonians being stationed on their own right, Darius, who held his own left in sway, flung his mounted kinsmen against them in his sight. These were men selected for bravery and loyalty, all one thousand of them being bound into a single chiliarchy.[142] Conscious that the king was overseeing their conduct, they faced all the missiles chucked his way with alacrity. Attached to them were the Apple Bearer infantry, as valorous as they were numerous, and additionally the Mardians and Cossaeans, famed for their dynamism and audacity, together with the entire palace guard and the bravest and best of the Indian soldiery. Collectively, they raised a resounding battle cry and engaged their opponents valiantly. Then the Macedonians were hard pressed by the enemy on account of Darius' numerical superiority.*

5.83 In the interim Aretes, having cut down the leader of the Scythians who were pillaging the baggage, set into them the more seriously since they were cowering. Then, directed by Darius, the Bactrians came upon the scene and tipped the fortune of the fighting. Hence many Macedonians fell at their first onset and still more fled back to the king. Thereupon the Persians gave a yell of such a sort as victors are wont to expel and fell fiercely upon their enemy there as though they had been put to flight everywhere. But Alexander upbraided those that were intimidated and exhorted his men, single-handedly reviving their contention of the tussle that had already begun to slacken. **Considering the successive successes of the opposition,** Alexander *knew that now was the moment for him to repair the fortunes of his forces by his personal intervention. Having finally restored the resolve of his troops, he* **led the royal squadron and the rest of the elite cavalry in a dashing charge** *towards Darius' position.* There had been a thinning of the Persian ranks facing his right wing, because the Bactrians had withdrawn from there to join the baggage fighting. Hence Alexander tore into their attenuated rows and burst through with a great slaughter of his foes.

---

[142] Greek term for a regiment of a thousand men.

Figure 5.8. Alexander's charge in the Battle of Arbela (~1880)

5.84 However, the leftmost Persians swung their lines up behind the focus of the fighting in the hope of being able to box in the king. And stuck in the middle, Alexander would have been in grave peril had not the Agrianian cavalry spurred on their steeds to assail the barbarians surrounding their ruler, compelling them to wheel and confront them by cutting into their rear. Their mutual battlefronts were in turbulence. Both before him and at his back Alexander faced opponents and those that beset him from behind, were themselves closely confined by the Agrianians. The Bactrians, who had been pillaging the baggage, were unable to reform their lines on their return. Several formations at once had broken away from the main fronts and were fighting wherever chance had clashed them together in the churn. The two kings, whose formations had virtually merged, gave fire to the fighting. Although the number of wounded was about the same on both sides, more of the Persians were perishing. **Darius was riding in a chariot *hurling javelins*,** whereas Alexander was mounted on horseback and both sovereigns were defended by crack troops, with no regard for their own preservation, for if their king were lost, they neither wished to survive nor had any hope of salvation. Each of these men reckoned it admirable to fall in battle before the eyes of his king. Yet they were exposed to the most peril whom their guards were best protecting, since everyone aspired to the distinction of killing a king.

Book 5: 14th October 332BC – 1st October 331BC

Figure 5.9. An eagle hangs over Alexander in the Battle of Arbela (1696)

5.85 Now, whether it was a mirage or the real thing, those around Alexander thought they spied an eagle hovering just a bit above the head of their king. It was unperturbed by either the din from the fighting or the shrieks of the dying, but seemed to be hanging around Alexander's horse rather than flying. Certainly, the seer Aristander, clad in a white robe and brandishing a laurel wreath in his right hand, persisted in pointing out the bird to the troops embroiled in the hostilities, deeming it undoubtedly an augury of their victory. In consequence, they, who shortly before had been filled with dismay, were inspired with confidence and fired with enthusiasm for the fray. And **as the kings converged, Alexander began to rain javelins upon Darius, whose charioteer,** *standing in front of him handling the horses,* **was transfixed by one such spear. And a great groan resounded amongst those that surrounded Darius, so that the Persians in the main and the Macedonians too did not doubt that the king himself had been slain.** *Therefore, his kinsmen and his guards with their doleful wailing and undisciplined shouting and moaning threw practically the entire Persian battlefront into confusion, though it had until that point proved a match for its opposition.* The chariot was exposed by the flight of the troops on its left flank, so those to its right received it and tucked it behind the banks of their densely packed ranks. It is said that Darius, his sabre drawn, wavered as to whether by an honorable death to shun the shame of flight.

But, conspicuous in his chariot, he thought it ignominious to forsake his forces, whilst they had not all abandoned the fight. And as he dithered undecided between hope and despair, **the Persians gradually gave ground and their lines began to tear.** Alexander, who had changed his horse again, having exhausted several steeds that day, was stabbing at the faces of those that still resisted and at the backs of those running away. So now *with the complete disintegration of his ranks, Darius became exposed on both his flanks, so it had already ceased to be a battle and become butchery, as* Darius himself wheeled his chariot to flee. The victor was hot on the heels of the rout, but the dust kicked about by the Persian cavalry billowed up into the sky clouding visibility. It was just as if they were roaming around in darkness, and only at the sound of a signal or a known voice could they coalesce. *Yet amidst the cries of the dying and the thunder of the cavalry,* they could clearly hear the cracking of the reins, with which the horses *that drew the chariot* were lashed repeatedly. *These were the only traces they could discern of the fleeing king, so they were unable to tell which way he was heading.*

5.86 *Yet on the Macedonian left wing, which, as previously stated, was in the charge of Parmenion, the affairs of the respective sides were in quite a different condition.* Mazaeus, the commander of the Persian right, had charged powerfully with virtually his entire cavalry and was pressing upon the flanks of the Macedonians quite severely. *Parmenion fought back fiercely with the Thessalian cavalry and for a while even seemed on the verge of victory, which was a testament to the Thessalians' fighting virtuosity. But Mazaeus had already begun to encircle the Macedonian battlefront through his numerical superiority, when* Parmenion ordered some horsemen to report to Alexander that they found themselves in a situation of considerable criticality: he would not be able to avert a collapse, unless he were reinforced rapidly. The king had already advanced a long way in the tracks of those Persians who were scuttling away and was close upon their backs, when he received Parmenion's dire communiqué. *He called upon his cavalry to rein in their mounts and the army checked its advance. The king gnashed his teeth that victory was being ripped from his grip, since Alexander was not so successful in his pursuit as Darius in giving him the slip. Meanwhile* Mazaeus had heard a rumour that his ruler had been bested by the Macedonian *and hence, despite being in the ascendancy, he was nevertheless alarmed by his side's situation, so he began to press his assault less vigorously.* Parmenion *was of course unaware of the cause for the spontaneous slackening of the attack, but he readily* took advantage of the opportunity to launch a fightback. He summoned the Thessalian cavalry *and queried: "Do you see that those, who were a moment ago savagely assailing us, are giving ground, scared by some sudden menace? Undoubtedly, some success of our sovereign has also secured us a chance to win. Slain Persians are strewn all about. Why are you lingering? Are you not even a match for such as have been put to rout?" The truth of what he was saying was plain to see and hope had even revived the weary, so they applied their spurs and surged upon the enemy. And these no longer gave ground gradually, but at a faster pace, so that they were fleeing effectively, except that they had not turned face. Yet still being unaware of the circumstances of his sovereign on the right wing, Parmenion held back his men. Being thus afforded a gap in the fighting, Mazaeus, ever the clever strategist, used the dust cloud to disappear and did not follow the other barbarians in withdrawing to the rear. Instead, he took a longer and therefore safer detour in the opposite direction and brought his troops into villages lying behind the Macedonian position.[143] Thence he crossed the Tigris via a circuitous course and entered Babylon with the remnants of his defeated force.*

5.87 *Darius had hastened with a handful of companions in his flight to reach the River Lycus, after crossing which he wondered whether he should break down the bridge, for it was reported that their foes were already approaching. But countless thousands of his men had not yet reached the rivercourse, so, if he destroyed the crossing, he saw that they would fall prey to the enemy force. Upon departing, having left the bridge standing, he is reliably reported to have said that he preferred to provide passage for his pursuers, than scupper the escape route of his survivors.* Thus, Darius himself, covering a vast distance in his flight, reached Arbela at about midnight.

5.88 Who could possibly grasp in his mind let alone verbally express such twists of fate: the wholesale slaughter of commanders and their contingents; the flight of the vanquished; the calamities that befell individuals and the entire state? Alas! Fortune congregated the events of practically an entire century onto one single date! Some fled by the shortest available route out of there, whilst others made for remote woodlands and tracks of which their pursuers were unaware. Cavalry and infantry were intermingled and unled; the armed were mixed up with the disarmed and the unscathed marched amongst many that bled. From then on compassion was consumed by dread and amidst mutual lamentation those that could not keep up were left for dead. **The fleeing Persians** were parched by thirst, particularly the injured and the spent, so that they sprawled facedown scattered along all the streams with mouths immersed as onwards the waters went. Since, when the water became muddy, they still gulped it avidly, the pressure of the slime distended their bellies quite promptly, such that their legs became sluggish and slack. Being then *overtaken by the enemy,* they **were goaded by renewed attack, so that the whole region became bedecked with bodies by**

---

[143] Diodorus 17.61.1 attributes this evasive manoeuvre to Darius, but it is obvious by analogy with Curtius 4.16.7 and in view of the clear statements that Darius rode straight to Arbela that Cleitarchus actually wrote this of Mazaeus. Most likely some intermediary misread or otherwise incorrectly transmitted the name. Mazaeus cannot readily have crossed the Tigris without crossing Darius's line of retreat except by going behind Macedonian lines, so this makes perfect sense.

the butchery. Some, finding the nearby brooks occupied, turned further aside, to glean whatever hidden moisture trickled anywhere. Thus, there was no pool so drained or so secluded that its thirsty trackers were eluded. And indeed, from the villages closest to the road there resounded the wailing of women and the pleas of old men, calling in the barbarian fashion upon Darius, their sovereign up until then.

5.89 As already related, Alexander had checked the charge of his forces and had arrived at the River Lycus, where the bridge was overladen, as the number of fugitives was enormous. Being hard pressed by their opponents, many of them threw themselves into the river's torrents. And heavily armed as well as fatigued by both the fight and their flight, they were consumed by the current's turbulence. Already the river, let alone the bridge, could not hold all those escaping, as regiment upon regiment kept gormlessly accumulating. For when men's minds are captured by consternation, they dread only that which initiated their trepidation. Being pressed by his men not to postpone the pursuit of his unpunished opponents, Alexander argued that their arms were either dulled or wearied, that their bodies were worn out from chasing with such persistence and that night would soon intercede. But really, he was anxious about his left wing, which he supposed still to be standing and fighting, so he was bent upon offering them the support of their king. And he had already wheeled about, when riders sent by Parmenion reported that he was the victor in that sector too. However, Alexander encountered no greater danger that day than whilst he was heading back to camp with his retinue. He was accompanied by just a disorderly few, who were exulting in their victory, since they thought that all of their foes had fallen in the fighting or had fled the field impetuously. Then quite suddenly he was confronted by a body of cavalry, who reined back initially, but spurred their squadrons against him with hostility upon perceiving the meagreness of the Macedonian tally. The king was marching at the head of his unit, disregarding the risk rather than scorning it. But neither was he then let down by the perpetual good fortune he enjoyed in every precarious circumstance. For when the leader of the cavalry, being keen for combat and consequently incautious, dashed towards him, the king transfixed him with his lance. And when he had toppled from his mount, the king skewered the next one and then several more men with the same weapon. His Friends too sailed in upon their disconcerted opponents. But the Persians were not slain without gaining recompense, for the entire battlefield saw no tougher contention than that engaged upon by this improvised battalion. When finally, in the fading light, flight seemed safer than prolonging the fight, the Persian formation split up and withdrew *into the encroaching night.* After coming through this exceptional jeopardy, the king led his men back to camp in safety.

5.90 *Combining cavalry and infantry casualties,* **ninety thousand of the Persians fell** *in this battle insofar as the victors were capable of determining the total.* **The Macedonians dead numbered** *fewer* **than five**

hundred, *but many more were wounded.*[144] Furthermore, this victory was attributable to the king's prowess rather than to his luck in the main. He won it with his brain rather than, as previously, through the intercession of the terrain. For he configured his forces most cleverly, as well as personally fighting most valiantly and with great perspicacity he disdained the loss of their baggage and personal property, since he perceived that victory would be decided at the front line of his army. And whilst the outcome of the contest remained in question, he behaved like the eventual champion. Thereafter, when he had daunted the enemy into stampeding, he pursued them judiciously rather than unrestrainedly, which is virtually incredible in view of his characteristic impetuosity. For, had he persisted in pressing upon the Persians as they withdrew, he would either have been defeated through his own fault or owed his victory to a viceroy's virtue. Lastly, had he been cowed in his confrontation with that considerable contingent of cavalry, he would, whilst on the crest of victory, have had either to flee disgracefully or to perish ignominiously.

5.91 *But neither should the commanders of Alexander's forces be defrauded of their share of the glory, for the injuries that they variously suffered are evidence of their bravery.* **Among the most eminent men, Hephaistion, who led the Bodyguards, was struck in the arm by a spear. Of the generals, Perdiccas and Coenus came near to being killed by arrows. So too was Menidas and others among the most senior fellows.** And if we wish fairly to assess the Macedonians that were present then, we shall allow that their king was wholly worthy of such men and his followers befitted so magnificent a sovereign. *And* **this was** *shown by* **the outcome of the battle near Arbela**, *for it was with this engagement that Alexander seized control of Asia on the twenty-sixth day of the month of Boedromion,*[145] *so the very next day was the fifth anniversary of the king's accession. This was so decisive a victory that none dared rebel thereafter, for the Persians after many years of their own mastery submissively accepted Alexander as their master.*

5.92 **Back in Greece many of the cities** *had become alarmed by the expansion of Macedonian dominance and* **had decided,** *whilst the Persian cause was still in existence,* **that they should seize the opportunity to recover their independence.** *They expected that Darius would support them and send them munificent moneys, so that they could enlist legions of mercenaries, whilst Alexander would not be able to divide his armies. If, alternatively, they looked on idly while the Persians were vanquished completely, the Greeks would stand alone and never again be able to reckon upon recovering their liberty. Additionally, a convulsion in Thrace*

---

[144] These figures are those given by Diodorus 17.61.3. Curtius 4.16.26 gives XL thousand Persian dead and fewer than CCC Macedonian casualties, but the numerical transmission in a Latin manuscript is more liable to corruption than the numbers expressed in words in Diodorus's Greek. For example, if XL in Curtius were a mistake for XC (which could very easily have happened), then Curtius would agree with Diodorus.

[145] Plutarch, *Camillus* 19.3.

that was quite timely appeared to grant the Greeks an ideal opportunity to make themselves free. Memnon, who had been made the marshal of Thrace, was a resolute fellow with a force of troops at his disposal. He suborned the barbarians, revolted against Alexander and raised a substantial army in no time at all, being blatantly bent on battle. Antipater was compelled to call upon his whole military and to cross Macedon and enter Thrace in order to campaign against Memnon. It was while the Regent was thus preoccupied that the Spartans, who had consistently denied the hegemony of Philip and Alexander, *considered the time ripe to launch hostilities, so they issued a call to arms to the Greeks for the united defence of their liberties. Nevertheless, the Athenians demurred, since, above all the other Greeks, it was they that Alexander had preferred. However, most of the Peloponnesians along with some others came to an accord and cemented a pact to resolve things through the sword. They enlisted the cream of their youths according to their availability from each city and recruited more than twenty thousand infantry and two thousand cavalry into their army. The Spartans had primacy* and inducted their entire military *with their king, Agis, holding the overall supremacy.*

5.93 *When* Antipater *learnt of the Greek aggression, he brought his Thracian offensive to an optimal conclusion and marched his whole force down into the Peloponnesian region. He incorporated troops from the loyal Greek cities and* augmented his army *to exceed forty thousand with ease. When a decisive battle took place* at Megalopolis in the Peloponnese,[146] **Agis** *charged into the focal point of the hostilities, cutting down his most resilient adversaries and driving back a large proportion of his enemies. Then the winners of this battle began to be put to flight, being cut down without reprisal, until they had led those too avidly hounding them right down onto level land. And there, at the first place they found in which they might stand and fight, they held their ground. Nevertheless, amongst all the Spartans their king retained pre-eminence, not just due to the splendour of his arms and person, but also in the vastness of his valiance, which was second to none. He was assaulted from all sides, sometimes hand-to-hand and sometimes from afar and for ages he swung his shield around to intercept every missile or else dodged them with a spar. But* his thighs were pierced by a lance in the end and haemorrhaging profusely they gave way whilst he still struggled to contend. *Therefore, his guards rapidly removed him from the field, carrying him back to camp by raising him up on his shield, though he could barely bear the agony from the jolting of his injury.*

---

[146] Curtius 6.1.1 opens here after a lacuna, introducing much more detail on the events. Probably Cleitarchus had given a lengthy introduction, explaining that Megalopolis was one of the few Peloponnesian cities to remain loyal to Macedon and that Antipater had come to its aid when it was close to surrender, engaging the army of the Spartan alliance in a narrow plain near the city.

Book 5: 14th October 332BC – 1st October 331BC

5.94 *Yet* the Spartans did not abandon the struggle, *but as soon as they had got to ground that was more defensible,* they closed ranks and received a torrent of their opponents upon their line of battle. *History records that no other contest was ever so ferocious. Well-matched were the forces of the two peoples whose prowess in warfare was most notorious. The Spartans were fixated by their past achievements, whilst the Macedonians were intent upon their current accomplishments. The former fought for their liberty and the latter for their hegemony. The Spartans lacked their leader, whilst the Macedonians wanted for room to manoeuvre. Additionally, so many reversals on a single day respectively raised the hopes and compounded the fears of either set of soldiers, as if Fortune were deliberately evening up this contest between the bravest of warriors. However, the constricted nature of the site where the battle continued to take its course did not allow either side to engage its entire force. Hence there were more men spectating than were actually exchanging blows and those who were beyond the range of javelins and arrows in rotation were bellowing to fire up their fellows.* At length, the lines of the Spartan allies began to exhibit exhaustion, *for they could hardly hold up weapons that were slick with perspiration. Then they began to retreat and, being harried by the opposition,* they gave way *more obviously with the victors closely pursuing the broken. And the Macedonians rushed across all the ground that had been held by the Spartans, hounding after* Agis *in person. That king,* upon seeing his men fleeing and the foremost of his foes approaching, bade that his bearers escape to serve Sparta by setting him down. *And upon trying his legs to see whether they would obey his will, but feeling them letting him down,* he sank to his knees donning his helmet hurriedly and brandished the spear in his right hand at his enemies using his shield to cover his body. Then he actually taunted his adversaries regarding which of them dared deserve to despoil him as a casualty. But there was nobody at all that would venture to engage him in close combat. So he was assailed from a distance by missiles, which he then hurled back felling some of his foes, until a long lance was implanted in his chest, which he had been forced to expose. When it was yanked from the injury, he leant his bowed and dazed head upon his shield momentarily, then, as breath and blood forsook him equally, *he collapsed dying to lie athwart his weaponry.* Thus, he perished *in the ninth year of his sovereignty.*[147]

5.95 Five thousand three hundred of the Spartans *and their allies* fell and another *three* thousand *five hundred* of Antipater's army as well, of whom

---

[147] Agis III succeeded his father, Archidamus III, to one of the dual Spartan kingships when the latter fell before the walls of Manduria in Italy in 338BC. It is possible that he ruled in 9 Attic years, if Archidamus died before the first New Moon after the Summer Solstice in 338BC (although Diodorus 16.63 & 16.88 suggests that it was on the same day as Chaeronea, which took place in August) and Megalopolis occurred after the same event in 331BC (which is likely).

fewer than a thousand were Macedonian.[148] However, hardly anyone returned to camp lacking any sort of laceration. This victory not only subdued the Spartans and those with whom they were allied, but all those who had been watching the outcome of the war from the sidelines were also thoroughly pacified. Nor was Antipater beguiled when those that offered him their congratulations betrayed dissenting sentiments in their facial expressions, but it was necessary that he allowed himself to be deluded, since he desired that the war be concluded. And although the outcome of the affair gave him some satisfaction, he nonetheless feared a grudging reaction, since he had exceeded the remit of a regent by such a major action. For despite that Alexander had desired the defeat of the enemy, he could not even manage to hold his tongue regarding the impropriety of Antipater's victory, reckoning that successes ceded to a deputy detracted from his own glory. Hence **Antipater**, who perfectly understood Alexander's psychology, did not dare personally **to impose the terms of his victory**, but **consulted a conference of the Greeks as to what it pleased them to decree.** Additionally, the Regent took as hostages a levy of the most prominent men among the Spartans totalling fifty.[149]

5.96 *Elsewhere in Europe, the uncle of the monarch of Macedon, that Alexander who was king of Epirus, had been invited into Italy, where the people of Tarentum had entreated his aid in combatting the Bruttii. He had been keen to charge in, as though the world had been partitioned, the East being allotted to Alexander the son of his sister, Olympias, and the West having fallen to him. And he considered that his opportunities would be no less in Italy, Sicily and Africa than those his nephew was encountering in Asia and Persia. Additionally, just as the Delphic Oracle had predicted a conspiracy against his nephew in Macedonia, so the Oracle of Zeus at Dodona had warned him to beware of the Acherusian River and the city of Pandosia. Since both lay in Epirus and Alexander was ignorant that identically named places existed in Italy, he had been the more eager to campaign overseas in order to dodge the dangers in his destiny. Therefore, when he arrived in Italy, he made war upon the Apulians initially, but he made peace and concluded an alliance with their king shortly, when he found out what was fated for their city.*

5.97 *Brundisium is a city held by the Apulians, though it was founded by the Aetolians, followers of Diomedes, that most glorious and noble leader, famed for his Trojan activities. However, they had been expelled by the Apulians. In consulting the oracles, the Aetolians had received a response that the place would belong in perpetuity to those that sought its return by embassy. Consequently, they had sent emissaries to propose with threats of belligerency that the Apulians should hand back their city. But the oracle became known to the Apulians, who slew every emissary and buried them within the bounds of the city, so that the site would indeed be theirs in perpetuity. Having thus fulfilled the prophecy, they had long held the city. When*

---

[148] Curtius 6.1.16 states fewer than a thousand Macedonians fell, but the figure of 3500 casualties in Antipater's army given by Diodorus 17.63.3 is a more likely total. Possibly, 2500 of the casualties in Antipater's army were among his allied troops, so there need be no real inconsistency here.

[149] Jacoby Fragment 4 of Cleitarchus (Harpocration s.v. *homereuontas*) attributed to Book 5; cf. Diodorus 17.73.6.

Book 5: 14th October 332BC – 1st October 331BC

Alexander heard this history, he refrained from further hostility towards them out of respect for ancient prophecy. Then he engaged the Lucanians and the Bruttii in warfare, seizing several of their cities. With the Metapontines, the Poediculi and the Romans he concluded alliances and treaties. But the Brutii and Lucanians gathered auxiliaries from neighbouring territories and with redoubled vehemence resumed their hostilities. In the course of this campaign the king was killed near to a Pandosia and a River Acheron as well, though he did not know the name of the fateful place before he fell and it was only as he was dying that he came to see that the threat of mortality that had led him to flee did not in fact lie in his home country. At public expense the citizens of Thurii ransomed and entombed his body.

5.98 Here ends the first part of the History Concerning Alexander, *which has recounted the events concerning that king up to the end of the fifth year of his reign.*

PART TWO

The world's an older place today
Than it ever used to be.
One time I heard a minstrel say:
It hurts to peddle melody,
For fatal tunes we people play
Echo still most violently:
Notes that kill and songs that slay,
Tones for turning flesh to clay
Make many men to melt away!
My music murders silently.

KEY
<u>**Underlined bold text for attributed Fragments of Cleitarchus**</u>
Bold text where there is overwhelming evidence
Bold italic text where there exists direct-firm evidence
Normal text where direct-weak evidence applies
Italic text where the evidence is conjectural

Book 6: October 2nd 331BC – July 330BC

The Escape of Darius and the Capture of Treasure at Arbela; Mennis and the Cave of Naphtha; The Occupation of Babylon; the Seizure of Susa; The Capture of the Susian Gates; Meeting with the Mutilated Greeks; The Burning of Persepolis; The Pursuit of Darius and his Murder by Bessus.

6.1 *Here begins the second part of the history concerning Alexander by Cleitarchus of Alexandria at the start of the sixth year of the king's reign, which commenced in the course of the second year of the one hundred and twelfth Olympiad on the twenty-seventh day of the month Boedromion as the Athenians reckon in accordance with the regulation of the Lunar phases by the goddess Selene.*[150]

6.2 It was almost midnight when **Darius reached Arbela following the nearby fight**. There he found that Fortune had fetched up a large fraction of his friends and soldiers in their flight. Gathering them about him, he explained that he was in no doubt that it was the major cities and the farmland fertile in all sorts of resources that Alexander would make towards, for both his troops and their ruler were fixated upon rich and readily reaped rewards. As things stood this should prove to be Darius' deliverance, since **he would head into the wastes** with disencumbered contingents. **The upper satrapies, the further reaches of his realm, from which he could readily extract fresh warriors, were still intact.** So, let that greediest of tribes go garnering his treasure and glutting itself with gold out of ravenous hunger, for they would soon become his plunder. Experience had taught him that fine furnishings, concubines and regiments of eunuchs were nothing other than burdens and impediments. Being likewise hindered, Alexander would be found wanting in those traits whereby he had formerly conquered.

6.3 This seemed a counsel of complete despair to everyone, since thereby they certainly forsook that wealthiest of cities, Babylon. Subsequently Susa would be seized and then the victor would overwhelm all his objectives in the war, the rest of the jewels of the realm. Yet Darius proceeded to construe that in episodes of adversity the course to pursue is not what is glorious to tell but what the practicalities compel. For war is waged with steel, not with gold, nor in the shelter of cities, but by the bold. Everything is ceded to the soldierly. So it was that their forefathers, though they had at first suffered regressions, had rapidly retrieved

---

[150] The mention in the manuscripts of Diodorus 17.63.4 that the first part of his account of Alexander's reign ended here strongly suggests that he had found a similar division in his source, Cleitarchus; the date was 2nd October 331BC in the Julian Calendar, but Cleitarchus would have specified dates using Attic months according to strict Lunar regulation (i.e. not the so-called Archon calendar, which often strayed from strict Lunar regulation) with years identified according to the count of 4-year Olympiads starting in 776BC following Timaeus of Tauromenium.

Book 6: October 2nd 331BC – July 330BC

their former possessions. ***Therefore***, either having bolstered their morale or because they accepted his authority rather than his strategy, **Darius entered upon the bounds of Media,** *so as to win a respite by far-flung flight.*

6.4 *He went first to Ecbatana and tarried there, mustering fugitives from the battle and refurbishing those that no longer carried their arms. He requisitioned the drafting of troops from the local inhabitants and despatched emissaries to his marshals and governors in Bactria and the upper satrapies asking that they reaffirm their allegiance.*

6.5 *In the wake of his victory* Alexander *arranged the burial of his dead and then, though Darius got there a little ahead, he reached* Arbela, *which had been abandoned to him.* On entering the town he found *it filled with a great stash of stocks together with Darius' gear and* a tremendous treasure including a profusion of foreign finery and between three and four thousand talents of silver.[151] As was said before, the valuables of the entire Persian host had been piled up in this post.[152] **Then, beset by a threat of contagion due to the stench of the corpses spread sprawled across the region, he hastened to advance his camp towards Babylon.** *Media was left on their left as they hurried on and* Arabia, renowned for its rich aromas, lay upon their right. Between the Tigris and Euphrates the route runs through cultivated country, which is so fecund and fertile that herds are kept from grazing lest they die of gluttony. The source of this productivity is the irrigation that flows from either river, for almost all the soil oozes with the water that canals deliver.

6.6 As for the rivers themselves, the mountains of Armenia are their sources, from which they pour forth like they arise on widely spaced courses. Around the Armenian ranges observers impart that they reach their greatest separation in running two thousand five hundred stades apart. When they start to slice through Media and the Gordyaean domains, they gradually converge, so that the further they flow the narrower is the intervening strand of land that remains. Where the rivers run closest together those that there abide call that land Mesopotamia,[153] since it is bounded by these watercourses on either side. Ultimately, after flowing through the Babylonian territory, these rivers empty into the Red Sea.[154] Upon the fourth day of his march Alexander reached the city of Mennis. At that place there is a chasm with a naphtha spring from which such a huge amount of

---

[151] Curtius 5.1.10 has 4000 talents whereas Diodorus 17.64.3 gives 3000 talents, probably respectively rounding up and down some intermediate figure cited by Cleitarchus; there is another example where Diodorus 17.80.3 rounds down a figure for Alexander's main treasure to 180,000 talents that is rounded up to 190,000 talents by Justin 12.1.3.

[152] Curtius 4.9.9.

[153] Mesopotamia means literally "the country between the rivers" in Greek.

[154] The Red (Erythraean) Sea was the name of the Persian Gulf in ancient Greek geography.

bitumen wells up as to corroborate the account that the vast walls of Babylon were mortared with tar from that fount.[155]

6.7 *Whenever Alexander was bathing, an Athenian named Athenophanes used to attend the king with the task of being entertaining. A boy called Stephanus, who could sing, but was not at all good-looking, was set to singing for the king during his Mennis bathing. Whereupon Athenophanes thought to suggest: "Why not make Stephanus the test of the naphtha's alleged zest? If it lights him up and is not straightaway put out, its potency would be shown beyond doubt." Amazingly, the boy agreed that this trial might proceed. Having smeared himself with naphtha in the bath he waited, while a lamp was lit so that he could be illuminated. When he quickly became engulfed in fire, the king was horrified and feared he would expire. And he might indeed have died, had the attendants at his side not used many ewers of water to quench the conflagration, though not without considerable exertion. Even so he was so badly burnt all over that it took a long time for him to recover.*[156]

6.8 Mazaeus accompanied by his adult offspring met **Alexander and his whole army** as the king **approached Babylon.** *As its satrap* he had fled from the battlefield to the city and now ceded its surrender and placed himself and his kin at Alexander's mercy. The king was thankful for his arrival, since the siege of so well fortified a city would have been an enormous operation. Moreover, Mazaeus was a famous fellow and a formidable fighter, whose exploits had distinguished him in the recent battle, so others would see him as an exemplar to spur their own surrender. Therefore, the king gave a welcome that was even cordial to him and his offspring. Nevertheless, he arranged his men in rectangular array with himself at their head and ordered them to advance as if they were going into combat.

6.9 A great number of the Babylonians had taken up vantage points on their battlements, being keen to catch a glimpse of their new king, yet even more of them had gone forth in order to greet him. Among the latter, Bagophanes, castellan of the citadel and the royal treasury, had strewn the entire route with flowers and garlands, so that Mazaeus should not surpass him in unction. He had set up silver altars in array along either side of the way and they were heaped, not merely with frankincense, but with all sorts of scents. As gifts there trailed in his train herds of horses and livestock. Leopards and lions too were borne forward in cages *under lock*. Next came the magicians chanting canticles after their manner and then the Chaldeans and of the Babylonians not just the seers but also the musicians with their local type of lyre. They customarily sing the praises of the king, whereas the Chaldeans make manifest the reasons for the motions of the

---

[155] Although the site of Mennis is unknown, such bitumen springs were historically to be found in the vicinity of Kirkuk, circa 100km south of Arbela.

[156] This story survives in Plutarch, *Alexander* 35 and Strabo 16.1.15 in association with other stories of the naphtha/asphalt/bitumen spring encountered by Alexander in northern Iraq including its use for mortar in the walls of Babylon and its emission from a chasm, both mentioned by Curtius 5.1.16. Hammond, *Sources for Alexander the Great* p.68-69, thinks Cleitarchus is the likely common source, although this is conjectural.

Book 6: October 2nd 331BC – July 330BC

stars and the status of the cycle of the seasons. Last came the knights of Babylon, whose trappings as well as those of their steeds were a demonstration not so much of grandeur as of ostentation. **Alexander** attended by his men-at-arms bade that the citizen bodies should parade after the hindmost of his foot. He himself **entered the city** in a chariot and installed himself in the royal residence. On the next day he acquainted himself with Darius' furnishings and with the evidence of his affluence.

Figure 6.1. Alexander's triumphal entry into Babylon (an engraving in the author's collection based on the painting by Charles Le Brun)

6.10 Yet *it was the splendour and antiquity of the city itself that drew the gaze not just of the king but also of his entire host and not without justification.* Babylon was founded by Semiramis, *rather than by Belus, as many have believed, though his basilica is among its sights. Her disposition made her eager for an exceptional deed and avid to exceed the fame of her predecessor on the throne.* She constructed the city wall from small baked bricks cemented with bitumen *that span a breadth of thirty-two feet* and it is claimed that a pair of four-horse chariots upon it can freely pass as they meet. This wall towers to a height of fifty cubits and its towers are ten feet taller yet. Three hundred and sixty-five stades are covered by its circuit and they recall that each individual stade of the wall was made in a single day, since it was her desire to match the days in a year, they say.[157] *There are a total of two hundred and*

---

[157] Jacoby Fragment 10 of Cleitarchus from Diodorus 2.7.3-4.

fifty towers, which might seem small in comparison with the length of the wall, but Semiramis saw that long stretches abut against marshland, which she considered a sufficient safeguard, so there no towers were planned. **The built-up area of the city does not extend to the base of the fortifications, but a corridor runs between of two-plethron dimensions.**[158] **Of the whole area within the city, housing occupies only eighty** *square* **stades,** *which are not merged into a single zone, but are strewn into many townships,* **the rest being farmed and sown,** *so that, if assailed by foreign forces, the besieged may receive from the city's own soil the requisite resources.*

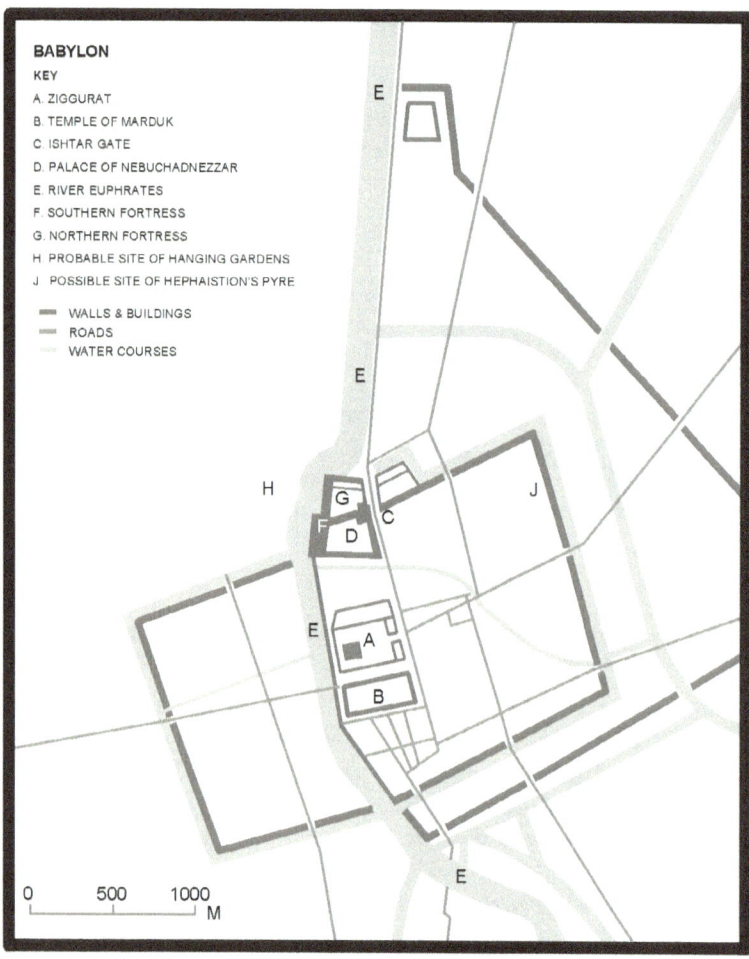

Figure 6.2. Plan of Babylon (based on the excavations of Robert Koldewey)

6.11 The River Euphrates courses through the middle of the metropolis, *being trammelled between vast dykes. Nevertheless, the whole of these*

---

[158] A *plethron* was about 30m.

huge works is encompassed by ditches, delved deep to receive the river's spate. For when it overspills the crest of the embankment, it would wash away the housing, were it not intercepted by culverts and reservoirs, which are built of baked bricks with bitumen cementing everything. A stone bridge five stades long spans the narrowest neck of the river, linking the two sides of the city. *This too is mentioned among the marvels of the Orient, since the Euphrates deposits a great depth of sediment and even when this was deeply dredged to lay a foundation, it was hard to find firm footings for supporting the construction. Moreover, sands continually accumulate against the stone piers that carry the causeway's weight, hence impeding the river's flow, which, being dammed back so, roils even more violently than if the streaming of its course were free.* The span is twelve feet between each pair of piers, of which the masonry tightly coheres, aided by iron cramps, with lead sealing their joints. And cutwaters streamline the current from their points. The deck of this bridge has a breadth of thirty feet with colossal palm trunks and beams of cypress and cedar paving its street.

Figure 6.3. A bull modelled in the glazed bricks of the Ishtar Gate of ancient Babylon (excavated by Robert Koldewey)

6.12 *Semiramis built two royal enclosures upon the banks of the river at either end of the bridge with tall curtain walls of baked brick. The precinct that faces west*[159] *over the river has a circuit of sixty stades. Beasts of every sort are figured in the glaze of its bricks and they are made to*

---

[159] This is ambiguous in Diodorus 2.8.4, but it should mean "faces west from the perspective of a viewer on the river," which is my clarification to agree with the archaeology (see plan in Fig 6.2.).

seem lifelike by the skilful use of colour. Within its walls stands **the citadel** *which* **has a perimeter of twenty stades and** *its fortifications* **are taller and thicker that the others. The foundations of its towers are set thirty feet beneath the surface and the crest of its wall reaches up eighty feet in all.** *These walls and towers too are embellished with wild animals over four cubits tall, realistically portrayed by the masterful use of tints in the glaze. The ensemble depicts a hunt with Semiramis shown mounted on the point of loosing a javelin at a leopard and Ninus, her spouse, in the act of spearing a lion. The citadel has a triple portal, two of its gates being forged in bronze and swung by mechanisms. Across the river the perimeter of the other precinct is merely thirty stades and adorned with scenes from battles and chases. Those that muse over them exhibit ecstatic feelings in their faces.*

6.13 *At the centre of the city Semiramis set up a sanctuary of Belus, which long lapse of time has left in a state of dilapidation, yet it was once toweringly tall and served the Chaldeans as their station for astronomical observation, since stellar transits of the horizon were clearly viewed by virtue of its elevation.*[160] **Beyond the citadel lie the Hanging Gardens, which match the loftiness of the walls** *and are made heavenly by the shade of many monumental trees.* **Semiramis did not create these, but it is told that a king of Syria**[161] **that reigned in Babylon of old performed the feat of their construction for the sake of his spouse's satisfaction. She, being Persian, pined for the woods and glades of her native mountain landscape and persuaded the king to shape and to plant in the plains of that place an imitation of its natural charm and grace.** *So now from a distance in the eyes of those seeing the sights, these gardens look like actual woodland hangers on their homeland's heights.*

6.14 *The park stretches for four plethra on each side and its terraces ascend tier by tier as in a theatre along the approach in semblance of a hillside.* **The great weight of the planted terraces is borne by galleries inside, the highest of which is fifty cubits tall and level with the battlements of the city's curtain wall.** *No expense was spared in constructing* **their piers, which** **are twenty-two feet thick with intervening passageways ten-foot broad.**[162] **These corridors are roofed over with squared stone beams** *sixteen feet long and four-foot wide, which underpin a damp-seal of reeds in a massive matrix of bitumen that is in turn covered by two cemented courses of baked bricks with a top-layer of lead that reinforces its ability to keep moisture in. For* **above** *it* **is set a sufficient bed of soil in which to rest the roots of the most tremendous trees in a terrace teeming with many spectacular species. The girth of their trunks reaches eight cubits and they soar to fifty feet high at their summits, fruiting as profusely as if they grew**

---

[160] This should be a reference to the Babylonian ziggurat, otherwise known as the Tower of Babel.

[161] It is a Cleitarchan quirk to refer to Assyria as Syria.

[162] Diodorus 2.10.4 has 22 feet and 10 feet; Curtius 5.1.34 gives 20 feet and 11 feet, but the Roman numerals in the Latin manuscripts are usually more vulnerable to corruption.

Book 6: October 2nd 331BC – July 330BC

amidst their native thickets. *And the staggering of the galleries permits the light of day to reach into their royal suites and garrets. One chamber has shafts ascending to the topmost stage with mechanisms to raise river water for irrigating the foliage. And despite that time gradually grinds down not merely the monuments of mankind, but also those that Nature's behind, this huge heap, though riddled with the roots of so many trees and stacked with the burden of such grandiose groves, nonetheless continues to survive intact.*

6.15 Alexander lingered longer than elsewhere in this city and in no other place was discipline more undermined amongst the military. Nothing is more corrupt than that city's immorality; nothing arouses illicit and unlimited lusts more systematically. Fathers and husbands condone the prostitution of their wives and offspring to guests, so long as a fee is forthcoming for such infamy. A fondness for frolicking at feasts among kings and nobles pervades the whole area of Persian domination, but the Babylonians are keenest of all on wine and what is entailed by intoxication. The feminine participants in these parties are initially modestly attired, but then stage-by-stage they divest their dress, progressively desecrating their demureness, until – with due respect to your sentiments – they slip out of their innermost garments.[163] Such entertainment is not left to the whores, but is delivered by ladies and lads, who consider it sociable to sell themselves as cheap paramours.

6.16 In the midst of such debauchery **the army that had conquered Asia was billeted and lavishly cosseted for thirty-four days,**[164] *since supplies were plenteous and the people were doting.* Yet in the aftermath it should undoubtedly have proven all the weaker in a crisis, had any enemy been forthcoming. However, continual refreshing of the army through augmentation mitigated such deterioration. *On the road after leaving Babylon* **Alexander was joined by Amyntas the son of Andromenes bringing six thousand Macedonian infantry and five hundred cavalry from the same country all sent by Antipater. These were accompanied by six hundred Thracian horsemen together with three thousand five hundred T**r*i*b**allian**[165] **foot from the same nation. There also arrived from the Peloponnese a mercenary force of about four thousand infantry and three hundred and eighty cavalry. At the behest of their fathers fifty adolescent sons of the king's Friends had**

---

[163] It would be easy for a modern reader to suppose that the expressed disapproval stems from prudery. Actually, the problem is not nakedness itself, but that wives and daughters are exposed to insemination by strangers. It was a social priority for high-status Greek males to ensure the legitimacy of their heirs and the eligibility of their daughters (which necessitated their virginity). It was the affront to these axioms of Greek culture that prompted our author's outrage.

[164] Diodorus 17.64.4 says "more than thirty days", whilst Curtius 5.1.39 and Justin 11.14.8 both state precisely thirty-four.

[165] Trallian in the manuscripts of Diodorus 17.65.1, but the Triballians were a Thracian tribe who are elsewhere said to have fought for Alexander.

journeyed with Amyntas to train to become Bodyguards.[166] *For such as these serve their king at meals as he feeds and when he engages in battle, they fetch him his steeds; they also escort him in the chase and take turns to stand sentry at the entrance to the royal resting place. These duties are the training and the apprenticeship for top commands and governorship.* Having welcomed every new recruit, Alexander continued on his route.

6.17 On leaving Babylon the king appointed Agathon of Pydna as castellan of the citadel with a garrison of seven hundred Macedonian soldiers *and three hundred mercenaries.* He also designated Apollodorus of Amphipolis and Menes of Pella as military governors of Babylonia and adjoining satrapies as far as Cilicia. They were assigned two thousand troops and one thousand talents with orders to enlist as many more soldiers as possible. *Alexander granted the Babylonian satrapy to the turncoat Mazaeus and ordered Bagophanes, who had surrendered the citadel, to serve under him.* Armenia was made over to Mithrenes, who had betrayed Sardis to the king. Then from the monies that had been relinquished to him at Babylon he made donatives of six hundred drachmae to each of the Macedonian cavalrymen, five hundred to each of his foreign horsemen, two hundred apiece to the Macedonian foot and two months' pay to every one of his mercenaries.

6.18 These matters being settled, *on the sixth day of his march* Alexander reached the region known as Sittacenê, a fecund land burgeoning with all sorts of supplies and provender, so during some days he protracted his stay. *He was keen to reconstitute his battle array, as well as to rest his warriors from the weariness of the way. But so that his soldiers should not mislay their mettle through lassitude,* he *set up a review board and* offered extraordinary commissions decided on the basis of military prowess and fortitude. *Those assessed to be the most valorous were each then to command a thousand of the men. They were dubbed chiliarchs*[167] *and this was the first time that their forces had been regimented into such divisions, for formerly there had been battalions five hundred strong and the courageous had not been accorded the key commissions. A huge crowd of troops had gathered to participate in the selection, both to attest to the records of the candidates and to the fairness of the adjudication, for so many could not but know whether a promotion were proper or a product of pretension.* The elder Atarrhias was adjudged the most resolute of all, who had single-handedly rallied the younger men at Halicarnassus, when they forsook

---

[166] The Greek of Diodorus 17.65.1 literally means "with a view to becoming Bodyguards", where the term for Bodyguards (*somatophylakes*) normally refers to the seven elite bodyguards, who were the highest officers of Alexander's court. Curtius 5.1.42 explains that these youths were in training to become the great commanders of the future, so Cleitarchus surely wrote that these were Pages looking to graduate as *somatophylakes* and not instant Bodyguards (as has usually been supposed.)

[167] Chiliarch is a Greek title preserved in Curtius' Latin and meaning literally lord of a thousand.

Book 6: October 2nd 331BC – July 330BC

the fight before its fall. Antigenes was ranked next after him and Philotas of Augaea took third place. Amyntas was given fourth and after him Antigonus followed by Amyntas Lyncestes, then Theodotus was given the seventh position and Hellenicus took the last commission. **Rewarding his captains with such preferments, he bound them to him by bonds of allegiance.**

6.19 Alexander also effectuated many wholly advantageous alterations in the military practices of his predecessors. For, whereas previously each cavalryman had been enrolled amongst members of his own tribe and segregated from others, he abolished racial distinctions and assigned them to commanders not necessarily of their own tribe but rather handpicked by him. The sound of the trumpet that gave the signal when he wished to move camp could scarcely be heard by most amidst the tumult and din. Therefore, he erected a pole above the headquarters that could be seen from every angle, from which a hoisted signal was always in sight: flame by night and smoke during daylight. **Hence, he honed his whole host into unhesitating allegiance to its leader and compliancy with his command, elevating its efficiency in consideration of what the coming contest would demand.**

6.20 And now the king *entered Susianê unopposed and as he* approached Susa *itself,* Abulites, the satrap of that region, sent *his son to meet him en route with* a promise of the surrender of the city. Perhaps he did this of his own volition, but some have written that he acted in accordance with an instruction from Darius to his faithful officials. They suggest the Persian sovereign hoped that the dazzling distractions and riches of the royal residences might retard Alexander's troupe, affording the fugitives a chance to regroup. The king extended a courteous welcome to the youth and under his guidance reached the River Choaspes, which is celebrated for the sweetness of the water that it conveys. There he was met by Abulites bearing gifts of regal richness. These presents included dromedary camels of exemplary swiftness and a dozen elephants acquired by Darius from India, now a buttress rather than the bane for the Macedonians that he had anticipated, now that the wealth of the vanquished was volunteered to the victors as Fortune had fated.

6.21 Upon entering the city Alexander took possession of a prodigious amount of money from its palace treasury, comprising forty thousand talents of gold and silver bullion and another nine thousand talents in minted gold darics. It had been hoarded over many reigns by successive sovereigns, so as to safeguard their descendants against the fickleness of Fortune. Or so they had supposed, yet but a single hour set it fully in a foreign sovereign's power. *Furthermore, he found phenomenal furnishings and fabulous things, including five thousand talents by weight*[168] *of purple cloth from Hermione,*[169] *which it*

---

[168] A talent was a weight of about 26kg (equal to 6000 drachmae or 60 minas) with its most common usage being the largest monetary unit, when the weight was composed (usually implicitly) of silver.

[169] A port on the eastern side of the Peloponnese.

appears had kept its freshness and brilliance despite having been stashed there for a hundred and ninety years. The reason is the use of honey in the purple tints and white olive oil in the white dyes, since these substances are seen to cleave to an unclouded clarity at corresponding antiquity. My father Deinon has also recorded that the kings of Persia had water carted from the Nile and the Ister and ensconced amidst their treasures as a kind of corroboration of the enormity of their empire and the totality of their domination.

6.22 A curious incident transpired whilst the king was being shown the precious artefacts. Alexander seated himself upon the royal throne, which stood too tall for his stature. Seeing his feet dangling well above its footrest, one of the royal pages substituted a table for his footstool. On finding that it fitted the king found it fitting, yet a eunuch standing at hand and who had served Darius was seen to be crying, being saddened by the transformations that Fortune was applying. On noticing him, Alexander queried: "What wickedness have you witnessed that you are weeping?" And the eunuch responded: "Now I am your servant as formerly I belonged to Darius and I am submissive to my masters by dint of my condition, so it grieved me to see Darius' prized possession, from which he was served his meals, reduced to such a disrespected position." On hearing this, the king recollected how vast a revolution had been visited upon the Persian realm and he felt remorse for having transgressed against the gods of hospitality and that kindness to captives that was his usual policy. Therefore, he called for the page that had put the table in place to take it away again. But Philotas was in attendance and he was moved to maintain: "This was not disrespect, for the thing was not done at your behest, but was engineered through the providential influence of some guardian angel. So do not undo his design, but accept as a propitious sign that the table from which your foe used lavishly to dine now forms your footstool." Hence the king chose to ordain that the table should remain so as to bolster his rule.

6.23 Alexander now aimed to enter within the bounds of Persia proper, so he set Susa in the hands of Archelaus with a garrison of three thousand. The custody of its citadel was consigned to Xenophilus and a thousand elderly Macedonian soldiers were assigned as his garrison. Callicrates was allocated the care of the treasury and Abulites was reinstated in the Susian satrapy. **Alexander** also **left the mother, the son and the daughters of Darius in the city of Susa, *furnishing them with tutors to teach them the tongue of the Greeks.*** And it chanced that the king had been sent a present of Macedonian clothing and a great deal of purple material from Macedon together with those women whose work they were. He bade that these be entrusted to Sisygambis, for he lavished every honour upon her and even dealt her the devotion due from a son. And he bade that she should be made aware that, if the clothing met with her approbation, she might have her granddaughters familiarised with its production and he had lent her ladies who could give instruction. But the welling up at these words of her tears exposed that her spirit spurned such a donation, since there is nothing that Persian ladies consider more humiliating than to have to set their hands to knitting.

6.24 Those that had presented the gifts reported Sisygambis' distress and it appeared proper to express regret and proffer solace. Therefore, Alexander visited her in person and explained: "Mother, in these garments that form my dress you behold not merely a gift from my sisters but also work of their own creation, so I was misled by the practices of my own nation. I implore you to be careful not to interpret my ignorance as insolence. Wherever I have been aware of your customs, I have, I hope, observed them with diligence. I know, for instance, that amongst you it is forbidden for a son to be seated within sight of his mother unless she has sanctioned it. Hence on each visit to you I have held back until you have gestured that I might sit. Though you have repeatedly wished to do me homage through proskynesis, I have not allowed you to do this, but I apply to you the title due to my most darling mother Olympias."

6.25 Having mollified the mother of Darius **Alexander marched on with his army and reached the River Tigris** *that the locals call the Pasitigris[170]* **at his fourth encampment. This river rises amidst the mountains of the Uxii and roils on rapidly for a thousand stades[171] through rocky gorges between forested banks in rough terrain. But then it slackens and becomes navigable by boats as it enters upon a level plain. After six hundred stades traversed tranquilly, it empties into the Persian Sea. The king crossed the river and entered the land of the Uxii** *accompanied by nine thousand infantry and archers from the Agrianians plus three thousand Greek mercenaries as well as a thousand Thracians. This territory borders upon Susianê but extends into the first part of Persia, leaving just a narrow corridor between the Persians and the Susians. This was a rich region, irrigated by widespread watercourses and fecund with multifarious fruits. At the harvest, by drying the ripe fruit, the merchantmen that ply the Tigris can convey to Babylonia all manner of sweetmeats to delight the gourmet.*

6.26 Alexander found that *the routes of* access had been secured *with many men* by Madates, *the governor of that region and a cousin of Darius. This man was no chameleon, for he had determined to extend his loyalty to the very end. The king could see instantly that the sheer cliffs posed a great deal of difficulty,* but a local man among the Uxii knew the country and confided the existence of a pinched and perilous path *that turned aside from their city.* If agreed, he would lead a few light-armed troops, who would ascend to a site above the heads of the enemy. When Alexander was pleased to approve this plan, he assigned a force *of fifteen hundred*

---

[170] This was the ancient Eulaeus, which is the modern River Karun.

[171] 1000 stades in Diodorus 17.67.2, but only 50 in Curtius 5.3.1. The word *chilious* in the former is less likely to have been corrupted than the L in Curtius and 1000 stades better fits the geography.

mercenaries and a thousand Agrianians to be taken with the guidance of the man *by the backways under the captaincy of Tauron and he ordained that they should set forth just after the setting of the sun.*

6.27 *The king himself* broke camp in the third watch and negotiated the narrows at about daybreak. After cutting canes for fashioning hurdles and breastwork, so that soldiers shifting up siege towers should be sheltered from missiles, he **instigated the investment of the city.** Every approach was sheer and riven by rocks and crags. Hence *the advance was repulsed* with many casualties, since they had to contend with the terrain as well as their enemies. **Nevertheless, they rallied and renewed the assault,** since their sovereign set himself amidst their front ranks, asking them whether the sackers of so many cities should not be ashamed to shirk from besetting so insignificant and unsung a citadel? Whilst he was chiding them, long-range missiles came marauding amongst them. His soldiers parried with a tortoise formation for his protection, when their efforts to urge his withdrawal met with rejection.

6.28 At last, Tauron manifested himself with his detachments at a vantage point overlooking the citadel of the city. The sight of him *both* **enfeebled their foes' nerve** *and also fired the Macedonians to fight with more verve.* **The defenders were crushed** *by the pincer movement, the impetus of their opponents being too powerful to repel. A few were of a mind to die, whilst many thought to fly, most of whom retired into the citadel.* Thence they sent thirty spokesmen to beg the king's pardon, but these received from him the grim response that there were no grounds for exoneration. Therefore, in trepidation of dire punishments as well, they sent persons by a hidden way unknown to their opponents to sway Sisygambis, the mother of Darius, into conciliating the king, since they were not unaware that he cared for her and indulged her as though he were her own offspring. Furthermore, Madates had married the daughter of her sister, so as to count as a kinsman of Darius.

6.29 For some while Sisygambis was loth to entertain the suppliants' petition, shaking her head to express that an appeal from her was inconsistent with her present position. She added that she was anxious not to compromise their conqueror's kind consideration and that she bore it more in mind that she was currently a captive than that she had been a queen of their nation. But being eventually converted to their cause, in a letter to Alexander she craved that he excuse her intercession in begging that he should excuse them too. Failing such lenity, then would he at least forgive her, for she was only pleading for the life of a relative and auxiliary, who no longer fought as his enemy but besought his mercy. In fact, this single act sufficiently portrays the moderation and clemency of the king in those days, for he not only granted Madates amnesty, but he absolved and set at liberty both those who surrendered and those that he held in captivity. Moreover, in quitting the city, he left it intact and untaxed in the tilling of its territory. Had Darius been the victor, his mother could not have expected better.

Book 6: October 2nd 331BC – July 330BC

6.30 *Thus* Alexander *won his way through and soon* received all the cities of Uxianê, *which he incorporated in the satrapy of Susianê.* Then he divided his forces between himself and Parmenion, whom he bade pursue a path through the plains, whilst **the king** accompanied by disencumbered contingents seized the range of mountains, of which the ridge **ran right the way on into the Persian domains.** Having ravaged this entire region **Alexander** entered Persia upon the third day and **reached the gorge that the Persians call the Gates of Susianê on the fifth day.** But Ariobarzanes held the passage with twenty-five thousand infantry *and three hundred cavalry.* Alexander at first thought to force the entry, filtering forward through fine defiles. The cliffs were everywhere sheer and precipitous and the barbarians lined their crests above the range of missiles. Practicing passivity and a pretense of apprehension, the Persians allowed him to reach the narrowest part of the pass without opposition. But when they perceived that he continued to proceed, whilst paying them no heed, then indeed they rolled colossal boulders down the mountain shoulders. These, in commonly colliding with projecting rocks, were responsible for avalanche generations, such that they crushed not just single soldiers, but packed formations. Stones were also flung from slings and arrows were showered upon them from all directions.

6.31 *Nor was this the most trying thing that these brave warriors were enduring, but rather that, in being butchered like beasts caught in a pit in that situation, they were denied any means of retaliation. Therefore, their rage turned rabid and they seized upon projecting rocks in order to reach their foes by attempting to lift each other aloft, yet these blocks, when simultaneously wrenched by the hands of many men, collapsed upon those that had disturbed them. Hence, they could neither stand nor struggle forward nor even be safe beneath tortoise formations, when such bulky blocks were being cast down by the barbarians. The king was anguished not merely by sorrow, but also by remorse, that he had imprudently pitched into that gorge with his whole force. Undefeated before that day, his every risk had been rewarded. He had careered into the conduits of Cilicia with impunity and in Pamphylia a novel pathway across the sea had been forded. But now his good fortune faltered and was held back, so that he had no other recourse but to retrace his track. Hence* Alexander, having issued the trumpet signal for retreat, bade his men *close ranks and evacuate the gorge by locking their shields overhead into a sheet.* For thirty stades they beat their retreat.[172]

6.32 The king encamped *in a place that was open on all sides,* but set about defending the site with a palisade. *There he not only commenced consultations on a course of action, but also made moves to summon seers out of a sense of*

---

[172] Diodorus 17.68.4 has 300 stades, but the difference between the words for 30 and 300 is small in Greek, so the xxx stades in Curtius 5.3.23 is preferable, also because it is more reasonable.

superstition. But what would Aristander, the most credible of his diviners, be capable of prophesying in the present situation? Therefore, sidelining sacrifices as inopportune, he commanded the convening of those familiar with the region. These locals proposed an unrestricted and risk-free roundabout route through Media at the expense of several days' journeying, but none knew of another road through the range ahead of him. Yet the king was ashamed to forsake his soldiers without burial, for it was conventional wisdom that scarcely any military duty was so sacrosanct as furnishing the dead with a funeral. But to beg for their bodies would have been discreditable, since it could convey that he had been bettered in battle. Hence, he ordered that such captives as he had recently seized should be summoned and amongst these there came forward a fellow fitted out in skins who was fluent in both the Greek and Persian tongues.

6.33 He was a Lycian long ago deported to those parts as a prisoner of war, who had been a shepherd in these mountains since some years before. He had come to know the region well and so concurred that to lead a large force into Persia across the ridges of that range would be absurd. But there were tracks barely passable in single file through the wood, where foliage and intermeshed branches masked everything by forming an unbroken forest hood. And indeed, Persia is upon that side ensconced by an unrelenting array of ridges. This range runs for a length of sixteen hundred stades with a breadth of one hundred and seventy, stretching all the way between the Caucasus and the Red Sea and, just where the mountains fade, the seething waves form a further barracade. A broad plain sinks down beyond the further foothills of the escarpments, where the fertile land is littered with cities and settlements. The River Araxes roils amidst those fields with the waters of many mountain spates, feeding the Medus, a less important river than that which it assimilates. Veering southwards to the sea, no other flow causes plants to flourish with more fecundity. Wherever it meanders is carpeted in flowers and its banks are plastered with plane trees and poplars, so that to those seeing them at some separation, they seem like a salient of the highland forestation. For the shaded stream is bound by a course carved deep into the ground, so the overhanging heights are lush with fronds and shoots due to the dampness that percolates to their roots. Asia in its entirety possesses no other region that is more salubrious, for its weather is abated upon the one side by the shading shelter of a range that is continuous and alleviates the swelter, and upon the other by the adjacency of the sea that tenders to the terrain its temperature stability.

6.34 *Having heard the internee's exposition, the king quizzed him as to whether he had learnt of the route through rumour or personal observation? He responded that, being a shepherd, he had traversed all those tracks and added that he had twice been waylaid, once by the Persians in Lycia and once again by Alexander's brigade. This caused the*

Book 6: October 2nd 331BC – July 330BC

king to recall a prophecy given out by the Delphic[173] *oracle* of Apollo. Whilst Alexander was still a boy, *in some or other consultation it had been its intimation that he would be led along lanes leading into Persia by* a wolf, which might mean *a person of Lycian extraction.*[174] *Therefore* Alexander piled such promises of presents upon this person as were in proportion to the pressure from his present predicament and his prosperity's ability to apportion. *And he ordered him to arm himself in the Macedonian fashion. Then, praying for success,* the king bade him show him the way. Whatever its steepness and severity, he would surmount it with a small party, so as to emerge behind the enemy, *unless by any chance the chap were to construe that what he for the sake of his flock had got through, Alexander for the sake of his glory and eternal renown could not negotiate too? And yet the captive continued to caution the king concerning the difficulty of the route, especially for armed troops.* Then Alexander retorted: "You can take it from me, indeed, that, wherever you may lead, none of those that follow shall refuse to go."

6.35 Hence *he relinquished the custodianship of the camp to Craterus* with his customary command of infantrymen accompanied by the contingents led by Meleager and a thousand mounted bowmen. *He instructed him deliberately to light more fires than were required in order to maintain the semblance of the encampment, the better for the barbarians to believe that the king himself was still present.* However, if it chanced that Ariobarzanes should realise that he was infiltrating via those tortuous tracks and tried to interpose part of his forces upon the adopted trail, Craterus should distract him with intimidatory attacks causing him to concentrate his troops against the more pressing peril. Conversely, if the king should succeed in seizing the wooded escarpment unnoticed by their foes, then when Craterus heard the uproar due to the throes of the natives in encountering the king, he should not hesitate to advance by that way whence they had been repulsed the previous day. It would be deserted, since contending with Alexander would have drawn their opponents away.

6.36 The king *himself* set out in *the third watch of* the night *upon the trail of the recounted route without even sounding any trumpet peals. He instructed his lightly armed troops to carry food for three days' meals.* But, as well as impassable reefs of rock and precipitous crags that repeatedly steered their steps astray, snowdrifts piled up by the wind frustrated their foray. *For they were swallowed up as if they had been pulled into imperceptible pits and when their fellow soldiers set about extricating them, they dragged in these rescuers more often than escaping with them. In view of the cloak of night as well as the obscurity of the territory and the*

---

[173] The information that this was the Pythia at Delphi comes from Plutarch, *Alexander* 37.1.

[174] This is a play on the Greek word for a wolf: *lykos*.

unproven probity of the guide their disquiet was much increased. If he had deceived his captors, they could each be trapped like a wild beast. The security of their sovereign and their personal safety depended upon both the loyalty and the life of a single detainee. ***But eventually they crested the ridge. To the right ran the route to Ariobarzanes himself, which Alexander assigned to Philotas and Coenus with*** Hephaistion Amyntoros[175] ***and Polyperchon, who were accompanied by a disencumbered contingent of troops.*** The king counselled them to advance gradually, since the land was most fertile and fecund with fodder and infantry were intermixed with their cavalry. He provided guides for their route from amongst those he held in captivity.

6.37 ***Alexander himself pressed on with the hypaspists and the squadron dubbed the agema via a precipitous path, where he hit many hazards, but bypassed the positions of his opponents quite widely. It was the middle of the day and their exhaustion dictated a delay for rest*** under cover of the wood, ***for as great a distance remained to be traversed as*** the eighty stades that ***they had already trod, though less arduous and steep. Therefore, the soldiers having recuperated by dining and dozing, they rose to their feet upon the second watch.*** The king traversed the rest of the route without inconvenience, except that, where the mountain ridge gradually gave way to level ground, the path was rent by a huge chasm carved out by a confluence of torrents. Beside this the branches of the trees were so intertwined and matted as to confront them with an unbroken fence. Hence, they were gripped by an intense sense of despair, such that they could hardly hold back their tears. The darkness especially fed their fears, since the stars could not be glimpsed, even if they pierced the clouds, for the trees were thick with leafy shrouds. They lacked even the use of their hearing, since the forest was thrashed by a wind that clashed the branches so as to redouble the din that was due to its howling.

6.38 At last the long looked for light alleviated all the terrors incited by the night. The cascade could be circumvented by a slight diversion and each man had begun to forge his own way on. Hence, ***they emerged upon a lofty elevation, whence they overlooked the enemy position.*** Upon a peal of trumpets, ***these warriors promptly appeared behind the back of the Persians, who had not thought to dread such an attack. Some few that faced about to fight back were cut down. Hence the combination of the groans of the dying and the pitiable appearance of those that were flying set in flight even those that still stood tight, before they had fought in the fray. The cacophony carried to the camp commanded by Craterus, who led forth his forces in a foray to seize those narrows in which the troops had faltered upon that previous day.***

---

[175] Manuscripts of Curtius 5.4.20 and 5.4.30 had Amyntas, but Polyaenus, *Stratagems* 4.3.27 appears to be following a Cleitarchan source in asserting that Philotas and Hephaistion were the commanders of the other pincer of the attack. Given that Hephaistion was the son of Amyntor (Arrian, *Indica* 18.3), it would seem possible that a reference to Hephaistion in Cleitarchus has been garbled by Curtius (cf. Arrian, *Anabasis* 3.18.6).

Book 6: October 2nd 331BC – July 330BC

Simultaneously, Philotas with Polyperchon, Hephaistion **Amyntoros** *and Coenus, who had been ordered to pursue the alternative way, beset the barbarians as a further threat.* But they made a memorable stand, despite that Macedonian arms flashed everywhere and disaster loomed both at their front and to their rear. It may be supposed that necessity hones even timidity and that despair spurs hope to appear. Though they were themselves unarmed, they surrounded and seized their armed adversaries, tumbling them to the ground with them by the great impetus of their bodies, and then they used their own weaponry to skewer many of these.

6.39 Nevertheless, *having slain the front ranks and seized the secondary positions, Alexander overran the rest, who abandoned their stations.* But Ariobarzanes, escorted by about forty knights and five thousand foot, shed much of his own men's blood as well as their enemies' in charging through the middle of the Macedonian lines and speeding off to seize possession of the city of Persepolis, the regional capital. However, its garrison denied him admittance and, being hotly pursued by his opponents, he resumed his armed resistance and was killed with all his fellow fugitives and adherents. Craterus too quickly came through by a forced march of his contingents.

6.40 The king stockaded a camp on the same site whence he had put his foes to flight, for despite that the rout of the enemy on every front had ceded him victory in the fight, his advance was arrested by the road, which was sundered by deep and steep-sided trenches in many a location. Hence, he no longer needed to proceed slowly and with caution just due to the duplicity he suspected in his enemies, but additionally because of his route's riven treacheries. **As Alexander edged forward** *on the road to Persepolis* **a letter was delivered to him from Tiridates,** *its governor and* **the custodian of the royal monies, advising him that those within the city having heard that he was coming were wishing to plunder its repositories. He urged him to hasten to seize this vulnerable treasure,** *for to surrender the city to Alexander would be his pleasure. He wrote that there was no hindrance on the highway except that between the king and Persepolis the River Araxes lay.* Of all the virtues of that sovereign, none merits more approbation than his expedition. *Forsaking his footsoldiers, he rode all night and reached the Araxes with his cavalry at first light, despite such a distance inducing exhaustion. He demolished the neighbouring hamlets, rapidly erecting a bridge using their timbers supported upon stanchions of stone.*

6.41 Having crossed the river and being now not far from the city, the king was confronted by the wretched spectacle of a piteous parade of persons bearing fronds in supplication. *Ranking among the worst ever cases of affliction,* these were about eight hundred[176] mainly elderly Greeks,

---

[176] Diodorus 17.69.3 and Justin 11.14.11 state "about 800", but Curtius, although seemingly following the same account, writes *ad IIII milia fere*. Most probably Curtius wrote "almost a thousand" and some other small word or mark has been corrupted to IIII, giving the numeral 4.

captured and carried away from their home nation by earlier kings of Persia. Each had suffered some sort of mutilation by their captors: some lacked feet and others were missing hands as a result of their amputation, whereas some had endured the severing of their noses and ears. *They had been branded with barbarian characters and detained for protracted oppression by their overseers. But when their masters found that they in turn were faced with foreign domination, they failed to forbid the desire of their Greeks to go to greet the new lord of creation. They looked like outlandish phantoms rather than men, for nothing but their voices could be recognised by their countrymen,* so they wrung more tears from those soldiers round about than they themselves had poured out. *To be sure, amidst so many and varied individual fates, which was the most wretched could not be discerned. For though they were actually dissimilar in their suffering, they seemed a lot alike as far as onlookers were concerned. But when* they yelled out in unison that Zeus himself, the avenger of the Greeks, had at last opened his eyes to events, *all that beheld them felt that they shared in the same chastisements.* In hearing their appeal for vengeance[177] and **succour Alexander was moved to weep more wantonly than any other. But having wiped away his tears, he respectfully called forward their leaders and bade them to be of good cheer, since he would guarantee that the chance for them to see their cities and wives was near.**

6.42 The king constructed his camp enclosure two stades from the city. **Then** *again* **the Greeks** came forth from its walls and **deliberated what it would be best to put to Alexander as their** *collective* **request.** *And when some favoured asking for a home in Asia, whilst others were pleased for each to be returning to his own homestead, Euctemon of Cymê addressed them in these words so it is said:* "*We, who were lately shy of emerging from darkness and imprisonment even to plead for succour, it seems now are desirous of exhibiting our mutilations (in which it is unclear whether our shame or our chagrin is greater) in Greece as though they were ornamentations. Indeed, he best bears a blight, who blots it out from sight and no refuge is so cosy for those in adversity as solitude and forgetfulness of their former prosperity. For those that confidently count upon their kinfolk being compassionate disregard how rapidly tears evaporate. No one's fondness is faithful for one whom he finds distasteful, for even as calamity causes us to complain, prosperity engenders disdain. Hence everyone considers his own predicament in deciding another's treatment. If we were not mutually marred by mutilation, we would long since have succumbed to mutual revulsion. What wonder is it that the fortunate only feel an attraction to people in the same situation?*"

6.43 "*I implore you, let us seek a site where we can bury these half-eaten bodies. What a welcome in a word we would receive in returning to the*

---

[177] See Justin 11.14.11.

wives whom we wedded in our youth! Will our offspring, at the peak of their deeds and their powers, in truth accept those debilitated in dungeons as their fathers? And what fraction of us is capable of traversing so many lands? Far from Europe, carted to the ends of the East, aged and infirm, missing most of our feet and hands, are we so sure that we shall be able to abide what has worn out the warriors from the winning side? What about the wives that chance encounters in captivity and keen necessity have wedded to us as our sole solace? Shall we drag them and their infants with us or shall we abandon them in this place? If they go with us, no one will want to know us.[178] Shall we therefore instantly forsake our current children, when it is uncertain whether we shall get to see our long-lost offspring? Instead, we should maintain our isolation among those who have begun to get used to our mutilation."

6.44 So spoke Euctemon, but the Athenian, Theaetetus, mounted some opposition: "No gentleman will judge his kin by their physical condition, especially when they were disfigured through the ferocity of their foes rather than at Nature's volition. He who is ashamed of his misfortunes is deserving of perdition. He thinks the worst of human nature and despairs of receiving a warm reception simply because he himself would confront his fellows with rejection. The gods are tendering you what you yourselves would never have dared to crave: your wives, your children, your homeland and whatever else men prize as much as their lives or will die to save. Why then do you not break out from this incarceration? At home they breathe another air and look at things in a different illumination. Even foreigners hanker for our customs, our cults and our common language. Yet you yourselves would voluntarily relinquish this heritage, although it is for no other cause that you suffer such desolation than that you are subjected to its deprivation. Emphatically, I would return to my household and my home country, availing myself of such regal philanthropy. But if a fondness for bedmates and their offspring that servitude has coerced you into adopting holds you in hesitation, you should forsake them if nothing is dearer to you than your own nation."

---

[178] Euctemon is not suggesting special coldheartedness among his Greek relatives. There would have been a practical, legal problem in that their fathers would thereby in effect have acknowledged these illegitimate foreign offspring. That would have given them inheritance rights under Greek laws, making them a threat to the grownup sons at home. The response of the Greek families might well have been to refuse to acknowledge their fathers in the first place.

Figure 6.4. Alexander meeting the mutilated Greeks (1696 edition of Curtius)

6.45 *Few shared in this view. The rest were swayed by their habituation, which is stronger than the ties of nation.* They agreed that they should petition the king to supply them with a substitute Asian settlement and a hundred were sent to seek the king's consent. *Reckoning that they would request what he himself had proposed to grant, Alexander announced: "I have bidden that beasts of burden be assigned to convey you and that a thousand drachmae be consigned to each of you. When you are back in Greece, my word ensures that none shall think his condition better than*

Book 6: October 2nd 331BC – July 330BC

yours, save in the matter of your sores." With welling tears, they fixed their eyes upon the ground, neither daring to raise their gaze nor to make a sound. Finally, the king coaxed them for the cause of their trouble and Euctemon answered in much the same words as he had spoken at their council. Then, pitying not merely their misfortunes but also their misgivings, the king commanded that they be gifted three thousand drachmae per person. To this were added ten garments apiece, five for a man and five for a woman, and they were given two teams of oxen, fifty sheep and fifty medimni[179] of seedcorn, so that they could farm and plant the land that they got by Alexander's grant. *They were also exempted from the king's taxation and he mandated his ministers to prevent their molestation. Thus, Alexander improved the propects of those preyed upon by adversity in line with his innate philanthropy.*

6.46 On the following day the king convened the commanders of his contingents. He asserted that *Persepolis was the imperial capital of the Persians:* "No city has been more aggressive towards the Greeks[180] than this, the ancient seat of the Persian kings. *It was from here that those huge hosts, firstly of Darius, then of Xerxes, wickedly waged war upon Europe.* Our forbears shall be avenged by its obliteration."[181] *In fact the barbarians had already forsaken their stronghold, being dispersed wheresoever dread had driven them, when* the king without lingering led in his phalanx. *He had stormed many cities stuffed with regal splendours, whilst others had submitted to his governance, but* the opulence of this metropolis surpassed all precedents. Here the barbarians had hoarded all of Persia's affluence. It was the wealthiest city under the sun: gold and silver were piled in heaps and there were vast numbers of vestments and furnishings that served no purpose but rank ostentation. Alexander allowed the looting of all but the palace quarter. In consequence the conquerors brandished their swords at one another, for he that had seized some more treasurable trophy was made their enemy *and of these they slew many.* Their lust for loot lasted from dawn to dusk *and when they could not cope with all that they had nabbed, spoils were appraised rather than simply grabbed.* They rent the royal robes of purple and gold by slitting with their swords *through a fold or crease* and vessels were vandalised with pick-axes, though each was a masterpiece. *Nothing stayed intact nor was carried off complete and many*

---

[179] A medimnus was around 55 litres.

[180] Alexander widens the scope of harmed Greeks to include victims of invasions of Europe launched from Persepolis, but coming immediately after the episode of the mutilated prisoners, it is clear that the king has them in mind as well.

[181] The implication of the timing is that Alexander was inspired to plan the destruction of Persepolis particularly as a result of the encounter with the mutilated Greeks, even if its eventual culmination at the instigation of Thais was decided on the spur of the moment (and in fact it may have been staged.)

statues were maimed as they hacked from its seat whatever could be claimed.

6.47 *Not only greed but also brutality rampaged through the captured city. Those weighed down with silver and gold butchered the cheap carcasses of their captives, killing wherever they encountered those who would once have been spared for ransom,* for now nobody cared. *Many therefore dodged the blows of their foes through suicides, donning their richest robes and plummeting from parapets along with their kids and their brides. Anticipating the evident intentions of their enemies, some set their buildings ablaze, so as to incinerate themselves with their families. In the end the king commanded his men to spare* the persons and the attire of the women, *who* were *merely* made into thralls, but the vast villas and huge halls, famed throughout creation, fell victim to vandalism and obliteration. *Even as Persepolis had eclipsed every other city in its prosperity, so now it similarly surpassed the rest in the extent of its calamity.*

6.48 Alexander went up onto the terrace of the citadel and took possession of its treasure that had been hoarded from the royal revenues, since the time of Cyrus, the first king of the Persians. The vaults were crammed with silver and gold. When they equated the weight of the gold to its value in silver, there were one hundred and twenty thousand talents all told.[182] In addtion, six thousand talents were taken at Parsagada, a city that Cyrus had founded, now given up by its governor, Gobares. **Alexander favoured ferrying some funds along with him to finance the forthcoming campaign and thought securely to stash in Susa whatever might remain. Hence, he commanded that innumerable mules and three thousand camels be summoned from Susa itself as well as from Mesopotamia and Babylon, by means of which the king conveyed each portion to its appointed destination.** *Alexander was irreconcilable against the local population: thinking them implacable, his plan for Persepolis was annihilation.*

6.49 The king detailed three thousand Macedonians to garrison the citadel of Persepolis and designated Nicarchides as its castellan. In addition, Tiridates was reinstated in the rank that he had held under Darius, since he had transferred the treasure. Furthermore, a large proportion of the army and its baggage were left there under the direction of Craterus and Parmenion. Alexander himself with a thousand cavalry and a disencumbered contingent of infantry set off into the Persian hinterland at around the evening setting of the Pleiades.[183] Though

---

[182] In September 2011 gold was at $59.64/g and silver at $1.33/g, so their price ratio by weight was 44.8. In Alexander's time this ratio was about 13. A talent was 6000 drachmae. On the Athenian standard (used for Alexander's currency) surviving silver coins show that a drachma was 4.35g. Hence 120,000 talents of silver weighs 3132 metric tonnes and has a Sept 2011 value of $4170M, but the treasure in Persepolis was mainly in gold, so its Sept 2011 value was $14000M.

[183] Plutarch, *Alexander* 37, states that Alexander was based at Persepolis for four months, which would be roughly February through May of 330BC. This 30-day roving expedition (southwards?)

Book 6: October 2nd 331BC – July 330BC

assailed by many storms and almost unendurable weather conditions, he nevertheless pressed on to fulfil his ambitions. He ventured upon a route perpetually packed with snow that had compacted to ice from being so far below zero. The wilderness of these tracts and their trackless desolation intimidated the tired troops, who thought that they beheld the end of civilisation. They peered in complete perplexity at an utterly barren landscape that was devoid of any trace of human activity and they insisted that they should turn back again ere the weather should worsen and the light too should wane.

6.50 The king refrained from reproving his frightened soldiers, but leapt from his steed and began on foot to forge through the snows and across the hard-packed ice. First of all, his Friends were shamed into pursuing him, followed by the commanders of his contingents and ultimately the rank and file. And the king was the first to cut himself some tracks by hacking at the ice with a pickaxe, whereupon the rest mimicked their monarch's style. At last, having passed through almost impassable forestation, they came back into contact with occasional traces of human occupation and scattered flocks of roving sheep and inhabitants who dwelt in isolated shacks, since they considered themselves secluded by the inaccessibility of the tracks. When these caught sight of the columns of their foes, they slew those of their fellows that were incapable of escape and fled into the trackless and snowbound mountain landscape. But then through the intercession of their countrymen in Alexander's custody they were gradually pacified and placed themselves at the king's mercy. Nor were those that surrendered dealt with severely.

6.51 After laying waste to the fields of Persia and putting in his power several settlements, the king next ventured among the Mardians, a truculent tribe greatly contrasting in their lifestyle with the rest of the Persian nations. They carve caves into the mountain features, wherein they conceal themselves with their wives and children, feasting upon the flesh of their flocks and of wild creatures. Even their women are not possessed of the gentler disposition that is Nature's tendency, but they wear their hair in shaggy tufts and the hems of their gowns hang above the knee. About their brows they bind a sling, which serves as a headdress as well as weaponry. Yet the same tide of Fortune also overwhelmed their community. Thus, it was that thirty days after parading forth from Persepolis, Alexander likewise returned to the metropolis. Then he rewarded his Friends with presents and the rest too in proportion to each person's importance. Virtually everything that he had seized in that city was shared out as bounty.

6.52 *Some account is called for concerning the part of Persepolis occupied by the palaces in view of their splendour. This citadel is immense and is walled by a triple enclosure. The first circuit rising to sixteen cubits in all is crested with crenellations and rests upon elaborate foundations. Though*

---

into the mountains during that period is dated by the evening setting of the Pleiades roughly to late March through April and is not explicitly recounted elsewhere than Curtius.

the second wall is twice as tall, it is otherwise identical. The third enclosure has a rectangular layout and a sixty-cubit stature. The sturdiness of its stone is stout with the intention that it should long endure. Each façade features a portal with a bronze door and twenty-cubit poles of bronze lie alongside it for the sake of spectacle, whereas the door is such as to make the place secure.

6.53 *The so-called Royal Crag that contains the sepulchres of the kings is situated some four plethra[184] to the east of the citadel. This is a cliff hollowed out halfway up to hold the tombs of many deceased sovereigns. These lack any other human access, save that they receive the burials of the dead by means of hoisting mechanisms. The sumptuously furnished lodgings of the kings and their marshals were spread across the citadel, which housed trusty treasuries for safeguarding the royal riches as well.*

6.54 But let us return to the course of events. Alexander's greatness of spirit was a trait in which he surpassed all other sovereigns: his steadfastness in the face of danger; his promptness and expedition in implementing his decisions; his conscientiousness towards those that capitulated and his clemency towards those that he had captured; he was not even enraptured by legal and general licentiousness. Yet his character was marred by a barely bearable infatuation with wine, *it would seem.* Just when his adversary and rival for the rule of the realm was preparing to renew hostilities and whilst the conquered, being but lately subdued, remained resentful of his new regime, **Alexander held celebrations of his victories by** *dedicating lavish sacrifices to the deities and* **feasting his friends freely at all-day festivities,** *which were also frequented by females, though not such ladies as it was illicit to violate, but courtesans accustomed to accompanying the warriors with more coupling than was temperate.*

6.55 *Whilst the banqueting was well underway and a drunken hysteria had begun to possess the intoxicated attendees,* <u>an Athenian hetaera named Thais declared that Alexander would be most lauded among all the Hellenes, if it should please him to order that the palace of Persepolis be set ablaze.</u>[185] *For there was an expectation that Alexander should raze the place among those Greeks whose cities had been obliterated by this barbarian race in former days.* Let the king lead them in a comus to set the palace aglow and allow women's hands in a trice to overthrow the famous feats of their foe. And when the boozy bawd had aired her thoughts on such a serious design before men that were yet youthful and well the worse for wine, predictably several voices concurred, saying it were a thing worthy of the king and a shout to form the comus and light up torches was heard. "Let us then avenge every last Greek shrine," the king answered,

---

[184] A *plethron* is about 30m.

[185] Jacoby Fragment 11 of Cleitarchus from Athenaeus 13.37 (576 DE).

Book 6: October 2nd 331BC – July 330BC

"Let us incinerate the city," for he too had drunk immoderately and was fired up by their every word. All being sozzled, they surged up from their couches, calling for the composition of a comus of conquest in commemoration of Dionysus. Hence in their intoxication they set about the incineration of a city *precinct* that they had spared when armed for confrontation.

6.56 *Immediately many a firebrand was brought to hand and female musicians from the banquet band accompanied the king as he led the throng with Thais the hetaera conducting the flutes, the pipes and the song.* Alexander was first to cast his blazing torch into the palace and Thais next, followed by the guests, the attendants and the courtesans. *A large proportion of the entire site had been built of cedar, which quickly caught alight, fueling the propagation of the conflagration.* When the army, encamped not far from the city, espied the inferno, they rushed to render assistance, supposing it was happenstance. But on reaching the courtyard of the complex, they beheld the king himself bringing brands. So, they set aside the water that they carried in their hands and themselves began to bung tinder upon the blaze. *And it was truly a sight to amaze and a startling thing that the sacrilege that Xerxes, the Persian king, had perpetrated upon the Acropolis of Athens was avenged in kind and in the course of revelling by a compatriot of its citizens, one woman alone, after so very many years had flown.*

6.57 Such was the demise of the seat of rule for the entire East, whither so many nations had looked for regulation, the home of such a succession of sovereigns and formerly a major menace to Greece. This was the city that had launched a fleet of a thousand vessels and had flooded Europe with her forces, bridging the sea with planking and digging defiles through mountains, then causing the sea to surge through the excavated courses.[186] *But not even the lengthy duration since its destruction has seen it rise again.* It was an embarrassment to the Macedonians that a city of such significance should have been razed by their ruler as a result of drunken revelling. Therefore, the deed was deemed rather a result of deliberation and they brought themselves to believe that such had been the most appropriate approach to its levelling. Certainly, as soon as rest and repose had restored his senses from the throes of inebriation, Alexander himself repented, saying that the Greeks would have been better avenged upon the Persians instead had they been compelled to behold him sat upon the throne within Xerxes' own royal homestead. The next day he donated a sum of thirty talents to the Lycian who had led him on that path by which Persia had been penetrated.

---

[186] The reference is to the carving of a ship canal through the isthmus of Mount Athos recounted by Herodotus 8.21-24.

Figure 6.5. Thais instigates the burning of Persepolis (G. Simoni)

Book 6: October 2nd 331BC – July 330BC

Figure 6.6. The ruins of Persepolis (an engraving published in 1685)

6.58 *All this having transpired, Alexander advanced upon the other cities of Persia, subduing some by force and winning others over through his clemency.*[187] Thence he moved into Media, where he was met by fresh reinforcements of troops from Cilicia, comprising five thousand infantry and a thousand cavalry with Platon of Athens commanding the combined body. Augmented by these forces, **Alexander set out in pursuit of Darius.**

6.59 *The Persian monarch* was then tarrying at Ecbatana, which was the capital of Media. From there he had *proposed to go directly to Bactra, but on account of Alexander's impetus* being fearful of interception*, he modified* his policy and changed *his direction.* For, though Alexander yet lay fifteen hundred stades away, no separation now seemed to supply sufficient space when measured against the Macedonian's pace. Hence **Darius** was readying himself to fight more particularly than preparing for flight. He **was backed up by thirty thousand infantry, including** four thousand **Greeks**, who to the last stayed steadfast in their loyalty. He had also recruited companies of slingers and archers totalling

---

[187] Alexander is now heading northwards past Parsagada and thence to Aspadana in southern Media, so there is no logic in associating the conquest of these Persian cities mentioned by Diodorus 17.73.1 with the late-winter campaign into the mountains (probably) south of Persepolis recounted by Curtius 5.6.12-20, which was explicitly antecedent to the incineration of the city.

four thousand men and additionally thirty-three hundred horsemen mainly of Bactrian origin. These were led by Bessus, who was satrap of the Bactrian region. With this array of troops Darius deviated a little from the military highway having bidden the baggage attendants and the sutlers to lead the way.

6.60 Having summoned an assembly Darius addressed them thus: "If fate had fastened me to the faint-hearted and to such as rate any sort of life above a distinguished estate among the departed, then I would rather maintain my silence than blather words of impotence. But having tested your faithfulness and your valiance further than I would have chosen, I ought all the more to strive to be worthy of such comrades, rather than doubt whether you remain of a like disposition. From among so many thousands you have stuck with me, though I was twice vanquished and twice forced to flee. It is your loyalty and your fidelity that lends my throne its credibility. Traitors and deserters now control my cities, not, by Heracles, because they are worthy of such dignity, but in order that their rewards should set your minds in a quandary. Yet you have preferred to bind yourselves to my fate rather than to the winner's destiny, making yourselves most deserving of rewards to be given by the gods on my behalf, if I should be unable to do so personally. And, by Heracles, you shall have your reward! No successors shall be so insensitive nor any record so callous as to fail to afford you fitting praise unto the Heavens!"

6.61 "Therefore, even if I had contemplated flight, from which my spirit completely cowers, bolstered by your bravery I would nevertheless have been roused to go to meet with these enemies of ours. Why indeed should I stay an exile in my own realm and flee before a foreign and alien ruler to the ends of my empire, when I have the chance to try the fortunes of warfare either to recover my losses or honourably to expire? Unless perchance it should prove more fulfilling to dance attendance upon the decisions of the victor and emulate the example of Mazaeus and Mithrenes by being insecurely relegated to the rule of regional territories, always supposing Alexander now favours fawning upon his fame rather than indulging his anger?[188] May the gods forfend that any man should either remove or reinstate this diadem upon my brow or that I should lose my throne whilst I still respire, but let them rather allow my reign to last until the moment that I expire."

---

[188] According to Diodorus 17.54.6 (see 5.60 above) Alexander had already offered Darius the opportunity to retain his throne, provided that he acknowledged Alexander's overlordship. An imputation from this comment is that an offer for Darius to retain the satrapy of Persia was still on the table in 330BC. Mazaeus had recently surrendered Babylon and retained its governance; Mithrenes had surrendered Sardis and had been given the Satrapy of Armenia in 331BC.

Book 6: October 2nd 331BC – July 330BC

Figure 6.7. The first and second panoramas of the ruins of Persepolis by Cornelius de Bruyn, who visited the site in 1704 (1730 edition)

Figure 6.8. The third and fourth panoramas of the ruins of Persepolis by Cornelius de Bruyn, who visited the site in 1704 (1730 edition)

Book 6: October 2nd 331BC – July 330BC

6.62 "If you adopt this spirit and this precept, there is not one of you for whom the promise of liberty will not be kept. None among you will be confronted by the disdain of the Macedonians or their haughty expressions. The right hand of each of you shall either reap vengeance for so many injuries or bring them to an end. In truth I am myself the living proof of Fortune's accidents and not unjustifiably I look for a milder turn in her trend. But if the gods do not side with just and righteous belligerency, they may nevertheless permit warriors to die with decency. By those auspicious ancestors of mine and yours, in their name, whose rule of the entire Orient has endowed them with enduring fame, by those warriors to whom these Macedonians once paid tribute, by those massed fleets of ships sent against Greece and all the many trophies amongst the royal loot, I beseech and implore you to embrace the courage befitting your reputation and that of your nation, so that you face up to whatsoever chance may bring with the same resolution with which you confronted all former suffering. I myself shall certainly secure enduring celebrity either through a notorious struggle or a glorious victory."

6.63 As Darius spoke, the awful prospect of their imminent peril impacted upon the hearts and minds of everyone at once, so that they were at a loss for anything to say or suggest, whereupon Artabazus, the eldest of the Friends, who had been a guest of Philip (as I have often reported)[189], asserted: "We shall in very truth follow our sovereign into the battle, clad in our costliest dress and outfitted with the most potent arms that we possess and truly of a mind to anticipate victory, although also willing to accept our own fatality." The rest greeted these words with assent, but Nabarzanes, who was attending this same council, had hatched a hitherto unheard-of plot with Bessus. They had resolved to arrest and fetter their sovereign with the support of the forces that they each commanded. Their thinking was that, should Alexander overtake them, surrendering the living king should win the victor's approbation, since he certainly set great store by the seizure of Darius. Conversely, if they could outrun Alexander, then, having done away with Darius, they themselves might rule the realm and revive the struggle for its defence.

6.64 Such treason having long been contemplated, Nabarzanes was preparing the way for their wicked intentions when he now stated: "I know that on first hearing, the opinion that I am about to express will not be such as pleases your ears, yet doctors too prescribe harsh remedies to cure the more serious diseases and a pilot apprehending the wreck of his ship rescues whatever can be saved by jettisoning it. However, my advice is certainly not intended to cause you injury, but rather offered in order that you may rescue your realm through a sound strategy. The gods were against us from this war's inception and Fortune persistently perseveres with Persian persecution. There is a need for a new beginning and different divination. Let you for a little while cede the leadership and your

---

[189] Perhaps a remark by Cleitarchus preserved by Curtius 5.9.1, who wrote "as we have often said". It is also mentioned at Curtius 6.5.2. But the implied earlier mention is lost.

sovereignty to another, who shall be called king only until Asia is abandoned by the enemy, then he shall restore the realm to you when he has secured victory."

6.65 "Moreover logic dictates that this shall soon come to be. Bactria remains unscathed and the Sacae and Indians are still subject to your authority: so many peoples, so many armies, so many thousands of infantry and cavalry standing ready to lend their strength for our recovery, such that more manpower remains to be deployed than has been destroyed from our military. Why should we like dumb beasts rush headlong into needless catastrophe? A valiant warrior rather spurns death than scorns his vitality. Frequently, cowards are caused by lack of tenacity to squander their lives cheaply, but nothing is left untried by bravery. Considering that death brings complete finality, it is enough not to die lazily. Accordingly, if we wish to proceed to Bactra, which is our safest sanctuary, let us appoint the satrap of that country, Bessus, to an emergency monarchy. Then, when matters are resolved, he shall hand back to you, the rightful ruler, this trust of his regency."

6.66 Hardly surprisingly, although it was still unclear just how much villainy lurked behind such disloyal language, Darius failed to contain his temper, yelling: "Most slinking of slaves, have you discovered the occasion that you have coveted for uncovering your treachery?" Drawing his sabre, it seemed he would have slain Nabarzanes, had not Bessus and his Bactrians hastily encircled the king, as if to intercede with him, feigning dismay, but actually intent upon restraining him, if he would not give way. Meanwhile, Nabarzanes slunk away and Bessus soon went off to join him. They bade the forces under their command to set themselves apart from the rest of the army in order to instigate a private consultation. Adopting an attitude in keeping with their current circumstances, Artabazus began to calm Darius, repeatedly prompting him to be mindful of the emergency situation. Darius should bear with equanimity either silliness or vacillation from any sort of person, if they nevertheless supported his position. For Alexander was bearing down upon him, a menacing prospect even with all his forces at his disposal. What would be the outcome, if his followers in his flight should become estranged? It appeared to the king that Artabazus had a point and, despite having meant to move his base, whilst the hearts of all were wavering, he kept to the same place. But being paralysed by a combination of desolation and despair, he secluded himself in his royal lair.

6.67 Therefore divided loyalties arose amongst those in the camp, which became subject to a degree of anarchy in place of the former consensus that had been in the interests of everybody. The commander of the Greek troops, Patron, called upon his men to snatch up their arms and stand ready to execute his instructions. The Persians had formed themselves into factions. Bessus was backed by the Bactrians, who sought to persuade the Persians to secede by reporting the riches of Bactra and its untouched territories, whilst also pointing out the impending peril for those that persisted in the performance of their duties. Practically all the Persians voiced the same objection: that it was treasonous to plot such a

Book 6: October 2nd 331BC – July 330BC

defection. In the meantime, Artabazus fulfilled all the leadership functions: he toured the tents of the Persians ceaselessly issuing exhortations, cautioning them individually and collectively, until it was sufficiently established that they would follow his command. Similarly, with some difficulty he induced Darius to eat and turn his mind to matters at hand.

6.68 But Bessus and Nabarzanes were burning with desire for dominance, so they plotted to implement the treachery of their earlier contrivance. They could not expect such supremacy, whilst Darius himself remained in authority, since among those peoples kingship confers exceptional majesty. At the mere mention of the king's name the barbarians are reduced to servility and the reverence he received in his heyday persists in his adversity. Yet the disloyal ambitions of the duo were inflated by the domain that was under their domination, which in arms and warriors as well as width of terrain was second to no other Persian nation. It made up a third of Asia and the multitude of its young men matched the armies that Darius had mislaid. Therefore, they not only despised Darius but even Alexander did not make them afraid, for thereby they would recover their empire's might, if they could but bring their satrapy in sight. After protracted consideration of every option, they favoured employing the biddably obedient Bactrian troops to arrest the king and then sending a message to Alexander declaring that Darius survived securely under detention. If, as they feared, Alexander despised their treasonous actions, they would deal death to Darius and fall back upon Bactra with the forces from their factions.

6.69 However, it was impossible publicly to pinion Darius, since so many thousands of Persians would spring to his defence and it was intimidating too that the Greeks maintained their allegiance. Hence, they adopted deception to proceed where force could not succeed by feigning contrition for their disaffection and excusing it to the king in terms of their consternation. However, they meanwhile introduced agitators amongst the Persians, who by turns utilised their aspirations and their fears to undermine the troops' affections, saying that they were exposing themselves to destruction and being dragged towards perdition, when Bactra beckoned beneficently to welcome them with wealth beyond their imagination. Whilst they were busied with this subversion, Artabazus came up to them, perhaps bidden by the king or else of his own accord, offering assurance that Darius had been mollified and that their former rank among his courtiers could be restored. At this they wept to wash themselves of suspicion, then implored Artabazus to plead their cause and convey their contrition.

6.70 Having thus reached the end of the night, Bessus and Nabarzanes in company with the Bactrian troops appeared in the courtyard of the headquarters just as it became light, veiling their secret treachery in the performance of a regular rite. Darius, having given the signal for getting underway, mounted upon his chariot in his familiar way. Nabarzanes and the other traitors prostrated themselves upon the ground, stooping to offer him reverence, whom they meant imminently to manacle, and even bursting into tears to protest their repentence. So readily indeed does the human conscience consent to pretence. In consequence, their humble pleas moved Darius, who was naturally kindhearted and sincere, not merely to believe their protestations, but even himself to shed a tear. Nevertheless, not even then did the conspirators conceive any compunction concerning their treasonous scheme, though they could perceive the mettle of the monarch and the man that they meant to deceive. He indeed, oblivious of this peril that neared, hastened to elude Alexander's grasp, his being the only hands that he feared.

6.71 However on the other hand, Patron, the leader of the Greeks, directed his men to don their panoplies that had until then been stowed amongst the baggage and to be alert and attentive to his every command. He himself was dogging the king's chariot, hovering for a chance to speak with him, since he could perceive the impending perfidy of the satrap of Bactria. But Bessus, being fearful of just such a cautioning, did not budge from beside the chariot, behaving as a warden rather than a companion of the king. Hence Patron dithered for ages, often biting his tongue as he wavered between faithfulness and faintheartedness, whilst scrutinising Darius. When eventually the king's gaze alighted upon the Greek, he bade Bubaces, a eunuch among the nearest of his entourage to his chariot, to query whether he wished to speak. Patron confirmed his wish to talk to him, but without an audience. He was bidden nearer to converse without an interpreter, since Darius was not ignorant of the Greek tongue *and heard these words in confidence*: "Your majesty, out of fifty thousand Greeks we few are all that have come through, your comrades in every difficulty. And even in your present adversity, we who followed you in your prosperity shall similarly make for whatever lands you may fancy in place of our own hearths and our home country. We have become bound to you through the vicissitudes of your affairs. By these unbreakable bonds, my men urge and implore you to erect your tent amidst theirs and to suffer them to serve as your bodyguards. We have forsaken Greece and we have no stake in Bactra, so all our hopes are vested in you. Would that this were true of the others too! I need not continue. As a foreigner and an outsider, I would not petition for the right to guard your person, if I believed that anyone else could assure your protection."

6.72 Despite that Bessus was ignorant of the Greek tongue, he was nevertheless spurred by the insight of an insider securely to assume that Patron had perpetrated an exposure. And that the Greek speech had been kept from the interpreters removed all doubt of the disclosure. But being, insofar as could be conceived from his countenance, scarcely distraught, Darius commenced querying Patron as to the cause of the advice that he had brought. Reckoning that this was not the occasion for further prevarication, Patron replied: "Bessus and Nabarzanes are intriguing against you. Your welfare and your life are in the utmost jeopardy and this day will be the last that either you or they see." And indeed Patron might have earned outstanding esteem by saving the king, although this thinking would indubitably be derided by those who are convinced that human affairs unfold and unwind by accident, else that a life runs its course consequent upon a combination of countless concealed causes long predestined according to laws with unalterable clauses.[190] As it happened, Darius answered that although he recognised the loyalty of the Greek legion, he would nonetheless never withdraw from among the men of his home region. For it was harder for him to vilify them than to allow them to beguile him. Whatever chance might instigate, he had rather suffer it among his countrymen than tergiversate. If his own soldiers did not wish to save him, then his end had come too late. Despairing of the king's welfare, Patron returned to those over whom he exercised authority, in order to prepare for every trial of loyalty.

6.73 But Bessus was possessed by a deep desire to despatch Darius right away. Yet fearing that he would fail to find favour with Alexander, unless Darius were delivered up alive, he arranged to delay his damnable design until the next night. Then he began to profess delight that Darius had diligently and prudently dodged the trap of a treacherous individual, who already had in view Alexander's might such that he would have made a present of the king's head to their opponent. He remarked that it was unremarkable that a man contracted for pay would make everything a matter of commerce. Without a hearth and family, an exile to all the world, he was a two-faced foe, trafficked at the dangling of a purse. As Bessus acquitted himself thus and invoked the gods of his country as testament to his loyalty, Darius's expression conveyed his acquiescence, though he did not doubt the veracity of the Greek intelligence. But matters had reached the point that it was as perilous that his followers should be disbelieved as for Darius himself to be deceived. Those whose treachery or infidelity was feared numbered thirty thousand, when Patron had a mere four thousand men. If he should entrust his preservation to them, blackguarding the trustworthiness of his countrymen, then he perceived that he would provide a proper pretext for regicide. Therefore, he preferred rather to be accosted undeservedly than justly. Nevertheless, when Bessus absolved himself of any subversive designs, Darius observed that it was clear that Alexander's sense of propriety was no less marked than his gallantry. They deceived themselves, who expected that he would reward them for perpetrating treachery, for there was none who would more vigorously vilify and avenge a violation of loyalty.

6.74 And night was now nearing, when the Persians after their normal fashion set aside their arms and dashed off to fetch provender from *Thara* the closest settlement. But the Bactrians, as Bessus had bidden, still stood in their equipment. Meanwhile Darius bade that Artabazus be summoned and when he had disclosed what Patron had exposed, Artabazus was convinced that the king should convey himself into the Greek compound and that the Persians too would accompany him once word of his jeopardy were spread around. But Darius was now resigned to his fate and no longer heedful of healthy counsel. His sole solace in his travails, Artabazus, he beheld for the last time, hugging him whilst they were both

---

[190] An intricate observation worthy of a Cynic, although Curtius 5.11.10 is slightly corrupt.

overwhelmed with weeping, but ordering that he be dragged away as he continued to cling. Then, veiling his brow so as not to watch as Artabazus went away wailing as if from his funeral pyre, he threw himself face down into the mire. Whereupon indeed those that customarily comprised his bodyguard, whom it behoved to protect the king even at the risk of their lives, slunk away, reckoning that they would be no match for the armed men that they supposed would arrive without delay. Hence an intense sense of solitude descended within the tent, where just a few eunuchs, who had nowhere else to go, still stood around their sovereign. But, dismissing even this audience, Darius long contemplated alternative expedients.

6.75 Finally, feeling oppressed by the solitude from which he had sought solace but a bit before, he bade that Bubaces to be summoned. Fixing his gaze upon him, the king gave this command: "Leave me and look out for your own welfare. As is befitting you have been faithful to your king to the last. Here I shall await the verdict on my fate. Perchance you wonder why I do not take my own life? It is because I desire my death to be due to another's villainy rather than have it stain me." Upon these words, not just the pavilion but also the entire compound resounded with the eunuch's lamentation. Then others burst in upon the scene and, rending their raiment, they began to lament their king with plaintive and alien ululation. When this pandemonium pierced the ears of the Persians, they were transfixed by their fears so that they dared neither to seize their arms, in case they were confronted by the Bactrians, nor to appear impervious, lest they should seem disloyal in deserting Darius. Raucous and diverse disturbances resounded spontaneously and without coordination all around the compound.

6.76 *Bessus* and Narbazanes heard from their adherents, whom the lamentation had misled, that Darius was dead by his own hand. Hence, they sped their steeds towards the scene with those they had appointed to perpetrate their perfidy in one band. And when they entered the royal tent, since the eunuchs disclosed that he had not died, they **ordered that Darius be seized and tied.** The king conveyed by a chariot but a little beforehand and reverenced by a sacred, sacrificial cult among the men of his land, had become the captive of his own lackeys without any foreign meddling **and was thrust into a dingy cart, wholly hidden by a hide awning.** The king's funds and his furnishings were looted as if legitimised by hostilities, then they made good their escape burdened by the booty from this last of their iniquities.

6.77 Artabazus headed for Parthia with those that accepted his authority and with him the Greek soldiers, considering anything safer than being stalked by traitors. The Persians, who had been plied with promises by Bessus, mainly for want of anyone else to follow, attached themselves to the Bactrians, catching up with their column the day after the morrow. Yet, lest the king should lack any respect, **they fettered Darius with a gold chain**, for Fortune formulated fresh mockeries for him again and again. And lest by chance he be recognised from any royal refinements, they had draped the wagon with shabby hides and the beasts were driven by peasants. In order that he could not be pointed out to the inquisitive amidst the column, his guards trailed at a suitable distance.

6.78 Upon hearing that Darius had decamped from Ecbatana, **Alexander** abandoned the route whereby he was roving into Media and ***pressed hard in the fugitive's pursuit.*** He reached Tabae, a citadel in the furthest reaches of Paraetacenê, where deserters declared that Darius was heading for Bactra in full flight. Thereafter he got more authoritative information from Bagistanes, a Babylonian, who asserted that, though the king had not yet been fettered, he nevertheless stood in peril of being bound or even murdered.

6.79 Having convened his commanders, Alexander declared: "The greatest of tasks but the briefest of labours remains to be undertaken. Darius is not far ahead, either deposed by his men or forsaken. Our victory is vested in his person and it is through velocity that such a prize will be won." All alike bellowed that they were ready to follow his lead: let him spare them neither toil nor peril in this deed. Hence, he led his forces forward rapidly rather as if racing than marching, not even stopping at night to recuperate from the day's dashing. **He went onwards in this way for five hundred stades** and reached the village *of Thara* where Bessus had apprehended Darius. There Melon, Darius' interpreter, was captured. His frail frame had not been able to keep pace with the Persian army and, when waylaid by Alexander's rapidity, he pretended to be a turncoat. From him **Alexander learnt of the events** of note. **But rest was required by** those driven to exhaustion, so he augmented the **six thousand elite cavalry that accompanied him** with three hundred horsemen that were dubbed dimachae.[191] These wore weightier armour and, though each rode upon a steed, they fought on foot, when the matter and the moment made for a need.

6.80 Whilst Alexander was thus engaged, there came before him Orsilos and Mithracenes. They had deserted by dint of their detestation for the treachery of Bessus and they announced that the Persians lay five hundred stades away and that they would show him a shorter way. The king was gratified that deserters were coming over to him. Accordingly, at the onset of dusk led by these men he set out upon the route that they pointed out, having bidden the phalanx to follow as fast as they could. The king, forging forward in rectangular arrays, regulated the rate of advance so that the van could keep in contact with the rear. He had progressed three hundred stades, when *Brochubelus*,[192] the son of Mazaeus, sometime satrap of Syria, came before him. He too had deserted and declared that Bessus lay hardly more than two hundred stades away and that his forces, being panicked, were withdrawing in a disorderly and disorganised rout. They appeared to be on the point of heading for Hyrcania. If Alexander were to press

---

[191] In the manuscripts of Curtius the word is *dimichas*, which is probably a slightly corrupted form of *dimachae*, Greek for "dual-fighters", since they evidently fought on foot as well as on horseback; Alexander is credited with having invented these troops by Pollux, *Onomast.* 1.10.

[192] The name of Mazaeus' son may be corrupt in the manuscripts of Curtius.

his pursuit whilst they were straggling, he would overwhelm them. And he specified that Darius was still alive. Ever expeditious, Alexander was galvanised by the renegade into completing the chase, so kicking their spurs they made it a race.

6.81 Straightaway the commotion made by their enemies on the march became audible, but the vista was veiled in a cloud of dust, so Alexander reined in their onrush for a little while, whilst the dust settled. At that point they were sighted by the barbarians and themselves beheld the retreating columns, for which they would by no means have been a match, had Bessus fought battles with as much alacrity as he perpetrated treachery. For the barbarians were superior in both armour and numbers, added to which their fresh forces would have tangled with tired soldiers. But both the name and the fame of Alexander weighed most massively in war, such that they turned tail due to an attack of terror. To be sure, Bessus and the rest of the partners in his perfidy came up to the cart that carried Darius and began to harangue him into mounting a steed in order to seize the opportunity to flee from his enemy. But Darius declared that divine vengeance was visited upon them and appealed for asylum with Alexander, repudiating any desire to consort with traitors. Then, truly, also fired with fury, they hurled their spears at their sovereign and left him lacerated by many an injury. And so that they would not be able to keep going, they maimed the beasts too that drew the wagon and slew two slaves who had accompanied their king.

6.82 The murder having been committed, so as to split up the tracks from their flights, Nabarzanes made for Hyrcania, whilst Bessus bolted for Bactra escorted by a small number of knights. Bereft of their leaders and being led by either their hopes or their fears instead, the barbarians became increasingly widespread. There hung together a mere five hundred cavalry, who were as yet undecided as to whether they should stand or flee. Upon discovering the consternation amongst his foes, Alexander despatched Nicanor with a section of the cavalry to stem the stampede, whilst he himself followed on with their fellows. Almost three thousand that fought back were killed, but the rest of their army were rounded up in the manner of cattle without blood being spilled, since the king's command to refrain from slaughter was fulfilled. None among those captured was able to identify the cart carrying Darius. Whenever a wagon was waylaid, it was individually scrutinised, but *as yet no observation of any trace of the king's disappearance was made.* Scarcely three thousand cavalry had kept pace with Alexander's rapidity. However, whole regiments of refugees gave themselves up to those that were following him more slowly. Though it is barely believable to tell, the captives outnumbered those into whose custody they fell. So completely had calamity deprived the petrified of all rationality that they were unable correctly to recognise either the sparsity of their enemies or their own numerical superiority.

6.83 Meanwhile, lacking a wagoner, *the beasts that were hauling Darius had strayed* off the military highway and wandered for four stades until they drew to

Book 6: October 2nd 331BC – July 330BC

a halt in one of the valleys, exhausted by both the baking heat and their injuries. **There was a spring that lay not far away, which was pointed out to Polystratus, one of the Macedonians**, by well-informed persons. Spurred by thirst he got to it and, whilst quaffing water from his helmet, he spotted the spears prodded into the body of each abandoned beast. Whilst he wondered why they had been stabbed instead of being nabbed, **he heard the moans of a man nearly deceased and discovered Darius lying within the wagon, his body perforated by many a javelin.**

6.84 *The king called for something to slake his thirst, so Polystratus proferred water from his helmet. When a captive was fetched, recognising him from his voice as a compatriot, Darius confided: "It is at least a solace in my present sorrows that my speech shall be understood and that my last words will not be wasted." Then* **he bade that the following message be conveyed to Alexander:** *"Though I have done you no favours, I die most deeply in your debt, since* **in your conduct towards my mother and other family** *instead of any hostility* **royal standards have been met.** *Indeed, I have been happier in my allotted enemy than in my kinsmen and the rest of those close to me. For my mother and children have been left alive by my foe, but I am slain by those I best know, to whom I have let my life and my lands go. And their reward for this shall be what you as victor wish to decree.* **I thank you in the only way the dying know, with my prayers to deities and regal gods on high and below that yours be the victory** *in every country and that your empire follow. For myself I seek the favour of a decent burial, which should be proper rather than impracticable. As regards revenge, now it is not mine alone but the common and particular cause of every king, which for you to ignore would be a perverse and perilous thing, since it is a question on the one hand of whether you are seen to act justly and on the other it is also a matter of expediency.* **Alexander, I offer my right hand to this soldier in your lieu, that he may convey this unparalleled pledge of royal loyalty to you." Then, in extending his hand to Polystratus, his spirit finally flew.**

6.85 **Alexander was told the story when he rode up presently and then he wept to see the body done to death so unworthily in view of its high dignity.** Therefore, unclasping his own cloak, he cast it upon the corpse of his erstwhile enemy. *Additionally,* **he ordered that his remains be** returned to Darius' mother to be **accorded a royal funeral**, then to be laid amidst the tombs of his forbears for his burial.

Figure 6.9. The death of Darius (by André Castaigne, 1899)

Book 6: October 2nd 331BC – July 330BC

Figure 6.10. Alexander cloaks the corpse of Darius (Antonio Tempesta, 1608)

6.86 Yet certain persons have written that Alexander reached Darius whilst he was still breathing and condoled the king on his misfortunes; and that, when Darius told him that he should avenge his murder, Alexander acceded and set off in pursuit of the regicide. But as Bessus had a huge headstart and was retiring through the Bactrian countryside, Alexander soon curtailed this campaign and decided to head back again.

6.87 *Such was the situation in Asia. Yet in Europe the Spartans were compelled by their defeat in the decisive battle* near Megalopolis *to seek terms from* Antipater, who convened the Council of the Hellenic League at Corinth *in order to refer a response to the Spartan diplomacy to its authority. But* after lengthy discussions *this body agreed no decisions save to allow the Spartans to send emissaries to Alexander* to expiate their indiscretions. *These were in addition to the* fifty hostages *who* were held by Antipater, selected from among the leading Lacedemonians and Spartans.[193] The Tegeans, excepting those that had incited their revolt, received pardons. The Achaeans and the Eleians were ordered to pay one hundred and twenty talents to the people of Megalopolis, whose city had been besieged by the

---

[193] According to Harpocration, Cleitarchus had already mentioned the fifty hostages in Book 5, but Diodorus 17.73.6 suggests that the matter was reiterated here, perhaps to distinguish them from the envoys sent to Alexander.

rebel forces. *Such was the settlement of a war that broke out suddenly, but had actually ended ere Arbela saw Darius cede Alexander the victory.*

6.88 ***These were the events concerning Alexander*** *in the sixth year of his reign.*

Book 7: July 330BC – June 329BC

The Advance to Hecatompylus; Description of Hyrcania and the Caspian Sea; Surrender of Artabazus & the Greek Mercenaries; Theft of Bucephalus; Surrender of Nabarzanes; Visit of the Amazon Queen; Adoption of Persian Dress; Revolt of Satibarzanes; The Philotas Affair; Assassination of Parmenion; The Euergetae; First Crossing of the Paropamisus Range.

7.1 *At the beginning of the seventh year of Alexander's reign, Darius being dead, Bessus accompanied by Nabarzanes, Barzaentes and many of their fellows eluded the king's grasp and bore towards Bactria. Bessus had been set up as satrap of this dominion under Darius and, being familiar to its folk in respect of his rule, he roused them to defend their freedom. He noted that the nature of their terrain would greatly aid them, since it was awkward of access and was settled with sufficient manpower to assert its independence. He proclaimed that he would personally prosecute the war and with the approval of the people he declared himself king. Then he engaged upon recruiting troops, forging abundant arms and keenly configuring to confront the encroaching crisis.*

7.2 Yet as soon as a mind that was more amenable to military matters than to peace and quiet was disburdened of bothers, Alexander succumbed to sensual pursuits and he who had not been worsted by the weapons of the Persians was vanquished by their vices. There were perpetual parties, the demented delight of drinking till dawn, sundry entertainments and herds of whores. Everyone lapsed into outlandish mores. By copying such customs, as though they were preferable to his own, he so offended the feelings of his folk and equally their gaze that many of his former friends found in him a foe. For his countrymen kept to their own schooled fashions and were inured to nourishing their natural longings with sparing and readily reaped rations, but he pressed upon them the depravity of foreign and defeated nations. Hence the hatching of conspiracies against his person occurred more often as also insurrections of his soldiers and more men resorted to resentment amidst mutual recriminations. Hence too he was for his own part at some points distrustful and at others exasperated due to groundless fears and suchlike sores as shall later be related.

7.3 Therefore when he was devouring days and nights alike in prolonged banquets, he used to introduce diversions at the conclusions of the courses. Yet he was not satisfied by the swarm of artists that he had gathered from Greece, since captive women were bidden to sing songs in the vernacular fashion that were dissonant and repellent to the ears of their visitors. Among them the king himself caught sight of one who seemed sadder than the rest in ashamedly resisting those who looked to lead her forward. She cut a fine figure that was accentuated by her bashfulness. Her eyes were downcast and her visage veiled inasmuch as was allowed, causing the king to sense that she was of too refined a pedigree to be exhibited amongst the entertainments in the revelry. Therefore, she was asked about her ancestry and she said that she was the granddaughter of Ochus, sometime sovereign of Persia. His son had fathered her and Hystaspes had been her husband, who was a kinsman of Darius and had himself led a large army.

7.4 The king still retained in his mind some modicum of his former morality. Thus, out of respect for the lady's royal roots and so celebrated an ancestor as Ochus, he not only released her from captivity, but also bade that her fortune be refunded and even that her husband should be sought, so that the king might hand his wife to him when he was brought.[194] Furthermore, the following day he instructed Hephaistion to order that every captive be convened at his headquarters. There one by one he looked into their lineages, segregating those of eminent descent from the commoners. He found a thousand of the former, including the brother of Darius, Oxathres, who was no less a luminary for his intellectual talents than for his family.

7.5 Alexander *performed the funeral rites for his fatalities in the flight of Darius with extra extravagance for he* **had garnered a great booty** *in the pursuit, including eight thousand talents taken from the* Persian *royal treasurers.* **What was dispersed as gifts among the** *surviving* **soldiers** *comprising such stuff as clothing and cups* **came to** *nearly* **thirteen thousand talents, whereas what fraudsters pilfered or purloined as plunder was perceived to match or even exceed this sum.** *Most of the mounts had also been lost or lamed due to the intense heat. However,* **Alexander's main monies, which amounted to between a hundred & eighty and a hundred & ninety thousand talents, were deposited at Ecbatana in the custody of Parmenion.**[195] A Persian nobleman named Oxydates, who was found in fetters due to having been condemned to death by Darius, Alexander set at liberty and made satrap of Media. The king also appointed a bevy of bodyguards and **Oxathres the brother of Darius was welcomed into the fraternity of his Friends** *with all the dignity due to his distinguished dynasty.*

---

[194] This event, though superficially trivial, has the significance of inaugurating the so-called "Persianising" phase of Alexander's career, but it happens that we are in the privileged position of being able to gain special insight into Alexander's thinking on this matter, even beyond what would have been apparent to most of his contemporaries. Essentially, it appears that the king was emulating the chivalric model of kingship presented by Xenophon in his *Cyropaidia*, specifically the episode at *Cyropaidia* 6.1.45-48 wherein Cyrus reunites Pantheia with her husband Abradatas and thereby wins the latter's allegiance. There are some hints that Alexander originally planned to reunite Darius with his wife according to this model, but being thwarted in that ambition, he evidently found a convenient substitute in the wife of Hystaspes.

[195] 180,000 talents according to Diodorus 17.80.3 and 190,000 in Justin 12.1.3 – perhaps respectively rounding down and up an intermediate figure in Cleitarchus.

Book 7: July 330BC – June 329BC

7.6 Alexander now reached Parthia, whereof the Scythians had seized the fertile fields. They have homesteads in both Europe and Asia. Those who dwell beyond the Bosphorus are attributed to Asia and those that are in Europe hold the land from the western strand of Thrace through to the Borysthenes and thence the stretches straight on to the Tanais.[196] This river runs down the boundary between Europe and Asia. There is no doubt that the Scythians that sired the Parthians penetrated into those parts rather by roaming from the region of Europe than from *beyond* the Bosphorus.

7.7 The king now headed for Hyrcania and halted near a city called Hecatompylus *on the third day. This wealthy town had been founded by Greeks and afforded a profusion of everything required for recreation and relaxation, so* he rested his army there for several days, *whilst supplies were gathered in from everywhere round about. Hence hearsay, the habitual sin of soldiers at leisure, whispered without warrant that the king, being content with his accomplishments, stood ready to return right away to Macedonia. They ran off as if raving mad to their tents and prepared their packs for the trek. It might have been believed that the signal to bundle up the baggage of the entire camp had been given. The cacophony carried to the king's ears as here they hallooed their tent-mates and there they weighed down the wagons.*

7.8 Alexander perceived from his perspective that the Macedonians saw the death of Darius as the conclusion of the campaign and yearned to return to their own land *and farms. In the mind's eye of each man, he was already enfolding his wife and children in his arms.* The king had convened an assembly of the allied levies from the Greek cities, at which he had commended their conduct and released them from soldiering service. As well as their awaited wages, he had awarded a talent to each of their cavalrymen and ten minas to each of their footsoldiers plus supplementary sums fully to fund their journeys home.[197] *Although* he had tendered retainers of three talents to any that would remain enrolled in the royal regiments, *the disbandments had lent credence to the view of the rest of the army that the end of their own service would duly ensue.*

7.9 *Being no less than duly alarmed by this, seeing as he was actually seeking to set off for India and the uttermost Orient, the king convened the commanders of his contingents in his headquarters. On the verge of tears, he loudly lamented that he was being recalled with his conquests but half accomplished, so as to carry back to his country a name more famed*

---

[196] These things are: the Cimmerian Bosphorus, which is the Strait of Kerch at the eastern tip of the Crimea; the River Borysthenes, which is the Dnieper; the River Tanais, which is properly the Don, but which Cleitarchus confused with the ancient River Jaxartes or modern Syr-Darya.

[197] A talent was a weight of 6000 drachms and a mina was one hundred drachms, where a drachm was approximately 4.3g (of silver) according to the Attic standard, which was popular at that time.

for its failures than its victories. Nor was it the war-weariness of his warriors that was thwarting him, but rather the spite of the gods, who had inspired fellows of the finest fortitude with a sudden desire for their land of domicile, whither they would withdraw more worthily and with better repute in just a little while.

7.10 *Then indeed each commander present proffered his efforts in Alexander's cause, ardently asking for the most awkward tasks and trumpeting the tractability of his troops* in the wars, *were the king willing to mollify the men's minds with a mellow and meet address. They had never withdrawn dispirited, dejected and in distress, so long as they had been able to elicit inspiration from Alexander's ardour and the valour of so sublime a spirit. To this the king responded that he would indeed inspire them: let them but ready the ears of the rank and file and he would speak fire in them. Hence when every appropriate preparation appeared to have been put in position,* the king commanded that his soldiers be summoned to a congress, at which he delivered a stirring address.

7.11 "When you study our stupendous successes, soldiers, it is little wonder that you hanker after peace and feel fed up with glory. Let me leave aside the Illyrians, the Triballians, Boeotia, Thrace and Sparta and the Achaeans in the Peloponnese, some of which I have myself subjugated, whilst others have been subdued in the name of my power and authority.[198] Instead let me commence my account of our campaign at the Hellespont, from which point we have freed the Ionians and Aeolis from servitude to despotic foreigners and we have put in our power Caria, Lydia, Cappadocia, Phrygia, Paphlagonia, Pamphylia and the Pisidians, Cilicia, Syria, Phoenicia, Armenia, Persia, the Medes and Parthia. Rivals have seized fewer cities than the number of countries that I have occupied and I am unsure whether in enumerating such a number of them I have detracted from the sum of the triumphs of our side. Therefore, if I considered that our control of the regions that we have so rapidly reduced were soundly secured, I myself, soldiers, would hurtle homewards to my mother, sisters and fellow citizens, though you strove to restrain me with cords. For there especially I might bask in the praise and glory that we have together instigated, where the most magnificent rewards of victory may be anticipated: the joy of our parents, wives and offspring, the ease of peace and the tranquil enjoyment of everything gained through our daring."

7.12 "Yet our rule here is recent and in reality, precarious, should we care to confess it, for the barbarians are still stiff-necked in yielding to its yoke. It will take time, soldiers, till they cultivate more congenial characters and healthier habits sap their savagery. Similarly, crops reserve their ripening pending the appointed date, since even insensate things mellow at their own rate. Well then, can you believe that so many nations inured to another monarch's name and

---

[198] Alexander means that he had personally led the campaigns against the Illyrians, the Triballians, Boeotia (Thebes) and Thrace in 336-335BC, whereas Antipater had defeated the rebellion of the Spartans and Achaeans in the Peloponnese in 331BC.

command and lacking any commonality of custom or communication or creed with us were tamed in the same combat in which they were overcome? Actually, it is your arms that restrain them rather than their own manners and those who are in dread of us while we are here, will emerge as enemies if we disappear. We are dealing with fierce beasts, which, being captured and confined, cannot calm their tempers save through a longer lapse of time."

7.13 "And up till now I have reflected, as if our arms have subjected all the domains that Darius directed. Yet Nabarzanes has seized Hyrcania and the murderer Bessus not only possesses Bactra, but also makes menaces against us. The Sogdiani, Dahae, Massagetae, Sacae and the Indians have fallen under their own jurisdiction. As soon as they see us turn tail, they will all of them be harrying our heels, since they are each of the same race, whilst we are outsiders bred in a foreign place. Everyone is more amenable to someone from his own society dominating, even though the outland lord can be more intimidating. It follows either that what we have seized must be forsaken, else we must also occupy what we have not yet taken."

7.14 "Just as a surgeon, soldiers, will leave nothing festering in the bodies of the ill, so let us cut away at whatever would withstand our will. There's many a time that a tiny, disrespected spark has kindled a colossal conflagration. And so, there is no such foe as may safely be spurned, for him whom you despise is made that much mightier when a blind eye's turned. Nor did even Darius receive the rule of Persia through inheritance, but rather he was set upon the throne of Cyrus by the beneficence of Bagoas the eunuch. So, let you not suppose that Bessus need greatly struggle to reap a realm that is rulerless. Certainly, we have sinned, soldiers, if we have defeated Darius simply to surrender his sovereignty to his servant, who has dared to commit the ultimate miscreancy. For when his sovereign was even in want of succour from foreigners, he set him in fetters like a common captive, though we the victors would assuredly have spared him.[199] And then in the end he slaughtered him in order that we should not be able to save him."

7.15 "So will you suffer such a wretch to reign? Personally, I am impatient to see him suffer crucifixion, since for the sake of every ruler and race and for his violation of loyalty he merits such a conviction. But, by Heracles, if you should shortly hear it heralded that he has annihilated the Greek settlements or even ravaged the Hellespont, what a massive sense of remorse will mortify you when the gains from your victories have been seized by such as Bessus? Then you will snatch up your arms. Then you will rush to recover the situation. But how much

---

[199] I have previously argued in *Alexander's Lovers* p.28 that the mention of Alexander having uncharacteristically halted his pursuit of Darius for 5 days when he reached the Caspian Gates (Arrian, *Anabasis* 3.20.3) suggests that Darius had agreed to surrender. The Latin of Curtius 6.3.13 (on which my Reconstruction relies at this point) could be translated to mean that Darius was known to have been considering seeking help from foreigners at the time that Bessus deposed him: most probably Patron's Greek mercenaries (7.19 below), but possibly even the Macedonians.

7.16 "There remains a march of four days for us, who have trampled so many snowfields, traversed so many rivers and surmounted so many mountain ranges. Neither can a surging sea that roils across the route cause us delay nor can Cilician gulches and gulleys box us in today, but rather it is smoothly downhill all the way. We stand on the very verge of victory. Before us but a few fugitives and murderers of their master remain at liberty. A lovely labour, by Heracles, that shall be enumerated amongst the most remarkable of the feats that you bequeath to posterity and the halls of fame. They will say that having ended your enmity towards Darius as soon as he was slain, you even avenged your foe by killing his killer in order that no faithless fellow should elude your grasp. And this being done, how much more compliant can you suppose the Persians will be, when they perceive that you crusade against disloyalty and that it is the betrayal by Bessus that riles you rather than his whole society?"

7.17 These winning words were heard with wholehearted acclaim by the troops, who bade Alexander to lead them wheresoever he wished for what remained of the campaign. *Nor did the king impede their impetus, so they pushed on through Parthia and reached the rim of Hyrcania on the third day.* He had left Craterus behind with the forces that were under his command and the company led by Amyntas augmented by six hundred cavalry and just as many bowmen with the mission of safeguarding Parthia against barbarian invasion. He ordered Erigyius to lead the baggage train on a route through the plain, assigning him an adequate escort. **Alexander himself advanced one hundred and fifty stades** *from Hecatompylus* **with the phalanx and the cavalry and established a fortified base in the valley that leads into Hyrcania, which is shaded by a lofty and dense forest of trees, where** streams *that flow out from beneath huge overhanging crags* irrigate the fertile soil of the dale. From a cavern at the very roots of the pinnacles the River Stiboeites[200] gushes forth on a torrential scale and rushes on in a single bed for *almost* three stades, until it swirls against the block of a breast-shaped rock and its confined current cascades into two channels, *so perpetrating a parting of its waters.* Roaring on from there, it is stirred to seethe more fervently by running over rocks, before falling forcibly into a fissure and foaming up from the thunderous shocks. Through three hundred stades it coasts along a concealed course and then surges back to the surface, *as if conceived from a second source.*

7.18 *These waters then spread into a new bed far wider than before, for their breadth broadens to thirteen stades, then again fades when forced between narrower banks once more. They eventually drain into another*

---

[200] Perhaps the modern Chesmeh-i-Ali about 25km NW of Hecatompylus: cf. P. Pédech, "Deux campagnes d'Antiochus III chez Polybe," *Revue des Études Anciennes*, 60 (1958), 67-81.

Book 7: July 330BC – June 329BC

river that is known as the Rhidagnus. The locals related that whatsoever were washed down the fissure nearer the source would emerge from the further orifice perforce. Therefore, Alexander bade that two *horses* be hurled in where the waters went underground and where the river resurges, by those he sent to see, their cast up carcasses were duly found.

7.19 Alexander had already rendered a rest of four days to his soldiers in this same vicinity, when he received a letter from Nabarzanes, who had been in league with Bessus in the detention of Darius. The gist of his epistle was that he had not been the enemy of Darius, but rather had contributed what he considered valuable advice, but for proffering this faithful counsel to his king, he had come close to being killed by him. Darius had discussed conveying the custody of his person into the hands of the foreign recruits in contravention of propriety and sanctity and vilifying the loyalty of his compatriots that they had maintained immaculately under consecutive kings for two hundred and thirty years. Nabarzanes had stood on a slippery slope, such that the pressures of his predicament had dictated his conduct. Darius too, when he had done away with Bagoas, had pacified the populace by explaining that he had been dispatched on account of his own treachery. Miserable mortals are more enamoured of nothing than the breath of life and it was love of life that had driven him towards deeds of despair. But he had simply collaborated in the affair rather than actively desired it. When catastrophe is everywhere, each man must look to his own welfare.

7.20 If Alexander should bid Nabarzanes to appear before him, then he would turn up without trepidation. He had no fear that so fine a king would violate his sacred pledge of safe conduct. It would be extraordinary for the gods to be deceived by a fellow divinity. However, if Nabaranes were deemed undeserving of Alexander's good faith, many lands lay open to him as a refugee. Wherever a brave man's chosen base stands defines his current home country. However, Alexander did not hesitate to grant assurances in the form in which the Persians conventionally embraced them, such that, should Nabarzanes come before him, he would not be harmed.

7.21 Nevertheless **Alexander advanced into Hyrcania** in tight formation and square array, repeatedly sending out scouts ahead of him, who reconnoitred the region. The light-armed levies led the order of march and the phalanx followed after them with the baggage trailing behind the infantry. Both the inaccessible nature of the territory and its hostile inhabitants caused the king to continue with caution. For in fact *there is a seamless valley that reaches as far as the Caspian Sea, where two tracts of land run out from it resembling arms, these being moderately flexed near their middles to make an arc most like the Moon when it has horns, whilst the face of its orb is far less than full. Leftwards lie the lands where the Cercatae, Mossyni and Chalybes reside, whilst the Leucosyri and the plains of the Amazons are on the opposite* side, the former where the land is northwards depressed and the latter where it leans towards the west.[201]

7.22 *Alexander took every town down to* the Caspian, *which is less salty than similar seas and* especially spawns sizable serpents in considerable numbers. Its fish too are truly distinguished from those elsewhere through their hue. <u>This body of water is known by numerous names nominated by the nations that inhabit its shores, the commonest being the Caspian or the Hyrcanian. In extent it is not inferior to the Euxine</u>[202] <u>and indeed there are those who hold that the Maeotic Marsh percolates into the Caspian.</u>[203] These base their case on the theory that it is fresher than many another sea due to dilution of its salinity by the inflow from its Maeotic tributary. *Further to the north stormy seas batter the shore shoving their waves far inland such that much of that strand is immersed beneath lagoons. But in calmer weather, these seas are expelled with the same seething with which they had swelled and the turf returns to its normal nature as the surf is dispelled. And some have deemed it credible that this might not be the Caspian Sea at all, but that the Ocean ranges round from India to enter upon Hyrcania, the Highlands of which dip down into an unbroken vale, as there has already been reason to retail.*

7.23 *From this place for twenty stades* the king proceeded *via a practically impassable path, which was overgrown with woodland, and torrents and floods further protracted his progress. Yet since no foe opposed him, he pushed on nevertheless and eventually came* into *more* cultivated country. These were the fields of the Favoured Villages as they are dubbed and indeed duly so designated, since their farmland is far more fecund in fine fare than is found elsewhere. For it is said that every vine furnishes a full metretes of wine, whilst some of their fig trees can provide ten medimni of figs, when dried.[204] *The grain that is missed during the reaping and*

---

[201] This location for the Amazon homeland (taken from Curtius 6.4.17) would suggest that Cleitarchus placed it on the steppe to the east of the Caspian Sea. His source on this is likely to have been Onesicritus, who seems to be the earliest of the sources listed by Plutarch (Life of Alexander 46.1) for Alexander having hosted a visit from the Amazon Queen.

[202] Jacoby Fragment 12 of Cleitarchus, in which Pliny, *Natural History* 6.36-38 describes the various names of the Caspian (e.g. Hyrcanian) as deriving from the peoples living upon its shores (cf. Curtius 6.4.18 & Diodorus 17.75.3), then attributes comparable sizes to the Euxine (Pontic Sea) and the Caspian on the authority of Cleitarchus.

[203] Jacoby Fragment 13 of Cleitarchus, wherein Strabo 11.1.5 says that Cleitarchus allowed that water of either the Euxine (Black Sea) or the Caspian might flood across the isthmus of land between them, which would appear to refer to these comments from Curtius 6.4.18 regarding the supply of water from the Maeotic Marsh (vicinity of the Sea of Azov) into the Caspian. The land is indeed very low lying between the Sea of Azov and the northern Caspian, but actual transfer of water would seem unlikely even in antiquity.

[204] Strabo 11.7.2 says sixty medimni; a metretes was about 40 litres, whereas a medimnus was around 55 litres, so each tree produced over half a cubic metre of dried figs (Diodorus 17.75.5).

Book 7: July 330BC – June 329BC

tumbles down upon the earth germinates without a sowing and leads to a second harvest of lavish worth. Another source of lusciousness in the lives of local folk is a type of tree that is common there with the characteristics of an oak and from each of its leaves there drips a honeydew cloak, but unless the natives gather it ere the sun rises, hardly any heat ensures that it volatilizes. A winged creature that infests the hill-country is called the anthredon, which, though smaller than a bee, is everywhere set eyes upon. It roves the ranges raiding nectar from all sorts of blooms and nests in lightning-struck trees and rock wombs. It fashions wax combs and secretes a syrup so sweet as our own honey can barely beat.[205]

7.24 *Alexander had gone forward a further thirty stades, whereupon Phrataphernes came before him surrendering himself and those who had deserted due to the death of Darius. The king gave them a kindly reception* and then progressed to the town of Arvae, where he was met by Craterus and Erigyius. They had escorted Phradates, the governor of the Tapurian people. Alexander also accepted him into allegiance, **and this was a model for many in pursuing a pardon from the king, because he became famed for his fairness.** Thereafter he assigned the Satrapy of Hyrcania to Manapis,[206] who had come to Philip as an exile during the reign of Ochus. He returned the Tapurian people to the rule of Phradates too.

7.25 Just when the king had come into the furthest reaches of Hyrcania, he was approached by *Artabazus in the company of his own offspring as well as the kindred of Darius and* a humble contingent of Greek troops. *His utmost loyalty to Darius has already been described. Upon his arrival Alexander proffered his right hand* in friendship, *for in the first place he had been a guest of Philip whilst in exile during the reign of Ochus, but more movingly he had kept faith with his king to the bitter end. Being therefore welcomed as a comrade, he said: "I pray to god, Sire, that you should prosper in perpetual happiness. I myself, though otherwise blessed, am tormented by this alone, that my impending dotage means I cannot long enjoy your kindness." He was soldiering through his ninety-fifth year and was escorted by nine youths, all of them his sons by the same mother. These he caused to clasp the king's right hand, praying that they should survive only so long as their lives were lived to the benefit of Alexander. The king generally went about on foot, but in this instance, he commanded that mounts be brought for both Artabazus and himself in order to spare the old man the shame, if he rode whilst his sovereign strode.*

---

[205] Jacoby Fragment 14 of Cleitarchus from Demetrius, *De Eloc.* 304, who criticizes the passage as repellent due to its overblown description of a mere wasp.

[206] Arrian, *Anabasis* 3.22.1 calls him Amminapes; he had been involved in the surrender of Egypt to Alexander and had then joined his entourage.

7.26 *Upon pitching camp,* Alexander bade that the Greeks, *who had been brought in by Artabazus,* be called to an assembly. *Yet they responded that they would have to consider their options, unless a pledge of safe-conduct were also extended to the men from Sparta and Sinope. These were the emissaries that had been sent by the Spartans to Darius. Following his defeat, they had joined forces with the Greek mercenaries serving on the Persian side.* But the king commanded that they come before him and take their chances as to what he would offer without either promises or assurances. After protracted hesitation and vacillation they eventually consented to come. But Democrates the Athenian, always to the fore in fomenting opposition to Macedonian power, despaired of pardon and ran himself through with his sword. All the rest, as they *had resolved,* put themselves in the power of Alexander. They numbered fifteen hundred seasoned soldiers *plus ninety men sent to Darius in delegations.* The troops were fully forgiven for their former enmity and were distributed as reinforcements across Alexander's army at the same pay rates as his own levies. *The others were sent home, except the Spartans, whom he commanded to be kept in custody.*[207]

7.27 Alexander marched westwards along the shoreline and reached the territory of the Mardians, who were a nation neighbouring upon Hyrcania. These people were scarcely civilized and had become habituated to banditry. They counted on their combat capability and deprecated the king's supremacy. Therefore, they alone disdained to dispatch delegates to him or to show any sign that they would respect his authority. Rather they occupied their passes with eight thousand men and audaciously defied Alexander's dominion. *Hence the king was vexed that a single tribe should deny him the name of invincibility, so, having left the baggage guarded, he advanced with an invincible vanguard in his company. The march being made by night,* their foes were found *at first light* and it was rather a rout than a real fight with most of them slain and the rest put to flight. *Hurled from the hills that they had held,* the barbarians were rapidly repelled *and the nearby towns were taken that the natives had forsaken.*

7.28 *However, their heartlands were hardly accessible without the army enduring a great deal of trouble. For* they were ensconced by *unscalable cliffs, towering forests and* mountainous massifs *and, where the way was flat, the barbarians had barricaded that with a fresh form of fortification. For this purpose, trees were designedly planted in thick array and whilst their stems were still pliable, they were pleated and thus twisted were bent back into the soil. Thence, seemingly out of another root, shoots sprang forth more vigorously. But these were not left to mature naturally, for the twigs are intertwined like a lattice. When they were cloaked in profuse foliage, they completely covered the land and hence their boughs,*

---

[207] At this time Alexander may not have been sure that the Spartan rebellion of Agis had ended.

Book 7: July 330BC – June 329BC

concealed like snares, choked the route with an unbroken fence. The only recourse was to cut a corridor through this coppiced cultivation, yet even this meant a major operation. For their numerous knots made the trunks intractable and the interlaced limbs of the timber, dangling like rings forming chains, cushioned the chopping with their springy canes.

7.29 *Moreover the natives were wont to burrow beneath the bushes in the manner of beasts. Thus, they had then too infiltrated the thickets and whilst well hidden were harrying their opponents with missiles. Alexander in huntsman mode tracked and transfixed quite a few of them in their hidy-holes and in the end, he ordered his troops to go around the woodland and to burst in through any opening that they found. But* being strangers in this district many stragglers went astray *whilst he was laying waste to the land with fire* and some were seized *by the foe.* The youths who escorted the monarch's mounts drifted a little apart from Alexander and were ambushed by the barbarians, who captured the king's most outstanding steed, which he esteemed above the rest of his herd. This beast was called Bucephalus. Alexander had acquired him as a gift from Demaratus of Corinth. He had carried the king into all of his combats in Asia. Whilst he was not caparisoned, he would only allow his groom to sit upon his back, but not even him when harnessed in the royal trappings. He stood still for Alexander alone thus arrayed and voluntarily bent his knees to aid the king's ascent, seeming to sense just whom he conveyed.

7.30 Such was the distinction of this steed that Alexander was aggravated into greater grief and aggression than was proper. He bade that his beast be tracked down and that proclamations be made by interpreters that none of the natives would survive were his horse not brought back alive. Cowed as he commenced to commit this threat, the Mardians returned the horse together with their most precious presents. Yet even this did not appease Alexander, but rather he directed that the forests be felled and he fetched earth from the fells to pile into the passes where they were choked with branches. The mounds had already been raised to a considerable height, when the barbarians abandoned hope of holding out in their haunts and put forward fifty of their fellows to surrender their nation and crave the king's pardon. Alexander held as hostages the most eminent of these *and made their people subject to Phradates.*

7.31 On the fifth day thereafter Alexander arrived back at his established basecamp. Thence he sent Artabazus back home after redoubling the distinctions that Darius had vested in him. At this time, he came to that Hyrcanian city that housed the palace of Darius,[208] where, having accepted the king's pledge of safe-conduct, Nabarzanes came before him proffering prodigious presents. Amongst these was Bagoas, a eunuch of uniquely lovely looks and just then in the very

---

[208] Perhaps Arvae as in 7.24, which is Zadracarta in Arrian, *Anabasis* 3.23.6 - possibly modern Sari.

flower of his youth, whom Darius had been wont to penetrate and with whom Alexander used later to mate. Mainly through this youth's pleas he was driven to agree an amnesty for Nabarzanes.

7.32 There is, as already mentioned, an Amazon people bordering upon Hyrcania and dwelling in the fields of Themiscyra on the banks of the River Thermodon and in the mountains beyond.[209] Their queen at that time was Thalestris, who ruled the entire region between the Caucasus Range and the River Phasis. She was distinguished by her combination of bodily strength with beauty and her Amazon army much admired her bravery. Being fired with desire to visit Alexander, she set forth from Thermodon and *for thirty-five days* she travelled *amidst the most truculent tribes* via the Caspian Gates and came to the Hyrcanian frontier. From here she sent emissaries ahead to make it known that she was keen to call upon and consort with him who held the throne. She was at once forwarded a welcome, whereupon she bade the bulk of her battalion to abide at the border and went on with an escort of three hundred women each armed as an Amazon. Sporting two spears in her right hand, she alighted from her steed as soon as Alexander was sighted.[210]

7.33 *The monarch and his men were amazed by the Amazons, for what they wore was weird for women. Amazon dresses do not drape the entire torso, since the left side of the chest is bared to beneath the breast, although they do veil all the rest. However, the hem of the skirt, which is girt with a knot, does not descend beneath the knee. They leave their left nipples intact so as to suckle their female offspring,* the boys being forwarded to their fathers for mothering. *But the right ones they sear, the better to bend a bow or cast a spear.* When one of these warrior women dies, her male partner is allowed to stay alive, so long as her corpse survives and he does not dally with other wives. But if this law be violated, he is summarily castrated and his genitals are incinerated at her tomb.[211]

---

[209] This was noted at the end of Section 7.21, but then placed to the east of the region. It is likely that Cleitarchus or his source (Onesicritus?) has attempted to reconcile traditional legends of an Amazon nation near the Thermodon on the southern shores of the Black Sea (i.e. west of Hyrcania) with the visit of a warrior queen from east of the Caspian Sea to Alexander's camp in this vicinity. This underlines the haziness of Cleitarchus' grasp of the geography of the area.

[210] The Jacoby Fragments are 15 (Plutarch, *Alexander* 46) and 16 (Strabo, *Geography* 11.5.4).

[211] This is Jacoby Fragment 32 of Cleitarchus from a scrap of papyrus (Pap. Oxyrh. II 218 col. II). It is uncertain whether it belongs with the account of Alexander's encounter with the Amazon Queen, although some of the historical review of Amazons in Justin 2.3-4 might have been sourced from Cleitarchus. A secondary possibility is that it is the corollary of *suttee* for men who murder their wives (cf. Cleitarchus Reconstruction 11.13). The papyrus co-attributes the report to "Zopyrus", probably Zopyrus of Magnesia, who seems to have written a history on *The Foundation of Miletus* perhaps around 300BC, which might have said something about Amazons.

Book 7: July 330BC – June 329BC

Figure 7.1. The meeting of Alexander with the Amazon Queen, Thalestris (from a French translation of Curtius by de Vaugelas, 1696)

7.34 *Displaying a dauntless demeanour Thalestris scrutinized the king, her perception of his appearance failing to match up to the fame of his achievements, for all the barbarians vest their veneration in individuals of vast stature. They consider that none is capable of colossal accomplishments, save him that Nature has favoured with a fabulous physique. But* Alexander *was bedazzled by her dashing dismount and by the dignity of the dame. Therefore, he* enquired as to whether she wished to present a request and she unabashedly confessed that she came to conceive offspring by the king. She was the strongest and most stalwart of women and he had made it manifest that he was the most remarkable of men through his achievements. The children of such a pair should surpass the rest of mankind in excellence, so with her he might beget a worthy heir. *Though she should retain any female child, any male would be forwarded to his father without fail. Then Alexander asked her whether she would like to set off soldiering with him?* But she excused herself on account of having left her realm lacking a guard, but pressed her appeal that he should not let her leave forlorn in her longing. *With the queen's wish for copulation being keener than the king's,* she obliged him to tarry there through the thirteen days that were required to indulge her desires. Finally, *when she believed that she had conceived,* Alexander allowed her to leave *laden with lavish presents* and thence he pursued his own path to Parthia.

7.35 It was actually at this juncture that Alexander gave vent to his inclinations and turned away from temperance and continence, venerable virtues at the peak of prosperity, veering *instead* towards loftiness and licentiousness. **From this point onwards the king** *considered that he incontestably possessed the throne of Asia. Hence, he regarded his own country's customs, the healthily restrained traditions of the Macedonian kings and their citizenlike dispositions, as too mean for the magnificence of his monarchy. Therefore, he* assumed the imperial pomp of the Persians that was on a par with the power and prestige of the gods. He anticipated that the conquerors of so many countries would prostrate themselves upon the ground in veneration of him and would gradually become used to servile obsequiousness. *In this* he welcomed their becoming equal to the conquered people.[212]

7.36 *First of all he installed Asiatic rod-bearers to orchestrate his court and he mandated that the most eminent of their men should serve as his sentries and among them was the brother of Darius, Oxathres.* Then Alexander donned the diadem such as Darius had once worn, which is a purple fillet interlaced with white *that no former Macedonian monarch's head had*

---

[212] To set Sections 7.35-37 in context the reader should appreciate that Cleitarchus was one of the Cynics, a sect that considered abstemiousness to be next to godliness. They were an early manifestation of the asceticism that later launched Christianity and Islam. By contrast Plutarch in his essays *On The Fortune Or Virtue of Alexander, Moralia* 329F-330A actually praised the king for his *rapprochement* with the Persians by adopting elements of their dress.

Book 7: July 330BC – June 329BC

borne. He also attired himself in the tunic *of purple* with a central white stripe and the cummerbund *and the scepter*. In fact, he adopted all of the Persian rulers' raiment, except for the trousers and the long-sleeved garment. *Nor was he even nervous about the portent in exchanging the victor's insignia for the routed realm's regalia. Actually, he used to say that he was displaying the spoils picked from the Persians, but he had seen fit to assume their customs as well as their costume and habitual hauteur came with the haute couture. Additionally, the letters that would be delivered to Europe he sealed with the device cut into the gem of his old ring, whereas he impressed those that he wrote to Asia with the ring of Darius, so as to suggest that a single charisma could not captivate both cultures.* He also distributed both Persian apparel and harnesses for their horses to his companions and to the cavalry, since these were his senior soldiers. Despite that they despised the cloaks with their purple hems *embroidered with gold*, they did not dare not to wear what the king would behold.

7.37 During the dominion of Darius there were kept at court three hundred and sixty-five women of such superlative loveliness as selection from all the lands of Asia could gather in. Nightly they processed around the king's bower, so he could choose which he wished to deflower. So, Alexander too retained in his retinue concubines as numerous as the days of the year *accompanied by herds of eunuchs, who, though not whole, were practised in performing the passive sexual role.* In fact, Alexander rarely employed their services and generally stuck to his established practices, for fear of offending his fellow Macedonians. *Finally, so as not to seem to stint or starve the extravagance, he convened vast banquets that he embellished with entertainments in keeping with kingly magnificence. For he had forgotten that great resources are not customarily produced by such practices, but rather rapidly reduced.*

7.38 *These activities, being tainted with ostentation and foreign tradition, were openly despised by the veteran troops of Philip, a faction who were unfamiliar with suchlike luxuries. And throughout the camp but a single sentiment and subject of conversation was rife: the thought that they had lost more in victory than they had gained during the strife. For now, they were most completely overcome, in giving themselves up to every alien and outlandish custom. How could they face returning home when they were dressed as if they were conquered men? Actually, they were already ashamed, since their sovereign resembled one of the vanquished rather than a victor, being recast as a Satrap of Darius instead of a Macedonian commander.* Indeed, the king perceived that both his principal friends and his forces were seriously aggrieved, so he sought to regain their goodwill through benefactions and *some* reforms *he had conceived*.

7.39 *So as not to seem isolated in succumbing to the corrupt customs of the conquered countries, he permitted his men to marry any of the captive women with whom they were sleeping. For he calculated that they would be less likely to hanker after heading homewards, if they had in the camp some semblance of a hearth and a household. He also held that the hardships of the campaign would make the blessings of marriage more amenable. Furthermore, to facilitate reinforcing his soldiery without stripping Macedon of manpower, he planned that the sons of his veterans should succeed their fathers in serving as recruits upon the palisades within which they had been born. He deemed that they would be the more steadfast for having spent not just their training but also their infancy within his own camp. Indeed, this policy even persists under Alexander's successors. Accordingly, as boys they received regular rations and as youths they were outfitted with arms and steeds and their sires were assigned premiums in proportion to the number of their sons. If the sire of any son were slain, the orphan still drew his father's entire pay, and they spent their boyhood engaged upon sundry military operations. Hence having been hardened by hardships and hazards from a tender age, they formed a force that was found invincible. They knew naught but the camp as their country and they fought no fight but that it led to victory. These progeny were proclaimed to be Alexander's Epigoni.*[213]

7.40 In order that the muttering not be magnified into mutiny, the king called for campaigning to curtail their leisures, because cause was conveniently mounting for measures. For **Bessus, *having* arrayed himself in regal raiment, *had* commanded that he be called Artaxerxes,**[214] ***and he was summoning up the Scythians and the rest of the races from the region of the Tanais. Satibarzanes, an accomplice of Bessus in the murder of Darius, announced this news.***[215] ***Alexander had accepted his fealty and reinstated him in the Arian Satrapy. But because the king's columns, being overladen with luxurious paraphernalia and plunder, were barely mobile, Alexander ordered that firstly his own and thereafter the entire army's baggage, excepting absolute essentials, be fetched into their midst. The weighed down wagons were wheeled whither there was a wide and level field. Whilst everyone was watching out for what he would next compel, the king bade that the draught animals be led away and touched a torch to his own baggage first, then required that the rest be fired as well. Kindled by their owners, there were combusted those riches that to rescue unwrecked from the cities of their foes they had often had to quench infernos. And though these rewards had been won with their blood, none dared voice laments, when the selfsame flames were consuming their king's own affluence. Soon after the sense of it assuaged their sorrow, since, set up for soldiering and ready for anything, they rejoiced that they had jettisoned their baggage instead of their fitness for fighting.***[216]

---

[213] Literally the "Afterborn" or alternatively the "Descendants": the Greek term is preserved in the Latin manuscripts of Justin 12.4.11. The original *Epigoni* were the sons of the *Seven Against Thebes*, who renewed the war of their fathers (e.g. the two plays with these titles by Aeschylus).

[214] The regnal name of several former Persian Great Kings.

[215] This occurred at Sousia (Arrian, *Anabasis* 3.25.1-3), which is probably the modern Tus.

[216] The detailed account of baggage burning in Curtius 6.6.14-17 is corroborated by Polyaenus 4.3.10 and Plutarch, *Alexander* 57.1-2; although the latter pair place the burning just prior to the entry into India, this is probably due to the fact that Cleitarchus counted southern Afghanistan as

Book 7: July 330BC – June 329BC

7.41 Therefore they were bound for the Bactrian territories, but then Nicanor, the son of Parmenion, was suddenly seized by death and a great grief for him enfolded everyone. More mournful than anyone, their monarch was minded to halt the march to attend his funeral, but a lack of provisions harried him into hurrying on. Hence, he left Philotas with two thousand six hundred men to furnish a fitting send-off for his brother and ***Alexander*** himself ***hastened to confront Bessus.*** But letters were delivered to him from the surrounding satraps ***whilst he was on his way***, from which ***he learnt that his foe was in fact faring forth to confront him in arms. Though bemused by the boldness of Bessus,*** Alexander *also* heard that Satibarzanes, whom he himself had placed in charge of the Satrapy of the Arians, had murdered his Macedonian minders and defected to Bessus. He was holed up in Artacana,[217] a considerable citadel of that satrapy that was situated upon a naturally tenable site. Therefore, though keen to cow Bessus himself, he rather reckoned he should first turn his attention to tackling Satibarzanes, who was the nearer of his enemies. Hence, he led his light infantry, comprising the Agrianians and the hypaspists, together with his contingents of cavalry via the mountains into Aria. Performing forced marches throughout the night, he came upon his opponents unawares. On realising that he had arrived and fearful of both the magnificence and the fame of his forces, Satibarzanes fled for Bactra with but two thousand mounted troops, because he could not muster more on the spur of the moment. He instructed the remainder of his men to hold out among the nearby mountains.

7.42 There is a towering rock in that range that is precipitous *on the side facing westwards but presents a slighter slope slipping down to the east and is thickly forested with a perennial spring, its circumference stretching to thirty-two stades. It has a grassy ground at its crest, upon which the Arians ordered all men unfit for war to rest. They themselves stacked up stones and tree trunks where the cliff edge was depressed. They numbered thirteen thousand men-at-arms, whom* Alexander *left Craterus to invest, whilst he himself pressed on in pursuit of Satibarzanes. But upon finding that his foe was far ahead in his flight, he* turned back *to overwhelm those who held the mountain height. Initially, he ordered his men to clear away*

---

part of India and it was true that Alexander was about to cross the mountains moving southwards into Afghanistan in pursuit of Satibarzanes at this juncture.

[217] Artacana in the manuscripts of Curtius 6.6.33 and Artacoana in Arrian, *Anabasis* 3.25.6, but Chortacana in Diodorus 17.78.1; its location remains uncertain: most have assumed that it lay at or in the vicinity of modern Herat, but Donald Engels has argued in *Alexander the Great and the Logistics of the Macedonian Army*, pp.87-91 that the "rock" in the nearby mountains was Kalat-i-Nadiri 60km north of Tus; a reconciliation of this with the order of events in the Cleitarchan tradition is not apparent, since, for example, Engels reverses the order of the attack on Artacana and the siege of the rebel stronghold in the mountains; it is easier to accept the traditional view, which would place Alexander on the borders of Bactria near Kushka immediately north of Herat when he heard of the defection of Satibarzanes; hence Artacana was near Herat, which is also the site of Alexandria in Aria (cf. *Geographies* of Strabo 11.10.1 & Ptolemy 6.17).

the barricade wherever headway could be made, but then, when they encountered sheer cliffs and unscalable scree, it seemed that Nature's opposition made for pointless industry. Since to advance was arduous and to retreat was risky, Alexander, being ever of a mind to wrestle with adversity, pondered plan after plan, resorting to every expediency, as is wont to happen when we ditch our initial strategy.

7.43 Whilst the king was in a quandary, Fortune put forward a scheme beyond the reach of rationality. There blew in a wild wind from the west and the troops had felled loads of lumber in looking to lay a causeway up the scree. This timber was now dessicated by the searing heat, so Alexander ordered other trees to be piled up to fuel a bonfire and it rapidly reached the mountain crest as the logs were raised higher. Then burning brands were cast in all around it, so that the whole heap was simultaneously lit. The gale flung the flames into the faces of their foes and the sky was veiled as if by clouds as voluminous fumes arose. The woods resounded with the roar of the conflagration and parts that the troops did not ignite caught alight, so that all about them suffered incineration. The barbarians sought to evade terminal torment, wherever the blaze had abated, but where the flames gave way, there their opponents waited. Therefore, they were dispatched by a medley of deaths: some rushed into the midst of the infernos; from the crags others went a-leaping; some consigned themselves to the arms of their foes, whilst a few, half-fried, came into their keeping. Thus, **by aggressing without cessation, the king compelled their capitulation.**

7.44 From there Alexander rejoined Craterus, who was besieging Artacana. Having completed the preparations, he was waiting for the coming of the king, so as to tender him the title of taker of that town in accordance with etiquette. Hence Alexander ordered that the siege-towers be trundled forward and the sight itself so intimidated the natives that they stretched their arms beyond their ramparts palms skyward. Then they began to beseech the king to focus his ferocity upon Satibarzanes, the fomenter of their defection, whilst sparing such suppliants as put their own selves into subjection. Alexander did pardon them and he not only lifted his blockade but saw that restitution of all the inhabitants' property was made. **Thus, thirty days after the rock's reduction, every Arian city was brought into submission.**

7.45 As he was quitting this city, he was met by reinforcements in the form of fresh recruits: Zoilus had fetched five hundred cavalrymen from Greece; Antipater had dispatched three thousand men from Illyria; a hundred and thirty Thessalian horsemen had come with Philip; two thousand six hundred foreign troops had arrived from Lydia and three hundred cavalry of the same country accompanied them. With his augmented army, **Alexander advanced upon the Drangians,** *a warlike nation, whose satrap was* **Barzaentes.** *He* **had been the accomplice of Bessus in his treason against their king.** Now he fled

Book 7: July 330BC – June 329BC

into India in dread of retribution,[218] *of which he was deserving. Alexander marched to the capital of Drangianê, where he paused to rest his army.*[219]

7.46 *It was on the ninth day that* the king *had been encamped in this locality that he* was *betrayed into perpetrating a dire deed, which was alien to his characteristic probity. When he was not simply safe from foreign forces, but actually invincible, he was assailed by insider villainy.* Dimnus was a man of modest influence and esteem with Alexander, a member of his monarch's circle of Friends, but on some account he became discontented with the king and incautiously conspired in a plot against his life.[220] Dimnus was fervently infatuated with his catamite called Nicomachus, *fixated by the favours of a body that was surrendered solely to him.* Virtually frantic, as was transparent in his countenance, he drew the youth aside unseen into a temple, first confiding that he had a secret and unrepeatable matter to reveal. With the young man held in suspense, Dimnus entreated him to swear in the name of their mutual love and the vows they had exchanged that he would keep silent concerning what Dimnus was about to share. So Nicomachus swore such an oath by the gods of that shrine, not reckoning on being obliged to expose, even at the cost of being forsworn, the secret that Dimnus was now to disclose. For what Dimnus divulged was that he was a member of a conspiracy comprising courageous and illustrious men that had planned upon the third day thereafter to attempt the assassination of their sovereign. Upon hearing this, the youth resolutely refuted that he had vowed to participate in a treasonous murder and asserted that no sacred oath could bind him to conceal treachery either. Out of his mind with both infatuation and fear, in tears Dimnus grasped the right hand of his beloved and first of all implored that he pledge himself to the plot and its implementation, but then begged, if he could not bear actually to be

---

[218] Barzaentes is called Ariobarzanes in *Metz Epitome* 3: "India" means Southern Afghanistan.

[219] This is very likely to have been at or close by the modern Farah (Phraa) in the west of Afghanistan. Strabo 11.8.9, Ptolemy 6.19.4-5 and Pliny 6.61 give the name Prophthasia to a site approx. 270km from Alexandria in Aria (Herat), which is about the correct distance for modern Farah (they give the route distances seemingly taken from the *bematists* of Alexander's expedition). Stephanus Byzantinus in his entry for "Phrada" states that Alexander called this place Prophthasia and that it was a town among the Drangians (a.k.a. Zarangians). Hence it is clear that Prophthasia was very probably at or near Farah, although Tarn has differed by placing it further south on Lake Seistan. The name Prophthasia ("Anticipation" in the sense of forestalling something) assigned by Alexander seems to refer to him having outrun fate here in the form of the Dimnus conspiracy, which ensues. The place is therefore believed to be the scene of the Philotas Affair.

[220] So began the Philotas Affair, a tragedy in three Acts, namely: *The Dimnus Conspiracy, The Trial & Execution of Philotas* and *The Assassination of Parmenion.* The account in Curtius is particularly full and vivid. Speculatively, Curtius found this quasi-judicial purgation especially interesting, since it bore comparison with the downfalls of some of the great political figures of his own time, such as Sejanus. Parallels with Diodorus suggest that Curtius's version is highly likely to be derived from Cleitarchus, hence it probably constitutes a near verbatim and barely abridged Latin translation of a large section of his text. However, I follow my standard practice of only using bold characters where relatively direct corroboration of a Cleitarchan source is available from Diodorus or elsewhere.

involved, that he should at least agree not to betray his lover. For the devotion of Dimnus to Nicomachus beyond everything else particularly had this strongest proof: that he had entrusted his life to the trueness of the untried youth.

7.47 However, in the end, when Nicomachus maintained his revulsion for the treason, Dimnus tried to terrify him with a threat of death, saying that the conspirators would inaugurate their most admirable enterprise with the murder of Nicomachus. Then, alternating between calling him an effeminate and womanish coward, the betrayer of his lover and promising lavish incentives even including a kingdom, Dimnus sought to warp a mind to which such a crime was utterly abhorrent. Thereupon he drew his sword and set it first to his beloved's throat, then to his own, combining begging with belligerence and thus at last **Dimnus extorted a promise from Nicomachus not just of silence but even of assistance.** Yet the youth possessed a staunchly steadfast spirit such as suits a person of conscience, so he had not veered from his previous view, but rather affected to feel such affection for Dimnus that he could deny him nothing. He then proceeded to gather intelligence as to the identities of Dimnus's associates in such a fateful undertaking. It mattered greatly, he said, what sort of men had agreed to put their hands to so distinguished a deed. Out of his mind with a mixture of amour and remorse, Dimnus simultaneously expressed his gratitude and his congratulations to Nicomachus for not having hesitated to ally himself with the bravest young men including Demetrius the Bodyguard,[221] Peucolaus and Nicanor. To these he added Aphobetus, Iolaus, Dioxenus, Archepolis and Amyntas.

7.48 When he was dismissed from this dialogue, *being as yet underage,* **Nicomachus related what he had learnt to his** *elder* **brother. This man was called Cebalinus** *and he was acutely concerned in case a conspirator should confess the plot to the king before they could.* It seemed best that Nicomachus should remain in the tent lest the conspirators realised that they were being betrayed, if he were uncustomarily conveyed into the royal quarters to see the king. Consequently, **Cebalinus himself went and stood at the entrance to the courtyard of the royal quarters,** *for he was not allowed any further forward. There he waited for anyone from the upper echelon of Alexander's Friends who would admit him to the king's presence. Of these by chance all had already gone save for* **Philotas the son of Parmenion, who had remained there** *for reasons known to none. Blithering and blatantly in a considerable state of consternation,* Cebalinus blurted out to him what he had heard from his brother and called for the king to be informed without demur. *Whereupon he was warmly praised by* **Philotas,** *who at once* went in to Alexander and engaged him in lengthy conversation on a variety of topics, but made no mention of what he had learnt from Cebalinus. *At twilight* the youth intercepted Philotas as he emerged *into the courtyard of*

---

[221] Demetrius was a *Somatophylax*, i.e. a member of the elite seven-man bodyguard of the king and therefore one of the most senior officers in the Macedonian court.

Book 7: July 330BC – June 329BC

the royal quarters and queried whether his mission had been accomplished? But Philotas, professing that he had found no opportunity to talk to the king, said that on the following day he would see Alexander alone on the matter *and went on his way.*

7.49 *It may be that Philotas was in fact a party to the conspiracy or perhaps he just failed to treat the matter sufficiently seriously. At all events,* the next day *Cebalinus was already at hand when Philotas arrived at the royal quarters and as he entered, he prompted him to recall the matter he had made known to him the day before.* Philotas *retorted that he was attending to it, yet* even then did not declare the affair to the king. Cebalinus grew suspicious and forsook his faith in Philotas. He deemed that there should be no further delay, lest another betray the plot and imperil *his brother and* him. Hence, he pestered one of the Royal Pages, a noble youth named Metron, who had charge of the armoury, and he apprised him of the planned perfidy, beseeching him to report it immediately. Having concealed Cebalinus in the armoury, Metron went at once to the king, who happened to be bathing, and revealed what his informer had imparted, adding that he had him in hiding. Alexander reacted with alarm, sending his attendants to apprehend Dimnus *and entering the armoury, where Cebalinus was exultant, exclaiming: "Sire, you are saved, rescued from the blows of faithless fellows." Thereupon the king interrogated him as to his whole story and put together a complete picture. And then he returned to the question of how many days it had been since Nicomachus had brought him this information? And when Cebalinus conceded that it had happened the day before yesterday, Alexander considered him hardly trustworthy in waiting so long to report what he had heard and ordered that he be fettered. But Cebalinus began to bellow that he had dashed off to Philotas the instant he had heard, so it was Philotas who had covered up what he had discovered.*[222]

7.50 *Then Alexander likewise interrogated the youth as to whether he had gone to Philotas and whether Cebalinus had pressed for them to approach the king. When Cebalinus resolutely reaffirmed his assertions, Alexander held his hands up to the Heavens and with his eyes flooding with tears he deplored that one who was formerly his fondest friend had rendered him such a reward.* Meanwhile, Dimnus, *not at all innocent of why he was summoned by his sovereign and happening to have his sword strapped on,* dealt himself a mortal wound. *Then the men from the royal retinue rushed to restrain him and conveyed him to the king's quarters. Glaring at him, Alexander asked: "What atrocity have I intended to commit against you that you should feel that Philotas is fitter than I myself to rule the Macedonians?"* But Dimnus was already rendered speechless and so he

---

[222] Adopting Jeep's emendation of Curtius 6.7.27 to read *ab eo operiri comperta* instead of the manuscript reading of *ab eo percomperta*.

simply sighed and, turning his face from the king's gaze, he at once collapsed and died. Yet the king had already learnt everything from his suicide.[223]

7.51 The king, *having* commanded that Philotas report to the royal quarters, *addressed him thus: "If for two days Cebalinus covered up a conspiracy primed to take my life, he has merited capital punishment. But he has shifted the blame for his felony onto Philotas through his claim that he immediately imparted the information to him. The closer your status of friendship ties you to me, the more villainous is your duplicity, although indeed I concede that this conduct better becomes a Cebalinus than a Philotas. You have a sympathetic judge, if you are at least able to absolve yourself, Philotas, of what should never have come to pass." To this Philotas responded without the least trepidation, if his emotions were to be measured by his expression, saying that Cebalinus had indeed retailed some talk from a tart to him, but that he himself had given scant credence to so fickle an informant. He had worried that he would not be able to tell of a tiff between a catamite and his lover without arousing derision from others. However, since Dimnus had done away with himself,* Philotas confessed that the information, *whatever its pedigree,* should not have been suppressed. *Then he embraced the king and commenced cajoling him to concentrate upon his career to date rather than this current misdemeanour, which was merely muteness rather than anything mutinous.* It is hard to say whether the king believed him or withheld his anger deep within himself. He proffered Philotas his right hand to seal their reconciliation and said that it seemed to him a case of spurning rather than hiding the information.

7.52 Yet the king convened a council of his Friends, to which however Philotas was not invited, and he bade that Nicomachus be brought before them, who set out the sequence of events just as they had been imparted to the king. Few were closer to Alexander than Craterus, who was consequently hostile towards Philotas as his rival for preferment. He was well aware that Philotas had often overburdened Alexander's ears by vaunting his valour and the value of his services excessively and hence was suspected of waywardness rather than criminality. Reckoning that there would be no better opportunity to disparage his enemy by obscuring his antipathy with a veneer of loyalty, he commented: "Would that you had discussed this affair with us from the start! If you had wished to forgive Philotas, we would have coaxed you to keep him in innocence of the degree of his debt to you, rather than have him meditate more often on his jeopardy, after having been put in fear of his life, than on your generosity. For Philotas will perpetually be in a position to conspire against you, yet you will not perpetually be in a position to pardon Philotas. There is no reason for you to imagine that a man who has manifested such audacity can be reformed by

---

[223] Diodorus 17.79.5 says Alexander learnt everything on arresting Dimnus, but must mean from his behaviour rather than from speech, since he agrees with Curtius regarding Dimnus's suicide.

Book 7: July 330BC – June 329BC

forgiveness. He knows that those who have exhausted one's clemency cannot expect any more mercy. But even if, overcome either by repentance or by your indulgence, the man himself should wish to shun strife, I am confident that his father Parmenion will be discontent to be indebted to you for his son's life. He heads so huge an army and holds such long-standing influence with the troops that he occupies a position scarcely inferior in authority to your own. There are such kindnesses as cause us to recoil. Since the man is dishonoured who declares himself deserving of death, Philotas will foster the feeling that he has received injustice rather than been reprieved. Therefore, be assured that you must make war on these fellows for your safety's sake. Sufficient foes remain amongst those whom we are about to pursue. Let you protect your flank against internal opponents too. If you but rid youself of these, I fear no foreign enemies."

7.53 So spoke Craterus and neither did the rest doubt that Philotas would not have stifled the story of the plot unless he were either its instigator or a conspirator. Indeed, what loyal and well-intentioned man - not necessarily a Friend *of the king*, but even the lowest of the low - on hearing the accusations made to Philotas would not have run off to his ruler right away? Yet the son of Parmenion, the commander of the cavalry and a consultant on all his sovereign's secrets, was not even inspired by the example set by Cebalinus, who had brought him everything from his brother's briefing. Philotas had even pretended that the king had not had a moment to talk to him, so that his informer should not seek an alternative intermediary. Nicomachus had hastened to disburden his conscience, despite being bound by an obligation to the gods. Yet Philotas had frittered away almost the entire day on mere horseplay, loth to introduce a few words pertaining his sovereign's preservation during such protracted and perchance inconsequential conversation. If indeed he had disbelieved such testimony out of the mouths of mere youths, why then would he have strung them along for two days as if he trusted in their allegations? Cebalinus should have been sent away at once, if Philotas had discounted his accusations. Chivalry should be shown in the face of one's own jeopardy, but, when there is concern for the sovereign's safety, there is a duty of credulity, such that even groundless allegations should be taken seriously.

7.54 They were therefore unanimous that Philotas should be put to the question in order to press him to name his accomplices in the treachery. Before dismissing them, the king bound them to silence concerning the outcome of the council. Then he ordered that that a march be announced for the following day, so that no signal of the council's decisions should be betrayed to the traitors. Philotas was even invited to what was to be his last banquet and Alexander deigned not merely to dine but also to gossip with the man he had condemned. Then in the second watch of the night with the extinction of every light there congregated in the king's quarters Hephaistion, Craterus, Coenus and Erigyius from among the Friends plus Perdiccas and Leonnatus from the Bodyguards together with a few others. Orders were issued by these that those on watch at the headquarters should stand to in arms. Cavalry detachments had already been deployed to all the exits from the camp and they had also been ordered to seal the roads in order that nobody should covertly abscond to Parmenion, who at that time commanded Media and vast contingents of troops. Furthermore, Atarrhias entered the royal quarters with three hundred men-at-arms. Ten deputies were seconded to him, each escorted by ten guardsmen. These were detailed to apprehend the other plotters, whilst Atarrhias was dispatched to Philotas with the three hundred. With the support of fifty of his readiest recruits he set about forcing the barred entrance to his house, for he had commanded the rest completely to surround the premises, lest Philotas should slip away via some secret access. But either on account of a carefree conscience or else overcome by fatigue he had succumbed to slumber and he was still only half-awake when he was seized by Atarrhias. When at last he was fully alert and fetters were fastened upon him, he groaned: "O Sire, your goodness has been soured by the bitterness of my antagonists!" And without further oratory he was led into the king's quarters with a hood over his head.

7.55 On the following day **the king decreed a general assembly of the Macedonians in arms in order to try Philotas.** Around six thousand soldiers as well as a crowd of camp-followers and servants congregated and were crammed into the royal enclosure. Files of guardsmen screened Philotas in order that he should not be glimpsed by the masses until the king had addressed his troops. It was the ancient custom of the Macedonians that the army - or the populace in time of peace - should try capital cases and the king's influence counted for nothing unless they had been swayed by his evidence before their decision. Accordingly, the corpse of Dimnus was introduced at the outset, the majority being ignorant of what he had plotted or how he had died. Thereupon the king made his entry to the gathering, his sense of sorrow being revealed in his expression and the solemnity of his Friends as well inspired no small apprehension of what was about to transpire.

7.56 For a long while **the king** seemed stunned and stupefied as he stood staring at the ground, then, recovering his self-possession, he **began to speak**: "I have very nearly been wrenched from you by the villainy of certain individuals and it is through the providence and mercy of the gods that I am still alive. The awesome sight of you so congregated has compelled me to be the more vehement in seeking vengeance against the traitors, since it is the primary or rather the sole profit of my existence to be able to render due rewards to such men of the utmost valiance and most meriting of my beneficence." Gasps and sighs from the assembled soldiers necessitated the suspension of his speech, whilst tears welled up in the eyes of each. Then their sovereign resumed: "How much more marked are the emotions I shall stir in your senses, when I expose the instigators of such foul offences. These I still shrink from defaming and, as if they could still be redeemed, I refrain from naming. Yet I must overcome the recollection of my former affection, since a conspiracy of corrupt countrymen requires revelation, for how can I keep quiet concerning such an abomination? Though behoven to me and to my father for so many favours, though the eldest of all our Friends

Book 7: July 330BC – June 329BC

and despite his age, **Parmenion proposed himself to lead this heinous outrage. His confederate, Philotas,** suborned Peucolaus, Demetrius and this very Dimnus whose body you behold before you together with the rest of the demented men who meant to murder me." All about him howls of indignant resentment broke out from the whole host, just as is wont to occur with a crowd, and especially an assemblage of soldiers, when it is aroused by partiality or fury. At that point Nicomachus and Metron and Cebalinus were led forward and each testified concerning his story. Yet none of the information from any of them fingered Philotas as a participant in the treachery. Therefore, following the first outburst of outrage, the evidence of the informants was absorbed in silence.

7.57 Thereafter the king continued: "What, then, does it seem to you is the mindset of a man, who, when the matter was disclosed to him, withheld the information, considering that the death of Dimnus demonstrates that the affair was not without foundation? Cebalinus was not intimidated by his liability to be tortured in reporting a deniable crime and Metron even burst into my bathroom, so as not to delay disburdening himself of the betrayal even for a short time. None but Philotas feared nothing and disbelieved everything. What a man of mettle! Yet should not such a man be stirred to action by his king's jeopardy? Should his expression not alter in anxiously hearing out the accuser of such a conspiracy? Assuredly it is perfidy that lies behind his silence and a keen craving for kingship sped his spirit headlong unto the ultimate treachery. His father is the master of Media and he himself covets more than he can properly command by dint of his overpowering influence with many commanders in my army. He would even have removed me whilst lacking heirs, insofar as I am without issue. Yet in this Philotas errs, for I do possess kindred, parents and progeny in all of you! Whilst you survive, I cannot be completely deprived of family." Then he read aloud a letter that Parmenion had written to his sons, Philotas and Nicanor, which had been intercepted, although it did not really reveal evidence that they had sinister plans in store. For this was the nub of it: "First of all concern yourselves with caring for your own advantage and then for the advantage of those close to you, since we shall thereby bring about what we envisage." And the king remarked that it was couched in such terms, so that, should it reach the sons, it could be understood by the conspirators, but should it be intercepted, it would not be decoded by outsiders.

Figure 7.2. The trial and execution of Philotas (from a 1696 edition of Curtius)

7.58 Alexander continued: "Yet it may be objected that Dimnus failed to finger Philotas, when he indicated the rest of his comrades in crime. This need not be evidence of his innocence, but rather of his influence, insofar as even those who could have disclosed his name were so much in dread of him that they still hid his identity, when they made known their own. But the history of his own behaviour in fact fingers Philotas. At that time back in Macedon that Amyntas,[224] who was my cousin, concocted a treasonous plot to murder me, Philotas was consorting with him as his ally and crony. And this is the man who gave his sister in matrimony to Attalus,[225] than whom I had no deadlier enemy. Then, when I wrote to him in the context of our close camaraderie and friendship regarding the response rendered to me by the Oracle of Zeus-Ammon, this is that very man who had the insolence to write back that, though he congratulated me on being recognized among the gods, he nevertheless pitied those that must live under one who transcends the bounds of humanity. These things indicate that his heart has long since been estranged from me and is jealous of my glory. These signs, soldiers, so long as was viable I suppressed in my mind. Indeed, it seemed to me as though I would wrench out part of my own guts, if I were to vitiate men that I had made so great. But now it is not mere words that must be punished: rash rant has reached the point of swords. If you believe me, Philotas has honed these blades against me, else, if you believe him, he has allowed them to be."

7.59 "Where shall I turn, soldiers? To whom shall I entrust my life? I have placed him in sole command of the cavalry, the finest force in my army, the flower of our young nobility. My safety, my aspirations and my conquests I have consigned to his good faith and guardianship. I have elevated his father to share the same pedestal upon which you have set me. I have made Media, than which no region is richer, subject to his mandate and authority, as well as so many thousands of our compatriots and confederates. Where I had sought support, a threat juts forth. How much happier to have fallen in the fighting, felled by a foe, rather than die by a countryman's blow! Now, preserved from the only perils that I feared, I am beset by threats that should never have appeared. Soldiers, you are accustomed repeatedly to plead with me to take fewer risks with my safety. Of this policy that you have urged upon me, you are now able to answer for the implementation. It is in your hands and through your arms that I seek my salvation. If you are unwilling to save me, I do not wish for safety, and you cannot intend my preservation, unless you act for my protection."

7.60 Then he bade that, with his hands tied behind his back and his head enfolded in a shabby cloak, Philotas be led in. It was plain to see that the men were moved by the wretched state of a man whom it had not been feasible to view without envy until that date. Just yesterday they had beheld him as commander of the

---

[224] This Amyntas was the son of Perdiccas III, the elder brother of Philip II, Alexander's father. Alexander had him executed some time between coming to the throne in the Autumn of 336BC and the Spring of 335BC (Justin 12.6.3 & Arrian, *Anabasis* 1.5.4) evidently for plotting the assassination of the king.

[225] Attalus had married his niece to Philip II, thereby threatening Alexander's succession in the case of male progeny. He managed to imply that Alexander was a bastard by loudly hoping for a *legitimate* heir at the wedding feast (Plutarch, *Alexander* 9.4 & Athenaeus 557B).

cavalry, whom they knew to have attended the king's banquet. Now, suddenly, they surveyed him as a defendant in fact, but already doomed, indeed even in bonds. The fate of Parmenion too loomed in their minds. What a giant of a general! What a coruscating countryman! But lately bereaved of two of his boys, Hector and Nicanor, he must now stand trial in his absence along with the sole son spared to him by calamity. Therefore, since the assembly was inclining towards mercy, Amyntas, from among the king's commanders, revived their antagonism towards Philotas through his oratory: "In fact Philotas sought to betray us to the barbarians. None of us would ever have made it back to our wives and parents in our home country, but like a decapitated body turned zombie, without identity and astray in strange lands, we should have made fine sport for the enemy." But this speech by Amyntas was by no means so pleasing to the king as its speaker had expected, because by reminding the soldiers of their wives and their homeland he had made them the more reluctant to endure the rest of their term of service.

7.61 Then Coenus, despite that he had wed the sister of Philotas, fulminated against him more fiercely than anyone else, bellowing that he was a traitor to his king, to his country and to the army itself. And scooping up a stone that happened to lie by his feet he prepared to hurl it at him – many surmised out of a desire to spare him from torture. But the king stayed his hand, declaring that the defendant ought first to be afforded an opportunity to deliver his defence and that he would not allow the trial to proceed otherwise. Then, when bidden to speak, Philotas was fuddled and stunned, neither venting his mouth nor raising his gaze, either due to a sense of guilt or the awfulness of his predicament. Thereupon he burst into tears and fainted into the embrace of him that held him. But his eyes being dried with his mantle, he gradually recovered his bearing and his voice and appeared to be on the point of speaking. Staring intently at him, Alexander thought to interject: "The Macedonians are ready to hear your case, so I would ask whether you will address them in their native dialect?" Philotas responded: "As well as the Macedonians there are many here, who will more readily appreciate what I have to say, if I use the same tongue as you yourself have been uttering today, for no other reason I believe than that your speech could be understood by more in the crowd." To this the king retorted: "Can anyone not see how Philotas loathes even the language of his patrimony, since he alone dislikes its study? But let him indeed speak in whatsoever way he deems wise, whilst keeping in mind that it is our ways as much as our speech that he seems to despise." And with that the king quit the assembly.

7.62 Then Philotas began: "It is easy for an innocent man to conceive of word after word, but for a wretched chap to choose them is awkward. Therefore, beleaguered between the clearest of consciences and the most perverse adversity, I do not know how to suit both my sentiments and the opportunity. In fact, the best judge of my case is no longer here, though, by Heracles, I cannot fathom why he should not wish to grant me his ear. When he is aware of both sides he may as legally condemn me as acquit me. But if he does not hear me, I cannot be set at liberty when he is absent, who condemned me whilst present. A defence by a fellow in fetters is not just in vain but also invidious, since he seems not to be enlightening but laying the blame upon his judge. Nevertheless, in whatever I am allowed to tell, I myself shall not falter nor foster the impression that I am guilty in my own opinion as well."

7.63 "In truth, I cannot see of what crime I am accused. None among the conspirators has named me. Nicomachus said of me not a word and Cebalinus could not know more than he had heard. Yet the king credits me with the leadership of the conspiracy. Could Dimnus have withheld mention of the man whom he abetted, especially since, being asked about his confederates, he ought to have named me, even if falsely, the more readily to recruit him whom he tempted? For when Dimnus laid bare their wickedness he did not omit my name in order to appear to have spared an accomplice. In confessing to Nicomachus, whom he thought would keep his own secret safe without doubt, all others being named, I alone was left out. Consider, comrades, if Cebalinus had not come to me, if he had wanted me to know nothing concerning those in the conspiracy, would I this day be delivering my defence, when none has named me in the offence? Definitely Dimnus so long as he lived forbore to name me, but how about the rest? Patently, those that currently incriminate themselves still maintain my anonymity! Adversity is vindictive, so a villain in torment will normally consent to the torture of another. So, can so many plotters fail to confess facts even when stretched upon racks? Just as nobody gives quarter to a condemned man, it is true that a condemned man gives quarter to nobody in my view."

7.64 "I need to return to the one true charge laid against me: 'Why did you keep silent concerning the matter that was reported to you? Why did you hear it with such serenity?' This, such as it is, being acknowledged by me was pardoned by you, Alexander, wherever you may be. I clasped your right hand to pledge our restored amity and even attended last night's revelry. If you believed me, then I was absolved. If you pardoned me, then the matter was resolved. Let you abide by your adjudication. What did I do last night after leaving your refection? What fresh villainy has been revealed to you to alter your conception? I lay deep in sleep oblivious of my troubles when my antagonists woke me as they set me in shackles. How did a traitor and betrayer come by such sound slumber? Miscreants cannot readily slip into sleep due to the nagging of their conscience. For the Furies harry them not merely after the perpetration of their treason but also in its anticipation. But my sense of security was founded firstly in my innocence and then bolstered by your right hand. I had no apprehension that you would allow others' inhumanity to outweigh your own inclination towards clemency."

7.65 "But let you not regret your belief in me, for the affair was unfolded to me through a mere boy who could produce neither proof nor any witness for his story and who could have caused comprehensive consternation, if people had begun to pay heed to his information. Unfortunately, it was my opinion that my ears had been taxed by a tiff between a lover and his minion and I doubted his good faith when he did not tell me to my face, but briefed his brother to act in his place. I feared that he would abjure what he had consigned to Cebalinus in that briefing and I would then be seen as a source of insecurity for sundry associates of the king. Even so, though I have denounced nobody, I have uncovered someone who would prefer to see me perish rather than secure safety. How much more resentment do you reckon I would have evoked, had I provoked the innocent? And yet, indeed, Dimnus slew himself. Do you honestly suppose that I should have been able to foresee that he would do so? Hardly! Hence the sole fact that has since confirmed the allegation could not convince me when Cebalinus cornered me with his information. But, by Heracles, had I really been in league with Dimnus in such treachery, I ought not to have kept it in the shade for those two days that we had been betrayed and Cebalinus himself could have been disposed of without difficulty. Furthermore, after the information, which I was to withhold, had been made known, I entered the king's bedchamber all alone and even girt with a blade. Why then would I have let the deed be delayed? Did I dare nothing without Dimnus? Then he was thus the leader of the escapade and Philotas, whilst manoeuvring to be monarch of Macedon, was sheltering in his shade. *Conspiring to be king!* Which among you have I bought with my presents? What captain, what commander did I cultivate at excessive expense?"

7.66 "There is even laid against me the accusation that I disdain to communicate in the language of my nation, that I recoil from the customs of the Macedonians, which would suggest that I covet the kingship of that which I detest. That native speech has long since faded out through our dealings with nations round about. Both the conquered and the conquerors must learn the language of foreigners. By Heracles, such charges made against me are no more scathing than that Amyntas the son of Perdiccas intrigued against the king. That I stood on friendly terms with him I shall not shy from defending, unless it was never our duty to adore a cousin of the king.[226] But if it was required that we even reverence such an exalted royal, am I indicted because I lacked foresight or is death also to be be dealt to the blameless friends of the disloyal? If that is just, why let me live so long? Else why am I now at last to die, if it is wrong?"

7.67 "It is indeed the truth that I wrote that I pitied those who had to live under one who believed himself to be Zeus's son. O faithful friendship with the perilous liberty to tender candid counsel, you have beguiled me! It was you that dispelled my reticence in revealing my sentiments. I confess that I wrote this thing for the king's own reading, though I wrote nothing of it to others about the king. For I sought not to expose him to odium, but rather I feared for him. It seemed to me seemlier for Alexander to acquiesce to his descent from Zeus without communication, rather than to broadcast it by public proclamation. But since we are convinced of the verity of the oracle, let its god bear witness in my case. Keep me fastened in fetters, whilst Ammon is asked whether I instigated a furtive and

---

[226] The Latin of Curtius 6.10.24 uses *frater* (brother), but the term extends to cousins, which was the actual relationship between Amyntas and Alexander.

Book 7: July 330BC – June 329BC

sinister disgrace. He who has distinguished our king as his son will not suffer the concealment of anyone who has conspired against his race. Yet if you consider torture to be more reliable than prophecy, even from that version of validating the truth I do not beg for mercy."

7.68 "Those accused in capital cases are accustomed to call upon their kin to come before you. But I have recently been bereaved of my two brothers and I am unable to present my father to you. Nor will I venture to invoke his name, since he himself has been implicated in this awful shame. For it is not enough that he, who was lately the father of many a son and now seeks solace in a single one, losing him too should be left with none, unless also he himself be put upon my pyre. So, dearest father, you are due to die due to me and with me. It is I who cause your life to expire. It is I who terminate your antiquity. Why indeed did you sire unhappy me against divine mandate? Was it in order to gather this harvest from me, which is now your fate? I do not know whether my youth or your age is the more distressing. I am reaped in my prime, whilst in your case the executioner will cut short a life, which, had fate been willing to wait, nature was already soliciting."

7.69 "Mention of my father has reminded me how timorous and hesitant I was obliged to be in divulging what Cebalinus had told me. For Parmenion, when he heard that poison was being concocted for the king by Philip the Physician, wrote Alexander a note to deter him from drinking the potion with which the doctor had decided to dose him. You will recall that my father was disbelieved and that his message was paid no heed. How often I myself have confided what I have heard and been rebuffed with derision for my gullibility. If our information attracts odium and our silence inspires suspicion, what ought our recourse to be?" And when one among the encompassing crowd had retorted, "Not to plot against your benefactors!" Philotas responded, "You are correct, whoever you may be. Hence, if I am guilty of such conspiracy, I do not entreat you for exemption from due sentence and I make an end of eloquence, since it appears that my final words have offended your ears." Thereupon he was led away by those in whose hands he lay.

7.70 There was among the commanders a certain Bolon, a formidable fighter, but unskilled in the arts of peace and urbane manners, an old trooper in fact, who had risen through the ranks to reach his current captaincy. He, when the host was hushed, began with discourteous and defiant audacity to remind them how frequently they had been kicked out of quarters they had requisitioned in the cause of accommodating the filth among Philotas's servants in the places whence his comrades had been evicted. His carts crammed with gold and silver had been parked throughout entire precincts, but not a single man among his fellow fighters had been admitted even to the vicinity of his lodgings. Rather they had all been banished into the distance by those he had disposed as wardens of his repose, so that that sissy should not be disturbed by the hush rather than the hubbub of their murmurings. Those that came from the countryside, whom he had nicknamed Phrygians and Paphlagonians, were martyrs to the mockery of him, who, though Macedonian by birth, was not ashamed that he had to hear men whose native tongue he shared through an interpreter. Now he desired that Ammon be consulted, the very same man who accused Zeus of lying when he recognized Alexander as his offspring, supposedly suffering anxiety lest this gift from the gods should engender jealousy. He never referred the matter to Zeus, when he conspired against the life of his sovereign and friend. Only now he wished to send to the oracle, whilst his father suborned those he commanded in Media and disbursed the funds consigned to his regency to induce outlaws to ally with him in his treachery. The army would indeed send envoys to the oracle, not to quiz Zeus on what they already knew from the king, but instead to tender their thanks and redeem the promises in their prayers for the preservation of their sovereign.

7.71 Then indeed the entire assembly was incensed *against Philotas*[227] and the Bodyguards made a beginning by bellowing that they should dismember the traitor with their bare hands. In fact, Philotas was scarcely scared on hearing this, since he feared far fouler suffering. But the king came back into the meeting and adjourned the proceedings until the following day, either in order to torment Philotas in confinement as well[228] or else to investigate the whole matter more thoroughly. And despite that the day was dimming into dusk the king convened a council of his Friends. **The consensus** of the rest **was that Philotas should be put to death according to the custom of the Macedonians *by stoning*, but** Hephaistion, Craterus and Coenus declared **that the truth should be extracted from him by torture first** and those who had argued otherwise came round to their view. Therefore, the council being dissolved, Hephaistion with Craterus and Coenus arose as one to subject Philotas to inquisition.[229] The king called Craterus aside and had a quiet word with him, the substance of which has not been published, before withdrawing into the private part of the royal quarters. There, having dismissed all onlookers, he waited up deep into the night for the outcome of the tortures.

7.72 The torturers arrayed all the tools of their brutality before the gaze of Philotas and he volunteered: "Why tarry in exterminating the king's enemy, who confesses he sought to assassinate him? What need is there for interrogation? I conceived the thing and wanted to bring it about." But Craterus required that he reiterate his confession under torture. Then he was seized and, whilst he was

---

[227] This constitutes the conviction verdict against Philotas: the verdicts of the Macedonian Assembly were by acclamation rather than a formal vote as is explained by Curtius 7.2.7.

[228] That is to say, as well as the preceding proposal by the Bodyguards that they should tear Philotas to pieces in public. The Penguin Curtius is wrong to give the translation "to subject Philotas to further torture in prison", since this infers earlier torture, which Curtius has not mentioned.

[229] The Latin of Curtius 6.11.11 grants primacy to Hephaistion among this group, because he was Commander of the Bodyguards (*Hegemon* of the *Somatophylakes*) according to Diodorus 17.61.3 and possibly already *Chiliarch*.

Book 7: July 330BC – June 329BC

being blindfolded and stripped of his clothing, he invoked the gods of his fatherland and human rights, but futilely in the face of deaf ears. He was mangled by the most excruciating torments, seeing as he was a condemned man being tortured by his bitter rivals for the favour of the king. Though assaulted successively with fire and the scourge, no longer for inquisition but to induce suffering, he initially curbed not only his screams but even his groans. But after his body had become swollen with weals, he could no longer bear the swipes of the scourges that cut to the bared bone, so he promised that he would tell them what they wished to know, if they would relent from tormenting him. But he wanted them to swear by Alexander's life that the interrogation would end and the torturers would withdraw. And when both things had been effectuated, Philotas said: "Tell me, Craterus, what you would have me say." However, when Craterus was indignant at such mockery and was calling the torturers back again, Philotas began to beg for time to recover his composure, whereupon he would divulge everything that he knew. Meanwhile, after they had got wind of the torturing of Philotas, the cavalry, including all those of the noblest birth and any with family ties to Parmenion in particular, were panic-stricken due to the Macedonian law that provided for the relatives of a traitor to share his death. Some did away with themselves whilst others fled into remote mountain ranges and desert wastes as abject terror stalked through the entire camp, until the king became conscious of the consternation and rescinded the law that allowed for the penalisation of the kindred of the convicted by a proclamation.

7.73 It is ambiguous whether **Philotas** sought to deliver himself from excruciation through truth or lies, inasmuch as both true confession and false disquisition held out the identical prospect of an end to his anguish. What he **confessed** was: "You are well aware how friendly my father was with Hegelochus. I mean the Hegelochus who fell in the fighting. He was the source of all our woes. For when first the king commanded that he be called the son of Zeus, he queried quite indignantly, 'Should we therefore recognize this ruler, who repudiates Philip's paternity? We are finished, if we can stand for this. A man who demands recognition as a deity doesn't only look down upon mankind, but also depreciates divinity. We have lost Alexander and are bereft of our king. We have become subject to an insolence that is intolerable either to the gods, to whom he equates himself, or to men, from whom he separates himself. Have we spilt our blood to raise up a god who disdains us and is loath to commune with mere mortals? Believe me, if we be men, we too should be the chosen of the gods.[230] Who avenged the killing of Alexander, the forbear of the current king, and

---

[230] At this point Hegelochus abandons overt criticism of Alexander's deification and launches into obscurely treasonous innuendo. Ostensibly, "chosen of the gods" parodies Alexander's adoption by Zeus, but in this context there is also an implication that they are to be chosen as instruments of divine retribution against Alexander.

Archelaus after him and Perdiccas's slaying?[231] However, the present Alexander pardoned his father's assassins.[232]'"

7.74 "This was what Hegelochus had to say over dinner and at dawn the next day I was summoned by my father. He was grimfaced and could see that I was troubled, for what we had heard had instilled disquiet into our hearts. Hence in order to check whether he had waffled whilst witless with wine or had imparted some deeper design, we decided to send for him. On arriving he recapitulated the same arguments of his own accord, adding that if we should dare to lead the endeavour, he would stand beside us as our ally, but if we were minded to drop the matter, he would keep the whole conception under wraps. The plot appeared untimely to Parmenion, while Darius were still alive, for we would have been doing away with Alexander rather on behalf of the enemy than to advantage ourselves. However, once we had disposed of Darius, the bounty on the head of the king would be that Asia and the entire Orient should be ceded to his assassins. This reasoning was ratified and relevant vows were exchanged. And though I know nothing regarding Dimnus, I realize that following this confession it shall not avail me that I had no part in his treason." At this they reverted to tormenting him, personally poking at his face and eyes with their javelins so as to compel his confession to that offence as well. Then, when they pressed him for the particulars of the scheduling of the intended outrage, Philotas explained that it had seemed that Alexander would be detained by Bactria for an age, in the course of which he had feared that his father being seventy years old might pass away. Parmenion commanded such colossal forces and was the custodian of so much money that he himself, stripped of such strong resources, would lack the backing to do away with the king. Hence, he had hastened to implement his plan, whilst the prize lay to hand. And unless they believed that his father had played no part

---

[231] The combined implication of the context and the names themselves is that these are former kings of Macedon, in which case they are Alexander I (reigned c495-c452BC), Archelaus (reigned c413-399BC) and Perdiccas III (reigned 368-360BC). The passage would suggest that the Macedonian nobility had avenged their murders in each case. The mode of death for Alexander I is not known, but Archelaus was slain by his *eromenos* Crateuas, who was then slain in turn (Aelian, *Varia Historia* 8.9). Perdiccas III died in battle against the Illyrians, but hostile writers suggested that his mother, Eurydice, was somehow implicated (NGL Hammond, *The Miracle That Was Macedonia*, p.56).

[232] It has sometimes been assumed that this is a reference to Alexander letting Alexander Lyncestes live, despite executing his brothers as accomplices in the assassination of Philip (Justin 11.2.2). However, Hegelochus must be speaking shortly after the visit to the oracle at Siwa, when Alexander Lyncestes had already been imprisoned on treason charges for a couple of years (Arrian, *Anabasis* 1.25). Hence the criticism that Alexander had pardoned him could not have carried much force in these circumstances. More cogently, it is the alleged involvement of Olympias in Philip's murder that is meant. She is explicitly accused of having arranged horses for Pausanias's getaway in Justin 9.7, but clearly Alexander took no action against her. Hence the sense of this passage is that Alexander was complicit in the murder of hs father and so should be a target for Macedonian nobles avenging regicide rather than the object of their protection.

Book 7: July 330BC – June 329BC

in the affair, he would not balk at further torture, though it was already more than he could bear.

7.75 On having conferred, they considered that sufficient inquistion had occurred, so they reported to the king, who ordered *at the assembly* the next day that the admissions made by Philotas should be recited and that he himself should be carried in, as he could not walk. After he had acknowledged everything, Demetrius was brought in, having been accused of complicity in the recent treachery. He strenuously denied equally by his disposition, his resolution and his expression that he had entertained any intention to act against the king, even demanding for himself vindication through torture. Whereupon Philotas swept his gaze around to either side letting it alight upon Calis, whom he bade move nearer, though he stood not far away. But when Calis was apprehensive and refused to approach him, he asked: "Will you endorse the deceit of Demetrius and the repetition of my torture?" Turning deathly pale, Calis was speechless and the Macedonians were suspicious that Philotas's intent was to incriminate the innocent, since neither Nicomachus nor Philotas during his torture had named this adolescent. Yet when the king's commanders stood around him in a ring, Calis confessed the complicity of Demetrius and himself in the plotting. Hence **in accordance with their country's custom, all who had been named by Nicomachus together with Philotas at a signal suffered extermination** *by stoning.*

7.76 Alexander had been freed from a frightful threat not merely to his wellbeing but even to his existence. For Philotas and Parmenion as the most senior among his Friends could not have been condemned without offence to the entire army, unless publicly shown to be guilty. Hence the outcome hung in the balance whilst the deed was denied and torture was viewed with abhorrence. But following his confession Philotas did not even merit the compassion of his adherents.

7.77 While Philotas's tracks in the treason were still fresh, **the soldiers** judged that he had been justly punished; yet after the object of their detestation had been despatched, their censure switched to remorse. They **were moved both by the illustriousness of the young Philotas and by the venerability of his father**, which was accentuated by the loss of his several sons. It had been Parmenion who had first established a bridgehead in Asia for the king and as his partner in every peril he had in battle always commanded the opposite wing. He had also been the foremost among Philip's Friends and so loyal to Alexander himself that the king had preferred him to any other agent in slaying Attalus. Suchlike rumination grew rife among the army, whose mutinous mutterings were recounted to the king. *Some said that they themselves could not count on better treatment from him.* But Alexander was unperturbed, since he was well aware that mischief born of idleness is dispelled by actual action and so he announced that everyone should gather in the court of the royal quarters. When he had determined that it was thronged, he strode into this assembly.

7.78 Doubtless by prior arrangement, **it was proposed** by Atarrhias **that Alexander Lyncestes, who had sought to assassinate their sovereign long before Philotas, should be arraigned before them.** He *had been denounced by two informers (as was mentioned above)*[233] *and* was currently in his third year of confinement in fetters. *It was also considered certain that he had been complicit with Pausanias in Philip's assassination. But since he had been the first to herald Alexander as king, he had been granted immunity from punishment rather than from incrimination. Furthermore, the appeals of Antipater,*[234] *his father-in-law, on his behalf had been staving off the king's righteous retaliation. However, the pain of this ulcer burst out again, since their current crisis called to mind the old threat.* Hence Alexander Lyncestes was led forth from confinement and bidden to speak. Yet *despite having had fully three years to prepare his defence,* he managed shakily and falteringly to pronounce just a few words *of what he had composed, until ultimately not merely his memory but even his mind forsook him. Nobody doubted that his agitation was an indication of a guilty conscience rather than impaired recollection.* Therefore, *whilst he still fought with his forgetfulness,* he was transfixed by the lances of *some of* those who stood nearby.

7.79 His corpse having been carted away, the king commanded that Amyntas and Simmias be led in. For Polemon, who was their younger brother, had fled upon learning that Philotas was being tortured. They had been the closest of all the friends of Philotas and they had been promoted into prominent and eminent offices especially through his sponsorship. The king recalled that he had recommended them with the utmost élan and did not doubt that they had also been participants in Philotas's final plan. He had long viewed them with suspicion on account of correspondence from his mother, which had cautioned him to keep himself safe from them. And although he was reluctant to give credence to defamation, he had been compelled by palpable evidence to command their incarceration. For there was no room for doubt that they had secretly consorted with Philotas the day before his treachery was laid bare. Furthermore, their brother, who had fled upon the news of Philotas's interrogation, had made it quite clear why he had run away from there. Of late, in semblance of doing their duty, yet contrary to established custom, they had removed the rest of his royal retinue to a distance and set themselves at his side for no plausible reason. Alexander had been bewildered that they were attending him out of their turn and alarmed by their nervous disposition, so he had promptly ensconced himself among his guards, who were trailing just behind them. He appended to this that when

---

[233] See 3.6 above: Olympias may be the 2nd informant. Curtius 7.1.6 refers back to the lost section at the beginning of his account, where the arrest of Alexander Lyncestes preceded the episode of the Gordian knot, which opens the surviving parts; cf. Diodorus 17.32 and Justin 11.7.1.

[234] Diodorus 17.80.2 speaks of Lyncestes' "relationship with Antigonus", but this is surely an error for Antipater, who was his father-in-law (Curtius 7.1.7) and rather more influential.

Book 7: July 330BC – June 329BC

Antiphanes, the clerk of the cavalry, had notified Amyntas the day before the detection of the treachery of Philotas that, as was customary, he should donate some of his steeds to those who were missing their mounts, Amyntas had arrogantly retorted that, unless he ceased his insistence, he would shortly discover the extent of Amyntas's influence. Moreover, the harsh language and rash verbage that had been vented upon the king himself was nothing other than a symptom and attestation of treacherous intent. If these charges were true, then they deserved to share Philotas's damnation. Else if they were false, then the king himself required that they provide a refutation.

7.80 Antiphanes was next led forward to attest to the failure to surrender the horses as well as the accompanying haughty menaces. Then Amyntas was granted the opportunity to speak and commenced: "If the king has no objection, I request that I should be freed from these fetters, whilst I speak." Alexander bade that both of them be released and when Amyntas also yearned for his guardsman's outfit to be restored to him, the king *even* commanded that he be handed a lance. Amyntas grasped this in his left hand and, keeping off the spot where the corpse of Alexander Lyncestes had lain a little beforehand, he began to declaim: "Whatsoever verdict is fated for us, Sire, we appreciate that we shall owe thanks to you, if it go in our favour; but we shall blame Fortune, if the outcome be graver. We are ourselves uncurbed in body and mind and our defence of the case is heard without prejudice. You have even restored the raiment in which we are accustomed to do our duty in your service. It is impossible that we should mistrust our defence and we shall cease to distrust providence."

7.81 "I crave that you permit me to counter the last of your charges initially. We, Sire, are quite ignorant of having uttered anything that was directed against your majesty. I would suggest that you long since transcended unpopularity, if there were no risk that you might suspect more malicious murmers were being flushed away by flattery. But even allowing that any of your soldiers might have been heard to mumble worse than a grumble either when wearied and worn out on the march or when imperilled in battle or when wounded and tending to his injuries in his tent, nevertheless we have deserved by our gallantry that you should choose to attribute it to the circumstances rather than to true dissent. When anything awful occurs, everyone is on trial. We turn harmful hands against our own selves, which are certainly not objects for revulsion.[235] Parents, in restraining their offspring, are met with both ingratitude and indignation. Conversely, when we are honoured with rewards and we come back laden with prizes, who can bear us? Who can cope with such elation? In soldiering neither exasperation nor exhilaration exists in moderation, but we are quickly carried away by every emotion. We scold, we praise, we pity or we rage as we are swayed by our current mood. At one moment we are looking to leave for India and the Ocean, but in

---

[235] This appears to be a reference to the Greek habit of self-disfigurement to express severe mourning or mortification – an example would be Alexander scratching his own face after killing Cleitus: see Section 9.12 below and Curtius 8.2.5.

the next we are checked by the recollection of our wives, our children and our own nation. But such reflections and such chatter amongst the men are curtailed by the peal of the trumpet, when we each rush to our station in the formation. Then whatever resentment has been pent up in our tents is poured down upon the heads of our opponents. Would that Philotas's transgression had been confined to conversation!"

7.82 "And so I return to the basis of the allegations against us: our friendship with Philotas, which I am so far from refuting that I confess that through it we both cultivated and reaped a great fruiting. Are you truly surprised that we have pursued the patronage of Parmenion's son, whom you saw fit to set next in rank to yourself, exceeding almost all your Friends in distinction? By Heracles! You, Sire, if the truth be told, are the cause of our present predicament. For who else instituted that he must treat with Philotas who would make you content? It is through his sponsorship that we have risen to our current rank in your fellowship. He stood so high in your estimation that we needed both to curry his favour and to fear his vexation. If not quite in your own words, have we not all recited the oath you have dictated that we should share as friends and foes the same such men as you propose? Bound by this pledge of loyalty, could we really turn against him whom you promoted above everybody? Hence if this is an offence, you have few men who can claim innocence. By Heracles! None in fact has any defence. For all coveted the friendship of Philotas, although not all who wished it could have it come to pass. Thus, if you do not distinguish between his accomplices and his companions, neither will you separate his associates from those that have sought such associations."

7.83 "So what evidence is offered that we were in the know? I suppose, it's that he had a cosey conversation with us on the preceding day without being overheard. Yet I'd be unable to exculpate myself, if on that day my lifestyle or habits had altered. So in fact, as we behaved the same way as on every other day upon that day in question, our adherence to routine relieves us of suspicion."

7.84 "Be that as it may, we did not hand over our horses to Antiphanes, and this just the day before Philotas's exposure. This shall be a case between Antiphanes and me. If he wished to incriminate us, because we did not surrender our steeds that day, he himself cannot evade suspicion, since it was just then that he wished to take them away. Indeed, it is ambiguous where the blame lies between the gripper and the grabber, except that his cause is nobler who hangs on to his own than his who would claim what is owned by another. As it happens, Sire, I had ten horses, out of which Antiphanes had already allocated eight to those who were bereft of theirs, so that two were all I had left. When this most insolent man - at any rate the most unjust - sought to commandeer these last, unless I were willing to fight on foot, I had to hold fast. I'll not deny that I spoke in the spirit of a free man addressing one of the most craven and a person who possesses the sole military role of assigning the steeds of others to fighting men. We are quite

Book 7: July 330BC – June 329BC

beset by adversities, when I must simultaneously excuse my words to Alexander and to Antiphanes!"

7.85 "But, by Heracles, your mother has denounced us in her letters as your enemies. Would that more prudence had tempered her fretting for her son and that her troubled mind had not evoked vague fantasies. Why indeed does she not impart the reason for her unease? And, finally, why does she not reveal her source? What deeds or words of ours prompted her to pen you such a fearful discourse? How dire a dilemma confronts me, since perchance it is less risky to hold my tongue than to speak plainly. But whatever the outcome may be, I would rather that my defence should displease you than have you doubt my fidelity. You yourself will confirm what I am going to relate, since you will recall that, when you sent me to fetch forces from Macedonia, you did intimate that there were many fit young fellows who were hidden on your mother's estate. Hence you instructed that I should pay heed to none save you, but rather bring to you those shirking soldiering service. Which is exactly what I did, executing your command with more willingness than was in my best interest. Thence I recruited Gorgias, Hecataeus and Gorgatas, who have been serving you with success. What, therefore, could be more unjust than that I, who would justly have been punished had your orders been betrayed, should now die for having obeyed? For the only cause your mother has for spiting us is that we favoured your acquisition over a woman's appreciation. I led hither six thousand Macedonian infantry and six hundred cavalry, some section of whom would not have followed me, had I been willing to collude with those who fought shy of service in the military. Therefore, since it is on this account that we are objects of her rancour, it follows that you should mollify your mother, since it is you who have exposed us to her anger."

7.86 Whilst Amyntas was stating his case, there chanced to arrive those who had given chase to his brother, Polemon, who having fled, as has been said, they were bringing back in shackles. Their hackles raised, the seething assembly could scarcely be restrained from instantly stoning him to death, as was ordained by custom *in such cases*. But he, entirely unterrified, said: "I do not ask forgiveness for myself, but beg only that the innocence of my brothers should not be impugned by my desertion. If this be deemed indefensible, mine is the culpability. Their own cause is actually the better for the fact that my flight diverts suspicion onto me personally." Yet by these words he won the approbation of the entire assembly. All were moved to shed a tear and they were so abruptly converted in their estimation that what had most undermined him became his sole source of salvation. He was a youth in the first flower of adolescence, who, when the cavalry was rattled by the torture of Philotas, had been carried away by others' consternation. Forsaken by his comrades and wavering between his options of desertion or reversion, he had been overtaken by his pursuers. Now he began to wail and thrash his face, not distressed for his own sake, but on behalf of his brothers, whose jeopardy was of his making. By this point he was also garnering the king's compassion, as well as the assembly's sympathy, but his brother alone was implacable and, glaring at him menacingly, he exclaimed: "When you spurred your steed in flight, cretin, that was the time that tears were due as the deserter of your brothers and the sidekick of deserters too. Whither did you think you'd flee and whom were you evading, villain? You have laid a capital charge against me on behalf of the prosecution."

7.87 Polemon lamented that he had let himself down, but repented that he had betrayed his brothers even more grievously. Then indeed those at the assembly neither withheld their tears nor the acclamations whereby such crowds express their favour. With one voice they collectively called upon the king to pardon these blameless and valiant fellows. Being afforded an opportunity to be merciful, his Friends too welled up as one and weepingly besought their acquittal. Having hushed them, Alexander announced: "I myself share the view that Amyntas and his brothers should be acquitted. To these young men I say that I would rather that they obliterate the memory of this kindness than ruminate upon their jeopardy. Amyntas, let you and your brothers favour me with the same loyalty with which I return you to favour with me. Failing having confronted you with these accusations, my furtiveness might have festered foetidly. It is better that you are vindicated than treated suspiciously. Be mindful that no one can be acquitted unless he states his case judicially. Now let you, Amyntas, pardon your brother, which shall also signify that you are unreservedly reconciled with me."

7.88 Thereafter **the king** dismissed the assembly and **bade that Polydamas be called.** He was by far the most familiar of Parmenion's associates, customarily fighting beside him in battle. And despite counting on his clear conscience in coming to the king's quarters, his assurance switched to nervousness and he began to fret when he was bidden to present his brothers, who, being juveniles, were as yet unfamiliar to the king on account of their age. He became more fixated by what could tarnish their good name than how they would shield themselves from such shame. By now the guards, who had been detailed to bring his brothers, were leading them forward, and Alexander, whilst waving everyone else away, ordered Polydamas, pale with apprehension, to draw nearer in order **to say:** "We have all equally been targets for the treachery of Parmenion, but especially you and I, whom he duped by masquerading as our companion. But see how much I trust in your loyalty: I have arranged to employ your services to **seek Parmenion out and impose our penalty.** Your brothers shall serve as surety, whilst you discharge this duty. You shall leave for Media carrying letters written by my own hand to my prefects there. **Speed is of the essence, so as to outrun rumour.** I wish you to reach the place at night and to implement what is written the next day. You shall also bear letters for Parmenion: one from me and the other written in the guise of his son. I have at my disposal his signet ring. If his father thinks the letter was sealed by Philotas, when he sees you, he will suspect nothing."

7.89 Freed from his frightful fretting, Polydamas promised his best efforts even more vehemently than they had been requested. Lauded and laden with reciprocal promises, he adopted Arab dress, his own being divested. **Arab guides,** whose

Book 7: July 330BC – June 329BC

wives and offspring were kept by the king to bind their loyalty, **were assigned as his company. They attained their destination on the eleventh day by riding racing camels across waterless desert territory**, *a journey of thirty or forty days normally.*[236] Ere his arrival were heralded Polydamas resumed his Macedonian attire and got to the pavilion of Cleander, one of the king's commanders, in the fourth watch *of the night*.[237] His letter being delivered, they arranged that they would go in company to Parmenion at first light, since Polydamas had brought royal mail for the rest as well. They were about to visit Parmenion, when he heard tell of the arrival of Polydamas. Whilst gratified to be able to greet his friend, he was simultaneously keen to learn what the king might intend, since he had received no message from him for a lengthy interlude, so he bade that the whereabouts of Polydamas be pursued.

7.90 The lodges in that land possess picturesque parks with grandiose groves planted by hand, which were the particular pleasure of their satraps and kings. Parmenion was pacing about in one such grove amidst those officers, who had been commanded to kill him by the king's written orders. They had scheduled the deed to be done during the time when he had begun to read the letters that Polydamas had brought. Parmenion perceived the approach of Polydamas from afar, scurrying forward to embrace him, his countenance portraying some semblance of delight. After they had greeted one another, Polydamas delivered to him the letter written by the king. Whilst fiddling with its fastening, Parmenion asked what things the king was doing? Polydamas responded that through the letter itself he would learn everything. On perusing it, Parmenion commented: "The king is readying a campaign against the Arachosii. Such a forceful fellow and quite unrelenting! But it is time he spared himself for the sake of his wellbeing, having already gleaned so much glory." Next, he read the other letter, ghostwritten in the name of Philotas, with obvious pleasure as could be judged from his expression.[238] At this Cleander cleaved his sword into his side, then slashed his throat and the rest also stabbed him, though he had already died.

---

[236] The distance from Prophthasia (Farah) to Ecbatana (Hamadan) is around 600 miles, so the rate of travel would have been in excess of 60 miles per day, which is just barely feasible on camels. Strabo 15.2.10 points out that it should normally have taken thirty to forty days to make this journey.

[237] Probably a few hours before dawn, as the Greeks usually divided the night into four watches.

[238] Although it is not explicitly stated, there is a strong implication that the letter seeming to come from Philotas contained some treasonous message and that the officers had been alerted to watch Parmenion's reaction as he read it. This would be why they awaited its reading before killing him.

Figure 7.3. The assassination of Parmenion (from a French translation of Curtius by de Vaugelas, 1696)

7.91 But the guards stationed at the entrance to the grove became aware of the killing and, being ignorant of its reason, they reached the camp and roused the troops to riot with their riveting tidings of treason. The soldiers seized their arms and marched en masse to the grove where the killing had occurred, threatening that, unless Polydamas and his accomplices in the crime were surrendered, they would demolish its encompassing wall and expiate the liquidation of their leader with the blood of all. Cleander commanded that the chief men among these

Book 7: July 330BC – June 329BC

troops be admitted and read aloud a letter to them from the king's own hand, in which were combined an account of Parmenion's machinations against Alexander with the king's invocations for vengeance to be planned. Consequently, recognizing the king's intent, their mutiny was suppressed, though not their sense of discontent. Though many of them drifted away, a few sought to stay, begging that they might be permitted to bury the body of Parmenion anyway. Warrant was withheld for a long while, on account of Cleander's anxiety not to offend the king. Then, when they pleaded more vehemently, reckoning that reasons for insurrection should be removed, Cleander consented to their interring the decapitated corpse, its head being conveyed to the king.

7.92 Thus Parmenion perished by assassination, having been an outstanding stalwart *of the regime* in war and peace. He had accomplished much without the king, whereas the king had achieved nothing significant without him. He ably served a most successful sovereign, who insisted that everything should match up to his own exalted condition. In his seventieth year he still discharged the duties of a youthful officer and often even those of a common trooper. A skilful strategist and forceful fighter, he was popular with his officers and even more so among the lower ranks of his soldiers. Whether this popularity impelled him to covet the kingship or simply subjected him to such suspicions may be deemed unresolved, since it was uncertain, even when the affair was fresh and it could more readily have been clarified, whether Philotas, broken by dire excruciation, spoke the truth about things that could not be verified or sought the termination of his torment through fabrication.

7.93 Alexander learnt that some among the Macedonians had openly deplored the death of Parmenion *and had made malign remarks about him*, *moaning that he had disowned the legacy of his father, Philip, and the customs of his country*. Reckoning that these should be separated from the rest of his forces, he sequestered them into a single company, which he called the Disorderly Division, *setting it under the leadership of Leonidas, who was himself a former close colleague of Parmenion*. This was more or less made up from those of whom the king had for various reasons formed a low opinion. *Alexander was concerned particularly that their criticism might be promulgated even unto Macedonia, sullying his glorious conquests with the stain of tyranny. And here is how he implemented his policy.* **Wanting to test attitudes among the troops, he alerted those who had penned letters to their loved ones in Macedonia to tender them to men he was sending back** *from among his Friends*, **who would faithfully convey them thither.** *He warned that such opportunities would diminish as they went on further.* **They had written frankly to their relatives revealing their true feelings. Most were willing warriors, but some considered their soldiering service onerous.** Thus, their sovereign *secretly* secured sight of the sentiments of *both the gratified and* the aggrieved *among the correspondents*. **So, the men who happened to have complained of weariness with the campaigning in their letters were ordered as a company to pitch their tents apart from the rest** *on account of their ignominy*.

Alexander would exploit their boldness in battle, whilst isolating their loose tongues from the ears of the gullible. *He planned to dispose of them either by the attrition of the campaign or by settling them as colonists in some distant domain.* This stratagem, though it might have appeared rash in that the bravest of young men were nettled by its slur, like everything else, the king's fortune caused to prosper. For none proved more dashing in war than these fellows. It was from a desire to diminish their disgrace that their valour arose and because small numbers necessarily expose bravery.

7.94 Having dealt with these matters and settled the situation among the Drangians *by appointing Arsaces[239] as their satrap,* Alexander bade that a march be made against the people once known as the Arimaspians, but now called the Euergetae.[240] They were renamed on account of that Cyrus, who propelled the primacy of the Medes into the hands of the Persians. For he was once warring in the wastes, where his warriors were worn out for want of warmth and rations, so that they were resorting to cannibalism in their desperation. Whereupon the Arimaspians manifested themselves with thirty thousand wagons weighed down with provisions. Preserved from perdition, Cyrus granted them exemption from taxation together with other tokens of his recognition and, spurning their previous appellation, preferred to know them as his Benefactors. Likewise, when Alexander led his columns into their country, they received him hospitably. *On the fifth day after he had arrived in that region,* he discovered that Satibarzanes, who had defected to Bessus, had surged back into Aria with a colossal corps of cavalry, renewing the revolt among its populace. Therefore, the king dispatched a task force against him under Erigyius *and Caranus supported by Stasanor, Artabazus and Andronicus. They led contingents of six thousand Greek infantry and six hundred cavalry. He himself devised government for the Euergetae in the space of sixty days and showered his funds upon them, since their superb service to Cyrus had earned his praise.* Alexander founded a town in their territory on the route into India, which he named Alexandria.[241] *He left Amedines, who had been Darius' secretary, to preside over them. Their neighbours, the Kedrosians, also proffered the king their fealty, so they too were rewarded with fitting generosity. Tiridates was made the marshal over both of these peaceable peoples.*

---

[239] The name/region is corrupted (*arianiorum*) at Curtius 7.3.1, but Arsames (*arsami*) is replaced by *tamsonor* (Stasanor?) as governor of the *dramearum* (Drangarum?) at Curtius 8.3.17; however, this is likely to be a mistake for Arsaces, who was also Satrap of Aria (Arrian, *Anabasis* 3.25.7 & 4.7.1).

[240] Which translates literally as the "Benefactors".

[241] Possibly this records the foundation of Kandahar, since *Metz Epitome* 4 is clear that it was within the Arimaspian territory.

Book 7: July 330BC – June 329BC

7.95 Thereafter, *in a few days,* Alexander subdued the Arachosii, *whose territory extends to the* River Indus.[242] The army that had been commanded by Parmenion caught up with him in Arachosia. It comprised six thousand Macedonians and two hundred knights; and five thousand Greeks with six hundred cavalry. They were without doubt the cream of all the king's chivalry. Menon was made governor of the Arachosii and a garrison of four thousand infantry and six hundred cavalry were left with him.

7.96 The king himself with his army invaded a nation not well known even to its neighbours, since it had no commerce to cultivate communion. They are called the Paropamisadae, a rude race of men, benighted even among the barbarians, the harshness of their habitat having hardened the habits of its inhabitants. Most of their landscape faces into the very wintry northern celestial pole, so it is snow-clad and inaccessible due to the cold. Westwards it borders on Bactria and to the south it verges upon the Indian Ocean. They construct their cottages with brick from their bases, but since their territory is timberless, even the lee of the mountains being bare, they extrapolate the same brickwork to the crest of each lair. That is to say, their build is broader at the base and gradually grows narrower as the structures rise, meeting much like ships' keels at the crests, where central apertures are left to vent smoke and let in light from the skies. *These homes afford sufficient shelter to those that reside in that land, being walled on every side to withstand the weather, since deep snow keeps them indoors most of the year with their stores at hand.* Those vines and trees that are able to survive in such icily solid soil, they heap up earth around leaving them buried throughout the winter and restoring them to air and sunlight only when the thaw begins to free the ground. Indeed, the snow lies so deep across this land, which a perpetual hard frost keeps fast bound, that not even traces of birds and beasts are anywhere to be found. The overcast skies, like dusk, more truly shade than light a concealed landscape, where even the foreground almost slips out of sight. *Marooned amidst this solitude, then devoid of human activity,* the army endured *every evil that it is possible to bear, including scarcity of supplies, perishing cold,* exhaustion *and deep despair. Being unaccustomed to the numbing paralysis of drifts, many were frozen to death, whilst many others got frostbitten feet and* an enormous number suffered snow-blindness, due to the glare of the snow and the harsh radiance of the reflected glow. It was particularly pernicious for those that were flagging, *for, when they collapsed, they splayed themselves upon the very ice and when they had ceased to move, the power of the cold so paralysed them that when they tried once more to rise, they found themselves immobilized. But their*

---

[242] The manuscripts of Curtius 7.3.4 read *ponticum mare* meaning the Black Sea, which is complete nonsense. It is clear from Strabo 11.10.1 that ancient geographers asserted that Arachosia extended to the River Indus (cf. Curtius 8.13.3, 9.7.14 & 9.10.7). The inference must be that the Greek word for a river (*potamos*) has somehow been corrupted to give Pontic in the Latin.

comrades shook them from their torpor, since there was no other remedy but to be made to march on. Only then did any energy return to their limbs, when the warmth of exertion came on.

7.97 *Those Macedonians that managed to reach the cottages of the natives were rapidly revived, but* the murk was so dense that the only feature that revealed the presence of the buildings was their smoke, even when they were stood upon them, *since they were steeped in a snowy cloak*. *The inhabitants had never before seen outsiders in their territory, so when armed men suddenly hove into sight, being breathless with fright, they proffered aught that they had in their habitations, beseeching the Macedonians to spare their persons. The king did the rounds of his columns on foot, setting some on their feet that he found lying and saving others that were struggling to keep up from dying by bearing them up with his own body. At one moment appearing in the van, in another at the center or tail of the column, he compounded his personal exertion. But eventually they reached more cultivated regions with ample supplies, whereby the army was revamped and at the same time the stragglers arrived where they were encamped. Soon the king had stamped his authority upon that entire nation.*

7.98 Thereafter the army advanced into the Caucasus Mountains, *a continuous chain of ranges that divides Asia, among those particular peaks* that some call Mount Paropamisus. The sea lapping Cilicia, the Caspian Sea and the River Araxes[243] together with the wastes of Scythia are all likewise overlooked by this Caucasus. The Taurus Mountains rise up in Cappadocia, skirt Cilicia and merge into the mountains of Armenia, meeting up with the Caucasus, though they are lesser in size. Thus, interconnected these ranges are arranged in an uninterrupted chain, from which almost all the rivers of Asia arise and empty into the Pontic or else the Caspian or Hyrcanian or else the Red Sea. **In the midst of that range there is a rock ten stades around and four in height, on which the natives denoted a cave as the immemorial site of the chaining of Prometheus** *as well as the eyrie of the eagle and the furrows of the fetters as in the fable*. Alexander selected a location for founding a city *at the foot of the range on the side of the pass that leads down into India.*[244] *The king also created additional settlements within a day's march of this city. Seven thousand natives, three thousand from the army's retinue and volunteers from among the mercenary soldiers unfit for active service the king consented to settle in the new foundations, the chief of which was named* by its inhabitants **Alexandria.**[245] *Then he advanced his forces towards*

---

[243] Probably the modern River Aras with its headwaters in Armenia and emptying into the Caspian Sea.

[244] The manuscripts of Diodorus 17.83.1 read *Media*, which must be an error. According to Strabo 15.2.10, the city was on the Indian side of the mountains, where Alexander wintered in 330-29BC.

[245] Alexandria-in-the-Caucasus: Arrian, *Anabasis* 3.28.4; Strabo 15.2.10.

Book 7: July 330BC – June 329BC

Bactria, since he received word of enrolment of an army and assumption of the diadem by Bessus. By the sixteenth day thereafter the army had traversed the width of the Caucasus.[246]

7.99 These were the concerns of Alexander *in the seventh year of his reign.*

---

[246] Strabo 15.2.10 has 15 days, Diodorus 17.83.1 has 16 days and Curtius 7.3.21 has 17 days.

Book 8: July 329BC – Autumn 328BC

Alexander's Advance to the River Oxus; Bessus Betrayed to Alexander; The Fate of the Branchidae; Alexander Wounded near Maracanda; The Revolt of Spitamenes; Alexander's Advance to the River Tanais; Annihilation of a Macedonian Column by Spitamenes and Alexander's Counterattacks; Capture of the Rock of Ariamazes.

8.1 *At the beginning of the eighth year of Alexander's reign,* **Bessus had had it heralded that he had become the king.** *Being absolutely alarmed by Alexander's dynamism and having performed the sacrificial rites for the gods of his fatherland in accordance with the customs of his countrymen, he was consulting with his comrades and the commanders of his contingents concerning the conflict in the context of a banquet. Well the worse for wine, they began to boast about their own potency and duly to disdain the audacity and then the paucity of their opponents. Above all, having become so conceited by a sovereignty won through wickedness as hardly to have kept his head, Bessus began with wilful words to denounce the indolence of Darius. This had fuelled the fame of their foes, for he had happened upon them in the most constricted confines of Cilicia, when a withdrawal would have drawn them unwarily into naturally defensible sites, where divers rivers ran across their route and there were so many crannies amidst the crags from which the ambushed enemy could not even have escaped, let alone opposed, their opponents.*

8.2 *It would please Bessus to retire towards Sogdiana. By way of a wall, he would waylay their foes with the Oxus River, whilst hefty reinforcements were mustered from the neighbouring nations. The Chorasmii would come as well as the Dahae & Sacae, the Indians and such of the Scythians as were settled on the far side of the Tanais River.*[247] *Not a man among these was so short that his shoulders were not at least level with the scalp of a Macedonian man-at-arms! His sozzled supporters yelled in unison that this was their sole sane strategy and Bessus bade that yet more pure wine be poured out for them as he devised the defeat of Alexander upon his dining table.*

8.3 Among the men at that meal there was a Mede named Bagodaras.[248] *Though he meddled in magic arts (if indeed they are arts and not the shams of the sharpest shysters), he was more famous for his pretentions*

---

[247] The Tanais is the Cleitarchan name for the ancient Jaxartes, identical with the modern River Syr-Darya: this stems from geographical confusion with the River Don (the Tanais proper).

[248] Bagodaras in the manuscripts of Diodorus, but Cobares in Curtius.

than his expertise, yet otherwise honest and mild-mannered. He introduced himself with the observation that he knew it to be more sensible for a servant to follow orders than to offer advice, since followers suffer no worse a fate than their fellows, whereas advisors particularly imperil their own persons. But **Bessus** advised him that he should make his counsel clear and even handed him the goblet in his own grip.[249] On accepting it Bagodaras began to speak: *"It is in the nature of mortals that they may be called capricious and contrary on this account also, that each of them is less effective in furthering his own affairs than in handling those of others. Those who advise themselves devise deranged designs. They are driven by dread, else distracted by desire or sometimes by a natural fondness for their own fancies, actual arrogance being unconscionable in your case, Sire. Your background leads you to believe at least that what you have yourself devised is either the only or the optimum approach. You bear a heavy burden upon your head, the symbol of sovereignty, which must be upheld with restraint, lest - may the fates forfend! - it should cause you to be crushed. Thus, there is need for due deliberation instead of an instinctive stampede."* Then he appended proverbs in common use among the Bactrians: that a cringing cur barks more vigorously than it bites and that the deepest rivers run least raucously.

8.4 By these words Bagodaras had his hearers holding their breath and thereupon he unveiled his advice, which was beneficial for Bessus rather more than gratifying to him: *"Upon the doorstep of your domains stands a most dashing king, who will fling his forces against you whilst you are still stowing that table. So now you would summon up an army from the Tanais and parry his arms with rivers. Obviously, you are fearless of your foe following wheresoever you may go, though the course is common to you both, yet more secure for the conqueror. Though you may deem that dread drives hard, hope is yet hastier. Why not ingratiate yourself with the greater power by devoting yourself to his cause? For, however affairs fall out, your fortunes shall fare more favourably as his devotee rather than as his enemy. A realm you have reaped from another may be relinquished all the more readily. Perchance you would arise as a rightful ruler, when he himself had raised you up, who can either confer a kingdom upon you or wrest your realm away. You have heard out devout advice that it would be vain to belabour at more length. A pure breed of steed is steered sheerly by the shadow of the lash, but even the spur cannot stir a mount of trash."*

8.5 Bessus, being bilious both by temperament and intoxication, came so close to boiling over that he was barely held back from butchering Bagodaras by his friends, since he had already unsheathed his sabre. At any rate he burst forth from the banquet beside himself with rage, whilst Bagodaras slipped away under cover of the confusion and swathed by

---

[249] Possession of the goblet symbolized that he had formally taken the floor.

night to switch his allegiance to Alexander. *The sanctuary that he received and Alexander's promises of presents were a temptation to the topmost captains of Bessus's battalions.*

8.6 Bessus had eight thousand Bactrians under arms. So long as they imagined the Macedonians would be moved to head for India instead by the wildness of their weather, they obeyed Bessus's bidding. But once they were wise to Alexander's approach, they vanished into their various villages, thus abandoning their boss. With a handful of his adherents whose loyalty had not lapsed, he got across the Oxus River, burning his boats to forestall their ferrying his foes. Then he sought to assemble substitute soldiers among the Sogdians.

8.7 Actually, Alexander had already clambered across the Caucasus, as related earlier, though he had come close to starvation through scarcity of grain. They barely kept *their gullets* greased with the sap squeezed from sesame as an inferior form of oil, but each amphora of this juice cost two hundred and forty drachmae, whilst each such jar of honey fetched three hundred and ninety drachmae and three hundred was charged for an amphora of wine. Little or no wheat was winkled out, for the barbarians keep caches that they call "siri", which they cunningly camouflage in such a way that none save those that dug them can discover them. Hence in these their harvests stayed hidden away. Faced with such famine, the soldiers subsisted on freshwater fish and greens. But when even these provisions were vanishing, they were commanded to kill the beasts of burden that carried their encumbrances. They eked out their existence on this meat until they met with the Bactrians.

8.8 The territory of the Bactrians has many and motley natures. One area is thick with trees and vines that nurture an abundance of soft fruits with widespread springs drenching the rich soil. They sow their grain in the more sheltered spots and the rest they render up to the foraging of their flocks. Beyond, a great stretch of the same land is taken up by desert sand. By dint of its dreadful dryness this region does not nurture either men or agriculture. When indeed the wind whistles in from the Pontic Sea, it sifts what sand is strewn about the land into dunes, which, when fully formed, appear from afar like huge hills, obliterating all trace of former tracks.[250] Hence, those that transit these tracts study the stars by night, on which they base the bearing of their course in the mode of mariners. Thus, the shade of night comes close to being clearer than the day's light. Therefore, they find those parts impassable during the days, since they lack a lead from any landmarks and the lustre of the stars is hidden in haze. Furthermore, if any be engulfed by a gale sprung in off the sea, then the sands smother them utterly. Yet, where the land is lusher, it accounts for a multitude of men and mounts. Therefore, the host of the Bactrian horse formed a thirty thousand strong force.

---

[250] The view that Bactria lay just to the east of the Pontic Sea (the Cleitarchan name for the Euxine, the modern Black Sea) is a Cleitarchan misunderstanding of the geography, which is also reflected in his concept that the Syr-Darya river was the Tanais (see note in Section 8.2); Alexander was actually >1000km east of even the Caspian Sea.

Book 8: July 329BC – Autumn 328BC

Bactra itself, the regional capital, sits beneath Paropamisus' mountain wall. The Bactrus River, which runs past its ramparts, gave its name to the city and surrounding parts.

8.9 Whilst Alexander was sojourning at Bactra news was announced from Greece regarding the revolt of the Peloponnesians and the Spartans[251] *(for they had not yet been decisively defeated, when those who were to announce the outbreak of that insurrection had set forth.)* But another cause for alarm was heralded to be at hand: that the Scythians that subsisted beyond the Tanais were on their way to bolster Bessus' band. **In the same period the accomplishments of Caranus and Erigyius in the region of the Arians were reported. The Macedonians had fought a battle with the Arians, in which the turncoat Satibarzanes had been the boss of the barbarians, since he was striking in his strategic virtuosity and valour. The Macedonians had encamped close to their foes, so that there arose repeated scattered skirmishes for a time with a multitude of tiny tussles. Then their full formations were engaged and became deadlocked in stalemate. Stirred by this state of affairs, Satibarzanes rode into his front ranks, raised his hands and removed his helmet so as to be recognized. After staying his missile chuckers, he challenged any Macedonian captain who cared to contest the outcome to duel with him in single combat, adding that he would give battle bareheaded.**

8.10 Erigyius could not tolerate the taunting of the barbarians' boss. Though virtually of venerable age, he would not be believed less robust in body and spirit than any of the youths. Doffing his helm to bare his greying hair, he declared: "The day has dawned for me to demonstrate either by predominating or else most dauntlessly dying just what sort of soldiers and friends Alexander possesses!" Then without additional eloquence, he steered his steed towards his opponent's, so a courageous contest could commence. *The impression given was that both battle-lines had been bidden to sheathe their weapons, for they fell back at once, forming a free space. They were fixated upon a fight that would not only allot their leaders' fates, but their own as well, since they too must fall who followed whichever of them fell. The barbarian began by launching his lance, which Erigyius dodged by a slight nod of his head, and then spurring his steed he sped his sarissa straight through the throat of his foe, so that it poked out of the nape of his neck. Though he hurtled from his horse, still the barbarian battled on. But having levered his lance out of the wound,*

---

[251] This may indicate the arrival of the Spartan envoys, whose departure from Greece had been delayed until the summer of 330BC (Aischines 3.133). It is scarcely credible that Alexander was still unaware of Antipater's triumph over Agis at the Battle of Megalopolis some two years after it took place. However, Megalopolis may not have been recognized at the time as the end of hostilities, since this passage seems to be saying that the envoys who had announced it to Alexander had not been able to confirm that the Macedonians had won the whole war.

Erigyius aimed it again into the face of his foe. Then Satibarzanes seized it in his grasp so as to speed his last gasp by guiding his enemy's blow.

8.11 The woebegone barbarians, being bereft of their boss, whom they had backed more out of kinship than for his own sake, and even then not unmindful of the rewards from Alexander, ceded themselves to Erigyius to seek their safety in surrender. Whilst rejoicing in this success, the king, though not at all flippant concerning the Spartans, yet tolerated their revolt with equanimity, saying that they did not dare to lay bare their designs until they knew him to have reached the rim of India.[252] Then he mobilized his men in pursuit of Bessus and was met on the way by Erigyius exhibiting the head of the barbarian as his spectacular spoil from the fray.

8.12 Accordingly, having entrusted the Bactrian tracts to Artabazus, **Alexander** left the luggage and the baggage there with a garrison. He himself **entered the desert spaces of Sogdiana** with a disencumbered contingent and he led this force forward by night marches. The aforementioned want of water fires a thirst, firstly through despair of its relief, even ere men are actually driven to drink. For four hundred stades not the merest modicum of moisture emerges. The searing summer sun incinerates the sands and when they are simmering, it is as though everything is cooked by a continuous conflagration. Thereupon, a haze evoked by the vicious heat of the terrain distorts the daylight, so that in vision the plain has a vast and boundless sheen like an ocean main.[253]

8.13 They noticed that nocturnal travel was tolerable; due to the dew and dawn chill recharging their bodies. But with the radiance itself the roasting resumed and their very saliva was sapped as they marched, so that their mouths and innards grew greatly parched. Consequently, firstly their verve and then their vigour began to flag: it troubled them either to push on or to lag. A few, forewarned by those familiar with this land, had furnished themselves with water beforehand, which

---

[252] This is not the outrageous anachronism that it might seem, because in Cleitarchan geography India began in southern Afghanistan in the region of the Helmand River, where Alexander had been during the previous year (cf. Curtius 8.9.10, who mentions the River Ethymantus, which seems to mean the Helmand, as being part of India). Some modern translations have interpreted this passage as Alexander being "not free of anxiety" about the Spartan revolt, but he must at this point have known that it had ended, so it is more apt that Curtius/Cleitarchus was defending him against a charge of flippancy. That such flippancy was an issue is shown by Plutarch, *Agesilaus* 15, where Alexander says of the Battle of Megalopolis: "It seems, my friends, that while we have been conquering Darius here, there has been a battle of mice in Arcadia."

[253] Anyone who feels that the Cleitarchan descriptions of the terrain are vague or exaggerated would do well to examine the route between Bactra (modern Balkh at Google coordinates 36.768352,66.901674) and the River Oxus (modern Amu-Darya at Google coordinates 37.359242,66.869316) on Google Maps in the Satellite images view. The overall distance is about 70km corresponding closely to the 400 stades mentioned by Cleitarchus. The last 30km just south of the river is a band of enormous dunes, some of them 100's of metres long and therefore tens of metres tall. On their leeward edge they would have been too steep to be negotiated by men in armour or carrying heavy packs, which would have compelled them to wend a winding course. Progress would have been terribly slow and the place a great trial for men on foot.

for a while withheld their thirst, but then their wish for wetness was rekindled when the heat reached its worst. Therefore, whatever wine and oil there was about was for each and all poured out and they were so besotted by this booze that their fear of thirst they were later to lose. After wine enough to be well the worse for wear, even their arms were more than they could bear and nor could they press on anywhere. And so, it was they came to think that they were happier who had had no drink, when those who had drunk without refraining were forced to spew forth all they were retaining.

8.14 Beset by such blights an anxious Alexander was encircled by his Friends, who begged him to bear in mind that his inspirational spirit was the sole succour for the failings of his forces. Thereupon, he was met by two scouts, who had gone ahead to select a site for the camp. They were lugging skins of water to support their sons, who were serving in the same sections and were understood to be suffering severe hardship from the shortage. When they came across Alexander, one of them unbound one of the bladders, filled a cup he was carrying and proffered it to the king. In accepting it, his sovereign asked for whom he had brought the water and discovered that he was carrying it for his sons. Then returning the brimming beaker, just as it had been handed to him, Alexander declared: "*Lest I pain my companions*, I cannot bear to drink alone and neither can I share such a trickle among all. So chivy along to your children and hand over to them what you have hefted for their sakes."[254]

8.15 *Eventually, the king reached the River Oxus* at around dusk, but the greater part of the army had not managed to keep up with him. Hence, he bade that beacon fires be lit upon a crag, so that those struggling to follow should know that they were not far from his camp. Those in the foremost formations being rapidly restored by food and drink, he had some fill skins and others of them use any vessels to hand that could hold water in order to carry aid to their comrades. **But those troops that drank too drastically choked and gave up the ghost in numbers that far exceeded the king's casualties in any conflict.**[255] As for Alexander himself, he stood, still encased in his cuirass and having tasted neither food nor drink, waiting beside the way by which his soldiers straggled in. Nor did

---

[254] A similar story is told by Arrian, *Anabasis* 6.26.1-3, in the context of the Kedrosian march, though he concedes that some accounts had placed it earlier in the general vicinity of the Paropamisus. However, Cleitarchus seems to have attributed the Kedrosian disaster to a shortage of food rather than lack of water, stressing that wells had been dug in advance along the army's route. It may be that Alexander regularly made a point of refusing water, if his men had to go without: Plutarch, *Alexander* 42.3-6, has him do so during the pursuit of Darius, although his otherwise resembles the Cleitarchan version in Curtius 7.5.9-12. Frontinus, *Stratagemata* 1.7.7, even places such an incident in Africa, but perhaps he was following Trogus and mistook the location.

[255] The circumstances were a classic case history for death through hyponatremia (loss of body salt) and "water intoxication". It is seriously dangerous to drink too much fresh water after severe, sweaty exercise, because the consequential sudden dilution of body salts can cause cells to swell, leading to death through seizures and coma. Such overindulgence is feasible, because there is a lag between the physical act of drinking and the psychological alleviation of thirst.

he stand himself down to pander to his own person until his entire force had passed before him. And he spent that whole night in sleeplessness with his mind in a mighty turmoil.

Figure 8.1. Alexander refuses a drink, whilst his army suffers from lack of water (from a 1696 edition of Curtius)

8.16 Nor was Alexander less dour the next day, since he lacked any launches and neither could a bridge be erected, by reason of the area around the river being bare and utterly devoid of timber. Therefore, he implemented the only plan that could be devised to meet his need. He distributed a great many skins stuffed with straw so that reclining upon these they could paddle their way across the river with the vanguard standing guard whilst the rest came over.[256] Eventually, by the sixth day he had managed to convey his whole host across to the opposite side.

---

[256] The use of such floats in crossing rivers was a standard tactic in Alexander's repertoire: Arrian, *Anabasis* 1.3.6, has him filling the leather tent covers with hay in order to cross the Ister (Danube) in 335BC. The straw/hay was necessary, because the skin bags could not be made completely airtight and so would have collapsed under the pressure of their load in the absence of stuffing. Furthermore, the hollow cores of the strands would have retained air, even if the skins became partially waterlogged. The floats were necessary not merely as buoyancy aids, but in order to get the soldiers' armour and baggage across. For this purpose and also because Curtius literally has the troops resting athwart them, they must have been quite large – perhaps half a cubic metre or more in volume.

Book 8: July 329BC – Autumn 328BC

8.17 At this point Alexander had resolved to continue to prosecute the pursuit of Bessus, when he heard what had occurred in Sogdiana. **Bessus held Spitamenes in the highest honour relative to the rest of his comrades, but treachery cannot be traded away by any manner of meed,** *though it could be deemed less damnable in his case, since it seemed that no sufficiently sinful deed could be done against Bessus, the murderer of his monarch.* And so Spitamenes vaunted the avenging of Darius as a *meretricious* motive for betraying his lord, *but it was Bessus's ascendancy rather than his villainy that he truly abhorred.* Prompted by the news that Alexander had crossed the River Oxus, Spitamenes invited Dataphernes and Catanes, *in whose lasting loyalty Bessus believed,* to be his accomplices in the plot he had conceived.

8.18 *To these and others who had been close to Darius he declared that the time had come to curry Alexander's favour by seizing Bessus and surrendering him as soon as they could to the king. They were no sooner told than enrolled, since day by day their desire to have Darius back grew, as an abomination of Bessus took hold. Rallying eight of their lustiest lads, they duly deployed a devious deception. Spitamenes went to Bessus and asked that the guards should leave, then in strict privacy averred that he had discovered that Dataphernes and Catanes had conspired to hand him over alive to Alexander. He, however, had forestalled their fickleness by fastening them in fetters.*

8.19 Bessus, *being obliged by such a superb service as he supposed it to be, was both thoroughly thankful and passionately impatient for their punishment, so he* bade that they be brought before him. *Their collaborators in the conspiracy then dragged them in with their arms voluntarily tied. Bessus sprang up, scowling scarily and unable to withhold his hands from them. At this* they shed their shamming and engirded him, frustrating his struggles by strapping him in bonds, ripping the royal coronet from his brow and rending the raiment that he had assumed from among the suits of his assassinated sovereign. *Bessus avowed that the divinities were visiting vengeance upon him for his villainy, but added that, though they were not opposed to Darius in so avenging him, they were especially well disposed towards Alexander, even whose enemies were ever aiding his victories. It is unclear whether the multitude might have militated for Bessus to be set free, except those that had fettered him feigned they had done it by Alexander's decree, thus intimidating them in their dubiety.* Then the plotters plonked Bessus on a horse and led him to be relinquished to Alexander.

8.20 Also at this time Alexander nominated nine hundred men due for discharge and donated two talents to each cavalryman and three thousand drachmae to each of the foot, then set them heading off homewards after goading them to beget offspring.[257] He gave his thanks to the rest, who had signed up to serve in all his coming campaigns with zealous zest.

8.21 *Whilst Bessus was leading him a merry chase,* **Alexander came upon an inconsequential citadel. Its populace comprised the Branchidae,[258] a race who had migrated from Miletus at the bidding of Xerxes,** *when he was on his way back from Greece. They had set themselves up in this seat, since they had profaned the sanctuary called the Didymeon to appease Xerxes. In the interim they had hardly lapsed from the habits of their homeland, though they were now bilingual, having little by little been lured from their own languange by the local lingo. Therefore, they were greatly gratified to greet Alexander and to set their city and themselves at his service.* Learning their history, **the king commanded that the Milesians who were serving in his forces should assemble. Against these Branchidaean folk, they nursed the ancient grudge. Hence, he allowed those whom they had betrayed freely to judge whether they wished to recollect the kinship or the crime of the Branchidae. Then, having received various views from them, he himself undertook to weigh up what had best be done.**

8.22 *The next day, when the Branchidae came before him, he called upon them to accompany him and, when they had come to the city, he himself got through its gate with a designated detachment. The phalanx he instructed to ring the ramparts of the fortress and to tear down the town at a given signal, since he said* it was an asylum for quislings and *these should be mown down to a man. Being defenceless* they were massacred everywhere and neither their shared speech nor the beseeching of the suppliants with olive branches and prayer could curb the cruelty. *Ultimately, they undermined the foundations of the walls so that they could be cast down in order that no vestige of the town should stand. And in order to leave naught but wiped out waste and lifeless land with even its roots eradicated, they not only felled the copses and sacred groves, but also extirpated the stumps. Had this been contrived against the traitors themselves, then it could have been vindicated as valid vengeance rather than rated as ruthlessness. As it was, the descendants suffered for the sins of their ancestors, though they had not even seen Miletus and hence never had the ability to betray it to Xerxes.[259]*

---

[257] A silver talent comprised 6000 drachmae, each weighing about 4.2g on the Attic standard.

[258] The important references on Alexander's destruction of the Branchidae are: Curtius 7.5.28-35; Diodorus, *Contents* of Book 17; Plutarch, *Moralia* 557B; Strabo 11.11.4 & 14.1.5; Suda (Aelian fragment 54) s.v. *Branchidae* (Adler number: Beta 514).

[259] By modern standards the destruction of the Branchidae was an atrocity. By the standards of Alexander's era, the issue is far more complex. It appears that contemporaneous religious law, which then enjoyed genuine respect, dictated that the descendants of serious religious criminals inherited the guilt (Plutarch's dialogue *On Delays in Divine Vengeance* in his *Moralia* attacks this religious law through examples, including the Branchidae, but it still treats it as axiomatic that such a law was

Book 8: July 329BC – Autumn 328BC

8.23 *From there Alexander progressed to the Tanais River, whither* Bessus was delivered *not just strapped* in chains *but also stripped of every scrap of his raiment. Spitamenes led him by a leash and collar of links, a sight that gratified the Persians as much as the Macedonians. Then Spitamenes spoke: "I have wreaked revenge on behalf of both Darius and yourself, my successive sovereigns, by leading this liquidator of his lord before you, after overmastering him in a manner for which he himself set the example. Would that Darius could awake to witness this spectacle with his own eyes! Would that he should arise from the Underworld, for his fate was unfitting and he deserves such solace!"* At this unexpected exposition, Alexander *specially praised Spitamenes, then turned to address Bessus directly: "Of what crazed creature did the insanity seize your soul that you could firstly bear to bind then butcher the sovereign who was your best benefactor? And yet you actually bribed yourself to commit monarch-murder with the pretended title of king!" Bessus did not dare to deny the misdeed, but said he had usurped the sovereignty in order to be able to surrender his society to Alexander, since some other would have seized the state, had he hesitated.*

8.24 *But* **Alexander** felt he had himself formed a friendlier foe for Darius than this supposed comrade, so he **bade Oxathres, the brother of Darius, whom he had incorporated among his bodyguards, to come forward and then he handed Bessus over to him together with the task of torturing the traitor by attaching him to a cross and mutilating his ears and nose, so that the Persians could pierce him with arrows.** *Yet Alexander also prescribed that his person be preserved even from the attentions of the birds. Oxathres averred that he and his family would assuredly take care of everything, adding that none other than Catanes should keep the birds at bay, since he desired to display and show his exceptional skill with a bow, for he shot so surely at anything that he even downed birds on the wing. It was an amazing marvel for those that saw it in effect, which reaped Catanes real respect.* **Thereafter** *ere they were dismissed* **presents were provided to all those who had delivered up Bessus.** *But his actual execution was deferred,*

---

applied and cites an attack upon the same principle by Euripides at *Moralia* 556E). It was a sacred duty of Alexander to uphold religious law, but he would have been conscious that this particular tenet was controversial and that the passage of 150 years could be seen as a major mitigation. It was probably his sense of a dilemma that led him to seek a sentence from his Milesians. Curtius is usually translated to the effect that these Milesians could not decide, so Alexander took the decision instead, but actually he need not mean more than that Alexander imposed a punishment in accordance with the preponderance of the varied views of the Milesians. Translations that make Alexander ignore his own consultations are unnecessarily implying irrationality and vindictiveness on the part of the king, which is not substantiated by the actual words of Curtius. Among the ancient sources Aelian and Strabo seem to endorse or accept the justice of Alexander's treatment of the Branchidae, whereas Curtius and Plutarch express doubts.

so that he should be slain in the same place, where he himself had done Darius to death.

Figure 8.2. The punishment of Bessus (André Castaigne, 1899)

8.25 In the meantime, some Macedonians who had fared forth on a foraging expedition in fragmentary formation were surprised by the natives, who careered down upon them from the contiguous crags. More of the Macedonians were captured than were killed and the barbarians harried their hostages into scurrying before them as they headed back into the highlands. These marauders amounted to twenty thousand men, who fell upon their foes with slings and bows. Whilst Alexander was blockading them with himself among the most prominent combatants, he was struck by an arrow, which left its head embedded in the middle of his shin.[260] The frantic and fretful Macedonians conveyed the king back to their camp, but it did not evade the notice of the natives that he had been freighted away from the front line, for they surveyed all the sights from their lofty heights.

8.26 Therefore the next day they sent emissaries to Alexander whom he instantly bade be admitted. Unbinding his bandages and making light of the largeness of the lesion, he showed his shin to the barbarians. On being bidden to settle down, they maintained that the Macedonians were not more miserable than they

---

[260] Curtius 7.6.3: this was a severe wound, as is confirmed elsewhere in the sources (Arrian, *Anabasis* 3.30.11; Plutarch, *Moralia* 327A-B & 341B and *Alexander* 45.3); splinters of one of the lower leg bones (most probably the tibia, but alternatively the fibula according to Arrian) are stated to have emerged from the wound.

Book 8: July 329BC – Autumn 328BC

themselves in being made aware of the wound. Had they been able to ascertain who had inflicted the injury, they would have handed him over, since solely the sacrilegious waged war against the gods. Furthermore, they offered him the fealty of their folk, being overwhelmed by his wound. Having promised them his protection and recovered his captured colleagues, the king accepted their surrender. Then the Macedonians struck camp and Alexander was lifted upon a military litter. The entire infantry and cavalry corps contended as to who should carry it. The cavalry, with whom the king customarily cantered into combat, considered it their prerogative. Conversely, since they were accustomed to carrying their incapacitated comrades, the infantry complained that a function that formally fell to them was being usurped most specifically when Alexander was to be borne about. Perceiving the two parties to be at loggerheads and reckoning a decision between them to be a dilemma and liable to be loathed by the losers, the king bade them take turns to bear him.

8.27 From there on the fourth day they reached the city of Maracanda,[261] *which is a matter of six days' journey from the River Tanais.* **This city is both sumptuous and secure, being bordered by the wide waters of its river and entirely encompassed by an uninterrupted rampart seventy stades in circumference.**[262] *A wall also surrounds the citadel inside.* **Alexander left a garrison** *of one thousand soldiers* **in the city** *and evacuated and incinerated the nearby shantytowns.*

8.28 Thereafter the envoys of the Scythian Abii appeared in order to place themselves at Alexander's disposal, though they had been independent since the death of Cyrus. They were generally judged the most just of the indigenous peoples, for they forbore from making war unless molested and the highest and the humblest persons had been put on a par by their balanced and leveling liberty. Alexander addressed them graciously and then dispatched Derdas from among his Friends to those Scythians who inhabit Europe. He was to instruct them not to stray across the Tanais River save at the king's command. This emissary also had the mission of scouting out the terrain as well as visiting such of the Scythians as were settled above the Bosphorus.[263] *Having arrived at the river and encamped beside it,* the king had selected a site for a city on the banks of the Tanais to act as a bulwark on which to belay both those already subdued and those he had

---

[261] Samarkand.

[262] Both Curtius 7.6.10 and Metz Epitome 7 agree that Alexander arrived at Maracanda "on the fourth day", that the circumference of its wall was 70 stades and that the king left a garrison. These are strong indications that the two authors had the same (Greek) text before them, despite the vast differences in scale, style and purpose between their respective Latin versions.

[263] This means (north of) the Cimmerian Bosphorus (the modern Strait of Kerch off the eastern tip of the Crimea in the the Black Sea); Alexander (or Cleitarchus) mistakenly thinks the Tanais is the River Don, so he seems to believe that the Scythians beyond its northern bank are Europeans!

determined duly to bring to bay.[264] However, his designs were delayed by news of insurrection among the Sogdians that also embroiled the Bactrians. All the rest imitated the example of seven thousand horsemen, by whom it was instigated.

8.29 Alexander called for Catanes and Spitamenes, who had surrendered Bessus, to be summoned, not doubting that the rebels might be reconciled to his rule through focusing their efforts upon the fomenters of the affair. But being in fact themselves the ringleaders of the revolt that he had invoked them to avert, they published the report that the king was calling up the cavalry from all over Bactria in order to quell the insurrection. But they said that they themselves could not stomach executing such an instruction, lest they should commit an inexcusable crime against their countrymen. And so, they asserted that they could no better bear the beastliness of Alexander than the regicide by Bessus. Thus, they readily incited armed insurrection from those already driven by dread of doom to contemplate such a reaction.

8.30 On becoming fully informed of the defection of these deserters, the king commanded Craterus to besiege Cyropolis. He himself took another town in that country after cordoning it off. The signal was issued that the adult men should be slain, but that the rest were to remain as the reward for their captors. That town was torn down, so that others might through the example of its extirpation stay steadfast to the crown. However, a powerful people called the Memaceni had resolved to sustain a siege as being not just more respectable but actually safer. Alexander sent ahead fifty cavalrymen to soften their stubborn stance by flourishing the king's clemency for those that capitulated whilst also brandishing his implacable displeasure towards those he had to subdue. They responded that they were in no doubt concerning either the king's clemency or his reliability and they directed the riders to rig their camp outside the fortifications of their town. Then they hosted them hospitably, but in the dead of night they sallied forth, when they were sleeping and sluggish from feasting, then they mowed them down.

8.31 Being suitably incensed by this incident, Alexander encircled the city with a cordon of troops, since it was too finely fortified to be taken at first onset. Hence, he enjoined Meleager and Perdiccas to invest the place, *whilst he himself continued on to Craterus at* Cyropolis, which was already besieged as has been said. However, he had ordained that this city established by Cyrus should be spared, since there were no other persons from their peoples that he admired more than that king and Semiramis: he believed the two of them far to have surpassed the rest both in the vastness of their vision and the distinction of their deeds. Yet the obduracy of its denizens left him so annoyed, that when it had been captured, he had it destroyed. On having wiped it away and feeling, not unreasonably, riled regarding the

---

[264] Although it is nowhere explicitly stated in the sources, the circumstances and analogy with the reaction of the Scythians to the foundation of the same city (Curtius 7.7.1 and 8.33 below) suggest that it was this decision to embed the Macedonian presence in the territory that instigated a renewed rebellion among the natives.

Book 8: July 329BC – Autumn 328BC

Memaceni, he returned to Meleager and Perdiccas. But no stronghold ever withstood a siege more stoutly, since the most resolute of his soldiers succumbed and the king himself endured dire danger. For the nape of his neck was struck by a stone so smartly that his vision was veiled and he tottered over hardly wholly conscious. Indeed, the army moaned as if they were already bereft of him. But being unconquerable in confronting things that unnerve others, he pursued the siege all the more insistently whilst his wound had not yet wholly healed, being roused to redoubling his regular rapidity. Therefore, having undermined its defences to broach a broad breach, he broke through into the town and as its captor he commanded that it be torn down.

8.32 *From this place Alexander despatched Menedemus to the city of Maracanda* with three thousand foot and eight hundred horsemen. *Having made Maracanda's Macedonian garrison forsake the city for its royal citadel,*[265] *the turncoat Spitamenes had ensconced himself within its walls* without its denizens having endorsed his design to defect, although afterwards it appeared as though they had, as they proved unable to inhibit him in any respect. Meanwhile **Alexander returned to the Tanais River and encompassed the countryside that had contained his camp with a wall, such that the circumference of this incipient city, which he commanded should be called Alexandria,**[266] **was sixty stades. Its founding was accomplished so swiftly that seventeen days after the fortifications were erected its dwellings had also been perfected.** *Since the work was apportioned piece-by-piece, considerable competition had arisen among the teams of troops over who would be the first to release its completed project.* **The king selected captives from the three cities founded by Cyrus to populate his pristine town, *freeing them by paying off their worth to their masters.*** They continue to be recognised among their countrymen as monuments to the memory of Alexander.

8.33 Yet the Scythian sovereign, *whose rule then ranged beyond the Tanais*, reckoned that this riverbank foundation of a fortified city by the Macedonians amounted to a halter around their necks. Hence, *he sent his brother, named Carthasis, with a huge horde of horsemen to eradicate it and to repel the Macedonian forces to far beyond the river.* The Tanais sunders the Scythians that are dubbed European from the Bactrians, since it is the same stream as separates the edges of Asia and Europe by its course.[267] Moreover those Scythian people settled not far from Thrace range right from the Orient to the North and are not the neighbours of the Sarmatians as some

---

[265] To agree with Arrian, *Anabasis* 4.3.6-7, *Metz Epitome* 9 (which is somewhat corrupt) might mean "the Greek force, which went to the garrison left in the royal citadel"; Curtius 7.6.24 is clear that the garrison had been ejected from the main part of the city, but says nothing of its citadel.

[266] Alexandria Eschate ("the Farthest") at modern Khujand: cf. Arrian, *Anabasis* 4.4.1; Justin 12.5.

[267] Reiteration of the >2000km confusion between the Tanais/Don and Jaxartes/Syr-Darya.

suppose, but rather a part of them.[268] Straight on from there they inhabit a further region ranging beyond the Ister[269] and reaching to the ends of Asia by Bactra. Their settlements occupy the nearer North, beyond which dense forests and wide wastes are encountered. On the other hand, their land hardly differs from farmed places, where they verge upon Bactra and the Tanais.

8.34 Being about to conduct an unplanned conflict with this people, given that they aggressively galloped before his gaze, Alexander convened a council of his Friends, though still troubled by the trauma that had especially spoilt his speech, neck-ache and meagre meals having mutually muted his voice. Yet it was not these foes that he feared, but the terrible times. The Bactrians had rebelled and the Scythians too were inciting him to action, whilst he himself could neither stand upon his feet nor bestride a steed nor even direct and exhort his men. Perched between pincers of peril and even blaming the gods, he bemoaned that he, from whose velocity nobody had previously been able to flee, lay thus languishing, such that his own men hardly held that his ill health was not a hoax. Consequently, though he had ceased to consult seers and diviners after his defeat of Darius, he relapsed into superstition, that mockery of the mind of mankind, and required Aristander, to whom he had consigned his credulity, to enquire through sacrificial rites what was going to transpire.

8.35 It was the practice of such prophets to examine their entrails in the absence of the king, then to regurgitate what they were portending. As Alexander waited while they investigated the guts of livestock to learn about obscured outcomes, he called upon his comrades to sit nearer him than normal, so that he should not rupture his raw lesion by straining his voice. Hephaistion, Craterus and Erigyius in the company of the Bodyguards had been admitted to his pavilion and ***the king counselled*** them ***thus:*** "This crisis has enmeshed me at a moment that is more opportune for my opponents than for me. But necessity supersedes careful calculation, particularly at the point of a lance, which rarely allows you leeway to pick and choose your chance. The rebellious Bactrians, on whose jugular we remain, mean to measure our mettle through a proxy's campaign. There is no doubt where our best interest lies. If we fail to answer the Scythians, when without prompting they have taken up arms against us, then we shall be contemptible in the eyes of the rebels when we turn back. *If,* however, *we transit the Tanais and vaunt our universal invincibility by slashing and smashing the Scythians, who will hesitate to obey us* when even Europe yields us the field? He errs who stints our accolades according to the breadth of the tract that we are about to traverse. A single stream intervenes, on passing over which, we shall have carried our conquest into Europe. And how much it must be admired that, in the course of capturing Asia, we should have made memorials to our might in what is almost another world. That which Nature has evidently divided

---

[268] Strabo 11.2.1 agrees in making the Sarmatians a species of Scythian.

[269] The River Danube.

Book 8: July 329BC – Autumn 328BC

by such substantial distinctions would all at once have become conjoined in a combined conquest."

8.36 "Yet, by Heracles, if we should faintly falter, the Scythians shall be harrying our backsides. Is it only we that can swim across rivers? Many stratagems that have availed us of victory will recoil upon us. It is the fate of warfare even to school those it scuppers in its skills. Having lately set them the example of traversing a torrent on stuffed hides, even if the Scythians cannot conceive how to copy it, the Bactrians shall be their guides. What is more, only the first force from these folk has yet arrived – others are to be anticipated besides. Hence by shunning a showdown we should simply aggravate the aggression and, when we might have seized the initiative, we would be forced onto the defensive."

8.37 "The sense of my plan is plain, but I worry whether the Macedonians will permit me to implement what I please, since, as a result of receiving this wound, I have neither been able to ride around on horseback nor get about on foot. But, if you will volunteer to follow me, I will be revitalized, my friends, and well enough to endure what I have proposed. Or else, if the end of my days be now nigh, in what such exploit were it better to die?" This was whispered in a waning and quavering voice that was barely audible to those beside him, whereupon everyone sought to dissuade the king from so cavalier a course. Erigyius was especially insistent, but when his own influence failed to reduce his ruler's resolution, he sought to subvert him with superstition, which Alexander was powerless to resist. Hence, he declared that even the deities disapproved of the plan and the king would be exposed to potent peril if he should traverse the river. On entering the royal pavilion Erigyius had encountered Aristander, who had said that the signs in the offal were awful. Thus, Erigyius was but announcing what he knew from the augur.

8.38 Having hushed him, Alexander was disconcerted not just due to annoyance but also by embarrassment that there were now revealed the superstitious ceremonies that he had concealed, but he bade that Aristander be called before him. When he had come, the king glared at him, complaining: "It was as a private client that I commissioned an augury rather than in my capacity as king. Why therefore did you disclose what was foretold to another rather than to me? Your indiscretion has exposed my private and confidential business to Erigyius, and, by Heracles, I am sure that he has extrapolated the entrails in the image of his own apprehensions. Yet you, who hedge in what you can, let you testify to me myself and publicly avow what the entrails have taught you, such that you may never gainsay what you say now."

8.39 Pastily pallid, Aristander stood as if stupefied, even his voice stilled by consternation, but finally the same fear prompted him not to protract the king's expectancy, so he responded: "I foretold an impending turning point of titanic yet not futile toil and it is not my art but my goodheartedness that discomfits me. I witness the weakness of your well-being and I know how much relies upon you alone, so I am apprehensive of whether you can cope with the present pressures."

But the king bade him: "Let you find faith in my famous fortune, for it is for further feats that the gods have ceded me such celebrity." Thereafter, whilst he was weighing up with these same stalwarts by what recourse they could cross the river-course, Aristander reappeared reporting that he had never otherwise witnessed such wonderful offal, it being besides quite at odds with the former insides. Then, cause for concern had been evident, but now, purely auspicious signs had been sent![270]

8.40 But the news that was announced to the king not long afterwards blotted his unblemished succession of blessings. As already related, **Alexander had sent Menedemus to besiege Spitamenes, the abettor of the rebellion of the Bactrians.** Being informed of the approach of the foe and so as not to become confined within the fortifications of the city, **Spitamenes concealed his soldiers by the wayside whereby he perceived his opponent must pass**, confident that he could catch Menedemus unawares. The way was swathed with woods as is apt for an ambush. Here he hid his Dahae, a duo of whose warriors ride upon each steed, disconcertingly dismounting in alternation, so as to sow confusion among the columns in a cavalry combat. The dash of these men matches the motion of their mounts. Having been bidden by Spitamenes to surround the woodland way, they managed all at once to appear at the front and the flanks and the rear of their enemy that day. Though boxed in on all sides and outnumbered, Menedemus long battled on, yelling that having been tricked by a treacherous trap no other option arose but a distinguished death through the solace of the slaughter of their foes.

8.41 Menedemus himself bestrode a hugely hefty horse, which he repeatedly rode in a rush against wedges of barbarians that he disintegrated with great carnage. But when all assailed him alone and a lot of lesions left him blanched of blood, he exhorted Hypsides, who was one of his friends, to alight upon his steed and save himself by flight. This being gasped out, he gave up the ghost and his corpse slid from his horse to the turf. Hypsides could indeed have fled, but having lost his comrade he resolved to die instead. His sole concern was that he should not perish unavenged, so, spurring on his horse with his heels, he hurtled into the heart of the hostile host and after faring famously in the fighting he was felled by a hail of missiles. On seeing this, **the survivors of the massacre ensconced themselves upon a hillock** a little loftier than the rest, **where Spitamenes beleaguered them**, looking to compel their capitulation through starvation. There fell in that fray two thousand foot and three hundred horsemen. Alexander disguised this disaster with shrewd intent, designating death for those delivered from the debacle, if they divulged the event.

8.42 Moreover **when the king could not any longer keep up his confident countenance in contradiction of his true feelings of uncharacteristic**

---

[270] In the tradition followed by Arrian, *Anabasis* 4.4.3, (Aristobulus?) Aristander's signs stayed bad.

Book 8: July 329BC – Autumn 328BC

inadequacy,[271] he retired into his tent, *which he had intentionally sited beside the bank of the river.* There *without witnesses* he weighed up his decisions one by one, whilst whiling the night away in wakefulness and worry over his woes. *Often, he lifted the skins of his tent in order to survey the fires of his foes, from which he could suppose how multitudinous their men were. But he persisted in perceiving his previous proposal as the most profitable one, so he determined to press on with what he had begun.*

8.43 *Presently* day dawned, whereupon he donned his cuirass and went forth to his troops *for the first time since receiving his recent wound. So vast was their veneration for their sovereign, that his mere presence readily eradicated the rumination upon the risks that had rattled them. Exultant therefore and shedding tears of joy in deploying their salutes, those that had formerly fought shy of the forthcoming fight now boldly beseeched him for a battle.* Their monarch announced that he would ferry the phalanx and the cavalry upon rafts, *but he bade the more lightly armed men to swim with the support of stuffed skins. The matter did not demand that more be spoken, nor could the king say more by dint of his debilitation.* Yet such was the enthusiasm of the soldiers by whom the craft were fabricated that within three days towards twelve thousand rafts had been created.[272]

8.44 Presently everything had been readied for the river transit, whereupon a score of Scythian emissaries careered through the camp upon their high horses, since such are the manners of their nation, bidding that it be announced to the king that they desired to deliver a decision to him in person. On their admission to the royal pavilion and having been bidden to be seated, each of them riveted his gaze upon the king's countenance[273] and the eldest of them delivered this speech: "If the gods had willed that your physical size were on a par with your avaricious aspirations, then the world would not contain you. You would touch its sunrise rim with one hand and its sunset brim with the other, and following upon nightfall, you would wish to know where such a divine shining had shaded itself. Thus, too you covet whatever you cannot capture. From Europe you assail Asia and from Asia you launch into Europe. Thereafter, if you have overcome all human races, you will wage war against woodlands, wild beasts, rivers and snowy places. To what end? For do you not know that tall trees take time to grow, yet are uprooted in an hour or so? He is a fool who ogles their fruit, but fails to judge how high they shoot. Watch that you don't dive down with the selfsame branches you seize, whilst trying to reach the tops of those trees. Just as the lion occasionally becomes the meat of the most minute of birds and iron is eaten by rust, nothing is so robust that it is not at risk even from feeble things."

---

[271] Alexander's feelings are derived by conflation of *Metz Epitome* 9 with Curtius 7.8.1.

[272] *Metz Epit.* 10 read *duo milia*, perhaps an error for *duodecim milia* given *XII milia* in Curtius 7.8.7.

[273] Curtius (7.8.9-11) interjects personal comments here, concluding that he will faithfully render the words of the Scythians "just as they have been passed down to us" despite their gracelessness.

8.45 "Of what concern are we to you? We have never touched your territories. Is it intolerable that the inhabitants of forsaken forests should claim ignorance of who you are and whence you came? It is impractical for us to obey anyone and neither do we desire to have aught to run. So that you may savvy Scythian society, the gifts given to us are the yoke for oxen, the libation bowl, the lance and arrows. These we employ for our friends and deploy against our foes. The fruits of the efforts of our oxen we furnish to our friends, with whom we offer wine to the gods with the bowl. With arrows we take a toll of our enemies from far away, whereas with the lance we bring them to bay. So it was that we subdued the sovereign of Syria[274] and later the overlord of the Medes and the Persians, such that the road as far as Egypt lay open to our incursions."

8.46 "Yet you, who vaunt your invasion as a pursuit of pillagers, you are yourself the marauder of every race that you have reached.[275] Lydia lies under you, Syria is seized and Persia is possessed by you, the Bactrians are bent beneath your sway and India is an intended target. Even now you are greedily grasping at our herds with ever hungering hands. What is the worth of wealth to you, when it aggravates your appetite? You are the first ever to have procured famine from profusion, such that the more you have possessed, the more obsessively you have coveted all the rest. Does it not strike you that you have lingered long about Bactria? And even while you have been subduing her cities, Sogdiana has commenced hostilities. Indeed, your wars are spawned by your victories. For though you be bravery's boldest incarnation, no one willingly suffers foreign domination."

8.47 "Just let you pass across the Tanais and you will find out how widely the Scythians range about, though you will never overhaul them. In our austerity we shall be swifter than your army, who are lugging the loot from so many lands. On the other hand, when you think we're far in the distance, we shall be seen among your tents. For we both chase and flee with the same rapidity. I hear it said besides that the isolation of the Scythians is satirized in the sayings of the Greeks.[276] But we haunt wilderness and desert strands rather than stalk through cities and lushly farmed lands. Hence hold onto your fair Fortune with a firm grip, since she is slippery and cannot long be kept against her will. Competent counselling shall be recognized more clearly in the future than upon the present day. Yet you should curb your successes, so as to make them more manageable *in every way*. Our folk

---

[274] It is a specific Cleitarchan idiosyncrasy to refer to Assyria as Syria: e.g. Athenaeus 530A (F2).

[275] The Scythian's speech (from Curtius 7.8.19) has a striking parallel in one of the references to Alexander's audience with the pirate, Aristonicus of Methymne. St. Augustine (*De Civ. Dei* IV, 4. 25) tells this story of Alexander and the pirate, which he probably took from Cicero, *De Republica*, who in turn is likely to have sourced this material from Cleitarchus. St. Augustine has: "Indeed, that was an apt and true reply which was given to Alexander the Great by a pirate who had been seized. For when that king had asked the man what he meant by keeping hostile possession of the sea, he answered with bold pride, 'What thou meanest by seizing the whole earth; but because I do it with a petty ship, I am called a robber, whilst thou who dost it with a great fleet art styled emperor.'" See Section 5.33 above.

[276] E.g. Aristophanes, *Acharnians* 704: "Cephisodemus, who is as savage as the Scythian desert…"

Book 8: July 329BC – Autumn 328BC

affirm that Fortune is footless, having hands and wings only. When she proffers her hands, also grasp her wings firmly!"

8.48 "In summary, if you be a deity, it is your duty to give gifts to mankind and not strip them away. But if you be a human being, you should bear that in mind day after day. It is folly to think only of those things that make you forget your humanity. Those that you refrain from waging war against, you can engage with in amity. For it is between peers that friendship is firmest and they appear equal who have not put each other's strength to the test. Have a care not to consider those you've conquered to be your comrades, for there can be no camaraderie between a serf and his lord, since even in times of peace a thrall is governed by the sword. And do not suppose that the Scythians consecrate a concord with an oath: their ratification grows from its observation. Such sacred precautions are a practice of the Greeks, who conclude their covenants with divine invocation. The keeping of faith is itself our creed: they, who disrespect their fellows, fail the gods indeed. Neither is a friend of doubtful goodwill of use to you in need. Yet we would be your rangers in both Europe and Asia. But for the intervention of the Tanais, we border on Bactria. Beyond the Tanais, we live in the lands as far as Thrace and rumour reckons that Macedon adjoins that place. With us being at the borders of your domains at both ends, think well on whether you wish us to be your enemies or your friends." So spoke the barbarian.

8.49 In reply **Alexander** retorted that he would rely on his own luck and upon their advice, since he would follow both Fortune, in whom he had faith, and the counsel of any who urged him not to act with rashness and recklessness. And having dismissed the delegation, he **embarked his forces upon the readied rafts** *that had been deployed along a designated stretch of the bank, commanding that they should cast off together at a given signal. He put hypaspists in their prows,*[277] *bidding them to crouch down upon their knees, so that they should be safer in the face of a hail of arrows. Behind them stood the men who cranked the catapults, encompassed on either flank and ahead by the men-at-arms. Being stationed behind the artillery, the rest of the armed men guarded the rowers, who lacked the cover of corselets, by forming a tortoise shell with their shields. The self-same arrangement was retained aboard the rafts that conveyed the cavalry. Most of these let their steeds swim at the stern trailing by their reins. However, those who skimmed across on skins stuffed with straw stayed sheltered to the rear of the rafts* until they reached the Scythian shore.

8.50 *The king himself with a crack crew was aboard the first raft to cast off, directing that it be steered straight for the far bank. Advancing over the*

---

[277] Curtius' term for these troops is *clipeatos*, which means shield-bearing soldiers. This is most probably a literal Latin translation of *hypaspists*. A secondary possibility would be *peltasts*, who were equipped with the smaller circular rimless shield (*pelte*) plus spears and long swords. These might specifically be the Agrianians, who were equipped as *peltasts* and are mentioned in this battle by Arrian, *Anabasis* 4.4.6.

deep channel they appeared with their vast array of rafts like a phalanx forging forward in formation on a battlefield rather than a river. However, the Scythians were resolute that the king's rafts should not even reach the land, so they arrayed ranks of riders at the rim of the shoreline with jutting javelins. *But besides the sight of such forces thronging the bank, the pilots were particularly perturbed, since the steersmen could not correct their course, which was canted by the current. Furthermore, in their anxiety to avoid being jettisoned the tottering troops hindered the helmsmanship of the pilots. Neither could the soldiers even poise themselves to cast their javelins, since their priority had to be to keep their footing rather than risk assailing their foes.*

8.51 *Yet upon a signal given at midway the Macedonians gave vent to rampant roars and the men's morale was right then raised by a peal of trumpets, the rhythmic rant of the rowers and the plash of the oars. However,* the Scythians *similarly shouted out and* started to shoot arrows and other missiles at the Macedonians, wounding many and causing some mortality, because, being hemmed in, the men could not elude their lethality. *Their salvation lay in the catapults, which flung their bolts, thus inflicting mayhem amidst the ranks of their compacted opponents who rashly rendered themselves as targets. But* the barbarians *too* rained such a heavy hail of arrows upon the rafts that scarcely a shield was not shot with a shower of shafts.

8.52 Shortly, the rafts were grounded upon the shore, *whereupon the hypaspists rose up in unison and being now sure of their stance took precise aim to volley their javelins from their vessels. As soon as they saw that the Scythian steeds were startled and starting to stampede, motivated by mutual exhortation they sprang ashore and set upon the disordered opposition.* Such squadrons of cavalry as had their mounts bridled broke through the disarrayed ranks of the barbarians. *Meanwhile, the rest readied themselves for combat in the cover afforded by the fighting formations. As for the king himself, what bodily vigour he was through infirmity denied, his resolute spirit supplied. Whilst his rousing words could not be heard, since his neck wound was not yet wholly healed, still everyone witnessed him fighting in the field.* Hence, as the phalanx also followed them forwards, they *themselves delivered their own leadership, each exhorting his fellows, so that they forgot their safety and* hurtled headlong at their foes.

8.53 Then, in truth, the Scythians could not cope with either the growls or the scowls or the arms and armour of the Macedonians, so slickly slackening their reins, for they were basically an array of riders, they all of them took flight. *Despite that he was unable to ride upright because of the bouncing of his debilitated body,* the king persisted with the pursuit *for eighty stades. And presently, when his spirit had expired, he specified that his men should dog the tracks of the fugitives so long as any light at all lingered. He himself, having exhausted even the resilience of his soul, returned to his base and remained there during the rest of the chase.* And now they went beyond the boundary of Dionysus, which was punctuated by rock pillars at frequent intervals[278] *and by lofty trees, the trunks of which were sheathed with ivy.* But the Macedonians were fired to press further forward by their fury, for it was almost midnight when they came back to camp on the Tanais having slain many, made even more captive and driven off eighteen hundred horses. *Of the Macedonians themselves sixty cavalrymen and around a hundred foot fell with a thousand being wounded.*

8.54 It was the repute of so convenient a victory in this excursion that subdued that far-reaching region of Asia, which had sought to secede. They had considered the Scythians to be unbeatable, but, when they were shattered, they conceded that no nation could match the Macedonians in military matters. Consequently, the Sacae sent envoys to proffer the fealty of their folk, being prompted less by Alexander's ascendancy than by his clemency towards the worsted Scythians: for he had repatriated all those taken prisoner without ransom, so as to curry confidence that his contention with the most provocative peoples was a question of chivalry rather than a tantrum. Therefore, he welcomed the emissaries from the Sacae and gave them his usher,[279] *Bagoas the Eunuch,* as their escort. He was as yet a mere youth and beloved by the king for his cuteness of those years, but, although he was equally as handsome as Hephaistion, he could not match his masculine charm, being barely manly at all it appears.[280]

8.55 *Three days after returning to the Tanais* the king made a forced march to the metropolis of Maracanda in order to surprise Spitamenes, *having bidden Craterus to bring the bulk of the army after him by steady stages.* But when Spitamenes was apprised of Alexander's arrival, he *aborted his*

---

[278] Perhaps Alexander's expedition observed immense glacially deposited monoliths/boulders in the plain north of the Syr-Darya River. During the Ice Ages an area of glaciation spread forth from the various northern Himalayan Ranges into that region.

[279] The best reading from the manuscripts of Curtius 7.9.19 is *excipinon* (in B, F, L, M & V, whereas P has been read as *escipinon*): despite confusion sown by modern editors, inspired by Hedicke's hugely imaginative emendation to *Euxenippon* and Foss's frankly weird *Elpinicon*, it is clear that this is a reference to the individual elsewhere known as Bagoas the Eunuch; he was the young, unmanly male, who had a sexual relationship with Alexander at this time; Diodorus 17.77.4 has Alexander appointing "Asian born rod-bearers to his court" just at the time that Bagoas had joined his retinue; presumably these officials resembled what we would call court ushers; hence the name/title might derive from *excipio* to greet or *excido* to castrate; it is likely that Bagoas spoke Greek as well as Persian, which is why Nabarzanes used him as his apologist before Alexander (Curtius 6.5.23) and why he would have been an appropriate escort for the Sacae at this point.

[280] The obvious sexual innuendo here accurately reflects the Latin in Curtius, where *lepore* for charm is also the ablative case of the word for a hare, which was a traditional love-gift between an older and a younger man in the ancient world (e.g. as depicted on Greek vases).

beleaguering of the Greeks and fled *to Bactra.*[281] In consequence, the king covered a considerable compass of the country in four days, reaching that locality where he had lost two thousand foot and three hundred cavalry under the leadership of Menedemus. He ordered that a mound be made to accommodate their bones and gave offerings to the spirits of the dead according to the customs of their country.[282] Presently, Craterus, who had been ordered to follow with the phalanx, caught up with the king. And so, in order that all who had rebelled should similarly suffer the sorrows of insurrection, he divided his forces, fired the fields and called for the killing of adult men. *It is claimed that over twelve myriads were slain.*

8.56 The most substantial section of Sogdiana is desert. An area almost eight hundred stades wide is occupied by empty waste and that region runs onwards for a vast space, through which the river that the locals call the Polytimetus is traced. There are rapids where it is constricted into a gorge by its banks and then it is consumed by a cavern and courses underground. The only sign of its suppressed progression is the sound from the sloshing of its waters, since the soil itself, beneath which such a torrent has snaked, is not the slightest bit slaked.

8.57 *There were led before the king thirty of the noblest Sogdians, chieftains of rare robustness of body. When they realized through an interpreter that they were being escorted to their execution by command of the king, they started to sing songs as if in celebration and rhythmically to stamp their feet and lewdly to jerk their bodies so as to display a species of spiritual joy. Watching with wonder as they went to meet their death with such magnanimity, Alexander bade that they be recalled and requested the reason for such rapture, when the spectre of extermination stood before their gaze? They confided that they would have been desolated to die by order of any other, but seeing as they were to be reunited with their forbears by so mighty a monarch, the conqueror of every country, they were celebrating with their customary merrymaking and choir a distinguished death, to which heroes might even aspire.*

8.58 Then, admiring their gallantry, Alexander responded: "I wonder whether you would wish to live without hostility towards me, in whose gift your welfare lies?" They replied that they had never been inherently hostile towards him, but when goaded into hostilities they were necessarily hostile towards the aggressors. If a person had preferred to approach them with presents rather than provocations, they would have fought not to be surpassed in civility. And when Alexander asked by what pledge their fidelity might be affirmed, they replied that what life were granted to them

---

[281] Presumably the Greek garrison of Maracanda had held out in its citadel for the whole period or (less probably) the survivors of Menedemus' forces were still holding out on their hillock.

[282] Entombment with Macedonian rites was also later granted to Alexander himself by Ptolemy in Memphis according to Pausanias 1.6.3, which may be sourced from Cleitarchus (see 13.87 below).

they would pledge to his cause. They would be at his service whensoever he should call. Nor did they revoke this avowal. For those who were sent home have led their population into alliance by their allegiance and four of them, whom he kept as bodyguards, were no less loyal than any of the Macedonians in their care for the king.

8.59 Having left Peucolaus in Sogdiana with three thousand foot, since indeed he had no need for a greater contingent, **Alexander relocated to Bactra. Here he had Bessus brought before him and bade that he** *be led to Ecbatana to* **pay through capital punishment for dealing death to Darius.** *There he was killed according to the custom of the Persians by being suspended, split and diced into little bits that were subjected to dispersions.*[283]

8.60 During virtually these same days Ptolemaeus and Menidas brought a thousand cavalry and four thousand foot to serve their sovereign as mercenaries. Asander arrived too with a comparable count of foot and five hundred cavalry. Just as many accompanied Asclepiodorus from Syria and Antipater had sent eight thousand Greeks incorporating six hundred cavalry. With his army thus augmented, the king set forth to pacify those parts that had been convulsed by the revolt and, after having executed the instigators of the disturbances, he arrived at the River Oxus on the fourth day. Due to conveying silt, its current is always cloudy and hence unhealthy to drink. Therefore, the soldiers started to sink wells, but, though they dug down deep in the earth, no source was seen to seep forth. Finally, a fount was found right beside the tent of the king himself. Then the men made out that it had only just begun to spout, since they had been slow to scout it out. And Alexander himself was desirous that it be deemed a donative from the deities.

8.61 *On the eleventh day* after leaving Bactra **the king reached and crossed the River Ochus. Subsequently, he traversed the River Oxus** *and reached the city of Margania.*[284] *In its environs Alexander selected six sites for the foundation of citadels: two to its south and four to its east. They were near neighbours of one another, so that mutual aid might be conveyed without being delayed by distance, and all of them were established upon high*

---

[283] With slight emendation *Metz Epitome* 14 can agree with Plutarch, *Alex* 43.3 & Diodorus 17.83.9 on the manner of Bessus's execution.

[284] A cogent explanation of Alexander's itinerary at this point has been put forward by A. B. Bosworth, "A Missing Year in the History of Alexander the Great", *Journal of Hellenic Studies*, Vol. 101, pp. 17-39, 1981. Bosworth points out that the readings *marganiam* or *marginiam* in the MSS of Curtius should not have been emended to read *margianam* (i.e. Margiana, the modern Merv). The Ochus must be a major tributary of the Oxus in the east of Bactria, which makes it most probably the modern River Surkhab. Hence Alexander travelled east from Bactra until he met the Oxus and continued eastwards along its southern bank (i.e. without crossing). Somewhere north of Kunduz, he crossed the Ochus (Surkhab), and then he headed on into the Kochka region, where he crossed the Oxus heading northwards somewhere near Ai Khanum. Margania must have been an otherwise unknown ancient city in the region to the north of the Oxus, which was the SE part of ancient Sogdiana. It cannot have been Margiana (Merv), since it does not fit the geography.

hills. *To these and six other of his foundations in Bactria their ruler relegated those he regarded as rebels within the ranks. Back then these citadels served as curbs upon those conquered in this land, but now, oblivious of their origin, they serve those that they used to command.*[285]

8.62 And so the king had imposed peace upon all other parts, but impelled by panic a multitude of men from the province had sought the protection of a towering pinnacle. **This rock was occupied by the Sogdian Ariamazes with *thirty thousand warriors and* previously hoarded provisions, *so as to provide for such prodigious numbers for as long as two years*.** The altitude of this pinnacle presented an intimidating sight, for it soars up in excess of twenty stades in height *with a circumference of a hundred and fifty*.[286] *None but the birds may inhabit it, for* **it is** *thickly forested*, **sheer on every side and approached by a** *precipitous and pinched* **pathway.**[287] **At about the halfway point in the ascent** the path passes into a cavern *with a narrow and shadowy mouth,* **which is the only way up to the heights. But bit-by-bit it broadens further in and ultimately even develops deep alcoves. Springs spout virtually throughout the cavern and the waters that course forth collectively source a stream that cascades down the crags.**

8.63 Having observed the obstacles that the place displayed, the king considered that it could not be captured by storm. *He had decided to depart, when he was inspired by a yearning even to harass Nature's art. Nonetheless, before gambling his Fortune on an investment, he sent Cophes, who was a son of Artabazus, to the barbarians to persuade them to surrender their craggy emplacement.* From the supposed security of his surroundings, Ariamazes made many a haughty reply, culminating in the question of whether Alexander could even fly?

---

[285] Cleitarchus was writing half a century after these events, which is a sufficient perspective for Curtius to have found these comments in his text: it would alternatively be surprising, if Curtius, writing some four centuries after their foundation, even knew precisely where these citadels were.

[286] Manuscipts of Curtius have *XXX eminet stadia*, whereas the Metz Epitome had *XX stadiis*.

[287] Polyaenus, *Stratagems* 4.3.29 provides the details that the rock was accessible only to the birds and heavily forested, although it is slightly surprising that neither Curtius nor the Metz mentioned the forest, if it was in Cleitarchus.

Book 8: July 329BC – Autumn 328BC

SOGDIANI AD SVPPLICIVM TRACTI LÆTANTVR.

Figure 8.3. The Sogdian prisoners are joyful on their way to execution, leading Alexander to spare them (from a 1696 edition of Curtius)

8.64 *When this was relayed to* **Alexander,** *it so fired his spirit that he convened his customary counselors, to whom he reported the arrogance of the barbarian, who had lampooned them for lacking wings. But he* said that he himself in the next night would make the man maintain that Macedonians were even capable of flight, adding: "Let you fetch me three hundred of the fittest young fellows from your respective forces, such as at home herd their flocks up mountain tracks and across crags that are practically impassable." They readily recruited those who were outstanding in both agility and dauntless daring. *Scrutinising them* the king confided: "*It is beside you, O youths that are my comrades, that I have surmounted the palisades of cities, which were erstwhile deemed invincible; that I have passed through peaks perpetually swathed in snow; that I have negotiated the narrows of Cilicia and suffered the fierce frost of India without indolence.*[288] *Thus I have presented you with proof of my princeliness and you have provided me with proof of yours!"*

8.65 "*As you can perceive, the pinnacle posesses but one portal, which the barbarians infest, whilst neglecting all the rest. They have set no sentinels, save those that contemplate our camp. You will ferret out a route, if you sedulously seek for fissures to see you to the summit. Nature has set nothing so high that it cannot be conquered by courage. We have taken Asia by attempting what has intimidated others.* Let you soar up to that summit. When you have seized it, issue me a signal with white banners, which you will wear as belts. *Then I shall shift up our forces to fend the focus of our foes off you and onto us.* The prize for him who first scales the crest shall be ten talents with one fewer for the next to follow and the same again until ten men have met the mission. *But I am sure you shall be motivated not so much by my munificence as by my ambition.*"

8.66 *They heard out their sovereign with such exultation that it seemed as if they had already seized the summit. When they were dismissed,* in accordance with the king's counsel, **the men made ready rugged ropes and tapering iron pegs to wedge between the slabs. Then their ruler rode around the rock and at its rear,** *where the access seemed least severe and precipitous, bestowing his blessings* **he bade them begin their ascent in the second watch of** the night.[289] *Packing provisions sufficient for two days and armed only with swords and spears, they started their climb. And at first they forged forward on foot, but then* upon reaching the cliffs some levered themselves aloft by grasping handholds in the rock, whilst others hauled themselves up on ropes with nooses cast ahead to snag on protrusions. *Still others* wedged the tapering iron pegs into crevices between the slabs,

---

[288] This is a reference to the blizzard conditions that the Macedonians had encountered in the highlands of central southern Afghanistan as they approached the passes across the Paropamisus Range (Curtius 7.3.12-14; Diodorus 17.82.2-7): Cleitarchus regarded this region as a part of India.

[289] The Greeks usually divided the night into four watches.

threading their ropes through them, so as to establish a ladder up which they could clamber. And each of them helped out the rest, as step by step they crept to the crest.

8.67 *A day was taken up between terror and toil. After struggling up hard stretches, still more arduous parts lay ahead and it appeared as if the pinnacle were elevating. It was a really wretched spectacle, when* those that were fooled by infirm footings tumbled down from the rockface, *for their fellows' fate foreshadowed what likewise awaited the watchers.* Yet they fought through these threats to surmount the summit, *all weakened by the weariness of relentless labour and some maimed in some section of their limbs. And there they were simultaneously overcome by night and slumber. With their bodies stretched and strewn about upon the impassable, jagged rocks, oblivious of their perilous perches* they dozed until dawn. *And then at last as if stirred from a stupor they studied the concealed vales that were revealed beneath them, uncertain in what part of the pinnacle a foe in such force might be confined, whereupon they spotted smoke coiling up from a cavern below them. Hence, they deduced that their enemies' lair lay there, so* they used their spears to raise the white banners *clear of the trees, the manner of signal that had been agreed. Then* they counted the climb's cost and found that thirty-two of their number had been lost.

8.68 *The king spent the whole day peering at the peak of the pinnacle, more anxious about the fate of those that he had consigned to such palpable peril than on account of his ambition to put the place in his power. Not till nighttime, when darkness veiled his view, did he retire for rest and repose. The next morning, whilst day was still dawning, he was the first to behold the banners that signalled the seizure of the summit. Yet the interplay of sunshine and shade from the shifting cloudscape made the king wonder whether it had fooled his eyes. But as brighter light filled the skies, no further doubt could arise,* despite Alexander's surprise that success had come so soon.

8.69 And having called for Cophes, through whom he had *previously* sounded out the resilience of the barbarians, he sent him *back* to them with the warning that they should now as a minimum adopt a stance that was more in their interests. But should they remain resolute in their faith in their fastness, he bade that those that had seized the summit at their rear should be exhibited to them. On being admitted, Cophes commenced urging Ariamazes to relinquish the rock and thereby curry the king's favour through not diverting him in the siege of a single crag, whilst he was setting such mighty matters in motion. However, he, speaking more haughtily and arrogantly than before, commanded that Cophes should depart. But Alexander's emissary grasped the hand of the barbarian, begging that he come outside the cavern with him. This request being granted, Cophes pointed out the presence upon the peak of the young men and, in a not unjustified jest at Ariamazes' arrogance, agreed that Alexander's warriors were indeed winged.

8.70 At this juncture there were heard from the Macedonian camp trumpet peals and the roar of the entire corps. These things, though vacant and hollow like many other events in war, pushed their opponents into capitulation, for being fixated by fear they were incapable of gauging how few were those that threatened their rear. Therefore, *out of panic* they promptly recalled Cophes, who had left them in their alarm, sending thirty of their chieftains with him to barter the surrender of the pinnacle for safe passage for their departure. *Though nervous that the natives on noticing the negligible numbers of his climbers might annihilate them,* the king was *nevertheless* both riled by the arrogance of Ariamazes and confident of his own good fortune, hence he held out for capitulation without conditions. *In consequence, more out of despair than from his real ruin in the affair,* Ariamazes was *escorted by his kindred and the most noble of the natives down towards the king's camp, and they themselves collectively commanded that he be* scourged and crucified *at the base of the pinnacle.*[290] Ariamazes having been killed, Alexander willed that the lives of the rest be spared when they surrendered. A huge host of those who handed themselves over were given as gifts to the settlers in the new settlements together with monies taken in the matter and Artabazus was left in charge of the rock and the region around it.

8.71 These were the concerns of Alexander *in the eighth year of his reign.*

---

[290] Although the Latin of Curtius implies that Alexander ordered the execution of Ariamazes, this is flatly contradicted by the *Metz Epitome*, which is clear that this was the act of Ariamazes' own men. The latter version is far more likely to be correct, firstly because it is incredible that Sisimithres would have surrendered only months afterwards (as is also related by Curtius) had Alexander been in the habit of executing those that put themselves in his hands; secondly because small tweaks to the Latin of Curtius can reconcile his version with the *Metz Epitome*.

Book 9: Autumn 328BC – May 327BC

The Hunt in Basista; The Killing of Cleitus; The Treaty with Sisimithres; The Decapitation of Spitamenes; The Proskynesis Experiment; The Conspiracy of the Pages; The Army Caught in a Blizzard; The Marriage to Roxane.

9.1 *At the beginning of the ninth year of his reign,* having acquired more notoriety than admiration through putting in his power the pinnacle *of Ariamazes,* Alexander strewed his strikes in answer to his errant enemies by splitting his army into three columns. He entrusted the command of one to Hephaistion, of another to Coenus and led the last himself. But the barbarians were not all of like mind: whilst some were subdued by force of arms, yet more submitted to his sovereignty ere a contest could occur. And he ordered that the latter be allotted the land and lodging-places of those who had proved dogged in their defection. But the Bactrian evictees in league with eight hundred horse of the Massagetae laid waste to the surrounding settlements. Aiming to thwart them, Attinas, the prefect of that province, led forth his three hundred cavalry quite ignorant of the trap that was being contrived for him. For their enemies ensconced armed troops within the forest that chanced to verge upon the meadows, where a few foes drove forth livestock, such plunder as to entice Attinas whilst unaware into the snare. Therefore, he charged after the chattels in fractured and fragmented formation and as he wended his way past the woods those who waited within unexpectedly sprang out upon him, so that he perished with his whole host.

9.2 Repute of their ruin rapidly reached Craterus, who came upon the place with his complete corps of cavalry. Though the Massagetae had already fled, a thousand of the Dahae were left dead and their extinction extinguished the insurrection in that entire region. Having crushed the Sogdians afresh, Alexander too returned to Maracanda.[291] There Derdas, whom he had sent to the Scythians dwelling beyond the Bosphorus, met him with emissaries from that people.[292] Additionally, Phrataphernes, who presided over Choras, which was contiguous to the territories of the Massagetae and the Dahae, had sent representatives to proffer his allegiance. The Scythians petitioned that Alexander should wed a daughter of their king or else, if such nuptials were beneath his dignity, that he should allow the Macedonian nobility to forge marriage alliances with the aristocracy of their people. They further affirmed that their king would presently appear in person. **Alexander** listened to both delegations with courtesy whilst in

---

[291] Samarkand.

[292] See 8.28 above: this means the Cimmerian Bosphorus, lying off the eastern tip of the Crimea; so these Scythians were thought to dwell in the Ukraine, but actually lived beyond the Syr-Darya.

quarters awaiting Hephaistion and Artabazus. When they had rejoined him, he *proceeded to the region called Basista.*

9.3 There is no vaster evidence of the affluence of the barbarians in those bounds than their aggregations of grand and brutal beasts enclosed within great groves and parklands. For this purpose, they reserve wide woodlands lushly laved by lots of ever gushing springs. They ring these woods with walls and they have havens to harbour the hunters. One such forest infiltrated by **Alexander** with his full force had lain undisturbed for four successive generations when he *ordered an assault from every side upon its savage beasts.* Amidst this slaughter it chanced that Lysimachus (he that later reigned) stood beside Alexander when a lion of singular size careered towards the king. Hence, he aimed to thrust his hunting spear into the crazed creature, but his ruler shoved him aside and said he should back off, adding that he himself had as much skill as Lysimachus to liquidate a lion at a stroke.

9.4 Indeed, once when they had been prowling for prey in Syria, Lysimachus had single-handedly slain just such an exceptionally sizeable beast, but had had his shoulder sheared through to the bone, so that he had nearly lost his life. This was the reason for Alexander's reproach to Lysimachus, but the king's actions spoke louder than his words, for he not only confronted the colossal cat, but also slew it with a single puncture.[293] But despite Alexander achieving a choice outcome in this instance, the Macedonians nevertheless let it be known that in accordance with the customs of their country he should neither hunt on foot nor *alone* without the company of a select band of officers and Friends.[294]

9.5 Alexander returned thence to Maracanda, where, having agreed that Artabazus might retire on grounds of age, he assigned his satrapy to Cleitus, who was a veteran trooper of Philip and famed for his prolific exploits in warfare. Whilst keeping the king in the shelter of his shield as Alexander fought bareheaded at the River Granicus, it was he who had hewn off the hand of Rhosaces with his saber, when the man had menaced the king's life. Furthermore Hellanice, *the sister of Cleitus, who had reared Alexander as his nurse, the king cared for no less than for a mother.* These were the counts on which he committed to the conscientious care of Cleitus the most powerful part of his empire.

---

[293] Curtius 8.1.17 comments that he thought this incident the basis for the story that Alexander exposed Lysimachus to a lion. His comment was probably not taken from Cleitarchus, since Pliny, *Natural History* 8.16.21 accepts the exposure story as true, despite also being a source of Fragments of Cleitarchus. NB. *Basista* in Diodorus, but *Bazaira* in Curtius.

[294] I doubt that it is sensible to read into this (as some translators have) that the Macedonian Assembly voted on the matter there and then. Rather this looks like an existing custom to which they drew Alexander's attention: it explains why Alexander & Philip in the mural on the façade of Tomb II at Vergina and Alexander, Abdalonymus & Hephaistion in the hunt scene on the Alexander Sarcophagus are all mounted.

Book 9: Autumn 328BC – May 327BC

Figure 9.1. Alexander slays the lion in Basista (Antonio Tempesta, 1608)

9.6 Then, having been bidden to prepare to set forth on the morrow, *Cleitus and others among the Friends were summoned by their sovereign to celebrate a festival at an opportune party. There the king, glowing with much unmixed wine and waxing uninhibited in his self-esteem, commenced commending what he himself had accomplished, which grated on the ears even of those who could vouch for the validity of his reminiscences. Nevertheless, the elder veterans held their peace, until he ventured to disparage the deeds of Philip, bragging that the brilliant victory at Chaeronea had been his own work, but that such a superb success had been stinted him by the stinginess and jealousy of his father. What was more, when a brawl had broken out between the Macedonian troops and the Greek mercenaries, being incapacitated by a wound, Philip had flung himself to the ground, lacking any other recourse than to play dead. Then Alexander had kept his carcass in the shelter of his shield and had slain his assailants with his own hand. But this Philip could never acknowledge with equanimity, being unwilling to owe his safety to his son. Also, after Alexander had launched a victorious expedition against the Illyrians in his father's absence, he had written that his foes were in full flight, for Philip was nowhere to be found. Let not those be praised, asserted Alexander, who had beheld the ceremonies of Samothrace when it would have been becoming to burn and batter Asia, but instead exalt those the magnitude of whose deeds defied belief.*

9.7 *To this and the like the lads listened with alacrity, but it was odious to their elders, most of all concerning Philip, under whom they had the longer lived. Whereupon Cleitus, not being himself soundly sober, slewed towards those settled beyond him and recited a song of Euripides, such that only his tone rather than his text could be distinguished by the king. Its gist was that it was a perverse practice of the Greeks that solely the names of their sovereigns were inscribed upon their trophies, for thus these kings were commandeering the glory gleaned by the blood of others.[295] Hence Alexander, since he suspected that the murmuring had been malicious, began to query those about him as to what they had heard Cleitus mutter. Whilst they remained resolutely silent, little by little Cleitus declaimed louder and louder, recounting the campaigns and wars waged by Philip in Greece and accounting them all a cut above their current conflicts. This gave rise to recriminations between the younger and older soldiers. And the king had conceived a colossal rancour, despite appearing passively to overhear Cleitus disparaging his reputation. But just when it seemed that the king could keep control of his temper, if Cleitus should stem his impudent invective, he instead abandoned all restraint and greatly aggravated Alexander's anger.*

9.8 *For now Cleitus even dared to defend Parmenion and extolled Philip's vanquishing of the Athenians over Alexander's obliteration of Thebes, being not only incited by the wine but also inspired by a depraved spirit of provocation. In concluding he complained: "If a man must die for you, then Cleitus is foremost, but when you allot the rewards of victory, the foremost go to those who most mannerlessly mock the memory of your father. Sogdiana is assigned to me: repeatedly rebellious and not merely unpacified, but even ungovernable. I am being sent among brute beasts, bred for bravado. But I shall pass over my personal predicament. You scorn Philip's fighters, forgetting that if old Atarrhias here had not bellowed the youngsters back into battle when they broke, we should still be hunkered down around Halicarnassus. How therefore have you subdued Asia with such striplings? What your uncle is established to have stated in Italy is valid in my view: that he had to hack his way through men, whilst you had gone up against women."[296]*

9.9 *Among all the ill-advised and unwise words exclaimed by Cleitus, nothing annoyed his monarch more than his respectful reference to*

---

[295] Euripides, *Andromache* 693-698: "Alas, what perverse customs prevail in Greece! Whenever the army sets up a trophy over the foe, men no more consider this the work of those who really toiled, but the general gets the credit for it. He brandished his spear as one man among a myriad others and did no more than a single warrior, yet he gets more praise than they." Cf. Plutarch, *Alexander* 51.5.

[296] Alexander of Epirus, the brother of Olympias, had been killed on campaign in Italy in the winter of 331-330BC; Cleitus' quote is also referenced by Livy 9.19.10-11 and Aulus Gellius 17.21.33.

Parmenion, but suppressing his resentment Alexander was content to command Cleitus to quit the banquet. And he only added that had he prolonged his prattle, Cleitus might perchance have chided him with having saved his life, a haughty boast he had often trumpeted. Yet Cleitus was still stalling over standing up, so those reclined around him manhandled him, cajoling and cautioning him as they heaved to haul him away. Whilst he was being dragged off, anger augmented his inherent impetuosity, and he yelled that he had defended Alexander's backside with his own breast, but that after such a space of time the recollection of such surpassing service had become abhorrent. Then he even confronted the king with the killing of Attalus, and, finally, he ridiculed the oracle of Ammon, whom Alexander asserted was his father, quipping that he himself had declared more truths than the king's dad had done.

9.10 *By now Alexander had realized such wrath as he could scarcely have suffered whilst sober. Yet in fact, his senses having long since succumbed to unmixed wine, he suddenly sprang up from his couch. His frantic Friends did not even set down their cups, but, flinging them aside, surged simultaneously to their feet, fixated upon the outcome of an act instigated with such vehemence. Snatching a lance from a guard's grasp, Alexander strove to strike Cleitus, who still ranted with the same reckless rage, but their ruler was restrained by Ptolemy and Perdiccas. They clasped his waist, holding firm as he wrestled against their grip. Lysimachus and Leonnatus also relieved him of his lance. Then Alexander appealed to his loyal troops, for he said he was beset by his closest comrades, as had but lately befallen Darius, so he shouted for the trumpet peal to be sounded that would gather his guards to the royal rooms.*

9.11 *Then, to be sure, Ptolemy and Perdiccas sank to their knees, pleading that he should not pursue such aggressive anger. Let him spare a space of time to moderate his mind: everything could be effectuated more fairly on the following day. But his ears were impermeable, being filled with fury, so he dashed deliriously into the courtyard of the royal quarters, where he seized a sentinel's lance and lingered in the entranceway where those with whom he had dined must emerge. The rest had retired and Cleitus came out last lacking a lamp. "Who goes there?" the king demanded, even revealing in his voice the severity of the sin that he intended. Then Cleitus, now recalling his ruler's wrath rather than his own, replied that it was he that departed from the party. Even as he uttered this, Alexander lunged the lance into his lungs and was bespattered with the blood of the dying man. Then he taunted the corpse with Cleitus' praise for the prowess of his father, crying, "Now, begone to Philip, Parmenion and Attalus!"*[297]

---

[297] Alexander's taunting of the corpse regarding Cleitus' praise for Philip is only reported by Curtius 8.1.52 and Justin 12.6.4, which is a strong indication that Curtius is following the Cleitarchan version. Arrian, *Anabasis* 4.8.9 and Plutarch, *Alex.* 51 recount a variant version where Cleitus is

Figure 9.2. The killing of Cleitus (André Castaigne, 1899)

9.12 *Nature has neglected the mind of mankind, for we are wont to weigh repercussions retrospectively. Thus, the king, after the anger had seeped from his soul and even his drunkenness had dried out, on reflection realized too late the magnitude of his misdeed. He saw that he had*

---

successfully dragged from the hall, but returns reciting Euripides' *Andromache* 693 and is speared in the doorway by Alexander. Arrian states that he found this account in Aristobulus: it is circumstantially more credible than Curtius, who makes Alexander stalk Cleitus in the courtyard.

slaughtered a man who had carried candour into calumny on that occasion, but had otherwise been wonderful in warfare and had saved the king's own life, though Alexander were ashamed to admit it. The sovereign had assumed the vile vocation of an executioner, avenging wilful words that might have been ascribed to the wine with an accursed killing. The courtyard was completely covered with the gore of his guest of a moment before and the astonished sentinels seemed stupefied and stood well back from him, so that in solitude his remorse was manifested all the more emotionally. Weeping and wailing he cuddled the cadaver, wiped its wounds and admitted his madness to it, as if he could be heard. **And thereupon he levered the lance from the recumbent corpse and turned it upon himself.** He had already brought it to his breast when the sentinels sailed in and, though he grappled with them, they grabbed the lance from his grip, heaved him up and hauled him off to his hut. He flung himself down in the dirt and the entire royal residence resounded with his grievous groans and woeful wailing. Indeed, he disfigured his face with his fingernails, imploring those around him not to allow him to live on whilst suffering such shame.

9.13 Punctuated by such appeals, the entire night was dragged out. And in racking his brains as to whether divine retribution might have driven him to commit such an accursed crime, he recalled that he had omitted to make the annual offering to Dionysus on the appointed occasion. It followed that a killing carried out amidst wine and feasting was the unfolding of the fury of the god of those things. *But he was more upset because he was conscious that his comrades were cowering from him. None now would venture to converse convivially with him, but he must live a lonely lifestyle like a brute beast: sometimes instilling terror; at other times itself terrorised.*

9.14 *At first light he commanded that the corpse should be carried into his quarters, though it was ghastly with gore. When it was deposited before him, his tears welled up and he wailed: "This is how I reimburse my nurse, whose two sons gave their lives for my glory at Miletus: her sole solace in this sacrifice, her brother, I have butchered at my banquet. Where now shall she come by comfort in her misery? Of all those close to her, I alone survive, who alone she cannot look upon lovingly. For I, the assassin of my saviours, when I get home to my own country, shall never be able even so much as to proffer my right hand to my nurse without conjuring up her calamity!" And when his weeping and wailing continued uncurtailed, his Companions commanded that the corpse be carried away.*

9.15 *For three days the king confined himself to his quarters.* When by the fourth day he had not yet fed, *his Courtiers and Bodyguards realized that he had resolved to die, so they burst as one body into his hut and, though for ages he parried their pleas, through persistence they prevailed upon him to finish his fast.* They begged him not to allow his sorrow for a single soul to sink them all, for after piloting them to the furthest of foreign fields, he would be forsaking them amidst perilous peoples already roused to waging war. He was particularly persuaded by the entreaties of the philosopher Callisthenes, for they were fast friends from studying together under Aristotle and he had been commissioned by the king to record his accomplishments. ***To lessen Alexander's shame for the killing of Cleitus, the Macedonians ordained his death to have been lawful and would even have debarred his burial had it not been commanded by the king.*** *And indeed, Alexander deserves recognition for having regretted his error and repented his wrath, for,* **if you defend your misdeeds, you will double your disgrace.**[298]

Figure 9.3. The philosophers console Alexander regarding Cleitus (Pinelli, 1821)

9.16 Thence, having tarried ten days at Maracanda mainly to shake off his shame, **Alexander** sent Hephaistion into the territory of Bactria with a section of his soldiers to secure supplies for the winter. The province he had previously consigned to Cleitus, he handed over to Amyntas, whilst he himself ***proceeded to Xenippa.***[299] This region verges upon Scythia and is settled with many teeming townships, since the fertility of its farmland not only sustains its own society but

---

[298] Fragment 49 = Antonii Melissa I 13 p. 805 D, considered doubtful by Jacoby, but apposite here: with exactly this sentiment Arrian, *Anabasis* 4.9.6, concludes a passage giving the Cleitarchan stories of Alexander's attempted suicide, his guilt regarding his nurse and the omitted sacrifice to Dionysus. He may well have been inspired in all this by Cleitarchus.

[299] *Xeinipta* or *Xemipta* were read in the *Metz Epitome* 19 before its destruction in 1944.

Book 9: Autumn 328BC – May 327BC

is also a magnet for migrants. It had been the bolthole of the Bactrian renegades who had rebelled against Alexander, but when it was discovered that the king was coming, the people of those parts expelled them. There were two and a half thousand of them amassed, all of them mounted and habituated to banditry even in periods of peace. At that time their innate brutality had been brought out not just by the warfare but also by despair of pardon. So, they launched a surprise assault upon Amyntas, Alexander's commander, and the battle long wobbled in the balance. But eventually, with seven hundred of their side out of action, of which three hundred had been seized by their foes, they turned tail to their vanquishers, though the victors were scarcely unscathed, since eighty Macedonians had been slain and a further three hundred and fifty were wounded. Yet even after such a second insurrection they negotiated an amnesty.

9.17 After accepting their allegiance, *the king* accompanied by his entire army *entered the country that is called Nautaca*, a part of Bactria.[300] *Its satrap was Sisimithres, who had sired two sons* and three daughters *born from his own mother, since in that society there is sacred sanction for sexual violations between parents and their offspring.* He had armed his populace and protected the pass into his territory with firm fortifications where it became most constricted. A turbulent torrent tore past and the backside was blocked by a rockface, through which the inhabitants had hacked a passageway. Although the entrance to this tunnel let in light, unless lit by a lamp its core was cloaked in darkness. An endless warren known to none save the natives afforded access to the fields.

9.18 Notwithstanding the natural invulnerability of the narrows, which were guarded by a strong garrison of the barbarians, Alexander deployed his battering rams, demolished the manmade barricades and downed most defenders with archers and artillery. When they had been scattered and were scuttling away he scurried across the wreckage of the ramparts and fed his forces forward towards the rockface. But the river rent his route where the waters from the peaks ran together in a gorge and it seemed a titanic task to fill such a vast fissure: yet still he felled timber and aggregated rocks. And the barbarians, being unwitting of such wondrous works, were terribly terrorstricken when they witnessed a causeway suddenly summoned up. The king reckoned as a result that they could be driven by dread to surrender, so he sent Oxartes of their own nation but sworn beneath his sway to coax their captain into conceding the crag. *And Alexander asked Oxartes ere he went what manner of man was the master of this mighty mountain and, on being told he was entirely timid, retorted, "We shall have it then, for he lacks the strength to struggle against us."* Meanwhile to compound their consternation he both sent siege-towers towards them and bombarded them with bolts fired from torsion catapults. Therefore, they fled to the crest of the crag, despairing of any other defence. But now Oxartes began to beg Sisimithres, who was disturbed and discomfited by his predicament, to elect to experience the good faith rather than

---

[300] Nautaca may be Shakhrisyabz near the headwaters of the Kashka-Darya.

the forcefulness of the Macedonians, lest he should impede the impetus of an all-conquering army that was aiming its aggression against India. For whosoever got in its way would bring down upon his own head the mayhem meant for others.

9.19 Sisimithres himself was reluctant to reject submission, but his mother with whom he mated made known that she would rather perish than pass into the power of another and she steered the mind of the barbarian towards what was more reputable rather than less risky. So, he was ashamed that their ladies loved liberty more than their men. Hence, he expelled the apostle of peace and resolved to suffer a siege. But thereupon, on pondering the power of his opponent compared to his own, he began to repent pursuing the policy of a woman that he reckoned reckless rather than irresistible. So, he promptly recalled Oxartes and said that he would put himself in the king's power, pleading only that Oxartes should not advertise the attitude and advice of his mother in order that he might the more readily appeal for her pardon too. Therefore, sending Oxartes on before him, he followed in his footsteps together with his mother, his children and a coterie of his kindred, without even waiting for the confirmation of safe conduct offered by Oxartes. The king sent a rider to require them to return and await his arrival. Then he himself overhauled them and, upon sacrificing creatures to Athena Nike, he restored his realm to **Sisimithres**, instilling high hopes of still larger lands, if he faithfully **fostered alliance with Alexander.** And Sisimithres consigned his two sons to the king, who assigned them to serve him as soldiers.

9.20 Following this he forsook the phalanx and continued in the company of the cavalry in order to reduce the *rest of the* rebels. Their path was precipitous and blocked by rocks, though at first they managed to cope. Later, however, not only were the horses' hooves worn down, but the beasts were on their last legs. Many fell behind and their ranks gradually grew thinner as, typically, intolerable toil overcame their sense of shame. Yet the king, occasionally switching steeds, rode on relentlessly after the retreating rebels. All the noble youths who customarily escorted him had relinquished that role, with the sole exception of Philip, the brother of Lysimachus, who had reached the threshold of manhood. As was readily evident, he was a character of uncommon capabilities. Incredibly, he flanked his mounted monarch on foot for over five hundred stades, despite wearing a cuirass and bearing arms. Although Lysimachus often looked to lend him his horse, he could not be coaxed from the king's side.

9.21 When they went through woodland in which the barbarians had hidden, this selfsame youth made a famous fight of it, safeguarding his sovereign in hand-to-hand engagements with the enemy. But when the barbarians broke out of the woodland in full flight, the spirit that had inspired the youth in the heat of battle melted away and all of a sudden, he perspired profusely from every pore and slumped against a nearby treetrunk. Then, when even that prop failed to bolster him, he collapsed into the king's embrace, wherein he fainted and expired. And the monarch in his mourning was met with another and not lesser sorrow. Just before he got back to his camp, he learnt that Erigyius, one of the king's *most*

Book 9: Autumn 328BC – May 327BC

accomplished commanders, had passed away. The funerals of both these fellows were conducted with every honour and utter splendour.

9.22 At winter's end **Alexander aimed to direct his army against the Dahae, for he had heard that Spitamenes was with them.** Yet in this undertaking, as in endless others, Fortune, who never failed in favouring him, arranged everything in his absence. **Spitamenes felt a far too fervent infatuation for his wife, so he hauled her along with him in conjugal jeopardy, though she could scarcely cope with their continual escapes from successive sanctuaries. Harassed by these hardships, she persistently sought to persuade her spouse with womanly wiles finally to renounce flight and to make his peace with Alexander, since his clemency in victory had been vindicated and he could not be outrun.** *She was the mother of three grownup offspring by Spitamenes that she now ushered into their father's arms as she implored him to pity them at least – and her appeals were the more potent, since* she had heard that *Alexander was not far away. But Spitamenes thought that she sought to forsake rather than forewarn him, supposing that her faith in the power of her beauty had inspired her desire to be given up to Alexander as soon as possible. Hence, he drew his sabre and would have struck her down had her brothers not streaked to her defence.*

9.23 *Nevertheless, he ordered her to get out of his sight on pain of death should she stray within his gaze again and to alleviate his lust for her he started to spend his nights amidst mistresses. But his lingering long-term love for her was relit by repugnance for these partners. Hence, he reverted to devoting himself to her alone, but never ceased saying that she should refrain from suggesting surrender and tolerate whatever eventualities Fortune might fling at them, since for him perishing was preferable to prostration. Then she excused herself for what she had appraised as profitable proposals, but were perhaps womanish whims, though urged by loyal intentions. Henceforth, she would submit to the mastery of her man.*

9.24 *Being conquered by her counterfeit compliance,* **Spitamenes demanded that a daylit banquet be served, at which** *with his wife waiting upon him* **he washed down wine** *and victuals* **in surfeit and was carried semi-comatose to his bedchamber. As soon as she was sure that he had sunk into insensible** *and silent* **slumber, his wife** *arose from the bed, slid the pillow from below his head and* **slashed** *his extended gullet* **with a sword** *that she had hidden in her robes,* **hacking his head off. Bespattered with blood she handed the head to a slave** *who was complicit in the crime.* **In his company and still in her gory garments she came into the camp of the Macedonians and called for the king** *to be told that she alone should make a matter known to him. Then Alexander's guards conveyed her to the king, since she seemed decent, despite the bloodstains, due to her dignified demeanour and dress.* **He ordered that the barbarian be admitted** *at once,* *but the sudden sight of her bespattered with gore gave him pause. Who was she or more to the point why was she there? He supposed that she had come to complain of an assault, so he bade her state what she sought. But she craved that the slave, whom she had had stand in the lobby, should be led within.*

9.25 *Having* the head of Spitamenes *veiled within his vestments*, the slave was suspected and bared *it before his scrutineers. Pallor had suffused the features of its anaemic countenance, so it could not be recognized. Hence Alexander, on hearing that a human head had been brought to him, emerged from his pavilion to ascertain the nature of the thing, which he verified from the vouching of the slave. "Oh, most mutinous Spitamenes," the king exclaimed, "finally you have paid the penalty for your perfidy!" Then he held the hand of the wife whilst thanking her. But thereupon he pondered the connotations of the case and was caught in a perplexing dilemma. He perceived that it was a huge help to him personally that a deserter and defector had been destroyed, who, had he lived, would have delayed Alexander's prodigious designs. Conversely, he was revolted by the vast villainy of her surreptitious slaughter of a husband who had deserved her devotion, the father of her own offspring! So, in the end the savagery of her sin vanquished his thankful feelings for her and he banished her from his base, lest by her lesson in barbarity the morality and mellow mettle of the Greeks should be compromised.*

9.26 The Dahae, on discovering the killing of Spitamenes, fettered Dataphernes, his fellow defector, and surrendered both him and themselves to Alexander. *On this account the king concluded that he did not need to field his forces against their stronghold.* Being thus unburdened of the bulk of his current cares, he turned his attentions to avenging the grievances of those oppressed by the avarice and arrogance of his governors. Therefore, he assigned Hyrcania and the Mardians together with the Tapurians to Phrataphernes, and charged him with sending Phradates, who was the incumbent, to the king in custody. Stasanor succeeded Arsaces, the satrap of the Drangae, whilst Atropates[301] was sent to Media in order that Oxydates might be removed. Due to the demise of Mazaeus, Babylonia was placed under the direction of Ditamenes.

---

[301] MSS of Curtius had Arsaces, but this is clearly corrupted, cf. Diodorus 18.3.3 & Justin 13.4.13.

Book 9: Autumn 328BC – May 327BC

Figure 9.4. Spitamenes' wife presents his head to Alexander (1696)

9.27 *At this juncture* with everything in hand, **he reckoned the time was ripe for a contorted concept conceived some time before,** so he set about considering how he might commandeer divine honours for himself. He not only desired that it were said that he was the son of Zeus but even wished it were widely believed, as though he might master men's minds as well as their tongues. Hence, **he bade the Macedonians to honour him by greeting him with the Persian practice of prostrating their persons upon the soil,** instead of simply saluting him. To fuel such aspirations, he never lacked for flagrant flattery, the constant curse of kings, whose power is more often overthrown by fawning than by foes. Neither was it the Macedonians who were delinquent, for none of them would tolerate the least compromising of their country's customs, but rather it was Greeks who perverted the pursuance of the graceful arts with prejudicial practices. For example: there was Agis the Argive, who composed poorer poems than any, save Choerilus; then Cleon of Sicily, a flatterer not just from a flaw in his own character but from the character of his country; and also the scum of sundry other cities. These the king favoured before even his kinsmen and the commanders of his mightiest contingents, for these were then paving his pathway to Heaven, proclaiming that Heracles, Dionysus and Castor & Pollux would give way to the new deity!

9.28 Accordingly, the king convoked a feast furnished with profusion upon a festal day, to which were invited not merely those Macedonians and Greeks who were the foremost of his Friends, but even any man of rank. When the king was reclining amongst them, after feasting for a little while he quit the banquet. Then, as had been prearranged *by Hephaistion*, Cleon embarked upon a speech celebrating the successes of Alexander and counting their consequential blessings. There was but one way they could give thanks: if, since they had deduced his divinity, they were to acknowledge it, recompensing such benefactions at the paltry expense of incense. Indeed, the Persians were not purely pious, but also rational in reverencing their rulers along with the gods, for it was the awesomeness of the empire that secured their safety. Neither Heracles nor Dionysus had been deemed deities until they had overcome the envy of their contemporaries and posterity perceives only so much of a man as his own time testifies. If the rest were irresolute, he himself would prostrate his person upon the ground when the king came back to the banquet. The others owed it to him to do likewise and those endowed with wisdom foremost, for they should provide the precedent for reverencing their ruler.

9.29 This last declaration was undisguisedly directed against Callisthenes. The self-importance and outspokenness of this man were irritating to the king, as though he had single-handedly held back Macedonians who would have settled for such servility! So, in the ensuing silence, all the rest regarded **Callisthenes** expectantly and he **began to speak**: "Had the king experienced your speech himself, then verily there would be no need for anyone to voice a response, since he himself would have solicited that you not incite him to sink into foreign and outlandish habits nor diminish his most productive deeds with the odium of such obsequiousness. But since he is absent, I say to you on his behalf that no fruit can both last long and ripen over-early. You are not heaping heavenly honours upon our sovereign, but seducing them from him. It takes an interval of time to trust

Book 9: Autumn 328BC – May 327BC

in immortality; hence it will forever be posterity that offers this favour to famous men. But I pray that Alexander's apotheosis be delayed, so that he may both live long and enjoy eternal eminence. Divinity sometimes ensues upon a man's demise, but never imbues him in his lifetime."

9.30 "You referred to Heracles and Dionysus just now as cases of consecration to immortality. Do you suppose that their deification was decided by a single supper-party? Nay, for Nature seized them from the sight of men before their fame ferried them to Heaven. O Cleon, of course you and I can confer godhead and the king can accrue credentials for his divinity from us! And yet I would wish to put your powers to the test. Let you make a monarch of someone, if you are able to gift godhead. Is it any easier to hand over the heavens than to reassign realms? *May the gracious gods* have heard without hatred what Cleon exclaimed, but let them allow matters to move on in the same manner as till now. Let them *consent that we be content with our own customs.* I am not ashamed of my homeland and nor do I hanker for coaching by the conquered in the way in which I should pay homage to my monarch. In fact, I am ready to recognize them as our conquerors, if we learn from them the laws by which we live."

9.31 Callisthenes was heard with open ears as if he were the keeper of their communal liberty. He had elicited not just tacit assent but also vocal vindication from the veterans in particular, since the supplanting of their ingrained customs by those of foreigners was discomfiting. Nor was *the king* ignorant of aught that was uttered on either side, since he had drawn up behind the drapes that he had caused to curtain the couches. *In consequence* he sent word to Agis and Cleon to terminate the debate and *averred that none but the barbarians in accordance with their customs should perform prostration when he entered.* Then a little later, as if he had been occupied by more important matters, he came back to the banquet.

9.32 When the Persians performed their venerations of the king, Polyperchon, who was reposing up past Alexander, poked fun at one among them, who had grazed the ground with his chin, by goading him to scrub the floor more forcefully. Hence, he reaped the rage of his ruler, who had been unable to contain his temper for some time. The king enquired: "Do you then refuse me reverence? Do we seem solely to yourself to be deserving of derision?" Polyperchon responded that his monarch did not merit mockery, but neither did he himself deserve disdain. At that Alexander wrenched him from his bench and flung him flat upon the floor and when Polyperchon had fallen face down he queried: "Don't you see that you've done what you derided in another just now?" Then he commanded that Polyperchon be placed in custody and he put paid to the partying.

9.33 Actually, *Alexander* eventually pardoned Polyperchon after protracted reproof. But his wrath *was* more *resolute against Callisthenes*, whose insubordination had made him suspect for some while. An opportunity to sate his ire was soon to transpire. *It was the custom as already recorded for the main men among the Macedonians to cede their sons into the king's care on their coming of age for duties not distinctly different from the services of slaves. They took turns to keep watch each night just outside an access to the quarters in which the king slept. They used to convey concubines within by a different door than the gangway guarded by the men-at-arms. Similarly, when their monarch meant to mount, they got the steeds from the grooms and led them up. They comprised his company both in the chase and in battle, being diligently indoctrinated in all the noble arts. They enjoyed the outstanding honour that their sovereign consented for them to sit beside him to sup. And none had the power to punish them with a whipping save the sovereign himself. Among the Macedonians this coterie of Royal Pages was a kind of crèche for commanders and commissioners and some of them subsequently became kings.*

9.34 *So it happened that* Alexander ordered that Hermolaus, a highborn lad from the band of Royal Pages, be lashed, since he had skewered a wild boar earmarked by his monarch for his own spear. Hermolaus began bitterly to bewail his shaming to Sostratus, who was his fellow bandmember and fervent lover. When he beheld the body, for which he burned, so badly lacerated, being perchance already sore with his sovereign on some other account, Sostratus convinced the youth, who was vexed of his own volition, to exchange vows and to conspire with him in killing the king. Nor did they effect the affair with callow incaution, since they shrewdly selected those they would include as their partners in perfidy. They elected to enlist *Nicostratus,* Antipater the son of Asclepiodorus and Philotas, then through these Anticles, Elaphthonius and Epimenes were recruited. But no easy way to perpetrate the plot was at all apparent. It was a prerequisite that the entire cabal be keeping watch on the same night, so as to prohibit hindrance by those who had no hand in their intrigue, but it happened that they were all on duty on different nights. Hence thirty-two days were dedicated to shuffling their shifts and to other preparations for implementing their plan.

9.35 The night had come, on which the company of conspirators was due to keep watch, and they were celebrating their solidarity, demonstrated by so many days during which none had wavered through fear or foreboding, so sheer was their shared rage against their ruler or else their faithfulness to their fellows. Thus, they were stood by the door of the salon, in which the king was feasting, in order to escort him to his bedchamber when he quit the banquet. But by Alexander's own good fortune as well as the fellowship of the feasters, all of them grew more immoderate with their wine and time was also taken up with festal fun and games. At first the plotters were pleased at the prospect of assaulting an insensible king, then later grew alarmed lest the revelry last till it were light, since reliefs were due to deliver them from their duties at dawn. It would be seven days before the rota returned to them and they could not expect over that span of time that the faith of all their fellows would hold firm.

9.36 But as day was duly dawning, the banquet broke up and the conspirators collected the king, cheered that a chance to commit their crime had been created. Whereupon a woman out of her wits (or so it was supposed) who was wont to frequent the royal quarters since she appeared possessed and able to foretell the future, did not merely meet the monarch as he emerged, but even set herself in his way. In her countenance and her gaze, she displayed a disturbance of mind as she cautioned the king to return to his feasting. Alexander playfully replied that the gods gave nice advice and, recalling his comrades, he continued the carousal until almost the second hour of the day.

9.37 By now other youths from the royal band had relieved the guard-posts before the bedchamber door of the king, but the conspirators still stood by though their term of duty had expired: such is the hold exerted by hope once it is harboured in the human mind. Addressing them more kindly than in other cases, the king commanded that they should stand down and have a care for their own persons, since they had stood on station for the entire night. He gave each of them fifty drachmae and commended them, because they had continued on guard even after the duty had devolved upon others. And they, deprived of such high hopes, betook themselves to their billets. While the rest of them awaited the night of their next watch, Epimenes abruptly repented his participation, either because of the courtesy of the king in relieving him along with the other conspirators or because he believed that the gods were obstructing their objective. Hence, he revealed what had been arranged to his brother Eurylochus, whom he had previously preferred to keep clear of the conspiracy.

9.38 Everyone had the fatal fall of Philotas in view, so Eurylochus instantly seized his brother and arrived at the royal quarters, and having roused the Bodyguards, he assured them that what he had to say concened the safety of their sovereign. Ptolemy and Leonnatus, who were on watch at the threshold of the king's bedchamber, were galvanised both by the hour of their arrival and by their countenances, which hardly heralded settled souls, not to mention the sorrow exuding from the second of them. Flinging wide the doors and leading a lamp within, they woke the king from the stupefied slumber of strong wine. He gradually gathered his wits and asked what they wished to divulge. Without demur, Eurylochus declared that the gods could not completely have forsaken his house, because his brother, despite daring to dabble in faithless foul play, was nevertheless both remorseful and personally proposed to expose the conspiracy. The plot had been planned for that very night that was now vanishing and the perpetrators of this treachery were such as their sovereign would least suspect.

9.39 Then point-by-point Epimenes gave vent to everything he knew including the names of the conspirators. It is established that Callisthenes was not named as a participant in the perpetration of the plot, yet he was wont indeed to offer an affable ear to the youths when they ranted and raved against their ruler. And certain persons assert that when Hermolaus bewailed his whipping in his hearing, Callisthenes confided that it was incumbent upon them to recall that they were now men. But whether this was said in consolation for suffering the lashing or to arouse rancour among the youths remains in doubt.

9.40 When the king conceived what a dire danger he had dodged, losing his lethargy in mind and body, he at once rewarded Eurylochus with fifty talents and the prosperous property of a certain Tiridates. He also gave his brother back to him before he even begged for his deliverance, but *the authors of the outrage, and among them Callisthenes, the king commanded to be kept in fetters.*[302] When these persons had been pulled into the palace quarters, wearied by wine and waiting up the king rested right through that day and the next night. The following day the king convened a mass meeting intermingled with the fathers and family of those accused. Neither were these kindred confident of keeping themselves safe, for according to the killing custom of the Macedonian nation the lives of all who were related to those arraigned were liable to be taken. The king commanded that all the conspirators save Callisthenes be brought forth and they confessed without hesitation what they had been hatching. Then, when the crowd growled at them, the king himself grilled them as to what he had done to deserve the devising of such damnable designs against his person.

9.41 The rest being totally tongue-tied, Hermolaus replied: "As you ask as though you did not know, we did indeed design your death due to you beginning to bully us as if we were slaves rather than ruling us as your countrymen." His own father, Sopolis, reacted most rapidly among them all, moaning that he was morally the murderer of his dad and barging forwards to muffle his son's mouth with his hand, declaring that they ought no longer to listen to a man made mad by malice and misfortune. But, restraining his parent, Alexander told Hermolaus to tell them what he been taught by his tutor Callisthenes.

9.42 Hermolaus retorted: "I shall capitalize on your kindness by telling what I have been taught by our catastrophes. Not many Macedonians remain as a result of your ruthlessness! Not many at all, excepting those of most servile descent! Attalus and Philotas and Parmenion and Alexander Lyncestes and Cleitus as far as our foes have fathomed still thrive; still stand in fighting formation, their shields sheltering you, enduring injuries for your glory and for your victory. To these you have rendered remarkable requital. One garnished your table with his gore; another did not even die a clean death. The commanders of your contingents were racked in torment for the entertainment of Persians over whom they had prevailed. Parmenion, through whom you had exterminated Attalus, was hacked down without a hearing. Truly in turn you utilize the hands of unhappy people to perpetrate your purges, then you unexpectedly order others to annihilate those who have just served as your assassins."

9.43 At this the whole host howled at Hermolaus and his father drew his death-dealing blade and would undoubtedly have dispatched his son had his ruler not restrained him. Of course, the king called for Hermolaus to carry on and appealed for patience in hearing him out, as he was compounding the case for his condemnation. When with difficulty they had been calmed down, Hermolaus

---

[302] Strabo 11.11.4 locates the arrest of Callisthenes in Cariatae in Bactria.

Book 9: Autumn 328BC – May 327BC

continued, "How courteously you consent for boys inexperienced in speaking to spout forth. Yet the voice of Callisthenes is kept in confinement, since he alone is adept at discourse. Why else indeed is he not appearing, when even those who have confessed are granted a hearing? Doubtless you dread to hear free speech from a spotless speaker or even to look him in the face. However, I hold that he had no hand in anything. Those who devised the dashing deed are here with me. There is none among us who alleges that Callisthenes was in league with us, though each has been doomed to die by the most tolerant and righteous of rulers. Such therefore are the rewards of the Macedonians, whose blood you squander as if it were squalid and expendable. Thirty-thousand mules convey your captured gold, whilst your troops will traipse home with naught save the scars from uncompensated injuries."

9.44 "Still we could have stood all this before you abandoned us to the barbarians and as a novel vogue set the victors under the yoke. You revel in the rites and robes of the Persians and revile the customs of your own country. Hence, we wished to do away with a Persian potentate rather than a Macedonian monarch and we meant to molest you under martial law as a deserter. You desired the Macedonians to kneel before you and to venerate you as a god. You spurn Philip's paternity and, were any god exalted above Zeus, you would actually disdain *the kinship of* Zeus himself. Are you amazed that autonomous men cannot tolerate your arrogance? What hope can we have in you, if we must either suffer a sinless death or else survive in servitude sadder than death? You shall indeed owe much to me, if you can mend your ways. For from me you have begun to ken what cannot be borne by freeborn men. For the rest, be moderate and do not pile punishments upon those made childless in old age. But order us led forth to be liquidated, so that what we sought to gain from your death we may attain through our own." So said Hermolaus.

9.45 But Alexander responded: "It is patent from my patience how ridiculous the defendant's testimony is as taught to him by his tutor. For though he has confessed to the foulest of offences I have not only heard him out myself, but also had you hear him. For I well knew that when I allowed this delinquent to lecture you, he would manifest the madness that made him mean to murder me, when it was his duty to foster me like a father. Recently, when he behaved impertinently on a hunt, according to the custom of our country and the conduct of immemorial Macedonian monarchs, I ordered that he be disciplined. This is both proper practice and is also perpetrated upon pupils by their pedagogues and upon wives by their husbands. We even suffer slaves to whip boys of his age. Such then was the supposed savagery from me, which he sought to avenge with an insidious assassination. Yet the rest of the youths let me treat them according to my disposition, though my leniency is legendary and beyond suspicion."

9.46 "By Heracles! That Hermolaus disapproves of the punishment of traitors scarcely surprises me, since he has himself deserved the same penalty. Thus, indeed he serves his own cause in favouring Philotas and Parmenion with his applause. Actually Alexander Lyncestes I left at liberty despite him conspiring twice against my life by the testimony of two informants. When he was once more implicated in plotting, I still stayed my hand for three years, until you yourselves demanded that he duly die to atone for his duplicity. As for Attalus, you will recall that he posed a threat to my life ere I became king. Concerning Cleitus, I would he had not roused me to such rancour against him! Yet I tolerated his reckless tongue lambasting both you and me with abuse for longer than he would have let me likewise vilify him. The clemency of kings and commanders relies not solely on themselves, but also correlates with the characters of those they command. Compliancy cushions compulsion, but when deference dies in men's minds and the highest are jumbled with the humblest, then force must needs fend off force."

9.47 "But why would I wonder that the defendant has denounced me as a despot, when he has the audacity to accuse me of covetousness? I would not wish you to bear witness one by one, for fear of forcing my generosity to rebound on me, if I make it undermine your modesty. But behold our whole army: those that a bit beforehand had nothing but their arms now slouch on silver couches, burden their benches with gold, lord it over loads of slaves and cannot transport all the spoils they chose from our foes."

9.48 "But he states that the Persians stand high in my esteem, though we have vanquished them. In fact, it is the surest sign of my clemency that I do not even dominate the defeated with disdain. For I did not enter Asia intending utterly to dispossess its peoples nor to wipe out half the world, but rather conceiving that those I overcame in conflict should cease to resent my victory. And so, they serve as soldiers beside you, shedding their blood to shield your empire, whom harshness would have roused to rebellion. Possession secured through the sword is never lasting, whereas gratitude for graces is everlasting. If we wish to win over Asia, rather than just journey through it, we must convey our compassion to these people. Their loyalty to us shall establish a stable and enduring empire. And in reality, we have more territory than we can occupy. Indeed, it is insatiable greed to keep on filling what is already overspilling. Yet I am reproved for pressing the practices of the Persians upon the Macedonians. Certainly, I see in many peoples aptitudes that we should not blush to emulate and such an immense empire cannot correctly be ruled other than by both handing habits to its inhabitants and assimilating some from them."

9.49 "As for Hermolaus' assertion that I should spurn Zeus, whose own oracle acknowledged me, that almost merited mirth. Is it even in my power to determine what deities ordain? Zeus presented me with the sobriquet of son. Nor was accepting it at odds with the activities in which we are engaged. Would that the Indians should believe me to be a god, for warfaring feeds on fame and often even a false faith has gained the tribute of truth. *Do you imagine that I am having your arms emblazoned with silver and gold to suit my sense of extravagance? Actually, I wish to show to those used to nothing meaner than these metals that the Macedonians, who are invincible in everything else, cannot even be beaten in gold. Therefore, from the first I shall amaze the gaze of*

Book 9: Autumn 328BC – May 327BC

those that expect to see a wholly meek and meager host, inculcating that our coming is not due to our desire for silver and gold but in order to hold the whole world in our hands. Such is the triumph, traitor, that you have sought to forestall and by eliminating their king to set the Macedonians at the mercy of the conquered countries."

9.50 "Yet you exhort me to spare your kindred. It is not really right that you be made aware of my decision on this, so your deaths might be the more distressing, if indeed you have any respect and regard for your relatives. But in fact I long since suspended that particular practice of killing the guiltless kith and kin as well as the culprit[303] and I avow that they shall all now retain the same rank as they formerly merited. Concerning your Callisthenes, who alone sees in you a soldier though you are really a marauder, I well know why you wish him to be brought forth. It is so there might once more emerge from his mouth before this meeting those slurs that you have just slung at me and had earlier heard from him. Were he a Macedonian, I would have had him appear with you, a master most meriting such a student, but as an Olynthian he is not subject to the same jurisdiction."

9.51 After this Alexander dismissed the Assembly and commanded that the condemned be consigned to the custody of their colleagues from the same cohort. These tortured them to death, so that their ferocity might make manifest their faithfulness to the king. **Callisthenes** also ***succumbed to torment, despite being spotless in respect of any conspiracy against the king's life.***[304] But his character was not at all compatible with a court and its sycophants. Consequently, no other killing caused greater grievance among the Greeks against Alexander, for Callisthenes was furnished with the finest feelings and faculties and had coaxed back the king's capacity for life when he had determined to die after the killing of Cleitus. Yet Alexander not only slew but also harrowed him without even a hearing. Repentance of this persecution came too late.

9.52 All this being settled, **Alexander *fared forth with his forces*** after two months ensconced in winter quarters ***and* headed towards the territory known as Gazaba. *The first day provided for peaceful progress. The next, whilst not particularly tempestuous and miserable, was nonetheless gloomier than before and did not end without warning of impending blight. Then upon the third day, *in gathering gloom* lightning flashes flamed across the***

---

[303] In the context of the conviction of Philotas: Curtius 6.11.20 and Section 7.72 above.

[304] There is considerable diversity in the ancient accounts of the death of Callisthenes: Plutarch, *Alexander* 55 cites Chares for a relatively credible version, which had Callisthenes expire from obesity and infestation by lice after seven months in a cage; Aristobulus broadly concurred and the Cleitarchan account as reconstructed mainly from Curtius 8.8.21-23 is not explicitly inconsistent with Chares & Aristobulus; Justin 15.3.4 expands the caging version with antecedent mutilation and by having Lysimachus assist Callisthenes' suicide with poison, but Alexander's consequential punishment of his Bodyguard by exposing him to a lion appears anachronistic relative to the Cleitarchan version; Ptolemy's suggestion that Callisthenes was hanged (Arrian, *Anabasis* 4.14.3) may be a gloss on the less savoury truth. Callisthenes must have died in privacy for such disagreement to stem from the early sources. But hanging is a mode of execution that implies an audience.

whole scope of the sky, *alternately illuminating and eclipsing the landscape and beginning to sear the souls as well as the eyes of the forces forging forwards.* There were nearly continuous cracks of thunder and bolts of lightning were witnessed to fall far and wide. *Hence* the army, being both deafened and dazed, *dared neither to endure it where they were nor to press on, whereupon* they were *suddenly* hit by a hurricane of hail *that poured upon them with the power of a torrent.*

9.53 At first, they deflected the deluge *by sheltering beneath their shields,* but soon *these slippery* safeguards could no longer be held in hands stiffened by the storm. *Nor could they decide which way they should shift themselves, since* they were met on every side by a more tumultuous tempest than they cared to confront. *Therefore,* their ranks were ruptured and their formations straggled throughout the forest. *Being fatigued by fear even ere they over-exerted themselves,* many *among them* grovelled upon the ground, despite the fierce frost cohering the hail into hard ice. *The troops' tents and textiles too were rendered rigid by the intensifying frigidity. Though some sought shelter under cliffs and overhangs, others still were too stiff to stoop from their steeds.* Others *again* entrusted themselves to the trunks of trees, which provided a prop and protection for many. *Yet they knew that they might be choosing a spot to expire, since they would shed the warmth of vitality through inactivity. But dormancy was welcome in their weariness, so they failed to refuse to perish for the sake of being at rest. In fact, the force of this foulness was not just furious but also tenacious, and the light that is Nature's solace was filtered out by the forest shade, which combined with the murk of the maelstrom, leaving it little lighter than night.*

9.54 *None but the king was able to cope with such a calamity: by circulating amongst his soldiers, mustering the missing men, lifting up those that were languishing and indicating the smoke that twirled up from huts in the distance, urging each man to requisition the nearest refuge. Nothing was more crucial to their salvation than that they were ashamed to forsake their sovereign, who was, by redoubling his efforts, overcoming the calamity to which they themselves had succumbed. Furthermore, force of circumstances, which is more compulsive when in difficulty than cool calculation, discovered a cure for the cold: for they fought to fell the forest far and wide with their hatchets and set fire to the heaps and piles of lumber. It soon seemed as though the woods were an unbroken inferno with scarcely room to range their regiments between the flames. The heat from this blaze revived their numbed limbs and little by little their breath that had been curbed by the cold began to course more freely.*

9.55 Some settled themselves in the bothies of the barbarians *that in extremity they had hunted out, though they were hidden in the heart of the forest. Others kept to a camp that they had set up upon sodden soil, since*

Book 9: Autumn 328BC – May 327BC

the savagery of the skies was now abating. **That scourge massacred** as **many** as thirty thousand **military men** *including also servants and sutlers and* four thousand *beasts of burden. Many more men that made it back to camp were incapacitated by exhaustion or injury. Those that had collapsed upon the ground had found that their clothes stuck sound, rendering them helpless and no help to anyone. It is also attested that some were seen attached to the trunks of trees, seeming to be not only alive but even indulging in conversation, yet frozen in that attitude in which death had surprised them.*

9.56 *It chanced that an elderly man of the Macedonian rank and file had managed to reach the camp, though hardly able to hold himself upright let alone handle his arms. On catching sight of him, Alexander sprang from his seat, despite having just then been warming himself back up close to a fire. He relieved the lethargic and almost insensible soldier of his arms and bade him settle himself in the selfsame seat. For a long while he was unaware of where he was resting and who had rescued him. On eventually reviving to vitality with the warmth, he saw that he was sitting in his sovereign's seat in the king's presence and rose up in trepidation. Regarding him attentively, Alexander queried: "Do you appreciate, soldier, how much more comfortably you live under a king than the Persians? Among them your life would have been forfeit for resting upon the royal throne, yet in fact your life has been saved by it."*

9.57 The following day, having convened his Friends and the commanders of his contingents, the king ordered it to be announced that he would himself make restitution for all that had been lost. And he faithfully fulfilled this undertaking, since Sisimithres delivered loads of pack-mules and two thousand camels as well as flocks of sheep and herds of oxen, which were distributed evenly among the soldiers, saving them from suffering and famine. The king proclaimed his gratitude to Sisimithres for these services and instructed his troops to carry cooked food sufficient for six days in setting out against the Sacae. Having ravaged the whole region, he presented Sisimithres with thirty thousand looted livestock.

9.58 Alexander then pressed on in his progress towards Gazaba and entered the territory that was in the sway of the celebrated satrap Chorienes, who submitted himself to the mastery and magnanimity of the monarch. Alexander restored him to his rule, *requiring nothing more than that two of his three sons serve as soldiers in the king's campaigns. In fact in their friendship the satrap also surrendered the son he had kept into the custody of the king.*

9.59 Chorienes[305] convened a banquet equipped with outlandish luxury, to which he welcomed Alexander. Whilst this was being conducted with considerable conviviality, the satrap instructed that thirty thoroughbred virgins should be introduced *as dancers at the dinner. These included the satrap's own maiden daughters as well as those of his friends.* The most remarkably radiant among them was Roxane *and she was also distinguished in her deportment to a degree that is rare among the barbarians. Though she strode among a select band of beauties, yet* she garnered the gape of all and most especially engaged the gaze of Alexander, *who was no longer so much the master of his lust, having been fawned upon by Fortune, whom mortal men too little distrust.*

9.60 *Hence* he *who had beheld with hardly more passion than that of a parent Darius' queen and her pair of virgin daughters, to whom none except Roxane could compare in comeliness,* was *then so* infatuated with feelings for this *little* virgin *of vulgar roots relative to royalty that he at once* asked to know her name and her father. On discovering that she was the daughter of Oxyartes, *also a diner at the dinner,* the king *took up his cup and tipped a libation to the gods, then* began to declaim: *"Much that befalls many men and women commonly occurs against expectations. Thus,* countless kings have sired sons on women won in war *or dispatched daughters to distant domains to seal an alliance with wedlock. Indeed, it is conducive to the durability of my domains that Persians and Macedonians be matched in matrimony, for only so may the humiliation of the vanquished and the vanity of the victors both be banished.* And among my own ancestors, Achilles, of course, coupled with a captive wench."

9.61 Then the king focused upon the foreigners: *"In my view the Macedonians are not a better breed than you and nor do I believe you to be beneath intermarriage with us too, even though you look for an alliance with us as losers. Therefore,* to forestall all ill-feeling I would like by lawful wedding to take to wife Roxane and I shall ensure that the other Macedonians act accordingly." He himself having exhorted his Friends with these words, each of them led away a virgin that he wedded at the banquet. Oxyartes and the rest of the foreigners were happy beyond their hopes for this to happen *and Alexander, in the heat of his ardent desire, ordered that a loaf of bread be brought in accordance with his country's customs. This was sliced with a sword and tasted by the two of them, which is the most sacrosanct surety of marriage among the Macedonians.*

---

[305] "Cohortandus" in the manuscripts of Curtius, spuriously altered to Oxyartes by Aldus: the true error in Curtius is to state that Roxane was a daughter of Cohortandus; it is clear from Metz 28-29 that Cleitarchus wrote that Roxane danced among Cohortandus' daughters, but was herself the daughter of one of his friends.

Book 9: Autumn 328BC – May 327BC

9.62 *In this fashion, the King of Asia and Europe married a maid who had been paraded as a performer at a feast, so as to breed from the conquered a king to command their conquerors. His Friends were ashamed that Alexander should have decided the parentage of his bride from among the defeated whilst wining and dining, but after the killing of Cleitus freedom of expression was suppressed and assent was expressed by their facial expressions, which are the most submissive.*

9.63 These were the concerns of Alexander *in the ninth year of his reign.*

Figure 9.5. The marriage of Alexander and Roxane (André Castaigne, 1899)

Book 10: June 327BC – June 326BC

The Invasion of India; Feting by Nysa; The Siege of Mazaga; The Capture of Aornus and The Battle Against Porus on the Hydaspes.

10.1 *At the outset of the tenth year of his reign,* **Alexander aimed to press on to India and thence to reach the Ocean** *in order to establish the ultimate ends of the Orient as the boundary of his empire.* And so as to hinder any threat to these prospects that might emerge in his rear, the king commanded that thirty thousand youths should be recruited from among all his satrapies and brought to him in arms to serve as both soldiers and sureties for the good behaviour of their compatriots. The king also despatched Craterus to track down Catanes and Haustanes, who had rebelled against his authority. Of these Haustanes was duly captured, whereas Catanes was slain in battle. Furthermore, Polyperchon brought the region known as Bubacenê into submission. Having thus set everything in order, Alexander was able to divert his attentions to his Indian campaign.

10.2 India was held to derive its wealth not only from its gold but also from gemstones and pearls. It was a land where the art of extravagance was better developed than the taste for elegant splendour. Those who were familiar with the place reported that its warriors glinted with chryselephantine accoutrements. Consequently, **Alexander, in order that none should surpass him in distinction, embossed his troops' shields with silver,** hence dubbing them "Argyraspides"[306]; and he also had their corselets either silvered or gilded *and gave golden trappings to his cavalry.* A hundred and twenty thousand men-at-arms followed the king into that war.[307]

10.3 Most of India stretches out towards the east, since it is less extensive in latitude than in longitude. Those parts that face into the south wind rise up to an exceptionally tall ridge of land, but all the rest is flat and grants a smooth passage to numerous renowned rivers that spring down from this Caucasus range. The Indus retains an icier chill than the rest and conveys such waters as scarcely differ in their character from the open sea. The Ganges, greatest of all the rivers of the Orient, flows in a southerly direction, its unswerving channel grazing past the immense mountain ridges, until its course is deflected eastwards by cliffs that loom up in its path. The Ganges and the Indus too empty into the Erythraean Sea. The Indus carves away at its banks, dragging off many trees and great masses of soil. Its course is often obstructed by rocks, which cause it to meander this way and that. Wherever it encounters friable earth, its current slackens and it heaps up islands *of silt.* The Acesines is its tributary.

---

[306] "The Silver Shields".

[307] Cf. Arrian, *Indica* 19.5; Plutarch, *Life of Alexander* 66.2.

10.4 As it runs on down, the Ganges intercepts the Iomanes[308] and the confluence of these streams is quite turbulent, for the Ganges affords an uneven access to the influx, but the agitated waters are not held back. The Diardines[309] is less well discussed, since it flows through the ultimate extremities of India, yet it nurtures not only crocodiles like the Nile, but also dolphins[310] and other types of water-beast that are unknown to other regions. *Whilst at the near edge of India* the Ethymantus,[311] often arcing and winding, is sapped for irrigation by those who dwell thereabouts. On this account, scarcely any of it reaches the area where it seeps anonymously into a sea. Besides these many other rivers partition the entire territory, but they remain obscure, since they flow through unexplored landscapes.

10.5 Moreover the parts of India that are nearer to the sea are raked by the north wind, but the interior finds shelter in the lee of the mountain ranges, thus attaining a lush and luxuriant mildness. But in that zone of the world the natural sequence of the seasons is reversed, such that India is cloaked in snow whilst other places bask in the heat of the sun. Conversely, elsewhere being frozen stiff, India languishes under stifling heat-waves. Nor is there any motive for this deviancy of Nature. **Certainly, the sea that laps India does not even differ from others in the matter of its hue, despite that it is named after King Erythrus,[312] on which account naïve people imagine its waters to run to redness.** But the land is bountiful in cotton, which garbs most of its inhabitants. And the bark of the trees is supple, so that it may be written upon exactly like papyrus. They have birds there that can be coached to parrot the human voice. In general, their beasts are not found amongst other nations, except as exotic imports. Likewise, India spawns rhinoceroses, which are not indigenous elsewhere.[313] And **the Indian elephants are more powerful than those that are tamed in Africa: their size too matches their strength.**[314] **The rivers carry gold-dust,**[315] which settles out of

---

[308] The modern Jumna; note that *Iomanes* is an emendation of *in mare* by Hedicke.

[309] Seemingly the Brahmaputra; Strabo 15.1.72 calls it the Oidanes, citing the lost Periplus of Artemidorus of Ephesus (c. 100BC); probably the Doanas in Ptolemy's Geography 7.2.7,11.

[310] The Ganges River Dolphin or Susu.

[311] Possibly the Helmand: *Etymandros* in Arrian 4.6.6; *Hetoimandros* in Ptolemy 6.17.17; *Erymanthos* in Polybius 11.34.13; *Erymandos* in Pliny NH 6.25 – though McCrindle, *Invasion of India by Alexander*, p.184 queries this identification.

[312] *Erythros* being Greek for red: this probably came from Nearchus (Arrian, *Indica* 37.2) and is repeated at Curtius 10.1.13, hence Cleitarchus is a very likely source for the latter.

[313] An anachronistic observation under the Roman Empire, which was aware of African Rhinoceroses, e.g. depicted on a quadrans of Domitian and mentioned by Martial. As Proconsul of Roman Africa, could Curtius have been ignorant of African Rhinos? Or is he simply failing to correct his source? (Note however that this is an emendation by Hedicke, whilst Yardley reads that the rhino was not indigenous to India, though any such suggestion would seem very odd.)

[314] This matches a fragment of Onesicritus in Strabo 15.1.43, reaching Curtius via Cleitarchus.

[315] This was recorded by Megasthenes (Strabo 15.1.57) and by Onesicritus (Strabo 15.2.14).

Book 10: June 327BC – June 326BC

the water *where it* flows sluggishly in a slack current. And the sea encrusts its shore with gemstones and pearls. They have no richer basis for their wealth than these, particularly since the dissemination of such corrupting merchandise among other nations. For, of course, lust fixes a high price for this vomit of the retching surf.

10.6 In India, just as everywhere else, the specifics of their environment influence the behaviour of the inhabitants. They wind linen sheets about themselves all the way down to their feet, which they shoe with sandals. They also bind linen around their heads and dangle precious stones from their ears. Those among the populace who are distinguished either by nobility or wealth also adorn their arms and wrists with bands of gold. They groom their hair more often than they shear it and the chin is never shaved, but they razor the rest of the skin of their jowls to apparent smoothness. *Yet the extravagance of their kings, which they themselves term splendour, excels all other peoples in turpitude.*[316] *When the king condescends to appear in public, his servants bring forth silver censers and waft perfumes along the entirety of his chosen route. He reclines upon a golden litter, which is hung all around with pearls, and he is dressed in a linen robe embellished with purple and gold. Men-at-arms follow close upon the litter, forming his bodyguard.*

10.7 In these festal processions, four-wheeled carriages trundle among the bodyguards, bearing broad-leafed trees, of which the branches serve as perches for a variety of tamed birds that have been trained to sing so as to divert the king from prosaic concerns. Among these songsters, Nature has made the Catreus, an indigenous species, outstandingly gorgeous in its polychrome plumage, being about the size of a peacock with the tips of its feathers tinged emerald green.[317] When it looks askance, the hue of its eyes is imperceptible. But you would judge they were vermilion, should it stare straight at you, except that the pupil has the colour of an apple; and its gaze is quite piercing. That region of the eye that is white in other species is pale yellow in the Catreus. The plush plumage of its head is azure, but there are also splashes like saffron, whilst its legs are a shade of orange. Its voice is mellifluous and pure like a nightingale's. The Indians raise these birds in order that they may feast their eyes upon loveliness, thus they can witness them in their purple or as red as unsullied flame. And they flock in flight such as to seem like clouds.

10.8 Besides these there is a flagrantly amorous species that is called the Orion: as large as the largest Herons and likewise sporting maroon legs, but dissimilar in having blue eyes. This Orion is instructed by Nature

---

[316] For a Roman who ascended to prominence under the Claudian emperors to attack the monarchs of India as the world's leading exponents of the vice of luxury/extravagance would have been disingenuous: more probably, Curtius transcribed views he found in Cleitarchus, for these sentiments harmonise with the ascetic philosophy of the early Greek Cynics, with whom Cleitarchus is associated.

[317] Possibly the Monal Pheasant.

herself in the art of song, such that it warbles dulcet melodies like to bridal canticles or marriage madrigals in their charm and allure. Its arias reach such a pitch of perfection that it might be reckoned a sort of Siren, for we have the patter of the poets and the pictures of the painters to prove that Sirens were winged and maidens in myth with legs like birds.[318]

10.9 The king's palace has gilded columns twined about their length with a vine fashioned in gold and studded with silver effigies of birds, for they take the greatest delight in ornithology. When the king has his hair groomed and dressed, the palace stands open to all comers: at that time, he responds to foreign delegations and that is the occasion on which he dispenses justice to his people. His sandals being discarded, his feet are anointed with perfume. His main exercise is hunting, which consists in archery against penned beasts to the accompaniment of the prayers and songs of his concubines. Their arrows are two cubits[319] long, but the effort of launching them outweighs their effectiveness, for a missile of which the efficacy depends upon slightness is handicapped by unwieldy weight. The king mounts a horse for his shorter journeys, but on longer expeditions he processes in a chariot drawn by elephants and the whole hide of each monstrous beast is gilded. Furthermore, in order that he need not desist from any of his decadent habits, a long column of his concubines trails after him in golden litters. Though they are separated from the queen's column in the order of march, they enjoy an equivalent degree of luxury. Women prepare the king's meals and serve him wine, which all Indians imbibe copiously. As he sinks into a drunken torpor, his concubines convey him to his chamber, whilst performing a customary incantation to nocturnal deities.

10.10 Who would credit that there could thrive an appreciation of philosophy amid such decadence? But there does indeed exist a coarse and vulgar class of men that are called sages. These men consider it a splendid thing to anticipate their appointed end by ordering that they be burnt alive, should they be suffering from ill-health or the decrepitude of advanced age. To linger for the reaping, they consider a stain upon their life and no respect is paid to the corpses of any who pass away from old age: they suppose the flame to be defiled, unless it receives them with the breath of life still in them. Those of them who live at public expense in the cities are said skilfully to observe the passage of the stars and to foretell the future. And they believe that a person shall not bring forward the day of his death, if he look forward to it without fear. They regard as sacred anything that they have begun to foster, and this is especially true of trees, injury to which constitutes a capital crime. They describe their month as comprising fifteen days, though they keep the year at its full duration. *This is because,* although they mark the passage of time by the phases of the moon, they begin their months at the threshold of its curvature into horns, rather than when it fills its face as most

---

[318] Deinon, Cleitarchus' father, had suggested that there were Sirens in India (Pliny, NH 10.136).

[319] A cubit is about 45cm.

Book 10: June 327BC – June 326BC

others do. Their months are consequently shortened *to half the usual length*, since their term is reckoned by *recurrences of* that *quarter* phase…³²⁰

10.11 All being readied, Alexander advanced into the countryside of *Bactria*. He *passed the encampment and* crossed the river *Oxus*. For *thirty* stades he led the army across an uninhabited region, then **he marched within the bounds of India** *and reached Drapis*, where he was met by a King *Arines* with his young sons and the greatest quantities of supplies, which he divided up amongst the army. He presented Alexander himself with many barbarian vestments, three thousand horses and *fifty thousand* silver talents. When Alexander enquired as to his motivation, the Indian answered: "You are a great king, and I wish us to be friends." Alexander responded: "These monies passed to you from your father on his death and I hereby return them to you. The horses I shall use in my campaigns. Let you keep us in mind. The stewardship of this *region* shall be yours." ³²¹

10.12 From this place he advanced to *reach the River* Cophen, from which point it is nine days' voyage to the Indus. ***He was met by the minor kings of the neighbouring nations, who acceded to his governance. On witnessing Alexander's arrival, they rejoiced, saying that according to tradition*** he was the third Diogenes³²² who had reached their lands. They knew of reputed visits firstly of Dionysus and secondly of Heracles, *but Alexander had actually manifested himself before their gaze. Gladdened by this, the king crossed the river, received the minor kings in a friendly manner and bade them be his guides in reaching the River Indus.*

10.13 *Moreover, when no more of the local potentates presented themselves before him, he sent Hephaistion and Perdiccas ahead with part of his forces to subjugate those who repudiated his overlordship.* His orders were that they should advance to the River Indus and there fabricate boats by means of which the army could be ferried across to the region beyond. *Since multiple rivers needed to be traversed, these commanders constructed ships which could be joined together to bridge each river, then disassembled and transported by wagon to be reassembled where required.*

10.14 After directing Craterus to trail after him with the phalanx, Alexander led forth the cavalry and the lightly armed troops *following the river. On approaching Silex, the first fortified town of India,* armed men issued forth to oppose him, but after a skirmish they fled back within their gates, whilst

---

³²⁰ A lacuna in the reconstruction of Cleitarchus may be inferred at this point from Curtius' statement that he omitted further material describing India that was in his source.

³²¹ This derives from the Metz Epitome 32-3: the italicised figures must be corrupt, e.g. a stade is ~180m and a talent ~25kg. There is a possibility that Arines is Taxiles, cf. Arrian, *Anabasis* 4.22.6.

³²² *Diogenes* is Greek for one who is Zeus-born or sprung from Zeus: the Latin of Curtius 8.10.1 is *Iove genitum*. Alexander had received this appellation at Siwa (see 5.30 above).

the army eagerly gave chase. *Then Alexander set the town's stockade alight, by which time Craterus had arrived.* In order to instil proper dread of Macedonian arms into nations that still lacked experience of such might, the king ordered Craterus to slay all the adult men. *Whilst Alexander was riding up to the walls, he was struck by an arrow. Nevertheless,* the town fell to him and having cut down all of its inhabitants, he further vented his fury in destroying its dwellings as well. *From there he progressed to lay siege to another fortified town, but in that instance, he accepted hostages and installed a garrison.*

10.15 After having subdued an inconsequential clan, **Alexander** *advanced two hundred and thirty stades through Nysaean lands and* reached the city of **Nysa.** By chance he encamped in the woods virtually before its walls, whereupon a most bitterly frigid night afflicted them with shuddering chillness, yet the opportunity was at hand to relieve their discomfort with fires. Hence, they felled trees and set them aflame. However, fed by dead wood, the fire consumed the tombs of the townspeople. Constructed of aged cedar, these spread the incipient inferno over a broad area, until everything was razed to the ground. Initially the baying of dogs issued from the city, but straight afterwards the clamour of men was heard. And not until this point had *the unwary Nysaeans realised that their enemy had arrived*, nor had the Macedonians known that they had reached the city. So thereupon the king led forward his forces to besiege its walls and their missiles overwhelmed their enemies, who had sallied forth in an attempt to repulse them.

10.16 Then among **the Nysaeans**, some advocated surrender, whilst others favoured a trial of arms. When Alexander received word of their indecision, he held back from slaying them, ordering that they should merely be blockaded. And eventually, tired of the hardships of the siege, they **sent a delegation of elders to negotiate a peace with the king. These men,** *led by Acuphis,* **managed through their entreaties to appease the king by pointing out that Dionysus had established their city of Nysa and the state of Nysaea at the extremity of his rovings and settled it with fifty thousand of his followers. They directed his gaze upon a mountain in the distance, which the god had called Meros, because he himself had sprung from the thigh of Zeus.**[323] *And they attested to its exceptional delights. Then all at once they began to weep and to beseech him that the monument and good works of Dionysus should not be overthrown. In response Alexander granted the Nysaeans their freedom and returned everything to their care,* for he was pleased to believe not only that he had matched the exploits of Dionysus, but that he was even following in the god's footsteps. **And he ordained that Acuphis should govern Nysa, requesting that he should select a hundred of their most prominent men to accompany his expedition. But Acuphis** smiled and **retorted that no city could long survive, from which a hundred of its finest**

---

[323] In Greek μηρός is "thigh".

Book 10: June 327BC – June 326BC

men had been abducted: *"If you wish us to remain secure, let you lead away two hundred of the least worthy." Alexander recognised both the humour and the truth in this statement,* therefore he requested that Acuphis should send him both his own son and his daughter's son instead.

10.17 Afterwards Alexander *learnt the layout of the sacred mountain from the local people and sent provisions on ahead, and then he* climbed to the summit of Meros with his entire force. The heights abound in luxuriant vegetation with vines and a variety of ivy, which they call "scindapsos", growing wild, yet flourishing as though tended by unseen hands and watered by numerous perennial springs. There too thrive wholesome orchard fruits of diverse flavours, spontaneously sprouting forth from such of their seeds as chance to germinate in the rich humous. And copses of wild laurel, box and myrtle burgeon among the rocky outcrops.

10.18 *The Macedonians were seized by the frenzy of the god, plucking the foliage to wreath themselves in garlands of the vines and the ivy, then cavorting through the groves in a Dionysiac comus. And the crags and the dells rang with thousands of yells as the revellers invoked the spirit of the place in adoration of its divinity.* As though in the midst of peace they reclined upon grass and fronds that they had heaped together. And the king was not at all averse to these fortuitous festivities, but most generously furnished the feasting with everything needed to immerse his army in the practices of Dionysus for fully ten days. Who then could deny that fame and glory are more often gifted by fortune than gleaned through virtue? For neither in their feasting nor their sodden slumber did any enemy venture to assault them, being just as much intimidated by their holy howling as by the baying of their battle cry. Identical good fortune was to preserve the Macedonians in the course of their return from the Ocean, when they again drunkenly caroused before the faces of their foes.

10.19 Moving onwards, Alexander crossed the Daedalian Mountains, where the inhabitants had abandoned their homesteads and taken refuge among the remote and forested peaks. Therefore, the king swept on past Acadira, which had likewise been wasted and forsaken due to the flight of its denizens. Hence Alexander was obliged to modify his conduct of the campaign. By splitting up his forces, he caused his warriors to appear in many places at once, and having thereby assaulted his enemies where they least expected, all who opposed him were thoroughly subdued in the slaughter. Ptolemy took most cities, but the largest fell to Alexander. Afterwards the king recombined his scattered forces for the onward march.

Figure 10.1. Alexander's triumphal entry into Nysa (Antonio Tempesta, 1608)

10.20 Now Alexander entered *the satrapy of* Assacena *and traversed the River Choaspes.*[324] *He left the siege of a wealthy city, called Beira*[325] *by its inhabitants, in the charge of Coenus, whilst he himself descended upon the people of the fortified town of Mazaga.*[326] *Until recently this had been the realm of Assacenus, but he was lately deceased, so his mother Cleophis was ruling the city and territory* as regent *for his young son. Amminais, brother to the late king, had incited 9000 Indian mercenaries to take up arms against Alexander and he had now brought them into the realm. The city was garrisoned by 38,000 infantry and was secured not merely by dint of its location, but also by a ring of fortifications.*

10.21 *On its eastern aspect a torrential river, either bank being so sheer as to stymie any approach from that direction, girds Mazaga. Towards the south and the west towering crags loom up forming a bulwark, seemingly by the design of Nature. And cavernous chasms plunge down from its base, eroded out over endless epochs. This abyss has been extended with vast ditches* to *complete the dyke, within which a wall having a*

---

[324] Probably the modern River Swat.

[325] Arrian calls it Bazira, whilst Aurel Stein identifies it with Bir-Kot in the Lower Swat Valley.

[326] Possibly Chakdara or Malakand in the Lower Swat Valley: it is Massaga in Greek sources, but the Latin sources have Mazaga (Curtius has "Mazagas" and the Metz Epitome has "Mazanan"), perhaps reflecting phonetic transliteration.

Book 10: June 327BC – June 326BC

circumference of thirty-five stades encompasses the city. *Its lower courses are masonry, whereas its upper reaches are constructed in mud brick. This brickwork is mortared together by a mixture of stone and mud, such that the brittle material is reinforced by tougher stuff. Nevertheless, in order to prevent subsidence, robust logs have been embedded, upon which boarding was overlaid forming gangways, which also sheltered the structure.*

10.22 Alexander invested the city with a cordon of troops and prepared to launch an assault. He was encouraging his soldiers and surveying the fortifications - *being consequently undecided* as to his plan of attack, **since he could not bridge the chasm, save by filling it, and neither could he otherwise advance his siege-engines up to the walls** - whereupon someone loosed an arrow from the battlements. The missile chanced to strike the king in the calf of his left leg. *When* he wrenched forth its barb, *his wound bled copiously, yet he ordered that his horse should be led up. Mounting without troubling to bind his injury,* he refused to withdraw from the action, *but carried on as he had intended without tarrying. However,* he was increasingly afflicted with pain *as his leg drooped down and the wound stiffened after the flow of blood was staunched. Whilst he still exhorted his troops* in the prosecution of the siege, **he is said to have commented that, despite being dubbed the son of Zeus, he nevertheless suffered from the debilitation of bodily injury,** quipping: *"What issues from my wound is gore, not 'Ichor, such as flows in the veins of the blessed gods."*[327]

10.23 The king only returned to his camp after he had inspected the entire circuit and decreed what he wished to be done. Thereafter, in accordance with his orders, some of **his troops** demolished such dwellings as lay outside the fortifications and delivered enormous quantities of debris for heaping into the chasm, whereas others cast the boles and branches of great trees and masses of rubble into the gulf. And soon the level of the fill had risen up to the brink, so they **erected siege-towers** ready for the assault. **The Macedonians were ardent to avenge the injury inflicted upon their king,** so they had accomplished these labours by the ninth day.

10.24 Alexander ventured forth to inspect the results before his wound had scabbed over, and, having commended his soldiers, he issued orders that the siege-engines should be advanced. From these a heavy rain of missiles was poured upon their opponents. **Then, their escorts having interlocked their shields above their heads, the siege-towers were trundled towards the walls.** Their mobility was especially terrifying for folk who were ignorant of such contraptions. They believed that such massive structures, lacking help from perceptible exertions, were actually moved by supernatural forces. Similarly, they were sure

---

[327] The Ichor quote derives from Homer, *Iliad* 5.340, and is recorded by Plutarch, *Alexander* 28.2.

that mere mortal men could not have deployed the heavy bolts shot by the catapults and the javelins cast against the walls.

10.25 *As the Macedonians surged towards her walls with scaling ladders, Cleophis surveyed a scene filled with a multitude of siege-towers advancing upon her city and a storm of projectiles fired from the slings of Alexander's catapults and scorpion engines. And she was panicked by the uncanny nature of the assault, for it seemed to her that the rocks hurled by the siege-engines were truly flying. Crediting Alexander with wielding supernatural powers, she called together Amminais*[328] *and her other friends, exhorting them to surrender the city to Alexander. However, the mercenaries were vociferous in their opposition: they grew obstructive and sought to foment a mutiny.* Nevertheless, the defence of the entire city seeming hopeless, its defenders withdrew into their citadel. From there, *on the following day* Cleophis *covertly* despatched envoys to Alexander to negotiate terms of surrender and to seek his forgiveness for their behaviour, *for they had been coerced by their own armed hirelings!* Suspecting that such moves were afoot, the mercenaries themselves sent a delegation to treat with Alexander, seeking his permission to issue forth from the town bringing their possessions with them. *The king granted the requests of both parties.*

10.26 As soon as the truce was concluded, Cleophis, marvelling at Alexander's magnanimity, sent him rich gifts and swore to follow his commands in every respect. And straightaway in accordance with their terms the mercenaries emerged from the town *gate with their wives, their offspring and their baggage* and encamped upon a hilltop[329] at a distance of 80 stades from Mazaga, *oblivious of what was about to transpire.*

10.27 Alexander followed in the tracks of the mercenaries *with contingents of his lightly equipped troops, for he persisted in regarding these Indians as his enemies. Throughout the night,* he held his forces in readiness and the following day he announced to his men that the mercenaries were all to be put to the sword. When the Indians *realised what was underway, undaunted they* gathered their baggage and their families to their centre and arrayed themselves protectively in an armed ring, *prepared either to fend off the aggression or else steadfastly to give their lives in defence of their wives and children.* But initially they shouted out that the assault contravened their treaty with Alexander, invoking the gods *in whose names it had been sworn* to witness his impiety. In retort, Alexander proclaimed that he had given permission for them to come out of the city, but not for them to march clean away *as friends of the Macedonians.* And thereupon his onslaught began.

---

[328] The Metz Epitome manuscript (destroyed in 1944) was read as "ariplicem".

[329] That Cleitarchus mentioned the hill is implied by Polyaenus 4.3.20 (cf. Arrian, *Anabasis* 4.27.3).

Book 10: June 327BC – June 326BC

10.28 *The Indians were driven to mount a desperate resistance, drawing upon their combat expertise to make a robust and courageous stand, whereas the Macedonians feared to be bested by barbarians in the martial skills, and so the struggle caused carnage. They grappled hand to hand, every sort of injury and variety of death being dealt in their deadly contests. The Macedonians pierced through the flimsy shields of the mercenaries with their sarissas,[330] puncturing their lungs with shards of steel. The Indians in response cast their javelins into the densely packed ranks of their opponents at such close range that none could avoid its target.*

10.29 *Soon many mercenaries were disabled by wounds and quite a few lay dead, hence their women snatched up the weapons of these casualties, holding the line shoulder to shoulder with their menfolk, since the extremity of their plight and the ferocity of the fight forced them to feats of valour beyond their physiques. Some of them, fully armed, shared the shields of their husbands, whilst others leapt unarmed into the fray to seize the shields of their foes so as to hamper their assault. But in the end, despite their warrior women, the Indians were overwhelmed by superior numbers and cut to pieces, opting for glorious death rather than cowardly survival. Alexander rounded up the disabled, the disarmed and the remaining women and led them away in the custody of his cavalry.*

10.30 **The king returned to Mazaga and was met by Cleophis, who came** *down out of the citadel* **with a grand entourage** *of noble ladies, tipping libations of wine from golden goblets.* **To signal their supplication, her leading citizens bore before them veiled produce and fronds of foliage. She herself placed her little grandson at Alexander's knees and elicited not merely a pardon, but also reinstatement in her former rank - as some say by virtue of the king's appreciation for her fair features.** *But indeed, from her status and authority* among her people, *it was quite apparent that she was of noble breeding and worthy of regal power.* **Afterwards Alexander entered the citadel with a few of his retinue and tarried there for several days.** Furthermore, it is a matter of fact that Cleophis subsequently gave birth to a son, whom she named Alexander, whatever his paternity. *And it is said that Cleophis was thereafter called the Courtesan Queen by the Indians, yet her son eventually became a king among them.*

10.31 Polyperchon was sent hence with a task force against the city of Hora, where he triumphed in an engagement with a rabble of its citizens. Following on their heels when they fled within their walls, he soon subjugated the place. Numerous benighted towns, which had been abandoned by their inhabitants, now came into Alexander's power, but moving onwards he reached the citadel of *Bagasdaram*. Its natives together with **the surviving Indians from many** other **towns had snatched up their arms and fled to seek refuge on a pinnacle**

---

[330] A sarissa was the Macedonian pike-cum-lance, which was over 4m long.

called Aornus, which was virtually impregnable. Indeed, Heracles in olden times was said unsuccessfully to have besieged this fortress crag, having been *thrice* forced to abandon the endeavour by a succession of earthquakes *and other portents from the gods. When he heard this, Alexander was inspired by a keen yearning to outdo the deeds of his divine ancestor.*

10.32 The base of Aornus has a circumference of 100 stades and it soars to a height of sixteen stades above the valley of the Indus, the greatest river in India, which flows between sheer banks beneath its southern flank. On its other sides it is hemmed by plunging gorges and towering cliffs. *Neither does the pinnacle itself reach its lofty elevation, as many others do, via a succession of moderate inclines, but rather it soars from its base in the fashion of an acute cone tapering to a sharp crest.* It gets its name from the observation that **it teems with birds that parrot the human voice,** a quite unbirdlike habit.[331] On reconnoitring the obstacles Alexander was frustrated to find that a direct assault was impracticable, but thereupon an aged native came before the king with his two sons. He had long subsisted in penury in that neighbourhood, sharing a cave containing three rock-cut beds with his offspring. In consequence he had grown intimately familiar with every detail of the terrain. Explaining this, he now offered to guide Alexander up through the foothills so as to bring him to a spot that overlooked the crag occupied by the Indian defenders,[332] *provided it were made worth his while.* Alexander offered him a bounty *of eighty talents, and, retaining one of the young men as a hostage, he sent the father to shepherd a body of lightly equipped troops, led by Myllinas,*[333] *a royal scribe, in ascending a tortuous route to the summit, chosen to elude detection by the enemy.*

10.33 Following the guidance of the old man, Alexander's advance force soon occupied the only viable route from the summit of Aornus, hence cornering its defenders in a siege. However, a steep ravine separated the Macedonians from the pinnacle itself. *Alexander assessed that* this chasm had to be filled for the storming of the summit to be practicable. *A forest grew thereabouts, which the king commanded be felled and the trunks stripped of their branches, such that his troops might heave them into the ravine unhampered by the foliage. Alexander personally hacked the first tree and cast it into the gulf and the ensuing acclamation from the army announced their enthusiasm, for none could shirk a task that had been begun by the king.* Through seven days and nights they toiled ceaselessly at this labour,

---

[331] The Greek ἄορνος is translated as "birdless", but it might mean "unbirdlike" in a name.

[332] Aurel Stein has convincingly identified Aornus with Pir-Sar: it is separated from a slightly higher peak to its west (Una-Sar) by the Burimar Ravine.

[333] Perhaps Myllenas son of Asander, honoured in an Eretrian decree together with Tauron son of Harpalus (*IG* xii.9).

Book 10: June 327BC – June 326BC

operating in relays *under enemy fire. Meanwhile the Indians kept yelling from the heights for Alexander to come on up, if he thought himself mightier than Heracles!* At first the defenders had the advantage of overlooking the Macedonian positions and they slew many who rashly sought to assault them. But before the seventh day was done, the causeway had risen to the brink of the ravine.

10.34 Now Alexander ordered the Agrianians and the archers to strive to scale the pinnacle. In addition, he picked out thirty of the most resolute men from his own squadron, appointing Charus and *another* Alexander as their captains. The king urged the latter to recall their shared name *and therefore to be brave in conducting the mission.*[334] *This was faithfully promised by his eager captain.* Initially, in view of the patent perils, **the king** judged that he should hold himself back from the fray, but when the trumpet blared to signal the attack, that audacious dare-devil turned to his bodyguards, ordered them to follow him and **was the first to assail the crags, *creeping upwards little by little*.** Thereupon none of the Macedonians could restrain himself, but as one man they abandoned their stations and surged impulsively after their king. Many met a miserable end, for they slipped from the steep rock-face and were engulfed by the stream that cascaded down *the ravine*. It was a tragic spectacle even for those who watched from safety, but for those who were reminded of their own peril by witnessing others perish, pity turned to dread. They did not so much mourn the dead, as their own predicament.

10.35 By this point they had reached a situation, such that they could not return without catastrophe, unless as victors, for the barbarians were rolling massive boulders down among them as they clambered up. Their footholds being precarious and slippery, those who were struck went hurtling headlong downhill. However, Charus and that other Alexander, whom the king had sent ahead with his select band of thirty men, had now climbed onto the crest and were starting to grapple hand to hand with their foes, but since the barbarians were showering missiles upon them from yet higher ground, they were themselves smitten more often than they inflicted wounds upon the Indians. Alexander, remembering his name and his promise and consequently fighting with more passion than caution, was skewered from all sides and fell. When Charus saw him lying slain, oblivious of aught but vengeance, he hurled himself upon the enemy, transfixing many with his lance and slaying others with his sword. But when a host of foes assailed him, he collapsed lifeless athwart the corpse of his friend. *Sorely* distressed, as was natural, by the slaughter of these most valiant youths and by his other casualties, the king signalled a retreat. Then they preserved themselves by withdrawing gradually and avoiding panic. The barbarians, being satisfied at having repulsed their antagonists, neglected to harry them as they retired.

---

[334] This is from Curtius 8.11.10, but is also mentioned by Plutarch, *Alexander* 58.3.

Figure 10.2. The assault on Aornus across the ravine (Antonio Tempesta, 1608)

10.36 Although **Alexander** had decided to desist from the assault – for there seemed to be no prospect that he could seize the pinnacle – he nevertheless made an ostentatious display of persevering with the siege. He **ordered** the trails to be blockaded and **the siege-towers** *with the bolt-firing torsion-catapults* **to be advanced** with fresh troops replacing the weary. *When* **the king's persistence was recognised by the Indians,** *they were disconcerted,* but they staged a show of confidence, even of triumph, by feasting through two days and nights with a rhythmic percussion of drums, as was their custom. *Sensing a viable stratagem, Alexander cunningly removed his guards from one track, so that any Indians who wished might escape from the pinnacle.* Hence on the third night the beat of the drums was no longer heard, but instead the entire peak gleamed with the flame of torches, lit by the barbarians safely to light their flight across rocks that were impassable **in darkness.** The king sent Balacrus to reconnoitre, thereby confirming that **the summit was deserted and the Indians were scuttling away** *in fear of the fighting resilience of the Macedonians.*

10.37 Then Alexander signalled his soldiers to bellow in unison, thus striking terror into the Indians as they fled in disorder. Believing their opponents to be upon them, many perished through casting themselves headlong down slippery rocks and pathless, flinty crags. Others yet, disabled by injuries, were forsaken by those still sound in limb. **Thus, Alexander** *used feints to outfox the Indians and* **took possession of the pinnacle.** Although he had conquered the place rather than its defenders, he celebrated the victory with sacrifices and

Book 10: June 327BC – June 326BC

thanksgiving to the gods, erecting altars to Athena Nike on the peak. **The contracted reward was faithfully paid to the trail-guides of his lightly equipped troops,** *though their assistance had accomplished less than they had promised.* **Finally,** the custodianship of the pinnacle and the surrounding territory was granted to Sisocostus, before *Alexander marched away.*

10.38 The king proceeded onwards to Ecbolima. **An Indian named Aphrices[335] was encamped nearby with twenty thousand men-at-arms** *and fifteen elephants. Discovering that this fellow was blockading a defile in his path, Alexander left the bulk of his forces marching at a moderate pace under the command of Coenus, whilst he himself forged ahead and deployed slingers and archers in driving off those who held the pass against him, thus opening the way for the force that followed. Either detesting their leader or seeking to ingratiate themselves with Alexander,* **the Indians overthrew Aphrices** *as he fled,* **slew him and delivered his head** *together with his panoply of arms* **to the king. Being granted immunity from punishment for the deed, they preserved their lives,** *but Alexander refused to condone such behaviour. He enrolled them in his army and rounded up their elephants, which were roving about in the countryside.*

10.39 Sixteen days after his departure from there, he reached the Indus, where he found that everything had been readied by Hephaistion *for the campaign beyond the river* **just as he had directed: a fleet of triacontors[336] had been constructed and fully outfitted; a pontoon bridge** *of linked boats* **spanned the stream and a substantial stockpile of supplies had been accumulated.** *The king rested his army for thirty days and offered up magnificent sacrifices to the gods.*

10.40 Mophis son of Taxiles dwelt beyond the river. Even prior to his father's death, whilst Alexander was in Sogdiana, he had persuaded Taxiles to place the kingdom of Taxila at Alexander's service in the conduct of his Indian campaign, since he was keen to ally their realm with the Macedonian, having been impressed by his accomplishments. After his father's demise, he sent a delegation to enquire of Alexander, whether he desired that Mophis should reign in the interim *at Taxila* **or else preferred to send a viceroy pending his own arrival? On hearing this, Alexander admired the remarkably fine sense and sensibility exhibited by Mophis. But despite Alexander allowing that he should assume the rulership, he could not yet endure fully to exercise its powers, declining to adopt the royal raiment or the title of Taxiles, but** *still* **awaiting the arrival of Alexander.** And although he had given a courteous reception to Hephaistion,

---

[335] Arrian, *Anabasis* 4.30.5 speaks of a brother of Assacenus, whose elephants Alexander was pursuing at this time, but it is unclear whether he is Aphrices; the suggestion that Aphrices might therefore be the Ariplex mentioned at Mazaga (Metz Epitome 42) is even more venturesome.

[336] Thirty-oared galleys.

freely issuing grain to his forces, he nevertheless had not met with him in person, not wishing to test the good faith of any save the king.

10.41 Alexander now *furnished provisions to his men and* conveyed his forces across the River Indus. *Receiving word of the king's approach,* Mophis was pleased to come forth with his army and elephants, *equipped as for war.* Whilst Alexander was yet at a distance of forty stades, Mophis, ensconced among his courtiers, arrayed his forces as if for battle, *the elephants being distributed among his formations of soldiers at measured intervals, giving from a distance an impression of castles.* Observing the approach of this vast and warlike host, Alexander immediately suspected that the Indian's pledges were deceptions in order that the Macedonians might be assailed in a state of unreadiness. He commanded the buglers to sound the call to arms *and deployed his cavalry to the wings. Though disturbed by this turn of events,* his troops confronted the Indians *in silence,* once they had reached their battle stations.

10.42 Mophis noted the agitated activity among the Macedonians and surmised its misconstrued cause. He ordered his men to raise their lances and to halt their advance, but spurred his own steed far forward escorted by a mere handful of horsemen. Alexander followed suit, considering himself safe whether he went to meet a friend or a foe: *by virtue either of the good faith of the Indian or else his own prowess in arms, for he reckoned himself to be a match for Mophis in single combat. But* they met in a spirit of friendship *insofar as their expressions could tell, though they could not converse without an interpreter. When one had been fetched and* Alexander asked why Mophis had mobilised, the barbarian explained that he had brought his army to meet Alexander, so as to place all the men under his command at the king's immediate disposal, *without tarrying whilst heralds delivered pledges of safe conduct. He was yielding up his person and his realm to him whom he understood to be pursuing glory in arms; to him who was most wary of staining his reputation with treachery.* Much relieved *and gratified by the candour of the Indian,* Alexander proffered Mophis his right hand as a token of friendship and fidelity and restored him to the rule of his kingdom.

10.43 Mophis relinquished fifty-*six* elephants into Alexander's hands together with teeming herds of prodigiously proportioned livestock and three thousand bulls bedizened as for sacrifice; such cattle being prized in that region and considered worthy of the prestige of potentates. *When Alexander queried whether his yeomen outnumbered his troops,* Mophis observed that he had more work for soldiers than for farmers, since he was at war with two kings. *Alexander asked the identity of these marauding monarchs. Mophis answered that* they were Abisares, whose abode lay among the mountains across the River Hydaspes, and Porus, who ruled over the plain on the far bank of the same waterway. Of these Porus was

Book 10: June 327BC – June 326BC

the more powerful, but both had determined to test the fortunes of war against any who bore arms. Then Alexander endorsed the assumption of the royal insignia by Mophis, as well as his adoption of his father's name in accordance with the custom of his nation. Thenceforth he was known as Taxiles by the people, for such was the title inherited by their sovereign.

10.44 *Then Taxiles hosted Alexander as his guest, whilst the king rested his army* at Taxila *for three days. During his stay Alexander sent Onesicritus to converse with the Indian sages near this place and one of them, who was called Calanus, consented to follow Alexander and did so to the end of his days.*[337] **Thereafter, on the fourth day Taxiles announced the tally of grain that he had furnished to Hephaistion's forces and gifted golden crowns to Alexander and each of his Friends, as well as bestowing eighty talents of minted silver upon them. He even made presents of several strange jungle beasts. Being extraordinarily delighted by his generosity,** Alexander gave *back what had been given with the addition of a thousand talents from such spoils of war as he had brought with him, plus* many gold and silver banqueting vessels, numerous Persian vestments *and thirty of his own steeds, caparisoned as when he himself rode them.* Though it placed the Indian under a debt of gratitude, Alexander's largesse deeply shocked his Friends. Among them, Meleager, being the worse for wine, offered Alexander his congratulations on having in India at last identified a person worthy of a thousand talents! Not having forgotten the depth of his remorse over slaying Cleitus for his rash tongue, the king curbed his temper, but commented: "People who allow themselves to be consumed by envy subject themselves to torment." *And indeed,* **just as iron is eaten by rust, so are the envious corroded by their own characters.**[338]

10.45 *The next day* a delegation arrived from Abisares, *led by his brother. They had been mandated by Abisares to concede Alexander's suzerainty and* to negotiate friendly relations *with him. They gave pledges of good faith and in turn received similar assurances from the king, who sent them back to Abisares accompanied by Nicocles as his own emissary.*[339] Reckoning that Porus might also be coerced into submission *by the notoriety of his reputation,* Alexander sent him Cleochares as his envoy. *Both embassies were* to seek to arrange the payment of tribute and the surrender of hostages to the king, *whilst* Cleochares also conveyed a demand that Porus should meet Alexander in person at his frontier.

---

[337] It is virtually certain that Cleitarchus mentioned the self-immolation of Calanus in his twelfth book; he also used material from Onesicritus' *On the Education of Alexander*, who in turn told that he met Calanus near Taxila (Strabo 15.1.63-64), so Cleitarchus may have introduced Calanus here.

[338] This is Fragment 48 of Cleitarchus (Maximi, *Eclogae* LIV 962 A), considered doubtful by Jacoby, but it might be fitted to this context. But see also Section 8.44 above.

[339] Probably Nicocles the son of Pasicrates of Soli, a Friend of Alexander (Arrian, *Indica* 18.)

10.46 *Abisares prevaricated, since he* **did not wish to send the king's envoys back to him. But, on hearing Alexander's demands, Porus was seized by fury and inflicted a gory scourging upon Cleochares. Concurrently, he composed the following letter and had it delivered to the king:** "Porus, Monarch of India, says this to Alexander: *whosoever you may be – and I have heard it said that you are a Macedonian – I suggest that you steer clear of me and contemplate your own wretchedness, rather than look ill upon another.* The fate of **Darius does not disturb me: therefore, moron, do not presume to give me orders! If you but set one foot upon my land in enmity, then you shall know me as ruler in India, for none save Zeus can call himself my lord. And Porus swears by the great** *ball of* **fire that governs the skies, if I should apprehend any man of yours in my territory, then I shall slake my lance with his blood and I shall spread the spoils among my slaves, for I am already replete with spoils.** One thing alone that you command, I shall enact. I shall stand ready to meet you where you enter my realm, but I shall stand in arms."

10.47 On reading this letter, Alexander was incensed and considered it settled that he would traverse the River Hydaspes. But at this juncture Barzaentes, who had fomented an insurrection among the Arachosians, was led before Alexander in chains and thirty elephants captured at the same time accompanied him. The latter were opportune reinforcements against the Indians, since their hopes and strength were vested more in these monstrous beasts than in their soldiery. Samaxus, king of a meagre portion of India, was also delivered in fetters, since he had been in league with Barzaentes. Having secured the traitor and the minor king in his custody, **Alexander approached the near bank of the Hydaspes in the company of Taxiles,** to whom he had handed over the thirty elephants. **From there they observed that Porus' forces had occupied various defensive positions in the plain on the opposite bank in order to thwart any crossing by his opponents.**

10.48 On enquiring of Taxiles as to the nature of the forces in the enemy camp, Alexander was told that Porus had arrayed eighty-five exceptionally mighty elephants against him, with three hundred four-horse chariots and over thirty thousand infantry backing them up.[340] *Archers who shot cumbersome* two-cubit Indian *arrows were interspersed among the foot soldiers.* **Porus** *himself rode upon an elephant that loomed above the rest of those monstrous beasts. His armour, chased with silver and gold, clad an almighty physique, for he* **stood five cubits tall and the girth of his chest was twice that of his warriors.** *His spirit matched the stature of his body and he was as wise as anyone to be found among ignorant people.* But

---

[340] The precise agreement between Curtius and the Metz Epitome on these figures confirms that they were in their common source (very probably Cleitarchus); Diodorus has larger numbers (50,000 infantry, 3000 cavalry, 1000 chariots & 130 elephants), but he cites them in a context such that they may be rounded-up combinations of the forces available to Porus and Abisares.

Book 10: June 327BC – June 326BC

notwithstanding Taxiles' disclosures, Alexander began fervently to investigate where he might cross the river.

10.49 The Macedonians were not only deterred by the spectacle of the enemy forces, but by the proportions of the river that they must traverse. It spread over a breadth of four stades with a deep bed and no sign of any fords, giving the appearance of a desolate sea. Nor was the impetus of its current slackened by the width of its channel, but, as though pinched by its banks into a narrow course, it swept past in a roiling torrent, and in many spots rebounding billows betrayed the presence of rocky shoals. Yet more forbidding was their prospect of the far bank, which was packed with men and steeds. There too stood a huge mass of monstrous hulks, which, when purposely goaded, trumpeted hideously, such as to exhaust the ears. The river and their foes between them suddenly set their hearts to trembling in breasts that could usually embrace optimism and had often seen it justified. For they now believed that their rocking rafts could neither be steered to the bank nor protected during the landing.

10.50 The middle of the channel was crowded with islets, to which both Macedonians and Indians waded and swam, whilst holding their weapons over their heads. Here they engaged each other in skirmishes, and both kings sought to deduce from the results of these minor actions how the overall outcome would be settled. Conspicuous among the Macedonians for recklessness and daring were the noble youths Hegesimachus and Nicanor, who were spurred by their side's unending successes to scorn every peril. With naught but their lances for weapons, they led the most eager youths in swimming out to an island held by a throng of foes and thereupon slew many of the Indians, though armoured by nothing better than their audacity. They might have quit the scene with glory, if successful rashness were capable of showing discretion. But while they lingered with disdain, not to mention arrogance, to meet any who might come against them, they were encircled by Indians who covertly swam behind them and they fell beneath a hail of long-range missiles. Those who managed to elude the enemy were either swept away by the force of the current or engulfed by whirlpools. This clash greatly bolstered the confidence of Porus, who watched the whole thing from the riverbank.

10.51 In frustration, ***Alexander*** eventually ***devised*** such ***a stratagem* as *to fool his foe. There was an island in midstream*** that was more substantial than the rest. Being wooded, it was ideal for concealing a covert attack. Furthermore, not far back from the bank he held, there was a ditch of great depth, wherein not just infantry but also cavalrymen and their mounts might be hidden. Therefore, ***in order to avert his enemy's gaze from guarding this propitious place, he ordered*** Ptolemy with ***his*** entire troop of ***cavalry to ride to a point far downstream from the island and there to panic the Indians by raising a clamour and even to canter into the shallows, as though they were about***

*to swim across the river.*³⁴¹ ***For many days*** Ptolemy's ***cavalry squadrons repeated these manoeuvres at various spots, and by this tactic Porus was driven to array his forces against the zone from which the feints were made. Hence the enemy's watch upon the island lapsed and Alexander further directed that his pavilion be erected on a part of the bank downstream from it. His personal squadron stood guard before it and all the royal paraphernalia were conspicuously flaunted before the eyes of the enemy. Attalus scarcely differed from Alexander in age, build and general appearance - at least when seen from a distance - so he was robed in the royal chlamys***³⁴² ***and accoutrements and ordered repeatedly to make excursions to the edge of the river with his retinue during daylight hours. Thereby the king sought to convey the impression that he himself was directing operations from that spot and was not organising a crossing.***

10.52 ***Now Alexander received word that Abisares was*** encamped ***just four hundred stades away*** with his army, ***so he determined to attack Porus forthwith, before his*** potential ***ally could unite with him. When darkness fell, the king assembled a select force of infantry and cavalry*** *and bade them follow him for 150 stades to a wild and wooded area* opposite the island, **having ordered Craterus to take the main army across the river as soon as he saw that Alexander's task force had occupied the far bank.**³⁴³ Alexander was at first delayed but then assisted in putting his scheme into effect by the occurrence of a storm, for Fortune even turned troubles to his advantage. As *he made ready to cross over to the island with the rest of his task force, whilst the enemy's attention was focussed on the riverbank downstream where* Ptolemy and *his cavalry had been manoeuvring,* there poured forth such tempestuous rains as were barely tolerable beneath shelter. Swamped by the downpour, the soldiers fled back onshore in panic, forsaking their boats and rafts. Yet the wailing of the wind masked the uproar of their tumult, so their foes could not hear them.

10.53 Then in a trice the rain ceased, yet such dense clouds blanketed the heavens as to block all their light, so that those who spoke together could not discern each other's faces. Such a night of blacked-out heavens would have unnerved any other commander, when he sailed upon an unfamiliar river and his enemies might have chanced to occupy the shore to which his blind and reckless course was directed. But **the king** reckoned on evoking glory from peril and deemed that a darkness that disconcerted the wary was his opportunity. Thus, he **gave the signal for his forces to embark upon the rafts,** *which were fashioned from inflated hides with wooden decking,* and ordered that his own vessel should be launched first.

---

³⁴¹ Their presence in Frontinus, *Strategemata* 1.4.9 & 1.4.9a tends to confirm that the cavalry manoeuvres and the island were in the Vulgate and therefore were very probably described by Cleitarchus.

³⁴² A Greek cloak of medium length.

³⁴³ The distance of 150 stades (~27km) between the main camp and the island is given in Metz Epitome 59, but Arrian, *Anabasis* 5.11.2, precisely confirms it.

Book 10: June 327BC – June 326BC

The bank for which they were making was empty of the enemy, since Porus' attentions were still fixated upon the zone where the cavalry under Ptolemy *had made feints.* Therefore, apart from a single ship that was struck by a wave and stuck upon a rock, all the vessels got across unscathed. **On the far side Alexander ordered his soldiers** to take up their arms, then he deployed them for action and began *to advance upon the enemy.*

10.54 And now Alexander's forces were arrayed in a winged formation with himself at their head, whereupon **it was announced to Porus that armed men had occupied his own bank of the river** and that a crisis was impending. *Initially,* through that flaw in human psychology that entertains false hopes, *he ventured to believe that Abisares was coming as his ally, as had indeed been agreed. But* soon *enough,* as the dawning light of day unveiled his foe's formations, **he deployed** *one hundred four-horse* **chariots** *and four thousand cavalry* **against the oncoming ranks.** Those contingents that he sent forward were commanded by his brother, Hages[344], with the greatest threat being posed by the chariots, each having a complement of six men. Two of these bore shields and a second pair were archers, stationed on either side of the vehicle. The others were the charioteers, though not disarmed by their duties; for in close combat, they would lay aside the reins and fling showers of javelins upon their enemies. However, on that particular day these squadrons were rendered virtually impotent, since the extraordinary cloudbursts of the preceding evening had left the fields slimy and impracticable for horse-drawn vehicles. The weighty and sluggish chariots became bogged down in the mud and the marshy patches. Conversely, Alexander with his wieldy and lightly armed lines charged them with verve. The Scythians and the Dahae were the first to engage the Indians.[345] Then **Alexander unleashed** Perdiccas with **his cavalry against** the right wing of **the enemy.**

10.55 Now battle was joined right across the front, and those who drove the chariots began as the last recourse for their side to swerve their vehicles with unbridled speed into the midst of the mêlée. This was a two-edged blow that fell on both sides. Whilst the Macedonian foot were trampled in the collisions, the chariots in hurtling forward over slippery and uneven ground ejected those who directed them. In other cases, the maddened steeds yanked their vehicles not just into the quagmires and the swamps but even into the river itself. A few, goaded by the missiles of their foes, plunged back through their own ranks as far as Porus, who was energetically invigorating *his men in* the fighting. *But* **soon all the chariots were out of action.**

---

[344] There appears to exist no manuscript authority in the Vulgate for Anspach's emendation of the name to Spitaces the Nomarch, who dies at the Hydaspes in Arrian, *Anabasis* 5.18.2, though Pittacus in Polyaenus 4.3.21 tries to ambush Alexander's advance for Porus and is his nephew.

[345] These were probably mounted archers (*hippotoxotae*), cf. Arrian, *Anabasis* 5.14.3.

10.56 *Craterus, who had been left in command at the Macedonian camp, saw that Alexander had crossed and was advancing upon the Indians. Therefore, he conveyed his forces across the river on rafts and ships, of which he had a great fleet.* **Porus, perceiving that he was unexpectedly confronted by two armies** and seeing his chariots wandering driverless over the entire front, *determined to engage Alexander at close quarters. Hence, he distributed his elephants* among those of his courtiers who were nearest to him. *Then, deploying his cavalry to either flank, he* spaced the monstrous beasts *between them* in a single rank at fifty-foot intervals, *so as to strike fear into his foes.* Himself he stationed with the leading elephant on his left wing. **His infantry were posted** *behind the elephants and* in the intervening gaps *with the task of supporting them and impeding javelin attacks upon their flanks.* The archers were interspersed with the foot and so were the usual drummers; whose tattoos serve the Indians as substitute for the blaring of buglers; neither did this din bother the elephants, whose ears had long since been inured to the sound. An effigy of Heracles was borne before the ranks of the infantry, which was a sharp spur to these warriors: to forsake its bearers was a martial disgrace and death had been decreed for failure to fetch it back from the field of battle; for fear of this former foe had been sublimated into religious veneration.[346]

10.57 *For a little while the Macedonians were awed into halting not just by the monstrous beasts but also by the spectacle of their ruler. For* the array of elephants resembled the towers and the troops between them the curtain walls of a fortified city, *whilst Porus himself seemed almost superhuman, so great was his stature. And this impression was reinforced by the fact that* the elephant Porus rode loomed over the rest of the herd *by as much as he towered above his men.*

10.58 Surveying the Indian king and his forces, Alexander declared: "At last I behold a trial worthy of my spirit, since I am up against both monstrous beasts and warriors of prowess." He stationed his cavalry *with himself* on his right wing, *the rightmost* half of them being angled forward. He deployed his phalanx and the light infantry on his left with some *at the extreme left* bent away from the enemy. Gazing intently at Coenus, the king said: "When I, supported by Ptolemy, Perdiccas and Hephaistion, have charged against the enemy's left wing, and you see me embroiled in the midst of the fighting, yourself edge to the right, then bear down upon the enemy where they are in turmoil. Thereupon, you, Antigenes, and you, Leonnatus and Tauron will advance against the centre and engage their front. The length and strength of our sarissas will never prove more effective than against these monstrous beasts and their drivers: topple the riders and stab their steeds! The elephant is a two-edged type of weapon in warfare, which slashes

---

[346] Possibly Heracles was equated with the Sanskrit term Heri-cul-eesh, meaning the Lord of the clan of Hari, i.e. Vishnu alias Krishna, or some such syncretism.

Book 10: June 327BC – June 326BC

more sharply against its own side; for it is goaded against the enemy by command, but against its own ranks by panic."[347]

10.59 This speech having been spoken, Alexander was the first to spur his mount and he led the cavalry hard to his right hoping to outflank the enemy's left wing. Porus moved to intercept him, but his beasts broke formation at many points, since Alexander's manoeuvre was unforeseen. When, as planned, Alexander drove into the ranks of the enemy, Coenus charged with great impetus into the Indian left wing, where gaps had emerged in their line. The phalanx *under Antigenes and the others* also broke through the Indian centre at their first onslaught. And indeed, Porus ordered that the elephants should be goaded against Alexander's cavalry, when he realised where they were attacking, but such was the sluggishness and relative immobility of these animals that they could not match the speed of the cavalry manoeuvres.

10.60 Neither were even their arrows of any use to the barbarians. Since they were long and ponderous, unless the foot of the bow were braced against the ground, they could not be properly fitted and nor could the bow be readily drawn. As the soil was slimy, it hampered bow-bracing, so that whilst struggling to shoot they were overrun by their impetuous opponents.[348] Therefore the Indians spurned the orders of their ruler, as tends to happen, when fear begins to supplant leadership by issuing sharper commands to those in turmoil. And so there were as many generals as there were stray clusters of warriors: one voice would bid them to reform the line, another to dissolve it; some urged them to stand fast and others to ride around to the rear of their opponents. Thus, they lacked any cohesion. Meanwhile Alexander had virtually succeeded in bringing his cavalry against their rear.

10.61 *On observing his formations disintegrating into disorder* **under the Macedonian onslaught, Porus** *with a few of his men, whose honour conquered their fear,* **rallied his scattered soldiers and gathered about forty of his elephants that were still manageable. Instructing that these elephants be arrayed ahead of his massed troops and himself mounted upon the largest of the beasts, the Indian king led these combined forces against his foes. The monstrous brutes were trained to employ their size and strength to best advantage, so they instilled great fear and inflicted many casualties.** *Their strident trumpeting not only panicked the horses, which are naturally nervous of everything, but even threw the Macedonian warriors and their formations into turmoil.*

---

[347] Coenus, Ptolemy, Perdiccas & Hephaistion commanded cavalry, whilst Antigenes, Leonnatus and Tauron led the infantry; cf. Arrian, *Anabasis* 5.16.3 naming Seleucus instead of Leonnatus.

[348] That the foot of an Indian bow was rested on the ground is confirmed by numismatic evidence; especially the Porus medallions of tetradrachm weight with the elephant & archer designs on their obverse and reverse.

10.62 *Victors but a little while before, the Macedonians were now looking around for escape routes, whilst against the elephants Alexander unleashed his lightly armed Agrianians and Thracians, since they were better at hit and run tactics than his close combat troops. These fighters cast great showers of missiles against both the beasts and their mahouts. Their* javelins began to pierce the hide on the elephants' flanks, racking them with pain. And the Macedonians were coping manfully with the menacing crisis, as *the contingents brought by Craterus entered the field so that* the phalanx began relentlessly and tellingly to bring their sarissas to bear upon the maddened monsters and the Indians stationed beside them, evening out the contest. *But some were so zealous in stalking the beasts, that they rounded upon them, incensed by their wounds.* The elephants stomped their tormentors underfoot, so that they perished with their bones crushed and even their armour crumpled. Many Macedonians were impaled upon the tusks and rapidly expired, being skewered right through their bodies. It was an especially awful spectacle when they grabbed men and armour in their trunks and lifted them over the heads of their mahouts, then dashed them upon the ground, where they died a dire death. These horrifying examples served to teach the rest the merits of a more cautious approach.

10.63 Thus the tide of battle ebbed and flowed: now chasing the elephants, then being chased by them. And the protracted conflict remained undecided until late in the day, when at last they began to hack off the beasts' feet with axes, such implements having been readied in advance. With the softly curving blades of kopis swords they slashed at the trunks of the monsters.[349] Fear familiarised them with novel types of torment, not only in meeting but also in meting out death.

10.64 Therefore the elephants, *overwrought by their injuries,* could no longer be curbed by their drivers, but veered about and careered into their own ranks, trampling friendly warriors. *And their mahouts too were flung to the ground and mangled underfoot. Hence like livestock, more panicked than aggressive, they were herded off the battlefield. But* Porus, *though forsaken by most of the other elephants, began to hurl spears from his copious cache upon those foes that now swarmed around his own beast. He* cast his javelins so forcefully, that they were scarcely less lethal than the bolts from the mechanical catapults. The Macedonians who were confronting Porus were astounded by his heroic defiance, but Alexander summoned his hippotoxotae and other light-armed troops, ordering them to concentrate a barrage of projectiles upon the Indian king.[350] *Despite wounding many at a distance,* Porus *himself* presented a substantial target to strikes from every direction, so few missiles missed.

---

[349] A *kopis* is a single-edged Greek hacking sword, more commonly known as a falcata.

[350] *Hippotoxotae* = mounted archers (probably Scythians and Dahae).

Figure 10.3. The phalanx attacks at the Hydaspes (André Castaigne, 1899)

10.65 By now **he** had **suffered** nine **wounds,** some to the chest and others to the back. **They bled profusely** and the javelins rather fell than were propelled from his enfeebled grasp. Though still uninjured, his own elephant had been incited to frenzy and charged into the Macedonian ranks with undiminished verve, up to the point at which the mahout noticed that his king had gone limp and had dropped his weapons, being barely conscious. Thereupon, he wheeled the monstrous beast into rapid flight with Alexander in close pursuit. But *Bucephalus, the king's steed, having been gored by many gashes, was on his last legs and collapsed from under Alexander, gently setting him upon the ground rather than throwing him.* Consequently, the chase was briefly delayed whilst his attendants rushed to the king's aid and he swapped to another mount.

10.66 Meanwhile, the brother of Taxiles, the Indian king, having been sent forward by Alexander, began to counsel Porus not to persist with his last stand and to give himself up to the victor. But he, though **his strength had been sapped with loss of blood,** was roused by the familiar voice to retort: "I know well that you are the brother of Taxiles, the betrayer of his sovereignty and his throne." It chanced that there was just one javelin he had not yet relinquished, which he now flung at Alexander's emissary, piercing the middle of his chest and emerging from his back. After executing this last deed of bravado, Porus accelerated his flight. But his elephant too had now received many missile strikes and was faltering. Therefore, he ceased to retire and arrayed his foot soldiers against the posse of his foes.

10.67 By now the king had caught up with Porus and, recognising his stubbornness, Alexander forbade that any who fought on should be spared. Therefore, flights of missiles hurled at both the Indian infantry and their monarch converged upon them from every direction. Hence **Porus finally slumped over and began to topple from his monstrous beast.** The Indian who directed the elephant supposed him to be dismounting and set the beast to crouching down on its knees in the usual fashion. *Then, not wishing to delay the surrender, he held his hands high asking for his life.*[351] When the king's elephant bowed down, the other beasts followed its example, in accordance with their training, and settled down upon the ground. By this deed both Porus and the others *still with him* were delivered up to the victors. Believing that Porus had perished, Alexander ordered that his body should be stripped of its appurtenances, and men were hurrying over to remove his cuirass and robe, when the elephant began to stand guard over him and to menace the despoilers, lifting his body and setting him back upon its back. Therefore, the beast was overwhelmed by a hail of missiles from every quarter and, when it had been slaughtered, Porus was laid in a chariot.

---

[351] This phrase follows a lacuna in Metz Epitome 60, where it is unclear who performs this action.

Book 10: June 327BC – June 326BC

10.68 *Word now spread that Porus was dead, so the Indians all fled. Many were being slain in the rout, but then Alexander, being satisfied by his outright victory in the battle, ordered that the bugles should sound the recall.* Over twelve thousand of the Indians had fallen, *including the two sons of Porus and his generals and his most illustrious commanders.* More than nine thousand Indians *with their beasts of burden* and eighty of the elephants were captured alive. The Macedonian losses were two hundred and eighty cavalry plus over seven hundred infantry *and a multitude of them were wounded.* In the aftermath Alexander instructed that the dead be given burial according to the customary rites: *both his own men and the most valiant of his foes.*

10.69 When Alexander saw Porus lift his eyelids, roused to pity rather than hatred, he enquired: "What awful folly was it that drove you to try the fortunes of war, in full knowledge of the fame of my deeds, when Taxiles was at hand as an example of my clemency to those who place themselves beneath my sway?" And Porus responded: "Since you ask, I shall reply with the same candour with which you have posed your question. I had considered that nobody stronger than I existed. Though I knew my own power, I had not yet tested yours. The outcome of the conflict attests that you are the stronger. But I am not too unhappy to be second to such as you!" *When Porus was* further *asked how he believed that the victor should treat him, he responded: "As advised by your conscience as a king* this day, on which you have witnessed the frailty of fair fortune." *Alexander promised that he would do so.* Indeed, Porus profited more by his cautionary advice, than if he had resorted to pleas, for the greatness of his spirit, neither cowed nor shattered by misfortune, moved Alexander to respond not merely with compassion, but even with respect.

10.70 The king had Porus' injuries cared for *just as if he had fought on his own side*, turning him over to the Indians for medical attention. When, *against the expectations of everyone,* he recovered, Alexander *ranked him among the number of his Friends and* not only restored his kingdom to him, but also thereafter extended his domains across adjoining territories. Truly, there was no more enduring and steadfast trait of Alexander's character than his admiration for genuine merit and glorious deeds. Yet he was more candid in his assessment of excellence in his opponents than in his countrymen, for he believed a fellow citizen might overshadow his own greatness, whereas it would beam forth more brightly, the greater were those whom he conquered.

Figure 10.4. Alexander receives the surrender of Porus (Charles Le Brun, 1673).

Book 10: June 327BC – June 326BC

10.71 *Also in that year, thinking Alexander safely distant in India*, a Mede called Baryaxes launched a rebellion back in Persia together with certain associates. **Although their tiara may be worn by any of the Persians, he ventured to wear it upright, which is the prerogative of their monarch** and indeed he styled himself King of the Persians and Medes. He was arrested by Atropates, Satrap of Media, and later delivered up to Alexander, who had him and his associates executed.[352]

10.72 *These were the concerns of Alexander* in the tenth year of his reign.

---

[352] Cf. Arrian, *Anabasis* 6.29.3.

Book 11: July 326BC – Late Spring 325BC

Eastwards Through India; The Mutiny On The Hyphasis and the Return to the Kingdom of Porus; The River Voyage Downstream; The Siege of the Town of the Oxydracae; Alexander's Wound and his Recovery.

11.1 *As the eleventh year of his reign began,* **Alexander** was elated by his remarkable victory over Porus, which he considered to have laid open the uttermost east to his advance, so he **slaughtered various sacrificial animals as a dedication to the Sun,** *in return for its gift of the Orient for his taking.* Then he convened an Assembly of his troops in order to set their spirits upon the continued prosecution of his campaigns. After lauding their prowess, he asserted that any will possessed by the Indians to resist them had been broken in the recent struggle. The rest of the campaign would be fine plunder, since the prodigious opulence of the region towards which they were headed was universally famed. In comparison, the booty from Persia was mean and tawdry. There would be enough gems and pearls and gold and ivory not merely to cram their own houses, but to sate all Macedonia and Greece too. The soldiers were greedy for both riches and glorious deeds and neither had any prospect presented by Alexander failed to live up to his promises, so they dedicated themselves to the venture *en masse,* and were all buoyed up by great expectations, when the Assembly was dispersed.

11.2 Alexander intended to advance to the ends of India, so as to bring all the peoples of Asia beneath his rule, but afterwards he planned to sail downstream to reach the Ocean at the edge of the world. *He thought to voyage thence to the Red Sea and onward even as far as the Pillars of Heracles.* To this end he commanded that a fleet of many vessels should be constructed on the river. This was facilitated by a plentiful supply of timber in the nearby mountains, including stately firs, abundant cedar and pine and other sorts of wood well suited for shipbuilding. *The first vessel was finished in just thirty-three days.*

11.3 In the course of felling the timber, the men encountered various curiosities among the mountain forests. There were innumerable <u>serpents of exceptional length, some extending to sixteen cubits.</u>[353] They also saw a great beast distinguished by a single horn protruding from its nose, which they consequently named "rhinoceros", but the Indians know it by a different name, and it is rather rare elsewhere.[354]

---

[353] Probably pythons.

[354] This is the Indian Rhinoceros (a.k.a. Great One-Horned Rhinoceros), which is now an endangered species: it does indeed dwell among the southern foothills of the Himalayas.

Book 11: July 326BC – Late Spring 325BC

11.4 Also in these mountains the Macedonians found many species of monkey in a range of sizes. <u>In one instance Alexander and his men suddenly came across a huge troop of the larger type confronting them and crowded into an array</u> upon a group of bare eminences. <u>The apes happened also to be standing erect when first seen, thereby conveying an impression of an army waiting in ambush.</u> Therefore, Alexander ordered his soldiers to prepare to defend themselves, but Taxiles was then with the king and was able to reassure him that these animals presented no real threat.

11.5 <u>The Indians dispense with the use of nets or scent-tracking hounds in the hunting and snaring of these apes,</u> *asserting that the beasts themselves have taught how they may be caught. They cannot readily be captured by brute force, due to their combination of brawn and wit, but they habitually mimic the antics of mankind. Thus,* <u>if he should see a person dance, then the ape becomes a dancing animal, and he would play the flute too, if anyone were to teach him to blow it. Therefore, in plain view of their quarry,</u> which watches from its refuge among the boughs, <u>the ape-hunters dab honey on their lower eyelids. They put on sandals and bind them around their ankles, and they hang hand-mirrors from thongs about their necks and admire their reflections. Afterwards they move well away having covertly swapped birdlime for the honey, having anchored the sandals by means of both weights and fastenings and having substituted a rugged slip-noose for the thong of the mirror. Then the ape fails to resist its urge to imitate the actions of its stalkers and thereby incapacitates itself, for its eyes become glued, its feet are held fast and its whole body becomes tightly leashed as it gazes in the mirror. Being thereby reduced to a helpless state, its capture is made easy.</u>

11.6 Alexander now exploited a plentiful supply of labour by speedily founding two cities, the first sited on the western bank of the River Hydaspes opposite the island, where he had crossed with his troops in launching his attack on Porus; the other on the eastern bank at the field of battle. He also rewarded those of his men who had performed well in this engagement. He presented a crown of gold and also a thousand gold coins to each of his commanders, and to all the rest he gave honourable gifts in proportion to their status in his entourage or to the merit of their services.[355]

11.7 *Alexander rested his army on the eastern side of the Hydaspes for thirty days, since supplies were plentiful in the kingdom of Porus.* **By this time** to the surprise of everyone **Porus himself had recovered from his many wounds,** *so the king commanded that he be brought before him. When he came, Alexander invited him to accompany him, when he set out for his own land. Porus replied: "O great Alexander, I would be willing to put*

---

[355] It has been suggested by Frank Holt (AtG & the Mystery of the Elephant Medallions, p.148) that this was the occasion of the issue of Alexander's Porus Medallions.

aside half of my life in order to see your homeland, except that you cannot persuade me *to appear as a captive before your countrymen. I have no desire to continue to defy death. If you wish to take me away to serve as an exhibit, then you can carry me off as a corpse."* Hence Alexander assured him that nothing would be done against his will. *Furthermore,* **in recognition of his virtuous excellence,** the king enrolled him in the fellowship of his Friends and **reinstated him as ruler of his former domains.** Indeed, Alexander subsequently extended Porus' realm quite considerably.

11.8 At this time Alexander received fresh envoys from Abisares, the king of the neighbouring realm, *who had been allied with Porus, yet had also previously sent a delegation to treat with Alexander and indeed Porus had received no reinforcements from him.* Now he promised to do anything that Alexander might command, excepting only that he refused to appear before the king in person, *for he could not bear to risk the loss of his royal power or liberty.* Alexander sent back a threat, that if Abisares should persist in his reluctance to manifest himself, then he would undertake to visit Abisares *together with his army.* This resulted in the capitulation of Abisares.

11.9 Then Alexander led his army eastwards and, after crossing the river in Porus' realm,[356] he penetrated into *the heart of India through* a territory of exceptional fecundity. It was shaded by *vast forests of seemingly limitless extent and comprising* weird trees that reached a height of seventy cubits. The girth of their trunks could barely be encompassed by a ring of four men with arms outstretched and they spread to shade an area of three plethra. *Most of their branches dipped down into the soil, then reared up again from the earth, so that the impression was not of boughs, but rather of a tree risen up on its own roots.*[357] *The air was temperate and salubrious, for the forest canopy filtered the intense sunlight and streams gushed forth from a profusion of springs.*

11.10 <u>In this region they again encountered a multiplicity of snakes, but quite distinctive from those seen in the mountains, being far shorter in length and having brightly coloured skin of many hues, as though their scales had been daubed with dyes. Some of them resembled bronze wands decorated in bands all the way from head to tail, whilst others were silver-tinged and still others were ringed with red.</u>[358] <u>A few even glinted with a golden sheen.</u> The worst of them displayed broad hoods.[359] <u>Their bites were most deadly and mortality was swift.</u> The victims were wracked with

---

[356] Perhaps the Acesines.

[357] The banyan tree (1 plethron is an area of 30m square, i.e. 900m²).

[358] Perhaps kraits and coral snakes.

[359] Cobras.

Book 11: July 326BC – Late Spring 325BC

agony and exuded bloody perspiration. The Macedonians were greatly plagued by snake attacks, so they resorted to slinging hammocks between trees and maintaining vigilance throughout the night. Eventually, however, they learnt from the local people of the curative usage of a plant root, which *functioned as an antitoxin and* relieved them from incessant anxiety.

11.11 *As Alexander marched on, he received intelligence that another king named Porus, who was cousin to him he had already subdued, had forsaken his realm and sought the protection of the people of Gandara. This so incensed Alexander that he delegated Hephaistion to lead an army into his territory with the objective of transferring those lands into the governorship of the Porus who had become his ally.*

11.12 Proceeding onwards through stretches of desert, they arrived at the River Hiarotis,[360] which was fringed by water meadows and woodland glades with shady trees of a type that they had not seen elsewhere and the clearings were crowded with peacocks. Having moved his camp beyond the river, **Alexander campaigned against the local people who were called the Adrestians, and gained control of their towns, sometimes through force of arms, but often through negotiation.** He surrounded and besieged their city[361] not far from the Hiarotis, inducing the surrender of the inhabitants, and afterwards imposing tribute payments and seizing hostages.

11.13 Next he entered the country of the Cathaeans, **who are notable for their custom that the wives are cremated together with their husbands, if the latter should die.**[362] **This law had been enacted following an incident in which a wife was found to have poisoned her husband,** because she had fallen in love with a younger man.

11.14 Alexander advanced upon Sangala, **the largest and best-fortified city of the Cathaeans,** since it was defended by a marsh as well as its ramparts. The barbarians came forth to give battle in wagons that had been yoked together, casting javelins and brandishing pikes. They would vault athletically from vehicle to vehicle, whenever they needed to reinforce their compatriots. Initially, these alien tactics intimidated the Macedonians, since they were taking casualties at long range, but soon they learnt to scorn such cumbersome conveyances and hemmed them in from either side, slaying any who fought back. Alexander ordered that the lashings that linked the wagons should be slashed, in order that they might be encircled and picked off individually. Hence the Cathaeans suffered 8000 casualties and the survivors scuttled back into their city. But the very next day its

---

[360] Hydraotis in Arrian, the modern Ravi.

[361] Probably Pimprama.

[362] Suttee – Cleitarchus is evidently following Onesicritus: cf. Strabo 15.1.30.

walls were taken in an assault with scaling-ladders propped simultaneously against every stretch, and so *the city was sacked and razed to the ground.*

11.15 A few rescued themselves by their quick reactions, and, on realising that their city had been obliterated, waded through the swamp and petrified all the settlements in the vicinity by avowing that an invincible host, undoubtedly composed of divine beings, had come among them *to wreak havoc*. In consequence, the Indians spread an adverse report that Alexander's forces fought savagely and viciously. On receiving word of this, Alexander began to look for opportunities to moderate his reputation with the native peoples. Nevertheless, the king sent forth Perdiccas with a mobile task force to ravage the surrounding territory, though he also assigned a detachment of his troops to Eumenes with the mission of persuading the barbarians to submit.

11.16 *Alexander himself led the deployment of the rest of his army to invest a well-fortified city,* whither the inhabitants of other towns had fled to seek refuge. The citizens sent a delegation to plead with the king, though without slackening their preparations for resistance. For a dispute had broken out, which had split the populace into two factions: one party deemed any alternative preferable to surrender, whilst the other believed that they could not defend themselves effectively. Neither did it prove possible for them to reconcile their conflicting views, but instead the party advocating surrender opened the gates to admit their enemy. Although Alexander could reasonably have punished the members of the faction that had wished to fight him, he chose rather to pardon everyone and to arrange a treaty, under the terms of which **he received hostages from them.**

11.17 **Then the king moved his camp to the next** *hostile* **city,** which was large and populous. **As the army advanced towards its walls, the hostages,** who included old men, women and children, **were sent forward ahead of the phalanx.** From their ramparts **the defenders recognised that the hostages were members of their own tribe,** so they invited them to parley and learnt of Alexander's leniency, and of his invincibility too! Interpreting also the release of the hostages as conciliatory behaviour, **the populace** *opened their gates to the king and* **welcomed him by waving suppliant branches,** *so he aborted his assault. Afterwards, news of Alexander's clemency quickly spread throughout the region, such that the rest of its cities were readily induced to place themselves under his protection as well.*

11.18 Alexander next moved against the cities that were governed by Sopeithes. His realm has the reputation among the Indians **of being wisely ruled in accordance with high moral principles. In particular, the administration directs its policies towards the acquisition of moral eminence and physical perfection is esteemed above all else.** *For example*, from the moment of their birth the fate of their children is *relinquished by their parents and* consigned to the discretion of examiners, who determine the physical condition of the infants. Those who are handsome, healthy

Book 11: July 326BC – Late Spring 325BC

and vigorous, they select for rearing, but any who are crippled or who exhibit any conspicuous bodily defect, they subject to infanticide, considering them unworthy of raising. *Furthermore,* they arrange their marriages without consideration of dowries or the wealth and prestige of their families, but rather with the objective of breeding beautiful and athletic children from especially comely couples. *By virtue of such practices most of the denizens of these cities rejoice in a prevalent sense of their superiority among the Indians.*

11.19 *Alexander arrayed his army before the town occupied by Sopeithes himself, since its gates were closed against him. Observing that its walls and towers appeared deserted, the Macedonians supposed either that its citizens had abandoned the place or else that they lay in hiding to take them by surprise. But suddenly a portal was flung wide and the Indian king emerged, flanked by his two adult sons.* He was a paragon of physical attractiveness *and further surpassed his countrymen in height, being over four cubits tall. His raiment, which draped his entire body down to his ankles, was embellished with gold and purple and he was shod with bejewelled and gilded sandals. Pearls adorned his arms from wrist to shoulder and huge gemstones of dazzling lustre dangled from his ears. His golden sceptre, which was garnished with beryl, he yielded to Alexander with an invocation that good fortune should attend its transfer. Thereby* he surrendered himself, *his offspring* and his kingdom, *but through the benevolence of his conqueror he was immediately reinstated in his former rank and responsibilities. With corresponding beneficence, Sopeithes entertained Alexander's entire force royally for some days.*

11.20 Alexander was pleased to receive numerous grand gifts from Sopeithes, including 150 large hunting dogs of a *famously* valiant and relentless breed. *They are reputed also to refrain from barking when they sight their quarry and they are especially aggressive towards lions.* Sopeithes was keen to demonstrate their strength and quality to Alexander, so he had a full-grown lion brought into a ring-fenced arena and set two of the least impressive dogs upon it. As the lion began to prevail over this pair, Sopeithes released two more of the hounds into the fray. Now *the advantage was shifted in favour of the dogs and* the lion showed signs of succumbing, so Sopeithes sent in an expert handler *who sought to restore the evenness of the match* by yanking a dog off the lion by its right leg. But the animal refused to release its jaws from its opponent, so the handler hacked away its leg with a curved knife. Alexander protested vociferously at this, and his guards rushed forward to stay the hand of the Indian, but Sopeithes *craved Alexander's indulgence,* promising three fine replacements for the maimed beast, which still would not relax its grip on the lion. *Hence the handler resumed his attack, slicing elsewhere at the dog, and, when it yet kept its teeth clenched upon its foe, slashing indiscriminately* until it fainted and died from loss of blood athwart the lion without having uttered the merest yelp or whimper *for fear of lessening its hold.* Such is the passion for the chase that Nature is reputed to have cultivated in these beasts.[363]

11.21 *The king enquired as to the secret of the tenacious bravery of these dogs. Sopeithes replied that* it was rumoured that they had inherited a strain of tiger blood, *for in that region this animal is most extraordinarily fierce and powerful with a great turn of speed. It gets its name from its swiftness, for the Persians call an arrow "tigris". On the same basis the River Tigris derives its name from having the most rapid of all currents. It was the custom to truss the bitches, which were the forbears of these dogs, and to leave them out overnight in the woods, such that some of them were slain by the tigers, whilst others were impregnated.*[364] From the offspring of these matings, a most exceptionally fierce breed of dog was spawned, as had been demonstrated.

11.22 At this time Hephaistion brought his army into camp to recombine with Alexander's forces, having *successfully* fulfilled his mission by subduing another *great* region of India, *including the lands of the rebel Porus, by force of arms. Alexander was pleased to commend him on his victories.*

11.23 Leaving Sopeithes in control of his realm, Alexander marched his forces on to the River Hyphasis. Phegeus, the king of that region, *had commanded his subjects to carry on working in their fields as normal when the Macedonians arrived, so* the inhabitants greeted their *actual* appearance with alacrity. Phegeus himself came to welcome Alexander with numerous presents and placed himself under the king's authority. Consequently, Alexander endorsed the governance of this nation by Phegeus, who generously entertained the Macedonians as his guests for two whole days. On the third day Alexander planned to cross the River Hyphasis *near the citadel of Altusacra,* although it was a great barrier, being seven stades wide, six fathoms deep *and strewn with rocks* with treacherous currents *flowing between them.*

11.24 Accordingly, the king sought information from Phegeus regarding the territory beyond the far bank of the river. Phegeus confided that a journey of twelve days through desert wastes would bring Alexander before a still greater river, which was thirty-two stades in breadth and deeper than any other stream in India. It was called the Ganges and beyond it lay the lands of the Prasii and the Gangaridae, whose king was Xandrames. He had barricaded the highways with an army comprising **20,000 cavalry, 200,000 infantry, 2000 chariots and,** so Phegeus believed, up to **4000 elephants** caparisoned for war, *the latter constituting a particular source of dread for*

---

[363] Curtius thought this might be a shaggy dog story, but Pit Bull Terriers exhibit similar reluctance to unclamp their jaws from their victims, so it may be an injustice that this story has been used to impugn the probity of Onesicritus, its probable ultimate source (cf. Strabo 15.1.31).

[364] Cf. Isidore of Seville, Etymologiae 12.2.28, but this story is not biologically credible.

Book 11: July 326BC – Late Spring 325BC

the Macedonians. Alexander was dubious of the accuracy of these figures, so he sent for Porus, *who was near at hand,* and asked whether he could confirm their validity. Porus firmly endorsed the information on the numerical strength of Xandrames' forces, but he disparaged their ruler as a lowly and mediocre serf. For he was said to be the son of a barber, who had barely scraped a living through this trade, but had traded more profitably with his good looks by seducing the queen. *She had promoted him into a close companionship with the king, her husband, whom he had proceeded foully to murder, seizing the regency of the kingdom on the pretext of protecting the succession of the dead king's offspring. But instead, he had slaughtered the legitimate heirs and sired Xandrames, who was reviled and despised by his people on account of a disposition better suited to his father's humble origins than his royal status.*

11.25 *Alexander was troubled by Porus' corroboration on several counts. Although he felt only disdain for the enemy and his monstrous war-beasts,* he *nevertheless* realised that a campaign against the Gangaridae would be arduous, *for he especially feared* the defensive advantage afforded by *the terrain with its fast-flowing rivers. It would be a tough task to hunt down and extricate people who dwelt virtually at the edge of human existence. Conversely, his feverish thirst for glory and his ever-burning desire for fame would not allow him to brook any obstacle nor to consider anything beyond his reach.* Therefore, he was not downhearted, for he had faith in the prowess of his troops, and he believed the promises of the oracles that had forecast his triumph. He recalled that the Delphic Pythia had dubbed him invincible and that Ammon had granted him the rule of the entire Earth.

11.26 *However, the king was also concerned about the willingness of his soldiers to advance further, for* he was well aware that they were showing signs of fatigue from the rigours of the campaign. They had endured nearly eight years of unremitting toil and peril. *Many had grown aged, whilst traversing vast tracts of the Earth in Alexander's service.* It would be vital to lift their morale with a rousing exhortation, if they were to be motivated to march against the Gangaridae. *Else he worried that they would rest content with the piles of plunder that they had already garnered instead of exhausting their lives in pursuit of ambitions no longer compatible with their own.*

11.27 *Whereas the king continued to covet the dominion of the world, his troops wished to settle down to enjoy the fruits of their endeavours as soon as practicable.* Many of their comrades were already dead, and no respite from *the toll of* warfare was on offer. The ceaseless trekking had ground thin the hooves of their steeds. Their weapons and panoplies had become dilapidated and not a thread survived of their original Greek vestments. They had resorted to adapting foreign clothing: for example, tailoring

Indian garments to suit. Unfortunately too, this was the monsoon season of relentless rains, which had been drumming down for seventy days with the accompaniment of continual percussions of thunder and lightning.

11.28 Recognising all these impediments to the undertaking, Alexander realised that the only hope of fulfilling his aspirations would be specially to ingratiate himself with his troops. *Therefore, he permitted them to forage through the land alongside the river, which was crammed with all kinds of bounty.* Whilst the soldiers were occupied with their pillage in the ensuing days, the king assembled their wives and sons. He awarded a monthly grant of provisions to the women and he announced a cadet bursary commensurate with the service records of their fathers for each of the youths. Then, when his veterans returned to camp sated with the spoils of their expedition, he called an Assembly and delivered a rousing oration concerning the campaign against the Gangaridae.

11.29 "Soldiers, I am well aware that worrying rumours have been spread about by the Indians in recent days with the aim of demoralising you. I know too that you are familiar with the tricks of such propagandists. For the Persians sought to deter us with grim accounts of the passes of Cilicia, the fields of Mesopotamia and the Tigris and Euphrates rivers, though we readily forded one and bridged the other. Reputations are invariably inflated: all such hearsay exceeds the truth. Even our renown, though founded on solid deeds, grows greater in the telling. Who, even now, would believe the tales of us tackling monstrous beasts arrayed like turreted ramparts in breaching the defences of the Hydaspes and all other such reports that embellish upon reality? By Heracles, we should long since have fled from Asia, if we could be intimidated by fables."

11.30 "Are you so credulous as to believe in a horde of elephants in India more numerous than the oxen of other *armies*, despite the rarity of these beasts and the difficulties presented by their capture and training? The same mendacity imbues the rumours of our opponent's strengths in cavalry and infantry. Consider too that wide rivers run smoothly, for it is the narrowing of their channels that induces torrential currents in order to balance their flow. And, besides, the true danger lurks at the further bank, where the enemy stalks us as we land our craft. Hence no matter what breadth of river confronts us, the risk does not alter, since it awaits our coming ashore. But suppose the rumours are true: need we allow the enormity of our enemy's war-beasts or his vast hosts to discourage us? Regarding elephants, we have witnessed their propensity to inflict more harm on their own side, when we hacked their gargantuan hides with our axes and kopis swords, whereupon they launched a frenzied charge back into their own ranks. What does it matter, whether they have as many as Porus or even four thousand such, when you know from recent experience that all will panic and flee, if but one or two be maimed? Furthermore, even small numbers of elephants can only be directed and coordinated awkwardly. If thousands were aggregated *in battle*, they would trample one another, being neither able to stand their ground nor to bolt. I myself had

Book 11: July 326BC – Late Spring 325BC

the use of these animals *after Arbela*, but, being contemptuous of their utility in warfare, I refrained from deploying them, knowing well that they would prove fratricidal."

Figure 11.1. The Mutiny at the River Hyphasis (Antonio Tempesta, 1608).

11.31 "You may say that it is our enemy's myriads of horse and foot that saps your confidence. Should I suppose it your custom only to fight little battles, whereas now shall be your first experience of holding the line against an immense rabble? In fact the invincible robustness of the Macedonians in the face of hostile hosts is well-attested by the river of blood at the Granicus and the flood of Persian gore in Cilicia, and also by Arbela, whose fields are filled with the bones of those we routed. It is a bit late to begin to quantify the enemy's legions, when you have already emptied Asia through the destruction of your foes. The time to worry about the sparseness of our forces was when we first sailed across the Hellespont. Now Scythian warriors follow our lead, Bactrian auxiliaries campaign at our side and confederates from the Dahae and Sogdiani serve in our ranks. Yet I do not rest my faith in those throngs, but rather I place myself in your hands. In your valour lies the surety of my success. Grant me, therefore, your spirits filled with eager faith and, so long as you stand by me in the fight, I need count neither my allies nor my foes. We stand not at the outset of our endeavours, but rather at their culmination. We have reached the birthplace of the Sun and the Ocean. Provided dispiritedness does not hold us back, we shall win control of the ends of the Earth, before returning thence to our homeland as famous victors."

11.32 "Do not like lazy peasants let slip the ripe fruit through sloth, for the rewards exceed the risks, since the country is both prosperous and peaceable. Thus, I lead you rather to riches than to glory. It is right and proper that you should salvage the pearls that are washed up on the shore of the Ocean and convey them to our homeland, for no opportunity *for profit* should elude you or be relinquished through timidity. For the sake of yourselves and your glory, which ascends beyond the ceiling of human achievement, and in the name of the favour I have shown to you and the matching favour you have shown for me, I implore you not to forsake your protégé and comrade (I will not mention king) as he approaches the boundary of human existence. All else I have commanded, but in this matter, I shall place myself in your debt. It is I that asks this of you; I, who has always been at the forefront of any peril to which I have exposed you; I, who joins your battle line with interlocked shield. Do not snap the palm frond that I grasp in order, if Nemesis be assuaged, to emulate Heracles and Dionysus. O grant my entreaties and shatter your delinquent silence. Where's the clamour that signifies your enthusiasm? Where's that Macedonian countenance of old? I do not know you anymore, soldiers, nor perhaps do you know me. You closed your ears to me some while ago and I have sought in vain to inspire broken and cowering spirits."

11.33 Yet each Macedonian obstinately kept his peace and locked his gaze upon the soil at his feet, so Alexander continued: "Have I in some unsuspected manner wronged you, that you refuse even to look me in the face? It is as though I were alone in a wasteland. No one answers me, yet neither does anyone refuse me. With whom do I speak? What do I propose? It is your power and glory that I strive to defend. What has become of the men that erstwhile vied for the privilege of bearing the body of their wounded monarch? Now I am abandoned, forsaken and betrayed to the enemy. Nevertheless, I shall march onwards all by myself. Consign me to the rivers, the monstrous beasts and those peoples whose very names make you quake. Though deserted by you, I shall find fresh followers. The Scythians and Bactrians will be with me. Though they were our foes but a little while ago, now they are my *loyal* soldiers. Glorious death is preferable to a mutinous command. Go and skulk back to your homes! Go glean what acclaim you can, having forsaken your king! For here I shall stay either to win the victory of which you despair or else to find a place to die with unblemished honour."

11.34 Even these words failed to coax any speech from the troops, who deferred to their senior commanders in the thankless matter of responding: their message being that, grown haggard through relentless toil and scarring wounds, they did not deny their duties, but were no longer capable of performing them. Yet their officers, being frozen with trepidation, still kept their gaze fixed upon the earth. Then an initially barely audible whisper spontaneously erupted to beset their ears with groans and sighs, as gradually their dolorous mood was openly expressed in floods of tears, which soon indeed dissolved the king's anger into a corresponding effusion of compassion. For Alexander himself, though he fought back against a wave of emotion, failed nevertheless to keep his eyes dry. At length, when **all at**

Book 11: July 326BC – Late Spring 325BC

the Assembly were weeping uncontrollably and despite his fellows persisting in hanging back, Coenus alone dared to approach the rostrum signalling his wish to be heard. As soon as the troops saw him doff his helmet, which is the custom when addressing the monarch, they petitioned him insistently to plead the army's cause with the king.

11.35 So Coenus began to speak: "Let the gods forfend that we should think rebellious thoughts, and surely they do forbid them. The sentiment of your soldiers is as it has always been: to go whither you command; to fight and to encroach upon danger *on your behalf*; to vaunt your name to posterity written in our blood. Hence, if you ultimately insist upon it, we shall still traipse after you wherever you may lead us, though we be disarmed, disrobed and bled white *from our many wounds*. But if you are prepared to listen to heartfelt truths, rent from your soldiers' mouths by force of circumstances, then lend a compassionate ear to those who have most diligently enacted your orders and respected your guidance and will forever do so, wherever you may go."

11.36 "Sire, through the immensity of your deeds, you have not merely triumphed over the enemy, but over your own soldiers as well. Insofar as human beings could withstand the rigours, we have done your bidding. We have journeyed across lands and seas, such that their geography is better understood by us than by their inhabitants. Now we are convened virtually upon the far edge of the Earth. You are about to enter and explore a different world, another India that is mysterious even to the Indians. You will strive to extricate from their dens and lairs people who lurk among serpents and brute beasts, so that you may cleanse by your conquests more lands than the sun beams down upon. It is an entirely fitting ambition for your exalted spirit, but it soars above ours. For your courage will expand indefinitely, but our strength is now almost spent. Just **examine our bodies,** which are bled white, **fissured with wounds and decayed by so many scars.** Many of us are grey-haired with barely enough lifespan left to get ourselves back to our homes, for, alone in your army, we Macedonians have served successively under both your father, Philip, and yourself. If any of us should die before our homecoming, then we beg only that you should return our remains to the tombs of our fathers."

11.37 *"Our weaponry is blunted and our armour is decrepit. We have sunk to adopting foreign ways and donning Persian attire,* having long been beyond the reach of supplies from our own country. How many of us still have a corselet or a steed? Let it be admitted how few of us retain their servants and how little is left to us of the booty from our campaigns. Though we are victors over all, we lack every comfort. Nor does the explanation for our destitution lie in profligacy, but rather it is warfare and the tools for warfare that have swallowed our wealth. So will you place this lovely army defenceless before monstrous beasts? Though the barbarians must deliberately have exaggerated the number of their elephants, their lies would not be plausible unless the true number were substantial. But if your intent to drive on deeper into India remains firm, consider that the southerly expanse of this continent is less vast and, when the intervening territory has been subdued, you may still run down to that great sea with which Nature has bounded human affairs. What's the point of stretching your luck by going the long way round, when a shorter southerly route to the Ocean lies open to you? Unless you would wish to wander for the sake of wandering, we have reached the point from which your best fortune leads you back."

11.38 "I have chosen to speak these truths to your face, rather than foment dissension behind your back. It is not my purpose to ingratiate myself with the army, but that you should hear the voice of those who *seriously* debate these matters, instead of the mere moans of grumblers." As Coenus concluded his oration a clamour arose in every quarter pierced with wails of lamentation: "O king", "O father", "O lord" yelled a cacophony of voices. Then, finally, Coenus' pleas were endorsed by the other commanders, especially the elderly for whom it was more respectable to ask to be relieved and whose views carried more weight.

11.39 *Alexander* could neither bring himself to rail against their intransigence nor to relax his own resentment at their stance. In a quandary, he leapt down from the rostrum, **ordered the royal quarters to be sealed and denied admission to all but his retinue of attendants. Two days were spent in ill temper, but on the third** the king emerged and issued orders that twelve altars of dressed stone, each fifty cubits high, should be erected **along the river** in honour of the twelve Olympian gods as a lasting memorial of this limit of his campaign. He further directed that the perimeter of their camp should be extended to thrice its original dimensions and that a ditch should encompass it, measuring fifty feet wide by forty deep, the earth being heaped up on its inner margin to form a formidable rampart. The infantry were required to construct huts containing pairs of bedsteads each five cubits in length; the cavalry, additionally, had to erect pairs of mangers at double their usual height *and even to scatter about bridles with bits of extraordinary weight, as if made for massive mounts.* Similarly, everything that they left in that place*, also including outsize shields and weaponry,* was scaled up in proportion. The king's purpose was to fabricate evidence for an encampment of heroes of giant stature and phenomenal strength as a wonder to deter the defiance of the native peoples and to amaze posterity.

11.40 *The men undertook the enlargement of the camp with alacrity. Then, after the conduct of propitious sacrifices,* **the expedition retraced its steps and encamped in the vicinity of the River Acesines.** There by the hand of fate Coenus fell sick and died. Though Alexander was grieved by his death, he could not resist commenting that Coenus had given a lengthy speech to gain but a short span of days *homeward bound*, as if *Alexander supposed* Coenus alone had wished to see Macedonia again! **Alexander found the fleet, which he had commissioned before marching eastwards, afloat in the river awaiting him.** *These ships he arranged to have fitted out for the voyage downstream, whilst he had still more vessels constructed.* At this juncture, reinforcements arrived in

Book 11: July 326BC – Late Spring 325BC

camp comprising allied and mercenary troops from Greece *and elsewhere* led by various commanders. *Memnon had brought* over 5000 cavalry *from Thrace, whilst Harpalus had dispatched 7000 of the infantry, who totalled over 30,000 men.* They had escorted a consignment of 25,000 splendid panoplies *inlaid with silver and gold* together with 100 talents of medicaments. Alexander distributed the supplies and the armour to the soldiers, *ordering that their worn-out battle dress should be burnt.*

11.41 It was Alexander's intention to row downriver to the southern Ocean aboard his fleet, which now incorporated over a thousand ships including 800 bireme-galleys and *300* cargo vessels. *As reward for their aid in building his armada, he left Porus and Taxiles as kings of separate realms, but reconciled with each other through a marriage alliance,* for they had been reviving their former rivalry and feuding. He also gave names to the two cities that he had earlier founded either side of the river near the site of his battle against Porus, calling one Nicaea in commemoration of his victory and the other Bucephala as a memorial to his horse, who *had borne him to victory in all his battles, but* had perished in that engagement. Indeed, Alexander suffered another personal bereavement at this time, when his little son by Roxane died. *After the funeral and the performance of sacrifices,* having ordained that the bulk of the army *with the elephants and the baggage train* should march down the banks under the command of Hephaistion and Craterus, Alexander himself embarked *upon his flagship* accompanied by his Friends and sailed *his fleet* downstream *with its multicoloured sails unfurled.* However, he advanced only about 40 stades each day in order that he might frequently put task forces ashore at convenient spots.

11.42 Not long after the start of their voyage they reached the kingdom of *another* Sopeithes. The most remarkable feature in this region is a mountain made entirely of salt, sufficient to supply the whole of India. Not the least wondrous feature of the mines that exploit this resource is the way in which **the salt-rock is naturally replenished within the excavations over time.**[365]

11.43 When the fleet reached the confluence of the Acesines and Hydaspes, Alexander disembarked his troops opposite to Eleumezen and marched them against the Sibi, who occupied the country around the unified river. It is recorded that these people claimed to be descendants of the army deployed by Heracles during his unsuccessful siege of Aornus. The lion-caped club-wielder had been forced to settle their forbears in this vicinity, *since they had been incapacitated by sickness. Their origins were betokened by their garbing themselves in the skins of savage beasts and their brandishing of clubs as weapons as well as many other vestiges, although proper Greek customs had died out among them.* Alexander advanced for 250 stades, ravaging the country so as to induce its

---

[365] Probably the ancient salt mines at Khewra 15km north of the Hydaspes in the Salt Range.

inhabitants to flee, until he invested an illustrious town and its leading citizens emerged to treat with him. They presented him with splendid gifts and recalled their common descent from Heracles, vowing therefore to assist his expedition by every means in recognition of their shared ancestry. The king graciously welcomed their support for his cause and pronounced that their cities should retain self-rule.

11.44 Alexander proceeded against the next nation *downstream*, who were called the Agalasseis, and found them drawn up in a strength of 40,000 infantry and 3,000 cavalry *on the opposite bank of the river*. Alexander *crossed the river and* launched an assault, mowing down the greater part of their forces and driving the survivors to seek refuge within the walls of the nearby towns, but these were besieged and stormed. The males of fighting age were killed, but the remainder of **their inhabitants were sold into slavery.** *Others among the natives had also congregated to oppose him,* leading the king to attack another substantial fortified city, where 20,000 people were sheltering. **The Indians fought back manfully from barricades in their streets, driving back the Macedonians and slaying a significant number of Alexander's men.** But when the onslaught was resumed, the Indians abandoned all hope of successful resistance and began to set light to their houses, roasting themselves within them together with their spouses and offspring. Ironically, therefore, the aggressors found themselves fighting to extinguish the flames, whilst the defenders sought to spread the conflagration in a perverse inversion of normal fighting conditions. **Most of the inhabitants were incinerated, but three thousand had escaped to the citadel. These waved fronds in supplication and were pardoned by Alexander.**

11.45 **The king** occupied the citadel of this great stronghold with a garrison of his sick and injured troops, before sailing on past **with his fleet to the** *nearby* **confluence of the conjoined Acesines-Hydaspes with the Indus river,** for this city had been protected on its northern side by the latter stream as well as on its southern margin by the former.[366] *These are the mightiest rivers in India with the exception of the Ganges, so* **the turbulence at their union is** *correspondingly* **intense, generating surges and deadly vortices** *like a stormy sea. Boats may only pass via constricted channels, since the riverbed is heaped with numerous banks of viscid sludge, which are constantly shifting about through the action of the current. The fleet met these shoals at speed whilst under sail,* causing many vessels *to be buffeted by successive violent swells and* to career out of the control of their helmsmen *before their canvases could be furled. Some of the ships collided and* two of the galleys were sunk whilst all looked on. Many of the vessels of a lesser draught *were also rendered unmanageable by the wild waters, but* were driven aground *intact at the riverbank.*

---

[366] Probably therefore located in the vicinity of modern Sitpur.

Book 11: July 326BC – Late Spring 325BC

11.46 Alexander's flagship was swept headlong into the most dangerous area of rapids, *which twisted it sideways-on to the current, such that its pilot could no longer steer it. The king had stripped with the intention of throwing himself into the torrent and his Friends were ready to swim beside him in order to rescue him* from drowning, *but it seemed just as risky to take to the water as to press on in their careening vessel. Therefore, they set to their oars in a concerted strenuous effort, and fought against the surges that sought to overwhelm them with as much force as humans can exert. It seemed as if the waves were rent asunder and the eddies retreated before them. When finally their ship was extricated from the maelstrom, they could not manage to dock it at the bank, but rather grounded it on the nearest sandbar.* On getting safely to shore, Alexander sacrificed to the gods for his deliverance from dire danger, *erecting altars in equal number to the channels of the divided watercourse and* comparing his own battle with a river to that of Achilles.

11.47 *Meanwhile Indian philosophers, natives of this region, who made do with a folded over cloak and no other clothing, dispatched the following letter to Alexander: "From the Indian philosophers to Alexander of Macedon,* Greeting. *We have heard that your Friends are endeavouring to persuade you to make war against us and our region, so as to bring it into your hands, though not even in their sleep have they dreamt of our mode of life; if you attempt to follow their advice, you will only be able to herd our bodies around, for our spirits can neither be led astray nor made to do anything unwillingly, though you bring the greatest force to bear upon us;* nay, no more than you would be able to make rocks or trees converse with you.[367] We can inflict the greatest pain and the greatest injury upon ourselves, for **our living bodies can triumph over fire: we walk upon it of our own volition and a part of our bodies** ascends in the flames. No king or prince **throughout the land has the power** ever to succeed in compelling us to do what we do not choose to do. *That which is actually bestowed through divine inspiration is most of all in the hands of god. We strive hard fully to comprehend that which we hold dear and consider to be profitable in life and we have the free use of other men's property. We are gladly praised, since investments* made by others *end up proving worthless. And we are not at all like the philosophers of the Greeks, who are only mighty in their speeches: when we venture to speak, our actions always correspond to our words. Hence the greatest value is vested in us, for we embody the truth and liberty of our most ancient past. Therefore, refrain from applying force in this matter, since nothing can be taken away from us against our will. But if, nevertheless, you direct yourself against us, it will be seen as unjust and foreign to that virtue, which good men strive to cultivate."*

---

[367] Perhaps this quip, inferred from Philo, Every Good Man Is Free 96 and St Ambrosius, Letter 37.35, was the inspiration for the story in the Romance about Alexander's conversations with trees in India.

11.48 *Being disturbed by this letter,* Alexander *advanced with his army for thirty stades and* entered upon the lands of the Oxydracae and the Malli. Both were bellicose, teeming tribes, who traditionally fought each other, but at this time, in view of their mutual peril, they had formed an alliance *to oppose Alexander.* In order to cement this pact, they exchanged 10,000 virgin brides between them. United, they fielded *the most powerful army in the Indus River region, comprising* 80,000 infantry *recruited from their younger men* and 10,000 cavalry with 700 chariots besides.

11.49 But when the Macedonians, who had believed themselves relieved from deadly duties, learnt that that they were confronted with renewed campaigning against the most ferocious people in India, they dreaded this unforeseen peril and rounded on their king with seditious recriminations: their leverage had but shifted the battle-ground from the River Ganges and beyond rather than ended the war. They were being put up against fiercely independent natives, so that their blood would clear a path to the Ocean. They were being drawn beyond the Sun and the stars and driven to approach that which Nature herself had concealed from mortal gaze. Again and again new enemies were manifested to meet their refurbished arms. And even if they routed and dispersed all of these, what recompense awaited them? Glooming darkness and eternal night extending to cloak a sea swarming with schools of gargantuan monsters and channelling irresistible currents, via which expiring Nature is swept away.

11.50 Not for his own sake, but stimulated rather by his soldiers' anxiety, the king convened an Assembly, reassuring his men that those they dreaded were irresolute warriors. After them no other tribe obstructed their traversal of wide-open country to reach the end of both their travails and the world itself. As a concession to their fears, he had forsaken the River Ganges and the populous nations that lay beyond its torrent. He had turned aside to lead them whither undiminished glory might be won with less peril. Before them lay the prospect of the Ocean. Already the taint of the sea blew upon the breeze. Let them not begrudge him his quest for renown. They would surpass the limits set by Heracles and Dionysus, thereby assuring their king of everlasting fame at scant risk to themselves. Let them permit him simply to withdraw rather than flee from India.

11.51 All crowds are easily swayed, and crowds of troops especially so; hence an outbreak of sedition may be cured as trivially as it was instigated. Never before had such a joyful clamour resounded among the ranks of the army. They called upon him to lead them onwards and, with divine favour, to match the glory of those in whose footsteps they trod. Buoyed up by their acclamation, Alexander straightaway broke camp and deployed against the enemy. These were the mightiest nations of the Indus region and they were making strenuous preparations for war, so they had picked a man of proven valour from the Oxydracae as their commander. He had chosen to establish his base among the

Book 11: July 326BC – Late Spring 325BC

foothills of a mountain,[368] distributing his campfires over a wide area, so as to convey an impression of a vast host. Furthermore, the Indians sought to instil fear by means of their customary bellows and war cries, though to no avail in the face of the resilience of the Macedonians. Then, as day was dawning, a blithely confident and optimistic Alexander issued the order for his cheery troops to take up their arms and advance to battle. *Yet the barbarians spontaneously took to their heels, fleeing into the nearby cities* or taking inaccessible refuge among the peaks, ostensibly **due to a quarrel regarding the leadership, else perhaps inspired by terror of the Macedonians, when their commander, whose name was Sambus, happened to be transfixed through both his thighs by a three-foot bolt from a Macedonian catapult.** The king captured their baggage train during the pursuit, but failed to overtake the bulk of their forces.

11.52 Next Alexander approached *and surrounded* the principal city *of the Oxydracae wherein many of the enemy had sought refuge, though they trusted in its walls no more than in their weapons.* Alexander was on the verge of launching his attack, when one among the seers, a man named Demophon, came forward and announced to the king that many omens had foretold a great danger to Alexander's life from a wound he would sustain in the action. He besought Alexander to abandon the operation or at least to divert himself elsewhere for the time being. *But the king glared at the prophet, challenging him: "If someone were thus to interrupt you, whilst you were intent upon your craft and busied with interpretation of the signs, I do not doubt that you would regard that person as a tactless irritant."* And when Demophon conceded that it would absolutely be so, he rebuked the seer for having disconcerted the soldiers, *inquiring: "When I have before my gaze weighty matters, rather than animal offal, could anything be a greater nuisance than a soothsayer obsessed with superstitions?"*

11.53 Loitering no longer than needed to dismiss the seer, *Alexander deployed his forces and personally led the advance, being keen to capture the city in this assault. His war engines lagged behind, but he battered down a side gate and led the break-in, felling many opponents and chasing the rest into their citadel. Therefore,* he ordered scaling ladders brought up and, since the rest of the Macedonians were dawdling *in the attack upon the wall,* he himself seized a ladder, propped it against the rampart of the citadel and clambered up to its parapet, *whilst holding a rimless shield*[369] *over his head. He moved so quickly, that he gained the parapet before the defenders could oppose him. Due to the crest of the wall being narrow and lacking in crenellations, but obstructed by a continuous breastwork, the king clung there precariously,* **raising his shield to parry a rain of arrows and**

---

[368] Perhaps Gendari Mt.

[369] A πελτη a round shield only 60cm or 70cm in diameter.

javelins flung at long range *from the various towers of the citadel, for the Indians did not dare grapple with him hand to hand*. At first his soldiers were impeded from supporting him by a storm of missiles, but shame vanquished their *sense of* peril, as they perceived that Alexander was being given up to the enemy through their hesitation. Whilst the king staggered under the onslaught, they raised two ladders and surged up them, but in such numbers that both collapsed, causing all upon them to plummet to the ground.

11.54 Hence Alexander stood utterly alone upon the battlements; isolated, though in plain view of his vast army, and his left arm bearing his shield was already tiring from the continual need to fend off the enemy's projectiles. *His Friends below screamed for him to leap down into their waiting arms, but* it seemed to him quite at odds with his reputation for valorous victory that he should impotently retreat from even so dangerous a predicament. Instead, he had the astonishing temerity to vault down within the ramparts of the citadel with naught but his armour to protect him from his seething opponents. *Had he stumbled in landing, he might instantly have been overwhelmed and captured, but by good fortune he alighted upon his feet, poised to defend himself.* Fortune had *also* thwarted his encirclement, for an ancient tree was rooted upon his right close by the wall, *its branches thick with foliage, as though designed for the purpose of securing his flank*. Thus, he ensconced himself between the huge girth of its trunk and the wall, blocking every bolt hurled by the Indians and putting up such a courageous resistance as befitted a king with so many illustrious deeds to his name. *His fame was itself a kind of haven, since none of his foes dared approach him, all being content merely to fling missiles from afar*. Despairing of his safety, he remained resolute that his final feats should secure him a supremely glorious death.

11.55 *Though most of the enemy's projectiles were deflected by branches*, the king received a great many strikes upon his shield and his helmet was battered and dented by stones. *As he wearied under the relentless pressure, he sank to his knees, thereby tempting his less cautious assailants to close in upon him. Two of these he slew with his sword, leaving them slumped lifeless at his feet. This sapped the courage of the rest, who again kept their distance, but persisted in pelting him with missiles from a safe range. Despite everything he maintained a stout defence, until* at last an Indian archer shot an arrow two cubits long so well aimed that it pierced his cuirass and lodged just beneath his breast *slightly above his right lung* not far from his gullet. *A great jet of blood gushed forth from the wound,* the shock of which caused him to *lower his guard and* topple onto one knee *as if mortally injured. Vainly he sought to pluck the shaft from his chest with his right hand, on seeing which* the archer sprang forward eager to despoil his victim. *But the indignity of the Indian's hands grappling with him*

Book 11: July 326BC – Late Spring 325BC

revived Alexander *sufficiently for him to* thrust his sword upwards into his enemy's exposed flank, inflicting a fatal gash.

11.56 *Now a triad of bodies were laid low around the king, whilst* most of *his surviving antagonists stood back in stupefaction,* but another Indian scurried out of a mill and thwacked Alexander's head from behind with a cudgel, leaving him dazed. Nevertheless, *the king struggled to rise to his feet by using his shield as a prop, thinking to die fighting, ere he drifted into unconsciousness. Yet lacking the strength to get upright,* he grabbed with his right hand for support from the branches hanging over him. *Even so he could not manage to stay on his feet, but sank once more to his knees, gesticulating defiance at his assailants and daring them to take him on hand to hand.*

11.57 At this juncture, Peucestes, one of the hypaspists, arrived in Alexander's footsteps to raise his shield over the king, having used a ladder to surmount a section of wall *that he had swept clear of defenders. Alexander looked to him rather for camaraderie in death than for preservation of his life, allowing his exhausted body to slump over his shield. But shortly afterwards more Macedonian guardsmen appeared: Limnaeus next, then successively Leonnatus and Aristonous. Nevertheless, word of Alexander's plight within their walls had spread to the other Indians, who now abandoned the defences in other sectors and sped to join the assault upon his handful of protectors. Of these, Limnaeus suffered many injuries in the course of a magnificent fighting stand and eventually perished in the onslaught. Peucestes, despite being gouged by three javelins, persisted in holding his shield over the king, rather than protect himself. Leonnatus valiantly repelled the frenzied charges of the barbarians, until he was gravely stricken in the neck* and pierced through his right thigh, *collapsing semi-conscious at the feet of the king. As Peucestes, enfeebled by many gashes, permitted his shield to droop, their sole hope of salvation rested in Aristonous, yet he too had received severe wounds and could no longer resist such an aggressive horde of opponents.*

Figure 11.2. An overloaded ladder breaks at the siege (André Castaigne, 1899).

Book 11: July 326BC – Late Spring 325BC

Figure 11.3. Alexander's lone defence within the Indian citadel (anon. 1696)

11.58 *In the interim a rumour had reached* the Macedonians *that Alexander had perished. Though this news might have deterred another army, it drew* *an incensed reaction from the Macedonians. Insensible of any peril, they hacked their way through the defences with pick-axes,* even adapting their swords to the task. **Having broken open a gateway, they surged into the citadel with Ptolemy to the fore**, *whereby he merited his later title of "saviour".*[370] **Hardly any of the Indians stood their ground in the face of so many invaders, but instead they fled in panic,** *including those surrounding Alexander.* **Considering that any of the occupants might have been complicit in the wounding of their king and seized by a fury of vengeance, the Macedonians slew all that they found, sparing neither the women, nor the aged, nor even the very young. Only when they had filled the city with corpses** and levelled its buildings over them *did they feel that their righteous malice had been sated.*

11.59 Alexander was conveyed to his pavilion, where the medics sliced off the wooden shaft of the arrow embedded in his body, whilst avoiding disturbing its head. *Thereby they were able to remove his breastplate, which had been pinioned to him.* With his body bared, they determined that the arrowhead was barbed; hence it could not be extracted without massive trauma to the body, unless the wound were surgically widened. But they were fearful that they would be unable to staunch the haemorrhage from the surgery, for the arrowhead was enormous, *perhaps three finger-widths broad and four in length,* and it appeared to have penetrated through to the internal organs. The doctor, Critobulus, though he was a paragon of the physician's art, was yet horrified by the magnitude of the risk. He dreaded engaging upon the task, lest the consequences of his skills proving inadequate should rebound upon his own head. Noticing that Critobulus was tearful and turned deathly pale with anxiety, Alexander asked: "What are you waiting for? Why not release me from this agony as soon as possible, even if it mean my death? Why should you fear any blame, if I have received a mortal wound?" At length, having set aside his fear or at least concealed it, Critobulus implored the king to allow himself to be held down, whilst he withdrew the point, since even a slight shift of his body could be harmful. After having assured the doctor that no restraint was needed, Alexander kept still as instructed, without the least flinching.

11.60 Therefore the wound was enlarged and the arrowhead was extracted, whereupon a copious effusion of blood induced the king to lose consciousness. With darkness veiling his vision, he lay supine as if at the verge of death, whilst the medics sought in vain to stem the flow of blood with poultices. All at once Alexander's Friends began to wail and lament, believing that their king had expired. But eventually the haemorrhaging ceased and Alexander gradually regained consciousness, becoming aware of those gathered around him. Throughout that day and the ensuing night, the army invested the royal quarters in battle dress, acknowledging that all of them survived through their king's inspiration. Nor were they persuaded to depart, until they ascertained that he had

---

[370] I.e. "Soter" in Greek; see Arrian, *Anabasis* 6.11.8 – perhaps actually awarded by the Rhodians.

Book 11: July 326BC – Late Spring 325BC

been sleeping comfortably for a little while, whereupon they returned to camp with good hopes for his recovery.

11.61 After seven days of care and convalescence, his wound had not yet scarred over, but Alexander heard tell that exaggerated rumours of his death were spreading among the Indians. Therefore, he instructed that two ships should be fastened alongside each other with his tent erected so as to be conspicuous in the middle. Hence, he could show himself alive to those who had believed the false reports that he had perished. And being thus manifested before the eyes of the inhabitants, he dashed the misconceived hopes of those who opposed him. Afterwards he sailed on downstream, keeping a short space ahead of his fleet, in order not to disturb the tranquillity essential to his recuperation with the incessant plashing of the oars.

11.62 During the fourth day after setting out, Alexander reached an area that had been evacuated by its natives, but was plentifully stocked with grain and cattle. The place appealed to him for resting both himself and his troops. It was customary for the leading Friends and the Bodyguards to stand watch in front of the royal lodgings whenever the king was in poor health. Since this practice was being observed at that time, they were all of them able to enter his bedchamber together. And since they all entered at once, Alexander was concerned in case they intended to impart some grave tidings, querying whether the enemy had launched a surprise attack? However, Craterus, who had been appointed spokesman for supplications from the king's Friends, responded thus:[371] "Do you suppose that we could be made more anxious by the approach of the enemy, even if they now stood before our palisades, than we already are through our duty of care for your well-being, which you deem inconsequential? However great a strength every nation may join in fielding against us, though they cram the world with arms and men and strew the sea with their fleets, even if they goad alien monsters into harrowing us,[372] you stand as guarantor of our invincibility. Yet what divinity may promise that this pillar and Star of Macedon will endure, when you rampantly expose your person to manifest perils, oblivious to having thereby dragged so many of your countrymen to the brink of disaster? Who among us, indeed, would be either desirous or capable of surviving your death? Following your guidance and your commands we have reached this place, whence none of us can return without you to lead us back home."

---

[371] Arrian, Anabasis 6.13.4, mentions that Nearchus recorded the ensuing admonition of Alexander by his Friends; if so, then Curtius probably found it in Cleitarchus, since his Fragments strongly suggest that Nearchus was one of his sources.

[372] "Alien monsters" (invisitatas beluas) is of course a reference to elephants, yet these beasts are unlikely to have been unfamiliar to Curtius, who was probably Proconsul of the Roman Province of Africa in the mid-first century AD: this terminology therefore hints that Curtius is paraphrasing an early source, most probably Cleitarchus.

Figure 11.4. The wounded Alexander sails past troops (André Castaigne, 1899).

11.63 "Were you still disputing the rule of Persia with Darius, though none of us would wish it, nobody would be astonished by your readiness to deal audaciously with every hazard. For when the prize is equal to the peril, not only are the fruits of success more honourable, but there is also nobility in defeat. Yet who could bear that the taking of a humble hamlet should cost you your life? Not even those among the foreigners that recognise your greatness, let alone your own soldiers! My spirit quails in recollecting the drama, which we witnessed a little while ago. I fear to speak of how those most cowardly hands might have tarnished the armour stripped from your invincible corpse, had not Fortune taken pity on us and brought about your rescue."

11.64 "We're just a gang of villains, a bunch of deserters, all of us who were unable to catch up with you. Branding all your soldiers to signal their disgrace would be entirely justified and none will shirk his punishment for the offence, even though none had any chance of forestalling it. However, I beg you to allow us to become your villains in its other sense. Wherever you direct us, we shall go. Abject perils and ignominious skirmishes we crave for ourselves. Let you reserve yourself for matters suited to your eminence. Nothing is more disreputable than wasting a reputation where it cannot be flaunted, for fame fades fast in fighting filthy foes!" Ptolemy too spoke in this vein and the rest of them likewise. By then a jabber of voices were bewailing Alexander to refrain from becoming a glutton for glory and to take due care of his personal welfare, which was identical with the security of the state.

11.65 The king was gratified by the devotion of his Friends, being moved to embrace them individually with special fondness. Then, having invited them to be seated, he began nobly and reflectively to address them: "Particularly to you, my most loyal compatriots and truest companions, I offer my sincere gratitude,

Book 11: July 326BC – Late Spring 325BC

not just by virtue of your concern this day for my welfare above your own, but also because you have stinted me neither pledges nor proofs of your goodwill towards me since the outset of our campaign. So much so that I confide that I have never before held my life so dear as henceforth: in order that I may take protracted pleasure in your friendship. Yet my views are at odds with those who wish to die in my stead, for I actually judge that it is through my valour that I have merited your continuing goodwill. Though indeed you may aspire to long-lasting benefits through me, perhaps even perpetual profits, it is not the length of my life by which I measure myself, but rather by the endurance of my fame.[373] It was an option for me to have been satisfied with my father's realm, idly lurking within Macedonia's bounds pending an obscure and dishonourable dotage. Yet even the unadventurous cannot prescribe their fates, for premature death often seizes those who suppose length of days to be the only true blessing. But I, who count my victories rather than my years, if Fortune's favours be rightly reckoned, have already lived a long while."

11.66 "Starting out with Macedonia, I have retained the dominion of Greece; I have subjugated Thrace and the Illyrians; the Triballians and the Maedi obey my commands; from the Hellespontine shore to the Red Sea surf, Asia lies in my possession. And now I am not far from the end of this world, upon going beyond which I plan to open up another Nature, a different Earth. I once passed from within the confines of Asia across to Europe in a single hour.[374] Having become the conqueror of both sides of the continental divide[375] in the ninth year of my reign and the twenty-eighth of my life, can you conceive of my relinquishing the pursuit of fame, which has been the sole object of my existence? I'll not deviate from my true path, and wherever I may fight, I shall consider that I am performing within the theatre of the entire Earth. I shall grant distinction to wretched places and I shall open up to all peoples lands which Nature has set apart."

11.67 "To lose my life in these enterprises, as chance may have it, would be a splendid way to go. I am sprung from such a lineage that I am bound to seek a crowded life rather than a long one.[376] I implore you to ponder upon our having reached a territory where a woman is famed for her gallantry. Semiramis founded such cities, brought so many nations beneath her sway and accomplished such great deeds! Are we already nauseated by a surfeit of fame, when we have still not matched a woman in renown? If the gods be willing, even greater feats lie before us. Yet those future accomplishments shall never be ours, unless we reckon nothing trivial, in which there is actually scope for great glory. Therefore, let you

---

[373] This is "The Choice of Achilles", cf. Iliad 9.410-416.

[374] Curtius 9.6.21, *ex Asia in Europae terminos*, refers to the crossing of the supposed Tanais in 8.50.

[375] Curtius is rather ambiguous, but this looks like a reference to Alexander's crossing of the Hindu Kush into India in 327BC.

[376] A clear reference to his putative descent from Achilles.

but preserve me from perfidious plots and court conspiracies and I shall confront the crises of war and Ares himself undaunted."

11.68 "Philip was better guarded in battle than in the theatre: he often dodged the clutches of his enemies, but could not escape those of his own subjects. Also, if you review the deaths of other monarchs, you will count more who were slain by their own people than by foes. Aside from this, I'll take this opportunity to air a matter that I've long been turning over in my mind. I shall obtain the greatest gratification from my labours and exertions, if my mother Olympias should be accorded divine honours upon her demise.[377] If I get the chance, I shall personally put this into effect; but if fate should forestall me, recall that I have laid this onus upon you all." Then he excused his Friends, but he kept camp in that place for many days thereafter.

11.69 Whilst these things transpired in India, **the Greek troops whom Alexander had recently settled around Bactra** *and in Sogdiana, received word that the king had died of his wounds. Disgruntled by their life among foreigners, they hatched dissension among themselves. After* they heard that the king yet lived, **they launched a full rebellion against the Macedonians**, though more from fear of castigation than from animosity towards Alexander. For, having slaughtered some of their fellows, the dominant faction began to look to their weaponry. Then, having seized the citadel of Bactra, which had been guarded somewhat negligently, they managed to compel the barbarians to defect to their cause. Their leader was Athenodorus, who actually assumed the title of king, though not so much because he coveted power, as to provide himself with the authority to lead his countrymen back to their homeland. However, jealousy inspired hostility towards him in a fellow Greek, named Biton, who concocted a plot whereby Athenodorus was invited to a feast by Boxus, a Bactrian, and slain in the course of the entertainment. During the ensuing day, Biton convoked an assembly and persuaded most of the Greeks that Athenodorus had in fact been conspiring to take his life; but others felt that Biton was deceiving them and little by little the suspicion began to spread to more of them. Hence the Greek soldiers took up their arms, intending to kill Biton at the earliest opportunity. However, the rest of the leading men managed to quell the anger of the crowd.

11.70 Despite having been snatched from impending peril, much against his apprehensions, just a little while later Biton authored a conspiracy against his deliverers. But when his treachery was detected, they arrested both him and Boxus. The rest of the leadership were satisfied to have Boxus executed

---

[377] Curtius 10.5.30 also notes Alexander's wish that Olympias be accorded divine honours, hence this request is probably historical and Alexander truly made it in the aftermath of his near-death experience, perhaps seeking to bolster his own claim to divine honours through inheritance. Curtius 10.5.11 records that the Macedonians had refused such honours to Alexander himself, whereas it appears that Philip had received divinisation prior to his assassination in the light of Diodorus 16.92.5 & 16.95.1 (Philip's statue paraded with the Olympians) and M. N. Tod, Greek Historical Inscriptions 191.6 (altars erected to "Zeus Philippios" at Eresus on Lesbos).

Book 11: July 326BC – Late Spring 325BC

straightaway, but Biton they chose to torture to death. And they were already instigating his torments, when the Greeks, as if driven mad (for their reason is uncertain), rushed to take up their arms. With the roars of the mob resounding in their ears, those assigned to contort Biton let him go, fearing that the tumult was directed at inhibiting their task. When their victim, stripped naked as he was, appeared before the Greeks, the pitiful figure of the condemned man inspired them with forgiveness, so they issued orders for his release. In this fashion Biton was once again reprieved from due punishment, so he returned to Greece with **a band of three thousand men** who *abandoned the colonies founded by Alexander and* **underwent great hardships during their homeward trek.** Such were the events in the vicinity of Bactra and the marches of Scythia.

11.71 *These were the concerns of Alexander* in the eleventh year of his reign.

Book 12: Late Spring 325BC – June 324BC

Southern India and its Ocean; The March through the Kedrosian Desert; The Dionysiac Comus and The Return to Persia.

12.1 *As the twelfth year of his reign began, Alexander completed his recovery from the chest wound that had so nearly proved fatal.* **When the king had been made better,** a delegation of **the Malli and Oxydracae** a hundred strong presented themselves before him. They all arrived in chariots and were powerfully built men with an air of proud dignity. Their dress was of linen, chased through with threads of gold and purple. They **conceded the subjugation of** their towns, their lands and **their persons to Alexander's authority**, thus relinquishing their accustomed liberty and placing their faith in the king's protection and good government. They asserted that it was an oracle of their gods that had motivated their submission, for their strength in arms remained undiminished. Alexander took counsel with his Friends before granting them his protection in exchange for their fealty. He further directed that a tribute, which these nations had paid to the Arachosii, should instead be delivered to him and he ordered that they should furnish 2500 cavalrymen to augment his forces. These commands were faithfully performed by the Indians.

12.2 *Alexander sacrificed to the gods for his salvation and arranged a sumptuous banquet for his Friends and the Indian envoys and magnates.* A hundred golden couches were arrayed side by side, each draped about with purple tapestries glinting with strands of gold. *After much wine had been drunk at this magnificent feast, there transpired a notable incident.* There was present one of Alexander's Companions, a Macedonian called Corragus, who possessed great bodily strength and was a gallant veteran of numerous battles. Spurred by the alcohol he challenged Dioxippus of Athens to a duel, *saying he should agree to meet him in armed combat if he were a man.* The Athenian was a renowned athlete, who had been crowned as victor in the boxing contest at the Olympic Games. Naturally the drunken guests encouraged their rivalry; therefore, Dioxippus accepted the challenge, *contemptuous of the soldier's bravado. On the following day the king sought to dissuade them, yet their resolve had hardened, so* Alexander fixed a date for the contest.

12.3 When the appointed day came tens of thousands of men turned out to witness the spectacle. Many of the troops, especially the Greeks, backed Dioxippus, but Alexander and the Macedonians favoured Corragus, because he was their countryman. The pair progressed to the field of combat, the Macedonian arrayed in his costly panoply and bearing a shield and his usual weapons: a sarissa in his left hand, a javelin in his right and a sword slung from a strap, as if he were up against a whole team of

Book 12: Late Spring 325BC – June 324BC

opponents. But the Athenian came naked and gleaming with oil, garlanded and carrying a purple drape in his left hand, whilst bearing a well-proportioned club in his right. Both exhibited splendid physiques and their bodily strength was regarded with wonderment. The crowd looked forward to a battle of the gods, for the Macedonian by his bearing and his shining armaments evoked trepidation as though he were Ares, whilst Dioxippus through his surpassing strength and fitness and particularly on account of the club bore close comparison with Heracles. *The audience was thrilled with keen anticipation by the disparity, since it seemed not merely rash, but actually insane for a nude man to confront an opponent in full armour.*

12.4 As the two closed the Macedonian, believing that the Greek could be dispatched at range, hurled his javelin, but Dioxippus dodged its impact with a slight twist of his torso. Then Corragus charged, whilst swapping his sarissa into his right hand, but the Greek too leapt forward and shattered the shaft of the sarissa with a single blow of his club. Having suffered twin setbacks through the loss of both of his spears, Corragus was forced to resort to his sword. But even as he sought to draw it, Dioxippus grasped the Macedonian's right wrist with his left hand and pushed with his own right to cause his foe to lose his balance, then tripped and butted Corragus, so that he tumbled to the ground. Snatching away the sword, the Greek set his foot upon the Macedonian's neck, as he lay recumbent. Finally, he raised his club poised to crush his defeated adversary and looked to the spectators to decide Corragus' fate.

12.5 The crowd was in tumult at the paradoxical and overwhelming nature of the Greek's skill, but the king signalled that he should release Corragus, and then ordered the gathering to disperse. Alexander was clearly displeased, for the spectacle had exposed the Macedonian reputation for valour and prowess in arms to ridicule in full view of the barbarians. Yet Dioxippus freed his fallen foe and departed the scene of his triumph bound about with ribbons by his fellow Greeks, who basked in the reflected glory from their countryman. But Fortune curtailed his opportunity to brag about his victory.

12.6 Alexander grew increasingly hostile to Dioxippus, for his ears were opened to the resentful lies of his Friends and other Macedonian courtiers. A few days later these men persuaded one of the attendants at a feast to conceal a golden cup beneath the pillow of Dioxippus' couch. During the banquet the staff reported its loss and the Macedonians pretended shock at its discovery, accusing the Greek of its theft. Thus, Dioxippus was placed in a shameful and embarrassing quandary. Perceiving that the Macedonians were united against him, he could not endure the stigma of theft, so he quit the banquet.

12.7 A little later on reaching his personal quarters he composed a letter to Alexander exposing the ruse of which he had been the victim. This he placed in the hands of his servants for delivery to the king. Then he took his own life by running himself through with his sword. Though he had been indiscreet in accepting the challenge to single combat, it was downright foolish of him to commit suicide in these circumstances. For many who had despised him, now mocked his folly, joking that it was hard to live with his fate of being endowed with great bodily strength, but a tiny mind. **Let us learn from this not to allow the body's strength to become the soul's weakness; let us consider wisdom to be the soul's strength.**[378]

12.8 Alexander read the letter and was moved to grief and anger by Dioxippus' death, *which he recognised to have been inspired by indignation and despair rather than guilt.* Afterwards, he frequently mourned the virtues of the man whom he had neglected in life, but whose death he now regretted. Only when it was futile did he appreciate the excellence of Dioxippus contrasted with the calumny of his detractors.

12.9 The Indian envoys were given leave to return home *to report the success of their mission*, but they returned a few days later bringing tributary gifts for Alexander. These comprised 300 cavalrymen, 1030 chariots each drawn by four horses abreast, a substantial amount of linen cloth, 1000 Indian shields, 100 talents of white iron, remarkably large lions and tigers, but all trained for handling, and also the skins of gargantuan lizards and the shells of tortoises. *Afterwards Alexander issued orders to Craterus to march the main army downstream, whilst maintaining contact with the river. But those who had been escorting him in the fleet he re-embarked and sailed with them towards the Ocean through the territory of the Malli.*

12.10 The king next reached the lands of the Sambastae, a people who were the equal of any in India in numbers and breeding. Their cities were ruled in a democratic fashion and hearing of the approach of the Macedonians, they gathered an army of 60,000 infantry, 6000 cavalry and 500 armoured chariots, *which they placed under the command of three generals, distinguished in the conduct of warfare. Yet the folk in the fields on the banks of the river, inhabitants of a multiplicity of villages, watched amazed as the entire sweep of the stream within their gaze became crammed with vessels each scintillating with the arms of innumerable troops. Astounded by the novelty of the scene, they believed they saw a heavenly host led by a new Dionysus, a god whose name was hallowed among those nations. And so the bellows of the soldiers and the plashing pulse of the oars and the sailors' chant of mutual exhortation flooded the ears of the natives filling them with terror. They fled to their own men-at-arms shouting that*

---

[378] This is Fragment 39 of Cleitarchus (Maximi, *Eclogae* II 734 B), considered doubtful by Jacoby, but it might be fitted to this context.

Book 12: Late Spring 325BC – June 324BC

they were mad to seek battle with so many divine and invincible heroes. The Indian troops being thus disconcerted and the elders of their nation also counselling against a risky fight, the Sambastae dispatched an embassy of fifty of their chief men to Alexander to seek favourable treatment from him. The king praised them for the wisdom of their submission to his authority **and concluded a peace treaty with them, being heaped with lavish presents and heroic honours in return.**

12.11 *Four days travel downstream tribes living on either side of the river, who were called the Sodrae and the Massani, submitted to Alexander.* At this place the king founded a city, Alexandria-beside-the-river, and designated ten thousand persons as its populace. Afterwards he entered the lands of **King Musicanus,** *at which juncture he held a trial for the satrap Terioltes, due to charges laid against him by the people of the Paropamisus range, of whom Alexander had made him the governor. Finding him guilty of many acts of avarice and tyranny, the king ordered his execution. Yet Oxyartes, leader of the Bactrians, was not merely absolved of guilt, but was thereby granted the rule of more extensive territories among the Paropamisadae, due to his bond of affection with Alexander.* A campaign was undertaken to complete the subjugation of the Musicani and the king left a garrison to secure their principal town. *Also at this time Alexander sent Craterus and Polyperchon back to Babylonia with a great part of the army, whilst he himself sailed on downstream towards the shore of the Ocean with select regiments.*

12.12 Alexander next launched an invasion through the forests to a wild part of India, where lay the kingdom of Porticanus. He stormed and captured two cities, allowing his troops to ransack their dwellings prior to setting them ablaze. Porticanus together with a great section of his population ensconced themselves in a fortified city, but Alexander overwhelmed its defences after a siege lasting three days. Porticanus retreated to its citadel *and sent out envoys to seek terms of surrender from Alexander, but, before they had a chance to treat with the king, two towers collapsed with a resounding boom and the Macedonians surged across their ruins into the stronghold.* After its fall, Porticanus was slain as he made a last stand with a few loyal followers. *Having demolished the citadel,* Alexander *sold those captured into slavery, and then* went on to capture the other cities of the kingdom, razing them all and thereby inspiring much fear of him throughout those lands.

12.13 Afterwards Alexander ravaged the realm of King Sambus, where many towns submitted to his authority, but the strongest city of the nation was taken by digging beneath its ramparts. *The barbarians were ignorant of military engineering tactics, so it seemed to them a supernatural horror when armed men rose up out of the earth near the centre of their city, since they had not noticed any prior sign of the mining operation.* Most of the cities of this region were obliterated and the king sold their inhabitants at auction, though more than 80,000 of the Indians were cut down *in the fighting.*

The sect known as the Brahmins shared in this catastrophe, but their survivors came before Alexander as suppliants waving fronds of foliage, so he absolved them, punishing only the worst culprits. King Sambus himself abandoned the struggle and escaped with thirty elephants into the territory on the other side of India.

12.14 At this time the Musicani launched a rebellion. Alexander entrusted Pithon with the task of suppressing their revolt, which he accomplished by capturing its leader: King Musicanus himself. Pithon arraigned his prisoner before Alexander, who had the man crucified, before rejoining his fleet, where it lay moored upon the river.

12.15 Three days later whilst travelling downstream Alexander reached a town at the far end of the kingdom of Sambus. *He had reached Harmatelia, the last city of the Brahmins, whose citizens were so confident of its invulnerability and so proud of their own valour that they forswore the submission of the realm and closed their gates against the king.* But Alexander sent a force of five hundred of his fleet-footed Agrianians to assault the ramparts, considering that their sparse numbers would be deemed contemptible. Their orders were to lure the enemy into an engagement beyond their walls, then steadily to retreat once they had been counter attacked. Around 3000 fighters spewed forth from the city, whereupon Alexander's contingent *turned their backs and* rushed away in feigned flight. The barbarians leapt after them in a hot pursuit, but were subsequently intercepted and surprised by forces led by Alexander himself. Charging furiously into the fray, the king's troops slew 600 of the barbarians and captured 1000 more, the remnants being chased back within their defences.

12.16 *Yet this was not so splendid and joyful a victory as at first appeared, as events went on to show.* Those among Alexander's forces who had suffered wounds were now exposed anew to mortal danger. The Brahmins had smeared their weapons with a deadly toxin, which indeed had been the basis of their confidence in joining battle. The potency of the poison was derived from a species of snake, which was hunted down and its carcass placed in the sun. The scorching radiance melted the flesh of the creature such that it sweated moisture and through this liquefaction the animal's venom was gleaned. By its action the bodies of the wounded at first became numbed, then little by little sharp pains developed and the victims were racked by shivering and convulsions. Their skin became clammy and grey and they began to vomit bile, whilst a dark spume seeped out of their gashes, which started to putrefy. The gangrene spread rapidly to overwhelm key parts of the body, thus inflicting a wretched death upon the sufferer. Whether the wound was great or small or even just a scratch, the outcome was the same. *The physicians were perplexed and confounded.*

Book 12: Late Spring 325BC – June 324BC

12.17 *It had been the hope of the barbarians that the rash and fearless Alexander could thus have been eliminated, but though he fought in the thick of the action, the king came through unscathed.* However, Ptolemy, the future king, had been injured *in the left shoulder, and, though the wound was slight, as the casualties began dying,* Alexander was greatly upset, since this man ranked high in his affections. He was a close relative and some said he was a son of Philip: indeed, it was known for sure that he was the son of a woman who had been one of Philip's mistresses. *Furthermore, he was one of Alexander's elite Bodyguards and a most resolute warrior, but even more accomplished and illustrious in the arts of peace than in military crafts. Temperate and courteous in his manner, notably generous and approachable, he had adopted nothing of the arrogance of royalty. Hence it was dubious whether he was more popular with the king or the people, for* his virtues were appreciated by all.

12.18 *So great was the concern of the Macedonians for Ptolemy's well-being that it was as if they had foreseen his later enthronement.* But indeed, on this occasion he received a just reward for his many kindnesses, some said through the intervention of divine Providence. For when Alexander came to visit Ptolemy, *exhausted by the battle and fatigued by worry, he commanded that a bed should be fetched for his own use and he slipped into slumber as soon as he lay down upon it.* On awakening he told of a serpent that had visited him in his dreams gripping a plant between its jaws and of how it had taught him the curative properties and the habitat of this herb. *The king gave out that he would know this plant were it brought before him. Therefore, many joined the search that tracked it down.*

12.19 Alexander ground a poultice from the herb and smeared it on Ptolemy's wound. *The pain was eased straightaway and soon a scab formed over the gash.* The king also brewed a tea from the leaves and had Ptolemy drink it, thus restoring him to health. Now that the virtue of the remedy had been vindicated by Ptolemy's recovery, the therapy was extended to all the afflicted troops and they were similarly cured. Then Alexander renewed his preparations to assault and subjugate Harmatelia, notwithstanding its formidable defences. But its inhabitants, *being thwarted in their hope of inflicting a decisive blow upon the Macedonians,* emerged waving branches in supplication and surrendered.

12.20 *At this same fortified town* **Alexander captured ten of the Indian** naked **philosophers, who had done most to encourage the resistance of King Sambus.** They were reputedly adept at producing witty and concise retorts to all manner of queries. Alexander therefore challenged them: **"Since, Indian philosophers, your enmity to us is manifest,** *and your lives are therefore forfeit,* it would be best to pay attention to what I say. **I will question you one by one, and you will respond** *as best you can.* The first man who gives a wrong answer, I shall put to death, and then according to quality of response *the rest of you shall die.* One among you I shall appoint to judge the replies, and if his adjudication be correct, then he himself shall be granted his life." *Then the chief of them requested whether each of them might be permitted to add explanations to their responses. This Alexander allowed.*

12.21 *Alexander proceeded to pose the question to the first of them of whether the dead or the living were greater in number. The Indian responded: "The living, of course, for those who do not exist cannot have any number."*

12.22 *Alexander asked the second whether the beasts of the land or the sea were more numerous. The Indian responded: "Of the land, of course, for the land contains the sea."*

12.23 *Alexander asked the third: "Which is the most cunning animal?" The Indian responded: "That, of course, which has appeared to no man up until now."*

12.24 *Alexander asked the fourth: "For what reason did you counsel King Sambus to make war against me?" The Indian responded: "So that he might either live or die with his self-respect intact."*

12.25 *Alexander asked the fifth: "Which of night or day was born first?" The Indian responded: "Night was born before day by one day." Alexander was dubious about this response, but noticing this the Indian explained: "Riddling questions will usually elicit riddling answers."*

12.26 *Alexander asked the sixth: "What must a man do in order to make everyone happy?" The Indian responded: "If, being powerful, he looks after them, without being seen to be severe with them."*

12.27 *Alexander asked the seventh, "On what basis can a man seem to be a god?" The Indian responded: "If, whilst being mortal, he does what no man can do."*

12.28 *Alexander inquired of the eighth whether life or death were greater in strength? The Indian responded: "Life, for this reason, that life makes things to exist out of nothing; whereas death makes nothing out of these things."*

12.29 *Alexander asked the ninth: "How long is it beneficial for a man to live?" The Indian replied: "So long as he himself does not perceive death to be more beneficial than life."*

12.30 *Next Alexander asked the last of them, which of those who had spoken appeared to have responded worst, at the same time conjuring him not to exhibit any favour for their cause in his judgement. And he, unwilling to voice his judgement of which of them should perish, said that each of them had answered worse than the others. Alexander retorted: "It is thus clear that all must die including you firstly, who has judged so*

Book 12: Late Spring 325BC – June 324BC

badly." The chief Indian responded: "But, surely, Alexander, it is not kingly to lie, for you said: 'Whichever of you whom I command to judge, if he judge correctly, he will be set free.' I said that each answer was worse than those already given, so I judged myself to have given the worst answer of all, which you have agreed. It was not therefore false, but true judgement. It is not in fact fair to condemn any of us through my judgement. None of us therefore according to your rules should meet with death, for indeed *to avoid* unjustly killing us, not so much to us, but to you yourself is providential." **When Alexander heard all this, he judged them to be wise, so he ordered** gifts and **garments to be given to them and let them go.**

12.31 *It is said that* **Heracles sired** but **one daughter and named her Pandaea. He granted her the rule of the southernmost part of India stretching as far as the Ocean and he divided up the inhabitants of her realm to dwell among 365 villages. He commanded that one village should pay a tax to the queen on each day of the year, his purpose being that those that had recently paid this tribute would support Pandaea in claiming from those whose payment was about to fall due. The people of this region are called the Mandi and the females of their race are mature enough for bearing children at just seven years of age whereas the males do not live beyond forty.**

12.32 Alexander commanded his forces to re-embark upon the ships and ordered them regularly to observe the constellations in order to resolve whether the river Indus issued into the Atlantic and thence into the Erythraean Sea.[379] **When they had voyaged onwards for some days, they came to the distinguished city of Patala and its island. It was governed in a fashion resembling the constitution of Sparta: the heads of two leading dynasties inherited a joint-kingship from their fathers, which accorded them the leadership in military matters. Conversely, a council of elders was responsible for the civil administration.** One of the kings, whose name was Moeris, had lately evacuated his city to seek refuge in the hills. Therefore, Alexander occupied the town *and ordered that it be fortified*. Through pillaging the fields, he amassed a great plunder of grain, flocks of sheep and herds of cows, which **he took onboard** as **provisions together with guides, who were familiar with the river. Then he sailed to the island, which arose in midstream,** *being formed by the branches of the Indus Delta*. **In that region on the right-hand branch of the river dwelt the Bigandar, whilst living upon the left were the Mamalces.**

12.33 Due to the laxity of their guards, the guides managed to escape. **The island appeared deserted, but Alexander ordered that, if anybody existed in that place with knowledge of the area, they should be rounded up. Eventually, when nobody could be found,** his burning ambition to reach the Ocean and

---

[379] By the Erythraean (or Red) Sea is meant the Persian Gulf (and the Arabian Sea by extension).

visit the limits of the world persuaded him to consign his own fate and that of his many brave warriors without guidance to a mysterious waterway. *After praying together to god, they departed from the island*, sailing on into the unknown, in ignorance of the native tribes, the distance to the sea and the navigability of the channel for the warships. Conjecture was their blind, two-faced augur and their sole solace lay in the perpetual good fortune of their king.

12.34 *Already they had hastened on for 400 stades, when suddenly they sensed sea air, a thing of which they were not ignorant. Hope inspired the king and filled him with joy,* so that he urged the oarsmen to row with renewed vigour, declaring: "The avowed objective for which we have all striven is at hand; now nothing shall sully our glory nor stain our valour; the world shall fall to us without further bloodshed or intercession from the God of War; Nature herself cannot advance further and, shortly, things unknown to any save the immortals shall be revealed." *And so between them they all encouraged one another, whilst rowing ever onward with the sea not far away.*

12.35 *Then,* when they spied natives wandering about, *Alexander ordered boats to be sent to the bank, having instructed them to seek out informants on the region. Searching all day, they finally discovered several peasants* skulking in their huts. *These they led before the king, who asked, how far away the sea lay? They denied any knowledge of the sea, but said that three days' further sailing would bring them to polluted waters. It was clear that this was a reference to seawater by persons ignorant of its nature. Their spirits lifted, the army rapidly embarked, so as to reach the sea as soon as possible.* So, the sailors rowed on eagerly as the consummation of their hopes drew near and each successive day the fire in their souls burnt brighter. *By the third day* they had reached salt waters and *they began to notice tidal undulations,* which were at first quite gentle.

12.36 Now they edged towards another island in the middle of the stream, their progress being retarded by a contrary current. Mooring the fleet on its shore, they rushed off to garner provisions in blissful ignorance of the calamity that was about to befall them. At approaching the third hour, the Ocean in its habitual alternation began to swell and surge against the current. The flow of the stream was first arrested and then reversed with escalating force, generating a torrent with more impetus than a cascade in spate. The common soldiers lacked experience of the temperament of the sea, so they imagined that they were witnessing a portent of divine displeasure as *the surge of salt water streamed into the fields, rapidly flooding* a vast expanse of erstwhile well-drained land.

12.37 The ships were buoyed up *and they felt the force of the flow tugging upon them and wrenching them into violent motion,* such as to cause the entire fleet to be dispersed. Those onshore were aghast at this malign turn of events and so from every quarter they raced frantically back to their vessels. Yet in the face of panic even haste is tardy: thus, some sought to punt their ships along, whilst others obstructed the deployment of the oars by squatting down in

Book 12: Late Spring 325BC – June 324BC

a mass. Some rushed to set sail without their full complement, thus incapacitating their vessels, which wallowed laboriously, whilst others crammed multitudes onboard. Hence both under-manning and overcrowding undermined their expedition. Here and there some yelled that they should linger, but others clamoured for departure, so that their contradictory cries confounded the ears and compounded the confusion that lay before their eyes.

12.38 Nor could the pilots rescue the situation, since their voices were drowned in the tumult and the sailors were anyway in such a state of consternation that they were uncontrollable. And so, the ships began to collide, each obstructing the course of another and shearing off whole banks of oars. You might have supposed them to be two fleets engaged in battle, rather than a single army embarked upon its own vessels. Prows crashed against sterns as ships, which struck those before them, were themselves rammed in their rears and angry words even led to fistfights.

12.39 And now the tide had inundated their entire panorama with just a few slight mounds protruding like miniature islands, whither many swam vigorously, being driven by terror to abandon the ships. One part of the divided fleet floated on a great depth of water, where before there had been depressions in the landscape; another part was stranded among shoals created where the flood had barely covered uneven stretches of higher ground. At this point a fresh source of even greater alarm was visited upon them: the sea began to ebb away with a huge dragging force as the waters returned to their former channels, draining the submerged terrain. Hence some ships were left high and dry, tilted onto their prows or leaning upon their sides. The fields were strewn with baggage, arms and fragmentary oars and planks. The troops feared either to land or remain aboard, since they anticipated that further and worse calamities might strike at any moment. They could scarcely trust their own eyes as they witnessed ships wrecked on dry land and the sea vanishing into streams.

12.40 Nor was this the end of their suffering, for, since they were ignorant of the fact that the sea would shortly return to re-float their ships, they expected hunger and dire deprivations to ensue. Vile sea-beasts deposited by the flood were roving around and night was fast approaching, so that even the king was grieved by the desperation of their plight. Yet *these troubles could not* so *overwhelm his invincible spirit, but* that *he* kept watch throughout the night and *stationed cavalrymen at the river mouth* in order that, on perceiving a resurgence of the sea, they might race back ahead of it. Furthermore, he issued orders that the damaged ships should be mended and that those which had been capsized by the flow should be righted, and that all should remain vigilant against a recurrence of the flood tide. When the whole night had been spent in watchfulness and exhortation, **all at once the cavalry pickets came charging back, and yet the swelling flood following on their heels came close to cutting them off from the fleet.**

Figure 12.1. Disaster strikes Alexander's fleet during the journey to the Ocean.

12.41 Then as the water began to seep beneath the ships, they were each lifted afloat and when the fields were entirely inundated, the whole fleet was freed to sail on. The riverbanks echoed with the unrestrained cheers of the soldiers and sailors as they joyously hailed their unexpected deliverance. Whence had the sea returned and whither had it sped hence the day before? They could only wonder at this natural phenomenon, which sometimes obeyed and sometimes breached the constraints of time. However, the king conjectured from its recurrences that the surge was due after sunrise each day, so he set off down the river with a flotilla in the middle of the night in order to reach the estuary ahead of the tide. *Escorted by his Friends,* **he sailed out** 400 **stades into the Ocean, where he encountered two islands. Here he performed opulent sacrifices,** *having set up altars to Tethys and Oceanus,* **the gods who presided over the sea.** *Pouring libations from many a golden cup, he also cast these chalices into the waters, proclaiming his campaign to have achieved its end,* the objective of his prayers.

12.42 *After rejoining the main fleet, Alexander headed back upriver towards Patala.* On the second day of the return journey his ships were moored near a briny lake, the innocent appearance of which deceived those who rashly bathed in its waters. They contracted an itchy mange, which proved communicable to others, but oil was found to cure it. Since the route by which Alexander intended to lead the army passed through an arid region, Leonnatus

Book 12: Late Spring 325BC – June 324BC

was sent in advance to dig wells along the line of march. The king held back with his main contingents *waiting for the monsoons to abate*, whilst taking the opportunity to found several cities.

12.43 As the stormy season drew to a close, **the king burnt such of his ships as were damaged or unserviceable and placed the most seaworthy vessels from his fleet in the hands of Nearchus** *and Onesicritus, who were master navigators.* **He ordered them to voyage out into the Ocean** *as far as safety permitted,* **taking careful note of everything they saw. They were to seek to meet him at the mouth of the Euphrates,** or alternatively, *if that were impossible,* to sail back to the Indus and rejoin him from there. *Alexander himself got the army underway on a march across vast tracts of land, befriending friendly natives, but vanquishing any who opposed him.*

12.44 *After marching for nine days* the army entered the land of the Arabitae and after *nine more* they came to the territory of the Kedrosians. These independent nations decided *in council* to accept Alexander as their overlord, *but the king, whilst welcoming their allegiance, asked nothing of them but the provisioning of his forces. On the fifth day thereafter, he crossed a river known locally as the Arabus. Beyond its further bank* he entered a wide stretch of virtual desert, which having traversed, he arrived at the frontier of the Oreitae. At this point, the king divided the lightly armed contingents between Ptolemy, Leonnatus and himself. *Leaving the bulk of the army in the care of Hephaistion,* he ordered Ptolemy to raid the coastal areas and Leonnatus to plunder the central region, whilst his own party pillaged the upland districts and the hills. Hence the entire country was simultaneously laid waste and every settlement was lit with flame and carpeted with corpses, for the death toll climbed to tens of thousands. But the troops garnered vast spoils and the devastation intimidated the neighbouring tribes, so that they proffered prompt submission. In the same region Alexander conceived a desire to found a seaport. Discovering a sheltered harbour in the vicinity, *called Rhambarce,* he constructed an Alexandria *and populated it with citizens from Arachosia.*

12.45 *Alexander advanced further into the land of the Oreitae via the passes and speedily subdued the whole territory. For the most part these people share the customs of the other Indians, save in one peculiar and incredible respect. Relatives of their deceased disrobe, then, when completely naked and brandishing spears, they bear away the body and deposit it in one of the copses scattered around their countryside. They similarly divest the corpse of its clothing, exposing it to the depredations of wild beasts. After sharing out these robes of the dead, they offer sacrifices to their Heroes in the Underworld and celebrate by holding a feast for their friends.*

12.46 Thence the king moved into Kedrosia, marching with the sea on his flank and encountering a primitive Indian race, *who dwelt along a vast and desolate stretch of the coast,* where only a few palms and a kind of thorn bush and tamarisk grew. *Complete isolation from their neighbours had made this people* hostile and aggressive towards visitors. But indeed, they are savage and brutish in their very nature, for their nails become talons, through never being trimmed from birth to senescence and they allow their hair to grow shaggy and to become matted like felt. Their complexion is seared black by the radiant sun, though they drape themselves in the hides of beasts. <u>Their sole fodder is fish</u> and the flesh of beached whales, <u>which they are wont to shred with their talons and to dry in the sun,</u> then to grind it in mortars made from whale vertebrae and mix in a little flour, <u>so as to make a sort of bread.</u> They *fabricate and* decorate the walls of their dwellings using oysters and other **shells and anything suitable that may drift ashore. The roof beams of these huts can span up to eighteen cubits, being formed from the ribcages and tiled with the scales of gargantuan whales,** whose jaws serve as portals.

12.47 A scarcity of provisions *among the fish-eaters* **began to place the supply of the army in jeopardy, but Alexander led them on into a region of sterile desert, where shortage became famine and hunger turned to starvation.** *Though they had sweet water from the wells Alexander had ordered dug by advance parties, the lack of food meant that* the Macedonians were soon reduced to grubbing up the roots of palms, the only tree that continued to flourish in their path. When eventually even this meagre sustenance failed, they were compelled to slaughter their beasts of burden, not even sparing the cavalry mounts. Bereft of any means to transport their baggage further, they simply burnt the gorgeous plunder stripped from their opponents, so that all the rich rewards for their campaigns in the uttermost east were merely fuel for the conflagration. And sickness stalked their famished condition, for the noxious succulence of their revolting nourishment together with the exhaustion from the march and the mental stress of their plight combined to spread illness among their ranks. Their deadly dilemma was that lingering meant starving, whereas progress risked debilitation and a surer death.

12.48 Therefore their tracks across this landscape became strewn with their incapacitated comrades more so than their stoical dead, since even mild infirmity sufficed to cause men to fall behind in the forced marches. For the army advanced at the fastest pace that the healthy could maintain, as they felt impelled to pursue their hope for safety with all their vigour. But those whose energy had failed appealed desperately for aid to their friends in the column and to strangers also, yet neither to any avail. There were no more beasts to bear the infirm and the marchers were challenged even to manage to carry their arms. Indeed, the pathetic sight of their fallen fellows was a constant reminder of their own peril. Hence, despite frequent entreaties, they looked away from the dropouts as fear conquered their compassion. Those abandoned called upon the gods to be their witnesses and invoked the sacred bonds of fraternity and the duty of care owed to them by the king. But in the end, realising that their breath was wasted on deaf ears, despair made them utter irrational curses that those who had refused them succour should suffer as cruel a fate as theirs and with equally faithless friends.

Book 12: Late Spring 325BC – June 324BC

12.49 Thus starvation claimed many victims and the army was greatly dispirited. Alexander himself experienced a mixture of dolour and anguish, *also tinged with shame, since his personal leadership had brought about the disaster.* It seemed a detestable irony that men who had surpassed all in the art and practice of warfare should perish ignominiously for want of basic rations in an empty land. Therefore, the king took action by dispatching fleet emissaries to *Phraphaphernes, Satrap of* Parthia and to Drangianê and Aria and to all his provinces bordering on the desert. The governors were commanded with the utmost urgency to send racing camels and other trained beasts of burden to him via the passes of Carmania, each to be loaded with cooked food and other essentials for the relief of his forces. These messengers were swift to reach their objectives and the response of the satraps was equally expeditious, such that large quantities of supplies soon arrived at the specified rendezvous. Therefore, the army was rescued from hunger, though not without losses, *and came through to a more fertile region of Kedrosia. Alexander encamped for some time at that place in order that his traumatised troops might gently recuperate.*

12.50 *There he received a letter from Leonnatus, describing a victory won against* the Oreitae. *They* had attacked Leonnatus' brigade *in a strength of 8000 infantry and 400 cavalry,* but the Bodyguard had forced them to flee back to their own country, though he had suffered significant casualties in the battle. News also reached him from Craterus, that he had subdued Ozines and Zariaspes, Persian aristocrats who had fomented a rebellion, and clapped them in irons. Menon, the satrap of Kedrosia having lately died, Alexander appointed Sibyrtius to the office in his stead, before advancing into Carmania, where the satrap was Astaspes. There were suspicions that this man had sought to revolt whilst Alexander had been in India, but the king suppressed his anger in greeting his governor pleasantly and retaining him in his office, pending an opportunity to investigate the accusations properly.

12.51 Following further orders from Alexander, the provincial governors now requisitioned huge stocks of cavalry steeds and beasts of burden from throughout their domains, so that Alexander was able to replace the chattels of those who had lost them *in the desert.* This included armaments as magnificent as those that had been discarded, for the entire wealth of conquered Persia was now at the king's disposal. He therefore conceived an ostentatious extension of his rivalry with Dionysus. In a spirit of ascending above and beyond the mere imitation of the god's triumph over the subject nations, **Alexander decided also to emulate the festal procession and carousal for which Dionysus is especially renowned.** To this purpose he arranged that his path through the villages *of Carmania* should be carpeted with blossom and hung with garlands. Cauldrons and even vats of wine were set upon the threshold of every dwelling on his route *to fuel the festivities* and he had carriages extended to accommodate large parties of soldiers, enclosed beneath canopies formed from dazzling white sheets or precious *purple* fabrics, *richly embroidered, or else shaded by fresh green fronds.*

12.52 Alexander himself led the pageant in the company of his close friends and the rest of the royal party, each of them crowned with a wreath woven from a diversity of flowers. To one side the flautists trilled; on the other strummers plucked melodies from their lyres, *so that the air was filled with music and song.* Trundling in their tracks came the rest of the army conveyed by *innumerable* wagons garnished with displays of their most impressive weaponry. The king's own chariot was *drawn by eight horses, being* particularly heavily laden, for it bore basins and beakers of solid gold as well as his personal guests *and a lofty dais, on which he banqueted day and night.* **In this state of revelry, feasting and intoxication the entire army progressed for seven days,** virtually defenceless against any among the local inhabitants who might have summoned the courage to attack. Yet none dared, for Fortune, whose gift is fame, turned even this militarily imprudent behaviour to glory. And now it is considered a wonder that Alexander paraded a drunken army through lands not yet purged of enemies and that the barbarians mistook his rashness for invulnerability.

12.53 But the executioner stalked at the tail of this Dionysiac comus, for shortly afterwards it was ordered that Astaspes, the governor of Carmania, should be put to death. Indeed, **at this time Alexander discovered that many of his officials had abused their powers and committed serious crimes** *in his absence,* **and so he inflicted punishment upon a number of his satraps and generals.** *For example,* around this time Cleander and Sitalces, and Heracon accompanied by Agathon joined the king. These were the officers who had assassinated Parmenion at Alexander's behest. They brought with them a force of 5000 infantry and 1000 cavalry, but complainants from the provinces that they governed also followed on their heels. Although the king was greatly appreciative of the service, which they had rendered by eliminating Parmenion, this could not compensate for the numerous offences that they had since perpetrated. Having despoiled everything in the temporal sphere, they failed to exclude even sacred things from their depredations. Virgins and noblewomen, whom they had raped, came *before Alexander* to bewail the defilement of their bodies. The grasping and libidinous misbehaviour of these men had blighted the reputation of the Macedonians among the native peoples. Yet Cleander excelled the rest in lechery, for after having forcibly deflowered a virgin of noble family, he consigned her to become the harlot of his slave.

12.54 It was not so much these accusations of atrocities as remembrance of their slaughter of Parmenion that influenced a large number of Alexander's Friends against these men, though this might privately have favoured their cause with the king himself. The courtiers were glad that the king's wrath had recoiled upon the instruments of his wrath, so that no power acquired through acts of infamy should prove lasting. After considering the case, Alexander pronounced his judgement: "The prosecution has overlooked the greatest treason, and that was

Book 12: Late Spring 325BC – June 324BC

the abandonment of hope for my safe return. For it is inconceivable that the accused should have lapsed into such misconduct, if they had either believed or desired that I should come back unscathed from India." Accordingly, he had them fettered and ordered that 600 of their soldiers, who had been the agents of their ferocity, should be put to death. On that same day the captured leaders of the Persian rebellion, Ozines and Zariaspes, who had been brought in by Craterus, paid the price with their lives. *As the news spread that Alexander was righteously disciplining his delinquent commanders, many of his generals were disturbed by recollections of their own extravagant or criminal behaviour. Some instigated insurrections with the backing of mercenary armies, whilst others absconded with substantial hoards of treasure. When Alexander ascertained these reactions, he dispatched letters to each of his generals and satraps in Asia, commanding them instantly to disband their private armies.*

12.55 At this time Alexander was resting in a city called Salmous, not far *upriver* from the sea. He was presiding over stage contests in the theatre, when the fleet was brought into the *nearby* harbour by its officers, *Nearchus and Onesicritus*. They immediately came *into town* to greet Alexander in the theatre and to report upon the progress of their mission, for the king had ordered them to explore the sea-lanes and the coastal waters on the Ocean route from India back to Persia. The Macedonians were overjoyed by their deliverance from the perils of their voyage and welcomed them with a rousing ovation, so that the whole arena resounded with unrestrained jubilation.

12.56 *The mariners told of wonders they had themselves witnessed and of others that were merely rumoured.* They had observed astounding ebbs and surges of the Ocean waters, so that many great islands were unexpectedly revealed along the coast by the former, only to be submerged by the latter with a vigorous landward flow, its surface white with roiling foam. <u>They described an island opposite the mouth of the river that was rich in gold but wanting in steeds, for which its inhabitants would pay a talent apiece to anyone who ventured to ship them from the mainland. Another island had a sacred mountain, which was shaded by a grove of trees that exuded a marvellously dulcet perfume.</u>

12.57 They said that their most extraordinary experience was an encounter with a multitudinous school of unbelievably huge whales, *each of them the size of the largest of ships. They drifted with the flow of the current, converging upon the course of the fleet.* The crews were terrified and fearful for their lives, believing that the beasts were about to dash their vessels to smithereens. But when they all yelled in unison, striking their shields to generate a great cacophony and when this was further augmented with the trumpeting of their bugles, then the beasts were discomfited by the strange din and promptly dived into the depths of the Ocean *with a great crashing of the waves as they closed over them, just like the roar from a foundering ship.*

12.58 *They also recited a legend of the natives that the Red (or Erythraean) Sea did not take its name from the hue of its waters, as was commonly supposed, but was called after a King Erythrus. The grave of this king was to be found on an island not far offshore in the centre of a dense palm forest at a site marked by a lofty column with an inscription in the native alphabet. It was added that merchant-venturers, pursuing their pilots' reports of a golden treasure, had sailed to the island, but had never been heard of again.*

12.59 *All these stories enthused the king to complete the exploration of the sea-route.* He therefore requested that his fleet should continue its voyage by navigating a coastal course to the mouth of the Euphrates *and thence upriver to Babylon.*

12.60 *At these same contests in Carmania, after wine had warmed the mood, it is recorded that Alexander's lover, Bagoas the Eunuch, won the prize for singing and dancing, whilst the king presided. Decked in his festal adornments, the champion quit the stage and went across the theatre to sit down right next to Alexander. On seeing this, the Macedonians clapped their hands and shouted for the king to kiss the victor, until their persistence was rewarded by the spectacle of Alexander embracing the eunuch and kissing him passionately.*

12.61 Having brought all the eastern coastal regions beneath his sway, the king conceived plans that were unbounded in their ambition. He intended to cross from Syria into Africa in pursuit of his animosity towards the Carthaginians for their aid to Tyre *during his siege*. Thence he would trek through the wastes of Numidia, directing his course towards Gades, for it was widely reported that the Pillars of Heracles lay thereabouts. Next, he aimed to cross to Iberia, named after its eponymous river. Afterwards he would march up to the Alps, but detour around them along the coast of Italy, whence it is but a short voyage to Epirus *and his homeland*. To these ends he issued commands to the governors of Mesopotamia to fell timber on Mount Lebanon and to convey it to the Syrian city of Thapsacus; there to lay the keels of 700 ships, all septiremes[380], for delivery to Babylon *via the Euphrates*. The kings of Cyprus were ordered to supply the requisite bronze, hemp and sails. Whilst Alexander concerned himself with these matters, letters from the Indian kings, Porus and Taxiles, were brought to him, advising that Abisares had ailed and died and Alexander's viceroy, Philip, had perished from a wound, though the culprits had been punished. Accordingly, the king appointed Eudamas, a commander of the Thracian troops, in Philip's stead and endorsed the inheritance of Abisares' kingdom by his son.

12.62 Afterwards the king arrived at Parsagada, where the people are Persians. Their satrap was Orsines, pre-eminent among all the inhabitants due to a

---

[380] Probably two tiers of oars with three and four men per oar respectively.

combination of noble ancestry and wealth. His family were descended from that Cyrus who had once reigned over the Persians. He had inherited the family fortune, which he had considerably augmented in the course of a lengthy tenure of the Satrapy. He showered gifts upon Alexander and purposefully directed his largesse upon the king's Friends as well. Herds of ready-broken horses trotted in his train, together with gilded chariots, magnificent furniture, flawless gems, massive golden vases, rich purple robes and three thousand talents of silver coin. Yet this immense profligacy of the barbarian was to lead to his death. For having bestowed presents exceeding all expectations upon the rest of Alexander's Friends, he conspicuously neglected similarly to honour Bagoas, the eunuch who had won Alexander's affection by making himself sexually available to the king. Orsines was actually cautioned by certain individuals that Bagoas was very dear to Alexander, but he quipped: "I wished to show my respect for the king's noblemen, rather than for his whores, for it is not the Persian custom to treat as men those who adopt the female sexual role."

12.63 On hearing of this, the eunuch *directed all his power and energy towards the downfall of the satrap. By making surreptitious enquiries he discovered Persians who were willing to bear witness to the misdeeds of Orsines, but he counselled them to refrain from making their accusations public until he should order it.* Meanwhile in private he began to undermine Orsines' reputation with the king, so that although the satrap had not yet been charged, he was already less highly regarded. Bagoas even began to take advantage of the opportunities afforded by his sexual liaisons with Alexander, so that whenever he had aroused the king's passion for him, he made accusations of acquisitiveness or even of sedition against the satrap.

12.64 Then it happened that Alexander ordered that the tomb of Cyrus should be opened, since he wished to reverence the corpse of the former monarch, which had been laid to rest within. He had supposed it to be a treasury crammed with gold and silver, for such was its widespread repute among the Persians. Yet in fact Alexander found nothing, save the king's decaying shield, two Scythian bows and a sabre. He set a golden crown upon the sarcophagus containing the body and draped it with his own cloak, musing that it was surprising that a monarch of such power and fame had been entombed with no more splendour than many an ordinary man. The eunuch, who was close beside him, gazed intently at Alexander: "What's so surprising about the tombs of kings being bare, when the mansions of satraps cannot hold all the gold gleaned from them? As for myself, I have never seen inside this vault before, but I heard from Darius that three thousand talents were buried with Cyrus. So, the generous donations that Orsines has made to you were designed to purchase your favour using funds that he knew he could not anyway retain with impunity."

12.65 Thus Alexander already harboured some antipathy towards Orsines, when the witnesses to the satrap's criminality procured by Bagoas came before him. On the one hand Bagoas and on the other the testimonies of Orsines' own subjects filled the king's ears with capital charges. Before he even suspected that allegations had been made against him, the satrap found himself arraigned in fetters. Bagoas himself manhandled Orsines to his execution. At the same time Phradates was put to death, since he was suspected of having sought the throne *and Baryaxes too was executed, since he had worn the tiara upright, which is the prerogative of the Persian king.*

12.66 **The king had progressed with the army as far as the borders of Susianê, when the Indian Calanus, who was an adept philosopher and greatly respected by Alexander, decided to terminate his own life in an amazing ceremony. He had achieved the age of seventy-three without ever having suffered from sickness and considered that he had reached the limits of happiness in terms of both health and good fortune. Recently he had been ailing** from a bowel complaint **and was growing weaker day by day. He therefore petitioned the king to construct a vast pyre and to order the royal attendants to set it alight once he had clambered atop it.**

12.67 Although Alexander sought to dissuade Calanus from this end, the philosopher proved resolute, so the king eventually agreed to arrange the matter. When word of the event had spread and the pyre had been erected, crowds gathered to witness the astonishing spectacle. The *naked* philosopher rode to his death on a fine steed, but dismounted at the base of the pyre to offer prayers. After also sprinkling himself *with holy oil* and casting a lock of his hair upon the edifice, **Calanus contentedly climbed to its apex and turned to salute the Macedonian spectators, exhorting them to celebrate the day in revelry with their king. Yet he declined to bid farewell to Alexander himself, saying only that he would see him again soon in Babylon.** Then he lay down and covered his head and did not stir at all as **he was swallowed by the flames and perished. Thus, he sacrificed himself in accordance with the ancient custom of the wise men of his country,** *for they consider it a sacred duty when their bodies become polluted by disease to purify themselves in fire.* **Some of those who attended considered him insane; others again considered it an arrogant exhibition of pride in his indifference to pain; others still simply marvelled at his strength of spirit and** his contempt for death. **But Alexander himself duly proceeded to celebrate the funeral of Calanus with splendid festivities.**

Book 12: Late Spring 325BC – June 324BC

Figure 12.2. The weddings at Susa (late 19th century, after Andreas Müller).

12.68 *The king continued onwards to Susa,* where he held magnificent wedding ceremonies. *He himself took Stateira, the elder daughter of Darius, as his wife, whilst marrying her younger sister Drypetis to Hephaistion. He also persuaded the most influential of his Friends and noblemen to take Persian brides selected from the most aristocratic families.* Thus, he forestalled criticism of his union with the former enemy by making all the senior men complicit in his policy.

12.69 *At this juncture a band of thirty thousand Persian youths arrived at Susa,* the cream of their generation, *chosen for their comeliness and strength. They had been recruited* as boys three years beforehand *at Alexander's behest and had since completed a course of military training under expert tuition. All were elaborately outfitted with Macedonian panoplies and weaponry and they set up their camp in front of the city, where the king came to review them. They performed their military exercises and utilised their weapons with such skill, vigour, agility and discipline that Alexander was greatly pleased and issued them a commendation. However, the Macedonian troops were downcast, fearing that their king would be freed from his reliance upon them,* now that he had these young war-dancers with whom he could go on to conquer all mankind. *Indeed,* it was recalled that *the Macedonians had not merely refused to march on to the Ganges in India, but were regularly insubordinate at assemblies and lampooned Alexander's adoption of Ammon as his heavenly father. Indeed, it was as a counter-*

weight to the power of the Macedonian phalanx that Alexander had conceived and formed the new cadre from a single age-stream of Persian youths.

12.70 These were the concerns of Alexander *in the twelfth year of his reign.*

Book 13: July 324BC – July 323BC & Beyond

The Flight of Harpalus; The Exiles Decree; The Mutiny at Opis; The Death of Hephaistion; The Cossaeans; Death in Babylon; Aftermath & Entombment.

13.1 *At the outset of the thirteenth and final year of his reign,* **Alexander received a letter from Coenus**[381] ***recounting events in Europe and Asia*** *Minor,* **whilst the King had been engaged upon the conquest of India.** *Zopyrion, Alexander's governor of Thrace* and *Pontus,* **had launched an expedition** *comprising 30,000 men* **against** *the Scythians and had attacked* **the Getae**, *for he reckoned himself a loafer, if he stayed inactive.* **But sudden gales and tempests had overwhelmed his entire force** *and engendered its destruction.*[382] *Hence Zopyrion paid the ultimate price for an unprovoked assault upon an inoffensive nation.* **On receiving word of this debacle, Seuthes had compelled the Odrysians, who were his subjects, to revolt. Thrace being all but lost, not even Greece** *was secure.*

13.2 Alexander had entrusted Harpalus with the custody of the treasury in Babylon and of the revenue streams that flowed into it too. Yet once he heard that Alexander had carried his campaigns into India, Harpalus supposed his sovereign to have ventured beyond returning, so he abandoned himself to a life of luxury. Though charged as satrap with the governance of vast territories, he made his priorities the debauching of women and lawless lechery with the foreigners, thereby frittering away much of the treasure on wanton pleasure. He had a great freight of fish fetched from as far as the Erythraean Sea and adopted an exorbitant lifestyle, hence making himself the object of widespread criticism.

13.3 Thereafter <u>he engaged Pythionicê,</u> the most celebrated courtesan of her time, shipping her in from Athens. Whilst she lived, he showered her with queenly gifts, <u>and when she died,</u> he gave her a fabulous funeral and erected an extravagant monument in the Attic style for her tomb. Afterwards <u>he imported another Athenian courtesan named Glycera and upon her arrival he ensconced her in the palace at Tarsus, where she</u> lay in the lap of luxury at vast expense and <u>received royal dignities</u>[383] <u>from its denizens, who addressed her as their queen. Furthermore, it was decreed that none might honour Harpalus with a crown unless another were</u>

---

[381] Probably either that Coenus who was later governor of Susianê or else Curtius has mistranslated a phrase such as ἀπὸ τοῦ κοινοῦ meaning the government in Macedon.

[382] Cf. Macrobius, *Saturnalia* 1.11.33.

[383] I.e. *proskynesis*.

<u>likewise accorded to Glycera. At Rhossus[384] he stood her effigy in bronze next to his own and ventured so far as to set up a third statue depicting Alexander beside them.</u>[385] But with a view to the vicissitudes of fortune, Harpalus also lavished favours upon the citizenry of Athens with the object of procuring asylum in adversity.

13.4 When Alexander did in fact return from India and executed numerous satraps, who had been accused of delinquency in the conduct of their duties, Harpalus likewise feared parallel punishment *for his similar indiscretions*. Therefore, he garnered five thousand talents *of silver*, engaged six thousand mercenary troops and quit the shores of Asia, setting sail for Attica *with a fleet of thirty ships. Hence, they rounded Cape Sounion and determined to head for the port of Athens, but* the citizens would not allow them to dock *in such force*. Therefore, Harpalus sent his soldiers to land at Taenarum in Laconia,[386] but, retaining some part of his riches, he himself sought sanctuary with the Athenians.

13.5 *Alexander received word of these matters and was equally enraged by the conduct of Harpalus and* the complicity of *the Athenians. Antipater and Olympias demanded that the renegade should be delivered up to them and Alexander commanded that an armada be made ready, meaning to proceed at once against Athens. But whilst he was covertly fomenting this strategy, he received a letter reporting that* Harpalus, having managed to gain admission to Athens, had won over its demagogues with his money, *notably buying a bout of laryngitis for Demosthenes at the cost of a cup of gold.*[387] **But a little later, an assembly of the citizens had decreed his departure, so that** he had been obliged to creep away to rejoin his mercenaries at Taenarum. Thereafter, he had voyaged to Crete with his fleet, where he had perished at the perfidious hands of Thibron, one whom he had counted among his Friends. *An inventory of Harpalus' treasure was performed at Athens, in consequence of which Demosthenes and others among the orators were convicted of having accepted bribes from Alexander's erstwhile treasurer.*

13.6 *Jubilant at this outcome,* Alexander *abandoned his plan to sail over to Europe. However, he* issued orders that the Greek city-states should accept the return of their own exiles, save for those either charged with sacrilege or having the blood of citizens on their hands. This decree he had proclaimed at Olympia, whilst the Olympic Games were being

---

[384] In Syria.

[385] Jacoby fragment 30 of Cleitarchus = Athenaeus 12.50 or 586CD.

[386] A promontory of the Peloponnesian peninsula due south of Sparta.

[387] Plutarch, *Demosthenes* 25-26, attributes this story to Theopompus, who also seems to be Cleitarchus' source for his information on Pythionicê and Glycera.

Book 13: July 324BC – July 323BC & Beyond

celebrated.[388] *Lacking the temerity to spurn Alexander's command, although they deemed him to be beginning to undermine their laws, the Greeks even restored such of their property as remained to those they had condemned to banishment.* The Athenians alone, championing not only their own interests but also the public good, would not suffer such a sewage of humanity, being accustomed to government according to their ancestral laws and traditions, rather than the edicts of a king. Hence, they barred the exiles from the bounds of their territory, being willing to endure anything but the former excretions of their own city, that had latterly befouled their places of exile.

13.7 Alexander now convened an Assembly at which he **announced that 10,000 of his older Macedonian veterans were to be released from service and would return to their native land.** *Conversely,* he ordered that 13,000 infantry and 2000 cavalry should be designated for ongoing service in Asia, calculating that the continent could be held by a force of moderate size, since garrisons had been established at many sites and his newly founded cities were packed with colonists, who were strongly motivated to keep matters in order. Yet prior to making his selection of which of them he would retain, he proclaimed that all his troops should make a declaration of their debts. **The king had learnt that many were heavily encumbered by their borrowings** and, despite their debentures having been pledged for their dissipations, **he had determined to discharge them of these obligations**, so that they might retain their spoils and their plunder, when they went home. The soldiers suspected an ensnarement, such that the spendthrifts could be threshed from the thrifty, hence they long prevaricated *in providing their accounts.* Being wise to the fact that it was shame rather than insubordination that withheld their admissions, **Alexander ordered** tables to be set up throughout the camp and **ten thousand talents to be brought forth.** Then, finally, **they declared their debts** in good faith *and the remarkable beneficence of the king in settling them at his own expense was appreciated by their creditors as much as by themselves, since collection had proven as trying as repayment.* Of so much money, **after but a single day just one hundred and thirty talents were left unspent.** Emphatically, that army, though it conquered so many of the richest realms, nevertheless gleaned more glory than booty from Asia.

13.8 It being known that, despite some being sent home, the rest of them would be retained and it being reckoned that the king planned permanently to vest the seat of his government in Asia,[389] **the troops grew heedless of military discipline** and fell into folly, filling the camp with seditious slander. **When summoned to an Assembly, they heckled the king** and began insistently to petition him for their collective discharge, showing their faces disfigured by scars and their greying heads of hair. *They demanded that he assess their length of service rather*

---

[388] Cf. Diodorus 18.8.2-7; Justin 13.5.2-5.

[389] Many of the tetradrachms of Alexander minted at Babylon bear a mu-tau-rho monogram, designating it as the *metropolis* or mother-city; this and Strabo 15.3.9-10 suggest that Alexander intended that it should be his capital.

than their age, asserting that fairness required that those who had enlisted together should all be released at the same time. **Undeterred either by the reprimands of their officers or any sense of respect for the king,** with maddened militaristic clashing and clamour **they drowned out Alexander as he sought to speak**, openly asserting that they should not be shifted a single step from that spot save towards their homeland. *And they jeered that he should prosecute his wars alone with his father Ammon, if he disdained his soldiers.* **When at last quiet was restored**, though not so much because their position could be shifted, but rather because they thought that the king had been swayed and they were waiting to see what action he would take, **Alexander addressed them.**

13.9 "What then does this sudden turmoil and such shameless and unrestrained anarchy signify? I dread to say, when you have openly flouted my commands and my crown is tottering, for I evidently lack the prerogative either to address or to acknowledge or to admonish you, or even so much as to look you in the face. Admittedly, I have resolved to send some home and a little later to take others onwards with me, and now I witness as much of an outcry from those headed homewards as from those whom I have decided shall follow my vanguard. Where's the sense in this? - Contrary cases causing common clamour! I should like at least to know whether it is those who are staying or those who are going who are moaning at me?" It might have been believed that they all bellowed their response through a single mouth, so concerted was the answer of the entire Assembly: "We are all of us complaining!"

13.10 "No, by Heracles!" Alexander retorted, "I cannot agree that everyone shares your professed grievance, in which the greater part of the army can have no part, seeing that I have parted with more men than I plan to retain. Assuredly, there is some underlying ill that turns you all against me. For when else has an entire army deserted from its king? Even serfs do not desert their lords en masse, for even they feel ashamed to abandon masters forsaken by the rest. But in truth I am forgetting how rabid your riotousness was and I am striving to administer cures to incurables. By Heracles! All the high hopes I have conceived in you, I consign to ruin, for I have decided to deal with you not as my soldiers - which you have patently ceased to be - but rather as the worst of whinging workmen! In grasping at the liquid assets that flow around you, you are slipping into madness, oblivious of the lowly status from which you were raised up by my generosity. By Heracles! You deserve to grow old in such penury, since you find it easier to aim for adversity than to follow favourable fortune."

13.11 "Behold! Those who were tributary subjects of Illyria and Persia just a short time ago now disdain Asia and the spoils of all its nations. Those who went about half bare as recently as under Philip, now think purple mantles mean. Their eyes cannot endure the gleam of gold and silver, but they hanker after wooden pots, wicker shields and rust-eaten swords. Such was the lustre of your lifestyle, when I took charge of you together with a national debt of five hundred talents, when all the royal chattels were not worth more than sixty. Such were the foundations

Book 13: July 324BC – July 323BC & Beyond

for the great deeds thereafter: the basis on which nevertheless – may it not tempt fate to utter it – I established my rule across the greatest part of the world. Are you so disenchanted with Asia, which through the glory of your achievements has set you on a par with deities? You are forsaking your king and scurrying back to Europe, when many of you would not have been able to pay your way, had I not liquidated your loans using riches gleaned from Asia! Neither are you ashamed, whilst parading your gross gluttony for the spoils of the conquered peoples, to wish to return to your wives and offspring, to whom few among you will be able to display the rewards of victory. Others among you have even pawned your arms, in the cause of realising such hopes."

13.12 "Fine soldiers I shall be losing! Servicers of their paramours: for this is the sole pleasure left to them from such rich treasure and in this their outlay is not yet spent! Therefore, let the roads lie open to my deserters. Get you gone at once! The Persians and I shall protect your rear as you scamper off and I shall detain none of you. O most ungrateful compatriots, relieve me of the sight of you! Gladly will your parents and children welcome you back, when you turn up without your king! They shall come surging forth to meet deserters and renegades! But, by Heracles, I shall transcend your flight and, wherever I may be, I shall see you suffer for it by favouring and preferring those left with me. Furthermore, you shall soon realise how much an army is worth when it lacks a leader and also what resources are vested in my sole self." Thereupon, *deeming further words ineffectual despite* **having cowed the crowd, an incensed Alexander vaulted from the dais into the midst of the ranks of armed troops. Having noted the most outspoken rebels, he seized them one after another, consigning to the custody of his attendants a total of thirteen,** *none of them daring to offer any resistance.* **Who could credit that** *a gathering that had been so mutinous a little while before was now* **so** *petrified by sudden dread* **on** witnessing colleagues whose conduct had been no more rebellious than the rest being dragged off to chastisement?[390]

13.13 *Alexander now ordered his Persian attendants to cast the thirteen men he had arrested into the river, whilst still fettered. As he was being led away, one among the condemned men addressed the king:* "For how long shall you impose your will through executions and in foreign fashions too? Your soldiers and fellow citizens led away, alas, by their vanquished opponents and dragged to their doom on untried charges. If you judge that we deserve death, at least exchange the executioners." It was a conciliatory reproach, had Alexander been amenable to the realities, but his anger had turned to madness. Therefore, since those to whom the order had been issued had momentarily hesitated, he reiterated that the bound prisoners were to be plunged into the torrent. Yet not even these sentences moved the troops to mutiny. Instead, they came before their regimental officers and the king's Friends squadron by squadron craving that if Alexander judged that any were implicated

---

[390] Freinshem inferred a lacuna at this point, whereas it appears to me that the material of Curtius 10.4 belongs here, since it follows the arrests, but precedes the executions.

in the earlier offence then they should be slain. They offered their corpses to appease his anger: let him slaughter them *and be assuaged*.

13.14 Whether out of worship of his title, since people ruled by kings are wont to reverence them among the gods, or else out of personal veneration for Alexander, or perhaps out of habitual faith in such assertive enforcement of his rule, they were thoroughly intimidated. At all events, they gave an extraordinary display of humility and in addition were so **far from being riled by the punishment of their comrades-in-arms, when their executions were confirmed** at dusk**, that they omitted nothing in manifesting the increased dutifulness and compliancy of each of them.** For upon the following day, when they had been denied access to Alexander, admission being confined to Asiatic troops, they wailed mournfully throughout the entire camp, declaring their desire to perish promptly, if the king should persist in his anger. But **Alexander**, being obdurate in everything he set his mind upon, **ordered that an Assembly of the foreign troops should be convened**, whilst the Macedonians were confined to their camp. **Then, when a great throng of the Persian auxiliaries had gathered together, he** engaged an interpreter and **delivered a speech.**

13.15 "When I crossed over from Europe to Asia, it was my hope that I should augment my empire with many renowned nations and mighty men. Neither was I misled in giving credence to their reputations. But to this it may also be added that *I behold bold men of unshakeable devotion towards their kings.* I had believed that luxury imbued everything here and that excessive bountifulness had overwhelmed you with pleasures. Yet, by Heracles, such is your resilience in mind and body that you cope equally efficiently with military duties and, whilst being brave men indeed, you cherish loyalty no less than valour. Though indeed I now proclaim this for the first time, it has long been my perception. Therefore, *I have both recruited a levy from the younger men among you and also introduced them among my regiments.* You have the same arms and the same outfits, but in obedience and compliance with orders you far excel those others."

13.16 "Hence *I joined myself in marriage to the daughter of the Persian Oxyartes, not scorning to raise offspring with a captive. Then afterwards, when I wished to propagate the shoots of my family tree more broadly, I took to wife the daughter of Darius and encouraged my closest friends by my example to beget children with captives, in order through these sacred unions to erase all division between the victors and the vanquished. And consequently, you may consider yourselves my compatriots rather than foreign recruits.* Europe & Asia is now one and the same realm. In assigning Macedonian arms to you, I have made you traditional troops instead of outlandish newcomers and *you are my fellow-citizens as well as my soldiers.* All are acquiring the same outward appearance and *it is neither improper for the Persians to adopt the customs of the Macedonians nor for the*

Macedonians to emulate Persian practices. Those who are to live as subjects of the same king should enjoy the same rights."[391]

Figure 13.1. Alexander seizes the leading mutineers (André Castaigne, 1899)

13.17 "Therefore from now on I propose to divide the duties of my personal bodyguards among you as well as my Macedonians." Thereafter, **Alexander selected a thousand of the Persian youths and assigned them as his lifeguards** *in the palace regiment of the hypaspists, in every sense showing the same trust in them as in his Macedonians.* **And he appointed**

---

[391] A long lacuna in Curtius begins here and lasts until the soldiers' tears at the king's deathbed.

handpicked Persian commanders and granted them elite ranks *within the army*. He also incorporated the division of the Persian auxiliaries who had received Macedonian training into his army. **When they saw the king escorted by the Persians,** *whilst they themselves languished in disgrace,* **the Macedonian troops** were much vexed, complaining that the king had transposed their foes to fulfil their own functions. Then they **began to repent their behaviour,** *considering that they had been crazed by jealousy and ill temper.* Thus, they went, *unarmed and dressed only in their tunics, to the king's pavilion* **and with tears and wails begged an audience with Alexander,** *beseeching him to chastise them as rude ingrates* **rather than prolong their humiliation.**

13.18 *At first* **Alexander** *would not see them, though he had begun to be mollified. Yet the men would not disperse, but stood for two days and nights before the entrance, blubbering and appealing to him as their lord, until at last on the third day he emerged and seeing them in so abject and distressed a condition he himself wept awhile. Then he reproved them mildly, but afterwards addressed them fondly and* **finally received them back into his favour.** By their conciliatory behaviour they persuaded the king to retire 11,000 of the veterans, whilst generously providing that they should continue to draw active service pay. *And he wrote to Antipater that at all the games and in every theatre, they should be wreathed and seated to the fore.* He also discharged Polyperchon, Cleitus *the White*, Gorgias, Polydamas and Antigenes, who were elderly among *the circle of* his Friends. He appointed Craterus to preside over those whom he had released with orders to govern Macedon in place of Antipater, whom he summoned to join him in the stead of Craterus with a force of fresh recruits.

13.19 *Alexander proceeded to induct Persians into the army to make up the shortfall created by the departure of the discharged veterans. At this time Peucestes arrived in camp with a force of 20,000 Persian archers and slingers, whom Alexander implanted in companies among his other troops, and by the innovation of this reform he developed an army melded and attuned to his own ideals.*

13.20 *There now being sons of the Macedonians born to women taken in the course of his campaigns and orphaned either by the death or the departure of their fathers, the king assessed their precise number and found that they totalled around ten thousand. Therefore, he apportioned sufficient funds to finance their upbringing in a manner befitting the freeborn and assigned them to tutors to provide them with an appropriate education.*

13.21 *Afterwards Alexander set forth from Susa with his army, crossed the River Tigris and encamped among the hamlets known as Karai.*[392] *From there he proceeded on through Sittacenê for four days and arrived at the place called Sambana. He tarried there for seven days, then, marching the army onwards, reached the Kelones, as they are called, on the third day. A*

---

[392] It is likely that the mutiny took place at Opis on the River Tigris, but this may not have been mentioned by Cleitarchus; we are now detouring through Babylonia en route to Ecbatana.

Book 13: July 324BC – July 323BC & Beyond

settlement of Boeotians, who were transplanted during Xerxes' campaign, continues to thrive there through to the present time, still remembering their ancestral customs. They are bilingual, being as fluent as the natives in the local tongue, whilst retaining most of the vocabulary in their Greek and also preserving some Hellenic institutions.

13.22 Eventually, after a sojourn comprising a number of days,[393] the king resumed his progress, deviating from the highway for the purpose of taking in the sights. Thereby he came within the bounds of Bagistanê, as that divine district is named, which is forested with fruitful orchards and bounteous in every requisite for an indulgent existence. *At about this time Hephaistion allocated quarters to Euios the flute player that had been assigned to Eumenes, who therefore went with Mentor to complain to Alexander. In anger Eumenes declared that the route to regard was to discard their arms and to resort to piping and theatricality. At this Alexander thought to reproach Hephaistion, but in conferring with him became annoyed with Eumenes for having questioned the royal authority and prevailed upon him to settle his quarrel with Hephaistion. He also persuaded a reluctant Hephaistion to agree to reconciliation with Eumenes.*

13.23 Thereafter he came to a country capable of nurturing huge herds of horses, *including the royal Nesaean mares as Herodotus tells us,* **where anciently they say a hundred and sixty thousand head were grazed. Yet at the time of Alexander's inspection a mere sixty thousand could be mustered,** *the majority having been rustled by thieves. There too Atropates, the Satrap of Media, made Alexander a present of a hundred Amazon women. They were outfitted like cavalrymen, except that they bore hatchets rather than spears and bucklers instead of shields. Some say that their right breasts were smaller than their left and were bared in battle. Alexander soon sent them away from the army, lest they should be raped by either his Macedonian or barbarian levies. But he first told them to tell their queen that he planned to pay her a visit in order to sire progeny by her.* **After spending thirty days in this region, he resumed his march.**

13.24 On the seventh day Alexander arrived at Ecbatana in Media, of which it is said that the circuit of its perimeter measures two hundred and fifty stades.[394] It is the royal seat for the whole of Media and its vaults are replete with riches. Here he rested his army for some time and held a theatrical festival in concert with perpetual drinking parties among his Friends. In the course of this merry-making Alexander's *dearest* **Friend Hephaistion drank a great deal and fell sick** *with a fever. Glaukos, his physician, being absent at the festivities, he had forsaken his dietary restrictions by consuming a boiled fowl and quaffing a full flagon of wine,* **soon after** *which* **he expired. The king was profoundly grieved,** *for he had greatly cherished Hephaistion, not only on account of his outstanding good looks and boyishness, but also by virtue of his compliancy with Alexander's desires. He mourned*

---

[393] It would appear that Cleitarchus specified the duration, but the exact number of days has accidentally been omitted from the manuscripts of Diodorus.

[394] About 30 miles!

immoderately, for straightaway he ordered that the tail and mane of every mount and mule should be shorn and he demolished the battlements of the surrounding citadels. He also crucified the unfortunate physician and for a long while banned the blowing of flutes and the sound of music in the encampment. **Alexander commanded that the cadaver be conveyed in the care of Perdiccas to Babylon, where he planned to stage a funeral of remarkable magnificence.**

13.25 At this time Greece was gripped by tumult and the hatching of political convulsions, which were the genesis of the Lamian War. This had come about following Alexander's edict that his satraps should disband their mercenary militias, for, when they complied, many of the discharged troops rampaged throughout all Asia, pillaging to furnish their supplies. After a while they began from every quarter to congregate at Taenarum in Laconia. Thither too came the dregs of the Persian satraps and other leaders together with their funds and their forces, so that they amounted to an assembled army. Eventually, they appointed as their general plenipotentiary Leosthenes the Athenian, a man of supremely radiant spirit and most antagonistic towards Alexander's policies. He conferred covertly with the Council of Athens, who contributed fifty talents towards paying his troops and stocking up on arms sufficient to supply immediate requirements. Aiming for an alliance, he dispatched envoys to the Aetolians, who were ill disposed towards the king and in general he did everything to make ready for war. Having foreseen the magnitude of the forthcoming struggle, Leosthenes applied himself *vigorously* **to all these preparations.**

13.26 *Making warfare a salve for his sorrow,* **Alexander took a task force against the insubordinate Cossaeans, a stalwart race** *of brigands,* **who infested the mountains of Media. They had counted on the cragginess of their country and their fighting prowess in order never to become vassals of a foreign overlord, having held their impregnable heights throughout the period of the Persian principate. Hence at the outset they were too vainglorious to be panicked by the proficiency of the Macedonian troops. Yet the king seized possession of the passages through their purlieus and ravaged the bulk of the Cossaean territory. Alexander was foremost in every fracas, slaying many,** *which he said were sacrifices to the shade of Hephaistion,* **and shackling countless more. Thus, the Cossaeans were vanquished everywhere and, being distraught that so many were fettered, they were compelled to save these captives by conceding the subjugation of their nation. Hence they gave themselves up to Alexander and secured peace in exchange for compliance with royal commands. It took the king no more than forty days to reduce this race; then he established exceptional citadels among the crags and stood down his forces.**

13.27 After subduing the Cossaean nation, Alexander marched away with his army and headed for Babylon, progressing at a gentle pace with

Book 13: July 324BC – July 323BC & Beyond

encampments at frequent intervals so as to rest his forces. *He planned to grant audience to the embassies from Europe and to fête Hephaistion with a fitting funeral, but* **whilst he was still three hundred stades distant from the metropolis, the magi known as Chaldaeans, who have grown greatly esteemed for their astrology by foretelling the future through perpetual star-gazing, put forward the most eminent and learned amongst them. From the configuration of the constellations, they had foreseen the forthcoming demise of the king in Babylon, so their envoys were delegated to alert him to his impending peril. They were to exhort Alexander to avoid entering the city and to advise him that he could avert the danger by reconstructing the tomb of Bel, which had been demolished under the Persians, but that he must also relinquish his route and bypass the metropolis.**

13.28 The pre-eminent emissary among the Chaldeans, who was dubbed Belephantes,[395] lacked the nerve to address Alexander directly through dread of him, but privately conferred with Nearchus, one of the Friends of the king. He divulged every detail and besought him to relate the matter to the king. Consequently, Alexander was apprised of the prophecy of the Chaldeans by Nearchus and the king became ever more concerned and disquieted as he contemplated the skill and repute of these men. Ultimately, he sent most of his Friends on into the city, but altered his own course so as to avoid Babylon and established his camp at a range of two hundred stades *across the Euphrates in the long-abandoned city of Borsipa.*

13.29 This behaviour caused widespread wonderment, such that many of the Greeks approached Alexander on the matter, in particular Anaxarchus from among the philosophers. When they discovered its cause, they harangued the king with rationales drawn from philosophy and converted him to the extent that he grew scornful of all the arts of augury and most of all those arts extolled by the Chaldeans. *Their predictions were doubtful and deceitful, for what is ordained by Fate is hidden from humans and what is owed to Nature may not be altered.* **It was as though his soul had been savaged and his sages had healed it through discourse, in consequence of which he now made an entry into Babylon with his army. Just as previously,[396] its inhabitants hosted his troops convivially and everyone eagerly embraced loose living and licentious revelry, since the requisite services could be procured in profusion.**

13.30 <u>Nearly every nation of the known world had sent envoys to Alexander</u> **with multifarious missions in mind: some to congratulate the king on his conquests, some by awarding him crowns; others to arrange pacts of amity and alliance; many conveying gorgeous gifts; and also some seeking to refute allegations that had been lodged against them. In addition to the**

---

[395] *Belephantes* is essentially Greek for Mouthpiece of Bel.

[396] I.e. just as at the end of 331BC.

races, cities and dynasts of Asia, many *such* from Europe and Libya[397] had also sent embassies. *From the latter came Carthaginians and the Libyan colonists of the* **Phoenicians together with those that live upon the Libyan littoral as far as the Pillars of Heracles.** The European delegations represented the Greek cities, the Macedonians, the Illyrians and most of those dwelling around the Adriatic Sea. The latter incorporated *a few from Italy, amongst whom were* **the Romans.**[398] *Emissaries from Spain, Sardinia, Sicily and* **the Thracian tribes swelled the throng and there were even representatives of their neighbours, the Gauls: the first occasion on which that people came to prominence in Hellenic affairs.** *Alexander was eager to preside over a congregation that seemed assembled from almost every abode on Earth.*

13.31 *Alexander compiled a list of the delegations and scheduled audiences according to the priority with which he wished to respond. First of all he heard those pursuing sacred missions; secondly, those who came bearing gifts; next those who were disputing borders with their neighbours; fourthly, those suffering internal ructions; and fifth in order, those who wished to air arguments against the restitution of their exiles. He received the Eleians initially, and then successively the Ammonii, the Delphians and the Corinthians ahead of the Epidaurians followed by the others: hearing their petitions in order of eminence of their sanctuaries.*[399] *In every instance he strove earnestly to deliver gratifying responses to the emissaries, letting them leave well pleased insofar as was in his power.*

13.32 *When the emissaries had been excused, Alexander became obsessed with the obsequies of Hephaistion. Such was his fervour for this funeral that it not only eclipsed every earthly precedent, but also denied any scope for posterity to transcend its magnificence. Hephaistion had been most beloved amongst those considered his dearest Friends, so he was surpassingly exalted after his passing away. Whilst he had lived, Alexander had favoured Hephaistion above the rest of his Friends, despite Craterus' rating a rival right to his affections. Hence, for example, when one of the Companions had remarked that Craterus was not inferior to Hephaistion in devotion, Alexander had responded that Craterus was devoted to the king, whereas Hephaistion was devoted to Alexander.*

13.33 *On the occasion of their first visit to the mother of Darius, she had mistakenly performed obeisance towards Hephaistion just as if he were the monarch. Her error having been imparted to her, she had been*

---

[397] By Libya is meant all of Africa west of the Nile Valley.

[398] Jacoby fragment 31 of Cleitarchus = Pliny NH 3.57; this hints that Cleitarchus wrote after 280BC, when Pyrrhus first made the Romans renowned in the Greek world.

[399] Presumably the Eleians represented the sanctuary of Zeus at Olympia; the Ammonii the oracle of Ammon at Siwa; the Delphians their oracle of Apollo; the Corinthians Poseidon and the Epidaurians Asclepios, so this was a pecking order of the gods.

Book 13: July 324BC – July 323BC & Beyond

disconcerted, but the king had said: "Don't worry, mother, for indeed he too is Alexander." And indeed, it may be agreed that **one should view one's friends' misfortunes as one's own and share one's own good fortune with them. Yet it is improper to mourn** *immoderately for* **dead friends, but instead the diligent devote their care to the welfare of their** *living* **household.**[400]

13.34 *In general, so much authority and latitude of self-expression was vested in Hephaistion through this relationship that when jealousy made Olympias antagonistic towards him, penning invective and menaces against him in her letters, he responded by writing reprovingly. Thus, he closed his own letter: "Let you cease your calumnies against us and forswear fulmination and threats. Even if you persist, we shall pay scant attention. You are well aware that Alexander is more important to us than anything else."*[401]

13.35 *In pursuing preparations for the funeral, the king commanded the surrounding cities to furnish it with finery to the best of their means. He also directed every Asian community diligently to extinguish the flames that the Persians call sacred, pending the finish of the funeral. Such was the custom of the Persians upon the demise of their king, so the masses thought the order an awful augury, whereby they supposed the gods foretold the death of the king himself. There were manifested at this time other supernatural signs alluding to Alexander's end, which we shall relate a little later in the wake of our words concerning the funeral.*

13.36 *Each of the Commanders and the Friends sought to humour the king by commissioning idols of Hephaistion fashioned in ivory, gold and such other materials as men deem marvellous. Meanwhile Alexander assembled engineers together with a multitude of artisans, and then razed the ramparts along a stretch of ten stades. He aggregated the baked bricks and evened out a level space to support the pyre, which he erected on a base a stade square. He divided the place up into thirty chambers, supporting the ceilings upon the trunks of palm trees and employing quadrangular forms to fashion the entire edifice.*[402] *Finally, he applied adornments to every outward facing wall.*

13.37 *From around its base there projected the gilded prows of quinqueremes in tight array and totalling two hundred and forty all told.*

---

[400] Fragment 41 of Cleitarchus = Maximi, Eclogae 6.761A; considered doubtful by Jacoby, but apposite in this context.

[401] Hephaistion seems to be represented as having used the *pluralis majestatis* (the royal we) here.

[402] Since $30 = 4^2 + 3^2 + 2^2 + 1^2$, this was presumably a four-stage step pyramid with 4x4 chambers for its square base, 3x3 chambers for the 2nd stage and so on: the ensuing description of the decoration would be congruent with two bands per step (excepting the topmost), but the lower band in each such pair might easily have been projected outwards so as to give the impression of 7 stages, perhaps matching the Babylonian ziggurat.

Upon each of their bows there knelt a pair of bowmen, each four cubits high, with effigies of fighting men five cubits tall and red felt flags filling the intervening voids. Above these on the second-tier torches towered fifteen cubits in all with golden crowns wreathing their hafts. Eagles with wings splayed ascended from the flambeaus, squinting down at serpents that peered up from around the toes. Adorning the third band bevies of beasts were harried by hordes of hunters, whilst in the fourth field was fought a Battle of the Centaurs wrought in gold and for the fifth lions and bulls alternated in bold gilt. The band above was bedecked with both Macedonian and Asian armaments commemorating the courage of the conquerors and the conquest of the conquered. Sirens sitting at the summit had been hollowed to hold hidden humans, who descanted dirges for the departed, and the altitude at the apex of this edifice exceeded a hundred and thirty cubits.

13.38 *It was universal among the commanders and every class of troops and also the envoys and even the denizens of the district that all strove to compete in embellishing the funeral, hence it is said that the cumulative monetary outlay exceeded twelve thousand talents. As the culmination of these sumptuous obsequies and other distinctions for the deceased, Alexander announced at the finale of the funeral that all should make offerings to Hephaistion as a demigod.*[403] *By chance at this time, Philip of the Friends arrived bearing a pronouncement from Ammon that Hephaistion be hallowed as half-divine. Gladdened that the god had endorsed his own estimation, Alexander was foremost in offering sacrifices and he entertained the crowd coruscatingly, for the slaying of all sorts of sacrificial victims entailed a tally of ten thousand.*

13.39 *In the wake of the funeral the king diverted himself in revels and recreation, seeming set at the summit of power and prosperity, yet Fate now sundered the span allotted to his life. Hence Heaven forthwith foretold Alexander's end, as sundry supernatural signs and portents transpired.*

---

[403] The manuscripts of Diodorus had *theos proedros*, but this is corrected to *theos paredros* on the basis of Lucian, *Calumniae non temere credendum* 17, which speaks of sacrifices to Hephaistion as *paredros kai alexikakos theos*; this use of *paredros*, which literally means "one who sits beside", is unusual and in this context seems to mean an assistant god or collaborating deity, which is not greatly inconsistent with the versions of Arrian and Plutarch, which state that Ammon approved honouring of Hephaistion as a hero: the oddity of *paredros* is suggestive of authentic terminology.

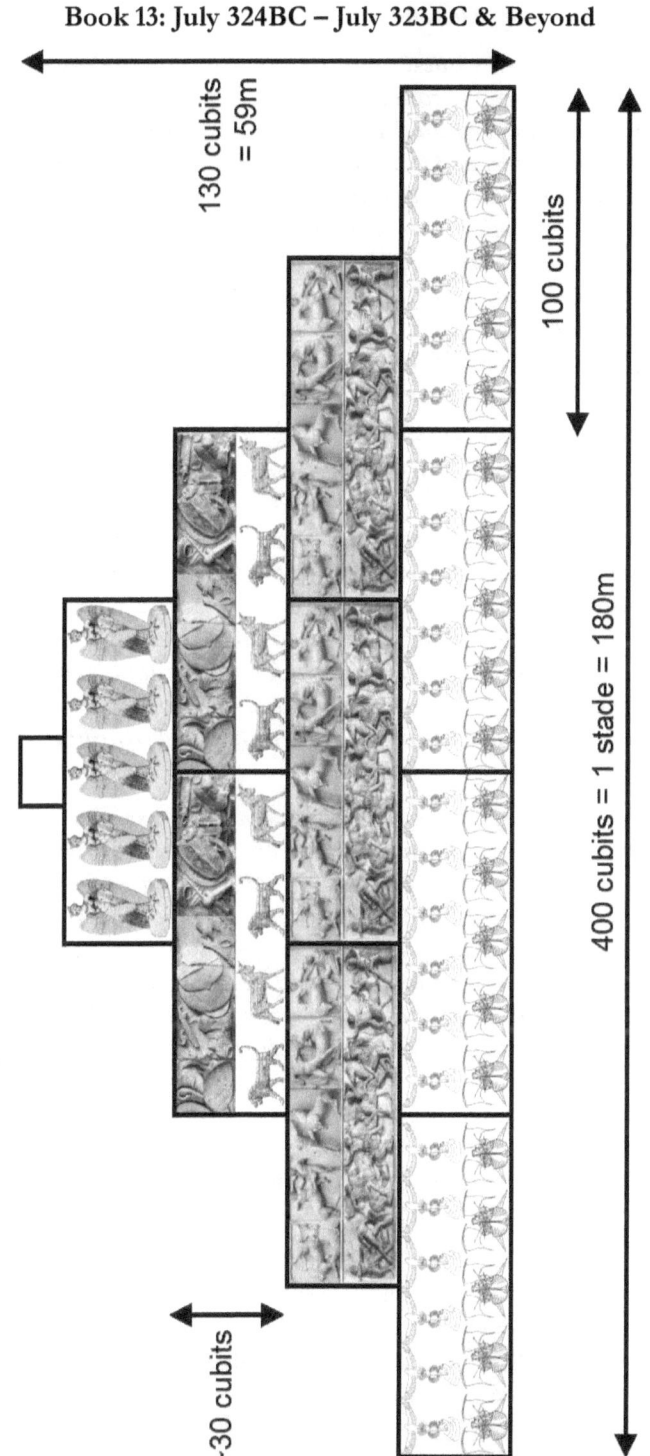

Figure 13.2. A conceptual reconstruction of Hephaistion's Pyre by the author.

13.40 *Whilst the king was oiled up for exercising, so that the royal robes rested with the diadem upon a throne, a shackled detainee from the hinterland slyly slipped his bonds, eluded his guards and passed through the portal of the palace unhindered. He approached the throne, arrayed himself in the royal raiment, bound the diadem about his brow and set himself upon its seat, where he sat silent and still. The king was alarmed on learning of this illogical lapse, but strode to the throne and concealed his consternation in calmly questioning the fellow as to his identity and his motive in the matter. But he could elicit absolutely no response.* Hence **the ruler strove to be mild, whilst his subject practiced hauteur, for the diadem does not render its wearer regally wise, but rather it is the mind that makes the monarch and without learning obedience, none should try to rule.**[404]

13.41 *Therefore Alexander presented this prodigy to the prophets for prognosis and put the perpetrator to death in conformity with their verdict, hoping that the catastrophe that the culprit's conduct foreshadowed had thereby rebounded upon the man himself. The king retrieved his robes and made offerings to propitiate the gods that ward off wickedness, but his consternation continued unassuaged. He pondered anew the premonition of the Chaldeans and castigated the philosophers that had inveigled him into entering Babylon, for he was bedazzled by the Babylonians' crafts and their clairvoyance, so he commonly cursed those who quibbled in querying the force of Fate.*

13.42 *Shortly thereafter the sacred spirits sent him a second sign regarding his reign. He conceived a yearning to survey the swamps surrounding Babylon, so he set sail in several skiffs with a party of his Friends. His vessel became separated from the rest and strayed by itself during some days, such that he despaired of deliverance. Whilst his boat navigated a narrow channel, where fronds flourished densely and dangled down over the swill, one of them snagged Alexander's diadem and swept it into the swamp. One of the rowers swam to fetch it and, desirous of assuring its safety, laid it upon his own head before swimming back to the boat. After three days and the same number of nights astray Alexander sailed to safety, just as unexpectedly as he had retrieved his diadem. Then he again consulted the seers concerning the symbolism of these signs. They exhorted him to perform elaborate sacrifices to the gods and with wholehearted haste.*

13.43 *But the king now resumed his erstwhile custom of convening formal feasts and entirely immersed himself in merry-making for a day and a wakeful night. As at last he was retiring from the revels,* **Medius the Thessalian, one of his Friends, encouraged him to come to a comus** to continue to carouse in company with his companions.

---

[404] Fragment 52 of Cleitarchus = Antonii, Melissa 2.1, p.1005C; considered doubtful by Jacoby, but apt in this context.

Book 13: July 324BC – July 323BC & Beyond

Thereat he downed a great deal of undiluted wine in commemorating the demise of Heracles[405] and ultimately sought to drain a brimming, gargantuan goblet, but had only gulped half of it, **whereupon he bawled a bellow** *as if he had been skewered* by a spike *piercing his back*. **His Friends lifted and led him away,** for he was in such excruciating pain that he begged for a blade as his remedy and to be touched by anyone was as agonising as a wound. His Friends spread the word that he was suffering from overindulgence in alcohol and *his attendants put him straight to bed and tended him attentively, but his sickness worsened and the medics were mustered. None was able to do anything to aid him, so he endured awful agony and anguish.*

13.44 By the fourth day Alexander sensed his certain death upon him *and he adduced that he detected the doom of his dynasty in it, for the Aeacidae were mostly deceased by their thirtieth year.* **Then the troops were in a ferment,** surmising that their prince was perishing through perfidy; **but Alexander** himself assuaged them all, when, laid out in the loftiest location in the city, he **allowed them all to look upon him. Weeping welled up as they beheld him** proffering his right hand for their kisses. *As their tears burst forth, they appeared not as an army visiting its king, but one attending his funeral. And greater grief gripped those prominent at his bedside.* Yet **Alexander** did not weep but **surveyed them** and asked: "After my passing, how shall you come by a king worthy of such men?" *All were mute, yet he gave no hint of depression, but rather consoled some who could not contain their sorrow and gave others instructions for their parents. His spirit was as invincible in the face of death as it had been in confronting the enemy.* **As incredible to say as to hear, he persisted with that posture, into which he had settled himself ere admitting the military, until he had taken a last salute from the entire army. He then dismissed the lower orders and, as though freed from all life's cares, flung back his limbs in languor.**

13.45 *He bade his Friends draw nigh, since* after six days *even his voice was now vanishing, and despairing of living he* then removed his ring from his finger and ceded it to Perdiccas. He also issued instructions that they should command that his corpse be conveyed to Ammon *and Ptolemy undertook the task.* **And when his Friends asked him, "To whom do you bequeath your realm?" he responded, "To the strongest."** But he added that he foresaw that his foremost Friends would stage famous funeral contests *in his honour.* **Then again, when Perdiccas inquired when he wished divine honours paid to him, he said that he wished for them when they themselves were happy.** These were the last words of the king, *for Alexander expired shortly afterwards, having reigned for twelve years and seven* complete **months.** His feats were the finest, not just judging by earlier reigns, but also looking at later leaders down to our day.

---

[405] A festival of the death of Heracles was held annually on Mt Oeta in southern Thessaly.

Figure 13.3. The death of Alexander (1696)

13.46 Initially, the entire palace resounded with woeful wailing, loud lamentation and plaintive plangency. But soon enough, all were numbed by mute melancholy as if in a desolate waste, when in dejection they turned to pondering what might now transpire. The noble youths who customarily cared for his person could neither restrain their gargantuan grief nor keep within the courtyard of the royal quarters. Roving around in semblance of fury, they saturated the city in sorrow

Book 13: July 324BC – July 323BC & Beyond

despite its immense extent, omitting no moaning that mourning mouths in such a dire disaster. Accordingly, those who had stood vigil outside the palace, Macedonians and foreigners alike, swarmed together. And neither could the victors and the vanquished be differentiated in their shared distress, for the Persians commemorated the mildest and most just of lords, whilst the Macedonians bewailed the best and bravest of monarchs, such that between them they staged a kind of contest in grieving.

13.47 Not merely mutters of mourning, but also voices of vexation could clearly be heard to complain that it was the jealousy of the gods that had hauled from the human sphere such a forceful fellow in the flower of his youth and fair fortune. His vigour and his visage as he led his troops into battle, besieged cities, scaled ramparts and at assemblies presented prizes to the valiant were as a vision before their eyes. Then the Macedonians repented having refused him divine honours, confessing their disloyalty and ingratitude in swindling his ears out of an epithet they should have enjoyed. And after lingering long between revering their king and pining at his passing, they turned their pity upon themselves. It was their perception that they had been marched forth from Macedon and forsaken beyond the Euphrates amidst enemies not yet reconciled to their recent rule. Lacking a legitimate heir for their monarch and in the absence of a sure successor to his sovereignty, every contender would be vying to draw the resources of the state to himself.

13.48 Thence they conceived a foreboding of the civil conflicts that were to come. Once more their blood would spurt forth as fresh wounds rent old scars, not now for the rule of Asia, but rather in disputing their own leadership. Decrepit and debilitated, those who had recently requested release from a rightful ruler would perchance perish to preserve the power of some piddling pretender. As they mulled this over in their minds, dusk descended to darken their disquiet. The soldiers stood at arms, whilst the Babylonians peered forth, some from the walls and others from their rooftops, as if they might thus perceive a resolution. Yet none dared set their lanterns alight, so their vision was veiled, but their ears caught the calling and the clamour. Being often possessed by pointless panic, they collided in careering down dark alleys and were mutually shaken and suspicious in such encounters.

13.49 The Persians sheared their shocks and locks in accordance with their custom and got themselves garbed for grieving with their wives and offspring, for they mourned their monarch not as their vanquisher and former foe, but rather with real regret as a most righteous ruler of their own nation. Though accustomed to abiding under kings, they conceded that none other had more deserved to command them. And the lamentation was not confined within the walls of the city, since such terrible tidings had irrupted into the region round about and thence percolated through a prodigious part of Asia on the near side of the Euphrates.

13.50 *Word rapidly reached* the mother of Darius too, *who* was dolorous over Alexander's demise. *Therefore, she ripped away her raiment, replacing it with garments for grieving, tearing her tresses and flinging herself to the floor. Settled with her was the second of her granddaughters, but lately bereaved of Hephaistion, whom having married she now mourned, so that the communal despondency accentuated her personal pain. But solely Sisygambis herself suffered for the injuries to her entire kindred: she wept in turn for the ills that had befallen her and her granddaughters. And these fresh frets evoked the pining of the past. You might have thought the woebegone woman had just lost Darius and was about to conduct the last rites for two of her own sons:* she wept for both the dead and the living. *Who now would be the guardian of her girls? Who would be the Alexander of tomorrow? They were prisoners once more and robbed of their royal rank all over again. After Darius had died, they had discovered a defender, but in the aftermath of Alexander it was clear that none could be found to care for them.*

13.51 *In this context she was conscious that her eighty brothers had been slain in a single day by that most savage sovereign, Ochus, and that the felling of their father had augmented the massacre of so many sons. Of the offspring that she herself had borne, but a single one of seven survived.*[406] *Darius himself had prospered for a little while, merely that he could meet with a more pitiless passing.* So, ultimately, Sisygambis succumbed to sorrow. *Veiling her head* and *turning away from her granddaughter and grandson, who sank down in supplication at her knees,* she spurned *both* sustenance *and sunlight and* she was deceased five days after determining to die. *Assuredly* her death is a *tremendous* testament to the tenderness of Alexander towards her *and for his virtuous treatment of all those taken in his wars:* for she, who allowed herself to live beyond Darius, was ashamed to outlive Alexander.

13.52 And, by Heracles, it is evident to those who evaluate the king evenly that his excellence was innate, whilst his errors were the fault of fate or else immaturity. He exhibited an astounding strength of spirit and nearly inimical tolerance of toil. His bravery was not merely remarkable among rulers, but exemplary even among individuals in whom valour is a singular virtue. Often his generosity rendered richer rewards than are implored from the immortals. His lenity towards the losers led him to release many realms into their rule, either kingdoms captured from them in conflict or else given as gifts. He always disdained the dread of death that paralyses other people. His yearning for praise and glory was more than was modest, but was excused by his youth and such superlative deeds. Then there was his devotion towards his parents, of whom he had determined to designate Olympias as a deity and had avenged Philip. Then again there was his beneficence towards almost all of his friends and his

---

[406] Oxathres.

Book 13: July 324BC – July 323BC & Beyond

benevolence towards his troops. As prudent as he was courageous; wily well beyond the wisdom of his years; self-controlled in his crude cravings and indulging love's longings within limits set by nature, he sampled no sensual pleasures save such as were licit. Indeed, these endowments were his natural disposition.

13.53 In consequence of his career prospering, he put himself on a par with the Pantheon and aspired to divine honours, being credulous of corresponding oracular advice. And he was more maddened than was meet by those who refused him reverence. He adopted foreign dress, thus copying the customs of the conquered countries that he had despised before defeating them. As for his irascibility and his lust for wine, seeing as they were exacerbated by his youth, more maturity might have moderated them. Yet it ought to be owned that, though he owed much to his virtue, he owed yet more to Fortune, over whom he alone among mortals held sway. How often she redeemed him from the threshold of Hades! How often, when daring drove him into danger, she guarded him with guaranteed good luck! She also ordained the same end for his life and his glory. The Fates deferred his demise whilst he overwhelmed the Orient and accessed the Ocean, fulfilling every feat that a mortal can manage.

13.54 Such was the sovereign and seignior for whom a successor was sought; yet the burden proved too great to set upon the shoulders of a single soul. So it was that his mere name and the fame of his feats raised rulers and realms across virtually the whole world. And those who kept control of even the slightest slice of his huge heritage were reckoned most renowned.

13.55 But back in Babylon, *whence indeed the discourse has digressed*, **the king's Bodyguards summoned his senior Friends and the commanders of his contingents to** *a parley at* **the palace.** There followed in their footsteps a mob of the military, desirous of discovering who would inherit Alexander's heritage. Quite a few commanders could not reach the royal quarters, being blocked by the teeming troops, despite a declaration debarring any not convened by name from a herald: for, being unwarrantable, his authority was spurned. Initially a sonorous sobbing and sighing resounded anew, but soon silence descended upon them and they tempered their tears as they wondered about what was to come. At this point Perdiccas put in public view the throne, upon which rested the raiment and the diadem of Alexander together with his arms, and he took the ring which had yesterday been yielded to him by the king and set it on the same seat. At such a sight the Assembly once more burst into bawling and fresh gales of grief.

13.56 And Perdiccas declared: "I hereby return to you that ring with which the king customarily endorsed edicts concerning his kingdom and his commands, which he himself consigned to my keeping. And, although even the gods in fury could not contrive a calamity comparable with that which has afflicted us, yet, considering the cardinal accomplishments of the king, it is conceivable that such a famous fellow was transfigured by divine will to work in the world of men until his destiny was done and thereupon rapidly reverted to his immortal roots.

Therefore, since naught endures of him save what is always sloughed off by immortality, it is firstly fitting that we should perform the rites due to his corpse and his name, being mindful of what municipality and which men we are among and of what kind of president and prince we are deprived! We must manage the matter, my fellow fighters, and consider how we can keep our conquests in the midst of the men we have mastered. We require rulership: whether by one or several is your prerogative. But it is incumbent upon you to realise that a swarm of soldiers without a leader is a body without a soul. **Roxane has been pregnant since** six **months ago. It would be for the best if she should bear a boy, who shall reign over us by the grace of the gods when he comes of age.** Let you lay down by whom you would like to be led in the interim."So spoke Perdiccas.

13.57 Then Nearchus responded that none could wonder that only the blood-kin and lineage of Alexander were well matched to the majesty of the monarchy. However, **to hold out for a king as yet unborn and to overlook him that already existed suited neither the circumstances nor the mood of the Macedonians, for there was a son of the king by Barsine**, *namely Heracles at Pergamon*, who ought to be endowed with the diadem.[407] This peroration pleased nobody. In accordance with their custom, they continually clashed their spears upon their shields in agitation and they were almost moved to mutiny, when Nearchus proved dogged in his dogma. At this point Ptolemy intervened: "*Despite that Alexander did not decree it as he died, it is claimed that* either **Roxane's** or Barsine's **son** is such a suitable successor to rule the race of Macedon! **Being the better part spawned from the spoils, even to speak his name will be an** *unholy* **shame for Europe. Is this why we have prevailed over the Persians: so that we can pander to their progeny?** Their rightful rulers, Darius and Xerxes, endeavoured ineffectually to accomplish this end with endless thousands of troops and immense armadas. Here's my opinion: the throne of Alexander should be placed in the palace and those he used to call upon to counsel him should convene there whenever communal concerns demand due deliberation. Whatever action the majority move should be mandated and the commanders and captains of contingents should comply with their will."

13.58 Some sided with Ptolemy, whilst fewer favoured Perdiccas; at which juncture Aristonous began to address them: "When Alexander was asked to whom he relinquished his realm, he desired the designation of the mightiest man. Furthermore, he himself appraised Perdiccas as the finest fellow by surrendering his ring into his hands. For he was not the only one who was sat nearby as the king lay dying, but rather Alexander chose him to whom he would hand it by casting his gaze around the throng of his Friends. Therefore, it pleased him to place Perdiccas at the pinnacle of power." None doubted that his view was true. Now all called upon Perdiccas to come to the fore and retrieve the ring of the

---

[407] Justin 13.2.6-7 attributes the remarks about Heracles to Meleager, but it is easy to see that Trogus might have summarised to "Meleager and others", hence Justin's further epitomisation; Nearchus married a daughter of Barsine at Susa in 324BC, so he was Heracles' brother-in-law.

Book 13: July 324BC – July 323BC & Beyond

king. But he was in a quandary between desire and dishonour and reckoned the more reluctantly he clutched at that which he craved, the more insistently they would define it as his duty. After hesitating in indecision over how to proceed, in the end he drew back and moved to stand behind those gathered around the throne.

13.59 But Meleager, one of the commanders *who had been sent to suppress the furore amongst the phalanx*, his spirit inspired and spurred by the prevarication of Perdiccas, now proclaimed: "May the gods forefend that Alexander's heritage and the rank of running such a remarkable realm should be shoved upon such shoulders. Certainly, people will not permit it. I speak not of those better born than this fellow, but of blokes such as need not long endure any outcome against their will. In truth it does not matter, whether you recognise as ruler Roxane's son, whenever he be born, or Perdiccas, since that man will seize sovereignty even in the guise of a guardian. That is why he does not wish to accept any king, except one as yet unborn. In the context of our mutual haste, which is not just justified but even essential, he alone would defer the matter for months and already divines that it is a boy that has been conceived. Which of you could doubt that he would even be prepared to provide an impostor? By the god of my faith, if Alexander had left us this man as our monarch in his stead, then this alone of all that he ordered ought not in my opinion to be enacted. Therefore, why should you not rush to raid the treasury? For certainly his citizens are the apparent heirs to the wealth of the king." This speech being spoken, he barged through the midst of the men-at-arms and those who ceded him passage as he departed proceeded to pursue him to the promised plunder.

13.60 So now there was a thick throng of armed troops gathered around Meleager, and the convention veered toward dissension and discord, whereupon a man of the merest rank, not known to very many of the Macedonians, inquired: "Why should there be any work for weapons in civil strife, when **you have the sovereign whom you seek**? There is in the camp **Arrhidaeus, son of Philip and brother to Alexander** that was king just a little while ago and lately his collaborator in ceremonies and sacrifices, and now his only heir, yet overlooked by you. What has he done to deserve this? What deed did he do that he is robbed of rights recognised by all realms? If it's that you seek a second Alexander, you shall never know such again. Else if you wish for one of his kin, there exists only Arrhidaeus." Having heard this, the whole host was hushed at first, as if under orders, but then they clamoured in concert for Arrhidaeus to be called, yelling that those who had convened the conference without him deserved death.

13.61 Then **Pithon**[408] in torrents of tears started by saying how Alexander was most to be commiserated on having been defrauded of the friendship and fellowship of such superb citizens and soldiers: for they were so single-minded in

---

[408] Or possibly Ptolemy: manuscripts of Curtius had *phiton*, but Justin has *ptolomeus* object to Arrhidaeus.

their surveillance of the laurels and legacy of the king that all else was veiled from their view. And he *was not at all ambiguous in speaking against the man to whom the realm was being rendered*: "*It is not just on account of his disreputable dam, for he was born of a bawd from Larissa,*[409] *but also because of the intense imbecility that afflicts him, and lest, were he king in name, some other should wield the authority.*"[410] Through throwing in their faces such vehement vitriol, he stirred up more antagonism towards himself than disdain for Arrhidaeus. For their sense of sympathy began to sow their support. Hence with relentless roaring they insisted that they should suffer no sovereign save such as had been sired into the succession and thus they bade that Arrhidaeus be summoned. Meleager promptly propelled him into the palace out of hostility and hatred towards Perdiccas and so *the soldiers saluted him as their sovereign under the pseudonym of Philip after his father.*

13.62 Such was the cry of the crowd, but **the foremost fellows** felt differently. Among these Pithon **began to pursue the policy of Perdiccas by proposing Perdiccas and Leonnatus,** *both related to the royal line,* **as guardians for any future son of Roxane; adding that Craterus and Antipater should be assigned the administration of affairs in Europe.** Then an oath *of obedience* was exacted from each of them that they should acknowledge any king begotten by Alexander.

13.63 Not without just cause, Meleager was worried he would be punished; hence he had withdrawn with his faction. But now he burst back into the palace dragging Philip along with him, proclaiming that he was of tempered maturity well suited to the public duties of a new monarch as they had envisaged just a little while ago. Let them merely audition this scion of Philip, son and brother to a brace of kings: let them favour their own feelings foremost.

13.64 Neither oceanic depths nor vast, storm-swept sounds can summon such surges as are seen in the emotions of a mob, especially if it is revelling in a recent yet transient autonomy. Few favoured the freshly picked Perdiccas, whereas many were minded to make their master Philip, whom they had disdained. But they were incapable either of opposing or approving anything for long, at some points repenting their plans, at others repenting their repentance. But in the final analysis their affiliation inclined towards the royal line. Arrhidaeus had quit the Assembly having been mightily alarmed by the lordliness of the leading men, yet the effect of his departure was more to muffle rather than diminish his support among the troops. And upon being now recalled, he wrapped himself in the raiment of his brother, the self-same suit as had been set upon the throne. Meleager donned a

---

[409] Arrhidaeus was the son of Philip and Philinna, a "dancing-girl" from Larissa, but he seems to have been formally acknowledged by Philip, perhaps in the context of the Pixodarus affair.

[410] The actual words of the denunciation of Arrhidaeus are missing in the surviving text of Curtius, which shows signs of corruption at this point, but a partial reconstruction may be read in from Justin 13.2.11; it is a reasonable hypothesis that Curtius omitted the invective, because he was drawing a parallel between the accession of Arrhidaeus and that of his own emperor, Claudius; cf. Curtius 10.9.3-6.

Book 13: July 324BC – July 323BC & Beyond

cuirass and clutched his arms to act as escort to the new king. The phalanx followed suit, smiting their shields with their spears to signal that they would spill the blood of any who aspired to the throne without warrant. They rejoiced that the imperial power would remain with the same house and family. The royal dynasty would duly appropriate their heritage of empire. They were accustomed to respecting and reverencing the name itself and none assumed it save such as were born to reign.

13.65 Therefore in consternation Perdiccas commanded that the chamber in which the corpse of Alexander lay should be bolted. With him were six hundred supporters of proven prowess. And also Ptolemy and the retinue of Royal Pages had coupled themselves to his cause. But the barriers were readily ruptured by so many thousands of men-at-arms. The king too burst in, beset by a cortège of collaborators, among whom Meleager was pre-eminent *with Attalus acting as his accomplice*. Perdiccas, in a rage, rallied any who wished to ward the body of Alexander, but those who had forced their way in flung their javelins at him from afar. And many were wounded, when eventually the veterans doffed their helms, the better to be known, and began to beseech those who were with Perdiccas to refrain from fighting and to defer to the king and force of numbers. Perdiccas was the first to sheathe his arms and the rest followed suit. Then, when Meleager confided that they should not forsake the corpse of Alexander, they supposed he sought to snare them there, so they stole away, passing through part of the palace facing the Euphrates. **The cavalry,** which was constituted from the best-born youths, **fully followed Perdiccas and Leonnatus and favoured faring forth from the city and fighting from the fields.** But Perdiccas did not despair of the foot following him as well. Hence, so it should not seem that he had severed himself from the rest of the army by withdrawing with the cavalry, he stayed within the city.

13.66 Moreover Meleager repeatedly reproached his ruler, saying that his right to reign would best be ratified, if Perdiccas were to perish, since, if his unbridled spirit were not crushed, he would subvert the situation; for Perdiccas knew full well what treatment he deserved from the king and no one was fully faithful to one whom he feared. The king rather heard him out than concurred; and so **Meleager** simply supposed his silence to constitute a command and **arranged** *for Attalus* **to send henchmen to arraign Perdiccas** in the king's name. **They were commissioned to kill him**, if he were to demur. When the approach of these henchmen was heralded, **Perdiccas posted himself** in the entrance to his residence **attended by** a total of sixteen of the retinue of **Royal Pages**. From there he castigated those who came for him, calling them Meleager's minions, and *inviting them to take him on, but* **the determination** of his demeanour and countenance **so cowed them that they fled in consternation**. Thereupon Perdiccas directed the Pages to mount their steeds and got through to Leonnatus with a few of his friends, so as to stage a sturdier stand against any force of foes that might be brought to bear.

13.67 On the following day the Macedonians deemed it a damnable deed that had put Perdiccas in peril of perishing, so they decided to set out in arms to retaliate for the recklessness of Meleager. But he, having foreseen such an insurrection, when he came before the king commenced to coax him as to whether he had not himself commanded the capture of Perdiccas? The king conceded that he had instructed it at the instigation of Meleager, but there was no cause for commotion, since Perdiccas still lived! Therefore, when the gathering had been dispersed, Meleager was panic-stricken in perplexity, particularly due to the defection of the cavalry, for the peril he had previously projected at his opponent had now recoiled upon his own person. He squandered three days as he pondered improbable plans.

13.68 Yet actually even the palace preserved a semblance of its former functioning, for envoys of state still came before the king and the commanders of the forces still stood about him and the antechamber was still stuffed with stewards and armed guards. But the atmosphere of deep despondency was an indication of their dire predicament, and through mutual distrust they did not dare draw together nor discuss matters amongst themselves. Rather they mulled over in their minds their private presumptions and through comparison with the new king they nourished their nostalgia for him whom they had lost. Thus, they longed for him whose leadership and guidance they had *formerly* followed, for they were forsaken amidst perilous, unpacified peoples, who would risk retaliating for their many injuries whenever they were availed of an opportunity. Such cogitation was corroding their morale when it was proclaimed that the cavalry commanded by Perdiccas, having seized the countryside surrounding Babylon, had begun to detain the grain being moved into the metropolis. Therefore, firstly frugality then famine set in and those within the city supposed that they had either to reach for reconciliation with Perdiccas or else to resolve the wrangle with their weapons.

13.69 Unintentionally, it so happened that the folk in the farmland, fearing that their villas and villages would be laid waste, were seeking sanctuary in the city, whilst the failure of their food supply moved the townsmen to migrate from the metropolis: to each community the abode of the other seemed safer. Having misgivings of mutiny amongst these migrants the Macedonians met in the palace and gave vent to their views. It was accepted amongst them that they should despatch a delegation to the cavalry to curtail the discord and discuss the discarding of arms. Therefore, the king so commissioned Pasas of Thessaly and Amissus of Megalopolis and Perilaus. When they had conveyed the monarch's message, they returned with the response that the cavalry would not set aside their arms unless the king surrendered the sowers of dissension.

13.70 This being promulgated, the soldiers impulsively seized their weapons and the ruction roused Philip forth from the royal quarters, declaring: "There's no use raising a rumpus, for those who rest in repose shall reap the riches of those who vie amongst themselves. Furthermore, be mindful that this is a matter of dealing with compatriots and hastily to hew away their hope of appeasement is to hurtle into civil war. Let us investigate whether they can be assuaged by a second delegation. As the corpse of the king has not yet been buried, I believe all will be allied in discharging this duty to him. As far as I am concerned, I would rather surrender my sovereignty than dispose it through spilling the blood of citizens. So, if there be no other hope of harmony, I beg and beseech you to pick a better man."

13.71 Then with welling tears he took the diadem from his head with his right hand and proffered it, so that he who professed to be a fitter fellow might relieve him of it. Such a sober speech inspired high hopes for his character, which had hitherto been bedimmed by the brilliance of his brother. Therefore, all present began to prompt him to proceed as he had proposed. Hence, he sent back the selfsame emissaries to solicit that Meleager be recognised as a third leader. This was conceded without difficulty, for Perdiccas also desired to distance Meleager from the monarch and he calculated that one would prove unequal to two. Therefore, when Meleager came forth at the fore of the phalanx to meet with him, Perdiccas received him at the head of his cavalry contingents. And each formation hailed the other, united in perpetual peace and staunch solidarity, or so they supposed.

13.72 *But now the Fates were forcing fratricidal conflict upon the Macedonian people, for monarchy brooks no rivals, yet was coveted by many. Hence at first they clashed their men together, then they scattered them about. And when they had burdened the body with more than it could bear, its peripheral parts began to break away and an empire that could have stood sound under a single sovereign was wrecked through being run by sundry rulers.*

13.73 Perdiccas vested his sole hope of salvation in the demise of Meleager, believing his brashness, faithlessness and readiness to revolt as well as his most malign enmity motivated a pre-emptive move against him. But he diligently disguised his designs, the better to catch Meleager unawares. Hence, he privately persuaded some from among the forces over which he presided publicly to bemoan the parity of Meleager with himself, as if Perdiccas himself were innocent of their complaints. When Meleager was informed of their invective, in a fuming fury he related what he had learnt to Perdiccas, who, as if horrified by an unheard of happening, began to seem surprised and to groan and to show some semblance of sorrow. In the end, they agreed that they ought to arrest the authors of such seditious prattle. Meleager was moved to thank Perdiccas and to enfold him in his arms, blessing his good faith and goodwill towards him. Then they took counsel together and plotted a plan to crush the culprits.

13.74 **They were pleased to perform a purification of the army** according to the custom of their country and the preceding dissension seemed to provide a plausible pretext for it. The Macedonian monarchs customarily lustrate their troops in the following fashion: they rend a bitch asunder and deposit a part of its flesh on either side at the far end of the field into which they parade the army.[411] All the soldiers stand within this land: hither the horse and thither the phalanx. Accordingly, **on the day** set aside for this sacred rite, the king accompanied by **the cavalry** and the elephants **arrayed themselves facing the foot** commanded by Meleager. As the cavalry contingents came on at them, the foot felt a frisson of fear and anticipation in view of the recent rift, not wholly healed, and they dithered awhile as to whether they should withdraw into the city, since the field favoured the cavalry. Yet reckoning they ought not rashly to refute the good faith of their fellow fighters, they stood their ground, readying their resolution to repulse any assault upon them.

13.75 Now the columns were converging and just a small space separated their foremost files. At this juncture the king commenced to canter up to the infantry with a single squadron of cavalry. Prompted by **Perdiccas** he **insisted that the instigators of the discord,** whom he was actually obligated to protect, **should be given up for punishment,** threatening that he would charge them with all his regiments and the elephants to boot should they refuse. The infantry were stunned by this unforeseen aggression and neither could Meleager himself contribute either counsel or courage to their cause. It seemed for the moment safest to await what might transpire rather than push their luck. Then, perceiving that they were paralysed and punishable, Perdiccas segregated thirty[412] men, who had followed Meleager in sallying forth from the Assembly held just after Alexander's death, and in the sight of the entire army he cast those chosen before the elephants. Every one of them was trampled to death beneath the feet of the monstrous beasts, whilst Philip neither hindered nor sanctioned it and it was evident that he would only endorse happy outcomes.

13.76 This was both a sign and the inception of civil war amongst the Macedonians. Belatedly perceiving the perfidy of Perdiccas, Meleager still stood stiff amidst his formations, since no force was focussed upon his own person. Yet soon afterwards he forsook all hope of salvation, since he saw that his enemies were manipulating the name of the man he had himself made king to procure his destruction *through charges that he plotted against Perdiccas*. Hence, he sought asylum in a sanctuary, but not even so sacred a site saved him from being slaughtered.

13.77 Having led the army into the metropolis, **Perdiccas convened a council of the main men, at which they were disposed to divide the direction of their dominions thus:**[413] *that the king should assuredly hold the whole*

---

[411] The same Macedonian ceremony is described in more detail by Livy 40.6, but in the context of the reign of Philip V over a century later.

[412] Manuscripts of Curtius 10.9.18 gave CCC (300), but Diodorus 18.4.7 has "thirty", which is preferable: e.g. manuscripts of Curtius 9.8.15 gave DCCC for LXXX (i.e. 10x exaggeration.)

[413] What follows is the Cleitarchan version of the First Division of the Satrapies, for which the sources are: Curtius 10.10.1-4, Diodorus 18.3 & Justin 13.4.9-23, although Justin becomes muddled for the Eastern Satrapies, which Curtius omits; there are also some significant commonalities with Metz Epitome 116-122; a slightly variant tradition is preserved by Photius.

Book 13: July 324BC – July 323BC & Beyond

empire in his sway; that Ptolemy the son of Lagus **should be Satrap of Egypt and of such Libyan peoples as were subject to the Macedonians;** that Syria **should be ceded to Laomedon** of Mytilene together with Phoenicia; **Cilicia was for Philotas; Antigonus was assigned to hold Greater Phrygia with** Nearchus to assist him in **Lycia and Pamphylia;** they sent Cassander[414] **to Caria and Menander to Lydia; Hellespontine Phrygia was designated as the province allotted to Leonnatus;** to Eumenes were granted Paphlagonia and Cappadocia plus the associated **coast of the Pontic Sea and he was empowered to protect that region as far as Trapezus**[415] **and to contest its rule with Ariarathes,**[416] **who alone had eluded the dominion of the empire,** since pressing problems elsewhere had diverted Alexander after the fall of Darius; Greater **Media was assigned to Pithon** the Illyrian; **in Europe, Thrace and those nations adjoining the Pontic Sea were given to Lysimachus** and Antipater was appointed to govern Macedon and the neighbouring nations.

13.78 Concerning the leadership of India, Bactria, Sogdiana and those others who inhabit the territories near either the Ocean or the Red Sea, it was decreed that those who had hitherto held command should keep it. In this vein they revalidated the reign of Taxiles and that of Porus as arranged by Alexander himself. Pithon *the son of Agenor* was sent to secure *the satrapy and* the Indian outposts *running alongside their lands*. The satrapy that stretches along the Caucasus range that is called Paropamisus was assigned to Oxyartes *the Bactrian, whose daughter, Roxane, Alexander had wed.* Sibyrtius was recognised as running Arachosia and Kedrosia; Stasanor of Soli in Aria and Drangianê; *Philip for Bactria*[417] *and Sogdiana; Phrataphernes had Hyrcania and Parthia; Peucestes was reappointed to Persia; Tlepolemus retained Carmania;* Atropates, *the father-in-law of Perdiccas,* held Lesser Media *and Coenus received Susianê;* Archon *of Pella* controlled Babylon and Arcesilaus managed Mesopotamia. They set Seleucus in command of the Companion Cavalry, *a most exalted status, for first of all Hephaistion had led them followed by Perdiccas. To construct the catafalque and convey the corpse of the king who had deceased unto Ammon they assigned Arrhidaeus. Finally,* Perdiccas was to remain with his monarch and to command the forces that followed him.

13.79 *It has been believed by some that the satrapies were distributed according to the Will of Alexander, but we have established that this is an unfounded rumour, despite its having been*

---

[414] Probably an error for Asander (cf. Photius: 92 Arrian 156.1.6 & 156.9.37; 82 Dexippus) but common to Curtius, Justin & Diodorus and therefore derived from their common source (Cleitarchus). This suggests that they are all still following Cleitarchus. The same error occurs in the Metz Epitome 117 – did Cleitarchus source his list from the prototype of the Metz Epitome?

[415] I.e. Trebizond (modern Trabzon in NE Turkey); *trapeiunta* or *trapeiuncta* in the MSS of Curtius.

[416] Ariarathes is interpreted from MSS readings: *araba, arbate* and *harbate*.

[417] On the matters of Philip for Bactria and Phrataphernes for Parthia, Diodorus agrees with solely the Metz Epitome.

reported by some authorities.[418] Yet indeed **they had each established themselves in power bases, which after the division of the dominions they defended as their own**, as if demarcation could ever endure in the face of unrestrained ambition.[419] **Thus those who had but recently seemed servants of another sovereign**, safeguarding his suzerainty, **seized sizable realms in their own right;** thereby removing reasons for rivalry, since all were on the same side by nationality and the headquarters of each was isolated from the rest. Yet it was hard to be happy with what opportunity had apportioned, for high hopes make first gleanings seem mean. Hence it appeared to each of them expedient to expand their realms, rather than be satisfied with them as they were.

13.80 It was the seventh day during which the king's corpse had reposed in a receptacle, as the attention of all had been distracted from due death rites by the stabilisation of the state. And nowhere else than in the domain of Mesopotamia does any more searing summer heat set in and to such a degree that crowds of creatures caught in open ground expire, so severe is the scorching of sun and sky, whereby the world is withered as if with fire. Springs of water are both scarce and disguised through the deceit of the denizens, by whom they are accessible to exploitation, whilst unnoticed by newcomers. *Hence hereafter is related what is recorded rather than reckoned reliable:*[420] when finally his Friends found leisure to look after Alexander's lifeless body, those who entered could discern no decay nor even the least livid grey of corruption.[421] Neither was his visage yet bereft of the vitality evoked by the breath of life. Therefore, on being commanded to care for the corpse according to their customs, the Egyptians and Chaldeans, as if he still respired, did not at first dare to set their hands upon him. Then, praying that it were proper and pious for mortals to manhandle an immortal, they eviscerated the cadaver, gorged the golden coffin with spices and set the symbol of his status upon his head.

---

[418] This is an intriguing sentence, uniquely sourced from Curtius 10.10.5; although some have seen it as a comment originated by Curtius himself, it is odd that he uses the first person plural here, having used the first person singular of himself at 10.8.7; in fact, the related sentiments in the ensuing paragraph were probably not devised by Curtius himself, since Curtius 10.10.6-8 is rather similar to Justin 13.4.24-25 in the same context; possibly "we" means Cleitarchus and Curtius or else is simply a direct translation of Cleitarchus' text; the sentence might equally derive from some kind of *scholium* on the standard text of Cleitarchus; however, the commonalities between the Division of the Satrapies according to Cleitarchus and Metz Epitome 116-118 strongly suggest that Cleitarchus was aware of the "Will of Alexander" as recited by the Metz Epitome.

[419] Every editor proposes some unique variant of the elliptical Latin prototype at Curtius 10.10.6.

[420] This phrase is usually given as a personal comment in the first person singular as if by Curtius himself in modern versions of his text, but the crucial verb *refero* is actually *refert* in the manuscripts, so there is no strong evidence that the comment does not originate with Cleitarchus.

[421] The freshness of Alexander's corpse is related by Curtius 10.10.12-13 and Plutarch, *Alex.* 77.3.

Book 13: July 324BC – July 323BC & Beyond

13.81 *Craterus, who was among the leading lords, had earlier led away ten thousand discharged veterans up to Cilicia at Alexander's behest.*[422] *Concurrently, he carried written commissions that the king had charged him to consummate. But after Alexander's passing his Successors were minded not to proceed with his projects. For when Perdiccas perused plans for the completion of Hephaistion's mausoleum in the memoranda of the king, which demanded much money, and also the rest of his schemes, which were many and magnificent and meant matchless munificence, he decided that it was wise to set them aside. But in order not to detract from Alexander's prestige at the whim of his personal opinion, he asked the Assembly of the common Macedonians to pronounce upon all these projects.*

13.82 *These were the most magnificent and meet of memory among the matters in the memoranda: the construction of a thousand galleys of greater size than triremes in Phoenicia, Syria, Cilicia and Cyprus for the purposes of the campaign against the Carthaginians and such others as dwell beside the shores of Libya and Iberia and the contiguous coastal countries all the way around to Sicily; to hew a highway along the Libyan littoral as far as the Pillars of Heracles; to establish six costly shrines, each at an outlay of fifteen hundred talents; to hatch harbours and develop dockyards at suitable spots as entailed by such enormous expeditions; and lastly to found cosmopolitan cities and expatriate populations out of Asia into Europe and contrariwise out of Europe into Asia, so as to lead the largest landmasses into loving kinship and communality through intermarriage and consanguinity.*

13.83 *The aforementioned shrines were to be erected at Delos, Delphi and Dodona, then in Macedon: a temple of Zeus at Dium; of Tauropolus at Amphipolis; and of Athena at Cyrrhus.*[423] *Likewise for the latter goddess at Ilium there was planned to be built a shrine that should never have been surpassed by any other. For his father Philip he intended a tomb paralleling the greatest of the pyramids of Egypt, such as some tally among the seven most magnificent masterpieces of mankind. When these memoranda were recited before the Macedonians, despite acknowledging the nobility of Alexander, they nevertheless perceived the projects to be overblown and impracticable, so they determined to put none of those mentioned into effect.*

13.84 Since some writers dispute the circumstances of the death of Alexander, declaring that he died by a deadly drug, it would seem necessary not to neglect narrating their notions.[424] They say that Antipater, who was Marshal of Europe under Alexander, quarrelled with Olympias, the mother of the king. At first he paid her no heed, since Alexander did

---

[422] Sections 13.81-83 derive exclusively from Diodorus 18.4.1-6 dealing with Alexander's "Last Plans": direct evidence for their ultimate derivation from Cleitarchus is weak, but all other material in Diodorus 18.1-4 seems to be Cleitarchan, hence it looks as though Diodorus did not switch sources to Hieronymus until 18.5.

[423] Russel M. Geer in the Loeb edition of Diodorus 18 makes Tauropolus a manifestation of Artemis, but the son of Dionysus associated with the Thracian Chersonese would seem possible, given that Amphipolis borders on Thrace; Cyrrhus is Cyrnus in the manuscripts, but it seems preferable to assume that the known Macedonian town is intended.

[424] Sections 13.84-86 are based on various matches between Curtius 10.10.14-19, Diodorus 17.117.5-17.118.2 & Pausanias 9.7.2-3; cf. Justin 12.14, Plutarch, *Alex* 77.1-3 & Metz 87 *et seqq*.

not swallow her slanders against him. But, later, as their hatred kept hardening and the king became anxious to mollify his mother in all matters out of filial reverence and when his own great deeds in Greece had reaped his ruler's rivalry rather than respect, **Antipater exhibited sundry signs of estrangement. Then, too, the slaying of Parmenion and Philotas** and the execution of his son-in-law Alexander Lyncestes **sent shudders through Antipater as through all Alexander's Friends.** Finally, there were the cold-eyed killings of the governors of the conquered countries not so many days beforehand. On the basis of these things Antipater supposed he had been summoned from Macedon not to participate in campaigns but to experience punishment. **So,** to forestall the king's plans, **he assigned his own son, Iollas, who was Alexander's cupbearer, to dose him with the deadly drug.**

13.85 *Certainly, Alexander was often heard to exclaim that Antipater coveted kingship; that he was more powerful than was proper in a viceroy; that he was conceited concerning his renowned victory over the Spartans and made all that was given him his own. They even credited that Craterus and a detachment of the veterans had been sent to slay Antipater. But it is a fact that the potency of the poison produced in Macedon is such that it* consumes crockery and bronze and *even eats through iron, so that solely the hoof of a beast of burden can contain* and convey *the liquor. The spring, whence wells up this vitiating venom, they call the Styx. Thus, this was carried by Cassander and brought to his brother Iollas,* that used to wait upon the king, *alongside their other brother, Philip. Antipater had enjoined his son to trust in none save Medius the Thessalian and his own brothers. Hence it was that the partying was resumed in the Thessalian's quarters* **and Iollas,** *who customarily tasted and diluted the king's drinks,* **introduced the poison into** *chill water and, after undertaking the tasting, poured this into* **Alexander's last draught.**

13.86 *These rumours, whatever their credence, were soon suppressed by the power of those whom the tales tainted. For* after Alexander's death Antipater reaped the rule of Macedon and also of Greece, *such that he was in complete control of Europe.* Thereafter his son Cassander succeeded him, so that many commentators lacked the resolution to write about the drug. But Cassander is manifestly revealed by his own deeds to have had an antagonistic attitude towards Alexander's legacies and he successively exterminated the whole house of Alexander. Olympias he murdered *through throwing her before the exasperated Macedonians to be obliterated,* and he cast her body out of its grave. With zestful zeal he raised up Thebes that had been razed to the ground under Alexander. *And he also slew the sons of Alexander, Heracles by Barsine, and Alexander by Roxane, whom he despatched with a drug.* Yet he did not end his own existence exulting. He swelled up with dropsy, from which maggots emerged whilst he still lived. And not long after succeeding as sovereign, Philip, his eldest son, was stricken with a wasting disease, which did away with him. Antipater, the next in line, murdered his mother Thessalonike, the daughter of Philip the son of

Amyntas and of Nicasipolis, accusing her of overly favouring Alexander, who was the youngest of Cassander's sons. Bringing in Demetrius the son of Antigonus, with his aid Alexander deposed and disciplined his brother Antipater. However, it transpired that in Demetrius he discovered his murderer rather than an ally.[425] So some god wreaked righteous retribution upon Cassander.

Figure 13.4. Ptolemy (obverse) and his badge of an eagle grasping a thunderbolt (reverse) on a silver tetradrachm coin by the Delta Engraver minted in Alexandria between 305-285BC (author's collection).

13.87 However, Ptolemy, to whom Egypt had been ceded, conveyed the corpse of the king to *this country, where he entombed it with Macedonian rites at* Memphis. Thence it has been transported these few years afterwards *by our sister-loving sovereign Ptolemy the son of Ptolemy* to Alexandria, where every respect is rendered to the remembrance and the renown of Alexander.

13.88 *These were the events concerning Alexander* in the last year of his reign and its aftermath.

---

[425] Cassander died in 297BC and his son Alexander was murdered in 294BC by Demetrius Poliorcetes, who then became King of Macedon.

Explicit liber Cleitarchi

"I should like, Onesicritus, to come back to life for a little while after my death to see how men read these present events then. If now they praise and welcome them, do not be surprised, for they think, every one of them, that this is a fine bait to catch my goodwill."

Alexander quoted by Lucian in Section 40 of his essay on How to Write History

Key Historical Issues

Alexander's Ancestry

Alexander's putative paternal ancestry from Heracles and maternal ancestry from Aeacus are mentioned at the outset of their accounts of Alexander by Plutarch, *Alexander* 1.5 and Diodorus 17.1.5; the only likely common source for these details in these authors would be Cleitarchus.

It is essential to understand that neither Alexander nor his biographers invented these genealogies. They were at least two centuries old in Alexander's time and probably much older still. Virtually all Alexander's contemporaries treated them as factual. Certainly, Alexander himself had no reason to question the stories concerning his ancestry that he would have been taught from infancy.

Regarding Alexander's descent from Heracles and thence from Zeus himself: the Macedonian Royal Family claimed descent from Temenus, king of Argos in the Peloponnese. Temenus was a great great grandson of Heracles, whose heavenly father was Zeus himself. Thus, the entire dynasty called themselves Temenids or Argeads. The first Temenid king in Macedonia was Caranus (reigned 808-778BC). The dynasty also put a portrait of Heracles wearing the Nemean lion skin on the obverses of their coins from at least as early as the fifth century BC and the reign of Archelaus (413-399BC). The Royal Family of Macedonia were recognised as Argives and Temenids by Herodotus 5.22[426] & 8.138.2[427] in the early fifth century BC and by Thucydides 2.99.3[428] in the late fifth century BC.[429] Manolis Andronikos found an inscription in the tholos room of the royal palace at Aegae reading ΗΡΑΚΛΗΙ ΠΑΤΡΩΙΩΙ, which means "Father Heracles", recognising him as the ancestor of the royal family of the Macedonians.[430]

---

[426] "...when Alexander [the first king Alexander of Macedon, reigned c498-454BC] chose to contend and entered the lists for that purpose [at the Olympic Games], the Greeks who were to run against him wanted to bar him from the race, saying that the contest should be for Greeks and not for foreigners. Alexander, however, proving himself to be an Argive, was judged to be a Greek. He accordingly competed in the stade race and tied step for first place."

[427] "This river, when the sons of Temenus had crossed it, rose in such flood that the riders could not cross. So the brothers came to another part of Macedonia and settled near the place called the garden of Midas son of Gordias, where roses grow of themselves, each bearing sixty blossoms and of surpassing fragrance."

[428] "The country on the sea coast, now called Macedonia, was first acquired by Alexander, the father of Perdiccas, and his ancestors, originally Temenids from Argos."

[429] See also N. G. L. Hammond, "The Miracle that was Macedonia", 1991 and "Philip of Macedon", 1994.

[430] Manolis Andronicos, Vergina: The Royal Tombs (1994) p.38.

Concerning Alexander the Great by Andrew Chugg

Regarding Alexander's maternal ancestry: tradition had long associated Neoptolemus, the son of Achilles, with the rule of Epirus (see Pindar, *Nemean* 4.51–53, 7.38–39). Perhaps as early as the days of Pindar (late sixth to early fifth century BC), but certainly by the time Euripides composed his Andromache (in the 420s BC), the rulers of the Molossian kingdom within Epirus asserted that they were the descendants of Neoptolemus through his son by Andromache, widow of Hector (Euripides, *Andromache* 1246–49). By the era of Olympias, Alexander's mother, an extension of her genealogy made Priam, through his son Helenus, an ancestor of the Aeacidae as well. In this version the Royal Family were also descended from a son of Andromache by Helenus. As the fourth century progressed, the name choices of the dynasty for their offspring indicated growing emphasis on this heroic Trojan genealogy: for example, Olympias was originally named Polyxena after the youngest daughter of King Priam of Troy. In the reign of Olympias' father, himself named Neoptolemus, they became standard. The peculiarly Trojan quality of the names of Neoptolemus' children has led some to conclude that their mother must have been Chaonian since the ruling house of that Epirote tribe claimed descent from Andromache and Helenus (Justin 17.3.6). This Aeacid genealogy for the Molossian Royal Family gained wide credence in the Greek world.[431]

It is also pertinent that Neoptolemus the son of Achilles is alternatively called Pyrrhus. This is a name meaning literally "flame" in the sense of the hair colour of the individual. It works rather like the nickname Ginger in English, but most likely indicated strawberry blonde hue rather than auburn. Such is the colour of Alexander's hair in a mural painting of him with a queen, probably Thalestris, from Pompeii (fresco in Regio 6 Insula Occidentalis 39). The great nephew of Olympias was also called Pyrrhus and ruled Epirus in the early 3rd century BC. Furthermore, the Persephone figure in the pebble mosaic recently unearthed in the Kasta Mound at Amphipolis has strawberry blonde hair and should be recognised as a portrait of Alexander's Epirote mother, Olympias.

Further evidence for the association between Achilles and Epirus is provided by Plutarch, *Pyrrhus* 1.3, who states that Achilles was worshipped in Epirus under the cult name of "Aspetus."

In mythology Achilles was the son of Peleus, who was the son of Aeacus the son of Zeus. Thus, it may be concluded that Alexander was legitimately regarded and legitimately saw himself as a descendant of Zeus via both his father's and his mother's family trees.

---

[431] See also Elizabeth Carney, "Olympias: Mother of Alexander the Great", 2006, Women of the Ancient World Series, Taylor and Francis, p. 5.

Key Historical Issues

The Date of Alexander's Birth

This matter is treated in some detail under the sub-section concerning the reliability of Arrian, so it suffices here briefly to assert the correctness of the date given by Plutarch in his Life of Alexander, which is likely to have been taken from Cleitarchus. That is the 6th Hecatombaeon in the Attic calendar corresponding to the (same day in the) month of Loios in the Macedonian calendar. In general Greek calendars in Alexander's time began months at the New Moon. However, there was a special version of the Attic calendar run by the Archon and used to fix the start of festivals, which was sometimes deliberately moved out of step with the Moon by the Archon for political and social purposes. Nevertheless, Plutarch implies that the date of Alexander's birth was on the same day of the month in the Macedonian calendar as in the version of the Attic calendar that he is using, which is suggestive of a lunar synchronised date. Elsewhere, he gives the date of the Battle of Arbela/Gaugamela and that was definitely lunar synchronised. This is important, because we can calculate the exact dates in the Julian calendar of dates in the lunar synchronised Attic calendar, since the dates of historical lunar and solar eclipses, which occur at Full Moon and New Moon respectively, have been tabulated for the whole of recorded history (e.g. by NASA). Hence, we can say that Alexander was born on 20th July 356BC in the Julian calendar

The only reason that this has ever seriously been doubted is that Arrian states that Alexander lived for thirty-two years and eight months. Since it is certain that he died on 10th (announced on 11th) June 323BC also in the Julian calendar, that dates his birth to October 356BC. However, Arrian appears to be erroneously conflating a rough age for Alexander of twenty years at his accession (which he took from Aristobulus) with a correct duration for Alexander's reign of twelve years and eight months. Furthermore, there is a test for the correctness of Plutarch's date, because both he and Justin note that Philip announced the victory of his team in the chariot race at the Olympic Games and the birth of Alexander to his troops at the same time. The two events would need to have occurred within a month or so of one another for that to be possible. Recent research on the ancient Olympic festival has confirmed that it climaxed at the second Full Moon after the Summer Solstice, which was 30th July in 356BC. The chariot race probably took place up to a few days before that climax. Consequently, the separation in time of the two events was only about a week. That means that Plutarch's date easily satisfies the test, whereas Arrian's inferred date completely fails it.

In the information in Plutarch on Alexander's date of birth, we may be seeing the influence of Eudoxus of Cnidus, who was an important Greek astronomer active in the first half of the 4th century BC. He visited Egypt to study astronomy. He was head of the Academy in Athens at one point and is said to have taught Aristotle, Alexander's tutor. He is also credited with introducing Babylonian information to Greek astronomy including astrology and probably the zodiac and its twelve divisions and associated constellations. Eudoxus was a polymath and indeed travelled from his home city of Cnidus to Athens, Halicarnassus and Egypt, as mentioned by Diogenes Laertius. Eudoxus wrote on many subjects including mathematics and astronomy. For example, he wrote a treatise (Okaeteris) on the eight-year calendar cycle (probably while in Egypt around 360BC). His Phaenomena, on the constellations and their myths, was the basis for Aratos of Soli's similarly named poem.

As a pupil of Eudoxus, it is quite likely that Aristotle was responsible for inspiring Alexander regarding his birth on a day when the sun was in the constellation of Leo and for Alexander's subsequent adoption of the lion as a personal motif.

Alan Samuel in his book on Greek & Roman Chronology has a section on Eudoxus[432] and cites various Greek sources, notably Aristotle, to show that Eudoxus promulgated a basic rotating spheres theory of the motion of the Moon and other celestial bodies, which in later elaborations led to the Almagest of Claudius Ptolemy and the amazingly advanced celestial modelling work of Hellenistic astronomers such as Hippocrates. Obviously, the immediate objective of such models was to calculate and predict the motions of the Moon and other bodies for calendrical purposes. Even the relatively primitive model of Eudoxus would have sufficed to predict the day of the next New Moon with very good accuracy, subject perhaps to occasional observational tweaks, which need not have been made at the actual time of New Moon. This is in total contrast to misty Babylonian religiosity in its literal observations of first crescent or last crescent, often delayed by cloudy conditions. It is clear that the more scientifically-minded Greeks of Alexander's time were calculating and predicting New Moon, Full Moon and other phases long in advance. The supposition that Greek calendars relied upon crescent observations after the middle of the 4th century BC is incorrect. For example, we know that the date for the Battle of Gaugamela/Arbela is correctly given by Plutarch, Camillus 19.3 (probably using Timaeus, perhaps via Cleitarchus) as happening on the twenty-sixth day after the preceding New Moon. We know this to be correct due to accurate modern calculations of ancient New Moon dates by NASA combined with the fact that the date of the battle is also fixed by a preceding lunar eclipse, which is mentioned in our sources. However, Babylonian Astronomical Diaries appear to place the battle twenty-four days after the New Moon, evidently because the first visibility of the New Moon by the Babylonian priests was delayed by a couple of days due to cloud or some other observational obscuration. This is a confirmation that Greek chronologists in the later 4th century BC were employing Eudoxus's Lunar motion modelling work to calculate rather than observe the New Moons. A corollary is that the dates in Cleitarchus including Alexander's birthday are accurate Lunar-regulated dates.

---

[432] Samuel, Alan E., "Greek & Roman Chronology", (Munich, 1972) pp.29-31.

Key Historical Issues

The Date of Accession of Alexander the Great

I have incorporated a mention by Cleitarchus that Philip died on the autumnal equinox in 336BC in section 1.5 of my reconstruction. He had been born in 382BC and had (effectively) ascended the throne in 360BC, so the reign duration of 25 years and the 47-year lifespan given Section 1.7 of my reconstruction and taken from Justin 9.8.1 are relatively accurate given that Greek chronologists sometimes included parts of years in their tallies. However, the reasoning underlying the dating of Alexander's accession to the equinox is derived by me from inferences concerning the book structure of Cleitarchus combined with our specific knowledge of the date of the battle of Arbela/Gaugamela. I first published this argument in Alexander the Great in Afghanistan in 2011 and a slightly expanded and revised version is given below.

On the best evidence the assassination of Philip took place in October of 336BC. The key arguments may be summarised as follows. Alexander's death is fixed to 10th June 323BC (Julian Calendar) according to Plutarch citing the *Ephemerides* (composed by Eumenes of Cardia)[433] or 11th June according to Aristobulus and the Babylonian Astronomical Diaries.[434] Arrian attributes a reign of 12 years and 8 months to Alexander, whilst Diodorus approximately concurs with 12 years and 7 months.[435] Hammond has further argued that the festival at which the assassination took place should be identified with the Dia held in honour of Zeus, which took place in the eponymously named Macedonian month of Dios.[436] E. Grzybek pointed out in 1990 that Josephus (*Antiquities of the Jews* 19.1.13 [19.95]) might indicate that the day number within the month was 24, because Josephus writes that the day of Caligula's assassination was the same day as Philip's assassination, but I am convinced that Josephus only meant that the events of the two days were the same.[437]

Specifically, the passage at issue reads:

ὁμολογεῖταιδὲ καὶ τὴν ἡμέραν ἐκείνην γενέσθαι, ἐν ᾗ Φίλιππον τὸνἈμύντου Μακεδόνων βασιλέα κτείνει Παυσανίας εἷς τῶν ἑταίρωνεἰς τὸ θέατρον εἰσιόντα.

"It was also confessed that this was the same day wherein Pausanias, a friend of Philip, the son of Amyntas, who was king of Macedonia, slew him, as he was entering into the theatre."

---

[433] Plutarch, *Alexander* 76.4; A. E. Samuel, *Ptolemaic Chronology* (Munich 1962) 46-47.

[434] Plutarch, *Alexander* 75.4; L. Depuydt, "The Time of Death of Alexander the Great: 11 June 323 BC, ca. 4:00-5:00 PM," *Die Welt des Orients* 28 (1997) 117–135.

[435] Arrian, *Anabasis* 7.28.1; Diodorus 17.117.5; other ancient accounts rounded the reign to either 12 years (in two instances) or 13 years (also two instances.)

[436] Hammond, *The Regnal Years of Philip and Alexander*, 358.

[437] E. Grzybek, *Du calendrier Macédonien au calendrier Ptolémaïque* (Basel 1990) 21-28.

Concerning Alexander the Great by Andrew Chugg

The date of Caligula's assassination is known to have been the 24th of January in the Julian calendar, so enthusiasts have believed that, if only they could work out the way in which Josephus was equating the Greek and Roman calendars, they would also know the date of Philip's death. Nobody seriously believes that Philip could have died in January. Nor is any equation between the Macedonian or Attic lunar calendars and the solar calendar introduced by Julius Caesar at all straightforward. Indeed, it would be surprising for Josephus to have attempted such a complex equation in the context of an offhand remark of this nature.

Nevertheless, numerous ingenious solutions have been proposed, although none is at all convincing and they all contradict one another. This is not surprising, because they are all founded on a misunderstanding of Josephus's intentions. It is actually obvious that Josephus is trying to say that the *events* of the two days were the same: that the monarch was assassinated by being cut down by one of his bodyguards on his way into a theatre on a festival day in both cases. Since the passage bears this interpretation, it must be the correct interpretation. It would be too much of a coincidence for it to bear both interpretations (i.e. such a possibility is improbable in the extreme.) Consequently, any attempt to derive the date of Alexander's accession from the comment by Josephus is altogether futile.

There is a further supporting argument for Philip having died in the autumn based on Arrian, *Indica* 21.1, where it is stated that Nearchus set sail from India on 20th Boedromion in the Attic Calendar in 325BC and that this was within the eleventh year of Alexander's reign. Hence the anniversary of the accession was after 20th Boedromion, which occurred on about 18th September (Julian calendar) in 325BC (assuming that Nearchus was having to resort to direct lunisolar observations to derive calendar dates in Southern India, so was not using the Attic archon calendar, which sometimes strayed from strict agreement with the lunar phases).[438] However, this has been the limit of our knowledge of the date of the assassination of Philip and its exact day in the Julian calendar has never previously been precisely established (which is the same as stating that it has only been located to within tens of days on the standard axis of Universal Time).[439]

I argue in the discussions of Cleitarchus' book structure (in the next main section) that there are strong reasons to suppose that Cleitarchus ended his fifth book with the Battle of Arbela (Gaugamela). Furthermore, Justin 11.14.6 comments on

---

[438] The Attic Calendar was lunar, so its months drifted backwards and forwards slightly from year to year relative to the fixed dates in a solar calendar, such as the Julian scheme, which we use for dates in Antiquity; but Boedromion was always within the range of late August to mid-October.

[439] In fact there are even voices (K.J. Beloch, W.W. Tarn, J.R. Hamilton, R. Lane Fox…) that have argued vociferously for a date of accession in the summer of 336BC, despite the consequential complete inconsistency with the reign durations given independently by Arrian and Diodorus, which should be accurate to within a month or so, and the fact that Nearchus specifically placed 20th Boedromion 325BC within Alexander's 11th regnal year. It seems that these authors base their case on the several references that make Alexander twenty at his accession (Arrian *Anabasis* 1.1.1; Plutarch, *Alexander* 11.1; Justin 11.1.9), but he was still twenty in the autumn and none of the ancient souces suggests that he was *exactly* twenty when Philip died.

Key Historical Issues

this battle, "It was with this engagement that [Alexander] seized control of Asia, in the fifth year after his accession to the throne." This implies that Cleitarchus (Justin's probable ultimate source) had made a special point of noting that the day of the battle fell within the fifth year of the reign. Furthermore, Cleitarchus' book boundaries appear to coincide with the anniversaries of the accession at least up to this point in the first part of his two-part history. It is therefore highly significant that the next definite event recorded by Cleitarchus, which is Alexander's arrival in the town of Arbela on the day after the battle, he evidently placed at the beginning of the sixth book of his history, which is also the start of the second part of the work. Diodorus recounts this at 17.64.3 *after* boundary phrases signifying the end of the fifth book of Cleitarchus. Arrian 3.15.5 states that Alexander reached Arbela on the day after the battle, which is perfectly consistent with a hot pursuit on horseback.[440] Curtius actually takes up the story with Darius' flight from *midnight* on the day of the battle at the very beginning of his fifth book, implying that he too was reflecting a major division in his source between the day of the battle and the following day with midnight as the specific point of division. *Thus, it may reasonably be inferred that Cleitarchus believed the day after the Battle of Arbela to be the fifth anniversary of Alexander's accession.*

This is highly significant, because we have incontrovertible dates for the Battle of Arbela in both the Julian and Attic calendars. The Julian date comes from the lunar eclipse that was observed by Alexander's forces at around 21:00 local time on the evening of 20th September 331BC. It is easy to calculate from analysis of the various sources that the battle itself took place eleven days later on 1st October.[441] Furthermore, Plutarch, *Camillus* 19.3 states that the battle took place on the Attic date of 26th Boedromion. It is important to notice that these dates are entirely independent in their derivation, since the Julian derives from modern astronomical calculations. Yet they agree with one another in a highly specific way. The date of the eclipse is of course also the date of the Full Moon in that month. The synodic lunar month (the month as defined by repetition of the phases) has a duration of 29.53 days. The New Moon had therefore occurred 14.765 days before 21:00 on 20th September in 331BC, i.e. on 6th September.[442] In principle, for Greek lunar calendars (as in the case of most lunar calendars) the New Moon (more strictly the first evening observation of the crescent after the New Moon) defines the first day of the month. We can see that the 6th September was indeed the 1st Boedromion from Plutarch's date for the battle, so Plutarch's

---

[440] The distance was in range 500 to 600 stades according to Arrian, *Anabasis* 6.11.5; the precise site of the battle remains controversial, see Bosworth, *Commentary on Arrian*, I, 293-294. I would place it just 50-60km from Arbela (see discussion on the site of the battle below).

[441] See of Brunt, *Loeb Arrian*, Section 5 of Appendix VIII for the details.

[442] In fact, the orbit of the Moon is slightly elliptical, which results in the Moon having a slightly higher angular velocity around the Earth in the half of its orbit where it is slightly closer to the Earth. Hence the New Moon does not in general occur precisely halfway between two successive Full Moons, but the discrepancy will only be of the order of a few hours. It is doubtful whether the ancients could establish the precise time of the New Moon any more accurately than this.

date gives exactly the correct lunar phase as predicted from the eclipse. But actually, this is rather surprising, because the standard Attic calendar used by the Archon for setting the date of festivals and also used for most other practical purposes was demonstrably normally out of synchrony with the lunar phases (mostly due to tampering by the Archons for social and political reasons). There was also an Attic Lunar Regulatory Calendar, which *was* strictly based on the lunar phases, but it was hardly ever used for practical purposes.[443] Nevertheless, it would appear that Plutarch did indeed use the Attic Lunar Regulatory scheme for his date, because Arrian, *Anabasis* 3.15.7 states that Gaugamela took place in the next Attic month of Pyanepsion and he is presumably referencing the standard Attic Archon/Festival Calendar, which was as usual out-of-step with the lunar phases. In fact, it was quite normal for the various *civil* lunar calendars in the Greek world at the time to be out of precise synchrony with the lunar phases. This tampering usually constitutes a difficult problem for the translation of Greek dates into the Julian calendar, unless it can be established that the particular Greek dates were Lunar regulated.

Why might Plutarch have used such a specialised and punctilious dating scheme? There is a straightforward answer. He was probably getting his dates directly or indirectly from a famously rigorous Greek chronologist and historian of the late 4th and early 3rd centuries BC: Timaeus of Tauromenium. Though originally from Sicily, Timaeus was educated in Athens and spent most of his life there. Diodorus and Polybius record his special attention to matters of accurate chronology.[444] There is strong evidence from elsewhere that both Cleitarchus and Plutarch were virtually disciples of the work of Timaeus. Hammond has shown that Plutarch's date of 6th Hecatombaeon for Alexander's birth comes from Timaeus, because Cicero gives many of the same details in his mentions of the stories about Alexander's birth and he names Timaeus as his source in one instance.[445] Cleitarchus himself definitely used Timaeus, since Fragment 7 of Cleitarchus couples him with Timaeus as its co-source and it mentions the Heracleidae, Alexander's putative ancestors.[446] Then Fragment 36 from the Suda seems to make Cleitarchus a follower of Timaeus and Anaximenes.[447] This makes it rather likely that Plutarch got 6th Hecatombaeon from Cleitarchus (although Plutarch did also use Timaeus directly, for example, in his Life of Timoleon.) There is also a strong possibility that Plutarch's date for Gaugamela came from Cleitarchus –

---

[443] Alan E. Samuel, *Greek & Roman Chronology* (Munich 1972) 57-58.

[444] Diodorus 5.1.3 & Polybius 12.11.1.

[445] N. G. L. Hammond, *Sources for Alexander the Great* (Cambridge 1993) 19-20; Jacoby FGrHist 566 F150a of Timaeus (Cicero, *N.D.* 2.69); Cicero, *Div.* 1.47; Hammond also believed that Timaeus was born in the same year as Alexander; it is an obvious corollary that Alexander was born on the sixth day after a New Moon in July of 356BC and a New Moon occurred on 15th July (Julian), so Alexander was born on 20th July 356BC in the Julian Calendar.

[446] Jacoby FGrHist 137 F7 (Clement of Alexandria, *Strom.* 1.139.4).

[447] Jacoby FGrHist 137 F36 (Suda s.v. ἔχετον).

Key Historical Issues

for instance, when he gives its date in his Life of Camillus he calls it the Battle of Arbela, which is the Cleitarchan name. Certainly, Plutarch had read Cleitarchus and it may be inferred that Cleitarchus gave a date for the battle, since otherwise it would have been difficult for him to demonstrate his point that it fell within the fifth year of Alexander's reign in view of its adjacency to the anniversary.

It being established that Cleitarchus considered 2nd October 331BC (=27th Boedromion in the Attic Lunar Regulatory Calendar) to be the fifth anniversary of Alexander's accession, how can we calculate the Julian date of the accession itself in 336BC? The obvious date of 2nd October 336BC is probably incorrect, because Cleitarchus is not likely to have had a source for the key dates in a solar calendar. Rather we need to identify the Julian date for 27th Boedromion in 336BC. If the Attic date had been given in the official Archon/Festival Calendar, then the situation would be difficult, because the Athenians regularly and arbitrarily added and subtracted days from that scheme to suit various social and political purposes. However, as I have argued, there are strong reasons to suppose that Cleitarchus was using Timaeus' astronomically regulated dating system and that this involved citing dates aligned with lunar phases according to the Attic Lunar Regulatory Calendar. Therefore, we need only establish the dates of the New Moons in the autumn of 336BC to calculate the possible Julian equivalents for the 27th Boedromion in that year. This is easily done: for example, NASA has calculated that a partial lunar eclipse and Full Moon occurred at around 04:30 (local time at Athens) on the morning of 14th December 336BC (Julian calendar).[448] Hence there would have been a New Moon on 1st September; so 27th Boedromion should be 27th September (Julian) in 336BC. According to a rule suggested by Plato, *Laws* 767C, the Attic year in the Lunar Regulatory Calendar began with the first New Moon after the Summer Solstice, which itself occurred on 26th June in 336BC.[449] This first New Moon occurred on about 3rd July in the Julian calendar in 336BC. Hence is is clear that 1st September was indeed the start of the *third* month, Boedromion.

This date has the additional attraction of giving Alexander just enough time to have made his reported expedition into Southern Greece as described by Arrian, *Anabasis* 1.1.1-3 and Diodorus 17.4 before winter set in. Furthermore, the date of 27th September gives Alexander a reign of 12 years 8 months and 14 days, which fits perfectly with all the other historical information. Finally, I note that 27th September 336BC in the Julian calendar is 22nd September 336BC in the retro-projected Gregorian calendar. This means that the festival of the gods at which Philip was assassinated was being held on the Autumnal Equinox. I believe this

---

[448] NASA Five Millennium Catalog of Lunar Eclipses.

[449] The solstice fell on ~26th June in the Julian calendar in that era, due to slippage relative to the Gregorian calendar of about 3 days in every 4 centuries: the two coincide in the early 4th century AD. Plutarch's date for Gaugamela does obey Plato's rule, but I am aware that there is ongoing controversy on Athenian practice regarding the date of the New Year: see W. Kendrick Pritchett, "Postscript: The Athenian Calendars," *ZPE* 128 (1999) 79-93.

significantly corroborates Cleitarchus' date for the event, since the Equinoxes have always been popular days for pagan holy festivals. Indeed, the Autumnal Equinox was especially significant in Macedon, because the Macedonian calendar began its year on the first New Moon after the Autumnal Equinox.[450]

Alexander's Half-Brothers

Justin 11.2.3 states that Alexander arranged the murder of his half-brother Caranus on his accession to the throne, saying that he was the son of his stepmother and had made himself a rival for the throne. It is highly improbable that this Caranus (named after the putative progenitor of the Argead dynasty) was an infant son of Philip and Cleopatra: she had just one child by Philip, a girl named Europa (Athenaeus 13.557e; Justin 9.7.12; Diodorus 17.2.3; Pausanias 8.7.7; cf. Plutarch, *Alexander* 10.4) and there was not time for another. Furthermore, an infant was not likely to have been a serious rival to Alexander in these circumstances, when the Macedonians were looking for dynamic and proactive leadership by a capable adult scion of the royal line. Furthermore, it is highly probable that Philip had other sons in addition to Alexander and his half-brother Arrhidaeus by Philinna of Thessaly (Athenaeus 13.557c). Indeed, this is stated explicitly by Justin 9.8.3: "Philip had, by a dancing girl of Larissa, a son named Arrhidaeus, who reigned after Alexander. He had also many others by several wives, as is not unusual for princes, some of whom died a natural death and others by the sword." It is suggested that Ptolemy was Philip's illegitimate son with a woman called Arsinoe by several sources (Pausanias 1.6.2; Curtius 9.8.22; *Armenian Alexander Romance* 269) and there is no significant evidence to contradict them. Whereas Arrian frequently refers to Ptolemy as the son of Lagus, that would be correct terminology whether Ptolemy were Lagus's natural or adoptive son, so it simply does not provide any evidence on his natural paternity. Although Caranus is not mentioned by Satyrus in his list of Philip's wives and their children (Athenaeus 13.557b-e), neither is Ptolemy. It must be our guiding principle that absence of evidence is not evidence of absence and there is no cogent reason to believe that Satyrus's list was comprehensive. I would therefore suspect that Caranus was a grown-up son of Philip most likely by some woman with whom his relationship was of dubious legitimacy. Justin 11.2.3 uses the word *noverca* (step-mother) to describe this woman's relationship to Alexander, but he does so as a way of identifying Caranus as both a son of Philip and Alexander's half brother. It is, for example, possible that Justin's source stated that Caranus was a son of Philip and a half-brother to Alexander and that Justin (or Trogus) inferred that his mother was Alexander's *noverca*. It is additionally possible that Philip had recognised Caranus as a legitimate son, even if his mother had not been formally married to Philip at the time of his conception or birth. This may well have been

---

[450] Samuel, *Greek & Roman Chronology*, 142; Hammond, *The Regnal Years of Philip and Alexander*, 355 & 358.

the way in which Arrhidaeus achieved legitimacy. It is possible that Arrhidaeus was only recognised by Philip, when the king sought to use his son as a pawn by marrying him off to the daughter of the satrap Pixodarus in order to cement a strategic alliance. Otherwise, it is hard to explain the mentions of Philinna which describe her as a dancing girl and a prostitute (Justin 13.2.11). It is alternatively possible that Caranus was the son of another wife among those listed by Satyrus (e.g. Meda). In short, there is no substantive basis to challenge the evidence of Justin 11.2.3 that Alexander had a half-brother called Caranus, whom he had killed at the time of his accession, because Caranus had made himself a rival for the throne. It was standard practice for Macedonian royals to execute challengers for the throne without compunction despite them being fellow members of the royal family. Examples abound: Alexander's grandmother, Eurydike, was reputed to have plotted the murder of her husband, Amyntas III and actually to have murdered two of her sons, Alexander II and Perdiccas III (Justin 7.4.7 & 7.5.4-8); Olympias killed Philip Arrhidaeus and Adea-Eurydike on behalf of her grandson Alexander IV (Diodorus 19.11.5-7); Antipater the son of Cassander killed his mother Thessalonike and warred with his brother Alexander to secure the throne of Macedonia (Justin 16.1).

Alexander and Diogenes

Although not mentioned in the Cleitarchan epitomes of either Diodorus or Justin, the story of the meeting of Alexander and Diogenes is told by a couple of sources related to the Cleitarchan (Vulgate) tradition including Valerius Maximus 4.3 ext. 4a and Plutarch, *Alexander* 14.1-3 and in Plutarch's *Moralia* 331E-332C & 605D. There is a slightly different version of the same event in Diogenes Laertius, *Diogenes* 6, whilst Arrian, *Anabasis* 7.1.5-7.3.6 draws a parallel between Diogenes of Sinope and the *gymnosophists* whom Alexander encountered in India. The ultimate source for the meeting is almost certainly Onesicritus, who was both Alexander's chief pilot (e.g. Arrian, *Indica* 18.9), a pupil of Diogenes (e.g. Diogenes Laertius 6.84; Strabo 15.1.65) and the author of one of the earliest accounts of Alexander's campaigns (e.g. *Liber de Morte* 97). It is also nearly certain that Cleitarchus used Onesicritus as a major source and Cleitarchus was himself associated with the Cynics and took a keen interest in the *gymnosophists* and Calanus in particular. For all these reasons, it is likely that he included an account of this meeting in his history of Alexander's reign and Plutarch's version is the best model for his original. The version in Valerius Maximus may suggest it was also in Trogus and that he took it from Cleitarchus (or else from Timagenes, who in turn took it from Cleitarchus). I have argued in Appendix A of the 2nd edition of my book on *Alexander's Lovers* (2012) that Alexander in saying, "Were I not Alexander I would like to be Diogenes" mainly meant that he would like to be known by the Homeric epithet of Diogenes meaning roughly "sprung from Zeus" and was not really suggesting that he thought that he had an alternative vocation as a cynical naked philosopher. Plutarch seems to recognise this in his

Moralia, but pretends that Alexander was emulative of Diogenes' condition in his Life of Alexander. Perhaps he was joking, but more credibly his source, being either Onesicritus or Cleitarchus, chose to misrepresent Alexander's quip as implying that Alexander admired Cynical philosophers, because that source was himself a Cynic. One thing is clear, however: the quip was not invented, because the double meaning is actually closely associated with Alexander's personal sensibilities, yet was misrepresented by the sources. We have the words actually spoken by Alexander here.

The Delphic Oracle and Alexander

We can be confident that the story of Alexander's consultation of the Delphic Oracle was in Cleitarchus, despite it being omitted from the Cleitarchan epitomes of Diodorus and Justin, because the story is mentioned retrospectively by Diodorus 17.93.4 in a way that agrees with the more detailed surviving account in Plutarch, *Alexander* 14.4. Furthermore, it seems that this incident was the basis on which Alexander was known as the invincible (*aniketos*) Alexander long before he was called Alexander the Great (initially by the Romans: Plautus, *Mostellaria* 775). The Cleitarchan sources regularly use this epithet for the king subsequent to the Delphic consultation (e.g. Curtius 4.7.27, 6.5.11, 7.7.12, 9.6.7 & 9.6.12, 9.9.23; Justin 12.15.4). Additionally, Hypereides (5.31-32) the Athenian orator in a speech of 323BC directed against Demosthenes referred ironically to the erection of a statue in Athens of Alexander as the "invincible god" and later Livy 9.18 called Alexander invincible. Hypereides was speaking at or around the time of Alexander's death, which suggests that the Oracle story had some popular influence in Alexander's lifetime. The historicity of Alexander's visit is also supported by an inscription from Delphi recording a gift to the shrine at about the right time of 150 gold coins minted in the name of Philip II [SIG³ 251H, col. II, lines 9-10 (p.436-7)]. (See also Section 6.34 of the reconstruction.)

Justification of the Invasion of Asia

According to Jacoby Fragment 7 of Cleitarchus from the Stromata of Clement of Alexandria 1.139.4, Cleitarchus stated that Alexander crossed into Asia 820 years after the invasion of Greece by the Heraclidae.

This Heraclid invasion of Greece, which Cleitarchus dated to 1154BC (i.e. 820 years before 334BC), was allegedly the return from exile of the descendants of Heracles, Alexander's paternal ancestors. This traditional event is commonly identified in modern times with the Dorian invasion of Greece. The motive for Cleitarchus mentioning the return of Alexander's ancestors from Asia would appear to be a desire to legitimise Alexander's Asian conquests. Since his ancestors had formerly inhabited Asia, it is implied that he was merely reclaiming lands that had once been occupied by his forebears. It should be borne in mind that Cleitarchus was writing as a Greek citizen of Alexandria in approximately the second quarter of the 3rd century BC. In Hellenistic geography Egypt, defined as the black land of the Nile valley, was the last nation of Asia before entering upon the third continent of Libya, which was considered to begin at the edge of the desert on the Nile's western bank and to continued westwards as far as the Pillars of Heracles (e.g. Strabo 17.3.1). There was no Suez Canal to provide an alternative to the Nile as a physical boundary between Asia and Libya. Thus, the legitimisation potentially extended even as far as to cover the Greek rule of Ptolemaic Egypt.

Cleitarchus was probably following Timaeus for the dating of the Heraclid invasion, because his fragment notes that both Cleitarchus and Timaeus gave the figure of 820 years. Timaeus is independently renowned as a chronologist and on the best evidence he wrote a little before Cleitarchus in the late 4th or early 3rd century BC. There are also separate indications that Cleitarchus used Timaeus for dating evidence on other matters, for example in respect of Alexander's birth (as discussed in the context of the reliability of Arrian).

Alexander's Emulation of Achilles

It is quite clear in the main Cleitarchan sources (Diodorus, Justin & Plutarch) that Alexander sacrificed at the tomb of Achilles at Troy. But that much could be expected in view of the tradition of his mother's family that Achilles was their ancestor. It is the report that Hephaistion sacrificed at the tomb of Patroclus at the same time that begins to show that Alexander wished to draw a parallel between Achilles and Patroclus and himself and Hephaistion. For that perspective it is necessary to refer to the report by Aelian, *Varia Historia* 12.7, although Plutarch, *Alexander* 15.4 also makes Alexander allude to Patroclus at Troy. Aelian is a source of fragments of Cleitarchus, so he had probably read his *History Concerning Alexander*. Cicero, *Pro Archias Poeta* 24 is another reader of Cleitarchus who mentions the sacrifice at Troy. It is therefore a reasonable conjecture that Aelian took his story from Cleitarchus.

That Cleitarchus reported Alexander's emulation of Achilles is clearer in the execution of Betis at Gaza (according to Curtius 4.6.29), when Betis was dragged behind his chariot as Achilles had dragged the corpse of Hector. Then Curtius 8.4.26 has Alexander point out a parallel between his marriage to Roxane and Achilles' relationship with a captive woman, Briseis. Furthermore, Diodorus 17.97.3 is almost certainly following Cleitarchus when he makes Alexander claim to have emulated Achilles by doing battle with a river. Finally Curtius 9.6.18 has Alexander make the choice of Achilles in preferring fame over length of days (c.f. Iliad 9.410-416).

Cleitarchus is undoubtedly accurate in pointing out repeatedly that Alexander saw himself as a second Achilles. For example, we have Aischines, *Against Ctesiphon* 160, revealing in 330BC that Demosthenes had ridiculed Alexander as a Margites before he had led his army out of Macedonia. Margites was a comedic parallel to

Achilles in Homer's writings, so the implication is that Alexander was already known to be emulating Achilles by the time that he came to the throne, else Demosthenes' joke would not have worked.

Alexander's Forces at the Granicus

Cleitarchus evidently gave a very detailed account of Alexander's forces at the battle of the Granicus, which is substantially preserved by Diodorus. His contingents may be itemised as follows:

Infantry totalling 32000 comprising:

12000 Macedonians

7000 Greek Allies

5000 Mercenaries

7000 Odrysians, Triballians & Illyrians

1000 archers & Agrianians

Cavalry totalling 4500 comprising:

1800 Macedonians under Philotas

1200 Thessalians under Calas the son of Harpalus

600 Greek Allies under Erigyius

900 Thracian Scouts and Paeonians

A fleet of 182 Ships

(12000 foot and 1500 cavalry left with Antipater in Macdonia)

One point particularly requires clarification. Diodorus 17.17.4 ostensibly implies that the six hundred other Greek cavalry were separate from the eighteen hundred Thessalians, but he then agrees with Justin 11.6.2 that the cavalry totalled four thousand five hundred, despite having seemingly listed five thousand one hundred. The solution is obvious: very probably in Diodorus's source's text the six hundred other Greeks were a component of the second block of eighteen hundred cavalry, of which the remaining twelve hundred were Thessalians. Justin and Diodorus agree exactly on the totals of both cavalry and infantry, but they disagree in the fine details with Plutarch, *Alexander* 15.1 [30,000-43,000 foot & 4000-5000 horse], Arrian, *Anabasis* 1.11.3 [not much more than 30,000 foot & 5000 horse] and numbers deriving from Aristobulus [30,000 foot & 4000 horse], Ptolemy [30,000 foot & 5000 horse] and Anaximenes [43,000 foot & 5500 horse] cited by Plutarch, *Moralia* 327D-E. There is therefore a strong implication in this evidence that the figures in Diodorus and Justin are taken from Cleitarchus, who is the only likely common source of Diodorus and Justin.

Key Historical Issues

The Date of the Battle of the Granicus

There are indications that Cleitarchus gave a date in terms of the Attic Lunar calendar for the Battle at the Granicus. Firstly, it is to be expected that he gave a date in the Attic Lunar calendar, because he seems to have given Attic dates in strict accordance with the lunar phases for other major events, such as Alexander's birth and the Battle of Gaugamela/Arbela. It appears he may have taken his dates from a work by Timaeus, who was a famous chronologist based in Athens, because there are connections with Timaeus in the fragments of Cleitarchus and the date for Alexander's birth is specifically connected with Timaeus. There are also mentions of the date of the Granicus by two Roman period writers, Plutarch and Aelian, whose works contain fragments of Cleitarchus and who had probably read his *History Concerning Alexander*. Plutarch notes that the battle took place in Thargelion in his *Life of Camillus* 19.4 and, separately, Plutarch, *Alexander* 16.2 confirms that the Macedonian month was Daisios, which is equivalent to the Attic Thargelion. Most importantly, Aelian, *Varia Historia* 2.25 implies that the Battle of the Granicus took place on 6th Thargelion. He does not actually name the battle that took place that day, saying only that Alexander defeated the Persians, but the Granicus is the only such major engagement that occurred in Thargelion. It is possible to use modern astronomical calculations of ancient lunar phases to show that 6th Thargelion in that year was 20th May 334BC in the Julian calendar (or possibly a day or so either side of that date allowing for slight discrepancies in the interpretation of lunar phases by different observers.)

Alexander's Route between the Granicus and Sardis

Alexander's route from the Granicus to Sardis has been a matter of dispute. Donald Engels in *Alexander the Great and the Logistics of the Macedonian Army* p.33 argued that he doubled back to Troy and then continued southwards hugging the coastline. This was mainly because Engels believed that Alexander had founded Alexandria Troas near the coast fifteen miles south of Troy just after the Battle of the Granicus, since that was the only time that the Macedonian army might have marched past its site. But this seems to be mistaken for at least two independent reasons. Firstly, Pliny *NH* 5.124 says that the name of the town was changed from Antigonia to Alexandria. This suggests that it was founded by Antigonus Monophthalmus, then renamed in honour of Alexander by a subsequent ruler of the area, perhaps Lysimachus after the defeat and death of Antigonus in 301BC at the Battle of Ipsus. Secondly, if it had been founded by Alexander, it is not necessary to infer that he marched the Macedonian army past it. It would equally be possible for Alexander to have visited the spot whilst encamped at Troy before the Granicus. The site of Alexandria Troas was within range of cavalry patrols from his camp on the Scamander River. Furthermore, it is most unlikely that Alexander would have retreated from the site of his victory at the Granicus. That would have put in question whether it actually had been a victory! Rather we should expect him to have pursued the main bulk of the retreating Persian forces. That was standard practice in such circumstances, because failure to do so risked the enemy re-grouping and resuming hostilities. Diodorus states that the fleeing Persians made for Miletus, perhaps by cutting up the mouths of the river valleys leading towards the southwest from behind their left flank on the Granicus and coming back down to the Aegean coastline near Adramyttium. Alternatively, and I think less credibly in view of the ruggedness of the terrain, the Persians might have made a beeline southward straight towards Sardis with Alexander on their heels, before continuing on to Miletus. Additionally, it should be noted that some Persian forces may have retreated due east to Dascylion, since Alexander sent Parmenion off that way (Arrian, *Anabasis* 1.17.2) in the aftermath of the battle. But they could not easily have got back to Miletus from there and Alexander may mainly have been concerned that Parmenion should secure the towns and strongpoints in that direction, whilst he himself pursued the bulk of the Persians southward.

The Passage of Mount Climax

I have based my reconstruction of the famous episode of the passage of the coastline at the foot of Mount Climax on Plutarch, *Alexander* 17.3, which is probably alluding to the Cleitarchan version, together with Jacoby Fragment 31 of Callisthenes, whom Cleitarchus himself probably followed. However, the degree to which Plutarch used Cleitarchus is uncertain and Cleitarchus's reliance on Callisthenes for the earlier parts of his history is not confirmed. Hence this part of the reconstruction must remain relatively conjectural. Arrian, *Anabasis* 1.26.1 notes that it was necessary for the north (i.e. offshore) wind to blow to keep the sea off this beach, which suggests that he used a more practical and less romantic account of this episode than Cleitarchus.

The Arrest of Alexander Lyncestes

Arrian, *Anabasis* 1.25 locates the arrest of Alexander Lyncestes at Phaselis, which is also consistent with its approximate timing in the Cleitarchan tradition. Arrian also names the informative prisoner as Sisines, Darius's messenger to Lyncestes, who was intercepted by Parmenion. This might be the same Sisines, whom Alexander subsequently had eliminated just before the Battle of Issus according to Curtius 3.7.11 and Section 4.6 of this reconstruction of Cleitarchus, according to which he had previously defected to Philip II, having been sent to his court by the Persian Satrap of Egypt. Therefore, he may in fact have deliberately betrayed his mission to Alexander upon his interception by Parmenion (or perhaps even sooner). This might explain why Alexander evidently distrusted his loyalty. Arrian, *Anabasis* 1.25.3 notes that Darius's message offered Lyncestes a thousand talents in return for assassinating Alexander and that Lyncestes had previously sent a letter to Darius. Darius's letter may have incorporated an offer of the hand of

Darius's sister or daughter in marriage, since that was the offer that Parmenion subsequently warned Alexander was available to Philip the Doctor. Reading between the lines we might infer that Alexander allowed Sisines' message from Darius to be delivered to Alexander Lyncestes and waited to see whether he would reveal it to Alexander. Failure to do so could legitimately be considered evidence of treasonous intent. Philotas subsequently likewise failed to alert Alexander to the existence of a plot to murder Alexander and was executed as a traitor. Alexander eventually had Alexander Lyncestes tried and executed on the same occasion as Philotas, for indeed how could he let Lyncestes live, when he was essentially guilty of the same crime for which Alexander and the Macedonian Assembly had determined that Philotas should be executed? In both cases a judicial death sentence required the acclamation of the Macedonian Assembly. It is interesting that Alexander seems to have decided not to bring the case against Lyncestes before the Assembly at the time he was arrested in 333BC, but went to the trouble of keeping him in custody for four years. Lyncestes had important connections: he was the son-in-law of Antipater. It is likely that Alexander considered it risky to bring a case before the Assembly on the available evidence in 333BC. Perhaps this suggests that Lyncestes did not go so far as to send a positive reply to Darius's proposition. The whole matter remains extremely murky.

Geographical Eccentricities: Turkey as a Peninsula

As Alexander's expedition advanced into Asia it entered successively upon regions where the Greek conception of the geography became increasingly hazy and distorted. Perhaps the first of these misconceptions to be manifested in the account of the expedition given by Cleitarchus is the curious case of the Anatolian isthmus. The geographical concept of an isthmus in eastern Turkey derived from the view that there was a substantial narrowing of the width of the landmass between the Mediterranean and the modern Black Sea (the ancient Euxine or Pontic Sea) created by the northerly extension of the Mediterranean produced by the Gulf of Issus. This was the position taken by Strabo 12.1.3 and Pliny, *NH* 6.2.7 as well as Cleitarchus. However, the concept is not very accurate. There is no more than a slight narrowing of Anatolia between the Gulf of Issus and the Euxine (Pontic Sea) and the landmass is 300 miles wide at its narrowest. The true position is however reflected relatively accurately by Claudius Ptolemy, whose map of Asia Minor in his *Geographia* does not exhibit anything so pronounced as an isthmus.

Why Did Alexander Head North from Pisidia?

Alexander's northward progression in the early months of 333BC could be seen as a move to secure the hinterland of Asia Minor or to meet up with reinforcements from Macedonia or to find a smoother route into Cilicia. I find none of these explanations wholly convincing. Instead, the historical context seems to be as related here in the Vulgate: Memnon was posing an acute threat to Alexander's rear and even an invasion of Macedonia seemed credible. Under such pressure the king wished to hedge on whether to return to Macedonia or confront Darius directly. Adopting this northwards route allowed Alexander to keep both options open for a while at least. It appears particularly to have been the news of Memnon's death (in late Spring) reaching Alexander (circa June) not long after he left Gordion that was decisive in moving the king at the head of his army rapidly through the passes in the Taurus range and down into Cilicia with the purpose of confronting Darius and the imperial Persian army directly.

Was Philip the Doctor Suborned by Darius?

It is clear from our sources that Parmenion did issue a note to Alexander warning him against trusting in medication from his doctor, Philip, on the grounds that Philip had been corrupted by Darius's rewards to anyone who did away with Alexander. However, it would seem very unlikely that Parmenion was actually revealing fresh intelligence against Philip or that he meant that Philip personally had received a secret offer from Darius. Had Parmenion had specific evidence of any such direct contact between Darius and Philip, it is obvious that the doctor would immediately have been arrested and would have had no further hand in the treatment of the king. The true situation was that it seems to have been public knowledge at that point that Darius had offered a thousand talents to anyone who disposed of Alexander, due to the publication of Darius's offer to Alexander Lyncestes recounted in Section 3.39 of the reconstruction, which derives from Curtius 3.5.16. Additionally, Arrian, *Anabasis* 1.25.3 notes that Alexander Lyncestes had been offered 1000 talents to betray Alexander. An offer of the hand of the sister of Darius may have been read over from a codicil to the reward for Lyncestes. It is interesting that it is Darius's daughter's hand in Plutarch, *Alexander* 19.3, but Pseudo-Callisthenes 2.8.5 agrees with Curtius that it was his sister and names her as Dadipharta. In actuality, at this point Darius was too far away even to have received news of Alexander's illness let alone to have had time to order an attempt to bribe his physician. Plutarch, *Alexander* 19.1 says that Darius thought Alexander lingered in Cilicia due to cowardice, which testifies clearly as to the lack of intelligence regarding the situation in Alexander's camp among his Persian opponents. Therefore, Parmenion must instead have raised *general* concerns regarding trusting in a single physician who knew of Darius's public offer. Parmenion seems to have been on hand in the Cleitarchan text: he had led the advance party into Tarsus at Curtius 3.4.15, though Justin 11.8.5 strangely puts him in Cappadocia. Hence the question also arises as to why he chose to communicate his concerns by letter instead of in person. Most probably, it was simply impossible to speak to Alexander privately during his illness, because he was constantly attended. Therefore, a note may have offered the most secure means for communicating what was intended as secret advice. Parmenion would not have wished to advertise himself to Alexander's attendants as a source of suspicion regarding the trustworthiness of those attendants. That Alexander effectively made Parmenion's warning public must have been embarrassing to Parmenion, but it enabled Alexander to check the physician's response to the warning before the king took the risk of taking the draught. I would assume that the story in Cleitarchus that the king drained the cup before showing the letter to the doctor is a distortion to enhance the drama, since it would have served no purpose other than to make Alexander seem unquestioningly trustful of his physician. Presumably Philip's outrage seemed suitably genuine.

The Three Peace Offers from Darius

It would seem that Cleitarchus recorded three peace offers between the battles of Issus and Arbela/Gaugamela. The first two took the form of letters, but the last was conveyed by an embassy. However, in the aftermath of Issus when the first letter was sent, Diodorus 17.39 appears to describe details from the *second* letter of Darius to Alexander, which Curtius 4.5.1-8 places after the siege of Tyre and which Diodorus omits at that point. Curtius 4.1.7-14 cites a ransom for the Persian Royal Family and a suggestion that Alexander return to Macedonia for the first letter. Since Justin 11.12.1-5 broadly confirms Curtius' version, it appears likely that Diodorus has become confused between the two separate letters. This is probably also what led him to suggest that Alexander presented a forged version of the first letter to his council – a story of which there is no hint elsewhere. This is further supported by Diodorus 17.39.3-4, where he gives an account of Darius' renewed preparations for war, which match details given by Curtius 4.6.1-2 just before the siege of Gaza together with Curtius 4.9.1-5 after Alexander's return from Egypt. I am therefore inclined to acquit Cleitarchus of responsibility for the confused account presented by Diodorus 17.39 on the combined evidence of Curtius and Justin, who were assuredly also following the Alexandrian on the matter of these letters.

Dating Issues Including the Fall of Tyre and Arbela

The duration of the siege of Tyre is stated to have been seven months by Diodorus 17.46.5 and Plutarch, *Alexander* 24.3. Similarly, Curtius 4.4.19 notes that the town was taken in the seventh month after the start of its investment. Arrian, *Anabasis* 2.24.6 states that Tyre fell in the Attic month of Hecatombaeon, which began on the day of the first New Moon after the Summer Solstice; Plutarch, *Alexander* 25.2 tells the story that Tyre fell on the last day of the month, which was originally designated the 30th, but that Alexander redesignated it as the 28th in support of a prophecy of Aristander. This suggests that this month was "hollow", meaning that it had only 29 days and the 29th day was therefore called the 30th, since it was the last. In 332BC the Summer Solstice fell on about 26th June and the next New Moon occurred on about 20th July, so the last day of

Concerning Alexander the Great by Andrew Chugg

Hecatombaeon would be about 17th August (all these dates being given according to the Julian Calendar: the fall of Tyre would be on 12th August in the Gregorian calendar, because there was a five day offset between the two calendars in the late 4th century BC.)

Alexandria was founded on 7th April (25th Tybi) 331BC according to Pseudo-Callisthenes and Alexander had returned from Egypt and reached Thapsacus on the upper reaches of the Euphrates in Hecatombaeon (8th July – 7th August) in the same year according to Arrian, *Anabasis* 3.7.1.

The Battle of Arbela/Gaugamela can be precisely dated, because a Lunar eclipse occurred on 20th September 331BC (Julian) with totality beginning at around 9pm local time. This was eleven days before the battle (Plutarch, *Alexander* 31.4). This is precisely consistent with the emendation proposed by Kinch (and adopted by me) to Curtius 4.9.14 to the effect that Alexander reached the Tigris fourteen days before the battle (see Reconstruction section 5.44 below).

We also have an exact lunar date for the battle in the Attic Calendar recorded by Plutarch, *Camillus* 19.3: he gives 26th Boedromion (in 331BC). Since the battle occurred eleven days after a Full Moon (Lunar eclipses necessarily occur at Full Moon, of course), it must also have occurred on the 26th day after a New Moon (there being nearly 15 days between the New and Full Moons). Hence Plutarch's date is also validated by the eclipse. Arrian's assertion that the battle occurred in the next Attic month (Pyanepsion) is similarly shown to be false by the eclipse observation (at least insofar as it was given in a version of the Attic Calendar that was matched to Lunar phases – however, the Athenian Archon did operate a festival calendar, which he often nudged to and fro relative to the Lunar phases for political reasons: hence in his calendar the Battle of Arbela might have occurred in early Pyanepsion.)

Plutarch, *Alexander* 37, states that Alexander was based at Persepolis for four months, which would be roughly February through May of 330BC. He also made a thirty-day roving expedition (southwards?) into the mountains during that period, which can be dated by Curtius 5.6.12 mentioning the evening setting of the Pleiades. This puts it roughly in the range of late March through April. The story of this mini-campaign is not explicitly recounted elsewhere than Curtius.

Arrian, *Anabasis* 3.22.2 states that Darius died in the Attic month of Hecatombaeon in 330BC, which was 28th June – 27th July in the Julian calendar.

As I have argued elsewhere,[451] Cleitarchus began his first five books on Alexander's accession and its respective anniversaries: hence books four and five began on the third and fourth anniversaries of his accession (27th Boedromion according to the Attic Lunar calendar). The third anniversary occurred on 25th September (Julian) 333BC and came between Alexander's recovery from illness and the Battle of Issus. Arrian, *Anabasis Alexandrou* 2.11.10, states that this battle

---

[451] *Alexander the Great in Afghanistan*, A. M. Chugg, 2011, Section 8, pp. 157-185.

was fought in the Attic month of Maimacterion, which corresponded to 28th October – 26th November in 333BC.[452] The fourth anniversary took place on 13th October 332BC and came between the fall of Tyre and the siege of Gaza. The latter held out for two months according to Diodorus 17.48.7, so Alexander's entry into Egypt should be dated to mid-December of 332BC. Cleitarchus ended his fifth book and the first of the two parts into which he divided his entire *History Concerning Alexander* on the day of the Battle of Arbela, the 26th Boedromion, just because the next day was the fifth anniversary of Alexander's accession. The 27th of Boedromion in 336BC happened to coincide with the Autumnal Equinox, which was the occasion for the festival at which Philip II, Alexander's father, was assassinated.

The fixed points established by these dates form the framework for the chronology of this key period. Other events may be dated by interpolating them appropriately within this framework.

The Appointment of the King of Sidon

Diodorus 17.47 recounts the story of the appointment of "Ballonymus" (i.e. Abdalonymus, as given more correctly by Curtius 4.1.15-26 and Justin 11.10.8 and meaning "Servant of the gods" in Phoenician) following the siege of Tyre after noting that the rulership of Tyre was given to Abdalonymus after its fall (Diodorus 17.46.6). It has long been supposed that the differences between the correct story of the initial appointment of Abdalonymus at Sidon in Curtius and Justin and the version in Diodorus, which is relocated to Tyre, mean that Curtius and Justin were following a different source than Diodorus on this matter, whilst Diodorus was following Cleitarchus, who was therefore giving a completely garbled account of events. However, I infer instead that Diodorus was prompted to tell the story of Abdalonymus's installation as King of Sidon retrospectively by the *additional* award of the territory of Tyre to Abdalonymus. Indeed Curtius 4.1.26 confirms that Alexander did indeed add an adjoining territory to Abdalonymus's domains. I would suggest that Diodorus himself told the story correctly of Sidon, but that an early editor of an archetypal manuscript of Diodorus subsequently incorrectly corrected the name of the city (which occurs just twice in Diodorus 17.47) to Tyre, because Diodorus' earlier omission of the matter together with his failure to explain clearly why he was referring back to events at Sidon made it seem to that inexpert editor that all Abdalonymus's territory should properly be located at Tyre. This rectification of an incorrect emendation has the effect of reconciling Curtius-Justin with Diodorus through

---

[452] There was an eclipse of the Sun on 27th October 333BC, which had evidently been predicted in the cuneiform tablets known as the Babylonian Astronomical Diaries; it is argued by some that Darius, out of deference to astronomical omens, would not have started the final stages of his march to Issus until after the eclipse and that the final stages would have taken around ten days to complete; hence it is argued that Issus might have taken place on 5th or 6th November; but this argument is rather weak and uncertain.

inferring a single point error, which inherently incorporates a logical explanation of how it could easily have come about. This is a much more straightforward explanation of the conundrum than to suppose that Curtius and Justin independently abandoned their usual source (Cleitarchus) on the matter of Abdalonymus and that Cleitarchus relocated the whole story to Tyre. My suggestion is also bolstered by the fact that Diodorus would otherwise appear to have made Straton (king of Sidon in Curtius 4.1.16) the king of Tyre during Alexander's siege, whereas Arrian, *Anabasis Alexandrou* 2.24.5 writes that the king of Tyre was called Azemilcus.

Did Alexander Visit Upper Egypt?

It is generally supposed that Alexander never got much further upstream on the Nile (i.e. further south) than Memphis. That is what is shown on virtually every modern map of his itinerary. This assumption is mainly based the silence of most sources on the matter coupled with the view that he had insufficient time to allow for the exploration of Upper Egypt. Nevertheless, in what seems to be the only actual surviving statement on the issue (excluding the fact that the *Alexander Romance* 3.18-23 (Kroll) implausibly tells the story of a visit by the king to Queen Candace in Meroë), Curtius appears to report that Alexander did in fact penetrate further upstream immediately following his arrival in Egypt and prior to returning and undertaking his famous visit to the Temple of Ammon at Siwa:

Curtius 4.7.5: *A Memphi eodem flumine vectus ad interiora Aegypti penetrat conpositisque rebus ita, ut nihil ex patrio Aegyptiorum more mutaret...*

"From Memphis he sailed on up the same stream [the Nile], penetrating into the interior of Egypt and he settled its affairs without tampering with any Egyptian national custom."

Secondly, after the king's return from Siwa, Curtius is clear that Alexander wished to visit Ethiopia, but did not have the time.

Curtius 4.8.2-4: *...et... Memphim petit. Cupido haud iniusta quidem, ceterum intempestiva incesserat, non interiora modo Aegypti, sed etiam Aethiopiam invisere: Memnonis Tithonique celebrata regia cognoscendae vetustatis avidum trahebat paene extra terminos solis. Sed imminens bellum, cuius multo maior supererat moles, otiosae peregrinationi tempora exemerat. Itaque Aegypto praefecit Aeschylum Rhodium et Peucesten Macedonem quattuor milibus militum in praesidium regionis eius datis...*

"Alexander made for Memphis. He was afflicted by a desire that was not so much unjustified as inopportune to travel not just to Upper Egypt but to Ethiopia as well. Being eager to investigate the vestiges of antiquity, the renowned palace of Memnon and Tithonus was drawing him virtually beyond the limits of enlightenment. However, the impending war, of which by far the most challenging phase was yet to come, curtailed his time for sightseeing. Hence, he gave the government of Egypt to Aeschylus of Rhodes and Peucestes of Macedon, allotting them four thousand troops to garrison the region."

In Greek mythology, Memnon was the son of Tithonus and an Ethiopian king, who came to the aid of Troy during the Trojan War. It therefore appears that Curtius is implicitly confirming that Alexander had already visited Upper Egypt at this juncture, but was thwarted in an ambition *additionally* to visit a famous "palace" complex in Ethiopia.

Alexander appears to have arrived in Egypt in December of 332BC (as has been argued above). If Curtius is correct, then any visit to Upper Egypt must have been concluded prior to the beginning of the expedition to Siwa. Alexander is also stated by Curtius, Diodorus and Justin to have founded Alexandria in the course of his return journey from Siwa to Memphis. The Alexander Romance (a.k.a. Pseudo-Callisthenes) 1.32.10 concurs and is clear that the Alexandrians celebrated the anniversary of the foundation of their city on the 25th day of the Egyptian month of Tybi. In the Ptolemaic Period immediately after the foundation, it can be shown that 25th Tybi equated to 7th April in the Julian Calendar. However, some smoke has been generated around the issue by P. M. Fraser (Ptolemaic Alexandria, Vol 2, page 3, note 9) amongst others by noting that the Alexander Romance appears to have been compiled in Roman Egypt (most probably in Alexandria itself) and that 25th Tybi equated to 20th January (Julian) in the calendar used in the Roman period. Nevertheless, I side with C. Bradford Welles in finding it implausible that anyone would have changed a traditional date in order to keep an anniversary in the same place in the solar year (i.e. relative to the equinoxes) and even more implausible that the date was originally calculated in the Roman period, as though the anniversary of the city's foundation only became interesting to its citizens at that time! Furthermore, P. M. Fraser also notes the existence of another ancient codex, the "Horoscope of Alexandria", which furnishes a date of 16th April 331BC for the foundation of Alexandria. It is not unusual for the complexities of translating between various calendars to lead to an error of a week or so, but it is much harder to account for a discrepancy of several months.

The Vulgate (i.e. Cleitarchan) chronology would seem to place Alexander's departure from Egypt shortly after his return to Memphis, as it asserts that he had no opportunity for further exploration of the country. Furthermore, Arrian *Anabasis* 3.6.1 states that Alexander left Egypt "when Spring began to show itself". This places his departure no later than around early May of 331BC and that is relatively consistent with Arrian's statement (*Anabasis* 3.7.1) that Alexander reached Thapsacus in Hecatombaeon (8th July – 7th August 331BC) and with the Julian date of 1st October 331BC for the Battle of Arbela/Gaugamela, which is precisely fixed by an antecedent Lunar Eclipse.

There is in consequence a considerable expanse of time (at least two months) between December of 332BC and the departure of the Siwa expedition some time in March of 331BC, during which Alexander might indeed have travelled further up the Nile. If he did so, it would be reasonable to infer that he left the main army near Memphis and transported an expeditionary force upstream in a flotilla of boats. The Nile so far outstripped the roads as a means of transport to Upper Egypt that no other route merits serious consideration. By such means Alexander might easily have travelled upstream by several tens of miles per day and downstream at twice that pace.

Even in the so-called "Official Tradition" represented by Arrian's *Anabasis Alexandrou*, there is no substantive reason to exclude the possibility of a trip to Upper Egypt. The main reason for apostles of Arrian's infallibility to have doubted the occurrence of the reported trip upstream is that this stance better suits their case for a foundation of Alexandria prior to Siwa and a return route eastwards via the other oases (chattering serpents and all) Archaeological evidence is very limited, but the existence of the famous chapel dedicated to Alexander at Karnak might hint that he actually reached the spot in person, although there is no reason strictly to require his presence for its creation to have been instigated.

It has also been noted by Catherine Lorber that Alexander is depicted participating in the Opet festival in some reliefs at Luxor.[453] This was a procession from Karnak to Luxor in the second month of Akhet (the four-month long season of Nile inundation) which was roughly July. Despite the anachronism, it being impossible that Alexander was there in July, the fact that his physical presence was depicted at all, is, I feel, enough to tip the balance of the evidence in favour of Alexander having travelled as far upstream as Luxor in roughly January-February of 331BC.

The Location of the Battle of Arbela or Gaugamela

The matter of the location of the Battle of Arbela (aka Gaugamela) is still disputed. Disproportionate reliance has been placed on Arrian, *Anabasis* 3.8.7 & 6.11.4-6, who states that the battle took place near a village named Gaugamela on the River Boumelus, where Darius camped, and that this was 600 stades (on the best authority and at least 500 stades according to all accounts) away from Arbela (modern Arbil in Iraq). However, a stade is about 180m, so 600 stades is 108km. Even allowing for some winding of the route, that implies a radius of ~100km from Arbela. As shown in Figure B, this is most unlikely. In the light of all other information on the battle, Arrian's distance from Arbela would put its site beyond Nineveh and near the Tigris, very close to the point at which Alexander forded the river.

---

[453] C. Lorber, "Theos Aigiochos: The aegis in Ptolemaic portraits of the divine king," in P. Iossif, A. Chankowski, and C. Lorber, eds., More than Men, Less than Gods. Studies in Royal Cult and Imperial Worship, Studia Hellenistica 51 (Leuven, 2011), p.296.

Key Historical Issues

There are two main rival theories for the actual site, between which scholarship has as yet been unable to decide.[454] Aurel Stein back in 1938 argued for a site just east of Mosul in the expansive plains on the direct route from Mosul to Arbil.[455] But F. Schachermeyr (recently supported by Micheal Wood in a TV documentary on the battle) has argued for Tel Gemel located north of Mount Maqloub (see Figure B).[456] Schachermeyr wrote to local contacts to confirm the location of Tel Gemel, which, it seems, is named for a camel. Aurel Stein had told a story of how a Mr Taylor, Chief Engineer of the Iraq Petroleum Company in Kirkuk, had informed him that "Tel Gomel" was marked on a War Office Map at 1:125,000 scale, No. J38/T about 6 miles due north of the confluence of the Khazir with the Greater Zab. However, it appears that Schachermeyr's later information was correct on Tel Gemel's site, which nevertheless constitutes something of a red herring, since the value of the evidence from such a vague name association across twenty-three centuries is slight.

The particular relevance of the camel is explained by Plutarch, *Alexander* 31.3, who asserts that Gaugamela means Camel's House and Strabo 16.1.3-4 elucidates further: "Now the city Ninus (Nineveh) was wiped out immediately after the overthrow of the Syrians. It was much greater than Babylon, and was situated in the plain of Aturia. Aturia borders on the region of Arbela, with the Lycus River (Greater Zab) lying between them. Now Arbela, which lies opposite to Babylonia, belongs to that country; and in the country on the far side of the Lycus River lie the plains of Aturia, which surround Ninus. In Aturia is a village Gaugamela, where Darius was conquered and lost his empire. Now this is a famous place, as is also its name, which, being interpreted, means "Camel's House". Darius, the son of Hystaspes, so named it, having given it as an estate for the maintenance of the camel, which helped most on the toilsome journey through the deserts of Scythia with the burdens containing sustenance and support for the king. However, the Macedonians, seeing that this was a cheap village, but that Arbela was a notable settlement (founded, as it is said, by Arbelus, the son of Athmoneus), announced that the battle and victory took place near Arbela and so transmitted their account to the historians. After Arbela and Mt. Nicatorium (a name applied to it by Alexander after his victory in the neighbourhood of Arbela), one comes to the Caprus River (Lesser Zab), which lies at the same distance from Arbela as the Lycus." The more important detail than the camel to be gleaned from this is that the village of Gaugamela lay in the plains of Aturia *surrounding* ancient Nineveh.

---

[454] E.g. P. A. Brunt's Loeb translation of Arrian's *Anabasis Alexandrou*, App IX, section 2.

[455] Aurel Stein, Limes Report, Geographical Journal vol 92, 1938, pp.62-66 & vol 95, 1940, pp. 428-438 and subsequently Geographical Journal, 1942, vol 100, 155 ff.

[456] F. Schachermeyr, Alexander der Grosse, Salzburg, 1949, p.511, note 153; cf. Streck, RE, VII, cols 861ff and E. W. Marsden, The Campaign of Gaugamela, Liverpool 1964, p.20 and Donald W. Engels, Alexander the Great and the Logistics of the Macedonian Army, 1978, p.70 and A. B. Bosworth, Commentary on Arrian's History of Alexander, Vol 1, 1980, pp.293-295.

Concerning Alexander the Great by Andrew Chugg

Diodorus 17.53.4 similarly states that Darius wished to fight in the plains around Nineveh (adjoining modern Mosul – see map of Figure B) and Curtius (at 4.10.8) says that Alexander advanced after fording the Tigris "keeping the Tigris on his right and the mountains that are called the Gordyaeans on his left" and (at 4.9.9-10) that Darius advanced from Arbela, bridged the River Lycus (almost certainly the modern Greater Zab) then moved on 80 stades (~15km) to the River Boumelus, where he encamped. Since the modern River Khazir is about 15km from the Greater Zab on the modern road from Mosul to Arbil, this strongly supports Aurel Stein over Schachermeyr and Wood, since the two rivers are 30km apart near Tel Gemel. It is also hard to see how Tel Gemel could be described as situated in "a plain surrounding Nineveh", since there is a not insignificant intervening mountain range, including Mt Maqloub, where lies the Mar Mattai monastery. It is also difficult to understand how Alexander could be said to have kept the Tigris on his right, if he actually marched directly away from that river towards Tel Gemel. Neither does Tel Gemel even match Arrian's six-hundred stade range from Arbela: it is about 70km or 390 stades from Arbil. In short, Tel Gemel matches none at all of the ancient descriptions of the battle site.

But there is an extraordinarily flat plain, which Alexander would inevitably have encountered, if he actually kept the Tigris on his right, in the vicinity of the modern village of Karemlesh between Mosul and the River Khazir. This looks a perfect match for the ground chosen by Darius. Indeed, its extreme flatness may be partly explained by the fact that Darius is said (Curtius 4.9.10 & Arrian, *Anabasis* 3.8.7) to have had every hillock on his chosen battlefield levelled. This site is very much among the plains immediately surrounding Nineveh and the separation of the rivers on the road to Arbela is very close to 15km here. There is also a tall ridge on the northern edge of the site that might be the Mt Nicatorium mentioned by Strabo and another ridge just to the left of Alexander's line of march as he passed the site of Nineveh might be the hill that Alexander took over from Mazaeus in the days preceding the battle and where he established his fortified basecamp (Curtius 4.12.15 & 4.12.18-19 & 4.12.24). It is even possible to see just why Mazaeus abandoned this hill: Alexander's line of march through the plain below it threatened to cut him off from the main body of the Persian army. Additionally, this explains why Alexander "fretted whether he should launch his attacks from the crest of the ridge against the Persian right wing" as noted by Curtius 4.13.16, for his elevated encampment lay very much towards the right of the Persian lines. Finally, it makes clear why, during the battle itself, it was Mazaeus on the Persian right wing who sent one thousand cavalrymen around Alexander's left flank to attack Alexander's encampment (Curtius 4.15.5), because the camp was behind Alexander's left.

Alexander was only marching for about five of the fourteen days after he crossed the Tigris (forded c. 18th or 19th September 331BC prior to a lunar eclipse on

Key Historical Issues

20th September with the battle fought eleven days later on 1st October).[457] Hence if he crossed at the most likely ford at Abu Wijam, as also proposed by Aurel Stein,[458] the battlefield should be about 60km south and west of that ford, which is highly consistent with a site a little beyond Nineveh.

The geographical and topographical considerations therefore overwhelmingly favour Karemlesh over Tel Gemel. But neither candidate (nor any credible candidate) is close to being consistent with Arrian's 600 stades, which simply seems wrong. And the argument from the modern place name of Tel Gemel does not weigh significantly in the matter, not least because Karemlesh also claims to have had a camel-derived place name in the past. Its Wikipedia entry under "Karamlish" states: 'Karamlish at the time [of the Battle of Gaugamela] was called Ko-Komle, which meant in Aramaic "The Camels' Square."'[459] The implication is that the Greeks rendered Ko-Komle as Gaugamela. However, the authority for this may be no more than the evidence of Plutarch and Strabo mentioned above taken together with the modern association with the site of Alexander's battle. In fact, Arrian, *Anabasis* 3.8.7 would seem to locate the original Gaugamela at Darius' camp at the point where the traditional route from Nineveh to Arbela forded the Khazir/Boumelus, which is about 12km east of Karemlesh. It would certainly appear unlikely that Darius would have encamped such a huge host very far from a major watersource.

The great *Geographia* of Claudius Ptolemy provides the clinching evidence. This gives latitudes and longitudes for both Arbela (80E, 37.25N) and Gaugamela (79.5E, 37.25N) under its list of towns for Assyria in Chapter 1 of Book 6. Claudius Ptolemy placed Gaugamela half a degree of longitude due west of Arbela. For identifiable locations between Rome and Samarkand it can be shown that 1 degree of longitude in the *Geographia* is about 0.75 modern degrees of longitude. A modern degree of longitude translates to a distance of about 90km at the latitude of Arbela, so Ptolemy placed Gaugamela about 35km due west of Arbela. This is very close to the confluence of the Khazir (Boumelus) with the Greater Zab (Lycus). Clearly it is overwhelmingly likely that Gaugamela lay on one or other of these rivers, most probably on the Boumelus, just north of their confluence. Equally transparently, this dramatically confirms the rest of the evidence in supporting a battlefield just west of the Khazir and south of Mt Maqloub in the vicinity of modern Karemlesh. Conversely, since Tel Gemel lies as far north as it is west of Arbela, it is most unlikely to be situated anywhere near the ancient town of Gaugamela.

---

[457] See Plutarch, *Alexander* 31.4 for the eleven days and the eclipse, which took place on 20th September 331BC (Julian) and Curtius 4.9.15-21 & 4.10.2 for fording the Tigris and the subsequent eclipse.

[458] Aurel Stein, Geographical Journal, vol 100, 1942, p.157.

[459] http://en.wikipedia.org/wiki/Karamlish

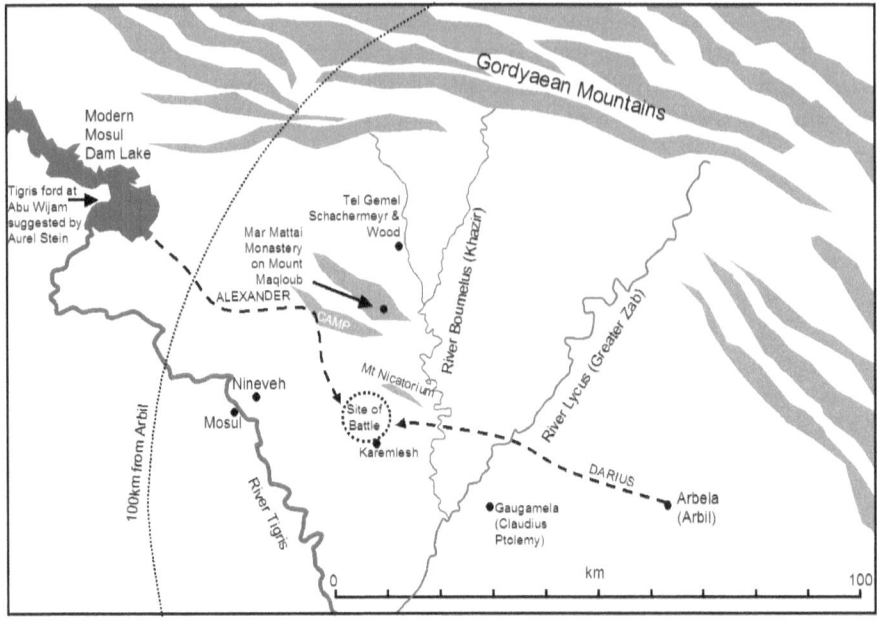

Figure B. The site of the Battle of Arbela/Gaugamela

The Sack and Burning of Persepolis

It is important to distinguish between two separate events: firstly, the sack of the lower town of Persepolis when Alexander first arrived at the city and secondly the incineration of the palace area some months later and not long before the king's departure from the vicinity. Indeed Curtius has Alexander undertake a month-long campaign in the mountains surrounding the city between the two events.

There were obvious motivations for the initial sack. Alexander had clearly been incensed by the treatment of the mutilated Greeks from the workshops of Persepolis, who had met him on the road just prior to his arrival. Furthermore, armies in the ancient world expected to be afforded opportunities to sack enemy cities, when they had triumphed in the battlefield. Alexander had held back his Macedonians at Babylon and Susa, because these cities had surrendered, but Persepolis was the very heart and soul of the Persian kingdom and it had fought on to the end. Alexander would therefore have been under enormous moral pressure to allow a sack: it was simply the done thing in the particular set of circumstances. Denying his army its traditional right to indulge in rape and pillage in such a situation risked the disgruntlement of the troops, which in turn risked the future of the expedition. Nevertheless, the king ordered the preservation of the magnificent palace complex, partly because the immense treasures contained within it were properly now the property of the Macedonian crown and partly because he planned to winter there and so had need of comfortable accommodation.

The incineration of the palace is a more complicated matter. Arrian makes it a cold-blooded decision (*Anabasis* 3.18.11-12), whilst the Cleitarchan Vulgate explains that it was done on the spur of the moment in the context of a drunken comus and was inspired by Thais the Athenian hetaera. However, both traditions agree that Alexander excused it as symbolic revenge "for the injuries done to the Greeks", presumably including the mutilations, but especially focussing upon the incineration by the Persians of Greek shrines, notably those on the Athenian Acropolis, a hundred and fifty years beforehand.

It is of course entirely possible that both the Official and the Vulgate accounts are simultaneously true. There is no reason to think that Alexander had abandoned his antipathy towards the principal seat of the Persian kings during his stay there and the fact that Persepolis was razed just as Winter was ending and the mountain passes were opening up allowing the Macedonians to resume the pursuit of Darius may not have been a coincidence. Either Thais may have known that she was pushing at an open door in urging the conflagration or the entire comus may have been stage-managed as a piece of political theatre. Alexander might well have deemed it poetic justice that his enemy's capital should be desroyed at the bidding of an Athenian courtesan, whether it came about through planning or upon a whim. Thais herself said as much according to Diodorus 17.72.2 by vaunting the irony of women's hands being seen to destroy the greatest architectural masterpiece of the Persians.

It is yet more ironical, however, that Alexander speedily regretted the act (Curtius 5.7.11), but the greatest irony of all was that the blaze actually engendered the preservation of the stone skeleton of Achaemenid Persepolis until our own day, since the destruction was so complete that no attempt was ever made to reconstruct the site or to re-use its masonry.

Did Darius Agree To Surrender in July 330BC?

Alexander appears to have been familiar with the works of Xenophon. Arrian, *Anabasis* 2.7.8-9 records that he cited matters from Xenophon's *Anabasis* in addressing his troops and there are many instances where his behaviour seems to have been inspired by the example of Cyrus in Xenophon's *Cyropaidia*. A particular instance would be Cyrus' reuniting of Pantheia, the Lady of Susa, with her husband, Abradatas, in return for the latter's submission to his rule (*Cyropaidia* 6.1.45-49). Alexander appears to have adopted this as a model for his own policy towards Darius and his captured wife, Stateira, and other family members after Issus. At any rate in Alexander's first letter to Darius, as quoted by Arrian, *Anabasis* 2.14.8, he states: "You must then regard me as Lord of all Asia and come to me… Ask for your mother, wife and children and what you will, when you have come, and you will receive them. You shall have whatever you persuade me to give." Cyrus won the fealty of Abradatas, who became Cyrus' loyal lieutenant. Similarly, according to Diodorus 17.54.6, Alexander offered Darius the opportunity to retain his kingship over the Persian Empire, provided that he acknowledged Alexander's overlordship.

Such was the background to the circumstances in the Summer of 330BC when Alexander was in hot pursuit of Darius between Ecbatana and the Caspian Sea. At this point Curtius 5.8.12-13 has Darius remark in a speech to his council: "Unless perchance it should prove more fulfilling to dance attendance upon the decisions of the victor and emulate the example of Mazaeus and Mithrenes by being insecurely assigned the rule of a single province, always supposing Alexander now favours fawning upon his fame rather than indulging his anger?" Mazaeus had recently surrendered Babylon and retained its governance and Mithrenes had surrendered Sardis and had been given the Satrapy of Armenia in 331BC. Hence Darius appears to be alluding to the earlier offers that he might retain the rule of Persia and even its empire, if he accepted Alexander as his overlord. Darius therefore seems to have believed that such terms were still available in 330BC, though he still maintained here before his courtiers that he would not accept them.

Arrian, *Anabasis* 3.20.3 states that Alexander halted for five days at about this time, abruptly and mysteriously suspending his hot pursuit of Darius. The only likely reason for this is that he thought he had reached an arrangement with Darius, for he was normally quite relentless in his conduct of military operations. Therefore the possibility arises that Darius did ultimately decide to accept Alexander's terms and to become a sort of glorified Satrap of Persia within Alexander's all-encompassing dominions.

Curtius 6.3.13 has Alexander confide to his men: "…when his sovereign was even in want of succour from foreigners, Bessus set him in fetters like a common captive, though we the victors would assuredly have spared him. And then in the end he slaughtered Darius in order that we should not be able to save him." This is partly based on the fact that Darius was known to have been considering seeking help from foreigners at the time that Bessus deposed him. Ostensibly the foreigners were Patron's Greek mercenaries, but possibly Darius's hopes extended also to the Macedonians. These words certainly tend to confirm that Alexander saw himself as the potential saviour of Darius rather than his persecutor at the end and that Alexander believed that Bessus understood and appreciated the political implications of this odd role reversal.

If Darius made a surrender plan known to his subordinates or if they otherwise discovered that Darius was treating with Alexander, then this may have provided the immediate motive for Bessus dethroning and arresting Darius. It is particularly significant that Bessus chose to kill Darius, forever staining his reputation with the crime of regicide, instead of simply leaving his sovereign to be dealt with by Alexander. Clearly, Bessus did not believe that Alexander would kill Darius for him. The compulsion for him to murder his king must have derived from a real fear that Darius would otherwise have become a puppet ruler of Persia under Alexander, which would undoubtedly have undermined Bessus's potential support as the new Great King.

Alexander's Route: Battle of Issus to Death of Darius

Between the Battle of Issus and the death of Darius a number of questionmarks hang over Alexander's route. This subsection briefly reviews the main points at issue.

The first major difficulty arises regarding Alexander's route for his return from Ammon (Siwa) - also discussed later in the context of Arrian's errors. I conclude that Arrian's curt statement that Alexander travelled directly east across the desert to Memphis is not very credible. In particular, it is inconsistent with the best evidence on the timing of the foundation of Alexandria. The accounts in both the Vulgate and the Alexander Romance traditions show that Alexander returned via the Mediterranean coast by retracing the route he indisputably took to get to Siwa. On this point the evidence of the Romance (Pseudo-Callisthenes) carries more weight than usual, because its author was Egyptian and most probably lived in Alexandria itself.

The next point concerns how far north up the Mediterranean coast Alexander marched on his return from Egypt before striking inland. Arrian, *Anabasis* 3.6.4 notes that Alexander marched inland to Thapsacus immediately after having devoted a paragraph to Alexander's return to Tyre. There is no reason to infer that Alexander struck inland from Tyre itself, but that is nevertheless what many have done due to a supposed lack of other evidence on the route at this point. However, Engels has observed that it would have made much more sense for Alexander to have marched up the coast as far as possible, roughly to the vicinity of Seleucia, the port of Antioch, in order to take maximum advantage of support from the fleet in supplying his army.[460] Furthermore, Jacoby Fragment 3 of Cleitarchus from Stobaeus *Florilegium*, IV 20, 73 is connected with the town of Byblos on the Levantine coast north of Tyre and is stated to be from the fifth book of Cleitarchus corresponding to the fifth year of Alexander's reign. Since the king's first visit to Tyre was in the fourth year of his reign, this fragment constitutes significant evidence that Alexander returned to Byblos on his journey back north. Hence Alexander did not strike inland from Tyre (as almost all modern maps of his route would have us believe). Instead, he continued up the coast until he was as close as possible to the upper reaches of the Euphrates and only then did he strike inland to reach that river.

Alexander is reported by Arrian, *Anabasis* 3.7.1-2 to have crossed the Euphrates at Thapsacus. This city is known to have lain on the upper reaches of the

---

[460] Donald W Engels, Alexander the Great and the Logistics of the Macedonian Army, University of California, 1978, p.65 & Map 8.

Euphrates, but there are several alternative candidates. However, Ptolemy's *Geographia*, Chapter 18 of Book 5, places Thapsacus on the Euphrates just east of the modern town of Ar Raqqah and the ancient town of Nicephorion. Furthermore, Pliny, Natural History 5.21 states that Thapsacus later became known as Amphipolis. In their 1855 translation of this text, John Bostock and Henry Thomas Riley note that Amphipolis' "ruins are to be seen at the ford of El Hamman, near the modern Rakkah". The Dictionary of Greek and Roman Geography (1854, ed. William Smith, LLD) notes that: "About 36 miles below Balls (the Alalis of Ptolemy), following the course of the river, are the ruins of Sura; and about 6 miles lower is the ford of El-Hammam, which Col. Chesney identifies with the Zeugma of Thapsacus, where, according to local tradition, the army of Alexander crossed the Euphrates (Expedition for Survey, &c. vol. i. p. 416)." Hence the best information seems to point to a site close to modern Ar Raqqah.

There is also some uncertainty regarding which ford over the Tigris was used by Alexander, but the most likely on the basis of its position relative to the battlefield at Gaugamela seems to be that at Abu Wijam, as also proposed by Aurel Stein.[461]

In discussing the location of the Battle of Arbela/Gaugamela I have concluded that Alexander's route ran past modern Mosul and ancient Nineveh and continued through the plain to the south of Mt Maqloub, where the battle took place. The alternative theory that Alexander marched round the north of Mt Maqloub has been promoted by Schachermeyr, because he discovered that the modern Tel Gemel lay to the north of Mt Maqloub. The irony is that Aurel Stein had promoted Tel Gemel as a place name that could be (rather loosely) associated with the battle site, because he had received garbled information that it lay south of Mt Maqloub, his own preferred location for the engagement. In fact, the place name connection is so remote as to be unworthy of any weight in the matter. All the useful evidence, mainly from Curtius, Diodorus and Strabo, but also supported by Claudius Ptolemy's *Geographia* (as discussed above), suggests a location for the battle in the plain to the south of Mt Maqloub.

On quitting Susa, Alexander headed southeast with Persepolis as his objective. He crossed the river that our sources call the Pasitigris, but which seems also anciently to have been named the Eulaeus (e.g. in Ptolemy's *Geographia*). This is the modern River Karun. Ariobarzanes blockaded the route into Persis at the gorge that was called the Susian Gates in the Vulgate (Curtius 5.3.17, Diodorus 17.68.1, Polyaenus 4.3.27) or the Persian Gates in Arrian, *Anabasis* 3.18.2 and Strabo 15.3.6 (729). This seems to be the modern Tang-i Khas.[462]

---

[461] Aurel Stein, *Geographical Journal*, vol 100, 1942, p.157.

[462] Aurel Stein, *Old Routes of Western Iran*, London, 1940, p.25.

Key Historical Issues

In May 330BC Alexander resumed his pursuit of Darius, marching on Ecbatana by way of Parsagada and (probably) modern Isfahan. Darius having fled northwards towards Hyrcania, Alexander followed on his heels. Darius had just crossed the pass called the Caspian Gates (the modern Tang-i Sar Darrah on the southern flank of the Elburz Mountains) moving eastwards into Parthia, when he was arrested at the village of Thara (Justin 11.15.1 - possibly modern Lasjerd) by Nabarzanes and Bessus and placed in fetters in a covered wagon. The Persians then continued eastwards, heading for Bactria. But Alexander was threatening to overtake them, which prompted them to stab Darius, whom they left for dead somewhere near modern Samnan. One of Alexander's men named Polystratus found Darius still alive, but he had expired by the time Alexander himself reached the scene. Alexander continued on to Hecatompylus, probably the modern Sahr-i Qumis near Qusheh.

Alexander's Emulation of Cyrus and the Persianising

There are very strong reasons to believe that Alexander had read the *Cyropaidia* (Education of Cyrus) by Xenophon the follower of Socrates:

There are numerous anecdotal instances where Alexander appears to emulate Xenophon's Cyrus (visits to the wounded, *Cyropaidia* 5.4.18 & *Anabasis Alexandrou* 2.12.1; gifts of food and drink to those he wished to honour, *Cyropaidia* 8.2.4 & Plutarch, *Alexander* 23.5…).

Alexander's fond pilgrimage to the tomb of Cyrus at Parsagada and his furious reaction to its desecration upon his return from India are most readily explained by his having read the *Cyropaidia*. Strabo, *Geography* 11.11.4 actually describes Alexander as "a lover of Cyrus".

Diogenes Laertius 6.84 describes a parallel between Onesicritus, Alexander's chief pilot, who wrote perhaps the earliest complete account of Alexander's reign and entitled it How Alexander Was Led, and Xenophon the author of The Education of Cyrus. The parallel had probably been consciously and deliberately devised by Onesicritus himself, which suggests that Xenophon's *Cyropaidia* was a familiar point of reference among Alexander's circle of Friends.

Arrian actually has Alexander refer to episodes from Xenophon's *Anabasis* in his own *Anabasis Alexandrou* 2.7.8.

Alexander is known to have been widely read and it is obvious that he would have had a particular interest in books dealing with Persia, so it would be surprising, if he had ignored Xenophon's *Cyropaidia* and *Anabasis*, which were recent works about Persia by a writer of great repute, who had actually fought for Cyrus the Younger within the Persian Empire.

Xenophon's account bears only a passing resemblance to the true history of that Cyrus who had founded the Persian Empire. It seems instead to have been Xenophon's purpose, rather than penning an historically accurate work, to create an idealized model of kingship through the medium of a fictionalized version of the most influential recent king in his own time. It is the same species of motivation as stirred Plato to write the Republic. That is, a burning desire by an aristocratic Athenian, who had witnessed and suffered the excesses of Athens' democratic regime including the execution of his mentor, Socrates, to develop a nobler alternative to democracy. In Alexander, his philosophy found a willing and fervent disciple.

The relevance of Xenophon's influence upon Alexander in the matter of the Reconstruction of Book 7 of Cleitarchus lies in further connections with the *Cyropaidia* that may be discerned in the way that Alexander fell into the practice of so-called Persianising. For example, in Curtius 6.2.6-8 and Sections 7.3-4 of the Reconstruction, Alexander seeks to re-unite the captive granddaughter of Ochus, a former Great King (Artaxerxes III), with Hystaspes, her husband, who was a kinsman of Darius. This event, though superficially trivial, has the significance of inaugurating the Persianising phase of Alexander's career. However, it happens that we can use our knowledge of Alexander's enthusiasm for Xenophon's writings to gain special insight into Alexander's thinking on this matter, even beyond what would have been apparent to most of his contemporaries. Essentially, it appears that the king was emulating the chivalric model of kingship presented by Xenophon in the *Cyropaidia*, specifically the episode at *Cyropaidia* 6.1.45-48 wherein Cyrus reunites Pantheia with her husband Abradatas and thereby wins the latter's allegiance. There are some indications that Alexander originally planned to reunite Darius with his wife according to this model. He actually says so in his letter to Darius cited in Arrian, *Anabasis* 2.14.8: "If you are afraid you may suffer any harsh treatment from me when you come to me, send some of your friends to receive pledges of safety from me. Come to me then, and ask for your mother, wife, and children, and anything else you wish. For whatever you ask for you will receive; and nothing shall be denied you." But being thwarted in the ambition of perpetrating those reunions by the deaths of both Darius and his wife, he evidently found a convenient substitute in the wife of Hystaspes.

A further instance where Xenophon's influence seems to have been instrumental is Alexander's adoption of Persian dress. Cleitarchus recorded this with some disdain (Sections 7.35-36). To set this in context it is necessary to appreciate that Cleitarchus was one of the Cynics, a sect that considered abstemiousness to be next to godliness. They were an early manifestation of the asceticism that later launched Christianity and Islam. By contrast, Plutarch in his essays On the Fortune or Virtue of Alexander (*Moralia* 329F-330A) actually praised the king for his rapprochement with the Persians by adopting elements of their dress. But even more interestingly Xenophon made a special virtue of the adoption of Median dress by the Persian Cyrus, when he had won control of that kingdom in *Cyropaidia* 8.1.40. This also explains why Alexander gave his companions Persian accoutrements, for Xenophon had Cyrus persuade his comrades to wear Median dress too.

Key Historical Issues

The Cleitarchan sources show that Cleitarchus himself had given a particularly detailed account of exactly what it was that Alexander wore. However, it is a difficult matter to explain the appearance of clothing with a purely verbal description, so some clarification is appropriate. In fact, a good example of what the ancient Greek writers understood as Persian or Oriental dress is the attire of the ancient statue of Paris in the British Museum, which I have sketched in Figure C. However, Cleitarchus noted that Alexander did not actually wear the trouser-leggings or the long-sleeves. What we are left with is a heavily pleated chiton or tunic, which in Alexander's case was dyed purple with a broad white stripe down the front (a similar tunic is worn by Darius in the Alexander Mosaic from the House of the Faun in Pompeii.) The tunic was tied just beneath the breast with a sort of cummerbund or belt called a *zona* and an ankle-length cloak (probably purple like those given to Alexander's companions) completed the clothing proper. Paris wears a type of cap, but Alexander had a diadem of purple interlaced with white bound about his head. This was simply a sort of elaborate ribbon tied in a bow at the back. Alexander is depicted wearing it in the silver tetradrachm coins minted by his Bodyguard Lysimachus after the king's death (one of the author's Lysimachus tetradrachms is depicted on the dedication page).

Of course, the irony is that to modern eyes the dress of Paris looks quintessentially Greek and even more so if the long-sleeves and leggings are omitted. Even Alexander's own men must have recognized that his heavily edited compromise version of Persian dress was little more than a tweak to his previous range of raiment. But it seems that even the tiniest of Persian elements were deemed objectionable on principle. It was the symbolism of appeasing the Persians that mattered more than the reality.

Xenophon also gives a description of the Persian king's Royal Eunuchs in the Cyropaidia 7.5.60-65:

> *[Cyrus] knew that men with children or wives or favourites in whom they delight must needs love them most: while eunuchs, who are deprived of all such dear ones, would surely make most account of him who could enrich them or help them if they were injured or crown them with honour. And in conferring such benefits he was disposed to think he could outbid the world. Moreover the eunuch, being degraded in the eyes of other men, is driven to seek the assistance of some lord and master. Without such protection there is not a man in the world who would not think he had the right to over-reach a eunuch: while there was every reason to suppose that the eunuch would be the most faithful of all servants. As for the customary notion that a eunuch must be weak and cowardly, Cyrus was not disposed to accept it.... No men have shown more faithfulness than eunuchs when ruin has fallen on their lords. In bodily strength, perhaps, the eunuch seems to be lacking, but steel is a great leveller and makes the weak man equal to the strong in war. Holding this in mind, Cyrus resolved that his personal attendants, from his doorkeeper onwards, should be eunuchs one and all.*

Concerning Alexander the Great by Andrew Chugg

Figure C. Ancient statue of Paris in the British Museum wearing Oriental/Persian dress (sketch by the author)

Key Historical Issues

It is in this light that Alexander's appointment of Persian rod-bearers (ushers?) to his court (Diodorus 17.77.4 and Section 7.36 of the Reconstruction) should be viewed and, most particularly, his eager acceptance of Bagoas the Eunuch, formerly the lover of Darius, into his retinue, perhaps introduced among the rod-bearers, and soon into his bed too. Bagoas himself must surely have been influential in promoting the subsequent progress of the Persianising. This is probably why he is accused of being one of Alexander's most influential flatterers by Plutarch, Moralia 65D. Ultimately, however, the Persianising project ran aground, when Callisthenes refused to perform proskynesis.

Geographical Errors between the Caspian and India

There are several geographical errors and ambiguities arising between the Caspian Sea and the borders of India within Cleitarchus' account. They are potentially rather confusing to an unbriefed reader. However, a basic understanding of these issues will engender an appreciation that the Cleitarchan account is actually relatively accurate and self-consistent on matters concerning Alexander's route and itinerary. There are even some indications of the date and sources of Cleitarchus to be gleaned from his geography. It is therefore the purpose of this sub-section to furnish a suitable grounding in Cleitarchan conceptions of Asian geography.

1) Uncertainty whether the Caspian Sea was a gulf of the Ocean.

This doubt of "some" concerning the nature of the Caspian is expressed at Curtius 6.4.19 as part of a geographical discussion of the region that includes Fragments of Cleitarchus and parts of which are also echoed at Diodorus 17.75.3. Hence there is a strong implication that this material was sourced from Cleitarchus. Strabo 11.7.2 references Patroclus, who explored the Caspian for Antiochus I around 284-3BC and concluded that it was nearly as big as the Pontic Sea (Black Sea). The same view appears in Pliny, *Natural History* 6.36-38, who attributes it to Cleitarchus. Hence there may be some connection between Cleitarchus' writings on this topic and Patroclus' account of his explorations. It is difficult to believe that Cleitarchus considered it possible that the Caspian might be a gulf of the Ocean, because it would eliminate the possibility that the Jaxartes was the Tanais (which Cleitarchus evidently did believe – see below.) More probably, Cleitarchus was aware of Patroclus' explorations and was disparaging or at least questioning his view that the Caspian was a gulf.[463]

2) Flow of water between the Caspian and the Sea of Azov

Strabo 11.1.5 states that Cleitarchus allowed that water of either the Pontic Sea (a.k.a. Euxine, the modern Black Sea) or the Caspian might flood across

---

[463] On the connection between Patroclus and Cleitarchus, see W. W. Tarn, Alexander the Great, Vol II, Sources & Studies, pp. 12-19.

the isthmus of land between them, which would appear to match the very similar comments at Curtius 6.4.18 regarding the supply of water from the Maeotic Marsh (vicinity of the Sea of Azov) into the Caspian. The land is indeed very low lying between the Sea of Azov and the northern Caspian, but actual transfer of water would seem unlikely even in antiquity. Nevertheless, the fact that Cleitarchus was able to discuss geographical issues pertaining to the northern Caspian region is suggestive of an awareness of the explorations of Patroclus (as in the preceding point).

3) The Bosphorus in Cleitarchus is usually the Cimmerian Bosphorus

Curtius 6.2.13, 7.6.12 & 8.1.7 is probably following Cleitarchus in referring to the "Bosphorus". To avoid confusion, it is important to realize that he means the Cimmerian Bosphorus, the modern Strait of Kerch at the entrance to the Sea of Azov, and not the more famous Bosphorus at the SW corner of the Black Sea by Istanbul.

4) The Caucasus mountain range extended eastwards to the Hindu Kush

Curtius 7.3.19-21 is probably following Cleitarchus in describing the Caucasus range as extending from the region of Armenia in NE Turkey eastwards across the whole of Asia to the Hindu Kush, when Alexander was about to cross the latter in the spring of 329BC. This is corroborated by the fact that Diodorus 17.83.1 also deems these mountains a part of the Caucasus, but notes that the Hindu Kush section was known as the Paropamisus Range. This slightly inaccurate view that the mountains stretch in an unbroken chain from west to east right across the center of Asia from Turkey to the Himalayas was common to a number of ancient geographers, being echoed somewhat in the maps of Claudius Ptolemy, for example.

5) The Syr-Darya was the upper reaches of the River Don

This is the most serious geographical distortion in Cleitarchus, because it engenders the view that Soviet Central Asia (now the various "Stans") was part of Europe and lay vaguely just to the NE of the Black Sea. Plutarch, *Alexander* 45.4 states that Alexander himself supposed the River Orexartes (elsewhere called the Jaxartes in ancient sources and now known as the Syr-Darya) to be the Tanais, which is the modern River Don. This has the effect of shifting the entire landscape some 2000km to the west of where it actually lies on the globe. The expedition believed that the Scythian tribes that they encountered to the north of the Syr-Darya were identical to the Scythians with whom the Greeks had long been in contact to the north of the Black Sea (anciently the Pontic Sea or Euxine). It is quite probable that there were indeed pronounced similarities of language and culture, but this would have reflected the wide geographical range of the Scythian tribes rather than a contraction of the landscape. The implication that Bactria lay just to the east of the Pontic Sea at Curtius 7.4.27 is likely to be a further consequence of the same Cleitarchan misunderstanding of the geography, since Alexander was actually more than 1000km east of even the Caspian Sea when he was in Bactria. There is a strong connection to be drawn between the misidentification of the Syr-Darya as the Tanais, the spurious Cleitarchan link between the Caspian and the Sea of Azov and Fragment 7 of the work of the Alexander historian Polycleitus of Larissa (in Strabo 11.7.4), which also asserts these concepts. A strong possibility is that Polycleitus was among Cleitarchus' sources for this material (see Figure A at the end of the Introduction). Strabo himself knew these things to be in error, quite probably based on the geographical researches of Eratosthenes, whom he mentions in refuting the misconceptions. This tends to corroborate the view that Cleitarchus antedates Eratosthenes, who was active in the second half of the 3rd century BC.

6) India began in South Afghanistan in the vicinity of the Helmand River

According to Cleitarchan geography, India began in southern Afghanistan in the region of the Helmand River, which Alexander traversed towards the end of 330BC. This is most explicitly stated at Curtius 8.9.10, where the River Ethymantus, which appears to be the Helmand, is mentioned as being a part of India. There are many confirmatory instances of the same geographical concept. Polyaenus 4.3.10 and Plutarch, *Alexander* 57.1-2 corroborate the detailed account of baggage burning at Curtius 6.6.14-17 shortly prior to the entry of the army into Southern Afghanistan. Although the former pair place the burning just prior to the entry into India proper, the confusion might well have resulted from Cleitarchus counting Southern Afghanistan as part of India, for it was true that Alexander was about to cross the mountains moving southwards into Afghanistan in pursuit of Satibarzanes at this point. The reason that Southern Afghanistan had to be incorporated within India may have been that the territory of Arachosia extended from the vicinity of the Helmand as far as the west bank of the Indus. The manuscripts of Curtius 7.3.4 read that Arachosia extended to the *ponticum mare* meaning the Black Sea, which is complete nonsense. It is clear from Strabo 11.10.1 that ancient geographers actually asserted that Arachosia extended to the River Indus (cf. Curtius 8.13.3, 9.7.14 & 9.10.7). The inference must be that the Greek word for a river (*potamos*) has somehow been corrupted to give Pontic in the Latin.

The Visit of the Queen of the Amazons

In the ancient world (as also today), Alexander's putative encounter with the Queen of the Amazons was one of the more controversial episodes in his career. The issue is neatly addressed by Plutarch in chapter 46 of his Life of Alexander:

Here [beyond the River Jaxartes] *the Queen of the Amazons came to see Alexander, as most writers say, among whom are Cleitarchus, Polycleitus, Onesicritus, Antigenes and Ister; but Aristobulus, Chares the royal usher, Ptolemy, Anticleides, Philo the Theban, and Philip of Theangela, besides Hecataeus of Eretria, Philip the Chalcidian, and Duris of Samos, say that this is a fiction. And it would seem that Alexander's testimony is in favour of their statement. For in a letter to Antipater, which gives all the details minutely, he says that the Scythian king offered him his daughter in marriage, but he makes no mention of the Amazon. And the story is told that many years afterwards Onesicritus was reading aloud to Lysimachus, who was now king, the fourth book of his history, in which was the tale of the Amazon, at which Lysimachus smiled gently and said: "And where was I at the time?" However, our belief or disbelief of this story will neither increase nor diminish our admiration for Alexander.*

It is certainly true that the daughter of the king of the Scythians dwelling beyond the Cimmerian Bosphorus was offered to Alexander in marriage, since this is also recorded by Arrian, *Anabasis* 4.15.2 and Curtius 8.1.9. Notionally, these were the Scythians dwelling in the vicinity of the Ukraine, but this may well be entangled with the geographical misconception that the Syr-Darya or Tanais or Jaxartes River was the border of Europe. If so, then the offer, which was received whilst Alexander was at Maracanda, may have come from a Scythian king perhaps based north of the Jaxartes. Some have supposed that Alexander's encounter with the Amazon queen was derived through embroidery of this incident, which is certainly a possibility. There is archaeological evidence for warrior women on the Russian Steppes in Alexander's era in the form of female ice-mummies preserved with their weapons in elaborate tombs dug into the Siberian permafrost. Hence the suggestion that Alexander encountered high status warrior women in this general vicinity may have some validity.

Curtius 6.4.17 appears to be following Cleitarchus in locating an Amazon homeland to Alexander's right as he approached the Caspian from the southeast. This would suggest that Cleitarchus placed it on the steppe to the east of the Caspian Sea. His source on this is likely to have been Onesicritus, who seems to be the earliest of the sources listed by Plutarch for Alexander having hosted a visit from the Amazon Queen. Subsequently, in giving the specific story of the visit of Thalestris, Cleitarchus suggested that she had travelled from the traditional Amazon homeland near the River Thermodon on the southern shores of the Black Sea (i.e. west of Hyrcania and very far to the west of the Caspian Sea.) It is likely that Cleitarchus or his source (Onesicritus?) has attempted to reconcile traditional legends of the Amazon nation with a visit to Alexander's camp of a high-status warrior woman from east of the Caspian Sea. This was perhaps facilitated by the haziness of Cleitarchus' grasp of the geography of the area.

Whatever the degree of its authenticity, the story of the meeting between Alexander and Thalestris seems to have gripped the imagination of his readership in antiquity. A fresco found in Pompeii depicting Alexander with a queen (Figure D) must surely have been intended to illustrate his meeting with Thalestris. She is a queen in her own right, since she bears a scepter and the helmet at her feet appears more likely to be her own than Alexander's.

Figure D. Alexander with Thalestris (author's sketch of a fresco in Pompeii)

Prophthasia

Prophthasia is the Greek for "Anticipation" (in the sense of forestalling something) and it is the name given to a town in the land of the Drangians by Alexander. It therefore seems to commemorate his having outrun fate in the form of the Dimnus conspiracy and hence it is considered to have been the site of the Philotas Affair, which is otherwise merely said to have transpired at the palace of the Drangians (Arrian, *Anabasis* 3.25.8).

Concerning Alexander the Great by Andrew Chugg

Prophthasia is very likely to have been at or close to the modern city of Farah (Phraa) in the west of Afghanistan. Strabo 11.8.9, Claudius Ptolemy, *Geography* 6.19.4-5 and Pliny, *Natural History* 6.61 give the name Prophthasia to a town approximately 270km from Alexandria-in-Aria. If the latter is assumed to have been at or close to the modern city of Herat, which is likely, then 270km is about the correct distance for modern Farah. The specific distances cited by Strabo and Pliny give the route lengths abstracted from the records of the *bematists* (i.e. "pacers") of Alexander's expedition, the so-called Stages or *Stathmoi* in Greek. "Prophthasia" is listed among towns of Drangiana by Ptolemy[464] and Strabo 15.2.8 speaks of "Prophthasia in Drangiana", so it is clear that it lay south of Alexandria-in-Aria. Stephanus Byzantinus in his entry for "Phrada" states that Alexander called this place Prophthasia and that it was a town among the Drangians (a.k.a. Zarangians) and there is also a mention by Isidorus of Charax, F2, 16 = Jacoby III C781. Hence it is beyond reasonable doubt that Prophthasia lay at or quite near Farah, despite that Tarn has gone against the grain by placing it considerably further south on Lake Seistan.

It is however a distinct possibility that Alexander's fort of Prophthasia was separate from the Farah that is the Phrada of Stephanus Byzantinus. Modern Farah lies down in the valley beside the river, but it is overlooked by crags of the nearby mountains, some of which are the sites of ancient fortresses. An adjacent refoundation could simultaneously explain the name change and the enduring association.

The old town of Farah, now in ruins, stood on the western bank of the river at a strategic point commanding the northern entrance into the province of Seistan. It used to be a major staging point and tollhouse mid-way on the caravan road from Kandahar to Herat. A modern town, built on the opposite (eastern) bank, is now the centre of all activities and accommodates the main population.

Farah was for centuries an important stronghold on the eastern frontier of the Sassanian Empire, possibly rebuilt by Peroz (AD457-84), since the province thereabouts was once named Fraxkar-Peroz. This might also have been the occasion of its refoundation on a fresh site. The ancient citadel within Farah is seemingly Sassanian and there is scant evidence that much material of greater antiquity than the era of Peroz exists in its immediate vicinity.

---

[464] Ptolemy assigns Prophthasia coordinates of 110 pseudo-degrees of longitude and 32.33 degrees of latitude, whereas he places Alexander-in-Aria at 110 pseudo-degrees of longitude and 36 degrees of latitude. Ptolemy's longitude for Bactra (modern Balkh) was at 116 pseudo-degrees of longitude, which means that his longitude for Alexandria-in-Aria and Prophthasia is roughly consistent with Herat and Farah. The actual latitudes of Herat and Farah are 34.37N and 32.38N respectively and Farah is due south of Herat, so Ptolemy's separation is in the correct direction, but its magnitude is too large, although he has the latitude (which can be precisely derived from solar observations) almost exactly correct for Farah.

Key Historical Issues
The Culpability of Philotas and Parmenion

The Philotas Affair, as it is commonly known, constitutes a real-life tragedy in three Acts, namely: The Dimnus Conspiracy, The Trial & Execution of Philotas and The Assassination of Parmenion. The account in Curtius is particularly full and vivid. Speculatively, Curtius found this quasi-judicial purgation especially interesting, since it bore comparison with the downfalls of some of the great political figures of his own time, such as Sejanus. Parallels with Diodorus, especially in the matter of how the plot of Dimnus and his fellow conspirators came to light, suggest that Curtius' version is highly likely to be derived from Cleitarchus, hence it probably constitutes a near verbatim and barely abridged Latin translation of a large section of Cleitarchus' text.

Alexander is often particularly deprecated for his treatment of Philotas and Parmenion by both ancient and modern authorities and these critics often base their opinions on the Cleitarchan version of the affair, but it appears to me on the basis of the same account that Philotas was legally guilty of treason beyond reasonable doubt and that Alexander had no better option than to act as he did. However, the matter seems plagued with misunderstandings, which require explication.

There is no real doubt that Philotas concealed the existence of the Dimnus Conspiracy from the king, firstly, because he was stated to have confessed this much to Alexander by Cleitarchus and secondly, because Arrian, *Anabasis* 3.26.1-2 (citing Ptolemy and Aristobulus) reaches the same conclusion in his brief account of the matter:

Here also [at the palace of the Drangians] Alexander discovered the conspiracy of Philotas, son of Parmenion. Ptolemy and Aristobulus say that it had already been reported to him before in Egypt, but that it did not appear to him credible, both on account of the long-existing friendship between them, the honour, which he publicly conferred upon his father Parmenion, and the confidence he reposed in Philotas himself. Ptolemy, son of Lagus, says that Philotas was brought before the Macedonians; that Alexander vehemently accused him, and that he defended himself from the charges. He says also that the divulgers of the plot came forward and convicted him and his accomplices both by other clear proofs and especially because Philotas himself confessed that he had heard of some sort of conspiracy, which was being formed against Alexander. He was convicted of having said nothing to the king about this plot, though he visited the royal tent twice a day.

Neither is there any doubt that the Dimnus Conspiracy was a very real threat to Alexander's life, for Dimnus himself made dubiety impossible by committing suicide, when men were sent to arrest him. Legally speaking, the fact of having concealed the existence of a genuine assassination plot against the sovereign constitutes treason. However, there might be some moral mitigation, if Philotas' defence that he had not taken the plot seriously could be considered to have any credibility. However, this is not really a viable defence at all, because Philotas was at liberty to divulge the plot to Alexander, thus covering himself against accusations of concealment, whilst still expressing his personal scepticism about the matter, so there was actually no innocent motive for concealment. Conversely, Plutarch, *Alexander* 48.1-49.2 backs the comments of Arrian to the effect that Philotas' loyalty was already seriously suspected long before the Dimnus Conspiracy:

Now, Philotas, the son of Parmenion, had a high position among the Macedonians; for he was held to be valiant and able to endure hardship, and, after Alexander himself, no one was so fond of giving and so fond of his comrades. At any rate, we are told that when one of his intimates asked him for some money, he ordered his steward to give it him, and when the steward said he had none to give, "What meanest thou?" cried Philotas, "hast thou not even plate or clothing?" However, he displayed a pride of spirit, an abundance of wealth, and a care of the person and mode of life which were too offensive for a private man, and at this time particularly his imitation of majesty and loftiness was not successful at all, but clumsy, spurious, and devoid of grace, so that he incurred suspicion and envy, and even Parmenion once said to him: "My son, pray be less of a personage." Moreover, for a very long time accusations against him had been brought to Alexander himself. For when Darius had been defeated in Cilicia and the wealth of Damascus had been taken, among the many prisoners brought into the camp there was found a young woman, born in Pydna, and comely to look upon; her name was Antigone. This woman Philotas got; and as a young man will often talk freely in vaunting and martial strain to his mistress and in his cups, he used to tell her that the greatest achievements were performed by himself and his father, and would call Alexander a stripling who through their efforts enjoyed the title of ruler. These words the woman would report to one of her acquaintances, and he, as was natural, to somebody else, until the story came round to Craterus, who took the girl and brought her secretly to Alexander. He, on hearing the story, ordered her to continue her meetings with Philotas and to come and report to him whatever she learnt from her lover. Now, Philotas was ignorant of the plot thus laid against him, and in his frequent interviews with Antigone would utter many angry and boastful speeches and many improper words against the king. But Alexander, although strong testimony against Philotas came to his ears, endured in silence and restrained himself, either because he had confidence in Parmenion's good will towards him, or because he feared the reputation and power of father and son.

The glaring motivation for Philotas' concealment of the plot that remains was that he quietly hoped the conspiracy would succeed in eliminating Alexander, in which case his father was in an excellent position to seize power. Everything that we know about the circumstances drives towards the conclusion that this thought was exactly what kept Philotas' lips sealed. If so, then morally he was as culpable as the conspirators themselves and deserving of his fate. Note, however, that I very much distinguish between Philotas and the conspirators, for it is very unlikely that he was part of the plot. As he pointed out himself during his defence speech, if he had been the leader of the conspiracy or even just a member, he should both have set about having Cebalinus silenced and he should have advanced the timing of the perpetration of the plot, whereas he actually simply sat on his hands and did nothing. He seems to have believed that he could thereby exculpate himself, if the plot were discovered. He was almost correct, for Curtius suggests that Alexander's first instinct was to accept his excuses and forgive him.

Key Historical Issues

However, the king's Friends, notably Craterus, cogently made clear that Alexander simply could not afford to do so in the ensuing private council session. The recriminations had already gone too far, such that Philotas and Parmenion would now be driven to rebel by the perilousness of the cloud of suspicion that hung over them, even if they had not indeed already contemplated insurrection.

The next matter that is disputed is the fairness of the ensuing trial. It is indisputable that such a trial took place before the Macedonian Assembly and that both Philotas and Parmenion (*in absentia*) were convicted, because, as we have seen, Arrian endorses the Cleitarchan version from Curtius using largely independent sources. Regarding its equity, Curtius 6.9.30-31 makes a point of having Alexander defend the right of Philotas to put his defence to the Assembly:

Then Coenus, despite that he had wed the sister of Philotas, fulminated against him more fiercely than anyone else, bellowing that he was a traitor to his king, to his country and to the army itself. And scooping up a stone that happened to lie by his feet he prepared to hurl it at him – many surmised out of a desire to spare him from torture. But the king stayed his hand, declaring that the defendant ought first to be afforded an opportunity to deliver his defence and that he would not allow the trial to proceed otherwise.

Hence Alexander himself apparently showed such meticulous attention to fairness as to insist that a man who had failed (by his own admission) to report a genuine assassination plot against the king's life should nevertheless be given a hearing before the entire army. However, the king's critics assert that he subsequently had Philotas tortured to elicit a confession, but this is mistaken. The torture did indeed take place, but according to Curtius (who gives by far the most detailed account) its purpose was not to secure a confession. Philotas gave a confession before the torturers began work in the hope of forestalling them. But in fact, it appears firstly that torture was a normal part of the punishment for those convicted of treason, since, for example, the Royal Pages were tortured to death after their conviction (Curtius 8.8.20), and secondly that it was designed to try to extract any further information about the plot that might not yet have been uncovered. In this particular case, it is clear that Alexander needed further evidence against Parmenion. He could not execute Philotas, Parmenion's last surviving son, without incurring the enmity of the general, so he was compelled to act against him. According to Curtius, Philotas did indeed provide evidence of Parmenion's treasonous intentions by describing an earlier pact with Hegelochus to kill Alexander after the death of Darius. Curtius also notes (and I agree with him) that such evidence given under torture was of doubtful validity. But that misses the point. Alexander had to move against Parmenion anyway, so it was better to do so on the basis of questionable evidence than on none at all.

Furthermore, Philotas had already made his defence and been condemned by the Assembly before the torture was applied to him. The torture occurs at Curtius 6.11.13-34, whereas Philotas was condemned with the Assembly having been roused against him at Curtius 6.11.8. That is the way the Assembly delivered its verdicts - by acclamation rather than an explicit vote. At this point all the evidence against Philotas had been heard and he had completed his defence, so the verdict was due. In the ensuing trial of Amyntas, Simmias and Polemon (who were acquitted), Curtius 7.2.7 actually states this by speaking of "the acclamations by which crowds express their favour". This is why the Bodyguards are starting to propose a sentence for Philotas (tearing him to pieces with their bare hands). It is true that the trials of the other suspects and Parmenion were conducted the following day. That was why Alexander only adjourned the Assembly. The next day, Philotas was merely a witness in the trial of his father, since the main evidence then available against Parmenion came from his testimony about Hegelochus given under torture the previous evening.

Unfortunately, additional confusion has been sown by a slight mistranslation of Curtius 6.11.9 in the Penguin version of his text, which states that Curtius was about to experience *"further* torture in prison". There is in fact no word in the Latin of Curtius that translates as "further" in this passage, which is:

rex in contionem reversus, sive ut in custodia quoque torqueret, sive ut diligentius cuncta cognosceret, concilium in posterum diem distulit...

The word at issue is *quoque*, which means "also" or "as well". It is only necessary to look at the immediate context (the preceding sentences) to see what this torture/torment was as well as. A correct translation would be:

Then indeed the entire assembly was incensed and the Bodyguards made a beginning by bellowing that they should dismember the traitor with their bare hands. In fact, Philotas was scarcely scared on hearing this, since he feared far fouler suffering. But the king came back into the meeting and adjourned the proceedings until the following day, either in order to torment Philotas in prison as well or else to investigate the whole matter more thoroughly.

So in fact it is perfectly clear that the torture/torment in the prison is in addition to the proposal by the Bodyguards that they should dismember Philotas with their bare hands. The meaning of *torqueo* in Latin is actually literally to wrench or twist, so the dismembering would very much have been recognised by a Latin reader as another instance of it. There is also a strong reason in the structure of the Latin phrase, which means that it must really be a reference back to the proposed tearing to pieces. This is because *quoque* has a meaning very similar to the English "too" and just like "too" it almost always emphasises the word preceding it: in this case "in prison", so the meaning is "***in prison*** too". Hence Curtius is explicitly implying some kind of earlier mention of torment in a context outside of prison. The only thing this could possibly have been is the tearing to pieces, which would have formed part of a public execution. Thus, there is no basis for the translation "further" in the Penguin Curtius, which infers something for which there is no evidence in the Latin.

It may also be noted that there has been no mention of Philotas having been tortured before, merely a proposal that he eventually should be. Hence, the translation "further" would make Curtius refer back to an event that he had not actually stated to have happened. So the Penguin translator (by the artifice of

Key Historical Issues

mistranslating a Latin word) would have us swallow that Curtius referred back to an episode of torture that he had forgotten that he had not already mentioned a few a pages earlier, which is preposterous.

Using "further" instead of "as well" was an artifice to give a particular slant to the Latin. But I do not at all suggest that the translator was committing a deliberate distortion. He probably put this slant on the Latin, simply because it was the only interpretation that he saw at the time. He simply did not notice on the spur of the moment that *quoque* should refer back to the tearing to bits by hand. However, the effect of this accident is unfortunate in seeming to provide evidence for pre-conviction torture where there is none.

It should be remembered that shortly after the trial of Philotas, Amyntas and Polemon were acquitted by the Assembly, so it is clear that trials before this body were not a foregone conclusion. But Philotas had the special problem that he had freely admitted to having concealed a genuine assassination plot against his sovereign, which would be sufficient to convict him of treason in most jurisdictions today.

There remains the question of the guilt of Parmenion. Many commentators, both ancient and modern, have assumed that he was innocent, since it is fairly unlikely that either he or Philotas were actually members of the Dimnus conspiracy. Two things, however, weigh significantly against him. Firstly, it is likely to be true that Philotas alleged under torture that Parmenion had consented to espouse Hegelochus' proposal that an opportunity should be sought to depose Alexander, once Darius had been dealt with. Although the truth of this accusation is in doubt, since it was made under torture, its falseness is equally in doubt, since it was credible to those present at the time and is relatively consistent with other information that has come down to us about the general context. For example, Hegelochus' reported accusation that Alexander had pardoned his father's assassins should probably be connected with the report at Justin 9.7 that Olympias had arranged getaway steeds for the assassin, Pausanias. It cannot refer to the pardoning of Alexander Lyncestes, because Alexander had long since imprisoned him on suspicion of treason at the time when Hegelochus spoke.

Secondly, Alexander seems to have made an additional effort to secure evidence of Parmenion's disloyalty. Curtius 7.2.27 makes a point of the fact that Cleander and Polydamas waited until Parmenion was reading the letter purportedly penned by Philotas before slaying him. It was precisely at the point that he exhibited pleasure with the contents of this correspondence that the execution was perpetrated. Assuredly, the explanation must be that Alexander had included some treasonous material in this letter and had instructed his officers to await Parmenion's reaction before imposing the death sentence. Hence Parmenion's pleasure in learning of this treason from his son, as he supposed, provided Alexander and furnishes us too with some valid corroboration of the general's disloyalty.

The Condemnation of the Branchidae

It will be helpful to begin with a review of the more significant elements of the copious ancient source material on Alexander's destruction of the Branchidae.

Firstly, Strabo 14.1.5:

Next after the Poseidium of the Milesians, at the distance of 189 stadia from the seacoast, is the oracle of Apollo Didymeus among the Branchidæ. This, as well as the other temples, except that at Ephesus, was burnt by the order of Xerxes. The Branchidæ delivered up the treasures of the god to the Persian king, and accompanied him in his flight, in order to avoid the punishment of sacrilege and treachery.

Strabo 11.11.4:

And near these places [in Bactria and Sogdiana], they say, Alexander destroyed also the city of the Branchidae, whom Xerxes had settled there - people who voluntarily accompanied him from their homeland - because of the fact that they had betrayed to him the riches and treasures of the god at Didyma. Alexander destroyed the city, they add, because he abominated the sacrilege and the betrayal.

Plutarch, *Moralia* 557B, *De sera numinis vindicta* (On delays of divine vengeance):

Again, not even the greatest admirers of Alexander, among whom I count myself, approve his wiping out the city of Branchidae and his general massacre of young and old because their great-grandfathers had betrayed the temple near Miletus.

Curtius 7.5.28-35 (which is essentially the version used in this Reconstruction):

Whilst Bessus was leading him a merry chase, Alexander came upon an inconsequential citadel. Its populace comprised the Branchidae, who had migrated from Miletus at the bidding of Xerxes, when he was on his way back from Greece. They had set themselves up it this seat, since they had profaned the sanctuary called the Didymeon to appease Xerxes. In the interim they had hardly lapsed from the habits of their homeland, though they were now bilingual, having little by little been lured from their own languange by the local lingo. Therefore, they were greatly gratified to greet Alexander and to set their city and themselves at his service. Then the king commanded that the Milesians who were serving in his forces should assemble. They nursed the ancient enmity against the Branchidaean folk. Hence, he allowed those whom they had betrayed freely to judge whether they wished to recollect the kinship or the crime of the Branchidae. Then, having received various views from them, he himself undertook to weigh up what had best be done. The next day, when the Branchidae came before him, he called upon them to accompany him and, when they had come to the city, he himself got through its gate with a designated detachment. The phalanx he instructed to ring the ramparts of the fortress and to tear down the town at a given signal, since it was an asylum for quislings and these should be mown down to a man. Being defenceless they were massacred everywhere and neither their shared speech nor the beseeching of the suppliants with olive branches and prayer could curb the cruelty. Ultimately, they undermined the foundations of the walls so that they could be cast down in order that no vestige of the town should stand. And in order to leave naught but wiped out waste and lifeless land with even its roots eradicated, they not only felled the copses and sacred groves, but also extirpated the stumps. Had this been contrived against the traitors themselves, then it would have been vindicated as

Key Historical Issues

valid vengeance rather than rated as ruthlessness. As it was the descendants suffered for the sins of their ancestors, though they had not even seen Miletus and hence never had the ability to betray it to Xerxes.

Diodorus, Contents of Book 17 (his main account is lost in a lacuna):

How the Branchidae, who of old had been settled by the Persians on the borders of their kingdom, were slain by Alexander as traitors to the Greeks.

Suda (Aelian fragment 54) s.v. *Branchidae* (Adler number: Beta 514):

Those living in Milesian Didyma, who, in seeking favor with Xerxes, betrayed the temple of the indigenous Apollo to the barbarians: the temple offerings, of which there were a great number, were plundered. The traitors, fearing vengeance from both the laws and the inhabitants of the city, asked Xerxes to pay them for this wretched betrayal and settle them in some Asian land. He agreed, and in exchange for what was evil and unholy, allowed them to live where they would never again set foot upon Greece and both they and future generations would be removed from the fear besetting them. Then, having obtained the land with birds of ill-omen, they established a city and gave it the name Branchidas, thinking they had not only escaped the Milesians, but also justice itself. But the watchfulness of the god was not asleep. For Alexander, when he obtained mastery of the Persian empire upon conquering Darius, heard of their daring and conceived a hatred for them and their successive generations; so he killed them all, judging that the offspring of evil is evil. He overthrew their pseudonymous city and razed it to the ground.

Given this wealth of source evidence, those that deny that this event ever happened are bound to expose their reputations to the taint of disingenuousness.[465] It is no excuse that Arrian omitted mention of the matter, for he omitted mention of many things that he considered distasteful.

By modern standards the destruction of the Branchidae was an atrocity. By the standards of Alexander's era, the issue is far more complex. It appears that contemporaneous religious law, which then enjoyed genuine respect, dictated that the descendants of serious religious criminals inherited the guilt. Plutarch's dialogue On Delays in Divine Vengeance in his *Moralia* attacks the application of this religious law through various examples, including the case of the Branchidae, but it nevertheless treats it as axiomatic that such a law was applied and even cites an attack upon the same principle by Euripides at *Moralia* 556E. It was a sacred duty of Alexander to uphold religious law, but he would probably have been conscious that this particular tenet was controversial and that the passage of 150 years could be seen as a major mitigation. It was probably his sense of a dilemma that led him to seek a sentence from his Milesians. Curtius is usually translated to

---

[465] For the denial of the historicity of the event see W. W. Tarn, *Alexander the Great*, Vol II, Sources & Studies, "The Alleged Massacre of the Branchidae", pp. 272-275; Frank Holt, *Alexander the Great and Bactria*, p. 74, refutes Tarn's case, which is essentially that the temple and oracle had already been burnt and plundered by Darius I in 494BC (according to Herodotus 6.19), so there was nothing left for Xerxes to deal with 15 years later. However, there is reason to believe that the temple was re-constructed in the interim. Alternatively, there may be some undetected confusion between Darius and Xerxes among the Alexander historians.

the effect that these Milesians could not decide, so Alexander took the decision instead, but actually he need not mean more than that Alexander imposed a punishment in accordance with the preponderance of the varied views of the Milesians. Translations that make Alexander override his own policy of consultation are unnecessarily implying irrationality and vindictiveness on the part of the king, which is not substantiated by the actual words of Curtius. Among the ancient sources Aelian and Strabo seem to endorse or accept the justice of Alexander's treatment of the Branchidae, whereas Curtius and Plutarch express doubts.

The Killing of Cleitus

The killing of Cleitus was arguably the worst thing Alexander ever did. Certainly, he seems to have thought so himself, even reportedly attempting suicide, as he realized the full horror of what he had done. Cleitus had ranked among the most senior of his Friends, and, what was worse, was the brother of Alexander's nurse. Worst of all, the man had saved Alexander's life at the Battle of the Granicus. The killing was utterly dishonorable and the king found his shame hard to bear.

Nevertheless, the behaviour of Cleitus himself in the matter was also foolish and disgraceful. Just how biting some of the taunts with which he provoked Alexander were likely to have proven requires some explanation.

Cleitus began by quoting Euripides, *Andromache* 693-698:

Alas, what perverse customs prevail in Greece! Whenever the army sets up a trophy over the foe, men no more consider this the work of those who really toiled, but the general gets the credit for it. He brandished his spear as one man among a myriad others and did no more than a single warrior, yet he gets more praise than they.

The particular passage may be firmly identified by the snatch quoted by Plutarch, *Alexander* 51.5. It argues that generals were too eager to claim too much of the credit for victories won by the exertions of their troops. It is plain enough how this might needle Alexander in itself, but Cleitus may additionally have been parodying a habit of Alexander, who is himself frequently cited as having quoted passages from Euripides to make pointed observations. Plutarch, *Alexander* 10.4 reveals that Alexander quoted an equivocal line from the *Medeia* to Pausanias, before the latter assassinated his father, whilst Nicobule (Athenaeus 12.537D) has the king recite an entire scene of *Andromeda* during the banquet at which his fatal illness began. Plutarch, *Alexander* 53.2-3 also records Alexander quoting from the *Bacchae* and another, unidentified play of Euripides in criticism of Callisthenes. Arrian, *Anabasis* 7.16.6 cites Alexander reciting Euripides to express cynicism to the Chaldean priests, who were warning him against entering Babylon.

As the tension rose, Cleitus suggested that Alexander of Epirus, the brother of Olympias, who had been killed on campaign in Italy in the winter of 331-330BC, had had to contend with much stiffer opposition than the Persians, who were

Key Historical Issues

women by comparison. Cleitus' quote is also referenced by Livy 9.19.10-11 and Aulus Gellius 17.21.33. It was an outright assault on Alexander's self-esteem. To add insult to injury, Cleitus combined this dig with praise for Parmenion, who was officially a convicted traitor. But perhaps the most stinging insult of all was his last, when he ridiculed the Oracle of Ammon and Alexander's official status in Egypt as Ammon's son. This was an attack on Alexander's religious sensibilities and was just as incendiary then as such things are apt to prove nowadays.

The sources are united in attributing this uninhibited and unrestrained foolishness to mutual inebriation, which rings very true. However, Plutarch and Arrian do differ markedly from Curtius in the precise circumstances of the killing itself. The version found in Curtius gives a more cold-blooded account of the killing by making Alexander wait for Cleitus outside the hall, where they had been banqueting. Also, Alexander's taunting of the corpse regarding Cleitus' praise for Philip is only reported by Curtius 8.1.52 and Justin 12.6.4, which is a strong indication that Curtius is following the Cleitarchan version. Arrian, *Anabasis* 4.8.9 and Plutarch, *Alexander* 51 recount a variant version where Cleitus is successfully dragged from the hall, but bursts back in reciting Euripides' *Andromache* 693 and is speared in the doorway by Alexander on the spur of the moment.

Arrian, *Anabasis* 4.8.4-9:

It was well known that Cleitus had long been vexed at Alexander for the change in his style of living in excessive imitation of foreign customs, and at those who flattered him with their speech. At that time also, being heated with wine, he would not permit them either to insult the deity or, by depreciating the deeds of the ancient heroes, to confer upon Alexander this gratification which deserved no thanks. He affirmed Alexander's deeds were neither in fact at all so great or marvellous as they represented in their laudation; nor had he achieved them by himself, but for the most part they were the deeds of the Macedonians. The delivery of this speech annoyed Alexander; and I do not commend it, for I think, in such a drunken bout, it would have been sufficient if, so far as he was personally concerned, he had kept silence, and not committed the error of indulging in the same flattery as the others. But when some even mentioned Philip's actions without exercising a just judgment, declaring that he had performed nothing great or marvellous, they herein gratified Alexander; but Cleitus being then no longer able to contain himself, began to put Philip's achievements in the first rank, and to depreciate Alexander and his performances. Cleitus, being now quite intoxicated, made other depreciatory remarks and even vehemently reviled him, because indeed he had saved his life, when the cavalry battle had been fought with the Persians at the Granicus. Then indeed, arrogantly stretching out his right hand, he said: "This hand, O Alexander, preserved thee on that occasion." Alexander could now no longer endure the drunken insolence of Cleitus; but jumped up against him in a great rage. He was however restrained by his drinking companions. As Cleitus did not desist from his insulting remarks, Alexander shouted out a summons for his shield-bearing guards to attend him; but when no one obeyed him, he said that he was reduced to the same position as Darius, when he was led about under arrest by Bessus and his adherents, and that he now possessed the mere name of king. Then his companions were no longer able to restrain him; for according to some he leaped up and snatched a javelin from one of his Bodyguards; according to others, a long pike from one of his ordinary guards, with which he struck Cleitus and killed him. Aristobulus does not say whence the drunken quarrel originated, but asserts that the fault was entirely on the side of Cleitus, who, when Alexander had got so enraged with him as to jump up against him with the intention of making an end of him; was led away by Ptolemy, son of Lagus, the Bodyguard, through the gateway, beyond the wall and ditch of the citadel where the quarrel occurred. He adds that Cleitus could not control himself, but went back again, and falling in with Alexander who was calling out for Cleitus, he exclaimed: "Alexander, here am I, Cleitus!" Thereupon he was struck with a long pike and killed.

Arrian states that he found this account of the killing in Aristobulus: it is circumstantially more credible than Curtius, who makes Alexander stalk Cleitus in the courtyard in a more pre-meditated mode of action.

Plutarch, *Alexander* 50-51:

Not long after [the Philotas Affair] came the affair of Cleitus, which those who simply learn the immediate circumstances will think more savage than that of Philotas; if we take into consideration, however, alike the cause and the time, we find that it did not happen of set purpose, but through some misfortune of the king, whose anger and intoxication furnished occasion for the evil genius of Cleitus. It happened on this wise. Some people came bringing Greek fruit to the king from the seaboard. He admired its perfection and beauty and called Cleitus, wishing to show it to him and share it with him. It chanced that Cleitus was sacrificing, but he gave up the sacrifice and came; and three of the sheep on which libations had already been poured came following after him. When the king learnt of this circumstance, he imparted it to his soothsayers, Aristander and Cleomantis the Lacedaemonian. Then, on their telling him that the omen was bad, he ordered them to sacrifice in all haste for the safety of Cleitus. For he himself, two days before this, had seen a strange vision in his sleep; he thought he saw Cleitus sitting with the sons of Parmenion in black robes, and all were dead. However, Cleitus did not finish his sacrifice, but came at once to the supper of the king, who had sacrificed to the Dioscuri. After boisterous drinking was underway, verses were sung which had been composed by a certain Pranichus, or, as some say, Pierio, to shame and ridicule the generals who had lately been defeated by the Barbarians. The older guests were annoyed at this and railed at both the poet and the singer, but Alexander and those about him listened with delight and bade the singer go on. Then Cleitus, who was already drunk and naturally of a harsh temper and wilful, was more than ever vexed, and insisted that it was not well done, when among Barbarians and enemies, to insult Macedonians who were far better men than those who laughed at them, even though they had met with misfortune. And when Alexander declared that Cleitus was pleading his own cause when he gave cowardice the name of misfortune, Cleitus sprang to his feet and said: "It was this cowardice of mine, however, that saved thy life, god-born as thou art, when thou wast already turning thy back upon the spear of Spithridates; and it is by the blood of Macedonians, and by these wounds, that thou art become so great as to disown Philip and make thyself son to Ammon." Thoroughly incensed, then, Alexander said: "Base fellow, dost thou think to speak thus of me at all times, and to raise faction among Macedonians, with impunity?" "Nay," said Cleitus, "not even now do we enjoy impunity, since such are the rewards we get for our toils; and we pronounce those happy who are already dead, and did not live to see us Macedonians thrashed with Median rods, or begging Persians in order to get audience with our king." So spake Cleitus in all boldness, and those about Alexander sprang up to confront him and reviled him, while the elder men tried to quell the tumult. Then Alexander, turning to Xenodochus of Cardia and Artemus of Colophon, said: "Do not the Greeks appear to you to walk about among Macedonians like demi-gods among wild beasts?" Cleitus, however, would not yield, but called on Alexander to speak out freely what he wished to say, or else not to invite to supper men who were free and spoke their minds, but to live with Barbarians and slaves, who would do obeisance to his white tunic and Persian girdle. Then Alexander, no longer able to restrain his anger, threw one of the apples that lay on the table at Cleitus and hit him, and began looking about for his sword. But one of his Bodyguards, Aristonous, conveyed it away before he could lay his hands on it, and the rest surrounded him and begged him to desist, whereupon he sprang to his feet and called out in Macedonian speech a summons to his corps of guards (and this was a sign of great disturbance), and ordered the trumpeter to sound, and smote him with his fist because he hesitated and was unwilling to do so. This man, then, was afterwards held in high esteem on the ground that it was due to him more than to any one else that the camp was not thrown into commotion. But Cleitus would not give in, and with much ado his friends pushed him out of the banquet-hall. He tried to come in again, however, by another door, very boldly and contemptuously reciting these iambics from the Andromache of Euripides: "Alas! in Hellas what ill government!" And so, at last, Alexander seized a spear from one of his guards, met Cleitus as he was drawing aside the curtain before the door, and ran him through. No sooner had Cleitus fallen with a roar and a groan than the king's anger departed from him. And when he was come to himself and beheld his friends standing speechless, he drew the spear from the dead body and would have dashed it into his own throat, had not his bodyguards prevented this by seizing his hands and carrying him by force to his chamber.

Alexander's distress initially proved intractable, despite the fact that an Assembly of the Macedonians retrospectively exculpated his actions by declaring the killing to have been lawful. They had missed the point. It was not the legality of the killing that troubled the king so much as the consequential dishonour. Perhaps, therefore, it was the arguments of the courtiers and philosophers that were more successful in eventually persuading Alexander to abandon an attempt to starve himself. They seem to have argued that the expedition could not afford to be deprived of his leadership. His loss in such perilous territory would endanger all of them, so it was the more honourable course that he should rise above his shame.

The Culpability and Fates of Callisthenes and the Pages

Some commentators have sometimes sought to argue or imply that the fact that there were two assassination plots launched against Alexander during his reign shows that he was an unpopular monarch. However, history actually teaches us that there is no clear correlation between the popularity of a ruler and the number of attempts on his or her life. Many popular rulers have suffered assassination (e.g. Abraham Lincoln or John Kennedy) or attempted assassination (e.g. President Reagan or Pope John Paul II). James Garfield was shot by a man (Charles Guiteau) who had supported his presidency and who mistakenly believed that his support had earned him a political appointment. Conversely, unpopular rulers have often been removed by legitimate means instead. Nero, having made himself unpopular through excessive taxation, was removed by a vote of the Senate, whereas Gaius Caligula, who remained popular with the Roman masses, could only be removed by assassination when he upset certain narrow sections of the Roman elite. It is a false syllogism to argue that assassins dislike their victims and Alexander was a victim of assassination attempts, therefore Alexander was generally disliked.

Regarding the second assassination attemp against Alexander's life, commonly known as the Conspiracy of the Pages, the instigators seem to have been inspired by special personal motives in the first instance. It is clearly reported by our sources that it came about simply because Alexander had Hermolaus flogged for having slain the king's prey (a boar) in the hunt, which was in itself a perfectly proper punishment by Macedonian standards for a significant offence against royal etiquette.

According to Macedonian custom Hermolaus needed to kill a boar to achieve the right to recline at supper, but was short of opportunities. Instead of talking the matter through with Alexander, he simply slew the first boar that came his way, despite the embarrassment caused to the king. This is classic misbehaviour by teenagers. Alexander had no choice but to treat it as insubordination. It could be argued that in an ideal world he should have been more sensitive to the issue beforehand, but that would be to apply 20:20 hindsight.

Subsequently, the complaints and moans of the Macedonian traditionalists concerning Alexander's Policy of Fusion were raised by Hermolaus during his trial in an attempt retrospectively to justify his unjustifiable behaviour. But are even these motives to be condoned? The basic premise of the traditionalists was that Persians were barbarians and should be treated as second-class citizens in their own country. Their central complaint against Alexander was that he treated the Persians too well and even admired aspects of their culture.

Others argue that the pages were partly motivated by the recent refusal of their tutor Callisthenes to perform *proskynesis* before Alexander. Although Callisthenes does not appear to have actually been in the plot, he does seem slyly to have encouraged Hermolaus in his rebellious tendencies – possibly due to his disillusion over the *proskynesis* issue.

The coterie of six or eight conspirators among the Pages (more accurately the "Royal Youths", who served as squires to the king) seems to have been selected either because they were boyfriends or ex-boyfriends of existing conspirators or because they also harboured known grudges against the king. Of course, the plot was rationalised in terms of the widespread dissent over the Policy of Fusion. Of course, there was a large traditionalist faction (probably even a majority) among the Macedonians that opposed Fusion. But the latter were not fundamentally disloyal and would not have supported killing Alexander (indeed the associated crisis would have been acutely dangerous for everyone). They would on the other hand have been unscrupulous in exploiting Alexander's premature death to seek the enslavement of the Persians.

It would be overly to rationalise the circumstances even to assume that this group of conspirators believed that they could necessarily avoid death, if successful. They felt personally outraged – Sostratus, the lover of Hermolaus, was said to be even more outraged than Hermolaus himself. It seems that Alexander was normally rather mild in his treatment of the Pages (the king says so himself at Curtius 8.8.4), so the flogging and horse-deprivation imposed upon Hermolaus rankled all the more bitterly. Teenagers are not normally perfectly rational in their behaviour and these teenagers do not seem to have thought much beyond their immediate objective: simple revenge. It is unlikely that the conspiracy would ever have happened without the flogging. That was what transformed mild resentment into murderous intent. The significance of the flogging was that it was the essential catalyst for a variety of less burning resentments to be formulated into tangible treason.

The greater area of controversy in the context of the Conspiracy of the Pages is the implication of Callisthenes in the plot and his ensuing arrest and maltreatment. Hephaistion claimed that he had agreed to perform *proskynesis* (a form of obeisance practiced by the Persians) before Alexander at a specially convened formal dinner held perhaps just weeks beforehand (Plutarch, *Alexander* 55.1). However, he had made a point of refusing *proskynesis* at the actual event and instead had delivered an oration defending his stance. This had probably damaged his standing with the king. He was Alexander's officially appointed historian of the expedition, but as a leading scholar had also been assigned responsibility for the education of the Pages. Callisthenes was said to have heard Hermolaus' complaints against Alexander and his whipping with sympathy. He had reportedly made ambiguous remarks to the Page that he should remember that he was a man and that he might become the most illustrious of men by killing the most illustrious (Curtius 8.6.25 & Plutarch, *Alexander* 55.2). Although none had named him as a participant, Callisthenes was arrested and imprisoned following the betrayal of the plot on the basis that he had used his position to influence the conspirators against the king.

Hermolaus called for Callisthenes to be brought before the Macedonian Assembly at his trial in order to employ his oratory in their mutual defence. However, Alexander refused, explaining his decision with the Latin phrase: *nunc Olynthio non idem iuris est*. It is unfortunate that this has been given a pejorative spin in the Penguin translation: "He is an Olynthian and does not enjoy the same rights". The word "enjoy" supposes that Callisthenes rights were inferior, which is not implied by the Latin, which literally has the meaning that "being Olynthian he does not come under the same jurisdiction." It was in fact a neutral statement of the legal position that the Macedonian Assembly was not the correct body to try Callisthenes, since he was not Macedonian. It specifically does not mean that he had no right to a trial: that is the whole point of *idem*, which would be unnecessary, if Alexander were trying to say that Callisthenes had no rights. The Penguin translation would almost be correct, if it were read as: "He does not enjoy *the same* rights." But, of course, everyone reads it incorrectly as: "He does not enjoy the same *rights*."

Immediately thereafter Curtius 8.8.20-21 reports:

With that Alexander closed the meeting and had the condemned men [the Pages] transferred to members of their own unit. The latter tortured them to death so that they would gain the king's approval by their cruelty. Callisthenes also died under torture. He was innocent of any plot to kill the king, but the sycophantic character of court life ill-suited his nature.

But again, it is worth referring back to the Latin in Curtius for Callisthenes' fate: *Callisthenes quoque tortus interiit.* This does not have to mean more than that "Callisthenes also died in torment". It is not inconsistent with the most credible of the various extant ancient accounts of Callisthenes' end, which is attributed to Chares, Alexander's chamberlain. Plutarch thought him reliable on this matter and I concur, because Chares was uniquely in a position to know the truth. Plutarch, *Alexander* 55.5 wrote:

Chares says that after his arrest Callisthenes was kept in fetters seven months, that he might be tried before a full council when Aristotle was present, but that about the time when Alexander was wounded in India, he died from obesity and the disease of lice.

Thus, Alexander evidently intended a trial should take place. Chares seems to have been the manager of Alexander's court. This and the fact that we find him making authoritative and detailed statements on Callisthenes' disagreement with Alexander and his ultimate fate would suggest that he was probably responsible for royal prisoners, in which case he would have had privileged knowledge on the matter. However, there is one notably dissonant version in Arrian, *Anabasis* 4.14.1-3:

As for Callisthenes, Aristobulus says he was bound with fetters and carried round with the army, but at length died of sickness, Ptolemy son of Lagus that he was racked and put to death by hanging. Thus, not even those whose narratives are entirely trustworthy and who actually accompanied Alexander at the time agree in their accounts of events which were public and in their own knowledge. There are many other varying accounts of the same events in different histories, but I must be content with what I have recorded.

My view is that Ptolemy's history bore the hallmarks of having been sanitised prior to publication, especially because it exhibited significant blandness and surprising omissions of scandalous anecdotes etc. Where possible it seems to have suppressed embarrassing details. In some cases, the event was too prominent to gloss over and then we see signs of whitewash. The suspicion should be that Ptolemy or his editor (Philadelphus?) has substituted a clean death for Callisthenes, because the truth was embarrassing.

The fact that disparate contemporaneous accounts of Callisthenes' death exist means that it must have happened in private. If he had been publicly executed, then there could not be room for doubt. But hanging is only likely to have been used as a public means of execution in Alexander's era. Private killings are dominated by stabbings (e.g. Eumenes), but also include poisonings (Alexander IV and Roxane) and strangulations in familiar cases (e.g. Heracles the son of Alexander and Barsine). It is difficult to prove a negative, but secret hangings do not seem to have been common in Alexander's world and it would seem unnecessarily elaborate. If you believe that secret hanging is unlikely, then it is similarly improbable that Ptolemy's account gave the truth on this matter.

The Marriage to Roxane

The marriage to Roxane formed the finale of Book 9 of Cleitarchus. It comes as a rather abrupt surprise, stimulating intense discussion of Alexander's motives anciently as well as today. Why wed this girl, when he could simply have taken her as his mistress? However, Alexander could simply be regarded as seeking to emulate his father, Philip, who took on new wives as an extension of his war policy, the idea being to build a victory by the formulation of pacts with suitable allies as much as by the defeat of irreconcilable enemies in battle. This is explained by Athenaeus 557B:

And Philip the Macedonian did not take any women with him to his wars, as Darius did, whose power was subverted by Alexander. For he used to take about with him three hundred and fifty concubines in all his wars; as Dicaearchus relates in the third book of his Life in Greece. "But Philip," says he, "was always marrying new wives in war time. For, in the twenty-two years, which he reigned, as Satyrus relates in his History of his life, having married Audata the Illyrian, he had by her a daughter named Cynna; and he also married Phila, a sister of Derdas and Machatas. And wishing to conciliate the nation of the Thessalians, he had children by two Thessalian women; one of whom was Nicesipolis of Pherae, who brought him a daughter named Thessalonice; and the other was Philinna of Larissa, by whom he had Arrhidaeus. He also acquired the kingdom of the Molossians, when he married Olympias, by whom he had Alexander and Cleopatra. And when he subdued Thrace, there came to him Cothelas, the king of the Thracians, bringing with him Meda his daughter, and many presents: and having married her, he added her to Olympias. And after all these, being violently in love, he married Cleopatra, the sister of Hippostratus and niece of Attalus. And bringing her also home to Olympias, he made all his life unquiet and troubled. For, as soon as this marriage took place, Attalus said, 'Now, indeed, legitimate kings shall be born, and not bastards.' And Alexander having heard this, smote Attalus with a goblet, which he had in his hand; and Attalus in return struck him with his cup. And after that Olympias fled to the Molossians; and Alexander fled to the Illyrians. And Cleopatra bore to Philip a daughter who was named Europa."

Another factor was Alexander's pressing need to beget a legitimate heir, for which purpose marriage was a prerequisite. The successive threats to his life were perhaps making the matter seem more imperative. The king seems to have fathered Heracles on his mistress Barsine at about this time, but she was politically unsuitable for marriage, especially because she had children by her previous husbands.

Concerning Alexander the Great by Andrew Chugg

Before considering the Cleitarchan version of the marriage, it will be illuminating to review the accounts in Plutarch and Arrian. It was a final reason for his marriage (though perhaps not the most important) that Alexander had genuinely fallen for Roxane as Plutarch, *Alexander* 47.4 affirms:

His marriage to Roxana, whom he saw in her youthful beauty taking part in a dance at a banquet, was a love affair, and yet it was thought to harmonize well with the matters, which he had in hand. For the Barbarians were encouraged by the partnership into which the marriage brought them, and they were beyond measure fond of Alexander, because, most temperate of all men that he was in these matters, he would not consent to approach even the only woman who ever mastered his affections, without the sanction of law.

Arrian, *Anabasis* 4.19.5-6 & 4.20.4:

The wives and children of many important men were there [at the Sogdian Rock] captured, including those of Oxyartes. This chief had a daughter, a maiden of marriageable age, named Roxana, who was asserted by the men who served in Alexander's army to have been the most beautiful of all the Asiatic women whom they had seen, with the single exception of the wife of Darius. They also say that no sooner did Alexander see her than he fell in love with her; but though he was in love with her, he refused to offer violence to her as a captive, and did not think it derogatory to his dignity to marry her. This conduct of Alexander I think worthy rather of praise than blame… Oxyartes, hearing that his children were in the power of Alexander, and that he was treating his daughter Roxana with respect, took courage and came to him. He was held in honour at the king's court, as was natural after such a piece of good fortune.

Arrian is clear that Oxyartes was not present when Alexander met Roxane, but the reader will discover in most modern texts of Curtius 8.4.21 that it was he who introduced them. However, this is a horrible mistake, dating back to Renaissance attempts to disambiguate Curtius' text in a section where there are indeed some significant manuscript problems. In fact, the name rendered as "Oxyartes" in modern versions of Curtius read "Cohortandus" in the manuscripts. Aldus spuriously altered it to Oxyartes. This was done to reconcile Curtius' ensuing statement that Roxane was the daughter of this Cohortandus. But in fact, it was this latter statement that was the true error. The reason this was not clear to Renaissance editors like Aldus is that they were unaware of the parallel text (also from Cleitarchus) in Sections 28-29 of the *Metz Epitome*, which states that Roxane danced among Corianus' daughters, but was herself the daughter of one of his friends:

Corianus welcomed Alexander to be entertained at his place and brought in his own virgin daughters and those of his friends as dancers. Among these was the daughter of Oxiatris, Rhoxane, the loveliest of them all.

This Cohortandus/Corianus appears to be the chieftain called Chorienes by Arrian. It seems probable on balance that Arrian himself is in error in placing the meeting with Roxane at the Sogdian Rock rather than at the Rock of Chorienes.

My reconstruction of Cleitarchus' version of the marriage is therefore a synthesis of Curtius with the *Metz Epitome*, using the latter to correct and elaborate upon the former. The most important Cleitarchan detail that was omitted by Curtius was the fact that Alexander arranged parallel marriages between the daughters of the local dignitaries and his Friends. The mention of this by the *Metz Epitome* is validated as originating with Cleitarchus by the Contents List of Diodorus 17th Book (although his detailed account is lost in a lacuna):

How Alexander, enamoured of Roxane, daughter of Oxyartes, married her and persuaded numbers of his friends to marry the daughters of the prominent Barbarians.

This obviously presages the Susa marriages between the senior Macedonians and eligible Persian ladies. It is fascinating to learn that Alexander had already conceived and begun to implement this politically crucial policy years beforehand.

Alexander's Route Through Afghanistan

The problem of Alexander's route is at its most complex and controversial during his Afghan years (see Figure E). A recapitulation, let alone a resolution, of all the issues is beyond the scope of this relatively short review. Rather the objective is to identify some of the key interdependencies between the reconstructed text of Cleitarchus and Alexander's geographical whereabouts. In the rest of this Section, "Engels" means *Alexander the Great and the Logistics of the Macedonian Army* by Donald Engels and "Brunt" means Appendix VIII in Vol. I of P. A. Brunt's Loeb translation of Arrian's *History of Alexander and Indica*.

The *Stathmoi* or Stages of Alexander's journey are of central importance for the geography of Alexander's route in these years, as has been shown in the discussion of the location of Prophthasia in Section 2. The distances between major cities, towns and fortresses on their march seem to have been recorded by Alexander's *bematists* or pacers and some of their data has been preserved in surviving ancient texts, notably Strabo's *Geography* 11.8.9 and Pliny's *Natural History* 6.61-62. A detailed analysis of the *Stathmoi* is also beyond the ambitions of this volume, but the reader may refer to Table 8 in Appendix 5 of Engels and Appendix VIII of Brunt's Loeb translation of Arrian's *Anabasis* and *Indica* for the rudiments of their application to the problems of Alexander's itinerary.

Shortly after the death of Darius, Alexander sojourned at Hecatompylus, which has been associated with the excavated ruins of an ancient city 32km southwest of the modern Damghan at a site called Sahr-i Qumis (Engels p.83; Brunt p.495-6).

Regarding Alexander's subsequent advance into Hyrcania in the late summer of 330BC, Cleitarchus' vivid description of the River Stiboeites provides a promising landmark for determining the king's route. And indeed, the Stiboeites has been tentatively identified with the modern Chesmeh-i-Ali about 25km NW of Hecatompylus.[466]

Cleitarchus mentions an Hyrcanian town that housed the palace of Darius at Section 7.31. This might be another reference to Arvae, which had already been mentioned in 7.24. Arvae seems to be identical with Zadracarta in Arrian, *Anabasis* 3.23.6. The best available speculation (Engels p.84; Brunt p.497) is that this should be the modern Sari.

Satibarzanes surrenders to Alexander at Section 7.40. This occurred at Sousia according to Arrian, *Anabasis* 3.25.1-3, which is probably the modern Tus (Engels p.85; Brunt p.498) about 20km north of Meshed. If so, Alexander was already well on his way eastwards beyond Hyrcania, when the baggage was incinerated.

The next major destination on Alexander's march was the chief city of Aria, which is Artacana in the manuscripts of Curtius 6.6.33 and Artacoana in Arrian, *Anabasis* 3.25.6, but Chortacana in Diodorus 17.78.1. Its location remains unconfirmed. Most authorities have assumed that it lay at or in the close vicinity of modern Herat, but Donald Engels has argued that the "rock" in the nearby mountains was Kalat-i-Nadiri 60km north of Tus.[467] A reconciliation of this with the order of events in the Cleitarchan tradition is not apparent, since, for example, Engels reverses the order of the attack on Artacana and the siege of the rebel stronghold in the mountains; it is easier to accept the traditional view, which would place Alexander on the borders of Bactria near Kushka ~100km immediately north of Herat when he heard of the defection of Satibarzanes and took the major decision to divert his advance southwards instead of marching directly eastwards towards Bactria (although Brunt p.498 thinks that Alexander had always intended to visit Artacana). Hence the Cleitarchan tradition supports the traditional interpretation that Artacana was near Herat, which is also the approximate site of the king's foundation of Alexandria in Aria (cf. Strabo 11.10.1 & "Articaudna" in Claudius Ptolemy, *Geography* 6.17).

As has already been extensively discussed, the Philotas Affair seems to have taken place at Prophthasia, which was founded by Alexander at or close to the modern Farah (Brunt p.499). Afterwards Alexander headed on southwards into central Drangiana (Drangianê). It is overwhelmingly likely on logistical grounds that he reached the vicinity of Lake Seistan and then journeyed through the lands of the Arimaspians (a.k.a. Euergetae), following the Helmand River eastwards to the vicinity of Kandahar, which lay at the far edge of the Arimaspian zone (Engels p.91-3).

Metz Epitome 4 records that Alexander founded a town in the territory of the Arimaspians on the route into India, which he named Alexandria. This probably

---

[466] P. Pédech, "Deux campagnes d'Antiochus III chez Polybe," *Revue des Études Anciennes*, 60 (1958), 67-81.

[467] Donald Engels, *Alexander the Great and the Logistics of the Macedonian Army*, pp.87-91.

Key Historical Issues

records the foundation of Kandahar, since it is clear that it was a city foundation within the Arimaspian territory and Kandahar is on one of the main routes into India proper. Thereafter, the beleaguering of the army in deep snow (Sections 7.96-97) is likely to have occurred between Ghazni and Kabul, where such conditions are normal in winter, for Alexander reached this region in the winter of 330-329BC.

Arrian, *Anabasis* 3.28.4 and Strabo 15.2.10 as well as Curtius 7.3.23 and Diodorus 17.83.1 confirm the foundation of Alexandria-in-the-Caucasus at the foot of the Hindu Kush probably in the vicinity of Begram and Charikar. The manuscripts of Diodorus 17.83.1 read that the city was founded "in the pass which leads down to Media", which must be an error - perhaps "Media" should be "India". According to Strabo 15.2.10, the city was on the Indian side of the mountains, where Alexander wintered in 330-29BC (as discussed already, India incorporated southern Afghanistan in Cleitarchan geography.) Engels p.94-95 believes that Alexander crossed the Hindu Kush into Bactria via the Khawak Pass in the spring of 329BC, rapidly penetrating to Bactra (a.k.a. Zariaspa) as Bessus fled the scene.

Anyone who feels that the Cleitarchan descriptions of the terrain are vague or exaggerated would do well to examine the route between Bactra (modern Balkh at Google coordinates [36.768352, 66.901674]) and the River Oxus (modern Amu-Darya at Google coordinates [37.359242, 66.869316]) on Google Maps in the Satellite images view. The overall distance is about 70km, corresponding closely to the 400 stades mentioned by Cleitarchus 8.12. The last 30km just south of the river is a band of gargantuan dunes, some of them hundreds of metres long and therefore tens of metres tall (as can be seen by zooming in on the Google satellite image). On their leeward edge they would have been too steep to be negotiated by men in armour or carrying heavy packs, which would have compelled them to wend a winding course through these obstacles. Progress would have been agonisingly slow and the place a great trial for men on foot just as Cleitarchus suggests.

Thereafter Alexander progressed to Maracanda, which is very likely the modern city of Samarkand in Uzbekistan (Brunt p.504-505, Engels p.99 is skeptical about the identification of every site in Sogdiana). A deceptive pacification having been imposed upon Sogdiana, Alexander moved up to the river that his expedition (and Cleitarchus following them) identified as the Tanais (which is actually the Greek name for the River Don). This was in reality the Syr-Darya, more correctly called the Jaxartes by later ancient geographers. Here he founded Alexandria Eschate ("the Farthest"), which has been located at modern Khujand (Khodjend).[468] When revolts broke out, Cyropolis was besieged by Craterus (Cleitarchus 8.30). Cyropolis might be Kurkath (Engels p.103).

---

[468] Cf. Arrian, *Anabasis* 4.4.1 & Justin 12.5; Engels p. 103 is dubious about the exact location, although Brunt p. 505 embraces Khujand.

Concerning Alexander the Great by Andrew Chugg

After campaigning extensively across Sogdiana in order to quell the widespread revolts, which appear to have flared up in response to his city foundations and the air of permanence that they lent to the Macedonian presence, Alexander eventually returned to Bactra, where he wintered in 329-328BC. En route, as mentioned by Cleitarchus in Section 8.56, he crossed the River Polytimetus, which is probably the modern Zeravshan (see Engels p.100). The direction and course of the next campaign, when he set forth for a second time from Bactra in the spring of 328BC, has been a matter of particular controversy. This is recounted from Section 8.60 onwards in the reconstruction of Cleitarchus. A cogent explanation of Alexander's itinerary at this point, where the king eventually moves back into Sogdiana, has been put forward by A. B. Bosworth, "A Missing Year in the History of Alexander the Great", *Journal of Hellenic Studies*, Vol. 101, pp.17-39, 1981. Bosworth points out that the readings *margianiam* or *marginiam* in the manuscripts of Curtius 7.10.15 should not have been emended to read *margianam* (i.e. Margiana, the modern Merv), thereby diverting the expedition way out to the west across vast desert tracts. Instead, the River Ochus that is mentioned must be a major tributary of the Oxus River in the east of Bactria, which makes it most probably the modern River Surkhab. Hence Alexander travelled east from Bactra (rather than west) until he met the Oxus and continued eastwards along its southern bank (i.e. without crossing). Somewhere north of Kunduz, he crossed the Ochus (Surkhab), and then he headed on into the Kochka region, where he crossed the Oxus heading northwards somewhere near Ai Khanum (where the ruins of a major early Hellenistic town have been excavated not far from the confluence of the Oxus with the River Kochka). Margania must have been an otherwise unknown ancient city in the region to the north of the Oxus, which was the southeastern part of ancient Sogdiana (the hill country of modern Tajikistan). It cannot have been Margiana (Merv), since it does not fit the geography described by Cleitarchus in the least (see also Brunt p.506, who agrees that Alexander never visited Margiana, but wrongly blames Curtius for the confusion, which is actually modern in origin). This results in a site for the Rock of Ariamazes in the mountains on the northern margins of Bactria. It then looks as if the division of the army into several columns in the summer was in order that they should advance in parallel up the various valleys of, for example, the rivers Shirabad, Surkhan, Kafirnigan and Vakhsh, which are tributaries of the Oxus with their sources in the Hissar Range. Perhaps he crossed the mountains via the Anzob Pass and/or the Iron Gate Pass down into the valley of the River Zeravshan, which flows past Samarkand further to the west. Eventually the army was reassembled at Maracanda at the end of the summer.

After the killing of Cleitus at Maracanda in the Autumn of 328BC, Alexander cleared out the rebels from a region called Xenippa (Cleitarchus 9.16) that verged upon Scythia and then overawed Sisimithres (Cleitarchus 9.17) at the end of 328BC at Nautaca, where he seems to have spent most of the winter (Arrian,

Key Historical Issues

Anabasis 4.18.2). Nautaca may be Shakhrisyabz near the headwaters of the Kashka-Darya as suggested by Bosworth.[469]

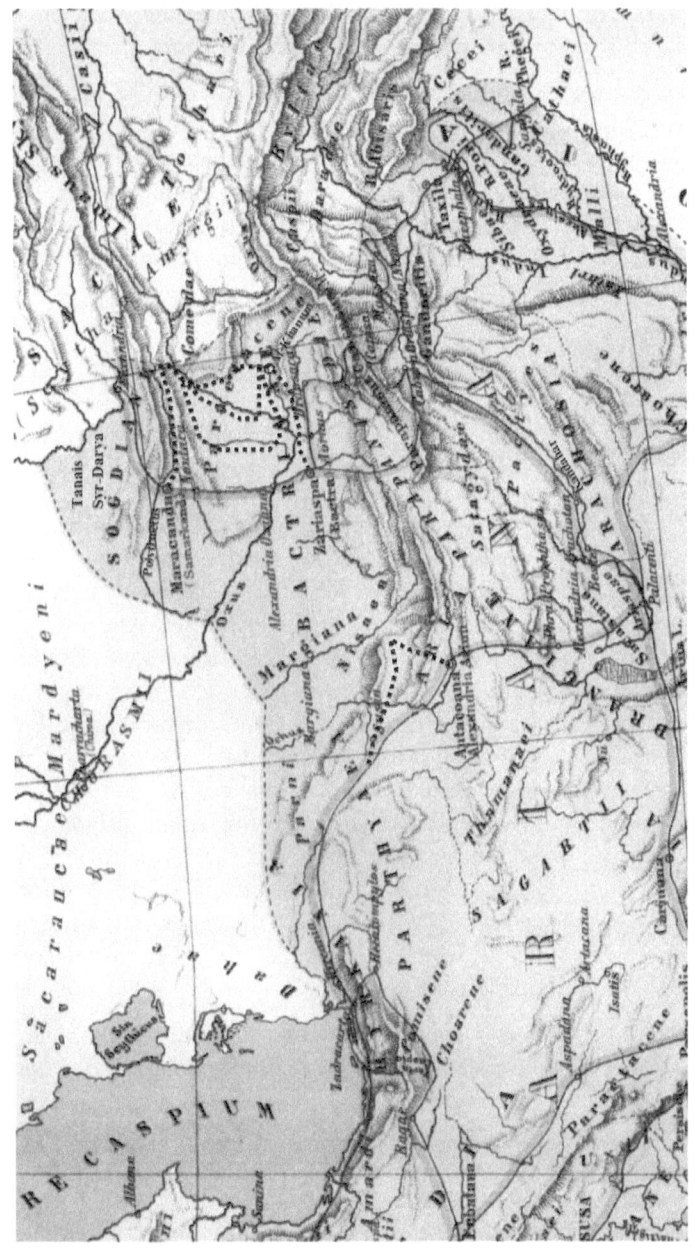

Figure E. Alexander's route in the vicinity of Afghanistan

---

[469] A. B. Bosworth, "A Missing Year in the History of Alexander the Great", *Journal of Hellenic Studies*, Vol. 101, 1981, p. 36.

In the winter of 328-327BC Spitamenes was slain by his wife and resistance collapsed. Alexander diverted himself with the *proskynesis* experiment and the Conspiracy of the Pages ensued. Strabo 11.11.4 locates the arrest of Callisthenes at Cariatae in Bactria, but we do not know where this was.

Afterwards, Alexander headed for Gazaba and was caught in an horrendous hailstorm en route. The army was rescued from destitution by Sisimithres (so they had not gone far from Nautaca). On reaching Gazaba, its ruler, Chorienes, surrendered to the king and convened the banquet, which engendered Alexander's marriage to Roxane. The location of Gazaba is unknown, but Alexander was probably heading back southwards into central Bactria on his way to India in the late spring of 327BC.

Alexander's Route Through India

Cleitarchus probably agreed that Alexander entered India (Figure F) via the River Cophen (Kabul River valley) and that the bulk of the army continued down this river under the command of Hephaistion until they reached its confluence with the Indus. Alexander operated separately with a large task force in the mountain valleys north of the Cophen, receiving the surrender of Nysa and capturing Massaga/Mazaga (in the Swat valley?) and Aornus (Pir Sar). After bridging the river, he advanced to Taxila and thence to the Hydaspes. After defeating Porus on its far bank, he proceeded eastwards crossing the Acesines and the Hydraotis/Hiarotis, but the army refused to advance beyond the Hyphasis and towards the Ganges. The king returned to encamp the army near the Acesines. Cleitarchus either stated or implied that he sailed down the Acesines (although he went down the Hydaspes in Arrian) with a newly constructed fleet, the bulk of the army marching along the banks. The most important difference on Indian geography between Cleitarchus and Arrian is that the former placed the conflict with the Malli and Oxydracae south of the confluence of the Acesines with the Indus. There is some support for Cleitarchus in the geography, since Gendari Mt could be the mountain from which the alliance of the Oxydracae and the Malli initially mounted their defence.

Craterus and Polyperchon evidently headed back towards Persia via Arachosia with a majority of Alexander's army from the vicinity of the kingdom of Musicanus, but only a mention of Polyperchon's return in Justin would suggest that Cleitarchus noted their departure. Alexander himself sailed on to Patala and thence into the western branch of the Indus Delta and out into the Ocean, where he visited islands up to tens of kilometers offshore, then retraced his course to Patala. Arrian mentions that Alexander afterwards led an exploratory expedition down the eastern branch of the delta, but there is no sign that this appeared in Cleitarchus.

Key Historical Issues

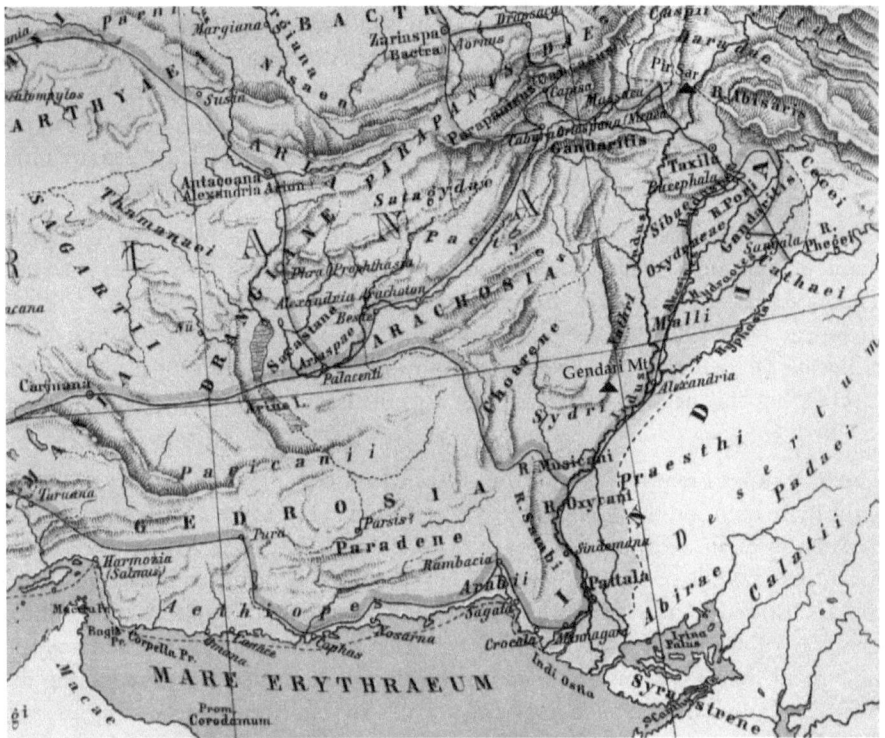

Figure F. Alexander's India

Nearchus and Onesicritus set sail for Persia via the Ocean and the Erythraean Sea from the vicinity of modern Karachi, whilst Alexander took the land route westwards, initially along the coast via Rambacia/Rhambarce (Bela). Cleitarchus was clear that Alexander's forces ran short of food on the coast of Gedrosia among the Fisheaters (Ichthyophagoi) and were reduced to a serious state of starvation after striking inland across desert wastes towards Pura. There is no sign that Cleitarchus attributed these travails to shortage of water, but rather he emphasized that Alexander had sent men ahead to dig wells. After celebrating a Dionysiac *comus* through a fertile region of Carmania, Alexander was re-united with the commanders of his fleet at Salmous, not far inland from the Strait of Hormuz according to Cleitarchus. Thereafter he journeyed in stages to Susa via Parsagada. He was there to greet the *Epigoni*, when Cleitarchus' twelfth book ended in the early summer of 324BC.

Fragments from Cleitarchus' Thirteenth Book

The longest Fragment to survive from Cleitarchus' final book is actually a passage cited from the work of Theopompus by Athenaeus concerning Harpalus' mistresses (Jacoby F30 of Cleitarchus = Athenaeus 12.50 or 586CD). However, Athenaeus concludes his quotation by noting that Cleitarchus had given the same account. Theopompus joined the court of Ptolemy in Egypt after Alexander's death, whereas Cleitarchus was a resident of Alexandria under Ptolemy. Hence it is likely that Cleitarchus was familiar with Theopompus' writings and borrowed from his material on Harpalus. Certainly, there is a close connection between the quotation from Theopompus in Athenaeus and the abridged Cleitarchan material on Harpalus' mistresses at Diodorus 17.108.5-6.

Theopompus seems to have been broadly hostile towards Harpalus. He was a pupil of Isocrates of Athens, a friend and supporter of Alexander's father. Theopompus also benefited from Alexander's patronage, which permitted him to return from exile to his home island of Chios. Hence, he was inherently politically aligned with Alexander in the context of Harpalus' flight and the Exiles Decree, but this need not detract from his criticisms, which may well have been justified.

The only other Fragment from Book 13 of Cleitarchus that is considered reliable is the mere mention that Cleitarchus wrote about an Embassy sent by the Romans to Alexander in Babylon (Jacoby F31 = Pliny, *NH* 3.57). Arrian 7.15.5 also mentions a couple of obscure writers (Aristus and Asclepiades) who had recorded that the Romans had sent representatives to Alexander, although Arrian omitted mention of Cleitarchus in this context. The ancient sources are generally in agreement that other envoys from central Italy (e.g. Etruscans) were among the throng in Babylon, so it need not be controversial that Romans were also present. What is more curious is the impression that Cleitarchus particularly drew attention to the Romans among so many disparate delegations. This is because the Romans were not well known in the Greek world until Pyrrhus' campaigns in Italy from 280BC. The implication is either that Cleitarchus' list of envoys was very lengthy and comprehensive or that he finalised his text after 280BC and highlighted the Romans because they had recently figured prominently in Pyrrhus' dispatches from Italy. Badian has also suggested that Pliny's comment that Cleitarchus' account was "more than mere rumour" may mean that Cleitarchus actually witnessed the Roman audience with Alexander, but this is surely to read too much into an ambiguous phrase.[470]

There are also two Fragments attributed to Cleitarchus by name that Jacoby has nevertheless considered doubtful, but which fit quite neatly in specific contexts within the reconstructed text of Book 13.

1) A short passage on not mourning friends excessively (Jacoby F41 = Maximi, *Eclogae* 6.761A[471]) is very much the sort of comment that Cleitarchus might have made concerning Alexander's elaborate arrangements for the funeral of Hephaistion, hence I have fitted it to Section 13.33 of the reconstruction.

---

[470] E. Badian, "The Date of Clitarchus", Proceedings African Classical Associations 8 (1965), p.10.

[471] A.k.a Maximus Confessor, *Loci Communes*.

2) A comment on kingly behaviour not being inculcated by royal trappings, specifically the diadem (Jacoby F52 = Antonii, *Melissa* 2.1, p.1005C) provides an extraordinarily apt addendum to the episode where the prisoner sat in the throne and donned the diadem, which is covered in Section 13.40 of the reconstruction.[472]

Having managed to fit nearly half of the "doubtful" Fragments of Cleitarchus to a range of the books within my reconstruction, *Concerning Alexander the Great*, it has come to seem highly likely to me that all the moralizing comments attributed to Cleitarchus by Antonius (a Greek monk of the 11th century AD) in his Melissa and by Maximus Confessor in his *Eclogae* (Anthology) are indeed abstracted from the *History Concerning Alexander* by our author, despite Jacoby's expression of dubiety.

Babylon as the Metropolis

Curtius 10.2.12 makes the interesting assertion that Alexander's Macedonian troops believed at the time of the Opis Mutiny that the king planned to establish the permanent seat of his government in Asia (incorporated in the reconstruction of Cleitarchus in Section 13.8). In fact, there are several strands of evidence that point to Alexander having regarded Babylon as the chief city of his Empire. Tangible evidence survives in the form of many of the tetradrachms of Alexander, which were minted at Babylon and which bear a mu-tau-rho monogram on their reverses, designating the city as the *metropolis* or mother-city (Figure G). Furthermore, Strabo explicitly attests to the significance of Babylon in Alexander's eyes:

Strabo 15.3.9-10: "Alexander carried off with him all the wealth in Persis to Susa, which was also full of treasures and equipment; and neither did he regard Susa as the royal residence, but rather Babylon, which he intended to build up still further; and there too treasures lay stored… At all events, Alexander preferred Babylon, since he saw that it far surpassed the other [cities], not only in its size, but also in all other respects."

Above all, perhaps, Alexander's decision both to hold Hephaistion's funeral in Babylon and also to build his friend's permanent memorial in the ashes of the pyre is an important indication that he viewed the metropolis as his de facto capital.

---

[472] Some (e.g. Michael Wood, *Footsteps of Alexander*, 1997, p.225) have linked the prisoner on the throne incident to the ritual of having a scapegoat king to divert the bad luck in times of ill-omen, although this is supposition, since our sources instead report the matter as an unfavourable sign from heaven.

Figure G. Posthumous tetradrachm of Alexander minted in Babylon – the city is designated as the Metropolis ("Mother City" = Capital) by the Mu-Tau-Rho monogram in a wreath at the left edge of the reverse (Author's Collection).

Re-Ordering Curtius on the Mutiny at Opis

There is a peculiarity in the manuscript tradition of Curtius regarding the placement of the fragmentary chapter 10.4. The surviving paragraph of the Latin text appears to be a reproach to Alexander by one of the thirteen condemned mutineers swiftly followed by their collective execution by drowning in the river (Tigris). This is incongruous and anachronistic, because we have already read at Curtius 10.3.4 that news that the executions of the mutineers had been carried out had reached the troops. Obviously, it looks as though the material in Curtius 10.4 has been misplaced and should actually be positioned somewhere between the arrest of the thirteen mutineers at 10.2.30 and news of their execution a few sentences later at 10.3.4. As John C. Rolfe has noted in the Loeb edition of Curtius, an important early 17th century editor of Curtius, Johann Freinshem, inferred a lacuna between 10.3.2 and 10.3.3, which precisely suits the insertion of the material in 10.4.

It is understandable that modern editors of Curtius have not felt at liberty significantly to re-order the manuscript tradition in this respect, although I am surprised that most modern editions do not even draw the reader's attention to the anomaly. Nevertheless, since my purpose is the reconstruction of Curtius' source, Cleitarchus, I have felt obligated to make the obvious correction in the present work. Thus, I have inserted the material of Curtius 10.4 into Cleitarchus 13.13, whereas material from Curtius 10.3.3 onwards follows it in Cleitarchus 13.14.

Key Historical Issues

The Palace *Hypaspists* and the *Somatophylakes*

Diodorus 17.110.1 mentions that Persian recruits a thousand strong were appointed to a palace regiment of the *hypaspists* (literally "shield bearers") in the wake of the mutiny of the Macedonian troops [at Opis] evidently scheduled to perform duties at his court. This must be derived from Cleitarchus and is incorporated in Section 13.17 of my reconstruction, where it is merged with a matching account from Justin 12.12.4. It appears that this unit derived its royal association from its provision of *doryphoroi* (literally spear-carriers) who performed traditional palace guard duties for the king of the type where one man stood either side of an entrance, so that they could cross-spears to bar entry to interlopers. The implication of the Persian appointments is that the original Macedonian members of the regiment had sided with the mutinous troops and were to be replaced by loyal Persians.

It would be reasonable to infer that this is the same body of troops that Arrian regularly refers to as the *Royal Agema of the Hypaspists* (e.g. Arrian, *Anabasis* 1.1.11, 1.8.4, 2.8.3, 3.11.9, 3.13.6, 5.13.4…).[473] In addition to the shared name and royal duties, both regiments seem to have had a nominal strength of a thousand men. And yet an extraordinary modern orthodoxy would have it that Diodorus elsewhere refers to these palace *hypaspists* as *somatophylakes* (literally "bodyguards"). This engenders considerable confusion due to this latter term also being used to refer to the seven elite personal bodyguards of the king, who were his highest-ranking courtiers. Yet, if *somatophylakes* was his normal term for the guards' regiment, why should Diodorus (and Cleitarchus?) have anomalously referred to them as *hypaspists* with palace duties in the context of the mutiny?

The orthodox interpretation particularly derives its ambiguity concept for the term *somatophylax* from a range of four instances in Arrian where it has been supposed that it refers to a unit within the overall brigade of *hypaspists*. Let us review these instances, which are interpreted by Heckel[474] (and others) to show that Arrian uses *somatophylakes* to mean the unit that he elsewhere refers to as the *Royal Agema of the Hypaspists*. Is it really impossible or even merely unlikely that these *somatophylakes* are instead references to the seven elite Bodyguards?

a) Arrian, *Anabasis* 1.6.5: "As Alexander saw only a few of the enemy still occupying a ridge, along which lay his route, he ordered his *somatophylakes* and *hetairoi* to take their shields, mount their horses, and ride to the hill; and when they reached it, if those who had occupied the position awaited

---

[473] It has been argued (e.g. Heckel, *Marshals*, p.245-6) that Arrian uses the Greek term *agema* as a name for a particular regiment of guards. But in fact *agema* seems to have been phonetically equated to the Latin military term *agmen* for a regiment or an arrayed block of troops (there is a similar pairing between *ile* [Greek] and *ala* [Latin] for a wing of cavalry). Other instances (Diodorus 19.27-29, Plutarch, *Eumenes* 7) indeed suggest that *agema* merely means a regiment and only refers to a particular regiment when given a qualifier such as "Royal" (e.g. Polybius 5.65.2).

[474] E.g. W. Heckel, *The Marshals of Alexander's Empire*, Routledge, 1992, s.v. The Somatophylakes.

them, he said that half of them were to leap from their horses, and to fight as foot-soldiers, being mingled with the cavalry. But when the enemy saw Alexander's advance, they quitted the hill and retreated to the mountains in both directions. Then Alexander, with his *hetairoi*, seized the hill, and sent for the Agrianians and archers, who numbered 2,000. He also ordered the *hypaspists* to cross the river, and after them the regiments of Macedonian infantry, with instructions that, as soon as they had succeeded in crossing, they should draw out in rank towards the left, so that the phalanx of men crossing might appear compact at once."

b) Arrian, *Anabasis* 3.17.2: "[Alexander] then took the royal *somatophylakes*, the *hypaspist* infantry, and 8,000 men from the rest of his army, and, under the guidance of the Susians, marched by night along a different road from the frequented one. Advancing by a route rough and difficult, on the same day he fell upon the villages of the Uxii, where he captured much booty and killed many of the people while still in their beds; but others escaped into the mountains."

c) Arrian, *Anabasis* 4.3.2: "But when [Alexander] observed that the course of the river, which flows through the city when it is swollen by the winter rains, was at that time nearly dry and did not reach up to the wall, and would thus afford his soldiers a passage by which to penetrate into the city, he took the *somatophylakes*, the *hypaspists*, the archers, and Agrianians, and made his way secretly into the city along the channel, at first with a few men, while the barbarians had turned their attention towards the military engines and those who were assailing them in that direction."

d) Arrian, *Anabasis* 4.30.3: "[Alexander] remained quiet until they began their retreat; then taking 700 of the *somatophylakes* and *hypaspist* infantry, he was the first to scale the rock at the part of it abandoned by the enemy; and the Macedonians ascended after him, one in one place another in another, drawing each other up. These men at the concerted signal turned themselves upon the retreating barbarians, and killed many of them in their flight."

It may be conceded that these *somatophylakes* seem to be mentioned in the same task forces as very large units and that it is strange that seven men should matter among forces of hundreds or thousands. But is this enough to conclude that a larger body is meant? It needs also to be recalled that Arrian's source is probably Ptolemy, who was himself a member of the seven elite Bodyguards. Homeric principles of celebrating the heroism of warfare, which Ptolemy is likely to have espoused, would allow that special attention should be paid to the exploits of key warriors and commanders. Hence some good reasons to suspect that these references actually refer to the Seven may be posited:

1) The first reference 1.6.5 makes it clear that its *somatophylakes* were mounted. Whereas it is not impossible that Alexander had given horses to some of his *hypaspist* infantry, it does stretch the meaning of the term

infantry in what was evidently a battle situation. In fact the only other unit involved in this particular action is the *hetairoi* (literally "companions"), which could mean the fifty or so Friends of the king in this context. Furthermore, the enemy upon the ridge are "few", so it is not necessary to envisage vast numbers in this action.

2) In extracts b) to d) the *somatophylakes* are mentioned in combination with the *hypaspists*, but as though they were a separate unit, which is slightly strange if they were in fact a regiment from within the *hypaspist* corps as some scholars have advocated.

3) In passage d) the very curious number of 700 men are included in the task force. This does not correspond to the probable strength of 1000 for an *hypaspist* regiment. In fact, chiliarchs (commanders of 1000 men) and pentakosiarchs (commanders of 500 men) are mentioned as attending on Alexander at his deathbed (Plutarch, *Alexander* 76.3 and Arrian, *Anabasis* 7.25.6). This comes from the *Ephemerides*. Hence, we have evidence for units of 500 and 1000 men in Alexander's army, but never 700 men. Therefore, the specific figure of 700 begs explanation and the desired rationalisation is to hand, since we know that there were precisely seven elite *somatophylakes*. What if Ptolemy had actually written that Alexander took the *somatophylakes* with seven centuries of the *hypaspists* on this mission? We have both an explanation for the total and an explanation of just why the *somatophylakes* were mentioned, for they commanded the individual hundreds for the purpose of this special mission.

4) If point 3) were correct and reflected standard practice, then it could explain the combination of mentions of the *hypaspists* and the *somatophylakes* in extracts b) & c) too.

In summary, I cannot accept that it is at all necessary to believe that a different unit than the Seven is meant in these four standard references.

Several instances of the use of *somatophylax* in the text of Diodorus have been deemed to reinforce the orthodox concept of ambiguous terminology.

1) Firstly, the incoming recruits to the *paides basilikoi* (literally "King's Youths" a.k.a. "Royal Pages") in Asia at Diodorus 17.65 are stated in C. Bradford Welles' translation to be "sent by their fathers to serve as bodyguards [*somatophylakes*]". This has led to the supposition that Royal Pages could also be referred to as a third species of *somatophylax*. However, the Greek text actually reads *pros ten somatophylakian*, for which a more literal translation would be "sent by their fathers *with a view to becoming bodyguards*". This is far more ambiguous. It could mean that they would soon have the responsibility of personally guarding the king (which was within the scope of their duties). But it could also easily mean that their fathers hoped that they would ultimately graduate from the

2) In the context of the assassination of Philip II the term that is used to describe Pausanias at both Diodorus 16.93.3 and 16.93.9 is *somatophylax of the king*. In the eyes of the advocates of ambiguous terminology this means that he was among a group of *hypaspists* on guard duty as *doryphoroi* (spear-bearing sentries) at the festival. *Doryphoroi* are indeed mentioned as being in the background in the theatre when Pausanias slew Philip, but Pausanias is obviously not one of them. If he had been, he would not have needed to conceal a dagger beneath his cloak, but would have been better armed. In the same context, Leonnatus, Perdiccas and Attalus are called *somatophylakes*, when they pursue and kill Pausanias. Yet at this time Leonnatus at least cannot easily be one of the seven elite Bodyguards of Philip, for he was only appointed as one of the king's elite Bodyguards much later under Alexander, replacing Arybbas, who died of illness in Egypt (Arrian, *Anabasis* 3.5.5). But there is a simple solution: Alexander as Crown Prince must have had a set of personal bodyguards as well as Philip. It would be fitting for Leonnatus to have been one such in 336BC. Actually, Diodorus speaks of two groups of bodyguards, one of which pursued Pausanias with the other staying by the king. This is usually interpreted as describing a splitting of the king's bodyguards into two groups, but perhaps it literally reflects the existence of two teams of bodyguards: one for the king and the other for the prince.

3) Diodorus 17.61.3 states that Hephaistion was *Hegemon of the Somatophylakes* (literally "Commander of the Bodyguards") at Gaugamela. The advocates of ambiguous terminology insist that this must mean that he led the Palace Regiment of the *Hypaspist* infantry, even though it is likely on general grounds that Hephaistion was a member of the Seven at that time. They argue that the king himself was the commander of the seven elite Bodyguards, although this is nowhere stated in our sources and there is evidence of a gradation of rank among the Seven when Diodorus 16.93.9 says that Philip gave Pausanias a more senior position among them. A bigger problem for his putative *hypaspist* command is that Hephaistion is stated to have fought with Alexander and the Companions in an isolated cavalry engagement at Gaugamela (Arrian, *Anabasis* 3.15.1-2), which is very hard to explain, if he commanded a regiment of infantry in that battle. He had previously commanded the Mediterranean fleet (Curtius 4.5.10), which would have been awkward, if his rank was more junior than many of its existing officers (if he had been commander of the Palace *Hypaspists*, he would have reported to Nicanor, Parmenion's son, who led the entire *Hypaspist* Brigade according to Arrian, *Anabasis* 3.21.8). Hephaistion is never otherwise given an explicit military rank in any source until after the fall of Philotas, which is

perfectly explained if he was an elite *somatophylax* rather than an army officer. As Bosworth has noted, there is no evidence for any of the seven elite Bodyguards having had an army rank until after Gaugamela.[475] In summary, it appears that Alexander did not gradually elevate Hephaistion through the military hierarchy. Instead, Hephaistion was one of the seven elite Bodyguards from the beginning of Alexander's reign and he was the most senior among them by the time of Gaugamela.

In conclusion, although orthodoxy would have us regard *hypaspist* and *somatophylax* as interchangeable terms, thus creating a deep vein of ambiguity and confusion at the heart of our key sources, we are equally at liberty to regard this as an entirely modern misunderstanding, such that *somatophylax* always means a personal elite bodyguard of some senior individual (usually the king) and no *hypaspist* is ever called a *somatophylax*, even though many *hypaspists* served as *doryphoroi* (spear-bearers, meaning sentries) It is clear to me that the latter viewpoint constitutes the most straightforward interpretation of the evidence. As a matter of principle, confused terminology should not be read into ancient sources unless the evidence clearly dictates it: in other words, this is not merely a matter of taste.

The Large Lacuna in the Tenth Book of Curtius

There is a vast lacuna in the manuscript tradition of Curtius, which corresponds roughly to the sections from the beginning of 13.17 to the middle of 13.44 in my reconstruction of Cleitarchus. This equates to about a third of the entire length of Cleitarchus' thirteenth book, but, fortunately, Diodorus is particularly full and detailed for many of the key events in this interval and some supplementation from Plutarch and Justin has been feasible. Nevertheless, it is likely that the accounts of the following events in my reconstruction are more compressed relative to the archetype than the rest of Book 13:

The induction of Persians into elite guards regiments; Alexander's reconciliation with the Macedonian troops; the arrival of Peucestes and his archers; funding the upbringing of the orphaned sons of the troops; the onward march through Karai, Sittacenê and Sambana; visiting the Kelones, an old Greek settlement; sightseeing in Bagistanê; the quarrel between Hephaistion and Eumenes; the visit to the Nesaean mares; Atropates' pretend Amazons; festivities at Ecbatana and the death of Hephaistion; digression on Leosthenes' preparations for war back in Greece; the campaign against the Cossaeans; the warning from the Chaldeans and how the Greek philosophers persuaded Alexander to enter Babylon anyway; audiences with the envoys; preparations for Hephaistion's funeral and reprise of his status in Alexander's affections; description of the pyre; sacrifices to Hephaistion as a demigod; the omen of the prisoner on the throne; going astray in the marshes and the omen of the snagged diadem; Alexander falls ill at the party hosted by Medius; the doomed Alexander allows the troops to file past his sick-bed.

---

[475] A B Bosworth, *Conquest & Empire*, Appendix C, Section IV, "The Structure of Command".

Hephaistion's Pyre

The Cleitarchan account of Hephaistion's pyre at Babylon has mainly to be derived from Diodorus 17.115, which is, however, by far the most detailed description in any source. But other ancient writers also alluded to its magnificence, novelty and exceptional cost: in the Cleitarchan sources this amounted to 12,000 talents, although this perhaps included the subsequent erection of a permanent memorial. A silver talent constituted 6000 drachms, each weighing ~4.2g, so this sum exceeded 300 tonnes of silver, equivalent to about 25 tonnes of gold in Alexander's day. Arrian and Plutarch give a figure of 10,000 talents, which is not seriously divergent, but which may indicate that they employed a source other than Cleitarchus on this point.

Plutarch, *Alexander* 72.3, adds that Alexander desired that Stasicrates should be its architect. This seems to be the same man who is elsewhere attributed with having restored the Temple of Artemis at Ephesus, designed Alexandria in Egypt and proposed a plan to carve Mt Athos in Thrace into a giant representation of Alexander with an entire city nestling in his left palm, although this last concept was rejected by Alexander. Whereas the name Stasicrates has the literal meaning of "one who triumphs over strife", he is elsewhere called Deinocrates (Vitruvius, *De architectura* 2, *praefatio* 1-4; Valerius Maximus 1.4 ext 1), which means "Master of Marvels" or Cheirocrates (Strabo 14.1.23), which is "Master of Hand-Skills": these apt appellations were presumably nicknames or possibly honorific titles.

Diodorus describes a structure erected upon a base of bricks a stade (=400 cubits) square and supporting itself upon palm trunks with the bricks having been gleaned by demolishing a ten-stade stretch of the city wall. He states that it comprised precisely thirty quadrangular chambers and that its exterior faces were decorated in six horizontal bands with the addition of an array of sirens hollowed out to accommodate human singers at its summit, which reached a height of 130 cubits.

Unfortunately, the precise form of this structure is not instantly unveiled by Diodorus' words. The matter of the configuration of the thirty chambers is especially obscure. C. Bradford Welles in the Loeb translation of Diodorus 17 suggests 30 transverse compartments each 22 feet wide and 220 yards long. Some have supposed that this edifice was a box-like tower with sheer sides, but major pyres are normally stepped pyramidal structures in Roman art. For example, they feature on coins, notably a denarius of Antoninus Pius. Furthermore, the stability of a simple rectangular structure a stade wide and 130 cubits tall that was entirely constructed of wood is dubious, for the force exerted upon its windward side in even a moderate breeze would have been tremendous. It might also be inferred that Stasicrates' inspiration was the ziggurat in Babylon, which probably also had seven pseudo-step-pyramidal stages. This concept is illustrated in the reconstruction of the pyre in the late 19th century engraving reproduced as Figure H, where Hephaistion's pyre echoes the ziggurat depicted on the horizon of the panorama.

Key Historical Issues

The solution to the conundrum probably lies in the geometrical significance of the number thirty, for $30=4\times4+3\times3+2\times2+1\times1$. Hence a square pyramidal structure comprising a four-by-four array of sixteen chambers on its foundation course, three by three on it first storey, two by two on its second and a single chamber at the summit precisely fits the description. This arrangement is illustrated in Figure 13.2, which shows that this suggests that each chamber measured 100x100x30 cubits, assuming that the final 10 cubits of height were provided by a plinth for the corpse. Diodorus' ensuing description of the decoration would be congruent with two bands per storey, excepting the topmost, where the sirens would have the full height of the crowning chamber. It is a strong confirmation of the width of the individual bands of decoration that Diodorus specified the overall height of the torches in the second frieze as fifteen cubits. The lower band of decoration on each storey might well have been projected outwards so as to give the impression of seven steps. Such projection might incidentally be helpful in accommodating the large reported total of sixty quinquereme prows per side at the base level of the decoration.

It is interesting to examine the iconography of the decorations in some detail, so I shall proceed from the base to the summit in the given order beginning with the galley prows in the first band. It is stated that each had a pair of archers on its catheads and five-cubit tall fighting men on its deck. Olga Palagia has speculated that these vessels might represent Hephaistion's command of Alexander's Mediterranean fleet in 332BC (Curtius 4.5.10) and has noted that ships readied for a naval battle also appeared in the fourth decorative tablet on Alexander's funeral carriage (Diodorus 18.27.1).[476] But in fact the clue to decipherment of the symbolism probably lies again in the number of prows, for there were precisely sixty on each side of the structure, which matches the "sixty fighting ships" with which Alexander sailed across the Hellespont (Diodorus 17.17.2).[477] Hence we may infer that the armed men whom Diodorus notes to have been standing in each prow were probably actually Alexander and Hephaistion, with the former in the act of casting the famous spear, whereby Asia was won (see also Justin 11.5.10). Certainly, Hephaistion was a key participant in the ensuing ceremonies at Troy itself, where he played Patroclus to Alexander's Achilles (Aelian, *Varia Historia* 12.7; Arrian, *Anabasis* 1.12.1). In fact, Alexander's ceremonial crossing of the Hellespont looks very much like a re-enactment of the arrival of Achilles and Patroclus at Troy with the fifty ships that Homer attributed to the Myrmidons (Iliad 2.685).

---

[476] Olga Palagia, *Hephaestion's Pyre and the Royal Hunt of Alexander*, pp. 167-206 in "Alexander the Great in Fact and Fiction", edited by A. B. Bosworth & E. J. Baynham, Oxford, 2000.

[477] Probably this was only a section of Alexander's total fleet at the time, for Arrian, *Anabasis* 1.11.6 gives 160 triremes, Justin 11.6.2 has 182 ships and Curtius 4.5.14 gives Alexander a fleet of 160 vessels a couple of years later; indeed, Arrian's account states that Parmenion led the main crossing from Sestus to Abydos, whereas Alexander crossed from Elaeus at the tip of the Hellespont directly opposite Troy nearly thirty km further south.

On the second level there were arrayed flaming torches with a serpent wound about each of their hafts, which gazed up at an eagle ascending from the flames. It is hard not to see the torch itself as symbolic of Hephaistion, because he was named for the Greek fire god, Hephaistos. According to Herodotus 8.98.2 the Greeks (e.g. the Athenians) held torch races in honour of Hephaistos. Notably, Hephaistion himself bore a torch in a named representation of the Chiliarch in a lost painting by Aetion (Figure I), of which a detailed description has been preserved by Lucian (*Herodotus sive Aetion* 4-7). This explains exactly why each torch was wreathed, since the wreath was explicitly placed upon the badge of Hephaistion. The serpent and eagle are strongly associated with Ammon and Zeus respectively, but they might also represent Alexander himself insofar as he had been publicly recognized as the son of Zeus-Ammon. Perhaps the tableau could be interpreted as Hephaistion acting as a support and inspiration to Alexander. We should expect to find such special and personal compliments to the deceased from the king in the iconography of the decoration of the pyre.

Figure H. Reconstruction of Hephaistion's Pyre by F. Jaffé (late 19th century – Author's Collection)

Figure I. The Marriage of Alexander and Roxane by Sodoma, based upon the description by Lucian of a painting by Aetion and depicting Hephaistion bearing a torch (19th century engraving from the Author's Collection)

Regarding the hunting scene on the third tier of decoration, a fairly direct parallel survives in the hunt depicted on one of the long sides of the Alexander Sarcophagus found in the royal cemetery of Sidon in 1887 (Figure J). This truly wondrous work of art appears to have been the tomb of Abdalonymus, who had been appointed king of Sidon by Alexander on the recommendation of Hephaistion (e.g. Curtius 4.1.15-20). In the hunting scene the rider behind the lion may be Hephaistion; the mounted man being attacked by the lion may be Abdalonymus and the third horseman may be Alexander, since he wore a diadem. In all probability the hunting scenes on the pyre were also an opportunity to commemorate the prowess and dynamism of the deceased in the chase as well as his camaraderie with his king in such pursuits.

The fourth band depicted a Centauromachy or fight of the Centaurs, which refers to the mythological battle between the Lapiths and the Centaurs. Its most renowned precedent was the Centauromachy shown in the metopes of the Parthenon in Athens, which Alexander would have visited in 338BC after the Battle of Chaeronea, probably in the company of Hephaistion. It is generally considered that the mythical Centauromachy often served to symbolize the struggle between the Greeks and the Persians, which is the most likely explanation for its inclusion on Hephaistion's pyre.

Figure J. The hunting scene on one of the long sides of the Alexander Sarcophagus from Sidon (from an albumen photo of the late 19th century in the Author's Collection).

The alternating bulls and lions in the fifth tier of adornment strongly recall the glazed brick reliefs of the Ishtar Gate and the adjoining Processional Way in Babylon, which were recovered by the German archaeological expeditions of Robert Koldewey in the early 20th century and used for a reconstruction displayed in the Pergamon Museum in Berlin. Alexander would certainly have seen them virtually every day he was in Babylon. The lions represent the goddess Ishtar and the bulls (technically aurochs) symbolize the god Adad. In the Babylonian Pantheon Ishtar was the goddess of love and war, whilst Adad was the god of storms. Lions also stood either side of the doorway of Alexander's catafalque, which was constructed in Babylon a little after the pyre (Diodorus 18.27.1). Similarly, a group of lions guarded one of the entrances to Alexander's probable first tomb at the Memphite Serapeum.[478] The main function of that temple was to house the mummified Apis Bulls in the famous subterranean galleries. Lion and bull motifs are also prominent in the decoration of other early Hellenistic tombs, such as, for example, Tomb No. 69 at Myra, which has a lion attacking a bull in the pediment of its façade.

A yet more widespread element of Greek funerary iconography was the panoply of arms, of which a fine example formed the sixth tier of ornamentation on Hephaistion's pyre. There are numerous surviving parallels in Hellenistic artworks from tombs and mausoleums. An interesting example with which I myself have had some involvement is the starburst shield sculpture discovered embedded in the foundations of the main apse of the Basilica di San Marco in Venice (Figure K). In the course of associating the sculpture with a Macedonian tomb, Eugenio Polito suggested in 1998 that the spear shaft extending to the upper lefthand corner of the front face of this block is a sarissa. He did not explain his reasoning, but it may be noted that the point of the spearhead appears to extend precisely to the square upper lefthand corner, which is an original corner. Obviously, the corners on the righthand edge of the block are not original, since it has been fractured away from another part on this side. However, symmetry

---

[478] See *The Quest for the Tomb of Alexander the Great*, Andrew Chugg, 2007, pp. 62-66 & 134-145 (especially p.143).

arguments would suggest that the spear shaft should have terminated at the original bottom righthand corner. The scale of the other arms shows that the intention of the sculptor was to depict them all at precisely lifesize: for example, the shield appears to be a lifesize phalangite type (diameter 70cm). If so, then the spear-shaft was around three metres in length both in art and reality, which is about correct for a Macedonian cavalry sarissa or xyston. Alexander himself wields such a weapon in the mosaic depicting his charge against Darius at Issus, which was found in Pompeii and is now in the Naples Museum.

The spearhead on the block in Venice is rather similar to a spearhead discovered in a warrior grave at Aegae together with a connector circlet and a sauroter. These elements are believed to be the remains of the inorganic parts of a sarissa comprising two wooden shafts joined by the connector with a spike at one end and a leaf-shaped spearhead at the other.

The sculpture also depicts a pair of greaves in high relief, although they are now badly damaged. They are staggered in height on the block just to the right of the shield and the individual greaves are to scale: the bottom of the upper greave is at approximately the level of the lowest part of the star design on the shield. There is also a *kopis*, a single-edged hacking sword popular with Alexander's troops, which is suspended from a tasselled belt on the lefthand side and is also precisely lifesize in scale. Its surface has however been seriously abraded.

Eugenio Polito assumed that the block had been imported to Venice from "the Eastern Mediterranean" and dated it to the third or early second century BC. It is sculpted from late Cretaceous limestone with rudist fossils, which may be found in the Roman Aurisina quarry seventy miles from Venice or in the vicinity of the lost pyramid at Abu Roash on the Nile, which was destroyed to provide sculptural stone in Ptolemaic Egypt.

The starburst design embossed upon the shield is perhaps its most striking feature, redolent as it is of the starburst emblem of the Macedonian monarchy, most famously emblazoned upon the lid of the larnax that held the cremated bones of King Philip of Macedon in Tomb II at Aegae. Starburst shields like this one appear on Macedonian coins and in several Macedonian wall paintings, notably in a mural depicting a Macedonian panoply in the tomb of Lyson & Kallikles located within Macedon itself. Phalangite and hoplite shields are commonly interspersed on Macedonian monuments.[479] A pair of rimless phalangite shields are depicted either side of the entrance on the façade of Tomb III at Aegae, which is probably the tomb of Alexander's son, Alexander IV, in which case it will have been constructed at the beginning of the third century BC.

---

[479] See "A Shield Monument from Veria and the Chronology of Macedonian Shield Types", Minor Markle, *Hesperia* 68.2, 1999.

Figure K. Macedonian arms sculpted upon two faces of a block from the foundations of the Basilica di San Marco in Venice (photo by the author.)

In practice, the trophy of arms motif was the core symbolism for the tomb of a Macedonian warrior. It was roughly the equivalent of a cross on a Christian grave. Here is a contemporaneous quotation that makes the point:

It is fitting for the Macedonian spirit to bear witness to exploits with arms in fighting, and to fairness of the soul, so that trophies may proclaim the valour of the body, but opinions may testify to the soul's nobility.

FrGrHist 2.153 F4 = Freiburg Papyrus 7-8

Therefore, this kind of symbolism is what an expert would expect to find in closest association with the corpse of a Macedonian notable, so it is no surprise to read that trophies of arms formed the penultimate band of decoration on Hephaistion's pyre.

At the summit of the pyre there stood statues of Sirens that had been hollowed out to accommodate human singers. Clearly, there is an allusion to the Sirens of

Homer's Odyssey with their impossibly lovely yet baleful voices. Only the most movingly mournful laments could be deemed worthy of the deceased. It is worth noticing that effigies of Sirens were also found among the statuary near Alexander's probable first tomb at the Serapeum in the Memphite necropolis at Saqqara: it is most likely that these were set up by Ptolemy Soter, who was undoubtedly an eyewitness at Hephaistion's funeral.

The archaeologist Robert Koldewey located a possible site for Hephaistion's pyre during his excavations of Babylon in the early 20th century (see Figure 6.2). He uncovered a scorched and reddened platform beneath a mound of brick rubble close to the inner wall of Babylon due east of the "Southern Palace" of Nebuchadnezzar.[480] Koldewey even described having found the imprints of incinerated palm trunks on the platform, recalling Diodorus' description quite evocatively.

It seems likely that it was Alexander's intention to build a mausoleum echoing the architecture of the pyre in its ashes, although this was thwarted by the king's premature demise. Among the Last Plans of Alexander, which are outlined in Diodorus 18.4 based on documents read to the Assembly of the Macedones by Perdiccas, there was an item calling for the "completion of the pyre of Hephaistion" at great expense. It is important to understand that in Greek the term used, which is *pyra*, can mean either a funeral pyre or a temple altar (i.e. a place where fire is kindled) or the permanent memorial erected on the site of a pyre (it was so used by Euripides in his *Hecuba* line 386 and by Sophocles in his *Electra* line 901). Hence it can reasonably be used to refer both to the incinerated pyre and the altar of a permanent memorial, where a flame was to be kept alight for the Chiliarch. There is evidence for permanent memorials having been erected upon the cinders of funeral pyres in the case of other major Macedonian tombs: for example, a monument from the late 4th century BC has been excavated at Salamis on the coast of Cyprus, where a funeral pyre had been built upon a brick platform and a stone pyramid was subsequently erected in its place as a permanent memorial – this may be associated with the naval battle at Salamis between Ptolemy and Demetrius Poliorcetes in 306BC.[481]

Hephaistion the Demigod

The manuscripts of Diodorus had Alexander decree that Hephaistion should receive sacrifices as *theos proedros*, but this is corrected to *theos paredros* on the basis of Lucian, *Calumniae non temere credendum* 17, which speaks of sacrifices to Hephaistion as *paredros kai alexikakos theos* (assistant and guardian divinity); this use of *paredros*, which literally means "one who sits beside" (as opposed to *proedros*,

---

[480] See "Hephaestion's Pyre and the Royal Hunt of Alexander" by Olga Palagia in *Alexander the Great in Fact and Fiction*, edited by A. B. Bosworth and E. J. Baynham, Oxford 2000, p. 173; R. Koldewey, *The Excavations at Babylon*, London 1914, p. 310-11.
[481] Plutarch, *Demetrius* 17.1; V. Karageorghis, *Cyprus*, London, 1969, pp. 171-199.

which means "sitting in front of"), is unusual and in this context seems to mean an assistant god or collaborating deity, which is not greatly inconsistent with the versions of Arrian, *Anabasis* 7.23.6 and Plutarch, *Alexander* 72.2, which state that Ammon approved the honouring of Hephaistion as a hero. Perhaps the very oddity of *paredros* is suggestive of authentic terminology. The only surviving named portrait of Hephaistion from antiquity is a stele from Thessalonike in Macedonia, which depicts him standing beside a horse with a libation being poured by a woman into a bowl that he holds out (Figure L). It bears a dedicatory inscription from a certain Diogenes to the hero Hephaistion (*DIOGENES HEPHAISTIONI HEROI*). Hence it probably represents a tangible consequence of the semi-divine status accorded to Hephaistion by the Oracle of Ammon.

Figure L. Stele dedicated to the hero Hephaistion found near Pella (sketch by the author).

The Cause of the Death of Alexander

There are three main causes for Alexander's premature demise for which significant evidence is attested by the ancient sources:

1) Excessive indulgence in alcohol
2) A feverish illness
3) Poisoning by Iollas at the instigation of Antipater

Cleitarchus seems to have been aware of the controversy, but to have had no firm favourite among them. Instead, he chose to present evidence for all three. Thus, he mentioned (section 13.43) that Alexander's Friends had spread the word that the onset of his fatal illness had been caused by drinking too much wine. But his actual description of the illness is highly reminiscent of escalating disease symptoms, especially since it agrees with other sources in stretching the duration of the sickness over a week or more. The Iollas poisoning theory is then related as an addendum to the description of the events themselves (section 13.84) with a noncommittal introduction from our author, which verges on a disclaimer. Cleitarchus' description of the plot follows the conspiracy described in the *Liber de Morte* section of the Metz Epitome (87-123) in some detail, so it would seem that Cleitarchus had read its notorious source pamphlet, yet had not been convinced by its assertions of foul play.

Although I recognize that the true cause of Alexander's death remains controversial to this day, I have argued in *The Quest for the Tomb of Alexander the Great* that the ancient evidence in fact presents an overwhelming probabilistic case for death through infection by the deadliest strain of malaria. It is apposite to reprise the case in summary with a view to showing that the version of events given by Cleitarchus is not at all inconsistent with this diagnosis.

Of key significance is Alexander's expedition through the marshes just a week or two before he fell ill. Falciparum malaria has been endemic to the Mesopotamian marshes through to modern times. The local population always acquires a degree of resistance to such deadly diseases, but they are especially pernicious for newcomers to an infected region. The combination of its prevalence with its dire deadliness means this was overwhelmingly the most perilous threat from a feverish disease to which Alexander was exposed. The statistical argument alone is virtually decisive, for death by this strain of malaria is more than ten times more probable than such other rare and exotic syndromes as have been contrived to fit the evidence: for example, the typhoid theory with the rare complication of ascending paralysis and coma, as proposed by Oldach & Richards (*New England Journal of Medicine*, 11th June 1998). In September 2017 at the *Disease and the Ancient World Symposium* held in Green Templeton College, University of Oxford, I used data on malaria, typhoid and other infections in the British Army in Mesopotamia in the First World War to show that malaria falciparum and a coma induced by cerebral malaria is overwhelmingly likely to have been responsible for Alexander's death.

But we need not rely upon statistics, since the interval between the marshes and the famous party at which Alexander collapsed is precisely consistent with the incubation period for falciparum malaria. This disease also has a characteristic and pronounced pattern of fever peaks, for it presents as a quotidian fever, which means that it has a twenty-four-hour cycle of peaks and troughs. In the first few days the fever will virtually vanish at one time of day and yet rage mercilessly twelve hours later. As the disease progresses the hatchings of broods of the parasite that are responsible for stimulating these fever bouts start to overlap and the fever rages more continuously. Hence, we should expect a pronounced intermittency of Alexander's fever in its initial stages and indeed there is no difficulty in finding evidence of this in the accounts of Plutarch and Arrian, both of which are stated to have been based of Alexander's own journal, kept by Eumenes his secretary and known as the *Ephemerides*. We read of a fever raging though the nights, whereas the king long continued to conduct normal matters of business during daylight hours. After four or five days Arrian explicitly states that Alexander "no longer had any rest from the fever", which shows that he had experienced marked remissions up to that point.

The onset of the illness is most comprehensively described in the Cleitarchan sources, which speak of Alexander experiencing stabbing pains in his back and all over his body after quaffing a large beaker of wine at Medius' party. It is ironic that the Cleitarchan authors believed that they were relating evidence of poisoning, when in fact just such stabbing pains in the limb joints and between the vertebrae of the spine are typical of the onset of falciparum malaria. Furthermore, there are clear indications of a profound terminal coma in the fresh and lifelike appearance of the corpse reported by Curtius 10.10.12-13 and Plutarch, *Alexander* 77.3 some days after the pronouncement of death. Cerebral malaria leading to terminal coma is absolutely the normal outcome in untreated cases of falciparum malaria among newcomers to the region of infection. We even have the detail deriving from Aristobulus that Alexander became delirious before the end, which is perfectly congruent with the onset of cerebral malaria (although Aristobulus sought to explain it as a consequence of Alexander having drunk some wine.) Falciparum malaria will also progressively attack a range of organs including the lungs, which readily explains the weakness of Alexander's voice, which is recalled by several sources, including Justin 12.15.12 from among the Cleitarchan authors. Even the least of Alexander's symptoms – e.g. indications of a weak appetite in that he is said to have been eating "lightly" – are consistent with malaria. I know of no recorded symptom that is at all inconsistent with malaria and overall, Alexander's demise is a near casebook account of a falciparum malaria fatality.

In summary, there is an immensely strong case for falciparum malaria in the reported evidence. It seems to be the only statistically credible explanation that is not contradicted by any evidence from any of the ancient sources. Perhaps the most impressive point in its favour is that it happily reconciles the supposed poisoning symptoms reported by the Vulgate sources (including Cleitarchus) with the sober description of death through an escalating feverish disease from the Ephemerides. In fact the onset of falciparum malaria in its standard case history would have looked very much like a case of poisoning to any ancient observer with a less than thorough familiarity with the finer points of tropical medicine.

Yet the fact that death occurred more than a week after the supposed poisoning symptoms renders actual poisoning highly improbable, for the simple reason that any poison capable of producing such a dramatic reaction should have killed Alexander right away. It is almost impossible that he should have lingered for ten days before dying, unless there had been repeated applications of the drug. The *Liber de Morte* author (Holcias?) seems implicitly to have recognized this in formulating the story of a poisoned feather used to repeat the dosing at a late stage in Alexander's illness. Although it may be allowed that feathers were used in antique medicine to induce vomiting, this story is very hard to swallow (please excuse any perceived pun). Neither the concept of Alexander gulping a sticky or dripping wet feather nor the idea that something intended to bring poison up would have seemed a good way of getting it down makes any sense.

One modern attempt to rescue the poisoning theory has been to suppose the "Styx water in a mule's hoof" (section 13.85) to have been actual water contaminated by some biological disease, but this would not of course have produced any of the prompt poisoning symptoms reported at Medius' party. It also ascribes quite a detailed practical knowledge of bacterial biology to the putative poisoner, which is equally dubious.

It is not feasible to be absolutely certain of the cause of Alexander's death unless and until a post mortem is performed upon his remains. However, it is impossible that the tight fit between the case history in our sources and the contraction and progression of a case of falciparum malaria could have been forged. Even if such a fit did not exist, the mere fact that Alexander had visited the Babylonian marshes a few weeks before his death would be sufficient to make falciparum malaria statistically its most likely cause.

How Did the Leading Men Split after Alexander's Death?

A dramatic explosion of factional politics dominates the picture that Cleitarchus seems to have painted of the situation at Babylon in the immediate aftermath of Alexander's death. Yet in principle the pecking order among the senior men was relatively clear. In particular, the seven or eight *somatophylakes* of the king stood at the apex of the court hierarchy and held many of the most senior army commands. Furthermore, they were all Macedonians, which gave them a crucial advantage over the broader elite of the king's Friends comprising around fifty men, of whom at least a third were not Macedonians. Since the ultimate power to acclaim a new king was vested in the Assembly of the Macedonian troops, narrow nationalistic considerations suddenly came swingeing to the fore.

The *somatophylakes* at Babylon in June 323BC were: Perdiccas of Orestis, Leonnatus of Pella & Lyncestis, Aristonous of Eordaea & Pella, Pithon of Alcomenae, Peucestes of Mieza, Lysimachus of Pella & Crannon in Thessaly and Ptolemy of Eordaea. Seleucus of Europus, probably the commander of the Silver Shields (*argyraspides* - formerly the hypaspists) may have been an eighth, assuming that the vacancy created by the death of Hephaistion had been filled. Among these officers, Perdiccas seems to have enjoyed acknowledged pre-eminence: he was evidently the most senior *somatophylax* and Alexander had been seen to hand him his signet ring.

There additionally survives an explicit list of the key men in Babylon at Alexander's death as preserved in the opening section of Photius' Epitome of

Arrian's *Events after Alexander*. It states that Perdiccas, Leonnatus and Ptolemy were the top-ranking cavalry officers, whereas Lysimachus, Aristonous, Pithon, Seleucus and Eumenes were cavalry officers of the second rank. It also notes that Meleager led the infantry faction, which is amply corroborated in my reconstruction of Cleitarchus.

Curtius, probably following Cleitarchus, provides us with a profound insight into the lines along which opinions and sentiments were divided among the *somatophylakes* as they met to discuss the future without Alexander. It is particularly striking that *somatophylakes* from the eastern cantons and townships of Macedonia (Orestis, Lyncestis, Eordaea and Alcomenae) lined up volubly behind Perdiccas, for Leonnatus, Aristonous and Pithon explicitly supported him in the Cleitarchan account. The only exception was Ptolemy of Eordaea, but he was probably only an Eordaean by adoption[482] and he anyway soon reverted to supporting Perdiccas' cause, when his own proposals were seen to lack significant backing and the cavalry faction as a whole united in the face of Meleager's abortive attempt to seize power in the name of Philip-Arrhidaeus. Justin further suggests that Attalus supported Meleager. If so, the former managed somehow to make his peace with the cavalry *hipparchs* before or after Meleager's fall, since he did not share in Meleager's fate. It is possible that he was estranged from Meleager by the offer of the hand of Perdiccas' sister Atalante, since Diodorus 18.37.2 later names her as his wife. He subsequently led the pursuit of Alexander's catafalque on behalf of Perdiccas, when Ptolemy had diverted it towards Egypt.

The position of Nearchus of Amphipolis & Crete is intriguing. He evidently chose to espouse the cause of Alexander's illegitimate son by Barsine, probably because he had married a daughter of Barsine at Susa the previous year. Unsurprisingly, advocacy of Heracles proved politically unpopular among the Macedonians, so Nearchus merely managed to isolate himself. This may be reflected in the fact that, despite his eminence under Alexander, he was not awarded outright control of any territory in the First Division of the Satrapies, although he may have been appointed as a deputy to Antigonus in Lycia and Pamphylia.

Eumenes of Cardia does not have any prominent role in the Cleitarchan version of events at Babylon, although he had inherited Perdiccas' hipparchy of the Companion Cavalry after the death of Hephaistion (Plutarch, *Eumenes* 1.5; Nepos, *Eumenes* 1.6). However, Plutarch, *Eumenes* 3.2 states that he stayed in Babylon maintaining neutrality, when the other cavalry officers went out into the surrounding countryside and that he was thereafter influential in persuading the infantry to reach an accommodation with Perdiccas.[483]

---

[482] He seems to have been an illegitimate son of Philip II, who was adopted by Lagus, when the latter married his mother Arsinoe: Pausanias 1.6.2; Curtius 9.8.22; *Armenian Alexander Romance* 269; Plutarch, *Moralia* 458A-B; *Suidae Lexicon* s.v. Lagos..

[483] Jane Hornblower, *Hieronymus of Cardia*, p.88, thinks Plutarch used Hieronymus on Eumenes.

Key Historical Issues

The stance of the other *somatophylakes* (Lysimachus, Peucestes and perhaps Seleucus) is not explicitly stated by our sources, but their backing for Perdiccas may be inferred from the fact that they all received important and desirable appointments in the First Division of the Satrapies.

Considering that Perdiccas enjoyed such broad support among the elite men, it is remarkable that the infantry managed to cause him so much trouble. The Cleitarchan analysis was that he did well in making a show of giving up Alexander's ring at the crucial meeting in the aftermath of Alexander's death, but that he was too hesitant in retrieving it, when the meeting had been rallied behind him by his supporters, thereby ceding the troublemakers their opportunity. I find this a rather compelling human explanation of the events, which is not significantly contradicted by any other account. Indeed, no other version provides anything approaching the same degree of detail at this juncture.

Arrhidaeus the Fool

There is virtual unanimity among the ancient sources on the fact that Arrhidaeus suffered from some form of mental impairment. Plutarch, *Alexander* 77.7-8 even goes so far as to allege that this had resulted from a drug administered to him by Olympias in his childhood. One of the most explicit references on this matter is the Heidelberg Epitome 1-2, which states:

"When Alexander died, he left behind his wives and an unborn son by Roxane. His followers quarrelled about who should become king, but Alexander's half-brother Arrhidaeus, who was later called Philip, was appointed king until the son of Alexander reached an appropriate age. Because Arrhidaeus was dull-witted and also epileptic, Perdiccas was appointed to be guardian and overseer of the royal government."

There are further attestations of Arrhidaeus' affliction in: Plutarch, *Alexander* 10.2 & 77.7-8; Diodorus 18.2; Justin 13.2.11 & 14.5.2. Justin 13.2.11 (backed up by Diodorus) is the sources for the mention of Arrhidaeus' incapacity in the reconstruction of Cleitarchus at 13.61. Curtius appears to have edited out the hostile invective, probably because he was drawing a parallel with the accession of his own emperor, Claudius. The ensemble of evidence on Philip-Arrhidaeus and especially the lack of any contrary indications from any ancient source leaves little room for doubt that he was conspicuously sub-normal. Thus, it would be appropriate to read a certain element of disingenuousness into the advocacy of Arrhidaeus' succession by Meleager and his cronies.

Plutarch, *Alexander* 10.2, has Alexander describe Arrhidaeus literally as a bastard in the context of the Pixodarus affair. However, some have supposed that Philip's attempt to marry off Arrhidaeus to the eldest daughter of Pixodarus, the satrap of Caria, in the cause of recruiting him as an ally must mean that Philip had married Arrhidaeus' mother, Philinna, since Arrhidaeus must have had the status of a legitimate son to be an acceptable groom. This relies on a Christian concept of illegitimacy as a sanction against indulgence in sex outside of marriage, which is of course a way of thinking that would have been utterly alien in the Greek world of the 4th century BC. Instead, the social function of illegitimacy for the Greeks was as a legal device to inhibit the division and disintegration of the assets and estates of wealthy families among the many illegitimate offspring sired by their senior male members. Consequently, the emphasis in deciding your legitimacy status in that culture does not seem to have been on whether your father had married your mother (although legitimacy was automatic and implicit, if he had), but rather on whether your father had publicly acknowledged you as his son or daughter.

It is likely that Philip had to acknowledge Arrhidaeus as his own in order to make a marriage with Pixodarus' daughter viable, but he did not need to have married Philinna: the quote of Alexander from Plutarch strongly suggests that he had not; also Satyrus (Athenaeus 13.5 [557C]) states that Philip fathered Arrhidaeus on Philinna, but conspicuously avoids saying that he married her. However, the official acknowledgement of Arrhidaeus explains why the troops were so ready to accept his claim to the throne in Babylon, despite his mother having been an unmarried dancing girl from Larissa. It also explains just why the Pixodarus marriage so upset Alexander: his bastard half-brother was now his official half-brother through this marriage, thereby becoming a theoretical threat to Alexander's succession. Philip probably calculated that Arrhidaeus' impaired mental faculties guaranteed that the threat to Alexander would remain hypothetical, but Alexander could not afford to feel so relaxed about the matter, for Arrhidaeus could yet be played as a pawn against him. Events after Alexander's death show that Alexander was right to fear the consequences of Arrhidaeus being adopted by a faction as a puppet king and that Philip miscalculated the risks of legitimizing an imbecile into the official Royal Family.

The First Division of the Satrapies

The reapportionment of control of the satrapies of Alexander's Empire effectuated by Perdiccas in June of 323BC at Babylon survives in three main traditions that I will term the Photian, the Cleitarchan and the Metz. The first derives from Photius' summaries of Dexippus and of Arrian's lost work on *Events After Alexander*. Secondly, each of Curtius, Diodorus and Justin cite lists that appear to preserve the version from Cleitarchus. Finally, the *Liber de Morte* section at the end of the Metz Epitome has a variant of the list, which it attributes to the spurious *Will of Alexander*, but which nevertheless generally encapsulates the outcome of the Perdiccan division. Some parts of the Metz tradition also appear in Pseudo-Callisthenes, although in an even more garbled form. The Cleitarchan tradition is summarized in Table 1, including my reconstruction of Cleitarchus himself in its final column; whereas the Photian and Metz versions are cited for comparison in Table 2, which also incorporates a version of the Second Division

Key Historical Issues

that was implemented by Antipater a few years later, the latter also being abstracted from Photius' summary of Arrian.

It is initially striking how much agreement there is to be found between these disparate sources. Once allowance has been made for various errors of transcription and transliteration, there is a great deal of commonality between them all. Particularly intricate details are shared by the Photian and Cleitarchan traditions: for example, both apparently mentioned that Eumenes' remit should extend specifically to the town of Trapezus (Trebizond) on the Euxine Sea; furthermore, the satrapies are dealt with in a similar order in each case and the eastern section is prefixed with the observation that its existing satraps were generally allowed to remain in office. These commonalities strongly suggest that all these traditions had their origins in a single contemporaneous, archetypal document.

Nevertheless, a focussed review of aberrant details of the First Division may help assuage the doubts aired by some, such as N. G. L. Hammond, as to whether the vivid, blow-by-blow account of the succession of Philip III in the latter half of the tenth book of Curtius is actually derived from Cleitarchus. In general, the differences between the traditions, though relatively few, bear close examination, because they may well serve to define the interpretation of the archetypal list by intermediary authors, notably Cleitarchus.

Perhaps the clearest instance is that the satrapy of Caria is awarded to Asander in the Photian lists, but consistently to Cassander in the Cleitarchan and also the Metz traditions. This was actually Asander the son of Agathon from Beroea, probably a relative of Antigonus, so we can say that there is a consistent error in the Cleitarchan version, which may therefore most credibly be traced back to the prototype variant of Cleitarchus. Certainly, the observation that Curtius, Diodorus and Justin all share in this error is a strong indication that they are all still following Cleitarchus at this point, despite the fact that the First Division occurred at an interval of a week or two after Alexander's death.

A second variation is that the reinstatement of Atropates as Satrap of Lesser Media seems only to be mentioned in Cleitarchan versions. He is cited among the examples of an existing eastern satrap, whose associations with the new regime have enabled him to retain his position, even though the satrapy of Greater Media is assigned to Pithon in the first half of the list dealing with the western and central satrapies. In Justin, Atropates is noted to have retained Lesser Media as the "father-in-law of Perdiccas", a relationship that he had achieved through the Susa marriages of 324BC. The Photian tradition evidently omitted mention of Atropates, whereas Cleitarchus seemingly saw fit to draw attention to this evidence for the nature of the patronage dispensed by the Perdiccan regime.

It would also appear that the Cleitarchan list gave Seleucus command of the Companion Cavalry in the First Division, whereas both the Photian and Metz traditions granted him immediate governance of Babylonia. In fact, it seems that Seleucus was not given control of Babylonia until the Second Division and that the Cleitarchan tradition correctly recalls that Archon of Pella initially received Babylonia.[484] This shows that the Cleitarchan tradition is certainly no less accurate overall than the Photian sources: a case might even be made that the Cleitarchan in fact provides the most accurate and detailed surviving account.

There is a slight difference of emphasis between the Cleitarchan and Photian traditions in that the former asserts that Ptolemy was to replace Cleomenes, whereas the latter suggests that Cleomenes was to become Ptolemy's deputy. It is tempting to explain this as political correctness on Cleitarchus' part, since he is believed to have written in Egypt under Ptolemaic rule, where the first Ptolemy had actually executed Cleomenes. It certainly harmonises with the assumption that Cleitarchus is the source of First Division details in Curtius, Justin and Diodorus.

It is interesting that Justin uniquely assigned Nearchus as the Satrap of Lycia and Pamphylia. This has been considered an error influenced by Alexander's earlier award of these territories to Nearchus (Arrian, *Anabasis* 3.6.6). However, we do know that Nearchus was active in Pamphylia and southern Asia Minor in the years following Alexander's death (Polyaenus 5.35) and it is mildly strange that someone so eminent as Nearchus lacks any role elsewhere in the First Division. The alternative interpretation would be that Nearchus was indeed awarded his former satrapies in the First Division, but that he was also required to report to Antigonus in this capacity. Hence, he acted as a deputy to Antigonus, who most ancient writers therefore recognized as the true ruler of Lycia and Pamphylia. Certainly, by 317-316BC Nearchus is explicitly operating as a lieutenant of Antigonus in leading a force of lightly armed troops into the Cossaean territory (Diodorus 19.19.4-5).

There is some additional evidence to be gleaned across the traditions that the archetypal source on the First Division recorded significant appointments in assistant or deputy posts against some of the satrapies and other high offices: as well as Cleomenes' status in Egypt, there is a sense in which Craterus is presented as Antipater's assistant in Europe. It is a possibility that Atropates was subordinate to Pithon in Media: perhaps it was only the nepotism interest that persuaded Cleitarchus to mention his appointment. In general, the surviving sources may have edited out much information on subordinate appointments in the cause of epitomizing a morass of data, which was to be found in the archetype.

There is huge scope for confusion in that two men named Pithon were awarded satrapies in the First Division and this problem was compounded by the fact that the Pithon who took Greater Media and was a Bodyguard of Alexander had a father named Crateuas, which is deceptively close to Craterus – hence in all probability the award of Greater Media to "Craterus" in the Metz version. The other Pithon was the son of Agenor and he seems to have been awarded control of those parts of India that did not fall within the domains of Taxiles and Porus.

---

[484] Arrian, *Events after Alexander* Fragment 10A.3-5, R24.3-5.

Key Historical Issues

Pithon the son of Crateuas came from Alcomenae in Deuriopus[485] on the borders of Illyria, which probably explains why he is called "Illyrius" in Justin. This is likely to be the epithet employed by Cleitarchus to distinguish him from the son of Agenor. Unfortunately, some editors have instead interpreted this as a reference to the "satrapy" of Illyria. In fact, the fate of Illyria seems only to be mentioned by the Photian tradition, which includes it among Antipater's territories, and the Metz Epitome, which assigns it to Holcias. The prominence of Holcias in the Metz has been held to suggest that he may have been the original author of the *Liber de Morte*. The indications that the original assignments extended to deputy roles would suggest that the archetype of the First Division list might have granted him subordinate control of Illyria reporting to Antipater. He is certainly a real historical character of some prominence, since he appears in Polyaenus 4.6.6 as one of the leaders of three thousand troops, who had revolted from Antigonus.

However, the key conclusion must be that Cleitarchus gave a well-informed and mostly accurate summary of the First Division of the Satrapies, which he probably abstracted from an archetypal published list. It subsequently became the basis for the surviving summaries in Diodorus, Curtius and Justin. The First Division was destined to have vast repercussions: it established the Ptolemaic Dynasty in Egypt and set Antigonus Monophthalmus and Seleucus Nicator upon their paths to glory. It also provided the model for successive divisions by Antipater at Triparadeisus (see also Diodorus 18.39.5-7) in 320BC and Antigonus in the aftermath of Gabiene (Diodorus 19.48) in 316BC.

---

[485] Strabo 7.7.8.

Concerning Alexander the Great by Andrew Chugg

TABLE 1: The First Division of the Satrapies – Vulgate Sources

TERRITORY	DIODORUS 18.3	JUSTIN 13.4.9-25	CURTIUS 10.10.1-4	CLEITARCHUS
"WEST"	-	-	-	-
ARABIA (PART)	-	Ptolemy	-	-
LIBYA/AFRICA	-	Ptolemy	Ptolemy	Ptolemy
EGYPT	Ptolemy	Ptolemy	Ptolemy	Ptolemy
SYRIA	Laomedon	Laomedon	Laomedon	Laomedon
COELE-SYRIA	-	-	-	-
PHOENICIA	-	-	Laomedon	Laomedon
CILICIA	Philotas	Philotas	Philotas	Philotas
GRT. MEDIA	Pithon	Illyrian Pithon	Pithon	Illyrian Pithon
PAPHLAGONIA	Eumenes	Eumenes	Eumenes	Eumenes
CAPPADOCIA	Eumenes	Eumenes	Eumenes	Eumenes
EUXINE COAST	(Eumenes)	-	(Eumenes)	Eumenes
PAMPHYLIA	Antigonus	Nearchus	Antigonus	Antigonus
LYCIA	Antigonus	Nearchus	Antigonus	(deputy Nearchus)
GRT. PHRYGIA	Antigonus	Antigonus	Antigonus	Antigonus
LYCONIA	-	-	-	-
CARIA	Cassander	Cassander	Cassander	Cassander
LYDIA	Meleager	Menander	Menander	Menander
HELL PHRYGIA	Leonnatus	Leonnatus	Leonnatus	Leonnatus
THRACE	Lysimachus	Lysimachus	Lysimachus	Lysimachus
CHERSONESE	-	-	-	-
EUXINE (EURO)	-	Lysimachus	Lysimachus	Lysimachus
MACEDONIA	Antipater	-	-	Antipater
EPIRUS	-	-	-	-
GREECE	-	-	-	-
ILLYRIA	-	-	-	-
INDIAN REALMS	Taxiles & Porus	Taxiles	"retained"	Taxiles & Porus
(CAUCASUS of) PAROPAMISUS	Oxyartes	Oxyartes	-	Oxyartes
INDIA (rest of)	Pithon	Pithon, son of Agenor	-	Pithon, son of Agenor
ARACHOSIA	Sibyrtius	Sibyrtius	-	Sibyrtius
KEDROSIA	Sibyrtius	Sibyrtius	-	Sibyrtius
ARIA	Stasanor	Stasanor	-	Stasanor
DRANGIANA	Stasanor	Stasanor	-	Stasanor
BACTRIA	Philip	Amyntas	"retained"	Philip
SOGDIANA	Philip	"Sulceos Staganos"	"retained"	Philip
PARTHIA	Phrataphernes	Philip	-	Phrataphernes
HYRCANIA	Phrataphernes	Phrataphernes	-	Phrataphernes
PERSIA	Peucestes	Peucestes	-	Peucestes
CARMANIA	Tlepolemus	Tleptolemus	-	Tlepolemus
LESSER MEDIA	Atropates	Atropates	-	Atropates
SUSIANA	-	Coenus	-	Coenus
BABYLONIA	Archon	Archon of Pella	-	Archon of Pella
MESOPOTAMIA	Arcesilaus	Arcesilaus	-	Arcesilaus
ARBELITIS	-	-	-	-
COMPANIONS	Seleucus	~Seleucus	-	Seleucus

Key Historical Issues

TABLE 2: The First Division of the Satrapies – Arrian & Others

TERRITORY	ARRIAN 1st F1.5-9 (PHOTIUS)	DEXIPPUS 82.62B (PHOTIUS)	ARRIAN 2nd F9.34-38 (PHOTIUS)	METZ EPITOME 116-122
"WEST"	Ptolemy	-	Ptolemy	-
ARABIA (PART)	(deputy	-	-	-
LIBYA/AFRICA	Cleomenes)	Ptolemy (deputy	Ptolemy	-
EGYPT		Cleomenes)	Ptolemy	Ptolemy
SYRIA	Laomedon	Laomedon	Laomedon	Pithon?
COELE-SYRIA	-	-	-	Meleager
PHOENICIA	-	-	-	Meleager
CILICIA	Philotas	Philotas	Philoxenus	Nicanor
GRT. MEDIA	Pithon	Pithon	Pithon	"Craterus"[486]
PAPHLAGONIA	Eumenes	Eumenes	-	Eumenes
CAPPADOCIA	Eumenes	Eumenes	Nicanor	Eumenes
EUXINE COAST	Eumenes	Eumenes	-	-
PAMPHYLIA	Antigonus	Antigonus	Antigonus	Antigonus
LYCIA	Antigonus	-	Antigonus	Antigonus
GRT. PHRYGIA	Antigonus	Antigonus[487]	Antigonus	Antigonus
LYCONIA	-	-	Antigonus	-
CARIA	Asander	Asander	Asander	Cassander
LYDIA	Menander	Menander	Cleitus	-
HELL. PHRYGIA	Leonnatus	Leonnatus	Arrhidaeus	Leonnatus
THRACE	Lysimachus	Lysimachus	-	-
CHERSONESE	Lysimachus	Lysimachus	-	-
EUXINE (EURO)	Lysimachus	-	-	Antipater to hold everything west of River Halys
MACEDONIA	Antipater & Craterus	Antipater	-	
EPIRUS		-	-	
GREECE		Antipater	-	
ILLYRIA		Antipater	-	Holcias
INDIAN REALMS	-	Taxiles & Porus	Taxiles & Porus	Taxiles & Porus
PAROPAMISUS	-	Oxyartes	Oxyartes	Oxyartes
INDIA (rest of)	-	Pithon	Pithon, son of Agenor	-
ARACHOSIA	-	Sibyrtius	Sibyrtius	Sibyrtius?
KEDROSIA	-	Sibyrtius	-	Sibyrtius?
ARIA	-	Stasanor	Stasander	Stasanor?
DRANGIANA	-	Stasanor	Stasander	Stasanor?
BACTRIA	-	-	Stasanor	Philip
SOGDIANA	-	Philip	Stasanor	-
PARTHIA	-	-	Philip	Prataphernen
HYRCANIA	-	Radaphernes	-	Prataphernen
PERSIA	-	Peucestes	Peucestes	Peucestes
CARMANIA	-	Neoptolemus	Tlepolemus	Phtolomeo
LESSER MEDIA	-	-	-	-
SUSIANA	-	Oropius then Coenus	Antigenes	Coenus
BABYLONIA	-	Seleucus	Seleucus	Seleucus
MESOPOTAMIA	-	Archelaus	Amphimachus	-
ARBELITIS	-	-	Amphimachus	-
COMPANIONS	-	-	Cassander	-

---

[486] It is likely that this originally read Pithon Crateuae (Pithon the son of Crateuas).

[487] Photius' summary of Dexippus has: "Cilicia as far as Phrygia".

Last Plans

Sections 13.81-83 of my reconstruction are derived exclusively from Diodorus 18.4.1-6 dealing with Alexander's "Last Plans": direct evidence for their ultimate derivation from Cleitarchus is weak, but all other material in Diodorus 18.1-4 seems to be Cleitarchan due to close and particular matches with Curtius and Justin. Hence, it would appear that Diodorus did not switch sources to Hieronymus of Cardia until 18.5.[488] The geographical review of Asia in Diodorus 18.5-6 is a strong indication of a switch to a new source, since such scene setting at the opening of their books was common among Hellenistic historians. For example, Cleitarchus himself seems to have given a geographical and cultural review of India by way of introduction to the tenth book of his work at the outset of Alexander's invasion of the sub-continent.

The fact that the genuineness of the Last Plans has so often been impugned[489] is arguably a clearer reflection of the sceptical loading of some scholars' scales rather than their balanced verdicts, for it can scarcely be deemed to mirror the weight of the evidence, which inclines towards authenticity. The key point is that nearly all of Alexander's plans as rejected by Perdiccas and the Assembly and which Diodorus lists as "memoranda" (*hypomnemata*) have close parallels in the actions and objectives of Alexander recorded elsewhere among our sources. Furthermore, there is copious evidence that an extensive body of Royal Papers existed, including also the journal known as the *Ephemerides* and the distances for stages in Alexander's marches, called the *Stathmoi* (see my paper on *The Journal of Alexander the Great* in *Ancient History Bulletin* 19.3-4, 2005 and reprinted in *The Quest*). It is hard to imagine that Perdiccas would have wished to invent spurious Plans merely to have them set aside by the Assembly and it is even harder to see how the existence of these Plans offered political advantage to any faction. In other words, forgery would have been a motiveless crime.

Let us consider the corroborative evidence for the individual plans:

1) Completion of the memorial altar of Hephaistion

Plutarch, *Alexander* 72.3, reports essentially the same plan: "[Alexander] proposed to expend ten thousand talents upon a tomb (*tumbos*) and obsequies for his friend, wishing that the ingenuity and novelty of the construction should surpass the outlay." Arrian, *Anabasis* 7.14.8, concurs, even using the same ambiguous term as Diodorus: "[Alexander] ordered a *pyra* (pyre/altar) to be made ready for [Hephaistion] at Babylon at a cost of ten thousand talents – by some accounts

---

[488] Jane Hornblower, *Hieronymus of Cardia*, pp.80-97, broadly supports the view that Cleitarchus was the source of the Last Plans and much of the other material in Diodorus 18.2-4 and she agrees that the geographical review comes from the opening of Hieronymus' account of the history of Alexander's successors.

[489] Perhaps most notably by W. W. Tarn, *Alexander the Great, Vol II: Sources & Studies*, p.378f.

Key Historical Issues

even more." The extraordinary expense militates in favour of a permanent memorial being envisaged in addition to a combusted funeral pyre.

2) A thousand warships larger than triremes to be built in Phoenicia, Syria, Cilicia and Cyprus for a campaign against Carthage

According to Arrian, *Anabasis* 7.19.4, Alexander had recently assembled various fleets at Babylon for the purposes of the Arabian circumnavigation in a harbour that he had dredged out to accommodate a thousand warships. That the whole space was needed is shown by Curtius 10.1.19, who records that 700 vessels were to be built at Thapsacus on the Euphrates to be sailed down to Babylon and added to Nearchus' fleet. It is an obvious corollary that the same size of fleet would have been required to support the North African campaign in the Mediterranean, since in Alexander's day there was no practicable sea-route to take the Arabian fleet into the Mediterranean. The campaign against the Carthaginians is also outlined by Curtius 10.1.17.

3) A road along the coast of North Africa as far as the Pillars of Heracles

The *Metz Epitome* 63 notes that Alexander planned ultimately to reach the Atlantic (in fact the manuscript read *adlanticum montem*, which might mean the Pillars of Heracles). Curtius 10.1.17 is explicit that Alexander wished to march to the Pillars of Heracles.

4) Six shrines at a cost of 1500 talents each to be set up at Delos, Delphi & Dodona in Greece and three in Macedonia: a temple of Zeus at Dium, of Tauropolus at Amphipolis[490] and of Athena at Cyrrhus[491]

This must have been among the written instructions given to Craterus, when he set off for Greece, for Plutarch, *Moralia* 343D, evidently cites the same programme of temple construction: "Alexander captured the riches of barbarians and sent them to Greece with orders that ten thousand talents be used to construct temples for the gods."

5) Ports and shipyards to be constructed to support Alexander's expeditions

Curtius 10.1.17-19 effectively corroborates Alexander's entire plan to march around the Mediterranean littoral in a clockwise direction starting from Syria. The practical need for suitable harbours and shipyards was an inevitable corollary.

---

[490] W. W. Tarn and also Russel M. Geer in the Loeb edition of Diodorus 18 make Tauropolus a manifestation of Artemis and there are some coins of Amphipolis with a goddess astride a bull; but Tauropolus the son of Dionysus and Ariadne is associated with the Thracian Chersonese and would seem an alternative possibility, given that Amphipolis lay near the Thracian border – but perhaps Tauropolus was manifested as the bull that Artemis rode.

[491] Cyrrhus is Cyrnus in the manuscripts, but it seems preferable to assume that the known Macedonian town is intended.

Concerning Alexander the Great by Andrew Chugg

6) To establish cities and to transfer populations from Asia to Europe and from Europe to Asia

There is copious evidence for Alexander's policy of settling Greeks in newly founded cities in Asia. For example, Polybius 10.27.3 writes: "Media is the most notable principality in Asia… On its borders a ring of Greek cities were founded by Alexander to protect it from the neighbouring barbarians." Then Pausanias 1.25.5 and 8.52.5 has: "All the Greeks who had served as mercenaries in the armies of Darius and his satraps Alexander had wished to deport to Persia, but Leosthenes was too quick for him, and brought them by sea to Europe… Leosthenes, in spite of Alexander's opposition, brought back safe by sea to Greece the force of Greek mercenaries in Persia, about fifty thousand in number, who had descended to the coast." Also, Diodorus 17.99.5-6 states: "The Greeks who had been settled in Bactria and Sogdiana, who had long borne unhappily their sojourn among peoples of a different race, now received word that the king [Alexander] had died of his wounds and they revolted against the Macedonians. They formed a band of three thousand men and underwent great hardships on their homeward route." There is little evidence for the colonizing of Europe by Asiatic people, but this is mainly because the European campaigns had yet to happen at Alexander's death. We should have to suppose a radical shift of policy by Alexander, if he had no intention of founding cities and populating them with suitable groups from among his followers in the context of the forthcoming European expedition. Alexander probably believed that he was emulating his forebear, Heracles, who was said by the Alexander historians (Onesicritus?) to have settled the ancestors of the Sibi in India, because they had been unfit for the onward march (Curtius 9.4.2 & Diodorus 17.96.2).

7) A temple of unsurpassed magnificence to be dedicated to Athena at Troy

Strabo 13.1.26 refers to the same project: "It is said that the city of the present Ilians [Trojans] was for a time a mere village, having its temple of Athena, a small and cheap temple, but that when Alexander went up there after his victory at the Granicus River he adorned the temple with votive offerings, gave the village the title of city, and ordered those in charge to improve it with buildings, and that he adjudged it free and exempt from tribute; and that later, after the overthrow of the Persians, he sent down a kindly letter to the place, promising to make a great city of it, and to build a magnificent sanctuary, and to proclaim sacred games."

8) A tomb for Philip emulating the Great Pyramid (at Giza)

There is no direct statement of this plan in any other source, but there are circumstantial strands of evidence that make it highly credible. Firstly, Alexander had undoubtedly seen the Giza pyramids, since his route in Egypt passed by them and it would hardly be surprising, if they inspired emulation in him. We also know that the pyre and tomb of Hephaistion seems to have had a stepped pyramidal design. Finally, modern archaeology has revealed that a little while after Alexander's death a very large earth tumulus was indeed heaped over the royal Macedonian tombs at Aegae, one of which probably belonged to Philip. Thus, it would appear that Alexander's ambition to aggrandize Philip's tomb was shared by his successors.

In summary, we find that the great bulk of the material in the Last Plans is echoed elsewhere in the sources. It would also be fair to say that many of these echoes occur in sources that we know to have used Cleitarchus, which is supportive of the view that Diodorus took the Last Plans from Cleitarchus. Insofar as any aspects of the Last Plans are not precisely corroborated elsewhere, they are nevertheless in conformity with what we know of Alexander's policies and motives. I know of no convincing argument against the authenticity of any of the Last Plans.

Antipater & Cassander as Regicides

As has already been argued in discussing the cause of Alexander's death, the theory that Antipater had instigated a poisoning conspiracy holds little water. Indeed, it seems as though Cleitarchus himself had doubts about its credibility and merely cited it for completeness. Antipater seems in fact to have shown some considerable loyalty to Alexander's house above his own, for he conspicuously avoided making his son Cassander his own successor, instead appointing Polyperchon. Subsequent events suggest that he may have acted out of concern for the safety of Alexander's wife and son in Cassander's power. Hence I am inclined to acquit Antipater of the charge of treason.

Conversely, it is hardly even controversial that Cassander became a serial murderer of Macedonian royalty just as suggested by Cleitarchus' closing paragraphs. Firstly, he orchestrated the execution of Olympias, as detailed by Justin 4.6 and Diodorus 19.51.4-5:

As Olympias refused to flee, but on the contrary was ready to be judged before all the Macedonians, Cassander, fearing that the crowd might change its mind if it heard the queen defend herself and was reminded of all the benefits conferred on the entire nation by Alexander and Philip, sent two hundred soldiers who were best fitted for such a task, ordering them to slay her as soon as possible. They, accordingly, broke into the royal house, but when they beheld Olympias, overawed by her exalted rank, they withdrew with their task unfulfilled. But the relatives of her victims, wishing to curry favour with Cassander as well as to avenge their dead, murdered the queen, who uttered no ignoble or womanish plea.

Six years later he perpetrated the murder of Alexander the son of Alexander together with his mother Roxane as related by Diodorus 19.105.2-3:

Now Cassander perceived that Alexander, the son of Roxane, was growing up and that word was being spread throughout Macedonia by certain men that it was fitting to release the boy from custody and give him his father's kingdom; and fearing for himself, he instructed Glaucias, who was in command of the guard over the child, to murder Roxane and the king and conceal their bodies, but to disclose to no one else what had been done.

Not long afterwards he bribed Polyperchon to extinguish the breath of the last of Alexander's sons according to Plutarch, *Moralia*, On Compliancy 530D:

Polyperchon agreed with Cassander for a hundred talents to do away with Heracles, Alexander's son by Barsine, and proceeded to invite him to dinner. When the youth, suspecting and dreading the invitation, alleged an indisposition, Polyperchon called on him and said: "Young man, the first quality of your father you should imitate is his readiness to oblige and attachment to his friends, unless indeed you fear me as a plotter." The youth was shamed into attending; and they gave him his dinner and strangled him.

It is no wonder that Cleitarchus seems to have commented that the subsequent sufferings of Cassander and his own sons were a species of divine retribution.

The Itinerant Corpse

The intricate and protracted adventures of Alexander's corpse after his death constitute a story on the same scale as his exploits whilst still alive. I have given full accounts in my earlier books, *The Lost Tomb of Alexander the Great* and *The Quest for the Tomb of Alexander the Great* (3rd Edition, 2020), to which I must refer any reader desiring more than a bare outline of how the remains reached Alexandria, which is the limit of my ambition here.

According to my reconstruction, Cleitarchus would appear to have made three important contributions on the matter:

1) In Section 13.45, Cleitarchus states that Alexander had asked on his deathbed that his corpse should be delivered to Ammon in Egypt. Other early sources (notably the *Liber de Morte* in the *Metz Epitome*, Section 111, and Lucian, *Dialogues of the Dead* 13) seem to agree at least that he had requested conveyance of his remains to Egypt.

2) In Section 13.78 Cleitarchus probably incorporated the appointment of Arrhidaeus (not Philip III, but a Macedonian officer) to oversee the preparation of a catafalque and to escort the corpse to Ammon in Egypt among the list of decisions regarding the *First Division of the Satrapies* made at Babylon in June 323BC. Other sources (notably Arrian in the epitome of his *Events after Alexander* made by Photius) agree that Arrhidaeus had been appointed to perform such escort duties, but they differ on the intended destination: in particular, Pausanias 1.6.3 states that the body's objective was Aegae in Macedon.

3) In Section 13.87 Cleitarchus seems to have concluded with a statement of the undoubted truth: that Alexander was initially entombed at Memphis in Egypt, but subsequently transferred to Alexandria, where he lay when Cleitarchus wrote.

It is rather likely that some further information filling the gap between items 2) & 3) has been edited out from Cleitarchus' full version by the intermediaries, but a judicious conflation of numerous fragmentary pieces of information from

Key Historical Issues

elsewhere has enabled me to compile the following probable outline of the journey travelled by Alexander's body.

It seems most probable that Cleitarchus was correct in reporting that Alexander's expressed wishes were respected in the impassioned atmosphere of the immediate aftermath of his death. Hence, a plan to send the corpse to Egypt was hatched and Perdiccas appointed Arrhidaeus, perhaps because he was close to Ptolemy, who was appointed to govern Egypt. A splendid catafalque was duly fabricated over a period straddling two Attic years. In the meantime, Perdiccas would have been in communication with Olympias back in Europe. She would have been horrified at the prospect of an Egyptian funeral with mummification and burial instead of a traditional funeral pyre: there is a hint of this in Aelian, *Varia Historia* 13.30, where Olympias groans on hearing that her son had lain unburied for a long period. Perdiccas badly needed her support. Aelian, *Varia Historia* 12.64 tells a story that Aristander of Telmissus gave a prophecy that the land that received Alexander's body would forever remain unconquered. It is tempting to see in this an artifice to persuade the Macedonians that the corpse should be re-directed to Macedon. At any rate, sending it to Aegae became Perdiccas' policy.

The exact date is quite uncertain, but most probably in the Autumn of 322BC the catafalque set forth from Babylon heading NW towards Syria, ostensibly bound for Macedon in accordance with Perdiccas' instructions. Diodorus 18.28 gives a thrilling description of its splendours, which is the basis for the reconstruction shown in Figure M. Some time around the turn of 322BC into 321BC the procession reached northern Syria and suddenly turned southwards towards Damascus, for Ptolemy, who still wished the corpse to be taken to Egypt, had suborned Arrhidaeus. Ptolemy's motive is uncertain, but what evidence there is (Lucian, *Dialogues of the Dead* 13 and the *Alexander Romance* in its Armenian manuscripts) suggests that Ptolemy had made a faithful promise to the dying Alexander to fulfil his wishes in this matter.

Perdiccas was wintering in Pisidia some seven hundred miles away, but couriers brought him word within a week or two. He sent his lieutenants Attalus and Polemon in hot pursuit with a large contingent of cavalry. However, Ptolemy had already met up with Arrhidaeus at Damascus, having come north by arrangement to escort his prize back to his satrapy. The stories in Aelian tell us that Perdiccas' men clashed with Ptolemy's somewhere in Palestine, but that Ptolemy used a decoy hearse to thwart his opponents. It is certain that he was successful in safely conveying Alexander's mummy to Memphis in Egypt, then still its capital.

A wrathful Perdiccas invaded Egypt with the Grand Army in the Spring of 321BC, but he was assassinated by his own men having twice failed to force the crossing of the Nile, whilst sustaining huge casualties through drowning and the marauding of the river's crocodiles. Ptolemy attended a tearful assembly of reconciliation with the survivors, before sending them back north and turning his attentions to the business of Alexander's funeral and entombment.

Concerning Alexander the Great by Andrew Chugg

Figure M. A reconstruction of Alexander's catafalque (19th century engraving from the author's collection).

Various strands of evidence are suggestive of the following scenario for Alexander's first tomb at Memphis. It seems that there existed an empty sarcophagus and a partially complete tomb on the eastern side of the Serapeum temple complex in the Memphite necropolis of North Saqqara, which had been prepared for the last native Egyptian pharaoh, Nectanebo II (or Nakhthorheb). This man had been forced to flee south to Ethiopia in about 341BC to escape a Persian invasion. As far as we know, he never returned, so his intended tomb still lay vacant in 321BC. The empty sarcophagus was found in Alexandria in 1801 by Edward Daniel Clarke and shipped to the British Museum, where it remains on display (Figure N). Clarke recorded that the Alexandrians had asserted that it had once been the sarcophagus of Alexander the Great.

This makes sense, if Ptolemy had adapted Nectanebo's empty tomb to serve for Alexander. The hypothesis is corroborated by the fact that Auguste Mariette uncovered a temple with cartouches of Nectanebo II at the eastern end of the Serapeum in 1850-1851. Its main entrance was guarded by a lifesize semicircle of statues of Greek poets and philosophers (see a photo taken during the excavations in Figure O). A side-entrance was guarded by an array of four lions. A windowless chamber unearthed at the end of a side-passage neatly fits the sarcophagus in the British Museum. The statues include several figures of relevance to Alexander's career: especially Homer, Alexander's favourite poet, Pindar, whose house and descendants Alexander protected at Thebes, and Plato, who was the mentor of Aristotle, Alexander's own tutor.

Key Historical Issues

Figure N. The sarcophagus found in Alexandria and made for Nectanebo II: it may have housed Alexander's corpse after it reached Egypt (photo by the author).

Figure O. The semicircle of Greek philosophers and poets excavated by Mariette in the Serapeum at Saqqara (photo circa 1851).

It is, however, certain that Alexander's tomb was subsequently relocated to Alexandria as reported by Curtius 10.10.20 and therefore incorporated in the penultimate sentence of my reconstruction of Cleitarchus. Several ancient sources (Strabo 17.1.8, Aelian, *Varia Historia* 12.64 & Diodorus 18.28.3) fail even to mention the sojourn at Memphis, notwithstanding the fact that it probably lasted around forty years. But there is a clear indication of the duration of the first entombment at Pausanias 1.7.1, where it is stated that Philadelphus, the son of Ptolemy, transferred the body from Memphis to Alexandria. This cannot have happened before ~290BC, since Philadelphus was not born until 309-8BC. Most probably it happened shortly after his father's death at the beginning of 282BC. Presumably the sarcophagus was transferred with the corpse, thus explaining its presence in Alexandria two thousand years later.

If, therefore, Curtius was still following Cleitarchus at the end of his work, which is the most likely scenario, then Cleitarchus cannot have published his account of Alexander's career much earlier than 280BC. Furthermore, if we were to seek an historical event, which might have prompted Cleitarchus to publish his volumes *Concerning Alexander*, then we should be looking for something that concerned Alexander in Alexandria around 280BC, which I previously concluded in *Alexander the Great in India* were the most likely place and time for the instigation of Cleitarchus' work. Clearly, the transfer of Alexander's tomb to Alexandria is the outstanding candidate. Hence it is consistent and fitting that the move to Alexandria is the latest and last event in the present reconstruction of Cleitarchus' history.

In time for the second impression of this book, I have published an exciting new strand of evidence on Alexander's tomb in a third edition of my book on *The Quest for the Tomb of Alexander the Great* (January 2020) and in an article in the Egyptology Journal, Kmt, which appeared in its Fall 2020 issue.[492] For the details, the reader must refer to those accounts. However, in summary: I have been able to show that the Star-Shield Block from the foundations of the Basilica di San Marco in Venice (Figure K) is an exact fit as part of a tomb casing for the sarcophagus of Nectanebo II (Figure N). Both objects are 118cm tall. Furthermore, the original length of the Star-Shield Block may be inferred by assuming that its diagonal lance terminated in its missing lower right corner. This length too is exactly right for the Block to have formed a section of a tomb casing closely fitted to the sarcophagus. I have previously associated the Block with Alexander's tomb in Alexandria, because the Basilica di San Marco was originally built to house a set of mummified remains brought from Alexandria in AD828. This set of remains, supposed to belong to St Mark the Evangelist, had appeared in Alexandria in the last decade of the 4th century AD, whereas Alexander's corpse is last mentioned by Libanius (Oration 49.11-12) at the beginning of the same decade. That decade also saw the outlawing of paganism by the Christian Emperor Theodosius, which posed a problem for the Alexandrians, since Alexander had become recognised as a pagan god. I have argued that the fit between the Star-Shield Block and the sarcophagus supports my theory that the Alexandrians conveniently re-labelled Alexander's mummy as that of St Mark when paganism was outlawed.

---

[492] A. M. Chugg, "Was Alexander the Great Originally Interred in the Usurped Sarcophagus of Nectanebo II?" in Kmt: A Modern Journal of Egyptology, Vol. 31, Number 3, Fall 2020, pp.66-74.

Key Historical Issues

Is Arrian Reliable?

For many present and past aficionados of Alexander's story the infallibility of the "Official" tradition of Alexander historiography as represented by Arrian and the *Itinerarium Alexandri* has been and continues to be an article of faith. Since the Vulgate tradition, and Cleitarchus in particular, represents the main source of evidence for challenging this conviction, the particular question of Arrian's reliability is a cogent issue in pursuing the reconstruction of Cleitarchus, as he is the Vulgate's archetype.

Consequently, I will here discuss a list of cases where evidence from the Vulgate and elsewhere might appear to cast serious aspersions on Arrian's credibility. As a strong believer in the prioritisation of evidence over opinion, I am pleased to present this list here with some preliminary discussion of each point in the hope of at least chipping, if not cracking, the veneer of Arrian's plausibility. My objective is to rescue my readers from the trap that ensnares those faithful to the concept of Arrian's infallibility. Practitioners of this creed are progressively and inexorably compelled to disparage the accuracy of every other source of evidence, even and indeed often when they all agree. Those who adhere to this faith find themselves in the uncomfortable position of having to assert that Arrian alone managed to dissociate himself from a hideous conspiracy utterly to mislead posterity regarding Alexander's motivations and behaviour, which embroiled every other surviving authority from ancient times, despite that they wrote independently over a period of many centuries and were spread geographically right across the Graeco-Roman world.

However, the alternative view is not that Arrian is a bad source, for it is overly simplistic to describe any source as exclusively good or bad. Rather, to be specific: (a) he deliberately censored information concerning Alexander's personal life; (b) he had a rather poor grasp of the geography of Alexander's itinerary and the chronology of his campaigns; (c) he sometimes missed key strategic features in battles and sieges and misunderstood Persian and Macedonian terminology through sheer remoteness from the context of the events. He was after all more distant from Alexander in time than we are from the era of Elizabeth 1 and some of the things he read in his sources were as obscure to him as much of the language used by Shakespeare is to us: what are bilboes, bolters and bombards, for example? Neither are all Arrian's flaws his alone. As I have suggested elsewhere (originally in *Alexander the Great in India*, p.39), there are reasons to suppose that the account of Alexander's campaigns by Arrian's most important source, the memoir of Ptolemy Soter, was substantially censored by the Ptolemaic regime in the aftermath of Ptolemy's death and prior to its posthumous publication.

1)   Arrian gives an incorrect lifespan for Alexander at *Anabasis* 7.28.1

The facts are straightforward. Arrian, *Anabasis Alexandrou* 7.28.1 asserts: "According to Aristobulus, Alexander lived thirty-two years and eight months;

his reign lasted twelve years and the same eight months." He had previously introduced his *Anabasis Alexandrou* at 1.1.1 with the words: "We are told that the death of Philip occurred in the archonship of Pythodelus at Athens; then around about twenty, Alexander succeeded, as Philip's son, and arrived at the Peloponnese."

The date of Alexander's death is well known: Plutarch, *Alexander* 76.4 relates that the king's own journal, known as the *Ephemerides* and kept by his secretary, Eumenes of Cardia, stated that Alexander died towards evening on the 28th day of the Macedonian month Daisios. Because this is a lunar date, which can be back-calculated astronomically, we are certain that this was 10th June 323BC in the Julian calendar (or 5th June 323BC in the Gregorian calendar).[493] Plutarch also mentions that Aristobulus stated that Alexander died on the 30th Daisios. Because a lunar month is 29.53 days long on average, nearly half the months in Greek lunar calendars only had 29 days. In such months, the Greeks gave the 29th day the name of the 30th day (i.e. thereby indicating that it was indeed the last day of the month). It appears that Daisios in 323BC was just such a "hollow" month, so Aristobulus meant that he heard of Alexander's death on 11th June 323BC. Similarly, a contemporaneous Babylonian astronomical record has been shown to give 11th June 323BC for Alexander's death. The proper inference is that Alexander died late on 10th June and that Eumenes, being a member of Alexander's inner circle of Friends, was aware of this and recorded it in the *Ephemerides*. However, the news was not made public until the next day. It is quite credible that it was concealed for a matter of hours by Alexander's Friends and Bodyguards, because we are also told (Plutarch, *Alexander* 76.4 and Arrian, *Anabasis Alexandrou* 7.26.1) that a few days beforehand the troops had insisted on being let in to see Alexander, **because they believed that news of his death was being suppressed by his Friends and Bodyguards.**

Thus, if Arrian were correct about Alexander's lifespan of 32 years and 8 months, Alexander would have to have been born in October of 356BC. But in fact, this is flatly contradicted by a considerable weight of evidence from elsewhere. In particular, Plutarch, *Alexander* 3.2 provides an explicit date for Alexander's birth that is at odds with Arrian: "Alexander was born on the sixth day of the month Hecatombaeon, which the Macedonians call Loios, the same day on which the temple of Artemis at Ephesus was burnt down." Hecatombaeon was the first month of the Attic year, which began at the first New Moon after the Summer Solstice. The Julian calendar date can therefore easily be reckoned (e.g. from modern calculations of ancient Lunar eclipses, which necessarily occurred at Full Moon) to have been 20th July 356BC.

The burning of the Temple of Artemis at Ephesus was very much an historical event in the Summer of 356BC. An arsonist called Herostratus set it ablaze in a

---

[493] That Plutarch really is using a very old citation from the *Ephemerides* is amply supported by the fact that he uses an antique Athenian format for specifying the days of the month, which fell out of fashion within a quarter of a century after Alexander's death.

Key Historical Issues

bid to immortalise his name amongst posterity: an objective that he achieved at the cost of his immediate execution. The incident was related in some detail by Theopompus in his lost work on *Hellenics* and the circumstances are also mentioned in some surviving ancient texts (e.g. Strabo 14.1).

Both Plutarch, *Alexander* 3.4-5 and Justin 12.16.6 tell the story that news of Alexander's birth reached his father, Philip, whilst he was besieging Potidaea on the isthmus of the westernmost peninsula of Chalcidice. They note that two other pieces of good news reached Philip at about the same time: a Macedonian victory over the Illyrians and the triumph of Philip's team in the Olympic four-horse chariot race.

Fortunately, there is now a basis to date the Olympic victory quite closely. A. E. Samuel concluded that "we are probably safe in accepting the evidence that the festival culminated with the full moon"[494] and subsequently Stephen G. Miller[495] argued convincingly that the Olympic festival culminated with religious ceremonies at the second full moon after the Summer Solstice. That can be accurately calculated as 30th July (Julian calendar) in 356BC (the solstice was on about 26th June in that era). The contests would most probably have preceded this date by a few days.

We should suppose that the event that instigated the story of the triple news in Plutarch and Justin was Philip's announcement of the three happy happenings to his troops at Potidaea. He would have done this partly to boost morale, but also because the occurrences were all public events that would have become known by other avenues of communication within a month at the outside. Furthermore, the troops would have known that Philip had had news of all of them directly. As a matter of trust therefore, Philip needed publicly to announce the news before it leaked out. Otherwise, his troops would have thought he was keeping secret things that they had a right to know from him: the succession, for example, was a matter of keen concern to all Macedonians.

It follows that the credibility of the triple news story requires principally that the events actually occurred sufficiently close together that there was not enough time for news of one to leak out before another had happened. This was necessary for Philip to be able to announce all three together as news items. If any event took place more than about a month from any other, this criterion could not be met (and even a separation of two weeks would be dubious). This is a stringent criterion. For example, it is completely broken by Arrian's implied autumnal date for Alexander's birth: it is quite impossible that Philip's Olympic victory could have been considered news three months after the event. But it is closely obeyed by Plutarch's date, because the gap between Alexander's birth and the subsequent Olympic victory does seem to be only about one week.

---

[494] A E Samuel, Greek & Roman Chronology, Munich 1972, p.194.

[495] Stephen G Miller, "The Date of Olympic Festivals" MDAI(A) 90 (1975) 215-31.

Innumerable satisfactory reasons might be postulated for the simultaneous announcement of Alexander's birth and the Olympic victory despite the former preceding the latter by a week. Here are some (not exhaustive) examples: (a) we don't know exactly where Alexander was born – if it was somewhere remote or isolated then news of it might have been delayed; (b) a weather event might have flooded or otherwise damaged the highways in Macedonia; (c) Olympias may have wished to wait to ensure that the child was healthy before sending a messenger or some post-natal crisis may have delayed the dispatch of a messenger; (d) Philip may have wished to await confirmation that the boy was healthy before announcing his birth (since the announcement would also have constituted his official acknowledgement of the boy as his heir and he may have had a cautionary experience in this respect with his mentally defective son, Arrhidaeus, previously); (e) Philip may have expected good news from the Olympics and deliberately delayed announcing Alexander's birth and his other victory for a few days in the hope of having a triple good news story for the sake of the extra boost to morale; (f) something untoward may have befallen the first messenger carrying the news of Alexander's birth… this list could be extended endlessly. The point is that exact simultaneity is not necessary for the story to be true, but the story does constrain the time range sufficiently to show that Plutarch's date is the correct birthday for Alexander.

If Justin and Plutarch used different primary sources, then Arrian's error is quite certain. However, supposing that Cleitarchus (the acknowledged common source of Plutarch and Trogus, whom Justin was epitomising) was the source of both of our accounts of the triple news story, is it at all likely that he made it up or got it from a bad source and failed to check it? He was probably writing in Alexandria just after 280BC. Given that it is inconceivable that the triple news was not publicly announced to the army (either directly by Philip or via briefing of his officers who in turn briefed their men), it would have to have been a famous event from recent history with some Macedonians still alive who had been at Potidaea. In these circumstances a complete invention stretches credulity. Cleitarchus cannot reasonably have been so careless of his credibility as to publish inventions that were so easily refuted.

Aelian, *Varia Historia* 2.25 also supports Plutarch's date. He discusses famous events that occurred on the sixth day of the month. He means the sixth day after the New Moon, because he references the Attic month of Thargelion, which strictly speaking began with the New Moon. Aelian concludes with a remark that Alexander's life both began and ended on that day of the month. He would seem to be wrong about Alexander's death (although a story was told that Alexander's body still seemed lifelike when the embalmers came to deal with it seven days after his death, which would have been the sixth day after a New Moon), but Aelian's comment accords well with Plutarch's date of the sixth day of the Attic month Hecatombaeon for Alexander's birth.

Key Historical Issues

There is even a third strand of evidence that bolsters Plutarch's date for Alexander's birth. There are circumstantial reasons to believe that Plutarch probably got many of his dates directly or indirectly from a famously pedantic Greek chronologist and historian of the late 4th and early 3rd centuries BC: Timaeus of Tauromenium. Though originally from Sicily, Timaeus was educated in Athens and spent most of his life there, so dating by the Attic calendar is to be expected of him. Diodorus and Polybius record his special attention to matters of accurate chronology.[496] There is strong evidence from elsewhere that both Cleitarchus and Plutarch were virtual disciples of the work of Timaeus. N. G. L. Hammond has argued that Plutarch's date of 6th Hecatombaeon for Alexander's birth comes from Timaeus, because Cicero gives many of the same details when he mentions the stories about Alexander's birth and he names Timaeus as his source in one instance.[497] Cleitarchus himself definitely used Timaeus, since Fragment 7 of Cleitarchus couples him with Timaeus as its co-source and it mentions the Heracleidae, Alexander's putative ancestors.[498] Then Fragment 36 of Cleitarchus from the Suda seems to make Cleitarchus a follower of Timaeus and Anaximenes.[499] This secondary path of association makes it quite likely that Plutarch got 6th Hecatombaeon from Cleitarchus (although Plutarch did also use Timaeus directly, for example, in his Life of Timoleon.) It should be noted that Plutarch also gives the correct Attic lunar date of 26th Boedromion for the Battle of Arbela/Gaugamela in his Life of Camillus (confirmed by eclipse evidence), so he is verified to be trustworthy on Alexander's dates. Conversely, Arrian thought that Arbela took place in the next Attic month of Pyanepsion (although he might be following a special festival version of the Attic calendar that was tampered with by the Athenian archon.)

Thus, firstly, Plutarch is supported by Aelian and, secondly, only his date is consistent with the simultaneous announcement of Alexander's birth and Philip's Olympic victory. Thirdly, the evidence suggesting that Timaeus was the ultimate source of Plutarch's date bolsters its credibility. Finally, the only other implied date for Alexander's birth from Arrian is not only non-specific in merely suggesting the month and at odds with all the other evidence, but it is also inherently flawed, because Arrian should not have stated that Alexander was "around about twenty" at his accession, but exactly twenty to the nearest month. The last point actually tells us what may in fact have occurred: Aristobulus, Arrian's source for these chronological details, probably stated that Alexander was "around about twenty" at his accession and separately noted that he reigned for twelve years and eight months. Both of these statements are correct. But

---

[496] Diodorus 5.1.3 & Polybius 12.11.1.

[497] N. G. L. Hammond, Sources for Alexander the Great (Cambridge 1993) 19-20; Jacoby 566 F150a of Timaeus (Cicero, N.D. 2.69); Cicero, Div. 1.47; Hammond also believed that Timaeus was born in the same year as Alexander.

[498] Jacoby 137 F7 (Clement of Alexandria, Strom. 1.139.4).

[499] Jacoby 137 F36 (Suda s.v. εχετον).

Arrian misleadingly took the initiative to combine the two statements together to reach a lifespan for Alexander of thirty-two years and eight months, when the truth is thirty-two years ten months and twenty days.

In a last-ditch defence of their idol, some Arrian disciples have even tried to argue that birthdays did not matter in Alexander's time, so that all our information on Alexander's birthday was compiled a long time after the event and may therefore be doubted in favour of Arrian's *non sequiter*. However, this too is untrue. The date of birth always mattered greatly to the ancients not so much for the purpose of the celebration of birthdays as due to the need to be able to cast horoscopes accurately! You needed to know the configuration of the heavens at the time of birth to be able to do this. For this reason, the date of birth was even more crucial to them than it is to us for modern birthday anniversary celebration purposes.

2) Arrian suppresses the existence of Barsine, Alexander's mistress.

Arrian never mentions the existence of Barsine the daughter of Artabazus in either his *Anabasis*, his *Indica* or in his *Events after Alexander*. It is however beyond reasonable doubt that she existed, that she became Alexander's mistress after her capture at Damascus and that she had the very special distinction of being the mother of Alexander's elder (though illegitimate) son, Heracles. Both she and her son are widely referenced in the rest of the antique historical sources covering the period.

Arrian does mention Alexander's marriage to a daughter of Darius, whom he calls Barsine at *Anabasis* 7.4.4, but it is clear that this is actually a reference to the princess named Stateira in all other sources.

It is particularly astonishing that Arrian seems to have managed to maintain his silence on the existence of Barsine in the aftermath of Alexander's death. Admittedly we have only the summary by Photius of his *Events after Alexander* together with a few other fragments, but it is probably still significant that neither Barsine nor Heracles gains any mention at all. Other sources (Nepos, Strabo…) speak of the children (plural) of Alexander (i.e. Alexander IV, the son of Alexander and Roxane, *and* Heracles). Curtius (very probably following Cleitarchus) provides a gripping blow-by-blow account of the Macedonian Assembly held after Alexander's death at which Alexander's admiral, Nearchus, urged that Heracles should be made king.

Thirteen years later, after Alexander IV had been murdered on the orders of Cassander in 310BC, Polyperchon led another attempt to award Heracles the crown, which ended with Cassander bribing Polyperchon to do away with his protégé.

Devoid of these key elements the history of the era lacks proper coherence. It is as though the Civil War period had been edited out of English history. This constitutes an appalling degree of economy with the truth on the part of Arrian.

Key Historical Issues

Why did he do this? Seemingly, as a matter of principle, Arrian believed that history should remain silent on the "private" lives of public figures and he determinedly maintained this stance, even when their "private" activities had major ramifications on the public stage. Such censorship should have no place in the work of an authoritative historian, because it completely undermines the balanced treatment of historical subjects.

3) Arrian suppresses the existence of Bagoas, Alexander's eunuch lover.

Parallelling his treatment of Barsine, Arrian similarly omits all mention of Bagoas, the Persian eunuch, except that he includes "Bagoas the son of Pharnuches" in his list of trierarchs of the major vessels in the Indus river fleet (*Indica* 18.8). As I have explained in detail in *Alexander's Lovers*, "Bagoas the son of Pharnuches" was probably actually "Bagoas the Eunuch" in the original list, which Arrian appears to have transcribed from Nearchus's lost account. It would seem that Arrian stopped short of summarily editing out a name on the list, but nevertheless it may have been Arrian himself who disguised the identity of the individual by adapting his epithet into a patronymic (in Greek the two are fairly similar).

There is no appreciable doubt that Bagoas became a senior courtier and Alexander's lover shortly after his first meeting with Alexander in Hyrcania just after the murder of Darius. Bagoas was subsequently influentially involved in some significant historical events. Curtius 10.1.22-37 names him as the prosecutor and executioner (under Alexander's orders) of Orsines in 324BC. Arrian, *Anabasis* 6.29.2 also records the execution of Orsines, whom he calls Orxines, but deliberately avoids naming Bagoas by instead refering to Orsines having been hanged by "persons appointed by Alexander".

The start of Alexander's liaison with Bagoas more or less coincided with the beginning of the "orientalising" phase of Alexander's career. If, gentle reader, you are, as Arrian intended, denied all knowledge of this steamy love affair with Darius' most beautiful eunuch, you are, I fear, placed in a very poor position to comprehend and assess Alexander's ensuing behaviour!

4) Arrian deliberately understates the relationship between Alexander and Hephaistion

As well as censoring the existence of Barsine and Bagoas, key characters in Alexander's personal life, Arrian is highly economical in his comments on the relationship between Alexander and Hephaistion. He never actually mentions in his works on Alexander that they had been lovers. The closest Arrian gets to revealing the amorous aspect of their relationship is to draw a parallel between Alexander & Hephaistion and Achilles & Patroclus at *Anabasis* 7.16.8. Yet he does refer to the lover (*eromenos*) of Alexander in his *Discourses of Epictetus* 2.22.17 and he demonstrably means Hephaistion. He writes that Alexander burnt down the Temple of Asclepius when his lover died, whereas Arrian also confirms in his *Anabasis* 7.14.5 that Alexander razed this sanctuary at the time of Hephaistion's death. This shows that Arrian deliberately avoided being clear about the relationship in his *Anabasis*, since he clearly knew the truth. The Chiliarch was such an important figure on the public stage that Arrian could hardly avoid mentioning his career and the fact that he and Alexander were close, but anyone reading Arrian in isolation from the Vulgate sources and other incidental records of the relationship receives a misleadingly understated impression of the affair.

5) Arrian completely confuses the order of events in 328-327BC

There is a magnificent article by Bosworth that cogently argues the case for Arrian's account of Alexander's campaigns having become completely confused for the year beginning in the middle of 328BC.[500] Bosworth points out that Curtius gives a coherent account of that year's activities, provided we avoid the temptation to emend Curtius 7.10.15 to read *Margianum*, where the manuscripts read either *Marganiam* or *Marginiam*, and thereby to send Alexander off on a wild goose chase to Margiana (modern Merv) some 450km westwards, when Curtius and the Metz Epitome actually appear to be suggesting that the king was marching eastwards from Bactra. Then in Section III of his article, Bosworth shows that all sources other than Arrian treat the three great Rocks (that of Ariamazes, that of Sisimithres and that of Chorienes) similarly and that the sieges of two of them should be placed in the campaigning season of 328BC rather than in the spring of 327BC as in Arrian. He concludes that Arrian has become confused due to switching between his main sources, Ptolemy and Aristobulus, and that Ptolemy confused Chorienes with Sisimithres. He summarises the issue as follows: "Ptolemy has confused two different native leaders, who were both confirmed in their dominions by Alexander. It is a disturbing testimonial to the erratic nature of this contemporary source, and Ptolemy's deficiencies are made worse by Arrian's method of switching from source to source without any critical discussion of variants or contradictions. The errors and exaggerations of the one are compounded by the uncritical and negligent approach of the other."

6) Arrian repeatedly misinterprets the title Chiliarch used for Hephaistion and others in that role by terming it a cavalry command

The Chief Minister of the Persian Great King was known as the *Hazarapatis* (or *Hazarapatish*), which roughly translates from the Persian as "commander of a thousand". The Greeks in turn rendered this title fairly literally as *Chiliarch* on translating it into their own language. The incumbent was second only to the Great King himself in rank and prestige and he is stated to have been responsible for the running of the royal court, including admissions to audiences with the king. Cornelius Nepos, *Conon* 3.2-3 gives Tithraustes the title of Chiliarch serving the Persian King Artaxerxes II at the time of the audience of Conon early in the 4th century BC and Nepos goes on to assert that "without him, none could gain audience". Aelian, *Varia Historia* 1.21 describes probably the same Tithraustes as

---

[500] A. B. Bosworth, A Missing Year in the History of Alexander the Great, The Journal of Hellenic Studies, Vol. 101, 1981, pp. 17-39.

Key Historical Issues

the court official "who took messages to the king and presented petitioners" in the context of the embassy of Pelopidas in 367BC. Furthermore, a decade before Alexander's conquest, a eunuch called Bagoas had for a while virtually ruled the Persian Empire, whilst bearing the title of Chiliarch. The eunuch Bagoas is assigned the title of Chiliarch (e.g. by Diodorus 17.5.3) in the context of his kingmaking in Persia in the years 338-336BC: initially poisoning Artaxerxes III Ochus and placing his youngest son, Arses, on the throne, then in turn murdering Arses and replacing him with Darius III.

It is quite certain that Alexander appointed Hephaistion to this exalted rank, probably sometime after Gaugamela, though the exact date is uncertain. Arrian accords Hephaistion the title of Chiliarch in his *Anabasis*, but he associates it with Hephaistion's command of the senior regiment of the Companion Cavalry, which is odd, since the proper title for such an appointment was Hipparch.[501] It is likely that Arrian is mistakenly conflating Hephaistion's separate (and separately awarded) offices of Chiliarch (of the empire) and Hipparch of the senior regiment of the Companion Cavalry (the latter seems also to have entailed overall command of the Companion Cavalry, for Hephaistion is so described by Appian, *Syrian Wars* 57.)[502] However, Photius has provided an epitome of Arrian's lost *Events after Alexander*, which states that, after Alexander's death, Perdiccas was appointed "to command the Chiliarchy which Hephaistion had originally held" and that this "entrusted him with the entire kingdom" in the context of the joint-kingship of Alexander's infant son and imbecilic half-brother, who were of necessity mere puppets.[503] It looks as though Arrian knew that Hephaistion had commanded the senior regiment of the Companion Cavalry *and* had acted as Alexander's Chief Minister in his court by virtue of his title of Chiliarch, but that he failed to distinguish clearly between the two roles, perhaps because he did not understand the Persian origins of the title and consequently thought that "lord of a thousand" had to refer to Hephaistion's cavalry command in some way. In other contexts, the Greeks did use the word chiliarch to mean the commander of a military unit of a thousand men, so there exists some real potential for confusion.

Happily, Diodorus 18.3.4 removes any possible ambiguity by stating that Perdiccas, when he became Chiliarch after Alexander's death, relinquished command of the Companion Cavalry in favour of Seleucus:

---

[501] Arrian, *Anabasis* 7.14.10.
[502] NGL Hammond, Sources for Alexander the Great, Cambridge 1993, pp.296-7 reaches this conclusion and is supported by Jeanne Reames in her treatise on Hephaistion; James Romm notes in the Landmark Arrian in respect of Arrian, *Anabasis* 7.14.10 that, "It seems possible that Arrian has confused this newly created Chiliarchy with a separate office, command over the Companion cavalry..."; PA Brunt reaches the same conclusion in App. XXIV.4 of the Loeb Arrian, II p.511.
[503] This is Photius 92, Epitome of Arrian's Events after Alexander; Photius 82, Summary of Dexippus' Events after Alexander also mentions this (it is likely that Dexippus used Arrian's work or that they had a common source).

[Perdiccas] placed Seleucus in command of the cavalry of the Companions, a most distinguished office; for Hephaestion commanded them first, Perdiccas after him, and third the above-named Seleucus.

This makes it unambiguously clear that the cavalry command (Hipparchy) and the ministerial role at court (Chiliarchy) cannot have been indissolubly one and the same, as Arrian seems to have believed. Furthermore Diodorus explains:-

Antipater also made his own son Cassander Chiliarch and second in authority. The position and rank of Chiliarch had first been brought to fame and honour by the Persian kings, and afterwards under Alexander it gained great power and glory at the time when he became an admirer of this and all other Persian customs. Diodorus 18.48.5

Obviously, Alexander's Chiliarch can only have been Hephaistion. Furthermore, Diodorus' statement that Alexander revived this title at the same time as he embraced other Persian customs makes it difficult to date Hephaistion's appointment later than the time of the proskynesis experiment (i.e. 328BC). His court management responsibilities as Chiliarch would also help to explain why it was Hephaistion who organised this experiment. It might further be argued that Hephaistion seemed already to be acting with the authority of a Chiliarch in the case of the Philotas affair. The common source of Diodorus 17.77.4 and Curtius 6.6.1-8 on the subject of Alexander's imitation of the kings of Asia[504] was Cleitarchus and it is clear from their accounts that Cleitarchus placed Alexander's main phase of "Persianising" in the immediate aftermath of the death of Darius in around August 330BC. This was also the period in which the previous Chiliarch, Nabarzanes,[505] surrendered to Alexander in Hyrcania, so this was the most opportune occasion for the appointment of Hephaistion as his replacement, since Nabarzanes was sent off into retirement.

However, as already noted, Arrian, *Anabasis* 7.14.10 erroneously suggests a combination of the Chiliarchy with Hephaistion's cavalry command in the immediate aftermath of the Chiliarch's death:

Alexander made no one else chiliarch of the Companion cavalry in Hephaestion's place so that Hephaestion's name would not disappear from that unit. The Chiliarchy was still called Hephaistion's, and the standard went before it which had been made by his order.

Note that Arrian had previously termed Hephaistion a Hipparch at *Anabasis* 3.27.4, when he was appointed to joint command of the Companion Cavalry with Cleitus.

However, Plutarch, *Eumenes* 1.2 records that during Alexander's lifetime, just after the death of Hephaistion:

---

[504] Cf. Plutarch, *Alexander* 45; Justin 12.3.8-12.

[505] Arrian, *Anabasis Alexandrou*, 3.21.1 & 3.23.4; Curtius 6.5.22-3.

Key Historical Issues

...[Eumenes] received the command in the cavalry which Perdiccas had held, when Perdiccas, after Hephaestion's death, was advanced to that officer's position.

This must mean that, whilst Alexander still reigned, Perdiccas received the command of the senior hipparchy (regiment) and thereby became overall commander of the Companion Cavalry, whilst Eumenes took over Perdiccas' original hipparchy. Consequently, it is clear that Hephaistion's cavalry command was filled by Alexander, but it does seem to be true that Hephaistion's *ministerial role* as Chiliarch was never filled until after Alexander's death.

Arrian repeats his association of the Chiliarchy with a cavalry command in his work on *Events After Alexander*,[506] where he speaks of Cassander having been granted the title of Chiliarch "of the cavalry". Similarly, in *Anabasis* 3.21.1 Nabarzanes is described as "Chiliarch of the cavalry" (and as Darius' Chiliarch at 3.26.4). It is therefore quite clear that the mistake is Arrian's, rather than being due to an error in transcription of some archetypal manuscript of his works. A transcriptional error is unlikely to have occurred three times in two different works. The double meaning of the term chiliarch must have confused Arrian. The alternative would be that the reports of a separation of the command of the Companion Cavalry from the Chiliarchy are inventions and that the completely consistent description of the Chiliarchy independently provided by all the other surviving ancient sources on the subject is wrong.

A recent scholarly article on the Chiliarchy potently illustrates the danger of trying to maintain that this obvious misunderstanding by Arrian concerning the nature of the Chiliarchy was in fact the correct view.[507] The author is led to infer that Arrian's epitomiser, Photius, flagrantly misrepresented the *Events after Alexander*, which he had just read, in stating that the Chiliarchy entailed the rule of the whole empire (in circumstances where the joint kings were not capable of exercising power in their own right). Furthermore, he invents the existence of two different Chiliarchies among the Persians, though the many ancient sources on the Persian Chiliarchy always refer to a single person. He makes the Chiliarchy basically a military command of cavalry, though all sources save Arrian describe it essentially as a court position. And he maintains Arrian's confusion between the Chiliarchy and command of the Companion Cavalry and in so doing makes Seleucus the Chiliarch when he led them after Alexander's death, though no source awards Seleucus the title. In other words, he infers many and varied mistakes and distortions concerning the Chiliarchy by practically every other source and invents several different sorts of Chiliarchy in order to avoid even contemplating the possibility of an understandable single point error by Arrian. He fails even to point out that, without Arrian's unilateral association of the Chiliarchy with a cavalry command, everything else available from all the other sources on the

---

[506] F1.38 epitomised by Photius 92 [72a or 9.38].

[507] Alexander Meeus, Some Institutional Problems Concerning the Succession to Alexander the Great: Prostasia and Chiliarchy, Historia, Band 58, Heft 3, 2009, pp. 287-310.

subject of the Chiliarchy is in complete agreement to the effect that the Chiliarch was a court official in both the Achaemenid and the subsequent Macedonian regimes, who acted as the deputy of the monarch and controlled the running of the monarch's court.

7) Arrian's location of the homeland of the Malli/Oxydracae north of the confluence of the Acesines with the Indus is dubious and his account of Alexander's chest wound is misleading

There is a direct contradiction between Vulgate sources and Arrian regarding the location of the war between Alexander and the Malli in alliance with the Oxydracae. The Vulgate tradition reports that the Oxydracae mounted their resistance from the foothills of a mountain (*sub radicibus montis castra posuit*, Curtius 9.4.24) located south of the confluence of the River Acesines (modern Chenab) with the River Indus, whereas Arrian places Alexander's near fatal chest wound to the north of the same confluence. The proximity of the mountains during this confrontation is an important geographical clue. The nearest substantial hills to the part of the Acesines just north of the confluence are of the order of 80km west of the Acesines and well beyond the Indus itself. However, about 50km downstream of the confluence the mountain foothills come within a couple of tens of km of the western bank of the river. Furthermore, Arrian, *Anabasis* 6.6.1 has Alexander march his troops through a waterless country to launch a surprise attack on the Malli. Although there are arid areas to the east of the confluence, the dry country approaches the river most closely between 50km and 100km downstream of the confluence. Also, in this war, Alexander was struck in the chest by an arrow. Arrian, *Anabasis* 6.10.1 cites Ptolemy for the observation that breath as well as blood spurted from the wound, which would indicate a perforated lung. Alexander would have been very lucky to survive such a wound and recovery would have been a protracted process, yet our sources have him on his feet and mounting a horse within a couple of weeks.[508] This rapid a recovery is much more consistent with an alternative tradition that the arrow lodged in Alexander's breastbone or a rib "in front of the heart" and therefore did not perforate his lung (Plutarch, *Moralia* 327B, 341C-D, 345A and Plutarch, *Alexander* 63.6).

8) Arrian locates the theft of Bucephalus among the Uxii against the weight of the evidence from other sources

Arrian, *Anabasis* 5.19.6 only mentions the theft of Alexander's steed, Bucephalus, in the context of a brief retrospective after the horse's death at the time of the Battle of the Hydaspes. However, to quote A B Bosworth[509]: "[Arrian] dates it erroneously to the Uxian campaign." All other surviving accounts (Curtius 6.5.18-21, Diodorus 17.76.5-8, Plutarch, *Alexander* 44.3) place the theft among the Mardians near the southern shores of the Caspian Sea. Bosworth subsequently

---

[508] Arrian, *Anabasis* 6.13 and Curtius 9.6.1-3.

[509] A. B. Bosworth, Commentary on Arrian's History of Alexander, Vol 1, OUP, 1980, p.353.

allowed the possibility that Arrian was correct on the grounds that all the other surviving sources might have obtained their information from Cleitarchus.[510] He further observed that there was another tribe called Mardians, who occupied a region south of Persepolis, whereas the Uxii were based northwest of Persepolis. Since the two tribes were near neighbours, the Uxii might perhaps have been regarded as synonymous with the Persian Mardians and Cleitarchus might have confused the Persian Mardians with the Caspian Mardians. Of course, it is equally true that the confusion between the Persian Mardians and the Caspian Mardians might have been perpetrated by Arrian or his source (Ptolemy or Aristobulus) and the fact that he mentions the matter only briefly and out of context militates in favour of this being the case. Plutarch, Curtius and Diodorus all tell the tale in its historical context and were all well aware of many primary sources on Alexander and so were in a position to correct any error in the story. Furthermore, N. G. L. Hammond concludes that Plutarch did not use Cleitarchus for the tale of the theft due to differences in his account relative to Curtius and Diodorus.[511]

9) Arrian's account of Persepolis is so contracted as seriously to mislead and his omission of Thais is highly suspect.

Arrian, *Anabasis* 3.18.10-12 does not mention Persepolis by name at the time Alexander went there, but merely speaks of Alexander capturing the treasure of Persia before the garrison could plunder it and confusingly refers to Alexander capturing a treasure from Parsagada in the next sentence. He then mentions the burning of the palace, without saying exactly where the palace was, but notes that Parmenion opposed this decision. Arrian's account is especially misleading in that it glosses over the undoubted fact that Alexander only burnt the palace about three or four months after he arrived at Persepolis and Arrian also omits mention of the role of Thais in inciting the conflagration, which is a famous story from the Vulgate (Curtius 5.7.3-7, Diodorus 17.72, Plutarch, *Alexander* 38.2). In particular, Athenaeus 13.576E cites Cleitarchus directly on the matter of the incineration of Persepolis, saying that Thais subsequently married Ptolemy after Alexander's death and bore him two sons and a daughter. Since Cleitarchus seems to have been a resident of Alexandria when he wrote his *History Concerning Alexander* between 280-250BC, it is rather unlikely that he made this story up. It follows that Arrian again wrote economically and sanitisingly concerning the truth regarding the burning of Persepolis.

---

[510] A. B. Bosworth, Commentary on Arrian's History of Alexander, Vol 2, OUP, 1995, pp.314-315.

[511] N. G. L. Hammond, Sources for Alexander the Great: An Analysis of Plutarch's 'Life' and Arrian's Anabasis Alexandrou, Cambridge, 1993, p.78.

10) **Arrian (in following Ptolemy) has Alexander led to and from the oasis at Siwa by talking serpents and he places the foundation of Alexandria prior to Siwa and cites an implausible return route directly to Memphis.**

Ptolemy's talking serpents (*Anabasis* 3.3.5) are an obvious absurdity. Hardly anyone argues otherwise. However, Arrian, *Anabasis* 3.4.5 notes that Aristobulus recorded that Alexander returned from Siwa via the same route by which he got there, but then asserts that Ptolemy had written that Alexander returned by a different route directly to Memphis. He does not say what that route was, but there are a couple of oases almost in the path of a return route directly eastwards across the desert, so that route is not entirely impracticable. Therefore, a return route via these oases to Memphis has been defended by Arrian's advocates. However, it would have been very dangerous relative to a return to the Mediterranean coast. It would have risked getting lost again, as had happened on the way to Siwa, whereas a return to the coast had the merit that any vaguely northward bearing would eventually contact the Mediterranean.

More importantly, most sources (Curtius 4.8.1-2, Diodorus 17.52, Justin 11.11.13, Pseudo-Callisthenes 1.30-32) state that Alexander founded Alexandria on the way back from Siwa, in which case he *must* have returned along the coast. Nevertheless, Plutarch has been read as supporting Arrian by describing the foundation of Alexandria prior to the visit to Siwa, but this support is of little value in that Plutarch often departs from strict chronological order and does not actually state that the foundation preceded the oracle visit. Furthermore, (as I explain in more detail in addressing whether Alexander visited Upper Egypt below) the date of 25th Tybi (7th April in the Julian calendar) given by Pseudo-Callisthenes 1.32.10 for the foundation of Alexandria tends to support a foundation subsequent to the Siwa visit.

11) **Arrian gives Porus a preposterously widely spaced formation comprising too many elephants at the Battle of the Hydaspes**

Arrian, *Anabasis* 5.15.4-5 claims that Porus deployed 200 elephants each spaced at least 100 feet from its neighbours at the Battle of the Hydaspes, whereas Curtius 8.13.6 and the *Metz Epitome* 54 mention only 85 elephants and Polyaenus 4.3.22 states that they were distributed at 50-foot intervals. The Cleitarchan elephant formation is therefore a very reasonable 1275m long, whereas Arrian's figures imply an Indian front line over 6km long! It does not even require any military expertise to realise that Arrian's figures are absurd. Arrian's source (probably Ptolemy for this material, since he is named as the source at the start of *Anabasis* 5.15) would seem to have indulged in rounding up and doubling of the numbers for the sake of impressing his readership.

Key Historical Issues

12) Arrian says that troops died of thirst in the Gedrosian desert, whereas Alexander had wells dug in advance and in actuality the troops starved to the point of lacking the energy to march on due to shortage of provisions

The Vulgate account of the Gedrosian disaster is quite clear, logical and persuasive. Firstly, Alexander had realised that water supplies would be a critical factor on some of the drier sections of his route, so he sent teams ahead to dig wells to supply the army. Secondly, it is implicit in the Vulgate account that Alexander had also realised that a shortage of provisions might be encountered: hence his plan was that the fleet should help to supply the army and potentially vice versa as the need arose. The main factor to upset this plan was that the fleet became trapped in port in India by persistently adverse winds until Alexander and the army had already completed the majority of the trek. Out of concern for his missing fleet, Alexander tried to keep the army's route in touch with the exceptionally barren coastline. This policy in combination with the absence of supplies from the fleet led the army to run short of provisions. Eventually, Alexander was forced to march inland in search of food, either to be obtained from the territory itself or by bringing his forces within range of re-supply from Alexander's eastern Satrapies. However, it took weeks of marching across >200km of virtual desert to reach a location (apparently the Gedrosian capital of Pura) such as to relieve the supply shortage. By that time many troops, non-combatants and baggage train attendants had literally succumbed to starvation. They fell by the wayside because they lacked the energy to keep up with the forced march, not due to dehydration. There is no evidence in the Vulgate of any real difficulty with water supplies. The territory is not even nowadays so dry that the policy of digging wells would not be satisfactory and it appears to have been wetter, if anything, in antiquity. Arrian seems to have indulged in a false supposition regarding his statement (*Anabasis* 6.24.4-6) that the troops died of thirst: he simply had not grasped the strategic situation or the vast size of the Gedrosian wastes, in which it was indeed feasible for troops literally to starve to death even when their need for water had been catered for.

The severity of the disaster has been overstated due to Plutarch's statement (*Alexander* 66.2-3) that only a quarter (~30,000 troops) of the army that had entered India came through Gedrosia. Plutarch points out that Alexander had gone into India with an army of 120,000 men, so he draws the naïve equation that the casualty rate on the march back was 75%. However, we know that the majority of Alexander's forces returned with Craterus via a longer and relatively safe inland route through Arachosia. Furthermore, there appears to have been almost no attrition among the senior men during the Gedrosian march, so the death rate among the rank and file was probably not so dramatic as some of the rather sensationalist rhetoric found in the Vulgate would imply.

13) **Arrian says that Gaugamela took place 600 stades from Arbela, but that would put it on the western side of the Tigris – actually it appears to have been no more that 300 stades from Arbela**

A full analysis of the site of the Battle of Arbela/Gaugamela has been given above, but even a cursory look at the undisputed aspects of the geography (e.g. location of Arbela relative to the River Tigris) makes it obvious that Arrian's assertion that the battle took place 600 stades from Arbela is completely wrong. Both of the feasible alternatives for the battle site are about 300 stades from Arbela as the crow flies and no more than 400 stades as the roads may have wound.

14) **Arrian fails to mention the Persian deployment of caltrops at Gaugamela as the reason for Alexander's move to the right as noted in Polyaenus 4.3.17 & Curtius 4.13.36**

It is well attested that Alexander performed a very peculiar maneuver in the early stages of the Battle of Arbela/Gaugamela. He advanced his right wing, including his own position with the Companion Cavalry, at an oblique angle, so as greatly to extend his position to the right. Normally, this would have been to court disaster, due to the potential consequential thinning of his own centre rendering him extremely vulnerable to a frontal cavalry charge by the Persians. However, the explanation in the Vulgate sources makes complete sense of this curious situation. Curtius 4.13.36-37 tells us that Alexander had received intelligence from a Persian deserter (named Bion) that Darius had planted iron spikes to bring down charging cavalry (technically known as caltrops) over a large area of the battlefield confronting Alexander's right wing. Alexander moved rightwards towards unprepared ground in the first instance simply to evade these obstacles. He did not need to worry about the thinning of his centre in consequence, because they in turn were protected from a Persian cavalry charge by the same caltrop field. In fact, Darius had unintentionally made it more difficult for the Persians to use their superior numbers to outflank the Macedonians by his planting of the caltrop field.

Arrian's account of the battle is, however, completely devoid of any mention of the caltrops. He is clear that Alexander advanced to the right so as to get his right wing clear of the ground prepared by the Persians, but he notes only that the rougher ground was more difficult for Darius's chariots. He does not explain the more pressing reason for Alexander to have avoided the prepared ground. This has the effect of making Alexander's strategy seem arbitrary and rather serendipitous, for, as all the sources make clear, his troops had to confront the scythed chariots anyway. It leaves Arrian's benighted readership in a complete state of incomprehension regarding what was really going on.

Key Historical Issues

15) Arrian places the final peace offer from Darius during the siege of Tyre, whereas it actually came just before Arbela

Arrian, *Anabasis* 2.25 records that a delegation from Darius offered Alexander all the territory to the west of the Euphrates during the siege of Tyre. But other sources (Curtius 4.11.1 and Diodorus 17.39.1) state that this offer was made only much later, just a matter of days before the Battle of Arbela/Gaugamela. Alexander could have used such a letter in the context of the siege of Tyre to compel the capitulation of the city, since it would have shown the Tyrians that resistance in the name of Darius was pointless. Furthermore, he could have secured his territories in the Levant whilst he visited Egypt by accepting and still have found some cause to resume the war a year or two later. For these reasons it is not strategically credible that Darius made such an offer during the siege or that Alexander refused it at that juncture, whilst Tyrian resistance was proving so determined.

16) Arrian claims that Alexander wore the tiara and Median dress, whereas Plutarch and Eratosthenes state explicitly that he did not and the Cleitarchan sources say only that he wore the diadem

Concerning Alexander's adoption of some features of the Persian king's attire, Arrian writes:

Nor do I at all approve the fact that, though a descendant of Heracles, Alexander exchanged the dress of the Medes for that traditional amongst the Macedonians and that he substituted the tiara of the Persians, whom he himself had conquered, for the headgear he had long worn.

Arrian, Anabasis Alexandrou 4.7.4

This is directly contradicted by Plutarch with more authoritative details:

Alexander did not adopt the famous Median fashion of dress, which was altogether barbaric and strange, nor did he assume trousers, or sleeved vest, or tiara, but carefully devised a fashion which was midway between the Persian and the Median, more modest than the one and more stately than the other.

Plutarch, Alexander 45.2

In support of Plutarch, the other Vulgate Tradition sources refer only to the diadem without mention of the tiara (or *kitaris* or *kidaris*): see *Metz Epitome* 2; Diodorus 17.77.5; Curtius 6.6.4; Justin 12.3.8; Ephippus in Athenaeus 537E.

Furthermore Fragment 30 of Eratosthenes in Jacoby FGrHist 241 also confirms that Alexander did not adopt the tiara, making it enormously probable that Arrian is again mistaken on this point:

Alexander did not favour the Median raiment, but preferred the Persian, for it was much simpler than the Median. Since he deprecated the unusual and theatrical varieties of foreign adornment, such as the tiara and the full-sleeved jacket and trousers, he wore a composite dress adapted from both Persian and Macedonian fashion as Eratosthenes has recorded.

Plutarch, Moralia 330A

For a full discussion see P. A. Brunt, *Loeb Classical Library: Arrian, History of Alexander and Indica* 1 (Harvard 1976) Appendix XIV.2 533.

In each of these instances it can clearly be seen that there is a great weight of evidence that refutes Arrian's version. In many further instances, the balance of probability and good sense would appear strongly to favour the Vulgate over Arrian, although it is also the case that in a wide range of other areas there is no meaningful disagreement between the Official and Vulgate traditions.

The Nature and Genesis of Cleitarchus' Account

Introduction

The history of the reign of Alexander the Great composed by Cleitarchus of Alexandria ranks as perhaps the most influential of all the many accounts of the King's career, despite the loss of the original text of Cleitarchus' work and the paucity of the attributed fragments collected by Müller and Jacoby. Cleitarchus was evidently the principal source for the authors of the so-called Vulgate tradition of Alexander historiography, which survives in the works of Diodorus, Curtius and Justin as well as in the anonymous *Metz Epitome*. Even Plutarch's writings on Alexander incorporate substantial Cleitarchan elements, and there are recognisable, though unattributed, fragments of Cleitarchus in a host of other ancient sources, such as Pliny, Aelian and Polyaenus.

The most important structural issues regarding Cleitarchus' work are the questions of the number of books into which it was divided and the periods that were covered by each book. Prior to the present research, no clear answer had been proposed even on the matter of the number, although it is apparent that there were at least twelve, since Jacoby's Fragment 6 of Cleitarchus is attributed to his twelfth book. Pearson thought that there were "two or three books more" beyond Book Twelve, whilst Bosworth has commented that there were "perhaps as many as fifteen" and Heckel has speculated that Cleitarchus' work was published "in 15 books?"

It is the purpose of this discussion to present a revised analysis of the structure of Cleitarchus' work and to propose a specific book structure that is consistent with all the available evidence. This will proceed in the first instance through a fresh look at the Fragments of Cleitarchus with a focus on resolving the problem that it has not been precisely clear where all of these Fragments, including some of those with Book Numbers, fit into the overall history. Secondly, it will be argued that echoes of many of the Book termini of Cleitarchus exist within the text of the seventeenth book of Diodorus. The combination of these two types of evidence will then be shown to imply a thirteen-book structure for Cleitarchus' work corresponding to one book for each year of Alexander's reign. This in turn will permit some pertinent observations on Cleitarchus' organisational principles as well as his quality and fidelity as an historian. Furthermore, it transpires that Cleitarchus located his book termini at the anniversaries of Alexander's accession at least as far as his fifth book and this has enabled me to propose a date for the assassination of Philip II of Macedon for the first time. It now appears that Alexander the Great acceded to the throne of Macedon on 27th September 336BC and that the duration of his reign was 12 years 8 months and 14 days in the Julian calendar.

Concerning Alexander the Great by Andrew Chugg

The lines of argument that are employed in fitting the fragments of Cleitarchus back together to discover the overall structure of his work are very much analogous to the methods employed by archaeologists to reconstruct fragmentary ancient vases and pots. Such reconstructions are necessarily guided by an hypothesis of the overall form in their early stages, but there is continual testing and sometimes adaptation of this hypothesis as the individual pieces are placed. The tension is whether the small-scale fitting of the individual sherds is consistent with the large-scale form and any design painted or impressed upon it. If such self-consistency between the various fitting criteria can be established, then that constitutes overwhelming evidence for the correctness of the reconstruction. The fitting requirements are so stringent and multi-faceted in practice that there will rarely be more than one viable reconstruction. If any scholars were to suggest that the evidence for the validity of the reconstruction derived from the self-consistency of the reconstructed object itself amounts to a circular argument, then there are thousands of reconstructed vases in museums around the world to demonstrate the fallacy in their position. So too, in the reconstruction of Cleitarchus, it is necessary to find a structure that accommodates a very large number of Fragments and other pieces of evidence. If such a structure can be established, then it gains much credence from the fact that it is extremely statistically improbable that so many strands of evidence could by chance all be found to fit an incorrect structure.

A successful reconstruction of a vase should also be expected to reveal additional design features that fit the object yet more intimately within the cultural and archaeological context in which it was discovered. So too the reconstruction of Cleitarchus presented here reveals many additional triangulations with the rest of the source evidence on Alexander. For example, the date of 27th September 336BC implied by the reconstructed structure of Cleitarchus' work for Alexander's accession turns out to be the autumnal equinox. (There is a five-day offset between the Julian and Gregorian calendars in Alexander's epoch, so 27th September in the Julian is 22nd September in the back-projected Gregorian calendar.) We know from the sources that Philip II was assassinated at a great festival of the gods to which he had invited delegates from around the Greek world.[512] Holy festivals at the equinoxes are particularly common and likely, because of the traditional linkage between astronomy and astrology. For Philip it served the additional purpose of providing a clear way of communicating the date of the event around Greece at a time when every city-state maintained a slightly different calendar system.

The order in which these structural analyses will proceed may be outlined as follows:

    a) Firstly, an analysis of the structure of Cleitarchus' book, because this permits an early review of the identified fragments and an understanding

---

[512] Diodorus 16.91.4-6.

of how they fit into the work (surprisingly, some have not previously been placed and the book divisions have not previously been established.)

b) An analysis of Cleitarchus' sources, since this is a key ingredient in addressing the vexed questions of the date and character of his work.

c) General considerations regarding the date of composition of Cleitarchus based on the Vulgate manuscripts and the fragments published by Jacoby.

d) Decisive clues on the dating and career of Cleitarchus from the newly published papyrus fragment POxy LXXI 4808.

e) The character of Cleitarchus' work and how to recognise Cleitarchan material.

f) A review of the main sources of extant Cleitarchan material.

g) Definition of the *modus operandi* followed in the reconstruction of Cleitarchus' work.

Connecting the Timespan and the Number of Books

Relative to his fame and influence, the attributed fragments of Cleitarchus are surprisingly sparse.[513] Nevertheless, it will prove relevant to note by way of introduction that we are well-informed on the matter of the title of his history of Alexander, which is his sole attested work. Athenaeus thrice mentions that it was known, albeit blandly, as Περὶ Ἀλεξάνδρου or Περὶ Ἀλέξανδρον Ἱστορίαι, which I translate as *Concerning Alexander* or *The History Concerning Alexander*.[514] Since Athenaeus is corroborated in this matter by the *Florilegium* of Stobaeus[515] and the Scholia on Apollonius Rhodius,[516] there is little doubt that he is correct.

Only six of Jacoby's Fragments preserve any mention of the book numbers whence they were abstracted. The key evidence for the total number of books is presented by the last and latest of these: Fragment 6 describes the disdain for death professed by the Indian gymnosophists and is attributed to Book 12 by Diogenes Laertius.[517]

There are only two occasions when this topic is at all likely to have been discussed by Cleitarchus: either in the context of Alexander's meeting with the gymnosophists in India or else at the ceremony for the self-immolation of

---

[513] F. Jacoby, *Die Fragmente der griechischen Historiker (FGrHist)*, Part II B (Berlin 1929) no. 137.

[514] Jacoby FGrHist 137 F1, F2, F30 (Athenaeus, *Deipnosophistae* 148D-F, 530A, 586CD).

[515] Jacoby FGrHist 137 F3 (Stobaeus, *Florilegium* 4.20.73).

[516] Jacoby FGrHist 137 F17 (Scholia on Apollonius Rhodius 2.904).

[517] Jacoby FGrHist 137 F6 (Diogenes Laertius 1.6).

Calanus (a gymnosophist, who is erroneously called Caranus in Diodorus[518]), which took place in Susianê early in 324BC. The estimate of a total of as many as 15 books for Cleitarchus, which is countenanced by some modern experts,[519] might be justified on the assumption that Fragment 6 refers to the meeting in India, but actually the suicide of Calanus is inherently more likely, because there is a detailed account of Calanus' end in Diodorus, which makes specific reference to the theme of his indifference to his death (note however that this event falls within a large lacuna in Curtius):

True to his own creed, Caranus cheerfully mounted the pyre and perished. Some of those who were present thought him mad, others vainglorious about his ability to bear pain, while others simply marvelled at his fortitude and contempt for death.[520]

In fact, the vocabulary of Diodorus (θανάτου καταφρόνησιν) and that of Diogenes Laertius (θανάτου καταφρονεῖν) in Fragment 6 are identical.

It is also notable that, were the total 15, the effect of the distribution of the other Fragments that possess book numbers would be to concertina the first half of Alexander's reign into the first third of Cleitarchus' books. For instance, Fragment 4 mentions the 50 Spartan hostages surrendered after the defeat of the rebellion of King Agis, which occurred in the late fifth or early sixth year of Alexander's reign and is attributed to Book 5 of Cleitarchus.[521] Conversely, placing the first half of 324BC in Book 12 engenders a total of about thirteen books up to the point of Alexander's death, which results in an even distribution of Alexander's regnal years across Cleitarchus' books. Furthermore, a 13-book total has the particular attraction of giving virtually exactly one regnal year per book, since the total reign was only a few months short of 13 years. The other book-numbered fragments are all broadly consistent with the hypothesis of one book per year. Later in the reign Cleitarchus may slightly have expanded the duration of some books and contracted others to suit the pattern of events or perhaps because the precise chronology of events in Bactria and India was mysterious even to him. However, it can be shown that the Cleitarchan book termini were consistently located in the early autumn in the first five years of the

---

[518] Plutarch, *Alexander* 64.3 explains that Calanus was the nickname of the gymnosophist Sphines, which was derived from his use of the Indian greeting "Kale"; Caranus was the name of one of Alexander's Friends, who was killed by Spitamenes (and also of an apocryphal son of Phillip II in Justin 11.2.3); Arrian, *Anabasis* 3.5.6 has the inverse error of Calanus for Caranus.

[519] E.g. L. Pearson, *The Lost Histories of Alexander the Great* (Philological Monographs XX: Am. Phil. Ass. 1960) 213 recognises that Book 12 is the suicide of Calanus, but thinks there were "two or three books more"; A. B. Bosworth, "In Search of Cleitarchus: Review-Discussion of Luisa Prandi: Fortuna è realtà dell'opera di Clitarco, Historia Einzelschriften 104 (Steiner Stuttgart, 1996)," *Histos* 1 (August 1997) notes that there were "at least 12 books and perhaps as many as 15"; J.C. Yardley & W. Heckel, *Justin: Epitome of the Philippic History of Pompeius Trogus, Vol I, Books 11-12, Alexander the Great* (Oxford 1997) 34 speculate that Cleitarchus' work was published "in 15 books?"

[520] Diodorus 17.107.5 (trans. C. Bradford Welles).

[521] Jacoby FGrHist 137 F4 (Harpocration, s.v. ὁμηρεύοντας) & section 5.95 of this book.

The Nature and Genesis of Cleitarchus' Account

reign and up to the end of the first of the two parts of Cleitarchus' work. The termini only seem to have shifted into the summer from the death of Darius onwards. In general terms, this scheme is not very different from the book-divisions at the end of each campaigning season that were seemingly adopted by Thucydides, Xenophon and Hieronymus.[522] More specifically, the book termini in the first half of the work appear to coincide closely with the anniversaries of Alexander's accession. It may also be added that there is evidence from his fragments that Cleitarchus had a fondness for associating things with calendar divisions: for example, he made the walls of Babylon 365 stades in circumference[523] and also seems to have asserted that Darius' harem comprised 365 women (Curtius 3.3.24 & 6.6.8; Diodorus 17.77.6; cf. Justin 12.3.10). In this trait he may be emulating his father, Deinon.[524]

Implicit in this discussion is the view that Cleitarchus' work opened with Alexander's accession, which I date to the autumnal equinox in 336BC, and closed with his death, which Plutarch dates to the early evening of 10th June 323BC (Julian calendar) on the basis of an entry that he read from Alexander's official journal compiled by Eumenes and known as the *Ephemerides*. This timespan for the work is relatively orthodox and appears in general to be supported by the evidence. For example, it seems that Diodorus mainly used the universal histories of Ephorus and Diyllus as his sources for his sixteenth book, which proceeded as far as the assassination of Philip.[525] He may only have switched to the considerably more detailed account of Cleitarchus at the beginning of Alexander's reign in Book 17. Then he began to use Hieronymus of Cardia from early in Book 18,[526] most probably from the geographical digression in 18.5. Furthermore, although his first two-and-a-half books are now lost, the indications are that Curtius originally opened his main account at Alexander's accession. In fact Jacoby's first fragment of Cleitarchus shows that the destruction of Thebes was described in Book 1, so it is unlikely that there was space for a fully detailed account of Alexander's youth.[527] Since Thebes fell no earlier than mid-September 335BC, it is clear that the first book must have incorporated the entirety of the first year of the reign. Nevertheless, Hammond may well be correct in believing that Cleitarchus also outlined Philip's last summer by way of a

---

[522] Jane Hornblower, *Hieronymus of Cardia* (Oxford 1981) 101.

[523] Jacoby FGrHist 137 F10 (Diodorus 2.7.3-4).

[524] Deinon gave 360 concubines in the Royal Harem: Pearson, *The Lost Histories of Alexander the Great* 221 & 228-229; Plutarch, *Artaxerxes* 27.

[525] E.g. Diodorus 16.76.6, though the Philip mentioned there is probably Cassander's son.

[526] For example, the account of Alexander's catafalque in Diodorus 18.26-27 is a fragment of Hieronymus, because Athenaeus 206E attributes it to him: see Jacoby FGrHist 154 F2.

[527] Jacoby FGrHist137 F1 (Athenaeus, *Deipnosophistae* 148D-F).

prologue.[528] This would be vaguely consistent with an overall plan of describing the events of thirteen years across thirteen books, since Alexander died in early June. Furthermore, there are significant indications that Cleitarchus provided an introduction to his history that recounted stories concerning Alexander's birth and ancestry, especially because Plutarch was probably utilising Cleitarchus in his introductory account of Alexander's descent from Achilles and Heracles (Plutarch, *Alexander* 2.1). Finally, there are good indications that Cleitarchus gave a detailed account of the events in Babylon in the aftermath of Alexander's death down to at least the First Division of the Satrapies in late June or July 323BC and that he may also have outlined the transport of Alexander's corpse to Egypt and its eventual transfer to Alexandria by way of an epilogue.

Locating Jacoby's Fragments and the Book Boundaries

The next step is to assign Jacoby's book-attributed fragments of Cleitarchus to their correct contexts within each book.

Fragment 1 (Athenaeus 148D-F), which is attributed to Book 1,[529] self-evidently relates to the fall of Thebes in early October of 335BC. This date is relatively well fixed, since both Plutarch, *Alexander* 13.1 & *Camillus* 19.6, and Arrian, *Anabasis* 1.10.2, mention that news of the fall of Thebes became known in Athens just after the celebration of the Great Mysteries had begun in Attica. These are known to have taken place between 15th-23rd of the Attic month Boedromion.[530] Boedromion began near the New Moon on 19th September (Julian) in 335BC, hence Athens heard of the fall of Thebes perhaps as early as 5th October 335BC and the event itself occurred a day or two earlier. Consequently, we know that Thebes fell between 3rd-10th October 335BC (Julian calendar). This Fragment mentions the wealth of Thebes as having amounted to just 440 talents. The same sum is mentioned by Diodorus 17.14.4, who states that Alexander sold the Theban prisoners and realised a sum of 440 silver talents. Bosworth has pointed out that it is not strictly necessary to read Diodorus as stating that the sale of the prisoners raised the entire sum, but that Diodorus may be abbreviating a longer account, which had listed further resources realising the total.[531] However, I note that this fragment takes the view that 440 talents was a small sum for so many

---

[528] N. G. L. Hammond, *Three Historians of Alexander the Great* (Cambridge 1983) 92-93; for the chronology of Alexander's accession see N. G. L. Hammond, "The Regnal Years of Philip and Alexander," *Greek, Roman and Byzantine Studies* 33 (1992) 355-373.

[529] Note that the attribution to Book 1 only occurs in the full manuscript of Athenaeus brought to Venice from Constantinople by Aurispa in 1423 (St Mark Codex A); the Epitome manuscripts from Paris and Florence published by S. P. Peppink, *Athenaei Dipnosophistarum Epitome: Pars Prima* (Leiden 1937) 45 attribute the matter to Cleitarchus but omit the Book number.

[530] A. B. Bosworth, *Commentary on Arrian's History of Alexander* I (Oxford 1980) 92.

[531] Bosworth, "In Search of Cleitarchus: Review-Discussion of Luisa Prandi: Fortuna è realtà dell'opera di Clitarco, Historia Einzelschriften 104 (Steiner Stuttgart, 1996)," *Histos* 1 (August 1997).

The Nature and Genesis of Cleitarchus' Account

prisoners and attributes this to the poor nutrition of the Thebans, so I have reconstructed Cleitarchus as giving 440 talents as the sum raised specifically from the enslavement of the captives. It is anyway clear that the first book of Cleitarchus extended to early October of 335BC, which just antedates the first anniversary of the accession on 16th October 335BC (i.e. 27th Boedromion in the Attic Lunar Calendar).

Fragment 2 (Athenaeus 530A), which mentions the death of Sardanapalus[532] and derives from Book 4, is almost certainly associated with an historical visit by Alexander to the Assyrian king's tomb at Anchiale near Tarsus in October 333BC, which is attested elsewhere in fragments of Aristobulus and Callisthenes.[533] It can easily be fitted into the 13-book annual scheme, since it occurs near the beginning of the fourth year of Alexander's reign, which began on 25th September 333BC. Cleitarchus is probably echoing this story from his father Deinon's *Persica*, which might in turn have followed Ctesias' *Persica*.[534]

Fragment 3 (Stobaeus, *Florilegium* 4.20.73) from the fifth book tells of Theis Byblios' passionate love for his daughter, Myrra, which is a legend of Byblos, a city on the Lebanese littoral, where Adonis, the son of Theis and Myrra, was worshipped and which Alexander reached in about January of 332BC.[535] This is some nine months ahead of the start of the fifth year of Alexander's reign, which is the context implied by the 13-book scheme. There are also strong indications that the epic siege of Tyre, which was so protracted as to extend into the second half of 332BC, was entirely accommodated within the 4th book of Cleitarchus with Book 5 opening after its conclusion. However, the concept of one book per year can be rescued by the observation that Alexander passed along the Levantine littoral *twice*. Logically, the only way to reconcile Fragment 3 with its placing in Book 5 is to suppose that it pertains to Alexander's *return* to Syria in the summer of 331BC. From this we learn that Alexander was probably in Byblos some time in the late summer of 331BC. The sources are clear that Alexander lingered at Tyre at this time, for he held athletic and musical contests there from around mid-June to early July of 331BC. He subsequently crossed the Euphrates at Thapsacus (circa early August) – see Arrian, *Anabasis* 3.6.1-4, Curtius 4.8.16 and Plutarch, *Alexander* 29. Engels has noted, "There were essentially two routes the

---

[532] Cf. Plutarch, *Moralia* 326F & 336C.

[533] Jacoby FGrHist 139 F9a (Athenaeus 530A-B); Jacoby FGrHist 139 F9b (Strabo 14.5.9); Jacoby 139 F9c (Arrian, *Anabasis* 2.5.2-4); Jacoby FGrHist 124 F34 (Photius & Suda s.v. *Sardanapalos*) - this mention is attributed to Callisthenes' *Persica*, but it may be a garbled reference to his history of Alexander; see Pearson, *The Lost Histories of Alexander the Great*, 26; Jacoby FGrHist 122 F2 (Amyntas the Bematist in Athenaeus 529E-530A);

[534] Ctesias, writing in the early 4th century BC, had described the reign of Sardanapalus (see Diodorus 2.23); Cleitarchus seemingly contradicted Ctesias on certain points - see L. Pearson, *The Lost Histories of Alexander the Great*, 230, probably in consequence of his father Deinon having written a *Persica* to rival Ctesias' work on the same theme.

[535] See T. S. Brown, "Clitarchus," *American Journal of Philology* 71 (1950) 149.

Macedonians could have followed to the Euphrates: through Coele Syria via Damascus, Homs, Hamah, and Aleppo, a region which was much more agriculturally productive in antiquity than at present; or up the Phoenician coast to Seleucia, the port of Antioch, and inland by the route essentially followed by Cyrus the Younger, Crassus, Trajan, and Julian through the Amuq Plain to the Euphrates. The latter route would, of course, simplify the army's logistic organisation by utilizing sea transport."[536] We now have an independent argument from the third fragment of Cleitarchus to show that Engels was correct to prefer the coastal route, since that was the one that passed through Byblos. Admittedly the inland route has been the orthodox assumption and will be found marked as the reality on most modern maps of Alexander's itinerary. However, it is actually inspired by the thinnest of textual evidence: specifically, Arrian, *Anabasis* 3.6.4 speaks of Alexander "starting inland towards Thapsacus" immediately after discussing his sojourn at Tyre. In the absence of anyone previously having noticed the evidence of the Cleitarchus Fragment on the matter, this seems to have been held to imply the inland route from Tyre onwards. But of course, Arrian's statement is actually in no way inconsistent with the coastal route either, since it would eventually have been necessary for Alexander to move inland in order to reach Thapsacus at all. In fact, it emerges that Fragment 3 of Cleitarchus is the only *solid* textual evidence on the road taken from Tyre northwards and it supports the more practicable coastal route. However, even if the army did take the inland route to Thapsacus, since Byblos is only 70 miles north of Tyre (just a couple of days by ship), the possibility would nevertheless still exist that Alexander made an otherwise unreported personal expedition to Byblos during his second visit to Tyre. Therefore, this Fragment is actually perfectly reconcilable with the one-book-per-year scheme for Cleitarchus, despite the superficial contradiction.

Fragment 4 (Harpocration s.v. ὁμηρεύοντας), which is also attributed to Book 5, mentions the fifty Spartan hostages received by Antipater after he quelled the rebellion of King Agis.[537] This revolt against the Macedonian Hegemony in Greece took place in the summer of 331BC, which is the later part of Book 5 according to the 13-book scheme. The implication is that Fragment 4 is drawn from a digression on the fighting back in Greece, which closed Book 5 of Cleitarchus.[538] Now Diodorus 17.62-63 precisely gives just such a digression on

---

[536] D. W. Engels, *Alexander the Great and the Logistics of the Macedonian Army* (California 1978) 65.

[537] The number of 50 is not present in the text of Harpocration (*Lexicon of the Attic Orators*), but is restored from the epitome of Harpocration used by the author of the Suda, of which only the best manuscript has 50 as the numeral ν' (in agreement with Diodorus), whilst others have eight as either the numeral η' or the word ὀκτώ.

[538] The departure of Spartan envoys to Alexander to ask forgiveness for the rebellion seems to have been delayed until the next year, since Aeschines 3.133 records that they were preparing to leave in the Summer of 330BC; their departure from Greece may have been recorded by Cleitarchus at the end of his 6th book, which prompted Diodorus 17.73.5-6 to mention the matter; their arrival with

The Nature and Genesis of Cleitarchus' Account

this rebellion in the aftermath of Gaugamela, although Curtius and Justin postpone mentioning the matter until after the death of Darius, which fitted in better with their book structures: Curtius 5.1.1-2 actually states his intention to delay interrupting his Asian narrative with an account of events back in Europe, evidently at the point that he found the account of the rebellion in Cleitarchus.[539] The date of Gaugamela is fixed to 1st October 331BC (Julian Calendar) by a lunar eclipse mentioned as having occurred eleven days before the battle. This astronomical phenomenon has been reliably calculated to have happened on 20th September 331BC. It looks as though Gaugamela was the climactic event of Cleitarchus' fifth book and that it closed with the digression on events in Greece immediately afterwards. This is strongly supported by a comment in Justin 11.14.6, which places Gaugamela within the fifth year of Alexander's reign. Since Cleitarchus via Trogus (and perhaps Timagenes) was the ultimate source of most of the material in Justin, if Cleitarchus had one book per regnal year, then a comment referring an event to the fifth year of the reign should also place the event in the fifth book of Cleitarchus. It is hardly likely that Cleitarchus could be the source of such a comment unless the battle was in his fifth book.

Fragment 5 (Scholia on Aristophanes Av. 487): the greatest conundrum among the fragments with book attributions is presented by the fifth, which assigns a comment about the law that permitted only the Persian monarch to wear the tiara upright to the tenth book of Cleitarchus. According to the 13-book scheme, this cannot have been related earlier than the middle of 327BC and should fit between the summer of 327BC and the summer of 326BC. The most obvious context for such a comment would be an account of a rebellion against Alexander's rule of Persia, for Alexander did not himself wear the tiara.[540] However, this occurs too late in Cleitarchus to be associated with the revolt of Bessus, who had been dead for two years. Nevertheless, we do know of a more obscure, subsequent rebellion in Persia led by a certain Baryaxes. Arrian specifically relates that he assumed the title of King of the Persians and Medes and wore the tiara upright. This rebellion evidently occurred whilst Alexander was in India, since Baryaxes was arrested by Atropates, the satrap of Media and presented to Alexander for punishment upon his return in early 324BC according to Arrian, *Anabasis* 6.29.3. The outbreak of this rebellion is the probable context of Fragment 5. A corollary is that Cleitarchus probably did not write that Bessus wore the tiara upright. Bessus' assumption of

---

Alexander may be reflected by the comment in Curtius 7.4.32 that Alexander received announcements out of Greece about the Spartan rebellion in about July 329BC.

[539] Apart from Diodorus 17.62-63 the main digressions on the revolt of Agis in the Vulgate authors are: Curtius 6.1.1-20; Justin 12.1.4-11; Diodorus 17.73.5-6.

[540] Plutarch, *Alexander* 45.2 and Fragment 30 of Eratosthenes in Jacoby FGrHist 241 = Plutarch, *Moralia* 330A; Arrian, *Anabasis* 4.7.4 seems to be mistaken on this point, for which see P. A. Brunt, *Loeb Classical Library: Arrian, History of Alexander and Indica* 1 (Harvard 1976) Appendix XIV.2 533; excepting Plutarch, the Vulgate sources refer only to the diadem without mention of the tiara (*kitaris* or *kidaris*): *Metz Epitome* 2; Diodorus 17.77.5; Curtius 6.6.4; Justin 12.3.8; Ephippus in Athenaeus 537E.

the upright tiara was reported by Arrian (from Ptolemy?)[541] But Curtius 6.6.13 writes more generally of his adoption of "regal attire" and Diodorus 17.83.3 notes that he "had assumed the diadem". Many points suggest that Cleitarchus usually adopted the tidy principle of placing digressions on events elsewhere at either the start or the end of a book (the matter of the rebellion of Agis as related in the discussion of Fragment 4 is a case in point), so these are the two alternative placements for this fragment. The end is preferable, since Baryaxes probably waited for Alexander to become safely embroiled in his Indian campaigns. This conclusion reveals the history of Cleitarchus in a startling new light, for it provides evidence that his work treated events elsewhere in more detail and in a more chronologically correct order than did Arrian.

Fragment 6 (Diogenes Laertius 1.6): as has already been argued, the sixth and final book-attributed fragment comes from Cleitarchus' account of the self-immolation of Calanus when Alexander was progressing towards Susa in the spring of 324BC. It was reported in Book 12 of Cleitarchus and falls in the middle of Alexander's twelfth regnal year. Hence it is precisely consistent with the one book per year scheme.

Vestiges of Cleitarchus' Book Structure in Diodorus

It is an important axiom for the discussion in this section that the seventeenth book of Diodorus' *Bibliotheke* is largely an epitome of Cleitarchus' account of Alexander's career. This concept had its origins in the application of the so-called *Einquellenprinzip* (single source principle), which was pursued by German scholars, such as Schwartz and Jacoby and has more recently been reasserted by F. Schachermeyr.[542] In its original 19th century form the *Einquellen-theorie* asserted that Diodorus slavishly epitomised a succession of earlier historians with little modification of their language or perspectives in compiling his *Bibliotheke*. In so doing, he confined himself to a single source over long sections of his work, often extending to an entire book or more. In the 20th century, Schwartz advocated relaxation of the strict *Einquellenprinzip* to the effect that Diodorus generally based his narrative upon a single main source, but sometimes intermingled material from another source and occasionally offered personal contributions.[543] This seems to me fairly to reflect the truth.

It is beyond the scope of this discussion to argue the point in fine detail, but it is pertinent to outline the main strands of the case that Cleitarchus was the major source for Diodorus 17:

---

[541] Arrian, *Anabasis* 3.25.3; cf. Xenophon, *Anabasis* 2.5.23.

[542] F. Schachermeyr, *Alexander der Grosse: Das Problem seiner Persönlichkeit und seines Wirkens*, (Vienna 1973) Anhang nr. 2: Der Weg zu Kleitarch 658-662.

[543] For a good discussion of the use of sources by Diodorus see Hornblower, *Hieronymus of Cardia*, 18-32.

The Nature and Genesis of Cleitarchus' Account

1. Because Cleitarchus had already been a named source for Diodorus in Book 2, so Diodorus had definitely read Cleitarchus' *History Concerning Alexander*.

2. Because of the high proportion of the fragments of Cleitarchus, which are closely echoed in Diodorus 17: more than are echoed among the fragments of any of the other early Alexander historian.

3. Because Jacoby's testimonies reveal that Cleitarchus' history was extremely popular in Italy in the late Republican period: very many episodes in Diodorus have detailed parallels in Curtius, who therefore seems independently to have elected to use the same source as Diodorus for much of his account of Alexander and Cleitarchus would have been the obvious choice for both of them.

These facts make it almost unavoidable that Cleitarchus was the principal source for both Diodorus 17 and Curtius. Hammond's conjecture that Diyllus was a significant secondary source for Diodorus 17 proves untenable, because it requires (on his own admission) that Curtius independently chose Diyllus as a secondary source for exactly the same set of episodes as Diodorus, which is a statistical impossibility. Similarly Luisa Prandi's advocacy of Duris as a secondary source for Diodorus is unconvincing, because her reasons for rejecting Cleitarchus do not stand up to scrutiny (e.g. the response of Bosworth) and because she cannot escape the same *impasse* as encountered by Hammond: i.e. arguing that two writers independently selected the same mix of episodes from a pair of shared sources. In fact, Diodorus 17 appears overwhelmingly to be dominated by Cleitarchus, but it is epitomised down to only ~10%-20% of the length of the original.[544]

The main chronological scheme utilised by Diodorus is Athenian Archon-years, which have seemingly been applied retrospectively (and rather clumsily) by Diodorus himself and are not derived from his sources. There are many errors and Diodorus often instigates an Archon-year among events that happened at a very different time of year than the beginning of the Archon-year in mid-summer (notionally at the first New Moon after the Summer Solstice).

However, there is another type of sub-division that seemingly occurs even more erratically within Diodorus' text in the form of a variety of curiously bland boundary phrases that contain no historical details, but simply indicate the end of one account and the beginning of another. Are they mere rhetorical flourishes or do they have some ulterior significance?

---

[544] Diodorus 17 is an exceptionally long book for a Greek work, so it is unlikely that Cleitarchus' 13 books averaged more than 75% of its length – conversely, Cleitarchus' work seems to have been substantial, so it seems improbable that his books averaged less that 40% of the length of Diodorus 17. My best estimate is that my reconstruction of Cleitarchus is about two-thirds the length of its archetype.

Concerning Alexander the Great by Andrew Chugg

In general, we can see that this type of formula is used by Diodorus to indicate major changes in the focus of his account, not only in Book 17, but also in parts of his history based on different sources than Cleitarchus. For example, he gives "This was the state of affairs concerning Philip," at Diodorus 16.89.3 before moving on to deal with Timoleon's activities in Sicily. Diodorus himself provides strong clues as to his inspiration for these curious phrases. For example, Diodorus 16.76.4 closes his account of the siege of Perinthus with Καὶ τὰ μὲν περὶ Περινθίους καὶ Βυζαντίους ἐν τούτοις ἦν ("Such was the situation at Perinthus and Byzantium"). But most interestingly he immediately goes on to comment that this was the point at which his source, Ephorus of Kyme, had closed his history. The obvious inference is that such phrases may often mark book boundaries or other significant termini in Diodorus' source texts, most of which are now lost.

This hypothesis is particularly rewarding for the question of the book termini relating to Cleitarchus in Diodorus 17. Starting from the hypothesis that Cleitarchus wrote one book for each year of Alexander's reign, it transpires that at least some and probably all of these boundary phrases in Diodorus 17 can be associated with Cleitarchan book termini as follows:

Diodorus 17.47.6 gives Ἡμεῖς δ' ἐπεὶ τὰ περὶ τὸν Ἀλέξανδρον διήλθομεν, μεταληψόμεθα τὴν διήγησιν ("Now we have described things concerning Alexander, we shall turn our narrative in another direction") and this appears to be in about the right place for the end of the narrative of Alexander's activities in Cleitarchus' Book 4 at the appointment of "Balonymus" as King of Tyre. It is followed by a digression on events in Europe and then the material of the next book began with Diodorus' Archon-year boundary and mention of the siege of Gaza.

Diodorus 17.63.5 has Ἡμεῖς δὲ διεληλυθότες τὰ πραχθέντα κατὰ τὴν Εὐρώμην ἐν μέρει τὰ κατὰ τὴν Ἀσίαν συντελεσθέντα διέξιμεν ("Now that we have run through the events in Europe, we may in turn pass on to what occurred in Asia"). This ends the digression on the rebellion of Agis in Greece, which seems to have closed Cleitarchus' Book 5.

Diodorus 17.73.4 concludes with Καὶ τὰ μὲν κατὰ τὴν Ἀσίαν ἐν τούτοις ἦν ("That was the situation in Asia"). This is very likely to have been the end of the narrative of Alexander's activities in Cleitarchus' Book 6 with the death of Darius. Again, it is followed by a short digression on events in Europe.

Diodorus 17.83.3 gives Καὶ τὰ μὲν περὶ Ἀλέξανδρον ἐν τούτοις ἦν ("These were the concerns of Alexander"). This is a plausible juncture for the end of Cleitarchus' Book 7 with Alexander's crossing of the Paropamisus range. The narrative focus then shifts from Alexander himself to the activities of his generals in Aria.

Diodorus 17.108.3 also has Καὶ τὰ μὲν περὶ Ἀλέξανδρον ἐν τούτοις ἦν ("These were the concerns of Alexander"). This is a plausible location for the end of Cleitarchus' Book 12. Again, it marks a shift in the narrative focus from Alexander himself to the activities of Harpalus.

The Nature and Genesis of Cleitarchus' Account

Virtually all of the boundary phrases of this type in Diodorus 17 (such that the narrative focus shifts from Alexander's activities to a digression on events elsewhere or back again) can be closely associated with a Cleitarchan book terminus.[545] It looks as though Diodorus is faithfully echoing these scene shifts from Cleitarchus' work. The phrases themselves may have been read from Cleitarchus' text, especially since the first, fourth and fifth incorporate the title of Cleitarchus' work, "Concerning Alexander" (Περὶ Ἀλεξάνδρου). Cleitarchus himself seems frequently to have followed the tidy policy of placing digressions on events remote from Alexander's operations at either the end or occasionally the beginning of his books. This is why these scene-shifting boundary phrases are evidently giving good indications of the Cleitarchan book termini. It is a corollary that significant digressions in Diodorus may mark Cleitarchan book termini, even where there is no boundary phrase, especially if the same digression occurs at the same point in Curtius. An excellent example would be the digression on events in Bactria at Diodorus 17.99.5-6 and Curtius 9.7.1-11, which appears to mark the end of Cleitarchus' Book 11.

Two other types of boundary phrase occur in Diodorus 17, but appear to be less significant:

Diodorus 17.61.3 has "This was the outcome of the battle near Arbela" at the end of the narrative of Alexander's activities in Cleitarchus' Book 5. However, there is a similar phrase at Diodorus 17.36.6: "This was the result of the battle at Issus in Cilicia". This latter cannot easily have been a book boundary in Cleitarchus, because Jacoby's Fragment 2 shows that the fourth book dealing with the fourth year of the reign had already opened and had another ten or eleven months to run.

There are four instances of "This is what happened in this year" at Diodorus 17.28.5 (autumn 334BC), 17.39.4 (January 332BC), 17.86.7 (April 326BC) and 17.112.6 (April 323BC), which all immediately precede Diodorus' own Archon-year boundaries. It is possible that the first of these is at the terminus of Book 2 of Cleitarchus, since it occurs just after the Siege of Halicarnassus, which probably ended just before the second anniversary of the reign. But the others are widely displaced from the expected Cleitarchan book boundaries.

The dates of the termini of Books 1, 2, 4 and 5 can all now be recognised to occur in late September to October of their respective years, so they appear specifically to be marking the anniversaries of Alexander's accession. From Book 6 onwards, the termini seem to shift into the summer months. On this point it may be relevant that the manuscripts of Diodorus declared an end to the first part of his 17th book at the same point as Cleitarchus' Book 5 closed. It is likely that this

---

[545] With the sole exception of the phrases at Diodorus 17.5.1 and 17.7.10, which bound a passage giving historical background on the Persian Empire: this appears to have been embedded in Book 1 of Cleitarchus, since it is also echoed in Book 10 of Justin; Cleitarchus' father, Deinon, had written a history of the Persian Empire.

reflected a division of Cleitarchus' work at this point. If so, then it could help to explain the change in practice regarding the end points of the books, although Cleitarchus nevertheless held to the pattern of one book per year. Obviously, the termini needed to shift into the summer at some stage, since the reign ended in June. It is also possible that Cleitarchus was unable precisely to locate the anniversaries of the accession accurately among the events once Alexander had moved into the wilds of the eastern satrapies.

The ends of Cleitarchus' Books 8 & 9 are lost in the Great Lacuna in Diodorus 17 and there are no boundary phrases to be found for the expected termini of Books 1, 3, 10, 11 and 13. However, at least five of the book termini of Cleitarchus seem to be marked by the boundary phrases associated with digressions. The hypothesis that Diodorus 17 is essentially an epitome of Cleitarchus is greatly strengthened by the presence of these vestiges of his book structure.

Book Boundaries and Fragment Locations in Cleitarchus

The location of the boundaries between Cleitarchus' books is a topic that is intimately intertwined with the fragment locations. It is clear that the starting point for seeking book boundaries for the first five books should normally be the anniversary of Alexander's accession at around the start of October. This is most clearly signalled by the division between the Battle of Arbela itself at the end of Book 5 and the subsequent advance to the town of Arbela, which occurs in Book 6. However, from the death of Darius onwards, it appears that Cleitarchus allowed the book boundaries to be brought forward broadly into summer. Although he successfully retained the scheme of one book per year, many of the later book boundaries significantly antedate the anniversary of the accession. It seems that Cleitarchus may have been especially vague on chronology in India, where even the familiar Winter-Summer cycle of the weather was largely missing as a guide. Throughout the texts of Diodorus and Curtius a helpful additional indication of the Cleitarchan book boundaries is the occurrence of digressions, since Cleitarchus seems mainly to have pursued the orderly practice of placing them preferentially at the beginnings or ends of his books. Due to the secondary authors in some cases having relocated the digressions to suit their own book structures, their Cleitarchan locations can only be reliably identified wherever Diodorus and Curtius relate a particular digression at the same juncture. However, the boundary phrases marking digressions in the text of Diodorus 17 do appear to be reliable indications of Cleitarchan boundaries even in isolation. Indeed, the occurrences of digression boundary phrases in Diodorus 17 can safely take precedence as the primary guide in the few cases where they are available. The normal book and chapter divisions in Curtius and Justin and the chapter ends or Attic year boundaries in Diodorus 17 do not, in general, follow Cleitarchus' scheme. Yet in some instances, particularly where a boundary is found at the same point in all the extant followers of Cleitarchus, there may nevertheless be evidence

The Nature and Genesis of Cleitarchus' Account

of a Cleitarchan boundary: e.g. Curtius' fifth book opens where Cleitarchus began his sixth and this is also the division between the two parts of Diodorus' Book 17. The detailed conclusions on the book structure of Cleitarchus and the locations of his Fragments are discussed below and summarised in Table 3.

Book 1: Cleitarchus seems to have begun with an outline of Alexander's birth and ancestry resembling Plutarch, *Alexander* 2.1 & 3.3-5. Hammond has shown that Plutarch's date of 6th Hecatombaeon for Alexander's birth comes from Timaeus, a rough contemporary of Cleitarchus, because Cicero gives many of the same details and names Timaeus as his source. However, there is good evidence that Cleitarchus himself used Timaeus, who was the leading authority on chronological issues in the early 3rd century BC. Fragment 7 of Cleitarchus couples him with Timaeus as its co-source and it mentions the Heracleidae, Alexander's putative ancestors.[546] Then Fragment 36 from the Suda seems to make Cleitarchus a follower of Timaeus and Anaximenes.[547] In this context Plutarch also gives Hegesias as the source of a quip about the conflagration of the Temple at Ephesus on the day of Alexander's birth.[548] Hegesias is another near contemporary of Cleitarchus, but immediately precedes him in a list of ancient writers given by Philodemus, who usually arranged his lists in date order.[549] A famous fragment of Hegesias describes the killing of Betis at the siege of Gaza, but fairly similar details of this event are given by Curtius, who usually followed Cleitarchus for such histrionic anecdotes.[550] Furthermore, Curtius' version of Gaza emphasises Alexander's emulation of Achilles, which is a familiar Cleitarchan theme. The end of Plutarch's passage on Alexander's birth cites a prophecy that Alexander would be *aniketos* (= Latin *invictus* = invincible), an epithet for the king, which is strongly associated with the Cleitarchan tradition.[551] Finally, Hegesias was renowned for being perhaps the earliest author to employ a curious metrical device known as Asianic rhythms and there are some hints among the fragments of Cleitarchus that he too occasionally practised this type of prose poetry.[552] In summary, there are indications that both Timaeus and Hegesias were sources for Cleitarchus, so when material is found from both, which is also linked to familiar Cleitarchan themes such as *aniketos*, descent from Heracles and Achilles and a fascination for chronology and the calendar (all these

---

[546] Jacoby FGrHist 137 F7 (Clement of Alexandria, *Strom.* 1.139.4).

[547] Jacoby FGrHist 137 F36 (Suda s.v. ἔχετον).

[548] Jacoby FGrHist 142 F3 of Hegesias.

[549] Jacoby FGrHist 137 T12 (Philodemus, *Rhet.* 4.1 col. 21).

[550] Jacoby FGrHist 142 F5 of Hegesias; Curtius 4.6.12-16.

[551] Plutarch, *Alexander* 3.5 & 14.4-5; Diodorus 17.93.4 & 17.51.3-4; Curtius 4.7.27; Livy 9.18; Justin 11.11.10; Cleitarchus' use of this epithet may reflect contemporary practice, since Hypereides I, col.32, 5 referred to a proposal to erect a statue of Alexander as θεὸς ἀνίκητος according to the interpretation of H. Berve, "Review of W I" *Gnomon* 5 (1929) 376 n.2.

[552] Pearson, *The Lost Histories of Alexander the Great*, 213, n.9 & 227, n.59.

things being found together in a short passage), then there are cumulatively strong grounds to suspect that Cleitarchus is Plutarch's immediate source of inspiration. Book 1 evidently extended as far as the end of the campaigning season in 335BC and the sack of Thebes, since Fragment 1, dealing with the aftermath of its fall, is from Book 1. The last known event of the season in the Vulgate tradition was Alexander's visit to Delphi whilst heading back towards Macedon.[553] Thebes fell at the beginning of October and the anniversary of Alexander's accession (27th Boedromion) fell on 16th October in 335BC leaving ample time for the visit to Delphi in Book 1.

Book 2: The second book appears to have opened with Alexander's return to Macedon and various stories telling of Alexander's somewhat theatrical preparations for the campaign against the Persian Empire during the winter of 335-334BC. Surviving versions of the stories are found in Justin and Frontinus (transmitted via Trogus) and in Plutarch (probably directly from Cleitarchus).[554] Fragment 7, noting that Alexander's invasion came 820 years after that by the Heracleidae, must be derived from the opening of this book.[555] I infer that Cleitarchus mentioned an otherwise unreported visit of Alexander to the tomb of Themistocles at Magnesia, because Fragments 33 and 34 are from a digression on the career of Themistocles.[556] We should expect this book to have closed in early October 334BC after the conclusion of the siege of Halicarnassus. It is likely that Alexander's encounter with the Marmares on the frontier of Lycia, which is uniquely recounted by Diodorus 17.28, was virtually the last event described by Cleitarchus in his second book. The accession anniversary was 6th October in 334BC, which would be a credible date. The boundary phrase at the end of 17.28 ("This is what happened in this year") possibly marks the end of Cleitarchus' second book. This is underscored by the opening of the next Attic Archon-year in the ensuing section – several months late! Perhaps, having admitted this incongruity into his epitome, this was where Diodorus gave up trying to coincide his Archon-year ends with Cleitarchus' book boundaries.

---

[553] Plutarch, *Alexander* 14.4-5; Diodorus 17.93.4; W. Dittenberger (ed.), *Sylloge Inscriptionum Graecarum, editio tertia* vol 1 (Leipzig 1915) 251H, col. II, lines 9-10 436-7 is an inscription from Delphi recording a gift to the shrine at this time of 150 gold coins minted by Philip II, but Alexander is the only likely donor of Macedonian coinage on this scale at this juncture.

[554] Justin 11.5.1-9; Plutarch, *Alexander* 15.2-3; Frontinus, *Strat.* 2.11.3 & 1.11.14.

[555] Jacoby FGrHist 137 F7 (Clement of Alexandria, *Strom.* 1.139.4).

[556] Jacoby FGrHist 137 F33 & F34 (Plutarch, *Themistocles* 27.1-2 & Cicero, *Brut.* 42-43); the surrender of Magnesia (Arrian, *Anabasis* 1.18.1) is the most likely occasion for Cleitarchus' digression on Themistocles, since his tomb lay there. Cleitarchus' father Deinon had evidently told the story of Themistocles, since Plutarch cites Deinon for the same story in Fragment 33. It is possible that Cleitarchus drew a comparison between Themistocles' submission to Xerxes and Charidemus' allegiance to Darius, since they were both exiled Athenians serving Persian kings. Arrian, *Anabasis* 1.18.2 may implicitly be contradicting Cleitarchus when he makes a point of stating that Alexander stayed at Ephesus when Magnesia surrendered.

The Nature and Genesis of Cleitarchus' Account

Book 3: Opened with winter campaigning in Pamphylia. Cleitarchus seems to have inserted a group of digressions on the activities and death of Memnon (see Diodorus 17.29, Plutarch, *Alexander* 18.3 and Curtius 3.2.1) and the preparations of Darius at Babylon (Diodorus 17.30.1-31.2 and Curtius 3.2.2-19). The surviving part of the account of Curtius opens just before the episode of the Gordian knot. Alexander probably arrived at Gordion in April of 333BC, but lingered during midsummer, departing perhaps as late as the end of July.[557] Diodorus omitted Gordion along with most of the other events from this book in his epitome: the only part of Alexander's activities that he included from Cleitarchus' third book seems to be the passage at Diodorus 17.31.3-6, mainly dealing with Alexander's illness. Alexander arrived at Tarsus in Cilicia early in September of 333BC and immediately fell seriously ill. His recovery may have been the last major event of this book, because Fragment 2, relating to Alexander's campaign in western Cilicia immediately after his recovery, was in the fourth book. The accession anniversary was 25th September in 333BC.

Book 4: Fragment 2 shows that Alexander's Cilician campaign towards Soli and Anchiale, west of Tarsus, was related at the beginning of this book. This is from Curtius 3.7 and Diodorus 32.2. This book's major events must have been firstly the Battle of Issus (Fragment 8)[558] on around 5th November 333BC and subsequently the siege of Tyre (Fragment 9).[559] It ended with the story of the appointment of "Balonymus" as King of Tyre. This has been believed by some to be an error by Cleitarchus for the appointment of Abdalonymus as King of Sidon. Curtius gives what seems a correct version of the story with Abdalonymus appointed King of Sidon *before* the siege of Tyre on the recommendation of Hephaistion, whereas the manuscripts of Diodorus do not mention Sidon. Prandi, Bosworth and others have highlighted and discussed the case of Abdalonymus,[560] because it appears to present an intractable local difficulty for the reconstruction of the Cleitarchan version. However, Curtius 4.1.26 mentions that an area surrounding Sidon was added to Abdalonymus' dominions by Alexander. Perhaps Cleitarchus therefore mentioned that he was given control of Tyre after its fall and that was what prompted Diodorus to tell the story of his original appointment as a king in the context of the fall of Tyre. Perhaps Diodorus in his original manuscript correctly referred the story of Abdalonymus' appointment back to Sidon in Section 17.47, having noted his appointment as King of Tyre in Section 17.46.6. If so, given the curious order in which Diodorus presents the matter, an ancient editor of Diodorus would obviously have assumed that the mentions of Sidon were errors for Tyre and incorrectly corrected them

---

[557] D. W. Engels, *Alexander the great and the Logistics of the Macedonian Army*, 37.

[558] Jacoby FGrHist 137 F8 (Cicero, *Ad f.* 2.10.3).

[559] Jacoby FGrHist 137 F9 (Schol. Plato *Resp.* 337A cf. Photius: Σαρδόνιος γέλως).

[560] Luisa Prandi, "Fortuna è Realtà dell'Opera di Clitarco" *Historia Einzelschriften* 104 (Stuttgart 1996) 102; Bosworth, Review of the Prandi monograph in *Histos* 1, 1997.

in some later manuscript that became the prototype for our surviving versions of Diodorus. This seems to constitute a logical and viable way of explaining the confusion through an understandable rather than a crass error, which also allows that Diodorus, Curtius and Trogus (Justin) were all still following Cleitarchus. Although it might be objected that Philotas was made garrison commander in Tyre according to Curtius 4.5.9, I cannot see that this excludes Abdalonymus as its king, since Macedonian military commanders were often appointed in parallel to local rulers in Alexander's domains. The end of the narrative on Alexander in Book 4 in the aftermath of Tyre is clearly marked by a boundary phrase "Now we have described things concerning Alexander, we shall turn our narrative in another direction" at Diodorus 17.47.6.

Book 5: Opened from the accession anniversary on 14th October 332BC. Its narrative probably began with a digression on events elsewhere including Agis' activities in Crete in Diodorus 17.48.1-2.[561] The focus returned to Alexander with an account of the siege of Gaza, the advance into Egypt, the visit to Siwa and **afterwards** the foundation of Alexandria. Cleitarchus probably described Alexander's return up the Levantine coast after Egypt, because this would explain why Fragment 3, which seems to relate to a visit of Alexander to Byblos on the Lebanese coast, is located in Book 5 by Stobaeus. The narrative of Alexander's activities within Book 5 seems to have ended on schedule on 1st October 331BC with the Battle of Arbela (Gaugamela). This account terminated with the boundary phrase "This was the outcome of the battle near Arbela". Book 5 then concluded with a digression on events in Europe and specifically the rebellion of Agis, since Fragment 4 attributes mention of the 50 Spartan hostages received by Antipater to Book 5. Conjecturally, other events in Europe were related by Cleitarchus at this point, such as the death of Alexander of Epirus, given in Justin 12.2.1-15. For example, Curtius 8.1.37 mentions a complaint by Alexander of Epirus (whilst he died of a wound according to Livy) that he had encountered men in Italy, whilst his nephew was up against women in Persia.[562] The relevant section of Livy has some Cleitarchan elements, such as referring to the "Invincible Alexander".[563] The final close of Book 5 is indicated by the boundary phrase "Now that we have run through the events in Europe, we may in turn pass on to what occurred in Asia" at Diodorus 17.63.5. This is immediately preceded by a declaration of the end of the first of the two parts of Diodorus' Book 17.

Book 6: Opened with the immediate aftermath of the Battle of Arbela, including the flight of Darius from midnight on 1st-2nd October and Alexander's arrival at Darius' base in Arbela the day after the battle. This book incorporated Fragment

---

[561] As well as Diodorus 17.48.1-2, see Curtius 4.1.39-40; note that there are additional digressions in Curtius 4.5.11-22 immediately following Curtius' account of Tyre and including the tale of Aristonicus the Pirate.

[562] Aulus Gellius, *NA* 17.21.33; Livy 9.19.10-11.

[563] See N. G. L. Hammond, *Three Historians of Alexander the Great* (Cambridge 1983) 112 on Cleitarchus as Livy's probable source.

The Nature and Genesis of Cleitarchus' Account

10 (description of Babylon) and Fragment 11 (the razing of Persepolis).[564] The narrative on Alexander's activities seems to have ended in July 330BC with the death of Darius, which was also the end of Curtius' fifth book and the 11th book of Justin/Trogus. Diodorus 17.73.4 concludes with the boundary phrase, "And that was the situation in Asia", before catching up with the diplomatic aftermath of the defeat of the Spartans, which Cleitarchus had described at the end of his fifth book. It looks as though Diodorus related the matter here, because Cleitarchus recorded the departure of the Spartan envoys to Alexander at this point (Diodorus 17.73.6 & Curtius 6.1.20). Perhaps the actual arrival of the Spartan envoys in Alexander's camp is indicated by Curtius 7.4.32, when Alexander receives news from Greece of the Spartan rebellion.

Book 7: The first events must have been the advance to Hecatompylus and the persuasion of the troops to continue the war, but Fragments 12-14,[565] Diodorus 17.75 and Curtius 6.4.1-22 show that Cleitarchus provided significant digressions on the geography of the Caspian region and the natural history of Hyrcania near the beginning of this book. Fragments 15 and 16 relate the visit of Thalestris, Queen of the Amazons, and Fragment 32 on the castration of a transgressing male also best fits the context of a digression on Amazon customs.[566] Following Alexander's first crossing of the Hindu Kush in the summer of 329BC Diodorus 17.83.3 has the boundary phrase, Καὶ τὰ μὲν περὶ Ἀλέξανδρον ἐν τούτοις ἦν ("These were the concerns of Alexander"), which probably indicates the end of Book 7 of Cleitarchus.

Book 8: Began with a digression on events in the camp of Bessus echoed in both Curtius 7.4.1-19 and Diodorus 17.83.7, followed by news reaching Alexander from Greece and elsewhere (Curtius 7.4.32-40 and Diodorus 17.83.4-6), then the march to the River Oxus (Diodorus, List of Contents for Book 17; Curtius 7.5.9-12; Frontinus, *Strat.* 1.7.7). The end of Book 8 falls in the great lacuna in Diodorus 17, but the *Metz Epitome* has opened and continues to provide corroboration of Cleitarchan material in Curtius down to Alexander's arrival in the Indus Delta. The closing event of this book seems to have been Alexander's capture of the Rock of Ariamazes (i.e. the Sogdian Rock), which Cleitarchus treated as the climax of the campaigning year of 328BC (*Metz Epitome* 15-18; Curtius 7.11.1-25; Polyaenus 4.3.29; Diodorus 17 – Contents List; Strabo 11.11.4.). This also ended the seventh book of Curtius.

Book 9: Apparently opened with Scythian peace overtures including the offer of the Scythian king's daughter to Alexander in marriage (Curtius 8.1.1-10). It continued with the first campaign against the Massagetae and the Dahae,

---

[564] Jacoby FGrHist 137 F10 & F11 (Diodorus 2.7.3-4 cf. Tzetzes, *Chil.* 9.569; Athenaeus 576D-E).

[565] Jacoby FGrHist 137 F12 (Pliny, *N.H.* 6.36-38), F13 (Strabo 11.1.5), F14 (Demetrius, *De eloc.* 304 cf. Tzetzes, *Chil.* 7.49, 11.832).

[566] T. S. Brown, "Clitarchus," *American Journal of Philology* 71 (1950) 149; Jacoby FGrHist 137 F15 (Plutarch, *Alexander* 46), F16 (Strabo 11.5.4), F32 (*Pap. Oxyrh.* 2.218 col. 2).

incorporating Alexander's 3-column campaign through Sogdiana. This book seems to have climaxed in a similar way to Book 8 with the capture of the Rock of Chorienes. It therefore closed in the late spring of 327BC with the marriage of Alexander to Roxane, who had fallen into his hands with the surrender of this strongpoint (*Metz Epitome* 28-31; Curtius 8.4.20-30; Diodorus - Contents List).

Book 10: Commenced with Alexander's preparations for the invasion of India and also mentioned his orders for the training of native youths in Macedonian arms to augment the *Epigoni*. Several Fragments (20-22) seem to be from an introductory description of Indian royal processions by virtue of parallels in Curtius.[567] A little later Alexander's visit to Nysa and the discovery of the ivy of Dionysus were related by Cleitarchus (Fragment 17).[568] This was the first book of the Indian campaigns. Its climax was the battle against Porus (beside the River Hydaspes) and it closed with the re-instatement of Porus as king in the same place as the close of Curtius' eighth book and the 89th chapter of Diodorus (Curtius 8.14.5; Diodorus 17.89.6; Justin 12.8.7; *Metz Epitome* 61). This was in June of 326BC. Jacoby Fragment 5 of Cleitarchus, which is stated to be derived from Book 10, was likely part of a digression on the revolt of Baryaxes that ended this book.[569]

Book 11: Opened with a discussion of Alexander's plans to reach the ends of India and to visit the Ocean (*Metz Epitome* 63; Curtius 9.1.1-6; Diodorus 17.89.3-90.6). There is copious evidence from the Fragments and other Vulgate sources for digressions on the geography and natural history of India near the beginning of this book: specifically, sixteen-cubit serpents in Fragment 18[570] (Diodorus 17.90.1 and Curtius 9.1.4) and troops of monkeys and their ensnarement in Fragment 19[571] (Diodorus 17.90.2-3). A visit to salt mines in Fragment 28 probably relates to the start of the voyage down the Hydaspes, when the expedition would have passed the famous and ancient salt mines at Khewra.[572] There is also a fragment of Onesicritus at Strabo 15.1.30, which mentions a mountain of salt in the kingdom of Sopeithes. According to Arrian 6.2.2 Hephaistion was ordered to hurry to the capital of King Sopeithes at the start of the river voyage. Fragment 24 suggesting that Ptolemy was present when Alexander was wounded at the Mallian town was part of the climax of this book.[573] The best indications are that Cleitarchus' 11th book closed soon after the

---

[567] Curtius 8.9.23-26; Jacoby FGrHist 137 F20 (Strabo 15.1.69l), F21 (Aelian, *N.A.* 17.23), F22 (Aelian, *N.A.* 17.22).

[568] Jacoby FGrHist 137 F17 (Scholia on Apollonius Rhodius 2.904).

[569] It is also feasible that it was in a digression at the beginning of Book 10.

[570] Jacoby FGrHist 137 F18 (Aelian, *N.A.* 17.2).

[571] Jacoby FGrHist 137 F19 (Aelian, *N.A.* 17.25).

[572] Jacoby FGrHist 137 F28 (Strabo 5.2.6).

[573] Jacoby FGrHist 137 F24 (Curtius 9.5.21).

The Nature and Genesis of Cleitarchus' Account

successful treatment of Alexander's Mallian chest wound by Critobulus in the Spring of 325BC. The main evidence for this is the insertion of a digression on a revolt of the Greeks settled in Bactria by both Diodorus and Curtius at this point (Diodorus 17.99.5-6; Curtius 9.7.1-11). Conversely, the Vulgate narrative is relatively seamless through Alexander's visit to the Ocean and subsequent march into Gedrosia, despite this seeming perhaps to modern sensibilities to be a more logical point to close the second book of the Indian campaign.

Book 12: Began with the capitulation of the Malli and Oxydracae and a celebratory banquet after which the contest between Coragus and Dioxippus took place.[574] F25 relates the killing of 80,000 Indians in the Kingdom of Sambus.[575] F23 telling of Mandi women bearing children at age 7 and being old at 40 is difficult to place exactly, but most probably comes from a digression during the progress down the Indus.[576] It is co-attributed to Megasthenes, suggesting that Cleitarchus took some of his stories about India from Megasthenes' account of his later visit. Fragment 26 clearly refers to the tidal bore in the Indus Delta described also by Curtius.[577] The location of F27 among the Oreitae and the Ichthyophagoi in Gedrosia is self-explanatory.[578] F29 cites stories told to Alexander about the Indian Ocean voyage and may securely be placed at the return of Nearchus and Onesicritus, since there are matching tales related by these men at Curtius 10.1.11.[579] F6 shows that Book 12 extended at least as far as the suicide of Calanus. Its end is clearly indicated following the arrival of the Persian *Epigoni* in summer 324BC (Diodorus 17.108.3) with a recurrence of the terminal sentence, Καὶ τὰ μὲν περὶ Ἀλέξανδρον ἐν τούτοις ἦν, incorporating Cleitarchus' title.

Book 13: Opened with a digression on the extravagance of Harpalus towards his mistresses (Fragment 30) and an account of his flight to Athens.[580] Subsequently, Cleitarchus evidently claimed that a Roman delegation met Alexander at Babylon in April-May of 323BC (Fragment 31).[581] There is significant evidence that Cleitarchus' account extended beyond Alexander's death in June 323BC in an epilogue focussed on the fate of his corpse. A similar version of the suicide of Sisygambis is found in Diodorus 17 and Curtius. Pausanias 1.6.3 speaks of

---

[574] Exclusively a Cleitarchan story: Diodorus 17.100.1-101.6; Curtius 9.7.12-26.

[575] Jacoby FGrHist 137 F25 (Curtius 9.8.15), which had 800,000 (DCCC milia) in the manuscripts, which is usually amended to 80,000 (LXXX milia) on the basis of Diodorus 17.102.5-7, which speaks of "more than eight myriad of the barbarians".

[576] Jacoby FGrHist 137 F23 (Pliny, *N.H.* 7.28-29).

[577] Jacoby FGrHist 137 F26 (Strabo 7.2.1-2); Curtius 9.9.9-21.

[578] Jacoby FGrHist 137 F27 (Pliny, *N.H.* 7.30).

[579] Jacoby FGrHist 137 F29 (Pliny, *N.H.* 6.198).

[580] Jacoby FGrHist 137 F30 (Athenaeus 586C-D); Diodorus 17.108.4-8; Curtius 10.2.1-3.

[581] Jacoby FGrHist 137 F31 (Pliny, *N.H.* 3.57); cf. Arrian, Anabasis 7.15.5-6.

Concerning Alexander the Great by Andrew Chugg

Alexander's body being laid to rest with Macedonian rites at Memphis in about 321BC and he does so shortly after giving a Cleitarchan version of the story that Ptolemy had saved Alexander's life in India. Curtius 7.9.21 similarly describes Macedonian funerary practices in writing that the bones of dead Macedonians were laid to rest in accordance with the rites of their fatherland in a passage likely to be derived from Cleitarchus. Furthermore, Curtius' account closes with a mention of Alexander's entombment at Memphis. This raises the possibility that both Pausanias and Curtius are following a description of how Alexander's body reached Memphis provided by Cleitarchus. There is more evidence that Curtius and Pausanias were using a common source (Cleitarchus): Curtius 9.8.22 shares the statement in Pausanias 1.6.2 that Ptolemy was not actually sired by Lagus, who was therefore only his adoptive father. Another significant indicator for Cleitarchus' account having extended beyond Alexander's death is provided by closely matching comments on the suppression of poisoning rumours under Antipater and Cassander in Diodorus 17.118.2 and Curtius 10.10.18-19 with further echoes in Pausanias 9.7.2. There are also 3-way matches between the accounts of these authors encompassing Cassander's actions: murder of Olympias; restoration of Thebes and the slaughter of all Alexander's relatives. Schachermeyr has also argued that Curtius was still drawing on Cleitarchus for his account of events after Alexander's death.[582] It is additionally pertinent that Jane Hornblower has concluded in the context of a detailed study of Book 18 of Diodorus[583] that the historian continued to follow his source for Book 17 (i.e. Cleitarchus) in several chapters near the beginning of Book 18 culminating in the review and shelving of Alexander's Last Plans (*hypomnemata*). She saw the geographical review of Asia in Diodorus 18.5 as the start of the material drawn from Hieronymus of Cardia. I tend to share the view that the Last Plans are from Cleitarchus, but for different reasons: specifically, I find many echoes of the Last Plans in other Cleitarchan material (notably: Hephaistion's memorial in Plutarch, *Alexander* 72.3; a proposed campaign against the Carthaginians, a march to the Pillars of Heracles and a return via Spain and Italy in Curtius 10.1.17-19; 10,000 talents to be spent establishing temples in Greece in Plutarch, *Moralia* 343D; temple of Athena at Troy in Strabo 13.1.26). Hornblower also suspected that Cleitarchus might be the source for Diodorus' version of Alexander's entombment in Alexandria at 18.28.3-6, but I consider that Diodorus was drawing on his personal experience of having visited the tomb in Alexandria for this, since Cleitarchus could not have implied that Ptolemy Soter created the Alexandrian tomb as early as 321BC. Nevertheless, Curtius also mentions the transfer from Memphis to Alexandria in his last sentence. It is likely that Cleitarchus' account extended at least as far as the entombment at Memphis in 321BC and a significant possibility exists that he finished with the transfer of the

---

[582] F. Schachermeyr, *Alexander in Babylon und die Reichsordnung nach seiner Tode* (Vienna 1970) 92.

[583] Hornblower, *Hieronymus of Cardia*, 92-97.

body to Alexandria by Ptolemy Philadelphus in ~280BC.[584] Indeed it is that event that may have prompted him, as a resident of Alexandria and a subject of Philadelphus, to compose his history.

Other Fragments: As regards F35 and F36 and also the aphorisms attributed to Cleitarchus by several Christian writers in the doubtful Fragments 37-52, none can be placed with certainty. However, some may be placed tentatively. There are echoes of the philosophy of the Cynics and mentions of the diadem in F37-52, which is enough to make it seem credible that they were indeed extracted from Cleitarchus' work. F48 might be associated with Curtius 8.12.17-18 and Meleager's complaints at Alexander's largesse towards Taxiles in section 10.44 of my reconstruction; F39 with Diodorus 17.100.1-101.6 & Curtius 9.7.12-26 describing the suicide of Dioxippus, so it has been incorporated in section 12.7 of my reconstruction; F41 with Diodorus 17.114.2 and Alexander's mourning for the death of Hephaistion and has been included in section 13.33 of my reconstruction; F52 with Diodorus 17.116.3 and the prisoner who sat in Alexander's throne and donned the diadem, so it has been added to section 13.40 of my reconstruction; F49 seems connected with Arrian, *Anabasis* 4.9.6, so I have fitted it to the episode of Alexander's remorse at the killing of Cleitus in section 9.15 of my reconstruction. In addition, F36 from the Suda is helpful in that it extends the evidence for Cleitarchus having used Timaeus as a source.

Sources of Cleitarchus

Several strands of evidence make it seem inherently unlikely that Cleitarchus actually accompanied Alexander's expedition.

1) Diodorus 2.7.3 speaks of Cleitarchus and separately of those who "went over [to Asia] with Alexander" in the same sentence, which implies that Diodorus did not believe that Cleitarchus had been a member of Alexander's expedition.

2) Cleitarchus makes some mistakes of a nature that would not be expected of a writer who had actually been present as events unfolded. For example, Cleitarchus seems to have written or at least implied that the river voyage in India set off from the River Acesines, whereas it actually began on the Hydaspes (according at least to Aristobulus and Nearchus).[585] Others have found errors in Cleitarchus' descriptions of Babylon, Hyrcania and the Caspian region, which make it seem improbable that Cleitarchus ever visited these places in person.[586]

---

[584] A.M. Chugg, "The Sarcophagus of Aleander the Great?" *Greece & Rome* 49.1 (April 2002) 14-15.

[585] Diodorus 17.95.3-5; Curtius 9.3.20-24; *Metz Epitome* 69-70; Justin 12.9.1; corrected by Arrian, *Anabasis* 5.29.5-6.1.1 & *Indica* 18; Strabo 15.1.17 & 15.1.32; Yardley & Heckel, 255.

[586] J. R. Hamilton, "Cleitarchus & Aristobulus", *Historia*, 1961, Vol. 10, 449.

3) There is no evidence of Cleitarchus' participation in any stage of the expedition, whereas most of the primary sources seem to have been only too keen to emphasise their roles in what was generally regarded as a glorious and illustrious campaign. Although this is an argument from silence, the silence seems significant in this instance, since Aristobulus, Ptolemy, Nearchus and Onesicritus are all known to have given prominence to their own activities.[587]

4) There is copious evidence that Cleitarchus incorporated material from a wide range of primary sources on Alexander's expedition (see below) and it seems improbable that he would have relied so extensively on the testimony of others, if he had direct experience himself.

5) Recently, papyrus evidence (described below) has emerged, which tends to suggest that Cleitarchus was still active a century after Alexander's expedition.

On the assumption therefore that Cleitarchus is not himself a true primary source in the sense of being an eyewitness, it is pertinent to examine whence he drew his material. A list of various writers who may have been among Cleitarchus' sources is presented in Table 4. In each case, there is either direct evidence from the ancient sources themselves or else some modern scholar has proposed the writer as featuring among Cleitarchus' sources. The overall picture is that Cleitarchus probably drew on at least ten early or primary sources and may well have used material from twenty or more ancient writers. Table 4 also presents my judgement of the degree of probability that Cleitarchus used each listed source.

Onesicritus of Astypalaea – It is almost certain that Onesicritus was a major source for Cleitarchus. For example, T. S. Brown has observed, "The evidence for Cleitarchus' having used Onesicritus… is irresistible."[588] Nevertheless, there is scarcely any direct overlap in the attributed fragments, although both authors are reported to have told the story of the visit of the Amazon queen.[589] Onesicritus is often supposed to be its originator, since he seems to be the earliest writer to relate this tale.[590] It is certain that Cleitarchus wrote after Onesicritus, because Cleitarchus also uses stories from Nearchus, who wrote partly to refute Onesicritus. Fragment 28 of Cleitarchus and Fragment 21 of Onesicritus both speak of Indian salt mining. But stronger evidence comes from multiple instances where stories (usually digressions) from Onesicritus are echoed by Diodorus and

---

[587] Aristobulus told of his work to restore the vandalised tomb of Cyrus (Arrian, *Anabasis* 6.29.10, Strabo 15.3.7); Ptolemy related his mission to arrest Bessus (Arrian, *Anabasis* 3.29.6-30.5); Nearchus concentrated on his command of the fleet for the return voyage from India, especially to correct Onesicritus, who had implied that he had himself led the fleet in his writings (Arrian, *Anabasis* 6.2.3 & *Indica* 18; see Brown, *Onesicritus* 7-11).

[588] Brown, *Onesicritus* 6.

[589] Jacoby T8 & F1 of Onesicritus and F15 & F1 of Cleitarchus.

[590] E.g. Tarn, *Alexander the Great II, Sources & Studies*, 328.

The Nature and Genesis of Cleitarchus' Account

Curtius. For example, the Cathaean custom of *suttee* and admiration for beauty in the kingdom of Sopeithes are mentioned in Fragment 21 of Onesicritus[591] and appear in the same context in Diodorus 17.91.3-7. Curtius 9.10.3 and 10.1.10 mention respectively the departure and return of the fleet and give the names of *both* Nearchus and Onesicritus as its officers. Since both incidents are covered in similar terms by Diodorus 17.104.3 and 17.106.4-7, their common source is likely to be Cleitarchus, despite the failure of Diodorus to mention the names of the officers. However, Cleitarchus' source is very probably Onesicritus, since Nearchus does not seem to have reported Onesicritus' presence by name in his account of these events.[592] Some at least of the wonders of Hyrcania mentioned in Diodorus 17.75 would seem to be sourced from Onesicritus. For example, the honey-dripping tree of Diodorus resembles the *occhus* tree from which honey distils for two hours each morning in Fragment 3 of Onesicritus and both authors highlight the prolific harvests from Hyrcanian fig trees. Diodorus 17.90.5 appears to refer to the banyan tree, saying that its trunk could barely be embraced by four men. Fragment 22 of Onesicritus in Strabo 15.1.21 says it could scarcely be embraced by five men (although Strabo also notes that Aristobulus mentioned this tree and it also appears in Arrian, *Indica* 11.7 in a fragment of Nearchus). There is an account at Diodorus 17.90.2-3 and in Fragment 19 of Cleitarchus describing a curious technique for capturing monkeys, but this occurs also in Strabo 15.1.29 in a context that makes it look like a fragment of Onesicritus (however, Aristobulus and Nearchus cannot be ruled out as Strabo's source).[593] Cleitarchus' story of Alexander's visit to Delphi may have been sourced from Onesicritus, since Plutarch relates it immediately after the meeting with Diogenes, of whom Onesicritus was a student.[594] The stories of Lysimachus and of the death of his brother Philippus in Curtius 8.1.11-19 and 8.2.34-39 might well have originated with Onesicritus, since he later read his book at the court of Lysimachus, so he had a special motive to celebrate the latter's deeds.[595] Schachermeyr speculated that Cleitarchus took the story of Abdalonymus from Onesicritus, because he considered the story to have a colouring of cynical philosophy (especially in Curtius).[596] Finally, the interview with the Indian gymnosophists, which probably originated in Onesicritus' account,[597] though

---

[591] Strabo 15.1.30.

[592] E.g. Arrian, *Indica* 34.6 following Nearchus; see Brown, *Onesicritus* 10-11 for a detailed argument of the point.

[593] See Pearson, *Lost Histories* 223-4, Hamilton, *C&A* 451 and Brown, *AJP* 71, p144, n9.

[594] Diogenes Laertius 6.75-76, 6.84; Strabo 15.1.65; Plutarch, *Moralia* 331E & *Alexander* 65.

[595] Plutarch, *Alexander* 46: see Hammond, *THA* 145-7 on the origins of the stories relating to Lysimachus in Onesicritus.

[596] Schachermeyr, *Alexander der Grosse* 214, n234; cf. Pearson, *Lost Histories* 238; Atkinson, *Commentary on Curtius III & IV*, 283.

[597] Strabo 15.1.63-65; Plutarch, *Alexander* 65.

missing from Diodorus and Curtius, nevertheless appears in the *Metz Epitome* 78-84, which is virtually entirely derived from Cleitarchan material.

Deinon of Colophon – He was the father of Cleitarchus according to Pliny.[598] He was also the author of a *Persica* (History of Persia).[599] These facts predispose us to expect that Deinon would have been a formative influence on Cleitarchus' conception of the Persian Empire. Nor does the evidence contradict this inference. Cleitarchus seems to have incorporated extensive background material on Asia and on the relationships between certain historically prominent Greeks and the Persians. At least some of this material matches the fragments of Deinon's *Persica*. For example, Cleitarchus seems to be the source for the suggestion that Darius had a concubine for every day of the year and he appears to have inherited this notion from his father.[600] Then Fragments 21 & 22 of Cleitarchus compare Indian birds to Sirens, potentially in homage to his father's assertion that the Sirens were to be found in India.[601] It also appears clear from Fragment 33 that Cleitarchus' stories about Themistocles were extracted from his father's writings, since Plutarch cites both as sources for the same version of Themistocles' career. It should also be suspected that the digressions on Persian history in Diodorus 17.5.3-7.3 and Justin 10 were sourced by Cleitarchus from Deinon. So too the story of Sardanapalus in Fragment 2 (although Alexander's actual visit to the monument of Sardanapalus at Anchiale was told by Callisthenes, Fragment 34). Plutarch, *Alexander* 36.2 has a direct quote from Deinon, which may in this context have been transmitted via Cleitarchus. Hammond suggests that an explanation for the name *Euergetae* given by Diodorus 17.81.1-2 may have come from Deinon via Cleitarchus.[602]

Nearchus of Crete – There are two strong matches between the fragments of Cleitarchus and Nearchus. Firstly, Cleitarchus' Fragment 27 in speaking of the Gedrosians making bread from sun-dried fish matches a fragment from Strabo 15.2.2, which may be from Nearchus, since he is named as a source a few lines above. The only difference is that whereas Nearchus spoke specifically of the Ichthyophagoi (Fish-Eaters), the fragment of Cleitarchus used the more general term Oreitae. Secondly, Cleitarchus' Fragment 18[603] mentions snakes 16 cubits in length and a serpent of the exact same length appears in Fragment 10 of Nearchus.[604] Nearchus and Cleitarchus both gave accounts of the Banyan tree,[605]

---

[598] Jacoby, *FGrHist* 137 T2 = Pliny, *Natural History* 10.136 (where he is "Dinon").

[599] Cornelius Nepos, *Conon* 5; T. S. Brown, *Clitarchus* 135.

[600] Diodorus 17.77.6; Curtius 6.8.8; Plutarch, *Artaxerxes* 27.

[601] Pliny, *Natural History* 10.136.

[602] Hammond, *THA* 60.

[603] Aelian, *NA* 17.2.

[604] Arrian, *Indica* 15.10.

[605] Diodorus 17.90.5 & Curtius 9.1.9-10 vs. Arrian, *Indica* 11.7.

The Nature and Genesis of Cleitarchus' Account

but it is perhaps more likely that Cleitarchus was following Onesicritus in this instance, because mention of the number of men required to embrace the trunk was common to Onesicritus and Cleitarchus. The account of whales in Cleitarchus[606] matches closely the Fragments of Nearchus,[607] especially in the use of trumpets to frighten them into diving out of the course of the fleet. However, Onesicritus evidently also mentioned the whales, though terming them "sea-serpents". It is also just feasible that Cleitarchus drew his tale of the capture of Indian monkeys (F19) from Nearchus, but again Onesicritus (or even Aristobulus) is a more probable source.

Callisthenes of Olynthus - Callisthenes told a story that the sea gave way to Alexander during his march along the coast of Pamphylia.[608] The same story recurs in Plutarch[609] and Hammond has argued that this whole section of Plutarch dealing with signs of divine favour for Alexander's cause was drawn from Cleitarchus.[610] Then Fragment 2 of Cleitarchus suggests that he told the story of Alexander's visit to the monument of Sardanapalus at Anchiale, but Callisthenes had previously related this, as shown by his Fragment 34. Thirdly, Cleitarchus told the story that crows guided Alexander on the road to Siwa,[611] which derives from the account by Callisthenes.[612] Furthermore the Cleitarchan version in Diodorus 17.50.6, that the oracular responses were conveyed via nods and signs, seemingly derives from Callisthenes as in his F14a. Pearson has adduced that Callisthenes was a source for Cleitarchus[613] and this must be correct insofar as story elements originally told by Callisthenes appeared in Cleitarchus. What is less certain is whether Cleitarchus used Callisthenes directly or indirectly through Onesicritus or even Aristobulus.

Timaeus - He is twice coupled with Cleitarchus as a co-source in the context of Jacoby's Fragments of Cleitarchus. According to Fragment 7 both of them cited 820 years as the interval between the invasion of Europe by the Heracleidae and that of Asia by Alexander, whilst other authorities gave shorter periods. Cleitarchus was almost certainly following Timaeus in this, since the latter was especially renowned for his work on chronology. Then in Fragment 36 Cleitarchus is specified to have followed Timaeus on a linguistic point.

---

[606] Curtius 10.1.12 and Diodorus 17.106.7.

[607] Strabo 15.2.12 and Arrian, *Indica* 30.4-5.

[608] Jacoby Fragment 31 of Callisthenes.

[609] Plutarch, *Alexander* 17.2-3.

[610] Hammond, *Sources* 46-7.

[611] Diodorus 17.49.5.

[612] Jacoby Fragment 14a/b of Callisthenes = Strabo 17.1.43 & Plutarch, *Alexander* 27; we know from Arrian, *Anabasis* 3.3.6, that Aristobulus also gave this version, so he would be a possible intermediary.

[613] Pearson, *Lost Histories* 231.

Furthermore, Hammond has shown that Plutarch's date for Alexander's birth probably comes from Timaeus,[614] because Cicero attributes the associated stories concerning the conflagration of the temple at Ephesus on the same day to Timaeus.[615] However, given that Timaeus was a source for Cleitarchus, who was in turn a major source for Plutarch's *Life of Alexander*, the suspicion must be that Plutarch found this information in Cleitarchus. If so, then Cleitarchus must have opened his work with a summary of Alexander's birth and ancestry. Finally, Tarn notes that Diodorus 17.75.7 uses a peculiar phrase μεγίστην ἐπιφάνειαν and a rare verb κηροπλαστεῖν in describing a bee-like creature which he calls an *anthredon*.[616] The same combination occurs in one other place: Diodorus 19.2.9 in a passage Tarn attributes to Timaeus. Tarn poses the question of whether Cleitarchus is using Timaeus, since Diodorus took the matter of the *anthredon* from Cleitarchus (for it is described in Fragment 14 of Cleitarchus). Tarn's observation coupled with the other evidence does indeed support the view that Timaeus was a major source for Cleitarchus.[617]

Liber de Morte [Holcias(?)] – As Heckel[618] has noted, it is clear from Justin 12.14, Curtius 10.10.14 and Diodorus 17.118.1-2 that Cleitarchus was aware of the rumour that Alexander was poisoned at Antipater's instigation by his sons Cassander and Iollas using toxin transported in an ass's hoof in the tradition of the *Liber de Morte*.[619] However, Cleitarchus seems to have given the poisoning rumour as an alternative possibility, rather than as the literal truth, much as the matter is presented by Diodorus.

Megasthenes - According to Fragment 23 of Cleitarchus, both he and Megasthenes mentioned an Indian tribe called the Mandi and attributed three hundred villages to them, saying that their women could bear children from the age of seven and became old at forty. Megasthenes is the source for a parallel description in Arrian's *Indica* 9.1-8, which adds the story of Pandaea.[620] Then Polyaenus 1.3.4 gives the Pandaea story in what has been considered a fragment of Megasthenes,[621] but the usage of the figure of 365 for the number of villages in his version is highly characteristic of Cleitarchus, who was fond of calendar values. Plutarch, *Alexander* 64 and the *Metz Epitome* 78-84 describe Alexander's

---

[614] Hammond, *Sources* 19-20.

[615] Cicero, *N. D.* 2.69 & *Div.* 1.47.

[616] Tarn, *Alexander the Great II, Sources & Studies* 90, n.3.

[617] Also endorsed by Pearson, *Lost Histories* 216.

[618] W. Heckel, *The Last Days & Testament of Alexander the Great*, Historia Einzelschriften, Heft 56 (Stuttgart, 1988), p.2.

[619] E.g. *Metz Epitome* 88-89.

[620] See also Phlegon. *Mirab.* 33: *Of the Pandaian Land*.

[621] Jacoby *FGrHist* 715: Fragment 58 of Megasthenes in J. W. McCrindle, *Ancient India as Described by Megasthenes and Arrian* (1877).

The Nature and Genesis of Cleitarchus' Account

interview with the Indian gymnosophists. Cleitarchus is their likely common source, yet elements at least of this version derive ultimately from Megasthenes according to Hammond.[622] Conversely, on the width of the Ganges, C. Bradford Welles[623] attributes the details in Diodorus 2.37.2, 17.93.2 and 18.6.2 to Megasthenes, but Strabo 15.1.35 and Arrian, *Indica* 4.7 cite Megasthenes in giving a width of 100 stades, whereas the Cleitarchan figure was 30 or 32 stades.[624] In his digression on India Curtius 8.9.8 mentions the River Iomanes (Jumna), which elsewhere (e.g. Arrian, *Indica* 8.5-6) is mentioned by Megasthenes.[625] Hammond observes that Curtius 8.9 includes material that was not known until after Alexander's time, such as Megasthenes' information on the region of the Ganges.[626] Yet it looks as though at least some of it comes from Cleitarchus, because this chapter of Curtius subsequently mentions the processions of the Indian kings with singing birds on branches, which are in Fragments 20-22 of Cleitarchus. It remains possible that Curtius consulted Megasthenes or another later geographer directly, but it is more likely that he found the geographical material on India in Cleitarchus. Posing the question of whether Cleitarchus used Megasthenes as a source for geographical and ethnographical information on India or the reverse, the former seems more probable, since Megasthenes had personally visited India, whereas Cleitarchus almost certainly had not. Megasthenes lived with Sibyrtius, Satrap of Arachosia and (later?) with Seleucus Nicator.[627] He visited the court of Chandragupta as an ambassador, so he was an authority on the region in his own right and is likely to be the originator of his information in most cases.[628]

Hegesias of Magnesia - Part of the description of Alexander's conduct at the siege of Gaza in Curtius 4.6.13-16 closely parallels Fragment 5 of Hegesias,[629] yet some disparities suggest that Curtius was not following Hegesias directly, but via an intermediary, who is likely to be Hegesias' contemporary, Cleitarchus (since he was Curtius' main source). Pearson has noted some tentative evidence that Cleitarchus sometimes used a metrical scheme known as Asianic rhythms,[630]

---

[622] Hammond, *Sources* 121.

[623] C. Bradford Welles, *Loeb edition of Diodorus*, Vol, 8, 389 note 2.

[624] Diodorus 17.93.2; Plutarch, *Alexander* 62.1; *Metz Epitome* 68-9.

[625] Though the mention of the Iomanes relies on a textual correction by Hedicke.

[626] Hammond, *THA* 148.

[627] Arrian, *Anabasis* 5.6.2 & *Indica* 5.3; Clement of Alexandria, *Stromateis* 1.72.4.

[628] Strabo 15.1.36.

[629] Jacoby, *FGrHist* 142 F5 = Dion. Hal., *De comp. Verb.* 123-126 R; Hammond, *THA* 127 notices the resemblances to Curtius' account.

[630] Pearson, *Lost Histories*, 213, n9 & 227, n59 notes evidence of Asianic rhythms especially in F19 (Aelian, *NA* 17.25) & Diodorus 17.13.6.

whereas Strabo suggests that Hegesias was virtually the originator of this style.[631] Cleitarchus' style is also seemingly considered comparable to that of Hegesias in Jacoby's T9 & T12 of Cleitarchus. Finally, having noted that some of Plutarch's information on Alexander's birth seems to come from Timaeus via Cleitarchus, by association it is likely that the rest of this passage, which actually cites Hegesias, was also sourced from Cleitarchus.[632]

Polycleitus of Larissa – He probably accompanied Alexander's expedition and he wrote a substantial history of Alexander's reign in around eight or nine books (since his Jacoby Fragment 1 from the 8th book reads like a story from the end of the reign circa 324-323BC).[633] There is uncertainty regarding when he published and his exact identity (although two historical figures of the same name are candidates). Tarn thinks Polycleitus wrote after Megasthenes, because he mentioned the size of tortoises in the Ganges, but Onesicritus seems to have written about the size of elephants in Ceylon, though he never saw the place.[634] Polycleitus seems to make similar geographical errors in his Fragment 7 as Cleitarchus in his Fragments 12 & 13 (e.g. confusing the Aral Sea with the Sea of Azov).[635] The sweetish water and sea serpents of the Caspian occur in Plutarch, *Alexander* 44 and Diodorus 17.75 respectively, as also in Polycleitus Fragment 7. Plutarch, *Alexander* 46 couples him with Cleitarchus and others in having told the story of the Queen of the Amazons.[636]

Herodotus - Hammond argues that Plutarch, *Alexander* 17.2-18.2 was mimicking Herodotus in his account of Xerxes being swayed by dreams and oracles, in recounting Alexander's uncertainty regarding his future strategy and in explaining how the ensuing oracles and miracles influenced his policy.[637] Hammond also infers that Plutarch found this idea in Cleitarchus, although he may alternatively have added information from other sources. Furthermore, Hammond suggests that Cleitarchus repeated the same formula for the indecision of Darius regarding the conduct of the campaign that culminated in Issus.[638] At the parade of Darius' forces before Babylon, Charidemus of Athens was pessimistic about their chances against the Macedonians and was executed.[639] This passage has features in

---

[631] Jacoby, *FGrHist* 142 T1 = Strabo 14.1.41.

[632] Plutarch, *Alexander* 3.3-5.

[633] Jacoby, *FGrHist* 128 F1 = Athenaeus 539A.

[634] Tarn, *Alexander II Sources* 8; tortoises in the Ganges - Jacoby, *FGrHist* 128 F10 = Paradox. Vat. Rohd. 10; elephants in Ceylon - Jacoby*GrHist* 134 F3 = Pliny, *NH* 6.81.

[635] Jacoby, *FGrHist* 128 F7 = Strabo 11.7.4.

[636] T. S. Brown, *Onesicritus*, 166, n. 84 to Ch. 4 confidently asserts that "Cleitarchus certainly used Polycleitus".

[637] Hammond, *Sources* 45-9.

[638] Hammond, *Sources* 45-9 and *THA* 40-1 & 116.

[639] Curtius 3.2.2-19; Diodorus 17.30.1-31.2.

The Nature and Genesis of Cleitarchus' Account

common with the conference of Xerxes in Herodotus 7 and Curtius 3.2.2-3 actually refers to Xerxes (as described in Herodotus 7.59) for the method of counting the Persian forces by herding them into an enclosure just large enough to accommodate 10,000 troops. According to Plutarch, *Alexander* 20.1-3, Amyntas, the son of Antiochus, gave good advice to Darius, which was ignored, as similarly Herodotus 7.235 & 7.237.1 had presented Demaratus, the Spartan king in exile, as giving good advice to Xerxes, who then disregarded it to his cost. Hammond traces this to Aristobulus and/or Ptolemy, since the same details are given in Arrian 2.6.3-7, but it is not impossible that Cleitarchus adopted this story from Aristobulus.[640] Both Curtius 4.1.27-33 and Diodorus 17.48.2-5 later recount Amyntas' raid on Egypt and they agree so closely that their mutual source must be Cleitarchus. According to Curtius 3.8.1-2 the advice of Amyntas that Darius should fight in open territory was given by Greek troops from the former army of Memnon, but it is likely that Amyntas was already their officer, for he led the Greeks on the Persian side at Issus.[641] It has sometimes been argued that Callisthenes was influenced by Herodotus, in which case the possibility arises that Callisthenes is the source of Herodotean echoes in Cleitarchus.[642]

Theopompus of Chios – Cleitarchus evidently gave the same account of the mistresses of Harpalus as Theopompus according to Fragment 30 of Cleitarchus. Since Cleitarchus post-dated Theopompus,[643] there is a good chance that Cleitarchus took his account from Theopompus. This is accentuated by the fact that after Alexander's death Theopompus joined the court of Ptolemy in Egypt, where he died shortly after 320BC.[644] His memory and influence would still have been strong in Egypt when Cleitarchus was active in Alexandria a few decades later.

Aristobulus of Cassandrea - There are undoubtedly significant similarities between the *History of Alexander* by Aristobulus and some aspects of Cleitarchus' work. Tarn tried to use them to prove that Aristobulus was a source for Cleitarchus, thereby pushing the date of Cleitarchus forward into the 3rd century BC.[645] However, this argument has been vigorously disputed, notably by Hamilton, essentially on the basis that the similarities are more readily explained by Aristobulus and Cleitarchus having had a common source, who was probably Onesicritus.[646] Specifically, Alexander's visit to a monument and statue of Sardanapalus at Anchiale, 12 miles SW of Tarsus, is told by Athenaeus 530A-B as

---

[640] Hammond, *Sources* 49.

[641] Curtius 3.11.18; cf. W. Heckel, *Who's Who in the Age of Alexander the Great*, s.v. Amyntas [2].

[642] L. Prandi, *Callistene. Uno storico tra Aristotele e i re macedoni*, Milan 1985, pp. 82-93.

[643] E.g. according to Pliny, *NH* 3.57 = Fragment 31 of Cleitarchus.

[644] Photius, *Life of Theopompus*.

[645] Tarn, *Alexander II Sources*, 31-36.

[646] J. R. Hamilton, *Cleitarchus & Aristobulus*, Historia 10, 448-458, 1961.

a fragment of Aristobulus.⁶⁴⁷ However, Athenaeus coupled this story with Jacoby Fragment 2 of Cleitarchus (Athenaeus 530A), which gives some historical background on Sardanapalus. It therefore appears likely that Cleitarchus also told the story of the visit to Anchiale, though he was probably echoing his father Deinon's *Persica* (which may in turn have followed Ctesias' *Persica*) for the background history. Tarn points to various Indian names having similar forms in Diodorus and in fragments of Aristobulus, but Hamilton has done much to undermine Tarn's arguments, mainly by proposing Onesicritus as the originator of these forms for the names.⁶⁴⁸ The issue revolves especially around alternatives such as Hypasis/Hypanis and Sudracae/Oxydracae. In fact, it is hard to discern the Cleitarchan forms in most of these cases, since Diodorus, Curtius, Justin and the *Metz Epitome* generally give different versions. Sometimes alternative manuscripts of the same author (or even different passages of the same manuscript) have different forms (e.g. variations for the River Hyphasis among manuscripts of Diodorus include: Ὕπανιν, Ὕφασιν, Ὕπανσιν). Consequently, it is difficult to attach much weight to arguments from the name forms. Perhaps the most striking potential parallel between Aristobulus and Cleitarchus is a description of apes appearing to confront Alexander like an army and curious techniques for the capture of monkeys by exploiting their habit of aping humans to persuade them to glue their eyelids shut or to trap themselves in special leggings. A rather garbled and corrupt version of this tale appears in Jacoby Fragment 19 of Cleitarchus, which is from Aelian, *NA* 17.25, and there is a further Cleitarchan rendering in Diodorus 17.90.2-3. A more intelligible version is found in Strabo 15.1.29 and Tarn argues that Strabo got it from Aristobulus, though his case owes much to the supposedly Aristobulan name forms in Strabo's text.⁶⁴⁹ However, Pearson and Hamilton agree that Strabo might be following Onesicritus for this tale.⁶⁵⁰ Neither can Nearchus be ruled out as Strabo's source. Even if Tarn is correct that Strabo found this material in Aristobulus, then it is still possible as suggested by Brown that both Aristobulus and Cleitarchus took the story from Onesicritus.⁶⁵¹ There remain various instances in which Hammond believes that he detects Aristobulus as the underlying source of passages in the 7th book of Curtius.⁶⁵² As Curtius lacks any attributed fragments of Aristobulus

---

⁶⁴⁷ Jacoby Fragment 9a of Aristobulus, with 9b (Strabo 14.5.9) and 9c (Arrian, *Anabasis* 2.5.2-4) also being related; cf. Plutarch, *Moralia* 326F & 336C.

⁶⁴⁸ Hamilton, *Cleitarchus & Aristobulus*, 457-8; both Tarn and Hamilton might be criticised for having underplayed the variations in the forms among authors, their various manuscripts and even within manuscripts and they overlook the *Metz Epitome*, which is helpful in supporting Oxydracae as the Cleitarchan form, for example.

⁶⁴⁹ Tarn, *Alexander II Sources*, 30-36.

⁶⁵⁰ Pearson, *Lost Histories*, 223-4; Hamilton, *C&A* 451

⁶⁵¹ Brown, *Clitarchus*, AJP 71, 144, note 9.

⁶⁵² Hammond, *THA* 151 suggests Aristobulus as the source for Curtius 7.4.22-31, 7.5.1-18, 7.5.27, 7.6.21-3, 7.9.20-1, 7.10.10-14, 7.11.1-26.

The Nature and Genesis of Cleitarchus' Account

and since some of Hammond's attributions to Aristobulus also seem to me to show evidence of derivation from Cleitarchus, these cases potentially indicate the use of Aristobulus by Cleitarchus. For example, Hammond discusses Aristobulus as the source of Curtius 7.6.11-23 & 7.6.25-27 for the advance to the Tanais and the foundation of Alexandria on the Tanais with a circumference of 60 stades in 17 days. This is mainly due to a general (though not detailed) similarity with events as reported by Arrian 4.1-4.[653] However, the detailed correspondence of Curtius with Justin 12.5.12 and the fact that some aspects are mentioned in the *Metz Epitome* 8-9 are clear indications of Cleitarchus and "Tanais River" is a Cleitarchan name for the river. For the rock of Ariamazes, Hammond thinks much of Curtius' account (7.11.1-25) is from Aristobulus,[654] but commonalities with the *Metz Epitome* include a cavern on the ascent path, an altitude of 20 (*Metz Epitome*) or 30 (Curtius) *stadia* and 300 climbers signalling with white cloths and using iron wedges and ropes. Hence, this would appear to be Cleitarchan material. Hammond also cites similarities between Curtius and Arrian 4.18.4-4.19.3 and suggests that Alexander's *cupido* in Curtius is a Latin equivalent of *pothos* in Arrian, where such *yearning* is believed to be a characteristic applied to Alexander particularly by Aristobulus.[655] Nevertheless, it might be countered that Hammond is taking advantage of the lacuna in Diodorus speculatively to attribute some of the more historically cogent passages in Curtius to Aristobulus. Finally, the key role for Aristander's prophecies in Arrian seems to be derived from Aristobulus, but Aristander's influence was also reported by Cleitarchus.[656] In summary, there are enough hints as to justify a suspicion that Cleitarchus was influenced by Aristobulus, but none is sufficiently clear as to establish high confidence in the matter.

Patroclus – Tarn[657] noticed that a geographical observation that the Euxine (Black Sea) is equal to the Caspian (in length) is common to Fragment 12 of Cleitarchus (Pliny, *NH* 6.36-38) and to a fragment of Patroclus.[658] Tarn made this point into the lynchpin of his theory of a late date for Cleitarchus, since he supposed Patroclus, who explored the Caspian in c. 280BC, to have originated the statement. However, Pearson and Brown do not accept this as proof that Patroclus was a source for Cleitarchus.[659] It remains possible that the comments are independent of one another or that Cleitarchus inspired Patroclus.

---

[653] Hammond, *THA* 142.

[654] Hammond, *THA* 144.

[655] It also seems to have been used of Alexander by Nearchus, e.g. Arrian, *Indica* 20.1.

[656] Diodorus 17.17.6; Curtius 4.2.14, 4.4.12, 4.13.15, 4.15.27, 5.4.2, 7.7.8-29.

[657] Tarn, *Alexander II Sources*, 16-19.

[658] Strabo 11.7.1, probably via Eratosthenes.

[659] Pearson, *Lost Histories*, 227; Brown, *Clitarchus*, AJP 71, 140.

Ephippus of Olynthus - Hammond suggests that Trogus (Justin 12.12.11-12) may have followed Cleitarchus, who in turn followed Ephippus, for the death and funeral of Hephaistion (since Ephippus is known to have written a lost book on the subject).[660] Similarly, Hammond attributes the elaborate description of the funeral of Hephaistion in Diodorus 17.115 to Ephippus, noting that the extravagant funerary dedications from Alexander's Friends in Diodorus 17.115.1 & 17.115.5 are comparable to the gifts made to Alexander himself in Jacoby Fragment 5 of Ephippus (Athenaeus 537E-538B).[661] Strangely, Hammond argues that Diodorus could not have taken the description of Hephaistion's pyre from Cleitarchus on the basis that the description of Alexander's catafalque in Diodorus 18 might have come from the same source, which is Hieronymus of Cardia.[662] However, this is illogical and inconsistent. If Justin is reporting Hephaistion's funeral from Ephippus via Cleitarchus, then so is Diodorus.[663] Nevertheless, despite the fact that Ephippus is the best-attested primary source on the death and funeral of Hephaistion, he was probably not the only early writer to treat the subject in detail, so it is far from certain that he was the source used by Cleitarchus. However, Ephippus also mentioned that Alexander quaffed from a giant cup before collapsing at his final party, which recurs as the "Cup of Heracles" in the Cleitarchan tradition.[664] There is one other hint that Cleitarchus may have followed Ephippus: the description of the dress adopted by Alexander after the death of Darius given by Ephippus closely matches details given in the Vulgate authors (diadem and purple tunic with the central white stripe etc.)[665]

Berossus - P. Schnabel long ago published a rather intricate argument[666] to the effect that Cleitarchus may have used Berossus, a Chaldean Priest of Bel, as a source on Babylon. In outline, Diodorus within his account of Babylon in his second book states that he sometimes corrects Ctesias from Cleitarchus and others. One such correction in 2.10.1 was to deny that Semiramis constructed the Hanging Gardens in favour of a "later Syrian king". Since Curtius 5.1.35 makes exactly the same statement, including the Cleitarchan "Syrian" instead of the more correct "Assyrian" and the matching detail that the king made them for his wife, there are good grounds to think that both writers took this from Cleitarchus. But

---

[660] Hammond, *THA* 107-8 & 114; Athenaeus 120D, 146C, 434A & 537D for Ephippus' work.

[661] Hammond, *THA* 75; Droysen, *Hellenismus*² II 126, note 2 has the same suggestion.

[662] Athenaeus 206E.

[663] Hammond, *Sources* 137 attributes the parallel account of Hephaistion's death and the funeral arrangements in Plutarch, *Alexander* 72.1-3 to Cleitarchus, but I suspect that Plutarch drew on other sources as well, since his figure for the funeral costs of 10,000 talents agrees with Arrian as opposed to the 12,000 talents in Justin and Diodorus, which should be the Cleitarchan value.

[664] Athenaeus 434A-B; Diodorus 17.117.1-2; Plutarch, *Alexander* 75.3; Justin 12.13.8.

[665] Ephippus in Athenaeus 537E; *Metz Epitome* 2; Diodorus 17.77.5; Curtius 3.3.17-19 & 6.6.4; Justin 12.3.8; Plutarch, *Alexander* 45.2 & *Moralia* 329F-330A (though the latter is attributed to Eratosthenes).

[666] P. Schnabel, *Berossus*, 1923, ch. 3 – this chapter had earlier been published as a separate study.

The Nature and Genesis of Cleitarchus' Account

whence did Cleitarchus obtain this information? Schnabel pointed out that the *Babyloniaca* of Berossus[667] is the earliest authoritative source for asserting that Nabukodrossoros (Nebuchadnezzar?) was the builder rather than Semiramis and for terming them a present for his queen. However, Berossus dedicated his work to Antiochus I, who came to the throne in 293BC (initially jointly with Seleucus Nicator), so this would push Cleitarchus well into the third century BC. It is possible that an earlier authority made the same statement, but no such source is known.[668]

Demetrius of Phalerum – Richard Billows has argued that Cleitarchus' attention to Alexander's *Tyche* (fortune) was inspired by a work *Peri Tyches* by Demetrius of Phalerum, which is cited by Polybius as having discussed Alexander's career.[669] However, the influence of Demetrius could have been indirect or Cleitarchus may have taken up this theme independently.

Chares of Mytilene - Pearson expresses confidence that Chares was a source for Cleitarchus, but he fails to offer any specific evidence and such evidence is hard to detect.[670] Nevertheless, Hammond thinks Curtius 8.11.1-25 supplemented his account of Aornus from Chares especially for the heroic acts of the King, another Alexander and Charus.[671] This is mainly because Curtius mentions the filling of *cavernas* with tree-trunks, whilst Fragment 16 of Chares (Athenaeus 124C) speaks of pits being filled with snow and covered with oak boughs in the context of Aornus (which he calls Petra, since it was known as The Rock in Greek). This would raise the possibility that Cleitarchus took these details from Chares, though it seems more likely that the rather vague similarities between Curtius and Chares are merely coincidental. Fragment 18 of Chares (Aulus Gellius 5.2.1-5) has Bucephalus die of his wounds after carrying Alexander from the midst of the enemy in the Battle of the Hydaspes and also mentions the foundation of the city of Bucephala at the site to honour the King's steed. This is also broadly the story told by Cleitarchus as reflected in the Vulgate sources.[672] It is therefore a possibility that the Cleitarchan version was inspired by the account of Chares. Conversely, Chares' versions of the proskynesis experiment (F14 – Plutarch, *Alexander* 54; Arrian, *Anabasis* 4.12.3-5), the death of Callisthenes (F15 - Plutarch, *Alexander* 55) and the funeral of Calanus (F19 – Athenaeus 437AB; Plutarch, *Alexander* 70) are not strikingly similar to the Cleitarchan versions.

---

[667] In the Fragment of Berossus in Josephus, *Contra Apion* 1.141-142.

[668] See also Pearson, *Lost Histories* 230-231.

[669] Richard Billows, "Polybius and Alexander Historiography" in *Alexander the Great in Fact and Fiction*, ed. A.B. Bosworth and E.J. Baynham, Oxford 2000, 297-299; Polybius 29.21.2.

[670] Pearson, *Lost Histories*, 61 & 131.

[671] Hammond, *THA* 149

[672] See Hammond, *Sources* 111 & 257; Curtius 8.14.34, 9.1.6, 9.3.23; Justin 12.8.4-8; Stephanus Byzantinus, s.v. *boos kephalai*; Diodorus 17.89.6 & 17.95.5; Strabo 15.1.29 and *Metz Epitome* 62.

Hieronymus of Cardia - Hammond gives a curious argument that Hieronymus should be seen as the source of the accusation in Diodorus, Curtius, Justin and other Vulgate sources that Antipater, Cassander and Iollas had conspired to poison Alexander.[673] He notes that Curtius 10.10.18-19 and Diodorus 17.118.2 both said that the subsequent power of Antipater and Cassander had caused this rumour to be suppressed. He concludes that it cannot have been published until after Cassander's death in 297BC. He infers that Hieronymus was the likely source, since he wrote his History dealing with events following on from Alexander's death in the early 3rd century BC (but completed it after the death of Pyrrhus in 272BC[674]) and because he was Diodorus' main source in his next book.[675] However, the *Liber de Morte* may well be the original written source for the poisoning of Alexander on Antipater's orders. Heckel dates it to ~317BC, before the fall of Eumenes.[676] The close correspondence between Diodorus and Curtius on the matter of the suppression of the story is in fact good evidence that both are still following Cleitarchus, but Cleitarchus is likely to be getting his information from the *Liber de Morte*, rather than from Hieronymus. It is sometimes argued that Curtius 10.6-10.10 is based on Hieronymus,[677] but the similarities between Diodorus 17.118.2 and Curtius 10.10.18-19 and between Diodorus 17.118.3 and Curtius 10.5.19-25 are indications that Curtius may have found at least some of this material in Cleitarchus. If so, then there is a vague possibility that Cleitarchus drew on Hieronymus.

One early history of Alexander's campaigns that Cleitarchus virtually certainly did not use was that compiled by Ptolemy, because Cleitarchus disagrees with Ptolemy's account on too many issues. For example, they specifically differ on whether Ptolemy was present when Alexander received his chest wound in India[678] and on many points regarding Alexander's activities in Egypt.[679] There is also no sign that Cleitarchus had direct access to the *Ephemerides* (Alexander's

---

[673] Hammond, *THA* 78 & *Sources* 146.

[674] Jacoby, *FGrHist* 154 F15.

[675] Hornblower, Jane, *Hieronymus of Cardia*, OUP, 1981.

[676] W. Heckel, *The Last Days & Testament of Alexander the Great*, Historia Einzelschriften, Heft 56 (Stuttgart, 1988), p.71-75.

[677] E.g. R. M. Errington, "From Babylon to Triparadeisos, 323-320BC," *JHS* 90 (1970) 72-75.

[678] Curtius 9.5.21.

[679] E.g. return route from Siwa - Arrian, *Anabasis* 3.4.5 versus Curtius 4.8.1: timing of the foundation of Alexandria - Arrian, *Anabasis* 3.1.5 versus Curtius 4.8.1, Diodorus 17.52: dragons versus crows guiding Alexander in the desert - Arrian, *Anabasis* 3.3.5 versus Diodorus 17.49.5.

Journal, kept by his secretary, Eumenes of Cardia), although he might have had indirect access if he used Ephippus, who made extensive use of the *Ephemerides*.[680]

The Date of the *Indica* of Megasthenes

The date at which Cleitarchus wrote and published his history of Alexander is of considerable interest, since it is a key determinant of his relationship with his own sources, the men who were friends and companions of Alexander. However, there seems to be significant evidence that Cleitarchus also sourced material from the *Indica* of Megasthenes, which was based upon its author's experience of India after Alexander's death. The date of composition of the *Indica* is therefore potentially a *terminus post quem* for Cleitarchus' work. But this issue is controversial: in particular A. B. Bosworth has recently argued for a revision of Megasthenes' publication date from circa 290BC to circa 310BC.[681]

It is stated by Strabo that Megasthenes visited Palimbothra (Pataliputra) on the Ganges, for the purpose of an embassy to the Indian king, Chandragupta Maurya.[682] It is separately stated by Clement of Alexandria that Megasthenes lived together with Seleucus Nicator, implying he was a member of Seleucus' court.[683] From these attestations and other circumstantial details, it has long been believed that Megasthenes was the ambassador of Seleucus in his negotiations with Chandragupta in 304/3BC. Such is the orthodoxy that Bosworth has disputed. At the core of the issue lies a single sentence from Arrian's *Indica* (5.3): συγγενέσθαι γὰρ Σανδροκόττῳ λέγει, τῷ μεγίστῳ βασιλεῖ Ἰνδῶν, καὶ Πώρου ἔτι τούτου μείζονι. Bosworth offers the translation: [Megasthenes] *says that he met Sandrocottus* [Chandragupta] *the greatest king of the Indians, and also met Porus, who was yet greater than him*. Although the Greek is good, this creates a paradox, since Porus was undoubtedly also an Indian king and was recognized as such by Megasthenes and his contemporaries. For this reason, it has become standard practice for modern editors to amend the final phrase to: Πώρου ἔτι τούτῳ μείζονι, giving the translation, [Megasthenes] *says that he met Sandrocottus the greatest king of the Indians, even greater than Porus*. However, Bosworth notices that Arrian, *Anabasis* 5.6.2, states that, *Megasthenes lived with Sibyrtius, satrap of Arachosia, and often speaks of his visiting Sandracottus, the king of the Indians*. He suggests that the paradox may be resolved by supposing that Megasthenes actually acted as the ambassador of Sibyrtius to Chandragupta in the context of the alliance of the eastern satraps against Peithon between 320BC and 318BC. He would have met Porus, who was not murdered by Eudamas until 317BC, *en route*. If he then compiled his *Indica*

---

[680] A. M. Chugg, "The Journal of Alexander the Great", *Ancient History Bulletin* 19.3-4 (2005) 155-175.

[681] AB Bosworth, "The Historical Setting of Megasthenes' *Indica*," *CPh* 91 (1996), 113-27.

[682] Strabo 15.1.36.

[683] Clement of Alexandria, *Stromateis* 1.72.4.

after Porus' death, but before Chandragupta took over the satrapies of the Indus river system, Megasthenes might have written that Porus had been the greatest ever king of the Indians, but that Chandragupta enjoyed that distinction at the time that he wrote. Bosworth supposes that Arrian has then garbled the meaning of his source (by failing to reflect the time distinctions) to generate the received manuscript reading. Bosworth adopts this reasoning to argue that Megasthenes probably wrote before Chandragupta's territories became larger than those of Porus at their greatest extent. Bosworth further observes that Porus had achieved control of virtually the entire Indus river system by the time of Alexander's death, so the critical juncture (at least from a Greek perspective) would be Chandragupta's acquisition of Porus' territories to augment his kingdom on the Ganges. The evidence is scant, but Justin remarks that Chandragupta came into possession of India whilst Seleucus was laying the foundations of his future power.[684] Bosworth places the extension of Chandragupta's control into the Punjab after 309BC. His acquisitions in the Indus river system were seemingly recent in 305BC, when Seleucus launched an expedition across the Indus and fought with him.[685] We are explicitly told of an alliance negotiated between them in 304/3BC involving an interrelationship by marriage and the gift of 500 elephants to Seleucus,[686] which he deployed to great effect at the Battle of Ipsus in 301BC.

On balance I support Bosworth (and T. S. Brown before him)[687] in rejecting the manuscript emendation of Arrian's *Indica*, even though it is textually minor. As Bosworth points out, it is in general bad practice to impute errors where the Greek of our manuscripts is good and in this case the manuscript reading is contextually superior to the emendation. However, it seems to me that there is a more straightforward way to resolve the apparent paradox, which does not involve the imputation of any kind of error on the part of our ancient sources. I would offer instead a translation of the manuscript reading with a variant nuance: [Megasthenes] *says that he met Sandrocottus the king of the Indians of the greatest stature, and also met Porus, who was of yet greater stature than he*. To appreciate that this is essentially a quip or pun, it is only necessary to know that Porus' most famous attribute was his exceptional tallness. Arrian himself introduces his description of Porus by noting his reported height to have been above 5 cubits.[688] In fact the paradox in this English version of the sentence *requires* that "stature" should be interpreted in its sense meaning greatness when it refers to Chandragupta, but in its sense meaning height when it refers to Porus. But in the Greek, μέγας has

---

[684] Justin 15.4.20.

[685] Appian, *Syriaca* 55; Justin 15.4.12.

[686] Strabo 15.2.9 & 16.2.10; Plutarch, *Alexander* 42.2; Appian, *Syriaca* 55.

[687] T. S. Brown, "The Merits and Weaknesses of Megasthenes," *Phoenix* 11 (1957) 13.

[688] Arrian, *Anabasis* 5.19.1.

exactly the same duality in its possible meaning. Indeed, Arrian uses its counterpart noun μέγεθος to describe Porus' height in his *Anabasis*.

This interpretation has the opposite effect to that suggested by Bosworth. It is seen to be necessary for Megathenes to have been aware that the territories of Chandragupta exceeded those that had been controlled by Porus. Probably, that would put the composition of his *Indica* after the negotiations in 304/3BC, because it would have been offensive to his patron Seleucus to imply Chandragupta's acquisition of the Punjab before that time. It also makes it very likely that Megasthenes' embassy to Chandragupta was indeed conducted on behalf of Seleucus. Although I concede that Megasthenes *could* have represented Sibyrtius in India, it seems strange that Sibyrtius should have conducted direct negotiations with a kingdom on the Ganges at a time when his ally Eudamas would have been in a better position to engage in diplomacy with his neighbour Chandragupta on behalf of the eastern satraps and there is of course no actual evidence of such diplomacy anyway. Consequently, I am compelled inexorably to accept the canonical publication date for Megasthenes' *Indica* in the first decade of the third century BC.

Dating Cleitarchus from the Vulgate & Fragments

Quintilian stated that Timagenes, who flourished in the middle of the 1st century BC and arrived in Rome from Alexandria in 55BC, was born long after Cleitarchus, who tends also to be listed among other writers of the late 4th and early 3rd centuries BC in various of Jacoby's Testimonies (e.g. T12, T14).[689]

We are told by Philippus, quoted by Diogenes Laertius in his *Life of Stilpo of Megara* (2.113), that Stilpo succeeded in poaching Cleitarchus as a pupil from his rival Aristotle the Cyrenaic sophist. It has been argued by Zeller[690] by analysing the list of his known pupils that Stilpo, though born around 380BC, only began actively teaching in around 322BC, yet when he met Demetrius Poliorcetes in 307BC he was said to be living a "life of tranquillity and study".[691] From this it has been argued that Cleitarchus' studentship probably occurred between these two dates. More recently it has been suggested that a possible specific occasion for Cleitarchus' recruitment by Stilpo was the visit to Corinth in the summer of 308BC of Ptolemy Soter, when he presided at the Isthmian Games. It is supposed that Aristotle of Cyrene and his pupils, Cleitarchus and Simmias, were among Ptolemy's retinue, since Cyrene was among Ptolemy's possessions and

---

[689] See Heckel in the Introduction to *Yardley's translation of Curtius*, 7; Jacoby, *FGrHist* 137 T6 = Quintilian, *Inst.* 10.1.74; Jacoby*GrHist* 137 T12 = Philodemus, *Rhet.* 4.1 col. 21; Jacoby*GrHist* 137 T14 = Pliny, *NH* 1.6, 1.7, 1.12-13.

[690] Eduard Zeller, *Die Philosophie der Griechen*, 4th ed., Part II, 1 (Leipzig, 1889) 248, n. 2; T. S. Brown, "Clitarchus," *American Journal of Philology*, 1950, Vol. 71, 137.

[691] Plutarch, *Life of Demetrius* 9.

Cleitarchus himself is called an Alexandrian by Philodemus.[692] Diogenes Laertius 2.111 mentions that Stilpo defeated a rival, Diodorus Cronos, in dialectic in the presence of Ptolemy, but he also states a little afterwards that Stilpo refused Ptolemy's invitation to visit Egypt, whereas the Suda observes that Stilpo was "entertained" by the first Ptolemy.[693] It has been argued that a visit by Ptolemy to Megara at only ~20 miles from Corinth during 308BC is the only recorded occasion such that all these references can be correct.[694] Since Diogenes Laertius seems to expect his readers to recognise Stilpo's Cleitarchus and since his era is reasonably consistent with all other evidence on our Cleitarchus, it is likely that Philippus was referring to the famous author of the history of Alexander. If this reasoning were correct, the Stilpo connection would have the effect of confining Cleitarchus' publication date to between about 320-250BC and is most consistent with a date towards the centre of this period.

The *terminus post quem* for Cleitarchus' work may be 310BC if the mention at Diodorus 17.23.2-3 of Agathocles' activities in that year was derived from Cleitarchus, which seems probable.[695] At any rate, few authorities would support a date outside this range, but within it scholars may be sub-divided into two main camps. One party (e.g. F. Jacoby, J. R. Hamilton, W. Heckel…) favour a date in the approximate range 310-300BC, whilst the other (e.g. W. W. Tarn, L. Pearson, N. G. L. Hammond…) would prefer a range of 280-260BC. The manuscript evidence for the earlier range may be summarised as follows:

1. Pliny suggests that Cleitarchus wrote before Theophrastus and it is on balance likely that Theophrastus published within a few years either way of 300BC.[696]

---

[692] *FGrHist* 137 T12 of Cleitarchus; Cleitarchus was probably an immigrant to Alexandria, firstly, because he was probably born before its foundation and, secondly, because his father may have been the Dinon of Colophon mentioned in the list of sources of Varro, R.R. 1.1.8 and Pliny, *N.H.*, sources for books 10, 14, 15, 17 & 18, but there are manuscript difficulties, on which see L. Pearson, *Lost Histories*, 226, n.56.

[693] Suidae Lexicon s.v. *Stilpon* – Adler number: sigma 1114.

[694] Luisa Prandi, *Fortuna è realtà dell' opera di Clitarco*, Historia Einzelschriften 104, Steiner, Stuttgart 1996; A. B. Bosworth, "In Search of Cleitarchus: Review-discussion of Luisa Prandi: Fortuna è realtà dell' opera di Clitarco," *Histos* (University of Durham, electronic journal of historiography), Vol. 1, Aug. 1997.

[695] Diodorus might in principle himself have introduced the example of Agathocles out of personal familiarity with the exploits of a fellow Sicilian; however, he is explicit that Agathocles was imitating Alexander's strategy in ridding himself of his fleet, a motivation which probably needed to be sourced from a contemporaneous writer, given the inexactitude of the parallel; yet Diodorus fails to mention the connection with Alexander when recounting Agathocles' boat burning in more detail using a different source (Timaeus?) at 20.7. That Agathocles is called a king at 17.23.2, whereas Diodorus assigns him the title of Dynast or Tyrant elsewhere in books 16, 18, 19 and 20, may be a consequence of sourcing from Cleitarchus.

[696] Pliny, *N. H.* 3.57; see J. R. Hamilton, "Cleitarchus & Aristobulus," *Historia*, 1961, Vol. 10, 452-3 for a detailed analysis of this point.

The Nature and Genesis of Cleitarchus' Account

2. Cleitarchus appears to have written in ignorance of Ptolemy's mention (penned before his death in 282BC) of his presence elsewhere during the Mallian siege at the time that Alexander received his chest wound; furthermore, it has been suggested that Ptolemy might have been implicitly contradicting Cleitarchus in recording his absence.[697]

3. Cleitarchus (F11) made Thais responsible for the burning of Persepolis, whereas Arrian's account, presumably deriving from Ptolemy, effectively denies her any role in the matter.[698] Since Thais was Ptolemy's mistress and the mother of his daughter Eirene and his sons Leontiscus and Lagus, it should have been dangerous for an Alexandrian to contradict Ptolemy regarding her biography. It is therefore argued that this is a further indication that Ptolemy's official version was not known to Cleitarchus when he wrote.[699]

4. It is relatively uncontroversial that Cleitarchus used both Onesicritus and Nearchus, who had probably both published by 310BC, but advocates of an early date for Cleitarchus have also been at pains to point out that it is strangely difficult to *prove* that Cleitarchus used Aristobulus, who wrote between 301BC and about 270BC, despite Aristobulus' history having been second only to Cleitarchus' own in popularity.[700]

Conversely, there are significant reasons to assign a date in the first half of the 3rd century BC to the publication of Cleitarchus' work:

1. The close similarity between Curtius 10.10.18-19 and Diodorus 17.118.2 in speaking of Antipater and Cassander having suppressed the rumour that they had caused Iollas to poison Alexander is a significant indication that these authors found this comment in Cleitarchus.[701] If so, then this

---

[697] Curtius 9.5.21; Arrian, *Anabasis* 6.11.8; F. Jacoby, *Real-Encyclopädie* 11, 625 argued that Ptolemy had probably contradicted Cleitarchus, but J. R. Hamilton, "Cleitarchus & Aristobulus" 451-452 considered the evidence inconclusive; Tarn, *Alexander the Great II, Sources & Studies*, 26-28, pointed out that our sources suggest that Ptolemy did not explicitly contradict Cleitarchus and sought to argue that Ptolemy wrote first and Cleitarchus deliberately distorted the truth to glorify Ptolemy's memory: the value of this evidence for the problem of the date of Cleitarchus is further undermined by arguments from Errington, "Bias in Ptolemy's History of Alexander", *Classical Quarterly* 19, pp233-242, and others that Ptolemy wrote soon after Alexander's death, although the more orthodox view that he wrote in the 280's BC remains preferable.

[698] Arrian, *Anabasis* 3.18.11-12.

[699] E.g. A. B. Bosworth, "In Search of Cleitarchus: Review-discussion of Luisa Prandi: Fortuna è realtà dell' opera di Clitarco," *Histos* (University of Durham, electronic journal of historiography), Vol. 1, Aug. 1997, paragraph 6.

[700] J. R. Hamilton, "Cleitarchus & Aristobulus"; however this is essentially an argument from silence and should therefore carry little weight.

[701] Diodorus 17.118.2 (Loeb trans.): *"After Alexander's death, Antipater held the supreme authority in Europe and then his son Casander took over the kingdom, so that many historians did not dare write about the drug. Cassander, however, is plainly disclosed by his own actions as a bitter enemy to Alexander's policies. He murdered Olympias and threw out her body without burial, and with great enthusiasm restored Thebes, which had been destroyed*

is suggestive that Cleitarchus published after the death of Cassander in 297BC, since the perspective of the comment seems to be an overview of the entire reign and it would indeed have been dangerous to promulgate such an accusation whilst Cassander lived. Nevertheless, Heckel has recently argued that Diodorus' mentions of Cassander's restoration of Thebes and murder of Olympias at the same juncture suggest that his source, Cleitarchus, wrote before the killings of Roxane, Alexander IV, Barsine and Heracles, since he should otherwise have been expected also to refer to them.[702] However, this is an argument from silence, which should therefore carry little weight. Furthermore, Pausanias 9.7.2 is another author who couples Cassander's rebuilding of Thebes with his role in arranging the execution of Olympias.[703] It is relatively unlikely that these two incidents were coupled in the same way independently by two different writers, so we should suspect that Pausanias is also following Cleitarchus. This is reinforced by our earlier observations that Pausanias 1.6.2-3 probably drew on Cleitarchus for Ptolemy having saved Alexander in the land of the Oxydracae and for Alexander's entombment at Memphis. Yet Pausanias 9.7.2 *does* proceed immediately to note the murders of Alexander's sons and he continues with details of Cassander's death and the fates of Cassander's sons. It appears likely that Cleitarchus gave these details, but that Diodorus abbreviated his source rather arbitrarily.[704] As regards the proposition that Pausanias might be merging other sources with Cleitarchus' account,

---

by Alexander." Curtius 10.10.18-19 (Yardley trans.): *"Whatever credence such stories gained, they were soon scotched by the power of the people defamed by the gossip. For Antipater usurped the throne of Macedon and of Greece as well, and he was succeeded by his son, after the murder of all who were even distantly related to Alexander."*

[702] Waldemar Heckel, "The Earliest Evidence for the Plot to Poison Alexander" in *Alexander's Empire: Formulation to Decay*, California 2007, 271; F. Schachermeyr, *Alexander der Grosse: Das Problem seiner Persönlichkeit und seines Wirkens*, (Vienna, 1973) 155, n. 149 also thinks Cleitarchus did not know of the murder of Alexander IV and Roxane, but Curtius 10.10.19 is suggestive of awareness of the murders on the part of Cleitarchus; N.G.L. Hammond, *THA* 78 notices that the implication is that the poisoning story was not reported by Diodorus' source until after the death of Cassander in 297BC and he uses this to argue that Hieronymus was Diodorus' source, yet this contradicts the *Einquellenprinzip* given the similarity of context and language found in Curtius.

[703] Pausanias 9.7.2 (Loeb trans.): *"My own view is that in rebuilding Thebes Cassander was mainly influenced by hatred of Alexander. He destroyed the whole house of Alexander to the bitter end. Olympias he threw to the exasperated Macedonians to be stoned to death; and the sons of Alexander, Heracles by Barsine, and Alexander by Roxane, whom he killed by poison. But he himself was not to come to a good end. He was filled with dropsy, and from the dropsy came worms while he yet lived. Philip, the eldest of his sons, shortly after coming to the throne was seized by a wasting disease, which proved fatal. Antipater, the next son, murdered his mother Thessalonice, the daughter of Philip, son of Amyntas, and of Nicasipolis, charging her with being too fond of Alexander, who was the youngest of Cassander's sons. Getting the support of Demetrius, the son of Antigonus, he deposed with his help and punished his brother Antipater. However, it appeared that in Demetrius he found a murderer and not an ally. So some god was to exact from Cassander a just requital."*

[704] There is a parallel instance in the misleading arbitrariness with which Diodorus seems to have summarised the matter of the 440 talents raised at Thebes.

The Nature and Genesis of Cleitarchus' Account

it should be noted that Curtius 10.10.19 mentions that all Alexander's relations were killed, whilst Pausanias states that all members of Alexander's house were destroyed by Cassander: virtually the same observation in the same context. There is in effect a three-way correspondence between Diodorus, Curtius and Pausanias on these points. Thus, it is difficult to evade the conclusion that Cleitarchus was the underlying source for every detail in all three accounts. This amounts to a cardinal argument for pushing his date forward into the 3rd century BC.

2. It has been argued that Cleitarchus would have been more likely to mention the Romans after Pyrrhus' campaigns against them in around 280BC, which was the first time that they came to prominence on the stage of Greek history.[705] (Badian's suggestion that Cleitarchus actually saw the Roman delegation, because he was present in Babylon, is not persuasive: his argument that Cleitarchus' information had to be based on autopsy, because Pliny *implies* that it was better than hearsay [*fama*] but less good than close study [*diligentius*] is a *non sequitur*.)[706]

3. There is evidence of varying strength that Cleitarchus drew on a range of writers of the early 3rd century BC for aspects of his account of Alexander's reign. These include (as a minimum) Aristobulus, Patroclus, Berossus and Megasthenes.

To show how the multiple, individually inconclusive strands of evidence that Cleitarchus used 3rd century writers can accumulate to make a strong case for a third century date for Cleitarchus, I have assigned conservative probabilities as to whether Cleitarchus used each source as follows (see also Table 4): Megasthenes 80%, Aristobulus 40%, Patroclus 35%, Berossus 30%. Thus the probability that Cleitarchus did not use Megasthenes is 1 - 0.8 = 0.2. For Cleitarchus to have a 4th century date, it is necessary that he actually used none of these writers. The probability that he used none of them p_{none} is the product of the probabilities that he did not use each one:[707]

$$p_{none} = (1-p_{Meg}) \times (1-p_{Aris}) \times (1-p_{Pat}) \times (1-p_{Ber}) = 0.2 \times 0.6 \times 0.65 \times 0.7 = 0.05$$

Hence the cumulative evidence suggests high confidence (~95%) that Cleitarchus published in the 3rd century BC, even though none of the individual sourcings

---

[705] E.g. Pearson, *Lost Histories*, 233.

[706] E. Badian, "The Date of Clitarchus," *Proceedings African Classical Associations* 8 (1965) p.10.

[707] On the basis that the evidence for his use of each writer is independent of the evidence that he used any other.

can be considered decisive. Clearly, there is room for argument about the exact probabilities that Cleitarchus used each source, but the general point that multiple independent strands of weak evidence combine to provide strong overall evidence will always be valid.

Given that no single strand amongst the manuscript evidence establishes a definite date for Cleitarchus, my judgement on the matter was originally guided by the collective preponderance of the evidence. It seemed to me that it was not unlikely that Pliny was led into assuming that Cleitarchus published soon after Alexander's death by the vividness and detail of his reports and that Ptolemy's history was not widely disseminated until some while after his death.[708] Conversely, the internal evidence that Cleitarchus had some knowledge of contemporaneous authors *and* events down to perhaps 280BC seemed to be emerging from a wider range of evidence and more forcibly than I had expected at the instigation of the reconstruction project. This led me to favour a date shortly after 280BC, whilst conceding that any time in the range 320-250BC remained feasible. However, I noted that in siding with Tarn and his followers on the matter, I did so for rather different reasons than theirs: it was the Cleitarchan comments on the poisoning plot, the extirpation of Alexander's family and the restoration of Thebes combined with the likely use of Megasthenes and other early third century sources that weighed particularly strongly in my evaluation. This conclusion also tended to support the suspicion of Jane Hornblower that Cleitarchus ended with the transfer of Alexander's corpse to Alexandria, though again she reached this view by a different route than that which I followed.[709] If Cleitarchus wrote in Alexandria under Philadelphus, then the celebration of the transfer of Alexander's remains to his own city by its monarch was by far the most obvious flourish on which to conclude his history of Alexander.

Conclusive Clues in a Papyrus on Cleitarchus' Career

The analysis of the dating of Cleitarchus provided by the preceding sub-section was originally drafted in the period 2005-2007. An early version appeared in *Alexander the Great in India*, the first part published (Books 10 to 12) of my *Reconstruction of Cleitarchus* in February 2009. Somewhat in parallel and unknown

---

[708] It is a normal practice throughout history for prominent individuals to suppress the publication of controversial works, especially autobiographies, until after their deaths: e.g. Procopius, Copernicus, Lord Byron, Charles Darwin, Mark Twain. If Philadelphus eventually published his father's memoirs, might he have sanitised them for public consumption? Is this why Ptolemy's history seems to have been so coldly devoid of characterisation, opinion and anecdotal information? Ptolemy's distortions seem mainly to have been achieved through omission, which is suspiciously characteristic of sanitisation by an editor: for Ptolemy's omissions see Errington, "Bias in Ptolemy's History of Alexander", *Classical Quarterly* 19, pp233-242.

[709] Jane Hornblower, *Hieronymus of Cardia*, OUP, 1981, p.93.

The Nature and Genesis of Cleitarchus' Account

to me at the time, a papyrus fragment was published, which potentially definitively dates Cleitarchus and provides us with some further clues regarding his career.

This was Oxyrhynchus papyrus 4808, "On Hellenistic Historians", the full publication reference being: Oxyrhynchus Papyri, Vol LXXI, ed. R. Hatzilambrou, P. J. Parsons & J. Chapa, Egypt Exploration Society Graeco-Roman Memoirs, No. 91, 2007, Papyrus Number 4808, pp. 27-36, A. G. Beresford, P. J. Parsons & M. P. Pobjoy.

It dates to the late 1st or 2nd century AD and was written in uncial script with sigmas in the lunate form C. Its key lines (column i, lines 9-17) describing Cleitarchus are shown in Figure P at the end of this section. This document appears to be a discussion of the merits of a number of Hellenistic historians together with a few details of their respective careers. Its modern editors produced the following transcription and reconstruction (reconstructed parts within square brackets) of its key lines concerning Cleitarchus:

νει.] Κλείταρχος δὲ κομπω-
δῶς] μὲν καὶ αὐτὸς τὴν ἱσ-   10
τορί]αν γέγραφεν, ἄμεμ-
πτο]ς δ' ἐστὶν τὴν διάθε[σι]ν.
[γέγ]ονε[ν] δὲ καὶ ἐπὶ τοῦ κ[α
[ταλ]ογεί[ου] καθά φησιν Φ[ί-
[λιπ]πο[ς] καὶ διδάσκαλος [γεγο-   15
[νὼς] τοῦ [Φ]ιλοπάτορος τε[
[λευτ]αι   vacat

An English translation would be:

[C]leitarchus himself also wrote his history vaingloriously, but its composition is faultless. He also became [head of the record-office(?)] according to Philip [*of Megara*] and [he passed away after becoming] tutor to [*Ptolemy IV*] Philopator.

A translation of a transcription and partial reconstruction of the whole of POxy LXXI.4808 is given in a footnote.[710] It is virtually impossible that the Cleitarchus

---

[710] *[Onesikritos]...who had been a pupil of Diogenes the Cynic. Chares, in addition to the fact that he himself also told many lies, for very many things are narrated in an [even] stranger way, shows malice; for example, you catch him blackening Parmenion and his friends. [C]leitarchus himself also wrote his history vaingloriously, but its composition is faultless. He also became [head of the record office?] according to Philip [of Megara] and [he passed away after becoming] tutor to Philopator.*

[Hieronym]os [who wrote about the D]iadochoi was a... historian and a gentleman(?)...experienced... since indeed he wrote about those things he followed closely... mediator... he offered himself(?)... writing... in favour..., and if he did

mentioned is other than the author of the *History Concerning Alexander*, because of the context, for the papyrus also discusses other famous writers on Alexander and Hellenistic historians: certainly Chares and Polybius and probably Onesicritus and Hieronymus, the latter being the author of the most important account of Alexander's immediate Successors.

The fragment suggests (lines 9-12) that its author considered that Cleitarchus treated the subject of Alexander's career boastfully or possibly bombastically, but that he nevertheless composed his material perfectly. It goes on (lines 13-14) to make a statement concerning an office that Cleitarchus held according to some writer called Philip. The editors suggest that "Head of the *Katalogeion*", i.e. the Record Office, provides a good fit to the surviving letters and gap sizes. The editors note that a *Katalogeion* in Alexandria is often mentioned in Roman period documents and (much more rarely) in Ptolemaic papyri (cf. P. Heid. IX 429 introd.) They point out that this gels with the report by Philodemus that Cleitarchus was an Alexandrian. Furthermore, the Philip mentioned is probably the philosopher, Philip of Megara, from whom Diogenes Laertius took the information that Cleitarchus studied under Stilpo of Megara.

However, the real bombshell comes in lines 15-17, which appear quite definitely to assert that Cleitarchus was tutor (*didaskalos*) to Ptolemy IV Philopater and, less securely, to suggest that he performed that office shortly before he died. The birth of Ptolemy IV Philopator is currently believed most probably to have taken place circa May/June 244BC as argued by C. J. Bennett in ZPE^{711}, but Bennett subsequently conceded that up to two years earlier is feasible, so 246BC is the *terminus post quem*. This makes it difficult for Cleitarchus to have served as Philopator's tutor before ~236BC at the earliest. That means that it is virtually impossible that Cleitarchus participated in Alexander's campaigns or that he wrote his *History Concerning Alexander* before the start of the third century BC.

In further support of a conclusion that would anyway seem hard to avoid, the editors note that in a famous papyrus list of the Librarians of the Royal Library in Alexandria (POxy X.1241 ii; FGrH 241 T7) both Apollonius Rhodius before Eratosthenes and Aristarchus after Eratosthenes are additionally credited with the tutoring of the royal princes. But this list conspicuously fails to note any such duties for Eratosthenes himself, although he had succeeded Apollonius as Chief Librarian by about 240BC. The statement in POxy 4808 that Cleitarchus, rather

---

not take pleasure in speeches, [something which is alien to] true history(?) and [any kind of] utility... [he would not be inferior] to any other historians... first... to the... by Alexander.... twenty-five... with E[umenes]... Antig[onos]... Dem[etrios].... [Antig]onos... he lived for over ninety years, [presenting] an example of sobriety... From all of which [it will be clear] that he was a [useful?] historian and a good man. Polybios, from the... order, himself took part in affairs and went on campaign with [Scipio] and was an eye-witness of most things and wrote them up truthfully. And he was more knowledgeable in... and especially in politics... knowledgeability...

[711] C. J. Bennett, ZPE 138 (2002) 141.

The Nature and Genesis of Cleitarchus' Account

than Eratosthenes, became the royal tutor in the later 230s is therefore implicitly corroborated by POxy 1241.[712]

If indeed Cleitarchus tutored the young Philopator in his old age, then there is still no contradiction with the statement that he was a pupil of Stilpo of Megara, because Stilpo may well have lived until ~280BC.[713] However, the previous guess that Cleitarchus met Stilpo during Ptolemy I Soter's meeting with Stilpo in Megara in 309BC probably falls. Instead, his studies under Stilpo should be placed some time during the first two decades of the third century BC.

In short, the revised and extended chronology of the career of Cleitarchus is that he was born in the last quarter of the 4th century BC; that he became a pupil of Stilpo some time in the first two decades of the 3rd century BC; that he wrote his *History Concerning Alexander* circa 280-250BC. He may have become famous on account of his work on Alexander and been appointed to head the Alexandrian *Katalogeion*. Finally, in the last years of his life in the late 230s, he was honoured with the position of Royal Tutor to the future pharaoh, Ptolemy IV Philopator.

The view held by some scholars prior to the publication of POxy 4808 that Cleitarchus wrote his *History Concerning Alexander* before 300BC and most probably around 310BC is not tenable, if Cleitarchus also served as tutor to Philopator. One of the more recent and detailed discussions leading to a 4th century BC date for Cleitarchus is Luisa Prandi's 1996 monograph in Italian on the subject, *Fortuna e realtà dell'opera di Clitarco*.[714] Consequently, Luisa Prandi has also led the defence of the 4th century BC dating in the face of the new papyrus evidence with the publication of an article entitled "New Evidence for the Dating of Cleitarchus (POxy LXXI. 4808)?" in *Histos* in 2012.[715] In particular, she puts forward a variant and less complete reconstruction of lines 13-17 of POxy 4808 as follows:[716]

νει.] Κλείταρχος δὲ κομπω-
δῶς] μὲν καὶ αὐτὸς τὴν ἱσ-   10
τορί]αν γέγραφεν, ἄμεμ-

---

[712] P. M. Fraser, *Ptolemaic Alexandria*, Vol 2, Oxford 1972, p. 477, note 127 argues that the omission of the role of Royal Tutor for Eratosthenes in POxy 1241 should indeed mean that he never held that post.

[713] Stilpo's life spanned approximately c. 360-c. 280 BC: ref. Tiziano Dorandi, Chapter 2: Chronology, in Algra et al. (1999) The Cambridge History of Hellenistic Philosophy, page 52. Cambridge.

[714] Luisa Prandi, Fortuna e realtà dell'opera di Clitarco, Historia Einzelschrift 104, Stuttgart (1996).

[715] Luisa Prandi, "New Evidence for the Dating of Cleitarchus (POxy LXXI. 4808)?" *Histos* 6 (2012) 15–26.

[716] This is stated to be the authorised version of the papyrus to appear in *Corpus dei Papiri Storici Greci*, edited by Luisa Prandi & F. Landucci Gattinoni.

πτο]ς δ' ἐστὶν τὴν διάθε[σι]ν.
ἐγέ]νε[το] δὲ καὶ ἐπὶ τοῦ κ[
] . γε . [ ] καθά φησιν . [
]πο . [κ]αὶ διδάσκαλος [15
]του [Φ]ιλοπάτορος τε [
] . .   vacat

Even so there remains a strong imputation that the papyrus makes Cleitarchus the tutor of Philopator and Prandi essentially concedes that that is its claim, but she prefers to believe that the scribe of POxy 4808 had become confused between Ptolemy Philopator and some earlier[717] Ptolemy, presumably either Euergetes or Philadelphus. However, in fact it appears from POxy 1241 that Apollonius Rhodius was tutor to Euergetes and Philitas of Kos (see his Suda entry) and Straton of Lampsacus[718] tutored Philadelphus.

Prandi also stresses the problem presented by the fact that Cleitarchus would appear to contradict the version of events given by Ptolemy I Soter in some parts of his history. She questions whether a resident of Alexandria potentially active in court circles could possibly have appeared to contradict or correct Ptolemy after he had published his account. But this objection presumes that Ptolemy's account was published before his death. As I have argued previously, there are good reasons to believe that his memoirs remained unpublished for some time after Ptolemy's passing and were only ever published in an edited and sanitised form by his successor.

I had already concluded even without POxy 4808 that the balance of the evidence dates Cleitarchus' history to after 280BC. With the advocacy of the new evidence to further cement the case, I believe that a date after 280BC and (probably) before 250BC is now inexorable.

---

[717] Prandi states "later" but must mean "earlier", since "later" merely exacerbates her difficulties.

[718] See Diogenes Laertius 5.58.

Figure P. Lines 9-17 of col i of POxy LXXI.4808 describing Cleitarchus.

Unattributed Fragments: the *Einquellenprinzip*

A fundamental tool for identifying unattributed fragments of Cleitarchus is the application of the so-called *Einquellenprinzip* (single source principle), which has been pioneered by German scholars, such as Schwartz and Jacoby and more recently reasserted by F. Schachermeyr.[719]

In its original 19th century form the *Einquellen-theorie* asserted that Diodorus slavishly epitomised a succession of earlier historians with little modification of their language or perspectives in compiling his *Bibliotheke*. In so doing, he confined himself to a single source over long sections of his work, often extending to an entire book or more. In the 20th century, Schwartz advocated relaxation of the strict *Einquellenprinzip* to the effect that Diodorus generally based

---

[719] F. Schachermeyr, *Alexander der Grosse: Das Problem seiner Persönlichkeit und seines Wirkens*, (Vienna, 1973), 'Anhang nr. 2: Der Weg zu Kleitarch', 658-662.

his narrative upon a single main source, but sometimes intermingled material from another source and occasionally offered personal contributions.[720]

In the specific context of Diodorus' account of Alexander in his 17th book the *Einquellenprinzip* concept may be adapted to mean that wherever any pairing among Diodorus 17, Curtius, Justin, the *Metz Epitome* and to a lesser extent Plutarch agree on incidental details (not just on the broad historical outline), then they have a common source, which is Cleitarchus.[721] The reason the common source should be Cleitarchus is that (conservatively) around a third of the attributed fragments of Cleitarchus are found to be closely echoed in Diodorus 17.[722] This is too many for there not to be an intimate connection between Cleitarchus and Diodorus 17. Insofar as it was Diodorus' regular practice to use a single main source for each book/section of his history, then his 17th book is essentially an epitome of Cleitarchus and there is indeed only occasional and questionable evidence that he supplemented Book 17 from alternative writers. Furthermore, it is clear from Jacoby's Testimonies that Cleitarchus was the most widely read account of Alexander's career under the later Roman Republic and the early Empire, which was the era of Diodorus, Trogus and (probably) Curtius. Finally, in this present analysis it has emerged that Diodorus 17 appears to incorporate certain echoes of Cleitarchus' book endings. Consequently, it may reasonably be assumed that Diodorus is mainly following Cleitarchus in his 17th book.

That Cleitarchus was also the principal source for Curtius is suggested by the numerous instances where he is seen to use the same source as Diodorus. A list of such matches was initially formulated by Schwartz and has since been significantly expanded by later scholars.[723] I give such an extended version of this list of matches in Table 5. Since Diodorus 17 is a highly summarised version of Cleitarchus' voluminous original, it is likely that many episodes in Curtius, though lacking extensive parallels in Diodorus, were nevertheless sourced from Cleitarchus. An example would be the eulogy of Ptolemy in Curtius 9.8.22-24. It should be noted that it has been argued that Curtius had read Trogus, whose

---

[720] For a good discussion of the use of sources by Diodorus see Jane Hornblower, *Hieronymus of Cardia*, OUP, 1981, pp 18-32.

[721] For example, J. R. Hamilton, "Cleitarchus & Diodorus 17" in *Greece & the Eastern Mediterranean*, 146 has concluded, "Much of Cleitarchus may be recovered from a comparison of the narratives of Diodorus and Curtius, provided that this is carried out with a proper appreciation of the individual characteristics of the two writers."

[722] See Hamilton, "Cleitarchus & Diodorus 17" in *Greece & the Eastern Mediterranean*, 137-142; E. Badian, "The Date of Clitarchus," *Proceedings African Classical Associations* 8 (1965) 5-11 for minimalism.

[723] E. Schwartz, *Paulys Real-Encyclopädie*, Vol. 4, 1901, s.v. Q. Curtius Rufus, cols. 1871-1891, & Vol 5, 1905, s.v. Diodoros, cols. 682-684; for expansion of Schwartz' list see for example J. R. Hamilton, "Cleitarchus & Diodorus 17" in *Greece & the Eastern Mediterranean*, 127, note 7.

The Nature and Genesis of Cleitarchus' Account

Philippic History was also the source for Justin's *Epitome*.[724] However, it is clear that Cleitarchus was a major source for Trogus, so it is not really clear that commonalities between the two accounts are not due to them both having followed Cleitarchus closely.

Various scholars have launched assaults on the application of the *Einquellenprinzip* to identify Cleitarchan material. A subtle line of criticism has been to postulate the existence of intermediaries between our surviving ancient sources and Cleitarchus himself. For instance, it has been postulated that Trogus got his Cleitarchan material via Timagenes, a Greek writing in Rome in the second half of the 1st century BC.[725] This has the effect of weakening the *Einquellenprizip* by introducing additional conduits for cross-contamination from other historical traditions (see Figure A at the end of the Introduction for interrelationships between lost and extant sources). However, the exceptional degree of detail in the agreements between Diodorus 17, Curtius and the attributed fragments of Cleitarchus, the fact that both Diodorus and Curtius cite Cleitarchus by name and the evident popularity and wide dissemination of Cleitarchus' history in their epoch militate in favour of them both having known his work from its original text.[726]

A more aggressive mode of assault has been to argue that Diodorus made significant use of a second source for his 17th book. It is instructive in this respect to examine Hammond's attempt to demonstrate that Diodorus continued to resort extensively to the universal history of Diyllus (who had been his principal source for large parts of Book 16) in parallel with Cleitarchus throughout Book 17.[727] Hammond began by expressing a low opinion of Cleitarchus as an historian. He was therefore minded to attribute the more sensible and measured passages in Diodorus 17 to Diyllus and to assign only those episodes that exhibited a degree of sensationalism to Cleitarchus. This *modus operandi* immediately confronted Hammond with the problem that many of the sober passages in Diodorus which he attributes to Diyllus also have close parallels in Curtius. He therefore inferred that Curtius too had resorted extensively to the history of Diyllus in formulating these parts of his narrative. But this was a cardinal error, for, whereas it is just about feasible that both Curtius and Diodorus might have used a combination of Diyllus and Cleitarchus as sources on Alexander's expedition, it is utterly implausible (especially on statistical grounds) that both authors independently made the same choice between Cleitarchus and Diyllus as their common source for every single episode. It may be added that some of the

---

[724] Yardley & Heckel, *Justin – Epitome of the Philippic History*, 7 & 34-36.

[725] E.g. Yardley & Heckel, *Justin – Epitome of the Philippic History*, 30-34.

[726] See Hamilton, "Cleitarchus & Diodorus 17" in *Greece & the Eastern Mediterranean*, 144-146.

[727] Hammond, *THA* 32-35.

material in Curtius that Hammond felt compelled to assign to Diyllus is simply too detailed to have been found in a universal history.

Similarly, Luisa Prandi's attempt to assign Duris as a co-source for Diodorus 17 cannot be sustained in the evidence as has been amply demonstrated by Bosworth in an extensive review published in Histos.[728]

Cleitarchan Style & Themes

Another useful tool in identifying material originating from Cleitarchus is a survey of particular stylistic features, quirks and themes that were characteristic of Cleitarchus' work. The identification of such features in pertinent ancient writings (e.g. those relating to Alexander) can then be recognised as indicating potential lost fragments of Cleitarchus. To this end, a proper starting point is a brief review of the testimony on the style and quality of Cleitarchus' writing from a range of his readers in antiquity:

1. Pliny, *NH* 10.136 (Jacoby T2) calls Cleitarchus "a celebrated writer".

2. Quintilian, *Inst.* 10.1.74 (Jacoby T6) writes "Cleitarchus is admired for his talent, but his accuracy has been impugned."

3. Cicero, *Ad f.* 2.10.3 (Jacoby F8) & *Brut.* 42-43 (Jacoby T7/F34) & *De legg.* 1.7 (Jacoby T13) implies that his friend Caelius Rufus was fond of Cleitarchus and mentions Cleitarchus in noting that "It is the privilege of rhetoricians to exceed the truth of history, that they may have an opportunity for embellishment…" and also asserts that Cleitarchus was the only Greek work read by Sisenna, who had sought to imitate him: "and even had he succeeded in this, he would still be considerably below the highest standards."

4. Curtius 9.5.21 (Jacoby T8) criticises Cleitarchus as one of the "framers of ancient histories" who are either negligent or too credulous.

5. Jacoby T9 (anonymous): "And some of the expressions of Callisthenes which are not sublime but high-flown are ridiculed and still more those of Cleitarchus, for the man is frivolous and blows, as Sophocles has it, 'on pigmy hautboys: mouthpiece have they none.' Other examples will be found in Amphicrates and Hegesias and Matris, for often, when these writers seem to themselves to be inspired, they are in no true frenzy, but are simply trifling."

6. Demetrius, *De Eloc.* 304 (Jacoby T10) relates, "Often objects which are themselves full of charm lose their attractiveness owing to the choice of words. Cleitarchus, for instance, when describing the wasp… This might

---

[728] Luisa Prandi, *Fortuna è realtà dell' opera di Clitarco*, Historia Einzelschriften 104, Steiner, Stuttgart 1996; A. B. Bosworth, *Histos*, Vol. 1, Aug. 1997; M. Fontana, "Il problema delle fonti per il XVII Libro di Diodoro Siculo," *Kokalos* I (1955), 155-190, also argued for Duris.

The Nature and Genesis of Cleitarchus' Account

have served for a description of some wild ox, or of the Erymanthian boar, rather than a species of bee. The result is that the passage is both repellent and frigid."

7. Philodemus, *Rhet.* 4.1 cols. 7 & 21 (Jacoby T11-12) in a rambling passage, essentially suggests that his own style is not dissimilar to that of Cleitarchus and that this is not a bad thing.

8. POxy LXXI.4808 accuses Cleitarchus of having been boastful (perhaps meaning overstated or bombastic) in the *History Concerning Alexander*.

In summary, these commentators considered that Cleitarchus' style was highly rhetorical and sometimes overblown and tasteless. Some were also dubious concerning his accuracy, but the sceptical views are mitigated by Cleitarchus' evident popularity in terms of emulation and citation by others: Philodemus implies that his own style is Cleitarchan and Caelius Rufus quotes Cleitarchus frequently. It is hard not to empathise with the mixed feelings among the ancient writers. Then as today, it was difficult to identify instances where Cleitarchus could be said to be unambiguously in error. For the most part, we can merely prosecute a charge of sensationalism regarding stories that were nevertheless founded in truth.

Certain characteristics frequently recur in recognisable fragments of Cleitarchus. The following features and themes may provide additional grounds to suspect a direct Cleitarchan influence in cases where there is uncertainty:

1. Alexander's emulation of his putative maternal ancestor Achilles (e.g. visits Achilles' tomb at Troy [Diodorus 17.17.3; Justin 11.5.12; cf. Arrian, *Anabasis* 1.12.1-2; Aelian, *VH* 12.7; Strabo 13.1.32], drags Betis behind his chariot [Curtius 4.6.29, cf. Diodorus 17.48.7, Arrian, *Anabasis* 2.25.4, Homer, *Iliad* 22.395-404], does battle with the River Indus [Diodorus 17.97.1-3, Curtius 9.4.8-14; cf. Homer, *Iliad* 21.228-382]).

2. Alexander's rivalry with his putative paternal ancestor Heracles, especially in the invasion of India (Curtius 8.10.1), in the conquest of Aornus (Curtius 8.11.2, Diodorus 17.85.2, Justin 12.7.12-13, *Metz Epitome* 47, Strabo 15.1.8), in defeating the Sibi or Ibi who were descendants of Heracles (Diodorus 17.96.2, Justin 12.9.2, Curtius 9.4.2), in capturing the land settled by descendants of Heracles' daughter (Polyaenus 1.3.4), in planning to advance to the Pillars of Heracles (Curtius 10.1.17), in quaffing from a Cup of Heracles (Plutarch 75.3, Diodorus 17.117.1-2, Justin 12.13.8, cf. Athenaeus 434A-B).

3. Alexander's emulation of legendary invaders of India: Semiramis (e.g. Curtius 9.6.23), Heracles and Dionysus (Curtius 8.10.1, *Metz Epitome* 34).[729]

4. Alexander's interest in tombs of heroes and kings: Achilles (Diodorus 17.17.3, Justin 11.5.12), Themistocles (F33-34 of Cleitarchus), Sardanapalus at Anchiale (Athenaeus 530A, cf. Plutarch *Moralia* 326F & 336C), Cyrus (Curtius 10.1.30).

5. Alexander's fascination for and honouring of oracles: Delphi (Diodorus 17.93.4, cf. Plutarch 14.4-5), Didyma (Curtius 7.5.28-35, cf. Strabo 17.1.43), Siwa (Curtius 4.7.25-28, Diodorus 17.49.3-17.51.4, Justin 11.11.2-10, Plutarch 26.6-27.4, Val. Max. 9.5 ext 1).

6. Alexander's exposure to omens: e.g. spring at Xanthus (Plutarch, *Alexander* 17.2-3); Demophon's warnings before the attack on the citadel of the Oxydracae (Curtius 9.4.27-9, Diodorus 17.98.3); return to Babylon (Plutarch, *Alexander* 73.1-4 Diodorus 17.112 Justin 12.13.3-5).

7. Alexander as the "World Ruler" (e.g. Plutarch, *Alexander* 18.1 & 27.4, Diodorus 17.51.2, Curtius 4.7.26, Justin 11.11.10).

8. Alexander hailed with the epithet "Aniketos" meaning invincible (Plutarch, *Alexander* 3.5 & 14.4-5, Diodorus 17.93.4, 17.51.3-4, Curtius 4.7.27, Livy 9.18, Justin 11.11.10, cf. Hypereides: Alexander as θεὸς ἀνίκητος).

9. Interest in Persian history and society based on his father Deinon's book on the subject (e.g. Diodorus 17.5.3-7.3 & 17.81.1-2, Justin 10); this seemingly inspired Cleitarchus to provide relatively more information on events at the court of Darius than given by Arrian.

10. Lauding of Greek figures (especially relative to Macedonians): e.g. Charidemus of Athens (Curtius 3.2.10-19, Diodorus 17.30), Thimodes son of Mentor (Curtius 3.3.1, 3.8.1, 3.9.2), Patron (e.g. Curtius 5.11), Dioxippus (Diodorus 17.100.1-101.6, Curtius 9.7.12-26).

11. Supplication of Alexander's enemies through the display of fronds or branches (e.g. the Branchidae [Curtius 7.5.33], at Massaga [*Metz Epitome* 45], the Indus River tribes [Diodorus 17.96.5] and the Brahmins [Diodorus 17.102.7]).

12. Alexander conceals himself behind curtains (torture of Philotas [Plutarch, *Alexander* 49.6], proskynesis experiment [Curtius 8.5.21]).

13. Fascination with chronology, the calendar and astronomy: making quantities equal to the number of days in the year (Diodorus 2.7.3-4, 17.77.6, Curtius 5.1.26, 6.6.8, Polyaenus 1.3.4); one book per year; lunar

---

[729] Tarn, WW, *Alexander the Great, Vol II, Sources and Studies, Part One, The So-Called 'Vulgate' and its Sources*, Cambridge 1948, 43-51.

The Nature and Genesis of Cleitarchus' Account

eclipse (Curtius 4.10.2); poetic reference to the pole star (Curtius 7.3.7); astronomy and calendar of the Indians (Curtius 8.9.33-6).

14. It has been argued by Pearson that Cleitarchus often modified the figures and units he found in his sources.[730] He notes that Cleitarchus appears to have changed 360 concubines into "one for each day of the year" and that he mitigated Ctesias's value for the height of Babylon's walls from fifty fathoms (a preposterous 90m) to fifty cubits (a much more credible 23m). In general, Cleitarchus seems to have striven to provide credible and rationalised figures rather than the ridiculous exaggerations found in some other sources, including Arrian. Another example would be the number and distribution of Porus' elephants in the Battle of the Hydaspes.

15. Emphasis of the role of fortune (*Tyche*) in Alexander's successes (which may have been inspired by a work *Peri Tyches* by Demetrius of Phalerum).[731]

16. Frequent examples of *thaumasia* (wonders) – this is perhaps an inevitable characteristic, since Cleitarchus embraced the writings of Onesicritus, described by Strabo 15.1.28 as the "Chief Pilot of Marvels", as a major source.

17. Use of Asianic rhythms.[732]

18. Sensationalism and prurience (especially in contrast with the censorial attitude of Arrian): e.g. in some instances Cleitarchus seems to have speculated pruriently a little beyond the facts, e.g. Alexander's adoption of Darius' harem (Diodorus 17.77.6, Curtius 6.6.8), an amorous liaison with Thalestris (Curtius 6.5.29-32, Diodorus 17.77.3) an amorous liaison with Cleophis (Curtius 8.10.35-36, Justin 12.7.9-11).

19. Evident influence of the Cynical philosophers consistent with Cleitarchus having been a pupil of Stilpo (Diogenes Laertius, *Stilpo* 2.113); stalwart veterans versus young shirkers (Diodorus 17.27.1-2) - perhaps this is why Onesicritus, as a student of Diogenes, ranked among Cleitarchus' favourite sources; perhaps the aphorisms attributed to Cleitarchus by the Christian Fathers also reflect the cynical bent in his philosophy (F38-F52).[733]

---

[730] See Pearson, *Lost Histories*, 228-9.

[731] Richard Billows, "Polybius and Alexander Historiography" in *Alexander the Great in Fact and Fiction*, ed. A. B. Bosworth and E. J. Baynham, Oxford 2000, 299.

[732] Pearson, *Lost Histories*, 213.

[733] T. S. Brown, "Clitarchus," *American Journal Philology* 71 (1950) 154-155.

20. Cleitarchus was not hostile in his attitude towards Alexander, for Diodorus 17 shows no significant sign of such antagonism.[734] The negative spin that was superimposed on Cleitarchus' work by Trogus represented Roman (Republican) moralising. Cleitarchus' attitude to his subject seems to have been equivocal, for his work was certainly not a eulogy either.

21. Some distinctive name forms are characteristic of Cleitarchus, such as Syria used for Assyria (e.g. Athenaeus 530A).[735]

22. It appears likely that Cleitarchus coloured his History with quotations from various letters and embassies addressed to Alexander by key individuals: particularly the sequence of three peace offers from Darius (First offer: Curtius 4.1.7-14, Justin 11.12.1-2, Diodorus 17.39.1-3; Second Offer: Curtius 4.5.1-8, Justin 11.12.3-4, Arrian 2.25.2, Plutarch 29.4, Val. Max. 6.4 ext 3; Third Offer: Curtius 4.11.1-22, Diodorus 17.54.1-5, Justin 11.12.7-16); also letters from Olympias and Parmenion warning Alexander about Alexander Lyncestes and Philip the Doctor respectively (Diodorus 17.32.1-2, Seneca De Ira 2.23, Val. Max. 3.8 ext 6, Curtius 3.6.4-16); also letters in the *Metz Epitome* 56-58 & 71-74 from Porus to Alexander (cf. Curtius 8.13.2) and from the Indian philosophers to Alexander; letter from Tiridates to Alexander, which is one of the *Einquellenprinzip* commonalities between Diodorus 17.69.1-2 and Curtius 5.5.2-4; also letters from Porus and Taxiles, which reached Alexander after he had returned to Persia (Curtius 10.1.20).

Cleitarchus in Diodorus 17 and Curtius

It is clear that Cleitarchus was a major source for Diodorus 17, because:

1. He had already been a source for Diodorus 2.
2. A high proportion of the fragments of Cleitarchus are closely echoed in Diodorus 17.
3. Cleitarchus' history is known to have been extremely popular in Italy in the late Republican period.
4. It is also apparent that many episodes in Diodorus have detailed parallels in Curtius.

These facts make it almost inevitable that Cleitarchus was the principal source for both Diodorus 17 and Curtius. As already discussed, Hammond's conjecture that Diyllus was a significant secondary source for Diodorus 17 is untenable, because it requires (on his own admission) that Curtius independently chose Diyllus as a

---

[734] E.g. Borza, *PACA* 1968; T. S. Brown, "Clitarchus," 153-5.

[735] Pearson, *Lost Histories*, 230.

The Nature and Genesis of Cleitarchus' Account

secondary source for exactly the same set of episodes as Diodorus, which is a statistical impossibility. Similarly, Luisa Prandi's advocacy of Duris as a secondary source for Diodorus is unconvincing, because her reasons for rejecting Cleitarchus do not stand up to scrutiny (e.g. of Bosworth) and because she cannot escape the same *impasse* as encountered by Hammond. In fact, Diodorus 17 appears to be dominated by Cleitarchus, but it is epitomised down to only ~10%-20% of the length of the original.[736]

It is also likely that Diodorus reproduces some excerpts from Cleitarchus with a reasonable degree of fidelity. On the basis of a detailed analysis of Diodorus' sources for his entire *Bibliotheke*, Jane Hornblower has concluded: "Diodorus adhered very faithfully to his sources at least over limited sections… He did not copy them word for word… He seems however to be a reliable vehicle for the subject matter of the histories he used, taking over both facts and the inbuilt attitudes and assumptions, and his language frequently echoes, even when it does not repeat, the language of the original."[737]

Cleitarchus is Curtius' main source, but the question arises of whether elements may have been taken from other early authors (Ptolemy? Timagenes? Trogus?) Did Curtius personally contribute some rhetorical elements, such as speeches and did he also seek to show a progressive deterioration of Alexander's character, which was not present in Cleitarchus? It has been suggested that this might have been partly due to Curtius following Trogus, for he may well have read the *Philippic History*.[738] This issue is further explored in the ensuing section.

Curtius definitely dates to the early Roman Empire and most probably to the reign of Claudius,[739] whilst Diodorus belongs to the end of the Republican period (not long) before 30BC. Therefore, it is not feasible that Diodorus used Curtius. Since Curtius gives much more detail than Diodorus for most of their common episodes, it also follows that Curtius cannot have used Diodorus as his source. The *Einquellenprinzip* provides a sound basis for attributing matching episodes in Curtius and Diodorus 17 to Cleitarchus, wherever they agree on matters of incidental detail. It may safely be extended to other pairings of Vulgate authors in particular circumstances: especially, for example, in respect of the extensive commonalities between Curtius and the *Metz Epitome* (sections 1 to 86).

---

[736] Diodorus 17 is an exceptionally long book for a Greek work, so it is unlikely that Cleitarchus' 13 books averaged more than 75% of its length – conversely, Cleitarchus' work seems to have been substantial, so it seems improbable that his books averaged less that 40% of the length of Diodorus 17.

[737] Jane Hornblower, *Hieronymus of Cardia*, OUP, 1981, p.32.

[738] J. E. Atkinson, *A Commentary on Quintus Curtius Rufus' Historiae Alexandri Magni, Books 3 & 4*, Amsterdam 1980, 59-61; Yardley & Heckel, *Justin – Epitome of the Philippic History*, 7.

[739] J. E. Atkinson, *A Commentary on Quintus Curtius Rufus' Historiae Alexandri Magni, Books 3 & 4*, Amsterdam 1980, 19-39.

Is Curtius Mainly Translating Cleitarchus?

Orthodox wisdom has held that Curtius is an original author, who fashioned a unique history of Alexander's reign in gloriously rhetorical Latin in the early Imperial period, most probably under the first Claudius. The case for this view is superficially strong. In particular, there are several passages where it is indisputable that we hear the authentic voice of Curtius himself. Key examples would be Curtius' comment on the inaccuracy of Cleitarchus in reporting the presence of Ptolemy at the Mallian siege and Curtius' remarks at 10.9.3-6 drawing a parallel between the elevation of Arrhidaeus and the succession of his own emperor to the purple of Rome.

Furthermore, whereas many passages in Curtius have strong and direct echoes in Diodorus, whence we infer that they shared a common source in Cleitarchus, there are also a number of instances where the account of Diodorus appears wildly disparate from Curtius' version. Since Diodorus is known generally to have followed single sources closely over long sections of his "Library of History", it would seem to follow that Curtius must have interspersed his gleanings from Cleitarchus amidst material from other sources.

This reasoning made perfect sense to me at the outset of this reconstruction project, at which stage my opinions on the matter were relatively in line with the prevailing orthodoxy. However, having had cause to examine the source texts far more attentively in the course of the reconstruction, my original confidence in the conventional wisdom has been substantially undermined. It is apposite to try to explain why.

Firstly, I have become keenly aware that modern editors or translators have inferred a number of instances of the use of the first person singular by Curtius, which actually lack any manuscript authority. Examples in the context of my reconstruction of the Death of Alexander include: *comperimus* at Curtius 10.10.5, which is unambiguously first person plural, but is translated as "I have ascertained…" by John Yardley in the Penguin edition; then again at Curtius 10.10.12 Vogel changed the manuscript reading from *refert* to *refero*, and he has been followed by other modern editors, thus giving "I report what is recorded rather than believed" whereas "Here is related what is recorded rather than reckoned reliable" would be more faithful to the source material.

Evidently, orthodox views on the nature of Curtius' work have intruded so far as to insinuate subtle re-writes into the source text to make it fit the hypothesis of its being an original work more conspicuously. I do not even suggest that this tendency has been conscious, for in fact it generally seems to have been inadvertent and accretive. At the very least the question of the originality of Curtius has not been to the fore in the minds of the perpetrators. The reason that this should nevertheless disquiet us is the background context of the quasi-political mission of Tarn and others in the 20th century to disparage and

The Nature and Genesis of Cleitarchus' Account

marginalize Cleitarchus as a source on Alexander. Downplaying Cleitarchus' influence upon Curtius harmonises tunefully with Tarn's litigious approach.

There remain, of course, some valid instances where Curtius genuinely interjects comments, but it could be posited that these are generally of the nature of footnotes in a modern translation. Some may have been inspired by early scholia (ancient marginal notes) that became appended to the traditional text of Cleitarchus. For example, it is interesting that the observation that Ptolemy effectively contradicted Cleitarchus on the issue of his presence at the Mallian siege is also explicitly pointed out by Arrian, *Anabasis* 6.11.8. Conversely, Diodorus and the *Metz Epitome* avoid mentioning Ptolemy's presence, even though it must have been in the text of Cleitarchus that they were following. An obvious way in which several authors could have been led to highlight or suppress this error would be for a scholium to have appeared in some early manuscript of Cleitarchus that happened to become the prototype for many subsequent manuscripts of his work disseminated within the Roman Empire. Curtius additionally realised that that Timagenes had made the same error, but he could have known this through familiarity with the work of Trogus.

More hints that the very sentiments of Cleitarchus pervade the words attributed to Curtius may be inferred from the pronounced vein of cynicism in his text. This is often manifested in ways that are hugely incongruous, in the light of the biographical evidence on Curtius. It is not feasible to review all the issues here,[740] but it is likely that he was the same Curtius who was the Roman Proconsul of Africa under Claudius. Yet this wealthy and influential servant of the Claudian dynasty speaks of pearls as the "vomit of the retching surf" (8.9.19) in railing against their supposed corrupting influence on society, which he also seems to regard as recent, despite trade between Europe and India having flourished for nearly four centuries in Curtius' era. Even more out of place is his vigorous condemnation of the luxurious lifestyle of the Indian kings, where most of his complaints refer to behaviour that would seem quite modest relative to the outrageous antics of his own imperial masters. Modern authorities on Curtius have seen all this as evidence for a covert streak of asceticism in this pillar of the imperial state, but, when we do hear Curtius' own voice clearly at 10.9.3-6, it is ringing in its support for the emperor and clearly intended to be publicly disseminated. It is a much more straightforward explanation for the overtly cynical sentiments in Curtius that they were understood by his audience to be mere Latin translations of the Greek words of the philosopher and rhetorician Cleitarchus, who is actually known to have associated with the Cynics (e.g. Stilpo) and even used them among his own sources (e.g. Onesicritus, the student of Diogenes).

---

[740] For discussions of the dating and identity of Curtius see Atkinson's Commentaries on Curtius and Waldemar Heckel's Introduction to the Penguin translation of Curtius.

Concerning Alexander the Great by Andrew Chugg

If indeed Curtius was the Quintus Curtius Rufus who was Proconsul of Roman Africa at the time of his death in AD53, then there are potentially yet more absurd incongruities, which I can only resolve by supposing him to have operated simply as Cleitarchus' translator. In particular, it is instructive to examine in detail a problem with some ancient rhinos in Curtius 8.9.16-17. The manuscript readings (with a few alternatives indicated) seem to have been:

Aves ad imitandum humanae vocis sonum dociles sunt. Animalia invisitata/inusitata ceteris gentibus nisi invecta. Eadem terra et rynocerontas/rinocerotas/rinocerontas alit non generat. Elephantorum/elefantorum maior est vis quam quos in Africa/Affrica domitant et viribus magnitudo respondet/respondit.

The statement regarding the elephants is also in Strabo 15.1.43. He attributes it to Onesicritus (Alexander's helmsman on the Indus river voyage), who was also undoubtedly a major source for Cleitarchus. By the 17th century Freinshem was giving the passage as:

Aves ad imitandum humanae vocis sonum dociles sunt. Animalia inusitata ceteris gentibus, nisi invecta. Eadem terra et rhinocerotas alit, non generat. Elephantorum maior est vis, quam quos in Africa domitant; et viribus magnitudo respondet.

The same form persisted through to C. H. Weise in 1840, but by 1841 Julius Muetzell had dropped the *et* in front of the rhinos. E. Hedicke (Teubner 1908) saw that it is fairly preposterous for the text to suggest that the rhinos were not native to India. In fact the Great One-Horned Rhino is native to the foothills south of the Himalayas and was certainly encountered by Alexander's expedition. It is at least unlikely that an eyewitness source like Onesicritus would have suggested that it had been imported. Furthermore, the preceding sentence has alluded to Indian animals that were unknown (or at least uncommon) elsewhere, so one would naturally expect the rhinos to have been mentioned as a specific example. Hedicke therefore proposed a rather heavy-handed emendation:

Aves ad imitandum humanae vocis sonum dociles sunt. Animalia invisitata ceteris gentibus nisi invecta. Eadem terra rhinocerotas aliis ignotos generat. Elephantorum maior est vis quam, quos in Africa domitant, et viribus magnitudo respondet.

Which was translated by John Rolfe (Loeb 1946) as:

"There are birds which can be taught to imitate the sound of the human voice. The animals are unknown to other nations, except such as are imported from that country. The same land produces rhinoceroses, which are unknown to other peoples. The strength of its elephants is greater than those which men tame in Africa, and their size corresponds to their strength."

Other 20th century editors took a different approach. Bardon in 1947 seems to have sought to lessen the difficulty by arbitrarily dropping the entire sentence beginning *Animalia*, even though it exists on perfectly good manuscript authority:

The Nature and Genesis of Cleitarchus' Account

Aves ad imitandum humanae vocis sonum dociles sunt. Eadem terra rhinocerotas alit, non generat. Elephantorum maior est vis, quam quos in Africa domitant; et viribus magnitudo respondet.

Yardley followed Bardon's text in the 1984 Penguin translation:

"Birds can be trained to imitate the human voice and the country also supports a population of rhinoceroses, though this is not indigenous. Its elephants possess greater strength than those trained in Africa and their size matches that strength."

The logic here seems to be that Curtius believed African rhinos to have been imported to the Himalayan foothills from Africa in the 4th century BC, which is a little preposterous. But Curtius probably did know about African rhinos: a rhino was exhibited at Pompey's games[741] in 55BC and Martial[742] mentioned the African rhinoceros, which also appears on a quadrans of Domitian. Why then would he have written, as Hedicke would suggest, that they were unknown outside India? I think the likely answer would be that he considered that he was translating his Greek source (Cleitarchus) rather than compiling a fresh account.[743]

Although I feel Hedicke had the right idea regarding what this corrupted passage is trying to say, his particular emendation is rather too gross to be easily credible. I suspect instead that the *et* in front of the rhinos that was dropped so long ago, might be a mistake for *est* (i.e. copulative use of the verb *esse*, as also occurs for the elephants in the ensuing sentence), in which case we would not be very far from: "The same land possesses rhinoceroses, elsewhere not indigenous."

How, then, would I explain gross disparities between Curtius and Diodorus? I cannot address every instance here, but let us take the passages on the accession of Abdalonymus as an example case. Curtius gives what seems a correct version of the story with Abdalonymus appointed King of Sidon before the siege of Tyre on the recommendation of Hephaistion, whereas Diodorus does not mention Sidon, but has Abdalonymus instead appointed to rule Tyre *after* its fall. Prandi, Bosworth and others have highlighted and discussed the case of Abdalonymus,[744] because it appears to present an intractable local difficulty for the reconstruction of the Cleitarchan version. It has been believed that Cleitarchus mistakenly made Abdalonymus king of Tyre and Diodorus followed him, whilst Curtius and

---

[741] Pliny, *NH* 8.71, whose description, despite a solitary horn, appears to be following Agatharchides, *De Mari Erythraeo* 72, who described a rhino from Eritrea or Northern Somalia.

[742] Martial, *Liber de Spectaculis* 9.2 & 22.1; other early mentions of rhinos in Rome include Suetonius, *Augustus* 43.4 and Dio Cassius 51.22.5 & 55.33.4.

[743] According to Athenaeus 5.201C a rhino from "Ethiopia" was displayed in the Grand Parade of Ptolemy Philadelphus in Alexandria in 275-274BC; however, Cleitarchus may have written at an earlier date and was himself probably closely following the primary account of Onesicritus.

[744] Luisa Prandi, "Fortuna è Realtà dell'Opera di Clitarco" in *Historia Einzelschriften* 104, Steiner, Stuttgart, 1996, p.102; A.B. Bosworth, "In Search of Cleitarchus: Review-Discussion of Luisa Prandi: Fortuna è Realtà dell'Opera di Clitarco" in Histos (University of Durham, electronic journal of historiography), Vol. 1, Aug. 1997, pages 6-7 of 9.

Trogus used a more correct source in placing events at Sidon. However, Curtius 4.1.26 mentions that an area surrounding Sidon was added to Abdalonymus' dominions by Alexander. Perhaps Cleitarchus therefore mentioned that his rule was extended to include control of Tyre's territory after its fall and that was what prompted Diodorus to tell the story of his original appointment as a king in the context of the fall of Tyre. Perhaps therefore Diodorus in his original manuscript correctly referred the story of Abdalonymus' appointment back to Sidon in Section 17.47, having noted his appointment as king of Tyre in Section 17.46.6. If so, given the curious order in which Diodorus' text presented the matter, an ancient editor of Diodorus would obviously have assumed that the mentions of Sidon were an error for Tyre and incorrectly corrected them in some later manuscript that became the prototype for our surviving versions of Diodorus. This would seem to constitute a logical and viable way of explaining the confusion through an understandable rather than a crass error, which also allows that Diodorus, Curtius and Trogus were all still following Cleitarchus in these matters. Although it might be objected that Philotas was made garrison commander in Tyre according to Curtius 4.5.9, I cannot see that this excludes Abdalonymus as its king. I would submit that this scenario makes more sense of the matter than the conventional suppositions and serves as an illustration of my point that holding fast to the view that Curtius is almost entirely Cleitarchus yields credible reconciliations of textual problems and avoids the need to infer deliberate, yet absurd, distortions of history by the early sources.

The question might, however, be posed of why exact parallels between the texts of Diodorus and Curtius are not more numerous, if they are both essentially epitomes of Cleitarchus? In response I would point out that the *virtually* exact parallels *are* in fact quite numerous (they are listed in Table 5 for the convenience of the reader). However, I would go on to note that Diodorus rarely precisely translates Cleitarchus, but continually paraphrases and contracts him. Indeed this case has been made for me by Bosworth, who notably and correctly points out that where the Fragments of Cleitarchus are echoed in the text of Diodorus, we can see evidence that Diodorus perpetrated some serious mangling: Bosworth particularly employs the example of the 440 talents that Alexander gleaned from the fall of Thebes.[745] My final comments on this issue are that the work of Curtius was on a grander scale across the period of Alexander's reign than that of Diodorus and they had quite different objectives for their texts: Curtius delighted in the rhetoric and cynicism of Cleitarchus' style, whereas Diodorus sought to extract a sharply pared down *precis* of the bare facts of the history of Alexander's conquests.

---

[745] He also informatively flourishes the actual mangling in a case where Diodorus is known to have used extant passages of Polybius as his source: A.B. Bosworth, "In Search of Cleitarchus: Review-Discussion of Luisa Prandi: Fortuna è Realtà dell'Opera di Clitarco" in Histos (University of Durham, electronic journal of historiography), Vol. 1, Aug. 1997, pages 4-5 of 9.

The Nature and Genesis of Cleitarchus' Account

Several scholars of Curtius' work have been at great pains to demonstrate that he resounds with reverberant echoes of his predecessors Trogus and Livy.[746] Their case seems well made, but it cannot greatly detract from the hypothesis that he is translating Cleitarchus for the simple reason that both Trogus and Livy were themselves demonstrably influenced by Cleitarchus. Hence it would be difficult to contradict the view in the case of any significant match between Curtius and either of them that both Latin writers were simply imitating Cleitarchus. To those who have said that Curtius borrows and retouches Roman history from Livy, I propose that Livy borrowed and retouched Greek history from Cleitarchus.[747] If so, then the readiness with which Livy's plagiarism can be recognized through the text of Curtius becomes a testament to the fidelity with which Curtius reproduced Cleitarchus.

It is beyond the scope of this sub-section to treat this issue comprehensively, since there are many lines of evidence that could be scrutinised in detail. Instead, the ambition of this short tract is to challenge the casual assumption that the orthodox view of the nature of Curtius may be regarded as secure. That Curtius is essentially a Latin translation and abridgement of Cleitarchus now seems to me to be the most defensible hypothesis in the light of the available evidence.

Cleitarchus in Trogus

The last datable event mentioned by Trogus is the surrender of Phraates' sons and grandsons as hostages to Augustus in 10BC (Justin 42.5.11-12), but a date of compilation as late as AD9 (as given by the medieval writer Radulfus de Diceto) is possible.[748] Indirect transmission and the curtness of the summarisation make it difficult absolutely to prove that Trogus used Cleitarchus: for example, Justin lacks the detail to prove that Trogus echoed any fragments of Cleitarchus. However, he did mention the ivy at Nysa and he used Thalestris, the Cleitarchan name for the Amazon Queen, whilst also giving Minythyia as a variant. It is nevertheless even more difficult to prove that Trogus did not use Cleitarchus either directly or indirectly and Trogus was unambiguously a part of the Vulgate Tradition, for it is easy to recognise overlap between Trogus and Cleitarchan material from Curtius and Diodorus. Yet there are significant circumstantial reasons to suspect that Trogus was inspired and guided by a lost work *On Kings* by Timagenes of Alexandria, who wrote in Rome some time after his arrival there in 55BC.[749] It is therefore possible that Trogus got his Cleitarchan material via Timagenes. Militating in favour of direct use of Cleitarchus, however, is the fact

---

[746] E.g. W. Heckel in Section C of his Introduction to the Penguin translation of Curtius (1983).

[747] R. B. Steele, "Quintus Curtius Rufus", *AJP* 36 (1915), p.409.

[748] Yardley & Heckel, *Justin – Epitome of the Philippic History* 5-6.

[749] J. C. Yardley & W. Heckel, *Justin: Epitome of the Philippic History of Pompeius Trogus, Vol I, Books 11-12, Alexander the Great*, Oxford 1997, 30-34.

that Trogus adopted the death of Darius as the endpoint of his 11th Book, which coincides with the end of Cleitarchus' 6th book and the midpoint of his work. (Conversely, Darius is murdered in the middle of Book 3 of Arrian.) Whereas Curtius may have read Trogus, the two books of Trogus that dealt with Alexander's reign were too short to have formed the entire basis for Curtius' *Deeds of Alexander*.[750] Similarly, there were strong parallels with Livy's works in Trogus: the two were contemporaries and may well have been influenced by one another's literary outputs.[751] But it is also possible that we are merely detecting how profoundly all these Roman writers were influenced by Cleitarchus.

Cleitarchus in the *Metz Epitome*

Much of the *Metz Epitome* (specifically sections 1-86) falls clearly within the Cleitarchan tradition, although the *Liber de Morte* (sections 87-123) seems to be derived from a different source: the same as used for the closing sections of Pseudo-Callisthenes. Perhaps this latter author was the Macedonian commander called Holcias.[752] Details are telling: for example, the *Metz Epitome* mentions that Alexander persuaded his companions to wed daughters of the Sogdian aristocracy at the time of his marriage to Roxane. The only other place where this information is to be found is the contents list for Book 17 of Diodorus (the actual details being lost in the great lacuna in Diodorus' Book 17). In general, events in the *Metz Epitome* closely parallel the corresponding episodes in Curtius.[753]

Ostensibly, a particular problem for the view that the *Metz Epitome* is Cleitarchan is the fact that its standard text[754] mentions Chorienes, a figure elsewhere found only in Arrian and believed by some (e.g. Heckel & Brunt)[755] to be an official title of Sisimithres, who fulfils a very similar role in the Vulgate Tradition. However,

---

[750] J. E. Atkinson, *A Commentary on Quintus Curtius Rufus' Historiae Alexandri Magni, Books 3 & 4*, Amsterdam 1980, 59-61.

[751] Yardley & Heckel, *Justin: Epitome of the Philippic History of Pompeius Trogus, Vol I, Books 11-12, Alexander the Great*, Oxford 1997, 6-8 & 333-336.

[752] P.H. Thomas accepted Pfister's conclusion that the *Liber de Morte* is a separate work from the rest of the *Epitoma Mettensis*, although Otto Wagner treated it as part of the *Epitoma*; see C. L. Howard's review of the Teubner edition in *Classical Philology* 58, 129; Elizabeth Baynham, "An Introduction to the *Metz Epitome*: its traditions and value", *Antichthon* 29 (1995) 60-77, points out that Lellia Ruggini's philological study of the *Metz Epitome* text shows that the two pieces were both the work of the same epitomist, who probably developed them from separate source documents, but intended that they should provide complementary coverage of Alexander's career.

[753] The parallels are often so close that J. M. Hunt, "An Emendation in the Epitoma Metensis", *Classical Philology* 67, 287-288, uses the phraseology of Curtius to determine the correct reading of a corrupt passage in the *Metz Epitome*.

[754] P. H. Thomas (editor), *Incerti Auctoris Epitoma Rerum Gestarum Alexandri Magni cum Libro de Morte Testamentoque Alexandri*, Teubner, 1966.

[755] W. Heckel, *Who's Who in the Age of Alexander the Great*, Blackwell 2006, s.v. Sisimithres; P. A. Brunt, *Arrian: History of Alexander and Indica*, Loeb, Harvard, Vol. 1, 1976, 407, note 1.

The Nature and Genesis of Cleitarchus' Account

it is instructive that on careful examination of the manuscript evidence this anomaly emerges as an invention of modern textual editors. The manuscript of the *Metz Epitome* read "corianus", which was corrected to Chorienes through comparison with Arrian by Otto Wagner. Conversely, a satrap named "cohortandus" in the manuscripts of Curtius 8.4.21 (or "cohortanus" according to Freinshem's older reading) has conventionally been emended to "Oxyartes" since the Renaissance edition of Aldus. However, it is clear from the context (i.e. hosting of the meeting of Alexander and Roxane) that "corianus" in the *Metz Epitome* is the same individual as "cohortanus" in the manuscripts of Curtius. Therefore these names almost certainly reflect separate Latinisations (and corruptions) of a similar name given in Greek by Cleitarchus, which may well have been Chorienes. The manuscripts, when analysed jointly, therefore seem to vindicate the common (Cleitarchan) derivation of the *Metz Epitome* and Curtius and it would appear that Cleitarchus considered Sisimithres and Corianus to be distinct persons. The correction of "cohortanus" to "Oxyartes" should therefore be rejected; despite the fact that Curtius implies a few sentences later that Roxane is the daughter of "cohortanus". It is easy to see that Curtius (or one of his transcribers) has probably garbled the complex statement found in the *Metz Epitome* that "corianus" invited his own virgin daughters *and* those of his friends to appear before Alexander, who was entranced by the daughter of "oxiatris" among them. This perspective also has the virtue of rescuing us from the need to make Cleitarchus (through Curtius) contradict the clear statements elsewhere (e.g. Arrian 4.20.4) that Oxyartes was not present when Alexander first met Roxane.

In another similar case, it may be argued that the *Metz Epitome* gives the correct Cleitarchan version where Curtius resorts for some reason to a variant. This is the surrender of the rock of Ariamazes. Section 18 of the *Metz Epitome* relates the complex outcome that the occupants of the rock were so much intimidated by the appearance of 300 of Alexander's men at its summit that they slew Ariamazes then surrendered to Alexander, who pardoned them all. Yet Curtius 7.11.28 suggests that Ariamazes himself together with his family and nobles surrendered to Alexander who then scourged and crucified them all at the foot of the rock. It should be noted that, if Alexander had truly brutally executed the high-status occupants of the Rock of Ariamazes after they had surrendered to him, then it would be astonishing that Sisimithres and his family readily surrendered to Alexander in his turn following a siege of his rock a few months later, as is also related by Curtius 8.2.28-33. It appears that small tweaks to Curtius' Latin can reconcile his text with my reconstruction in line with the *Metz Epitome*: "...**more out of despair than from his real ruin in the affair,** Ariamazes *was escorted by his kindred and the most noble of the natives down towards the king's camp, and they themselves collectively commanded that he be* **scourged and crucified** *at the base of the pinnacle.*"

Another name in the *Metz Epitome* that might superficially appear to follow Arrian's usage is "oxudrac" or "oxidragas" for the Indian tribe that Arrian himself calls the "Oxydrakai" in his *Anabasis* (6.4.3 and 6.11.3), but the "Oudrakai" in his

Indica 4.9.[756] However, Arrian uses "Oxydrakai" particularly in the context of refuting unnamed "Vulgate" sources, which stated that Alexander had received his chest wound among them. We know that Cleitarchus was prominent among these sources, so it is feasible that Arrian was actually following Cleitarchus' spelling of the tribe's name in order to make the target of his criticism the more apparent. This is supported by the fact that Pausanias 1.6.2 uses "Oxydrakai" in citing the Cleitarchan version of Alexander's wounding as true history and similarly Plutarch, *Moralia* 343D. Conversely, Curtius (9.4.15 and 9.4.26) uses "Sudracae", although he states that he was aware of Ptolemy's divergent account for this episode in his history (9.5.21). The manuscript readings for Diodorus 17.98.1 (Συρακοῦσαι) and Justin 12.9.3 ("Sugambri") are so wildly variant that they can scarcely be used to decide the issue. Furthermore, the various manuscripts of Strabo arbitrarily used either spelling at 15.1.8 and 15.1.33 and several used both forms in different places e.g. one gave ὀξύδρακας at 15.1.8 and συδράκαι at 15.1.33.[757] A rather mixed range of spellings is found among various other ancient texts.[758] In the light of this impenetrable confusion in the manuscripts, it is altogether unsafe to assume as many have that "Oxydrakai" is from Ptolemy/Aristobulus and "Sudracae" derives from the Cleitarchan Vulgate. In actuality, there is a strong possibility that "Oxydrakai" is the authentic Cleitarchan spelling and that the confusion arose later.[759] Again it must be concluded that there is no sound basis to question the Cleitarchan nature of the *Metz Epitome*.

The *Metz Epitome* also has some things we might expect to have been in Cleitarchus, but which are absent from Diodorus and Curtius. For example, Alexander's interrogation of the ten gymnosophists is exactly the type of tale that would have appealed to Cleitarchus and would certainly have been known to him, since it originated with Onesicritus.[760] Furthermore, Arrian, *Anabasis* 5.2.3 tells as a story that when Alexander asked Acuphis, chief negotiator on behalf of Nysa, to surrender a hundred of his "best men" to him, the Indian retorted that he could more readily spare two hundred of his worst people. When Arrian refers to such items as "stories", it usually means that he found them elsewhere than in his two main sources, Ptolemy and Aristobulus. Exactly the same story occurs in the

---

[756] Yardley & Heckel, *Justin: Epitome of the Philippic History of Pompeius Trogus, Vol I, Books 11-12, Alexander the Great*, Oxford 1997, 20 have excluded one of Seel's fragments of Trogus found in Ampelius, because the latter used Oxydracae "the form used by Arrian".

[757] Manuscript *Athous Vatop.* 655; this is despite the fact that all the main manuscripts are believed to have derived from a single, relatively late prototype.

[758] Strabo 15.1.6 (*Hydrakai* after Megasthenes); Pliny, *NH* 12.24 (*Sudracae* in modern texts, but just *Sydra* in the *Codex Moneus*); Stephanus Byzantinus s.v. *Oxydrakai*; Ampelius 35.2 (*Oxydracae*).

[759] It is feasible that by the early Roman imperial era both *Oxydrakai* and *Sydrakai* existed in manuscripts of Cleitarchus: we could imagine that, when the copiest had multiple orders for this popular work, he might have recited the text to a group of scribes; the corruption of *Oxydrakai* to *Sydrakai* is among a range of observed errors that would fit this scenario.

[760] Jacoby, *FGrHist* 134 F17a-b = Strabo 15.1.63-65; Plutarch, *Alexander* 65.

The Nature and Genesis of Cleitarchus' Account

Metz Epitome 36-38 and a slightly curtailed version is given by Plutarch, *Alexander* 58.5. These circumstances make it very likely that Acuphis' quip was in Cleitarchus, one of whose fragments relates to the Nysa episode. Nysa is mentioned in the contents list of Diodorus 17 but falls in the great lacuna in his text. Curtius would appear to have cut any mention of Acuphis from his account of Nysa, although he records that its citizens gave themselves up to Alexander. Perhaps Curtius' omissions of certain Cleitarchan episodes in India were motivated by a wish to emphasise the deterioration of Alexander's character.

Merkelbach has analysed the sources of the *Metz Epitome* and agrees that much of the material in Sections 1-86 is essentially Cleitarchan in character.[761] However, he further supposes that the epitomist interpolated two letters to Alexander and also the exchange with the gymnosophists from a separate ancient collection. This is curious, since it presupposes that Cleitarchus did not himself quote from letters sent to Alexander, whereas there are in fact many indications that he did (as noted in item 22 under Cleitarchan Style and Themes above). In fact, the letter from Porus in *Metz Epitome* 56-58 is reported in summary at Curtius 8.13.2: the parallels are so close that it is overwhelmingly likely that the two accounts are based on the same source, who is almost certainly Cleitarchus. It is transparent that Merkelbach is simply wrong in this instance at least. Furthermore, as already noted there is nothing surprising in the possibility that the exchange with the gymnosophists was recorded by Cleitarchus, since it probably originated with Onesicritus, who was one of Cleitarchus' main sources. It would seem to be superfluous to believe that the otherwise distinctly unsophisticated epitomist chose to adulterate his episodic Cleitarchan gleanings with letters from an entirely separate document.

There seem to be good reasons to suppose and no good reason to doubt that Sections 1-86 of the *Metz Epitome* were relatively directly derived from Cleitarchus. Baynham agrees that it was based on early historical sources and notes strong parallels with Cleitarchus.[762] It has too few parallels with Arrian to have been substantially derived from Aristobulus and it appears to have been adapted from too conventional a history to be based directly on the book entitled *On the Education of Alexander* by Onesicritus (which seems itself to have been modelled on the *Cyropaidia* of Xenophon), for Strabo 15.1.28 described Onesicritus ironically as the Chief Pilot of Marvels.

In the context of the reconstruction of Cleitarchus the *Metz Epitome* is primarily important as a control on Curtius within the great lacuna in Diodorus 17. By an *ad hoc* extension of the *Einquellenprinzip*, wherever the *Metz Epitome* agrees with Curtius in matters of detail, then we can be reasonably confident that Curtius is

---

[761] Reinhold Merkelbach, "Die Quellen des Griechischen Alexanderromans," *Zetema Monographien zur Klassischen Altertumswissenschaft*, Heft 9, Munich 1954, 118-121.

[762] Elizabeth Baynham, "An Introduction to the *Metz Epitome*: its traditions and value", *Antichthon* 29 (1995) 60-77.

following Cleitarchus. The secondary importance of the *Metz Epitome* lies in its mentioning a few Vulgate stories that are absent from both Curtius and Diodorus and would therefore otherwise be difficult to associate with Cleitarchus. Additionally, it clarifies the Cleitarchan version of some episodes, notably events at the Rock of Ariamazes and at Mazaga.

Cleitarchus in Plutarch

The use of Cleitarchus by Plutarch is probably more extensive than has generally been realised, perhaps especially on the events of Alexander's youth, although Heckel & Yardley note cogently that Plutarch's "basic narrative of Alexander's campaigns is the same as that used by Diodorus, Trogus and Curtius."[763] Hammond concludes that Plutarch used many early writers on Alexander, but that Cleitarchus, Aristobulus, Onesicritus and Chares exerted an especially strong influence upon his work.[764] Among these, as we have seen, only Chares is unlikely to have been an influential source for Cleitarchus. Hammond's attribution of material in Plutarch's *Life of Alexander* to Cleitarchus therefore represents a minimalist viewpoint, since some of the items attributed to other writers may in fact have been extracted from Cleitarchus, even when Plutarch explicitly cites another source. For example, as argued above in discussing the contents of Cleitarchus' first book, there are indications that Plutarch took some of his information on Alexander's birth from Cleitarchus, though he only mentions Hegesias as a source, presumably therefore following Cleitarchus in doing so. Nevertheless, it is difficult to identify Cleitarchan material unambiguously, since Plutarch evidently mixed together information from various early authors. But Hamilton has usefully identified a shortlist of instances where Plutarch was very probably following Cleitarchus in his *Life of Alexander*.[765]

Plutarch's essays on the *Fortune or Virtue of Alexander* in the *Moralia* are also regularly imbued with Cleitarchan character. For example, at 343D and 344D Alexander leaps down inside the walls of a town in the country of the *Oxydrakai* and is rescued by Ptolemy amongst others, which is the version of Cleitarchus. However, at 327B Plutarch had noted that the event occurred among the Malli, in agreement with Arrian and sourced from Ptolemy and/or Aristobulus. Plutarch actually cites Aristobulus, Onesicritus, Ptolemy, Chares, Duris, Anaximenes and others as sources for various stories in these essays, but never Cleitarchus. Consequently, it is relatively difficult firmly to attribute material in them to Cleitarchus, except where there are strong connections with Cleitarchan stories known from elsewhere. Even in these cases, the rather rhetorical and opinionated

---

[763] Yardley & Heckel, *Justin – Epitome of the Philippic History*, 35.

[764] Hammond, *Sources* 149-151.

[765] J. R. Hamilton, *Plutarch, Alexander: A Commentary*, Oxford 1969, lix.

character of the essays clouds our ability to discern exactly what Plutarch had read in his source.

There are also important mentions of Alexander's career in other parts of the *Moralia* and in various other of Plutarch's *Lives*. A few of these may be associated with Cleitarchus' work.[766]

Other Anonymous Fragments

In addition to material from those ancient texts specifically dedicated to the history of Alexander, stories pertaining to the King that would appear to have been inspired by the Cleitarchan Vulgate appear frequently in a host of other surviving sources from antiquity. Prominent among these are Polyaenus, Athenaeus, Aelian, Pausanias, Cicero, Pliny the Elder, Frontinus, Ampelius and Valerius Maximus. Many Greek and Roman writers between the 1st century BC & the 4th century AD seem to have been familiar with Cleitarchus and this is often reflected in their works. Cicero, Athenaeus, Aelian and Pliny are sources of named fragments of Cleitarchus, but they also mention Alexander's career in other contexts, and, in general, it is productive to seek further fragments of Cleitarchus in authors known to have read his work.

For example, St Augustine *De Civ. Dei* 4.4.25 cites a lost passage of Cicero, *The Republic* 3.24 describing Alexander's interrogation of a captured pirate (Aristonicus of Methymna) at Alexandria, which is likely to have been sourced from Cleitarchus.[767] Additionally, Pausanias is especially interesting, because he combines the Cleitarchan story of Ptolemy rescuing Alexander in the town of the *Oxydrakai* with details of the arrival of Alexander's corpse in Egypt.

Conversely, the 4th century epitome known as the *Itinerarium Alexandri* is generally recognised to be derivative from Arrian in its character[768] and some Hellenistic authors seem to use other first generation sources: for example, Polybius appears particularly to use Callisthenes, Hieronymus and Demetrius of Phalerum.[769]

Poetical Devices in Cleitarchus

Pearson has noted that there is some evidence that at least part of Cleitarchus' work may have been written in a type of blank verse known as Asianic

---

[766] E.g. Plutarch, *Life of Themistocles* 27.1-2.

[767] Cf. Curtius 4.5.19-22; Arrian, *Anabasis* 3.2.4.

[768] The *Itinerarium Alexandri* was published by Müller in his *Fragmenta*; see Yardley & Heckel, *Justin – Epitome of the Philippic History* 34.

[769] See Richard Billows, "Polybius and Alexander Historiography" in *Alexander the Great in Fact and Fiction*, ed. A.B. Bosworth and E.J. Baynham, Oxford 2000; but Jane Hornblower, *Hieronymus of Cardia*, OUP, 1981, p. 236 is uncertain whether Polybius used Hieronymus.

Rhythms.[770] He cites several passages in Diodorus 17, where tiny tweaks reveal snatches of lyric verse, and adds a couple more instances found in Fragments 19 and 22 of Cleitarchus. In addition, it is known that the so-called Asianic style was briefly popular around the beginning of the 3rd century BC and was extensively employed by other contemporaneous historians of Alexander: notably by Hegesias of Magnesia. The use of metrical devices by Cleitarchus also provides a possible explanation for the existence of numerous poetical turns of phrase and much highly rhetorical material in Curtius and Diodorus 17.

It has been impractical to attempt to reproduce any consistent metre in the reconstruction of Cleitarchus in English: my view is that it would have interfered too much with the accurate translation of the meanings in the source material. However, I have insinuated certain rhetorical and poetical devices in a less systematic and more fitful fashion insofar as may be accommodated within a faithful reproduction of the source texts. In particular, I have injected a fair amount of alliteration, verse and metre. Hopefully, this gives an impression of the lyrical pretensions of the original to those looking for a colourful read, whilst allowing those readers more concerned with the information contained in the text to ignore these evocations of its original artistic ambitions.

The Character and Value of Cleitarchus

The key tension in the ancient source traditions of Alexander historiography is the contrast between the sensationalism of the Cleitarchan Vulgate versus the censorial attitude of Arrian. The latter exudes worthiness and appears to be sincere in his pursuit of the unadorned facts in most circumstances, nevermind how prosaic and dull this may render parts of his text. But he is often economical with the truth: the destruction of the Branchidae is altogether missing, and, more seriously, there are clear indications that he suppressed information on Alexander's personal life. For example, he fails to mention Alexander's mistress, Barsine, and takes some trouble in avoiding naming Bagoas in the *Anabasis*, especially when referring to the hanging of Orxines. Trying to interpret Alexander's personality through the medium of Arrian's filtrations is sometimes scarcely more fruitful than attempting to formulate an impression of the character of a modern politician from a calendar of meetings, events and visits that he/she has attended (though it would overstate the case to suggest that Arrian is entirely devoid of information on Alexander's character.)

Conversely, Cleitarchus' attitude to Alexander's private life seems to have been downright prurient. Few rumours were too exotic to be incorporated and he hardly ever overlooked a good story. Consequently, it is possible to regard the two dominant traditions of Alexander historiography as being substantially complementary to one another. As far as concerns the details of the events

---

[770] Lionel Pearson, *The Lost Histories of Alexander the Great*, American Philological Association, 1960, p. 213.

themselves, the Cleitarchan tradition is occasionally demonstrably inferior to Arrian, but it nonetheless provides a good control on the relative authoritativeness of Arrian's version of each episode. In a few cases, where there is irreconcilable disagreement, it may well be Arrian who is mistaken. Furthermore, it appears that Cleitarchus probably treated the revolt of Baryaxes more thoroughly than Arrian. Another illustration that Cleitarchus is relatively more reliable than has often been suggested is the fact that he correctly stated that the River Pasitigris lay four days' march from Susa, whereas Diodorus 18.17.3 (following Hieronymus?) wrongly gives the distance as a march of a single day. Furthermore, some of the deficiencies in the Vulgate may have been introduced by intermediaries and cannot safely be deployed to denigrate Cleitarchus himself: for example, Diodorus' text seems to have been incorrectly corrected by a transcriber in antiquity to suggest that Abdalonymus was king of Tyre and Curtius (or a transcriber of his work) inadvertently suggested that Cohortanus was the father of Roxane.

In many Western nations there exists today a similar dichotomy among daily newspapers: on the one hand the sensationalist, popular titles, which habitually focus on the ephemeral antics of celebrities and on the other the more sober publications (formerly termed "Broadsheets"), which seek to focus and deliberate on events and issues which they deem to have a proper degree of significance for our lives. Yet from the perspective of a future historian, it would be difficult to achieve a fully rounded comprehension of our society without examining examples of both types of journal. In the same way, the Cleitarchan reportage and Arrian's meticulous, but nevertheless flawed, efforts to detail campaigning dispositions are both essential in formulating a relatively balanced, accurate and human portrait of Alexander and his times.

Feasibility of Reconstruction

Wherever Curtius and Diodorus agree *in detail*, then the *Einquellenprinzip* establishes a confident basis for the reconstruction of Cleitarchus. A particular problem arises within the great lacuna between Diodorus 17.83 and 17.84, however we have seen that the *Metz Epitome* can largely be used as a substitute for Diodorus in this period. It validates a great deal of material in Curtius as Cleitarchan in its origin. The weakest area in the reconstruction must inevitably be the period between the beginning of Cleitarchus' account and the opening of the surviving books of Curtius. In this range it is best assumed on the basis of incomplete evidence that the early part of Book 17 of Diodorus is essentially Cleitarchan. Occasionally, Diodorus may be supplemented from Plutarch's *Life of Alexander* and Justin's *Epitome of the Philippic History of Pompeius Trogus*. Similarly, Curtius has many significant lacunae in the period 324-323BC, though it is more securely established that Diodorus was mainly relying on Cleitarchus for this part of Alexander's reign.

It has also been possible to feed in a great deal of manuscript material from other sources to bolster the overall framework as well as the detail of many episodes.

Naturally, it has not been feasible to reconstruct the exact phraseology of Cleitarchus, except in a few limited cases. Since Latin authors, particularly Curtius, must provide much of the detail, the Greek is obviously irretrievable. Therefore, the reconstruction must be confined to establishing the factual material together with the sense and flavour of Cleitarchus' account of each reconstructed episode. In view of this, there is little point in trying to recreate the work in its original Greek. Rather English is preferable due to its superior accessibility to a wide readership.

The Methodology of the Reconstruction

Firstly, it was necessary to compose a table of references to all the material with any claim to a Cleitarchan pedigree. The references needed to be grouped against each successive incident or episode of Alexander's career, together with a concise outline of the Cleitarchan version of the incident or episode. Where relevant, notes were provided to justify and to guide the Cleitarchan interpretation of the information in the references. The episodes needed to be correctly ordered and grouped into the appropriate Cleitarchan books. This document was compiled and is presented in the next main section: **Organisation & Sources**. It provides a basic framework for the reconstruction, which is further supported by the detailed analyses in this section. In providing an organized listing of the source material for the reconstruction together with some discussion of special issues, this Table serves as a substitute for copious annotations of the reconstructed text, thus avoiding overburdening the reconstruction proper with a morass of footnotes.

I have considered it essential to indicate a hierarchy of confidence within the reconstructed text to maximise its value as a source for historiographical studies. This has to be done in a way that is immediately interpretable by the reader and flexible enough to be reproducible as an element of any likely publishing format (especially the present book form.) In particular, it needs to be readily presentable within the constraints of a textual pdf file in standard black and white (or greyscale) fonts. In the light of these considerations and constraints the following range of six textual gradations was adopted:

<u>**Underlined bold text for Fragments**</u>

Bold text where there is overwhelming evidence

Bold italic text where there exists direct/firm evidence

Normal text where direct/weak evidence applies

Italic text where the evidence is conjectural

The Nature and Genesis of Cleitarchus' Account

Grey text for connecting passages, if Cleitarchus' version is indeterminate

However, it has transpired that the use of the grey text is nowhere necessary for the actual reconstruction. There is enough Cleitarchan material surviving as to provide a satisfactorily continuous account across the entirety of Alexander's reign.

Finally, the chapters and sections within the reconstructed books needed to be enumerated in a logical and self-consistent fashion, so as to facilitate referencing of episodes. Therefore, I adopted a simple two-level book-and-section numbering system, which permits referencing of items down to the level of their paragraph. Obviously, the sentence number within each paragraph could be added, if it were desired to provide that degree of specificity. However, I have not deemed it appropriate to clutter the text with actual enumeration down to the sentence level.

Conclusions

A revised analysis of the book-numbered fragments of Cleitarchus has shown that he organised his *History Concerning Alexander* into thirteen books, one for each year of Alexander's reign. Echoes of the *termini* of five of Cleitarchus' books have been discerned in Diodorus' seventeenth book in the form of boundary phrases marking digressions on events elsewhere that Cleitarchus placed at the ends of his books. Cleitarchus' work appears to have been divided into two parts in the same place as Diodorus 17 is so divided (between its 63rd and 64th chapters). The five books in the first part of Cleitarchus had *termini* located quite precisely on the anniversaries of the accession in the Attic Lunar Calendar corresponding to dates between mid-September and mid-October in the Julian calendar. However, Books 6 to 13 comprising the second part of the work generally ended in the summer months, probably in order to agree with Alexander's death in June at the end of the work.

This improved understanding of the structure of Cleitarchus' work has yielded startling new information on key details of Alexander's reign. Among various revelations on Alexander's itinerary, it has emerged that Alexander's route probably hugged the Mediterranean coast for as long as possible for the march between Tyre and Thapsacus in 331BC. This means that most modern reconstructions of his path are in error in making him march inland from Tyre. It has become clear that Cleitarchus paid detailed attention to events beyond the narrow focus of Alexander's expedition in a more comprehensive sense than has previously been realised and he was scrupulous about chronology. For example, he appears to have given a detailed account of the revolt of Baryaxes in Persia in its correct context, whilst Alexander was in India. It has also been demonstrated that Cleitarchus believed the Battle of Arbela (or Gaugamela) to have taken place on the day before the fifth anniversary of Alexander's accession. Since this battle can be dated accurately in the Julian Calendar using an antecedent lunar eclipse and Plutarch has provided an Attic date for the event, which is synchronised with the lunar phases, it has been possible for the first time to calculate a Julian date for the festival of the gods at which Philip was assassinated. This is 27th September 336BC, which was the autumnal equinox (for it was 22nd September in the back-projected Gregorian calendar).

The first book of Cleitarchus opened with some details of Alexander's birth and ancestry. The last book probably extended to note Alexander's entombment at Memphis and seems briefly to have alluded to attempts by Antipater and Cassander to suppress rumours that they had poisoned Alexander. Possibly it closed (as Curtius closes) with the transfer of Alexander's corpse to Alexandria in ~280BC. It appears virtually certain that Diodorus' seventeenth book is essentially solely an epitome of Cleitarchus' work, despite some modern speculation that he incorporated a significant admixture of a second early author. Furthermore, Curtius' *Deeds of Alexander* is essentially a translation and abridgement of Cleitarchus, notwithstanding its author having interjected a few personal comments and references to scholia that he found in his manuscript of Cleitarchus.

With the additional help of an analysis of the recently published papyrus fragment *On Hellenistic Historians* (POxy LXXI 4808) it is now possible to be reasonably confident that Cleitarchus wrote *Concerning Alexander* between around 280-250BC. Thus the transfer of Alexander's corpse to Alexandria was a relatively recent event when Cleitarchus began, so it is possible that it formed part of Cleitarchus' inspiration. Additional inspiration probably derived from the fact that Cleitarchus' father, Deinon, had previously written a history of Persia, so Cleitarchus may have considered that he was extending and completing the work that his parent had begun. Although it is now clear that Cleitarchus himself did not accompany Alexander's expedition, he nevertheless based his account on the works of Onesicritus, Nearchus, Callisthenes and others, who had been eyewitnesses of the events and he was writing at a time and in a place (Alexandria), where it was possible to access a comprehensive range of earlier writings and to interview elderly eyewitnesses of the events. However, virtually all the key participants in Alexander's campaigns were recently, safely dead, so Cleitarchus had the opportunity to produce a fairly uninhibited critique of Alexander's reign for the first time. His position was similar to that of modern historians, who needed to wait four decades for the revelations concerning the importance of the code-breaking at Bletchley Park before they could compose a remotely valid history of the Second World War.

It has also been found that Megasthenes wrote at the beginning of the third century BC and was probably a source for Cleitarchus. Furthermore, there are strong reasons to consider that the *Metz Epitome* (sections 1-86) is essentially a crude and incomplete but nevertheless direct epitome of Cleitarchus, covering roughly the period between Alexander's adoption of items of Persian dress in the

The Nature and Genesis of Cleitarchus' Account

latter part of 330BC to the expedition's arrival at the mouths of the Indus in the autumn of 325BC.

This investigation has shown that it is generally inadequate to pursue a single strand of evidence in addressing the key problems presented by Cleitarchus, for such strands are almost invariably individually inconclusive. Nevertheless, a connected reconstruction has proved possible by recognising the intersections and mutual reinforcements between multiple independent strands of evidence aided by a detailed appreciation of Cleitarchus' style, method and approach. The salvation of the Cleitarchan tradition has therefore relied on the agglomeration of disparate hints, clues and fragments into concrete foundations.

I believe that the completed reconstruction casts considerable light on the full extent and magnificence of Cleitarchus' work. Whereas he occasionally incorporated and even magnified the faults of his sources, thus leaning towards sensationalism and an uncritical acceptance of embroideries of the original facts, Cleitarchus also gave a better rounded and more chronologically ordered version of Alexander's career than any other ancient author. It has also become clear that a large proportion of the faults and discrepancies in the extant Vulgate Tradition are not due to Cleitarchus himself, but have been perpetrated by his disciples or have arisen through accreted manuscript defects.

In accordance with the principles that have emerged from this analysis, a relatively complete and generally accurate reconstruction of Cleitarchus' work has been completed. It should prove to be a valuable and useful document for scholars, despite necessary imperfections. Much stands to be learnt simply from reading the reconstruction, whilst bearing in mind the process of its creation. In my view, it is also a fascinating and gripping epic of the remote past, which stands to capture the imaginations of its future readers just as much as it once thrilled their ancestors in antiquity.

Concerning Alexander the Great by Andrew Chugg

TABLE 3: The Books and Fragments of Cleitarchus

bk	START	END	FRAGMENTS
1	**Spring 336BC** Alexander's birth & ancestry; Philip sends a vanguard under Parmenion & Attalus into Asia	15th October 335BC Razing of Thebes Alexander's visit to Delphi(?)	F1* - the wealth of Thebes was just 440 talents
2	**16th October 335BC** Alexander's preparations for the invasion of Asia	5th October 334BC Capture of Halicarnassus The Marmares(?) "This is what happened in this year" Diodorus 17.28.5	F7 – 820 years between invasion of the Heracleidae and Alexander's invasion F33 & F34 – Themistocles at the court of Xerxes (the context is Alexander's visit to the tomb of Themistocles at Magnesia)
3	**6th October 334BC** Pamphylian campaigns	24th September 333BC Alexander's recovery from illness at Tarsus	
4	**25th September 333BC** Campaign in western Cilicia and visit to Anchiale Battle of Issus	13th October 332BC Balonymus appointed king of Tyre "Now we have described things concerning Alexander…" Diodorus 17.47.6,	F2* - Death of Sardanapalus (the context is Alexander's visit to his tomb at Anchiale near Tarsus) F8 – Battle of Issus (November 333BC) F9 – Tyrian sacrifice of a boy
5	**14th October 332BC** Digression on events elsewhere: Agis conquers Crete… Siege of Gaza	1st October 331BC Battle of Arbela (Gaugamela) "This was the outcome of the battle near Arbela" D 17.61.3 Digression on Agis' rebellion in Greece: "Now that we have run through the events in Europe, we may in turn pass on to what occurred in Asia" D 17.63.5	F3* - Story of Theias Byblios F4* - 50 Spartan hostages given to Antipater
6	**2nd October 331BC** Capture of Darius' base at Arbela	Late July 330BC Pursuit & death of Darius "That was the situation in Asia" Diodorus 17.73.4, digression?	F10 - Description of Babylon F11 – Razing of Persepolis
7	**August 330BC** Advance to Hecatompylus	June 329BC First crossing of the "Caucasus" (actually Paropamisus – modern Hindu Kush) "These were the concerns of Alexander" Diodorus 17.83.3	F12 – Caspian Sea equal to the Euxine F13 – Flooding of isthmus between Euxine and Caspian F14 – a wasp in Hyrcania F15 & F16 - Visit of Thalestria, Queen of the Amazons F32 – Castration of man (spouse of an Amazon?) for adultery

The Nature and Genesis of Cleitarchus' Account

8	**July 329BC** Digression on quarrel of Bessus & Bagodaras at a banquet	**Autumn 328BC** Capture of the Rock of Ariamazes	
9	**Autumn 328BC** Scythian king offers Alexander his daughter in marriage	**May 327BC** Marriage to Roxane	
10	**June 327BC** Preparations for the invasion of India. Alexander orders the formation of the Epigoni	**June 326BC** Re-instatement of Porus as king following his defeat at the Hydaspes Report of the revolt of Baryaxes in Media	F20-22 – Indian processions with trees drawn on carriages and tame birds in their branches F17 – Ivy of Dionysus at Nysa F5* - Only the Persian king may wear the tiara upright (revolt of Baryaxes)
11	**July 326BC** Foundation of Bucephala Digression on wonders of India and Alexander's geographical objectives	**Late Spring 325BC** Treatment of the Mallian wound by Critobulus Digression on the revolt of the Greeks in Bactria	F18 –16 cubit serpents F19 – Troops of monkeys and an entrapment technique F28- A salt mine F24 – Ptolemy saves wounded Alexander at the Mallian town
12	**Late Spring 325BC** Surrender of Malli & Oxydracae Contest between Coragus & Dioxippus	**June 324BC** The arrival of 30,000 Epigoni at Susa "These were the concerns of Alexander" Diodorus 17.108.3	F25 – 80,000 Indians slain in the Kingdom of Sambus F23 – Mandi women bear children at 7 and are old at 40 F26 – Tidal bore in Indus Delta F27- Oreitae & Ichthyophagoi F29 – Nearchus & Onesicritus arrive with stories of the Ocean F6* - Gymnosophists scorn death
13	**July 324BC** The extravagance of Harpalus & his flight to Athens The exiles decree & the mutiny	**June 323BC (Epilogue 280BC?)** Death of Alexander First Division of the Satrapies Entombment in Alexandria?	F30 – The courtesans of Harpalus F31 – Roman Embassy at Babylon

* Fragment with the book number in Cleitarchus

Concerning Alexander the Great by Andrew Chugg

TABLE 4: Sources of Cleitarchus

SOURCE	DATE	EVIDENCE	PROBABILITY
Onesicritus	Before 310BC	Amazon Queen; Indian salt mines; suttee & Indian beauty; departure & return of fleet; wonders of Hyrcania; Banyan; monkey capture; Delphic oracle; interview with gymnosophists; death of brother of Lysimachus	99%
Deinon	Father of Cleitarchus	365 Persian concubines; sirens & Indian birds; Themistocles; story of Sardanapulus; Euergetae; details of Persian history	99%
Nearchus	Before 310BC	Oreitae/Ichthyophagoi make bread from fish; 16 cubit snakes; trumpets to scare whales	95%
Callisthenes	After 336BC Before 327BC	Sea withdrawal in Pamphylia; visit to tomb of Sardanapalus at Anchiale; crows *en route* to Siwa & oracle responds in nods & signs	95%
Timaeus	Late 4th to early 3rd century BC	Invasion 820 years after Heraclidae; terms to describe anthredon; date of Alexander's birth; follows Timaeus' use of language	95%
Holcias(?) *Liber de Morte*	317BC Heckel or 308BC Bosworth	Poisoning of Alexander by a conspiracy instigated by Antipater and perpetrated by Cassander & Iollas	90%
Megasthenes	c.290BC	Mandi & Pandaea; Gymnosophists; River Iomanes & details of the Ganges region	80%
Hegesias	Early 3rd century BC	Siege of Gaza; Asianic rhythms; fire in Ephesian temple at Alexander's birth	75%
Polycleitus	Late 4th – early 3rd century BC	Confusion between Aral Sea and Sea of Azov; sweet water and sea serpents in the Caspian; Amazon Queen	70%
Herodotus	Early 5th century BC	Parallels between Darius/Charidemus/Amyntas and Xerxes/Demaratus	65%
Theopompus	324-320BC	Mistresses of Harpalus	50%
Aristobulus	After 301BC	Visit to Anchiale; apes & monkey capture; Alexandria on Tanais; Rock of Ariamazes; Aristander's prophecies	40%
Patroclus	After 380BC	Common statement comparing size of the Caspian to the Euxine – but may have been originated by Onesicritus or Polycleitus	35%
Ephippus	Late 4th century BC	Death & funeral of Hephaistion Giant cup at final party Parallel descriptions of Alexander's dress	30%
Berossus	After 293BC	Semiramis did not build the Hanging Gardens in Babylon	30%
Demetrius of Phalerum	318-310BC	Cleitarchus' attention to Alexander's fortune may derive from Demetrius' *Peri Tyches*	30%
Chares	Late 4th century BC	Heroism at Aornus; Bucephalus died of wounds	20%
Hieronymus	Shortly after 272BC	Conspiracy of Antipater, Cassander & Iollas?	10%

The Nature and Genesis of Cleitarchus' Account

TABLE 5: The *Einquellenprinzip*: close matches between Curtius and Diodorus 17

C=Curtius, D=Diodorus, J=Justin, S=Schwartz, H=Hamilton in Cleitarchus & Diodorus 17, cf.=vergleiche in Schwartz

C3.2.1=D17.30.7 S
C3.11.7-11=D17.34.2-6 S
C3.11.20,23-6=D17.35.2,36.5,2,4 cf.J11.9.11-12 S
C3.11.27=D17.36.6 H
C3.12.15-17=D17.37.5-6 H
C3.12.26=D17.38.2 H
C4.1.15-26=D17.47.1-6 H
C4.1.27-33=D17.48.2-4 S
C4.1.39-40=D17.48.1-2 S
C4.2.7=D17.40.4 S
C4.2.12=D17.41.3-4 S
C4.2.18=D17.40.5 S
C4.2.20=D17.41.1 S
C4.3.6,9,11-12=D17.42.5-6,43.3 S
C4.3.20=D17.41.2 cf.J11.10.14 S
C4.3.22=D17.41.8 H
C4.3.25-26=D17.44.1-3 S
C4.4.1-2=D17.45.7 S
C4.4.3-5=D17.41.5-6 H
C4.4.10-12,17=D17.46.2-4 S
C4.5.11=D17.48.6 S
C4.6.30=D17.49.1 S
C4.7.1,5,9=D17.49.2-4 S
C4.7.12-14=D17.49.4-5 S
C4.7.16-17,20-28=D17.50.3-51.3 S
C4.9.4-5=D17.53.1-2 H
C4.13.26-29=D17.57.1-4 S
C4.15.9-11=D17.59.6-7 S
C4.15.16-17=D17.58.4-5 S
C4.15.28-29,32=D17.60.2-4 S
C4.16.31-32=D17.61.3 S
C5.1.10-11=D17.64.3 S
C5.1.40-42=D17.65.1 S
C5.1.43-45=D17.64.5-6 S
C5.1.25-26=D2.7.3-4 (Jacoby F10) S
C5.1.34-35=D2.10.4,1 S
C5.2.1-7=D17.65.2-4 cf.D17.27.1-2 S
C5.2.8, 12-15=D17.65.5,66.2-7 S
C5.3.1.2,4-5,10=D17.67.1-2,4-5 S
C5.3.17-18,23&C5.4.2-4,10,12,18=D17.68.1-6 S
C5.5.2-4=D17.69.1-2 S
C5.5.5-9,12,23-24=D17.69.2-8 cf.J11.14.11-12 S

C5.6.1-5,8,9=D17.70.1-71.2 S
C6.2.15=D17.75.1 S
C6.4.3-6=D17.75.2 S
C6.4.18,22=D17.75.3,6 S
C6.5.11-12,18-21=D17.76.3-8 S
C6.5.24-26,30-32=D17.77.1-3 cf. J12.3.5-7 & Strabo11.5.4 S
C7.1.5-9=D17.80.2 S
C7.2.18=D17.80.3 S
C7.2.35-37=D17.80.4 cf. J12.5.4-8 S
C7.3.1,3=D17.81.1-2 S
C7.3.5-18=D17.82 S
C7.3.22-23=D17.83.1-2 S
C7.4.33,38=D17.83.4-6 S
C7.5.28-35 cf. Dκ S
C7.10.4-9 cf. Dκβ S
C7.10.15-16 cf. Dκδ S
C8.1.11-19 cf. Dκς S
C8.5.4 cf. Dλα, J12.7.5 S
C8.10.5-6 cf. Dλβ S
C8.11.2=D17.85.1-2, J12.7.12 S
C8.11.3-4=D17.85.4-5 S
C8.11.7-8,25=D17.85.3,8-9&D17.86.1 S
C8.12.1-3=D17.86.2 S
C8.12.4-10,14=D17.86.3-7 S
C8.14.3=D17.87.5 S
C9.1.1,3-4,6=D17.89.3-6&D17.90.1 S
C9.1.8-12=D17.90.4-7 S
C9.1.24-33=D17.91.4-D17.92.3 S
C9.3.10-11=D17.94.2 S
C9.3.19=D17.95.1-2, J12.8.16 S
C9.3.20,23=D17.95.3,5 S
C9.4.1-2,5=D17.96.1-3 S
C9.4.8-14=D17.97.1-3 S
C9.7.16-26=D17.100.2-D17.101.6 S
C9.8.4-8=D17.102.1-4 S
C9.8.13-15(Jacoby F25)=D17.102.6 S
C9.8.17-28=D17.103, J12.10.2-3 cf. Cic. de divin. 2.135 S
C9.10.5-11,17-18,27=D17.104.4-D17.106.1 S
C10.2.4,8-12,30=D17.190.1-2 S
C10.5.21-25=D17.118.3, J13.1.5-6 S
C10.10.14,18-19=D17.117.5&D17.118.2 cf. J12.13.10 S

Organisation and Sources

Tabulated References for the Reconstruction of Cleitarchus
Book 1: Spring 336BC – 15th October 335BC

Summary	Sources	References	Comment
Prologue: birth and ancestry of Alexander. Razing of the temple at Ephesus and descent from Aeacidae and Heraclidae.	Plutarch 2.1&3.3-5 Justin 12.16 Diodorus 17.1.5	Hammond THA 91 Sources 19-20	It has been thought that Cleitarchus opened his history with the assassination of Philip & Alexander's accession. However, a summary dealing with Alexander's birth & his youth may have been included. Hammond shows in *Sources* 19-20 that Plutarch's date for Alexander's birth comes from Timaeus, a contemporary of Cleitarchus. But Jacoby F7 of Cleitarchus from Clement of Alexandria says that both Timaeus & Cleitarchus gave 820 years for the period from the invasion of the Heraclidae to Alexander's crossing into Asia, whereas other Greek historians, such as Eratosthenes, gave wildly variant figures (cf. Jacoby F 36). This strongly indicates that Cleitarchus made use of Timaeus' work (cf. Pearson 216). If so, then Plutarch & Cicero are likely to be getting Timaeus' information on Alexander's birth via Cleitarchus. Perhaps Cleitarchus attributed the information to Timaeus. Hammond also attributes stress on Alexander's Aeacid ancestry to Cleitarchus & Jacoby F7 mentions the Heraclidae (cf. F36)
Philip sends his generals Parmenion, Amyntas & Attalus into Asia Minor	Justin 9.5.8-9	Hammond THA 93	Spring of 336BC
Philip celebrates marriage of daughter Cleopatra to Alexander of Epirus; Pausanias kills Philip in narrow passage, because he has ignored Pausanias' complaints against Attalus, who had raped him	Justin 9.6.1-8	Hammond THA 93	Summer of 336BC
Sons of Philip	Justin 9.8.1-3	Hammond THA 90-3	
Accession & funeral of Philip; rebelliousness of Thebes; appointed general by assembly at Corinth	Justin 11.1.1-11.2.7 Diodorus 17.3-4	Hammond THA 94; Yardley & Heckel on Justin 83-5	Yardley & Heckel rightly reject Hammond's view that Diodorus used Diyllus here and prefer Cleitarchus

Concerning Alexander the Great by Andrew Chugg

Summary	Sources	References	Comment
Visit to Diogenes of Sinope	Plutarch, Alexander 14.1-3 Plutarch, Moralia 331E-332C & 605D Arrian 7.2.1	Cf. Diogenes Laertius on Diogenes 6	Plutarch notes it after the fall of Thebes, but it should occur at Alexander's first appearance before the Corinthian League, since it is linked to his appointment to lead the war against Persia
Digression on the historical background in the Persian Empire: troubled prelude to the accession of Darius III to the throne	Justin 10 Diodorus 17.5.3-7.3		Hammond suggests this is from Diyllus in Diodorus and from Cleitarchus' father, Deinon, in Justin, but the material is similar and placed in the text in both such as to imply a common source. (cf. Jacoby F 33) Cleitarchus is the likely common source of Justin and Diodorus with a special interest in Persian events due to his father's work.
Evolution of the war in Phrygia after the death of Attalus: including Memnon's raid on Cyzicus and the stratagem of the hats and the activities of Calas	Diodorus 17.7.8-9 Polyaenus 5.44.5		Details of the raid on Cyzicus are given by Polyaenus in a way that is consistent with the thinner outline in Diodorus. Calas appears to have replaced Attalus at this time.
Balkan campaign: battle with Syrmus of the Triballi at the Danube	Plutarch 11.1-3 Justin 11.2.8 Diodorus 17.8.1	Hammond THA 94 & Sources 24; Yardley & Heckel on Justin 84-5	Spring-summer 335BC in extreme summary
Omens of the fall of Thebes	Diodorus 17.10 Arrian 1.9.8 Aelian VH 12.57	Hammond Sources 207	
Siege & destruction of Thebes & Council at which the destruction was proposed by the Plataeans and Phocians	Diodorus 17.8.2-14.4 Plutarch 11.4-6 Justin 11.3.1-11.4.6	Hammond THA 91-3 & Sources	
Alexander saves Pindar's house and descendants	Plutarch 11.6 Arrian 1.9.10 Aelian VH 13.7	Hammond Sources 207	
After razing of Thebes, its wealth (from selling Thebans into slavery…) just 440 talents & its citizens were stingy	Athenaeus 148 D-F (cf. Diodorus 17.14.4)	Jacoby, Fragment 1 of Cleitarchus	Attributed to Cleitarchus and Book 1 of Concerning Alexander – Diodorus *implies* 440 talents raised by selling the Thebans, but probably equals total proceeds
The freeing of Timocleia	Plutarch 12 Polyaenus 8.40		Story attributed to Aristobulus by Plutarch in his Moralia, but the version in his Life of Alexander has different details and may be from Cleitarchus
Alexander demands 10 prominent Athenian politicians as hostages – Demades persuades the king to relent, but generals exiled and defected to Darius	Diodorus 17.15 Justin 11.4.10-12 Plutarch, *Demosthenes* 23.5 Plutarch, *Alexander* 13	Hammond, Sources 27	

Organisation and Sources

Summary	Sources	References	Comment
Visit to Delphi: Alexander declared invincible by the Pythia	Plutarch 14.4-5 Diodorus 17.93.4 [Livy 9.18] [SIG³ 251H, col. II, lines 9-10 (p.436-7)]	Hammond Sources 29 THA	Alexander is *aniketos* (invincible) & promised world-rule, cf. Siwa & Ammon. Livy too refers to the "invincible Alexander", though also the attacks on Alexander by Athenian orators, eg Hypereides, who called Alexander "king and invincible god" (ironically). Historicity of oracle visit supported by gift to shrine at this time of 150 gold coins of Philip from Alexander(?) Perhaps read of Xenophon's consultation of Delphi for *his* campaign against Persia. Pearson (Lost Histories p. 92) thinks Plutarch got Delphic visit from Onesicritus, but Cleitarchus used Onesicritus.

Book 2: 16th October 335BC – 5th October 334BC

Summary	Sources	References	Comment
Council in Macedonia to plan the invasion of Asia and celebration of the festival of the Muses.	Diodorus 17.16; Plutarch, *Demosthenes* 23.5		Events back in Macedonia should be in the second book given the date on which the second year of the reign began
Crossing to Asia and preparations; Alexander's gifts to his friends, Alexander took with him the most capable Thracian kings, dye on priests hands left marks foretelling victory on victims' livers	Justin 11.5.1-9 Plutarch 15.2-3 Front. Strat. 2.11.3 & 1.11.14	Hammond THA 95-6 Sources 31	
820 years from the invasion of the Heraclidae to Alexander crossing into Asia	Clement of Alexandria, Strom. I 139,4	Jacoby, Fragment 7 of Cleitarchus	Early Spring
Alexander casts a spear into the Asian shoreline	Justin 11.5.10-11 Diodorus 17.17.2		Hammond makes no suggestion for this against Justin, but this story is common to Justin and Diodorus, so Cleitarchus is overwhelmingly likely to be its source
Troops ordered not to ravage Asia, because it was their own property	Justin 11.6.1	Hammond THA 96	
Honouring the tombs of Achilles and the heroes (Patroclus) at Troy	Arrian 1.12.1 Diodorus 17.17.3 Justin 11.5.12 Plutarch 15.4 Aelian VH 9.38 & 12.7, cf. Cicero, Pro Archia poet. 24		Hammond does not explicitly identify this anecdote as Cleitarchus, but he does point out that Alexander's emulation of Achilles was probably a Cleitarchan theme (THA 64-5, 91, 109; Sources 48 n11). The story is common to Justin and Diodorus, which strongly suggests that Cleitarchus is its source

611

Concerning Alexander the Great by Andrew Chugg

Summary	Sources	References	Comment
Troop numbers: 32000 infantry, 4500 cavalry and 182 warships. Contrasting Alexander's world conquest with a small band of experienced troops with Darius' reliance on overwhelming strength	Justin 11.6.2-9 Diodorus 17.17.3-5	Hammond THA 96-7	Abbreviated(?) to 40,000 men in Frontinus, Stratagems 4.2.4 & Ampelius 16.2
Battle of the Granicus	Diodorus 17.19.3-21.6 & 17.23.2 Justin 11.6.10-13	Hammond THA 16-17	Late spring - Thargelion according to Plutarch, *Camillus* 19.4 (~14th May to ~12th June 334BC) – Plutarch, *Alexander* 16.2 confirms that the Macedonian month was Daisios, equivalent to the Attic Thargelion - Aelian, VH 2.25 may suggest 6th Thargelion (20th May 334BC in the Julian calendar), but this is might be an inaccurate Archon date
Alexander heads for Sardis which is surrendered by Mithrines, its satrap	Diodorus 17.21.7		
Alexander takes the surrender of Magnesia, where lay the tomb of Themistocles (Athenian commander at Salamis) – digression on Themistocles at the court of Xerxes following his exile from Athens – he later drank bull's blood and died rather that lead Persian forces against Athens	Plutarch's Life of Themistocles 27.1-2 Cicero, Brut. 42-43	Jacoby, Fragments 33 & 34 of Cleitarchus	The surrender of Magnesia on the Maeander (Arrian 1.18.1) is the most likely occasion for Cleitarchus' digression on Themistocles, since the tomb of Themistocles was in the agora there. Cleitarchus' father Deinon had evidently told the story of Themistocles. It is possible that Cleitarchus drew a comparison between Themistocles' submission to Xerxes and Charidemus' allegiance to Darius, since they were both exiled Athenians serving Persian kings. Arrian (1.18.2) may implicitly be contradicting Cleitarchus when he makes a point of stating that Alexander stayed at Ephesus when Magnesia surrendered.
Miletus	Diodorus 22		Very heavily epitomised
Dismissed the fleet to encourage troops to fight more vigorously, when Darius reached the coast	Diodorus 23.1	Hammond THA 38	
Concentration of Persians at Halicarnassus. Memnon sends his wife (Barsine) and children to Darius for safety and trust	Diodorus 17.23.4-6	Hammond THA 39	
Halicarnassus	Diodorus 17.24.4-27.6	Hammond THA 39-40	Stalwart veterans and young shirkers – a Cleitarchan theme
Fortress of the Marmares on the border between Lycia and Pisidia	Diodorus 17.28	Hammond THA 40	Not recounted elsewhere – may be Chandir in Pamphylia
End of book 2	Diodorus 17.28.5		

Organisation and Sources

Book 3: 6th October 334BC – 24th September 333BC

Summary	Sources	References	Comment
Campaigns of Memnon culminating in his death	Diodorus 17.29		Events from the Autumn of 334BC through to Memnon's death in the Summer of 333BC
Alexander uncertain regarding future strategy	Plutarch 17.1-2	Hammond Sources 45-6	Alexander's policy is swayed by the ensuing oracles and miracles – mimics Herodotus in his account of Xerxes being swayed by dreams and oracles
Spring near Xanthus in Lydia casts forth a bronze tablet prophesying the overthrow of the Persians by the Greeks	Plutarch 17.2-3	Hammond Sources 46	
Crowns statue of Theodectas at Phaselis during a comus Arrest here of Alexander Lyncestes on charges of conspiracy due to information from a prisoner	Plutarch 17.2-3 & 5 Justin 11.7.1 Diodorus 17.32 Cf. Curtius 7.1.6	Hammond Sources 46-7, Tarn Sources 49	Tarn argues mentions of Alexander in a *comus* are from Cleitarchus. Justin's timing agrees with Curtius 7.1.6, who placed the arrest in his lost second book. Diodorus delayed mentioning the arrest of Lyncestes until after the recovery of Alexander from illness, seemingly to draw attention to the parallel between Olympias's letter about Lyncestes and Parmenion's letter about Philip. Hammond makes no attribution.
Sea gives way to Alexander on the Pamphylian coast;	Plutarch 17.3 & Jacoby F31 of Callisthenes		Cleitarchus following Callisthenes for the sea giving way?
Alexander cuts the Gordian knot with his sword	Arrian 2.3.7, Justin 11.7.3-16, Curtius 3.1.14-19, Plutarch 18.1-2	Hammond Sources 47 & 217 THA 97 & 128	Knot-solver "destined to become king of the inhabited Earth" in Plutarch – chimes with World-Ruler idea from Cleitarchus (cf. Siwa oracle below)
Reaction of Darius to the death of Memnon	Plutarch 18.3, Curtius 3.2.1, Diodorus 17.30.1	C3.2.1=D17.30.7 Schwartz	Completes the encouragement of Alexander to attack Darius
Parade of Darius' forces before Babylon: Charidemus of Athens is pessimistic about their chances against the Macedonians and is executed	Curtius 3.2.2-19 Diodorus 17.30.2-31.2	Hammond THA 40-1 & 116	Resembles conference of Xerxes in Herodotus 7; Curtius directly references Herodotus 7.59
Dream of Darius misinterpreted by magi	Plutarch 18.4-5, Curtius 3.3.2-7	Hammond Sources 48	Hammond does not assign this passage in THA
Marching order of the army of Darius	Curtius 3.3.8-25		Darius's dress (e.g. the diadem of interwoven white and purple and the purple tunic with a white stripe) is echoed at Curtius 6.6.4, Diodorus 17.77.5, Justin 12.3.8-12 & Metz 2
Advance to Cilicia across Mount Taurus by a forced march on hearing of Darius' approach	Justin 11.8.1-2	Hammond THA 113	By association with Justin's version of Tarsus

613

Concerning Alexander the Great by Andrew Chugg

Summary	Sources	References	Comment
Alexander tarries at Tarsus due to illness, after plunging into the Cydnus	Plutarch 19 Curtius 3.5.1-3.6.3 Justin 11.8.3 Val.Max.3.8 ext 6	Hammond Sources 48-9 THA 97-8 & 121	
Letter from Parmenion warning Alexander about Philip the Doctor and the successful potion provided by Philip	Diodorus 17.31.4-6 Seneca *De Ira* 2.23 Val.Max.3.8 ext 6 Curtius 3.6.4-16 Pseudo-Callisthenes 2.8	Hammond THA 41	Justin 11.8.5 places Parmenion in Cappadocia, but this is at odds with Curtius 3.4.15 placing him at Tarsus and it is incredible that he warned against Philip without knowing about Alexander's illness

Book 4: 25th September 333BC – 13th October 332BC

Summary	Sources	References	Comment
Alexander's visit to Anchiale; Sardanapalus died of old age after he had lost the sovereignty of the Syrians	Athenaeus 530A, cf. Plutarch *Moralia* 326F & 336C Cf. Curtius 3.7.2	Jacoby, Fragment 2 of Cleitarchus cf. Arrian 2.5.2-4	Attributed by Athenaeus to Book 4: context is Alexander's arrival before a monument and statue of Sardanapalus at Anchiale, 12 miles SW of Tarsus – here Cleitarchus is echoing his father Deinon's *Persica*, which may in turn have followed Ctesias' *Persica*. The story of Alexander's visit is also told by Athenaeus 530 A-B as a fragment of Aristobulus, so too Strabo 14.5.9 and Arrian 2.5.2-4 – this is also in Fragment 34 of Callisthenes. Curtius 3.7.2 recounts Alexander's arrival at Soli, whereas his visit to Anchiale immediately preceded his arrival at Soli
Battle of Issus: Darius defeated by Alexander	Cicero Ad f. 2.10.3 Curtius 3.8.13-3.11.27 Diodorus 17.32.3-17.38.2	Jacoby, Fragment 8 of Cleitarchus; Hammond THA 17 & 118; C3.11.7-11=D17.34.2-6 Schwartz; C3.11.20,23-6= D17.35.2,36.5,2,4 cf.J11.9.11-12 & C3.11.27=D17.36.6 Hamilton:C&D17	November 333BC
Alexander captures the chariot & bow of Darius	Plutarch 20.5-6	Hammond Sources 51	
Visit to the Persian Queens with Hephaistion, who is mistaken for Alexander	Arrian 2.12.6-7 Diodorus 17.37.5 Curtius 3.12.1-3.12.26 Justin 11.9.11-16 Plutarch 21.2-3 Val. Max. 4.7 ext 2	Hammond THA 19, 98, 118 Sources 50-52, 225; C3.12.15-17=D17.37.5-6 Hamilton:C&D17; C3.12.26=D17.38.2 Hamilton:C&D17	

Organisation and Sources

Summary	Sources	References	Comment
Alexander sends Thessalian cavalry to capture the Persian treasure & women at Damascus & the defection of its governor	Curtius 3.12.27-13.17 Plutarch 24.1-2	Hammond Sources 53-54	
Alexander seduced by Persian luxury and falls in love with Barsine and advances into Syria	Justin 11.10.1-3 Plutarch 20.6-8 cf. Curtius 3.13.14	Hammond THA 98 Sources 51	Given the coincident mentions in Justin and Plutarch, it is very likely that Alexander's liaison with Barsine was mentioned here by Cleitarchus and Curtius's note of her capture surely marks the occasion for this in Cleitarchus's text
First peace offer from Darius: Diodorus uniquely suggests that Alexander concealed the real letter and presented a forgery	Curtius 4.1.7-14 Justin 11.12.1-2 Diodorus 17.39.1-3	Hammond THA 42, 99, 122	Diodorus appears to have wrongly summarised the second letter from Darius (delivered after Tyre) in place of the first and consequently thought that Alexander had misrepresented Darius's letter to his council in devising his indignant response.
Balonymus (Abdalonymus in J & C, Aralynomus in P Moralia) appointed king of Sidon	Diodorus 17.47.1-6 Curtius 4.1.16-26 Justin 11.10.8-9 (cf. Plutarch Moralia 340C-E)	Hammond THA 98, 119, 121; C4.1.15-26=D17.47.1-6 Hamilton:C&D17	Diodorus recounted this story at the end of the siege of Tyre and cited "Balonymus" – Hammond's belief that he was using Cleitarchus is probably correct, but I conjecture that Tyre (and possibly Paphos in Cyprus) was incorporated into the kingdom of Sidon at that point and that Diodorus's text was incorrectly corrected by an editor to attribute Tyre as the site of Diodorus's whole story.
Siege of Tyre	Diodorus 17.40.2-17.47.6 Justin 11.10.10-14 Curtius (most of) 4.2.2-4.4.19	Hammond THA 42, 98, 121, 119; C4.2.7=D17.40.4 Schwartz; C4.2.12=D17.41.3-4 Schwartz; C4.2.18=D17.40.5 Schwartz; C4.2.20=D17.41.1 Schwartz; C4.3.6,9,11-12=D17.42.5-6,43.3 Schwartz; C4.3.22=D17.41.8 Hamilton:C&D17; C4.3.25-26=D17.44.1-3 Schwartz; C4.4.1-2=D17.45.7 Hamilton:C&D17; C4.4.10-12,17=D17.46.2-4 Schwartz	January-July 332BC

Concerning Alexander the Great by Andrew Chugg

Summary	Sources	References	Comment
Tyrian dreamt that Apollo wished to abandon them, so they chained his statue	Diodorus 17.41.7 Curtius 4.3.21 (Plutarch 24.4)	Hammond THA 42, 119 Sources 55-6	
Phoenicians (especially Carthaginians) worship Cronos by burning a child as an offering	Schol. Plato Resp. 337A (Photius: Sardonios gelos); cf. Curtius 4.3.23	Jacoby, Fragment 9 of Cleitarchus, Hamilton Cleitarchus & Diodorus 17	Curtius relates that Tyrians proposed to resume the sacrifice of a freeborn boy to Saturn just after the arrival of Carthaginian envoys
Sea monster (whale?) temporarily beached upon the causeway	Curtius 4.4.3-5 Diodorus 17.41.5-6	Schwartz; C4.4.3-5=D17.41.5-6	Diodorus places this much earlier in the siege than Curtius, but Diodorus's ordering of events is suspect
Balonymus appointed King of Tyre (also Paphos as in Plutarch's Moralia?)	Diodorus 17.46.6 & 17.47.1-6 (cf. Plutarch Moralia 340C-E)	Hammond THA 98, 119, 121; C4.1.15-26=D17.47.1-6 Hamilton:C&D17	This was probably an extension of Abdalonymus's kingdom, which Diodorus thought a convenient place to recount his installation in Sidon as well, i.e. Tyre in D 17.47.1&5 is a mistake for Sidon, but Tyre is correct at D 17.46.6
"Now that we have described activity *concerning Alexander*, we shall turn our narrative in another direction"	Diodorus 17.47.6		Looks like a book-end from Cleitarchus, because it incorporates the title of his work: Concerning Alexander – cf. the ends of books 7 & 12

Book 5: 14th October 332BC – 1st October 331BC (Julian Calendar)

Summary	Sources	References	Comment
Agis hires mercenaries who had escaped from Issus and invades and conquers Crete	Diodorus 17.48.1-2 Curtius 4.1.39-40	C4.1.39-40=D17.48.1-2 Schwartz	
The rebel Macedonian, Amyntas son of Antiochus led 4000 troops to Egypt and overcame the local forces in battle, but his forces were destroyed in a surprise counter-attack, when scattered for looting	Curtius 4.1.27-33 Diodorus 17.48.2-5	C4.1.27-33=D17.48.2-4 Schwartz	Hammond THA thinks this is Diyllus, but it is clear that Curtius and Diodorus used a common source and it is not tenable that they independently selected the same episodes from two separate sources as Hammond has suggested. This is therefore very likely to be Cleitarchus. Diodorus relates this episode after Tyre.
The delegates of the League of Corinth vote at the Isthmian Games to send Alexander golden crowns via 15 envoys	Curtius 4.5.11-12 Diodorus 17.48.6	C4.5.11=D17.48.6 Schwartz	Hammond THA thinks this is Diyllus, but the exact agreement of Curtius and Diodorus is suggestive of Cleitarchus
Capture of the pirate, Aristonicus of Methymna, at Chios	Curtius 4.5.19-22		This is Cleitarchus, because the delivery of Aristonicus to Alexander at Alexandria (see below) was related by Cicero, who is a source for other fragments of Cleitarchus

Organisation and Sources

Summary	Sources	References	Comment
Second peace offer from Darius: Parmenion suggests acceptance of terms offered in a letter from Darius	Curtius 4.5.1-8 Justin 11.12.3-4 Arrian 2.25.2 (Plutarch 29.4) Val Max 6.4 ext3 cf. Diodorus 17.39	Hammond THA99-100, 122 Sources 62, 225	Diodorus appears to edit out this offer, but implies it was in his source by speaking of other daughter of Darius under third offer (he gives some of the contents of the second letter when citing the first after Issus). Plutarch places his anecdote in the run-up to Gaugamela (i.e. where Cleitarchus probably recorded Darius' third offer).
Siege of Gaza: Alexander struck by an arrow, the city is stormed and Alexander is struck in the leg, Alexander emulates Achilles by dragging Betis behind his chariot	Curtius 4.6.1-12(?) & 4.6.17-30	Hammond Sources 57 THA 128;	Falls November 332BC – Curtius 4.6.12-16 resembles Fragment 5 of Hegesias, but this may be Cleitarchus using Hegesias as his source.
Alexander sends Amyntas son of Andromenes with 10 triremes to Macedonia Occupation of Egypt		C4.6.30=D17.49.1 Schwartz	Enthroned as Pharaoh in Memphis (Alexander Romance) December 332BC
Settles affairs in Egypt and decides to visit the Temple of Ammon (at Siwa) – meets envoys from Cyrene		C4.7.1,5,9=D17.49 .2-4 Schwartz	
Enters the desert - water gives out after 4 days - a great storm provides drinking water		C4.7.12-14=D17.49.4-5 Schwartz	
Description of the oasis, its people and its situation - visit to the oracle at Siwa: Alexander, son of Ammon, would be invincible (*invictus*[Lat] = *aniketos*[Gk]) and rule all lands	Curtius 4.7.25-28 Diodorus 17.49.3-17.51.4 Justin 11.11.2-10 Plutarch 26.6-27.4 Val. Max. 9.5 ext 1	Hammond THA 43, 92, 122 Sources 58-61; C4.7.16-17,20-28=D17.50.3-51.3 Schwartz	Plutarch's version is coloured with an item from Callisthenes, a letter from Alexander to Olympias and the confusion of Paidion with Paidios, but his reference to Cambyses might be from Cleitarchus
Foundation of Alexandria	Plutarch 26.5-6 Curtius 4.8.1-6 Diodorus 17.52.1-3 Justin 11.11.11-13 Arrian 3.2.1 Val. Max. 1.4 ext 1	Hammond THA 44, 99, 128 Sources 59, 226	April 331BC Cf. Strabo 792
Pirate (captured at Chios) brought before Alexander (by Hegelochus)	St Augustine *De Civ. Dei* IV, 4. 25 (from a lost passage of Cicero *The Republic* III .24), cf. Arrian 3.2.4, Curtius 4.5.19-22		The rhetorical style of the passage, its origins via Cicero (a source of other fragments of Cleitarchus) and the location in Egypt (Arrian says Egypt, probably at Alexandria, which was later Cleitarchus' home) all suggest Cleitarchus as source. The pirate is Aristonicus of Methymna, whose capture is mentioned by Curtius, probably following Cleitarchus

Concerning Alexander the Great by Andrew Chugg

Summary	Sources	References	Comment
Alexander's return march up the Levantine littoral: Story about the ultra-handsome Theias Byblios, who fell in love with his daughter Myrra	Stobaeus *Flor.* IV, 20, 73	Jacoby, Fragment 3 of Cleitarchus Brown, Clitarchus p.149	Attributed by Stobaeus to Book 5: presumably relates to a visit of Alexander to Byblos, an ancient Phoenician port to the north of Sidon – may reflect worship of Adonis at Byblos – must reflect Alexander's return to the vicinity after Egypt, if it is placed in Book 5
Darius hears news of Alexander's return from Egypt – his preparations for war including 200 scythed chariots		C4.9.4-5=D17.53.1-2 Hamilton: C&D17	
Run-up to Gaugamela, march into Mesopotamia	Diodorus 17.53.3-4, 17.55	Hammond THA 44-45	In Diodorus the 3rd peace offer precedes the Tigris crossing
Crossing of the Tigris	Diodorus 17.55 Curtius 4.9.14-21	Hammond THA 45	
Ariston, captain of the Paeonians, slays Satropates, cuts off his head and lays it at Alexander's feet	Curtius 4.9.24-25 Plutarch 39.1-2	Hamilton Plutarch Alex liii (lix in 2nd edition)	
Lunar eclipse	Curtius 4.10.1-8		20th September 331BC (Julian)
On the death of Queen Stateira - reported to Darius by a eunuch	Plutarch 30 Curtius 4.10.18-34 Diodorus 17.54.6	Hammond Sources 63-64	Gallantry with Darius' women as with meeting in Darius' tent after Issus
Third peace offer from Darius: an embassy	Curtius 4.11.1-22 Diodorus17.54.1-5 Justin 11.12.7-16	Hammond THA 45, 99, 122	Diodorus & Curtius have Parmenion urge acceptance on this occasion, but it is not unlikely he did so at both the second and third offers
Disposition and size of the Persian army	Curtius 4.12.5-13 Arrian 3.8.6 (Diodorus 17.39.4 & 17.53.2-3)	Hammond THA 42, 44 Sources 231	There is a distinction to be made between the host of up to a million raised by Darius at Babylon and the army of a quarter of a million that he fielded at Arbela/Gaugamela
Parmenion counsels a night attack	Arrian 3.10.1, Curtius 4.13.4-10 Plutarch 31.5-7	Hammond Sources 38, 232	
Alexander and Aristander sacrifice to fear	Curtius 4.13.15 Plutarch 31.4	Hammond Sources 38, 65	(Note however that many Aristander stories seem to come from Aristobulus)
Alexander oversleeps before Gaugamela	Justin 11.13.1-3 Diodorus 17.56 Curtius 4.13.16-24 Plutarch 32.1-2	Hammond THA 20, 100, 122-3 Sources 38	
The order of battle of Alexander's forces		C4.13.26-29 = D17.57.1-4	Schwartz parallel
Battle of Gaugamela (Arbela in Cleitarchus)	Curtius 4.14.1-26, 4.16.8-9 Diodorus 17.57.5-17.61 & parts of Plutarch 33.1-11, Arrian 6.11.4 (for use of Arbela) Front. Strat. 2.3.19	Hammond THA 20, 123, 128 Sources 39-40 & 270	1st October 331BC (fixed by Lunar eclipse) – Cleitarchus in particular located the battle close to Arbela, though it was ~70 miles away. Hamilton, "Cleitarchus & Diodorus 17", p128 thinks Curtius used Ptolemy for parts of his account.

Organisation and Sources

Summary	Sources	References	Comment
The attack of the scythed chariots and its defeat		C4.15.16-17=D17.58.4-5 Schwartz	
Attack on Alexanders's camp by Scythians – Sisyngambris remains aloof		C4.15.9-11=D17.59.6-7 Schwartz	
Darius' charioteer slain by spear (thrown by Alexander) – Persians suppose Darius slain – Persian flight instigated		C4.15.28-29,32=D17.60.2-4 Schwartz	
Wounds of Hephaistion, Perdiccas, Coenus & Menidas		C4.16.31-32=D17.61.3 Schwartz	
Persian casualties	Arrian 3.15.6	Hammond Sources 232	
Alexander proclaimed king of Asia, abolishes tyrannies in Greece, promises to rebuild Plataea, sends some spoils to Croton in Italy	Plutarch 34.1-2 (Justin 11.14.6-7 cf. Curtius 4.10.34)	Hammond Sources 66-68	
Uprising of the Spartans in Greece; heroism of King Agis of Sparta	Diodorus 17.63.4 Justin 12.1.6-11 Curtius 6.1.1-16 (& 6.3.2 in a speech) Front. Strat. 2.11.4	Hammond THA 46; Yardley & Heckel on Justin 37 & 183-8	Hammond's view (THA 113) that J's account is inconsistent with D is unconvincing
Antipater refers the fate of Sparta to the League of Corinth. Sparta receives permission to send envoys to Alexander. Fifty representatives sent to Alexander by the Lacedaemonians.	Harpocration: homereuontas Curtius 6.1.16-20 Diodorus 17.73.5-6	Jacoby, Fragment 4 of Cleitarchus Hammond THA 133	Attributed by Harpocration to Book 5: happened after Antipater defeated Agis at Megalopolis in 331BC – it is therefore certain that Cleitarchus gave an account of the Spartan rebellion in Greece at this point, which is when it probably actually took place (although 330BC is not impossible). C & J postponed mention of events in Europe until after the death of Darius (D until after Gaugamela); Curtius stated that he was deliberately doing so at 5.1.1-2. Hammond thought the matter of the League came from Diyllus, but the details are very similar in D & C, so it is likely to be from Cleitarchus

This was the end of the first of the two parts of Cleitarchus' history of Alexander. It was the fifth anniversary (according to Lunar reckoning) of Alexander's accession. Events in Europe, such as the death of Alexander of Epirus, given in Justin 12.2, may have been related by Cleitarchus at this point, but this is conjectural. It is however interesting that Curtius 8.1.37 mentions a complaint by Alexander of Epirus (whilst he died of a wound according to Livy) that he had encountered men in Italy, whilst his nephew was up against women in Persia (cf. Gellius, NA 17.21.33, Livy 9.19.10-11). This section of Livy has some Cleitarchan elements, such as referring to the "Invincible Alexander" (see Hammond THA 112 on Cleitarchus as Livy's likely source)

Concerning Alexander the Great by Andrew Chugg

Book 6: 2nd October 331BC – July 330BC

Summary	Sources	References	Comment
Capture of Persian camp and treasures at Arbela	Diodorus 17.64.1-3 Curtius 5.1.10-11	Hammond THA 54; C5.1.10-11=D17.64.3 Schwartz	
Visit to Mennis in Babylonia – the cave of Naphtha – anointing and igniting the boy Stephanus	Curtius 5.1.16 Plutarch 35 Strabo 16.1.15	Hammond Sources 68-69	
Babylon: description of the city – walls 365 stades in circumference and 50 cubits tall – the Hanging Gardens were built by "a later Syrian king" than Semiramis for his wife	Diodorus 2.7.3-4 & 2.10 Curtius 5.1.24-35	Jacoby, Fragment 10 of Cleitarchus, P. Schnabel, Berossus, 1923, Ch III, Pearson p.230; C5.1.25-26=D2.7.3-4 Schwartz; C5.1.34-35=D2.10.4,1 Schwartz	Cleitarchus corrects the wall height of 50 fathoms cited by Ctesias in his Persica - Nearchus fragment 3a/b notes Alexander's rivalry with Semiramis in marching across the Kedrosian desert
Dissolute nature of Babylonians; relaxation of army at Babylon for 34 days	Diodorus 17.64.4-17.65.1 Curtius 5.1.36-39 & 5.1.40-45, Justin 11.14.8	Hammond THA 54; C5.1.40-42=D17.65.1 Schwartz; C5.1.43-45=D17.64.5-6 Schwartz	Curtius 5.1.36-39 is attributed to Diyllus in THA 129-130, but Hammond is clearly mistaken, because the 34 days is common to Curtius and Justin and so must be Cleitarchus; the appointments of Agathon etc to commands at Babylon and the arrival of 50 sons of the Macedonian nobility are common to D & C, therefore Cleitarchus; probably all in C about Babylon is Cleitarchus
Reorganisation of the army in Sittacene	Diodorus 17.64.2 Curtius 5.2.1	C5.2.1-7=D17.65.2-4 cf.D17.27.1-2 Schwartz	Strong resemblance between C & D, though D is heavily summarised
Susa – Abulites sends forth his son – 40,000 talents found there, mother and children of Darius left there, Alexander uses a stool to rest his feet upon when sitting in Darius' throne	Plutarch 36.1-2 Diodorus 17.65.5, 17.66.3-5, 17.67.1 Curtius 5.2.13-17 Justin 11.14.9	Hammond THA 55 Sources 70; C5.2.8, 12-15=D17.65.5, 66.2-7 Schwartz	Plutarch quotes Cleitarchus' father Deinon in 36.2 – this probably follows such a quote by Cleitarchus himself. Hammond thinks Diodorus is following Diyllus at this point in THA, but the throne story is from the same source in C & D, which is therefore Cleitarchus
Alexander gives Sisygambis purple cloth	Curtius 5.2.18-22	Hammond THA 130-131	
Uxii and campaign against Madates – Sisygambis obtains a pardon for Madates	Curtius 5.3.1-15 Diodorus 17.67.2-5	Hammond THA 55-56, 130-131; C5.3.1.2,4-5,10 =D17.67.1-2,4-5 Schwartz	

Organisation and Sources

Summary	Sources	References	Comment
Campaign against Ariobarzanes – Susian Gates – a Lycian leads Alexander around them by a narrow path through the woods	Curtius 5.3.16-5.4.34 Diodorus 17.68.1-7 Plutarch 37.1 Front. Strat. 2.5.17 Polyaenus 4.3.27	Hammond THA 56, 131 Sources 70 Hamilton Plutarch Alex liii; C5.3.17-18,23&C5.4.2-4,10,12,18=D17.68.1-6 Schwartz	The story of the Lycian guide and the connection made with an earlier oracle is widespread in the sources
Advance to the Araxes	Curtius 5.5.1 Diodorus 17.69.1	Hammond THA 131	
Letter from Tiridates	Curtius 5.5.2-4 Diodorus 17.69.1-2	C5.5.2-4=D17.69.1-2 Schwartz	
Alexander meets 800 mutilated Greeks who do not wish to return home	Diodorus 17.69.2-9 Curtius 5.5.5-24 Justin 11.14.11-12	Hammond THA 56, 101, 131; C5.5.5-9,12,23-24=D17.69.2-8 cf.J11.14.11-12 Schwartz	
Capture of Persepolis followed by a Winter campaign in Persis	Curtius 5.6.1-20 Diodorus 17.70.1-17.71.7 & 17.73.1	Hammond THA 132; C5.6.1-5,8,9=D17.70.1-71.2 Schwartz	The campaign is only detailed by C, who places it at the evening setting of the Pleiades (April 330BC), and mentioned after the burning of the palace in one sentence by D
Burning of Persepolis incited by Thaïs the Athenian courtesan: a *comus*	Athenaeus 576D-E Diodorus 17.72.1-6 Curtius 5.7.1-7 Plutarch 38.1-4	Jacoby, Fragment 11 of Cleitarchus Hammond THA 56, 131-132 Sources 72-73 Hamilton Plutarch Alex liii	May 330BC
Pursuit and death of Darius	Curtius 5.8.1-5.13.25 Justin 11.15 Diodorus 17.73.2-3 Plutarch 42.3-43.3	Hammond THA 57, 101, 132-133 Sources 74-76 Hamilton Plutarch Alex liii	At the death of Darius Trogus ended his Book XI and Curtius ended his Book V, further vindicating the view that this was the conclusion of Book VI of Cleitarchus
Antipater refers the fate of Sparta to the League of Corinth. Sparta receives permission to send envoys to Alexander.	Curtius 6.1.16-20 Diodorus 17.73.5-6		Cleitarchus may also have reiterated the matter of the 50 hostages, perhaps to distinguish them from the envoys sent to Alexander

Book 7: July 330BC – June 329BC

Summary	Sources	References	Comment
Advance to Hecatompylus. Persuasion of the army to join in the pursuit of Bessus, who declares himself king and adopts royal regalia as Artaxerxes.	Curtius 6.2.15-6.4.1 Diodorus 17.74.3-17.75.1 Justin 12.3.2-3 (Plutarch 47.1-2) King Bessus: Diodorus 17.74.1 Curtius 6.6.13	(Hammond Sources 80); C6.2.15=D17.75.1 Schwartz	Hammond THA 58 & 134 argues Diyllus as the source for Curtius and Diodorus. But the details are very similar in Justin too, so the common source must be Cleitarchus. Hammond worries that Plutarch has a slightly different order of events and indeed Plutarch attributes his version to a letter from Alexander to Antipater, so it is doubtful whether Plutarch followed Cleitarchus here.

621

Concerning Alexander the Great by Andrew Chugg

Summary	Sources	References	Comment
Entry into and description of Hyrcania and the Caspian Sea	Diodorus 17.75 Curtius 6.4.1-22	Hammond THA 58 & 135; C6.4.3-6=D17.75.2 Schwartz; C6.4.18,22=D17.75.3,6 Schwartz	Onesicritus may be the ultimate source of the natural history details – Aristobulus is unlikely despite noting oaks in Hyrcania
Caspian Sea equal to the Euxine (Black Sea)	Pliny NH 6.36-38 Plutarch 44.1-2	Jacoby, Fragment 12 of Cleitarchus Hammond Sources 77	This resembles a comment by Patroclus, a geographer who wrote circa 280BC and was cited by Eratosthenes, but it is possible that the comments are independent of one another or that Cleitarchus inspired Patroclus.
The isthmus between the Caspian and the Euxine is subject to inundation from either sea	Strabo 11.1.5	Jacoby, Fragment 13 of Cleitarchus, Brown, Clitarchus p.140	The "isthmus" in question is the region of the Caucasus Mountains, neither low-lying nor narrow – Brown suggests this was inspired by Polycleitus' error of confusing the Sea of Azov with the Aral Sea
Wonders of Hyrcania: the wasp (*tenthredon*) of the hill-country	Demetrius, De Eloc. 304 Diodorus 17.75.7	Jacoby, Fragment 14 of Cleitarchus	Diodorus has *anthredon*; Tarn (vol 2, Sources, p.90 n.3) notes that Diodorus uses a peculiar phrase μεγίστην ἐπιφάνειαν and a rare verb κηροπλαστεῖν in describing this bee-like creature; the same combination occurs in one other place in Diodorus 19.2.9 in a passage Tarn attributes to Timaeus. Tarn poses the question of whether Cleitarchus is using Timaeus; our answer must be yes, given the other evidence of his doing so.
Surrender of Persian commanders (Phrataphernes, Phradates, Artabazus)	Curtius 6.4.23-24 & 6.5.1-5 Diodorus 17.76.1	Hammond THA 135	
Surrender of the Greek mercenaries	Curtius 6.5.10 Diodorus 17.76.2	Hammond THA 135	
Attack on the Mardi: theft and restitution of Bucephalus	Curtius 6.5.11-21 Diodorus 17.76.3-8	Hammond THA 135; C6.5.11-12, 18-21=D17.76.3-8 Schwartz	
Surrender of Nabarzanes: entry of Bagoas into Alexander's service	Curtius 6.5.22-23 (Diodorus 17.76.1)	Hammond THA 157	
Visit of Thalestris, Queen of the Amazons, who had journeyed from the River Thermodon to conceive a child by Alexander in Hyrcania	Plutarch 46.1 Strabo 11.5.4 Curtius 6.5.24-32 Diodorus 17.77.1-3 Justin 12.3.3-7	Jacoby, Fragments 15-16 of Cleitarch. Hammond THA 59, 102 & 135 Sources 81 (Jacoby Fragment 32?); C6.5.24-26,30-32=D17.77.1-3 cf. J12.3.5-7 & Strabo11.5.4 Schwartz	The Thermodon is in northern Asia Minor, which anomaly Cleitarchus explained by making the Caucasus region very narrow. The story may have originated with Onesicritus, but could have been embellished by Cleitarchus. (Brown, Clitarchus p.149 suggests Jacoby Fragment 32 was background to the Amazon story)

Organisation and Sources

Summary	Sources	References	Comment
Alexander's adoption of Persian dress (purple tunic with a vertical white stripe, zona belt, diadem, sceptre) and luxury: 365 concubines from Darius' harem. Macedonian resentments assuaged by gifts from Alexander.	Curtius 6.6.1-12 Diodorus 17.77.4-7 & 17.78.1 Justin 12.3.8-12 Metz 2	Hammond THA 59, 102-3, 136; Pearson 221 (Plutarch, Artaxerxes 27 for Deinon)	Here again is seen the Cleitarchan propensity for making things equal to the days in a year; probably inspired by Deinon - Pearson. The Metz Epitome opens here, replete with Cleitarchan stories. F. Dicaearchus (Athenaeus 13.5 [557]) citing 350 concubines
Alexander burns surplus baggage and wagons to avoid the encumbrance in crossing the mountains into India	Curtius 6.6. Plutarch 57.1-2 Polyaenus 4.3.10	Hamilton Plutarch Alex liii	Plutarch associates this with the invasion of India & Polyaenus likewise; but Curtius is more likely correct. The confusion is probably due to the geographical disparity that Cleitarchus regarded southern Afghanistan from the Helmand River eastwards as part of India. Hence in Cleitarchan tradition this really was the first transit across mountains into India.
Revolt of Satibarzanes, who flees to Bactra with 2000 cavalry. Alexander storms a rock occupied by rebels.	Diodorus 17.78.1 Curtius 6.6.20-34 (Justin 12.4.1) Metz 3	Hammond THA 59, 136	The Metz has Ariobazanes and states he fled to India – perhaps this is an error for Barzaentes as at Curtius 6.6.36 (which is suggested by Elizabeth Baynham in Antichthon 29, p.71).
Dimnus conspiracy: execution of Philotas	Curtius 6.7-6.11 Diodorus 17.79-80 Justin 12.5.2-3 Plutarch 49	Hammond Sources 87 Hamilton Plutarch Alex liii	Hammond THA 59 argues Diodorus is from Diyllus mainly because he differs from Curtius in saying Alexander "learnt everything" from Dimnus, but Cleitarchus probably said *behaviour* of Dimnus spoke eloquently of his guilt & Diodorus is summarising clumsily. Compelling points of similarity on incidental details between D & C are: Cebalinus hidden in the armoury; Alexander is informed while bathing & Philotas is executed "in the manner of his country, Macedon". Hammond concedes (in Sources) that Curtius must be from Cleitarchus: it is too vividly detailed for a general history, e.g. Diyllus or Duris. Plutarch's version resembles Cleitarchus, but not on Alexander hiding behind a curtain where Plutarch is less likely to be using Cleitarchus than Curtius 6.11.12, who has Alexander not present during the torture.

Concerning Alexander the Great by Andrew Chugg

Summary	Sources	References	Comment
Execution of Alexander Lyncestes	Curtius 7.1.1-9 Diodorus 17.80.2	C7.1.5-9 =D17.80.2 Schwartz	Hammond THA 138 suggests Diyllus, but his argument about the timing of Lyncestes' arrest being later in Diodorus than in Curtius overlooks the fact that Justin 11.7.1 suggests that the Cleitarchan tradition placed Lyncestes' arrest prior to the march to Gordion (as in Arrian). It looks as if Diodorus mentioned Lyncestes' arrest a few months late, perhaps connecting it with warnings in a letter from Olympias, which might have taken months to reach Alexander. Curtius & Diodorus follow the same source for Lyncestes' execution & the detail in Curtius seems too extensive for sourcing from a general history. (Hammond's view that C & D shared Diyllus as a secondary source is statistically implausible: it implies they independently made the same choice for most episodes between Cleitarchus & Diyllus: it is more likely that matches between C & D means both used Cleitarchus.)
Assassination of Parmenion: Polydamas' camel trek	Curtius 7.2.11-34 Diodorus 17.80.3 Strabo 15.2.10	C7.2.18=D17.80.3 Schwartz	Detailed correspondence between Curtius and Diodorus implies Cleitarchus was the source for the completion of the story of the downfall of Parmenion
Alexander forms a disciplinary regiment by reading the letters which the troops sent home to Macedonia to identify malcontents	Justin 12.5.4-8 Diodorus 17.80.4 Curtius 7.2.35-38 Polyaenus 4.3.19	Hammond THA 103; C7.2.35-37=D17.80.4 cf. J12.5.4-8 Schwartz	Hammond thinks that the version in Diodorus comes from Diyllus, but its close resemblance to the version in Justin is clear evidence that this material came from Cleitarchus. Hammond THA 139 fails to attribute the corresponding passage in Curtius, but it is Cleitarchus, since it is connected with the execution of Parmenion as in the other accounts.
The march against the Euergetae: origin of the name Euergetae (Benefactors) for the Ariaspi (Arimaspi in Cleitarchus) in their succour for Cyrus' army	Diodorus 17.81.1-2 Curtius 7.3.1-4 Metz 4	Hammond THA 60; C7.3.1,3=D17.81.1-2 Schwartz	From Deinon? Strong correspondences between Diodorus and Curtius
Land of the Paropamisadae	Curtius 7.3.5-18 Diodorus 17.82 Metz 4	Hammond THA 60, 139; C7.3.5-18=D17.82 Schwartz	

Organisation and Sources

Summary	Sources	References	Comment
Crossing the "Caucasus" (Hindu Kush) in 16 or 17 days; Rock of Prometheus; foundation of an Alexandria; advance into Bactria in pursuit of Bessus	Curtius 7.3.19-23 Diodorus 17.83.1-2 Metz 4 (for the foundation)	Hammond THA 60, 139; C7.3.22-23=D17.83.1-2 Schwartz	Diodorus 17.83.3 has a terminal one-liner, Καὶ τὰ μὲν περὶ Ἀλέξανδρον ἐν τούτοις ἦν ("These were the concerns of Alexander"), which may indicate the end of Book 7 of Cleitarchus. A similar formula ended Bk 6 at 17.73.4 and exactly the same formula ends Bk 12. Similar formulae are used in other books of Diodorus, but this one may echo Cleitarchus, because it contains the title of his history (Περὶ Ἀλεξάνδρου - Pearson p.213).

Book 8: July 329BC – Autumn 328BC

Summary	Sources	References	Comment
Bessus and Bagodaras (D) or Cobares (C) quarrel at a banquet	Curtius 7.4.1-19 Diodorus 17.83.7	Hammond THA 139	Digressions and accounts of events elsewhere often mark a book boundary in Cleitarchus.
Alexander receives news from Greece of the Spartan revolt, of Scythians coming to the aid of Bessus and of the combat between Erigyius and Satibarzanes	Curtius 7.4.32-40 Diodorus 17.83.4-6	Hammond THA 140 Heckel & Yardley on Justin 184; C7.4.33,38=D17.83.4-6 Schwartz	Spartan news is only in C: was this the arrival of the Spartan envoys/hostages in Alexander's camp? Their departure seems to have been delayed (preparing to leave in Summer 330BC - Aischines 3.133).
Advance to the Oxus: march through a desert with the loss of many men – anecdote of Alexander refusing water brought in skins	Diodorus, List of Contents for 17 Curtius 7.5.9-12 Front. Strat. 1.7.7		The anecdote being in Frontinus and Curtius tends to confirm that it is Cleitarchan
Betrayal by Spitamenes, Dataphernes & Catanes of Bessus and his dispatch to Alexander as a prisoner	Curtius 7.5.19-26 Diodorus 17.83.8-9 Justin 12.5.10-11 Metz 5-6	Hammond THA 61, 140-141	It appears that Curtius correctly reflects Cleitarchus by breaking up the downfall, torture and execution of Bessus into several mini-episodes. The Metz similarly divides the betrayal to Alexander from the eventual execution
Branchidae	Curtius 7.5.28-35 (in the long lacuna in Diodorus 17, but listed in contents), Strabo 11.11.4, Plutarch Moralia 557B(?)	Hammond THA 141; C7.5.28-35 cf. Dκ Schwartz Aelian, ap. Suda s.v. Branchidae Strabo 14.1.5	Perhaps Cleitarchus gave the Branchidae story as a doublet with the destruction of Bessus: Persian and Greek traitors similarly destroyed (so Pearson).
Bessus delivered to Alexander in fetters; Alexander hands him over to Oxathres for interim torture but postpones his execution.	Curtius 7.5.36-43 Diodorus 17.83.8-9 Justin 12.5.10-11 Metz 5-6		The handing over to Oxathres is explicit in Curtius, Justin and Diodorus

Concerning Alexander the Great by Andrew Chugg

Summary	Sources	References	Comment
Alexander wounded by an arrow of which the point remained fixed in the middle of his leg; the rebels sent envoys to apologise the next day; rivalry between the cavalry and the infantry over bearing Alexander's litter	Curtius 7.6.6-9	Hammond THA 142	
Advance to Maracanda – circumference of 70 stades with many rivers flowing around it	Curtius 7.6.10 Metz 7		With Diodorus missing in the great lacuna (and Justin being very thin and episodic here), the Metz Epitome (7-43) provides key corroboration that much of Curtius is from Cleitarchus, wherever there is close correspondence between Curtius and the Metz. This is vital, because it appears that Curtius sometimes resorted to other sources. This applies until the middle of Book 10, where Diodorus resumes.
Plan to found a stronghold on the Tanais to subdue the region	Curtius 7.6.13		News of this plan probably instigated the ensuing revolts.
First news of the revolt of Spitamenes & Catanes	Curtius 7.6.24 Metz 9	Hammond THA 143	Alexander destroys several rebel cities.
Foundation of Alexandria on the River Tanais (Alexandria Eschate) with a circumference of 60 stades in 17 days	Curtius 7.6.25-27; Justin 12.5.12 Metz 8		Hammond THA 142 discusses Aristobulus, but the detailed correspondence of Curtius with Justin is a clear indication of Cleitarchus. Tanais is a Cleitarchan name for this river (through confusion with the Don). Actually the Syr-Darya.
Emperor of the Scythians sends his brother Carthasis to prevent Alexander crossing the Tanais. Speech of Alexander & augury of Aristander in Curtius. Plan for an attack on the Scythians.	Metz 8 Curtius 7.7.1-29	Hammond THA 143-4	Carthasis is in Curtius and the Metz has "Carcasim"
Insurrection of Spitamenes: routing and destruction of the Macedonian column under Menedemus. (2000 infantry and 300 cavalry are dead.)	Metz 9 Curtius 7.7.30-39	Hammond THA 143	Alexander spends the night sleepless – watches Scythian fires in Curtius, reflecting upon wrongs against him in the Metz
Alexander's attack across the Tanais via 2000 rafts (Metz) or 12000 (Curtius)	Metz 10-12 Curtius 7.8.1-9.16 (Diodorus – contents)	Hammond THA 143-4, Pearson (Lost Histories) 222	X may have been dropped from XII in the Metz. Curtius gives Scythian envoys' words verbatim from his source – arrows, shouts, markers of Dionysus are common; Pearson notes parallels with aphorisms attributed to Cleitarchus
Visit of envoys of the Sacae	Curtius 7.9.17-19	Hammond THA 143-4	Escorted by Bagoas as Alexander's Greeter?
Alexander's return to Maracanda to counterattack Spitamenes who flees; burying of Greek dead and erection of a monument to Menedemus.	Metz 13 Curtius 7.9.20-22	Hammond THA 143	Reached Maracanda on the 4th day – bones covered with mound-monuments in the Metz

Organisation and Sources

Summary	Sources	References	Comment
Pardoning of Sogdian prisoners (chieftains) who sang on their way to execution	Curtius 7.10.1-9 (Diodorus – contents)	Hammond THA 144; C7.10.4-9 cf. Dκβ Schwartz	
Alexander defeated the Sogdiani & slew over 120,000	(Diodorus – contents)	Hammond THA 61	Hammond notes that Theophylactus Simmocata burnt 120,000 & Goukowsky thought Cleitarchus his likely source
Return to Bactria – orders Bessus to Ecbatana for splitting and chopping up – founds towns (6 or 12?) to curb the conquered nations (in SE Sogdiana near Margania)	Metz 14 Curtius 7.10.10-16 Justin 12.5.13	Hammond THA 103 on Justin; C7.10.15-16 cf. Dκδ Schwartz	Crosses rivers Ochus and Oxus at Metz 14 and Curtius 7.10.15 (Hammond THA 144 thinks this is Aristobulus) – emendations of Margania to Margiana (Merv) are wrong.
Sogdian Rock (Rock of Arimazes in C or Ariobazanen in M or Ariamazes in S or Ariomazes in Polyaenus)	Metz 15-18 Curtius 7.11.1-25 Polyaenus 4.3.29 (Diodorus – contents) Strabo 11.11.4	Hammond THA 144-145	Both Curtius and the Metz Epitome seem to make this a climactic event of the campaigning year in 328BC – hence this should close Book 8 of Cleitarchus as well as Book 7 of Curtius. Curtius 7.11.28 *appears* to differ from the Metz, but this is probably just a transmission error (Hammond THA 144-145 thinks Curtius' account is Aristobulus then Cleitarchus.) Commonalities with the Metz include a cavern on the ascent path, 20 (Metz) or 30 (Curtius) stadia high, 300 climbers signalling with white cloths, iron wedges, ropes.

Book 9: Autumn 328BC – May 327BC

Summary	Sources	References	Comment
Offer of daughter in marriage by the Scythian king. First campaign against Massagetae, Dahae – 3 columns through Sogdiana	Curtius 8.1.1-10	Hammond THA 145	
The hunt in Basista (Bazaira in Curtius) and the abundance of game there	Curtius 8.1.11-19 (Diodorus – contents)	Hammond THA 145; C8.1.11-19 cf. Dκσ Schwartz	Hammond thinks this is Onesicritus (but this is no bar to it being in Cleitarchus)
Killing of Cleitus at Maracanda – Alexander persuaded to forgive himself by Callisthenes	Curtius 8.1.19-8.2.12 Justin 12.6 Arrian 4.9.2-6 (Diodorus – contents)	Hammond THA 104,146 Hammond Sources 242	Arrian has legomena about Alexander's attempted suicide, concern over Lanike's reaction and a forgotten sacrifice to Dionysus
Winter in Bactrian Nautacene (Metz)	Curtius 8.2.13-18 Metz 19		
Treaty with Sisimithres, who had fathered 2 sons and 3 daughters through incest with his mother, after a siege of his rock.	Curtius 8.2.19-33 Metz 19 Plutarch 58.3 Strabo 11.11.4	Hammond THA 146	Hammond Sources is silent on the mention of Sisimthres by Plutarch
Death of Philippus.	Curtius 8.2.34-39	Hammond THA 146-7	Hammond THA thinks Philippus is from Onesicritus (but this is no bar to it being in Cleitarchus too)

Concerning Alexander the Great by Andrew Chugg

Summary	Sources	References	Comment
Beheading of Spitamenes by his wife assisted by a slave boy – delivery of head to Alexander and his gratitude and her expulsion from camp	Curtius 8.3.1-15 Metz 20-23	Hammond THA 147	
Dahae surrender Dataphernes (& Catanes?)	Metz 23 Curtius 8.3.16-17 Justin 12.6.18		Curtius 8.5.2 says that Catanes was subsequently killed in battle. Hammond is unsure of the source for this, but its presence in the Metz suggests Cleitarchus.
The proskynesis experiment	Curtius 8.5.5-24 Justin 12.7.1-3 Val. Max. 7.2 ext 11	Hammond THA 148 says speeches are Curtius' own invention, Alexander hides behind curtain like Agrippina in Tacitus Ann. 13.5.2 (but also like Alexander with Philotas [Plutarch 49], which suggests Cleitarchus) Hammond THA 103-4 for Justin: "most likely Cleitarchus"	This is postponed until the point of departure for India in Curtius. However Cleitarchus evidently placed it here, because Justin agrees with Diodorus by putting the award of silver shields to the hypaspists after Callisthenes' arrest, rather than before as in Curtius. Arrian gave the proskynesis experiment and the arrest of Callisthenes following on from the death of Cleitus, but points out (4.22.2) that the pages' conspiracy occurred at Bactra just prior to the invasion of India. It may be that Cleitarchus was correct in placing the proskynesis experiment at this point and chose to tell the whole story *en bloc*.
The conspiracy of the pages and the arrest and execution of Callisthenes	Curtius 8.6.1-8.8.23 Justin 12.7.2 (Diodorus – contents)		Hammond is unsure of the source for Curtius and Justin, but Diodorus' contents list confirms that this material was in Cleitarchus. It is possible that Curtius used other sources as well.
Campaign against the Nautaces and the destruction of the army in a hail storm	Metz 24-27 Curtius 8.4.1-15 (Diodorus – contents)	Hammond THA 147	
Saves a common soldier after the snow storm	Val. Max. 5.1 ext 1a Frontinus, Strat. 4.6.3 Curtius 8.4.15-17	Hammond THA 147	
Visit to (rock of) Chorienes (perhaps a re-visit to Sisimithres, but Cleitarchus now used his title rather than his name – yet it looks as though Cleitarchus believed him to be a distinct individual)	Metz 28 Curtius 8.4.21 has "cohortandus" in MSS wrongly changed to Oxyartes by Aldus		The Metz manuscript read "corianus"; Chorienes is from Arrian 4.21; Brunt & Heckel suggest that Chorienes is an official title of Sisimithres from the name of the area he ruled. Justin 12.6.18 mentions the surrender of the "Chorasmians"

Organisation and Sources

Summary	Sources	References	Comment
Marriage to Roxane	Metz 28-31 Curtius 8.4.20-30 (Diodorus – contents)	Hammond THA 146	Metz & Diodorus mention marriages of Alexander's companions – hence probably from Cleitarchus

Book 10: June 327BC – June 326BC

Summary	Sources	References	Comment
Orders formation of 30,000 "Epigoni"	Curtius 8.5.1		This is Cleitarchan, since their arrival at Susa in 324BC is in Diodorus 17.108.1-3
Preparations for India: distribution of silver shields etc. - 120,000 men followed Alexander into India (Curtius only)	Justin 12.7.4-5 Curtius 8.5.4	Hammond THA 104, 147-8; C8.5.4 cf. Dλα, J12.7.5 Schwartz	Hammond seems inconsistent in recognising that J is using Cleitarchus, but expressing uncertainty over C – the 120,000 men may have been derived from Nearchus by Cleitarchus (see Arrian Indica 19.5 – Plutarch 66.2 gives 120,000 foot)
Digression on India: mention of processions of the kings in which trees are drawn along on four-wheeled carriages and tame birds (the Orion and the Catreus) decorate their branches and sing – "…some birds are like sirens" may reflect Cleitarchus' father Deinon's belief that there were sirens to be found in India (Pliny NH 10.136)	Strabo 15.1.69 Aelian NA 17.22-23 Curtius 8.9.23-26	Jacoby, Fragments 20-22 of Cleitarchus, Brown, Clitarchus p.148	Curtius 8.9.8 mentions the River Iomanes (Jumna), which elsewhere (e.g. Arrian Indica 8.5-6) is mentioned by Megasthenes. Hammond THA 148 also notes that Curtius 8.9 includes material that was not known until after Alexander's time (e.g. Megasthenes' info on the Ganges region), yet at least some of it is from Cleitarchus. This is *suggestive* of use of Megasthenes by Cleitarchus, but Megasthenes dates to 1st decade of 3rd century BC. Cf. digression on Pandaea below.
Invasion of India: march from Bactra, Alexander greeted as third son of Zeus to enter India following Heracles and Dionysus, destruction of a city occupied by his initial opponents as an example	(Diodorus – contents) Curtius 8.10.1-6 Metz 32-35	Hammond THA 148; C8.10.5-6 cf. Dλβ Schwartz	
Alexander visits Nysa finds the ivy of Dionysus - citizens of Nysa intimidated into surrendering (probable mention of Acuphis and Alexander's request for 100 of his best men), then Alexander climbs Meron, the adjacent mountain, sacred to Dionysus with streaming waters and fruitful trees.	Schol. Apoll. Rhod. 2.904 Diodorus (in the great lacuna but listed in Contents of 17) cf. Arrian 5.1.1-6 Justin 12.7.6-7 Curtius 8.10.7-18, Metz 36-38	Jacoby, Fragment 17 of Cleitarchus Hammond THA 104 &148	See also Arrian's Indica 1.5-6, which has several mentions of Nysa and its legend of Dionysus – also Strabo 15.1.7-8 & Plutarch, Alex. 58.4-5
Dionysiac revels of companions (a *comus*)	Arrian 5.2.7, Justin 12.7.8	Hammond Sources 250	A legomenon

Concerning Alexander the Great by Andrew Chugg

Summary	Sources	References	Comment
Mazaga in kingdom of Assacenus & slaughter of the Indian mercenaries – Alexander wounded in leg - Cleitarchus especially noted that the siege engines and their missiles terrified the defenders into surrendering, since they seemed supernatural – Alexander may have been seduced by Cleophis and she had a son, whom she named Alexander – Cleitarchus wrote that the mercenaries opposed the surrender, but then requested that they be allowed to leave the town – Cleitarchus did not give an excuse for Alexander's attack on them	Diodorus 84 (emerging from the great lacuna), Metz 39-45, Justin 12.7.9-11, Plutarch 59.3-4, Curtius 8.10.19-36 Polyaenus 4.3.20	Hammond Sources 106 Hammond THA 52-3, 104 & 149	Arrian blamed the slaughter of the mercenaries on their plan to slip away without Alexander's leave
Aornus – Heracles' failure to capture it due to an earthquake & Alexander's longing to outdo his ancestor – 100 stades in circumference, 16 high – poor old local man with two sons guided Alexander's assault – filled chasm in 7 days & nights	Metz 46-7, Curtius 8.11.1-25, Diodorus 17.85.1-86.1, Justin 12.7.12-13, Plutarch 58.3 on other Alexander	Hammond THA 53, 104-5 & 149; C8.11.2=D17.85.1-2, J12.7.12 Schwartz; C8.11.3-4=D17.85.4-5 Schwartz; C8.11.7-8,25=D17.85.3,8-9&D17.86.1 Schwartz	Hammond thinks Curtius supplemented his account from Chares (see Jacoby fragment 16 of Chares) especially for the heroic acts of the king, another Alexander and Charus (Strabo 15.1.8 says Alexander's flatterers reported that Heracles had thrice failed to take Aornus)
Aphrices (D) or Erices (C) blocks Alexander's advance with an army of 20,000, but his own men bring his head to Alexander	Diodorus 17.86.2-3, Curtius 8.12.1-3	Hammond THA 53, 149-150; C8.12.1-3=D17.86.2 Schwartz	Aphrices may have been the brother of Assacenus
Hephaistion's bridge of boats across the Indus	Metz 48, Curtius 8.12.4, Diodorus 17.86.3		Not explicitly attributed by Hammond but subsumed into the adjoining Cleitarchan passages
Mophis ruler of Taxila and son of dead Taxiles advances against Alexander seemingly in battle array, but joins forces and donates treasure and 56 or 58 elephants	Metz 49-52, Curtius 8.12.4 – 18 Diodorus 17.86.4-7 Plutarch 59.3	Hammond THA 53-4 & 149-50 Hammond Sources 106; C8.12.4-10,14=D17.86.3-7 Schwartz	Mophis is the probable Cleitarchan form, since the Metz (Motis) and Diodorus agree (the form Omphis in Curtius may be from elsewhere) – Curtius 8.12.17-18 is attributed to Onesicritus by Berve & Hammond, but Cleitarchus may well have repeated it.

Organisation and Sources

Summary	Sources	References	Comment
The Battle Against Porus (Cleitarchus may not have named the battle after the river Hydaspes – modern Jhelum) initial diversionary tactics – precipitated by rumoured approach of Abisares (the name is probably corrupt in Diodorus, who gives both Embisarus 87.2 and Sasibisares 90.4) – Alexander's horse wounded (C, J, M), elephants arrayed like towers in a circuit wall, trampled or seized opponents with their trunks and dashed them to the ground, were attacked with missiles, axes and Kopis swords, then trampled their own men. Concentration of archers upon Porus – Porus slid off kneeling elephant, which was killed by missiles when it tried to protect its master. Porus asked how he wished to be treated – Porus replied that Alexander should consult his feelings as a king	Diodorus 17.87-88, Metz 53-61 (Justin 12.8.1-7) Curtius 8.13-14, Polyaenus 4.3.22 (cf. Strabo 15.1.42 on elephants protecting their masters in warfare) Front. Strat. 1.4.9 & 1.4.9a	Hammond THA 22-3, 54, 62, 150; C8.14.3=D17.87.5 Schwartz, Merkelbach thinks the letter from Porus in ME 56-58 is from a separate letter collection, but this is dubious	Perhaps the first half of May (Heckel & Yardley on Justin p.246), though Arrian 5.9.4 suggests late June after the solstice. Hammond's view that the version of the battle in Cleitarchus was as naïve as that in D is suspect, because of the details given by the Metz and Polyaenus. Hammond (THA 105) thinks J differs from D, but the Metz and D have common details such as concentration of bowmen on Porus and the Metz and J share the wounding/killing of Bucephalus: it seems more that D, J and the Metz are retaining different details from a lengthy original. Hammond thinks C supplemented his version from other sources. The Letter from Porus in ME 56-58 is faintly echoed in Pseudo-Callisthenes 3.2
Casualties	Metz 61, Diodorus 17.89.1-3		
Report of the revolt of Baryaxes in Media (Arrian 6.29.3) following the replacement of Oxydates as its Satrap by Arsaces (Curtius 8.3.17) or Atropates (Arrian 4.18.3) in early 327BC. Cleitarchus explained that Baryaxes had worn the tiara upright, which signified a claim to the throne of the Persians and Medes. (A location at the start of book 10 is also feasible, but Baryaxes probably waited for Alexander to be safely distant in India before he struck.)	Schol. Aristoph. Av. 487	Jacoby, Fragment 5 of Cleitarchus	The revolt of Baryaxes, though known to us solely through Arrian, is the only likely reason for Cleitarchus to have needed to explain the significance of the upright tiara at this juncture (the Fragment is specific that this was related in Book 10). A corollary is that Cleitarchus did not mention that Bessus had worn the tiara upright. Also Cleitarchus may have noted the arrest of Baryaxes by Atropates, who brought him to Alexander for execution at Pasargadae early in 324BC. This would place it in Book 12.

Book 11: July 326BC – Spring 325BC

Summary	Sources	References	Comment
Alexander plans to visit the ends of India and the Ocean – orders ships built with timber from neighbouring mountains – sacrificed to Helios – disbursements of gold coinage as reward to officers and proportionate rewards to troops (C only)	Metz 63, Curtius 9.1.3-4 Diodorus 17.89.4-5, 17.90.3-6	C9.1.1,3-4,6=D17.89.3-6&D17.90.1 Schwartz	This is evidence of a Cleitarchan discussion of Alexander's plans. Geographical and other digressions are characteristic of a new book in Cleitarchus. The coinage may be the famous Porus decadrachms (see Holt on the Elephant Medallions)

631

Concerning Alexander the Great by Andrew Chugg

Summary	Sources	References	Comment
Foundation of a city to honour the dead Bucephalus – the naming seems to have happened later just before the voyage down to the Indus	Arrian 5.14.4, Metz 62, Curtius 9.1.6, Justin 12.8.8 Diodorus 17.90.6 & 17.95.5	Hammond Sources 257	Some details in Arrian may be from Chares. Hammond's view (THA 54 & 62) that the foundation of Bucephala in D was from a different source is contradicted by the evidence of the Metz, which concludes this episode with the foundation.
The serpents of India reach sixteen cubits in length	Aelian, NA 17.2 Diodorus 17.90.1 Curtius 9.1.4	Jacoby, Fragment 18 of Cleitarchus	This is probably lifted by Cleitarchus from the account of Nearchus (Arrian, Indica 15.19)
Indian monkeys mistaken for an army: a curious technique using mirrors for the capture of monkeys (there may be confusion between arboreal monkeys and baboons here)	Aelian, NA 17.25 Diodorus 17.90.2-3	Jacoby, Fragment 19 of Cleitarchus, Brown, Clitarchus p.144	This probably derives from Onesicritus, because there is a more intelligible version in Strabo 15.1.29 (however, Aristobulus and Nearchus cannot be ruled out as Strabo's source – see Pearson 223-4, Hamilton C&A 451 and Brown AJP 71, p144, n9)
After he recovered from his wounds, Porus invited to Macedon in Metz Epitome: re-instatement as king & Friend of Alexander	Curtius 8.14.5 Diodorus 17.89.6 Justin 12.8.7 Metz 61 & 64		Curtius and Metz preview this at the end of the battle, but Diodorus & the Metz put the actual event here in Cleitarchus
Abisares sends envoys, but Alexander replies that he will pursue him if he does not come in person	Curtius 9.1.7-8, Metz 65-6 Diodorus 17.90.4	Hammond THA 62-3, 151	
Crosses a rapid river (the Acesines?) and marches east into forests: the height, extent and trunk circumference of the banyan tree, small multicoloured snakes with deadly bites	Diodorus 17.90.5-7 Curtius 9.1.9-12 Aelian, NA 17.2	Pearson 225; C9.1.8-12=D17.90.4-7 Schwartz, Jacoby F18 (on the snakes)	Cleitarchus is plagiarising Nearchus on the banyan (Arrian, Indica 11.7) and Onesicritus (Strabo 15.1.21)
Hephaistion sent to deal with the rebel Porus, a cousin of the conquered Porus	Diodorus 17.91.1-2	Hammond THA 63, 151; C9.1.24-33=D17.91.4-D17.92.3 Schwartz	
Marches on across a desert and across the Hyraotis (Hydraotis) past a grove of wild peafowl; campaign against the Adrestians (city surrenders) & campaign against Cathaeans (sacked city & 2 surrendered cities) – custom of cremating wives on the pyres of their husbands to forestall poisoning	Diodorus 17.91.2-4 & 19.33 Curtius 9.1.13-23 Justin 12.8.9 Polyaenus 4.3.30		Cleitarchus is again following Onesicritus (see Strabo 15.1.30) on the custom of Suttee - Polyaenus names the Cathaean capital of Sangala as the sacked city – supplication with fronds at third Cathaean city
Surrender of Sopithes with his sons: sets dogs on a lion	Curtius 9.1.24-36, Metz 66-7 Diodorus 17.91.4-92.3	Hammond THA 63, 151; C9.1.24-33=D17.91.4-D17.92.3 Schwartz	Cf. Strabo 15.1.31 & Isidore of Seville, Etymologiae 12.2.28.
Campaign of Hephaistion – his return.	Diodorus 17.93.1 Curtius 9.1.35		

Organisation and Sources

Summary	Sources	References	Comment
Realm of Phegeus: 12 days from the Ganges which was 32 stades wide (30 in M) – warnings of an army of 200,000 infantry, 20,000 cavalry, 2000 chariots and up to 3000 elephants under Xandrames (D) or Aggrammes (C) or Sacram (M), king of the Gandaridae (D & P) or Candaras (M) or Gangaridae (C & J) or Gandridae (P Moralia 327B) and also the Prasii (C) or Praisii (P) or Praesidae (J) or Tabraesians (D) or Persidas (M) beyond the Hyphasis (7 stades wide in D) and at the Ganges. Alexander asks Porus to validate these figures. Alexander is undeterred, recalling that the Pythia had called him invincible.	Metz 68-9, Curtius 9.2.1-9 Diodorus 17.93 Justin 12.8.9 (Plutarch 62.1 has the same width for the Ganges)	Hammond THA 63, 151	Plutarch & Diodorus are probably not getting the width of the Ganges from Megasthenes (pace Bradford Welles), because Strabo 15.1.35 quotes a width of 100 stades from Megasthenes. Xandrames was king of the Nanda kingdom, probably the same as Nandrus in Justin 15.4.16.
Mutiny on the Hyphasis and retreat to the Acesines – exhaustion of the soldiers is a Cleitarchan feature – speech to soldiers - armour wearing out – Greek clothing gone and replaced by Indian stuff – dressed stone altars of extraordinary size (50 cubits tall in D) were built and the camp was enlarged to thrice its size with 5 cubit long beds/couches in huts as wonders for posterity	Metz 69, Curtius 9.2.10-9.3.19 Diodorus 17.94.1-17.95.2 Justin 12.8.10-17 (Plutarch 62.3 also mentions the upscalings, but of different things)	Hammond THA 63-4, 151-2; C9.3.10-11=D17.94.2 Schwartz; C9.3.19=D17.95.1-2, J12.8.16 Schwartz; C9.3.19=D17.95.1-2, J12.8.16 Schwartz	Speeches of Alexander (9.2.12-34) and Coenus (9.3.5-15) might be Curtius' inventions, but Diodorus 17.94.5 agrees there was a speech to the troops (speech was to the officers in A). Unclear whether Alexander's sulk in tent was mentioned by Cleitarchus (it is in C, who may have taken it from Ptolemy or elsewhere, but not in D, J, M – it is also in A & P). Whether Cleitarchus noted Coenus' role is also uncertain.
Alexander retraces his advance to the Acesines and is joined by reinforcements who bring 25,000 suits of armour inlaid with gold and silver - a fleet has been built by Porus and Taxiles at the Acesines: 800 service ships and 200 open galleys (D), 800 biremes & 300 penarias (Metz); 1000 ships in Curtius – Alexander names the cities he had earlier founded on opposite river banks: Nicaea & Bucephala [Coenus dies (C only)]	Metz 70, Curtius 9.3.20-24 Diodorus 17.95.3-5 (Justin 12.9.1 also reports a return only to the Acesines)	C9.3.20,23=D17.95.3,5 Schwartz	It seems to be a Cleitarchan error to state that Alexander returned only to the Acesines, when in fact he went back to the Hydaspes (according to Aristobulus and others). Hammond (THA p.62 & 152) thinks this material is from Diyllus, but ship numbers and other details match between D, C & M, so this is still Cleitarchus
Death of Alexander's infant son (or child) by Roxane	Metz 70		The Metz is the sole surviving source for this

Concerning Alexander the Great by Andrew Chugg

Summary	Sources	References	Comment
Voyage down the Acesines to its junction with the Hydaspes with Hephaistion & Craterus commanding the bulk of the army which marched down the bank	Diodorus 96.1 Justin 12.9.1 Curtius 9.3.24-9.4.1		Alexander sailed down the Hydaspes, which flowed into the Acesines, which in turn flowed into the Indus (Arrian 6.14.4-5). Cleitarchus' confusion on this point is evidence that he was not with the expedition in India, else he would not have made such an error. Hammond thinks this is Diyllus, but D, C & J essentially agree, though all are brief and omit different details.
Digression on an Indian salt-mine	Strabo 5.2.6 (& 15.1.30)	Jacoby, Fragment 28 of Cleitarchus	Likely to have been occasioned by a visit of Alexander to the ancient salt mines at Khewra in the SE foothills of the Salt Range 15km north of the Hydaspes (Jhelum) River. A fragment of Onesicritus (Strabo 15.1.30) mentions a mountain of salt in the kingdom of Sopeithes. Arrian 6.2.2 says that Hephaistion was to hurry to the capital of King Sopeithes at the start of the voyage down the Hydaspes. (It is dubious whether Sopeithes is the same as the Sophytes/Sopeithes, who ruled an Indian kingdom further east.)
At junction of the Acesines with the Hydaspes Alexander took the surrender of the Sibi (C) or Ibi (D), who were descended from followers of Heracles – Defeated Agalasseis (Agesinas etc in MSS of J?)	Diodorus 17.96.2-5 Justin 12.9.2 Curtius 9.4.1-8	C9.4.1-2,5=D17.96.1-3 Schwartz	The footsteps of Heracles is a Cleitarchan theme. Hammond THA 153 thinks this is a mixture of Diyllus and Cleitarchus, but there is a good level of agreement between D & C and foundation by Heracles is also in J. Hammond's argument (THA 64) that D gives different accounts of the failure of Heracles to take Aornus is not credible.
Sailed to confluence with the Indus – near wrecking of the flagship in rapids – Alexander says he has done battle with the river like Achilles (Iliad 21.228-382)	Diodorus 17.97.1-3 Curtius 9.4.8-14	Hammond THA 64-5, 153; C9.4.8-14=D17.97.1-3 Schwartz	Emulation of Achilles is a Cleitarchan theme – D said Alexander jumped into the river and swam to safety, but Curtius that he merely disrobed to be ready to swim
Letter from the Indian philosophers	Metz 71-4; cf. Pap. Hamb. 129	Merkelbach thinks the letter from the Indian Philosophers in ME 71-74 is from a separate letter collection, but this is dubious	Similar letter in Philo of Alexandria, Every Good Man Is Free, Section 96. Similar letter among the letters of St Ambrosius XXXVII (11), 34/35, Migne, Patrologia Latina XVI col 1139 (letter in Pseudo-Callisthenes 3.5 differs substantially)

Organisation and Sources

Summary	Sources	References	Comment
Campaign against the Oxydracae & Malli - Alexander suffers an arrow wound to the chest when leading the storming of a town of the Oxydracae & Malli (Mandri/Mambros in J) – Cleitarchus said Ptolemy & Peucestas (A & C) & Limnaeus (P: wrongly Timaeus in C) & Leonnatus (A & C – Metz had Legatus) & Aristonus (C) saved Alexander (Syracousas in D; Sugambri in J; Sudracae in C; Sydracai or Oxydrakai Strabo; Oxydracae in A & Pausanias, oxudrac in Metz) - Alexander showered with missiles, jumps down inside wall, ladders collapse under weight of Macedonians, Alexander shelters next to tree, drops to knees	Curtius 9.4.15-9.5.21 Arrian 6.11.3 & 6.11.8, Metz 75-8 Plutarch Moralia 327B & 343D & 344D Diodorus 17.98.1-99.4 Justin 12.9.3-12 Pausanias 1.6.2	Jacoby, Fragment 24 of Cleitarchus Hammond Sources 270 Hammond THA 65, 153-4	c. November 326BC, the Metz mentions both the Oxydracae (oxudrac) and the Malli – so probably Cleitarchus – Oxydracae is probably Cleitarchan since it is in Arrian (where he disputes the "Vulgate" version), some manuscripts of Strabo. Pausanias (where he tells Cleitarchan stories) and the Metz – Timagenes also had Ptolemy present
Risky treatment: Alexander's wound enlarged by Critobulus to remove the barbed arrow – Alexander faints, then slowly recovers	Curtius 9.5.22-30 Diodorus 17.99.4 Justin 12.9.13	Hammond THA 154 (wrongly Critodemus in Arrian 6.11.1, cf. Indica 18.7)	D & J are very brief; Pliny NH 7.37.37 notes that Critobulus was even more famous for having extracted an arrow from Philip II's eye in 354BC.
Revolt of the Greeks settled in Bactria (since they heard tell that Alexander had died from the Mallian wound)	Diodorus 17.99.5-6 Curtius 9.7.1-11	Hammond THA 66 (for 99.5 only), 154	Diodorus confuses this rebellion with another after Alexander's death (probably due to his account of a subsequent rebellion of Bactrian colonists at 18.7.1). The version in C is probably Cleitarchus. Since Cleitarchus habitually ended books with news from elsewhere, this report from his work of events in Bactria is the best indication of the boundary between his 11th and 12th books. Also chapter 17.99 in Diodorus and chapter 12.9 in Justin end here.

Book 12: Spring 325BC – June 324BC

Summary	Sources	References	Comment
Surrender of Indians - Alexander held a banquet – the contest between Coragus (D) or Coratas (C) and Dioxippus and the latter's suicide	Diodorus 17.100.1-101.6 Curtius 9.7.12-26 Aelian VH 10.22	Hammond THA 66, 154-5; C9.7.16-26=D17.100.2-D17.101.6 Schwartz	The story of Dioxippus is exclusive to D & C among the main sources, so is clearly from Cleitarchus
Submission of Sambastae(D) or Sabarcae(C), 60,000 infantry, 6000 cavalry & 500 chariots – impressed by the fleet into thinking another Dionysus was coming - Sodrae & Massani – founds an Alexandria on Indus	Diodorus 17.102.1-4 Curtius 9.8.4-8	C9.8.4-8=D17.102.1-4 Schwartz	

635

Concerning Alexander the Great by Andrew Chugg

Summary	Sources	References	Comment
Subjugation of the Musicani. Trial of Terioltes and Oxyartes. Conviction & execution of the former – acquittal and enlargement of realm of latter.	Diodorus 17.102.5 Curtius 9.8.9-10	Hammond THA 155	The trials were probably in Cleitarchus, though only found in C (compare and contrast with Arrian 6.15.3) D subsumes the later revolt and crucifixion of Musicanus into a single sentence entry at the arrival of Alexander in his realm (is D following Cleitarchus or does Curtius better reflect Cleitarchus?)
Dispatch of Polyperchon (& Craterus) to Babylonia with an army	Justin 12.10.1	Yardley & Heckel on Justin 260-1	This mention in J is the only indication that Cleitarchus recorded the return of a large contingent of the army with Craterus to the west – probably from the kingdom of Musicanus and before the war with Sambus. Hammond THA 106 has a curious explanation that this line is misplaced in J
Invasion of the kingdom of Porticanus – storming and burning of two cities – capture and slaying of Porticanus as he sheltered within a stronghold	Diodorus 17.102.5 Curtius 9.8.11-12	Hammond THA 155	Porticanus is Cleitarchan – he is Oxycanus in Arrian 6.16.1
The kingdom of Sambus (Ambus in Justin 12.10.2): 80,000 Indians slain by Alexander (Curtius names Cleitarchus as his source for this) – Sambus escaped to the east with thirty elephants in D but surrendered (gave up the fight?) in C	Curtius 9.8.13-15 Diodorus 17.102.6	Jacoby, Fragment 25 of Cleitarchus, Hammond THA 67, 155; C9.8.13-15=D17.102.6 Schwartz	The Sambus at the Mallian siege in Metz 75 is almost certainly a different person. The number was DCCC *milia* rather than LXXX *milia* in manuscripts of Curtius, but is emended on the basis of Diodorus
Revolt and suppression of the Brahmins and their supplication with branches	Diodorus 17.102.7		Supplication with branches is recalls the surrender of Mazaga
Revolt, capture by Pithon and crucifixion of Musicanus	Curtius 9.8.16	Hammond THA 155	It is uncertain whether this was in Cleitarchus, but it is in the same paragraph as a direct quote of Cleitarchus
The Indian town of Harmatelia, the last city of the Brahmins, refuses to submit and is attacked by 500 Agriani. Ptolemy receives a wound from a poisoned hand weapon (sword in C or arrow in J) and his life was saved by Alexander who was shown an antidote herb in a dream – followed by a eulogy of Ptolemy	Diodorus 17.103 Curtius 9.8.18-28 Justin 12.10.2-3 (cf. Strabo 15.2.7 who places this among the Oreitae) [Cic. de divinatione. 2.66.135 – Schwartz on Curtius]	Hamilton Cleitarchus & Diodorus 17, Hammond THA 67, 105, 155; C9.8.17-28=D17.103, J12.10.2-3 cf. Cic. de divin. 2.135 Schwartz	Definitely Cleitarchus, because the eulogy is common to Diodorus and Curtius. The mention by Curtius that Ptolemy was believed to be an illegitimate son of Philip is echoed by Pausanias 1.6.2 in a Cleitarchan context and thus probably also goes back to Cleitarchus. Dreaming cures was a standard technique in Greek medicine. Alexander had been taught herbal medicine by Aristotle according to Plutarch 8.1.

Organisation and Sources

Summary	Sources	References	Comment
Interview with the Indian philosophers, who were asked why they had induced King Sambus to revolt *inter alia*	Metz 78-84, Plutarch 64-5, cf. Pap. Berol. 13044	Merkelbach thinks the interview with the gymnosophists is from a separate letter collection, but this is dubious	Plutarch mentions that the 10 gymnosophists were captured after instigating the revolt of King Sabbas (probably Sambus in Curtius & Ambus in Justin). Hammond traces some of Plutarch to Onesicritus & Megasthenes, but this may nevertheless be via Cleitarchus, since it is in the Metz
Digression on the Indians (called Mandi) of Pandaea(?) – their women can bear children from the age of 7 and become old at 40 – Pandaea is the southernmost part of India extending to the sea, which Heracles gave to his daughter of that name to rule: he divided it into 365 villages, one of which would pay the royal tax each day of the year	Pliny NH 7.28-29 Polyaenus 1.3.4 Arrian Indica 9 (cf. Solinus 52.6-17)	Jacoby, Fragment 23 of Cleitarchus	Pliny co-attributes this fragment to Megasthenes & he is the source for a parallel description in Arrian's Indica, which adds the story of Pandaea. Polyaenus gives the Pandaea story in what has been thought a fragment of Megasthenes, but the usage of the number 365 in his version is highly characteristic of Cleitarchus. Solinus has a garbled version linked with Nysa. (Mandi from Pliny is similar to Mandri, which is J's name for the Malli) – Tarn, Alexander the Great II, Sources & Studies p.52 appears to confuse Pandaea with the Panchaea of Euhemerus (Brown, Onesicritus p.66 ff.)
Patala and the Patalii – pursuit of their king Soeris and a sojourn upon an island in the channel of the Indus (the island of Patala – "insulam catacam" in the Metz?), whilst seeking fresh guides	Metz 84 Curtius 9.8.28-30 (Diodorus 17.104.2 mentions Patala when Alexander returns from the Ocean)	Hammond THA 155	Reached "Patalene" about the rising of the Dog Star, i.e. mid-July 325BC (Strabo 15.1.17 from Aristobulus)
Sailing on 400 stades to visit the Ocean: during a stop Alexander's cavalry have to gallop to escape the returning tide (evidently a tidal bore) which dashed ships together – Alexander's sacrifices to Oceanus and Tethys on islands (one in the river and one out in the ocean)	Strabo 7.2.1-2, Metz 85-6, Curtius 9.9.1-27, Justin 12.10.4-5, Diodorus 17.104.1	Jacoby, Fragment 26 of Cleitarchus	Hammond THA 67 & 155 thinks D follows Diyllus & fails to attribute Curtius' account, except to note that he used a different source to Arrian and probably did not use Diyllus. But that a fragment of Cleitarchus in Strabo recorded the bore makes it likely that Curtius used Cleitarchus & the Metz agrees with C on details.
Return to Patala (mooring at a salt lake which diseased the skin of swimmers – C only) Nearchus as admiral and Onesicritus as chief pilot appointed to lead fleet along the coast keeping India on their right as far as the mouth of the Euphrates recording all they saw – burnt damaged ships	Diodorus 17.104.3 Curtius 9.10.3-4		

Concerning Alexander the Great by Andrew Chugg

Summary	Sources	References	Comment
Submission of the Abritae (D) or Arabitae (C) & the Kedrosian tribesmen	Diodorus 17.104.4 Curtius 9.10.5	C9.10.5-11,17-18,27=D17.104.4-D17.106.1 Schwartz	
Three columns under Leonnatus, Ptolemy and Alexander himself – founds an Alexandria at a sheltered harbour	Diodorus 17.104.4-8 Curtius 9.10.6-7	Hammond THA 155-6; C9.10.5-11,17-18,27=D17.104.4-D17.106.1 Schwartz	The city at Rhambakia in Arrian 6.21.5 – perhaps "Barce" (*parcem/bartem/bastemostem*) in Justin 12.10.6
The Oreitae inhabit the land separated from India by the River Arabis/Arabus and expose their dead naked to be eaten by wild animals… on the coast of Kedrosia an unfriendly and brutish people eat nothing but fish, which they tear to pieces with their nails and dry in the sun to make bread – their houses are roofed with whale ribs and scales	Pliny NH 7.30 cf. Diodorus 17.105.1-5 Curtius 9.10.6-10	Jacoby, Fragment 27 of Cleitarchus, Hammond THA 70, 156; C9.10.5-11,17-18,27=D17.104.4-D17.106.1 Schwartz	?Autumn 325BC The story of the fish eaters seems gleaned from Nearchus (cf. Strabo 15.2.2)
The march through Gedrosia (Kedrosia in Cleitarchus) - many deaths in Kedrosia – Alexander had ordered wells to be dug at regular intervals to provide water, but the army was threatened by starvation - Alexander sent to the satraps who made supplies abundantly available – Leonnatus attacked by Oreitae	Diodorus 17.105.6-8 Arrian 6.24.4 Plutarch 66.2-3 Curtius 9.10.11-21 Justin 12.10.7	Hammond Sources 124-5 & 275 Hamilton Plutarch Alex liii; C9.10.5-11,17-18,27=D17.104.4-D17.106.1 Schwartz	Arrian legomenon – Plutarch says that only a quarter of the army survived the desert, but he may have read that 30,000 infantry came through and (wrongly) compared this figure with Alexander's army of 120,000 in India – it is not clear that the Cleitarchan vulgate mentioned the men who returned with Craterus
Festivities in Carmania – seven day comus	Arrian 6.28.1-2 Diodorus 17.106.1 Curtius 9.10.22-28 Plutarch 67	Hammond Sources 125 & 278 THA 156 Hamilton Plutarch Alex liii; C9.10.5-11,17-18,27=D17.104.4-D17.106.1 Schwartz	Arrian legomenon
The purging of the Satraps – first Astaspes – then Cleander & Sitalces and the rebels Ozines & Zariaspes	Curtius 9.10.19-21, 10.1.1-9, Diodorus 17.106.2-3 Justin 12.10.8		Hammond THA 70 &156 is unsure of D's & C's sources for the purging of satraps except that they were different to Arrian's
Return of Nearchus & Onesicritus – meeting with in theatre at Salmous - stories including: an island where a horse was worth a talent of gold, school of whales etc. – fleet ordered to sail to the Euphrates (kiss with Bagoas in this theatre may have been noted – Plutarch 67)	Pliny, NH 6.198 Diodorus 17.106.4-7 Curtius 10.1.10-16	Jacoby, Fragment 29 of Cleitarchus Hamilton Cleitarchus & Diodorus 17 Hammond THA 71, 156	Cf. Nearchus in Strabo 15.2.12 and Arrian, Indica 30.4-5 on whale spoutings. The use of trumpets to frighten the whales in Diodorus & Curtius matches the accounts in the fragments of Nearchus.

Organisation and Sources

Summary	Sources	References	Comment
Alexander orders ship construction at Babylon using Lebanese timber to support a campaign around the eastern sea coast (Arabia?) & across N Africa to the Pillars of Heracles then back through Spain and Italy – letters from Porus & Taxiles	Curtius 10.1.17-21	Hammond THA 156-7	Was this from Cleitarchus?
Bagoas prosecuted & hanged Orsines at Parsagada (perhaps included mention of the execution of Baryaxes, who had worn the tiara upright and was brought to Parsagada by Atropates – Arrian 6.29.3)	Curtius 10.1.22-38	Hammond THA 157, Brown, Clitarchus p.153-4	Brown concludes that Cleitarchus was not unfavourable to Alexander, so C's emotive treatment of this story probably reflects his own spin on the matter. A large lacuna begins at Curtius 10.1.45 after an account of the defeat of Zopyrion by the Getae
Alexander and the army progress to Susianê. Self-immolation of Calanus (Caranus in Diodorus) on becoming ill: the disdain of the Indian gymnosophists for death	Diogenes Laertius 16 Aelian VH 5.6 Diodorus 17.107.1-5	Jacoby, Fragment 6 of Cleitarchus Hammond THA 71	Diogenes Laertius attributes this to the 12th book of Cleitarchus
Calanus would greet Alexander at Babylon	Arrian 7.18.6 Plutarch 69.3-4	Hammond Sources 132-3 & 301	
The marriages at Susa	Diodorus 17.107.6 Justin 12.10.9-10		Hammond THA 72 thinks D is Diyllus
The 30,000 Epigoni arrive	Diodorus 17.108.1-2 (Plutarch 71.1)	Hammond Sources 134-5	Hammond THA 72 thinks D is Diyllus - Curtius had mentioned the instigation of their formation and training at 8.5.1
Καὶ τὰ μὲν περὶ Ἀλέξανδρον ἐν τούτοις ἦν ("These were the concerns of Alexander")	End of Diodorus 17.108.3		This seems to indicate the end of Book 12 of Cleitarchus: the same formula is found at Diodorus 17.83.3, where Cleitarchus' Book 7 closed. This is also the boundary between chapters 12.10 and 12.11 in Justin.

Book 13: July 324BC – June 323BC

Summary	Sources	References	Comment
Destruction of Zopyrion and his army in Europe	Curtius 10.1.43-45		Cf. Justin 12.1.16-17
The extravagance of Harpalus towards his courtesans – his flight to Athens & bribery of the demagogues – his ejection from Athens and his murder by Thibron	Athenaeus 586C-D Diodorus 17.108.4-8 Curtius 10.2.1-3 Plutarch, *Demosthenes* 25-26	Jacoby, Fragment 30 of Cleitarchus	Cleitarchus commonly began (or ended) his books with news from elsewhere. Curtius emerges from a major lacuna in the midst of the Harpalus story. Hammond THA 72 & 157 thinks this is Diyllus, but this is confuted by a close match between the Cleitarchus fragment in Athenaeus and D's version

Concerning Alexander the Great by Andrew Chugg

Summary	Sources	References	Comment
The Exiles Decree	Diodorus 17.109.1 Curtius 10.2.4-7	C10.2.4,8-12,30=D17.109.1-2 Schwartz	Hammond THA 72-3 thinks D is Diyllus
Paying of troops' debts at 10,000 talents (20,000 in J & A) on planning to send 10,000 veterans home to Macedon	Diodorus 17.109.2 Curtius 10.2.8-11 Justin 12.11.1-3 (Arrian 7.5.3?)	Hammond Sources 285; C10.2.4,8-12,30=D17.109.1-2 Schwartz	Hammond THA 72-3 & 157-8 thinks D & C are both from Diyllus, but I assert that all matches between versions in D & C are overwhelmingly likely to be from Cleitarchus – Hammond is probably wrong to suggest that Arrian used Cleitarchus
The Mutiny (at Opis) - troops taunt Alexander for claiming to be the son of Ammon – drowning of ringleaders of the mutiny in the river – Craterus to lead the veterans home – Antipater to come to Babylon with a force of fresh recruits	Plutarch 71.2-5 Justin 12.11.4-12.10 Diodorus 17.108.3 & 17.109.2-3 Curtius 10.2.12-10.4.3	Hammond Sources 134-6; C10.2.4,8-12,30=D17.109.1-2 Schwartz	There is no evidence that Cleitarchus located the mutiny at Opis – Diodorus implies that it took place at Susa - Curtius enters a further long lacuna during events at Opis - Hammond THA 72-3 & 157-8 thinks D & C are both from Diyllus, but I assert that all matches between versions in D & C are very likely to be from Cleitarchus
Arrival of Persian reinforcements; 20,000 archers and slingers arrive with Peucestes	Diodorus 17.110.1-2		This occurred nearly a year later in 323BC in Arrian - Hammond THA 73 thinks D is Diyllus
Arranges for the upbringing of 10,000 children of his veterans by captive women	Diodorus 17.110.3		Hammond THA 73 thinks D is Diyllus
March from Susa to Ecbatana via Karai, Sambana and the Kelones, where he saw a settlement of Boeotian Greeks	Diodorus 17.110.4-5		Hammond THA 73 thinks D is Diyllus
Quarrel of Hephaistion with Eumenes	Plutarch, *Eumenes* 2 Arrian 7.13.1		The only hint that Cleitarchus may have mentioned the quarrel between Hephaistion and Eumenes is that Arrian mentions their reconciliation as a "story", which usually means he did not find it in Ptolemy or Aristobulus (the main source on the quarrel is Plutarch's Life of Eumenes) – there is a similar dearth of evidence for the quarrel between Hephaistion and Craterus in India, so perhaps Cleitarchus avoided this topic
Sightseeing trip to Bagistane - 60,000 horses where once there had been 160,000 - Atropates gives Alexander 100 Amazons	Arrian 7.13.2-3 Diodorus 17.110.5-6	Hammond Sources 293	Strabo 505 Hammond THA 73 thinks D is Diyllus
Arrival at Ecbatana – holds a drama festival - the Death of Hephaistion and Alexander's mourning – orders Perdiccas to conduct the corpse to Babylon for a magnificent funeral	Plutarch 72.1-3 Diodorus 17.110.7-8 Justin 12.12.11-12	Hammond Sources 136-140 & THA 107-8	Hammond THA 73 thinks D is Diyllus, but that J is drawing on Ephippus, perhaps via Cleitarchus and "P's much more sensational account" is Cleitarchus

Organisation and Sources

Summary	Sources	References	Comment
Unrest in Greece fuelled by dissolution of Satrapal armies of mercenaries on Alexander's orders	Diodorus 17.111.1-3		Hammond THA 73-4 thinks D is Diyllus
Against the Cossaeans	Diodorus 17.111.4-6 Plutarch 72.3		January-February 323BC - Hammond THA 73-4 thinks D is Diyllus
To Babylon – ill omens – warnings from the Chaldean scholars	Plutarch 73.1-4 Diodorus 17.112 Justin 12.13.3-5	Hammond Sources 141-3 Hammond THA 108	March-April 323BC - Hammond THA 74 thinks D is Diyllus
Embassies at Babylon including the embassy of the Romans	Pliny NH 3.57 Diodorus 17.113 (cf. Arrian 7.15.5, Livy 9.18.6) Justin 12.13.1-2	Jacoby, Fragment 31 of Cleitarchus Hammond THA 108	Possibly suggestive that Cleitarchus wrote after campaigns of Pyrrhus made Romans famous in the Greek world, but could simply be true. Livy attacks "frivolous Greeks" who harped on about Romans bowing to Alexander in his digression on Alexander vs. the Romans - Hammond THA 74 thinks D is Diyllus
Hephaistion's pyre at 12,000 talents - anecdotes of Hephaistion's status in Alexander's affections – response from Ammon brought by Philip that Hephaistion should be worshipped as God-Coadjutor (Paredros)	Diodorus 17.114-115 Arrian 7.14.8 Plutarch 72.3 & 75.2, Jacoby Fragment 41	Hammond Sources 139 & 296 Hamilton Plutarch Alex liii	Cf. Lucian, Slander 17, Aelian, VH 7.8 - Hammond THA 74-5 thinks D is Diyllus & Ephippus (however, there are grounds to suspect that Cleitarchus used Ephippus' book on the Death of Alexander & Hephaistion)
Episode of the prisoner who sat on the throne	Diodorus 17.116.2-4, Jacoby Fragment 52	Hammond THA 76-7	Cf. Plutarch 73.3-4
Visit to the marshes – Alexander's boat becomes lost for three days – diadem catches on a reed, retrieved by oarsman	Diodorus 17.116.5-7	Hammond THA 76-7	
Drinking party hosted by Medius the Thessalian following a ceremonial banquet in honour of Nearchus - Cup of Heracles – Alexander falls ill	Plutarch 75.3 Justin 12.13.6-10 Diodorus 17.117.1-3	Hammond Sources 151 & THA 77-8 & 108-9 Hamilton Plutarch Alex liii	Cf. Ephippus in Athenaeus 434A-B
Death in Babylon (After 3 days troops filed past, Where to find a worthy king? Body to Ammon, Funeral Games, On 6th day voice failed and gave ring to Perdiccas, "To whom do you leave your kingdom?" - "To the strongest", Divine honours when happy)	Diodorus 17.117.4 Curtius 10.5.1-6 Justin 12.15 Arrian 7.26.3	Hammond Sources 309& THA 77-8 & 108-9	Towards evening 10th June 323BC – Hammond THA 158-9 thinks C did not draw on Arrian's sources, but he is unsure of the identity of C's source
Reaction in Babylon	Curtius 10.5.7-17		
Death of Sisygambis (D: Sisyngambris)	Diodorus 17.118.3 Curtius 10.5.18-25 Justin 13.1.5-6	C10.5.21-25=D17.118.3, J13.1.5-6 Schwartz	Hammond THA 78 & 159 thinks D & C are both from Diyllus, but all matches between versions in D & C are very likely from Cleitarchus
Obituary for Alexander	Curtius 10.5.26-37		

641

Concerning Alexander the Great by Andrew Chugg

Summary	Sources	References	Comment
Accession of Philip III: the dispute between the cavalry and the infantry and its resolution in the elephant parade	Curtius 10.6-9 Justin 13.2-13.4.8 Diodorus 18.2 & 18.4.7-8		
First Division of the Satrapies	Curtius 10.10.1-8 Diodorus 18.3 Justin 13.4.9-25		Cf. Metz Epitome 116-122
Preservation of Alexander's corpse	Curtius 10.10.9-13 Plutarch 77.3		
The Last Plans	Diodorus 18.4.1-6	Jane Hornblower, Hieronymus of Cardia, pp.80-97	The lengthy geographical review starting at Diodorus 18.5 probably marks his switch to his next source, Hieronymus of Cardia
Conspiracy of Antipater and his sons, Cassander and Iollas (and Philip) – poison from the Styx brought in a mule's hoof - the rumour was suppressed, because of the subsequent power of Antipater and Cassander; restoration of Thebes and murders of Alexander's family by Cassander; fate of Cassander and his family	Diodorus 17.118.1-2 Justin 12.14 Val Max 1.7 ext2 Curtius 10.10.14-19 Pausanias 9.7.2	C10.10.14,18-19=D17.117.5& D17.118.2 cf. J12.13.10 Schwartz	Cleitarchus may have given this as an alternative as in Diodorus – cf. Ampelius 16.2, which Seel thought a fragment of Trogus: it says it was thought unclear whether Alexander died of drunkenness or poison (cf. Pliny NH 30.16.53) – Hammond THA 78 thinks D's version inspired by Hieronymus and THA 109-111 thinks J's version is from Satyrus and does not identify C's source, but it is more likely (e.g. Heckel LD&T) that Cleitarchus took this rumour from the *Liber de Morte* – NB D & C 10.10.18-19 say this story was suppressed until Cassander died in 297BC
Entombment in Memphis and transfer to Alexandria by Philadelphus	Curtius 10.10.20 Pausanias 1.6.2-3	Jane Hornblower, Hieronymus of Cardia, p.93	There is reason to suppose Cleitarchus extended so far as to mention the entombment in Memphis and perhaps the move to Alexandria (how could he ignore it, if it had just happened when he wrote in Alexandria ~280BC?) The clues are that Curtius ended his history with this information and that Pausanias mentions the Memphite entombment and the transfer to Alexandria in the context of his having noted some Cleitarchan stories (e.g. Ptolemy's birth and Alexander's wound among the Malli/Oxydracae). Pausanias uses Cleitarchan phraseology in speaking of "burial with Macedonian rites" (cf. Curtius 7.9.21). This implies that most of the information in Curtius on the aftermath of Alexander's demise was taken from Cleitarchus.

Bibliography

Modern References

1) Algra, Keimpe et al., "The Cambridge History of Hellenistic Philosophy", 1999, Cambridge.

2) Andronicos, Manolis, "Vergina: The Royal Tombs", 1994.

3) Atkinson, JE, "A Commentary on Quintus Curtius Rufus' Historiae Alexandri Magni, Books 3 & 4", Amsterdam 1980.

4) Atkinson, JE, "A Commentary on Quintus Curtius Rufus' Historiae Alexandri Magni, Books 5 to 7.2", Amsterdam 1994.

5) Atkinson, JE, "Quintus Curtius Rufus' *Historiae Alexandri Magni*", *ANRW* II (H. temporini ed., Aufsteig und Niedergang der römischen Welt, Berlin), 34.4: 3447-83, 1998.

6) Atkinson, John E, "Curzio Rufo: Storie di Alessandro Magno. Volume I (Libri III-V) & Volume II (Libri VI-X)", tr. Virginio Antelami and Maurizio Giangiulio, Milan: Fondazione Lorenzo Valla/Arnoldo Mondadori Editore, 1998 & 2000.

7) Atkinson, JE, "Originality and its Limits in the Alexander Sources of the Early Empire" in *Alexander the Great in Fact and Fiction* (editors: AB Bosworth & EJ Baynham), Oxford 2000, pp. 307-25.

8) Atkinson, JE, & Yardley, JC, "Curtius Rufus: Histories of Alexander the Great, Books 10", Oxford 2009.

9) Badian, E, "The Date of Clitarchus" *Proceedings African Classical Associations* 8 (1965): 5-11.

10) Bardon, H., "Quinte-Curce: Histoires", Paris, Tome I (1947) & Tome II (1948).

11) Baynham, Elizabeth, "Alexander the Great: The Unique History of Quintus Curtius", Ann Arbor 1998.

12) Baynham, Elizabeth, "An Introduction to the *Metz Epitome*: its traditions and value", *Antichthon* 29 (1995) 60-77.

13) Bennett, C. J., "The Children of Ptolemy III and the Date of the Exedra of Thermos", ZPE 138 (2002) 141-5.

14) Beresford, A. G., Parsons, P. J. & Pobjoy, M. P., "POxy 4808", pp. 27-36 in R. Hatzilambrou, P. J. Parsons & J. Chapa, eds., *Oxyrhynchus Papyri*, Vol LXXI, Egypt Exploration Society Graeco-Roman Memoirs, No. 91, 2007.

15) Berve, H, "Review of W I", *Gnomon* 5, 1929.

16) Billows, Richard, "Polybius and Alexander Historiography" in *Alexander the Great in Fact and Fiction*, ed. A.B. Bosworth and E.J. Baynham, Oxford 2000.

17) Borza, EN, 1968, "Cleitarchus & Diodorus' Account of Alexander" *Proceedings African Classical Associations* 11:25-45.

18) Bosworth, AB, "A Missing Year in the History of Alexander the Great", *Journal of Hellenic Studies*, Vol. 101, pp. 17-39, 1981.

19) Bosworth, AB, "From Arrian to Alexander", Oxford, 1988.

20) Bosworth, AB, "Conquest & Empire: The Reign of Alexander the Great", Cambridge, 1988.

21) Bosworth, AB, "Commentary on Arrian's History of Alexander I", Oxford 1980.

22) Bosworth, AB, "Commentary on Arrian's History of Alexander II", Oxford 1995.

23) Bosworth, AB, "The Historical Setting of Megasthenes' Indica," *Classical Philology* 91, 1996.

24) Bosworth, AB, "In Search of Cleitarchus: Review-Discussion of Luisa Prandi: Fortuna è Realtà dell'Opera di Clitarco" in *Histos* (University of Durham, electronic journal of historiography), Vol. 1, Aug. 1997.

25) Bradford Welles, C, "Diodorus Siculus: Library of History", Vol. 8, Loeb, Harvard, 1963.

26) Brown, TS, 1949, "Onesicritus", Berkeley.

27) Brown, TS, 1950, "Clitarchus" *American Journal of Philology* 71: 134-55.

28) Brown, TS, "The Merits and Weaknesses of Megasthenes," *Phoenix* 11, 1957.

29) Brunt, PA, "Arrian: History of Alexander and Indica", Loeb, Harvard, 1976 & 1983.

30) Carney, Elizabeth, "Olympias: Mother of Alexander the Great", 2006, Women of the Ancient World Series, Taylor and Francis.

31) Chesney, F. R., "The Expedition for the Survey of the Rivers Euphrates and Tigris, Carried on By Order of the British Government, In the Years 1835, 1836, and 1837", Vol. I, London, 1850.

32) Chugg, AM, "The Journal of Alexander the Great", *Ancient History Bulletin*, 19.3-4 (2005) 155-175.

33) Chugg, AM, "The Sarcophagus of Aleander the Great?" *Greece & Rome*, Vol. 49.1, April 2002.

Bibliography

34) Chugg, AM, "The Tomb of Alexander in Alexandria", *American Journal of Ancient History*, New Series 1.2 (2002) [2003], pp.75-108.

35) Chugg, AM, "The Quest for the Tomb of Alexander the Great", AMC Publications, 2007 (2nd Edition 2012).

36) Chugg, AM, "The Lost Tomb of Alexander the Great", Periplus – Richmond Editions, London 2004.

37) Chugg, AM, "Alexander's Lovers", Lulu & AMC Publications, 2006 and revised 2012.

38) Chugg, AM, "Alexander the Great in India: A Reconstruction of Cleitarchus", AMC Publications, 2009.

39) Chugg, AM, "The Death of Alexander the Great: A Reconstruction of Cleitarchus", AMC Publications, 2009.

40) Chugg, AM, "Alexander the Great in Afghanistan: A Reconstruction of Cleitarchus", AMC Publications, 2011.

41) Chugg, AM, "Alexander the Great and the Conquest of the Persians: A Reconstruction of Cleitarchus", AMC Publications, 2013.

42) Chugg, AM, "Was Alexander the Great Originally Interred in the Usurped Sarcophagus of Nectanebo II?" *Kmt: A Modern Journal of Egyptology* Vol. 31, Number 3, Fall 2020, pp.66-74.

43) Depuydt, L., "The Time of Death of Alexander the Great: 11 June 323 BC, ca. 4:00-5:00 PM," *Die Welt des Orients* 28 (1997) 117–135.

44) Engels, Donald W, "Alexander the Great and the Logistics of the Macedonian Army", University of California, 1978.

45) Errington, RM, "Bias in Ptolemy's History of Alexander", *Classical Quarterly* 19, 1969, 233-242.

46) Errington, RM, "From Babylon to Triparadeisos, 323-320BC," *JHS* 90 (1970) 72-75.

47) Fontana, M, "Il problema delle fonti per il XVII Libro di Diodoro Siculo," *Kokalos* I (1955), 155-190.

48) Fraser, P. M., "Ptolemaic Alexandria", OUP, 1972.

49) Goralski, Walter J., "Arrian's Events after Alexander," *Ancient World* 19, 1989.

50) Goukowsky, P, 1969, "Clitarque seul? Remarques sur les sources du livre xvii de Diodore de Sicile" *Revue des Etudes Anciennes* 71: 320-6.

51) Grzybek, E., "Du calendrier Macédonien au calendrier Ptolémaïque", Basel, 1990.

52) Gunderson, Lloyd L, "Quintus Curtius Rufus: On His Historical Methods in the *Historiae Alexandri*" in *Philip II, Alexander the Great and the Macedonian Heritage*, eds. WL Adams & E N Borza, Lanham, 1982, pp.177-196.

53) Hamilton, JR, 1961, "Cleitarchus & Aristobulus" *Historia* 10: 448-59.

54) Hamilton, JR, "Plutarch, Alexander: A Commentary", Oxford 1969.

55) Hamilton, JR, 1977, "Cleitarchus and Diodorus 17" in *Greece & the Ancient Mediterranean in History and Prehistory*, ed KH Kinzl, Berlin, 126-46.

56) Hammond, NGL, "The Battle of the Granicus River", JHS 100, 1980, 73-88.

57) Hammond, NGL, "Three Historians of Alexander the Great", Cambridge 1983.

58) Hammond, NGL, "The Miracle that was Macedonia", London 1991.

59) Hammond, NGL, "The Regnal Years of Philip and Alexander," *Greek, Roman and Byzantine Studies*, Vol. 33, 1992, 355-373.

60) Hammond, NGL, "Sources for Alexander the Great", Cambridge 1993.

61) Hammond, NGL, "Philip of Macedon", 1994.

62) Heckel, W, "The Last Days & Testament of Alexander the Great", *Historia Einzelschriften*, Heft 56, Stuttgart 1988.

63) Heckel, W, "The Marshals of Alexander's Empire", Routledge, 1992.

64) Heckel, W, "The Earliest Evidence for the Plot to Poison Alexander" in *Alexander's Empire: Formulation to Decay*, California 2007.

65) Heckel, W, "Who's Who in the Age of Alexander the Great", Blackwell 2006.

66) Holt, Frank, "Alexander the Great and Bactria", supplement to *Mnemosyne* 104, 1989.

67) Holt, Frank, "Alexander the Great and the Mystery of the Elephant Medallions", California, 2003.

68) Hornblower, Jane, "Hieronymus of Cardia", OUP, 1981.

69) Howard, CL, "Review of the Teubner Edition of the *Metz Epitome*", *Classical Philology* 58, pp. 129-131.

70) Hunt, JM, "An Emendation in the *Epitoma Metensis*", *Classical Philology* 67, pp. 287-288.

71) Hunt, JM, "More Emendations in the *Epitoma Metensis*", *Classical Philology* 80, pp. 335-337.

72) Jacoby, F, "Kleitarchos", *FGrH* 137.

Bibliography

73) Karageorghis, V, "Cyprus", London, 1969.

74) Koldewey, R, "The Excavations at Babylon", London, 1914.

75) Lorber, C, "Theos Aigiochos: The aegis in Ptolemaic portraits of the divine king," in P. Iossif, A. Chankowski, and C. Lorber, eds., More than Men, Less than Gods. Studies in Royal Cult and Imperial Worship, Studia Hellenistica 51 (Leuven, 2011), pp.293-356.

76) Markle, Minor, "A Shield Monument from Veria and the Chronology of Macedonian Shield Types", *Hesperia* 68.2, 1999.

77) Marsden, E. W., "The Campaign of Gaugamela", Liverpool, 1964.

78) Meeus, Alexander, "Some Institutional Problems Concerning the Succession to Alexander the Great: Prostasia and Chiliarchy", *Historia*, Band 58, Heft 3, 2009, pp. 287-310.

79) Merkelbach, Reinhold, "Die Quellen des Griechischen Alexanderromans," *Zetema Monographien zur Klassischen Altertumswissenschaft*, Heft 9, Munich 1954.

80) Miller, Stephen G, "The Date of Olympic Festivals" *MDAI(A)* 90, 1975, pp.215-31.

81) Müller, Konrad & Schönfeld, Herbert, "Q. Curtius Rufus: Geschichte Alexanders des Grossen", Tusculum, Munich, 1954.

82) Oldach, David W. & Richard, Robert E., "A Mysterious Death", *The New England Journal of Medicine*, June 11, 1998, Volume 338, Number 24.

83) Palagia, Olga, "Hephaestion's Pyre and the Royal Hunt of Alexander", pp. 167-206 in *Alexander the Great in Fact and Fiction*, edited by A. B. Bosworth & E. J. Baynham, Oxford, 2000.

84) Pearson, Lionel, "The Lost Histories of Alexander the Great", American Philological Association, London and New York, 1960.

85) Pédech, P., "Deux campagnes d'Antiochus III chez Polybe," *Revue des Études Anciennes*, 60 (1958), 67-81.

86) Prandi, Luisa, "Callistene. Uno storico tra Aristotele e i re macedoni", Milan, 1985.

87) Prandi, Luisa, "Fortuna è Realtà dell'Opera di Clitarco" in *Historia Einzelschriften* 104, Steiner, Stuttgart 1996.

88) Prandi, Luisa, "New Evidence for the Dating of Cleitarchus (POxy LXXI. 4808)?" *Histos* 6 (2012) 15–26.

89) Prandi, Luisa, ed., "Corpus dei papiri storici greci e latini. Parte A. Storici greci. Vol. 2: Testi storici anepigrafi. I papiri e le storie di Alessandro Magno", 2010.

90) Pritchett, W. Kendrick, "Postscript: The Athenian Calendars," *ZPE* 128 (1999) 79-93.

91) Reames, Jeanne, "Hephaistion Amyntoros: Éminence Grise at the Court of Alexander the Great", *Thesis*, Pennsylvania State University, December 1998.

92) Rolfe, John C, "Quintus Curtius: History of Alexander", Loeb, Harvard, 1946.

93) Romm, James, (ed.), "The Landmark Arrian: The Campaigns of Alexander", Pantheon, 2010.

94) Samuel, Alan E., "Ptolemaic Chronology", Munich, 1962.

95) Samuel, Alan E., "Greek & Roman Chronology", Munich, 1972.

96) Schachermeyr, F, "Alexander der Grosse", Salzburg, 1949

97) Schachermeyr, F, "Alexander der Grosse: Das Problem seiner Persönlichkeit und seines Wirkens", Vienna, 1973.

98) Schachermeyr, F, "Alexander in Babylon und die Reichsordnung nach seiner Tod", Vienna, 1970.

99) Schwartz, E, *Paulys Real-Encyclopädie*, Vol. 4, 1901, s.v. Q. Curtius Rufus, cols. 1871-1891, & Vol 5, 1905, s.v. Diodoros, cols. 682-684.

100) Smith, William, (ed.), "The Dictionary of Greek and Roman Geography", 1854.

101) Steele, R. B., "Quintus Curtius Rufus", *AJP* 36, 1915.

102) Stein, Aurel, "Limes Report", *Geographical Journal*, Vol 92, 1938, pp.62-66

103) Stein, Aurel, *Geographical Journal*, Vol 95, 1940, pp. 428-438

104) Stein, Aurel, *Geographical Journal*, Vol 100, 1942, 155 ff.

105) Stein, Aurel, "Old Routes of Western Iran", London, 1940

106) Streck, *Paulys Real-Encyclopädie*, Vol. 7, cols. 861ff.

107) Tarn, WW, "Alexander the Great, Vol II, Sources and Studies", Part One, The So-Called 'Vulgate' and its Sources, pp. 1-133, Cambridge 1948.

108) Thomas, PH, Editor, "Incerti Auctoris Epitoma Rerum Gestarum Alexandri Magni cum Libro de Morte Testamentoque Alexandri" (The *Metz Epitome*), Teubner, Leipzig 1966.

109) Wood, Michael, "Footsteps of Alexander", BBC, 1997.

110) YardleyC & Heckel, W, "Quintus Curtius Rufus: The History of Alexander", Penguin Classics, 1984.

Bibliography

111) Yardley, JC & Heckel, W, "Justin: Epitome of the Philippic History of Pompeius Trogus, Vol I, Books 11-12, Alexander the Great", Oxford 1997.

112) Zeller, Eduard, "Die Philosophie der Griechen", 4th ed., Part II, Leipzig, 1889.

Selected Ancient Sources

Aelian, Varia Historia, N.G. Wilson, Loeb, Harvard, 1997

Aelian, On the Characteristics of Animals, trans. A.F. Scholfield in 3 volumes, Loeb, Harvard, 1958

Aischines

Agatharchides, Agatharchides of Cnidus on the Erythraean Sea, Stanley M. Burstein, Translator and Editor, Hakluyt Society, London, 1989

Arrian, Anabasis Alexandrou and Indica, P.A. Brunt, Loeb, Harvard, 1976 and 1983

Arrian, Discourses of Epictetus

Arrian, Epitome of the History of Events After Alexander, *Photius* 92, Photius, Bibliothèque, vol. II, René Henry, Paris, 1960

Athenaeus, Deipnosophistae, Charles Burton Gulick, Loeb, Harvard, 1927-41

Cicero, Ad Familiares, Brutus, De Natura Deorum, De Divinatione, Pro Archias Poeta

Curtius, The History of Alexander, John C. Rolfe, Loeb, Harvard, 1946; The History of Alexander, trans. John Yardley, Penguin Classics, 1984; Historiae Alexandri Magni, ed. E. Hedicke, Teubner, 1908; De Rebus Gestis Alexandri Magni, Freinshem et al., Petrus vander Aa, Lugduni Batavorum, 1696; Konrad Müller & Herbert Schönfeld, Geschichte Alexanders des Grossen, Tusculum, Munich, 1954; H. Bardon, Quinte-Curce: Histoires, Paris, Tome I, 1947 & Tome II, 1948

Dexippus, *Photius* 82, Photius, Bibliothèque, vol. I, René Henry, Paris, 1959

Diodorus Siculus, Library of History, vol. VII, Charles L. Sherman, Loeb, Harvard, 1952; vol. VIII, C. Bradford Welles, Loeb, Harvard, 1963; vol. IX, Russel M. Geer, Loeb, Harvard, 1947

Diogenes Laertius, Lives of Eminent Philosophers

Dio Cassius, Roman History, Loeb, translated by Earnest Cary, based on translation by H.B. Foster - reprints of the editions published from 1914-1927

Ephemerides, FrGrHist 2.117

Concerning Alexander the Great by Andrew Chugg

Frontinus, Stratagems

Hegesias, FrGrHist 2.142

Herodotus

Homer, Iliad, trans. A.T. Murray, revised William F. Wyatt, Loeb, Harvard, 1999

Itinerarium Alexandri, Didericus Volkmann, Naumburg 1871

Justin, Epitome of the Philippic History of Pompeius Trogus, Books 11-12, J.C. Yardley and W. Heckel, Oxford, 1997; Justin, Cornelius Nepos and Eutropius, Rev. John Selby Watson, London, 1853

Livy, History of Rome, Loeb Classical Library in 14 Volumes

Lucian, Dialogues of the Dead, XIII, vol. 7, M.D. MacLeod, Loeb, Harvard, 1961

Lucian, Essay on How to Write History, vol. 6, K. Kilburn, Loeb, 1959

Lucian, Calumniae non temere credendum, Lucian: Vol. I, A. M. Harmon, Loeb, 1913

Macrobius, Saturnalia, Macrobius: Opera: Band I Saturnalia, Saur Verlag, 1994

Martial, Liber de Spectaculis, De Spectaculis Liber, Shackleton Bailey, Loeb, 1994

Metz Epitome & Liber de Morte, P.H. Thomas, Ed., Incerti Auctoris Epitoma Rerum Gestarum Alexandri Magni cum Libro de Morte Testamentoque Alexandri, Teubner, Leipzig 1966

Nepos, Eumenes in Justin; Cornelius Nepos and Eutropius, Rev. John Selby Watson, London, 1853

Pausanias, Description of Greece, vol. 1, W.H.S. Jones, Loeb, Harvard, 1918

Pliny the Elder, Natural History, H. Rackham, W.H.S. Jones, D.E. Eichholz, Loeb, Harvard, 1938-62 and the 1855 translation by John Bostock and Henry Thomas Riley

Plutarch, Agesilaus, Lives vol. 5, B. Perrin, Loeb, Harvard, 1917

Plutarch, Alexander & Caesar and Cicero & Demosthenes, Lives vol. 7, B. Perrin, Loeb, Harvard, 1919; Plutarch: The Age of Alexander, trans. Ian Scott-Kilvert, Penguin 1973

Plutarch, Camillus, Themistocles

Plutarch, Eumenes, Lives vol. 8, B. Perrin, Loeb, Harvard, 1919

Plutarch, Demetrius, Antony & Pyrrhus, Lives vol. 9, B. Perrin, Loeb, Harvard, 1920

Plutarch, Moralia, especially vols. 3 and 4, Frank Cole Babbitt, Loeb, Harvard, 1931 and 1936

Bibliography

Pollux, Onomasticon

Polyaenus, Stratagems of War, trans. Peter Krentz & Everett L. Wheeler, Ares, Chicago, 1994

Polybius, The Histories, W.R. Paton, Loeb, Harvard, 1922-7

Pseudo-Callisthenes, Alexander Romance, e.g. Guilelmus Kroll, Historia Alexandri Magni, vol, 1, Weidmann, 1926

Claudius Ptolemy, Geographia, ed. C.F.A Nobbe, Leipzig, 1843-1845 and Claudius Ptolemy: The Geography, trans. Edward Luther Stevenson (1932), reprinted by Dover Publications, London, 1991

Stephanus Byzantinus, Augustus Meineke, Stephani Byzantii, Ethnicorum, Berlin, 1849

Strabo, Geography, H.L. Jones, Loeb, Harvard, 1917-32

Suidae Lexicon (a.k.a. The Suda), Ada Adler (ed.), Leipzig, 1928-35

Thucydides

Valerius Maximus

Xenophon, Anabasis

Acknowledgements

I would like to express my particular gratitude to the following for their assistance in the research reported in this book:-

Matthew Wofinden and Centonex for website support

Visitors to the Cleitarchus Reconstruction pages at www.alexanderstomb.com

The readership of the earlier volumes in the reconstruction for its support and encouragement

C. Bradford Welles for recognizing the usefulness of a reconstruction

A. B. Bosworth for endorsing the feasibility of reconstruction

Index

A

Abdalonymus..... 85, 86, 101, 272, 429, 485, 545, 553, 589, 615, 616
Abii 253
Abisares . 312, 313, 314, 316, 317, 328, 370, 631, 632
Abistamenes 56
Abradatas 196, 437, 442
Abu Roash 487
Abu Wijam 435, 440
Abulites 161, 162, 620
Acadira 303
Acarnania 59
Acarnanians 13, 52
Acesines. 297, 328, 338, 339, 340, 472, 522, 551, 632, 633, 634
Achaeans 132, 133, 193, 198
Achaemenid Empire 437, 522
Acheron, River 149
Acherusian River 148
Achilles v, 8, 13, 31, 32, 109, 294, 341, 351, 410, 421, 483, 517, 534, 543, 581, 582, 611, 617, 634
Acropolis 177, 437
Acuphis 302, 594, 629
Ada 40, 651
Adad 486
Adea 419
Adler, Ada 250, 457, 651
Admetus 97
Adonis 117, 535, 618
Adramyttium 37, 424
Adriatic Sea 386
Aeacidae 8, 391, 410, 609
Aeacus 8, 31, 409, 410

Aegae 487, 504, 506, 507
Aegean 37, 424
Aelian. 31, 34, 228, 250, 251, 421, 423, 457, 458, 483, 507, 509, 514, 515, 518, 529, 548, 554, 557, 560, 581, 597, 610, 611, 612, 625, 629, 632, 635, 639, 641, 649
Aeolia 104
Aeschylus 115, 431
Aesculapius 63
Aetion 484, 485
Aetolians 13, 52, 148, 384
Afghanistan .. v, 10, 210, 213, 246, 268, 413, 428, 447, 450, 467, 469, 471, 529, 623
Africa . 87, 93, 148, 298, 349, 370, 386, 474, 503, 587, 588, 589, 639, 643, 644
Against Ctesiphon 421
Agalasseis 340, 634
Agatharchides 649
Agathocles 39, 568
Agathon 160, 368, 497, 620
Agema 132, 477
Agenor 100, 403, 498, 500, 501
Agesilaus 650
Agis 102, 146, 147, 532, 536, 538, 540, 546, 604, 616, 619
Agis the Argive 284, 285
Agis, King 204, 245, 537
Agrianians .. 31, 68, 133, 140, 163, 164, 211, 261, 309, 320, 358, 422, 478
Ai Khanum 265, 470
Aischines ... 14, 245, 421, 625, 649
Ajax 31
Akhet 432
Alalis 440

Alcomenae 493, 494, 499
Aldus 294, 466, 593, 628
Aleppo 536
Alexander II 419
Alexander IV ... 406, 465, 487, 570
Alexander Lyncestes .iv, v, 12, 45,
  46, 60, 228, 230, 231, 288, 290,
  406, 424, 426, 455, 584, 613,
  614, 624
Alexander Mosaic 443
Alexander of Epirus 148, 274, 458,
  546, 609, 619
Alexander Romance 2, 12, 418,
  430, 431, 439, 494, 507, 617,
  651
Alexander Sarcophagus ... 485, 486
Alexander son of Cleophis 307
Alexander's Lovers 517, 645
Alexandria ... iv, 2, 30, 37, 83, 102,
  115, 116, 152, 211, 213, 238,
  240, 255, 357, 365, 407, 416,
  420, 423, 427, 428, 431, 432,
  439, 450, 468, 469, 474, 482,
  506, 508, 509, 510, 514, 515,
  523, 524, 529, 534, 543, 544,
  546, 550, 557, 559, 561, 564,
  565, 567, 568, 572, 574, 575,
  576, 589, 591, 597, 602, 605,
  606, 609, 611, 616, 617, 625,
  626, 634, 635, 638, 642, 645
Alexandria Troas 423
Alexandrians .. 431, 550, 568, 569,
  574, 575
Almagest 412
Alps 370
Altusacra 332
Amanic Gates 66
Amazon 206
Amazons 201, 202, 206, 207, 383,
  447, 448, 547, 552, 558, 591,
  604, 606, 622, 640
Ambraciots 13, 14
Amedines 238
Amissus 400

Amminais 304, 306
Ammon .. 110, 111, 112, 115, 221,
  224, 226, 333, 373, 378, 386,
  388, 391, 403, 430, 439, 459,
  460, 484, 490, 506, 611, 617,
  640, 641
Ammonians 386
Ammonii 112, 386
Ampelius 594, 597, 612, 642
Amphictyonic Council .. 14, 20, 23
Amphipolis 160, 405, 410, 440,
  494, 503
Amphoterus 49, 105, 106, 117
Amu-Darya 246, 469
Amuq Plain 536
Amyntas 10, 41, 51, 68, 74, 97,
  102, 103, 109, 110, 132, 159,
  161, 168, 200, 214, 221, 222,
  224, 230, 231, 233, 234, 278,
  407, 413, 419, 454, 455, 500,
  535, 559, 570, 606, 609, 616,
  617
Amyntas Lyncestes 161
Anabasis .. 1, 3, 10, 15, 32, 38, 41,
  43, 46, 51, 55, 60, 98, 100, 101,
  103, 106, 115, 125, 168, 199,
  203, 205, 210, 211, 221, 228,
  238, 240, 247, 248, 252, 255,
  258, 261, 275, 278, 291, 301,
  306, 311, 316, 317, 319, 325,
  348, 349, 413, 414, 415, 416,
  417, 419, 422, 424, 426, 427,
  428, 430, 431, 432, 433, 434,
  435, 437, 438, 439, 440, 441,
  442, 448, 449, 451, 458, 459,
  464, 466, 467, 468, 469, 471,
  477, 478, 479, 480, 483, 490,
  498, 502, 503, 511, 512, 516,
  517, 519, 520, 521, 522, 523,
  524, 525, 527, 532, 534, 535,
  537, 538, 544, 549, 551, 552,
  555, 557, 560, 563, 564, 565,
  566, 567, 569, 581, 587, 593,
  594, 597, 598, 649, 651

Index

Anacyndaraxes 63
Anatolia 425
Anaxarchus 385
Anaximenes 32, 416, 422, 515, 543, 596
Anchiale... 63, 535, 545, 554, 555, 559, 582, 604, 606, 614
Andromache .. 274, 276, 410, 458, 459, 461
Andromachus 104, 116
Andromeda 458
Andromenes 97, 159, 617
Andronicus 238
Andronikos, Manolis 409
Andros 103
aniketos... 113, 543, 582, 611, 617
Ankyra 50
anthredon 203, 556, 606, 622
Anticleides 447
Anticles 286
Antigenes 161, 318, 319, 382, 447, 501
Antigone 452
Antigonus 37, 103, 105, 161, 230, 403, 407, 423, 494, 497, 498, 499, 500, 501, 570
Antioch 439, 536
Antiochus 200, 445, 468, 559, 563, 616, 647
Antipater.... v, 29, 32, 46, 49, 102, 146, 147, 148, 159, 193, 198, 212, 230, 245, 265, 376, 382, 398, 403, 405, 406, 419, 422, 425, 448, 490, 497, 498, 499, 500, 501, 505, 520, 536, 546, 550, 556, 564, 569, 570, 602, 604, 606, 619, 621, 640, 642
Antipater the son of Asclepiodorus 286
Antiphanes 231, 232
Antiquities of the Jews 413
Antissa 45
Antixyes 72
Antoninus Pius 482
Antonio Tempesta .. 304, 310, 335, 381
Antonius 278, 475
Anzob Pass 470
Aornus 308, 310, 339, 472, 563, 581, 606, 630, 634
apes 327, 560, 606
Aphobetus 214
Aphrices 311, 630
Apollo 27, 94, 101, 167, 386, 456, 457, 616
Apollodorus 160
Apollonides 105
Apollonius 115, 531, 548, 574, 576
Appian 519
Apple Bearers 139
Apulians 148
Ar Raqqah 440
Arabia 90, 91, 153, 503, 639
Arabic 2
Arabs 109, 111, 234
Arabus river 365, 638
Arachosia 104, 128, 239, 365, 403, 447, 472, 525, 557, 565
Arachosii 235, 239, 354
Aradus 84
Aral Sea 558, 606, 622
Aramaic 435
Aratos of Soli 412
Araxes, River . 104, 166, 169, 240, 621
Arbela .... iv, v, 102, 118, 119, 140, 141, 143, 145, 152, 153, 154, 194, 335, 411, 412, 413, 414, 415, 417, 423, 427, 428, 429, 431, 432, 433, 434, 435, 436, 440, 515, 526, 527, 541, 542, 546, 601, 604, 618, 620
Arbelus 433
Arbil 432, 433, 434
Arcadians 13, 19
Arcesilaus 403, 500
Archelaus .. 29, 162, 228, 409, 501

Archepolis 214
archon 34, 152, 423, 428, 515, 612
Archon.. 1, 30, 403, 411, 416, 417, 498, 500, 539, 540, 541, 544
Ares 104, 352, 355, 651
Aretes 138, 139
Argeads 12, 25, 409, 418
Argives 13, 19, 409
Argos 409
Argyraspides 297, 493
Aria 211, 213, 238, 367, 403, 450, 468, 540
Ariamazes 266, 269, 270, 271, 470, 518, 547, 561, 593, 596, 605, 606, 627
Arian Satrapy 210, 211
Arians 211, 245
Ariarathes 403
Arimaspians 238, 468
Arines 301
Ariobarzanes 33, 128, 165, 167, 168, 169, 213, 440, 621
Aristander... 33, 88, 101, 107, 130, 132, 141, 166, 256, 257, 258, 427, 460, 507, 561, 606, 618, 626
Aristarchus 13, 574
Aristobulus 1, 23, 32, 82, 258, 276, 291, 411, 413, 422, 447, 451, 460, 464, 492, 511, 512, 515, 518, 523, 524, 535, 551, 552, 553, 555, 559, 560, 568, 569, 571, 594, 595, 596, 606, 610, 614, 618, 622, 626, 627, 632, 633, 637, 640, 646
Aristogeiton 83
Aristomedes 67
Aristomenes 103
Ariston 120, 618
Aristonicus of Methymna 105, 106, 115, 116, 597, 616, 617
Aristonous 345, 396, 461, 493, 494
Aristotle 9, 46, 278, 411, 412, 464, 508, 567, 636
Aristus 474
Armenia. 128, 153, 160, 180, 198, 240, 438, 446
Armenian Alexander Romance 494, 507
Armenians 2, 12, 128, 153, 418
Arrhidaeus ..... v, 10, 12, 397, 398, 403, 418, 465, 494, 495, 496, 501, 506, 507, 514, 586
Arrian. v, 1, 2, 3, 5, 10, 15, 32, 38, 41, 43, 46, 51, 55, 60, 73, 77, 98, 100, 101, 103, 106, 115, 125, 168, 199, 203, 205, 210, 211, 221, 228, 238, 240, 247, 248, 252, 255, 258, 261, 275, 278, 291, 297, 298, 301, 304, 306, 311, 313, 316, 317, 319, 325, 329, 348, 349, 388, 403, 411, 413, 414, 415, 416, 417, 418, 419, 421, 422, 424, 426, 427, 428, 430, 431, 432, 433, 434, 435, 437, 438, 439, 440, 441, 442, 448, 449, 451, 452, 453, 457, 458, 459, 460, 464, 466, 467, 468, 469, 470, 472, 474, 477, 478, 479, 480, 482, 483, 490, 491, 494, 496, 498, 501, 502, 503, 506, 511, 512, 513, 514, 515, 516, 517, 518, 519, 520, 521, 522, 523, 524, 525, 526, 527, 528, 532, 534, 535, 537, 538, 544, 548, 549, 551, 552, 553, 554, 555, 556, 557, 559, 560, 561, 562, 563, 564, 565, 566, 569, 581, 582, 583, 584, 587, 592, 593, 594, 595, 596, 597, 598, 599, 610, 611, 612, 613, 614, 617, 618, 619, 624, 627, 628, 629, 630, 631, 632, 634, 635, 636, 637, 638, 639, 640, 641, 644, 645, 648, 649
Arsaces 238, 282
Arsames 34, 57, 238

Index

Arsanes 16
Arses 15, 519
Arsinoe 10, 418, 494
Arsites 34
Artabazus. 82, 183, 184, 185, 187, 188, 203, 204, 205, 238, 246, 266, 270, 272, 516, 622
Artacana 211, 212, 468
Artacoana 211, 468
Artaxerxes 16, 17, 38, 82, 442, 518, 533, 554, 621, 623
Artaxerxes (Bessus) 210
Artaxerxes II 82, 518
Artaxerxes III 442
Artemis 9, 405, 482, 503, 512
Artemus of Colophon 461
Arybbas 480
Asander 265, 403, 497, 501
Asclepiades 474
Asclepiodorus 265, 286
Asclepius 517
Asia. iv, v, 8, 9, 10, 12, 15, 17, 29, 30, 31, 32, 35, 38, 48, 49, 50, 51, 53, 56, 64, 69, 76, 77, 84, 85, 92, 97, 102, 105, 125, 145, 148, 159, 166, 170, 172, 184, 185, 193, 197, 205, 208, 209, 228, 229, 240, 255, 256, 259, 261, 263, 268, 273, 274, 290, 295, 326, 334, 335, 351, 369, 375, 376, 377, 378, 380, 384, 386, 393, 405, 415, 420, 425, 437, 446, 475, 479, 483, 498, 502, 504, 520, 540, 546, 547, 550, 551, 554, 555, 604, 609, 611, 619, 622
Asianic rhythms 543, 557, 583, 606
Asians ... iv, 15, 27, 29, 33, 48, 92, 263, 387, 388, 420, 445, 457, 537
Asiatic officials 208
Aspetus 410
Assacena 304

Assacenus 304, 311, 630
Assembly .... iv, 8, 226, 272, 291, 326, 334, 337, 342, 377, 378, 380, 395, 398, 402, 405, 425, 453, 455, 461, 463, 489, 493, 502, 516
Assyria 158, 435, 562, 584
Astaspes 367, 368, 638
astrology 530
astronomy 530
Atalante 494
Atarrhias 43, 160, 218, 230, 274
Athena 33, 37, 63, 81, 130, 280, 311, 405, 503, 504, 550
Athenaeus 10, 12, 25, 63, 176, 221, 260, 376, 418, 458, 465, 473, 496, 523, 527, 531, 533, 534, 535, 537, 547, 549, 558, 559, 562, 563, 581, 582, 584, 589, 597, 610, 614, 621, 623, 639, 641, 649
Athenian Archon-years 539
Athenians ... 13, 14, 15, 19, 25, 27, 30, 38, 42, 48, 51, 69, 83, 117, 146, 152, 204, 274, 354, 355, 375, 384, 417, 420, 442, 539, 544, 610, 612
Athenodorus 352
Athenogoras 105
Athenophanes 154
Athens 1, 13, 14, 18, 25, 26, 27, 51, 101, 106, 147, 152, 154, 171, 174, 176, 177, 179, 354, 375, 376, 377, 384, 411, 416, 417, 420, 423, 427, 428, 429, 437, 442, 474, 484, 485, 512, 514, 515, 534, 549, 558, 582, 605, 611, 612, 613, 621, 639, 648
Athmoneus 433
Athos, Mt 177, 482
Atizyes 37
Atkinson, JE 587, 643
Atlantic 326, 361, 503

Atropates 282, 325, 383, 403, 481, 497, 498, 500, 537, 631, 639, 640
Attaginus 25
Attalus 10, 12, 13, 15, 18, 133, 221, 229, 275, 288, 290, 316, 399, 465, 480, 494, 507, 604, 609, 610
Attic calendar .. 411, 414, 416, 423
Attic Lunar Regulatory Calendar 416, 417
Attica 375, 507, 534
Attinas 271
Aturia 433
Audata the Illyrian 465
Augaea 161
augury .. 33, 49, 98, 107, 141, 257, 385, 387, 626
Augustine, St 597, 617
Augustus 591, 651
Aulus Gellius .. 274, 459, 546, 563
Aurisina 487
aurochs 486
Azemilcus 430
Azov, Sea of ... 202, 445, 446, 447, 558, 606, 622

B

Babylon .iv, v, 45, 53, 54, 83, 117, 118, 143, 152, 153, 154, 155, 156, 157, 158, 159, 160, 174, 180, 189, 370, 372, 375, 377, 384, 385, 390, 395, 400, 403, 433, 436, 438, 458, 474, 475, 476, 481, 482, 486, 489, 493, 494, 496, 502, 503, 506, 507, 512, 533, 534, 545, 547, 549, 550, 551, 558, 562, 564, 571, 582, 583, 604, 605, 606, 613, 618, 620, 639, 640, 641, 645, 647, 648
Babylonia . 50, 106, 160, 163, 282, 357, 382, 433, 497, 620, 636

Babyloniaca 563
Babylonian Astronomical Diaries 412, 413, 429
Babylonians ... 128, 154, 159, 390, 393, 620
Bacchae 458
Bactra..... 104, 179, 184, 185, 186, 189, 190, 199, 211, 245, 246, 256, 264, 265, 352, 353, 450, 469, 470, 518, 623, 628, 629
Bactria 69, 104, 106, 126, 153, 184, 186, 195, 211, 228, 239, 241, 244, 254, 260, 261, 265, 266, 278, 279, 301, 335, 352, 403, 441, 446, 456, 457, 468, 469, 470, 472, 504, 532, 541, 549, 605, 625, 627, 635, 646
Bactrians 34, 51, 106, 117, 128, 129, 139, 140, 180, 184, 185, 187, 188, 193, 243, 244, 254, 255, 256, 257, 258, 260, 336, 357, 403
Bactrus, River 245
Badian, E 474, 643
Bagasdaram 307
Bagistanê 383, 481
Bagistanes 189
Bagoas 15, 199, 201, 205, 263, 370, 371, 445, 517, 519, 598, 622, 626, 638, 639
Bagodaras 242, 243, 605, 625
Bagophanes 154, 160
Balacrus 105, 132, 310
Balkh 246, 450, 469
Balls.................................... 440
Balonymus...... 429, 540, 545, 604
Banyan tree.................... 554, 606
Barbarians...... 198, 204, 205, 208, 212, 222, 239, 244, 245, 246, 252, 258, 262, 266, 268, 269, 271, 272, 279, 280, 285, 289, 292, 294, 457, 460, 462, 466, 467, 549
Barcanians 51

Index

Bardon, H 588, 589, 643, 649
Barsine..... 82, 396, 406, 465, 494, 506, 516, 517, 570, 598, 612, 615
Baryaxes 325, 372, 537, 548, 599, 601, 605, 631, 639
Barzaentes 195, 212, 213, 314, 623
Basilica di San Marco.... 486, 488, 510
Basista 272, 273, 627
bastard 495, 496
Baynham, E ... 563, 583, 592, 595, 597, 623, 643, 644
Begram 469
Beira 304
Bel 385, 562
Belephantes..................... 385
Belitae......................... 128
Belus 53, 54, 155, 158
bematists 213, 450, 467
Benefactors 238, 624
Bennett, C 574, 643
Beresford, A 573, 643
Berlin 486, 643, 646, 651
Beroea........................... 497
Berossus.. 562, 563, 571, 606, 620
Berve, H........................... 644
Bessus.... 106, 128, 136, 152, 180, 183, 184, 185, 186, 187, 188, 189, 190, 193, 195, 199, 200, 201, 210, 211, 212, 238, 241, 242, 243, 244, 245, 246, 249, 250, 251, 252, 254, 265, 438, 441, 456, 459, 469, 537, 547, 552, 605, 621, 625, 627, 631
Betis 106, 108, 421, 543, 581, 617
Bibliotheke 2, 538, 577, 585
Bigandar 361
Billows, Richard.... 563, 583, 597, 644
Bion 133, 526
biremes 339
Bithynia 1
Biton 352

Bitter Lake 111
bitumen 90, 107, 154, 155, 157, 158
Black Sea 202, 206, 239, 244, 253, 425, 445, 446, 447, 448, 561, 622
boar 286, 462
Bodyguards 131, 145, 160, 214, 217, 226, 251, 256, 277, 291, 349, 359, 367, 395, 443, 454, 459, 460, 461, 477, 478, 480, 498, 512
Boedromion...... 10, 145, 152, 414, 415, 417, 428, 515, 534, 544
Boeotia............................. 14, 198
Boeotians....... 14, 20, 69, 383, 640
Bolon........................... 225
Borsipa......................... 385
Borysthenes....................... 197
Borza, EN........................ 644, 646
Bosphorus, Cimmerian... 197, 253, 271, 446, 448
Bostock, John.................. 440, 650
Bosworth, AB 1, 265, 415, 433, 470, 471, 481, 483, 489, 518, 522, 523, 529, 532, 534, 539, 545, 563, 565, 566, 567, 568, 569, 580, 583, 585, 589, 590, 597, 606, 643, 644, 647, 652
Boumelus, River..... 119, 432, 434, 435
Boxus 352
Brahmins 358, 582, 636
Branchidae 250, 456, 457, 582, 598, 625
Briseis 421
British Museum....... 443, 444, 508
Brochubelus 189
Brown, T. S. 552, 558, 560, 561, 566, 583, 644
Brundisium........................... 148
Brunt, PA 415, 433, 467, 468, 469, 470, 519, 528, 537, 628, 644, 649

Bruttii 148, 149
Bubacenê 297
Bubaces 186, 188
Bucephala 339, 563, 632, 633
Bucephalus 205, 322, 522, 563, 606, 622, 631, 632
bulls 388, 486
Burstein, SM 649
Byblios 535, 604
Byblos 85, 102, 117, 439, 535, 546, 618
Byzantium 540

C

cadet bursary 334
Cadmeia 13, 14, 19, 22
Cadusians .. 17, 128, 134, 137, 138
Caelius Rufus 580, 581
Caesar 650
Calanus ... 313, 372, 532, 538, 549, 563, 639
Calas 18, 31, 50, 105, 422, 610
Caligula 413, 414, 462
Calis 229
Callicrates 162
Callicratides 83
Callisthenes .... v, 2, 46, 60, 66, 68, 278, 284, 285, 287, 288, 289, 291, 424, 445, 458, 461, 462, 463, 464, 472, 524, 535, 554, 555, 559, 563, 580, 592, 597, 602, 606, 613, 614, 617, 627, 628, 631, 634
caltrops 526
camels 111, 161, 174, 433, 435, 624
Camillus ... 34, 145, 412, 415, 417, 423, 428, 515, 534, 612, 650
Candace 430
Cappadocia ... 50, 56, 60, 103, 198, 240, 403, 426, 614
Cappadocians 128
Caprus, River 433

Caranus 8, 12, 238, 245, 409, 418, 532, 639
Cardia 413, 494, 502, 512, 533, 562, 564, 572, 578, 585, 597, 642, 646
Caria 40, 198, 403, 495, 497
Carians 40, 41
Cariatae 288, 472
Carmania 367, 368, 370, 403, 473, 638
Carthage. 87, 88, 93, 94, 100, 386, 405, 503, 550, 616
Carthaginians 40, 370, 550, 616
Carthasis 255, 626
Caspian v, 51, 128, 195, 199, 201, 202, 206, 240, 244, 438, 441, 445, 447, 448, 522, 547, 551, 558, 561, 604, 606, 622
Caspian Gates 206
Cassander403, 406, 407, 497, 500, 501, 505, 506, 516, 520, 521, 533, 550, 556, 564, 569, 570, 602, 606, 642
Cassandrea 559
Castabalum 63
Castaigne, A .. 252, 276, 296, 321, 346, 350
Castor & Pollux 284
catafalque403, 486, 494, 506, 507, 508
Catanes .. 249, 251, 254, 297, 625, 626, 628
Cataonians 128
catapults 306, 310, 320, 343
Cathaea 553, 632
Cathaeans 329, 632
Catreus 299, 629
Caucasus 104, 166, 206, 240, 244, 297, 403, 446, 469, 604, 622, 625
Caunii 63
cavalry . 67, 68, 71, 72, 73, 77, 81, 118, 119, 120, 127, 128, 129, 132, 133, 134, 136, 138, 139,

Index

140, 142, 144, 146, 159, 165, 168, 169, 174, 179, 184, 189, 190, 200, 209, 211, 212, 217, 221, 222, 227, 231, 233, 238, 239, 253, 254, 258, 259, 261, 262, 264, 265, 271, 280, 459, 518, 519, 520, 521, 526, 612, 615, 623, 626, 633, 635, 637, 642
Cebalinus 214, 215, 216, 217, 219, 223, 224, 225, 452, 623
Celaenae 46
Centauromachy 485
Centaurs 388, 485
Cercatae 201
Ceylon 558
Chaeronea 24, 147, 273, 485
Chalcidice 513
Chaldaeans 385
Chaldeans 53, 154, 158, 385, 390, 404, 458, 481, 562, 641
Chalybes 201
Chandragupta.. 557, 565, 566, 567
Chaonians 410
Chapa, J 573, 643
Chares.... 106, 291, 447, 464, 563, 573, 574, 596, 606, 630, 632
Charidemus 51, 52, 544, 558, 582, 606, 612, 613
Charikar 469
chariots 71, 72, 73, 77, 83, 109, 110, 118, 128, 133, 134, 135, 136, 137, 138, 140, 141, 142, 155, 185, 186, 188, 314, 317, 318, 332, 342, 354, 356, 371, 513, 526, 614, 617, 618, 619, 633, 635
Charus 309, 563, 630
Cheirocrates 482
Chesmeh-i-Ali 200, 468
Chesney 440, 644
Chians 117
Chiliarch .. 64, 160, 484, 489, 518, 519, 520, 521, 647

chiliarchs 160, 479
Chiliarchy 519, 520, 521
Chios 45, 49, 56, 103, 105, 474, 559, 616, 617
Choaspes, River 104, 161, 304
Choerilus 284
Choras 271
Chorienes 293, 294, 466, 472, 518, 548, 592, 628
Chortacana 211, 468
Christianity 208, 442, 488, 495, 583
Chugg, AM 428, 486, 551, 644, 645
Cicero ... 31, 38, 73, 260, 416, 421, 515, 543, 544, 545, 556, 580, 597, 609, 611, 612, 614, 616, 617, 649, 650
Cilicia .... iv, 43, 45, 54, 56, 57, 59, 60, 63, 65, 102, 104, 105, 117, 120, 130, 134, 135, 160, 165, 179, 198, 240, 242, 268, 334, 335, 403, 405, 425, 426, 452, 501, 503, 541, 545, 604, 613
Cilician Sea 48
Cilicians 58, 200, 545
Cithaeron 14
Clarke, ED 508
Claudius .. 398, 495, 585, 586, 587
Cleadas 24
Cleander 46, 92, 235, 236, 368, 455, 638
Cleitarchus i, v, vii, 1, 2, 3, 4, 5, 6, 7, 8, 15, 23, 25, 27, 30, 32, 34, 38, 40, 43, 44, 46, 51, 63, 68, 73, 83, 88, 94, 95, 96, 117, 118, 122, 127, 132, 137, 143, 146, 148, 151, 152, 153, 154, 155, 160, 168, 176, 183, 193, 196, 197, 202, 203, 206, 208, 210, 213, 246, 247, 253, 260, 264, 266, 268, 272, 278, 294, 298, 299, 300, 301, 306, 313, 314, 316, 329, 349, 356, 376, 382,

383, 386, 387, 390, 403, 404, 405, 409, 411, 412, 413, 414, 416, 417, 418, 419, 420, 421, 422, 423, 424, 425, 427, 428, 429, 439, 442, 443, 445, 446, 447, 448, 451, 465, 466, 467, 468, 469, 470, 472, 473, 474, 475, 476, 477, 481, 482, 490, 491, 492, 493, 494, 495, 496, 497, 498, 499, 502, 505, 506, 507, 509, 510, 511, 514, 515, 516, 520, 523, 529, 530, 531, 532, 533, 534, 535, 536, 537, 538, 539, 540, 541, 542, 543, 544, 545, 546, 547, 548, 549, 551, 552, 554, 555, 556, 557, 558, 559, 560, 561, 562, 563, 564, 565, 567, 568, 569, 570, 571, 572, 573, 574, 575, 576, 577, 578, 579, 580, 581, 582, 583, 584, 585, 586, 587, 588, 589, 590, 591, 592, 593, 594, 595, 596, 597, 598, 599, 600, 601, 602, 603, 604, 605, 606, 607, 609, 610, 611, 612, 613, 614, 615, 616, 617, 618, 619, 620, 621, 622, 623, 624, 625, 626, 627, 628, 629, 630, 631, 632, 633, 634, 635, 636, 637, 638, 639, 640, 641, 642, 644, 645, 646, 647, 652
Cleitus .... v, 36, 43, 132, 231, 271, 272, 273, 274, 275, 276, 278, 288, 290, 291, 295, 313, 382, 458, 459, 460, 470, 501, 520, 551, 627, 628
Clement of Alexandria ... 420, 557, 565, 609, 611
Clement of Alexandria 30, 416
Clement of Alexandria 515
Clement of Alexandria 543
Clement of Alexandria 544
Cleochares 313, 314
Cleomantis the Lacedaemonian 460
Cleomenes 115, 498, 501
Cleon of Sicily 284, 285
Cleopatra 10, 12, 418, 465, 609
Cleophis .. 304, 306, 307, 583, 630
Climax, Mt .... v, 46, 424
Cnidus 411, 649
Codommanus 17
Coenus 68, 132, 145, 168, 169, 217, 222, 226, 271, 304, 311, 318, 319, 337, 338, 375, 403, 453, 500, 501, 619, 633
Cohortandus 294, 466
Colophon 554, 568
Companion Cavalry . 77, 403, 494, 497, 519, 520, 521, 526
Companions 277, 386, 480
comus 176, 303, 368, 390, 437, 473, 613, 621, 629, 638
Conon 518
conspiracy 213, 451, 452, 462, 463, 472
Cophen 301, 472
Cophes 266, 269, 270
Coragus 635
Corianus 466, 593
Corinth .... iv, 8, 14, 16, 105, 193, 205, 567, 609, 616, 619, 621
Corinthians 386
Corragus 354, 355
Corycus 57
Cossaeans 128, 139, 384, 481, 498, 641
Cothelas 465
cotton 298
Craneion 14
Crannon 493
Crassus 536
Craterus 68, 90, 92, 132, 167, 168, 169, 174, 200, 203, 211, 212, 216, 217, 226, 254, 256, 263, 271, 297, 301, 316, 318, 320, 339, 349, 356, 357, 367, 369,

Index

382, 386, 398, 405, 406, 452, 453, 469, 472, 498, 501, 503, 525, 634, 636, 638, 640
Crateuas 498, 501
Cretaceous 487
Cretans 64, 68, 102
Crete 64, 102, 117, 133, 376, 494, 554, 616
Critobulus 348, 549, 605, 635
Croesus 56
Cronos 95, 568, 616
Ctesias 535, 560, 562, 614, 620
cupbearer 406
Curtius v, vii, 1, 2, 3, 4, 12, 43, 46, 51, 56, 60, 66, 70, 73, 77, 83, 84, 85, 92, 94, 95, 96, 100, 101, 108, 118, 119, 122, 125, 127, 132, 136, 137, 143, 145, 146, 148, 153, 154, 158, 159, 160, 163, 165, 168, 169, 172, 175, 179, 183, 187, 189, 199, 202, 207, 210, 211, 213, 215, 216, 220, 224, 226, 230, 231, 236, 238, 239, 241, 242, 246, 247, 248, 250, 251, 252, 253, 254, 255, 259, 260, 261, 263, 265, 266, 267, 268, 270, 272, 275, 282, 291, 294, 298, 299, 301, 304, 314, 332, 349, 351, 352, 375, 379, 381, 397, 398, 402, 403, 404, 405, 415, 418, 420, 421, 424, 426, 427, 428, 429, 430, 431, 434, 435, 436, 437, 438, 440, 442, 445, 446, 447, 448, 451, 452, 453, 454, 455, 456, 457, 459, 460, 463, 464, 466, 468, 469, 470, 475, 476, 480, 481, 483, 485, 492, 494, 495, 496, 497, 498, 499, 502, 503, 504, 509, 510, 516, 517, 518, 520, 522, 523, 524, 526, 527, 529, 532, 533, 535, 537, 538, 539, 541, 542, 543, 545, 546, 547, 548, 549, 551, 553, 554, 555, 556, 557, 558, 559, 560, 561, 562, 563, 564, 567, 569, 570, 578, 579, 580, 581, 582, 583, 584, 585, 586, 587, 588, 589, 590, 591, 592, 593, 594, 595, 596, 597, 598, 599, 600, 602, 607, 613, 614, 615, 616, 617, 618, 619, 620, 621, 622, 623, 624, 625, 626, 627, 628, 629, 630, 631, 632, 633, 634, 635, 636, 637, 638, 639, 640, 641, 642, 643, 646, 647, 648, 649
Cyclades 45
Cydnus 57, 58, 614
Cymê 170
Cynical school 44
Cynics 2, 14, 15, 208, 299, 419, 420, 442, 551, 583, 587
Cynna 465
Cypriots 98, 117
Cyprus 92, 102, 370, 405, 489, 503, 615, 647
Cyrene 110, 567, 617
Cyropaidia 196, 437, 441, 442, 443, 595
Cyropolis 254, 469
Cyrrhus 405, 503
Cyrus .... v, 56, 128, 136, 174, 196, 199, 238, 253, 254, 255, 371, 437, 441, 442, 443, 552, 582, 624
Cyrus the Younger 441, 536
Cyzicus 17, 18, 610

D

Dadipharta 60, 426
Daedalian Mountains 303
Dahae 128, 199, 242, 258, 271, 281, 282, 317, 320, 335, 547, 627, 628
Daisios 34, 423, 512, 612

Damascus 63, 65, 81, 84, 126, 452, 507, 516, 536, 615
Damghan 467
Danube 18, 126, 248, 256, 610
Dardanians 11
Darius iv, v, 16, 17, 27, 33, 35, 37, 39, 40, 45, 46, 48, 49, 50, 51, 52, 53, 54, 55, 56, 57, 58, 59, 60, 63, 64, 65, 66, 67, 68, 69, 70, 71, 72, 73, 74, 75, 76, 77, 78, 80, 81, 82, 83, 84, 85, 87, 102, 103, 104, 105, 106, 107, 110, 117, 118, 119, 121, 122, 123, 124, 125, 126, 127, 128, 129, 130, 131, 133, 134, 136, 138, 139, 140, 141, 142, 143, 144, 145, 152, 153, 155, 161, 162, 163, 164, 173, 174, 179, 180, 183, 184, 185, 186, 187, 188, 189, 190, 191, 192, 193, 194, 195, 196, 197, 199, 200, 201, 203, 204, 205, 208, 209, 210, 228, 238, 242, 246, 247, 249, 251, 256, 265, 275, 294, 314, 350, 371, 373, 380, 386, 394, 396, 403, 415, 424, 426, 427, 428, 429, 432, 433, 434, 435, 437, 438, 439, 441, 442, 443, 445, 452, 453, 455, 457, 459, 465, 466, 467, 468, 487, 504, 516, 517, 519, 520, 521, 526, 527, 533, 537, 540, 542, 544, 545, 546, 554, 558, 562, 582, 583, 584, 592, 604, 606, 610, 612, 613, 614, 615, 617, 618, 619, 620, 621, 623
Dascylion 38, 424
Dataphernes 249, 282, 625, 628
de Vaugelas 207, 236
Deinocrates 482
Deinon 63, 162, 300, 533, 535, 541, 544, 554, 560, 582, 606, 610, 612, 614, 620, 623, 624, 629
Deipnosophistae 649
Delos 405, 503
Delphi iv, v, 8, 20, 26, 27, 28, 113, 148, 167, 333, 405, 420, 503, 544, 553, 582, 604, 606, 611
Delphians 386
Delphic Oracle 148, 167
Delta Engraver 407
Demades 26, 27, 610
Demaratus 205, 559, 606
Demetrius 203, 214, 219, 229, 407, 489, 547, 563, 567, 570, 580, 583, 597, 606, 622, 650
Democrates of Athens 204
Demophon 343
Demosthenes ... 13, 14, 15, 19, 25, 26, 51, 376, 420, 421, 610, 611, 639
Derbices 51
Derdas 253, 271, 465
Deuriopus 499
Dexippus. 403, 496, 501, 519, 649
Dia 413
diadem ... 180, 208, 241, 390, 395, 396, 401, 443, 475, 481, 485, 527, 537, 538, 623, 641
Dialogues of the Dead ... 506, 507, 650
Diardines 298
Dicaearchus 465, 623
didaskalos 574
Dido 88
Didyma 456, 457
Didymeon 250, 456
dimachae 189
Dimnus .. 213, 214, 215, 216, 218, 219, 220, 223, 224, 228, 449, 451, 455, 623
Dio Cassius 589, 649
Diodorus .. vii, 1, 2, 3, 4, 8, 10, 12, 13, 18, 23, 24, 27, 32, 36, 37, 39, 41, 43, 44, 51, 56, 73, 77, 83, 85, 89, 92, 94, 96, 97, 100, 101, 103, 118, 122, 127, 132,

Index

137, 143, 145, 147, 148, 152, 153, 155, 157, 158, 159, 160, 163, 165, 179, 180, 193, 196, 202, 211, 213, 216, 226, 230, 240, 241, 242, 250, 263, 265, 268, 272, 282, 314, 352, 377, 383, 388, 402, 403, 405, 409, 413, 414, 415, 416, 417, 418, 419, 420, 421, 422, 424, 427, 429, 431, 434, 437, 438, 440, 445, 446, 451, 457, 467, 468, 469, 474, 477, 479, 480, 481, 482, 483, 486, 489, 494, 495, 496, 497, 498, 499, 502, 503, 504, 505, 507, 509, 515, 519, 520, 522, 523, 524, 527, 529, 530, 532, 533, 534, 535, 536, 537, 538, 539, 540, 541, 542, 543, 544, 545, 546, 547, 548, 549, 551, 552, 554, 555, 556, 557, 558, 559, 560, 561, 562, 563, 564, 568, 569, 570, 577, 578, 579, 580, 581, 582, 583, 584, 585, 586, 587, 589, 590, 591, 592, 594, 595, 596, 598, 599, 601, 602, 604, 605, 607, 609, 610, 611, 612, 613, 614, 615, 616, 617, 618, 619, 620, 621, 622, 623, 624, 625, 626, 627, 628, 629, 630, 631, 632, 633, 634, 635, 636, 637, 638, 639, 640, 641, 642, 644, 646, 649

Diogenes..... iii, iv, v, 8, 14, 15, 16, 113, 115, 301, 419, 441, 490, 531, 532, 538, 553, 567, 573, 576, 583, 610, 639, 649

Diogenes Laertius..... 15, 412, 419, 441, 531, 532, 538, 553, 567, 574, 576, 583, 610, 639, 649

Diogenes of Sinope......... 553, 583

Diomedes............................... 148

Dionysus..... 69, 79, 177, 263, 277, 278, 284, 285, 301, 302, 303, 336, 342, 356, 367, 548, 582, 605, 626, 627, 629, 635

Dios 413

Dioscuri 460

Dioxenus 214

Dioxippus 354, 355, 356, 582, 635

Dirke 20

Discourses of Epictetus ... 517, 649

Disorderly Division 237

Ditamenes 282

Dium 29, 405, 503

Diyllus..... 533, 539, 579, 584, 609, 610, 616, 619, 620, 621, 623, 624, 633, 634, 637, 639, 640, 641

Dodona 148, 405, 503

Dog Star 17, 637

dogs 302, 331, 332, 632

dolphins 298

Domitian 589

Don, River...... 197, 242, 253, 255, 285, 446, 469, 626

Dorians 30, 420

doryphoroi 477, 480, 481

Drangiana 213, 367, 403, 450, 468

Drangians 212, 213, 238, 449, 450, 451

Drapis 301

Dropides 83

dropsy 406

Drypetis 373

Duris 447, 539, 580, 585, 596, 623

E

eagles.... 9, 54, 141, 240, 388, 407, 484

Ecbatana. 104, 153, 179, 189, 196, 235, 265, 382, 383, 438, 441, 481, 627, 640

eclipse 417

eclipses... 121, 415, 416, 428, 429, 431, 434, 435, 512, 515, 537, 583, 601, 618

665

Eclogae 387, 474, 475
Egypt...iv, v, 2, 30, 64, 72, 83, 97, 98, 102, 103, 107, 109, 110, 111, 115, 117, 121, 134, 203, 260, 403, 405, 407, 411, 421, 424, 427, 428, 429, 430, 431, 432, 439, 451, 459, 474, 480, 482, 487, 494, 498, 499, 504, 506, 507, 509, 524, 527, 534, 546, 559, 564, 568, 573, 597, 616, 617, 618, 643
Egypt Exploration Society 573, 643
Egyptians. 102, 103, 110, 121, 404
Egyptology 510, 645
Einquellenprinzip... 538, 570, 577, 578, 579, 584, 585, 595, 599, 607
El Hamman 440
Elaphthonius 286
Elburz Mountains 441
Eleians 13, 19, 193, 386
elephants 161, 298, 300, 311, 312, 314, 318, 319, 320, 322, 323, 332, 334, 337, 339, 349, 358, 524, 558, 566, 630, 631, 633, 636, 646
Eleumezen 339
Elimiotis 132
Elizabeth 1 511
Engels, D.. 37, 211, 423, 433, 439, 467, 468, 469, 470, 535, 536, 545, 645
England 516
English 454
Eordaea 493, 494
Ephemerides... 413, 479, 492, 502, 512, 565, 649
Ephesus 9, 298, 456, 482, 512, 543, 544, 556, 609, 612
Ephialtes 42, 43
Ephippus . 562, 565, 606, 640, 641
Ephorus 533, 540
Epidaurians 386

Epigoni .. 210, 473, 548, 549, 605, 629, 639
epilepsy 495
Epimenes 286, 287
Epirotes 410
Epirus.10, 148, 370, 410, 546, 619
equinox 10, 417, 418, 429, 431, 530, 602
Eratosthenes... 447, 527, 537, 561, 562, 574, 575, 609, 622
Eressos 45
Erigyius ... 32, 132, 200, 203, 217, 238, 245, 246, 256, 257, 280, 422, 625
Errington, RM 645
Ersilaus 116
Erymanthian boar 581
Erythraean Sea 297, 361, 370, 375, 473, 649
Erythrus 298, 370
Ethiopia . 111, 115, 430, 431, 508, 589
Ethiopic 2
Ethymantus, River .. 246, 298, 447
Etymologiae 332, 632
Euainetos 30
Euboea 45, 128
Euctemon 170, 171, 173
Eudamas 370, 565, 567
Eudoxus of Cnidus 411, 412
Euergetae 238, 468, 554, 606, 624
Euergetes 576
Euios 383
Eumenes 330, 383, 403, 413, 465, 481, 492, 494, 497, 500, 501, 512, 520, 521, 533, 564, 640, 650
eunuchs 56, 77, 79, 106, 122, 124, 125, 152, 162, 186, 188, 209, 443, 517, 519, 618
Euphrates 48, 53, 63, 83, 103, 104, 117, 118, 119, 125, 126, 127, 135, 153, 156, 334, 365, 370,

Index

385, 393, 399, 428, 439, 503, 527, 535, 536, 637, 638, 644
Euripides 251, 274, 276, 410, 457, 458, 459, 461
Europa 12, 418, 465
Europe 8, 9, 10, 30, 32, 33, 50, 69, 102, 148, 171, 173, 177, 193, 197, 209, 253, 255, 256, 259, 261, 295, 351, 375, 376, 379, 380, 385, 386, 396, 398, 403, 405, 406, 446, 448, 498, 504, 507, 537, 540, 546, 569, 587, 604, 609, 619, 639
Europus 493
Eurydike 419
Eurylochus 287, 288
Euxine 48, 202, 244, 425, 445, 446, 497, 561, 604, 606, 622
Events after Alexander .. 494, 496, 506, 516, 519, 521, 645
Exiles Decree 474, 640

F

Farah 213, 235, 450, 468
Fate 385, 388, 390, 395, 401
Favoured Villages 202
Fear 130, 132
figs 202
First Division of the Satrapies 402, 494, 495, 496, 497, 498, 499, 500, 501, 506, 534, 605, 642
flogging 463
Florilegium 531, 535
Fontana, M. 645
Fortune... 2, 35, 45, 59, 61, 66, 67, 76, 80, 82, 86, 99, 102, 103, 104, 105, 115, 135, 138, 143, 147, 152, 161, 162, 175, 183, 188, 208, 212, 231, 260, 261, 266, 281, 294, 316, 344, 350, 351, 355, 368, 395, 442, 596
Fraser, PM 431, 645
Fraxkar-Peroz 450

Freiburg Papyrus 488
Freinshem 379, 476, 588, 593, 649
Friends.. 10, 29, 30, 46, 51, 52, 54, 60, 61, 77, 97, 115, 131, 132, 144, 159, 175, 183, 196, 213, 214, 216, 217, 218, 226, 229, 232, 234, 237, 247, 253, 256, 272, 273, 275, 284, 293, 294, 295, 313, 323, 328, 339, 341, 344, 348, 349, 350, 352, 354, 355, 364, 368, 371, 373, 376, 379, 382, 383, 385, 386, 387, 388, 390, 391, 395, 396, 404, 406, 441, 453, 458, 467, 479, 490, 493, 512, 532, 562
Frontinus 247, 316, 544, 547, 597, 612, 625, 628
Full Moon 411, 417, 428, 512

G

Gabiene 499
Gades 370
Gandara 329
Gangabae 81
Gangaridae 332, 333, 334, 633
Ganges.... 297, 298, 332, 340, 342, 373, 472, 557, 558, 565, 567, 606, 629, 633
Garfield, James 461
Gaugamela ... v, 34, 411, 412, 413, 414, 416, 417, 423, 427, 428, 431, 432, 433, 435, 436, 440, 480, 515, 519, 526, 527, 537, 546, 601, 604, 617, 618, 619, 647
Gauls 386
Gaza .... iv, 83, 102, 104, 105, 106, 109, 110, 421, 427, 429, 540, 543, 546, 557, 604, 606, 617
Gazaba 291, 293, 472
Gedrosia 473, 525, 554, 638
Gendari Mt 343, 472
Geographia 425, 435, 440, 651

German 486
Getae 375
Ghazni 469
Giza 504
Glaucias 505
Glaukos 383
Glycera 375, 376
Gobares 174
Google 246, 469
Goralski, WJ 645
Gordian knot 230, 545, 613
Gordion .. 48, 49, 50, 56, 426, 545, 624
Gordius 48, 49
Gordyaean Mountains 121, 153, 434
Gorgatas 233
Gorgias 233, 382
Gortuae 128
Goukowsky, P 645
Granicus .. iv, v, 29, 34, 35, 37, 39, 48, 69, 120, 134, 135, 272, 335, 422, 423, 424, 458, 459, 504, 611, 612, 646
Great King 20, 439, 442, 518
Great Lacuna 542
Great Mysteries 534
Greece ... iv, 3, 4, 8, 18, 20, 22, 26, 30, 38, 45, 64, 67, 69, 81, 82, 84, 89, 92, 102, 103, 105, 117, 121, 122, 132, 135, 139, 145, 146, 153, 159, 160, 163, 165, 166, 167, 170, 171, 172, 176, 177, 183, 184, 186, 187, 188, 189, 195, 212, 245, 250, 274, 326, 339, 351, 353, 375, 384, 406, 417, 420, 431, 437, 438, 440, 456, 457, 458, 465, 481, 503, 504, 512, 513, 515, 517, 530, 536, 540, 547, 550, 551, 570, 578, 579, 604, 609, 619, 622, 625, 626, 633, 636, 641, 644, 646, 648, 650

Greek ... v, 2, 8, 10, 13, 14, 15, 17, 20, 21, 24, 25, 29, 30, 32, 40, 46, 49, 51, 52, 53, 56, 186, 195, 197, 199, 203, 204, 210, 231, 238, 239, 253, 255, 263, 264, 273, 298, 299, 301, 302, 304, 308, 316, 320, 333, 339, 348, 352, 355, 376, 383, 385, 386, 409, 410, 411, 413, 414, 415, 416, 418, 420, 422, 425, 443, 447, 449, 450, 460, 469, 474, 475, 477, 479, 481, 484, 486, 489, 496, 504, 508, 509, 530, 534, 539, 559, 563, 565, 566, 571, 579, 580, 582, 585, 587, 589, 591, 593, 597, 600
Greeks. iv, 1, 5, 12, 13, 18, 20, 23, 24, 25, 29, 32, 45, 48, 53, 64, 65, 74, 83, 84, 86, 102, 105, 117, 122, 145, 148, 152, 162, 169, 170, 172, 173, 176, 177, 179, 185, 186, 197, 204, 235, 239, 260, 261, 264, 265, 268, 274, 282, 284, 291, 341, 352, 353, 354, 355, 377, 385, 409, 422, 435, 436, 437, 446, 457, 461, 484, 485, 496, 504, 512, 518, 519, 549, 554, 559, 605, 613, 621, 635, 640, 641, 646
Gregorian calendar 417, 428, 512, 530
Grynion 18
Grzybek, E 413, 645
Guiteau, Charles 461
Gunderson, LJ 646
gymnosophist ... 15, 419, 531, 553, 557, 594, 595, 606, 637, 639

H

Hades 395
Hadrian 1
Hages 317

Index

Halicarnassus.... iv, 29, 40, 43, 63, 160, 274, 412, 541, 544, 604, 612
Halys, River................... 103, 125
Hamah 536
Hamilton 414, 551, 553, 559, 560, 568, 569, 578, 579, 596, 607, 614, 615, 616, 618, 621, 623, 632, 636, 638, 641, 646
Hammond 154, 228, 413, 416, 497, 515, 519, 523, 533, 534, 539, 543, 546, 553, 554, 555, 556, 557, 558, 559, 560, 561, 562, 563, 564, 568, 570, 579, 584, 596, 609, 610, 611, 612, 613, 614, 615, 616, 617, 618, 619, 620, 621, 622, 623, 624, 625, 626, 627, 628, 629, 630, 631, 632, 633, 634, 635, 636, 637, 638, 639, 640, 641, 642, 646
Hanging Gardens... 158, 562, 606, 620
harem 583, 623
harmamaxes................................ 55
Harmatelia 358, 359, 636
harpagones................................. 88
Harpalus. v, 18, 31, 308, 339, 375, 376, 422, 473, 474, 540, 549, 559, 605, 606, 639
Harpocration 532, 536, 619
Hatzilambrou, R 573, 643
Haustanes.............................. 297
hawks... 55
Hazarapatis 518
Heaven.................... 121, 284, 285
Hecataeus............ 13, 15, 233, 447
Hecatombaeon ... 8, 101, 411, 416, 427, 428, 431, 512, 514, 515, 543
Hecatompylus 197, 200, 441, 467, 468, 547, 604, 621
Heckel.... 529, 532, 551, 556, 559, 564, 567, 568, 570, 579, 585, 591, 592, 594, 596, 597, 606, 609, 610, 619, 625, 628, 631, 636, 642, 646, 648, 649, 650
Hector............ 116, 222, 410, 421
Hedicke, E............... 588, 589, 649
Hegelochus....... 49, 105, 106, 115, 227, 228, 453, 454, 455, 617
Hegesias 9, 108, 543, 557, 580, 596, 598, 606, 617, 650
Hegesimachus 315
Heidelberg Epitome 495
Helenus 410
Hellanice 272
Hellas 461
Hellenes.................. 176, 383, 386
Hellenics 513
Hellenicus 161
Hellenistic tombs 486
Hellespont ... iv, 17, 29, 30, 34, 49, 58, 79, 84, 103, 104, 125, 134, 198, 199, 335, 351, 403, 483
Hellespontine Phrygia............. 403
Helmand, River 246, 447, 468, 623
Heneti....................................... 50
Hephaistion .. v, 31, 79, 80, 81, 85, 104, 145, 168, 169, 196, 217, 226, 256, 263, 271, 272, 278, 284, 301, 311, 313, 318, 319, 329, 332, 339, 365, 373, 375, 383, 384, 385, 386, 387, 388, 389, 394, 403, 405, 421, 463, 472, 474, 475, 480, 481, 482, 483, 484, 485, 486, 488, 489, 490, 493, 494, 502, 504, 517, 518, 519, 520, 521, 545, 548, 550, 551, 562, 589, 606, 614, 619, 630, 632, 634, 640, 641, 647, 648
Hephaistos............................. 484
Heracles.. 8, 13, 25, 30, 40, 65, 69, 81, 82, 86, 89, 94, 101, 117, 123, 126, 131, 135, 180, 199, 200, 222, 224, 232, 233, 257, 284, 285, 289, 301, 308, 309,

669

318, 334, 336, 339, 342, 355, 361, 370, 378, 379, 380, 386, 391, 394, 396, 405, 406, 409, 420, 465, 494, 503, 504, 506, 516, 527, 534, 543, 562, 570, 581, 582, 629, 630, 634, 637, 639, 641
Heraclids .. 30, 416, 420, 421, 515, 543, 544, 555, 604
Heracon 368
Herat 211, 213, 450, 468
Hermione 161
Hermolaus 286, 287, 288, 289, 290, 462, 463
Herodotus ... 25, 50, 177, 383, 409, 457, 484, 558, 606, 613, 650
Herons 299
Herostratus 512
hetaera 176, 177, 437
hetairoi 477, 479
Hiarotis 329, 472
Hieronymus 405, 494, 502, 533, 538, 550, 562, 564, 570, 572, 574, 578, 585, 597, 599, 606, 642, 646
Himalayas 446, 588
Hindu Kush 351, 446, 469, 547, 604, 625
Hipparch 494, 519, 520
Hipparchy 520, 521
Hippocrates 412
Hippostratus 465
hippotoxotae 317, 320
Hissar Range 470
History Concerning Alexander 63, 149, 429, 523
Histos 532, 534, 545, 568, 569, 575, 580, 589, 590, 644, 647
Holcias ... 492, 499, 501, 556, 592, 606
Holt, F 646
Homer 15, 31, 105, 113, 305, 419, 422, 478, 483, 489, 508, 581, 650

Homs 536
Hormuz, Strait of 473
Hornblower, ... 585
Hornblower, J 533, 538, 550, 564, 572, 578, 585, 597, 642, 646
horoscopes 431, 516
House of the Faun 443
Howard, CL 646
Hunt, JM 483, 489, 646, 647
Hyacinthus 26
Hydarnes 105
Hydaspes 312, 314, 317, 321, 327, 334, 339, 340, 472, 522, 524, 548, 551, 563, 605, 631, 633, 634
Hydraotis .... *See* Hiarotis
hypaspists 132, 168, 211, 261, 262, 345, 381, 477, 478, 479, 480, 481, 493, 628
Hypereides 27, 420, 543, 582, 611
Hyphasis . 332, 335, 472, 560, 633
hypomnemata 502, 550
Hypsides 258
Hyrcania .. 68, 104, 189, 190, 197, 199, 200, 201, 202, 203, 204, 206, 282, 403, 441, 448, 467, 468, 517, 520, 547, 551, 553, 604, 606, 622
Hyrcanians. 34, 51, 202, 205, 206, 240, 468, 553
Hystaspes 196, 433, 442

I

Iberia 370, 405
Ichor 305
Ichthyophagoi. 473, 549, 554, 605
Ida 17
Ida, Mt 17
Idaean Dactyls 17
Iliad..305, 351, 483, 581, 634, 650
Ilians 504
Ilium 405
Illyria 69, 212, 378, 499

Index

Illyrians....... 9, 11, 18, 31, 69, 133, 198, 228, 273, 351, 386, 403, 422, 465, 500, 513
Imbros..................................... 106
Immortals................................... 54
India v, 15, 69, 104, 126, 132, 139, 161, 197, 202, 210, 213, 231, 238, 240, 244, 246, 260, 268, 280, 297, 298, 299, 300, 301, 308, 313, 314, 325, 326, 328, 332, 334, 337, 339, 340, 341, 342, 351, 352, 354, 356, 357, 358, 361, 367, 369, 373, 375, 376, 403, 414, 419, 441, 445, 447, 464, 468, 469, 472, 473, 475, 498, 502, 504, 510, 511, 524, 525, 531, 532, 537, 542, 548, 549, 550, 551, 552, 554, 556, 557, 564, 565, 566, 567, 572, 581, 582, 587, 588, 589, 595, 601, 605, 623, 628, 629, 630, 631, 632, 633, 634, 636, 637, 638, 639, 640, 645
Indians 51, 117, 128, 184, 199, 242, 290, 299, 300, 306, 307, 309, 310, 311, 312, 314, 315, 317, 318, 319, 320, 323, 326, 327, 330, 334, 337, 340, 343, 344, 345, 348, 349, 354, 357, 365, 549, 565, 566, 583, 605, 635, 636, 637
Indica... vii, 1, 168, 297, 298, 313, 414, 419, 467, 516, 517, 528, 537, 551, 552, 553, 554, 555, 556, 557, 561, 565, 566, 567, 592, 594, 629, 632, 635, 637, 638, 644, 649
Indus 239, 297, 301, 308, 311, 312, 340, 342, 361, 365, 447, 472, 517, 522, 547, 549, 566, 581, 582, 605, 630, 632, 634, 635, 637
Indus Delta...................... 361, 472
Indus, River 239
invictus 543, 617
Iolaus....................................... 214
Iollas....... 406, 490, 491, 556, 564, 569, 606, 642
Iomanes 298, 557, 606, 629
Ionia 34, 35, 84, 104
Ionians................................... 198
Iphicrates................................. 83
Ipsus 37, 423, 566
Iraq 154, 432, 433
Iraq Petroleum Company 433
Iron Gate Pass 470
Isfahan................................... 441
Ishtar 486
Ishtar Gate 157, 486
Isidore of Seville 332, 632
Isidorus of Charax.................. 450
Islam............................... 208, 442
Isocrates 474
Issus...... iv, v, 4, 36, 46, 48, 63, 64, 66, 68, 70, 71, 73, 75, 83, 102, 103, 105, 119, 424, 425, 427, 428, 429, 437, 439, 487, 541, 545, 558, 604, 614, 616, 617, 618
Istanbul................................. 446
Ister 126, 162, 248, 256, 447
Isthmian Games....... 105, 567, 616
isthmus 19, 48, 177, 202, 425, 446, 513, 604, 622
Italy 147, 148, 274, 370, 386, 458, 474, 539, 546, 584, 619, 639
Itinerarium Alexandri 1, 106, 511, 597, 650
ivy 263, 548

J

Jacoby ..vii, 25, 30, 38, 46, 63, 73, 95, 117, 148, 155, 176, 202, 203, 206, 278, 313, 356, 376, 386, 387, 390, 416, 420, 424, 439, 450, 473, 474, 475, 515, 527, 529, 531, 532, 533, 534,

535, 537, 538, 539, 541, 543, 544, 545, 547, 548, 549, 552, 554, 555, 556, 557, 558, 560, 562, 564, 567, 568, 569, 577, 578, 580, 581, 594, 607, 608, 609, 610, 611, 612, 613, 614, 616, 618, 619, 620, 621, 622, 629, 630, 631, 632, 634, 635, 636, 637, 638, 639, 641, 646
Jaxartes, River 197, 242, 255, 445, 446, 447, 448, 469
Josephus 413, 414, 563
Julian (Emperor) 536
Julian calendar 8, 34, 101, 121, 152, 411, 413, 414, 415, 416, 417, 423, 428, 431, 435, 512, 513, 524, 529, 530, 533, 534, 537, 601, 602, 612, 616, 618
Julius Caesar 414
Jumna 298, 557, 629
Justin 2, 3, 4, 10, 12, 23, 25, 29, 32, 34, 60, 77, 83, 85, 88, 103, 118, 122, 127, 153, 159, 169, 170, 196, 206, 210, 221, 228, 230, 255, 275, 282, 291, 377, 396, 397, 398, 402, 403, 404, 405, 410, 411, 413, 414, 418, 419, 420, 421, 422, 426, 427, 429, 431, 441, 455, 459, 469, 472, 477, 481, 483, 492, 494, 495, 496, 497, 498, 499, 502, 505, 513, 514, 520, 524, 527, 529, 532, 533, 537, 541, 542, 543, 544, 546, 547, 548, 551, 554, 556, 560, 562, 563, 564, 566, 578, 579, 581, 582, 583, 584, 585, 591, 592, 594, 596, 597, 599, 607, 609, 610, 611, 612, 613, 614, 615, 617, 618, 619, 620, 621, 622, 623, 624, 625, 626, 627, 628, 629, 630, 631, 632, 633, 634, 635, 636, 637, 638, 639, 640, 641, 642, 649, 650

K

Kabul 469
Kabul River 472
Kafirnigan River 470
Kalat-i-Nadiri 211, 468
Kandahar 238, 450, 468, 469
Karachi 473
Karageorghis, V 489, 647
Karai 382, 481, 640
Karemlesh 434, 435
Karnak 432
Karun, River 163, 440
Kashka-Darya 279, 471
Kasta Mound 410
Katalogeion 574, 575
Kedrosia 365, 367, 403, 549
Kedrosians 238, 365
Kelones 382, 481, 640
Kennedy, John 461
Kerch, Strait of 197, 253, 446
Khawak Pass 469
Khazir, River .. 119, 433, 434, 435
Khewra 339, 548, 634
Khodjend 469
Khujand 255, 469
Kinch 428
Kirkuk 154, 433
Kmt 510, 645
Kochka River 265, 470
Ko-Komle 435
Koldewey, R .. 156, 157, 486, 489, 647
kopis sword 320, 334, 487
Kos 43, 49, 576
Kroll, G 430, 651
Kunduz 265, 470
Kushka 211, 468
Kyme 540

L

Lacedemonians 193
Laconia 376, 384

Index

lacuna..... 108, 146, 379, 381, 476, 481, 625, 626, 629, 630, 639, 640
Lagos 494
Lagus 403, 418, 451, 460, 464, 494, 550, 569
Lamian War........................... 384
Lampsacus............................. 576
Laomedon............... 403, 500, 501
Lapiths................................... 485
Larissa 10, 398, 418, 447, 465, 496, 558
Lasjerd................................... 441
Last Plans 405, 489, 502, 505, 550, 642
Latin... 2, 3, 4, 55, 66, 70, 73, 125, 145, 158, 199, 210, 213, 224, 226, 239, 253, 261, 263, 270, 301, 304, 404, 447, 451, 454, 455, 463, 464, 476, 477, 543, 561, 586, 587, 591, 593, 600
Laurel..................................... 303
Laws... 417
Le Brun, Charles..................... 324
League of Corinth...... 24, 25, 105, 193, 616, 619, 621
Lebanon 370, 639
Leo... 412
Leonidas 237
Leonnatus 78, 108, 217, 275, 287, 318, 319, 345, 364, 365, 367, 398, 399, 403, 480, 493, 494, 500, 501, 635, 638
Leontiscus.............................. 569
leopards 154, 158
Leos 26
Leosthenes 384, 481, 504
Lesbos............ 45, 49, 56, 105, 352
Leucosyri 201
Leuctra............................... 21, 22
Levant..................... 439, 527, 618
Levantine littoral 535, 546
Libanius 510
Libanus, Mount............ 83, 89, 90

Liber de Morte 419, 491, 492, 496, 499, 506, 556, 564, 592, 606, 642, 650
Liber de Spectaculis........ 589, 650
Library................................ 649, 652
Libya .. 30, 39, 115, 117, 386, 405, 421
Libyans................... 386, 403, 405
lice................................... 291, 464
Limnaeus........................ 345, 635
Lincoln, Abraham 461
lions 154, 158, 331, 339, 356, 388, 486, 508, 632
Livy .. 27, 274, 402, 420, 459, 543, 546, 582, 591, 592, 611, 619, 641, 650
Locrians................................. 132
Loeb 405, 476, 482, 503, 519, 588, 644, 648, 649, 650, 651
Loios 8, 411, 512
London 650
Lorber, C 432, 647
Lucanians 149
Lucian 388, 408, 484, 485, 489, 506, 507, 641, 650
Luxor..................................... 432
Lycaonia................................ 105
Lycia .. 45, 46, 166, 403, 494, 498, 544, 612
Lycians 43, 166, 167, 177, 621
Lycurgus 25
Lycus....................................... 47
Lycus, River..... 47, 119, 143, 144, 433, 434, 435
Lydia .. 37, 56, 103, 104, 125, 198, 212, 260, 403, 613
Lydians.................................. 136
Lyncestians 46, 132
Lyncestis........................ 493, 494
Lyrnesus.................................. 57
Lysimachus 272, 275, 280, 291, 403, 423, 443, 448, 493, 494, 495, 500, 501, 553, 606
Lyson & Kallikles 487

673

M

Macedon. 8, 13, 25, 29, 30, 64, 65, 66, 67, 68, 69, 71, 72, 73, 74, 76, 78, 84, 86, 87, 88, 89, 90, 92, 93, 94, 95, 96, 97, 98, 99, 100, 102, 103, 105, 106, 107, 108, 109, 115, 119, 126, 129, 130, 134, 135, 136, 137, 138, 139, 141, 142, 143, 144, 145, 146, 147, 148, 159, 160, 161, 162, 164, 167, 169, 174, 177, 179, 183, 191, 210, 221, 224, 228, 261, 341, 349, 375, 382, 393, 396, 403, 405, 406, 407, 409, 418, 427, 431, 433, 436, 437, 438, 439, 487, 490, 494, 503, 505, 506, 507, 511, 512, 513, 514, 516, 522, 526, 529, 544, 570, 613, 616, 617, 620, 623, 624, 626, 632, 635, 640, 642, 646, 647

Macedones 489

Macedonia.. 15, 18, 19, 29, 33, 46, 50, 56, 59, 83, 197, 228, 233, 237, 326, 338, 351, 409, 413, 419, 421, 425, 611, 646

Macedonians v, 10, 12, 13, 14, 15, 17, 18, 19, 20, 21, 22, 24, 25, 30, 31, 32, 33, 34, 35, 36, 37, 38, 39, 41, 42, 43, 46, 49, 51, 52, 53, 56, 61, 197, 199, 204, 208, 209, 211, 214, 215, 218, 222, 224, 226, 227, 228, 229, 233, 235, 237, 239, 240, 242, 244, 245, 251, 252, 254, 255, 257, 262, 263, 264, 265, 268, 270, 271, 272, 273, 278, 279, 280, 281, 284, 286, 288, 289, 290, 291, 293, 294, 302, 303, 305, 306, 307, 309, 310, 311, 312, 314, 315, 317, 318, 319, 320, 322, 323, 327, 329, 331, 332, 333, 335, 336, 337, 340, 342, 343, 345, 347, 352, 354, 355, 356, 357, 359, 366, 368, 369, 370, 372, 373, 374, 377, 380, 381, 382, 383, 384, 386, 388, 393, 396, 397, 400, 401, 402, 403, 405, 406, 407, 409, 411, 413, 414, 418, 419, 422, 423, 425, 451, 452, 453, 459, 460, 461, 462, 463, 465, 467, 468, 470, 475, 477, 478, 481, 486, 487, 488, 489, 493, 494, 503, 504, 505, 506, 507, 527, 536, 544, 545, 546, 548, 550, 558, 570, 582, 592, 612, 645, 646

Machatas 465
Macrobius 375, 650
Madates 163, 164, 620
Maeander 38, 612
Maedi 351
Maeotic Marsh 202, 446
Magi 54, 106
Magnesia ...... iv, 29, 38, 206, 544, 557, 598, 604, 612
Maimacterion 429
malaria 491, 492, 493
Malis 132
Malli 342, 354, 356, 472, 522, 548, 549, 569, 596, 605, 635, 636, 637
Mallian siege 586, 587, 642
Mallus 63
Mamalces 361
Manapis 203
Mandi 361, 549, 556, 605, 606, 637
Mantinea 22
Maqloub, Mount 433, 434, 435, 440
Mar Mattai Monastery 434
Maracanda 253, 255, 263, 264, 271, 272, 278, 448, 469, 470, 626, 627
Marathus 84

Index

Mardians .. 81, 128, 139, 175, 204, 205, 282, 522
Mardonius 25, 84
Mareotic Lake 110, 115
Margania 265, 470, 627
Marganiam 518
Margiana 265, 470, 518, 627
Margianum 518
Marginiam 518
Margites 421
Mariette, A 508, 509
Mark Antony 650
Markle, M 487, 647
Marmares iv, 29, 43, 44, 544, 604, 612
marriage ... 82, 210, 271, 294, 296, 448, 465, 466, 472, 516, 547, 605, 609, 627
Marsyas River 46
Martial 589, 650
Massagetae 128, 136, 199, 271, 547, 627
Massani 357, 635
Matris 580
mausoleum 405, 489
Maximus 475
Mazaces 103, 110
Mazaeus. 118, 119, 120, 122, 127, 128, 129, 137, 142, 143, 154, 160, 180, 189, 282, 434, 438
Mazaga .. 304, 306, 307, 311, 472, 596, 630, 636
Meda 12, 419, 465
Medeia 458
Medes 34, 51, 128, 136, 198, 238, 242, 260, 527, 537
Media 68, 104, 128, 153, 166, 179, 189, 196, 218, 219, 221, 226, 234, 240, 282, 325, 383, 384, 403, 469, 497, 498, 504, 537, 605, 631
Median dress 442

Mediterranean .. 66, 425, 439, 480, 483, 487, 503, 524, 578, 579, 601, 646
Medius 390, 406, 481, 492, 493, 641
Medus, River 166
Megalopolis 146, 147, 193, 400, 619
Megara 567, 573, 574, 575
Megasthenes ... 298, 549, 556, 558, 565, 566, 567, 571, 572, 594, 602, 606, 629, 633, 637, 644
Meleager .. 68, 132, 167, 254, 313, 396, 397, 398, 399, 400, 401, 402, 494, 495, 500, 501
Melissa 278, 390, 475
Melisseus 17
Melon 189
Memaceni 254, 255
Memnon iv, 17, 18, 33, 34, 38, 40, 41, 42, 43, 45, 49, 50, 53, 56, 57, 82, 115, 116, 146, 339, 426, 430, 431, 545, 559, 610, 612, 613
memoranda 405, 502
Memphis 103, 110, 115, 264, 407, 430, 431, 432, 439, 486, 489, 506, 507, 508, 509, 524, 550, 570, 602, 617, 642
Menander 403, 500, 501
Menedemus 255, 258, 264, 626
Menes 160
Menidas ... 127, 138, 145, 265, 619
Mennis 152, 153, 154, 620
Menon 239, 367
Mentor 53, 82, 383, 582
mercenaries 65, 102, 133, 145, 160, 163, 164, 304, 306, 307, 438, 616, 622, 630, 641
Merkelbach 595, 631, 634, 637, 647
Meroë 430
Meros 302, 303
Merv 265, 470, 518, 627

675

Meshed 468
Mesopotamia ... iv, 50, 51, 64, 102, 117, 118, 153, 174, 334, 370, 403, 404, 491, 618
Metapontines 149
Methymna 45, 105, 115, 116
Metron 215, 219
Metropolis 377, 385, 400, 402, 475, 476
Metz Epitome ... vii, 2, 4, 213, 238, 253, 255, 259, 265, 266, 270, 278, 301, 304, 306, 311, 314, 316, 322, 402, 403, 404, 405, 466, 468, 491, 496, 497, 498, 499, 503, 506, 518, 524, 527, 529, 537, 547, 548, 551, 554, 556, 557, 560, 561, 562, 563, 578, 581, 582, 584, 585, 587, 592, 593, 594, 595, 596, 599, 602, 613, 623, 624, 625, 626, 627, 628, 629, 630, 631, 632, 633, 634, 635, 636, 637, 642, 643, 646, 648, 650
Midas 48, 49, 409
Mieza 493
Milesians .. 38, 103, 250, 251, 456, 457
Miletus iv, 29, 37, 38, 39, 40, 105, 206, 250, 277, 424, 456, 612
Miller, Stephen G. 513, 647
Minythyia 591
Mithracenes 189
Mithras 130
Mithrenes 37, 78, 160, 180, 438
Mithrobuzanes 37
Moeris 361
Molossians 410, 465
monkeys . 327, 553, 555, 560, 606, 632
Monophthalmus, Antigonus 499
Moon 101, 121, 152, 201, 411, 412, 415, 416, 417, 427, 428, 431, 512, 514, 534, 618, 619
Mophis 311, 312, 630

Moralia 2, 15, 23, 32, 85, 125, 208, 250, 252, 419, 422, 442, 445, 456, 457, 494, 503, 506, 522, 527, 535, 537, 550, 553, 560, 562, 582, 594, 596, 597, 610, 614, 615, 616, 625, 633, 635, 650
Mossyni 201
Mostellaria 420
Mosul 433, 434, 440
Muetzell, Julius 588
mule's hoof 406, 493, 642
mules 174, 642
Müller, K 529, 597, 647, 649
Munich 513, 647, 648, 649
Muses 29, 611
Musicani 357, 358, 636
Musicanus 357, 358, 472, 636
Myllinas 308
Myndii 63
Myra 486
Myrmidons 483
Myrra 117, 535, 618
Myrtle 303
Mytilene 45, 56, 106, 117, 132, 403, 563

N

Nabarzanes 64, 67, 183, 184, 185, 186, 190, 195, 199, 201, 205, 263, 441, 520, 521, 622
Nakhthorheb 508
naphtha 152, 153, 154, 620
Naples Museum 487
NASA 411, 412, 417
Nasamones 111
Natural History 202, 445, 450, 467, 650
Nature 91, 106, 159, 171, 175, 208, 212, 256, 266, 268, 276, 285, 292, 298, 299, 304, 332, 338, 342, 351, 362, 385
Nautaca 279, 470, 472

Index

Nearchus.... 1, 298, 349, 365, 369, 385, 396, 403, 414, 473, 494, 498, 500, 503, 516, 517, 549, 551, 552, 553, 554, 560, 561, 569, 602, 605, 606, 620, 629, 632, 637, 638, 641
Nebuchadnezzar 489, 563
Nectanebo 508, 509, 510, 645
Nemean 410
Nemean lion........................... 409
Neoptolemus......... 8, 41, 410, 501
Nepos.............. 494, 516, 518, 650
Nero 462
Nesaean mares 383, 481
New Moon. 8, 101, 147, 411, 415, 416, 417, 418, 427, 428, 512, 514, 539
Nicaea............................ 339, 633
Nicanor 68, 132, 190, 211, 214, 219, 222, 315, 480, 501
Nicarchides 174
Nicasipolis 407
Nicator, Seleucus.................... 499
Nicatorium, Mt 433, 434
Nicephorion 440
Nicesipolis of Pherae.............. 465
Nicocles 313
Nicomachus ... 213, 214, 215, 216, 217, 219, 223, 229
Nicostratus............................. 286
Nike 130
Nile .. 30, 102, 110, 115, 162, 298, 386, 421, 430, 431, 432, 487, 507
Nineveh . 118, 432, 433, 434, 435, 440
Ninus 54, 158, 433
Numidia................................. 370
Nysa 302, 304, 472, 548, 591, 594, 605, 629, 637
Nysaeans................................ 302

O

obeisance........................ 461, 463
occhus tree 553
Ocean 79, 104, 134, 202, 231, 239, 297, 303, 326, 335, 336, 338, 339, 342, 356, 357, 361, 362, 364, 365, 369, 395, 403, 445, 472, 473, 548, 549, 605, 631, 637
Oceanus........................... 364, 637
Ochus . 15, 82, 125, 136, 196, 203, 265, 394, 442, 470, 519, 627
Ochus River 265, 470
Odrysians 31, 375, 422
Official Tradition 1, 2, 5, 432, 437, 511, 528
Okaeteris 412
Oldach & Richards.......... 491, 647
Olympia........................... 376, 386
Olympiad......................... 8, 9, 152
Olympian gods 338
Olympias 8, 10, 148, 163, 228, 274, 352, 376, 387, 394, 405, 406, 410, 419, 455, 458, 465, 495, 505, 507, 514, 550, 569, 570, 584, 613, 617, 624, 644
Olympic Games.... 9, 10, 105, 354, 376, 409, 411, 513, 514, 515, 647
Olynthians 291, 463
Olynthus.......................... 555, 562
Onchae 83
Onchestus................................ 20
Onesicritus 15, 202, 206, 298, 313, 329, 332, 365, 369, 408, 419, 441, 447, 448, 473, 504, 548, 549, 552, 553, 555, 558, 559, 569, 574, 583, 587, 588, 589, 594, 595, 596, 602, 605, 606, 611, 622, 627, 630, 632, 634, 637, 638, 644
Onomas 83
Onomastorides 83

677

Opet festival 432
Opis Mutiny ... 382, 475, 476, 477, 640
oracle. iv, v, 8, 20, 26, 27, 87, 110, 111, 112, 113, 115, 148, 167, 221, 224, 226, 228, 275, 290, 354, 386, 420, 456, 457, 459, 490, 524, 606, 611, 613, 617, 621
Oracle of Ammon .. 221, 275, 459, 490
Orchomenians 23, 24
Oreitae 365, 367, 549, 554, 605, 606, 636, 638
Orestians 132
Orestis 493, 494
Orexartes, River 446
Orient ... 31, 52, 69, 157, 183, 197, 228, 255, 297, 326, 395
Orion 299, 629
Orontobates 128
Orpheus 49
Orsilos 189
Orsines ... 128, 370, 371, 517, 598, 639
Orxines 517, 598
Ostanes 16
Oxartes 279, 280
Oxathres 72, 82, 196, 208, 251, 394, 625
Oxus River 242, 244, 246, 247, 249, 265, 301, 469, 470, 547, 625, 627
Oxyartes . 294, 357, 380, 403, 466, 467, 500, 501, 593, 628, 636
Oxydates 196, 282
Oxydracae 342, 343, 354, 472, 522, 549, 560, 570, 594, 596, 597, 605, 635, 642
Oxyrhynchus 573, 643
Ozines 367, 369, 638

P

Paeonians ... 18, 32, 120, 129, 422, 618
Pages. 77, 215, 286, 399, 453, 461, 462, 463, 472, 479
paides basilikoi 479
Palagia, Olga 483, 489, 647
Palestine 507
Palimbothra 565
Pamphylia .. 45, 46, 165, 198, 403, 494, 498, 545, 555, 606, 612
Pamphylians 46, 604, 613
Pandaea ... 361, 556, 606, 629, 637
Pandosia 148, 149
Pantheia 196, 437, 442
Pantheon 395, 486
Paphlagonia 34, 50, 103, 105, 198, 403
Paphlagonians 226
papyrus .. 206, 298, 531, 552, 573, 574, 575, 576, 602
Paraetacenê 189
Parapanisadae 357
paredros 388, 489, 641
Paris ... 17, 31, 443, 444, 534, 643, 649
Parmenion .. v, 4, 9, 10, 12, 15, 18, 29, 31, 35, 38, 43, 46, 58, 60, 61, 63, 64, 68, 71, 73, 81, 82, 83, 104, 116, 122, 126, 129, 130, 131, 132, 133, 137, 142, 144, 165, 174, 195, 196, 211, 213, 214, 217, 218, 219, 222, 225, 227, 228, 229, 232, 234, 235, 236, 237, 239, 274, 275, 288, 289, 368, 406, 424, 426, 451, 452, 453, 454, 455, 459, 460, 480, 483, 523, 573, 584, 604, 609, 613, 614, 617, 618, 624
Paropamisadae 239, 624
Paropamisus ... 240, 245, 247, 268, 403, 446, 540, 604

Index

Paropanisum 357
parrot 298, 308
Parsagada 174, 370, 441, 473, 523, 639
Parsons, P 573, 643
Parthenon 485
Parthia.... 188, 197, 198, 200, 208, 367, 403, 441
Parthians 128, 197
Pasas 400
Pasippus 83
Pasitigris, River 163, 440, 599
Patala 361, 364, 472, 637
Patroclus .. 31, 421, 445, 446, 483, 517, 561, 571, 606, 611, 622
Patron 184, 186, 187, 438, 582
Pausanias 10, 11, 12, 26, 228, 230, 264, 405, 413, 418, 455, 458, 480, 494, 504, 506, 510, 549, 570, 594, 597, 609, 635, 636, 642, 650
peacock 299
Pearls 331
Pearson .. 529, 532, 533, 535, 543, 553, 555, 556, 557, 560, 561, 563, 568, 571, 583, 584, 597, 598, 609, 611, 620, 623, 625, 626, 632, 647
Pédech, P 200, 468, 647
Peleus 410
Pella 160, 403, 493, 498, 500
Pelopidas 519
Peloponnese 13, 46, 146, 159, 161, 198, 409, 512
Peloponnesians .. 19, 68, 132, 146, 245
Pelusium 103, 110
Penguin .. 586, 587, 589, 591, 648, 649
pentakosiarch 479
Perdiccas.... 22, 30, 32, 41, 68, 90, 132, 145, 217, 221, 224, 228, 254, 275, 301, 317, 318, 319, 330, 384, 391, 395, 396, 397, 398, 399, 400, 401, 402, 403, 405, 409, 419, 480, 489, 493, 494, 495, 496, 497, 502, 507, 519, 520, 521, 619, 640, 641
Pergamon 396, 486
Pergamon Museum 486
Perilaus 400
Perinthus 540
Peroz 450
Persephone 410
Persepolis 104, 152, 169, 173, 174, 175, 176, 178, 179, 181, 182, 428, 436, 437, 440, 523, 547, 569, 604, 621
Persia v, 14, 24, 63, 64, 66, 70, 71, 72, 73, 74, 77, 78, 79, 80, 81, 86, 99, 102, 103, 104, 105, 106, 110, 117, 118, 120, 121, 123, 128, 131, 135, 136, 139, 141, 142, 144, 145, 148, 153, 158, 159, 161, 162, 163, 165, 166, 167, 170, 173, 174, 175, 177, 179, 180, 185, 189, 196, 198, 199, 260, 325, 326, 350, 354, 367, 369, 378, 403, 427, 434, 436, 437, 438, 439, 440, 441, 472, 473, 504, 511, 517, 518, 519, 520, 521, 523, 526, 537, 546, 554, 584, 601, 602, 610, 611, 612, 614, 615, 618, 619, 620, 622, 623, 625, 640
Persian dress.... 442, 443, 444, 623
Persian Empire 441, 541, 544, 554, 610
Persian rod-bearers 445
Persian Sea 163
Persianising 196, 441, 442, 445, 520
Persians . iv, v, 2, 8, 10, 14, 15, 17, 18, 19, 24, 25, 27, 30, 31, 33, 34, 35, 37, 38, 40, 41, 45, 48, 50, 51, 52, 53, 54, 55, 58, 63, 64, 65, 66, 68, 69, 70, 71, 73, 74, 75, 78, 81, 83, 102, 103,

105, 106, 109, 110, 122, 128, 129, 130, 134, 136, 138, 139, 140, 141, 142, 143, 144, 145, 163, 165, 166, 168, 173, 174, 177, 184, 185, 187, 188, 189, 195, 196, 200, 201, 204, 208, 209, 210, 238, 251, 260, 263, 265, 284, 285, 288, 289, 290, 293, 294, 313, 325, 332, 334, 335, 337, 361, 367, 369, 370, 371, 372, 373, 379, 380, 381, 382, 384, 385, 387, 393, 396, 423, 424, 426, 437, 441, 442, 443, 444, 445, 456, 457, 458, 459, 460, 461, 462, 463, 467, 477, 481, 485, 504, 508, 521, 526, 527, 537, 541, 544, 549, 554, 559, 582, 602, 605, 606, 612, 613, 619, 631, 645

Persica 535, 554, 560, 614, 620
Persis 440, 475, 621
Peucestes 115, 345, 382, 403, 431, 481, 493, 495, 500, 501, 640
Peucolaus 214, 219, 265
Phaenomena 412
phalanx. 21, 22, 34, 42, 52, 68, 71, 74, 119, 129, 132, 138, 173, 189, 200, 201, 250, 259, 262, 264, 280, 301, 318, 319, 320, 321, 330, 374, 397, 399, 401, 402, 456, 478
Pharnabazus . 53, 64, 82, 103, 105, 106
Pharnaces 37
Pharnuches 517
Pharos 115
Phaselis 45, 46, 424, 613
Phasis River 206
Phegeus 332, 633
Phila 465
Philadelphus ... 464, 510, 551, 572, 576, 589
Philinna ... 398, 418, 465, 495, 496

Philip .... iv, v, 8, 9, 10, 11, 12, 13, 15, 17, 19, 24, 25, 27, 29, 32, 43, 45, 51, 59, 60, 61, 62, 64, 69, 84, 108, 113, 121, 132, 137, 146, 183, 203, 209, 212, 221, 227, 228, 229, 230, 237, 272, 273, 274, 275, 289, 337, 352, 359, 370, 378, 388, 394, 397, 398, 400, 402, 403, 405, 406, 409, 411, 413, 414, 417, 418, 420, 424, 425, 426, 429, 447, 459, 460, 465, 480, 487, 494, 495, 496, 497, 500, 501, 504, 505, 506, 512, 513, 514, 515, 529, 530, 533, 534, 540, 544, 570, 573, 574, 584, 602, 604, 609, 611, 613, 614, 635, 636, 641, 642, 646
Philip II 221, 529, 530, 544
Philip of Theangela 447
Philip the Chalcidian 447
Philip the Physician 225
Philip, brother of Lysimachus 280
Philippic History 579, 585, 591, 592, 594, 596, 597, 599, 649, 650
Philippus 553, 567, 627
Philitas 576
Philo the Theban 447
Philodemus 543, 567, 568, 574, 581
Philopator 573, 574, 575, 576
Philotas ...... v, 4, 19, 31, 104, 108, 132, 161, 162, 168, 169, 195, 211, 213, 214, 215, 216, 217, 218, 219, 220, 221, 222, 224, 225, 226, 227, 228, 229, 230, 232, 233, 234, 235, 237, 287, 288, 289, 291, 403, 406, 422, 425, 449, 451, 452, 453, 454, 455, 460, 468, 480, 500, 501, 520, 546, 582, 590, 623, 628
Philotas the Page 286
Phocians 20, 23, 24, 132, 610

Index

Phocion 26
Phoenicia . 45, 85, 86, 87, 90, 102, 104, 198, 403, 405, 429, 503, 618
Phoenicians 95, 96, 386, 616
Photius 95, 402, 403, 493, 496, 497, 498, 499, 501, 506, 516, 519, 521, 616, 649
Phraates 591
Phrada 213, 450
Phradates 128, 203, 205, 282, 372, 622
Phrataphernes 203, 271, 282, 367, 403, 500, 622
Phrygia 33, 34, 43, 48, 49, 198, 403, 501, 610
Phrygians 49, 82, 128, 226
Phrynon 25
Phthiotis 132
Pierio 460
Pillars of Heracles.. 421, 503, 550, 581
Pinarus, River 66, 67, 81
Pindar 25, 410, 508, 610
Pinelli 278
Pir Sar .... *See* Aornus
Pisidia 507
Pisidians 198
Pitanê 18
Pithon 358, 397, 398, 403, 493, 494, 497, 498, 500, 501, 636
Pixodarus 398, 419, 495, 496
Plataea 25, 619
Plataeans 23, 24, 610
Plato 417, 442, 508, 545
Platon 179
Plautus 420
Pleiades 174, 175, 428, 621
Pliny... 37, 48, 202, 213, 272, 298, 300, 386, 423, 425, 440, 445, 450, 467, 474, 529, 547, 549, 554, 558, 559, 561, 567, 568, 571, 572, 580, 589, 594, 597, 622, 629, 635, 637, 638, 641, 642, 650
Plutarch ....vii, 2, 3, 4, 5, 8, 12, 15, 23, 24, 27, 31, 32, 34, 38, 46, 51, 60, 77, 85, 101, 121, 122, 125, 130, 145, 154, 167, 174, 202, 206, 208, 210, 221, 246, 247, 250, 252, 265, 274, 275, 291, 297, 305, 309, 376, 388, 404, 405, 409, 410, 411, 412, 413, 414, 415,416, 417, 418, 419, 420, 421, 422, 423, 424, 426, 427, 428, 433, 435, 441, 442, 445, 446, 447, 448, 452, 456, 457, 458, 459, 460, 463, 464, 466, 477, 479, 481, 482, 489, 490, 491, 492, 494, 495, 496, 502, 503, 506, 512, 513, 514, 515, 520, 522, 523, 524, 525, 527, 529, 532, 533, 534, 535, 537, 543, 544, 545, 547, 550, 553, 554, 555, 556, 557, 558, 560, 562, 563, 566, 567, 578, 581, 582, 584, 594, 595, 596, 597, 599, 602, 609, 610, 611, 612, 613, 614, 615, 616, 617, 618, 619, 620, 621, 622, 623, 625, 627, 628, 629, 630, 633, 635, 636, 637, 638, 639, 640, 641, 642, 646, 650
Pnytagoras 92
Pobjoy, M 573, 643
Poediculi 149
Polemon . 115, 230, 233, 234, 454, 455, 507
Policy of Fusion 462
Poliorcetes, Demetrius 407, 489
Polito, E 486, 487
Polyaenus168, 210, 266, 306, 317, 440, 447, 498, 499, 524, 526, 529, 547, 556, 581, 582, 597, 621, 623, 624, 627, 630, 631, 632, 637, 651

Polybius 66, 68, 298, 416, 477, 504, 515, 563, 574, 583, 590, 597, 644, 651
Polycleitus 447, 558, 606, 622
Polydamas 137, 234, 235, 236, 382, 455, 624
Polyperchon ... 130, 132, 168, 169, 285, 297, 307, 357, 382, 472, 505, 506, 516, 636
Polystratus 191, 441
Polytimetus River 264, 470
Polyxena 410
Pompeii 36, 73, 410, 443, 448, 449, 487
Pompey 589
Pontic Sea. 48, 202, 239, 240, 244, 403, 425, 445, 446, 447
Pontus 375
Pope John Paul II 461
Porticanus 357, 636
Porus 312, 313, 314, 315, 316, 317, 318, 319, 320, 322, 323, 324, 326, 327, 328, 329, 332, 333, 334, 339, 370, 403, 472, 498, 500, 501, 524, 548, 565, 566, 567, 584, 595, 605, 631, 632, 633, 639
Poseidium of the Milesians 456
Poseidon 89, 98
pothos 561
Potidaea 9, 513, 514
Prandi, L. 532, 534, 539, 545, 559, 568, 569, 575, 576, 580, 585, 589, 590, 644, 647
Pranichus 460
Prasii 332, 633
Priam 17, 410
Pritchett, W Kendrick 417, 648
Pro Archias Poeta 31, 421, 649
Processional Way 486
Proconsul 587, 588
Prometheus 240, 625
Prophthasia 213, 235, 449, 450, 467, 468

proskynesis 163, 445, 462, 463, 472, 520, 563, 582, 628
Providence 359
Pseudo-Callisthenes .. 2, 426, 428, 431, 439, 496, 524, 592, 651
Ptolemaeus 68, 265
Ptolemaic Period 431, 511, 645, 648
Ptolemy 1, 4, 10, 12, 32, 211, 213, 264, 275, 287, 291, 298, 303, 315, 316, 317, 318, 319, 348, 350, 359, 365, 391, 396, 397, 399, 403, 407, 418, 422, 425, 435, 447, 450, 451, 460, 464, 465, 474, 478, 479, 489, 493, 494, 498, 500, 501, 507, 508, 510, 511, 518, 522, 523, 524, 538, 548, 550, 552, 559, 564, 567, 569, 570, 572, 573, 574, 575, 576, 578, 585, 586, 587, 589, 594, 596, 597, 605, 618, 633, 635, 636, 638, 640, 642, 643, 645, 651
Ptolemy, Claudius .. 412, 435, 440, 446, 450, 468, 651
Punjab 566, 567
Pura 473, 525
Pyanepsion 416, 428, 515
Pydna 160, 452
pyra 489
pyramids 405, 487, 489, 504
Pyramus, River 57, 63
Pyrrha 45
Pyrrhus ... 386, 410, 474, 564, 571, 641, 650
Pythia 333, 611, 633
Pythionicê 375, 376
Pythodelus 512

Q

quadriremes 92, 93, 98
quinquereme 387, 483
quinqueremes 92, 98

Index

Quintilian 567, 580

R

Radulfus de Diceto 591
rainbow 20
Rambacia .... *See* Rhambarce
Reagan, Ronald 461
Red Sea 51, 111, 128, 153, 166, 240, 326, 351, 370, 403
Renaissance 466
Republic 442
Rhambarce 365, 473
Rheomithres 34, 72
Rhidagnus 201
rhinoceroses 298, 326, 588
Rhodes 17, 34, 115, 431
Rhodians 33, 104, 117
Rhoeteion 18
Rhosaces 36, 272
Rhossus 376
Riley, Henry Thomas 440, 650
ring... 64, 107, 112, 133, 391, 395, 396, 493, 495, 504, 641
Rolfe, J 476, 588, 648, 649
Romans .. 1, 5, 149, 298, 299, 349, 386, 414, 416, 418, 423, 462, 474, 482, 487, 534, 549, 571, 573, 574, 578, 584, 585, 587, 588, 591, 592, 594, 597, 605, 641, 643, 646
Rome 88, 158, 431, 435, 440, 511, 513, 567, 579, 591, 644, 648, 649, 650
Romm 519, 648
Roxane v, 271, 294, 296, 339, 396, 397, 398, 403, 406, 421, 465, 466, 467, 472, 485, 495, 505, 516, 548, 570, 592, 593, 599, 605, 629, 633
Royal Crag 176
Royal Family 496
Royal Relatives 35, 36
rudist 487

Russian Steppes 448

S

Sabaces 72, 102
Sacae 199, 242, 263, 293, 626
Sahr-i Qumis 441, 467
Salamis 489
Salmous 369, 473, 638
Samaritans 116
Samarkand 253, 271, 469, 470
Samaxus 314
Sambana 382, 481, 640
Sambastae 356, 635
Sambus ... 343, 357, 358, 359, 360, 549, 605, 636, 637
Samnan 441
Samothrace 273
Samuel, AE 412, 413, 416, 418, 513, 648
Sandrocottus 565, 566
Sangala 329, 632
Sangarius 48
Saqqara 489, 508, 509
Sardanapalus 63, 535, 554, 555, 559, 582, 604, 606, 614
Sardians 37
Sardinia 386
Sardis v, 37, 43, 78, 160, 180, 423, 438, 612
Sari 205, 468
sarissa 487
sarissaphoroi 138
sarissas 307, 318, 320, 486
Sarmatians 255, 256
Sassanian Empire 450
Satibarzanes ... 210, 211, 212, 238, 245, 246, 447, 468, 623, 625
Satrapies 77, 525, 642
Satropates 118, 120, 618
Satyrus 12, 418, 465, 496, 642
sauroter 487
Scamander 37, 423
scepter 209, 448

683

Schachermeyr. 433, 434, 440, 538, 550, 553, 570, 577, 648
Schachermeyr, F 538, 550
Schnabel, P.............. 562, 563, 620
Scholia on Apollonius Rhodius 531, 548
Scholia on Aristophanes.......... 537
Schönfeld, H 647, 649
Schwartz..... 1, 538, 577, 578, 607, 613, 614, 615, 616, 617, 618, 619, 620, 621, 622, 624, 625, 627, 629, 630, 631, 632, 633, 634, 635, 636, 638, 640, 641, 642, 648
scindapsos 303
scorpion engines...................... 306
Scythia.... 240, 278, 335, 353, 371, 433, 470, 626, 627
Scythian king 448, 547, 605
Scythians 106, 117, 129, 134, 137, 138, 139, 197, 210, 242, 245, 253, 254, 255, 256, 257, 259, 260, 261, 262, 263, 271, 317, 320, 336, 375, 446, 448, 619, 625, 626
Second Division of the Satrapies 496, 497
Seistan 213, 450, 468
Sejanus 213, 451
Selene 152
Seleucia 439, 536
Seleucus ... 68, 319, 403, 493, 494, 495, 497, 499, 500, 501, 519, 520, 521, 557, 563, 565, 567
Semiramis 155, 157, 158, 254, 351, 562, 582, 606, 620
septiremes 370
Serapeum.......... 486, 489, 508, 509
serpents 432, 524, 632
Shakespeare............................. 511
Shakhrisyabz 279, 471
Shirabad River 470
Sibi 339, 504, 581, 634

Sibyrtius. 367, 403, 500, 501, 557, 565, 567
Sicily.94, 148, 386, 405, 416, 515, 540
Sidon.... 63, 71, 85, 100, 429, 485, 486, 545, 589, 615, 616, 618
Sidonians 85, 100
siege-towers 305, 306, 310
Silex.. 301
Silver Shields.................. 132, 493
Simmias 230, 454, 567
Simui 111
Sinope 14, 15, 204, 419, 610
Siphnos 103
Sirens 300, 388, 488, 554
Sisenna.................................... 580
Sisimithres 270, 279, 280, 293, 470, 472, 518, 592, 593, 627, 628
Sisines....................... 46, 64, 424
Sisygambis..... 55, 78, 79, 80, 122, 138, 162, 163, 164, 394, 549, 620, 641
Sitalces........................... 368, 638
Sittacenê 160, 382, 481
Siwa 102, 112, 228, 430, 431, 432, 439, 524, 546, 555, 564, 582, 606, 611, 613, 617
skins..97, 111, 166, 247, 248, 259, 261, 625
Smith, William 440
snakes 326, 328, 329, 337, 358, 359, 554, 555, 558, 606, 632
Socrates 104, 441
Sodrae............................. 357, 635
Sogdian Rock 466, 547, 627
Sogdiana 242, 246, 249, 260, 264, 265, 274, 311, 352, 403, 456, 469, 470, 504, 548, 592, 627
Sogdians .. 51, 104, 128, 199, 244, 254, 264, 271, 335, 627
Soli.................. 63, 403, 545, 614
Solstice .. 101, 147, 411, 417, 427, 512, 513, 539, 631

Index

somatophylakes...... 477, 478, 479, 480, 481, 493, 494, 495
Sopeithes 330, 331, 332, 339, 548, 553, 634
Sophocles................ 580
Sopolis 288
Sostratus 286, 463
Soter 348, 489, 511, 550, 567, 575, 576
Sounion, Cape......... 376
Source of the Sun..... 112
Sousia 210, 468
Spain............. 386, 550
Sparta..... 102, 147, 198, 204, 361, 559, 619, 621, 625
Spartan hostages 532, 536, 546, 547, 604
Spartans 13, 45, 83, 102, 117, 146, 147, 193, 198, 204, 245, 246, 406, 619, 625
Spear-Bearers 54
Spitamenes..... 249, 251, 254, 255, 258, 263, 281, 282, 283, 472, 532, 625, 626, 628
Spithridates 34, 35, 36, 460
St Mark 510, 534
stades ... 67, 77, 87, 111, 115, 119, 122, 128, 153, 155, 157, 163, 165, 166, 168, 170, 179, 189, 190, 432, 434, 435, 526, 620, 626, 630, 633, 637
Star-Shield Block..... 510
Stasanor .. 238, 282, 403, 500, 501
Stasicrates.............. 482
Stateira... 102, 103, 373, 437, 516, 618
Stathmoi................. 450, 467, 502
Steele, RB 591, 648
Stein, Aurel.... 433, 434, 435, 440, 648
Stephanus......... 154, 620
Stephanus Byzantinus.... 213, 450, 651
Stiboeites River 200, 467

Stilpo 567, 574, 575, 583, 587
Stobaeus 531, 535, 546, 618
Strabo . 34, 48, 154, 202, 206, 211, 213, 235, 239, 240, 241, 250, 251, 256, 288, 298, 313, 329, 332, 377, 419, 421, 425, 433, 434, 435, 440, 441, 445, 447, 450, 456, 458, 467, 468, 469, 472, 475, 482, 499, 504, 509, 513, 516, 535, 547, 548, 549, 550, 551, 552, 553, 554, 555, 557, 558, 560, 561, 563, 565, 566, 581, 582, 583, 588, 594, 595, 614, 617, 620, 622, 624, 625, 627, 629, 630, 631, 632, 633, 634, 635, 636, 637, 638, 640, 651
Straton 84, 85, 86, 430, 576
Stromata 30, 420
Stymphaeans 132
Styx 406, 493, 642
Successors 405, 574
Suda 250, 416, 457, 494, 515, 535, 536, 543, 551, 568, 576, 625, 651
Sudracae 560, 594, 635
Suez Canal 30, 421
Sura 440
Surkhab River 265, 470
Surkhan River 470
Susa 152, 161, 162, 174, 373, 382, 396, 436, 437, 440, 467, 473, 475, 494, 497, 538, 599, 605, 620, 629, 639, 640
Susian Gates.... 152, 165, 440, 621
Susianê ... 128, 161, 163, 165, 372, 375, 403, 532, 639
Susians 163, 478
suttee 553, 606
Swat River Valley 304, 472
Syracusans........... 39, 93
Syracuse 94
Syr-Darya 197, 242, 244, 255, 263, 446, 448, 469, 626

Syria 63, 65, 66, 81, 83, 86, 87, 104, 116, 128, 134, 135, 158, 189, 198, 260, 265, 272, 370, 376, 403, 405, 503, 507, 519, 535, 562, 584, 615, 620
Syriac 2
Syrians 84, 433, 614
Syrmus 18, 610
Syrticans 111

T

Tabae 189
Taenarum 376, 384
Tajikistan 470
Tanais River ... 104, 197, 210, 242, 243, 244, 245, 251, 253, 255, 256, 260, 261, 263, 445, 446, 447, 448, 469, 561, 606, 626
Tang-i Khas 440
Tang-i Sar Darrah 441
Tapurians 51, 203, 282
Tarn, WW .. 1, 213, 414, 445, 450, 457, 502, 503, 552, 556, 558, 559, 560, 561, 568, 569, 572, 582, 586, 587, 613, 622, 637, 648
Tarsus iv, 45, 58, 60, 63, 375, 426, 535, 545, 559, 604, 613, 614
Tauromenium 88, 152, 416, 515
Tauron 164, 308, 318, 319
Tauropolus 405, 503
Taurus 56, 57, 240, 426, 613
Taxila 311, 313, 472, 630
Taxiles 301, 311, 313, 314, 322, 323, 327, 339, 370, 403, 498, 500, 501, 584, 630, 633, 639
Taylor 433
Tegeans 193
Tel Gemel 433, 434, 435, 440
Telmissus 507
Temenids 409
Temenus 409
Tempesta, Antonio 273

Tenedos 105
Terioltes 357, 636
Tethys 364, 637
tetradrachm 407, 476
Teubner ... 588, 646, 648, 649, 650
Thais 173, 176, 177, 178, 437, 523, 569, 621
Thalestris 206, 207, 208, 410, 448, 449, 547, 583, 591, 604, 622
Thapsacus 370, 428, 431, 439, 503, 535, 601
Thara 187, 189, 441
Thargelion 34, 423, 514, 612
thaumasia 583
Theaetetus 171
Theagenes 24
Thebans 13, 14, 19, 20, 21, 22, 23, 24, 25, 26, 27, 534, 535, 610
Thebes .... iv, 8, 18, 19, 20, 21, 23, 24, 25, 51, 57, 198, 210, 274, 406, 508, 533, 534, 544, 550, 569, 570, 572, 590, 604, 609, 610, 642
Theis 535
Themiscyra 206
Themistocles 38, 544, 554, 582, 597, 604, 606, 612
Theodectas 45, 46, 613
Theodotus 161
Theophrastus 568
Theopompus .. 376, 473, 474, 513, 559, 606
Thermodon, River ... 206, 448, 622
Thermopylae 13
Thersippus 85
Thespians 23, 24
Thessalian League 13
Thessalians 13, 31, 32, 35, 37, 52, 68, 73, 142, 212, 390, 406, 422, 465, 641
Thessalonike 406, 419, 490
Thessaly . 67, 71, 73, 81, 132, 142, 391, 400, 418, 493, 615
Thibron 376, 639

Index

Thimodes 53, 64, 67, 582
Thomas, PH 648, 650
Thrace 19, 29, 50, 68, 69, 145, 197, 198, 255, 261, 339, 351, 375, 403, 405, 465, 482
Thracians ... 11, 18, 23, 24, 32, 57, 68, 69, 133, 146, 159, 163, 320, 370, 386, 405, 422, 465, 503, 611
Thrasybulus 42
Thucydides 533
thunderbolt............................ 407
Thurii 149
tiara 527, 537, 605
tigers 332, 356
Tigris 102, 104, 118, 119, 120, 121, 135, 143, 153, 163, 332, 334, 382, 428, 432, 434, 435, 440, 476, 526, 618, 644
Timaeus ... 88, 152, 416, 417, 421, 423, 515, 543, 551, 555, 558, 568, 606, 609, 622, 635
Timagenes.... 4, 15, 419, 537, 567, 579, 585, 587, 591, 635
Timocleia.................... 23, 26, 610
Timoleon 416, 515, 540
Tiridates. 169, 174, 238, 288, 584, 621
Tithonus.................. 115, 430, 431
Tithraustes 518
Tlepolemus 403, 500, 501
tortoises 164, 165, 356, 558
torture 96, 124, 125, 222, 223, 225, 226, 229, 233, 453, 454, 455, 464, 623, 625
Trajan...................................... 536
Trapezus 403, 497
Trebizond............................ 403, 497
triacontors............................... 311
Triballians... iv, 8, 18, 19, 31, 159, 198, 351, 422, 610
trierarchs................................. 517
Triparadeisus 499
Tripolis 102

triremes .. 92, 93, 98, 99, 105, 109, 115, 405, 483, 503, 617
Troad 10, 17, 18, 31, 33
Trogodytes 111
Trogus .... vii, 2, 4, 12, 15, 31, 247, 396, 418, 419, 514, 532, 537, 544, 546, 547, 562, 578, 579, 584, 585, 587, 590, 591, 592, 594, 596, 599, 615, 621, 642, 649, 650
Trojan War 31, 431
Trojans 31, 410
Troy ...... iv, 17, 29, 31, 37, 82, 148, 410, 421, 423, 431, 483, 504, 550, 581, 611
Turkey .... v, 48, 403, 425, 446
Tus......................... 210, 211, 468
Tybi 431, 524
Tyche............................... 563, 583
Typhon 57
Tyre .. 4, 63, 83, 85, 86, 89, 90, 91, 93, 94, 96, 97, 98, 99, 100, 101, 104, 117, 370, 427, 429, 439, 527, 535, 540, 545, 546, 589, 601, 604, 615, 616
Tyrians . 86, 87, 88, 89, 90, 92, 93, 94, 95, 96, 97, 98, 99, 100, 527, 616
Tyriotes 124

U

Underworld 251
Universal Time....................... 414
Uxianê 165
Uxii 163, 478, 522, 620
Uzbekistan............................ 469

V

Vakhsh River 470
Valerius Maximus 15, 419, 482, 597, 651

Varia Historia 31, 34, 228, 421, 423, 483, 507, 509, 514, 518, 649
Venice 486, 487, 488, 510, 534
Vitruvius 482
Vogel 586
Vulgate ..... vii, 2, 3, 4, 33, 56, 316, 317, 419, 426, 431, 437, 439, 440, 492, 500, 511, 518, 522, 523, 525, 526, 527, 528, 529, 531, 537, 544, 548, 562, 563, 564, 567, 582, 585, 591, 592, 594, 596, 597, 598, 599, 603, 635, 648

W

Wagner, Otto 592, 593
Weise, CH 588
Welles, C Bradford 1, 431, 479, 482, 532, 557, 633, 644, 649, 652
whales 366, 369, 555, 606, 616, 638
Wikipedia 435
Will of Alexander 403, 404, 496
Wood, Michael 433, 434, 475, 648

X

Xandrames 332, 633
Xanthus 45, 582, 613
Xenippa 278, 470
Xenodochus of Cardia 461
Xenophilus 162

Xenophon 196, 437, 441, 442, 443, 533, 538, 595, 611
Xerxes 24, 38, 50, 69, 84, 173, 177, 250, 383, 396, 456, 457, 544, 558, 604, 606, 612, 613
xyston 487

Y

Yardley .. 298, 551, 567, 570, 579, 585, 586, 589, 591, 592, 594, 596, 597, 609, 610, 619, 625, 631, 636, 643, 648, 649, 650

Z

Zab, Greater 119, 433, 434, 435
Zab, Lesser 433
Zadracarta 205, 468
Zarangians 213, 450
Zariaspa 469
Zariaspes 367, 369, 638
Zeller, E 567, 649
Zeravshan River 470
Zeugma 440
Zeus 7, 15, 29, 48, 49, 54, 81, 110, 113, 114, 130, 148, 170, 224, 226, 227, 284, 289, 290, 301, 302, 305, 314, 352, 386, 405, 409, 410, 413, 419, 484, 503, 629
ziggurat 387, 482
Zoilus 212
Zopyrion 375, 639
Zopyrus 206

www.ingramcontent.com/pod-product-compliance
Lightning Source LLC
Chambersburg PA
CBHW020117240426
43673CB00038B/511